Milestones

(a fifties "kid" looks back at his life)

Clint Brown

Printed in the United States of America.

ISBN: 978-1-4669-1777-4 (sc)
ISBN: 978-1-4669-1776-7 (e)

Trafford rev. 06/18/2012

 www.trafford.com

North America & international
toll-free: 1 888 232 4444 (USA & Canada)
phone: 250 383 6864 ◆ fax: 812 355 4082

Thanks to Linda, Andree, Caren, Cindy and Dianne,
for their inspiration and support

Contents

"In Dreams, I am with you . . . . Roy Orbison...1

(1955—"Rock Around The Clock . . . Bill Haley And The Comets)...................5

2003...10

1956-1958 . . . A Teenager In Love . . . Dion...12

(Young Love . . . Sonny James)...17

The Journey..19

"You Don't Have To Be A Baby To Cry" . . . The Caravelles.........................96

(The Party)..164

The Proms..193

Psycho...254

Young Love . . . (Tab Hunter/Sonny James)..266

Halloween, 1960...326

"Blue, Navy, Blue" (Diane Renay)...329

"Travelling Man" by Rick Nelson...404

College days..428

The Apartment...434

(You Were On My Mind . . . The Wee Five)..442

Lorraine...453

Epilogue...465

"In Dreams, I am with you . . . . Roy Orbison

Her short, dark red bangs were slightly tossled. The rest cascaded down each side of her head;

Spilling onto her creamy bare shoulders. Dark green eyes opened and closed with each of his thrusts.

Moans of pleasure escaped from her mouth, framed by luscious cherry red lips.

Sometimes, she bared her perfect white teeth. Their lips would meet in lustful frenzy,as their passion increased. When their lips parted, he'd lower his head to her perfectly formed breasts and kiss each one, saving the nipples for last. As he caressed each hard nipple with his tongue and lips,her moans would deafen his ear drums.

The calves and ankles of her legs crisscrossed across his lower back, keeping him inside her. He could tell she was beginning to "crest". She began to grind against him, urging him on; his thrusts increased.

"OH MY GOD!!!!!! He moaned, "YES, YES, YES" She cried!!! "Oh No. it can't be!!!" he cried. "What??"

She asked. "OMIGOD!!!! DON'T STOP!!!! She moaned. "I have to" He sobbed. "Why?" she asked. "I don't believe this" he said. "NO!!! she cried, squeezing her legs and thighs closer Against him. "I have to pee." He said. "WHAAAT??? She cried! YOU'RE KIDDING! NOW????" "Afraid so" he said. "Damn you" she hissed. Her eyes wide open and boring into his. He raised

1

himself up. Her beautiful face began to fade; her body, too, and then she was gone. He was staring at his pillow.

He rolled, gently, out of the bed, so as not to waken Lorraine. He, quietly crept out of the bedroom; into the hall and down to the bathroom. "Damn!" he muttered to himself. He couldn't believe she was just a dream. She seemed so real, it all seemed so real. He hadn't had a dream like that in a very long time.

As he came back into the bedroom, he noticed the morning sun filtering through the bedroom curtains. He really wanted to climb back into the bed and continue the dream. He knew it was too late! He looked over at Lorraine, still asleep, on her side of the bed. "How could she have slept through all that?" he asked himself. He sighed and went back into the bathroom, to get ready for his last day of work, in the classroom.

After showering, shaving, brushing his teeth and combing his hair, he took a long look at his reflection in the bathroom mirror. "What the hell happened to me?" He asked, aloud. Lorraine had risen and walked past him, as he spoke. "what's wrong, dear?" She asked. "I used to be a real good-looking guy." He said.

She came up behind him and put her left hand on his shoulder and her chin on his right shoulder; looked at his reflection. "You still are!" She said. "No, no, I'm not!" he argued. "My temples are gray, my nose is larger, ears are bigger and I've got wrinkles!" "It's called age, dear." She said. "Get used to it. Besides, you don't look like a man in his 60's, a man, who's retiring today." "How old do I look?" He asked. "OH." She said," at least 15 years younger." "For real?" He asked. "For real." She said. "Now get out of the bathroom, so I can get ready for work." He left and went back to the bedroom, to get dressed.

In the bedroom, he stopped and looked at a picture of the two of them, on top of her dresser. They were a lot younger, when the picture was taken. She hadn't changed that much. She was a little heavier in her hips, now. Her, once, jet black hair had gray streaks in it. She, too, had developed some wrinkles. He didn't think she looked her age either.

Once again, he looked at his reflection in the bedroom mirror; he really didn't like it. As a younger man, and teenager, he liked his reflection. But not now. His mind was still sharp as a 20 year old male. His dream proved that to him. As he got dressed, he hoped the dream would return to him that night.

Once clothed, he, again, stepped in front of the mirror, over the dresser. Tan pants, neatly pressed with a light blue, dress shirt; button down collar. His light brown hair with graying temples. Long on the top and short on the sides and back. Just the way, he liked it. His reflection would have been that of younger man, if not for the gray and the wrinkles! He heaved a large sigh of resolution and vowed to avoid the mirror, as much as possible. He did ask himself, "why does age have to affect the physical and leave the mental longing for youth." He was thankful that he still had the ability to maintain an erection and make passionate love. Even though, the erections were not as big and hard as those of his teenage years. The days were long gone, when girls would marvel at his manhood. He heaved another long sigh and stepped back from the mirror and slipped on a pair of tan cowboy boots. He did not put on a tie!

He walked out of the bedroom, down the hall, down the stairs, and into the kitchen, of the three story townhouse. He turned on the coffee maker and walked into the living room and turned on the TV, to catch the local news. He went back into the kitchen and plopped two pieces of bread into the toaster. He got some butter out of the fridge, peanut butter out of the cabinet and a knife out of a drawer. He buttered the toast with the peanut butter and butter, poured himself a cup of coffee and proceeded to the living room to watch the morning news.

Lorraine made her entrance from upstairs, into the kitchen. She always looked very sexy, when she was made up and ready for work. Her thick black hair with some gray streaks, blended well, with her dark, Cajun skin. Her short body was still quite petite. Her long dress covered her magnificently curved legs. Her ample breasts and short waist were hidden by her suit jacket. She still looked adorable and very cute to him now, as did, they day, they met. She still had the deep, dark, brown, eyes and small nose and ears. He never got tired of looking at her. He was proud at what she had accomplished! From an Associate's Degree, to a Bachelor' and then her Masters! Now, she was in charge of a clinic! He, always said that she was a dynamite mixture of beauty and brains! He felt very happy that she had accepted his proposal many years ago!

She said, "I still can't get over how you like to put peanut butter and butter on your toast! YCCHH! I should think you would like more variety in your breakfast." "And a good morning to you, too!" he exclaimed. They had the same morning conversation for the past 37 years! "You know what? Just for that, maybe we'll go out for breakfast tomorrow, my first day of retirement." "That would be nice." She said as she got a cup and poured herself some coffee. She joined him in the living room and they watched the morning news, together.

He finished his breakfast and got up off the couch and went back into the kitchen. He rinsed out his coffee cup and put it in the dishwasher. Lorraine turned her head way from the TV and asked him, over her right shoulder, "Any special plans for your last day at work?" "Not really!" He said. "Already packed most of the stuff into the truck and brought it home and put it in the store room behind the garage. Just have some personal things to pack, from my desk. Not much to do. Kids won't be around, as this is the last day of school, as well." He continued, "guess what? I won't have to work this summer. My first check should arrive in July." "Lucky you!" She said. He sensed some resentment in her voice. He went on "I've been working all my life, ever since I was thirteen years old!

Lorraine got off the couch and came up behind him. Her right hand on his right shoulder and turned him to face her. They hugged! She said, "I'm sorry. You have a great day. No guilt. You've worked hard; and it's time to relax." He nodded and gave her a kiss as she reached around him and placed her cup on the sink. "UGH!" peanut butter breath!" She hissed. "Sorry!" He said as she headed for the front door. He turned and looked out the kitchen window, as she drove her Subaru, off to work. He glanced over to the big, brand new red Ram pickup truck in the parking lot. "This is really it! Wow! Where did the time go? I can still remember the days, months; years, as if they happened yesterday. How is that possible?"

The morning sun beams were streaking through the stately Pines, as he walked out of the townhouse and across the lot and climbed into the cab of the truck. Once, behind the wheel, he put the key into the ignition and turned it on. He liked the sound of the 306 horses "roaring" to life! Something told him to turn on the radio and turn the dial to an "oldies" station. It didn't take him long to find one. He put the gear shift into "drive" and headed out of the parking lot. He began to sing with the song, on the radio.

(1955—"Rock Around The Clock . . . Bill Haley And The Comets)

He was thirteen years old, when he first heard the very song he was singing along with, "Rock Around The Clock, by Bill Haley and The Comets. Teenagers, in the very early fifties, were carbon copies of their parents. At least, he was. The clothes that he wore were the same styles as his father. Dress shirts, corduroy pants, wingtip shoes. The only clothes that weren't copies, were dungarees and T-shirts and sneakers, sometimes called "Tennis shoes." There were two colors of sneakers, black or white. The styles were high top or low top.

He, even, had to use his dad's Vasoline oil, on his hair. His haircut resembled his dad's too. Then, there was the music! Big bands, Patti Page, Frank Sinatra, Tony Bennett, Perry Como, Dean Martin, Nat King Cole, The Maguire Sisters, Ink Spots, Mills Brothers, The Lennon Sisters, Dinah Shore, Kay Starr. Even though he enjoyed listening to it and that one of his favorite songs was Nat King Cole's "Walking My Baby Back Home". It really didn't "talk" to him or "move "him.

The only excitement, in his young life, were his brother's pinup books and pictures. Magazines such as, "Flirt, Esquire, Snappy, Tempo, Nymph, Brief, Teaserama, and Jokes (cartoons)." Sex was very exciting to his young mind and body. He would sneak some of the books and pictures, out of his older brother's room and into his room, at night. He would place the magazine on his pillow, lay on his stomach, while looking at the pictures. It was during this "ritual" that he began to notice a "strange sensation" come over his body. His penis would stiffen. The sensation would intensify, when he put his hands on the headboard, of the bed, and pull himself towards it and then, push himself away from it. One night, while looking at a picture of completely exposed breasts, he increased the tempo of his "rubbings". The "quickened" pace resulted in an explosion, of sorts, that gave him the most incredible feeling of pleasure! He lay on the bed, with a complete sense of release and ecstacy. Followed by a wet mess! He knew he couldn't sleep in the wetness. He thought he might have "peed" in the bed, but the feeling was unlike any sensation, he got from peeing! He got out of bed, changed his pajamas, crept down the hall and got a towel out of the bathroom. Crept back down the hall, to his bedroom and put the towel over the damp area of the sheet. In the morning, he would strip the "soiled" sheet, towel, and pajama bottoms and put them on the floor of his closet.

When he got home from school, he would get the pajama bottoms and sheet, out of his closet and sneak them down into the basement and put them in the Bendix washer. He didn't know how much soap to use, so he put just a little in and ran the washer. He would do the same thing, every day, after school, before he went out, to the ball field, to play. He never asked him mom about them, but always found fresh sheets and pajamas, in his room.

The noise of the 'creaking' bed would get louder and louder. He was, at the point, where he needed to do something about the bed. He tried "oiling" the springs, but that didn't work. His dad, once questioned why three small cans of "oil" were missing, from the basement. He said that he didn't know. He had disposed of the cans, deep down inside the trash barrels, under the back porch. He was at a loss as to "enjoy" himself, without casting suspicion on his actions, from the other members of his family.

Then, one night, he found that by touching himself, and stroking "it". He got the same fantastic results. He, also, realized, that by lying on his back, he no longer soiled the sheets, just himself and his pajamas. Then, by simple deduction, he would place the towel over his penis and eliminate the mess on him and his pajamas. The only thing that got messy was the towel. He, also, found that performing his act was best done in the afternoon, after school. His mom thought that he was in his room, studying, but couldn't understand why his grades hadn't improved. He seemed to be obsessed with his discovery of masturbation, and the wonderful, fantastic sensations, it gave him.

He was in junior high school, when he really began to notice the girls. It was because they were beginning to develop breasts. The girls would wear tight skirts and tight V-necked sweaters. He could not help but notice them. They, sometimes, would catch him staring at them and their chests. The worst part, for him, was the effect it had on his penis. That part of his anatomy seemed to develop a "mind": of its own. It would harden, almost without any thought, from his brain. It would stretch the confines of his briefs and pants. Many was the time, he thanked God for large textbooks and notebooks, that when carried in front, would hide his "obvious" predicament.

It was a Saturday morning, sitting across from his dad, at the breakfast table, that he noticed an advertisement, in the lower right hand corner of the newspaper, his dad was reading. It was an ad for a movie. The ad showed two girls, with ripped skirts, halfway up their legs and torn blouses, revealing most of their breasts. He thanked God, that the table top hid his "excitement!" He had to know the name of the movie! His gaze went from the girls, to the top of the ad. "Blackboard Jungle." He made up his mind, then and there, that he was going to see that movie!

After breakfast, he left his house and went down the road to his friend John's house. He told him about the ad in the newspaper. The two of them decided that they would make plans to catch an early afternoon bus and go to the theater. He would break into his "bank" and take some money from his "caddy" and "pinboy" money. He wasn't supposed to take any of the money, except in extreme emergencies. He decided that the movie was one of those emergencies! They planned to meet in front of his house. After lunch, he went home and tried, in vain, to find the newspaper. He was unsuccessful! He looked all over the house, even in the wastebaskets and trash barrels. His father must have taken it with him. He was edgy. All he could think about was that "sexy" ad!

At last, it was time to eat his lunch. He was so excited, he barely ate any of the muffins and soup. He went back up to his room and put on a dress shirt and a nice pair of pants. He combed his hair and went downstairs. "Wow! Look at you!" his mom said. "What are you up to on a Saturday afternoon? You look like you are going to church or school!" "Movies" was all he could get out of his mouth. He was afraid to tell her that he was on his way to see a movie with naked girls, in it.

He and John met in front of his house. He checked his money and decided that he had enough, for the bus trip, there and back, and for the movie and some popcorn and a coke. They, quickly, walked to the bus stop. They had a difficult time containing their excitement. It seemed that the bus took forever to get them to the next town, where the theater was. When the bus finally got there, they were the first ones off the bus. They, practically, ran to the theater ticket window. Once, inside the theater, they found seats close to the large screen. They didn't want to miss anything! Especially, the naked girls! The lights dimmed as the black and white newsreel came on. After the newsreel, came the colored cartoon of Porky Pig. After the cartoon, were the words, in huge red letters, "OUR FEATURE PRESENTATION". The words faded into black. Music filled the theater. Music like they had never heard before! "One, two, three o'clock, four o'clock, ROCK"! It was electrifying! It captured their souls; moved their fingers and feet! The music rocked their world! When the music faded, into the black and white movie. They groaned! They didn't want see naked girls in black and white! They sat through the whole show. They felt cheated! There weren't any naked girls! But, that music kept going and going around, in his head! They sat through the newsreel and the cartoon, again, just to hear the music! Once the music faded, they left the theater and went looking for a record store. He had to have that song! They looked and looked and, finally, found one! They went inside and up to the counter. They asked the man, behind the counter, for the "Blackboard Jungle song." He told them it was called "Rock Around The Clock" and no he was completely sold out! He said he couldn't keep the records in the store. That as soon as they came into the store, they would sell out! They left the store, completely devastated! At least they knew the name of the song.

They walked back to the bus stop. As they waited for the bus, John said that maybe, just maybe the record store, in their small village, would have it. When the bus stopped back in their village, they got off and practically ran to the store. The man had only three copies left. He was glad that he hadn't bought popcorn and a coke, in the movie. The record cost him, his last 99 cents! The man handed him the small record with a large hole in the middle. He asked the man, "how do I play this?" The man called it a 45 rpm record. That it was the newest thing in records. The man held up a small yellow plastic disc that could be snapped into the center of the record, allowing it to be played on a record player. John bought a record and a disc. He asked how much did the disc cost? The man said "ten cents." He asked John to loan him ten cents. John gave him the money. Happily, they walked out of the store, with the records. They headed to his house, which was the closest.

When they got to his house, they went straight into his living room and over to the hi-fi. He lifted up the lid, turned it on and took other records off the spindle. He took the record out of its paper package and inserted the yellow disc into the hole. He placed it on the turntable and put the needle to it. When it began to play, it sounded "funny". Not at all like the song, in the movie. He took the "arm" with the needle off the turntable. He looked at the needle and ran his thumb over it. The needle sounded fine. Then John, who was looking at the turntable, said "It's the speed! Moved the lever to 45 rpm and try it!" He did as John instructed. He put the needle back onto the record. It was the same song! They played it over and over! They learned the lyrics and tried to dance to the "beat."

John had taken his record and disc and gone home. He had gone upstairs to his room and got a dime and gave it to John, before John left. His older brother, Dave came into the living room and watched as he tried to dance to his new record. "Pathetic!" Dave declared. "That's a jitterbug record." Dave went over to the hi-fi and stopped the record. Dave started the record, from the beginning. Dave taught him how to do a jitterbug. He kept playing the record and practicing the jitterbug, long after Dave left the room.

Even though he became quite proficient at the jitterbug, he still refused to go to any of the school dances. When his mom asked him why he wouldn't go to the dances, he told her that he did not have any of the "cool new" clothes that many of the kids were wearing. Most of the guys were wearing the latest styles, just for teenagers. Those were "tan, polished chino pants, button down collared Ivy League shirts, loafers instead of wing tipped shoes. That all changed, for him, Christmas of 1955. His Christmas gifts consisted of new clothes.

He received 4 Ivy League button down shirts, two solid and two pinstriped. Four cotton polished slacks, two tan, one light blue and one pair of black. Another box contained a pair of black loafers, while two others contained a pair of brown loafers and a pair of white bucs. He was, finally, going to be one of the "cool" dressers. With some of his Christmas money, he bought a yellow V-neck, long sleeved sweater, and a soft light blue button down sweater. He couldn't wait for school to start, so he could show off his new "duds."

As it turned out, he didn't have to wait for school to start. He got invited to a New year's Eve party. His friend, John knew about the new clothes and invited him. John had gotten a new record player for Christmas. It played 45's. John was able to stack ten records on the large spindle and did not have to go and change one record, at a time. When one record was finished, the arm would swing out of the way and another record would drop down and the arm would come back to the new record and lower the needle to it. With his new clothes, he had officially become a 50's teenager!

When "Rock Around The Clock" began to play, on the turntable, he asked a "cute" brunette, standing near him, to dance. She said that she didn't know how. He said, "just follow me!" She did pretty well! Soon, other girls were asking him to teach them. Soon everyone was jitterbugging! He was the "star" of the party! No longer did he harbor feelings of inferiority. The party got over around 10:30PM. They were, after all just thirteen years old! He did manage to "garner" three New Year's Eve kisses. 1955 ended on a great note, for him!

2003

The last drive to the high school was completely uneventful. No slow ups due to construction, no tie ups from accidents. He, even, caught three green lights. He surmised that listening to the oldies station must have relaxed him and caused the drive to be so easy.

Today should be very easy. There shouldn't be any students around, as today was the last day of school. Exams were over; report cards were being mailed out, yup, no students should be around. As he pulled into the back faculty parking lot; backed into his parking space. He noticed three students, three of his students, waiting by the back door. He turned off the truck, got out, and locked it. As he approached the large black, rear door, he said, "Good morning." They returned his greeting. "Why are you guys here?" He asked. "We came to help you clean up." One answered. "Okay" He said. He stuck his door key into the lock and unlocked the large door and pulled it open. The kids went in first. They walked down the hall, towards the TV studio, as the big door shut behind them. When they got to his room, he unlocked the door and the kids, again, went in before him; turned on the lights. One "student" went to his coffee pot and prepared the coffee. One went out of the room, to the office, to get his mail and newspaper. The other three went into the studio and started to unplug the three big cameras. "Where do you want to store these?" they asked. "in the storeroom." He answered. They unlocked the wheels after unplugging the cables and began to push them out of the studio towards the storeroom. One of the girls, "Sandy" told him his coffee was ready. He started to the back of the room, when the other girl, Jill came back into the room with his mail and newspaper. The other three stored the cameras and then went back into the studio and secured the camera cables. All he had to do was get his coffee and sit at his desk and read the paper. "You guys really don't have to do this.' He said. "We know" said James, one of the boys. "We want to." "Well, He replied. "I appreciate it, but I would think you would want to be anywhere but here, like the beach or something." "there's always time for that," Sandy said. "Okay guys, thanks!" he said. He open desk drawer and took out a pen; open the paper to the puzzles and began to do the Word Jumble. He didn't notice that the kids gathered into the control room. Just as he finished the Jumble, the TV came on in his room. He looked up and saw his picture on the screen. There were words underneath the picture, "Goodbye Mr. Chips, We love you and we will miss you. We wish you a long, happy and healthy retirement." A large lump appeared in his throat. He couldn't speak; tears came into his eyes. Just then, his fellow teachers entered his room, along with some students. They stood around him and applauded! The Vice Principal told them that everyone was invited to his office, around noon for cake and punch. Then they left as quickly as they had arrived. His "students" turned off the equipment in the control room. They told him that everything was secured and put away in the control room. He, literally, had nothing to do. The kids left and said they would be back at noon. He bid them goodbye and said he would see them later and, again, thanked them.

His friend, Tony, the CAD teacher, who had the room next to his, stayed behind. He went to the back of the room and poured himself a cup of coffee. He came back to the large desk and drew up a wooden chair. They had been friends for many years. They started at the Junior High School level together, and went to the high school level together. They found they both enjoyed NASCAR races and music of the 50's and 60's. It seemed that wherever one of them was, the other was there, too. In fact, the rest of the faculty termed them "the Dynamic Duo." They always worked together putting together a senior video yearbook. Theirs was a strong bond! Each attended their daughter's weddings; attended stock car races together. They barely talked about his leaving. "We're still going to the races, this summer, aren't we?" Tony asked. "Of course!" he responded. "Good!" Tony said and then left him alone to do his crossword puzzle. He couldn't concentrate on the puzzle. He got up from the desk and went into the store room. He found an empty cardboard box. He brought it out of the store room and placed it on top of his newspaper, on the desk.

The only things left to pack, were the personal things, in his desk. He began to open drawers and fill up the box. Once the box was full, he began to sift through it and look at all the things that he had accumulated over the years. There were pictures of his students, pictures of fellow teachers, pictures of his kids and his grandkids and artifacts from his past. He found an old tube of Brylcreem. He held it in his hand and began to think back, into the past, of his life as a teenager, in the fifties.

1956-1958 . . . A Teenager In Love . . . Dion

February,1956. He trudged through six inches of heavy wet snow, to the record store, in the square, to buy Carl Perkin's record of "Blue Suede Shoes." It was Guy Mitchell's record, "Rockabilly, Rock" that turned him to Rockabilly. He had already purchased Jimmy Bowen's "Party Girl". Rockabilly was a combination of Country/Western and Rock and Roll. He played those records more often than those of Bill Haley. He felt "moved" by the rockabilly sound.

It was the Spring of 1956, at the age of 14, that he saw a movie, that starred Marlon Brando as the leader of a motorcycle gang that took over a small town. It was the way Brando was dressed that grabbed his attention. Brando's sleeves of his white t-shirt were rolled up to his shoulders. A pack of cigarettes were encased in one of the t-shirt's rolls. His dungarees were rolled up at the bottom, showing his black motorcycle boots. He later learned that the boots were really called "engineer boots."

Brando looked and acted "cool." He, even, took note that Brandos' pants were slung low on his hips, not up on his waist. He decided that he, too, wanted to look "cool." His parents would not allow him to wear dungarees and a t-shirt to school. After school was different. With money from his "piggy bank" he had his Mom drive him to the store that would have the boots. He was set.

For school, he wore his "Ivy league styled clothes. After school, he wore his "Brando Look". His friend, John, was not into the "Brando" look. They didn't spend a lot of time together. John attended a private school, while he attended a public school. He was in the town square, when he met Carl, a friend he had known since elementary school. Carl was into the "Brando" look, as well. They began to spend a lot of time together, after school. It was Carl that introduced him to the world of hot rods and customized cars, Hot Rod Magazine, more pinup magazines and, actually, smoking cigarettes. He, also, learned how to swear from Carl. The first word he used was "shit". The reason he took up all these habits, was that he believed they made him "cool". They spent many an afternoon, at Carl's house, being "cool."

Carl's older brother, Alan, would purchase the cigarettes for them. He couldn't decide which brand he liked best. He tried them all, L&M's, Kents, Pall Mall's, Winstons, etc. He didn't care for Lucky Strikes or Chesterfields, because they didn't have filters. He didn't like getting bits of tobacco in his mouth. I t took him a long time to learn how to inhale and when he did, he, also, learned how to blow smoke rings. He really felt "cool", especially around girls.

When summer vacation arrived, He spent almost all the time at Carl's. Alan had bought a 1946 Ford sedan. He and Carl spent a lot of time, helping Alan customizing it. They stripped the chrome insignia's from the front hood (nosed it) and from the trunk (decked it). They lowered the rear end and replaced the mufflers with glass packs. The car looked very cool and when he went down a hill or slipped the car from third gear to second gear, the pipes would make a loud rumbling sound.

When they weren't helping Alan, with the car, they were at the playground, down the hill, from Carl's house. He would arrive on his bike, with his ball glove, sneakers, and bat on his handle bars. They would play baseball most of the day. In those days, it wasn't organized, no umpires, uniforms, just a bunch of kids getting together, choosing up sides and playing. If there was a dispute about a play. "do over' would take care of it. He either played first base or right field. They would play ball for most of the day. The only break would be to go home and have lunch and then go back to the field and either continue the previous game, or start a new one.

He and his folks would spend Saturday nights watching Jackie Gleason. It was July,1956. Gleason was "off" for the summer. Instead, The Dorsey Brothers Big bands were on. He joined his parents and watched the show. About halfway through the program, a young man named Elvis Presley was introduced. He had dirty, greasy blonde hair, with long sideburns. He strummed his guitar and sang a rocking rockabilly song; girating his hips to the music. He was mesmerized watching Elvis. Elvis performed two songs. At the end of the second song, he received warm applause from the audience, which consisted of people of his parent's generation. His father looked at him and made the statement that "that guy won't go far!" he disagreed and said he thought that Elvis was the signal that the big band era was coming to an end. At the end of the show, the announcer said that Elvis would be back the following week.

The next week, when he was introduced, the audience went absolutely wild! The audience consisted of teenagers, mostly girls. He could barely hear Elvis sing through all the screams. He would see

Elvis, again during the year. On Steve Allen's night show, Milton Berle's show and then on Ed Sullivan's show. Each time, the audience was filled with screaming teenage girls. Elvis was called by several names, "Hillbilly Flash",Elvis the Pelvis, and "Swivel Hips." After his first appearance, his hair had become jet black. The last time he appeared on the Sullivan Show, the censors took over and "blacked out" his hip swinging. It didn't hurt his career, at all. Elvis's records soared off the shelves. "Heartbreak Hotel", "I want you, I Need You, I Love You", "Don't", "Money Honey", "Love me Tender", just to name a few. He bought every one of Elvis's records, along with Buddy Holly, the Everly Brothers, and Little Richard. Watching the girls react to the Rock and Roll guitar players, he decided to learn how to play the guitar. His parents didn't mind him learning to play the guitar, but his Dad said a strong "NO!" to his having a DA haircut, and sideburns. He kept his hair long enough for a DA and combed it into one when he was at Carl's house.

One afternoon, he and Carl were walking, on the sidewalk, by the stores. He held a cigarette in his left hand and a yoyo in his right hand. He heard an adult remark that he couldn't make up his mind, whether to be a teenager or a little kid. He thought he was being "cool." That remark caused him turmoil. He wanted to be the one guy, the girls wanted. Unfortunately, the girls still avoided him.

Carl's brother, Allen, was very appreciative of their help. He, always, told them the car wouldn't look and sound as it good as it did, if it weren't for their help. To show his appreciation, he drove them to school. They would always get to school early, to get a good parking space. They would sit in the car, listen to the radio and watch the girls walk by. One day, Alan decided that he wanted to move the column shift to a floor shift. They tore up the floor board between the dashboard and the seats. They dismantled the column and attempted to make the switch. Unfortunately, they couldn't find a shifter.

For over a month, they searched for the right shifter. Meanwhile, Alan used a pair of vice grips to shift the gears. To this day, when he hears "I'm Available" by Margie Rayburn, he can still taste the exhaust fumes, that came up through the nonexistent floorboard of the car.

He began to dread Friday afternoons. For some reason, his Mom and Carl's Mom signed them both up for ballroom dance lessons, at the local community center, just what fourteen year old boys wanted to do. His Mom took him to the store, to buy his dark blue suit, white dress shirt, blue tie, black socks, black shoes, and worst of all, white gloves. They were not allowed to wear loafers. Had to be black wing tipped shoes. They were both, literally dragged by their hands to the first lesson. Once registration, by the front door, their Moms departed. They were looking for an easy exit, when a stern, rather large woman grabbed then by the arms and escorted them into the hall; directed them to chairs, on one side of the large hall. Once seated, they looked around at all the other poor, frightened, uncomfortable souls. Some of whom, he recognized from school. They acknowledged each other like prisoners of war. Each one looking, trying to find an easy escape. His attention was directed across the hall. Girls!! Girls of all shapes and sizes, sitting in large prink, white and light blue, or green dresses, down to their ankles. Bows in their hair, that matched the color of their dresses, black leather patent shoes, and, also, wearing white gloves. They all looked so prim and proper. His eyes took in each girl, from head to toe. Most were "flat chested" and offered no sexuality at all. They all had their hair tied in the back in a bun. They all looked as if they would pass out, if they ever knew he smoked and swore. His eyes found her in the third row. She seemed to be the only one who showed the existence of breasts, even in that dress. If he had to dance with one, it would be her.

Mrs. Ferguson, the extremely large teacher, stood on the stage, facing the empty dance floor. She stepped up to the microphone,in her large dress, that stopped just above her shoes; introduced herself and her slim-looking husband. His job was to play the record player, and demonstrate to the boys, how to approach the girls and ask for dance. The first thing she showed them, was how to bow, and ask for the dance. The boys would put their left arm behind their backs, extend their right hand towards the girl and bow from the waist. The girls would respond by doing a curtsey, bending their knees and putting both hands on each side of their dress and slightly pulling the dress away from their sides. The boy was, then, supposed to "May I have this dance?". The girl had to answer. "Yes, you may." Whether they wanted to dance with that particular boy or not. It took may practices for the students to accomplish the "deed."

Mrs. Ferguson, then announced, that they were going to learn the waltz. He kept his gaze upon the girls with the breasts. Little did he know, that he had competition. It appeared that every boy in the class had the same idea. The boys were told to get off their seats and walk to the girls and practice, once again, how to ask for a dance. He walked, quickly, towards the girl. When he reached her, a shoving match began between at least four boys. Mrs. Ferguson, obviously annoyed, announced that the boys return to their seats. She, then, announced that there were plenty of young ladies. They were, again, told to approach the young ladies. Again, he headed for the same girl. This time, he did not get to her in time. He ended up face to face with a small redheaded flat chested girl in a light pink dress. He swallowed hard and bowed to her and extended his hand and asked for the dance. She curtseyed and offered her white gloved right hand. He could tell she sensed his disappointment. They moved to a spot on the dance floor and faced each other at arms length, waiting for Mrs. Ferguson tell them what to do next.

Mrs. Ferguson bellowed her displeasure and had them all return to their respective seats. "A second chance." He thought to himself. Mrs. Ferguson admonished the boys for "rushing' towards the girls and told them that they were to walk normally, a lot slower, towards the girls. She picked up a whistle and said when she blew it the boys would walk towards the girls. "Fat chance." He thought. The teacher brought the whistle to her lips. He bolted from the chair and was halfway across the floor, headed for his first choice. "YOU!!! STOP!!" She yelled. He came to an abrupt stop. He was alone on the dance floor. All the other boys were still in their seats. She ordered him back to his seat. He wished there was a hole in the floor, big enough, for him to drop into and disappear. She told him when she blew the whistle, all the boys, but him, would walk to the girls. Only when all the others were paired, could he walk to the remaining young lady and take their place on the dance floor. He sat with his eyes fixed on the wooden floor by his feet. Then, Mrs. Ferguson told him to rise and go to the girl on the other side of the floor. He got up and walked over to the very same red-headed girl, that he was paired with the first time. The completed the "asking' ritual and proceeded to a spot on the dance floor. They did not speak to each other. They spent the rest of the lesson learning where and how to put their hands and arms and the box step to waltz. He did apologize to her, for his actions and for the pain he caused her. He could tell the pain had to be quite sufficient, by the scuff marks on the toes of her patent leather shoes. When the lesson, finally ended, he and Carl could not wait to get to their respective homes and get out of their "monkey suits."

Each week, the lessons got a little better. He found he was attracted to one girl. She was a thin blonde girl with bright blue eyes, and even though, she was flat chested, She had a laugh that made his heart race. It was obvious that she was attracted to him, as well. He found out, after one lesson, that she was the daughter of a radio/TV; movie celebrity. He was awestruck, the night he got to meet her father.

They learned many different ballroom dances. The Foxtrot, Samba, Tango; Mambo. They also learned some "fun' dances, ie: Bunny Hop and Hokey Pokey. He and Carl actually started to look forward to the Friday afternoon lessons. Carl had found a dance partner, as well. They continued the lessons all through junior high school and into the first year of high school. As they grew, so did the girls. Most of them developing well and the party dresses turned into strapless gowns. He always had a dance partner, even when it was ladies choice. Once, two young ladies even argued over which one had reached him, first, for a dance. That was a new experience, for him. He was, actually, sad, when the dance lessons ended.

Rock and Roll was in full swing, at the end of 1956. Elvis was dubbed "The King of Rock and Roll", followed at a close second was Pat Boone. Others who followed were, Fats Domino, Little Richard, The Diamonds, Lloyd Price, Jackie Wilson, The Platters, Four Preps, The Moonglows, etc. Rock and Roll was being played on most radio stations. Christmas of 1956, he received a wonderful gift of a portable radio. It was green, with one large AM dial and an on/off switch on the top, near the handle; a volume dial on the right side. It was powered by one very large battery inside the plastic case. He took everwhere he went, except school. The music became an important part of his life, as more and more new songs and artists exploded on to the music world.

(Young Love ... Sonny James)

1957 was going to be a year of milestones, for him. But not until the fall. He still was without a "real" girlfriend. Even though he was attracted to several girls from the dancing school, his lips had never touched theirs. There was a girl, younger than he, that lived down the road from him. He had known her ever since elementary school. She was a year younger than he. Her name was Joan. She had dirty blonde hair, always styled in a pony tail. Fair skin and dark blue eyes. He always considered her to be very pretty, even though mother nature had passed by her chest. He even thought she was quite "cute" at times. They were friends, nothing more. And never really showed any interest in each other. They attended different junior high schools. Their indifference to each other came to an abrupt change, one Saturday afternoon.

He and Carl were sitting on the small wooden fence in front of his house. Joan and a friend of hers, from school came walking up the road, towards them. They stopped and began to talk. Joan introduced Janice to them. Janice seemed to take quite an interest to Carl. Carl had just finished drinking a bottle of Coke. Janice made a "flirty" remark about the now empty glass bottle. Carl accepted the "flirt". Joan wanted To know if he and Carl wanted to walk with them to the playground. He and Carl said "sure". Janice continued the flirting with the bottle. "What are you going to do with the bottle?" She asked. Carl said, "Oh I guess I should throw it away." Janice said, "I've got a better idea." She looked at Joan. Joan said. "like spin the bottle?" Janice said, "why not?" He did not know what the girls meant, but Carl did and said. "let's go!" The four of them walked towards the woods, behind his house, instead of going to the playground. The girls walked ahead of the boys as Carl asked him if he had played the game before. He told Carl that he hadn't, so Carl explained the game to him. He, immediately became excited. Carl noting his obvious excitement, said "you better settle down or you'll scare them away."

They found a clearing, surrounded by large pine trees. It was perfect. The guys found some small branches and swept the pine cones and occasional leaves from the spot, leaving a small clear circle. The girls sat on one side of the circle and the guys on the other. Carl put the bottle in the center and gave it a spin. When the bottle stopped spinning, the opening, pointed at him. "No good." Said Carl and gave it another spin. This time, when the bottle stopped, it pointed at Joan. They both leaned, towards each other and shared a small kiss on the lips. It was Joan's turn. She gave the bottle s good spin and when it stopped, this time, it pointed at him. She had a slight grin on her mouth as they leaned towards each other and shared a slightly longer kiss, than hers and Carl's. He then took the bottle and gave it a spin. It stopped, pointing at Carl. "definitely not good." He said. They all laughed. He gave it another spin and it stopped, pointing at Janice. They shared a light kiss on the lips. Janice then spun the bottle and it stopped at Carl. The kiss, they shared, was longer than all the others. As the game progressed, the kisses lasted longer and longer and became more passionate.

On one turn, Janice's spin stopped at Carl. She reached across the center and grabbed Carl's shoulders, knocking him off balance. Now Janice was a very sexy looking girl, with short black hair, dark green eyes; long legs encased in extremely short shorts. She had a well defined bustline, that practically popped the buttons off her shirt. Carl fell flat on his back. Janice was on top of him, in an instant. Their lips pressed together, legs and arms intertwined as they rolled around on the pine needles. He was completely stunned, by the sight. He looked at Joan. She had a look on her face that he had never seen before. Her blue eyes were half closed. She moved across the circle towards him, as he moved towards her. Their lips crushed together, as they fell to the ground. They began kissing and hugging. He wished she wasn't flat chested. They were not as "into" each other as carl and Janice.

As suddenly as carl and Janice had started, they stopped. He and Joan broke from a hug. The girls got up from the ground and brushed each other off. Janice's shirt was unbuttoned and he could see everything but her nipples. They were covered by her small bra. His excitement rose again. He looked over at Carl, who was zipping his fly up. The girls thanked them and then walked out of the woods, Janice, nonchalantly buttoning her shirt. Carl had a bif grin on his face. As he and Carl left the woods, Carl described how Janice's breasts felt to his touch and he knew she had put her hands on his penis. He felt the strong pangs of jealousy overcome him. Anger grew from the jealousy. All he got from Joan was kisses and hugs, nothing like what Carl got! Still, he developed feelings for Joan. He wanted to see her again! The next time, he did see her, she was walking with another boy. That was his first "heartbreak" experience. He hoped it would never happen, again.

The summer of 1957 was spent "caddying" on the local golf course, during the day. Some days, he helped Carl's brother, Allen, work on the old Ford. The exterior of the car looked great and the floor shift was, finally, in. The rumbling of the twin glass packs gave a great rumbling sound like no other car.

The Journey

As a reward for helping Allen with the old Ford, Allen, along with another friend, took him and Carl to the local drive in movie. This was yet another "first" in his young life, another milestone. It was a Friday night. The four of them headed to the show. He was excited. Carl, too, kept wondering if they would park next to a car filled with girls. It was still "light' out when they pulled up to the entrance. Each one paid their two dollars. Allen found a spot near the concession stand. He said it was the best place to park, because when the place filled up with cars, it would be difficult to find the car, in the dark. They all agreed, except Carl. He was searching for a car with girls. They weren't the only "early birds". A few other cars had pulled in behind them. Allen said the show would start in about an hour, when dusk settled in. He and Carl occupied the back seat. Allen had just placed the speaker on the side window and was rolling it up, when Carl noticed a pink 1954 Oldsmobile convertible pull into a spot, not too far from them. It was a real beauty. Customized, with fender skirts and a continental kit on the back. He was looking at the car, while Carl was noticing the girl, with the driver. She glanced over at them and then the driver looked over, turned his head and looked at the dash. Then the top began to rise up from behind the back seats. When the top reached the top of the windshield, the guy reached up and attached it to the top of the windshield. The, things got interesting. The guy and girls heads began to slip down in the front seat, out of view. Allen said, "It's not even dark yet; the show hasn't even started!" All eyes were "glued" on the Olds, hoping to catch a sigh of some of the action.

More cars began filling into the spaces between them and the Olds. Pretty soon, they couldn't see the pink Oldsmobile, but they knew it was there. Darkness enveloped the area. Allen said that the show was going to start real soon and that it was time for a food run. He and Carl were picked to go get the food. There weren't too many people at the concession stand. It didn't take them long to get everything. He was carrying the drinks and a pizza. Carl was carrying the popcorn and candy. When he got to the Ford, he noticed he was alone. "Where's Carl?" asked Allen. "don't know." He replied. "was just behind me a minute ago!" he got in, distributed the drinks and placed the pizza beside him on the backseat. They were trying to find Carl, in the darkness, when the show started. The screen lit up the parking area like a giant spotlight. It was then that saw what Carl was doing. He was at the Olds. Just then, popcorn flew up in the air, along with the candy and tray. Carl came running towards them, followed by an angry guy, trying to keep his pants from falling down. Allen, quickly, rolled down his window, replaced the speaker, turned the car on, put it in first gear and began to move forward, just as Carl reached them. He opened the rear door as Carl jumped in beside him, right onto the pizza box. Carl hit the gas and the car raced out of their "spot", with the other guy still running after them. He finally gave up. He must have realized he had something better waiting for him back in that pink Olds. Allen drove around, until he finally found another spot close to the other side of the concession stand. After cussing out Carl, they made Carl go back to the concession stand and replenish the popcorn and candy and pizza, with his own money. Then, when he got back, Allen turned the speaker volume down and they sat and listened to what Carl had done. It seemed that Carl decided to go to the couple and offer them some popcorn. He was standing next to the Olds looking in the driver's side window. The girl had her head in the guy's lap. He had his hands on the top of the back if her head. Her head was slowly going up and down. The guy's eyes were closed, until he opened them and saw Carl looking in. Carl offered them popcorn, but obviously they didn't feel the need to have any, at that particular moment. The four of them had a good laugh and then settled down, munching on the snacks and watching the rest of the show. It was the first time, he went to the drive in, with guys and the last time he would go to the drive in with guys.

He was a high school freshman, in the fall of 1957. Steve sat behind him in homeroom. They became good friends. They had only been in school a couple of weeks, when Steve asked him if he wanted to double date to the football game. He explained to Steve that he wasn't dating anyone. So, Steve set him up with his first "blind" date. She was a friend of his girlfriend. He said "okay". Another first, another milestone. Steve's sister, Martha, drove them to the stadium, where they would meet the girls. When he met "Nanette", he had misgivings. She was short and skinny with light brown hair tied back in a ponytail. Her nose was a little too big, to suit him. He asked himself," Why do I always attract girls who are flatchested?" She was, also, a talkative girl, very expressive. She did have a great sense of humor, though and the "date" went well. After the game, they walked to Steve's girlfriend's house. The four of them ended up in the finished basement of her house. Steve and his girlfriend ended up on one couch, while he and Nanette ended up on the other couch. Steve got up and went to the record player and put a Johnny Mathis album on the turntable. He asked to use the restroom. When he returned, he could barely see, in the dimly lit room. The "Twelfth Of Never" was playing. He made his way to the couch, where Nanette was waiting. He glanced over at Steve. Steve and his girlfriend were locked in a passionate embrace. He looked at Nanette. She had moved closer to him and he noticed she applied more lipstick to her pursed lips. He sensed she was wanting to be kissed. He sighed to himself and moved to her. The kiss was sweet and short, followed by a big hug. They spent the rest of the afternoon, kissing and hugging. After what seemed like hours, Nanette said she had to go home. He offered to walk her home, but she told him no, that she only lived a couple of houses down the street. Steve called his sister to come and pick them up. Nanette wrote her phone number on a napkin and asked him to call her. Another short, sweet kiss, on the lips, and they parted.

The next two weeks were spent talking with Nanette, on the phone. Then, she asked him to a dance (record hop) at her school. He accepted. The "old" blue suit, from dancing school, still fit well. His mother made him get a corsage for Nanette He had to call her and find out what color dress she was wearing to the hop. "Light blue poodle skirt ". She replied. He got her a white wrist corsage.

The Saturday night, of the dance, arrived. He was nervous. His brother, Dave, drove him to her house. When he walked up and knocked on the front door, her father opened it. He told him that Nanette would be there soon. It was the most uncomfortable he had ever been, in his life. Another milestone. Finally, Nanette entered the room. He gave her the corsage and she placed it on her wrist, They said "goodnight" to her parents and walked to the car. They had to both sit in the back seat of the car. She informed him that the dress had a hoop under it. She told him that when they sit down, he would have to place his leg on one side of the skirt to keep it from rising up. He agreed, His brother, said he felt like a chauffer. He apologized and explained why they had to sit in the back seat. When they arrived, at the school, she put her hands on both sides of her skirt as he took her by the arm and they exited the car and walked to the school gym. Once inside, she introduced him to her friends. They jitterbugged, waltzed, and strolled. There was no tango, nor foxtrot nor mambo. The D.J. played nothing but rock and roll. He really enjoyed dancing, She, finally, asked if they go sit down for awhile. He agreed. They made their way to a row of folding chairs that bordered the dance floor. She sat down, first, then he sat beside her. She moved her hand from her skirt as his leg took it's place. The hoop was behaving itself. They chatted with her friends. All was going great. Then came the announcement that refreshments were being served. He asked her if she wanted something to drink and eat. She said "yes." He was famished. He jumped up, without thinking, and started to walk, quickly, to the refreshment table. The scream reverberated off the floor, walls and ceiling, of the gym. He turned in the direction of the scream. All he saw was her legs and underwear! The hoop covered everything else. He just stood there, looking, in her direction. Two hands were desperately trying to capture the sides of the hoop and bring it down over her legs. Then came the laughter, all male voices. He knew he was in trouble, a lot of trouble. Her girlfriends, finally, helped her to bring the hoop and skirt down over her legs. She, and her friends, got up from the chairs and she ran out of the gym! He tried to go after her. One of her friends stopped him. "haven't you done enough?" She asked. He went back to the chairs and sat, waited for her to come back. After what seemed like an eternity, one of her friends, came up to him and told him that her dad has just picked her up and took her home. If he knew what was good for him, he would leave, too. He didn't need a brick to fall on him. He went to the hall and found a pay phone and called his brother to come and get him. "Is the dance over, already?" Dave asked. "It is for me!" he replied. He told his brother what had transpired at the dance. Dave, apparently thought it was very funny, because he laughed all the way home. He tried calling her, to apologize, but she wouldn't come to the phone. He found out, much later, that she was dating another guy; another friend of Steve's.

1957 ended much the same way as 1956. With the exception of, finally, meeting girls. Christmas of 1957, saw him with a pair of brand new ice hockey skates, gloves and a hockey stick. He couldn't wait for the ponds and rivers to freeze, so he could try them out. He went to parties at Carls' sans any girlfriends. He, actually prayed that the new year, 1958, would be a better year. It began as a "stag" year. He spent much of the month of January, alone, listening to music on the radio; buying records. Anew TV show premiered, on the weekday afternoons, "American Bandstand." His mother had caught him a couple of times, stealing cigarettes from her pack of Kents. So, for Christmas, he had also, got a carton of L&M's.

February, saw the rivers and ponds finally freeze. He tried skating, at a pond, near him, but the ice was rough, and made hockey playing, a real challenge, Cracks and large bumps made it practically impossible to control the hockey puck. Both he and Carl decided that there had to be a better place to play. A couple of days later, Allen told Carl that he heard about the river, in Auburndale, was not only smoother but had boards set up for hockey. They made plans to go to the place, the following Saturday. He was a little anxious about going there, because Nanette lived in Auburndale. He really didn't want to run into her. She would probably create a scene and scream and curse at him.

The Saturday arrived. Allan picked them up and they drove to the river. Allen parked the car and they walked to the clubhouse. It cost a quarter to get a locker, to store his engineer boots and wallet. He sat on a bench and put on his skates, gloves; grabbed his new hockey stick and headed out of the clubhouse, down the ramp and onto the ice. The ice was, just as Allen had said, smooth. Allen, Carl, Jimmy,Andrew, and him began practicing. Puck handling and shooting. The felt like they were on a real hockey rink, because of the boards and goals. They, also, took turns at being the goalie. After a while, other guys came into rink. Introductions were made and, pretty soon, a game was set up. Other skaters began to gather along the outside of the rink, to watch the game. When it was his turn to be goalie, he heard his name being called. He scanned the crowd. Suddenly his eyes found her. He hardly recognized her. She was wearing a large winter coat and a stocking cap, that covered her entire head. She smiled and waved a mitten covered hand. He, halfheartedly, waved back. He thought she had thrown something at him, it had just missed hitting him on the side of the head. It practically parted his hair and knocked his ear muffs askew. It didn't come from Nanette, it was the hockey puck. Luckily, it didn't go into the goal. His teammates admonished him for not paying attention to the game. He looked again and saw she was actually smiling at him. She, probably, hoped the puck would have hit him. The game went on for another half hour, before everyone decided to take a break. They vowed to continue the game, in a half hour. He and Carl skated to the clubhouse. He went to his locker and got some money to get a sandwich and a cup of hot chocolate. He and Carl got separated. He got his lunch and found a vacant bench. He sat down and began to eat. "Hi" she said. He turned, saw her next to him, and nearly spilled his hot chocolate over both of them. "Nice!" She said, sarcastically. She did seem genuinely happy to see him. He could not understand why. "I called many times to try and apologize for what happened at the dance." "I know." She replied. He then asked how things were with her and Sandy. "Okay." She said. Then she asked if he was dating anyone. "Nope!" he said. "Good!" she answered. "A friend of mine would like to meet you." "Oh?" he answered. He thought, to himself, probably another skinny, flatchested girl. "Look, I'm here to play hockey, that's all." He said. She said, "I know, but it won't take long, to just say "hi". She got up off the bench and told him that they would be waiting for him at the end of the ramp, on the ice. He was wishing there was a back door to the clubhouse, that he could sneak out and avoid the girls. He was still sensing that she was planning some sort of revenge. The others came up and told him they were heading back to the rink, to continue the game. He told them he would join them, when he was finished with lunch. He lit a cigarette, when he finished and started out of the clubhouse and down the ramp. He noticed a group of girls standing at the end of the ramp. They didn't notice him, as he walked towards them. Nanette appeared to be the only short, skinny girl of the bunch. One girl really stood out from the rest. Short, dirty blonde hair, spilling out from the sides of a stocking cap. His eyes scanned her really cute face and then his gaze drifted down to see breasts, he glanced at her figure. Even with the bulky sweater, he could tell she had breasts. He hoped she was the one he was supposed to meet. He got to the end of the ramp and stepped onto the ice. The girls didn't notice his presence. He cleared his throat, loudly. Nanette turned around and said "Hi, again." She then introduced him to Abby. He was pleased. She was the girl, he had noticed. The other girls drifted away and left the two of them to get acquainted. The usual questions were asked, ie:" Where do you live?, likes and dislikes, subject in school, musical groups, etc. Their conversation was interrupted by Carl. Hey!" said Carl. "The others are wanting to leave, You coming?" he really did not want to leave. Carl looked at him and then at Abby. He nodded to him, knowing he didn't want to go home. "Okay, see you tomorrow." Carl said. As Carl went up the ramp to take off his skates, Abby smiled at him. The two of them skated away from the ramp, still engrossed in conversation. Before they realized it, they skated all around the skating area. He looked at his watch and realized they had been slowly skating for almost an hour. He told her that he probably should get back to the clubhouse and call his brother for a ride home. They skated to the ramp. She said that she should probably go home, too. They walked up the ramp and into the clubhouse. He went to his locker and retrieved his boots. He joined her on a bench.

She, already, had her skates off and was putting on her snow boots. He glanced over at the place where the public phone was and noticed a large line waiting to use the phone. Abby looked at the line, too. "I have an idea." She said. "I only live a few blocks from here. If you want, you can come to my house and call your brother from there." He looked at her and smiled. "Okay. If you don't mind." He took a lace of each skate and tied them together. He then put the skates over his hockey stick. He kept the gloves on. Abby did the same thing with her skates and was about to put them over her shoulder. He took the skates from her and put them on his stick, too. She, again, smiled at him. He liked her smile. They, then, exited the clubhouse and began the walk to her house. Again, they were lost in conversation, when they, finally, came to her house. At the front door, he handed her skates to her and put his skates, stick and gloves on her front stoop, by her front door. "Can you take your boots off, too?" She asked. "You can put them just inside the door." He would have walked across hot coals, if she asked him to. He was beginning to have feelings, he never experienced before. Not with Joan, not with Nanette. She introduced him to her mother and then the two of the walked from the front hall, through the livingroom, and into her den. He took off his jacket and earmuffs as she turned on the TV. She turned her back, to him, and slipped off her bulky sweater. As she brought it over her head, she turned to him. Three buttons on her white blouse came unbuttoned, revealing at least 80 percent of her milky white breasts. Her bra covered only the bottoms and the nipples. She didn't realize what had happened, until she followed his gaze to her chest. She, immediately, turn her back again and buttoned the buttons. She looked him in the eye, as he lowered his head and apologized. ":What are you sorry for?" She asked. "For not turning away." He said. She responded, "That's okay, accidents happen." He sat back on the large couch, as she joined him. The space between them could have been occupied by two more people. Hopalong Cassidy was on TV. Her mom came into the den with some hot chocolate and crackers. She mentioned the phone was on a small table, in the livingroom. He got up from the couch and went to the phone. Abby helped him give directions to her house. He, then came back and joined her on the couch in the den. He told her that his brother, Phil said that it would take about a half hour, before he would be there to pick him up. Abby smiled. She seemed happy that they would have some alone time. Abby moved closer to him, on the couch, She could tell he was a little nervous." My mom's in the kitchen and my Dad's in the basement." She said. "In the basement?" He asked." He's in advertising and he works, in the basement. He says it's his sanctuary." "Oh," he replied. She was now pressing up against his side. She backed off, just a little. "I was at the dance when Nanette's dress flew up and covered her front, but not her underwear." "Oh God!" he moaned. He began to blush and told her how sorry he was for that incident. Abby began to laugh. "You should have seen the look on your face! It was priceless!" Then she said that it was Nanette's fault for wearing a hoop under poodle skirt, in the first place. "I mean, it was a record hop!" She said, "She didn't need to wear the hoop." He began to feel more at ease with Abby. They hardly looked at the TV. They became more interested in each other. Their eyes locked on and he felt a strong desire to hold her in his arms and kiss her. Fear of rejection swept over him, so he backed off.

Abby got up off the couch and went to the TV and turned it off. She, then, went to the record player and turned it on. The first record to fall down the large "45" shaft was Elvis's "Playing For Keeps." She turned towards him and asked if he danced. He said "of course." He got up off the couch and moved towards her. He put his right arm around her waist; his left hand met hers halfway. She moved in close. He felt awkward. She was too close. It was not the way Mrs. Ferguson had taught him to waltz. She laid her face against his cheek; brought his left arm, around her waist, to meet the other. Their bodies were plastered together and they began to sway to the music. "Mrs. Ferguson would have a cow!" He thought to himself. But he was enjoying the close contact. Her left and right arms and hands were around him, meeting at the small of his back. They continued to sway together to music. They were lost in their own little world. Just him, Abby and Elvis. When the song ended, she brought her head back and looked at him. Again, their eyes locked. She, slowly, closed her eyes and moved her lips towards his. Their first kiss was sweet and long. Her arms left his back and tightened around the nape of his neck. It was the sweetest kiss he had ever had. His head was spinning. They just stood there, in the middle of the floor in her den, kissing. Pat Boone was next on the turntable, "Love Letters In The Sand." They slowly parted their lips and began to sway to the music. They moved their lips to each other's cheeks. He was falling very fast!

Even though time had stood quite still for them, it didn't for anyone else. The blare of the horn, on his brother's car, snapped them back to reality, They had just pulled apart from each other, when her mother came into the den and informed them that his ride was there. Abby, immediately, went into the living room, to the phone. She came back with a slip of paper. She had written her phone number on it. Her mother had gone back into the kitchen. He and Abby held hands, as they walked to the front door. She only released his hand, so he could put on his ear muffs, boots and jacket. Outside on the front stoop, he slung his skates over his hockey stick and put the same on his right shoulder. He turned to thank her and, once again, their lips met. Even though it was a brief kiss, it practically sent him reeling and, almost, off the front stoop, to the ground. She turned and walked back into the house. He regained his physical composure, but his mind was in a fog of love. He made his way down the walk, to his brother's car. He opened the rear door and slid his gear off his shoulder and into the car. He, then, remembered his hockey gloves. They were still on the stoop. He ran up and retrieved them, hoping she would open the door, for one more kiss. She didn't. He walked back to the car, opened the passenger door and got inside. He put the hockey gloves beside him. "Looks like you had a great afternoon!" Phil said. "yup!" he replied. He was hooked by the "love bug."

For the next few weeks, every weeknight, they tied up the phone line, for over an hour. Saturday morning s, he would walk to her house, from his. It took about an hour each way. He didn't care. He'd walk over mountains to get to her and her luscious lips. They would spend the whole day together. Walking around the town, holding hands, stealing kisses, when they felt no one was watching. Sometimes, they would end up at one of her girlfriend's house; meet up with her girlfriend and her boyfriend. They would spend the time, listening to records, dancing and making out. Saturday nights were spent at the movies, in the balcony, where they never seemed to watch the show. They just couldn't get enough of each other.

One day, at school, Charley, the guy who sat in front of him, in homeroom, mentioned that he not only had his license, but his own car. Charley trying to find another couple to go with him and his girlfriend, to the Totem Pole Ballroom. Charley asked him if he was dating anyone. He responded that he was. "Well, what about it?" "You, two want to double date to the Totem Pole?" He said he definitely wanted to go. He would have to ask Abby. He got Charley's phone number and said he would call and let him know. He forgot to ask him, When? . . . Charley yelled over his left shoulder as they filed out of homeroom, for their first period class, "This Friday night!" The rest of the day, in school, wad a blur. All he could think about was Abby in a sexy gown, dancing and making out in the back seat of Charley's car. When he got home, he, immediately, went to his room; turned on his portable radio and paced around waiting for the time he could call Abby. He prayed, real hard, that her folks would let her go. He rushed through his dinner and, quickly, left the dining room table. He took the stairs two at a time, to get to the phone on the second floor. He had to dial the phone three times, because his fingers moved faster that the dial on the phone. Finally, he took his time and dialed perfectly. Abby's mom answered the phone and told him they had to have a short conversation that Monday night, because she was expecting an important call. He could barely contain himself, waiting for Abby to come to the phone. "Hi baby!" she said. "Hi!" he replied. Then, asked the all important question." Want to go out this Friday night?". "guess so." She said. "Instead of Saturday?" "Well, I guess we can do both nights." He said. "Don't think my folks will let me go out both nights." She answered. "Why Friday instead of Saturday?!" She asked. He took in a large gulp of air and let it out slowly, as he told her. "A guy in school, Charley and his girlfriend, are going to the Totem Pole this Friday night and they asked if we wanted to go,too." Nothing, she said nothing. The dramatic pause was tearing his heart apart. She said, "hold on, I'll be right back!" His hands began to sweat on the receiver. Beads of persperation formed on his brow. The wait was like an eternity. She came back on the phone. "How will we get there?" She asked. "Charley has a license and his own car." He said. "hold on, again." She said. This was killing him, minute by minute. When she returned to the phone, she asked, excitedly, "What time?" Damn! He thought. He never asked Charley. "Not sure yet, but I'll know in a minute. I'll have to call Charley and ask him." She whispered into the phone, "yes." He wasn't sure he heard right. "What?" he asked. "YES!" She screamed. His heart felt like it was going to jump right out of his chest! "I'll call you back in a few minutes with the time." He said. She told him to call tomorrow night, because her Mom needed the phone. He agreed and as he said goodbye, she whispered, "I love you!". She had hung up before he responded. His heart was racing, his body tingled, he was, deeply in love! Now, he knew she loved him, too. He had not known such happiness before. Certainly not with Nanette. He could barely contain his gleefulness as he went to his room. He opened his "bank" and counted his "caddy/bowling pinboy "money. He had saved well over a hundred dollars. The excitement of going on a double date with Abby, in a car, caused him to toss and turn most of the night. This was to be another milestone in his life.

The next morning, he couldn't wait to get to school and home room. When Charlie walked into the room, he practically ran up to him. "We're all set for this Friday night!" He said. Charley gave him a deer in the headlights look. "Friday night? What's Friday night?" he asked. He felt his heart sink to the old wooden floor, of the ancient brick building. How could Charley forget? Then, he saw the big grin spread across Charley's face. He could have slugged him, right there in home room, in front of everyone. He forgot that Charley had a weird sense of humor. "Great!" said Charley. "I'll need directions to your house. I'll be by around 6 PM Friday night. "he said okay and calculated that they would get to Abby's about 6:30 that night. "You know it's suit and tie only, right?" Her didn't but he did now. "What should the girls wear?" he asked." Something dressy." He said. He went back to his desk and found some composition paper and wrote down all the details. Charley sat down in front of his desk. "Be nice if the girls wore something low cut in the front, huh?" he said. He thought about Charley's statement and grunted "yeah". But, he knew he wasn't going to ask Abby to wear a low cut dress. That night, after dinner, he called Abby. She answered the phone, on the second ring. "Hi baby!" she said. "Hi back!" he answered. He loved it when she called him that. He gave her the details about the coming Friday night date. She asked him what color was his suit. The only suit, he had, was the one he wore to Mrs. Ferguson's. He would wear that one, sans white gloves. He told her it was dark blue, almost black. She said that was good. Because, her dress was light blue. He, almost, asked her if it was low cut. But felt it would not be a good idea. Then, they started talking about how exciting the date was going to be. She said she that she had never been to the Totem Pole ballroom before. He told her the same thing. Another milestone. She told him that he wouldn't be able to call her, for the next two night, because she and her folks were going to visit some cousins and that Thursday night she was going to be busy getting her dress ready. She told him she wanted to look extra special for him, so he wouldn't be embarrassed to be with her. He told her that she could wear a burlap bag and still look fantastic. She told him that he was the sweetest guy she had ever known. As they said goodnight, he, quickly, told her that he loved her, too. "Oh baby, me, too!" He went to his room wondering how many guys she dated, before him. Then, he felt, it didn't really matter, because he was talking her somewhere she had never been before. The rest of the week seem to drag by and the nights were sleepless. Thursday afternoon, when he got home from school, he found his suit hanging, in his closet, wrapped in plastic. His mom had taken it to the dry cleaners. He went back downstairs, to the kitchen to thank her. "You're welcome. She said, then asked, "when do you plan to get her a corsage?" "A what?" he asked. His mom let out a big sigh and took off her apron, went and got her car keys. "Come on" she said. "We're going to the flower shop, in the square." "okay." He said. They went out and got in the car and began driving to the store. "Do you know what color her dress is?" His mom asked. "yeah, she said, light blue." Good, then at least we don't have to guess about the color of the corsage." When they got to the store, the clerk was very helpful and picked out a white flower, with very light blue little flowers around it. "Do you want one with a pin, so you can pin it on her dress or do you want a wrist corsage. He did not know the difference. Then, the clerk asked them. "Does the young lady have a bust?" He felt the redness enter his face. "yes" he replied. "Then a wrist corsage it is. It'll be ready after 3 tomorrow afternoon". His mom paid the ten dollars and ninety five cents and they left the store and headed home. He told her he would pay her back, as soon as they got home. His mom said "okay". He now felt that everything was falling into place for their fantastic date on Friday.

He couldn't wait till Thursday night. He called her right after dinner. "We should be at your house around 6:30." He said. "Morning or night?" She asked, with a chuckle. "Evening." He replied. "I can't wait!" She said. "Me either." He replied. They had never seen each other 'dressed up. "He was really looking forward to it. "I haven't had much sleep, thinking of you." He said. "I know." She replied. As they terminated the phone call, they both processed their love for each other.

Friday, at school, dragged on and on. He thought the day would never end. Charlie saw him at lunch and they went over the times again and parted with "cyas". When school, finally, let out, he ran to the car. Allen and Carl were late. He prayed that they didn't have detention or something. After what seemed like an eternity, he saw them approach the car. Even though his date was three hours away, he felt pressed for time and asked Allen if he could drive a little faster. "You know the cops are out on the roads on Friday afternoons." He said, "you want to pay the speeding ticket?" "No!" he sighed. He slunk back against the back of the back seat and closed his eyes and tried to envision what Abby would look like. When Allen dropped him off at his house, he jumped out of the car and ran into the house. He ran straight up the stairs, two steps at a time and down the hall to his room. There, on his bed, was a new white shirt with a button down collar, the kind he liked. Next to the shirt was a brand new light blue tie. He went to the top of the stairs and yelled to his Mom, "Thank you!!!" "You're welcome!" she hollered back. "We need to go and pick up your corsage." She said. "Oh yeah!" he yelled back. He went to his room and opened his bank and took out ten dollars. He left the room and went down the hall, down the stairs and joined his Mom, in the kitchen, as she grabbed her car keys and they went out the back door to her car. He handed her the money, he owed her for the corsage, as they drove to the store.

The clerk had just finished up with another customer, when they walked in. She went to the back of the shop and returned with the corsage. It was sitting in a plastic box. It looked beautiful! The clerk told him not to open it, until he gave it to his date. He promised. He cradled it in his lap, as if it were a fragile, expensive work of art. When they returned home, his mom put it in the refrigerator, to keep it cool. It was two hours until Charlie would be there. His mom insisted he have a sandwich or something to eat. He told her he wasn't hungry. She said the worst thing that could happen was to have his stomach start growling while they are dancing close. That made sense to him. He sat down and had a ham and cheese sandwich and some chips and milk. He checked his watch. An hour and a half till Charlie showed up. He thanked his mom and went upstairs, to his room. He took some black shoe polish out of his closet and sat on the edge of the bed and began to polish his shoes. It took longer than he thought it would. He must have put enough polish on them to last for days. His hands were covered with the black stuff. That made him decide to get in the bathtub. They didn't have a shower. He took off his clothes and walked to the bathroom. He turned on the water and tested it to make sure it was just the right temperature. He didn't like it too hot nor too cold. When he decided it was the right temperature, he got in. he took the bath soap and began to scrub the polish off his hands. When that was done, he proceeded to wash the rest of his body, especially behind his ears. His mother, always told him, to wash behind his ears. The last thing was shampooing his hair. He used more than the usual amount of shampoo. He wanted to be absolutely sure that every part of his body would smell clean. He leaned his head back into the soapy bath water and submerged till only his face was above the water. He dunked his hair, again, just to be certain that all the shampoo was gone out of his hair. He, then sat up, pulled the drain plug and climbed out of the tub. He grabbed the large bath towel and began to dry himself off. The last part, to dry, was his hair. He rubbed and rubbed his head until he was sure the hair was dry. He wrapped the towel around his waist and walked back to his room. He proceeded to get dressed. He checked his hands, to be absolutely sure they were devoid of any black shoe polish. He slipped the plastic cover off the shirt, took out all the pins, tissue paper, and cardboards and unbuttoned the shirt. He laid the shirt on the bed and put on a fresh pair of briefs and black socks. Then, he put on the dress shirt and buttoned it up, all except the buttons for the collar. Next, he donned the suit. Pants first, then the coat. Everything still fit. He took off the coat and laid it back on the bed. He took the tie and, standing in front of his mirror, attempted to tie a Windsor knot. He finally got it right, on the fourth try. He adjusted his belt, so the buckle was at the center of his pants and shirt seam. All lined up just right. The tie bar! He couldn't find the tie bar!!! He looked in his dresser drawers, on the top of the dresser, on the floor, beside the dresser; even under the bed! He began to panic! Then, he remembered, it was attached to his other tie in the closet. He looked in the mirror, all was right, except his hair. He walked back down the hall to the bathroom. He stood in front of the mirror and was looking at the tube of Brylcreem, lying next to the can of Right Guard Aerosol deodorant. Deodorant!!!! He forgot to put the deodorant under his arms. He loosened his tie and unbuttoned four top buttons of his short. He popped off the top of the can; put the can inside his shirt to his right under arm and pushed down on the nozzle. He had never used this product, before, so he was not used to icy cold spray that soaked his skin and underarm hair.

He held his right arm out straight, so the wet would not hit his shirt. When it started to dry. It began to sting! He danced around the bathroom floor, waving his arm and asking himself, "why didn't he put this shit on right after his bath?" The stinging didn't last long. He, then proceeded to deodorize the left armpit, but with a lot less spray. The cold and the stinging were not as bad as the right armpit. He rebuttoned the shirt and the buttons for the collar and readjusted his tie. Again, he checked out his reflection in the mirror. All was well, except the hair. He picked up the Brylcreem and unscrewed the top and put some of the white oily goo onto the palms of his hands. The ad said a little dab will do ya, but he wanted to be sure his hair stayed in place, so he put two dabs. He ran his hands through his hair, along the top, the sides, front and back. He grabbed another towel and whipped his hands free of the goo. Then, with his comb he proceeded to comb the sides back to the back of his head. His hair was not long enough for a "real" D.A., but long enough to make it look like the beginning of one. Then, he combed the top back and brought it forward just enough to cover the top of his forehead. It looked good. A cross between Tony Curtis and Elvis. He walked back to his room, sat on the edge of his bed and put on the newly polished black shoes; laced them up. OH No!! he looked sat his fingers. Black polish had returned to his fingers!!! He ran out of the room, down the hall, to the bathroom and, again, scrubbed the polish off his fingers. With a huge sigh, he checked himself out in the mirror. He was satisfied, he looked good. He went downstairs, to wait for Charley to drive up to the house. His mother said he looked very handsome and wished he would go to all that trouble for dancing school. He looked, at his wrist, to check his watch. NO WATCH!!! He forgot his watch!!!! He ran back upstairs to his room and retrieved the watch. It read 5:55PM. Charley would be there in five minutes. He went to the refrigerator and took out the corsage. He checked his back pocket to make sure his wallet and money were there. They weren't!!! He put the corsage on the kitchen table and went back upstairs and got his wallet from the top of the dresser and, then, took sixty five dollars out of his "bank", and put it in his wallet. He went back downstairs, to the kitchen and picked up the corsage. Another huge sigh and he was ready. His mom helped with a "checklist" he, finally had it all together. He, even, splashed some of his brother's Old Spice Cologne on his face. It was 6 o'clock; no Charley.

6:15PM, A horn signaled that Charley had arrived. He checked his hair, one more time, in the hall mirror. He said goodnight to his folks and went out the door to the car. He opened the car door and slid in next to Charley's date. He recognized Cheryl, from school. She had long, dark brown hair, cherry red lips, greenish eye makeup. A cute face; at a quick glance, he noticed a low cut light green dress, cut low in front, revealing enough cleavage, to show she had ample breasts. He said hi and quickly moved his glance to the front and looked out the windshield. Cheryl giggled. She moved closer to Charley as he started up the green and white Dodge and began to drive to Abby's house. He learned from Cheryl, that this was hers and Charlie's first dress up date, as well. They had talked about it, a lot, but did not want to go alone and when Charley found out that he was dating someone, that was when Cheryl told him to ask, if they wanted to double date. He told her, he was glad that Charley mentioned it. He had to talk with her, while looking out the windshield, as if he was driving. Every time he looked in her direction, his eyes went right to her cleavage. He hoped, in a way, that Abby's dress would be low cut as well, but he, also, hoped it wouldn't be. He did not want her to get angry at him for staring at her cleavage. It was like a double edged sword, a catch twenty two, mixed emotions. He heaved a sigh and went back to looking out the windshield. Charley turned the volume up on the radio and they all began singing along to "Don't be Cruel" by Elvis. Cheryl had gotten so caught up, by the music, she was unaware that her dress had hiked up above her knees. Now he really had to concentrate on not looking at her, but several glances at her cleavage and thighs had an obvious effect on him. He placed the corsage directly over his crotch and tried, in vain, to cross his legs. He began to pray hard, to himself, that his "excitement" would cease by the time they got to Abby's.

It was just before 6:45 PM, when they pulled up in front of Abby's house. His "problem" was ebbing slowly like the tide. He opened the car door and slowly exited the vehicle. With corsage in hand, he trodded up the walk to her front door. The corsage was still conveniently placed in front of him. He knocked on the door. A tall, burley, man opened the door. He looked very mean and threatening. "Yes??" Her father asked. "Hi," he gulped, "I'm here to pick up Abby." "And just who are you??" her father bellowed. He introduced himself and, meekly, added that he and Abby had a date. Her father let out a belly laugh and ushered him inside the house. "Abby will be down in a minute, have a seat in the living room. Her father was just what he needed to fix his problem. Her mother was sitting in an easy chair, by the fireplace, with a book, in her hand. She took off her glasses and remarked how nice he looked, in his suit. He sat on the edge of the couch, looking at her parents, as her father sat down in an easy chair on the other side of the fireplace, facing her mother. "When we were younger." He said, "We use to go to the Totem Pole, all the time. All the big bands played there, for example, Glenn Miller, Glen Gray, Benny Goodman, Artie Shaw, The Dorsey Brothers, Duke Ellington; Count Basie. Yup, those were the good old days, good times." He just nodded. His tongue seemed to have gotten so dry, that speech was impossible. "Here she comes, now." Her mother said. He stood up and turned as Abby stepped into the living room. She walked past him and kissed her parents good by and then turned to face him. He was blown away!! She was a vision of total beauty and sexiness!!! Her light brown hair was coiffed just enough to cover her ears. Her bangs came down to just above her eye brows, which gave her an expression of coyness. She had just the right amount of makeup that accentuated her beautiful face, her lips were colored in dark, luscious red. Her light blue, off the shoulders gown was cut low enough to show just the hint of cleavage. Enough to trigger the imagination, but not enough to cause him obvious embarrassment. He almost let out a slow wolf whistle, but her father's stern glare, at him, made him think better of it. He walked up to her and d handed her the corsage. She was thrilled! He leaned into her left ear and whispered. "You are absolutely drop dead gorgeous." He stepped

31

back as her mom helped put her corsage on her wrist. He, silently, thanked his mom for thing of the wrist corsage, instead of one that would have had to be pinned on. Her father had left the room and came back in with a small jacket and draped it over her shoulders. They said their "good nights" and went to the front door. As they walked down the walk, towards the car, he exclaimed, to her, "you take my breath away, you are so very, very, pretty!". She took his hand and squeezed it tightly. When they got to the car, he opened the rear door and helped her get in. Then, he slipped in beside her. Introductions were made and the four of them settled in as Charley started the car and headed for the Totem Pole Ballroom. She turned to him and told him how handsome he looked and she loved his Old Spice. He told her, that he was aching to hold her and kiss her, but that he didn't want to mess up her hair and makeup. "maybe we can do that after the dance." She whispered, to him. Once, again, he had to cross his legs.

He couldn't keep his eyes off her. He, again, whispered in her ear that he was the luckiest guy on Earth. He just knew she was the most beautiful girl in the world. She just squeezed his hand and smiled. His heart was bursting with love for her.

Charley parked the car in the parking lot, across the street from the amusement park. They all got our and waited for Charley to lock the car and they proceeded across the street towards the center of the amusement park, that housed the ballroom. They had to walk up a long sloping ramp to the entrance. Once inside, they knew why there was a slight incline. They guys paid the cover charge and they walked to the coat room and deposited Abby's wrap. They were on the top tier of a large amphitheater styled ballroom. The entire aisles were covered in carpeting. The aisles that led down to the polished dance floor were also carpeted. Each row had large backed sofas with a small coffee styled table. The sofas could hold three couples and insured privacy from anyone who was standing behind them. It was like a large movie theatre with high backed sofas instead of movie seats. The back of the large dance floor had a stage and on that stage was a seventeen piece orchestra. Behind the orchestra was a large silver shimmering scrim. The band leader was Bob Batchelder. The band was playing Glenn Miller's" Moonlight Serenade" when they found their sofa. As they snuggled in against the soft plush seats, Abby snuggled up to him. She wrapped both her arms around his left arm and laid her head against his shoulder. He felt like a Prince with his beautiful Princess. They sat for a few minutes, in awe of their surroundings. Then the girls both stated that the guys should go to the concession stand and get them all some cokes, while they, the girls, went to the ladies room. They would meet back, at the sofa, in a few minutes. It didn't take long for the guys to get to the concession stand, but the line kept them there, for a while. When the returned to the sofa, the girls were waiting for them. Abby, quickly, got up and took his hand, just as he placed the cokes on the table. "C'mon lover, let's dance." The four of them made their way down the aisle to the dance floor. The orchestra played "Stardust". He gathered Abby in his arms, both around her lower back. Her arms around his shoulders. They swayed, cheek to cheek. She whispered in his ear,

" I am so very much in love with you." He beamed, and answered, " I love you so much." He closed his eyes and drank in her perfume. The orchestra played four more slow waltzes, songs he had never heard of, but it didn't matter, he was hopelessly in love with the girl of his dreams. He opened his eyes as the last song ended. It was then that he noticed beams of light dancing off of them. He glanced up and saw suspended from the ceiling was a large crystal ball that reflected lights onto the dance floor and all who were dancing. She whispered , in his ear, again. "this is so wonderful! I've never been here before and I feel so very special!" He replied, "My first time, too and you are very special!" the orchestra began playing "Walking My Baby Back Home". He said, " my favorite song!" they began a slow jitterbug to it. He was thankful her dress was practically straight from her hips to just above her knees and NO HOOP!! They danced well together, like they had been doing it forever. When the song was over. They made their way back to the sofa. Charley and Cheryl were still on the dance floor. When they settled into the sofa, Abby cuddled up close to him and with her right hand, turned his face to hers. They pressed their lips together for the first kiss of the evening. It was long and semi passionate (no tongue). They only parted their lips when they heard a loud "AHEM!" Charley and Cheryl had returned from the dance floor ." Plenty of time for that, afterwards" Charley joked. He hoped so.

The night went on with a lot of dancing and a lot more cuddling. Sometimes, there was more cuddling than dancing. He was in heaven! He prayed the night would never end. Abby and Cheryl made another trip to the ladies room. Charley leaned over to him and asked if he and Abby wanted to go parking in the DFA, afterwards. He did not knows what the DFA was, but he knew what parking was. "I'll ask her." He said. When the girls returned, they all headed for the dance floor. As he and Abby swayed, clinging to each other, he asked, "What time do you have to be home?" She said "before midnight." "okay." He replied. They said nothing else as they enjoyed the closeness of each other's body. Charley and Cheryl saddled up next to them and Cheryl said, " Abby and I have been talking. It's almost 10:30 and the last dance is at 11:30, but we'd like to go somewhere else. Somewhere, we can all kinda be alone." He drew his head back and looked at Abby. She nodded "yes." Charley said, "ok, after this dance, we'll get the coats and be on our way." When the music stopped, they briskly made their way, up the aisle. The girls made one last stop at the ladies room; the guys got their coats. They quickly made their way out of the ballroom and across the street to the car. Charley quickly unlocked it and they all got in. Once the heat enveloped them, Abby doffed her wrap and snuggled up next to him. He turned his face to hers and leaned in for the second kiss of the night. Their arms wrapped around each other, their lips pressed harder and harder. He moved his lips slowly around hers. She tightened her grip on him with her arms. Their bodies pressed tighter and tighter together. They didn't even notice that Charley had brought the car to a stop. Somehow, his tie and jacket came off. Their kisses lasted longer and longer, only to be interrupted by short gasps, for air. She seemed to "glow" in the dim light. He felt as if he was kissing an "angel". She was so very pretty! He was alone with her in the backseat of a car! This was such a new experience for him. Her perfume engulfed him and the taste of her lips, urged him on .He wanted more than just kisses and hugs, but his inexperience caused him to exercise caution. His "excitement" grew and he didn't want her to notice. He was making out with a beautiful girl in a parked car!   Another milestone.

He brought his mouth and lips back up to hers. This time their lips pressed together and then opened just enough for her tongue to enter his mouth. His tongue had nowhere to go, but into her mouth. She , moaned through their passionate kiss.. After a while, she moved beside him on the seat, both lying down, facing each other, arms around each other, bodies pressing against each other, lips locked, slightly opened as tongues danced and swirled in each other's mouths. They stopped when they heard Cheryl say," hey you two, it's 11:45!" She sat up first and smooth out her dress. Then, he sat up and buttoned and tucked in his shirt. He put his tie back on, as Charley started the car. He noticed that Cheryl was actually putting her dress back on. Abby cuddled up next to him. "I hope you have a hankerchief." She said. "Why?" He asked." Because your face is probably covered in my lipstick" she said. Cheryl, once she had her clothes back on, turned on the overhead light. "You look like a circus clown!" She laughed. She took his hankerchief and spit on it and began to "wash" his face, chuckling all the time. He was so in love!!! The ride to Abby's house didn't take but about fifteen minutes. They got out of the car and walked up to her front door. They didn't care that front porch light was on. They ended the evening with another long passionate kiss and professions of deep love for each other. She went inside her house. He walked down the walkway to the car. He thought to himself. "Parking for the first time, first dress up date and first feel of breasts and pelvic grinding. Talk about first milestones!!!!"

He opened the rear passenger door and slid onto the seat. "You sure you want to sit back there?" Cheryl asked. " Yeah." He replied. "okay", Cheryl and Charley said. Charley started the car and proceeded to drive him home. He didn't tell them that he was afraid that, if he got into the front seat, next to Cheryl, she would have observed just how excited he was. " Besides" he thought to himself, "he wanted to be alone, in his thoughts about Abby. He took out the hankerchief and put it to his nose and drank in the aroma of her perfume.

Upon arriving home, He got out of the car, thanked them both for a great evening, and practically ran to the front door. He was thankful that no one was up to ask him a lot of questions about the date. He locked the front door, turned off the porch light and front hall light and made his up the stairs and down the hall to his room. He, softly, closed the door, to his room and crept over to his night stand and turned on the lamp, by his bed. He, quickly, stripped out of his clothes; grabbed his towel from under the bed, put the hankerchief to his nose; closed his eyes and reminisced about Abby as he brought relief to his aching body.

Afterwards, he disposed of the towel back under the bed and drifted off, still thinking of his fantastic date with Abby.

He slept in, most of Saturday morning. He was still "lost" in dreams of Abby and the previous night. It was past ten o' clock in the morning, when his Mom came into his room and picked up his clothes from the night before. He awoke with a start when she exclaimed. "Well, judging from your shirt and hankerchief, you had quite a date!" He could feel his face flushing. "Don't worry." She con" I won't tell anyone." "Thanks!" he said as he tried to open both eyes and shield them from the shimmering beams of bright sunlight that filled his room. He was beginning to wish his room faced West instead of East. "Looks like I'm going to have to use plenty of bleach. Oh and give me that towel under your bed. I'll wash that, too, with plenty of Clorox!" He could have died!!! "Come on!" She said, with a chuckle, "You think I didn't go through this with your brothers!" She left his room, still chuckling. He was mortified!!! How could he face her, now that she knew his secret. He closed his eyes and prayed that she would keep her word and not tell his Dad or his brothers. If she did, he would have to leave the house and become a "Lonely Teenager" like Dion. He never thought of his Mom as being "cool", but now that had changed. He got up and went down the hall, to the bathroom, to take care of "business" and get cleaned up for the day. He really wanted to call Abbey, but knew it was too early in the day. When he got back, in his room. He ,began to get dressed. He straightened out his bed and fixed his pillow. Holding it in his hands, he realized that Abby's "scent" from her perfume had rubbed onto it from his face. He held the pillow to his nose and ,once again, drank in her aroma. His mind raced back to the night before. He couldn't wait to see her and hold her in his arms again, to kiss her lips, and breasts and feel her body pulsate against his. "Phone!" his mother screamed. He, quickly, put down the pillow; put on his dungarees and t-shirt and went down the hall, to the landing, and answered the phone. He prayed it was Abby. It was Carl. Carl had just bought an old 1940 ford coupe. It was in parts, and he wanted to know if he could come up to his house and help him start to put it together. He told Carl he would have to call him back and let him know. He would rather spend the day with Abby. He hung up the phone and called Abby. Her mom answered and told him that Abby had just left the house and was going to Nanette's to spend the day. She told him that Abby should be home later that afternoon. He thanked her and asked her to please let her know that he had called. She said she would and they hung up. He called Carl back and said he would be up after breakfast. He hung up the phone; went back to his room and put on his socks and engineer boots and went back to the landing, down the stairs to the kitchen and ate breakfast. When he finished eating, he got up and disposed of his dishes in the sink and told his mom he was headed to Carl's for the day.

Joan's family had moved from the house, down the street, to the house across the street from his. Even so, he rarely saw her. Except for this Saturday morning. She and Janice were sitting on the steps of her front porch, as he went out the front door of his house. They both waved to him, as he started to walk by. He waved back. "Where are you going?" Joan asked. "Up to Carl's house." He answered. "Oh." She said. Then Janice asked, "Can we come with you?" He knew what the girls had on their minds. Probably more spin the bottle. If he wasn't passionately and madly in love with Abby, he would have said "yes!" but things were different. He was in love with Abby and the girls knew he was dating Abby. "Won't be much fun for you." He said, We're going to be working on an old car." "Oh!" They said, disappointed. Then Joan asked, "Are you and Abby going steady?" "No." he said. " well," She said, "When you and Carl get tired of working on that old car, why don't you come over? We'll probably still be here." "okay!" he said and started walking faster." She didn't want me, after the last time and now she does." He said, to himself. He wouldn't tell Carl, because Carl would want to drop everything and spend the day, makingout with Janice. That would cause a lot of trouble between Abby and him. He just knew Joan and Janice would definetly tell her.

He and Carl spent the day, sorting out all the small parts of the car and figuring out what went where. Even though he was working hard, his mind was on Abby and the date. Sometimes Carl got quite frustrated with him. "Do you realize you've cleaned that carburetor three times?" Carl said. He apologized and exclaimed that his mind was elsewhere. So, Carl gave him the simple task of replacing the old spark plugs with new ones. He kept wishing he was with Abby, instead of Carl. "Thank God, the week after next is vacation and we have all that week to work on this thing." Said Carl. "Vacation!" he said. His mind was racing with images of spending the entire week with Abby. He had completely forgotten about the upcoming vacation week. " I might be busy." He told Carl, "I'll let you know."

The sun began to set and they both realized they had worked the entire day without a food break. Carl invited him into the house for a sandwich. He thanked him, but declined. He wanted to get home and call Abby. He, almost, ran past Joan's house, for fear that they might still be sitting on the porch. He got to his front door and quickly went inside his house. Are you hungry?" His mom asked. "I've got chicken noodle soup and English muffins. They are all ready; you just have to eat them." He decided to eat and then call Abby. When he was finished, he went upstairs to the landing and picked up the phone and called Abby. Her Mom answered the phone, again, and informed him that Abby was still at Nanette's and would probably spend the evening. "I'll tell her you called." She said, and hung up the phone. Disappointment and a tinge of anger, coupled with frustration crept into his mind. He went back downstairs and into the den, to watch TV with the family.

Just as the Jackie Gleason show began, the phone rang. His Mom got up out of her chair and went to answer it. She called to him, "it's for you! I think you'll want to pick it up, upstairs." He jumped off the sofa and went to the stairs and went up, taking two stairs at a time. He grabbed the receiver and it almost left his hand. He juggled it and finally grasped it before it hit the floor. "I've got it!" he yelled to his Mom. " hello?" he asked. " Hi lover!" Abby said. "You have no idea how many people ,in the phone book, have the same first and last name as your Dad's. I've been trying to call you, for over an hour." Relief flooded over him as the anger, frustration and disappointment left his mind and body. He felt like the flood gates of despair had been opened. "Guess I should have given you my number." He said. "Would have helped and saved a lot of time." She replied. "I've been thinking about you all day." He said. "Me, too." She said. She, then asked him if his parents had noticed his shirt and hankerchief from last night. "uh huh." He said. "sorry!" She replied. "I'm not!" he answered. He heard another voice, giggling in the background. "You're not alone," he said. "No, I'm still at Nanette's." She replied. "Oh!" He said. He told her that he wished they were alone. "Sorry." She said, "I wanted to talk to you about February vacation." He told her that he had forgotten about vacation and hoped that they could spend a lot of it together. "Maybe." She replied, coyly. He was getting a little annoyed with the conversation. It appeared she was toying with him, because of Nanette. He wasn't expecting a "maybe". He heard her and Nanette giggle about the "maybe." He told her that if she didn't want to see him or be with him to just say so. He could ,always work on the old car with Carl. "Of course I want to see you!" She said. "Can we talk about this some more tomorrow afternoon?" he asked. "Why not now?" She asked. "I'd rather do it when it's just the two of us." He replied. " Okay." She said. "Great." He replied. "Are you okay?" She asked. She must have sensed he was a little annoyed. "I really missed seeing you, today." He said. Her voice softened. "I really missed seeing you, too." "I'll call you tomorrow afternoon." He said.

"Okay." She replied. They hung up without the love words. There was so much he wanted to say to her, but couldn't with Nanette listening in.

He called her around 2:30 that Sunday afternoon. This time they were both alone, on the line. They both expressed what a wonderful time they had had on Friday night. She told him that she just had to go to Nanette's Saturday to let her know how much she appreciated Nanette for introducing them. He said he was thankful, too. She, then , told him that she hoped they could spend every day of the vacation together. His heart nearly exploded. "Me, too!" he exclaimed. They would make plans during the week for vacation. They ended the call, professing their undying love for each other.

At school, he attempted to get Charley and Cheryl to double date, again. Charley explained the his car was going to be in the shop, all that week. He called her Monday night and explained about Charley's car. Even though she sounded disappointed, she suggested a movie, she wanted to see the following Saturday night. She, then, suggested that he could come over to her house Saturday morning, spend the day together, have lunch at her house and then, later, her Mom would drive them to the theater. He liked the sound of that plan. They knew that

Sunday would not be a good day, because of church and she always had relatives at the house on Sunday afternoons. He told her, he would think of something they could do on Monday. They hung up after, once again, professing their love for each other and that he would call her Monday night.

That Monday, at school, another one of his classmates handed him a party invitation. It was for Tuesday night, of vacation. It was his friend, Lenny's birthday. It was a skating party and would take place,at 4:30 PM on the pond, behind his house, with the rest of the party, inside and lasting until 10 or 10:30 that night. The invitation stated that it was "couples only" which was fine with him.

When he got home, that afternoon, he showed his mom the invitation and asked if she could drive him, first to Abby's, and then the party and then drive them back home. She said that she or one of his brother's would do it. After supper, he called Abby with the news of the party. She was very excited and told him it would be her first high school party. She, then, told him, that a bunch of them were going to spend that Monday together, just hanging around and she wanted him to come over, to her house, so they could spend the day together. He said that he would spring for lunch, for the two of them. So, Saturday, Monday and Tuesday were taken care, as far as plans went. She said she couldn't wait to be in his arms, again. He told her he missed her kisses. Again, the call ended with professions of undying love, for each other.

At school, he attempted to get Charley and Cheryl to double date, again. Charley explained the his car was going to be in the shop, all that week. He called her Monday night and explained about Charley's car. Even though she sounded disappointed, she suggested a movie, she wanted to see the following Saturday night. She, then, suggested that he could come over to her house Saturday morning, spend the day together, have lunch at her house and then, later, her Mom would drive them to the theater. He liked the sound of that plan. They knew that Sunday would not be a good day, because of church and she always had relatives at the house on Sunday afternoons. He told her, he would think of something they could do on Monday. They hung up after, once again, professing their love for each other and that he would call her Monday night.

That Monday, at school, another one of his classmates handed him a party invitation. It was for Tuesday night, of vacation. It was his friend, Lenny's birthday. It was a skating party and would take place,at 4:30 PM on the pond, behind his house, with the rest of the party, inside and lasting until 10 or 10:30 that night. The invitation stated that it was "couples only" which was fine with him.

When he got home, that afternoon, he showed his mom the invitation and asked if she could drive him, first to Abby's, and then the party and then drive them back home. She said that she or one of his brother's would do it. After supper, he called Abby with the news of the party. She was very excited and told him it would be her first high school party. She, then, told him, that a bunch of them were going to spend that Monday together, just hanging around and she wanted him to come over, to her house, so they could spend the day together. He said that he would spring for lunch, for the two of them. So, Saturday, Monday and Tuesday were taken care, as far as plans went. She said she couldn't wait to be in his arms, again. He told her he missed her kisses. Again, the call ended with professions of undying love, for each other.

All day, Wednesday, at school, he tried to think of something he and Abby could do together, on the Wednesday, of vacation. He was stumped. When he called Abby, that night, She told him that she was invited to a slumber party for the Wednesday night of vacation. She wanted him to come over to her house for at least the morning and early afternoon. "We can at least cuddle and watch TV." She said. "Okay," he answered, "What can we do on Thursday?" he asked. "I don't think much of anything. I won't get much sleep at the party and will probably be too tired." She said. To hide his obvious disappointment, he told her he promised to help Carl with the '40 Ford. Again, they ended the conversation with their "undying love" for each other. His heart felt very heavy. He really wanted to be with her all the time, to taste her kisses and love her body. He went to his room and did some homework and then, feeling tired, he got ready for bed. As his head hit the pillow, he thought he heard the telephone ring. It was 9:30." Who,' he wondered would be calling after 9? ". He heard his Mom pick up the phone in the downstairs hallway. She yelled out his name. he got out of bed, ambled down the hall and picked up the upstairs landing phone. "Hello?" He muttered. Whoever was on the other end, waited for the familiar "click" signifying that they were alone on the phone. "Hi Lover!" Abby said. She sounded quite excited. "My friend Annie called and invited us to a party at her house, the Friday night of vacation." He asked her which Friday night she was talking about. "This Friday!" She exclaimed. "Ok!" he said." What time?" he asked. "Be there around seven and oh, casual, but no dungarees. Wear what you normally wear to school." "okay." He said, again." We still have to make plans for the weekend, before we go back to school." He said. "We will!" She answered. As the conversation cam to it's normal close, she said something that really took him by surprise. "What are you doing now?" She asked. "Talking to you." He responded. "No, silly, I mean after we hang up." "Going back to bed." He said. "Wish I was with you right now!" She said. "Do you mean, what I think you mean?" He asked. "Maybe." She said with a giggle in her voice. "Good night, Lover, I love you!" "I love you, too!" he said. Her comment drew an immediate response to the front of his briefs. He hung up the phone and made a hasty retreat to his bed.

He was filled with mixed emotions about vacation week. He would call her again, after school, to get the directions for the party. He, also, needed to think what to do the weekend before school starts. Do they go out Saturday or Friday night? He would rather go out on Saturday night. He prayed that the week before vacation would pass very quickly and vacation week to go by real slow, though, he knew it didn't work that way.

When he called for the directions, she told him they could not talk too long, because her father was waiting for an important business call. After she gave him the directions to Annie's house, she told him that she would be staying at Annie's for another slumber party. "Great!" He said sarcastically. "That rules out Saturday . . ." "No, it doesn't, "She said. Annie's slumber parties usually end up with everyone falling asleep around eleven. Especially after the party." "Oh, okay!" he said. "Good!" He, then, ended the call by saying he wished he could tuck her into her bed. She responded, with a whisper, "Me, too."

She hung up the phone before he could respond. He couldn't believe that part of their conversation. That was the first time there was even the hint of anything sexual between them. They had never even joked about sex. Even though they got "carried away" in the back seat of Charley's car, they never talked about it. He went back to his room, quickly. He did not want his brothers to see his "excitement". Excitement that was stretching the cotton material of his briefs. He would have to pleasure himself before he fell asleep or he would never be able to sleep.

Thursday and Friday really dragged, for him. Especially since he was unable to talk to Abby on Thursday night. Her mom said she had a test on Friday and needed to study. He told her mom that he understood and asked if she would tell Abby that he called and he would see her at the party. She said she would relay his message to Abby. He thanked her and hung up the phone. He spoke to his mom about getting a ride to the party and a ride back home. His mom said "okay. I'll sure be glad when you get your driver's license this year." He had forgotten all about it. "I'll need to practice driving a stick shift; your car is the only one with a clutch." He said. His Mom said that he should start practicing in the driveway, during vacation week. He was excited about that and not the kind of excitement that Abby caused.

Friday afternoon, after school, couldn't come quick enough. Allen dropped him off, at his house and, again, he made a beeline for the front door. Once inside, he raced up the stairs, two at a time, he was getting pretty good at it. He, quickly, doffed his school clothes and went down the hall, to the bathroom, to get cleaned up and get ready for the party. Once he was back in his room, he went to his closet and picked out a pair of clean and pressed chinos and a red and white (small) checkered shirt. The checks were really small. Putting on clean briefs, the shirt and pants, he picked out a black, sleeveless, v-neck sweater to put over the shirt. Next, came the black socks and black loafers. Now, it was time for the "Old Spice" cologne and then it was time to tackle the hair. More" Brylcreem" and work with his comb. He spent the next twenty minutes on his hair. He looked at his watch. It read five thirty. With a heavy sigh, he realized he had at least an hour before he had to leave. "Are you eating supper with us?" his mom asked. "No, I'm too nervous!" he replied. This was to be his first "night" party and first party with Abby. Another milestone!

He spent the rest of his time, sitting on his bed and listening to the radio and singing along. When the Diamonds "The Stroll" came on, he got off the bed and practiced doing the stroll. Exactly like it was done on American Bandstand. He thanked God and Dick Clark for the TV show. That show taught teenagers, across America, how to dance. At six fifteen, he checked his hair, one more time, in the mirror, fletched his arms against his armpits to make sure there was enough Right Guard deodorant. He was fine. He sure didn't want wet armpits. Everyone was finished eating. His brother, Dave offered to do the driving, instead of his mom. They got in Dave's '49 Mercury sedan. As they drove to Annie's, Dave told him that he was going back to college and could not have a car on campus. He asked him to start the car up, at least once a day, to keep the motor from freezing up in the cold weather. He said, even with antifreeze, if the car isn't run for a few minutes a day, it could still freeze up. He was thrilled, but he just said a "humble, okay."

He didn't arrive to the party until well after 7:30. His brother had to, not only get gas, but made several other stops, along the way. He was not in a good mood. He hated being late, for anything. He got out of the car and told his brother that he would call, for the ride home. He walked up to the front door and rang the bell. No one came to the door. He could hear the music and thought, "who could hear the bell through the music." He put his hand on the door knob, turned it and pushed open the door. He walked into the living room and ran into Annie's parents. "Party is downstairs." Her Dad (he assumed it was her Dad) said. "Just follow the music." That's exactly what he did. "Who Wrote The Book of Love?" by the Monotones directed him to the stairs that led to the basement. "Some basement." He thought to himself. It was like another floor of the house. Even in the dim lights, he could make out a dance floor with couples swaying to the music. He shifted his glance around, trying to find Abby. There were couches and easy chairs against the wall, occupied by more couples. He could just make out an opening that was well lit. He ventured towards it and found it to be a small kitchen. There was an array of differe nt foods on the counter and a refridgerator, that, as some guy opened the door, housed many bottles of cold sodas. Still, no Abby. "Maybe she hadn't arrived yet." He thought. He went to the counter and grabbed a small egg salad sandwich and then over to the "fridge" and got a coke. He popped the top with a bottle opener. He leaned against the counter and consumed the drink and sandwich. The Platters were singing "Only You" when he made his way back into the "dancing room." His eyes were adjusting to the dim light, when he saw her. She had been there the whole time, dancing with another guy!! He rubbed his eyes to be sure it was her. Anger began to swell up inside him. He walked up to the couple, swaying tightly with the music. He tapped her on the right shoulder, as she turned around, he yelled "WHY?" Before she could answer, he stormed back into the kitchen. She was right behind him. She put her hand on his left shoulder and spun him around. Before she could speak, he bellowed, "I thought you were my girl! I thought we were in love with each other! Why did you want me here?" She put her hand to his mouth and began to explain. "I was waiting for you. Gary's girlfriend isn't here, yet, either, and he just asked me for a dance. I am in love with you! As far as being your girl and you being my guy, we aren't there yet, because we aren't going steady!" by now several others had gathered in the kitchen and by the doorway to the kitchen. A short blonde girl pushed her way through the others and asked Abby if everything was all right. His anger subsided, a little. He saw tears begin to gather under eyes. He held out his arms and gathered her in. She came to him, willingly. The others began to disperse. She introduced him to Annie. He asked Annie, if the two of them could be alone for a minute. "Do you want to go steady?" He asked. "I don't know." She said. She asked him why would he want to go steady. He replied, "so other girls and guys will know that we belong to each other." "Oh" she said. "Are you asking me to go steady with you?" She asked. "Yes." He said and took off his high school ring, which he had just got two weeks before, and offered it to her. She looked at him and said "Yes!" He put the ring on her left hand finger. It was too big. She gave him a kiss and told him to wait in the kitchen, that she would be right back. She went into the dance floor and found Annie and Nanette and the three of them left the basement. Gary, the one she was dancing with, came up to him, in the kitchen and apologized. He then introduced him to his girlfriend, Kathy. Kathy wanted to know what was going on and Gary explained to her. She gave Gary a look that told him that she was not crazy about him dancing with Abby either. Kathy took Gary, by the hand, and led him back to the other room. He heard her say to Gary, "We have to talk." He was to learn that no guy wants to hear those words from a woman/girl. Especially one he is dating.

Abby, Annie, and Nanette came back into the basement. Annie turned up the lights. A lot of groans were heard from the easy chairs and couches. "I have an announcement to make." Abby went into the kitchen and took his hand and brought him into the room. They stood side by side, holding hands. Annie went on. "This is Abby and her boyfriend. They are, officially, going steady! So, ladies and gents, hands off." He couldn't believe the applause. Annie dimmed the lights and party continued. He and Abby started dancing to Pat Boone's "Love Letters In The Sand." Nanette danced by with Sandy and, even in the dim light, he caught her winking at Abby. "What was that about?" He asked Abby. "Oh, nothing." She said and gave him a big hug. The next song was Sam Cooke's "You Send Me." Abby noticed a couple get up off an easy chair, to dance. She steered them to the chair. She pushed him down into it and then climbed on his lap. She began to lightly kiss him all over his face and then their lips met. It was a long, tongue lashing passionate kiss. They hugged and kissed for a long time. With each kiss, she would move her hips against him, side by side and back and forth. He was afraid he was going to make a mess. She had to feel his excitement through her skirt. He wanted to bite the buttons of her white blouse and kiss her breasts. She would, only, allow him to put his lips on the outside of her blouse. He wondered if she could feel anything through her blouse. If she did, she wasn't saying anything. He did manage to get two buttons undone with his teeth and put his mouth to her cleavage. She moaned a little and then whispered, "You gave me your ring and your heart. I give you my heart and these. He was hoping she meant her breasts. She put her lips to his both sides of his neck. He felt a little pain, which only increased her hip movements and his lips to her cleavage. If this was "going steady" then he was all for it, another milestone.

They did very little dancing and a lot of "making out." With every kiss and hug, he wanted more. She had him remove his black v-neck sweater. Which he did, without question. She unbuttoned four buttons of shirt and ran her hands over his chest and flat stomach. He caressed the outer edges of her blouse and bra covered breasts as she began kissing where her hands were. They were really getting "hot and bothered" when Annie turned up the lights. "Hey, it's stroll time!" She yelled. Everyone lined up, guys on one side, facing the girls on the other side, forming two rows. The "Stroll" by the Diamonds started. They all began to dance, side by side as one after another couple "strolled" down between the rows. The song kept playing over and over until everyone had strolled down the middle. He and Abby didn't miss a beat. It was obvious that they had been "making out", as many of the other couples, because they had failed to button up shirts and blouses. Some of the girls showed a lot more cleavage than Abby. Some of the guy's zippers were down, also. Most of the guys, himself included, looked like they were wearing red rouge and lipstick and the girls were not wearing any lipstick. After the dance, the lights dimmed again and this time they joined another couple on one of the couches. Again, she took up residence on his lap. Before he knew it, it was time for the guys to think about leaving. Abby and Annie and some of the other girls went into the kitchen, to clean up. Gary and Kathy came up to him and, again, Gary apologized. He said," I understand, it's okay." "No." Gary said. "You were set up. Abby had this planned all the time. We waited until she saw you coming down the stairs. She told Kathy to hide in the corner. We started dancing. You were supposed to see us right away, but you didn't. You went into the kitchen. She was getting nervous; afraid you would go back up stairs and leave. Then, you saw us. "I'm confused." He said. "It was all a plan to get you to ask her to go steady." Gary said. Kathy nodded, in agreement. "You're kidding!" He said. Gary said to him, "Where do you think she had the tape and chain to hold the ring? Upstairs! That's why the three of them ran upstairs, to put your ring on her chain." "Wow! He said, "I was going to ask her anyway, this week." Gary said, "Well I don't think she knew that." He thanked Gary and Kathy for the information. Gary said, "I was afraid you were going to belt me in the mouth." "I thought about it." He said. He left Gary and Kathy and went into the kitchen. The girls were just about done, cleaning up. "Just had an interesting talk with Gary and Kathy." He said. "OH!" Abby said. He put his arms around her and snuggled up to her back. "I was going to ask you to go steady, anyway. You really didn't have to do what you did." He said. "You were? Really?" She asked. "Uh huh" He said. He had buttoned his shirt and put the sweater back on. She had buttoned her blouse. He was glad they did, because Annie's parents came into the kitchen and told them the party was over. He went upstairs and called his brother to come and get him. He went back downstairs and helped the last remaining guys help the girls clean up. When it was all done, He and Abby sat in one of the easy chairs. Annie and her boyfriend sat in one of the others. Nanette and Sandy sat on a couch. Abby was twirling the chain that held his ring. She announced to the others, that He knew what had transpired. Nanette was surprised and asked him if he was going to take the ring back. "No." He said and explained that he had planned to ask Abby, anyway. They all just sat, cuddled and listened to Johnny Mathis sing "The Twelfth of Never". A voice called from the upstairs, "somebody's rides is here!" they got up and proceeded up the stairs. It was his brother. "Great!" he told Abby. "He takes his time getting here, for the party, and races here to take me home!" They gave each other a kiss and a hug and he told her he would be at her house, in the morning. The other guys rides had just arrived, as well. They all left the girls and proceeded to their rides.

"Looks like you had a great time," Dave said. "Yup!" he replied. "We better stop at a gas station so you can use the restroom to clean the lipstick off your face." Dave said. "Thanks," he said. "How come we're not driving Abby home?" Dave asked. "The girls are going to have a slumber party." He answered. They drove the rest of the way, in silence, until they found a late night gas station open. He went inside the men's room and proceeded to clean his face. He looked, in the mirror, to check everything out and that was when he noticed the red angry marks, on his neck. He, then, remembered Abby's "gifts".

He got back in the car. Dave turned on the overhead light to inspect his "work". "Well, the lipstick is gone, but those "hickeys" won't go away too soon. "Dave said. He felt the red creep out of the collar of his shirt and along his neck to his face. "Hopefully, everyone will be asleep when we get home." Dave said. He replied that he hoped so too. Dave laughed, as he started the car, and headed home. He unbuttoned the buttons on his buttoned down collar and flipped the collar up around his neck.

He arose early Saturday morning. He went down the hall, to the bathroom. While brushing his teeth, he surveyed Abby's handiwork on his neck. Something had to be done to cover it up. After taking care of "business" in the bathroom, he toweled himself off and began to pick out the clothes that he would be wearing all day, with Abby. He rummaged through his bureau and found a black, turtle neck jersey that would fit perfectly. He put it on and, then, in the closet was a newly ironed white long sleeved short, with the pair of black polished chinos and black loafers, he looked like he was dressed to kill. He combed his hair and added the Brylcreem and then combed it again. Be surveyed his image, in the mirror, and decided he liked what he saw. He went to the top of his dresser and splashed some Old Spice on his face and a little behind his ears. He made his way from his room, down the hall, down the stairs and through the front hall, to the kitchen. He sat down just in time for his Mom to put the scrambled eggs and toast in front of him. "Well, don't we look nice! And smell nice! Is this a leftover from last night or new this morning. "New." He muttered, between bites. "I take it you are going to Abby's today?" She asked. "Yup!" he replied. "How are you going to get there?" She asked. "Walking." He replied. "Good." She said, "because I have a lot of errands to do today." He finished his breakfast and got up and made his way to the front door. "I know you think you are "Superman" she said, "but you better, at least, wear a jacket. "He went to the hall closet and took out his black and pink reversible jacket. He put the pink side inside, and the black on the outside. He bid his farewell and went out the door and started his long trek to Abby's.

The walk didn't seem to take the hour that it was supposed to. He cut across the local golf course, where he had spent many a summer, caddying. He was not concentrating on the walk, but rather on Abby. He couldn't wait to get into her house and join her on the couch, in the den for some more loving. When he, finally, made the turn onto Abby's road, his heart began to race, in anticipation, of what was waiting for him, in her house. He walked up her walk and knocked on the front door. Her mom answered. "They are in the den, waiting for you." She said. He started for the den, "they." He thought to himself, "they?" As he crosses through the doorway, Abby jumped up from the couch, "Hi Lover!" and gave him a big kiss and hug. Then she turned around and he saw Ann and Tom (her boyfriend) sitting on the couch. Disappointment flooded his entire being. "So much for being alone," he thought to himself. It appeared the four of them were going to spend the day, together, including Nanette and her boyfriend, Sandy. He was informed that the four of them were going to walk to Nanette's and then all of them were going to walk downtown. The girls left the room, to get their coats. Tom whispered, to him, "not my idea, pal, I, too, was hoping for some alone time". They both heaved a heavy sigh of disappointment and went to the front hall. They said "Good bye" to her mom and headed out the front door. As they walked down the walk, hand in hand, Abby stopped and let go of his hand. She stepped in front of him and unzipped his jacket and with both hands rolled the top of his turtle neck jersey down his neck, revealing the "hickeys". Anne giggled and Tom just smiled. "I do good work, for my first time." Abby said. He replied that he was thankful that the next week was vacation week and hoped the hickeys would go away before school started up, again. She rolled the turtle neck back up and said with a slight chuckle, "don't count on it. You just might have some more to deal with." The others just smiled, as she took his hand in hers. He wasn't sure he liked her to be in control, as she seemed to be. But, he enjoyed making out with her. As they walked, he held her back from Anne and Tom, "I thought we were going to spend the day, alone, just the two of us!" he said. "I'm so sorry, lover, but they showed up just before you did and I couldn't very well tell them to leave." She said. He told her he understood. She squeezed his hand as they continued to walk towards town.

They walked around the town and looked in the store windows. He and Tom traded jokes, which made the girls laugh. He realized he was having fun, just the same. Holding hands with Abby felt so good. He really felt that they were, indeed, a couple.

After a while, he looked at his watch and knew why his stomach was beginning to ache. It was lunchtime. They were supposed to head back to Abby's for lunch. They were headed towards the town diner and he mentioned that instead of walking all the way back to Abby's, they have lunch at the diner. Tom and the girls liked that idea. They went inside and found an empty booth. Tom and Ann sat across from them. The waitress came and took their orders. Abby's left leg pressed tightly against his right leg. She moved her left hand and placed it on the top of his right thigh. The initial contact caused a rush of "excitement" to his groin. "Damn!" he thought, he really wished they were alone back in Abby's den. He asked the girls, if they were too tired from the party and the sleepover, to go the show. They both replied that they weren't tired at all. Seems the girls only stayed up for a little while and all fell asleep rather fast. They ate slowly and talked about mundane things, that teenagers talk about. He told Tom about the '40 Ford Coupe that he and Carl were working on and the girls talked about American Bandstand and the couples, on the show, like Bob and Justine.

When they finished and the guys paid the tab and left the tip, they proceeded to walk back through the town. Abby had both her arms wrapped around his left arm. Ann had noticed the clock on the town hall was showing that they should walk faster, if they were going to make the later afternoon matinee. He and Abby really didn't seem to care about the time, they were lost in their own little world, stealing small kisses from each other. It wasn't until Ann mentioned that if they didn't get to the theater early enough, the balcony seats would all be taken. They began to pick up the pace, walking back to Abby's. he did not want to sit down in the area where there might be a lot of little kids sitting. Iut didn't take too long to get back to Abby's house. Her mother was waiting and they, quickly, piled into her car. She drove a little too slow, for him. He whispered in Abby's ear, that in a few months they would be alone in a car and he would be doing the driving.

Once, they got inside the theater, the girls practically ran up the stairs, to the balcony, while the guys stopped at the concession stand and loaded up on popcorn and cokes. The theater lights were still on, quite bright, as they got to the balcony. The girls were seated in the very last row. Tom made the statement that they might have a difficult time seeing all the show, from the back seats. Ann made a face and asked him if he was really interested in seeing the movie. Tom smiled and said, "guess not."

The lights were a little dimmer, as people filed into the theater. The balcony was filling up with fellow teenage couples. Four small kids ran up to the balcony and went to sit in some seats. One of the teenage boys got up and went to them and told them to beat it and go back downstairs. He told them that the balcony was "reserved seating only." Every one chuckled as the kids beat a hasty retreat back down the stairs. The guy turned around and took a bow as they all applauded his actions.

The lights disappeared into darkness. It was a short period of total darkness, before the newsreel started. It was all the time they needed. Abby snuggled up against him as he placed their popcorns and drinks on the floor in front of them. She took his right arm and draped it around her right shoulder and placed it on her sweater, that covered her right breast. She turned her towards his and their lips met. This was the kiss, he had wanted all day. A long, tongue lashing passionate kiss. He wished her top was off and that his hand was massaging a bare breast. She placed her left hand on his right thigh and then moved it to the place where his penis was straining against the polished cotton fabric of his pants. Their lips began to crush together, tongues swirling in each other's mouths. She massaged his penis, through the thin fabric, as he massaged her breast. He could swear he felt her nipple harden, through the sweater and her bra. His hips began to move to her fingers, as they sucked on each other's tongues. All of a sudden, the screen lit up, as the newsreel started. It was like they were sitting under a street lamp. They parted their lips and Abby laid her head against his right shoulder. Their hands stayed where they were, but the massaging stopped. He was in heaven!! It was as if they were the only two people in the world. This was his first time. In the balcony of a theatre, with the girl, he was in love with. Another milestone, in his life.

They nibbled on the popcorn and sipped on their drinks. They only released their hands from the previous positions, to consume their treats. Once, they had eaten and drank enough, they clasped their hands together and entwined their arms together. Every now and then, they would steal a long and passionate kiss. They spent more time kissing than actually watching the movie. Some "realists" might consider it a waste of money, but not him. During the second show, their passion intensified and they were locked in a passionate kiss and her left hand returned to his crotch and his right hand returned to her breast. He wished they were alone on a bed, making long passionate love. When their lips parted and they nuzzled each other's cheek, he whispered his wish to her. She gave his penis a short squeeze. She told him that she couldn't wait until he got his driver's license, so they could really be alone. They found each other's lips, in the dark, once more, and resumed another long passionate kiss.

All, at one, the darkness was shattered by bright lights! The movies were over. They released their hands and lips from each other and began to get ready to leave. She smiled and told him, he should visit the men's room and wipe off her lipstick from his face. They got up and left the balcony. She said that she was going to call her Mom and to meet him at the public phones. He said he had to call home,too and tell his Mom to pick him up at her house. He, then, ran for the men's room. When he entered the room, he went right to the mirror. A boy with a bright red face stared back at him. It took a lot of cold water soap and paper towels to clear his face from her lipstick. He, then went to the urinal and relieved himself. He left the men's room and met her at the phones. He called his Mom and she told him that his brother would pick him up.

The rest of the vacation week was spent, going to parties was spent at various parties. They would do some jitterbugging, but spent most of the time on the dance floor, swaying to the slow ballads. Their bodies were pressed so tight together, he was sure she could feel his "excitement". When they weren't on the dance floor, they were in a chair, or on a couch, in a dark area of the room, making out. The kissing and the petting getting more intense each time. If it weren't for his "nightly" masturbations, he would have been in serious pain.

After vacation week, their time together went back to Friday afternoons, Saturdays and Saturday nights. Weekday evening were spent on the telephone. They were both waiting for him to get his driver's license. Weekday afternoons found him, in his driveway, practicing driving his Mom's Jeep Wagon and his brother Dave's '49 Mercury sedan. He was getting quite proficient with a standard shift. It took him a while to get used to just how much gas to give the car, before releasing the clutch. The first few times were not very good for either car's tires. One of the first times, in the Mercury, he burned rubber halfway up the driveway. In his mom's car, he stalled it many, many, times, by not giving it enough gas.

In the middle of March, he had to give up seeing Abby, Saturday mornings. He was attending driving school. During April vacation, he spent every morning at driving school. Abby understood, because she knew that with his driver's license, they would be free to be alone and go places, alone, that they had never been. The old phrase that" absence makes the heart grow fonder" was so very true for them. Their phone calls came very close to "phone sex." When they were able to spend time, together, the passion was so intense that they would actually be afraid that they would not be able to control themselves and get in trouble. He made up his mind that when he got his license, he would, also, find a way to buy some condoms.

At last his 16th birthday arrived. He had a family gathering, at his house; Abby was there, too. After dinner and the blowing out of the candles and cutting the cake, he opened his gifts. His brothers gave him a carton of Parliaments cigarettes, His dad gave him a set of hair brushes, his mom gave him an extra set of keys to her car; Abby gave him a two bottle set of Old Spice., One bottle was after shave and the other, cologne. She whispered in his ear, "I better be the only one you wear them for."

His brother, Phil, drove them to Abby's house, after the party. They hid in the shadows of her front stoop and shared a long passionate goodnight kiss. He would be taking his driver's license test the next Friday. She gave him another good luck kiss, before they parted. On the way home, Phil remarked how happy he and Dave and their mom were going to be, not having to chauffeur him around anymore. He could barely contain his excitement about driving. Of course, the main idea, was so, he and Abby could, finally be alone, in the car. He knew she was just as excited as he was. Thoughts of "parking "alone with Abbey, made him that more determined to pass the written test and the road test. He studied the book, practically, all night, Thursday. Friday morning with his mom in the car, he drove to the school. He, even, put the test booklet in between the pages of his textbooks, during classes. It looked like he was reading the textbook, when in reality, he was studying the driver's test. After school, his mom picked him up. She drove them to the driving school. his mom waited, in the car, while he went into the school building. He and ten of his "classmates" were ushered into a small classroom. A stern looking Registry of Motor Vehicles Cop stood at the front of the classroom. They took their seats. Pencils were passed out along with separate lank sheets of papers. Test booklets were passed out, along with answer sheets. They were to fill in the spaces next to the number of the corresponding question, by shading in the oval circle. There were 20 questions. To pass the test, they could only miss 5 questions. They were instructed to fill out their names and social security numbers, date of birth, height and weight, hair and eye color, on the top of the answer sheet. Dampness sprouted on his hands and face. He was glad that he remembered to put deodorant under his arms. They were warned to keep their own eyes on their own papers. The large cop said "Go!" he turned to the first question. Eureka! He knew the first answer! He went to the next and so on. He was thrilled! His nervousness abated. He blackened in the correct answers. He finished the test in ten minutes! He went back and checked and rechecked his answers. He didn't have to use the blank sheet of paper! He got out of his seat and walked to the front of the class and handed in his test booklet and answer sheet. He went back to his seat. Others began to get up and turn in their tests. The others took the whole thirty minutes that they were allotted. He wondered how his mom was doing, waiting for him. He thought about the test. The first ten questions were easy, for him. They were about the rules of the road. The next ten were a little harder and were hypothetical situations and required the best answer possible.

When all were finished, the surely cop stood up and began to read the list of names. He did not say pass or fail. His was the third name read! He began to wonder if he had failed. The cop only read six names! He, then, said the six names he read were to report to the side of the building to take the road test! He passed! He breathed a heavy sigh of relief, got out of his seat and the other five. He felt bad for the other four. As exited the building, he heard the cop chastise those that failed the test.

One by one, they were called to the driving school car. He was the last one. As he, again, waited, the nervousness enveloped his body. He sure didn't want the big, surly cop giving him the road test. Finally, the car pulled up. The girl, who had been driving it, got out and ran past him, tears streaming down her face. "Damn!" he thought, "wonder what she did wrong?" he walked to the car, opened the door and slid in behind the wheel. He looked at his passenger. It was a woman! As she read his name, he looked in the rearview mirror. In the back seat, was another one of his instructors. The woman cop said "before you start the car, tell me what you need to do." He went through the list. He watched her make notes on her clipboard. "Let's go!" She said. He started the car, checked his mirrors, put on his turn signal, checked the mirrors, again, and slowly pulled out into the traffic. She put him through his paces. Turns, stopping on hills, changing lanes. All the time, asking him the same questions that were on the written test. They returned to the driving school and he pulled up to the curb, behind his mom's car. They all sat, in silence, as the cop was busily writing. Finally, she turned to him and said "Congratulations!" She handed him his temporary license. She said his permanent license would arrive in the mail in about five days. The only restriction on the license, was motorcycles. He thanked her and got out of the car. His instructor got out and shook his hand. He, quickly, walked to his mom's car. She had witnessed everything and moved over to the passenger seat. He got in behind the wheel. He was now a licensed driver! Another major milestone, in his young life! It was just after 4PM when they got home. He really wanted to go to Abby's. His mom got out of the car, handed him some money, for gas, and some more, in case he wanted to get something to eat. Before she could say anything more, he told her that he would be careful. She smiled and walked into the house. He waited until she was inside, before he pulled away from the curb and headed to Abby's.

Freedom! What a strange feeling! Fear and excitement! For the first time, in his life, he was behind the wheel of a car on the open road, driving! No one else was with him. He was alone! Like a baby bird, the first time out of the nest, flying on its own! The young bear cub wandering away from its mother, for the first time! This was an adventure! All was right with the world! He was extremely happy! The walk to Abby's house used to take him an hour. He pulled onto her street and it only took him 30 minutes from his house. He drove past her house and pulled into the driveway, backed out and parked the car, in front. He put the car in first gear and set the emergency brake and turned off the car.

He was halfway up her walk, when the front door opened and she ran out to him, screaming, "You got it!" She gave him a big hug and a kiss. He looked beyond Abby and saw her mom standing in the doorway. She was smiling. She, too, must have thought, "no more chauffeuring!" her mom voiced her congratulations as Abby turned to her and asked if they could go to "HO-Jo's". "Where?" Her mom asked. "Howard Johnsons" Abby said. "Oh, okay, but please be careful!" They both said that they would. They went to the car. He opened the passenger side door, for her, as she slid in. He, gently, closed the door and walked around the back and came up to the driver's side. He opened the door and slid in behind the wheel. He noticed that Abby was, practically plastered, against the inside of the passenger door. "You okay?" he asked. "You can sit beside me, you know." She nodded and said "Wait until you get off my street." Once they left her street and started down the other road, she slid over to him and threw her arms around his neck and began to "rain" kisses on his cheek. He was on cloud nine! They came to red light. She turned his face to hers and their lips met. "That's my congratulatory kiss!" She said. He wished the light would stay red!

As they pulled into the parking lot at ho-Jo's, she told him to find a parking space behind the building. He obeyed. As soon as he turned off the engine, she wrapped her arms around him and they celebratedtheir freedom with a long, passionate kiss. They were so wrapped up in each other's arms, they forgot why they drove there. They, finally, parted their lips. He glanced at his watch and saw they had better go inside and order something to either drink or eat. They got out of the car and walked, hand in hand, around to the front of the restaurant. Once inside, they found a booth and sat down, across from each other, holding hands on the table. A waitress came and asked them what they wanted. They both ordered chocolate frappes. When the waitress left, he got out of the booth and came to her side and slid in next to her. They, again, shared sweet loving kisses. He got up and went back to his side when he heard the waitress coming back with their drinks. Even drinking the frappes, they couldn't keep their eyes off each other. When he finished his drink, he asked her if she wanted to go to the drive in, the following night. "Why?" She asked, "What's on your mind?" He was flabbergasted! "I thought one of the main reasons that I got my driver's license was so that you and I could be alone!" He said. She tilted her head slightly to one side and again asked, "Why do you want to be alone with me?" He was speechless!. She, then, giggled and told him she was kidding. Then she said, "Maybe we should double date?" "Damn! "He said. It was the first time he had ever used that word in her presence. She put her hand to her face and said, "What did you say?" He felt the rush of redness swarm over his face. She giggled again. "You are so cute!" Those words didn't help his complexion. She then told him that, of course, they would go to the drive in. Their only concern was their parents. He told her that he would tell his Mom that he was going with the guys. She said she would tell her parents that they were double dating with Annie and Tom. "Can we see each other during the day, too?" She asked. He pondered her question for a minute and told her that he wanted to surprise her. He was putting a radio in the car, in the morning. She smiled and said "good!" She finished her frappe; he paid the bill and they left the restaurant, holding hands as they got to the car. Once inside the car, they again moved to each other and wrapped their arms around each other and crushed their lips together in another long, French kiss. They couldn't get enough of each other. When they, at last, parted and gasped for air, he noticed that they had better head for her house. She put her left arm around his shoulders and her right hand just above his right knee. He started the car and they headed for her house. Once they were in front of her house, they shared another sweet loving kiss. He got out and walked around and opened the door, for her. They walked up her walk and shared another sweet kiss before she turned and opened the door and was gone. He drove home, thinking about their first night, alone, at the drive in.

His face was buried in his pillow, his arms wrapped around it. His pelvis pressed hard against the bottom sheet. He was dreaming of Abby. "Don't you think it's time to get up?" The voice seemed to penetrate his entire being from a great distance away. "I was hoping you would drive me to get groceries this morning." He realized it wasn't Abby's voice, but his Mom's. He cracked open one eye and muttered "okay." She left his room and said, over her right shoulder that breakfast was ready. He stumbled out of bed and went into the bathroom. After taking care of "business" he cleaned up and went back to his room. He put on his dungarees, t-shirt, boots; brushed and combed his hair and went out of his room. Once downstairs, he ate his breakfast. He asked his Mom if he could put a radio in her car. "As long as you pay for it." She said. He went back upstairs to his room and scraped together a hundred dollars from his "piggy bank." When he returned to the kitchen, she had just completed her grocery list. They went out the back door, to the car. He started it up and they headed out of the driveway. "Nice to have you chauffeur me around, for a change." His mom said. He smiled. When they arrived at the grocery store, he waited in the car, while she did her shopping. He thought to himself how great it was going to be to have a radio in the car. Something he could listen to, at times such as these. He, also, began to visualize how wonderful it was going to be, at the drive in, alone with Abby. His mom did not take as long as he thought she would. He got out of the car and helped her load the groceries in the back of the wagon. He, again, started the car and headed home. When they arrived he got out of the car and helped carry the groceries into the house and, finally, into the kitchen. "You go ahead and get that radio put in. It's just after 10:30. You'll want to get there before they shut down for lunch." His mom said. She didn't have to say it twice. He practically ran from the house and jumped into the car.

It was just after 11:00, when he drove into the car audio parking lot. He drove right up to the front entrance. Before he could shut the motor off, a tall balding, thin man approached the driver's side window. "Can I help you?" He asked. He told him that he would like to have a radio installed. The man told him to turn off the motor and exit the car. The man, then, got in and stretched out his lean body to look under the dashboard. When he got out of the car, he told him that it was going to be pretty easy. He then asked him to go into the showroom with him and pick out what kind of radio, he wanted. Once in the showroom, he couldn't believe the many different types and sizes of radios. He. Finally. Decided on a small AM radio. The man looked at it and told him that it would cost $49.95 plus the antenna and tax. The total would be close to $79.00. He shrugged at the total price, thinking that he would be left with only $21.00 for the drive in. His face gave away his disappointment. The man thought for a moment and said, "wait a minute, this radio is on sale for only $29.95 and I'll throw in the antenna of your choice." "You can do that?" He asked the man. "Yup." He said. "I can do anything I want. I own the place." He grabbed the man's right hand and shook it. "We got a deal!" he said. "Great!" said the man. "As I said it's an easy install. Should be done, before lunch." "Excellent!" he beamed. He left the building and went to the car and placed the keys in the ignition; and went back into the building to wait in the waiting room. He sat down and thumbed through a couple of "Hot Rod" magazines. He looked out the window, when he heard the sound of a drill. He, nervously, lit up a Parliament cigarette when he saw one of the workers drill a rather big hole between the firewall and windshield on the passenger side of the car. He turned around and began to pace back and forth, in the waiting room. Like an expectant father waiting for the birth of his first child. He glanced at his watch and realized it was almost 11:45. Fifteen minutes before the lunch break. He sat down and tried to read more magazines, but was unable to. He looked out at the car, again. This time, the hood was up. "Damn" he thought, "sure takes a lot to put a radio in." he turned around and started to go back toward the magazine rack, when he heard the unmistakable sound of "Be Bop A lula," emanating, from the dashboard of the Jeep. A big grin spread across his face. He, almost, felt like crying, he was so happy. The owner motioned his hand to him to come to the pay window. "You're all set. We even dialed in WMEX the new Rock and Roll radio station for you." The whole thing ended up costing him about $40.00. He was extremely happy and told theowner that he would tell all his friends where he got the radio. The owner told him, that for every person that came in and told him that they heard about the radio, from him, and bought one. He would send him a check for ten bucks. Before he left, he gave the owner his name and address. They shook hands and he went out to the car, got in and rolled down the driver's side window and drove out of the parking lot, singing along to Bill Haley's "See You Later, Alligator." He now was driving a car with a Rock and Roll radio in it. He noticed the large speaker had been put into the top of the dashboard and centered so all would be able to hear it, in the car. Driving around was going to be a blast! As he drove home, He sang along to the next song, Chuck Berry's "Johnny Be Good." He felt that this, too, was another milestone, in his life.

He was so excited, when he got home, he went right to the phone and called Abby. Her mom answered the phone and before she called Abby to it. She told him that she and Abby's Dad had some misgivings about the date, that night. He promised her, profusely, that he would be very careful. She said "okay" and called Abby to the phone. "hi!" Abby said. He sensed that her mom was nearby. She said that Anne and Tom were very excited about the date that night. "Right!" he said, "I can't wait for us to be, finally, alone." "Uh, we will pick them up at Anne's house." "okay." He said. "I'll be by around 5PM to get you." "okay." She said, "See you then." She hung up. He smiled, thinking that she really played it well, with her mom near her. He was heading to the kitchen for some lunch, when the phone rang. He turned around and went back and answered it. "Hi lover!" It was Abby. "My mom's out back. I had to call you and let you know that we really are double dating with Anne and Tom." He didn't respond right away. Disappointment flooded his entire being, followed by a whisp of anger. "What? Are you kidding me? Why?" He asked. She replied that her mom had spoken with Anne's mom and they made the decision for them. His heart sank like a lead balloon. "Oh lover, I am so sorry. I really wanted our first date, to be alone, in the car. I promise you, it will still be okay. They won't bother us." He, still, felt like he had sucker punched in the gut. He mumbled, "okay. See you at 5." She whispered, "I love you so much." She hung up the phone. He went into the kitchen and sat down to eat his chicken noodle soup and four English muffins. "You look like someone just stole Abby from you." His mom said. He, quickly, responded, "no, just that I'll miss her tonight, that's all." He didn't say another word and began to eat his lunch.

After lunch, he decided to wash and wax the Jeep. His mom couldn't believe he wanted to do it. She was glad that he wanted to do it. He went out the back door and moved the car closer to the back of the house, near an outside spigot. He went to the door that led to the basement and got a bucket, sponge, car wash soap, can of wax and two dry rags. He got the garden hose from under the porch and hooked it up to the spigot. He put a quarter of car wash soap in the bucket and filled the bucket to the top with water. He dropped the sponge in the soapy water. He, then, proceeded to rinse the car, from top to bottom, just as his dad had taught him, to do. He went under the porch, again and retrieved a small step ladder and proceeded to rinse the very top of the wagon. He couldn't understand why the top had to be done, no one could see the top, from the ground, but his dad said it was very important, so he did it.

Once rinsed, he began to wash it, again, from top to bottom. After he rinsed off the soap, he let it sit in the sun, to dry off. He went back into the house and up to his room, to pick out what he was going to wear. He decided on black polished chinos, white dress shirt and black loafers. Had he really been going with the guys, it would have been dungarees, t-shirt and boots. This was a special night. Abby's and his first drive in, alone, as a couple. He laid the clothes out on his bed. He went downstairs and out the back door to the car. He moved the car, out of the sun and in the shade of the large Oak tree by the back porch. He had to let it cool off before he could apply the wax. He turned on the car and turned up the radio. He was so happy to be driving a car with music! He began singing along to Carl Dobkins Jr's song "My Heart Is An Open Book." The next song, the D.J. played, was Johnny Horton's "All For The Love Of A Girl." Then, after a few commericals, was The ventures, "Walk Don't run." He whistled along to the instrumental. He made a mental note to by those records. He got out of the wagon and put his hands on the hood. He was amazed how quickly the vehicle had cooled off. He went into the basement, with one of the dry rags and dampened it in the sink by the clothes washer. He came back out and opened the can of Turtle Wax and began waxing the car. When he got to the driver's side door, he remembered the car was "running". He opened the door and turned off the ignition key as the Cheers record of "Black Denim trousers" was playing. "Damn!" He said, "Abby says she likes a guy in dungarees, white dress shirt, with the sleeves rolled up past his elbows, and engineer boots!" He thanked the D.J., in his mind, for playing the song and reminding him. He would, definetly change his wardrobe. He finished waxing and polishing the car. It was 2:45 PM. Next, he went into the house and got the vacuum cleaner and brought it outside and plugged it into the outside plug, under the porch. He got in the car and moved it closer to the house. This time he made sure to turn off the engine. He vacuumed all the seat cushions and the floors, and the backs of all the seats. Finished, he brought the vacuum cleaner back into the house and got an old dry rag and some window cleaner and went back to the car. Not only did he clean all the windows, outside and inside, but the rear view mirror and the side mirror, as well. He emptied the wash bucket in the driveway, and brought all the "tools" back into the basement. He rolled up the hose. He stepped back to admire his hard elbow rubbing work. The car actually sparkled! He was quite pleased with himself. It was 3:30 PM. He moved the car back onto the driveway. He turned off the ignition, only after singing along to the last verse of Ivory Joe Hunter's "Since I Met You Baby." He got out of the car and went back into the house and back to his bedroom. He put the black chinos back in the closet and opened the dresser drawer and took out a clean pair of dungarees. He put the loafers back in the closet and took off his boots, to polish them. As he applied the wax, he hoped Abby would be thinking of him, when she picked out her clothes, to wear. He told her he would love to see her in a low cut, off the shoulder peasant blouse and short shorts. She had just smiled, when he told her.

It was close to 4 PM. He realized he had very little time to bathe, brush his teeth, get dressed and comb his hair. He did it all in record time, except the hair. He wanted it just right. He used two dabs of Brylcreem. By 4:30, he was ready. He went downstairs, through the kitchen and out the back door, to the car. He got in and turned on the car, turned up the radio and drove out of the driveway, singing along to Tommy Edwards, "It's All In The Game." Followed by the flip side, "Please Love Me Forever."

As he drove along the road the Abby's, he was thankful that no one was in the front hall or the kitchen, when he walked through to go out to the car. He had, quickly, applied the "Old Spice" to his face and behind his ears. He knew he had to get gas, before going the rest of the way to Abby's. He pulled into a "Jenny" gas station, a few blocks from her house. The attendant came out of the station and walked up to the driver's side of the car. He rolled down the window to tell him to fill up the car and check the oil, when the attendant backed up away from him." What did you do? Bathe in Old Spice? " He asked. "Damn!" he said. "Is it that strong?" "Yup!" said the guy. He got out of the car, only after lowering all the windows to "air' out the wagon. He told the guy what he wanted. He walked around outside the car and around the lot of the station. The attendant was finished filling the car with gas and asked to him to get in the car and open the hood. He got in and took a long sniff. The car no longer "reeked" of his cologne.

He pulled the latch to pop open the hood. The guy checked the oil and said it was good and shut the hood. He paid the guy the five dollars for the gas and drove out of the lot.

He entered Abby's street and drove past the house and into her driveway. He backed up and turned to the car around, facing the direction he just came in, and pulled up in front of the house. He turned off the car and walked around the front of it and started up the walk. Anne, Tom and Abby were sitting on the front step. Anne and Tom got up and started walking towards him. Abby got up and went back inside the house. Tom and Anne walked closer to him. Tom said, "Whew, a little strong on the Old Spice aren't you?" "Crap!" he said. He was hoping most of it had dissipated in the air. Anne just smiled. Abby came out of the house, as the approached the front door. "I was just saying goodnight to my folks." She said. He gave her a low wolf whistle, showing his appreciation of her looks. She was wearing a white, off the shoulders, peasant blouse with tight short Bermuda shorts. He really wanted to see her in short shorts, but the ones she was wearing looked good on her, very good! Her light brown hair was showing blonde highlights which accentuated her fair skin and bright red lips. Lips, he knew, would not be that bright, after the show. She came up to him and gave him a light, sweet kiss on his right cheek. "Oh wow!, you smell fantastic!" She said. He could smell her perfume as well and told her she smelled wonderful, too. He took her by her right hand and escorted her to the passenger side of the car, opened the door and guided her into the car. He closed the door and walked around the front of the car wearing a broad grin on his face. He started the car and put it in gear and proceeded down her street to the main road. As soon as they were out of sight of her house, she slid over next to him. Her left hip, side and arm pressed tightly against him. She moved her left arm up and over his shoulders and turned her face to his cheek and "planted" another sweet kiss on his cheek. He was in heaven! He glanced in the rear view mirror and noticed that Tom and Anne were already getting comfortable and cuddling, in the backseat.

They arrived at the drive in, just as it opened. He drove in and looked for a good spot to park. Anne said, " let's park near the concession stand, not too close, but near it, maybe behind it and to the left side of it. That way the noise and lights won't bother us." He was about to say he would park where he wanted to, but, after, listening to her, he surmised it was a good idea. He found a spot, pulled up to the speaker stand. He stopped the car, set the emergency brake and left the car in first gear. He reached through his open window and took the speaker off the stand and placed it on the top edge of his window and cranked the window up as far as it would go. He turned up the volume. The speaker was tuned into WMEX radio and Elvis's voice filled the air with "Don't Be Cruel." Anne and Tom offered to go for popcorn and cokes. He reached for his wallet. Tom said "No, you paid for the movie and the gas, to get us here. The least I can do is pay for the food." He nodded "okay". Tom and Anne got out of the car and walked towards the concession stand. Abby put her hands on both sides of his face and drew his lips to hers. Their lips met in a sweet, loving kiss that lasted from the end of Elvis's song and into Pat Boone's "Love Letters In The Sand." That was their first kiss of the evening. Their second kiss, followed soon after and was more intense, more passionate. Between their kisses, Abby brought her hands around his neck and drew their lips tighter together. Between kisses, they hugged each other very tight. She exclaimed how wonderful it was to be together. She was so very happy that they were going steady. He couldn't help stealing glances at her slight cleavage. He really wanted to see more, but he respected her too much, to try anything.

They were so oblivious to their surroundings. Jack Scott was singing "Goodbye, Baby." In the speaker. They parted their lips, gasping for air! Once their lungs were "refilled", they, again, continued kissing. They were "lost" in paradise!. Their lips met in a fiery kiss! "Hey! You Two!" It was Tom and Anne, with the food. "Jeez!" said Anne, the movie hasn't even started yet." They parted and were breathing heavily. They didn't care that Tom and Anne had "caught' them.. They decided to consume the food, now ,before the show began. They were eating, drinking and chatting as darkness fill the lot. The large screen sprang from total blackness to blinding light as the cartoon came on. When they were through, Tom offered to take the trash to the trash can, by the concession stand. Anne didn't want him to go. He told Tom to just throw the garbage and trash over his seat and into the back and he would take care of it in the morning. They began to settle back, when Abby reached down to her pocketbook, on the floor, in front of them and brought up a roll of Canada Mints. She offered everyone a mint. Tom and Anne each took one. She looked at him and said "open up." She fed him a mint. She, then , snuggled close to him, as they sucked on their mints and watched the last cartoon. He heard Abby start to chew on hers and he decided to do the same. That way, they could continue where they had left off.

When they were through, with their mints, she pulled him away from his door and they began to slide down in the seat, away from the steering wheel and all other obstructions. They lay, side by side on the seat. Abby's back was against the back of the seat. She wrapped her arms around him and their lips met again. Sweetly, at first, but their passion for each other overtook them. Their lips were locked together. They could care less about the movie. They were only interested in each other. They felt so "free". He wished they were really alone! He wanted so much to hold her and caress her. As their passion increased, Abby pulled her lips from his and huskily told him that they needed to stop for a while. He did as she had asked. They looked into each other's eyes. She told him that she wasn't ready to go "all the way." He told her that he wasn't either. That wasn't entirely true, on his part. But he would never force her to do anything that she wasn't ready to do.

Once they had "calmed down", they began to "make out" again. Once again, their passion grew and he brought his hand to her knee. As their kissing and hugging increased, he moved his hand above her knee, sliding up her to her inner thigh. He didn't know if she could feel his hand or not. Maybe she didn't care. He kept his hand still, for the longest time, not wanting to "alarm" her. Their French kisses grew more fervent!!! Nothing ,in the world, mattered but them and their love for each other! He was "lost' in the scent of her perfume and the taste of her lips They held each other so tight, he was afraid he might hurt her.

When he wasn't kissing her lips, he was kissing her neck and cheek, and she did the same. When they weren't kissing, they were telling each other how much they truly loved each other! She vowed that they would never, ever break up! He felt like he was in heaven! He was so in love and felt so loved! He just knew that Abby was the girl of his dreams! He longed for the day when they would be "old" enough and mature enough to "consummate" their .love! She did tell him that she wanted him to be the one that made her a woman. When she told him that, he told her that he wanted her to be his "first' also. As they hugged each other and began kissing, his hand began to move closer up her thigh!

She ripped her mouth, from his and with eyes wide open, shook her head "NO". He brought his hand away from her leg. He had been so close. She snaked both her arms around him and held him as close as possible. He moved his hands away and did likewise. They were locked in a tight embrace, with their faces, cheek to cheek. He moved his lips closer to her hair covered ear and whispered, " I am so in love with you and you make me crazy." She reciprocated. " You, too drive me crazy. I want you so bad, but not in a car." He brought his lips back to hers. Again, their lips travelled over each others's lips . Their passion began climbing, once again. She maneuvered herself, so her back was flat on the seat.; the other against the back of the seat. He moved on top of her. Another new experience. It felt very good!

She pushed him up and off of her. She ,then, had him lie on his back, on the seat and she got on top. She was in complete control of him, and he enjoyed it. They were locked together in a passionate embrace!

They were unaware that they had been making out, not only during both movies, but intermission, as well. A bright light flooded the car and the movie lot. She raised her head from his and looked at him. "I think the movies are over." She said. "Damn!" he said. He did not want the night to ever end. She slid off him and sat up. He, too, sat up and moved over behind the steering wheel.WMEX returned to the speaker with Buddy Holly singing "That'll Be The Day." He was just about to start the car, when he heard Anne. Apparently, she and Tom were unaware that the show had ended. He did not start the car, right away, to do so, would have turned on the overhead lights and that would have been embarrassing for all concerned. He felt a wave of jealousy come over him. "Lucky Tom," He thought. Anne and Tom were still in the throws of their passion! He looked at Abby. She had a real stern look, on her face. She was not happy. He had not seen that look before and he did not like it. He was very happy that she was not angry with him. She moved over to him and cuddled next to him, with her left arm around his shoulders. Tom, finally, sat up, in the back seat. "I've got to go the men's room." He said. "Go with him!" Abby demanded. "uh, okay." He said. "But I really don't have to." "GO!" She said with a stern look, in her eye. He opened the his door and slipped out; closed the door and caught up with Tom as he maneuvered his way through the lines of cars, leaving the lot. "I've got to get to the men's room, before this damn 'safe" falls off." He said. Tom gave him a big grin. He said ,to Tom, " I guess you and Anne had a great time." "Yup," Tom said, as they both tried to avoid getting hit by any vehicles. "I think you two ruined the rest of my evening ." He said. When they finished their "business", they walked back to the car. The lot was practically empty and they didn't have to avoid any cars. As they approached the wagon, he could see Abby. She was really animated in anger, at Anne. "Don't think it's such a good time to go back to the car." He said. They made a left turn and walked a few rows away. They kept looking at the Jeep. Finally, it appeared that the girls were through. They headed back. When he got to his door, he looked through the passenger side window. Abby was sitting with her arms folded and staring out the windshield. He and Tom got back in the car. He heard Tom ask Anne, if she was okay. "NO!" she said. He looked at Abby and asked if she was okay. "NO!" She said. He notice the girls weren't talking to each other, either. He lowered his window and took off the speaker and replaced it on its' stand. He rolled up the window and started the car. They were one of the last cars to leave the lot. The temperature, in the car was in sharp contrast to the 68 degrees outside. He thought to himself, that if the air was any colder in the car, he would have to turn on the defroster. Abby sat a good distance away from him and wouldn't look at him. He thought " Thanks Tom. She probably blames all men for what you and Anne did."

Not one word was spoken, on the ride home. He turned up the radio and was humming along to Bill Doggett's "Honky Tonk". After that instrumental ended, he softly sang along to "Sh-Boom" by the Crew cuts. "Thank God for the radio" he thought. "In the Still Of The Night" by the Five Satins was playing , when he dropped Tom and Anne off at her house. As he pulled away, Abby slid over to him. She placed her left arm over the back of his shoulders and snuggled her head, to his. He turned the radio down and said to her, "I obviously screwed up and made you upset, I'm sorry, I'm really sorry." She raised her head and looked at him. "Oh, baby! It wasn't you! It was that "slut, Anne!" "Oh, he replied, "Oh! Okay!" Abby continued, "She promised me that she wouldn't go all the way and she did!" He did not know how to respond to her. He kept his mouth shut and turned the radio back up. Abby returned to her previous position. They both sang along, softly, to "Chantilly lace" by the Big Bopper.

When he got to her house, he pulled into the driveway and then backed out into the street and pulled up to the curb, in front of her house. He turned off the car, and looked over at Abby. Her head had moved from his, to rest on the back of the seat. Her lips were too inviting, not to kiss her. He turned and brought his lips to hers. Her arms snaked. Once again, around his neck and the back of his head, as their lips pressed together. When they broke for air, she , huskily, mentioned that the next time they will go alone to the show. He agreed. She gave him another sweet kiss on his lips and said." I really need to go in." "Okay." He said. He let go of her and got out of the car and walked around the front, to her side and opened the passenger door. "I could have slid out you side, you know." She said. " I know." He replied, " but I need to practice my chivalry." They both chuckled. As he helped her from the car, she whispered, " I am so crazy in love with you." "Oh, Abby, my life started anew, when we met." She gave him a big hug ,as they strolled up her walk. At the front door, they shared a long, passionate "good night" kiss. He promised to call her, as she turned and opened the door and went inside. He waited for the door to close. He walked back to the car. He got in and turned the car on and headedhome. He turned up the radio and sang along to Bobby day's "Rockin' Robin." He didn't really pay attention to the song as he was thinking of their next date, ALONE!!!

He turned off the motor and the headlights and coasted into the driveway. He did not want to wake anyone up and have to answer a lot of questions. He walked , very softly, up the back stairs, to the back door. He slowly opened it and then softly closed it behind him. He crept through the kitchen, into the front hall and up the stairs, down the hall and into his room. He softly closed the door and ,quickly, undressed. No briefs, no pj's, he slipped under the covers. He reached into the night stand drawer and took out the towel. He knew it wouldn't take long for him to release his pent up passion. The deed done, he slipped the "soiled' towel back in the drawer and fell fast asleep. His last few thoughts were of Abby. Her luscious lips, esquisite breasts and marvelous passion.

"Get up! Get dressed! You have a job interview!" his mom's voice shattered his ear drums and reverberated throughout his brain. "What?" he mumbled. His head face down in the pillow. She repeated herself. "But, it's Sunday." He said. "Shouldn't you be in church?" He asked. " Church was over at 10:45 this morning. It's now 12:30 on the afternoon. You have an interview for a summer job at 2:30, so get out of bed and get cleaned up. I've laid out some appropriate school clothes for you to wear. Now, get up!" he obeyed. He got up and got cleaned up and went downstairs, in the clothes his mom had picked out. " You can have a glass of orange juice. We'll have our Sunday dinner when we get back." "We?" He asked. "We." She said. "Your Dad and I are going with you to the interview." He groaned. He drank the orange juice and then the three of them went out the back door towards his dad's Mercury. "Why not the Jeep?" He asked. "Because it smells of stale popcorn and other things." His mom said. "Oh" he replied.

The interview went well. The job entailed helping a travelling salesman tote his sample suitcases across the state. It was a five day week job, with a couple of overnights, when they had to go to the western part of the state. The job paid a hundred dollars a week and included his food and, when needed, board. It certainly paid more than caddying. Mr. Stone, the salesman, sold ladies nightgowns. He wasn't too crazy about the job, because it meant only seeing Abby on the weekends. But the money was excellent for a sixteen year old, in 1958. Mr. Stone said that only he and two other boys had applied. They were very skinny and had trouble handling the suitcases. He asked him to come out of his house, to his car and see if he could handle the cases. Mr. Stone opened the trunk of his brand new 1958 Cadillac. The suitcases were huge black cases with large belt like straps holding the bottoms and tops together. There were four cases, in all. He lifted each one out of the trunk, with ease and placed them on the driveway. The cases had wheels on the bottom that would make them easy to push or pull along sidewalks and into stores. Mr. Stone seemed pleased and offered him the job. He would begin the Monday, after school got out for the summer. He accepted the job. His parents were pleased. They drove home, in silence. Normally, he would be listening to his radio station, but this was his dad's car and so he listened to Patti Page sing "Mockingbird Hill", and big band sounds.

How was he going to explain, to Abby, his summer job? He paced back and forth, in his bedroom, trying to come upwith best way to explain to her, why he couldn't see her during the week days, this coming summer. He waited, anxiously, until well after supper, to call her. "Hi Sweets." He said. "Hi lover!" She answered. She began by apologizing for her bad mood, at the end of the drive in, last night. He told her that he understood. That one of his pet peeves is people who say they are going to do something and then don't do it. She sighed and was happy that he understood. Then he hit her with the bad news about his new summer job. There was a long pause at her end of the line. "Well," she said, "we'll still have the weekends, right?" "Yes!" He said. He was amazed that she took the news so well. They made plans for the following Friday night to go play miniature golf and he mumbled "parking, afterwards?" She whispered, " of course." His heart leaped in his chest and his penis "jerked" alive. "I can't wait!" he said. "me either," she answered. They professed their undying love for each other and hung up.

Once again, the school week dragged on and on. He thought Friday night would never arrive. He got home ,from school, did some homework and then proceeded to get ready. They talked all week, on the phone, about how exciting and wonderful their "first" date, alone in the car, would be. He was happy about miniature golf and even decided to go to Adventure car hop, afterwards for burgers, fries and a coke. He was more excited about being with Abby, alone, in the car. In the tub, his penis was like the periscope of a submarine, peeking up through the soapy surface of the bath water, searching for a mate. He applied the Prell Shampoo to his hair and then dunked his head under the water, to rinse off the soap. He stepped out of the tub and gave himself a good look in the mirror. His lean torso and muscular arms, coupled with a full head of tossled dark brown hair, added to his ego. He knew he was very good looking. Yet, he never said it to anybody else. He never wanted anyone to think he might be conceited. He toweled off and wrapped the bath towel around his waist and waddled to his room. He put on a pair of freshly washed and dried briefs, black socks, black polished chinos, light blue dress shirt and black loafers. He thought he might be a little over dressed for miniature golf, but he wanted Abby to be proud to be in public with him. Next, it took about an hour, to get his hair, just right, with just the right amount of Brylcreem. This time, he was a little more lenient with the Old Spice. His brother, Dave, showed him how to use just the right amount. One more look in the mirror and he was ready. He pocketed his "pin boy" money from his "bank" and walked out of the room. His mom asked if he wanted any supper and he told her that he and Abby were going to grab a couple of burgers at the car hop. He checked the wagon, to make sure there weren't any stray popcorn smells from the last weekend. He had cleaned out the car, when he returned from the job interview. His mom had left him plenty of gas, in the tank, so he was ready for a night of love!

It was close to five o'clock, in the afternoon, as he drove to Abby's. He made a mental note, to never go out, at this time, on a Friday afternoon. He could not believe all the traffic. His driver education emerged from his brain and told him to take it easy, not to get upset with things he couldn't control. Still, he wished he had some kind of weapon that he could use that would pick up all the cars, in front of him, and deposit them behind me, giving him a clear road. It took longer than a half hour, to get to Abby's.

He made his usual swing into her driveway and pulled up to the curb, in front of her house. He turned off the car and got and walked up to her front door. He rang the bell. The door opened and once again, her father answered. "You again?"

He joked. "'fraid so." He answered. Her dad, then said, "You must really like her, though it's a mystery to me, why?" he couldn't understand why a father would say things like that about his only child. He ushered him into the livingroom. "She'll be down in a minute." He said. Her Mom asked, " Where are you two headed this evening." He replied, "miniature golf and then the car hop and maybe over to one of her girlfriend's house." "Oh" her mom said. " Which one?" " I'm not sure." He answered. He thought they were going to be in trouble if she asked Abby what friend's house. He was unaware that Abby was coming down the stairs and heard the question. " New friend from school, that I recently just met, invited us over." "Oh." Her mom answered, " well, have a good time." His mouth must have been wide open. He couldn't believe his eyes. She wore a pair of white short shorts and a blue, low cut, blouse. She grabbed his left hand and pulled him out of the living room, into the hall and out the door. They walked hand in hand to the car. He was speechless. She was a living doll!!!! A sexy, living doll! He knew concentrating on driving, miniature golf, the car hop, was going to very difficult. Her tan legs accentuated the whiteness , of her shorts.

When they got settled in the car and were on their way, he suggested they forget about the golf and the car hop and just the spend the date, parking. She smiled and chuckled and told him it was still too light out for parking. He accepted her logic. She did say that she was really hungry and that maybe they could go to the car hop, first. He, too, felt the pangs of hunger and agreed. So, they headed for the car hop. She snuggled up next to him and made it difficult for him to look at her beautiful tan legs and drive safely. He kept thinking how much he wanted to touch them and kiss them, all the way up. Ironically, Jimmy Clanton's record, "Just A Dream" came on the radio. His desire for Abby was raging, as they drove to the car hop.

As he pulled into the Adventure Car Hop, he ,quickly, found a spot in the front row, in front of the building. Abby asked him m" Why did you park so close?" he told her that it was the best place to watch the parade of hot rods and customs. He had just rolled down the window, when the roller skating waitress came up to the window. " Hi guys!, What can I get yah?" He ordered two cheeseburgers, two fries, and two large cokes. When the waitress left with their order, Abby leaned back against the front seat, next to him and raised her arms above her head and stretched. He couldn't take it! He wanted to throw himself on top of her and make mad passionate love to her. "You are driving me crazy!" He told her. She looked at him and told him that she, too, was getting hot and bothered. "I wanted to tear off your clothes, when you first walked into the house tonight." "Then why aren't we parked somewhere, all alone?" He asked. She turned her body towards him and held his right arm with her two arms. "Baby" She crooned, "Just think what a wonderful time we are going to have, after playing golf." She was really being a tease. The picture, in his mind, almost put him over the edge. He had to take his mind off her, quickly, but how? Then the "parade" began. The first car to come into view was a pink Oldsmobile, nosed and decked, with fender skirts, a lowered rear end and twin pipes. "Obviously glass packs, he said to Abby. The next car was a '32 Ford Deuce roadster, blue, with orange and yellow flames along the sides, that made them appear, as if, they coming from the motor. It was followed by a '46 Ford convertible, painted candy apple red. " I'm going to get my own car, soon." He said. "It'll have a souped up motor and skirts and duels and have at least 30 coats of paint on it. "When are you getting it?" Abby asked. "Probably after school starts in the fall. "Will you let me ride in it?" She asked. " You know it!" he said. Those were the only three cars in the "parade" so far. Abby brought her hands up to each side of his face and planted a soft sweet kiss on his lips. He put his arms around her and her and responded with a kiss of his own. "Ahem!" They both separated at the waitress's voice. "Hate to break you too up. "She said. As she told him to raise his window up about a quarter of the way, so the food tray would be secure. He raised it up and she put the tray on the edge and the bottom braces rested against the door , of the car. "That'll be three dollars and seventy five cents." She said. He handed her a five dollar bill and told her to keep the change. She skated away. Frankie Ford was singing "Sea Cruise" on the radio, as they ate the burgers, fries and drank their cokes. She was very careful not to get any ketchup on her clothes. Another car joined the parade, a 1940

Ford sedan, with what looked like a 1956 Chrysler motor in it. The car was jet black, in color and had fender skirts and dual exhaust. He had taken a large bite of his burger and it ,almost, lodged in his throat as the watched the car, slowly pass in front of them. Again, Abby was too interested with eating her food to notice.

The burgers and fries consumed. They sat and listened to Elvis sing, " Love Me Tender" on the radio, as they sipped their cokes. When they finished their cokes, he placed the empty cups on the floor, at their feet. She reached down and from her purse she brought up two pieces of Dentyne gum. "open your mouth." She said, as she unwrapped the small stick and placed it on his tongue. She, then, did the same with her stick, in her mouth. He turned on the motor and was very happy that the radio hadn't worn down the charge on the battery. They drove out of the car hop, listening to Charlie Ryan's "Hot Rod Lincoln" on the radio. The miniature golf course was about a half hour down the road. When he started the car. She half turned her back against his right side and laid the back of her head against his right upper chest. He ,almost, went into the passing lane, of the road, when he glanced at her and saw her slight cleavage. "You're going to be the death of us." He warned. She just giggled. She knew what she was showing him. "having trouble seeing the road?" She asked. "uh huh" he replied.

As they pulled into the parking lot of the miniature golf course, the lot's lights came on. Dusk was upon them. They got out of the car and walked up to the shed that held the putters and different colored golf balls and score cards. He recognized the guy behind the counter as a kid from school. Hal was his name. They exchanged greetings and he told him that he didn't know that he worked there. "All Right," he said. "So," Hal said, "you two ready to play?". "Yep." He said. "Hal said, " normally, it's a dollar fifty a piece, but you two can play for two bucks." Thanks, Hal," he said, "I owe you." He said, "I'll think of something." Abby picked out a pink golf ball and he got a green one. They got their putters and proceeded to hole number one. It had a waterfall, that they had to putt through. There weren't too many people on the course. They pretty much had the place to themselves. Abby said, "how about the one with the lowest score, on each hole gets to kiss the other. He thought it was a great idea. A win-win, for them both. As Abby placed her ball on the rubber tee, over

the loudspeakers came, The Paragons, "Hey Little School Girl." Hal had tuned in the radio station, WMEX and it was playing all over the course. She, practically, drove the ball completely over the waterfall, Instead of through it. They, both, laughed as she said, "oops." He dropped his ball and putted it through the waterfall. They walked around the waterfall to search for her ball. His was sitting about three feet from the hole. He looked around the grass next to the second hole. "Here it is!" Abby yelled. "It's in the hole." "Which hole?" He asked. "The one we are playing." She said. He came back to the first hole and, sure enough, there sat her pink ball. "Guess I won the first hole." She said. "Guess so." He said, softly. It took three tries for him to, finally, sink his putt. At the second hole, Abby went first. She, again, hit the ball, a little hard. It went through a loop de loop and ended up right next to the hole. He proceeded to put his ball on the rubber tee to hit it. "Wait a minute!" Abby said. She walked over to him and gave him a long, passionate kiss on his lips. When she was done, he tried to kiss her back. "uh uh!" She said. "You lost. You can't kiss me." He just smiled and thought, to himself, that he didn't care, if he lost every whole. He hit his ball and it, also, went through the loop de loop and came to rest right next to hers. They both dropped their balls into the hole for a two. She still had the "right" to go first on the third hole. As she placed her ball, on the tee, Johnny Horton's "The Battle Of New Orleans" came blaring through the speakers. They played the entire 18 hole course. She won 10 holes and he won 8. They laughed most of the time, when she wasn't collecting her winnings.

On the 18th hole, the balls disappeared through the hole and into a bucket next to the hole. They returned their clubs. They talked with Hal, for a few minutes and then walked hand in hand back to the car. He told her, the reason she had won, was he couldn't concentrate on the game, because of her short shorts. He didn't tell her, that every time she bent over to put her ball on the tee, he wanted to grab her by her hips and rub his groin right up against her. He, also, had problems, when she bent over to get her ball, out of the hole. He got a good look at her cleavage. He was lucky to win any holes, much less play the game.

They were settled, in the car. He turned it on and put it in reverse and backed out of his spot. He turned it around and headed out. She cuddled right up against him. "That was fun!" She exclaimed. He agreed. She asked him if they could go back to the car hop, because she had to use the ladies room. He said "okay". He thought he might use the men's room too. She asked him, if he could get a couple of frappes to go. He said he would. This time they parked next to the building. The spaces, there, were for folks who wanted to go inside the building. They got out of the car. He locked it and they walked inside. She went to the right, for the ladies room and he to the left. He was finished before her and went to the counter and ordered two chocolate frappes, to go. He just got them, when she returned and they went back out to the car. She held the frappes, while he unlocked the car and opened her door, for her. She got in with the frappes. He went around to the drivers' side and got in behind the wheel. He noticed she had refreshened her lips, with dark cherry. His heart was racing with anticipation of what was next. She cuddled up next to him as they drove to the parking area by the river. She sipped her drink as he drove and would hand him, his, when he had to stop for a red light. By the time they got to the area, the frappes were consumed. There were quite a few cars already there. He hated driving around to find a spot, with his headlights on. He knew he must be making a lot of couples upset with him. He, finally, find a spot and pulled in. he put the car in reverse, turned it off and set the emergency brake. He leaned back, with his right arm around Abby. She nestled her head against his the right side of his chest. They stared out the windshield at the reflection of the moon rippling across the water, in their direction. "We've waited a long time for this." She said. He agreed. She turned her face towards his. "You have no idea how much I really love you." She said. "Oh Abby, I'm so in love with you, nothing else matters in this world." He looked at her eyes and saw them glisten in the moonlight. "Are you crying?" he asked. "I'm just so happy." She said. They embraced each other so tightly, he was afraid he'd hurt her. They parted and she reached into her purse, on the floor of the car and brought out a tissue and dabbed her eyes. She, also, brought out two pieces of Dentyne gum. They unwrapped the small sticks and fed them to each other. After a few minutes, she took out her gum and wrapped it in the tissue. "Give me your piece." She said. "Too late." He said. "You swallowed it!" She said, in a loud voice. "Couldn't help it. Just happened." He said. She giggled and they embraced, again.

They were ready to start to make out. "The back seat is a lot bigger than the front, isn't it?" She asked. "Uh huh." He said. She got out of the car and went to the back door, opened it and got in the back seat. He, quickly, followed suit. They wrapped their arms around each other and fell onto the large seat. Their lips met. Sweetly and softly, at first, and then after the third kiss their passion began to rise. His lips traced every inch of her lips, as she responded with her lips. They began to "French kiss".. When she withdrew her tongue, he thrust his into her mouth and copied what she had done. Their hands began to move up and down each other's sides. He moved his hands over her back and up and over her bra strap, to her shoulders and then back down to the small of her back. They were lying on the back seat, facing each other. She put her right leg up and over his left leg. Their hands and kisses intensified. When they parted their lips, for air, they hugged each other tightly. They were so much in love with each other! They continued to make out, during the entire first feature. They would only stop kissing, to catch their breaths. She felt so good in his arms, he never wanted to let her go! From the way she hugged him, he could 'sense' she felt the same.

With intermission, they got out of the car and walked hand in hand, to the concession stand. She went to the ladies room, while he went to get a pizza and cokes. They met in front of the stand. She took the cokes and he carried the pizza, back to the car. They got back into the back seat and began to feed each other slices of pizza and drink the cokes.

He joked about never going to the drive in, again, with just guys. She laughed. "You mean you like being here with me, better than being here, with your friends?" He laughed. "You know it!" He said. They cuddled together, as they finished their food and drinks. Once they were "done", he put the "trash" back behind the rear seat. She, Again, reached into her purse and brought out two sticks of Dentyne gum. "Don't swallow it this time!" She laughed.

They held each other tightly, and began to 'french kiss" again. This time, they 'traded" their sticks of gum. When they parted their lips, they laughed about swapping gum. Then, they hugged each other and continued to make out. Once again, they "missed" the movie.

He really wanted to take "things" further in their relationship, but he knew she wasn't ready. He was not the type of guy to push it, or pressure her. They never really talked about it. She would talk about "other" girls that had" bad" reputations. Some had even gotten pregnant and had to leave school. She never mentioned names. He listened to her and decided that they would never get into that situation.

They got out of the back seat and into the front seat. He couldn't get over how quickly she went from "super" hot to "ice' cold. The radio was playing Fats Dominos' "Blueberry

Hill".forgot he left the radio on. He hadn't heard any music, just their own sweet music. He, silently, thanked God that the car started. As they drove, from the parking area, he finally spoke and apologized. She began to soften and moved closer to him. She slid over next to him. Little Richard was singing "Tutti Fruiti" on the radio. he put his right arm around her shoulders as she nestled in against his chest.

He pulled up, in front of her house. Before he got out to open her door, she looked at him and, tearfully, asked him not to tell his friends about the night. He promised her, with all his heart, that he was not that type. That he respected her too much and would never tell anyone. He ,even, told her that it was their business and no one else's. She gave him a big hug. When they separated with a soft , sweet kiss, he got out of the car and went to open her door. They walked up the walk to her front door. They ended the 'date" with a passionate kiss and hug and. Again, professed their love, for each other. When she was , safely, inside the house, he went back to the car and started it up and headed home. He was in heaven. Talk about milestones!

Abby was not very happy with him. For one thing, they only got together on the weekends, during the summer. Most of the time, they were not alone. They would be at the beach, with some of her friends, or at parties with his friends.

It was warm a August night, They were invited to a party, at a friend's house. The house was located in the wealthy side of town. When they arrived ,at the house, they were ushered to the basement. The basement was actually a bottom floor that had a living room, with a large dance floor, in the center, another large room, full of couches and easy chairs and a full size kitchen. Abby was feeling uncomfortable around "his" people. He tried to make her feel, at ease. By introducing her to everyone. Then, he saw Carl. Carl appeared to be alone. When he asked him "where his date was?" He said that he wasn't sure. She was one of the sisters whose family ownThe house. He said it was a blind date and that she hadn't shown up yet. Abby got right into the conversation and told him that he shouldn't worry, that the girl should show up soon and shouldn't leave a good looking guy like him unattended for too long. That statement really bothered him. "Was she flirting with Carl?" Abby turned to him and told him she was thirsty and would he get her a coke. He excused himself and went to the kitchen. He got two cokes out of the "fridge" and proceeded back into the dance room. The lights had been dimmed. Couples were swaying to the sound of the platters, "The Great Pretender." He couldn't believe his eyes! Abby and Carl were dancing so close, nothing , not even air could get between them. He walked up to them. They were oblivious to his presence. He grabbed Carl's hands from Abby and shoved him away. Carl fell on his back on the floor. "What the hell are you doing?" he yelled at Abby. She went over to Carl and helped him to his feet. "You're impossible!" She yelled back, at him. "I'll bet he'll find protection!" He was dumbfounded! She pulled the chain out of her shirt and ripped his ring from it and threw it at him. "I'm tired of waiting for you to make love!" She said, "We're Through!" She grabbed Carl's hand and pulled him off the floor and up the stairs. He couldn't believe what had just happened. The others, on the floor, began dancing again. He went back into the kitchen with the cokes. He put them back in the "fridge" and put his back to the door and stared down at his feet. His heart felt like it was made of "fragile" bricks, heavy, but cracking in two. He was still in shock!

Two open toed sandals stood in front of his loafers. They "housed" a pair of golden tanned feet with dark red nail polish. He glanced up from the feet to the ankles, the calves, up her dark tanned legs, past her knees , to her thighs and then , almost to the spot where everything comes together. He had never seen such a pair of tight short shorts, before. They were tighter than Abby's. his eyes continued to move up, over a black V-neck jersey to her neck and shoulders and her face. She was absolutely Gorgeous!!! Prettier than Abby! She had blonde hair that cascaded down the sides of her head to her shoulders. Her lipstick matched the color of her fingernails and toenails. She shook her head and her hair just swirled around. She was the sexiest angel he had ever seen. "Are you Carl?" She asked. "No, but I wish I was.," he said. "Hmm, he is my date, tonight." She said. "Well, then you and I are out of luck." He said, "Carl just took off with my ex-girlfriend. He showed her the ring that Abby had thrown at him. "Then it's you and I". She took his hand and led him out of the kitchen to the dance floor. "I'm Sherry and I really like your looks. I'll bet your better looking than Carl, anyway. I'm lonely and want to dance." "okay" he said. She turned around and came face to face with him . "You're really cute!" She exclaimed. She put his hands around her and placed them on the small of her back. She put her arms around him and put them on each of his bottom's cheeks. She gave his cheeks a tight squeeze, which sent him, tightly up against her. She lay the side of her face against his. Her perfume made his head spin. She whispered in his ear, "I love the smell of Old Spice. It really gets to me." They were swaying so close . She whispered again, "God, you are the sexiest guy here, you're driving me crazy." He couldn't believe his ears. He gulped, "You are the most beautiful, sexiest girl here," She stepped back and looked at him and said, "That's it." She grabbed his hand and led him into the dimly lit room with the couches and recliner chair. She found a recliner, away from the other couples who were making out. She pushed him into the chair and then moved onto his lap. She leaned in and put her luscious lips to his. They began to

move their lips together. Her hands went to his shirt and unbuttoned it. She ran her hands all over his chest. He began to lose all sense of reasoning. This was not love! Even though, he enjoyed her kisses, he felt "nothing' for her. She didn't seem to care, who she made out with! Yet, he was enjoying himself! He couldn't help but respond to her kisses. He knew that he probably would never see Abby, again. The anger, hurt and frustration seemed to come out with his kissing, Sherry! Their kisses began to intensify! When they parted their lips, for air, she exclaimed, "Wow! I like the way you kiss! I don't know if you like me, or you're angry about the girl that left with my ex -date!" He didn't say anything. Once again, they began to make out. Then a voice rang out loud and clear," Party's over! Everyone has to leave, NOW!" It was Sherry' older sister, Dottie. Sherry, immediately, got off him and brought her jersey back over her chest. He was unable to get out of the chair, right away, due to his erection. He was one of the last to leave the party and the house. Sherry had disappeared, as quickly as she had appeared. He found his way to the car, got in and turned it on and headed for home. Lloyd Price was singing, "Stagger Lee" on the radio. He just knew he had to see Sherry again and soon. He hadn't thought about Abby, at all.

He parked the Jeep in the driveway and made his way through the back door, into the kitchen, down the front hall and up the stairs to his room. He was surprised to see his folks in his brother Dave's room. They were both awake. "How was the party?" his Mom asked. "Interesting." He replied, then asked, "How come you are both in Dave's room.?" His father answered. "Your brother went back to college today. We moved our beds up here and his downstairs in our old room." "How come?" he asked, again. "This room is bigger than the other." "Okay." He said, " Good night." They both wished him a good night and went back to reading their books. "Damn!" He ,thought to himself. "I can't bring myself off tonight, they'll hear me." He just knew he was going to wake up , in the morning, with a serious aching feeling. Then, it hit him! He would go back downstairs and use the bathroom off of their old bedroom. He didn't waste any time. He made the excuse of wanting to see if there was anything on TV. "Don't think so dear." His Mom said, "It's after midnight and all the programs are off the air." He went downstairs, anyway. It didn't take him long to accomplish his mission. He came back up the stairs and, again said goodnight and went to his room.

He woke up early the next morning. It was a bright sunny, Sunday morning. He wanted to get in the car and drive over to Sherry's house. He knew had to wait to wait until ,at least, after the noon hour. His mom had jeep, anyway. She ,always drove it to church. After their Sunday dinner, he excused himself and, wearing polished chinos and a dress shirt, he drove to her house. He parked , in front, like he did last night, and walked up the walk to the big oaken doors. He rang the gold plated door bell. He waited for a few minutes and then rang it again. This time, the ring was answered. The door opened and a rather heavy black woman, in a light blue dress with a large white apron stood in the doorway. "Yes?" She asked. "Is Sherry home?" he asked. "Who?" she said. "Sherry." He repeated. "Do you mean Charise?" She asked. He did not know her by that name. "Dottie's sister." He said. "Charise." She said. "No, their folks drove them both to the airport this morning. They are going to be studying abroad this year , in Europe." She closed the big Oak doors, in his face. It hit him, as he stood there, last night was a going away party for them. His heart felt like it crashed around his loafers. He, slowly turned and walked back towards the car. Not only had he "lost" Abby, he, now felt like he lost Sherry, too. He ,suddenly, felt quite alone. He climbed into the car and proceeded to drive home. Laverne Baker was on the radio, singing " I Cried A Tear." She was followed by Fats Domino singing " Aint That A Shame." How appropriate! He said to himself. Finding another girlfriend had come "easy" to him, before. Somehow, he knew, it wasn't going to be easy, this time. He parked the car, in the driveway, and went back into the house. He couldn't remember when he felt so sorry for himself.

He walked into the den and sat in one of the easy chairs. His Mom came into the den and told him that since " this is your last week, working for Mr. Stone, we decided to all go to the lake, next Friday night." He liked that idea. He hadn't seen his "buddy" Danny, since last summer. "you better pack enough clothes for two weeks. We plan on staying over Labor Day." "Okay!" he said. Then his Mom hit him hard in the heart. "Why don't you ask Abby, if she wants to come with us." He mumbled, " we broke up last night." "Oh honey!" She said, "I'm so sorry.. well, maybe you'll meet someone , at the lake." He thought ,to himself, as he headed up the stairs, to figure out what he'll bring, maybe she's right, maybe I will meet someone.

His last week of work, with Mr. Stone, took him to the western part of the state. So. He was away from home, every night. He wouldn't have been able to call Abby anyway, if they were still together. Mr. Stone dropped him off at his house, that Friday, around noon. He handed him his weekly pay, in cash, and another hundred, in cash. "It's a bonus." Mr. Stone said, "You were a big help to me, this summer. You are a credit to your parents. You have a wonderful work ethic. I wish you well, in all you do." He thanked Mr. Stone and told him that it was a pleasure working for him. He stood on the sidewalk, in front of his house, and watched that gold 1958 Caddy pull away and drive down the street. He turned and walked into the house. "Get your bag and meet your Dad by his car. He's waiting for us." His Mom said. He went up to his room. Before he packed his stuff, he went to his "bank." He counted over seven hundred dollars. He felt very rich!. He put five hundred and fifty back into the bank, and pocketed one hundred and fifty into his wallet. He thought ,to himself, as he packed his bag. "Abby, we would have had a wonderful time, spending some of this money." He thought of Sherry and how he could have taken her on dates, she was accustomed to going on. He heaved a sigh as he put two dress shirts and two pairs of chinos in the bag, on top of his underwear and t-shirts and "polo"Shirts and dungarees. He put in five pairs of socks and underwear. He changed into a polo shirt and a pair of dungarees and his engineer boots. He put a pair of Keds and black loafers on top of the bag. He, then, picked up the bag, with his left hand and held the sneakers by the laces and cuddled the loafers in the crook of his right arm. He managed, somehow, to get out to his Dad's car, with the help of his Mom, opening doors. "Tell him, I only have two more small bags to pack." He said that he would relay the message to his Dad, who he knew, would not welcome the news. His Dad took his bag and placed it in the trunk. He was meticulous about packing a trunk. It had to be done just right, in order for the trunk lid to close properly. "We may have to put those two other bags of your mothers' in the back seat with you." He told his dad that he hoped not. "Sorry to hear about you and Abby." He said, "maybe now, you can concentrate more on your studies this year. You do know that colleges really look at your junior year grades, don't you?" he said that he knew and would really work at improving his grades. His Dad's smile didn't last too long, as he noticed his Mom carrying her last two bags to the trunk of the car. She laid the bags on the driveway and went and got into the passenger side of the front seat, of his dad's 1957 Mercury. He watched his dad, thinking, wondering how he was going to find room for the bags. He knew, if there was a way to do it, his dad would find it. He decided to get into the back seat and wait. His Dad did not like an "audience" while he was trying to figure out his packing. He knew that he figured it out, when he heard the trunk slam shut.

His dad got in behind the wheel and started the car. He looked at his watch and said, "We should make the Howard Johnson's just outside Pittsfield just in time for dinner, as long as we

don't run into heavy traffic." The only part of the trip that bothered him, was having to listen to his folks radio station. He really wished he could hear Rock and Roll. His dad turned up the radio, as they headed North. "Wait a minute!" he thought, to himself , " That's Nat King Cole and the song has a Rock and Roll beat. It was "Send For Me." He liked that song and made a mental note to buy the record. He had to admit that he liked Glenn Miller's " In The Mood." The next song was Kay Starr's " Rock and Roll Waltz." It, too had a great beat. " I can't believe that these singers are trying to get the kids, with these songs." His Dad said to his Mom. He sat back and decided that maybe this trip wasn't going to be so bad, after all. Then came Frank Sinatra with "Love and Marriage." He just sighed and settled back, hoping to take a nap. He didn't realize just how tired he was. The last thing he heard was Patti Page singing 'Tennessee Waltz."

He woke up, when the car came to a stop in the Howard Johnson's parking lot. They got the car and went in. He ordered his usual cheeseburger, fries and chocolate frappe. After their "dinner" , they were back on the road, again. His stomach full, he began to doze off again to Dean Martin's " Memories Are Made Of This." "Wake up! We're here!" His Mom said. It was pitch black. He stumbled out of the car and went to the trunk, to help unload the bags. His Mom went ahead of him and his Dad, to turn on the porch lights and inside lights of the living room. He picked up his bag and one of his mom's and waited for the porch light and pole light at the end of the path, to come on. The pole light illuminated the parking area. Once the lights came on, he headed for the cottage. Once inside, he went and deposited his Mom's bag in their bedroom and then went into his room and put the bag on his bed. His dad followed him into the cottage, carrying his bag and another of his mom's. He went back out to the car and grabbed his mom's last remaining bags and brought them out of the car and headed for the porch. His dad passed him on the path. He was going to lock the car up, for the night. He never could understand why he felt he had to lock the car, in the middle of the woods.

Once, back in his room, he unpacked the bag and put the empty case in the closet. He went back out into the living room. The place always seemed to have a "musty" smell to it, whenever they first arrived. He surmised it was because it was closed up for a couple of weeks. He asked his dad if they were going fishing, in the morning. "After my swim." He said. He went past the large open fireplace, into the kitchen and opened the door to the porch. He turned on the porch light and reached up to the brackets holding the fishing rods and reels. He took down his rod and checked to make sure, it would be ready for use, in the morning. It was ready. He went back into the cottage, to the hall closet and took out his tackle box , from the floor of the closet. He opened it up and made sure everything was just as he left it. He looked up at the shelf and found his old fishing hat. He brought it down and looked at it, in the light. He checked the fishing license. It was still "good." He took the tackle box and hat out to the porch and put it in the floor of the porch near the rods. He was ready. All he had to do, in the morning, was got to the shed, by the side of the cottage and get the Johnson 5 HP outboard, along with the gas tank and put the motor to the transom ,of the boat and hook up the gas can. His Mom and dad were already sitting in their respective chairs, in the living room. Mom was reading a book that she had left, from the previous time there. Dad was doing his crossword puzzle, in the paper. He was bored! If he had female companionship, they would be out sitting on the end of the dock, looking at the stars and probably making out ,too. He wasn't sure what time it was, because the sunburst clock on the living room wall had stopped working. He decided to go to bed early, so he could get things ready for the early morning fishing trip.

Wet water was spraying on him. He opened one eye and saw his dad, in a wet bathing suit, Spraying him with the residue of his early morning swim. "Get up!" he ordered. He rose up, slowly, put on the same t- shirt and dungarees that he wore yesterday. He dug his keds out of the closet floor and put them on and went into the bathroom to take care of "business" and brush his teeth. His mom was still asleep. He came out of the bath room and walked out into the living room and looked out the large picture window, facing the lake. A grayish white mist rose off the surface of the water. The sun would be rising very soon. He went to the porch and turned on the porch light. He went out onto the dock and noticed that his dad, in his swim, had brought the row boat into the dock, from it's mooring. How he could swim, so early in the mor ning, was beyond him. He joined him once. When he exited from the water, he had six or seven leeches on his legs. That was enough for him. He ,now, only swims, during the day, when the sun is out.

He went to the shed and unlocked the door and brought the Johnson over to the dock and the boat. He positioned it on the transom of the boat and turned the flat edged screws, to lock it in place. He, then, went back to the shed and got the gas tank. It was heavy. He carried it to the boat. He was glad it was heavy. One rule ,of the house was when someone was done with the motor, they were always to leave the cottage with a full tank of gas, for the boat. He hooked u[p the gas line and primed the pump, on the gas line. He, then, put the gear in neutral and pulled the starter cord. The Johnson came to life. The motor purred like a well fed kitten. He said to the motor, "you may not be fast, but you are dependable." His dad had changed into his fishing gear and came down the dock, carrying his rod and tackle box. He got out of the boat and went back onto the porch and retrieved his "gear." Once they were both in the boat. His dad untied the lines holding the boat to the dock cleats. He put the motor in reverse gear and slowly backed away from the dock . Once clear of the dock, he put it in forward gear and the y headed for their favorite spot. It was a small cove just across the channel, from the cottage. It was quiet and away from other boats. The bottom was littered with huge boulders that the bass liked to hang around. Dawn was beginning to break, as the mist dissipated. The water was so clear and calm, he could see the boulders on the bottom. He turned off the motor and let the boat, silently drift over the large rocks. His dad brought the anchor of the bottom of the boat and let it slip gently over the side and into the water, slowly sinking into the depths. It took the ,almost, all the rope. To the bottom. He could see it resting near a huge rock, but on the sand. They began to set up their rods. His dad liked to "fly fish", while he just used his spinning rod and artificial bait.

Sometimes, the fishing was really good. Other times, nothing. This was one of those times. They had a few 'bites" but were unable to "land" anything. They fished for quite a while. He thought, "they never really spoke to each other, on those trips." His dad ,always said, that conversation scared the fish away. He always hoped they would have some father and son conversations, but they never did. The sun was out and started to really beat down on them and the water. It was time to go in and get some breakfast. His dad pulled up the anchor as he put the gear in neutral and started the motor, and put it in forward. He turned the boat around and headed out of the cove, to open water and home.

Breakfast, always, seemed to taste better ,at the cottage. His Mom said, it was the cool crisp mountain air, that added to the flavor. He didn't know. He just liked the taste. After breakfast, he helped his mom wash and dry the utensils, skillet, and glasses. They never used real dishes. For them, must paper plates. It made cleanup easy. He left the dining area, by the kitchen and went out to the porch, down the steps ,to the dock. He stepped into the boat and got his fishing gear and brought it out of the boat and put it back on the wall, of the porch. He put his tackle box and hat, on the floor. His dad had already removed his stuff from the boat.

His folks were going into town and do some shopping. He declined to go with them. He was going to change into his bathing suit and sit on the dock. Gloom began to set it on him, as he sat in the deck chair, he bought from the porch. This was the first time he was really alone sans female companionship. "This really sucks!" he said. He got out of the chair, went to the end of the dock and made a shallow swan dive into the cool, sparkling water. He was just clearing the surface, when a large SPLOOSH sent water over his head and into his eyes, mouth and ears. He , again, reached the surface and yelled, "What the Hell!" he looked and saw another head break to the surface. It was Danny!" He was glad to see him, even with almost being hit by his "cannon ball" dive. They laughed and splashed each other, like two little boys. They took turns climbing up the ladder, by the side of the dock. He looked around the dock and the waters near the dock, no boat! "How did you get here?" He asked. "Car," answered Danny. "Oh." He assumed he meant he borrowed his Dad's truck. Danny went up to the porch and returned with another deck chair. They plopped themselves into each chair. "Didn't think I heard your boat pull up." He said. "No," said Danny, folks still aren't too crazy about me taking it out of winter harbor." "You mean, after all this time, they are still bringing that up." He said. "Ayuh." Said Danny. "Wow!" he said. "Well," said Danny, "we really shook them up, that time." "Guess so." He replied. "Shook us up, too." He remembered what they were talking about, as is it was yesterday. They , along with Keith, Danny's distant cousin, had decided to take Danny's runabout for a trip to town. It was late in the afternoon. They got to town okay and spent quite a bit of time there. The sun had set, by the time they got back in the boat and headed for home. Not only was the sky dark, but they could tell that they were riding into a storm. Waves crashed over the bow, sending water over the small deck and into the seating area. Danny backed the motor off to a real slow speed, so as to prevent the boat from being tossed too much. They could just make out the white caps, in the dark. Keith began to bail out the water, with a small bailing can. He tried to help Danny navigate through the waves and the heavy rains that whipped against their faces, causing their eyes to close a lot. They were all a lot younger then, and their inexperience didn't help. They weren't sure. Exactly where they were. As they plodded along. What should have taken minutes to get home, stretched into the hours. What made Danny turn to the left, when he did, was anybody's guess. They saw land, very close, to their left. "I think that may be the airport." He said. They hoped they were in Winter harbor. The storm grew worse, in intensity. If they were scared, they didn't show it, to each other. That would have meant 'weakness" on their parts. He thought, that, if they were inside Winter harbor, the waves should have subsided some, but they didn't. How they saw it, he still didn't know, but there it was. Through the pelting rain, a building. Was it a boathouse? Danny steered, as well as he could, towards it. As they got closer, they realized it was the Libby Museum! They were in Winter Harbor! The waves were now rocking the boat from side to side. If he turned the boat to the left, the boat would have been swamped and them in it. So he stayed the course. They made it to the museum dock. Danny turned off the motor and they grabbed the dock with their hands and held on tight. Danny told them, that the ropes probably wouldn't hold the boat, in the storm. So, he and Keith got out onto the dock, holding the ropes. Danny got out, next and the three of them battled the waves, rain, lightning and thunder and slowly brought the boat around to the boat launch, by the dock. It took the three of them, with all their might to drag the boat, heavy with water in it, up and out of the water on to the soaked land. When they felt it was far enough out of the water, Danny took a rope and tied the motor down to the transom. They made plans to come back, early in the morning , weather permitting, to retrieve the boat. They were drenched, but happy to be off the lake. They proceeded to walk home, along the road. It took them another 45 minutes to get to Danny's house. No one was home! They weren't sure why his folks would be out in the storm. For some reason, they decided to walk down the road, to the cottage, that his folks were renting. As they approached the door to the porch, they heard the cursing and yelling. It came from all their families! They weren't sure they should go into the house, or not, but his mother turned and saw them. "They're here!!!" She yelled. At first, everyone was glad to see them and then when

they realized that the they were okay, just soaking wet. The fury began. Danny's father. After "chewing him out" asked about the boat. Danny told him where it was and that they were going to go back in the morning and get it. His father told him that he was not going anywhere hear that boat, for a very long time.

"yep." He said. That was probably the worst trouble we ever got in." The, he asked Danny how he came to the cottage. " I got a car," Danny said. "Really? " he asked. "What kind?" Danny answered, " A 1954 Ford custom." "Where is it?" he asked. "In your driveway." Danny said. " I want to see it." He said. So, the two of them got out of the deck chairs and put on their sneakers and went to look at it. It was dark blue, a four door sedan, with a V-eight motor. It was real clean and when he started it up, the engine ran real smooth. "Very nice." He said, envious.

As they were looking at it, his folks drove up from shopping. They greeted Danny. His father remarked what a nice car it was. Danny thanked him, as he turned off the motor. His dad told the two of them, they were just in time to help unload the groceries. They went to the trunk and each grabbed two paper bags of groceries. "We're going to have a late lunch, Danny, you'll stay and eat with us." His Mom said. Danny tried to say "no", but his mother insisted.

She made tuna fish sandwiches and she put a large bag of chips on the table, in the eating space. They each had a bottle of coke. After they ate, Danny mentioned that a new record store had opened downtown and that they should go check it out. Danny gulped hard with a slight chuckle when his dad asked them, "You're not going by boat are you?" "No, dad", he said. " Good." His father said. Danny thanked his mom for lunch. He went to his room, to change into 'street' clothes. Danny had gone to his car and came back with his "street" clothes. He changed out of his suit, in the bathroom. When he said goodbye to his folks, he hung his damp suit on the clothes line by the side of the camp. Danny hung his off the radio antenna. They got in the car and Danny started it up and he put it in reverse gear and backed down the driveway, turned and faced the dirt road as the headed for town. The Coasters were singing "Searchin" on the radio. "That's the new station over in Laconia. They play all the latest stuff, plus old ones ,too." Danny said. To prove what he was saying, the station played The Cadillacs "Speedo, " next. As they drove along, he thought ,to himself, this is just what he needed to help him get over his blues."

When they got to town, Danny parked by the town docks. They exited the car and went into the small record store. Danny found the Coasters record of "Searchin." He found Nat King Cole's "Send For Me." He, also, found the Everly Brothers, "Bird Dog." They went to the counter with their records, paid the 89 cents a piece for them and went back to the car. Danny mentioned that there was, also, a new ice cream parlor, in town. They put their records on the back shelf, above the back seat, by the rear window; locked the car and headed to get some ice cream. The store had tables set up by the sidewalk. They got their cones and sat at one of the tables and slowly devoured their treats. When they had finished, they headed back to the car and got in and started for home. Danny said he wanted to stop by his house, on the way, and put his record away. On the way home, Jimmy Rodgers was on the radio, singing "Honeycomb". He mentioned to Danny that was the only record, he had that his father actually liked. Danny joked, "You mean, he doesn't like Little Richards' "Tutti Frutti"?" They laughed.

Danny pulled into his yard and parked in front of the large gray barn. They got out of the car. He climbed into the back seat to retrieve the records. When he picked them up, the sides folded up, like a Mexican Taco. The sun, beating down on the car and through the back window, melted the plastic records. They just stood outside the car and looked at the records. Danny thought since they were still quite warm, he could bend them back and straighten them out. He tried and got them somewhat flat, but they were still badly warped. He told Danny, "let's go back downtown and get some more. I'll pay for them, since it was my fault, for putting them on the shelf." Danny agreed. He went into his house and told his Mom, that they had to go back downtown for a while. They made a "pact" never to tell anyone what they had done to the records. When they got back to the store, the guy behind the counter recognized them. "Didn't you guys just buy the same records earlier?" They told him they had and that the records were warped and wouldn't play. The guy just shook his head and took his money and gave them the new records. They got back into the car and, this time, he held them on his lap. When they got back to Danny's, he, quickly, took his record into the house. While Danny was in the house, he found a trash barrel by the barn and he disposed of the warped ones. He had just returned to the car, when Danny's mom came towards him, from their screened in porch. "Tell your Mom and dad that the cookout on the beach tonight will be around six." "Okay." He answered. He found himself getting excited. He, always, enjoyed the cookouts and the stories that Danny's dad told. Danny came out and got into the car. He didn't ask what happened to the warped records. "Oh. My Mom asked if your mom can bring a bag of chips and a bowl of potato salad, and whatever you are drinking." He told Danny that he would tell her. When they got to the cottage. Danny stayed in the car, as he got out, with his records. "See you in a little while." Danny yelled out the driver's side window, which was rolled down. He walked into the cottage and put his records on top of his dresser. He went into the kitchen and told his folks about the cookout and what she was asked to bring.

He went out to the clothes line and checked his bathing suit. It was dry. He brought it back into the cottage and put that too, on the dresser. His dad asked him to give him a hand with the three folding deck chairs that were left on the dock. "Let's just put them in the trunk of my car, for the cookout." They carried the chairs to the car and put them in the trunk. He went back in to the cottage and to his room, to decide what he would wear, to the cookout. As he sat on his bed, he thought about what happened with the records. It seemed, to him, that when he and Danny get together, something goes wrong. He began to wonder if the two of them were being punished by God, for some of the things they did, in the past. The name, Tyler Martin came out of his subconscious and, practically, slapped him in his face.

Tyler Martin was a short, fat, little kid. He epitomized the term "nerd". He wore thick eyeglasses that sat, almost, at the end of his nose. His round face made him seem even shorter that he was. His voice had a distinct nasal quality, that seemed to ingratiate both he and Danny's nerves, especially when he "whined". Which was, practically, all the time. He and Danny picked on Tyler, a lot. Tyler always came back for more. Danny's mom insisted that the two of them, Danny and he, always included Tyler in their plans. Tyler was like the little brother that always had to "tag along" even when he wasn't wanted. They didn't "bully" Tyler, or insult him. They just wanted to be left alone and do their own thing. So, they would do things or have Tyler do things that would, eventually, cause Tyler to go home.

There was the time, he and Danny, asked Tyler to go to the back of one of the old rowboats, to check the transom. While, he leaned over to check it, they pulled the boat, quickly, up on the beach, catapulting Tyler over the transom and into the water. The time, they had him help them, catch some bullfrogs and Tyler ended up in the swampy water. Then, there was the time, he and Danny, invited Tyler to play baseball, in one of the fields. He was in the outfield and Danny pitched. Tyler was the first one up, to bat. Danny threw a "perfect" pitch and Tyler swung the bat and hit the ball, sending it over his head, into left field. Danny yelled at Tyler to run to first base and all the bases. While Tyler was running, Danny found a "fresh" cow flap and stood behind it, making it home base. He got the ball and threw it as hard as he could. The ball was on its' way to Danny. Tyler rounded third and was heading "home", as was the baseball. Danny yelled to Tyler, at the top of his lungs, "Slide, Tyler, Slide!!!!" Tyler slid into "home", right through the "fresh" cow flap. It covered his leg all the way to his waist and up the right side of his shirt. It was not a pretty sight and the odor was not so sweet either. Tyler went home and he and Danny went down, to the beach, to swim.

He doesn't remember seeing much of Tyler, after that summer. So, again, something always goes "a foul" when he and Danny get together. Some summers, it got worse, when his cousin Keith came, for vacation. Such was the time when Danny found an old outboard motor and gave it to Keith. Poor Keith tried, unsuccessfully, every morning, of his vacation, to try and start that motor. He and Danny, often wondered, how Keith's arm never seemed to tire from pulling the starter cord.

One year, Keith got even. Danny's dad had bought a 15 foot boat with a Scott Atwater motor. They had more fun, with that boat, except for the afore mentioned time, of nearly drowning in the storm. Along with the boat was a "homemade" heavy wooden surfboard. Not the type that surfers would use to ride ocean waves, but the type that was to be pulled behind a boat. It's bottom was two pieces. The back was flat, while the front was at an upward angle, so it would ride on the water and not "plow". Keith found some ropes. One set was attached, in a loop. To the front of the board. That loop was to be held by whoever was riding it. The second set of ropes were quite longer and attached to the back of the boat. Since, only, Danny was allowed to "drive" the boat, he went first, on the surfboard, while his Dad drove it. Next Danny drove, while Keith rode the board. He made a remark about Keith's weight, which didn't sit too well with Keith. Danny was not allowed to run at full speed, when pulling someone, on the board. They pulled Keith around the harbor a few times and then brought him back in towards the beach. Next, was his turn, on the board. Keith was in the boat, with Danny driving. He noticed that the rope. He was holding onto, was really quite "worn". He wondered why Keith hadn't mentioned it. As he looked at the "frail" rope, he was unaware that the boat was travelling at full speed. When Danny made a left turn, to go back in towards the beach, the board slipped out of the "wake" and picked up a tremendous amount of speed, slapping over the surface of the water, barely touching the surface. He loved it!!! Then, he looked down at the rope, just as it snapped. Unfortunately, the tow rope snapped, at the same time. For a few seconds, he and the surfboard were one and the same, slapping the water and careening out of control. When he was no longer on the board, he was skimming across the water on his back. He had no idea where the board was. He, finally, slowed down and came to a stop and began to sink into the depths of Lake Winnipesaukee. He, quickly, regained his senses and moves his arms and legs and brought himself back to the surface, just in time to be picked up by Keith and Danny, in the boat. Then, they went to retrieve the surfboard was bobbing in the water near them. They slowly towed the board back to the beach. Needless to mention, Danny's dad was none too pleased and the boat and the board were retired for the rest of the day.

These events and many stories would be told and retold at many, many, cookouts, for years to come. He was looking forward to going to the beach, that night. For one thing, it might help him to forget about Abby and Sherry. Laughter, and their friends, always managed to make "someone" forget bad times. Danny's father, always, seemed to have the greatest stories. His Mom handed him the large bowl of potato salad and told him to put on the floor of the back seats, of the car. When he got back to the cottage, to get his bathing suit and towel, his dad handed him a six pack of Coca Cola and told him to put them on the floor of the backseat. When he finished that, he went into the cottage and got a towel and walked outside to the clothes line and grabbed his bathing suit. He was ready.

They all got into the car as his dad started up the Mercury. He backed the sedan down the dirt driveway and turned it, at the end and proceeded up their dirt driveway. After a mile and a half, they turned onto the pavement and headed for the beach. When they got to the top of Danny's dirt road, his dad slowed the car, way down and slowly edged it down the road, avoiding the huge boulders that lined the sides, but, also, protruded out of the grassy medium strip. When they finally got down to the beach area, he parked it in such a way that they could easily just drive back up the road. His mom took the bowl, his dad, the cokes. He left the suit and towel in the back seat. As they walked towards the beach, he could smell the aroma of "dogs" and "burgers" on the grill. Danny's dad was at the grill, cooking. His Dad gave him the keys to the car and told him to get the chairs out of the trunk. Danny offered to go with him and help. As they walked, to the car, Danny implored him not to talk about the warped records. He promised he wouldn't.

They were sitting around in a horseshoe shape, facing the water, waiting for the meat to be done. He heard another car come down the road. When the people in that car, got out. He recognized Keith, his sisters and their folks. He said, to himself, "this was going to be a great party!" Everyone greeted one another and then Danny's father said "let's eat!" After everyone had ate their full, they gathered around a large pit that was full of wood and kindling. Danny's dad, lit the fire and the little kids got their marshmellows ready. Danny's father sat back, in his chair and began to tell the stories. The first one had "props." He reached into a paper bag and produced three "warped" records. He and Danny put their heads down towards their laps. "My 11 yr old daughter, Daryll found these in our trash barrel, this afternoon. I'm sure my son has a good story to tell about this. Danny glared at his sister. He felt that if Danny had his way, Daryll would not live to see 12. Danny explained what happened and everyone had a good laugh. His father mentioned that it wouldn't have been a big loss, if one of the records was "Tutti Fruiti." The rest of the evening centered around farm life in New Hampshire and cows. The adults had many laughs. He kept noticing Keith's sister, Kayla. She was cute and kind of sexy. She was a year younger than him, and Danny. Unfortunately, she never really showed any interest in him or Danny. All he ever got was a nice smile and that was about as far as it went.

Danny's Dad brought the conversation back to Danny and how the records warped, in the heat. He asked Danny, "Who drove the car to town?" Danny said that he did. His dad, then, told him that with the learner's permit, he was not allowed to drive without a licensed driver with him. He said to Danny's Dad that he was a licensed driver. "Okay." Danny's dad said, "but how did you and he get together?" That's when Danny had the keys to his car, taken away. The sullen mood didn't last long. Danny's aunt Pat produced a birthday cake from the back of their car. The candles were lit, at the table, and everyone sang "Happy Birthday" to Danny. He got the keys back, with the stipulation that he not drive over to his house, anymore, until he got his permanent license. He gave Danny 20 bucks, in a card, his mom had got, while shopping downtown. It was a great party. He just wished that he wasn't alone.

The rest of the vacation went well. He and Danny managed to stay out of trouble. They spent a lot of time, with Keith, playing baseball and swimming and listening to their records. The vacation went by too fast for him. He did look forward to school, that fall of 1958. Maybe, he would find another girlfriend. He hoped so. After the Labor day weekend, they all said their goodbyes and went their separate ways, until next summer.

It wasn't long, after school started, that his Mom traded in the Jeep and bought a 1957 Volkswagon Beetle. It was dark green, with a tan interior, a sunroof, that when opened, went from just behind the windshield to just behind the back seats. It came with a nice sounding radio. with one speaker, up front and one in back of the rear seat. He liked the fact that it had dual exhausts. The only problem was "reserve gear". He had to bring the shift up near him and press down on it, for it to go into reverse. It was difficult to do. It, also, did not have a gas gauge, but it did have a reverse tank. He had to put his foot up under the dashboard to switch tanks. The small car was fun to drive, but dating, in it, was a problem. He decided to look for his own set of "wheels".

October, 1958 was the month for a tremendous change, in his life. He still was without female companionship. A friend from school told him about a car that one of his friends was trying to sell or trade. It was a 1946 Ford sedan, four door. The friend had just bought a '51 Ford convertible and was looking for "things' to dress it up. One of the things was a set of Spun aluminum wheel covers called "Moon Disks". He just happened to have a set and didn't need anymore, because the fit the Jeep, which his mom no longer had. His friend told him that he would take him by the other friend's house and see if a deal could be made. They got together, on a Saturday morning, and went to the guy's house. He brought the disks with him and some cash from his "bank". The car was sitting, in the guy's driveway. It was black, with a light blue interior. He got in and started it up. The motor came to life and purred like a well fed kitten. The guy looked at the disks and gave him a price of one hundred dollars and the disks for the car. He liked the deal and handed him the cash and the disks. He got in the car and drove it to his house, with his high school friend, following him. When he parked it at the very end, of the driveway, he and his friend took off the license plates. His friend would take them back to the other guy. When the guy left, he took a good look, at his car. It had a three speed column shift. The interior was in good shape and the exterior needed a little work. He, already, made plans to alter the outside. He was going to "nose" it, by taking off all the chrome, on the nose of the hood and the trim alongside the hood. He walked to the rear and was making plans to "deck" the trunk lid, by taking all the chrome off it. That part would be easy. The difficult part was adding duel exhausts to the exhaust system. His own car, another milestone.

The following Monday, he called his Dad's insurance agent and worked out a monthly payment plan. He had to wait two days, for his insurance card, to arrive, in the mail. That Wednesday, after school, He drove the VW to the Registry of Motor vehicles and got the car registered. When he got home, he attached his new license plates. He got in the car and "burned rubber" going out of the driveway. He drove to the local gas station and filled it up. The attendant checked the oil. "You need two quarts of oil." He said. "okay." He told the attendant. He paid for the gas and oil and started it up. He noticed a bluish white cloud of smoke rise up from the back of the car where the tailpipe was. The attendant told him that it looked like the motor needed a set of new rings. His excitement faded. He knew that if he didn't get the motor fixed, it would mean he would need a new motor. He realized he needed to find an after school job.

His Mom and Dad were sympathetic, but offered no financial help. It was, also, during this time, that six of his friends, in high school, were forming a Hot Rod club. It was named the "Aladdins".

The logo showed Aladdin's lamp with a huge motor in the front and large wheels on the back. They asked him to join. He did. He, even, ordered a jacket with his name on the left shoulder and the logo, on the back. The jacket was black with gold trim. The club was working on a class "C" dragster that they wanted to race the following summer. They would meet, every Friday night, in a room over one of the guy's garage. At one of the meetings, he mentioned to Jack, the guy whose garage they met in, his problem with the motor of his car. Jack and the others said that wasn't a problem. They asked him if he wanted to keep the "flathead" in the car or put something with more power in it. He didn't think twice about answering that question. Ralph, another member, mentioned that a guy, he knew, was "junking" a 1957 Oldsmobile "Rocket" and would give anyone the motor, if they took it out of the car. He said that he wanted the motor. The adapters would cost less than a ring job. They all went over to the guy's house and found the Olds sitting behind the garage. Jack had a pickup truck and brought a chain fall set, to help take the motor out of the car. It didn't take them long to loosen and take apart the front motor mounts. The engine refused to come out of the car. Someone had a jack and jacked up the front passenger side of the Olds. He climbed under the car and located the rear transmission mounts. He would have to loosen them and take them off the frame. The engine and transmission would come out together. The others left him, to go get some burgers and would bring him some, while he worked on the mounts. He came out from under the car and placed his Craftsmen tool box by the jacked up front tire, under the frame. He opened up the box and took out the necessary tools. He closed the box and slid on his back, under the car, to work on the mounts. He slid, on his back, under the transmission, to the drivers' side and unhooked the linkages to the shifter. He, then worked on the mount. When he finished that mount, he slid back to the passenger side and began to work on that mount. It was harder that the first. He slid back out, opened his box and took out a hammer. He slid back under and placed the ratchet around the bolt and began to hit the end of the ratchet, to loosen the bolt. He heard a noise and, all of a sudden, the jack failed, sending the car down onto his stomach and chest. The car rested just inches from crushing him to death. He lay, quietly, not wanting to disturb whatever was keeping that big Oldsmobile from ending his life.

It seemed like hours, before the others returned with lunch. When they drove up, in the driveway, they knew something was wrong. They saw his feet and the car was not sitting high on the jack. They ran to where his feet were. "Hey man! You all right!" Jack yelled. ":Yeah." He said, "the jack failed and something saved my life." He heard them replace the jack and cranked the car back up. When there was enough room for his to slide out from underneath, he stood up beside the car and checked himself all over. When he realized he wasn't injured, he looked to see what had saved him being crushed to death. It was his Craftsmen tool box! He had placed it under the frame and when the jack failed, the box took the brunt of the weight. It had a huge horizontal dent along the top. The others gathered around him and told him how very lucky he was. This was the greatest milestone, so far! First, if he hadn't joined the club, and second, the box saving his life!

They put another jack on the drivers' side of the car, so the whole front end was off the ground. They didn't jack the car as high as they did the first time. He had just enough room to get under the car and by the transmission to "work" the last remaining mount. It was done! He got out from under the car and they all sat and ate their burgers, fries and drank their cokes. When they were finished, the hoisted the motor out of the Olds and swung it into the bed of jacks' pickup. They stored the chain fall behind the garage, out of sight and would come back for it later. They unloaded the motor on the floor of jack's garage and went back for the chain fall. Once back in Jack's garage, they set up the fall and hoisted the motor, off the floor, and secured it. His next plan, was to get the adapters he would need, to install the "rocket" into the Ford.

He began doing odd jobs to raise more money. He caddied on Saturdays, was a pin boy two nights a week; delivered the Sunday newspapers. He was able to raise enough money to continue work, on the Ford. He decided to use the transmission from the Olds, as well. His only concern was if the rear end could handle the torque of the motor. He took time off, one Saturday, to put the motor into the Ford. He adjusted and mounted the motor mounts. Next, was the transmission. He bought a floor shifter from a "49 Ford truck. It took some work to line up the linkages from the Olds transmission. After considerable "jury rigging", he was able to connect the shifter to the transmission. He had to put a hole in the floorboard, for the shifter. Everything was "set." He and the other "Aladdins" wired up the motor. He had purchased a manifold that was set up for two, two barrel carburetors. With the carbs in place, they hooked up fuel lines. Next, came the finishing touches to the motor. They primed the carbs as he sat behind the wheel. He put the key, in the ignition and turned it. The motor sputtered and sputtered and "coughed" and then died. They tried again with the same results. Then Jack said, "let me try." He got in behind the wheel and after they, again, primed the carbs, he put his foot hallway down on the gas pedal, and turned the ignition key. The motor "coughed" once and then roared to life! He was ecstatic! Jack took his foot off the gas, as the motor ran smooth in idle position. Jack warned him, that with a motor as powerful as the" Rocket". He needed to install a tachometer. He told Jack that he had asked for one for Christmas. They finished working on the car around 11:45 PM. They had worked all day. He drove his mom's beetle home. He was the happiest paper boy that next Sunday. He knew he would have to wait before he could buy the exhaust system for the duals. His only concern was if the hood would fit over the motor. Needless to say, his studies took a dramatic drop. He still had some time to bring up his grades, before report cards came out.

One afternoon, after school, he went to Jack's garage. He and Jack lifted the hood and gently lined it up and placed it over the motor. It fit! He was so happy! The car was the best thing to happen, to him. It enabled him to forget about girls, at least for the time being. Next came another big step. He and Jack got into the car and he turned it on. They crossed their fingers as he shifted the car into first gear. He gave it some gas and lifted his left foot off the clutch. The car began to move forward. The adapters held. He eased the car out of the garage and onto the driveway. He turned up the volume on the radio and as they headed for the street, the Olympics sang "Western Movies." He felt like a king! The car was his chariot. He thought to himself, as they drove down the street, "the girls are going to come running to me." They rode around for a while and then drove it back to the garage. He needed to make it "legal" in the eyes of the law. It was still, technically, a 1946 Ford, but the motor had to be changed, on papers.

As he drove the Beetle home, he was anxious to get to the registry and get all that paper work settled. He sang along to the Hollywood Argyles, "Alley Oop." When he walked into the house, his mom was surprised that he wasn't as greasy as he had been the other times, he came home from working on the car. He got cleaned up for supper. At the dinner table, his dad wanted to know how the car was coming along and when it was going to take up space in the driveway. "Soon." He said, "very soon." His dad, also, mentioned that he couldn't wait to see his report card for that term. After supper, he went to his room and actually, sat at his desk and did his homework.

Halloween came and went without any surprises or girlfriend. He was glad that the Ford was in a garage and not parked out in the open where vandals could get at it. He stayed home and answered the front door, for all the costumed kids. He would have liked to go to a party, but was not invited. In fact, not one of the" Aladdins" received an invitation. He thought that maybe people, at school, thought they were some kind of "gang." He had worked hard at improving his grades and was doing well. He had nothing else to do, until he could acquire the funds to reregister the car. He was hoping to be able to get some leftover candy, but even that was not to be. By ten o'clock that night, all the candy was gone.

By the end of the week, he had enough money to go to the registry and get the new plates for for the car. He had to wait, almost an hour, before he could see a clerk. The clerk looked over his paperwork. "This is a 1946 Ford sedan, four door, black, with a 1957 Oldsmobile engine. Is that right?" The clerk asked. "yes." He replied. "Boy! You kids sure do know how to mess things up." The clerk said. "Why can't you just use the motors that the cars come with?" It sure would make things simpler for me." The clerk was obviously not happy with all the work, she had to do. After forty five minutes or so, he had the proper paperwork, registration and plates. He walked out of the office, a happy 16 year old.

He drove his mom's VW right to Jack's. He got out of the Beetle and with all his stuff. From the registry, he opened the garage door and went right to the Ford. He took a screwdriver from the tool bench and affixed his new plates to the car. Just as he put the registration and other papers in the glove box, Jack walked in. "All right! She's legal! "He exclaimed. "Yep!" he said. Jack offered to drive the VW and follow him home. He tossed the keys to beetle to Jack and waited for Jack to move the VW out of the driveway, onto the street. He noticed that he wasn't the only one who had trouble putting that little car, in reverse gear. The path was clear. He put the key in the ignition and turned it. The "rocket" roared to life. He, slowly, eased the shift into first gear and began to drive out of the garage and onto the driveway. He gave it just a little gas, but that was all it took for the rubber to burn on the asphalt. He, quickly, left off the gas and eased it down the driveway, onto the street. Richie Valens was singing "Donna" on the radio. he really had the urge to "goose" the gas, as he drove home, but traffic was heavy and the last thing he needed, was to cause a wreck. When they reached his house, Jack pulled the VW into the spot, where he told him to park. When Jack parked the beetle and had exited it, he pulled the Ford in next to it. The Everly Brothers were singing "Bye Bye Love" on the radio. his mom came out the back door, of the house to look at it. He turned off the motor and exited the car. His mom walked around it and told him that it really could use a "paint job." She, also, unwittingly, named the car. "With a good paint job, it will be a real black beauty." He liked that name. "Thanks, Mom." He exclaimed. "That's her name, Black Beauty." Jack handed the keys to the VW, to his mom. She thanked him and was happy that she had two sets of keys. She turned and went back into the house. The hood and the deck still had primer paint on them, where he had removed the chrome. Jack stood looking at him, and finally, asked, "Well, sare you going to drive me home?" he felt kind of stupid. "Of course. Let's go!" They both got into the car and he turned it on and slowly backed it up, till he had space, in the driveway, to turn it around and head out to the street. As he pulled onto the street, in front of his house, he noticed Joan, sitting on the front steps of her house. He rolled down his window and waved to her. She got up off the steps and started to walk towards him. He stopped the car and turned down the El Dorados, "Crazy Little Mama (At My front Door)". "Is this yours?" she asked. "uh huh." He replied. She looked into the car and saw Jack. Apparently, she knew him from school. "Hi Jack." She said, then asked, "Where you going?" he replied that he was taking Jack home. "Can I come?" She asked. "Sure!" he said. Jack got out of the car and Joan went around the front and climbed into the front seat, next to him. Jack got in and sat by the passenger door. He put the car back into first gear and gave it a little more gas than was needed and let out the clutch. Once again, the power of the motor, sent the rear tires burning on the road. They took off down the road and he quickly eased off on the gas as he shifted into second gear and then third. "This is a neat car!" said Joan. "Thanks." He said. She leaned forward and turned up the radio. Little Anthony and the Imperials were singing "Shimmy Shimmy Ko Ko Bop." As he drove, he would steal a glance at Joan. Her blonde hair, tucked in a pony tail, her dungarees, with the bottoms turned up, revealing her lower calves, white socks and black and white Keds. Her dark blue sweatshirt, over a white shirt with the collar turned up. She was very cute! She sat back and put her left arm around his shoulders. He was in heaven! His heart was bursting with pride. Harold Dorman came on the radio with "Mountain Of Love." They all sang along, as he headed for Jacks' house.

Once they dropped Jack off, She slid over towards the passenger door. He wished she had stayed closer to him. He realized he missed that close contact with a girl. He looked at her and then he saw the high school ring, dangling at the end of a chain, around her neck. She was going steady! He shrugged, as he realized she wasn't "free". Laverne Baker sang "Tweedlee Dee." On the radio. She kept exclaiming how she liked the car and wished her boyfriend, Ken had his own car. "Took me a while," he said, "and a lot of work." They didn't say much, after that. They listened to the radio and Bill Doggett's "Honky Tonk". He stated that he really liked part two of the record. She said that she did, too.

He dropped her off, in front of her house. She thanked him and wished him good luck with the car. He, then, drove into his driveway and parked it next to the VW. He turned it off and got out and walked around it. He knew it needed a paint job, before winter came. He, also, wanted the dual exhausts, and he noticed it, also, would look good with fender skirts. He made a "mental" note that those were the things that would make "her' a real "black beauty."

He took on more jobs, at the bowling alley and worked Sunday afternoons, caddying. By Thanksgiving, he had enough funds to get the paint job. His Dad knew of a shop that would do a good job, for less money that he had expected to pay. The day, after thanksgiving, his mom followed him to the shop. The owner said he could have the car back, the middle of the next week. He gave the man his keys and got into his mom's car. She drove them home. He was lost without "Black Beauty". He was excited, as well. He couldn't wait to see how she would look with a new coat of paint. When they got home, he went up to his room and pulled out the note pad that had his "car" list. He checked off the paint job. Next, was the fender skirts and dual exhausts. The weekend dragged on and on. Sunday afternoon, he drove the VW to Jack's house. The "club" was having a meeting. He joined the guys in the backroom of the garage. Many of the guys felt that since they all helped him with the Ford, he should help them with the dragster. He agreed. They went to the other side of the garage, where the dragster was hidden under an old tarp. They pulled off the tarp and began to inspect the rail job. The suspension was still good, as were the tires, and the steering. The only things missing were the seat and the engine. Jack said that the best engine for that type of dragster was a Chevy. Some of the guys had hoped that the Olds wouldn't fit in his Ford and that they could have used that motor. Jack got some rags and handed them out to the others. They spent the rest of the "meeting" cleaning up the race car. They made a pact that they would be racing that machine by the following summer. A seat for the car was going to cost approximately fifty dollars. The motor was going to be considerably more. One of the group, Henry, said he knew where they could get their hands on a 1956 Chrysler engine, in good condition, for little money. They told Henry to check it out and get back to them. Once they had the rails all cleaned up and the back tires switched, along with the front ones, they called it a day. He drove home, realizing. He would get home in time for supper.

His mom let him take the VW to school on Monday and Tuesday, with the stipulation that he come right home from school, so she could go shopping. He did so. He used the afternoons to catch up on his school work. It helped him take his mind off Black Beauty. On Wednesday, he had to take the school bus. Something he hadn't done, for a very long time. Wednesday afternoon, when he got home, he went up to his room and collected the money, to pay for the car. His mom was already waiting for him, in the VW, when he came out of the house. They drove to the paint and body shop. His excitement was so strong, that he didn't even ask to listen to his radio station.

They pulled up to the shop. His Mom got out of the VW, with him. They walked into the shop. He went straight to the office. The owner got up from behind his desk and handed the bill to him. He paid the bill and followed the guy to the back of the shop. The owner said, "I think you're going to like the job." They got to the last booth. His jaw must have dropped right to the floor. She was absolutely beautiful! Her paint glistened under the lights. She looked like she must have looked when she came off the assembly line. The owner directed him to walk around her and make sure he was satisfied with the work. As he approached the back, the owner said, "your dad asked us to do something a little extra, which he paid for." He gulped! What did his dad have done to his car? Then, he saw "it". On the left hand side of the deck, just above the back bumper, at an angle, starting from the bumper and angling up towards the center of the deck, written in Italics, in small letters, but large enough to read, were the words, "Black Beauty." He stood there, staring in disbelief. A lump formed in his throat. He was unable to speak. He walked up to the owner and without saying a word, shook his hand. The owner gave him back his keys. His mom told him she had some Christmas shopping to do and she would see him at home. He got into the car, rolled down the driver's side window, turned up the radio and eased the car out of the garage and into the street. Wilbert Harrison was singing "Kansas City" on the radio. He just knew, people were admiring his car, as he drove through town, on his way home.

He pulled into the driveway and parked at the end. His Dad pulled in behind him and into the garage. He wished his Dad would let him park "Beauty" in the garage, but he knew that was "sacred" space, only for his Dad's Mercury. He got out of the car and greeted his dad with a hefty handshake and thanked him for his contribution to the Ford. His dad was not into hugging and so the handshake was it. They both walked around the Ford. His dad seemed pleased with the work, and was glad that he was happy, too.

Thursday, when he pulled into the student parking area, the "Aladdins" gathered around "beauty" and remarked how beautiful she looked. Others, who had hot rods, also came over and looked at her. George, who had a "41 Plymouth coupe with a Pontiac motor, in it, askedto what was powering the Ford. He put his hand under the front of the hood, by the top of the grill and opened it. George stepped back and let out a low whistle. "You know you and I have got to drag." George said. "maybe." He replied. The late bell rang. He slammed down the hood and went and locked up the car and headed into school, with the others. His heart was bursting with pride! To get a favorable whistle from George, the number one hot rodder, at school, was a big deal. All through the day, others came up to him and asked when was he going to drag George. He told them that he just wasn't ready yet. One even went so far as to call him "chicken", but he came back and told him that he would drag him, just not now. After school, it was obvious that word had got out about Black Beauty. When got to her, there was a crowd gathered around her. Again, he was asked to "pop" the hood. Gasps filled the air. One asked if it was an Olds Rocket. He replied that it was. Already, kids began to place bets that the Olds would "take" the Pontiac. He told them that he still had a lot of work to do on the ford, before there would be any racing. He unlocked her and climbed in. Then, he saw them, Joan and Ken.

They walked up to the car, holding hands. Joan asked if he would give them a ride home, seeing that they lived across the street from each other. He said, "sure" and they ran around the front and climbed in beside him, in the front seat. Joan sat next to him, while Ken sat by the passenger door. "The car looks fantastic!" Joan said. "thanks!" he said. Once again, to show the others her power, he "peeled out" and drove down the road. He heard applause through the screeching of the tires as rubber burned against the road. He had kind of hoped that Abby and Carl may have witnessed his exit. When he dropped Joan and Ken in front of her house, she gave him a quick "peck" on his cheek; thanked him and they were gone. He drove into his driveway and parked beside the VW. When he got out of the car, he noticed that clouds had moved in and obliterated the sun. The temperature had suddenly dropped. His mom came to the back door and opened it and yelled to him, to make sure his windows were up and to check hers, as well. "We are going to be hit hard tonight with the first snowstorm of the season." He did what she had told him to do. He, then, backed Beauty up the driveway and turned her around and backed her into his spot, facing out. His Mom came to the back door again and asked him to come and get her keys and do the same thing for her car as he did for his own. He got her keys and parked hers facing out, too. He popped the hood, on Beauty and checked the antifreeze. It was full. He closed the hood and locked her back up, and headed into the house. He hoped the snow would not harm his paint job.

He arose to the sound of his mom's voice, "No school today!" he got up and went to the window and looked out at the white cover over the yard. He couldn't believe his eyes. There was a lot of the white stuff over everything and it was still coming down, very heavy. He put on his dungarees, engineer boots; shirt. He went to the bathroom and took care of "business". He walked out of the bathroom and went downstairs. His mom already had his breakfast ready. "Nobody's going anywhere, this morning." She said. He went to the kitchen window and looked out at the driveway. "Beauty" was nothing but a large mound of white, with a radio antenna sticking up through it. The VW, next to it, was a smaller mound, with an antenna sticking up. He looked at the garage and noticed that the snow had drifted over half way up the doors. He went back and sat down at the kitchen table and ate his breakfast. After eating, he joined his folks in the den and watched the weather/news report. According to the report, the storm had already dumped over a foot of snow on them and the storm wasn't over. "No sense going out until it's over," his dad said. He went back up to his room and decided to do some catch up on his school work. He knew that if he didn't get his grades up, his dad would take away his carkeys. He opened up his history book and turned on the radio. he began to read about the Civil War, as he listened to Carl Perkins sing, "Blue Suede Shoes." The rest of the music fell on deaf ears, as he became engrossed in his reading. After about an hour, he put the book down and caught the middle of Chuck Berry's "Maybelline."

He got up and went, again, to the window. He surmised that it was going to be a white Christmas. He went back downstairs and into the den. The report said that the storm would last until the middle of the afternoon. "Could be at least two feet." His Dad said. He knew that there was going to be a lot of shoveling to be done. He went to the kitchen and grabbed some saltine crackers and a bottle of coke and went back upstairs to his room. The Teddy Bears were on the radio singing "To Know Him is To Love Him" on the radio, as he walked back in. He picked up his English book and workbook and began to work on his last two assignments. It was around noon, when he finished. He turned off the radio just as Jody Reynolds finished singing, "Endless Sleep."

His Mom was heating up the chicken noodle soup and toasting his English muffins, as he sat down at the table. His Dad came into the kitchen. "They say it is a heavy wet snow. So, we're going to have to take it easy and not exert ourselves." He nodded in agreement, as his Mom poured his soup into the bowl, in front of him. After he ate, he went to the window, again, and looked out. He could barely make out where the cars were. He was not happy. When he was younger, he'd be out playing in it, but not this time. He still had some gifts to get for his mom and dad and Christmas was a only a few days away.

He went back up to his room and took up his math book and began to do his geometry homework. His math skills were not good. He left the radio "off" so, he could concentrate on the work. He struggled through it and, finally finished it around two PM. He, again, went to the window and looked out. The storm had passed. It was no longer snowing. He went to his bottom dresser drawer and took out his heaviest sweater and put it on. He left his room and went downstairs, to the hall closet and took out his winter coat and gloves. He had a winter ball cap with ear muffs, built in. he walked through the kitchen and out the back door. The snow was well over his knees, as he slowly lifted his feet up and down, in the snow. His dad was already clearing off the VW. He got to "beauty" and stretched out his arms, holding his hands, making a big hole between himself and his hands. He put his hands into the snow and pulled it towards him. The snow slid easily off the slick black metal, leaving a beautiful shine. He got the hood and deck and sides done and then moved to get in the car and turn it on. The engine roared to life. He threw the switch, on the dashboard, for the windshield defroster. He sat in the car, waiting for the cold air to turn to heat. Ronnie Hawkins was singing "Mary Lou" on the radio. As soon as he felt the heat, on the windshield, he got out of the car. His dad was finished clearing off the VW and began to shovel the snow away from the front of it. He put his right arm into the snow and "plowed" it off of the right side of the windshield. He, then, went to the driver's side and did the same thing. The snow slid off the heated glass, easily. He went and took up the other shovel and began to help his Dad clear the driveway, in front of the VW. "Your mom needs to get out and do some shopping." His dad said. They, then began to shovel the whole driveway, to the street. They worked for almost an hour and a half. His mom came out of the house, looking like an eskimo and got into the VW, and drove it up the drive way, to a spot just before the street. He and his Dad had shoveled the snow away from the end of the driveway, just as the truck with the huge snowplow on the front, came plowing up the road. The road was almost bare, from snow, as he passed by. He and his dad, shoveled the "plowed' snow away from the end of the driveway. His mom drove the beetle out of the driveway and turned into the direction that the plow had come from. He and his dad went and continued to clear off the rest of the driveway. Then the cleared the snow away from the doors of the garage. They opened the doors. He wished it was his car that sat in the garage and was clear of any snow. He walked back towards "Beauty" with his shovel over his right shoulder. He deposited the shovel in the drift beside the car. He got in and put her in first gear and slowly lifted his foot off the gas. She slowly edged away from the encased drifts and into the driveway. He took the shovel and cleared the rest of the snow from his parking space. He put the shovel back into a drift and got back into the car and backer her into his spot. His dad had already gone back into the house. He took his shovel from the drift and went back towards the house. He put the shovel by the back door, where his dad's was and went into the kitchen. He took off his coat,hat, boots; gloves and went back to his room, to finish the crackers and coke and rest. He was tired. The shoveling took a lot out of him. He knew he was going to have to go out again to clear the end of the driveway, so his mom could get back in. he figured he had at least an hour.

He was watching American Bandstand, when he heard the horn of his Mom's VW. He got off the couch and went on put on his winter "gear" and went out the back door. He picked up the shovel beside the door and trodded through the snow, making a path from his boots to the driveway. He walked up the drive way and shoveled out the end. His mom drove in and parked in her spot. He helped her bring in the groceries.

A "Montreal Express" cold wave came in behind the snowstorm and kept the snow from melting. It hung around until way past Christmas. At Christmas, he gave his mom a nice blue sweater. His dad was given a box of his favorite cigars. His brother, Phil, who was away, in the Navy, he gave some money, and his brother, Dave away at college, he gave a carton of Lucky Strikes. The packages that were for him were small. He had hoped that he would have got spinner hub caps for the front wheels of the Ford and fender skirts. He opened the small packages, two of them. They contained money with notes that told him to go and buy the things he wanted for the car. He was thrilled!

Christmas came and went. By New Year's eve, the snow was almost completely gone. The cold wave gave way to a "thaw". He bought the fender skirts and took them to the same shop that had painted the car. He picked them up two days before the new year. The day before new years, he had the dual exhausts put on and on the 31st, he bought the spinners for the front wheels. The car looked fantastic! It looked just the way he imagined it should look. Not only was he proud of the car's looks, he was also happy that his report card allowed him to keep the keys.

When he got home, from the garage, where he got the exhaust system put on, his mom told him that Jack had called. He called Jack and was informed that the Alladins were going to have a New Year's Eve party that night, starting around 8 and he should be prepared to spend the night. He covered the mouth piece of the phone and informed his mom of the plans. She thought it was a good idea to spend the night, because of all the drunk drivers that would be on the road. Jack told him to wear school clothes and not to worry about trying to get a date. He said, "okay" and hung up the phone. This was his first party since not having a girlfriend. He was excited. The car looked and ran great, his grades were good and now he was going to a party. Life was good!

He started to get ready for the party around 6:30 PM. He showered and bathed and brushed his teeth, twice and then he picked out a red striped shirt, tan chinos, white socks, black loafers, and a black sleeveless v-neck sweater. He carefully combed his hair, checked himself out in the mirror and decided he looked good, he headed out of his room and down the hall, to the stairs. Once, downstairs, he put on his winter coat and wished his folks a Happy New year, they too, were on their way out, to a party. He made sure he put on the just the right amount of Old Spice and the right amount of Brylcreem. He felt good, he looked good and was really very happy! He got to the car, unlocked it and got in behind the wheel. He turned it on and listened to his twin pipes roar! He closed the driver's side door and turned up the heat. Bobby Helms was singing "My Special Angel" on the radio. He made a mental note to go and buy Bobby's "Jingle Bell Rock" before the stores put it away for next Christmas.

He pulled into Jack's driveway and put the car in neutral and "raced" the motor. Jack and the others came out onto the lighted porch and saw who it was and came over to the car. They exclaimed how beautiful the car looked and sounded. He turned it off and turned off the lights; got out and locked it and followed them back into the house. Music filled his ears, as he entered the living room. Sarah Vaughn was on the hi fi singing "Broken Hearted Melody". He noticed most of the guys had "dates". After he put his winter coat on a bed in one of the bedrooms, he went up to Jack and asked, "Why did you ask me? I seem to be the only one without a date." Jack said, "relax. Kelly brought a friend from school and she doesn't have a date, either." He was not very happy. The last thing he needed was a "blind date" on New Year's Eve. He went over to where Jack had set up a bar. Since he wasn't going to be driving that night, he poured himself a "seven and seven". He was standing at the bar, when he noticed Kelly walking towards him with a tall girl, with long red hair, wearing a dark green dress, that showed enough cleavage, to make his eyes water. She was the sexiest girl he had seen in a very long time. He hoped that she was his date.

Kelly said "Hi" and introduced the girl as Susan. She was indeed his date, for the party. She was a shade taller than him, but it didn't seem to bother her. Dinah Washington was on the hi fi. Singing ":What A Difference A Day Made". He asked her if she wanted to dance. She said "okay" he put his drink down on the bar and took her in his arms. It felt so good to be holding a girl, again. He, almost forgot just how good it felt. They stood still, their arms still around each other as they waited for the next song. He silently, prayed that it too would be a ballad. It was Carla Thomas singing "Gee Whiz". Troy Shondell was next with "This Time". As they danced some more, he felt that she was holding him a lot tighter than the first dance. He reciprocated. Elvis came on with "Love Me". As they swayed to "The King" she turned her lips to his ear and whispered. "will you?" He replied, "will I what?" She said, right into his ear, "love me". He gulped and whispered back, "sure". She moved her hands down from the small of his back and squeezed his ass cheeks. The move prompted him to push his pelvis into hers. She breathed into his ear. "Oh baby, I want you!" he couldn't believe what he was hearing. He wondered if this "date" was a joke, put on him by the others. He looked around at other couples dancing, talking, and some already in chairs, making out. No one noticed him and the tall gorgeous redhead, in his arms. "I am so glad to hear that." He said, his excitement growing between them. "We're going to have a great New Year's." She said. Brooke Benton's record, "It's Just A Matter Of Time" began to play. She brought her face to his and moved her lips to his. There wasn't any tongue, but the way she moved her lips over his, caused his heart to race. It hadbeen a very long time between girlfriends, for him. He decided not to rush this relationship. But see just how far it was going to go. After Brooke Benton' song was over, The Diamonds record of "The Stroll" dropped on to the turntable. The lights were turned up and Kelly said, loudly, "Come on guys, let's stroll." Susan stepped back from him and took his hand and led him out of the room. "let's not," She said. She led him to another room. The only light was from the TV. Guy Lombardo and the Royal Canadians were playing "Little Coquette". They found an empty easy chair. She pushed him into it and then sat sideways on his lap. Her dress rose high above her knees. She put her arms around him and pressed her lips to his. This time, she forced her tongue into his mouth. While their lips moved over each others', she pushed his black sweater up his chest. Their lips parted as he pulled the sweater up over his head and tossed it on the floor, next to the chair. She, again leaned and pressed her eager lips to his. This time, she unbuttoned all the buttons of his shirt, right down to his belt buckle. She put her hands on his naked chest and began to rub and explore. When their lips parted, again, she brought her head, mouth and lips to his chest. She kissed and licked every inch of his chest and finally began to lick and suck his nipples. This was a first, for him. He wanted to do the same to her. His hands went to her sides and moved up the dress, to her shoulders. He couldn't see through her red hair, but he tried to move his hands to her top. She brought her head up from his chest and put her hands on the top of his head and guided him to her cleavage. He ran his tongue between the sides of her breasts and the over the exposed flesh. She began to moan and move her shoulders. He wanted so much for the top of her dress to disappear, so he could gaze upon her naked mounds and kiss them all over, especially her nipples. She pushed his head from her cleavage and brought his lips, once again, to hers. He moved his left hand from her dress covered hip to her her naked thigh and began to massage it and gently squeeze. She parted her legs just enough to let him know she liked what he was doing. He moved his hand farther up her inner thigh. Her lips went wild on his, her tongue stabbing the inside of his mouth. He was almost "home" when their lips parted and he saw pure lust, in her eyes. She again, moved her head to his chest and started all over again on his nipples and skin. His hand moved up to the elastic trim of her panties. He was thankful she wasn't wearing a girdle. She was all over him, kissing his chest, then raising her lips, to his. She was completely uncontrollable and squirming all over his lap. Suddenly, they were bathed in a bright light. She jumped off his lap and straightened up her dress. He button up his shirt and retrieved his black sweater and put it back over his shirt. He knew his hair was a mess. He stood up and took his comb out of his pocket. She grabbed his hand and told him to leave his hair alone. That she liked his mussed up hair. It's very sexy." She said. Others piled into the room. Apparently, the "ball" was about to fall, signifying the New Year, 1959. They were all huddled together, watching the TV. The ball started to fall slowly and then picked up speed. When it hit the bottom, "1959" lit up in big numbers. Everyone yelled "Happy New Year!!" Everyone was kissing everyone with New Year kisses. He turned to Susan and she wrapped her arms around him and crushed her lips to his. It was his first tongue lashing, passionate, kiss of the New Year. They were "locked" in each others arms for what seemed eternity. He heard Jack's voice suggest they find a room. When their lips parted, Susan looked him in the eye and said in a husky voice, "good idea."

He couldn't believe what she said. They left the TV room and went into the "dancing" room and up to the bar. They each got a large glass and filled it with seven and seven. With drinks in one hand and their arms around each other's waist. They went into the hall and began to climb the stairs to the second floor. He couldn't believe that they were actually going to a bedroom. They found out that they weren't the only ones. After opening, at least, three doors, they found an empty room. He knew Jack's house was a large Victorian home, but he never knew it had so many bedrooms. They entered the room. He turned and locked the door, as she proceeded to the large bed. "Don't turn on the lights." She said. He went to her and they embraced. Their lips were moving all over each other. Their hands roamed over their bodies. Their passion intensified. They fell onto the bed. They rolled over and over, on the bed. Legs and arms intertwined. She pushed him off her and ordered him to undress her. His fingers trembled as he unzipped the back of her dress. She, in turn, took off his sweater and unbutton his shirt and pulled it out of his pants. Then, he slipped her dress off, revealing black bra and panties. She moved to unzip his pants and unbuckle them. Soon, they were both facing each other, in just their underwear. They moved to each other. Their lips slowly meshed together. Her hands went behind him and stroked the small of his back and then grabbed the elastic of his briefs and slid them off him. She pushed him onto his back and put both hands on his "shaft." She was in such a position, so he could slide her panties down to her thighs. "Oh God, Yes!" She cried, "Kiss me there!" he moved his lips and tongue to her. At the same time, she took him in her mouth. She began to move her lips up and down the shaft, from the "base" to the "tip". He couldn't help it. This was the very first time, in his life, that this had ever happened. He felt his eruption start and he was unable to stop it. She increased the tempo and he screamed, "Oh Shit!!!!" She pulled her lips from him just as he erupted. She didn't move her face away fast enough. "Goddam!" She said, angrily. "You sure know how to ruin a good time!" She got off the bed,grabbed her dress; slipped it on and zipped it up. She turned to him. He was still lying on the bed. "You certainly were a disappointment!" She went to the door, unlocked it, opened it and went through, to the hall, slamming the door, behind her. He was still in shock. He knew that, if she had been a little more patient, he would have been "ready" for more "action". He, slowly got off the bed and proceeded to get dressed. He checked himself and found that he was quite "dry". He, then, realized that she must have received most of his "climax". "Well," he thought to himself, as he left the room. "Happy New year, to me. It wasn't the best milestone, I've ever experienced, but it was climatic."

He was anticipating a lot of laughter, aimed at him, when he got to the bottom of the stairs. People were talking and dancing. No one seemed to notice him. He breathed a sigh of relief and went to the bar. He was about to mix himself a drink, when he realized that somewhere, in that bedroom were two seven and sevens. He went back upstairs to get the drinks. He was just about to enter the room, when he heard voices coming from within. He thought he recognized Jack's voice, but wasn't sure of the girl's. He surmised it was Kelly. He went back downstairs and to the bar. He had just poured himself a drink, when Kelly came up to him. "Have you seen Jack?" She asked. He was about to tell her that Jack was upstairs, but sensed better not to say. Then she asked him, "So, did you have a good time, with Susan the Slut?" He almost spilled his drink. "What?" he asked her. "Didn't jack tell you? Susan begged me, at college, to bring her home with me and to a party, so she could get laid on New Year's." He was in shock! "By the way." She asked, "Where is Susan?" He told her that when they were done, she left the room. Kelly left him, at the bar, and went looking for Susan and Jack. It had hit him that the voices he had heard were Jack's and Susan's. "This can't be good." He said to himself. He wondered if he should get his coat and leave.

His eyes were getting heavy. It was almost 3 AM. He needed to ask Jack where he could "crash". Jack appeared at the bottom of the stairs and saw him, at the bar. He walked up to him. "Man, I'm sorry. I couldn't say no to the girl. Weren't you able to satisfy her? I know I wasn't." He lied, when he said, "She is insatiable!" Jack agreed. Kelly walked up to them and demanded to know where jack had been. He told her that he was in the garage, looking at the dragster. She bought the story. She, then, wanted to know if they had seen Susan, because they had to leave. Just as she spoke, Susan descended the stairs. She had a look, on her face, that said she had just had a great evening. She gave Jack a wink and him a slight kiss on the lips. Kelly and Susan got their coats and left. He and Jack poured themselves a drink and sat down on one of the couches. "What a way to usher in 1959!" Jack said, he agreed, as they clinked their glasses and drank the contents.

"You Don't Have To Be A Baby To Cry" . . . The Caravelles

January started the year off, in typical fashion. Some snow and very cold temperatures. 1959 was beginning to be just another winter. He was in his junior year of high school. For the first time, he wasn't dating anyone. He felt alone, even at work, delivering newspapers around town. The work kept him busy and put gas in his car. As January came to a close, he was thankful that the heater in the Ford was working perfectly.

Then came February 3rd, 1959. He remembered that frigid February morning. He sat in the car, enjoying the warmth, from the heater, waiting for school to start. Hearing the late bell, he shut off the motor and braved the bitter, driving wind, to home room. It was a typical morning, at school. Kids talking, joking and discussing who they were going to the record hop with, that coming Friday night, in the gym. It was during first lunch, that the news hit them! He could, barely, hear the voice on the loudspeaker, over the noise in the cafeteria. Then someone screamed "QUIET!" A teacher's voice, shakily, described what had happened that morning, in a corn field, in Iowa. That was when he learned that Buddy Holly, Ritchie Valens, and J.P. Richardson, better known as The Big Bopper, had died in a small plane crash.

The shock waves spread through the cafeteria, as if a bomb had gone off! Girls were sobbing, guys were stunned. Other sounds were non-existent. The room was like a tomb! When the bell sounded, ending first lunch, everyone filed out, in silence. The elderly teachers were unaware of who had been killed, but the younger members of the faculty were very sympathetic with the kids. He was glad that his afternoon classes had younger teachers. They forgot about the lessons and discussed the tragedy. One of his teachers remarked that this was the first rock and roll tragedy of their young lives. They talked about feelings. It was a moving experience, for him.

When school let out for the day, he ran to the Ford, unlocked it and started it up. He sat and listened to the radio. The music was all Buddy Holly, Ritchie Valens and The Big Bopper. He had tears, in his eyes, as he drove home. All he heard was the music and the awful news.

When he got home, he went right into the house and to the den and turned on the TV. There wasn't any news. He would have to wait for American Bandstand and Dick Clark. He knew that show would have more news, plus the music. He turned off the TV and went up to his room to change into dungarees, a sweatshirt and boots. He went downstairs and waited for his newspapers, to be delivered.

As soon as the truck dropped the papers off on the sidewalk, in front of his house, he ran out the front door. The news and the pictures of the twisted wreck of what was once a plane, lying on the snow covered ground, shook him up. He just stared at the pictures and then read how Holly had chartered the plane, because the heater in the tour bus was broken. They were sick of freezing. Ritchie Valens chose to get on the plane, because he thought he had the flu and didn't want to ride in the cold bus, anymore. J.P. Richardson was tired of riding in the bus, too.

After reading the story, he sorted out the papers and put them in the back seat and front seat of the Ford. He started up the Ford and began to deliver them. All the while, Buddy Holly's music, along with the music of the others was being played over and over, on the radio. It was a "gut wrenching" sad day for Rock and Roll. He had one Boston newspaper left, after his route. He took it home and placed on the top of his dresser. He tried to do his homework, but just couldn't concentrate. At 6PM, after dinner, they all gathered in the den and turned on the news, on TV. His folks tried to be sympathetic, but had no ideas the impact, the three deaths would have on Rock and Roll.

The deaths of the three Rock and Roll stars lingered for quite a while, in his mind. It was not the kind of milestone that anyone would want. In the days that followed, the pain subsided and he began to think of things that he wanted to do, in his life, if for some reason, it would be cut short. He made a list. One of the things, on the list, was to lose his virginity, in the arms of a beautiful girl, or woman. That was on the top of the list. The other things didn't even come close.

Winter gave way to Spring. The warm temperatures meant girls would start wearing skimpier clothing and he would doff his heavy winter apparel, as well. It meant better times with "Beauty." Such as going to the beach, drive ins, etc. Hopefully, it meant finding someone to date. He wanted, so much, to fall in love, again. He was not having much luck, in that department. He joined a teenage church group. It consisted of, mostly, couples. Discouragement seemed to be the rule of the times. He hated being alone and feeling lonely! He had a great looking hot rod, but girls apparently weren't really interested. He did not want to face the summer, alone.

He spent a good deal of the warm, spring days, with the Aladdins, working on the dragster. They were getting it ready for the grand nationals race on Memorial Day weekend he didn't have much time to think about girls. Henry told the guys they could have the Chrysler motor for free! That the owner just wanted it out of the car and off his property. So, they opted for the Chrysler over the Chevy. Jack drove the truck, with the chain fall, disassembled, in the bed.

Henry rode with him and the others followed in Frank's car. When they reached their destination. They followed the owner to a spot behind the garage. The car sat in tall grass was without tires. The motor was still in the car. "Will it run?" Jack asked. The owner threw the ignition key to Jack. Jack got into the car and inserted the ignition key and turned it. The engine roared to life! Jack turned it off and got out of the car. Jack said, "Get the chain fall, guys!"

It took them most of the day to take the motor out of the car and then put it into the bed of the truck. They told the owner that they would be back, later, to pick up the chain fall. When they got back to Jack's garage, it took all of them to move the motor out of the bed of Jack's truck and onto the floor of the garage. He and Jack got back into Jack's truck and went back for the chain fall. Frank had found a "used" seat from a guy who used to race stock cars. So, everything was in place. All they had to do, was put it all together. It took all of Spring vacation and weekends to get the car ready for the drags.

He got a job at a local country club, as a "houseman". He would work three afternoons a week, after school and then, full time, during the summer. The pay was good and all he had to do was wax and buff the dining room floor, before the evening meal, vacuum the main rooms, on the first floor, and deliver the mail to the permanent guests, on the third floor and make sure all the ash trays were clean. His uniform consisted of black pant, white shirt, black bow tie (a cheater), black socks and shoes and a white jacket. He started work, after he was sure the dragster was "ready to run" for Memorial Day weekend. He made sure that he had that weekend off, form work.

The car was ready. The only problem they had, was transporting it to the races. They failed to obtain a trailer. Jack called everyone that he knew, but found nothing. Frank called some friends, to no avail. Then, Bobby, the newest member, remembered that he had an uncle, that once, transported racing cars. Jack got on him, to call his uncle. His uncle just happened to have an enclosed trailer that the car just might fit in. The uncle brought the trailer to them. The uncle, also, had ramps that the wheels would go up on. They pushed the dragster up the ramps and into the trailer. Bobby's uncle threw the keys to the truck, to Bobby and then asked for a ride home. Jack was dumfounded! "You mean we get to use the truck, too?" he asked. Bobby's uncle said "yes!" As long, as he could have the truck and trailer back, when they were finished with it. Henry put two empty five gallon cans in the bed of the truck. They, also, put an extra set of tires in the back of the trailer. When everything was packed, they stood back and congratulated each other on the job that they did. This was going to be a huge milestone, for him! His first time, being a member of a racing team!

As the big weekend neared, his excitement level increased. He could hardly wait. Ralph, one of the Aladdins, parents had a summer home 15 minutes from the drag strip. The plan was to go up the night before and stay over, race and come home the next day. All, he was going to pack, was enough underwear, socks, a couple of T-shirts, dungarees and toiletries. They had a meeting two days, before the trip. Ralph mentioned that his dad had stocked the refridgerator with beer. Jack cautioned them. That no one was to be in the pits. Either hung over or still drunk. They all agreed. They planned to meet at the garage at 4PM, that Friday and head up North. He offered to take some of the guys and follow the truck. They were all set for the big day.

That Friday, at school, seemed to drag on and on. He thought the day would never end. Finally, the last bell rang for the long weekend. He, practically, ran from the room, the building, down the road, where the students parked, to his car. He got in and started "Beauty" up. The Coasters were singing "Charlie Brown" on the radio. He drove home, just a little above the speed limit. He knew the cops would be out on the roads, because of the long weekend. He got home with time, to spare. He parked the Ford in front of the house, turned it off, opened and closed the door and ran up the walk and opened the front door, slammed it shut, behind him and ran up the stairs, two at a time, down the hall and into his room. He scooped up the small overnight bag. He, quickly, went back down the hall, down the stairs, into the kitchen, kissed his mom goodbye and headed to the front door. "We're going t0 be at the lake, opening the cottage, if you and your friends want to come by." His mom yelled after him, as he left the house. He got into Beauty, turned her on and headed to the garage, as Jackie Wilson was singing "Lonely Teardrops" on the radio.

He pulled into Jack's driveway. The others were already there. They lived closer to Jack, than he did. Henry, Frank and Charlie grabbed their bags and walked towards him. He got out of Beauty and opened the trunk. They all put their bags in it and he closed the trunk. Jack, bobby and Ralph got into the truck. The others got in the Ford. He backed it out of the driveway and pulled it over to the curb. The truck, with the dragster, pulled out into the street. They all headed North! Ricky Nelson was on the radio, singing "Travelling Man." They all joined in and sang along. When Doris day sang "Everybody Loves A Lover" he turned the volume down and they all started talking about what a great time, they were going to have. He said that it really didn't matter if they won any races, as long as they had fun! Ralph chimed in that it would be nice if they could, at least, win one race. They agreed. The excitement, in the car, grew with every passing minute. It was 7PM, when they pulled off the highway, to get something to eat. They began to discuss who was going to drive the dragster. Jack volunteered! They all agreed that Jack should do it. After all, he had the helmet and the "gear". As they ate their burgers and fries, a guy, in the next booth, leaned over and asked if they were going to the drags? They replied, "of course!" They were planning to race tomorrow, Saturday. The guy asked what kind of rod, they had. Jack said, "We have a class "C" dragster." The guy informed them that the dragsters were racing on Sunday, and that the hot rods were racing on Saturday. At first, they were disappointed. But, then, realized that they had an extra day to get the car ready. Henry said that they, also, had an extra day to party! Jack kind of groaned! He could tell that Jack was concerned that the wouldn't be "up" for the races. He assured jack that he would be all right to help him. Jack thanked him. They finished their burgers, paid and as they walked out, they thanked the guy for the valuable information.

They arrived at the cottage around 9PM. Jack was actually glad that they didn't have to race until Sunday. They had a full day of preparation. He turned off Beauty, got out and opened the trunk. They all took out their bags and he locked up the Ford. They waited for Ralph to unlock the front door. Ralph went in and turned on some lights. Then, they all went in. he and Jack picked the bedroom on the first floor. The others went upstairs and claimed the other rooms. He and Jack found the kitchen and the refridgerator and opened the 'fridge's door. They extracted two Buds from the fridge They sat at the kitchen table and began to discuss how they would set the car up for the first race. He told Jack that with the new tires on the back, jack would have to "burn" them, to "scruff' them up. Jack understood. The others soon joined them, after they got their beers. Henry reminded, whoever, was going to handle the fuel, to be very careful; not spill a drop! "That stuff is very expensive, at least $2.50 a gallon." They, then, decided who was going to have what job. He was picked to be the "checker". The checker made sure all the wires on the motor were where they were supposed to be, and hooked up properly. He, also, made sure that the tires were properly inflated and that the steering linkage was properly hooked up. It was a very important job! If anything went wrong, it would be his fault. They finished their beers and decided to call it a night.

The next morning, he woke up before anyone else. He got dressed and took care of himself, in the bathroom, before anyone else woke up. He went out of the cottage. The sun was just starting to break over the eastern horizon. He went to the truck and unlocked the back doors, of the trailer. He climbed up into the back and squeezed himself alongside the right side of the dragster. He had just enough room between the dragster and the side of the trailer. He went to the front and checked the fuel lines, from the small gas in the front. He checked the spark plugs and the spark plug wires. Everything seemed to have made the trip okay. He worked his way on the other side, towards the back. He put his right hand on the back of the driver's seat. It move under his hand! He stopped and in the dim light, he could see the bolts, holding the seat to the frame, had worked themselves loose. He made a mental note, to tighten them. "everything okay?" It was jack's voice. He told Jack about the seat and the bolts. Jack said, "we'll tighten them, as soon as it's light enough, to see. "Okay!" he said. He edged himself out of the trailer and the two of them walked back to the cottage and into the kitchen. "Can you cook?" Jack asked him. "I think I can scramble some eggs, fry bacon, and put toast in the toaster." He replied. "Good." Said Jack, "I'll put the coffee on."

The aroma of bacon and eggs and toast woke the others up! They all gathered, again, in the kitchen and "wolfed down" the food. "Guess I did all right!" he said. Jack said that he thought so, unless the others were so hungry, they would have eaten anything. Everyone laughed! They spent the rest of the day, drinking beer, eating sandwiches and making sure the dragster was ready for the raced on Sunday. He and Jack got in Beauty and drove over to the track, to register the team and the dragster. They found their way to the registration booth, paid their entry fee and picked up their I.D. badges, for everyone. They were walking back towards beauty, when a voice asked if he was going to race the Ford? He stopped dead in his tracks. The thought passed through his brain. Jack gave him a quizzical look. He didn't take him long to evaluate the pros and cons. The biggest con was if he wrecked, it would be a tight ride home, for all of them. He loved Beauty too much, to risk damaging her. "nope!" he said, "not today!" Jack breathed a sigh of relief as they got back in and headed back to the cottage. Lloyd Price was on the radio singing "Lawdy Miss Clawdy."

No one slept well that night. They were all up early, the next morning. They ate very little, at breakfast. They packed up their stuff and headed out to the drag strip. The place was buzzing with activity. They went to the registration desk, to find out what time they would be racing. They were told that they were the fourth race. They went back to the trailer and proceeded to unload the dragster. Once it was out of the truck, he began his checking, all over again. He told them about tightening the bolts of the seat. He checked limes and plugs, oil and gas. Henry and Bobby took the two empty gas tanks, to fill them up. He checked under the chassis and over the motor. He was satisfied that there weren't any leaks. He told Jack to "fire it up." Jack got into the seat and pushed the toggle switch up. The engine came to life! It sounded "perfect" to them. Jack "revved' it up. It sounded absolutely great! Jack "killed "the motor. Jack got out of the seat. They began to wipe the rails clean. He looked up as someone approached them. He couldn't believe who it was! It was Carl! They greeted each other, warmly, but not excitedly. Carl asked to see their paperwork. He worked at the strip. He handed Carl, their paperwork. As Carl looked at it, he asked how Abby was? "She's here." He answered. "Oh" was all he could say. Carl left and they went back to cleaning up the dragster. Henry and Bobby returned with the gas. "We don't have any change. The price went up to three dollars a gallon." "Well" said Jack, it is racing fuel." Bobby said that he had never seen pink colored gas, before. They laughed and put one of the cans in the truck and topped off the gas in the front tank of the car. He, then put the other can in the truck and helped clean the dragster. Jack got into his racing "togs". Clothes and helmet he bought a year ago. He said, "I just knew I'd be putting them on sometime." He and Jack walked to the concession stand, to get a sandwich. He thought Jack just wanted people to see him in his "attire". They got to the stand and had to wait. They were third in line. When they got to the counter, the girl behind the counter turned to face them. It was Abby! A look of genuine surprise flashed across both their faces! Then, she stepped back and her face took on a stern look. "What do you want?" She asked, coldly. They gave her their orders. She went to get their sandwiches and cokes. When she returned with them and they paid her. She didn't say another word. He thanked her and mumbled "nice to see you, too". As they walked back towards their pit, jack asked him what that was all about? He told jack that they had dated for over a year and that she was now with the guy who checked their papers. Jack said "oh." They sat on the back of the truck and ate their food. Ralph came back with some sandwiches and sat down. Then, Ralph blurted out, "Hey you guys see that hot chick in the food stand?" They nodded that they had. He told them that she was "taken". Ralph said, "figures." Their race was fast approaching! Jack began to pace around the pit. He tried to tell jack to relax, but it was useless. Then, they heard the call. Jack got into the seat and put on his helmet. They got behind the dragster and pushed it out of the pit and to the starting line. Excitement filled the air, around them. They looked to their right and saw their competition! The dragster had a massive motor! The blower was so big, the driver couldn't see over it. He had a sinking feeling, in the pit of his stomach. Somehow, he knew that they didn't stand a chance. Jack fixed his eyes forward, down the track. The order was given to "smoke" the tires. Jack threw the switch and the engine responded! He put it in gear and gave it just enough gas to burn the rubber. Jack released the clutch and the car stood still, for a few seconds and then screamed off the line, in a huge cloud of black and white smoke! When the smoke cleared, the dragster had stopped a few feet over the starting line. Jack turned it off. They ran to the front of the car and pushed it back to the starting line. Both cars were ready! Engines were on and roaring! The flagman stepped to the line between both lanes. He raised the green flag above his head and shoulders and in an instant, he brought the flag down. The roar of both engines and the thick smoke blocked everyone's view. When the smoke cleared, both dragsters were speeding down the strip! Then, all they saw was a huge plume of smoke, come from the motor of their dragster, accompanied by what appeared to be engine parts flying into the air! Their dragster veered to the left and went straight towards the wall. It scraped the concrete, sending sparks into the air, before it, finally came to a stop against the wall. The announcer said "Oh no! Another blown engine!" The emergency crew took off towards Jack and the dragster! They, also, took off running along the side of the strip. When they, finally, got to him, the emergency crew had already put out the fires and had Jack out of the dragster. We got to check him out." One of the crew said. A tow truck appeared and hooked up the front of the car. He jumped into the cab and told the driver, which trailer to take the car to. As the tow truck and the ambulance left, he saw the cleanup crew, from his passenger window, clean up the engine parts off the track. The others walked back up the side of the strip, to the trailer.

The tow truck dropped off the dragster, by the trailer. They all just stared at the twisted wreck and what was left of the motor. It was a big mess! They, with the help of some others, managed to get the dragster back into the trailer. By that time, Jack was released from the medical tent. He was okay! Bobby took the two cans back to where he had gotten the gas and sold it back to them, along with the cans. Jack took off the suit and helmet and put them in the truck. No one said anything. They were glad that Jack had not been injured! They got back into their vehicles and left the drag strip. They knew that their drag racing days had come to a quick end.

When they got back to the garage, they left, what was left of the dragster, in the trailer. He dropped his passengers off at their respective houses, and headed home. It was well, after dark, when he pulled into his driveway. He turned off the car and its headlights, got out and locked it and went up the backstairs, into the house and up to his room.

The next day, Memorial Day, he got up early and ate some toast. The phone rang, it was his mom, the cottage was open for the summer. He told her that he was working up to the last two weeks of August. He would have the same time off, as last summer. He hung up the phone and headed out of the house. He got into Beauty and headed for Jack's. When he got to Jack's the dragster was already out of the trailer and in the garage. They had pulled it out, with Jack's truck. He looked in the garage. The dragster was way in the back, under a tarp. Jack said, with a great deal of sadness, "Maybe we'll get to race something else, some day."

He drove beauty back home and decided that it would be a good time, to wash and wax, her. By the time he was finished, buffing off the last remnant of wax, he stepped back and admired her. He really loved his car. He got in and turned the ignition key to on. He moved her back to her space, in the driveway. The Everly Brothers were on the radio, singing "I Wonder If I Care As Much." He sat in the car and sang along, he turned off the engine as Ernie Fields, "In The Mood" came on. He really liked Glenn Miller's version better.

It was June and the class of '59 had departed the school. He was, technically, now a senior, a member of the class of 1960. All his classes were "reviews". Preparation for final exams. The only class that didn't have a final, was his speech class. His teacher, Mr. Sparks, wanted him to try out for the senior play. It would be put on in November, of 1959, just before Thanksgiving. The name of the play was Thorton Wilder's "The Matchmaker". He was skeptical about auditioning. The only acting, he had done, was in his church, when he was in elementary school. he played the lead in "Hans Brinker and The Silver Skates". Mr. Sparks asked him to come after school, Thursday of that week. He drove home from school, that day. When he walked into the kitchen, his mom asked him how school went. He said "okay." Then added, that Mr. Sparks wanted him to stay after and try out for the senior play. His mom got all over him! "Well what are you doing here? You get right back to the school and audition! If your teacher wants you to audition, it must be for a reason, now get!" He, reluctantly, went out the front door and got back into Beauty, started her up and headed back to school. Chuck Berry was on the radio, singing, "School Days."

He parked the car in front of the building that housed the auditorium. He turned her off and, slowly, walked into the building. He opened the door, to the auditorium and walked in. Mr. Sparks was closing up his briefcase, when he noticed him. "Well I wondered if you were going to show up." He ambled his way down the aisle towards Mr. Sparks. "Okay!" Mr. Sparks said and handed a small book. He asked him to read the line, "I'm too young Mr. Vandergelter!" Mr. Sparks Asked him to get up on the stage and do it with the student was trying out for Vandergelter. The "actor" read, "Boys, you are going to have a mistress!" To which he jumped in with his line. This time he put some emphasis on it. He heard laughter come from the others in the seats. He read one more line, with the "actor" trying out for the part of Cornelius Hackle. The role he was reading was that of Barnaby Tucker. Again his reading invoked laughter. Mr. Sparks thanked him for coming back and reading. Mr. Sparks said that he would put up the cast list on the door of his office, tomorrow. He left the auditorium, went out the building and got back into his car. He turned it on and Elvis was singing "Blue Moon" on the radio. he drove back home and once again parked the car, this time in the driveway. He went in the back door. His mom was cooking dinner. "Well?" She asked. "I did it!" he said. "Good!" She replied. He told her that he didn't think he did very well. She said that it didn't matter, the point was that he did what his teacher asked him to do.

He went upstairs to study for his final exam, in history. After about an hour, his mom called him to supper. The discussion, at the dinner table, was about the play. His dad questioned why his teacher would want him to try out. He said that he was sure he didn't know. After supper, he studied, most of the night, up to eleven. He, even, turned off the radio. he woke up, early the next morning. Got cleaned up, dressed, ate breakfast, and headed out to the driveway, got into Beauty, started her up and headed out of the driveway. Margie Rayburn was on the radio, singing "I'm Available". Listening to the song, brought back the memory of riding in Carl's brother's car, with the hole in the floorboard, tasting the exhaust fumes. He got to school early, parked the car and sat in it. He went over his history notes. It was Friday and history was his first exam. When he heard the bell, he turned off the car and got out, locked it and headed to the classroom. Once inside, he took his seat, and waited for the teacher to pass out the exam and answer sheet.

The bell sounded, signaling that all test should begin. He had two hours to complete the test. He opened the booklet, wrote his name and homeroom number on the answer sheet and began to answer the questions. He was extremely happy! The questions were easy; he thanked God, that he had studied. He finished the exam in an hour and twenty five minutes. He handed it into his teacher. His teacher corrected the test, in front of him. He had five answers wrong. His teacher told him that he could expect an A—for the term. His teacher congratulated him and called him "Barnaby." He walked out of the classroom, elated about the grade, but confused as to why the teacher "blew' his name. He only had the one exam, that day, and was able to go home. He headed out of the building, back to Beauty. He stopped and turned around, when he remembered that Mr. Sparks was going to post the cast list. He went to Mr. Spark's office. He stood in front of the door. He was in shock! There was his name, next to Barnaby Tucker! He got the part! He couldn't believe it! He knew it had to be a mistake. He was still standing in front of the door, when Mr. Sparks came down the hall, towards him, with a huge grin on his face! Mr. Sparks grabbed his right hand and shook it! Mr. Sparks told him to report to the auditorium, Monday, after his English exam. He would pass out the scripts and have a "read through." He was to study and learn his part, over the summer. He told Mr. Sparks that he would see him Monday afternoon. He left, a happy boy, and walked towards Beauty.

When he got home, he couldn't wait to tell his mom! She was so excited! She called his dad, his brother, Dave, his aunt, and his uncle! He spent the weekend, at work, at the country club. Sunday night, he studied for his English exam. The whole test was going to be on William Shakespeare. He liked the plays, but the language gave him problems. He studied until 11:30PM!

Monday morning, he again, woke up early and did his morning routine. After breakfast, he went out to the driveway and got into Beauty. As headed out the driveway, Ricky Nelson was on the radio, singing "Hello Mary Lou." He parked the car in the students area and turned "her' off. He went over his notes on William Shakespeare. At one point, he had the feeling that someone was watching him. He looked out the driver's side window. Joan, the girl who lived across the street, was standing next to Beauty. He rolled down the window. "Wow! You leave early for school!" She said. All he could say was "yup." He knew that they were in the same English class. "Are you ready for this exam?" She asked. "Hope so." He answered. "Want to go over some of the stuff?" She asked. "Sure!" he said. He leaned over to the passenger door and opened it for her. She went around the front of the car and climbed in. "Beauty looks really nice, really cool!" She said, "I'll bet Abby wishes she was riding around in it, with you!" "Don't think so." He said. She opened her book and they began to study together. They heard the warning bell and both exited the car. They ran together to the building and the room where the test was being given. They got to the room, just as the tests were being given out. The question sheet had ten questions on it. It was an essay exam. The teacher remarked, to them, "how nice of you, two to join us!" he sensed the sarcasm in her voice, but thought it best to ignore it. The bell rang and he opened the book. He looked at the first question. He was to identify the villain, who murdered all those they stood, in his way, to the throne of England and describe how each one was slain. He began to write. He took the whole two hours, to answer all the questions. When he was finished and passed in the test, he walked out of the room. He was walking down the hall, when Joan caught up to him. "Can I get a ride home?" She asked. He told her that he had to go to the auditorium for a "read through" for the senior play. She asked if she could sit in. He told her that she would have to ask Mr. Sparks. They reached the auditorium and Joan went up to Mr. Sparks, who was reluctant to let her, but let her "Just this once." She sat in the back row of the auditorium. Mr. Sparks handed him, his script and told him to learn it by the first school day, in September. When all the cast members had arrived, he passed out scripts and had them sit in a horseshoe, facing Mr. Sparks. He wanted them to be familiar with the play and not concerned with "emphasis." When they finished reading, Mr. Sparks wished them a safe and happy summer. He put away his chair and walked up to the last row in the auditorium. Joan got up out of her seat and followed him. Out of the auditorium and down the road, to Beauty. He unlocked the car and they got in. He started it up, rolled down his window, lit up an L&M, put it in gear and headed home. Dwayne Eddy was on the radio,

"I thought I would give it a shot." He said. His teacher gave him an exam and a blank worksheet. "If you pass this test, I'll raise your grade to a "C". He said, as he handed him a pencil and an exam booklet. The bell rang and he began to work on the first problem. He took the whole two hours and passed it in. "Have a good summer, Barnaby." His teacher said. He thanked him and headed out the door. Joan was in the hall, waiting for him. "Can I hitch a ride home?" She asked. He asked her if her boyfriend was around. "He doesn't go to this school." She said. "Oh" he replied. "I have to go and see if Mr. Sparks is around." He said. She said that was fine with her. They left the building and went across the street, to the auditorium. They entered through the door and found Mr. Sparks talking with an art teacher. He waited, patiently, for Mr. Sparks to finish with the other teacher. Then, he asked if he could mark the playbook. Mr. Sparks answered, "of course, it's your book." "great!" he said and they turned and left the auditorium.

When they got to black beauty, he saw Carl and Abby standing by the car. Carl lowered his head and asked, sheepishly, if they could get a ride to Carl's house. "What happened to the '40 Ford?" He asked. "Needs a new water pump." Carl said. Abby never uttered a word, except to say 'hi" to Joan. They all got into the car. He started it up. "Sounds good." Said Carl. "Thanks" he replied. He burned a little rubber, leaving Elm road. Connie Francis was on the radio, singing "Who's Sorry Now". Joan leaned over to him and said in a low voice, "an appropriate song." He grinned as they headed home.

He dropped Carl and Abby off at Carl's house and headed down the street, to Joan's home. He dropped her off in front of her house and drove across the street, into his driveway and into his spot. He had one more exam to study for, French. It was going to be an "oral" exam. The teacher would ask each student a different question, in French, and the would answer her in French. The only thing, he could study was vocabulary and then try and put the words into conversational French. He had a B minus, going into the final and he did quite well during the last "review class.

He spent the rest of the day, reading and rereading his lines for the play. His mother gave him a pencil to mark his lines. After supper, he went to his room and began to study his French vocabulary. He studied well into the night and finally put down his book around 11:30 PM. He woke up the next morning around 7 and took care of business, dressed, ate his breakfast and headed out to the driveway to go to school. Joan was not waiting by the car. He thought she might be running late, so he waited a bit. 7:45 AM and still no sign of Joan. So, he unlocked beauty and got in and started her up and headed out of the driveway. Conway Twitty was on the radio singing "It's Only Make Believe." He pulled into a spot on Elm road, just as the warning bell rang. He turned off the car, opened the door and jumped out. He locked her up and ran to the language arts building. He just made it in to the room, before the late bell. "Bonjour." She said. He gulped back, "Bonjour." He took his seat and waited his turn. The "oral exam" last exactly two full hours. He did well. His teacher smiled at him, as he left his seat. "Tres Bien." She said, and then in a thick French accent, "Barnaby." It seemed, to him, that the whole school knew about him being in the senior play.

When he got to the car, five Alladins were waiting for him. He was glad to see them. Jack said, "School is out!" let's go to Ho-Jo's. They piled into beauty, after he unlocked her. He started her up and, again, peeled out" of his parking space. Gary U.S. Bonds was on the radio, singing "School Is Out At Last, and I'm So Glad I Passed." They all sang along. His freedom was to be short lived, for he started his summer job, at the country club, the next day.

June and July, 1959 kept him very busy, with his summer job. He worked six days a week, which left very little time to do anything else. Things that a seventeen year old boy would want to do during the lazy days of Summer. It wasn't until the last weekend in July, that he got a "break". The main building of the country club was closing for four days, as new carpets and wallpaper was going to be put in. That gave him four days off. He started wondering how he was going to spend the time. He had many, many options, available to him. He could go to the lake. He could just stay home and relax, maybe go to the beach. He could go to the Grand Nationals Drags, in Maine. The last option was made available by the Alladins. They would stay at the same cottage and spend the days, at the drag strip. He decided to join the guys and go to the drags. His folks were disappointed with his decision. He told them that he would be at the cottage, with them, the last two weeks of August, like he always was. They accepted that. He called Jack and told him that he was coming with them. Jack was excited. They were going to take two cars, Black Beauty and Jack's car. They all met one night, after his "shift" and discussed their plans. He was going to be off Friday, Saturday, Sunday and Monday. He would be off work at 3 PM on Thursday. They decided to leave around 4 PM that Thursday. This was the most exciting thing to happen, to him, all Summer.

That last day, at work, seemed to drag on and on. Finally, he hung up his white work jacket and black bow tie and headed out to "beauty." He had packed his clothes, the night before. All he had to do was stop for gas and have the oil checked, on the way to Jack's house. He got to jack's around 3:45PM. All the guys were waiting for him. Bobby and Henry were riding with him and the other two with Jack. They threw their stuff in the trunk of his car. Bobby wanted to ride in the back, while he and Henry rode up front. They backed up and out of the driveway. Jack was in the lead. He put his arm out the driver's side window and gave the "Let's Go!" sign. The Five Satins were on the radio singing "To The Aisle."

They arrived, at the cottage, around ten that night. They unloaded their "gear" from the cars and went into the cottage. Ralph's folks were there and welcomed them in. He did not know that Ralph's folks were going to be there. They were sleeping in the bedroom that he and Jack had slept in, the last time. Ralph's dad told them they had set up cots with sleeping bags on the porch, for three of them. The other two could sleep in a bedroom, up stairs. Ralph said that room was his and Henry chimed in with "dibs" on it, as well. That left him, Jack, and Bobby on the porch. Ralph's parents bid them all a good night and walked off to their room. Ralph was sorry about his folks, but told them it was a lot cheaper than a motel. Henry made the comment that there wasn't going to be any beer being consumed in that house. Jack said, "but it doesn't mean it won't be in the back of our cars, at the track. They all laughed and then turned in to their respective bunks.

Friday, they all rode in beauty, over to the track. Nervous Norvus was on the radio with "Transfusion." They all listen to the radio and laughed along with the "song." When he pulled up to the main gate, Frankie Lyman and The Teenagers were singing "Why Do Fools Fall In Love?" They paid their admission fee and found a spot just down from the start line. They "cracked "open some beers and sat on the grass, by the strip to watch "warm ups." Friday was just a practice day. The hot rods would be racing on Saturday. It was Bobby that asked him, if he had ever really" opened up" beauty. He said, "No." Henry said that the strip would really be the place to see what beauty could do. Jack said that he had brought his helmet along just in case he found someone that wanted him to drive. It seemed to him, that the stage was being set. They ate the ham and cheese sandwiches, that Ralph's mom had made for them and along with their fourth beer, apiece, had all but convinced him to sign up for a race on Saturday. As the afternoon wore on, and the beer took effect, he 'caved" in. They got up off the grass and walked down to the registration stand. He paid the entry fee of twenty five dollars and was told that he would be the fifth race on Saturday. He had mixed feelings about racing beauty. He knew she was fast and that he knew how to "speed shift", but he still was worried about his safety. Jack sensed his concerns and told him that if he could survive the fiery wreck of the dragster, then he should be okay in beauty. They walked back to the car and, once again, sat on the grass and watched the rest of the "trials". They stopped drinking around 4 PM. They didn't want to drive drunk and they didn't want Ralph's folks know about the beer. By 9 PM, they felt sober enough to drive the short distance back to the cottage. Ralph's folks were already in bed, so they, quietly, went to their own beds. He tossed and turned all night. He did not have pleasant dreams about racing. He knew his car and that it was going to do well. He just lacked confidence in his ability.

Saturday morning arrived earlier than he wanted it to. Ralph's mom fixed them all breakfast. After which, they headed over to the drag strip. He pulled up to gate and showed the guard his papers and was directed to the pit area. Once inside the pits, he turned beauty off and raised her hood. They checked all the lines and wires. He checked his tires. Henry got under the car and looked at the brake lines. He got in the car and tested the brakes. He turned "her' on and Jack checked the dual carbs. They were in sync. Bobby came back from the safety shack with a seat belt. "It's mandatory." He said. They had to borrow some tools to attach the belt. He tried on Jack's helmet and it fit just right. He felt that everything checked out. He was extremely nervous. He paced around the car, wondering if there was something they forgot to check. He heard the call for the entrants to line up for the fourth race. The others left him to go and watch. He was alone with beauty. He turned the car off. It had sounded good and strong. He got in her and put his hands on her dash and uttered a "silent" prayer. He didn't care if he won or lost, he just wanted everything to go well. Jerry Lee Lewis was on the radio, singing "Whole Lotta Shakin Going On." When the song was over. He turned off the radio. He wanted nothing to distract his concentration. Then came the words from the announcer, "Fifth race entrants report to the starting line." The others had just come back. He checked the helmet and the seat belt. The helmet was fine, but the seatbelt felt uncomfortable. He had never worn one before. They all wished him well. He started up beauty and headed out of the pits, towards the starting line. Jack rode with him. When they got to the line, Jack got out and guided him up to the line. He stopped the car and put it in neutral. Jack moved away and went over to the others, just outside the ropes, that separated the crowds from the cars. The started stood in front of him. He looked over, to his right, at his competition. It was a cherry red 1932 Ford Deuce, coupe. It had a huge blower on top of the motor. He knew he would not be able to beat that car. The starter pointed the white flag at him and rolled it clockwise. He put the car in first gear and kept the clutch pressed to the floor, while he put his right foot on the gas and pressed it down just enough to cause the car to "shake'. He glanced at the "Deuce", as the started did the same thing to him. Both cars were ready. The started brought up a green flag. His adrenaline was pumping; he was shaking as much as beauty. The green flag dropped. He popped the clutch with his left foot and slammed his right foot, on the gas, to the floor. The rear tires screamed in agony as rubber burned against the asphalt. Smoke ballooned out the back of the car. Then, the tires grabbed the pavement and beauty roared off the line like her motor was called, "a rocket." The transmission "begged" to be let out of first gear. He threw the floor shift into second gear. The car responded by picking up the speed. Then the transmission wanted out of second and he shifted into third. He glanced at the "deuce" it was losing ground to him, he thought the driver may have missed a shift. The "rocket" was flying down the strip. He glanced at the speedometer, 98 MPH!!! Then, he noticed the "deuce" was next to him, its front end, even with his passenger door. Both cars sucking down the gas. Then it happened! Beauty began to shake! He grabbed the steering wheel with both hands, knuckles white, he held on. He felt the front end wobble and then the car veered to the right! He looked at the "deuce" and saw the grille and knew he was in trouble! The front end of the "deuce" struck the side of beauty! He saw sky through the passenger side window; and turned his head to his side window. The asphalt was rushing up to his side window and then all went black!!!

Faint voices entered his ears. His head felt like it was exploding. He tried to open his eyes, but bright lights blinded him, so he closed them, again. "I think he's coming out of it." A voice said. He had the sensation that he was lying on his back, but he couldn't move. He, again, opened his left eye, slowly. He waited for the his eye to adjust to the bright light. "Yup." Said another voice, he's regaining consciousness." He, slowly, opened his right eye. His eyes began to focus on where the voices were coming from. A face loomed down close to his. She had dark brown eyes and from what he could see. Black hair, pulled back. He lowered his eyes and saw she was wearing a uniform. "Well, hi." She said, "welcome back!" he tried to speak, but was unable to. Something was covering his face, with just a small hole for his mouth and one for his nostrils. She knew he couldn't talk. He felt he was moving. "You're in an ambulance and we're taking you to the hospital," She said. That's when his ears cleared enough for him to hear the siren of the ambulance. He heard the driver tell someone that he was awake. He could not comprehend what had happened to him. He closed his eyes and drifted into the darkness, again.

The next time he woke up, he was still on his back, on a something with wheels. The girl and a guy were on each side of him, rushing him down a hall, with more bright lights. He heard the guy say, "xray!". They put him next to a wall, in the hall. Then they moved him into a room with a huge machine. A woman, dressed in white approached him and wheeled him under the machine. He felt a heavy piece of material over his groin. Then he was alone, as the machine moved all over his body. Afterward, the "nurse" wheeled him back into the hall. Next, two more guys, dressed in white, wheeled him into an elevator. They stood on each side of him and when the elevator stopped and the doors opened. They wheeled him down the hall and into another room. They placed him next to a bed, but did not move him.

He was, totally, confused. He had no idea, why he was in what appeared to be a hospital. He lay on the bed, with wheels, for a few minutes. The two guys came back in and told him that he had no broken bones. So, they lifted him from the "guerney" to the bed. They, then told him that they were going to cut off his jeans and T-shirt. Before he knew it, the only clothing, he had on were his jockey shorts. They, then, put a thing, with no back, and like a skirt on him. They cranked up the back of the bed. His throat and mouth were very dry. The thing over his face was still there and beginning to bother him.

A man wearing a white jacket and a stethoscope around his neck, walked into the room. He came over to him and loomed over his face. He felt the 'thing" on his face being removed. "Nice, very nice." He said. He, then, stepped back and introduced himself as Doctor Johnson. "You are one very lucky, lucky, young man." He said. "The only damage, I see, so far, are the four stitches on the bridge of your nose. Your face must have hit the rim of the horn on your steering wheel. You, also, have two nasty black eyes, but they will heal well, as will your nose." My only concern is the distinct possibility of a concussion. Being unconscious, as long as you were, is going to keep you for observation. If all goes well, you may be able to leave, by tomorrow, We'll just wait and see. Oh, you have visitors, so I'll let you go and see you later." With that the doctor left the room. They all came through the door, happy to see that he was sitting up. All was clear, to him, now. The fog, in his brain, was clearing. He recognized the guys. "Hey!" they said. His throat and mouth were still very dry. He still couldn't speak. A nurse came in with a cup and a straw and a pitcher of ice water. She stuck the straw in his mouth and ordered him to take small sips. He did as he was told. The water felt really good, in his mouth and down his throat. After he sipped all the water out of the cup, he was able to speak. His voice was raspy, but he could speak. "What happened?" he asked the guys. They smiled, when they heard his voice. One by one, they told him about the horrendous wreck. Beauty, for some reason, was really wobbling. It looked like the front end was falling apart. Then, she crossed right into the path of the other car. When they hit, beauty rolled over and over, at least four times. His foot must have still been on the gas, because when she righted on all four tires, she slammed, head on into the retaining wall. Luckily, the guy, in the other car hit the brakes and steered away. The safety crew had to cut him out of the car. The guys thought that he was dead!

When he heard the story, he kind of smiled. Someone told them that the seat belt and helmet saved his life. He asked about Black beauty. The guys lowered their heads and told him she was "totalled". The car was a total mess. Tears came to his eyes, at the news. He really loved that car. They were all glad that he was going to be okay. They knew he was not doing well about beauty, so they decided to let him rest and told him they would be back, in the morning. He told him that if his head is okay, he'll be able to leave and for them to bring his clothes. They said they would and then left him to grieve beauty.

He slept through the night and, only woke up, when the nurse came in and asked him what he desired for breakfast. He gave her his "order" and she left. It was just after 8:30 AM when his breakfast arrived. He ate everything and realized that his headache was gone. His hearing and vision were back to normal. It was 9:30 AM, when the doctor came into this room and checked him out. He asked him about his headache, checked his ears and vision and with a smile, said, "Looks good, guess you can leave us. Your parents called and gave us your insurance information, so you are good to leave. When your friends get here, one of them better do the driving." He grinned and left the room. It was a half hour later, when Jack came into the room, with his bag. He got out of the bed, slowly, and went into the bathroom. When he came out, he was wearing a fresh pair of dungarees and a T-shirt, and white socks. A nurse came in and told him that his boots were in the closet. He went to the closet and brought out his boots and put them on. The nurse told him that he had to wait for an orderly, before he could leave. Jack didn't have much to say, as they waited. Soon, an orderly arrived with a wheelchair. He tried to tell them that he didn't need it. "Hospital policy." The orderly said. He got in and said to them, "why walk, when I can ride." They all chuckled. Jack told him that the guys were at the front door, with his car and that they were ready to go home.

He was "wheeled" out of the front doors, of the hospital, and deposited in the back seat of Jack's car. Jack opened the trunk and tossed his bag in. he walked around and got in behind the wheel and started up the car. It was a real tight fit, in the back seat. They were on their way home. He thought to himself. "Some milestones, his first attempt at drag racing on a real drag strip, his first and, hopefully, only bad wreck, and losing his first car, in a wreck." Not the kind of milestone he was hoping for. He really wanted it to be, losing his virginity, in the backseat of beauty. With a deep sigh, he now knew that was not going to be. He closed his eyes and listened to the radio, as Shirley and Lee sang, "Let The Good Times Roll." They were followed by Connie Francis and "Lipstick On Your Collar." He drifted off to sleep.

He woke up to The Olympics singing, "Western Movies." The car had come to a stop. They were in a Ho-Jo's parking lot. They asked him, what he wanted them to bring him? He said that he would go in with them. They all hesitated. Jack turned the rear view mirror, so he could see his reflection. He couldn't believe his eyes. Who was that grotesque creature staring at him?

A large bandaged nose and two dark black eyes! He mumbled, two cheeseburgers and fries and a chocolate frappe. He reached for his wallet. Henry told him, "I got it." They left him in the car, alone. Tears filled his eyes. He couldn't believe what he had done. He wondered, if he still a job at the country club, if he could face people, and what if he looked like this, when school started? Surely, Mr. Sparks wouldn't let him do the play. He was miserable!

When they returned, Henry handed him his lunch. He was so filled with self-pity that he really didn't feel like eating. His stomach growled in anticipation, so he satisfied his hunger. They started on the last leg home. Brenda Lee was on the radio, singing, "Sweet Nothings." Followed by Dee Clark and ":Raindrops." He dozed off, again, and only woke up when Jack stopped the car in front of his house. He looked out the window and saw his mom, come running from the front door, down the walk to the car. When he got out, she embraced him, with tears flowing. His dad was not one for affection. He thanked the guys for bringing him home. His dad got his bag and followed him and his mom, into the house. His dad couldn't wait to tell him what a foolish thing he did and that it would be a cold day in hell, before he got his own car, again.

He called the country club and was told that he didn't have to finish out his last two weeks and that they would look forward to him working with them, next summer. Two days, after that bit of news, he went to his own doctor, with his mom. Doctor Thompson took off his bandages and checked out his nose. He asked him, if he was in any pain. He told him, "no." he looked at it again and mentioned that the cartilage in his nostrils had slipped. He asked him, if he had any trouble breathing, especially, at night. He, again, answered in the negative. He told he and his mom that the stitches would probably fall out by themselves, but if they didn't by the end of the week, he would take them out. His eyes were bluish, black. Doctor Thompson told him they should clear up in five days. They thanked the doctor and went home.

He was going "stir crazy" at home, but he still didn't want to go out, where people would see him and ask a lot of "stupid" questions. His mom notice how "irritable" he was getting. She came into the den and turned off "Love of Life". She said, "Come on, we've got work to do." He got up and followed her out of the house, to the driveway. She tossed him her car keys. "If you fall off a horse, the best thing to do is get right back on it." He backed up and shook his head, "NO!" She insisted. "I have shopping to do and if we are going to eat tonight, then we need to get going." She got into the VW and sat in the passenger seat. He, slowly, walked over to the car and opened the driver's side door and got in. It felt very strange. He put the key into the ignition and stopped. Visions of the wreck came streaming out of his subconscious mind and into his consciousness. He recoiled against the back of the seat. His mom just sat there, not looking at him. He told her he couldn't do it. She told him that he could and would. She was getting angry. He turned the key and the motor started up. He, timidly, put the clutch in and stepped on the gas and shifted the car into reverse. He backed it up slowly and turned it around to face out towards the street. He put the car in first gear and slowly drove out of the driveway. He felt his confidence starting to come back. As he drove down the street, his confidence improved. By the time they got to A&P, he was driving as if he had never wrecked. His mom noticed his smile and relaxed and muttered "good."

She, then, told him that he was going to drive her car up to the lake. She and his dad would go in the Mercury. His Dad was only going to stay for a few days and she and him would stay for the month of August. They would go over his lines and relax, for the rest of the summer. He thought that he would like that. He, also, hoped the stitches would be out and his eyes would return to normal.

They had to wait until the second week of August, to go. His Doctor took out his stitches and said his eyes should clear up by then. He spent a good deal of time, going over his lines with his mom. She was concerned that he wasn't going out. He told her, he didn't feel like it. Joan came over a couple of times, to see how he was doing. She had noticed the absence of beauty and wanted to know what happened. His mom had told her. At first, he stayed in his room and wouldn't come downstairs to see her. But after the stitches were removed and his eyes looked better, he came down. She was very sympathetic. She tried, unsuccessfully, to get him to go to the beach with her "gang." He just wasn't ready to mix with other people. She said that she understood, but, also, said that he should get over it and get out of the house. His mother agreed with Joan. His mom, also, wondered why he never went out with Joan. She told him that Joan, obviously, liked him. He told his mom, they were too close, as friends. He failed to tell his mom that she was too "flat-chested" for him.

By the second week of August, his eyes were practically ":normal". His stitches had been removed and his driving confidence had returned. His family was packing, to go to the lake. He was ready. He hoped that Keith and his family, would, also, be there. He loaded his bag into the front of the VW, got in and turned it on and tuned the radio to WMEX. Santo and Johnny were playing "Sleep Walk." He didn't have to wait too long, for his folks to come out the back door and head for the Mercury. His dad told him that they were going to stop at Ho-Jo's in Pittsfield for supper. He told his dad that he would follow him, but if he did lose him, he knew where to stop.

His Dad "fired" up the Mercury and drove out of the driveway. He was right behind them, in the "bug". Dorothy Collins was on the radio, singing about "My Boy Flattop." He thought about getting a flattop, once, but Abby said, "no". So, he didn't. The ride to the lake was quite uneventful. They pulled into the restaurant and had supper. He had his usual, cheeseburgers, fries and chocolate frappe. His mom chided him about not trying anything different. He got back into the VW, turned it on, put it in gear and followed them out of the parking lot. Bill Justice was on the radio, playing "Raunchy." Once again, it was dark when they pulled up to the cottage. He waited until his mom got out of their car and went to open the door and turn on the lights. He took his bag, from the front of the "bug" and helped his dad with the other bags. The first thing his dad did, when they got settled, was to turn up the floor heater, in the hall. He was tired, so he said good night and went into his room. He still had trouble falling asleep. He would still envision the side of beauty coming up on the passenger's side and the asphalt rushing towards him. He wondered if he would ever be able to erase those images from his mind.

The next morning, he arose early, got cleaned up and dressed and walked through the living room, to the kitchenette. The aroma of bacon wafted through the cottage. He sat down, to eat, and looked out the window, in time to see his Dad climb back onto the dock, after his early morning swim. His mom asked what his plans, for the day were. He told her he was going over to Danny's and hang around with him. "We'll probably come by here around noon and go for a swim. I'm sure his folks will be at the beach this afternoon and we'll probably end up there, too." His mom mentioned that they were going downtown, to shop and would be back by noon. He finished breakfast, went to the shed and got the outboard and took it down the dock and put it on the back of the rowboat. His father had already retrieved the gas tank. "How about we do some fishing tomorrow morning?" his dad asked. "Sure" he said. He was, always up for fishing. Once the motor was secured, he said "so long" to his folks and went out the screen door, on the porch, and walked to the VW. He opened the door and got it and turned it on. The Chordettes were singing "Mr. Sandman." He could barely hear the station, through the static.

When he drove in the driveway of Danny's farmhouse, he noticed Danny's car was in the barn. He got out of the VW and walked up to their screen in porch. He opened the door and hollered in. "Hello!!!". Danny's mom hollered back, "Hello!" She came into the kitchen and gave him a hug, like she always did. She always seemed glad to see him. Danny walked in behind her. They shook hands. He asked him why his Ford was in the barn. "Needs a ring job." He said. "Oh." He replied. Danny, then, asked him, how he was doing? He said "okay." Danny leaned and took a long look at him. "Hmmm, never know you were in a wreck." Danny said. "How did you know?" he asked. "Your mom must have called everyone." Danny said. He asked Danny if he wanted to hang out. Danny looked at his mom. "You better check with your Dad." She said. He left the kitchen and went into the livingroom. When he returned, he said "Just today." They said good by to his mom and went out the door on the porch and into the driveway and got into the VW.

They got into the small car and he couldn't believe how Danny had to bend over. Danny wasn't that much taller than him, but the passenger seat was obviously higher that the driver's seat. It wasn't that noticeable, when there wasn't anybody sitting in it. He knew there must have been a lever to lower it, but they couldn't find it. So, he reached up towards the top of the windshield and took hold of the lever. He pushed it to the right and unlocked the canvas sun roof. He pushed it all the way back till it stopped over the rear seats. They were glad that it was a beautiful sunny and warm August day. Danny sat upright, in his seat, the top of his head, just over the top of the windshield. They headed for town.

They pulled into the parking lot, at the town docks. Danny asked him what radio station he was listening to. He told him. They could barely hear Perry Como singing "Dungaree Doll". Danny reached down and changed the station to a local one. It came in very clear. Smiley Lewis was singing "I Hear You Knocking". They were just about to turn off the car and go to the Dockside restaurant, to get an ice cream, when they saw a blue Chevy convertible, filled with three good looking girls, pull out of a parking space. Danny said, "let's follow them, maybe we can get a date!" He tried to put the car in reverse and met with resistance. When he finally put it in reverse and backed out of the space, turned and put it in forward gear, the girls were gone. He pulled onto the main drag and saw that the blue convertible was stopped, to let some pedestrians cross the road. They pulled up behind them. Danny tried to yell at them to pull over. They wouldn't. Instead, they hit the gas and drove off, out of town. He did the same. The chase was on. He backed off some. He was afraid the girls might think they were going to harm them. The Chevy sped up, when he backed off. "We're going to lose them!" Danny yelled. He told him that they would follow them and see where they lived and then they could talk with them and maybe spend the afternoon with them. Danny agreed. When both cars came down the hill by the museum, the Chevy barreled through the pedestrian crossing, barely missing some people, in the crosswalk. He had to stop. When it was clear, he took off after the girls. They could barely see the rear end of the convertible. He gave it some more gas. They came around a bend and the Chevy was nowhere in sight. Danny said they must have turned down one of the two side roads. They were now in a small town called "Melvin Village." He went down one of the side roads. He came to a fork, in the road. He turned left and drove to a clearing behind some summer camps. No blue convertible. He turned around and went back up the road, to the fork. He took the right and went down that road. Again, another clearing. There was the blue Chevy, parked by a big cottage with a farmer's porch. They girls were sitting on the porch. He parked beside the Chevy. Danny was able to see the girls over the windshield. He tried to talk with them. One of the girls got up from her seat and went inside the cottage. When she came out, she was followed by a large, older woman. The woman started to walk towards them. Danny got very nervous. "Put it in reverse, let's get out of here!" he said. He reached down and, desperately, tried to put the car in reverse. It wouldn't go. The woman was fast approaching the car. Danny was practically screaming at him. "PUT IT IN REVERSE!!!!" he slunk down, in his seat, so all the woman saw was Danny. He kept yelling at him. He finally got it into reverse, just as the woman approached the car. He hit the gas and sprayed dirt and pine needles all over the woman and the Chevy. He backed up as far as could he could go, without hitting a tree. He, then, turned it around and pit it in first gear and hit the gas, once again, and sprayed dirt and pine needles everywhere. They raced up the dirt road, past the fork and out onto the paved road. Once on the main road, he slowed down. Danny kept telling him that he had to do something about that reverse gear. They approached the town and saw a sign for ice cream. He took the right and went down the road, towards the water. They pulled into a parking spot, turned off the car and went up to the building's take out window. They got their ice cream cones and sat down on a bench. As they were enjoying their ice creams, they noticed the town's only police car come down the road. He parked by the VW and got out and walked to the back of the "bug," and looked in their direction and walked towards them. Both of their mouths were open, but they weren't eating. Ice cream was dripping onto the hands. The cop sat down across the table from the them. "You guys weren't just at the Mansfield place, down the road, were you?" he asked. Danny was the first to answer. "Don't know any Mansfields, sir." He said. The cop asked for their I.D.'s. They gave him their driver's licenses. Got a complaint that two guys in a green Volkswagon were harassing some girls at the Mansfield place. They both shook their heads, no! The cop handed him back his driver's license, but kept Danny's. he kept looking at it. "You any relation to Luther?" he asked. Danny said, "yes, he's my Dad." "Hmmmm" said the cop. "You're dad coached me in baseball. A real nice guy, I owe him a lot." "You guys aren't going to go near the Mansfield place, anymore, are you." "No sir!" they both chimed in together. "Good!" said the cop. "You tell your Dad, Billy Connors says Hi." "Yes sir" said Danny. They both heaved a big sigh of relief, when the cop got back in his cruiser and left. They ate was left of their cones and got back in the VW and proceeded to get out of Melvin Village. Perry Como was on the radio singing "Round and Round."

They rolled into the parking space, beside his Dad's Mercury. Guy Mitchell was on the radio, singing, "Rockabilly Rock." He turned off the car and they both got out and walked around the cottage to the dock. "Just in time for lunch, you two." His mom said. They had made a pact that they would never tell anyone about the day, with the girls.

After lunch, they decided to go to Danny's beach, to swim. His mom had him wait, while she put together some hamburger patties and two packages of hot dogs and rolls for both. She told them that they might as well stay there, for the afternoon and evening, because Danny's mom had called and invited them for a cookout, on the beach. He put the food in the back seat of the VW and went to the clothesline and grabbed his bathing suit. Danny said that no one was in the cottage that week, so they could change into their suits, there. As he started up the "bug" Clarence "Frogman" Henry was singing "Aint Got No Home."

He turned off the paved road, onto the dirt road, down to the beach. He drove very slowly, as as not to hit any rocks with the small car. Danny wasn't paying attention, he was too busy singing along with Danny and The Juniors, "At The Hop." They made it down the road, all right and parked in a clearing by the dark brown cottage with the farmers porch. They both remarked, as kids, they had shucked many an ear of corn, on that porch, for many a cookout. He turned off the car and got out and took the patties, hotdogs and rolls to Danny's mom. She handed both of them a bucket with about twenty four ears of corn. "You know what to do." She said. They looked at each other and grinned. They headed to the porch to schuck the corn. When they were done, he went to the car and got his bathing suit. Danny had already gotten his from his mom. They went into the cottage and changed. He changed in the first floor bathroom; Danny in the upstairs bathroom. They met in the living room and headed out the door onto the porch. They looked at each other, grinned and raced each other to the beach and into the calm, diamond crusted, sparkling water. They could only run so far, before they had to dive. He stopped himself, just in time, before heading head first into the water. Danny's head broke the surface and he hollered "I win." "yep," he said, "you won." He, then, told Danny he couldn't dive head first for a while, cause he might open the wounds on his nose. They swam out to the raft that Danny's Dad had built. He looked to the beach and noticed Danny's little sisters, playing in the sand and talking with each other. He told Danny, that his sister Darlene was really growing up. His other sister was still just a little kid. Danny dove off the raft, as he slipped over the side, feet first. They swam over to the large boulder that loomed just below the surface. He was, always, afraid that some large snapping turtle was going to come out from underneath the rock and bite him. He got up on the large rock and sat down. Danny got up on the other side and sat down, too. Danny, then told him that Keith and the family would be up the next week. Danny said, "you seen his sister, lately?" "nope." He said. "They were up in June, for a week. Man is she built!" I'd like to get a hold of them boobies!" Danny said. That was the first time he had ever heard someone refer to a woman's breasts as "boobies." It struck him funny and he began to laugh. He laughed so hard, he slipped off the rock and down under the surface, next to the rock. He looked at the monster side of the slimy boulder. It was frightening, to him. He propelled himself up to the surface and began to swim back towards Danny's beach. He really swam fast, so fast that Danny couldn't catch up to him. He walked out of the water and started to walk back to the cottage. Danny's dad threw him a towel. "Wipe yourself off, before you go in the house." He said. He walked to the steps, that led onto the farmers porch and sat down and wiped his feet and then the rest of him. Danny was right behind him. When they had changed and brought their respective suits out of the house, they saw his folks pull up in the Mercury. He was glad to see them, because that meant they would be eating soon. He went to the VW and hung his wet suit over the radio antenna.

His dad asked him to help him carry the lawn chairs, from the trunk of his car, to the beach. Danny's sisters were already helping themselves to the potato chips. He and Danny joined the girls and got some chips, too. Danny's dad was cooking the burgers and hot dogs. When he saw his Dad, he remarked, "I was in Melvin Village, today, and ran into a kid, I coached. He's now the cop in town." That was all he said, as he flipped the burgers and rolled the hot dogs over.

He and Danny almost choked on their chips. They went to the ice chest and got two cokes and started to walk towards the other side of the beach. "Don't you two wander off." Danny's dad said. "Charlie, our sons may have gotten into some more trouble." He heard his dad, groan. "Seems two young men in a green VW were chasing some girls and scaring them." Danny's dad continued. He and Danny looked at each other. Finally, Danny spoke, "we just wanted to talk to them and maybe get a date." Danny's dad smiled. He saw his dad stifle a laugh. He knew they weren't going to get a talking to. "There are better ways to meet girls than to scare them." His dad said. Danny's sisters were silently convulsing with laughter. "Guess so." Danny said. Danny's dad announced the meat was ready. They all got paper plates and plastic utensils for the salad and potato salad. He got two burgers, a hot dog, an ear of corn and some potato salad and went and sat at the long wooden table. Once they were all finished eating, it was time to light the logs, in the pit, and draw their chairs in a circle around the fire and get set to listen to Luther's stories. They were the highlight of the evening. Some they had heard before, like the cows that got drunk on green apples. The night came to a close. He went to the VW, took his dry suit off the antenna and threw it in the back of the car and headed home.

The next week, Keith and his family arrived at the cottage. That meant a lot of time on the beach and in the water. When not at the beach, they played baseball, in one of Danny's pastures. A lot of time, he and Keith spent together. Danny was working for his dad, haying. He was saving up money to get his car fixed.

One night, the three of them, piled into the VW and headed to town to the movies. It was a John Wayne western. As he drove to town, the Diamonds were on the radio, singing "Little Darlin." He told them that he really came to dislike that song. He said he liked the Del Vikings better. Ironically, the next song was the Del Vikings singing, "Come Go With Me," They laughed and sang along.

After the movie, it was the custom to go to Bailey's for ice cream. Keith was hungry, so they went inside and found a booth and sat down. Danny poked him in the ribs. "look who's sitting at the other booth." He said. He looked at the three girls. The girls did not look at them. Finally, he decided to say something. He looked at them and said," Hi, we just wanted to apologize for scaring you the other day." The girls looked at him and said, "Okay" and turned their attention to their menus. Keith was looking over the top of the menu, at them and then at the girls. He said, to he and Danny, "you guys don't stand a chance with them, they are out of your class. You can do much better than them, believe me!" he said it loud enough, for the girls to hear. The girls glared at Keith and yelled, "Oh Yeah!!!". They got up and moved to another part of the restaurant. Keith just laughed. He and Danny stared at him. Danny asked him why he said that.

Keith replied that either the girls were going to laugh and then join them, or leave. He said, "Well. Guess what? They left!" They got their orders, ate and left. When they got the VW, they noticed ":SCREW YOU" was written, in red lipstick, on the windshield. He was angry and wanted to have revenge, but, after what Danny's Dad had said, thought better of it. It was very difficult driving home, looking through the windshield, in the dark. Especially when other headlights came at them.

When they, finally, got back to Keith's cottage, he noticed that Keith's sister Carol, was still awake and sitting on the steps of the farmer's porch. He stopped the car; turned it off and got out and walked up to her. "Carol, do you happen to know what removes lipstick from glass?" he asked. She gave him a quizzical look and reached into her pocketbook, which she just happened to have with her. She bought out a bottle of nail polish remover. "Try this." She said. Danny got some paper towels, left over from one of the cookouts. They walked to the car and proceeded to try and wipe off the lipstick. Carol had followed them and when she saw what was written, dropped to her knees, in hysterics. It was the first time he had ever seen her really laugh at anything. It took three tries, but the lipstick was gone. He handed the bottle back to Carol, who had composed herself. "Boy you really pissed some girls off!" She said. Keith told her to watch her mouth She stuck her tongue out at Keith, like a little girl would, turned and went back to the steps. He yelled "Thanks!" to her. He and Danny said goodnight to Keith and got back in the bug and turned it on, this time it went smoothly into reverse gear. "Oh yeah," Danny said, "Now it shifts easy." He turned it around and put it in first and headed up the dirt road. The Moonglows were singing "Sincerely" on the radio. Danny said he liked the Maguire Sisters version better.

The rest of the summer went by too quickly and without any further "events". Before he knew it, it was Labor Day and time to head home. He couldn't believe that he knew all his lines and his "cues". He hoped Mr. Sparks would not notice the scars on his nose. He drove over to the cottage that Danny's folks owned and that Keith's family had rented. As he drove into the clearing by the cottage, Bo Diddley was singing "Bo Diddley" on the radio. He turned the volume down, when he noticed the stern look, he got from Keith's dad, who was loading bags into the trunk of his Chevy sedan. Keith and Danny were sitting in two deck chairs, on the farmers porch. He turned off the VW and got out of the car and joined them. The weather seemed to sense that summer came to an end. It was a gray, cold, morning. The guys talked about school and how "cool" it was going to be that they were going to be seniors. They, also, shared some apprehension about the following summer and what they hoped was going to be in their respective futures. Keith had plans to go to Holy Cross. Danny was looking at UNH. He didn't have any idea what he wanted to do. He knew his dad insisted he go to college. Keith's dad hollered at his family, that it was time to go. Danny and he shook hands with Keith and vowed that no matter what, they would get together next summer. He and Danny watched as Keith and the rest of them piled into the sedan and drove up the dirt road. They could hear Patti Page singing "Mockingbird Hill" on the car radio. he laughed and told Danny that Keith's dad turned up the volume, to get back at him. They both laughed. Then, they walked to the VW and got in and he turned it on. The Crew Cuts were on the radio, singing "Sh—Boom". He pulled into Danny's driveway. He turned the car off. They got out and walked into the house. He gave Danny's mother a hug and shook his dad's hand and bid them all goodbye until next summer. He walked out of the house and got back into the car. He turned it on, turned around and drove out onto the road and headed to his cottage. Bill Haley and The Comets were singing, "See You Later, Alligator." He thought that was appropriate.

He had a feeling that the winds of change were blowing, as he pulled into the clearing at their cottage. He turned off the beetle and popped open the hood. He went onto the cottage, to his room and packed his clothes, except the bathing suit. He took the packed bag out to the bug and put in the storage space and closed the hood. He opened the door and pushed the back of the front seat forward and retrieved the bathing suit. He pulled the back of the seat forward, closed the door and walked back into the cottage and into this room and deposited the suit in the top drawer of the dresser.

His Dad had taken the gas tank out of the boat and put it in the shed. He went around the house and to the dock, walked out on it and got into the boat. The wind had picked up and the waves were topped with white caps. The boat was savagely rocking beside the dock. He put his left foot on the rear seat, against the side, of the boat. He put his right foot, on the seat and against the other side. He bent down, from the waist and balancing himself., began to unscrew the toggles that held the motor to the transom. When the motor was loose enough, he braced his legs and back and proceeded to bring the motor up to his waist and out of the boat. Where the huge wave came from, he didn't know. All he knew was that he, lost his balance, and he and the motor pitched forward, over the transom and into the choppy water. When his head broke the surface, he was able to regain his stance in the four feet of rough water and hold the motor with the prop sitting on the sandy bottom. He hefted the motor out of the water and with every muscle screaming in his arms, pulled and pushed the five and a half HP outboard up and onto the dock. With the motor, safely out of the water and resting on the dock, he walked through the waves, around the front of the dock, up the side ladder. When he got on the dock and turned to face the porch, he saw them. His mom was sitting in one of the deck chairs, holding her sides and roaring with laughter. His Dad was leaning against the screen door, laughing hysterically. He was not amused. He walked up the steps to the porch and pushed his dad away from the door and entered. He sat down in one of the deck chairs and took off his "soggy" Keds and soaked socks. His mom, still laughing, went into the cottage, to the bathroom and got him a bath towel. He dried off his feet and walked through the living room to the hall and into his bed room. He went to the dresser, said a "silent" prayer and opened the bottom drawer. There, neatly folded was a "spare" set of clothes. Underwear, socks, dungarees, and an old shirt. He had put them in the drawer, for just such an occasion. He changed and took his car keys and wallet out of the wet dungarees and placed them on the dresser. He rolled up the wet clothes in the bath towel. He was glad that he hadn't packed his engineer boots yet. He put on the boots and with the rolled up wet clothes, went to the porch and retrieved his wet socks and keds. He left the porch and walked to the VW. He opened the door and, again, pushed the back, of the front seat forward. He placed the wet clothes, in the back storage area, behind the back seat. He got out of the car and pulled the back of the seat forward, and closed the door. He went back into the cottage, to his room and got his keys and wallet. He left the room and walked into the kitchenette. He opened the wallet and took out his license and insurance papers and the money he had left. He put it all plus his keys on the table. He, again, proceeded onto the dock. He picked up the motor, by its' handle and took it to the shed. He made a mental note, that whenever he was, either, bring the motor to the boat or taking it off the boat, that he would be sure and wear his bathing suit! When he returned to the kitchenette, his mom, still chuckling, was drying his papers with her hair dryer. He thanked her. He, then went to help his dad load the Mercury. His dad was still laughing, "That was the funniest thing I've seen in a long time." He laughed. He told his dad he was glad he enjoyed witnessing his misfortune. With the Mercury loaded. He went back into the kitchen. Everything was dry! He thanked his mom. She packed the dryer into a little bag, she had for it. He took it out to the car. His dad and mom did a final walk through of the cottage and made sure all doors were locked, all appliances were off, lights were off and all perishables. In the refrigerator were packed. He sat in VW and waited. He turned it on and heard the Danleers sing "One Summer Night." His folks got into Mercury and backed out of the driveway. Once they made the turn onto the dirt road, he backed out and turned and put it in drive and followed. Summer was, officially, over.

He did not have to report to school until the Thursday, after Labor Day. He had extra days to review his lines, for the play. His mother took the time to help him. He felt he was ready to hand the playbook, back to Mr. Sparks. His mother said she was proud of him, the way he stayed on "task." His dad wished he would do the same thing with his other subjects. He was both excited and anxious about the new year. This was his year. He was a senior, top of the hill, big man on campus, top dog, etc. It was, also, his last year in the public school system.

His mom did not have to wake him up for the first day of school. he got up early, took care of business and got dressed in some new "Ivy League" duds. He spent about 100 of the 500 hundred dollars, he got, for selling beauty. His dad had called him, during one of the times, he was home and he and his mom were still at the lake. The manager of the drag strip had called and wanted to know if he was going to get the 'wreck' or, if he wanted to sell it. Seems some guy was willing to give him five hundred dollars for it. He wanted it for parts. His dad gave him the number of the manager's office. He called him and said "okay" to the deal. The five hundred dollar check was waiting for him, when he got home from the lake. His mom cashed the check, for him, the day after Labor Day. He took one hundred and went and got new "school" clothes. Three pairs of different colored polished Chinos. Three new button down collared shirts, new underwear and socks and a new pair of white bucs shoes (the kind Pat Boone wore and a pair of "dirty bucs". He, also, got a light blue" Perry Como" button down sweater. He was ready, well, fashion-wise, anyway.

His mom let him drive the VW to school, that Thursday. The first person, he saw, on Elm road, was Carl. He had to explain what had happened at the track to him and "beauty." By the time third period rolled around, almost everyone in school knew what happened to him, over the summer. The first place, in school, he had to go, was the office, to pick up the year's schedule. Each "class" lasted about twenty minutes. Books were handed out and teachers went over what they expected of their students. He had first lunch, which he liked. He went with some guys, he had just met, in his last period class. When lunch was over, the seniors were told to report to the auditorium. When they were all seated, the Principal stepped up to the podium and welcomed them all back. "Take a look around you." He said. "There are over 1200 of you. This is the largest senior class in the history of this school. You are the last class to graduate from this school. Next year, it will be called Newton North. They are finishing up, building a new school; it will be called Newton South. I want to remind you that your underclassmen are looking up to you. Please give them the benefit of your knowledge of this school. Don't send the boys to the girls locker room. Don't send them to the roof, looking for the pool. Please be kind to them, remember, you were once, in their shoes." With that, he stepped aside from the podium. The class applauded him. Next to the podium, was the class President, Paul. He told them about all the dances, they were going to have, ever Friday night. He. Also, told them that they were looking to have the prom at TheTotem Pole ballroom. He, also, mentioned a lot of other things the officers had planned for their senior year. Paul got the most applause of anyone. When he stepped back, the class treasurer told them that their class had a lot of money to spend and they were going to make sure that everyone enjoyed their final year, at school. The last speaker was Mr. Sparks. All he said was that the cast of the senior play would stay behind, after the program, to start rehearsals for the play. With that, the Principal stepped back up to the podium and wished them all a great year!

When everyone had cleared out of the auditorium, the cast were the only ones left. Mr. Sparks had everyone join him on stage. He raised the curtain and the chairs, for them were set up just as they were, the last day of school. Mr. Sparks asked how many had learned their lines. They all raised their hands. "Really?" Mr. Sparks asked. "That's a first! If it's true. Everyone pass their play books to me and we'll see." He said. When he had all the books, in his hand, he said, "let's begin. Horace?" The student playing Horace began. When he came to the line, "boys you're going to have a mistress, he pipe up, without a pause and blurted out, "I'm too young! Mr, Vandergelter." It went smoothly from there. Mr. Sparks was very pleased. No one had to call for a line. When they were done, Mr. Sparks, with a huge grin, on his face, said, "we'll begin blocking on Monday." He passed back the books, just in case someone needed more studying. He left the auditorium, with a big grin on his face. He felt good about himself, even if he didn't have a very good summer and didn't lose his virginity. It looked like it was going to be a good year.

Rehearsals went well. The cast met every afternoon, except Fridays. By the third week, construction had begun on the various sets. The fourth week, the art classes had begun painting the sets. Mr. Sparks was more than pleased. It was during the fourth week, that measurements were taken, for costumes. He had only one costume, for the duration of the whole play. The best news, he got from Mr. Sparks, was to grow sideburns. He was thrilled. He wanted to grow sideburns, ever since he saw them on Elvis. He noticed how the girls reacted to Elvis. Some of the girls even called Elvis, "The sideburn King." His father was dead set against him having sideburns. So, when he was "ordered" to grow them. He told his folks, one night, at supper, reluctantly, that he had to grow them. His dad said "okay, but they come off, when the play is over." So, his "suppressed desire" came to fruition. When anyone asked "why" he said, "for the show." But, inside, he was excited to be growing them. They did seem to get him a lot of attention, from the girls. He enjoyed the attention. It was, at that time, that he began to hang around with Tina and her friends. Tina was the daughter of the TV celebrity, from dancing school. His brothers kept goading him to start dating Tina, so they could be rich and not have to work, for a living. They were quite upset with him, when he told them that he and Tina were must friends. He really fit in with them, even though his family didn't have a quarter of the wealth that hers had. Tina and her other friends were excited that he was acting in the play. They all told him that they couldn't wait to see him, on the stage. His ego was at an all time "high". He didn't even mind, when Shelly showed up, one night, at one of Tina's parties, with a new boyfriend, on her arm. She had met him, while studying abroad.

Friday and Saturday nights, he was at Tina's. During the day, on Saturdays and Sunday afternoons he was helping his dad, with yard work. His grades were good. The rehearsals were great. Then, came the night, a Thursday, for dress rehearsal. His costume fir perfectly. He, even, got to wear a brown derby. The technical rehearsal was set for the Saturday, before the play was to go up. He was at the school, all day. That was the longest rehearsal, ever. The lights had to be set, the sound system, in place and working, and the final blockings were set. Mr. Sparks had arranged for everyone to have pizza, for lunch. He was part of a happy cast and crew. Everyone got along, so well, like a well-oiled machine. Mr. Sparks never stopped smiling. Monday afternoon, after rehearsing Act two, each member of the cast was given 5 tickets for each night. 5 for Friday and 5 for Saturday. He knew his folks were going to be there, for

Friday, which left him 8 extra tickets. He called Tina that night and said he'd drop the tickets off at her house, the next day, Tuesday. She was thrilled and thanked him profusely. Classes that week were a real drag, for him. The anxiety and excitement, almost made him ill. He overheard Mr. Sparks, tell the Art teacher that he was really nervous, because there hadn't been one bad rehearsal. Apparently, every show has at least one very bad rehearsal, where nothing seemed to go right. That rehearsal came the Thursday before the first show. The "exploding cans of tomatoes failed to work, people messed up their lines, the blocking went wrong, and he rolled off the stage, with a lace tablecloth wrapped around his face. He rolled right into the orchestra pit. Everyone rushed to him. Luckily, he was only scratched. Mr. Sparks face turned a bright crimson. He threw his clipboard of "notes" down hard on the stage, turned and walked up the aisle, towards the doors, yelling, "I'm cancelling the play!" The cast and crew were horrified by his words. The silence, in the auditorium and on the stage was deafening. They all sat down. Girls began to sob. Lips were frozen down at the ends. But, no one moved. Finally, the art teacher, Mr. Hanson, walked into the auditorium and up onto the stage. "Relax, the show will go on." He said. "This was the rehearsal, Mr. Sparks wanted to see. Every show has, at least, one bad rehearsal. Now, ladies and gentlemen, please go to your dressing areas and neatly hang up your costumes. We will see everyone here, promptly after classes, tomorrow afternoon. You will be given something "light" to eat, before the show. Tell your families that you won't be home until after tomorrow night's performance. Good afternoon." Smiles returned to everyone. They did, as they were told. He hung up his costume and headed out of the building to where he had parked the VW. He got to the car and unlocked it, turned it on and headed home. Johnny Preston was singing "Running bear" on the radio.

As he walked in the door, of his house, his mom was on the hall phone. She said, "wait a minute, he just walked in." She handed the phone receiver, to him, "it's Mr. Sparks." He took the receiver, from his mom and spoke into it. Mr. Sparks told him that he meant to tell him to get a haircut," just a trim." He replied that he would go right away before the barbershop closed. He hung up the phone and went back out the front door. He got back into the VW and turned it on and headed to the "square". The (late) Big Bopper was singing, "Chantilly Lace." By the time the record ended, he had pulled into a parking space, in front of the barbershop. He turned off the car and got out and walked up to the door, opened it and went in. Vic was working on a customer. Vic said "hello, I'll be right with you. You got here, just in time. Normally I'm closed by now, but I'm working on a very special client." He answered, "okay. I just need a trim, for my role in a play, at school." Vic took the comb and clippers away from his customer and looked at him and said, "well, whadda ya know! Two actors in the same afternoon." He didn't understand what Vic meant. The customer asked him what character he was playing. He answered, "Barnaby Tucker, in The MatchMaker." The customer, who's head was tilted down, so Vic could trim the nape of his neck, said, "great part!" he replied. "yeah, I'm really enjoying it." The customer asked when the show would "go up." He answered, tomorrow night." "Where?" the customer asked. He answered, "at the local high school." Vic had a big grin on his face and then asked him, "Do you know who you are talking to?" "No!" he answered. Then, Vic swung the chair around; he was face to face with the actor, Robert Morse! He knew that he lived in town, but he had never met him. Mr. Morse stuck out his right hand, from underneath the cover, they shook hands. Vic told him that Robert played Barnaby Tucker on Broadway. His jaw mist have dropped so far, that is came close to the floor. Vic told him, that he would be finished with Robert in a minute or so. He couldn't talk; he just stood there, in awe, as Vic swung the chair around to finish Robert's hair. When he was done, Robert got out of the seat and gestured him to it. "Vic cut my hair for my role as Barnaby, so he knows just how to cut it. I'll stick around and give some pointers, if that's ok with you." Again, he was at a loss for words. Vic put the cover on him and put the comb and scissors to his hair. Robert asked him, his name and said that he would try and get over to the high school, to see the play. "I'd love to see it from an audience point of view." Then, out of the blue, he said, "Boys, you're going to have a mistress." Without so much as a small pause, he blurted out, "I'm too young! Mr. Vandergelter!" "Bravo!" said Robert. As Vic trimmed his hair, Robert and he talked about acting. Robert asked him, if he was considering a career in the theatre. He said that he wasn't sure, but that it certainly was an exciting line of work. "Well, I'll you" said Robert, "it's the kind of career, where you'll be eating steak, one week and peanut butter sandwiches, the next. Yep, you'll pay the rent and have plenty of money, one week and be dead broke, the next." He looked at his watch and thanked Vic, gave him two tickets to "Take Me Along" in which he was acting next to Jackie Gleason. He, also, told Vic that when he came to New York City, for the show, he wanted him to come backstage and give him another trim. "Be glad to Robert," Vic said. With that, Robert, again, shook his hand, "hope to see the show this weekend." Robert turned and walked out of the shop. Vic told him that Robert lived just up the hill. He, also, told him that Robert gave him so very good advice. He told Vic that he hoped that Robert would be able to come to the show. When he was "trimmed", Vic took the cover off him. He got out of the chair and reached in his pocket for the two dollars, for Vic. Vic refused take the money and told him that when he made it big on Broadway, to remember him, like Robert Morse does. He promised Vic, that he would. He left the shop and said to himself, "another milestone, meeting a famous actor and playing the same part he did." He couldn't wait to get home and tell his mom. He got in the VW, turned it on and backed out of the spot and drove home. The Crew Cuts were on the radio, singing "Crazy 'Bout Ya Baby".

When he arrived home and parked the car at the end of the driveway, he turned off the car, jumped out and ran into the house, through the front door, to the kitchen, his mom was cooking supper. He was so excited! He, practically, screamed, "I just met Robert Morse, the actor!" His mom, turned around and nonchalantly said, "well, he does live, here in town, and he's been over here, many times, with your brother, Dave." He couldn't believe it! Robert Morse was in his house. "When?" he cried. "Many times." His mom said. "Don't you remember? He and your brother used to squirt you with the garden hose." "That was him?" he asked. "Uh huh." His mom said and then told him to wash up for supper. He went to the bathroom, to wash up, in a slight case of shock.

Friday, "D" day, "red letter day," THE day. He got up early, washed up, got dressed and went downstairs, to eat breakfast. He handed his mom, their tickets, for that night's performance, and went out the back door, to the VW. His mom let him use it that week. She did her shopping when he got home from school and rehearsals. He got in and turned the car on, put it in gear and headed out of the driveway, to school. Elvis was singing, "I Don't Care If The Sun Don't Shine." He sang along. He pulled into the parking lot, on Elm road. He got out of the car, locked it up and bid "farewell" to it. He wouldn't be back in the car, until late that night. Again, a flood of mixed emotions swept over him. He, silently, prayed to God that he wouldn't make a fool of himself. He entered the building and went to his homeroom. He was the first one there. He went to his desk and sat down. His homeroom teacher entered, soon after. "Well, this is a first." She said. "Usually, you don't come in until just after the late bell." "I'm very nervous!" he exclaimed. "I'm sure you'll do just fine." She said. She sat at her desk and went through her mail. "Well, Barnaby." She said, "looks like you and the entire cast and crew are excused from classes, today. You are to report to the auditorium right after homeroom." "Really?" he asked. "Yes sir." She said. He felt a real sense of relief. He did not have to suffer through classes.

When the bell rang, signifying the end of homeroom, all the kids wished him well. He thanked each and every one of them. He grabbed his books and headed out of the room, down the hall, out the big oaken doors of building One and across the street, to building three and the auditorium. When he stepped through the large green doors, to the auditorium, the smell of fresh biscuits filled the air. He walked down the aisle, towards the pits. There was a long table that had fresh biscuits and juice on it. Pretty soon, the entire cast and crew showed up. Mr. Sparks walked in an bade them all a "good morning". He was one of the first to thank Mr. Sparks, for getting them out of classes. "Do it every year," he said. "Enjoy the food, now I want you to sit down and just relax, for the day. We have sandwiches coming in for lunch and dinner. All you have to do is relax, study, if you want. But, mostly, just relax." He couldn't hold back the news about Robert Morse. Everyone got excited and hoped that he would come to the performance. This day was one of the best days, at school, for him. Mr. Sparks came back into the auditorium, during lunch, and spoke to the cast. "This is the last time I will be speaking with you. My last instructions to you. Please. When you hear the audience laugh, you must not continue talking, wait till the laughter stops, then continue, especially, you Barnaby, you have some very funny lines. On the other hand, don't pause and wait for laughter. There is nothing worse than "dead air". You may think your line is very funny, but the audience may not. Tonight's audience may laugh at everything and tomorrow's audience may not. So, please be aware of them. Now, most important, tonight, have fun. When you are enjoying the play, the audience will enjoy it, too. Thank you." Then, he turned and left the auditorium.

The rest of the afternoon was nerve wracking, for him. He tried to go over his lines, but his mind would go blank. Others told him, not to try, that everything would be fine. He did a lot of pacing around the auditorium. Finally, school had let out and, soon, the building was quiet. It was after three PM. At around 4 PM. The cast was told to report to their dressing rooms, to be "made up". He had never had make up applied to his face and hands, before. When it was done, he got up and looked at himself, in the mirror, that someone had placed on the inside of the classroom door. He was warned not to touch his face. If he were to rub or scratch any part of his face, the lights would shine on that spot like a beacon.

5 PM came quickly, after being "made up". They were instructed to get into their costumes. The play was going up, precisely at 7PM. Once, he was in costume and had put his school clothes in one of the closets, he was really feeling nervous. He knew there was no backing out. The show was going to go on. This was what all the rehearsals had been about, this was the culmination of all the hard work. 6:30 PM came, without notice. One of the stage hands came into the boys dressing room and instructed them to go backstage, quietly. He said those that had to use the restroom, should do so now. He was one of those. After leaving the restroom, he quietly crept down the hall and through the backstage door. The stage manager whispered to the cast, that they had a full house. That really made him nervous. He, silently, prayed that he would do a good job and not embarrass himself nor his fellow cast members.

6:45 PM, he and the Howard (Cornelius) were told to go on stage and get inside the large landing. The landing was supposed to be the stairs to the basement of the store. They climbed inside the cramped space. They managed to take off their sport coats. They were supposed to be in just their shirts, with the garters on the upper part of their sleeves. They were quite still. He heard the curtain being opened. Large applause reverberated around the stage and the "theatre". Then he heard Barry's (Vandergelter's) voice calling. On the third screaming of their character's names, they threw open the hatch and came out. The audience roared their approval. Then Vandergelter said the line to them, "Boys, you're going to have a mistress!" He put his hand towards his mouth in schock surprise and uttered his first line, "I'm too young Mr. Vandergelter." The audience roared!!!!!! And so it went. The first night was a huge success!

This was, to him, the best milestone, so far, of his senior year. Being made up and acting on a stage, in front of a full house. When the called him, to take his bow, the audience gave him a standing ovation!! He couldn't believe it! After the first show was put to bed. They went back to their dressing rooms and hung up their costumes and proceeded to take off their makeup. Everyone was so happy and congratulated each other. A stage hand handed him a program. He took it and turned it over, there handwritten was a message, "Great job! From one Barnaby to another, signed, Robert Morse." He yelled to the others, "He was here, Robert Morse was here.

"Another milestone! Once, he was changed and cleaned up, he left the building and went out into the front hall, by the front doors. His parents and Tina and the others were there. They all congratulated him and Tina invited him, back to her house, with others. He accepted and told his folks that he would be home around midnight.

The second night's performance was another smash hit. That audience, though laughed at different lines, gave them all a standing ovation. As they were cleaning up, Wendy (who played Mrs. Malloy) handed out invitations and directions to the her house, for the cast and crew party. It was at the party that he met Charlene. She was short, stocky, dirty blonde hair, rosy cheeks and the largest chest, he had ever seen. She was a junior. They shared some dances and when he sat down, she joined him, on his lap. He asked her if she wanted to go out some time. She said that she was dating someone, but that she'd think about it.

He saw her, off and on, through the fall. They went out a couple of times. They went to parties and bowling and to the movies. Whenever they kissed, it was sweet little kisses. There wasn't any passion at all. She was still dating the other guy, as well. He would dream about holding her breasts and kissing them. He knew that if he did get the chance, he would probably be the first guy to do so.

Halloween, Thanksgiving, and Christmas came and went. He was invited to a New Year's Eve party. When he arrived, he realized that he was the only "single" person there. All the others were couples. He didn't think about bringing a date. He was absolutely miserable. He decided that he would drink away his "blues." Jim Lowe's record of "Talking To The Blues." Was on the Hi Fi. He said to himself that song was appropriate, as he poured himself a Seven and Seven. At one point, after several Seven and Sevens, he, through blurred vision saw Abby and Carl come through the front door. He wished he was invisible. He managed to avoid eye contact with them and found his way out the back door. He stumbled around to the front of the house and found the VW. He got in, turned it on and was thankful that he only lived a few blocks away. Somehow he made it home, without incident. He carefully parked the car, in the driveway, and crept quietly into the house and up to his room. He lay down on the bed and watched the room spin. He closed his eyes and prayed that 1960 would be a better year.

It was the first day, back at school, after vacation, that Charlene said she wanted to date him, exclusively. She told him that she had fallen in love with him. He didn't say it, but he didn't feel the same. She loved him and wanted to be with him and that made him feel good. He wasn't lonely anymore. Their "make out" sessions were sweet kisses and nothing else. One time, while she seemed to be "hot and bothered", he attempted to put his hands on her humungous breasts. She grabbed his hands and pushed them away and slapped his face. He apologized and vowed to never try it again. They went to the Friday night "record hops" at the school gym. They danced to The Stroll and jitterbugged. She would not dance any slow dances with him, because of her size. She only came up to his waist and didn't think it looked right. He tried to bend down, to her, once, but it hurt his back.

For the next three months, he "ached" for a passionate love affair. He knew she was not ready. She was too "pure" and had become quite 'religious". Then, one Saturday night, they double dated with his friend Fred and Fred's girlfriend, June. They went bowling. Afterwards, over burgers and cokes, Charlene heard Fred and June talk about going "parking." Charlene said "No" and insisted on being taken home. When he pulled up in front of her house, she leaned over and gave him a "peck" on the cheek and said "good night." She got out of the car, went up the walk and into her house. She didn't give him a chance to walk her to the door. He leaned over and pulled the passenger door shut.

Fred couldn't believe what he had witnessed. "After going out with her, for three months, all you get is a peck on the cheek?" He asked. "Yeah." He replied. June chimed in, "You like that? Is that all you want from a girl?" She asked. "No!" he said, emphatically, "I'm slowly dying! June, then remarked, "You need to meet my friend Ree (pronounced Ray)." "Wait a minute!" he cried, "I'm not into guys!" She and Fred howled with laughter. "Don't worry, Ree is a girl! And she's been without a boyfriend since Thanksgiving." She said and then asked "Would you like to meet her?" "What does she look like?" He asked. "Well, she's about your height, a great personality, a dynamite figure and very long legs." "Guys call her cute and very sexy." "Okay!" He said to Fred and June, "try and set it up." He, then, put the car in forward gear and drove off from Charlene's house, for the last time. The Drifters were on the radio, singing "Dance with Me." Fred and June were two involved with each other to notice.

He didn't hear from Fred for over two weeks. He kept making excuses, with Charlene, why they couldn't go out. He was losing interest, in her, fast and hoping for the date with Ree. Finally, the last week of March, Fred came up to him, in the school cafeteria. "June had finally convinced Ree to go out with you." He said. That statement did not help his "bruised" ego. Should he be happy or maybe she thought too much of herself, to go out with him. "We'll double date." Fred said. He, almost wanted to tell Fred to forget it, but he was feeling desperate. So, he agreed. "Great!" said Fred, "the drive inn opens up this Saturday.!" Great!" he said, sarcastically. Then he thought that is the date is a drag and she's a dog, at least he can watch the movie. Then, Fred reached in his pocket and produced a sheet of paper, with words written on it. Now, there are some rules, you'll have to follow. "Rules?" he asked. "you're kidding?" "Nope." Fred said. He looked at the sheet and the rules.

Rule#1. Play it cool. Don't pounce on her like a dog in heat.

Rule#2. Show a definite interest, in everything she says.

Rule#3. Don't stare at her.

Rule#4. Be a gentleman, open doors for her, walk her to and from the car.

Rule#5. Don't make the first move, let her make it, if there is to be a move.

Rule#6. Be courteous to her, even if the date doesn't go well.

Rule#7. Stick to rule #1. Don't scare her off!

Rule#8. She has a great sense of humor and likes to laugh, so jokes are good Riske is okay, but not real raunchy.

Fred handed the sheet to him and advised him to study the rules. He kept emphasizing the fact the he should keep hos "cool". He experienced mixed emotions about the upcoming date. Was she as good looking as Fred said? Was she out of his league? What if he liked her and she didn't like him or vice-versa? Several times, over the next few days, he, almost called Fred to call off the date, but changed his mind. The next few days, at school, dragged by. His anxiety grew, with each passing day. He had blind dates, before, and they were disasters! The words to describe a girl, he hadn't seen, were "great personality." Those words told him to say no thanks. But Fred assured him that Ree was good looking. In fact, he used a cartoon from the newspaper, to help describe her. The cartoon was" Long Sam". The girl had very long legs that went all the way up to a pair of very short shorts. She, also, was very cute with long black hair tied in a long pony tail. If Ree looked anything like the cartoon girl, he would have a difficult time with rule # 1. Every night, he went to bed, he dreamed of the cartoon girl and ended up needing his "towel." He looked for Fred, at lunch, everyday of the week. Fred must have taken a different lunch, than him. He wanted more information. Finally, the Friday, before the date. Fred called him and told him to pick up him, first, then June and then they would go pick up Ree. The drive in opened at 7 PM, so he was supposed to pick up Fred at 6, and then pick up the girls, so they could get to the show and get a good parking space. The actual show started at dusk. So, he and Ree would have plenty of time to get to know each other. He was hoping that the date would go well and that he, would once again, have a "steady girl".

He awoke that Saturday morning, of the impending date. Anxiety gripped his mind and body like a vise. After his "morning routine", he tried to sit in the den and watch TV. He just couldn't sit still. He got off the couch, went and turned off the TV and went outside, into the bright sunshine. He decided that it would be a good idea to wash the "bug." He went back into the house and retrieved the keys, to the car. He got in and turned it on, put it in reverse and backed it up just enough, to park it near the back of the house, near an outside faucet. Eddie Cochran was on the radio singing about the "Summertime Blues."

He attached the water hose to the faucet. Then, he went into the basement and found an empty bucket. He put a large sponge, some car wash soap, turtle wax, rags, and two large "old" towels, in the bucket. He went back outside, to the car. The car was still running and in neutral gear. Through the window, he heard The Johnny Otis Show, singing, "Willie And The hand Jive." He opened the door and reached in and turned off the car. He made sure the sunroof was closed tight and that all the windows were rolled up tight. He then turned on the water and proceeded to wash and then wax the VW. It took most of the morning, to get the job done. He finished buffing off the last remnant of wax, just before noon. He stepped back to look at the job, he had just done. The beetle shined like it just came off the assembly line. He opened the driver's side door and got in behind the steering wheel and peered out, through the windshield, at the front hood. It shined so nicely, in the noon day sun. he stepped out of the car and went back into the basement and got paper towels and window cleaner, and proceeded to clean the windows. He thought, if he was going to be stuck looking at the movies, it might as well be through clean windows. He cleaned up the tools, wrapped up the hose, emptied the soapy water out of the bucket onto the driveway. Put the remaining car was bottle, can of wax, towels, etc. into the bucket and returned them, where he found them, in the basement. When everything had been returned to its proper place, he went into the house and found the vacuum cleaner and brought it outside and plugged it into the outside receptacle. He vacuum the entire interior floors and seats of the car. He wanted the car, to look perfect. It was one thirty, in the afternoon, by the time, he was finished.

As he brought the cleaner, back into the house, his mom exclaimed, "I kept your soup warm, on the stove. Your English muffins are in the toaster. He thanked her and went to the kitchen sink to wash up. Just as he finished eating, the hall phone rang. He got up and went to the phone and picked up the receiver; It was Fred. "What are you wearing tonight?" Fred asked.

"A tuxedo!" he exclaimed. "Very funny," said Fred. "June just told me that Ree likes guys in white dress shirts and jeans." "Jeans?" he asked, "What the hell are jeans?" "Dungarees" said

Fred. "Oh" he replied. "And no boots! Shoes." Fred added. "Damn!" he said, "I haven't worn loafers with my dungarees, before. It will seem and look strange." "Don't care" said Fred. "Apparently, Ree thinks guys, in those clothes are real sexy." Fred, again, reminded him that Ree was worth the sacrifice. He said that he hoped so. "And what is the princess wearing?" he asked. Fred responded, "No idea." He said to call June and tell her, to tell Ree, that short shorts and low cut pleasant blouses are what he thinks look sexy on a girl." He heard Fred utter a big sigh and then asked him, "You really don't want me to do that, do you?" He thought a moment and then said, "No, I guess not. As long as she isn't wearing a big bulky sweater and huge pants that hide that magnificent body, you say she has."

When he got off the phone, with Fred, he went up the stairs, to his room and began to pick put the clothes, for the big date. He found a newly ironed white shirt, with button down collar, hanging in the closet. He opened up his bottom drawer, of his dresser and found a recently pair of washed dungarees. He looked in the top drawer and found a pair of white cotton socks and a new pair of black socks. He sat on the bed and looked at both pairs. Though he really wanted to wear the white ones, he decided that the black pair would look better.

He dug his black loafers, out of the closet floor and gave them the "once over". He decided that they could use some polish. He found a can of "CatsPaw" black wax, on his closet shelf and opened it up. It still had the polish rag still on top of the wax. He went back to the bed and sat on it and began to polish the shoes. When he was satisfied that they looked shiny enough, he put them down on the floor. He checked his watch. It read 4:17 PM. He was supposed to pick up Fred at 6. He would have to leave the house around 5:15, get the bug gassed up and be able to get to Fred's on time. He heaved a big sigh. He leaned across the bed and turned on the radio, on his bed stand. Larry Williams was singing "Bony Maroni." That was followed by Jimmy Dorsey's Band playing, "So Rare." He, almost drifted off, for a short nap, but was brought back to reality by Ritchie Valens singing "Come On Lets Go." He got up off the bed and laid his "date" clothes on the bed. He went to the dresser and retrieved a pair of 'fresh' briefs and headed to the bathroom to bathe and get ready.

After his bath, he applied a "stick" of Old Spice deodorant to his under arms. He was so happy that he no longer had to spray the cold 'Right Guard" and then wait for the pain. He wrapped a dry towel around him and headed back to his room, to get into his "date" clothes. Once dressed, he turned his attention to his hair. He wished he still had the sideburns. His dad made him shave them off, that Sunday, after the play. He took his time with his hair. When he felt it was just right, he applied two dabs of Brylcreem, then, he combed it again. He took toilet paper and cleaned the Brylcreem residue off his comb. He checked himself out in the mirror. He looked good! He topped off the grooming with light splashes of "Old Spice cologne". He wasn't going to overdo it this time. He went back into his room and "raided" his "bank". He took fifty dollars. He knew he probably didn't need that much, but he didn't want to get caught "short". Marv Johnson was singing, on the radio, "You've Got What it Takes." He danced in front of the mirror and sang along. He turned off the radio, when the song ended. He checked his watch, it read 5:10 PM. He put the money, in his wallet and placed the wallet inside his left rear pocket of his dungarees. He made a mental note to stop calling them dungarees, and start calling them "jeans". He walked out of his room, down the hall, downstairs, through the hall, into the kitchen. His mom and dad were seated at the kitchen table, talking. He told them that he was leaving and would probably be home before midnight. They wished him a "good time". He walked out the back door and out to the driveway. He opened the driver's side door, got in and turned on the VW. He put the car into reverse and backed up. Enough, to turn around and head out to the street. Bill Haley and the Comets were on the radio, "Rip it up". He sang along as he headed down the road to his first stop, the gas station. He wished the car had a gas gauge. It did have an emergency switch under the dash. He would have to slink down in the seat and stretch his left foot up to the switch and push it to the right. He did that once and was so afraid the guy behind him would hit him. To push the switch, he had to let his foot off the gas. That would make the car slow down, quickly. So, he always made sure there was enough gas in the tank, so he would not have to do that ever again. When he pulled into the gas station, he was third, in line, he wasn't expecting that. By the time, he got gassed up and headed out to Fred's house, he was running late. Danny and the Juniors were on the radio singing, "Rock and Roll Is Here To Stay." He arrived in front of Fred's house at 6:05 PM. Fred was waiting for him, on the sidewalk, in front of his house. Fred, quickly, walked up to the passenger side door, yanked it open and jumped in. "You're late!" he exclaimed. They headed for June's house. They both sang along to Roy Orbison's "Only The Lonely" on the radio. After the song, Fred mentioned that if he played his cards right, he wouldn't be lonely anymore. He liked the sound of that. "I know" he said, Rule #1, play it cool." Yep," said Fred, "exactly right."

They arrived at June's house, still about five minutes behind "schedule". He sat, in the car, with the motor running and the gear in neutral, waiting for Fred to escort June to the car.

Even though, he knew June, he had never really looked at her. The last time he saw her. She was encased in heavy winter wear. As she and Fred, finally emerged from her house, he had a chance to really see her. She was quite petite, with shoulder length, dirty blonde hair. She had a cute face and a small, but curvy figure. She wore a navy blue, low cut V-neck sweater that showed just the hint of cleavage. From what he could surmise, her breasts were a little larger than medium. She, also, had on a pair of white, tight, short shorts. He wondered how she got into them.

She said "hi" to him, as she and Fred climbed into the back seat. He, almost, felt like saying to them, "where to?" He felt like a chauffeur. She was talking a "blue streak" and would keep reminding him to be "cool" and let Ree make the first move, if there is to be one. He said that he would be "cool" and obey her wishes. The ride, across town, seemed to take forever, for him. Marvin Rainwater was on the radio, singing, "Gonna Find Me A Bluebird." That was followed by Bobby Day and "Rockin Robin."

They pulled up in front of Ree's house at about 6:35PM. He turned off the motor and looked out the driver's side window. The house sat up high off the road. There were about ten steps that lead to a long walkway, then three more steps, to the front door. She lived in a nice side of town. He opened the door, of the car, sighed a heavy sigh and got out of the VW. He closed the door and slowly walked up the steps and walkway to her front door. He stood in front of the door and located the doorbell. He pushed the bell. He could hear the chimes ring, in the house. He waited and waited for a response. It seemed like eternity before the door opened. He stood face to face with a girl who couldn't have been more that fourteen years old. He, quickly, turned and looked towards the car. "Was this a sick joke?" he thought. He heaved another heavy sigh and turned back to the girl. "Hi!" she said, "I'm Madge. You're really cute, Wow!" he knew he was blushing and didn't know what to say. She continued, "Ree will be here soon.!" He muttered "thanks." Then he saw her approaching him and her little sister. She was tall, with auburn hair that came down both sides of her head, to just below her ears. She had dark brown eyes and ruby red lips. She was the most beautiful girl he had ever seen! That included all the other girls that he had ever dated and knew. Her snow white blouse did little to hide her ample breasts. Her red and black plaid Bermuda shorts hugged her long and very tanned legs. Her smile revealed two rows of white, straight teeth. He was paralyzed! Mesmerized! He just knew that the magnificent creature that slipped past her sister was out of his class. She smiled, at him and extended her "perfect" right hand and said, "Hi, I'm Ree." He introduced himself and then shook hands. Her sister wished them a good time, as he led her down her walk and steps to the car. She waited while he opened the passenger side door and held her arm as she slid into the passenger's seat. He closed the door and walked around the car, towards the back. Fred looked at him, through the back window of the car. He gave Fred the "OK" sign. He reached the driver's side door, opened it and got in the seat, behind the wheel. He started the car and sat back against his seat and put it in first gear. He, almost, missed second gear, because her strong, sexy, perfume wafted it's way up into his nostrils, to his brain and signaling his excitement, to his penis. He could barely concentrate on his driving. Ree positioned herself in her seat, so she was facing him, but able to talk with June and Fred. Buddy Holly was singing "Maybe Baby" on the radio. he glanced towards her and she flashed him a big smile. Her voice was like soft velvet, to his ears. "Be Cool" he kept saying to himself, over and over.

Fred must have decided that it was time, to tell a joke, "This elderly couple were talking about when one of them passes, would the remaining spouse remarry. She said she wasn't sure if she would. She asked him, if he would. He said that yes, he would remarry. The wife became quite indignant and said that she would hope he wouldn't let her sleep in their bed, he said no, of course not, She said she would want him to get rid of her clothes that she wouldn't want his new wife, wearing her clothes. He said he'd get rid of them. She became quite agitated and said to get rid of jewelry, that she wouldn't want his new wife wearing her jewelry. Then she said, get rid of my golf clubs, that she wouldn't want the new wife, using her clubs. He said not to worry about the jewelry and as for the clubs, she wouldn't use them anyway, cause she's left handed." They all laughed, hysterically. That joke was just what they all needed. Everyone seemed to be relaxed, after that. Ree, then turned her face, towards him and wanted to know all about him. His likes/dislikes about food, music, clothing styles, sports, TV shows, etc. He was going to tell her, when Nat King Cole came on the radio, with "Those Lazy Hazy Crazy Days Of Summer". Ree asked him, if she could turn up the volume. He nodded "okay" and she reached over the emergency brake and stretched her hand to the radio and turned up the volume. They all began to sing along. When the song ended, he turned the volume back down and answered all her questions. He, then, asked her the same ones. They found that they had a lot in common. They smiled at each other, a lot, on the way to the drive in.

Dusk had not yet replaced darkness, when they pulled up to the ticket booth. He paid the two dollars and they drove in. He was instructed to find a parking spot near the back of the concession stand. He found the spot that everyone agreed on. It was near the stand, but far enough away, so the lights and the noise wouldn't bother them. As soon as he pulled in to the spot,he put the car in first gear, set the emergency brake, and turned off the motor. He lowered the window, and reached out and took the speaker, off the stand and attached it to the top of his window and rolled the window up. He turned up the volume on the speaker and settled back, in his seat. June and Ree told them that they needed to use the ladies room. He and Fred said they would get out, too and walk with them to the concession stand and get some food and drinks, while the girls were in the restroom. He, quickly, opened his door and squeezed between the car and the speaker post, ducking under the wire and made it around to her door and opened it and gave her his hand and helped her out of the car. She smiled and said "Thank you, kind sir," he, then, helped June out, too. Fred got out on his own. Ree, then, leaned in on him and gave him a sweet "peck" on his right cheek. He smiled.

Daylight was quickly turning to dusk. As the guys were waiting in line to get the popcorn and cokes, Fred asked him, what he thought of Ree? "I think she is way out of my class!" He said. Fred just smiled and reminded him to keep his "cool." Fred, also, told him that he believed Ree liked him, by the way she was acting, even with the kiss. "Maybe" he said. With food and drinks, in hand, they waited, in front of the concession stand, for the girls. As June and Ree approached them, he felt his lips turn up at the ends, into a great smile. He couldn't believe that the "goddess" walking towards him, could conceivably like him. He was beginning to have a stronger dislike for the rules. Fred bumped his right arm, slightly, and said, "you're staring at her." He replied that he just couldn't help it. The four of them walked back to the car. Ree and June took the popcorn from him, so he could open the doors and let everyone back into the car. Once they were all settled in,he walked around the back of the car and squeezed back in between the post and the door. Ree chuckled as he got into his seat. "I thought you might need some oil put on you, so you could get back in." "almost" he chuckled.

As they consumed their popcorn and drinks, he decided to relate the story of his first drive in experience about Carl and the pink Olds convertible. They were laughing so hard, Ree almost choked on a piece of popcorn, June sneezed coke out of her nose and Fred nearly spilled his food and coke. When Ree had composed herself, she asked if it was him that did it and not Carl. He told her that he thought about doing it, but that Carl beat him to it.

They had just finished their popcorn and cokes, when he noticed that night was upon them. Even though he was feeling very comfortable with Ree, he still kept his distance. When the newsreel came on, he was "aching" to make a move. He looked at her She was leaning against her door, watching the newsreel. She turned her head towards him and smiled. He smiled back. "Be cool" kept going around and around, in his head. He could tell that things were not so "cool" in the backseat, by the sounds that were emanating from that part of the car. He glanced into the back seat, through the rearview mirror, just as their heads disappeared from view.

The front seat of a Volkswagon Beetle is not conducive to romance. The backseat was a different place for romance. The motions of the backseat" romance" were being felt throughout the entire car, especially the front seat. He was becoming more and more "hot and bothered." The atmosphere made it increasingly more difficult for him to maintain his "cool." He couldn't help but wonder, if Ree was feeling the effects of what was taking place, in the back seat. He glared at the movie screen, knowing Fred and June could care less about the movie. He glanced over at Ree and saw that she was constantly shifting her hips, in the seat. She returned his glance. He could barely make out the questioning look, in her beautiful brown eyes.

"How do I adjust this seat back, for more room? My legs are starting cramp up." He told her about the lever, on the side of the seat, down a little from the cushion. She put her hand down and then told him "I can't seem to get it to move." Being a gentleman and being "cool", he moved closer to her. He moved over the gear shift and emergency brake. "Excuse me." He said, as he lay across her lap and reached his hand down, for the lever. It moved back, so fast that it threw him down and across her. He put his right arm up, over, and behind her shoulders. Using his hand on the back of her seat, he brought himself up and off her. His face came very, very close to hers. The space between their lips was very small. "To hell with being cool" he thought. She did lean back and away from him, but leaned closer, towards him. Their lips moved closer. Slowly inching to each other. Her arms encircled his shoulder and back, which brought his lips to hers. At first, their lips met in a sweet kiss. Then, they began to move their lips over each others'. They explored each others lips, as their kissing intensified. She parted her lips, just enough, for her tongue to move over his lips. He parted his lips and move his tongue to meet hers. Her tongue moved past his and entered his mouth; he reciprocated. He moved his left arm, from her lap and legs up to the right side of her waist, drawing her even closer to him. She came willingly. To this day, he has no idea how he maneuvered his whole body over the emergency brake and gear shift. He squeezed in next to her on her seat. Their bodies pressed together. Their passion began to intensify. Hands and arms held tight. Legs intertwined with each other. The, finally, separated their lips, just long enough to gasp some fresh air. Her arms released their hold on his shoulders and back. She brought her hands to his front and unbuttoned the buttons on his shirt, one by one, starting with the top button. She smiled, at him, when she discovered he wasn't wearing a T-shirt, underneath his dress shirt. He leaned back, just a little to give her access to his bare chest. She brought her fingers under the shirt and began to caress his chest. She twined her fingers through his small chest hairs, gently. He had never felt anything, like what she was doing to him. Another milestone!

Their kissing intensified. He began to unbutton the buttons, on her blouse. She allowed him to only unbutton the four top buttons. It was enough for him to place his hands on the tops of her heaving breasts. Their lips parted, again, as she moved her head to his chest and began to kiss his bare chest and nipples. He gasped with pleasure, as he allowed her lips to travel from his chest to his navel. She stuck the tip of her tongue into his navel. He couldn't believe the sensations he was experiencing. She spent a lot of time on his navel and chest. Then, she brought her head up and away from his body, to his face. Their lips crushed together in a lustful frenzy! His hands gently massaged her soft, but firm breasts, as they continued kissing. When, they, again, parted, for air. He brought his lips, to the places, where his hands had been. He began to kiss, lightly, the tops of her breasts; he ran his tongue gently over them and then into the valley between them. Stopping only at her bra. She moaned and ground her pelvis against his. Animal lust engulfed them. Her hands began to travel over the outside of his jean covered thighs, and then over the tops and to the insides. His hands moved under her shirt. Slid around and caressed her bare back. He really wanted to unsnap her bra strap and feast and caress her naked breasts and nipples, with his hands, tongue and lips.

Her hands moved up from his thighs, to the zipper of his jeans. She pulled the zipper down, opened access to his briefs covered penis, which felt "rock hard". They slipped further down into the seat. She was like a "Wildcat" in heat! She began to rub and stroke him. Their lips crushed against each other. Then, their lips parted and their tongues met and "danced" inside each other's mouths. He brought his hands from her back and put them on her bare legs, just above her knees. He copied what she had done to his thighs. He moved them up to within inches of the "treasure" between her thighs. She brought her hand, from his pants and placed it over his hand, stopping his from proceeding further. Their lips, once again, parted. They brought their hands to each others hips. Hers on his and vice-versa. The passion returned to their kisses. The began to grind their bodies against each other. He knew she could feel his hardness. They could not get enough of each other. They were like two "sex starved animals, in heat! Her tongue swirled around, in his mouth, as her hand left his hip and again went between them and found the opening, in his jeans. At the same time, his right hand left her hip and moved up to the front of her blouse, found the opening, just above her bra. His fingers strained to get under the stiff material of the cup, to reach the goal of a nipple. He, finally gave up the quest, and caressed the swells of the tops, that were still available to him.

When their lips, again, parted, for lack of air, she thrust her pelvis so hard against him, he thought she "flattened' his penis. She eased off the next thrusts and she brought her arms up around his sides, with her hands on his back, he reciprocated and with their cheeks touching they hugged each other, tightly. As they eased off each other, she brought her hands to each side of his head, grabbed his ears and pushed his face back to her breasts. He put his lips to first one and then the other, eliciting moans from her lips. She, then, brought his face back up to hers and began "raining" kisses all over his face. He had never experienced a girl like Ree before. Their clothing was the only obstacle that prevented them from having actual intercourse.

They continued their passionate "make out" through the rest of the first feature. Their arms and legs were tightly intertwined. Their lips fused together. Hands travelled over their bodies. Then, bright lights blinded them! The whole lot was bathed in spotlights. Intermission! They, slowly disengaged themselves from each other. She sat up and buttoned her blouse back up. He zippered up his pants and buttoned his shirt. Ree brushed her hair back and gave a loud "WHEW!" That was the only word uttered from each of them, they whole time, they were locked in each others arms. She reached over for her pocketbook, on the floor. He managed to find his way back to his seat, without causing injury to himself. She took a hankerchief from her pocketbook and spit on it. "Come over here!" She ordered. He did as he was told and she began to wipe her red lipstick from his face. He was speechless! Meanwhile, the sound of clothes rustling in the back, meant that Fred and June were emerging from their passion, too.

The girls decided that they needed to go to the ladies room to freshen up. They guys thought that was a good idea and they opted for the mens room. He opened his door and, once again, slid out between the speaker post and the door. He was a little wobbly, but managed to get around to her side of the car. He opened the door and helped the girls out. While Fred was getting out, he went around to his door and locked it and then came back and locked the passenger door. The girls had already started to walk to the restrooms. He grabbed Fred by the shirt, "I should slug you in your mouth!" he said. Fred backed away from him. "Be cool, be cool, be cool! You said, "I wasted the cartoon, the newsreel and a lot of the first feature!" he was, visibly upset with Fred. Fred just laughed and said, "well, from the sounds of things, you sure made up for it." His tone softened, "yeah, she is wonderful!" Fred asked him, "better than Charlene?" "Who?" he answered. They both laughed, as they walked to the men's room.

As they stood in line to use the "facilities", Fred told him that Ree told June, that if he kissed as good as he looked, she could easily fall for him. He smiled, at that news, and told Fred that he was not going to let Ree go. He wanted her, all for himself. He exclaimed to fred that he couldn't believe that a "Goddess" like Ree, could like him. They finished their business and left the men's room and headed back to the car. Ree and June were waiting for them, by the car. The girls were holding a large pizza and four cokes. He, quickly, went to them and unlockded the passenger door and took the pizza from Ree. Fred took the cokes. June got into the back seat, followed by Fred, who handed the cokes to June, before he climbed in. Ree got in and he handed the pizza back to her and closed the door. He walked back around the car and unlocked his door and squeezed back in. He told her that he didn't know they were buying the pizza and drinks. He would have, gladly, given her the money to get them. She replied that it wasn't fair that he should pay for everything. He said, "okay." His heart overruled his brain. She opened up the box and took a slice. "Open your mouth." She ordered, sweetly. He obeyed and she shoved the slice into his mouth; cheese oozed down from his mouth, over his chin. Everyone laughed. He silently, prayed that the night would never end.

The lights, throughout the lot, began to flicker a few times and then went out. The big screen came "alive" and lit up the cars that were closest to it. They were, again, in total darkness. Then the second movie began. They finished their slices of pizza and washed them down with their cokes. Fred asked him, "what do we do with the trash?" He responded, "just toss it over the back seat, I'll take care of it, in the morning."

As his eyes got used to the darkness, he saw Ree slide down in her seat. Her back was against the door, she opened her legs, just enough to give him room, to join her. He, safely, maneuvered himself over the gear shift and emergency brake. He sat, on the seat, and Ree lifted her legs and placed them over his lap. She, again, leaned towards him and told him to open his mouth. He did and she "popped" a Canadian Mint into it. As he sucked on the mint, She stretched out her arms and drew him to her. They cuddled very close to each other, as they chewed on their mints.

He knew he was falling fast, for this girl. This beautiful woman, in his arms, was everything he wanted in a woman. She was cute, pretty, with a wonderful sense of humor; and extremely passionate! He, also, liked the fact that they were the same age. He silently, prayed to God, that she felt the same about him.

They continued to "make out" with the same intensity as before. Their passion, for each other never subsided. The next time, the car and them was "bathed "in brightness, the movie was over. He was in no hurry to leave, nor was she. Fred and June were still "testing" the springs and shocks of that little car. He and Ree shared one more long "French" kiss. She, slowly, pulled away and whispered, "time to go." "I know." He said, sadly. He climbed back over the emergency brake and gear shift. He said, "a VW is not the car for romance." She laughed and then leaned towards him and said in a sultry voice, "we did all right." He nodded, in agreement. Once, back behind the steering wheel, he rolled down his window and took the speaker off and reached out and placed it back on the stand. He put the car, in neutral, and started the motor. The back seat "rocking" ceased. He turned on the headlights, put the car in first gear and released the emergency brake and gave the beetle enough gas to move forward. They began their way out of the drive in lot. Sam Cooke was on the radio, singing "Cupid." Ree moved over towards him, as close as she could get without injuring herself on the brake and gear shift. She placed her left hand on his upper, inner, right thigh; put her head against his right shoulder. He was in heaven! He couldn't believe that she really liked him! Maybe she, too, had fallen for him.

Fred and June's heads, finally, popped up from the back seat. He could tell, from their reflection, in the rearview mirror, that they were getting dressed. Ree lived closer to the drive in, so she was 'dropped" off first. He pulled up to the front of her house. He turned off the car and the headlights and got out of the car and went around, to her side, and opened the door and helped her out. As the stepped out of the car, she fell into his arms. They stood beside the car and shared another hot, passionate kiss. When, at last, their lips parted, he asked if he could call her the next night. She reached into her purse and brought out a small piece of paper with her phone number on it. He took it from her and placed it in the breast pocket of his shirt. She said, with a grin, "you better call or I'll hunt you down." He laughed. She put both her hands on the sides of his head and said, "I can't wait to see you again." "Good!" He replied and told her the same. They shared yet another good night kiss. Then, he, slowly, walked with her up the steps, hand in hand, up the walk, to her front steps. Once, on the small landing, they embraced, yet again. He wanted to keep on holding her and kissing her. When they parted their lips, again, for air. She said, "I really need to go in." "I know!" he replied. She turned and opened her front door and went in. When the door, closed, he turned and walked, briskly, back to the car.

When he got back in the VW, he didn't care that Fred and June were still in the back seat. He was happy and in love! Before, he started the car, he turned around and looked at Fred and June. He thanked June for introducing him to Ree. Then, he said, "You can stick your damn rules up your asses!" They all laughed. June told him that Ree liked him from the moment, she saw him. She didn't think he liked her, because he took so long to kiss her. "DAMN!"

he said, "that won't happen again!" June asked him if he was going to continue to "see" Ree. "Definetly!" he said. "Good," she replied, "because she is really crazy about you." Those were the sweetest words he had heard in a very long time. He turned back around and started the car, and left them to continue to "make out". As he pulled away from the curb, he turned up the radio and whistled along to Billy Vaughn's "A Swingin Safari" on the radio.

The next morning was Sunday and he slept in until after 10:30. He went into the bathroom and got cleaned up. Went to the kitchen and ate his breakfast. He, then, went outside, to the driveway and to the VW. He unlocked the car and opened the door. The stench of old pizza nearly knocked him down. he got into the car and opened the windows, and the sunroof, to allow the sun and fresh air, "air" out the car. He, then, disposed of the trash, from the back of the car, into the trash barrel, under the back porch.

His folks arrived back home, from church around 11:30. His mom told him that she had planned on taking her car to church, but the smell, of garbage, was too much for her. He told her that he had just taken care of it. She thanked him and went into the house, to change, and get Sunday dinner, ready. He went back in the house and up to his room. He lay down on the bed and dreamed of the previous night. He was so in love! He wanted to get out of the house and rush over to her house and hold her in his arms, forever! He tried to relax, but couldn't. He got up off his bed and went downstairs. He tried to watch TV, but couldn't sit still. He kept looking at the piece of paper, with her phone number on it. He was to call her, but knew he would have to wait until after supper. His folks always told him that Sundays were for families. He went back to his room and sat at his desk and opened his history book. He could not concentrate. He turned on his radio. The Lettermen were singing, "When I fall In Love." It seemed that every song he heard was appropriate, for what was happening in his life. He turned off the radio and went back downstairs. He told his folks that, after supper he would be using the phone. The afternoon dragged. He did manage to go back to his room and do his homework, though it was a strain, trying to concentrate on it. He felt like he was being torchered. At last, he checked his watch and noticed it was nearing 6PM. He smelled the roast beef waft its way to his room and his nose. He got up out of his chair, turned off the desk lamp, and went downstairs to eat his supper. He practically inhaled his food. He got up from the dining room table and took his dishes to the dishwasher, in the kitchen. He stuck his head back into the dining room and, again, informed them that he would be on the phone. He raced up the stairs, to the landing phone, unwrapped the piece of paper, and dialed the number. The phone rang six times, before he heard someone pick it up. A man's voice answered. "Hello? Is Ree there?" "Who?" the man asked. "Ree." He repeated. He thought, "oh no, I've dialed a wrong number." "Do you mean Andrea?" The man asked. "Guess so." He replied. "Just a minute," the man said. In the background, he heard the man say that someone wants to speak to a Ray. He heard a second voice say. "Dad, that's my nickname!" "Thank God!" he thought, to himself. She came to the phone and, quickly, said "Hi", and then asked if he could call her back in about 15 minutes, that they were just finishing up supper. "okay" he said and hung up. He went back, down the hall, to his room. He turned on his radio and listened to the Arnie Ginsberg show" on WMEX. He thought of Ree, as he listened to the Platters sing "Twilight Time". He danced around the room to Dave "Baby "Cortez' s "The Happy Organ." He laughed at Larry Verne's "Please Mr. Custer." He enjoyed listening to Arnie Ginsberg's "Night Train Show" with all the bells and whistles, etc. He thought it was strange that the show was on a Sunday night. It was, usually, on weeknights. He was glad that it was on, though, it helped him pass the time. He listened, intently, to Martin Dennings, "Quiet Village." When the song was over and the "Adventure Car Hop" commercial came on, he checked his watch. Ray Steven's "Ahab The Arab" was playing. He liked the way the song started and soon lost interest as "it" played out. His watch read that eighteen minutes had passed. He left his room and walked down the hall to the landing phone and picked it up and, again, dialed Ree's number. The phone was picked up, on the second ring. "Hello?" She asked. "Hi!" he said. "I've got it! It's for me!" Then she softly said, "hi". Before he could say anything else, she asked, "Do you have any idea, how many people have the same last name as you?" he laughed and then asked if she had a piece of paper and a pencil. She asked him to wait a minute and then she came back and said, "got it." He gave her his phone number. She asked him, if he was serious about seeing her, again. "Of course!" he answered. He, almost, blurted out that he was" head over heels" in love with her. She wanted to know when they could see each other. He told her, that his mother let him take her car to school every Wednesday and Friday. He, always had a last period study, and being a senior, was allowed to leave the building and go home. "Any chance you could come by my school and pick me up, say, this Friday?" she asked. His heart skipped, at the thought of seeing her so soon. "Sure!" he said, "just need the directions." He took a pencil, by the phone, and wrote down the directions on the piece of paper, she had given him, with her phone number on it. She sounded very happy. They made plans to talk with each other, on the phone, every night, during the week, after supper. She ended their conversation, by telling him that she had a wonderful time, with him, at the drive in. He told her that he did, too and couldn't wait to see her on Friday. "See you, then." She said and hung up the phone.

Their phone conversations were about what was going on at their respective schools. They never really discussed how they felt about each other. She did say that she wanted him to meet her best friend, Jane. He said that he thought June was her best friend. She replied that June was "just a friend." He said that he would be glad to meet Jane. She said that maybe they could double date with her and her boyfriend, John. He said "okay", even though, he, really wanted to be alone. On Wednesday, on the way to school, he told his passengers that they would have to find another way home, from school, on Friday. He told them he was leaving school, early, so he could go and meet his new girlfriend. They weren't too happy, but understood and thanked him for telling them. Fred "picked up" on the word, "girlfriend" right away. "So, you two are a couple?" he asked. "Not yet, Fred," he said. "Why not?" asked Fred, "June says all Ree does is talk about you all the time and how crazy in love with you she is." His heart nearly burst when he heard those words. "Well, she hasn't told me." He said. Fred said, "maybe she wants to hear it from you, first." "Maybe." He said. If Fred were right, then maybe he would tell her, how much in love with her, he was.

Friday, finally arrived. He drove to school early and found the closest parking spot to the building that he would be in, when it would be time, to leave. Ironically, it was next to Carl's 1940 Ford sedan. He gave a half-hearted wave to Carl. It wasn't returned. Carl was too busy "making out" with Abby. He really didn't miss Abby. The passion that he and Ree shared, saw to erasing any memory of her. He backed the "bug' into his parking space, so he could get out, as fast as possible. He turned off the motor, got out of the car, with his books, and waited till his passengers exited the vehicle. Then, he locked the car and headed down the road, to the building that 'housed" his home room.

The day seemed to really drag on and on. He kept looking at his watch. It didn't help. He had a lot of trouble concentrating on what his teachers were saying. Finally, lunch interrupted the day. He sat down at a lunch table with Fred. Fred asked him, if he and Ree would like to double date, that night. He told Fred that it was awful short notice, but he would mention it to Ree. Fred said that they could go and play miniature golf, get something to eat, afterwards and then go parking. He liked the idea of going parking, but still told Fred that he would run it by Ree and give him a call later.

The last two periods seem to take forever to end. Finally, came the bell signaling that last period. His study period. He leaped out of his seat and grabbed his books and, practically, ran out of the room, out of the building, down the road, to the VW. He, quickly, unlocked the driver's side door, opened the door, threw his books onto the back seat and got in behind the steering wheel. He put the key into the ignition and started the car. He headed out of the parking space, up the road and on his way to Ree's school. The Crests were on the radio, singing "Step By Step", he sang along. He arrived at her school, early and found a place to park, near other cars, in front of the school. He was happy that her school had only one building. Not like his school, that had three. The radio was playing Dion's "A Teenager In Love, "followed by Sil Austin's "Slow Walk."

Over the instrumental, he heard the bell, dismissing the students. Kids started streaming out the front doors like rats leaving a sinking ship. His eyes were focused on the big green doors. They were trained on the different faces, amongst the crowd. He was afraid that he would miss her and that she wouldn't see him. Then he saw her! She must have seen him, too. She walked towards him with a big grin on her pretty face. She held her books against her chest. They did little to hide the tight dark blue V-neck sweater. He was amazed she could walk as fast as she was, with the tight gray skirt, that hugged her hips, like it was painted on. She released one of her hands from the books and waved, at him. She seemed overjoyed to see him. He got out of the car and walked around the front, to the passenger door. She came up to the car, ust as he opened the door. She gave him a kiss on the cheek, as she hiked the skirt above her knees and slid onto the passenger seat. He made sure she was in the car, as he closed the door and walked back around the front and to the driver's side. He opened his door and got inside and closed the door. She asked him what should she do with her books. He told her to toss them onto the back seat, as he had done with his. "That'll work," She said. They leaned towards each other, across the emergency brake and gear shift and shared a "Hello." Kiss. Afterwards, he started the car, put it in first gear and pulled out of the parking space and down the street. "Where to?" he asked. "I'll show you." She said, as she put her left hand on his upper thigh and laid her head against his right shoulder.

She directed him down the old highway. As the road turned towards the river, she cautioned him to slow down. She showed him what appeared to be a dirt road, on the left. He turned down the road and slowly maneuvered the VW to a clearing. He brought the car to a stop, just before the bank of the river. She moved away from him and sat back in her seat and reached down with her right hand to the lever on the bottom of her seat and moved it back as far as it would go. She hiked her skirt higher up her legs to her thighs. She, then found another lever that moved the back of the seat back to almost a level angle. He moved toward her, over the emergency brake and gear shift. "Better set the brake, so we don't end up in the river." She said. She moved closer to her door, to make room for him on her seat. They opened their arms around each other, as their lips met. Their first kisses were sweet, short and very loving. He really wanted to move his hand up under the gray skirt, as they continued to kiss. Their lust soon began to intensify, their lips parted just enough for their tongues to intermingle. Her left hand left his back and moved down, between them, to his crotch. She began to trace his erection, through his pants, causing it to strain against the cotton fabric. He, finally, got up the nerve to move his left hand from her back and to the thigh of her left leg. He, softly massaged the soft, but firm flesh. She brought her right hand from his back and placed it on the back of his head and pressed her lips, harder, against his. He moved his hand farther up her thigh, to the hem of her skirt. She moved her legs, a little farther apart. Her hand unzipped his zipper and found its way inside his pants. Her hand found his penis, covered with the soft cotton fabric. "It" was straining to be let "free." He moved his hand under the hem of her skirt, to her inner thigh, still softly massaging the flesh. They were still locked, in a passionate embrace, wit their lips. He continued to move his hand up her inner thigh, until he came upon the thin fabric of her panties. Her fingers had found the opening of his briefs and were stroking his hard flesh. He moved his fingers over the fabric, sensing dampness and began to caress her "lips". He could feel the "cleft" between the "lips" and began to slowly massage the "area". She ripped her lips from his and buried her face against his chest, moaning, "OH GOD, YES, OOH, YES!!" Her strokes emitted moans from his mouth, too. He noticed, the more he massaged her, the wetter she got. His erection responded to her strokes, as well. She brought her face up from his chest and their lips met in a frenzied kiss. Their hips began to thrust and gyrate to their touch. Their tongues explored each other. He had never caressed a female vagina before. It was a fantastic milestone. The shock absorbers on the VW were, once again, being tested. Their passion was soon interrupted by the approach of another car. It was a police car. Through the fogged up windows, he could just make out the light bar, on top of the car. They, quickly, disengaged their hands from each other. He, quickly, zipped up his pants, as she brought the hem of her skirt to her knees. The cop approached his side of the car. He rolled down the window. He asked them both for their I.D.'s and driver's licenses. The cop noticed that they were both about to turn 18. He asked them what they were doing. He responded and said that they were just talking and enjoying the quietness of the area. They knew he did not believe them. The fogged up windows, probably gave that away. He handed them back their licenses and school I.D.'s and told them that they need to get out of the place. That he would be back in twenty minutes and if they were still there, they would be in a lot of trouble. The cop, then left; got back in the patrol car and turned around and left. "Damn cops!" They said in unison and laughed. She said, "We've got twenty minutes." He leaned against her and they began to kiss, again. The passion had subsided, but their kissing was still intense. They "made out" for another ten minutes and then decided to leave. As he backed the car away from the river bank, he mentioned, to her, what Fred had asked. "Okay!" She said, "Really?" he asked. "We'll get to spend some more time together." She said. ":Absolutely!" he said. He put the "bug" in first gear and headed up the dirt road, shifting, quickly, through the gears, as they headed to her house. When he pulled up in front and stopped the car, she wrapped her arms around his neck and pressed her lips against his. The kiss was short. She opened her door, reached into the back seat and retrieved her books and stepped out of the car. He was halfway out of his door, "That's okay baby, you don't have to open my door, all the time." She said, "see you in a couple of hours. He watched her walk up the steps and walkway. Her hips were swaying, under the tight skirt, sending signals to his penis. The song "Sways With A Wiggle, With A Wiggle, When She Walks." Came to his mind. He closed his door as he continued to watch her walk. When she entered her house, he drove home.

As soon as he got in the door, he told his mom that he would be going out, again, soon. She said she was glad that she did the week's shopping, when she did. He went to the phone and called Fred. Fred was glad that the date was on. Fred told him that he would call June and get back to him about times. He hung up the phone and walked into the kitchen and went to the cabinet that held the cookie jar. He found the jar and opened it and took out three chocolate chip cookies. He then opened another cabinet and took out a small glass. He started to go to the "fridge", when his mom told him to please close the cabinet doors. He went back to the cabinets and with his right shoulder, push the doors shut. He, then, put the small glass on the counter and went to the fridge and got out the glass bottle of milk. He went back to the counter and put the bottle on the counter, opened the cardboard top and poured some milk into the small glass. He put the cookies on the counter, next to the glass. He picked up the bottle and put the cap back on it and returned the bottle, to the fridge. He, then, sat down, at the table with his cookies and milk and proceeded to satisfy his hunger and thirst. As he finished, the phone rang. He got up and went to the hall and picked up the receiver and said "hello?" It was Fred. "Can you pick us up in an hour?" Fred asked. "Guess so!" He said. "I'll call Ree and get back to you." "ok" said Fred. He hung up the phone and called Ree. She had been expecting his call and picked it up on the first ring. "Hi" he said. "Can you be ready in an hour and fifteen minutes?" he asked. "For you, baby, I'll do it." He laughed, and almost said that he loved her. "See you then," he said. "I'm counting the minutes." She said and blew him a kiss, over the phone. He hung up the phone and then called Fred back. Fred must have been waiting by the phone as he never heard it ring, when Fred picked up. "All set." He said. "Great!" said Fred, see you in a while."

He hung up the phone and ran up the stairs, two at a time, and down the hall, to his room. He took off his school clothes and went down the hall and ran the bath. He figured he had just enough time to take a quick bath, get changed into "regular" clothes, brush his teeth and splash on some cologne, comb his hair and head out of the house. After he bathed and took care of the rest, he put on a pair of fresh briefs, jeans, white socks, Keds and a purple polo shirt. It was a warm April day, so he knew he would be comfortable, but he would grab his pink and black "Spring" jacket, just in case. He checked his hair, one more time and decided it looked okay and headed down the hall, to the stairs; down the stairs and out the front door. He walked down the driveway and unlocked the beetle and got in and started it up. He knew he would have to stop and fill her up with gas, before heading to Fred's. He backed up the beetle, turned her around to face the street, put it in first gear and headed out of the driveway. He was in third gear by the time he was halfway down the road and fourth gear as he "hit' the main road.

It was a good idea, to stop and get gas. The tank was close to the "reserve gallon." After filling her up, he headed to Fred's house. Little Jimmy Dickens was on the radio singing, ":May The Bird Of Paradise Fly Up Your Nose." He sang along. That song was followed by Connie Francis singing "Vacation". He sang along to that one, too. As he pulled up to Fred's house, Ray Charles was singing "What'd I Say?". He liked the part two the best. It sounded like a couple making love.

He stopped by the curb and was ready to get out of the car and go get Fred, when he noticed that Fred and June were walking down the steps of his porch and coming towards him. He kept the car running. When they got to the door, he had to reach across the passenger seat and open it, for them. Fred and June couldn't get in. The passenger seat was still tilted all the way back and the seat was still in the "far" back position. Fred leaned down and moved the levers, bringing the seat back to it's usual position. "Hmmmm" said June, as she got into the back seat. "seems as if you had someone with you today and you had some fun." He felt the blush fill his face. "Sorry", he replied. "Don't be." She said, "we won't say anything." He put the car in gear and headed for Ree's house. Little Willie John was, on the radio, singing his version of "Fever." As he pulled up to Ree's house, the Coasters were singing "Yakety Yak." He stopped the car, put it in neutral, set the brake and got out of the car. He closed the door and walked around the front, to go and get her. He looked up the walk and saw her coming down the walk, towards him. Her auburn hair was in sharp contrast to her dark green polo shirt. That was not what caught his attention. It was her white shorts. They weren't exactly short shorts, but shorter than Bermuda shorts. He meant to ask her how she kept her legs so tan. She was carrying a black jacket, on her right arm. He was paralyzed, just watching her come to him. He still could not believe that this gorgeous woman liked him. She came up to him and gave him a short sweet kiss on his lips. "Long time, no see" she joked. He could hardly speak, her perfume hung around his head like a shroud. He followed her to the car and opened her door for her. His eyes were "glued" to her legs and shorts, as she slid in. "Were you in this car earlier today?" June asked. Fred tried to stop June from asking, because he knew she was. "Uh huh." Ree said, "Why do you ask?" "Oh! No reason! "June said. "I forgot to put the seat back." He said. "Oh!" said Ree. I remember now, how it felt riding home, in that seat, I wasn't thinking about it, too much, my mind was elsewhere." "I'll bet." Said June. Everyone laughed. He put the car in first gear and headed out to the miniature golf course. Ree noticed how he liked to "speed shift" through the gears to the fourth gear. "Do you race cars?" She asked him. "used to." He said. "I'll tell you all about it sometime." "Okay." She said. Jimmy Jones was singing "Handy Man" on the radio. She moved closer to him and put her left hand on his right thigh, his inner right thigh. He loved having her hand there. Johnny Cash began to sing, on the radio, "I Walk The Line."

He pulled into the gravel surfaced parking lot of the miniature golf course. It appeared a lot of people had the same idea. Fred mentioned that it was "opening day." "That explains the people." He said. He put the gear in reverse and pulled the emergency brake and turned the motor off. Ree had opened the door and was out of the car, before he could get over to the passenger side. Fred got out and helped June get out. June was wearing tight blue shorts and a light blue shirt. Even though, she looked sexy, he thought, to himself, she didn't hold a candle to Ree. He locked the car and joined them, In the parking lot. The four of them walked over to the booth. Ree grabbed his hand, as they walked. He moved closer to her and whispered low, "How am I supposed to concentrate on the game? Looking at you and the clothes your 're wearing. You, the clothes, and your sexy perfume, are driving me crazy." "Good." She said, "then maybe I'll beat you." She grinned. He knew he lost, just by being next to her. He paid their admission and got their putters. Fred and June went before them. Fred had a red ball, June, a yellow ball, Ree, a green ball, and he had his usual blue ball. Ree asked him, if he always played with blue balls? Before he could answer, they burst into laughter. Ree turned to Fred and June and said, with a grin, "you're nasty!" They laughed some more, as they waited their turn on the first tee. When they were, finally, able to play, June bent down and placed her ball on the tee. He couldn't believe how tight her shorts were, until she bent over. He swore that he saw the crack of her "rear". Still his reaction was nothing, compared to when Ree bent over to place her ball, on the tee. He wanted to walk up behind her and grab her hips with both hands and press his groin up against her. If the place hadn't had a lot of families playing, he just might have. On the third hole, he was just about to putt, when Ree walked up behind him and pinched his right cheek, and not the cheek, on his face. His ball went flying through the air, hit a fan blade on the windmill and careened off the rocks, nearby and landed in a small pond. Fred, June and Ree all burst into uncontrollable laughter. He was embarrassed, to say the least, as the retrieved his ball, from the little pond. When it was her turn to putt, on the fourth hole, he walked up behind her and put his hand, between her cheeks. She stood straight up, turned and said with a straight face, "I'll give you 24 hours to stop." His jaw must have dropped at least a foot. Again, all three of them broke out in laughter. They weren't sure what each's score was, when they finished. It took, over an hour, to play the 18 holes. They were hungry, as they returned their putters to the shed. "Should we go up the road, to Adventure Car Hop", he asked. They agreed. She, again, took his hand, as they walked back to the car. "Did I embarrass you baby?" She asked. "Not really" he said. "But I've played better games that tonight's." "Oh, poor baby!" she mused. He just smiled and squeezed her hand. He didn't care, because he had a wonderful time with her. They joked and would steal short kisses and hold hands, as they played the course. He was just so in love!

They got to the car. He unlocked the passenger door, first as Fred helped June into the car and then he joined her in the back seat. He assisted Ree into her seat. Again, he couldn't help stare at her lovely tanned legs. The game left him with a raging erection. He walked around the car and unlocked his door and got in. He put the car in neutral, put the key in the ignition and started it up. He put the car in reverse, backed up and then put it in first gear and headed out of the lot, spewing loose gravel, behind him. She marveled at how fast he was able to through the gears. They found a parking spot in the front row, at the car hop. Ree asked him why he didn't want to park farther back. Fred answered her, before he could. "He has his reasons, he wants to watch the parade of hot rods," "Oh" Ree answered. She still wasn't exactly sure why. They weren't there very long, when the girl, In the short skirted uniform roller skated over to his side of the car. He rolled the window down, as the "waitress" took their orders. He turned off the motor and put the car in neutral and set the emergency brake. WMEX was blaring through the loudspeakers over the cars. Johnny Horton was singing, "The Battle Of New Orleans." Then, came the first car, a 1933 Ford Coupe, painted canary yellow, followed by a 1949 Mercury sedan. He just sighed, as the cars began to parade by. Fred leaned forward, close to his ear and said, "miss it, don't you!" "Yeah" he sighed. Ree had turned her head to look out her window. He wasn't sure if she heard Fred or not. But she squeezed his thigh, when Fred had said it. Pretty soon, the burgers, fries, and cokes arrived. As they ate, The Royal Teens were on the speakers with "Short Shorts." Followed by Sheb Wooley and "The Purple People Eater." When they had finished eating, he placed the trash on the tray that was sitting on his window and the side of the car. Ivory Joe Hunter was on the speakers, with "Since I Met You Baby." He looked at Ree and sang along. He noticed her eyes glistened, as he sang. He sensed that she knew he was singing about her. When the song was over, she leaned in towards him and their lips met, for a sweet, loving kiss. Johnny Mathis was singing "Chances Are" as their lips lingered on. Their lips parted with The Fendermen came on with "Mule Skinner Blues."

The "waitress" came and took the tray, from off the car and when the parade had left enough space between hot rods, he turned on the motor, put her in gear and drove out of the lot. Ree moved over towards him and put her left hand back on his thigh and laid her head against his right shoulder. "Can we go somewhere and just make out?" She asked. "You've been reading my mind." He said. "Good." She mumbled. He headed for the duck feeding area, by the river. Fred and June had already started making out. Jimmy Dean was on the radio, singing about "Big Bad John." Eddie Cooley followed with "Priscilla". The song, after that was Dale and Grace, "I'm Leaving It All Up To You." The Fireflies were next with "You Were Mine." He turned the radio down, so he and Ree could talk. He wanted so much to tell her how crazy in love with her, he was. She caressed his thigh and said that she could stay like "this" forever. He murmured back, to her, "me, too."

He pulled into a spot, in the area, that was near the back. There were a lot of cars, already there. "Popular place." Ree said. "Yeah," he said, "and unfortunately, the cops patrol it on a regular basis. "Damn cops." She said. She moved away, towards the door and made room for him to, once again, climb over the obstructions. They managed to sit, tightly, against each other. The arms embraced each other as their lips caressed each other's lips. In his haste, although, the car was in neutral and the emergency brake was on, the motor was still running. He heard Mel Carter begin to sing "Hold Me, Thrill Me, Kiss Me." He brought his arm from around her and reached to turn up the volume on the radio. "Sounds like a wonderful idea." Ree murmured. He returned to press his lips against hers. Their lips parted, just as the song ended. He, again, released her and reached out, this time to turn off the motor. When he brought his lips back to hers, she parted hers, to allow their tongues to meet. It didn't take long for their passion to rise. She brought her right hand to his crotch and unzipped his zipper. He, once again, brought his left arm from her back, to her legs and moved it quickly up past her knee to her inner thigh, to the edge of her shorts. She turned her body ever so slightly, bringing her right leg up and over his left hip. This move gave his hand better access to that place between her thighs. Her shorts were too tight, for him to slip his hand underneath, so he just caressed her, over her shorts. He felt her hand find his "steel" flesh. As she stroked and slowly rubbed him, he did the same, to her. He could feel her "lips'" and the "valley" between them. Their passion kept increasing. He was so afraid that he was going to climax all over her hand. When their lips broke free, he cautioned her to please take it easy with him, he didn't want to make a mess. She smiled and said "okay". She stopped stroking and just held him. He continued to caress her. She began to moan and moan. "Oh baby!" she whispered. You are so wonderful!" Then, she told him that he needed to stop

As well. She, then, with both hands, pulled his polo shirt from out of his pants and ran her hands up inside to his sides and chest. Her hands on his bare flesh. He did the same, to her polo shirt. He ran his hands up her sides, to her bare back. Oh! how he wanted to unsnap her bra strap and caress her breasts with his hands and lips and tongue. To feel her nipples come to "life" under his touch. She slid tighter against him, as once again, their lips and tongues met. The next time, they paused to breathe, they embraced each other and began to thrust their pelvis's together. They just couldn't get enough of each other. He moved his head to stomach and under her shirt and began to kiss every inch of her soft, but firm flesh. He started to move his lips up to where her breasts were encased by her bra. She took her hands from his flesh and lifted her shirt up over her bra, to bunch around her neck. She, then, lifted his shirt up and over his head and off of him. He did the same, with her shirt. The only thing that kept him from 'worshipping her breasts with his lips, tongue and hands, was her bra. They put their arms around each other's backs and held each other tight, all the while their pelvis's were still matching thrusts. Her nakedness felt so wonderful, to him. His hands caressed her naked back, as did hers to his. Even with her bra against his naked chest, he could feel the sides of her breasts against him. Their lips and tongues had a "mind" all their own. Their mutual lust engulfed them and took over. He could feel the wetness of her 'crotch' against his pants. He knew that he would probably erupt and make a big mess and bring their passion to an end. It was Ree that pulled her lips from his and, huskily, suggest they take a "break." He agreed. They still hugged each other, just not as tight, as before. He glanced past her, at the window, on her side. Then he realized that all the windows must be fogged up. Through the mist, he saw the red and blue lights flash. They sat up and each put their shirts back on. Fred and June were already sitting up and each enjoying a cigarette. "Good idea" he thought. He reached out to the glove box and retrieved his cigarettes. "Didn't know you smoked?" she said. "A little." He said, "You?" "A little "she said. He put both cigarettes in his mouth and lit them with his silver Zippo lighter. He handed one to her. They all were settled back, smoking when the cop knocked on the window. He rolled it down. The cop flashed his light at all of them. Then he turned to his partner and said, "just smoking." The cop walked away. They all breathed a sigh of relief. Ree said, "must be a record, twice in one day." They decided that it was probably a good time to go anyway. He turned on the car, turned on the headlights, put the car in gear, released the emergency brake and drove out of the lot. He had parked, in such a way, that he didn't have to back up. Pat Boone was on the radio, singing, "I'm In Love With You." The next song played as they headed down the road. It was Andy Williams, accompanied by Peggy Powers, "I like Your Kind Of Love." They sang along with the record. He and Ree looked at each other as they sang.

He dropped June off first and then Fred. He and Ree, were alone, as he drove her home. She was as close to him as she could possibly be. Without being on top of him. Dinah Washington was singing, "Unforgettable". The Paris Sisters followed with "I Love How You Love me." They hardly spoke to one another. They didn't have to. They knew they were, totally, in love with each other, yet no one said so. He knew that, someday, he would tell her, when the time was right. Still, he hoped she would be the first. He didn't have to do "downshift" the car, so, he was able to put his right arm around her. She nestled her head into the "crook" of his arm. Her hand remained on his inner right thigh. He had never felt such a strong love, as this before. Mickey and Sylvia were on the radio singing, "Love Is Strange."

He pulled up in front of her house and "killed" the motor and the headlights. He put the car in forward gear and left the emergency brake down and away from them. They reached for each other and held each other in each other's arms as their lips and tongues danced together. After a while, she pulled, slowly away and with a loud "whew!" She huskily said "I have to go in." "I know." He said. He released her and opened his door and got out and went around the front of the car, to her door. She was already out of the car. She closed the door and the two of them walked arms around each others' waists up her steps, up her walk and then climbed the last three steps to her door. They gathered each other in their arms and enjoyed a long 'good night' kiss. Then, she turned and opened the front door and was gone into her house. He waited for her to close the front door. He walked back to the VW and got in, started it up and drove home.

In order for him to get to sleep, he "pleasured" himself after each date with Ree. He hoped the day or night would come, when he wouldn't have to do it anymore. That would mean that he would lose his virginity with her. He fell asleep, afterwards, still dreaming of her. He couldn't stand being apart from her. The next day was Saturday. He would call her and see if they could spend the day together, alone, or, at least Saturday night.

He woke up around 10:30 AM, to the sound of his mom yelling that he had a phone call. When his senses realized that it wasn't a dream. He first opened his left eye and then his right. "Ree" he thought. "She's calling me!" he hopped out of bed and ran down the hall to the landing phone. He picked up the receiver and said, "Hi!" The voice on the other end was a voice he hadn't heard in a long time. "What's going on?" She demanded. It was Charlene.

"Oh God!" he thought. "what do I say?" "Charlene, I've been meaning to call you." He said. "Oh really!" she said, angrily. "I got a call from a friend of mine, who was playing miniature golf last night and swore she saw you and another girl there." "Charlene, "he said, "I'm really very sorry. I have met someone else." That was all he could say. She interrupted him and told him that she was very hurt and that he should have told her, before she had to hear it from someone else. He tried to apologize, again. But she screamed into the phone, "GO TO HELL! WE'RE THROUGH!" She, then hung up. He was still holding the receiver, listening to a "dead "line. The guilt at having hurt her was beginning to consume him. He wanted to call her back and tell her how really very sorry he was. He hung up the phone and started back down the hall, to his room. He was halfway there, when the phone rang, again. He turned and quickly ran to answer it. He hoped it was Charlene and that he could explain to her what had happened. He picked up the phone. "hello" he said, cautiously. "Hi baby." It was Ree. "Hi yourself." He said. She said, "remember I told you about my best friend Jane and her boyfriend, John." "Uh Huh" he said. "They want to know if we want to spend the day and evening with them." "Oh?" he said. "They are driving down to the Cape this morning and riding around and then, for dinner, we'll have lobster, before we come back, tonight. Want to spend the whole day with me?" She asked. "You know I do!" he said. Then, she whispered into the phone, "we, finally have the back seat. He drives a big old Plymouth sedan." "When do we leave?" he asked. "As soon as you are ready." "okay," I'll be over as soon as I get cleaned up." She said, "baby, we're going to come and pick you up." "Oh!" he said, "okay." He then waited while she got a pencil and paper and wrote down the directions to his house, from hers. "We are leaving in ten minutes." "Ok!" he said. He hung up the phone and ran down the hall to his room. He grabbed a fresh pair of briefs and ran back to the bathroom. Took a quick bath, brushed his teeth, combed his hair; ran back to his room. Put on a pair of tan chinos, a pin striped shirt, dark socks and his "new" dirty bucs. He grabbed a sweater, just in case, it got cold. He splashed on some ":Old Spice" and left his room and went downstairs, to grab something to eat. He had just bit into a piece of toast, when the doorbell rang. He left the kitchen and went to the door. Ree was standing there in tan slacks and a white shirt. He invited her inside. They shared a light kiss on the lips. He took her by the hand and led her into his living room. His dad was in his easy chair, reading his morning newspaper; his mom was on the couch doing a crossword puzzle. He introduced Ree to them. His folks took to her right away. This was another milestone, for him. Ree was the first girl that his folks got to meet. She told his folks that she was kidnapping him for the rest of the day and evening. They all laughed. As they turned to leave, his folks and Ree expressed how wonderful it was to meet. He felt like he was walking on air. They left the house, holding hands. She told him that his dad was a very good looking man. He looked at her, as if she had just lost her mind. They walked to the car and he held the back door for her as she slid in. Then he slid in next to her. She introduced him to Jane and then John. Jane turned her body to face them and began to ask him questions about his school and family, etc. After the questions, she turned around, as John drove away from in front of his house. Ree pulled him to her. They sat so close to each other, that a flea would have suffocated between them. He couldn't keep his eyes off her. Her dark auburn hair and dark red lips made it almost impossible, for him to believe that she really cared for him. He still felt like he was out of his "league". He, also, noticed that her white cotton blouse was strained by the size of her breasts. He was hoping that someday, he could not only see them, but feel and taste them, as well. It was still, pretty much, daylight, as they headed for the Cape. Ree and Janet were talking "girl" talk,so he wasn't paying much attention. His head was spinning from the scent of her perfume. He hoped she could, at least, get a hint of his Old Spice. Lonny Donegan was on the radio, singing, "Does Your Chewing Gum Lose it's Flavor On The Bedpost Overnight?" Janet reached forward and turned up the volume on the radio and they all began to sing along. The next song was an appropriate one, "Old Cape Cod", by Patti Page. The next song was Little Anthony and The Imperials, "2 People In The World." Followed by "Bongo Rock" by Preston Epps.

They were approaching the bridge that would take them over the Cape Cod Canal. She pretended to be scared and buried her head, in his right shoulder. He just laughed. He knew she was kidding around. He took his left hand and put it under her chin and brought her lips up to his. He had intended for the kiss to be short and sweet, but she had other ideas. She began to move her lips all over his and he reciprocated. Her right hand moved to his inner right thigh and squeezed the flesh under his pants. His right arm tightened around her shoulders. They moved their bodies, so they were facing each other. "Hey! You two!" cried Janet. "It's not even dark yet!" They released their lips from each other and were slightly gasping for air. She looked him straight in the eye and said, "You drive me crazy!" he responded that she too was driving him crazy. They gave each other a big bear hug and then settled back to the way they were, before the bridge. John asked everyone, "I'm starved, where do we want to stop for lunch?" They really didn't care. So, he took it upon himself to find a place. Being that it was early April, there weren't many places open. They did manage to find a small seafood restaurant open. John pulled up and parked the Plymouth. They all got out and went inside. Ree reminded him that they were eating lobster, for dinner. So, he ordered a fried shrimp box. She did the same. As they ate, Janet asked Ree, if she had mentioned Blinstrub's yet, to him. "No, not yet," she said. Janet said that Johnny Mathis was coming to Blinstrub's the end of June and she and John thought it would be fun to double date. He looked at Ree. She had a questionable look, in her eyes. He felt that she really wanted to go. He said that he started his summer job, after graduation, but that if they knew the exact date, he could get it off. Ree reached under the table and squeezed his thigh, tightly. "Okay!" said Janet," then it's a date!" He said, "okay, if Ree still wanted to be with him, by then." Ree looked at him and said, "baby, I'm not letting you go!" To which he responded, "good! Because I'm holding on to you, too." They put down their shrimp, that they were eating and shared a short, loving, sweet kiss. "Oh, come on you, two!" said Janet. Apparently, she and John had been dating a lot longer than he and Ree. He didn't care, as long as she liked kissing him, he enjoyed kissing her.

They finished their lunch and got back in the Plymouth and headed down the road. It was a cool gray April day. A good day to be cuddling in the back seat, as someone else drove. They arrived in Hyannis and John parked the car, right on Main street. John commented that he would not be able to park there, during the summer months. He told everyone that his grand parents once owned property, right on the water, over looking Hyannis Bay. "What do you mean "once owned" asked Ree. "My dad does not like the Cape. He'd rather be on Lake Winnipesaukee in New Hampshire." He said. Ree gave a disappointed "oh." They held hands as they walked along the sidewalk and looked in the windows of the various shops. "Do you like the Cape?" She asked. "Always did." He said. "Good!" She said. "I love it!" They walked along, some more. When they came to the end of the sidewalk, they walked across the, almost, deserted street. On the other side, some shops were open, while others were being readied for the summer crowds. As they began to walk up that sidewalk, Ree asked him, "Did you really mean, what you said, at lunch, that you want to be with me?" "Of course!" he said. "I don't want to imagine myself without you!" She grabbed his arm and told him how happy he made her feel. "I've never really felt this way about anyone else." She said. He stopped walking and turned her towards him. "I have never been this happy with anyone else, either." They hugged each other for a good minute or so and let go of each other, when Janet said, "Oh really!" They all continued walking along the sidewalk, looking in the windows of the shops. They got back to the car and decided to drive to the town beach. John followed the signs and pulled up to the entrance, which had a chain across it. He parked the car and the four of them got out of the car and walked past the chained entrance and through the parking lot, over the dunes and onto the deserted beach. John and Janet fell onto the sand and began making out. Ree grabbed his hand and pulled them away. "We have the back seat!" She said. "Yes, we do!" he said. They walked along the water's edge, holding hands. Stopping, every now and then, to hold each other and savor each other's lips. The wind began to pick up and sand began whipping against their faces and into their hair. They decided to walk back to the car. When they came upon John and Jane, it was obvious by the disarray of clothing, that John and Janet had "made love" in the sand. He was jealous, so jealous, that he didn't speak for a while. Ree thought he was angry with her. Then he whispered how jealous he was of John and Janet. Ree said that it was okay and that she understood. They decided to drive all the way to Provincetown. John found a gas station, along the way and stopped to fill up the car's gas tank. He pried himself from Ree and reached into his back pocket and pulled out his wallet and took out a five dollar bill and handed it to John, before he had a chance to get his wallet. "On me." He told John. "Thanks pal." John said and then told the attendant to fill it up. Ree smiled at him. Janet thanked him, too. When the car was "gassed "up, they headed back on the road towards Provincetown. "Ever been there?" Janet asked him. "Nope!" he said. Ree told him that he was in for a treat. She wouldn't say anymore. Ree repositioned herself by bringing her legs over his lap and sitting up straight with both her arms around his neck. She pressed her lips to his and gave him short sweet kisses. He, in turn, did the same. After about ten of the kisses, she nestled her cheek against his, then moved her lips to the side of his neck. He began to give short kisses to her neck, as well. She stopped and brought her face to his and said, "we'd better stop, or we may not be able to. It's still daylight. He agreed. The Mello Kings were singing, "Tonite Tonite" on the radio. Followed by The Elegants singing "Little Star". The song that followed, was "Alley Oop" by The Hollywood Argyles. Again, Janet turned up the volume as they all sang along. When it was over, they all laughed. Janet turned down the volume.

John pulled the car into a small parking lot and turned off the engine. They all got out. Ree took his hand and John and Janet held hands, too. Again, they walked the sidewalks and looked into the store windows. He noticed other couples walking around, holding hands, some with each others hands into each others back pockets. He did notice that those couples were either "boy/boy" or "girl/girl". He had never seen gay and lesbian couples before. Ree leaned in and whispered, "try not to stare, baby". He replied, softly "I'm trying, I'm trying." They stopped at a local bistro and went in and sat at a small table and ordered cokes. The four of them were the only heterosexual couples in the place. At first, he felt uncomfortable, but as time wore on and they drank their cokes, he realized that it was actually like any other coffee shop. When he paid Ree's and his bill, they walked back out onto the sidewalk. Ree snuggled up to him and said, "you did very well". John asked him if he ever encountered homosexuals before. He said that was the his first encounter. He wasn't going to tell them, that one time, at the country club, a man had made sexual advances towards him, which he politely rebuffed.

The late afternoon air was turning colder. They decided to head towards Dennisport and the Lobster Shack, where they would dine on lobsters. Ree resumed her position, on his lap, as John drove. The Platters were, on the radio, singing, "Twilight Time,". Once again, Ree nestled her head against his neck and kissed it several times, sending shivers up and down his spine. God! He loved that girl! Jack Scott followed the Platters with, "My True Love". Ree brought her face back to his and their lips began exploring every inch of each other's lips. She began to moan as their kiss intensified into pure passion. His arms encircled her waist and moved to her back, he exerted enough pressure, to bring her against him. Her arms went around his neck to the back of his head. Their lips pressed harder together. "You two should get a room." Said Janet. Ree retorted with "At least we didn't do it in broad daylight on the beach." Janet came back with "touché". They both laughed as Ree and he enjoyed a nice hug. The Chimes were singing "Once In A While".

John turned on the headlights, as they began to get closer to the restaurant. He felt his stomach begin to growl. Ree said "someone is hungry." "Only for you." He said. "You are so sweet. I could just eat you up!" Ree said, as she brought her lips to his, once again. She seemed to be in control, but he really didn't mind, in fact, he was enjoying it. The gray, of the day, was turning to the dark of the night, as the car pulled into the gravel parking lot. John turned off the car and the headlights. They exited the car and walked across the gravel parking lot, to the entrance of the restaurant. Once seated, he excused himself to use the restroom. When he returned to the booth, he noticed the girls were missing. He sat down. John told him that Janet told him that Ree was completely lost in love with him. He hoped that he felt the same for Ree. He told John that he was completely in love with her, too. John asked, "have you told her, yet?" "No." He answered, "Why not?" asked John. "because, the last girl, I expressed my feelings for, used them to walk all over me and dump me." He said, referring to Abby. "Oh" said John. "I don't see that happening with Ree, I've known her a while, through Janet and I've never seen her so much into a guy. Never seen her so affectionate with someone. I know that she would do anything for you. So, please, be good to her." "okay?" He was dumbfounded. He had never heard a guy talk about feelings before. He assured John that he loved Ree very, very much and would never hurt her. He noticed the girls returning from the ladies room. Ree slid in next to him and put her hand on his inner right thigh. "Miss me?" she asked. "You know I did!" he said. They shared a short, sweet loving kiss.

The waitress came over to their table and asked if they wanted to see a menu. "No!" they all said in unison. John told her that they all wanted two chicken lobsters with fries and lots and lots of melted butter. The waitress smiled and said "You got it,kids!" When she left. John checked his watch and noted the time. "We should be back by at least 8:30." Ree said, "That gives us plenty of time to go parking." They all laughed and agreed. He felt his excitement rising. He was put his hand on her left thigh and massaged it. She looked at him and smiled. The waitress brought their bibs, for the lobster. Ree placed his around his neck, before the others could get theirs on, a little kid, walked by their booth and looked at him and exclaimed to everyone in the restaurant, "Look Mommy! He's wearing a bib!" his face flushed as he ripped off the plastic covering from his neck. The three of them were laughing, hysterically. He told them that he didn't care if he ruined his shirt. Ree was laughing so hard, she put her head on his shoulder. The waitress returned with their cokes. When she looked at him, she asked if he would like another "bib." He, emphatically, said "no!" That started the trio laughing again. Ree told him that he was "priceless." The others had put their bibs on and waited, patiently, for their orders. The lobsters that they ordered were "chicken" lobsters. The lobsters that the waitress brought out were larger and had all their claws. John told the waitress that there had been a mistake. She told him that they were out of chicken lobsters and that they could have the ones she brought them and that they would be charged the chicken lobster price. They all, graciously, thanked her. Then the fun began. Cracking the shell and dipping the meat in the butter. He was very careful, not to ruin his shirt. Their meal last just about an hour. He and John left the waitress a very generous tip. They all used the restrooms and then meet by the front door of the restaurant. Hand in hand, he and Ree walked to the car. Night had definetly replaced day. He and Ree climbed into the back seat of the Plymouth. They cuddled right up next to each other. Ree told him to open his mouth and she popped two Canadian Mints into his mouth. He began to chew them, rather than suck on them. He wanted his breath to be fresh, right away. Ree got the hint and chewed hers, too. John started the car and pulled out of the parking lot. The Platters were on the radio singing, "You've Got The Magic Touch." Followed by Fats Domino and "Yes it's Me And I'm In Love Again."

They held each other so tight, they slid down onto the seat, facing each other. He put his lips to hers. Their lips, once again, moved all over each others lips. She moved her right leg over his left hip as their bodies pressed tighter to each other. Her hands, on his back, moved down to his waist and pulled his shirt out of his pants. Her hands began to stroke and massage his flesh. He put his hands on her blouse and pulled it out of her pants. He stroked her sides and back. She opened her mouth, just enough, for her tongue to protrude and stab his lips and teeth. He opened his mouth and her tongue stabbed his tongue. She began to grind her pelvis against his. He brought his hands up from her stomach to her bra covered breasts and began to softly squeeze and massage them. She groaned softly, through their kisses. Her right hand moved between them and began to squeeze his manhood, over his pants. He was "aching" to rip her pants and bra off and kiss her entire body and enter her. She raised her right leg just a little off his hip and began to rub his hip with it. He brought his left hand from her right breast and put it between them and moved it up her inner right thigh, all the way. He softly rubbed her vagina over her pants. She began to thrust and thrash against him and his manipulations. Somehow, their position changed, he was lying on top of her. Her legs splayed apart as his pelvis and legs went between hers. They began to thrust their pelvis's against each other, as their lips searched each others', tongues lashed together. They were lost in lust! He had to breathe! He brought his lips from hers and took a breath and began kissing the right side of her neck, then moved down to the top of her heaving right breast. "Oh baby! "She moaned. They acted as if they were all alone, in the car. She, apparently, realized that they were not alone. She brought her hands to his chest and gently pushed him off. "Not here, baby, not in the back of a car." He agreed. She brought her hands to his back and held him on top of her. He thought he was getting "mixed signals. She wouldn't let go of him, so, he brought his lips to hers and, again, they began to kiss. Short, sweet kisses, that soon, began to increase in passion. She moved her lips from his and let out a "Whew!" She increased the pressure on his back. God!!! He wanted her! He felt that she wanted him, too. Somehow, they moved, again and this time, she was on top of him, raining kisses all over his chest and face, finally, on his lips. His hands, were now under her shirt, caressing her back. He wanted to unsnap her strap and hold her magnificent breasts in his hands. Her bra was the only clothing between their chests and stomachs. She was the most passionate girl, he had ever met. They were all over each other. Legs and arms intertwined rubbing and massaging. They were, both, reaching a "fever" pitch. Again, she brought her lips from his and asked that they slow down and take it easy. She climbed off him. They looked, at each other, and could see they were both "shaking" from their passions. She buttoned her shirt, as he did his. They moved to each other and embraced, tightly. They put their cheeks together and "calmed down" together.

Janet turned her around and told them that they were getting close to "their" favorite parking place. They looked at each other and smiled. They were like two "sex addicts". John pulled off the "old" highway and pulled the car around the "unfinished road. It was like a cul-de-sac. John turned of the motor and the headlights. Ree whispered to him, "let leave them alone and go find our own little place. He agreed. "We're going for a walk." Ree told John and Janet. She wasn't sure they heard her. They were already embracing and falling down, on the front seat. He and Ree got out of the car and walked across the road. They climbed a small rise that looked down on the car. They found a clearing and she pushed him down on the pine needles. She climbed on top of him and straddled his waist. She unbuttoned her shirt and then unbuttoned his. "Now, where were we." She said. She leaned forward and, this time, there weren't any sweet kisses, just lustful lips and tongues. Her hands roamed all over his chest. He brought his hands back to her bra covered breasts. She moaned through their kiss. He thought that this was going to be the moment that they were going to "go all the way." They both were moaning and groaning with increased passion. Flashing red and blue lights caught their attention. She raised herself slightly off his chest and looked towards the car. "Damn!" She exclaimed, "Cops!" She put her finger to his lips. They lay very still and waited to see, what was going to happen. Apparently the cops were going to let John and Jane go. John started the car, turned on the headlights and drove out of the cul-de-sac. "Oh great!" Ree said. She saw the cops, in turn, leave. Ree got off of him. They stood up and were about to walk down to the road. He told her to wait. Then, they both saw the cops return. "Probably looking to see if they had beer." Ree said. The spotlight, on the police car, scanned the road. Then, they left again. "Guess we're safe now." He said. They sat down on the ground and waited. It took about ten minutes before the Plymouth returned. The stood up and ran down the incline, over to the car, and jumped into the back seat. John hit the gas, as they drove out of the cul-de-sac. He and Ree embraced each other very tightly. Janet sighed and said that it was probably be time to call it a day anyway. They drove him home, first. This time, it was Ree's turn to walk him to his front door. They laughed as they realized it as a "first." They embraced and shared a long, passionate kiss. Then, she turned and walked back to the Plymouth. He watched as the car pulled away from the curb. He glanced at his watch. 11:30 PM! He couldn't believe the time! He unlocked the front door and made his way, softly, up the stairs, to his room. He crept past his folks room and down the hall, to his room. He skipped brushing his teeth and shed his clothes. He put on his pajama bottoms and got into bed. He closed his eyes and dreamed about their wonderful day. It didn't take long for his "wet" dream to finish. He got out of bed, took off his 'soiled" PJ's and put on a pair of fresh underwear. Once, back in his bed, he drifted off to sleep, almost instantly.

The sound of his folks voices, awakened him. He glanced through a sleepy left eye, at his clock, on the bed stand. It read 11:45AM! He got up and went down the hall, to the bathroom and cleaned himself up. He went back to his room and threw on a pair of jeans and a T-shirt and a pair of white socks. He went down the hall, down the stairs, to the kitchen. He got himself a glass of milk and put two pieces of bread, In the toaster. After his breakfast, his folks asked how the day went. He, barely, heard them. He did hear his Dad say, "from the look, on his face, I'd say he was in love!" he just smiled. "Are we blessed with your presence today?" His mom asked. "Think so!" he said. His dad said "good! I'd like it if you could cut the grass, today." "Okay!" he said. He was glad that his dad had broken down and purchased motorized lawn mower. One, that was self-propelled. All he had to do was "guide" it. It didn't take long for him to cut the front and side lawn. But, the back would take a longer time. Before he got started kn the back, he refilled the gas tank. He was just about to star,. when his mom called him from the back porch. "Telephone!" He yelled back, "Okay!" he left the mower and went into the house, through the back door. He went to the front hallway phone. 'Hello?" He asked. "Hey! It's Fred."

"Hey!" he said. "Glad I caught you at home. Just got off the phone with June. She told me that her folks are going to be out of town, next weekend. She wants to have a party. Me and her, you and Ree and . . . her cousin. We need another guy for her cousin. Now, for the interesting part. It's an overnight party. If you get my drift." "You're not serious!" he said. "uh huh! I sure am." He couldn't believe his ears. Then, he thought that Ree wouldn't go along with it. "Sounds like a great plan, but I doubt if Ree will be up for it." He said. "June is talking with her, right now." "If she is okay with it, then I guess I am, too." Fred, then, asked, "Who can we get for her cousin?" "I don't know! Maybe Bert. I don't think he's dating anyone right now." He said. Fred said, I'll give him a call." He, then, said, "You know that next week is Spring Vacation!" "Yeah, that's why her folks are taking her sister on a vacation." "She's not going?" he asked. "Nope. She told them she had two term papers due, after vacation. So, she's staying home. I'm going to call Bert and I'll get back to you." "okay!" he said. He hung up the phone and went back outside to finish cutting the lawn. It took him about an hour, to finish the job. He came back in the house, after cleaning the lawnmower and putting it away. He went upstairs and changed out of his jeans and T-shirt and briefs and went to the bath room to take a short bath. When he finished, he went back into his room and changed into fresh jeans and another T-shirt and white socks. His Keds were grass stained, so he just went downstairs, in socks. He was excited about spending the entire afternoon and evening with Ree, but he didn't think she would go for it.

He had just finished supper, when the phone rang. He was apprehensive about answering it. He was afraid it was going to be an angry Ree, or an upset Fred, that he couldn't get Bert to join them. He, reluctantly, picked up the receiver. It was Fred. "The party is on!" he said. "You're kidding!" he said. "Ree is okay with it?" he asked. "Apparently" Fred said. "Bert isn't sure. He wants to know more about the cousin. So, I'm having June call him." "So," he said, to Fred, "everything hinges on whether Bert will come with us." "Yep!" Said Fred. "Let me know." He told Fred.

He waited, until after 7PM, to call Ree. She answered the phone on the sixth ring. "Hi" he said. "Hi baby!" she said, "so, what do you think about next Saturday night?" he responded that he was excited that he would get to see her again. She pressed him, "What are your expectations?" "I don't really have any." He said. "Are you sure?" She asked. "Uh huh." He said. "Good!" She answered. "Fred is getting the booze from a friend and the rest of us are getting a couple of pizzas and some chips and things." "What things?" She demanded. "I don't know, some other "munchies, I guess." "Oh!" She said. Her questioning began to bother him. He began to understand that she was thinking that he had plans to "consummate" their relationship. He respected her too much, to take it for granted that, Saturday night, would be the night. He knew that it was entirely up to her. From the sound of her voice, it wasn't going to happen. He kept telling her, that he was looking to a lot of dancing, and "eats" and maybe a beer or two. She began to "lighten up" and then told him that she was looking forward to seeing him, too. He told her, that, he would not be able to pick her up from school that week, because his mom needed her car. She understood, even though, she was disappointed. He told her that he, too, was disappointed. She, then, told him that she a wonderful time Saturday. He lowered his voice and told her it was the best ride to the Cape, he had ever had. She giggled and said "Me, too." He wanted so very much, to tell her about his strong feelings of love, for her. He was afraid to say those three little words, especially, on the phone. They hung up with the promise that they would talk, every night, during the week.

Monday, during lunch, he met with Fred and Bert. Bert was a "go" for the party. Fred assured him that he was going to get laid. June told Fred that her cousin loved sex. Bert said "okay" as long as the cousin didn't weigh at least two hundred pounds. Fred, again, assured him that he was going to have a great time. Fred asked him, if he wanted him to get some "safes" for him, too. He told Fred that he didn't think Ree would appreciate it, if he had some. He told Fred that he was too much in love with Ree, to lose her, over his wanting to have sex with her. Fred said, "But you do, don't you?" "Of course," he said, "but it has to be her idea. "understood." Said Fred. Bert replied, "guess you're the only one who won't be getting laid this Saturday night." He felt like it might be a big mistake not to, at least, have some protection, just in case. Though, he really didn't want to piss her off.

When he called her, Tuesday night, she, again, questioned his motives, for Saturday night. He told her that he would not force his "attentions" on her. He respected her, too much. She appeared to like his response. He, then, told her that he received a letter from Emerson College. She asked him, if he had opened it. "Not yet! And my folks are really bugging me, to open it." She said that she didn't blame them. She told him to take the letter and open it, in front of his folks and then to call her right back, even if it is bad news. He promised he would and hung up the phone. He went downstairs, to the den. They were watching "Sugarfoot" on TV. He stood by the TV and when the commercial came on, he opened the letter. His folks leaned forward, with interest, h read the first few sentences, "It is with great pleasure that I write you, to tell you that your application, to Emerson College has been accepted. We look forward to seeing you, among your colleagues, as we welcome your class of 1964." His mom screamed with delight. His dad came off the couch and grabbed his hand! They both congratulated him. He turned and ran back upstairs, to the phone and called Ree. She answered the phone with "well?" "I'm going to Emerson, I've been accepted!" he said. "Oh baby!" Congratulations!" She screamed. He heard her scream to her family, "he got accepted to Emerson! My folks send their congratulations,too!" She, then, said that he should bring the letter to the party, so she can read it. He said he would. Another "big" milestone.

Wednesday, during lunch at school, he, Bert and Fred started to formulate their plans for Saturday. Bert was going to drive. Fred would get the beer. He would buy the pizzas and snacks. Once, again, Fred asked if he wanted a pack of condoms. Once again, he declined, because he didn't think Ree was ready. Fred looked at him and said, "look! She is willing to spend the night with you, in bed! Don't you think she is thinking of having sex with you?" "Not from our phone conversations, no". he said. "Okay" said Fred, "I won't push it any further, but I think you're making a mistake."

When he called her that night, he asked her if she still had apprehensions about the party. She told him. No. She trusted him. That was all he had to know. He was not going to break, or do anything to destroy that trust. She asked him, if they were going to be able to spend much time together, during the next week of Spring vacation. He told her that he hoped so. She said she wanted to see him as much as they could. They decided they could talk about it and make their plans, at the party. She told him that she really had to study, Thursday night, that she had a lot of tests on Friday. He understood and told her that he would call her on Friday. "You better!" She said, laughingly.

They guys, once again, met during lunch, that Thursday. Fred was the man in charge. He went over the plans, once again. Bert asked Fred to get him a bottle of Seagrams, because he really didn't care for beer. Fred said, "okay." Fred told them that the girls would be at June's around 4 o'clock Saturday afternoon. June was nervous about her neighbors, seeing the guys pull up to the house. Fred told her that they would wait until it was dark, before they would arrive. They all agreed to meet for lunch, again, on Friday, to finalize their plans.

Thursday night, he tried to study for the history test, on Friday. He kept looking at his watch and wished he could call Ree. He turned on his radio, Julie Rogers was singing "The Wedding." He began to dream about the possibility of marrying Ree. Then, Johnny Horton came on with "The Battle Of New Orleans". He went back to studying. He began to fantasize about the party. He wondered just how far he and Ree would "go". He glanced at his watch and realized that he had been up "studying" for quite a while. "The Night Train" show was going off the air. He decided to call "it" a night.

The history test was an essay test. He, always, did well on essay tests. He surmised that it was because he usually "BSed" his way through. He was pleased that he knew the answers. He met the guys for lunch and they formalized their plans. Bert was driving. He would pick up Fred, first, then him. They would "pool" their money and head to Fred's friend's house to get the "booze". Then, they would go to the store and get the snacks. Fred told them not to pack any clothes. He reminded them that they told their folks they were going to the drag races. In Maine. All they needed to bring was a tooth brush, deodorant, toothpaste, any hair products and shaving gear. He told them that he wasn't shaving, yet. They laughed. They would pick up the pizzas, on the way to June's house. He noted that being April, it still didn't get dark until around 6PM. So, they had plenty of time. Still, if they left their houses in the late afternoon, their folks might get suspicious. So, Bert would have to pick them up in the "late" morning, around 11:00. They agreed. Bert asked, how they were going to hide the car from the neighbors. Fred said, "as we near the house, you kill the headlights, put it in neutral and coast into the driveway. June will leave the garage door open and we'll push the car, the rest of the way, into the garage. They agreed on the plan.

He "wolfed" down his supper and ran up the stairs to the landing phone and called Ree. She was so happy to hear from him. He asked how the tests went. She said, "okay." He told her that he had a history test and he did "okay." He, then, told her about the "guys" plans for Saturday and the party. She said that she had hoped the two of them could spend the day, together and then attend the party. His heart fell into the pit of his stomach. He apologized and told her, had he known how she felt, he would have told the guys. She said, sadly, that it was okay and that she couldn't wait to see him. Then she told him that it wasn't fair that the guys should pay for everything. He told her, it was worth every penny, just to be with her. "Oh! Is that all I'm worth, just a penny?" She laughed. He told her that she was priceless. She cooed, "you are so sweet." He wanted to reach through the telephone wires and give her a hug. He told her so. He could tell from the tone of her voice that she was smiling. He asked her about vacation, if she might want to go to the Totem Pole Ballroom. She said that she would like to, but that she was saving for a dress to wear to Blinstub's. 'Oh yeah! That's right!" he said. Then she asked, "My prom is coming up in May. You are going with me, aren't you?" He had forgotten all about the proms. He said "of course". She said, "great!" When is your prom?" He told her that it was near Memorial Day weekend. She said she hoped they weren't on the same day. She would check her date and he said that he would check his. They ended their conversation by saying howe much they were looking forward to Saturday.

(The Party)

He got up early that Saturday morning. He went into the bathroom and got cleaned up. He brought his toothpaste, toothbrush, Brylcreem, deodorant and comb, back to the bedroom. He put on a fresh pair of jeans and a yellow polo shirt. He, also, put a fresh pair of briefs on the bed with the rest. He, then, went downstairs and had his breakfast. He asked his mom for a small sandwich bag, to put some things in for the weekend. She said that she didn't have any sandwich bags left, but gave him a small paper bag, that was a little bit bigger than a sandwich bag. He went back upstairs and was able to put everything in it. He grabbed another comb. Off the top of his dresser and combed his hair. He checked out the cash, in his bank. He still had over two hundred dollars. He figured 65 would be enough. He opened up his wallet and put the money into it and stuck the wallet in his left back pocket. He checked his watch. It was 9:45 AM. He, also, put his "Old Spice "bottle in the bag. He was glad that everything fit in it. He rolled the top down over the bag, so no one could see what was in it. He wondered if he should call Ree. He went to the landing phone and picked up the receiver, then put it back down into it's cradle. He did not want to arouse any suspicion, from her folks. He went back to his room and turned on the radio. "Maybe" by the Shangri-las, was on. Followed by Laverne Baker and "C.C. Rider." She was followed by Sam Cooke and "You Send Me." He was singing along with Sam, when he heard his mom call, "Bert is here!" He looked at his watch. It was just after ten AM. Bert was early! He picked up his paper bag and turned off the radio and went down the hall and downstairs. Bert and Fred were waiting in the front hall. They said, "hi"; he responded. He said goodbye to his folks and all three walked out the front door, to the 1952 Plymouth. When they got inside. He said, "What gives? You are about an hour and a half early!" Bert responded that his folks got on his case about leaving too late for the drag strip. That they should get an early start to avoid the traffic and get a decent place to park. "Oh." he said, "great! Now what do we do?" "Well" said Fred, "let's go to a coffee shop and sit down and see if we can come up with a way to kill some time." They agreed and headed to a diner that was in the next town. Bert parked the car and they went into the diner. Fred ordered toast and coffee. He had already eaten, so he ordered just coffee. Bert ordered scrambled eggs, toast and coffee. He was feeling "edgy". He wanted to get the "show" on the road. When Fred and Bert had finished their breakfast, they paid and headed out to the car. Fred checked his watch. "Okay!" he said, "We're back on schedule." They pulled out of the parking lot and headed to Fred's friend's house. It took over an hour, to get to their destination. They met his Fred's friend and followed him to the garage. Fred paid for the beer and Bert paid for the Seagram's. They loaded the booze in the back of Bert's car and headed back to their town. "Still on schedule." Said Fred.

They headed to the local market. Fred said, "Whoa, wait a minute! May not be a good idea to go to our local market, seeing as that one of our moms may be in there." The others agreed. So, they headed to the next town, to buy the snacks. They got three different bags of chips, some coke and 7UP and two different kinds of dip, plus some crackers. The store was crowded, with Saturday shoppers. It was around 2:30 in the afternoon, when they got back into town. They were hungry, so they went up the highway to Adventure Car Hop, for some lunch. Seemed they, again, weren't the only ones having a "late" lunch. By the time, they finished their burgers and fries. It was well past 4PM. "Okay!" he said, "what do we do now, for the next two hours." Fred told Bert to drive back to the next town. He had to go to the drugstore, there. A friend of his worked there on weekends. He was going to buy the "protection." Again, Fred asked him, if he wanted to buy some. Again, he refused. "last chance." Said Fred. Bert gave him some money. "Not sure if I'll need them, but better to be safe than sorry." He pondered that statement, for a few minutes, but stuck to his guns, hoping that he wouldn't be sorry.

It was 5:30PM and the gray skies of the April day were starting to fade into evening. They got back into town and then "cruised" by June's house. It was still too" light" out. He noticed that he was just about out of cigarettes. "Cigarettes!" said Fred, "forgot to get cigarettes!" They drove into town and stopped at the local drugstore. He bought two packs of L&M's, one for pack for Ree and one pack for him. Fred smoked Pall Mall's and Bert was a "Marlboro man." They cruised by the house, again. It was getting darker. They went to the pizza parlor. He ordered two large pepperoni and cheese pizzas, When they, finally, got their pizzas, it was after six. Bert drove away from the store, with his headlights on. They were "hyped". "Next stop, paradise!" said Fred.

They came "cruising" up the road. When they got in front of the house, that was two houses away from June's, on the left, Bert turned off the headlights. When, they were in front of the next door neighbor's, he put the car, in neutral, and coasted into the driveway. It was a gravel driveway and the car coasted to less than halfway up it. They still had a way to go to get the car into the garage. He and Fred got out of the car. He whispered to Bert to keep the car in neutral, so they could push it into the garage. They had no idea that the girls were at the kitchen window, watching them. He and Fred, pushed with all their might, but the car didn't move an inch. He went back to Bert. He whispered, "It's in neutral, right?" "Yes." Whispered Bert. He went back to the rear of the car. He whispered "on three.". On three, they both pushed with all their muscles, heart and souls, the car didn't move. Fred whispered, "I know it's a heavy sedan, but it isn't that heavy." They looked under the tires, to see if anything was blocking them. The tires were clear. He, again, went back to Bert. "I don't get it!" he whispered. Bert then asked him, "when do you want me to release the brake?" "Whaat!" He, almost screamed. He stuck his face, through the open window, till it was practically touching Bert's, "NOW". Release it now!" He walked, quickly, back to the rear of the car. It was starting to roll backwards. Fred had all he could do to hold it, from running over him. He joined Fred and together, they gave a mighty push, which propelled the car forward and both of them, face down onto the driveway. The car rolled, easily, into the garage. They, quickly and silently unloaded he car and then pulled the garage door down and closed it tightly against the driveway. They carried all their "goodies" to the back door. June, opened the door and let them in. The shades of the kitchen windows were pulled down as they entered. They put the beer in the fridge and the snacks on the kitchen counter. He put his small paper bag on the counter near the door, to the living room. They hadn't notice that the girls were trying, desperately, to hide their laughter. Finally, they let it out. Ree had tears running down her cheeks. June was holding her stomach and the other girl was leaned over the counter. The guys, then realized, that the girls had witnessed their "stupidity" with the car, trying to put it in the garage. Ree was the first to speak, through her laughter, "It was like watching a Three Stooges Movie." He felt so stupid. He pointed to Bert and told the girls that Bert forget to take his foot off the brake. That excuse invoked more howls of laughter from the girls. Fred looked at him and then Bert and said, "I guess it did look, kind of dumb, at that. The guys began to laugh, too.

After they settled down, they all took the boxes of pizzas and drinks into the living room. He gave Ree, her cigarettes. "Thanks, baby, I was just about out." She said, then gave him a short kiss on his lips. Bert was introduced to June's cousin, Lucy. The Coasters were on the Hi Fi singing "Poison Ivy." He and Ree sat next to each other on one of two couches. She kept feeding him pieces of pepperoni. She showed no signs of apprehension, at all. He began to think that maybe he should have invested in a package of "rubbers." He, stupidly, mentioned that maybe he should go out to a drugstore. Her mood changed dramatically! "Why do you think you need to go to a drugstore, for?" He was thrown back against the back of the couch. He mumbled "protection?" She glared at him and said, "You don't need it!" He "meekly" responded, "ok". They went back to eating and drinking. When they had finished, Ree wanted to dance. She went to the Hi Fi and found a Johnny Mathis album and put it on the turntable. Johnny began to sing, "It's Not For Me To Say." They got on the dance floor and wrapped their arms around each other and just swayed to the music. Her perfume clouded his senses, he was "lost in Paradise." She apologized for snapping at him, and explained that she was afraid that if she gave herself to him, entirely, that she would never hear from him again and she did not want to be some guy's "conquest." He stepped back and looked her straight in her dark brown eyes, it just came out, without any forethought at all. "I am in love with you and would never treat you that way!" Her eyes, suddenly, got quite big; her mouth dropped open. "What did you just say?" He repeated himself. Her eyes got teary and her lush red lips quivered. "Do you have any idea, how long I have been waiting to hear those words from you? I have been in love with you, since our very first kiss!" They embraced, so tight, he thought she might crush his ribs. They must have stood there, on the living room floor, in their tight embrace all the way through the Johnny Mathis album. When they, finally parted, he turned and went into the kitchen and brought back two beers, one for her and one for him. She took her beer and said to him, "I know a better place to drink these." She led him by the hand, to the front hall and up the stairs. When they got to the top of the stairs, they walked down the hall, to the third room, on the right. They opened the door and went in. She walked ahead of him and turned on a lamp. She told him to lock the door.

He turned his back to her and proceeded to lock the bedroom door. When he turned around, she was standing in the center, of the room. He walked up to her. They embraced and shared their first kiss of the evening. It started out very sweet, but soon turned into a wet passionate kiss! She stepped back from him, when their lips parted. She brought her hands to the bottom of his polo shirt and pulled it up out of his pants, up over his chest and neck and it got stuck on his head and face. He brought his hands up to dislodge it from his head. He pulled the shirt up and over his head and tossed it on the floor. She, at the same time, had removed her tight V-neck sweater. They were both naked from the waist up, except for her bra, which was being tested by her large breasts. She smiled at him and said nothing as she reached her hands behind her back and he heard the snap of her strap. Her bra, immediately, slipped, a little from her breasts. She brought both hands across her chest to her shoulders and slipped the straps off her shoulders. The bra fell to the floor, by her sweater and his shirt. She, slowly, brought her hands away from her chest. His mouth must have fallen to the floor with the garments. He was staring at two of nature's perfect accomplishments! Her breasts were perfect in shape and even tilted up at the ends. her nipples were hard like the new, stiff erasers at the end of brand new pencils. He gulped and exclaimed, "you are so very beautiful!" He stepped closer and brought his hands to her breasts and, slowly caressed them, like they were magnificent works of art. He brought his mouth and lips to first the right one and then the left one. Kissing every inch, saving the nipples, for last. She put her hands on the top of his head and guided him. When he, finally, came to each nipple, he lightly sucked it into his mouth, his tongue circling it. She pushed her chest to him. He, once glanced up at her. Her eyes were rolling in her head, her tongue was off to the corner of her mouth. She was moaning and moaning. Her hands twisted and pulled his hair. Sometimes, causing pain, but he didn't care. His arms and hands were on her naked back as his mouth and lips lightly "feasted" on her wonderful orbs. She continued to arch her back, drawing his mouth and lips to every inch of her breasts. Her head was thrown back, moan after moan, loudly emerging from her lips. He brought his mouth away from her chest and with his hands, turned her around, placing her naked back against his naked chest. He reached around her and began to cup, massage and knead her breasts and nipples, while his mouth and lips caressed and kissed her neck. She began to rub her backside against his front. He knew she could feel his erection. Her hands were on his hips, moving him against her. They were as one body, in motion. Somehow, they had maneuvered each other to the bed. The back of his knees hit the edge of the bed and he went down onto it. Ree fell with him. On top of him, her eyes were clouded with lust! They rolled around on the top of the bed, their lips pressed tightly against each other. Their arms and hands tightly embracing, their naked chests rubbing against each other. He could feel her stiff nipples jab into his chest. His manhood, still encased in his pants, straining against the same. He knew she could feel it.

When, finally, they "broke" for air, she exclaimed, "I've never been loved like this before! You are amazing and absolutely wonderful! OH BABY, I AM SO HAPPY! ILOVE YOU SO MUCH!!!!!!" He "croaked" back, "I have never felt this much love for anyone!!!!!" She began to "rain" kisses all over his face,neck,chest and stomach. She, then, sat up and straddled his legs. Her hands went to his pants and "feverishly" undid his belt and unzipped his fly. She rolled off him as he slipped off boots and jeans. She got off the bed and stripped off her pants. The only clothing for them were his briefs and her panties. She had, also, kicked off her shoes. He was still on his back as she 'climbed "on top of him. Their tongues met way before their lips ever did. She was still doing a lot of moaning. He flipped her off him and onto her back. He, then, began to kiss her lips, tongue, face, neck, shoulders and upper chest. Her hands grabbed him by the ears, and began to "guide" him. He kissed her arms and then moved to her sides, leaving her breasts for last. He trailed kissed over her ribs and down to her navel and then moved back up to her breasts, where he spent a great deal of time. He ran his lips and tongue, again over every inch and then gave her nipples the same "treatment" as before. While his mouth and lips were busy on her breasts, his hands were massaging her legs and inner thighs. She was "thrashing" from side to side, on the bed. Her moans were clouding his ear drums. He moved his left hand up her thigh to that "magical" juncture between her thighs. Her panties were soaked, as he moved his middle finger over the lips and into the "crevice" covered by the thin cotton of her panties. She was, loudly, crying out his name, followed by "Oh my sweet sweet baby!!!!!. He, then. Slipped his finger inside the edge of her panties and found the flesh. He pushed his finger inside her. He began to explore her. All of sudden, his finger was flooded with juices. She arched her back, sending her left breast against his mouth. He heard a strange noise emanate from her lips. Almost like an "AAARRGGHH!" Then her body went limp. He withdrew his finger and his mouth. He thought she might be unconscious. He just looked at her. He was ready to get off the bed and get some help, when her eyes opened and focused on him. She had the biggest grin on her lips. In a husky, raspy voice, she muttered, "my turn."

He stretched out on the bed. She moved to his side and brought her lips to his forehead. She gave him short kisses all over his forehead and then moved to his cheeks, after which, she pressed her lips on his, exploring every inch of his lips. She moved from his lips to his chin, from his chin to the sides of his neck, then down across both shoulders. She paused, from her kissing to bring her breasts down, lightly across his chest, with only her nipples touching him. She, then, began, softly kissing his chest, stopping to lightly suck on his nipples. As she lowered her mouth down and around his torso, her fingers, lightly, raked where her mouth, lips and tongue had been. She brought her mouth to the elastic band of his briefs. She puckered her lips and as she moved down over his briefs, she blew a warm breath over him. This brought an instant reaction to his penis. The cotton fabric of his briefs was stretched almost beyond its' limits. She moved her lips and began to kiss his thighs, first the outer and then moved to his inner thighs, first the left and then the right. She brought her face back up to his. As their lips met and tongues "lashed", her fingers moved under the top of his briefs and found his throbbing flesh. She moved her left hand up and down and over him. She ran her fingers over its' head. Her hand was "making love" to "him". He began to groan and move his hips. "Oh baby! Do you like this?" she whispered. She, again, pressed her lips to his. He knew that it wouldn't take long for him to reach completion. She brought her lips off his, again, and whispered. "I love your penis, it isn't too big and certainly isn't small. I want to bring you off, are you ready, sweetie." All he could do was nod "yes." She continued to softly stroke her fingers up and down and over the head. Then, she held him in her hand and began to "pump" him. His moans and groans grew louder. He knew he was about to erupt, and then he felt it begin. He tore his lips from hers and cried "OH GOD! OH SHIT!". She covered her hand and him with his briefs to catch as much of his semen as she could. His hips kept bucking as he pumped his semen out. When he had finished, he realized that most of the "mess" was on his briefs and his flat belly. Ree got off the bed and went to her bag and came back to him, with a small face cloth. She proceeded to wipe him. When she was done, he got off the bed and went to his bag, threw the soiled briefs in it and took out the fresh pair and them on. He went back to the bed and Ree. He stretched out both arms and drew her to him. Their kissing, again, reached an intensity that caused his head to spin. Her hand went back to his penis and his hands encased her breasts. They were, again, reaching a "fever pitch" when they heard a loud crash! In the hall, outside their door. They were both gasping for air, when he rolled away from her and got off the bed and slipped into his jeans. He unlocked the door and opened it, to find a seriously drunk, Bert, lying on the floor. "What the hell?" he asked. Bert, with slurred speech told him that he got Lucy's clothes off and wanted to know what he supposed to do next. By that time, Fred had emerged from his room and came up to Bert and told him to go back in the room and get inside that girl. Bert said, "She passed out!" Fred told him, "So what? She's naked and wants you, so go get her!" They helped Bert to his feet and helped him back into the room. Lucy was lying on the bed, on her back, softly moaning. They helped put Bert on the bed, next to her. they got out of the room and closed the door behind them. They looked at each other and parted. He got back into the room and turned and locked the door and climbed back onto the bed. Ree was under the covers. He got off the bed and then climbed back in and joined her under the covers. They wrapped their arms around each other and tightly embraced. He loved to feel her hard nipples press against his chest. She lifted her right leg and put it over his left hip and drew their pelvis's together. She began to grind against him and, once again, his penis began to respond.He brought his lips from hers and bent down and found her right breast. He began to caress it, once again, with his lips and tongue. She brought her right hand from around his back and moved it between them, down to his crotch. He brought his left hand and did the same to hers. She pushed down his briefs and "liberated" his now, swollen, penis. He slipped his finger under the elastic edge on her right thigh and found her "wetness". He, again, caressed the outer "lips" and gently slipped his finger inside. She threw her head back and began to moan. He, too was moaning. The vibration of his moaning lips against her nipple, seemed to increase her passion. She began to writhe around and moan louder. "Oh My God! Where have you been all my life?" She cried. "I'm here now", he groaned," and I'm staying!" he moved his finger around inside her, in a circular motion. When he came to a certain spot on the left, she really reacted. Her gyrations increased and her moans were louder. He decided to stay on that area and massage it. She started thrashing her legs and arching her back, shoving her breast against his mouth and her nipple deeper, between his lips. Then, once again, she flooded his finger with her juices. Her body, practically, rose off the bed and then, once again, went limp. He wasn't sure what he had done, but apparently she liked it. She disengaged her leg from his hip and began to actively stroke him. He saw the face cloth was still on the bed. He reached for it, knowing he was going to need it, again. With the face cloth in his left hand, he brought his lips back to hers. He opened his, mouth, just in time for her tongue to drive into his mouth. He had never experienced a girl, like her. Her eyes moved to the left and saw the face cloth, in his hand. She withdrew her left hand from his back and took the face cloth from him. Now, she had both hands stroking him. She disengaged her lips and tongue from his and told him to tell her when he felt he was going to climax. He groaned that he would. It didn't take long. "OH Hell!" he cried. He felt her put the face cloth over him as he unloaded, again. This time the face cloth caught it all. She brought the face cloth up and deposited it on the bed covers. They embraced again and he told her, again, how much he was in love with her. She gave him a big squeeze. They continued making out for a long time, afterwards. He felt the sleep start to close in on him. She rolled over and placed her back against his chest. "Put your arms around me." He did as she said. She took his hands and placed them on her breasts. "Just hold them, please." They fell asleep, together.

The room was filled with the gray, of the morning, as they stirred from their slumber. His hands were still filled with her fantastic breasts. She turned her head backwards over her left shoulder and he moved his lips to hers. The kiss was sweet and full of love. "Good morning, baby." She said, as their lips parted. "Hi, babe!" he said. Then she said, "you are the very first boy I have ever slept with." He told her that she was his first, too. She moved to face him and they embraced. Then, her eyes grew large. "What time is it?" She asked. He reached behind him and fumbled for his watch. He had taken it off, when they fell onto the bed, the first time. "8:35." He said. "oh my God!" She cried. "I've got to get up!" "Why?" He asked. "We're meeting my folks for church!" "Church? We?" he asked. "Not you, the girls and I." She said. "Oh!" he said. "After this wonderful night, you're going to church?" he asked. She was already out of the bed and walking across the floor towards, what he saw, was a closet. He watched her walk. He couldn't believe how beautiful she was. "You are so very, very, beautiful!" he said. She turned to face him, showing him, once again, her beautiful breasts. She gave a slight "curtsy" then turned back to the closet. She slipped off her panties and reached into her bag and brought out an undergarment that looked like it had some elasticity to it. She bent over and began to pull it on, up her legs and over her thighs to her waist. She reached into her bag, again, and brought up stockings. She walked over to the edge of the bed. He was still in it, leaning on his left side and watching her. Her back was within reach of his right hand. He reached out and began to caress her back. She leaned back into his hand, as she brought one stocking up her bent leg and fastened it to the "girdle". She told him that he had stop massaging her back, because, if he didn't she was going to rip off the clothes she had on and "rape" him. He laughed. When both stockings were attached, she got off the bed and went to her bag and retrieved a "fresh" bra. She put it on and then bent over to the floor and picked up her "old" bra, his polo shirt and her sweater. She threw the shirt at him and put the other clothes in her bag. She then withdrew a dress from the closet. It was light blue, with small yellow flowers on it. She raised her arms and brought it over her head and let it fall over her body. She smoothed it out, with her hands and then bent over by the closet door and came up with light blue high heel shoes. She came over, once again, to the edge of the bed and sat down and put on her shoes. "Now, before I apply my lipstick and makeup, give me a kiss!" She turned around and put her right knee on the bed and leaned into him. He put his arms around her neck and the shared their last passionate kiss of the weekend. She said, "I have to go to the bathroom, so I'll meet you downstairs." He said, "okay." Then she took her bags, the little one and the overnight one and went to the door, put the small bag down on the floor and unlocked the door and opened it, and left. He jumped out of bed and straightened the covers, so it would look, like no one had been in it. He took the 'soiled' face cloth and put it in his paper bag. He, then got dressed and before leaving the room, made a quick inspection and made sure everything was as they found it. He, later, learned that he hadn't needed to do all that, because he and Ree had spent the night in June's room. She was in her sister's room and Lucy and Bert were in the guest room. Her parents weren't do back for a couple of days. So, she would wash the sheets and clean the house.

When he got downstairs, he found that the others had already been up. Fred and June had cleaned up the living room and the kitchen. He looked around and took note that he would never had known that there had been a party. Ree, finally, came down the stairs. She looked absolutely beautiful! He gave her a low wolf whistle. She turned herself around, spinning the lower part of her dress. "Thanks, baby!" She said. She looked out the living room window and turned to the other girls, "My folks are here!" Then, all three of them, dressed in church clothes blew kisses to the guys and walked out the front door. The guys hid behind the walls when Ree opened the front door. They went back into the kitchen. Fred had put the trash in large paper bags, including their garbage, pizza boxes, snacks and beer and the empty Seagram's bottle. Bert did not look at the bottle. In fact, he was surprised that Bert could see anything. He looked horrible. Lucy had not looked like her "radiant" self, either. He asked Bert if he was okay to drive. Bert said he was, but that he sure could use some coffee. Fred was a little on edge. "Guys, we were supposed to have been up and out of the house, before daylight, so the neighbors wouldn't see us!" he looked at Fred and said, "should have mentioned that earlier." Fred responded that he was going to, but that he and Ree went upstairs, too early. He just shrugged. Fred went to the back door, opened it and looked out, first to his left and then to his right. No neighbors were out in their yards. Fred hoped that they all went to church, too. The three of them, grabbed their bags and the bags of trash and headed for the garage. They, quickly, opened the garage door and then Bert unlocked the trunk, of the car, and put the trash in it and closed it. They got in the car and Bert started it up and backed it out of the garage and down the driveway and into the street. He stopped and put it in forward and off they went. Bert, again, noted that he needed coffee and plenty of it. They decided to head for the diner. He sat, alone, in the back seat. His memory of the previous night, filled his senses. He was totally in love with Ree! Even though, he hadn't, technically, lost his virginity, it was close and the milestones were many. Seeing naked breasts "live" not in a magazine, putting his lips and tongue on them, feeling a vagina, for the first time and inserting his finger, in one, and finally both of them experiencing a climax, not once, but twice. Then, actually sleeping with a girl. Yep, he thought, many milestones had been reached.

They pulled into the diner parking lot. Fred was the only one who seemed oblivious to the events of the last night. Bert was a "hurting" puppy and he was "lost" in love. They found a booth and sat down, as the waitress came over to them and asked what she could get them. Bert ordered "coffee and please, keep it coming." He and Fred ordered coffee and a full breakfast of scrambled eggs, toast, and bacon, and orange juice. She looked at Bert. Again, he said "coffee, just coffee." He sat and stared out the window, at the gray, cloudy morning. He was so lost in his thoughts of Ree, he hadn't really heard Tennessee Ernie Ford, on the jukebox, singing "Sixteen Tons. "Fred looked at him and said, "I know what's wrong with Bert, but for you not be listening to the songs on the jukebox, what's wrong?" "Nothing." He said. "Oh! "Fred said, "frustrating night, huh? I told you to buy some condoms." He looked at Fred and told him that the night was absolutely fantastic! Fred stared at him and then asked him if he got laid. He replied "no, not really." Fred gave him a quizzical look. He, obviously, didn't understand. He was not going to elaborate. He was a strong believer in the old adage of not kissing and telling. He believed that what happened between him and Ree was their business and no one else's.

They ate their breakfasts in silence. Again, for the second time that morning, he heard the Everly Brothers, sing "Cathy's Clown." The first time was in Bert's car, as they drove out of the driveway. Bert turned off the radio, before the song was over. They paid their bill and tipped the waitress and got up and left the diner. It was still too early to go home. They decided to just ride around town, and maybe head for Adventure car hop, for lunch and then head home. Bert was beginning to feel a little better. Bert turned on the car radio. Buddy Holly and The Crickets were singing, "Every Day."

It was getting close to noon, when they decided to head for the car hop. He and Fred weren't really hungry, but Bert was. They pulled into the second row, at the car hop, as Little Anthony And The Imperials were singing "Shimmy Shimmy Cocoa Puffs". The song was, also, playing over the loud speakers at the car hop. A girl roller skated up to the car and took their orders of burgers, fries, and cokes. The Teen Queens were singing "Eddie My Love" over the speakers, as the girl brought their orders. Again, they ate, in silence. Fred finally asked if they had a good time "last night." Bert said that he didn't remember too much of it. He and Fred laughed, as they "filled" him in. "You guys saw me naked?" he screamed. "Did the girls see me, too?" "No!" they said, just Lucy. Fred added, "well she may not have, she was passed out on the bed, naked, as well." Bert stared out through the windshield, "I wonder, if we did the 'nasty'?" He and Fred were unable to answer. They said that they didn't know. They remember leaving the two of them, lying naked next to each other, on the bed. Bert asked both of them to swear, never to tell anyone about the weekend. They promised.

He fell back into his mind and became "lost" in the images of the previous night. His heart was swelling with the love of Ree. He had, finally, told her how much he cared for her. He had used the "L" word. She used it, too. He knew that he never, ever, wanted to be, in the world, without her. He couldn't wait to talk to her, that night.

Fred looked at his watch and told them, that it was time to, finally go home. They would drop him off, first. They headed for his house. It was 1:40 PM, when they dropped him off at his house. He grabbed his little paper bag and climbed out of the back seat and opened the rear door. He bid his "so longs" to the guys and headed up the walk. He, almost made it to the front door, when he realized that he had the "soiled" face cloth in the bag. He, quickly turned to his right, ran across the front lawn, down the driveway and to the trash cans, under the back porch. He took out the face cloth, which had "crusted" semen on it and opened the trash can and stuffed the cloth way down inside. He, then, piled the other trash on top of it.

He walked up the back steps to the back door, of his house. He went into the kitchen, down the hall and into the den. "How were the races?" his dad asked. "great!" he replied. His mother looked up from, watching TV and said, "You look exhausted, very tired, didn't you get much sleep last night?" He told them, that he really didn't, because they stayed near the track and there was too much going on. "Well, his mom said, "why don't you take a nap? I'll call you when supper's ready." He thanked her and said that it was a good idea. He turned and walked out of the den and turned again, to his left and went up the stairs and down the hall to his room. He put his "toiletries" on the top of his bureau and cursed himself for not disposing of his "soiled" briefs with the face cloth. He put the bag, with the underwear on the floor of his closet. He would take care of it later. He lay down on the bed and closed his eyes and conjured up images of the time with Ree. It didn't take long for him to drift off to sleep.

"Dinner! Dinner's on the table!" his mom's voice shattered the image of Ree, taking off her sweater and bra. "Okay! Be right there!" he yelled back. He stretched and got off the bed. He felt a little groggy. As he walked down the hall, to the landing and then downstairs, his mind began to clear. He walked into the dining room and took his seat. His dad asked him if he had a chance to talk to Ree, during the weekend. He was quick to answer, "No! I am going to call her after supper." His dad said, "Good, I really like her; too bad, you didn't meet her towards the end of college, instead of high school." he told his dad that he was going to do whatever it took to keep her around. "Hope so, son" he said. He said nothing else, during supper. When the meal was over, he got up from the table and went into the kitchen and placed his dirty dishes in the dishwasher and walked down the hall to the stairs. He went up the stairs, to the landing and dialed Ree' s phone number.

Her sister, answered the phone and called her to it. He heard Ree ask," who is it?" He, also, heard her sister say, "your boy friend." He liked the sound of that. Ree got on the phone, and said, softly "Hi baby!" he liked the sound of that, too. "hi," he said. "I miss you!" She replied that she missed him, too. After heaving a heavy sigh, he started to talk about vacation week. "Do you like parties?" She asked. "Sure, why not? Especially if they are like the last one." He said. He heard her chuckle. "Even if, maybe, I'll be the only one you know?" She asked. "As long as you don't abandon me!" he said. She said "good! And don't worry, I wouldn't leave you alone for a second. Some gorgeous girl might steal you away." "Not me!" he said. "I'm taken!" "You better believe you are!" She said, "There are parties almost every night of next week and we've been invited to all of them." Any ones like last night?" He asked. "Shhh!" She said, "No, afraid not." "That's okay," he said, "as long as we're together." "The first one is at Janet's tomorrow night around 7, I promised her that I would be there early, to help her set up. Why don't you meet me there?" he said "okay." He tried to remember where Janet lived. Ree was quick to remind him. "You can come early, if you want?" She said. "Okay!" he said. I'll see you tomorrow night. While at Janet's party, a couple bumped into them, while dancing, she introduced him to them, and the guy asked what town he was from. He answered "Newton" and the guy looked at Ree and said, "out of towners, now, huh?" Ree responded "he is the best!" He told her that she made him feel very "special". She gave him a hug and told him that what she said, was true.

There was a party, every night of the April vacation. They did a lot of socializing and eating and dancing. He slept in, the mornings. He was having a lot of fun. Ree had a wonderful sense of humor and was such a "joy" to be around. They would steal kisses, whenever they could. As for going "parking" afterwards. They were both too tired and the parties lasted until 11:30PM. The Saturday, before school started again was 'void' of parties. When he spoke to Ree, at the Friday night party, she invited him to her house for a cookout, with her family.

He slept in, once again, and arose, with his mom telling him to wake up and go to the phone. He stumbled out of bed and looked at his watch. It read 11:30 AM. His eyes were barely open and his mind was still full of the dreams of Ree. He, slowly, walked down the hall, to the landing and picked up the receiver. "Hey baby!" It was Ree. "My folks said you can come over anytime, today." "Uh. Okay" He mumbled. "Are you okay, baby?" She asked. "Just got up." He said. "Oh. wish I could come over and help you get up." His eyes shot open and his mind cleared, quickly. "If you were to do that, we'd be in a lot of trouble." He said. "Oh why?" She cooed. "You know why!" he said, with a chuckle. "If my parents weren't home, I'd dare you to come over here." She laughed and said "maybe someday, I'll take you up on that dare. Now get dressed and get over here!" She ordered and then softly said "Okay?". "Okay!" he said. They hung up the phone and he went right into the bathroom and ran the tub, while brushing his teeth. He 'relieved' himself and got in the tub. He, quickly, bathed and wiped himself off and ran down the hall, to his room. He put on a fresh pair of jeans a white dress shirt, with the button down collar, white socks and Keds. He rubbed the deodorant under his armpits and combed his hair and put just a "splash" of Old Spice on.

His mom had already done her shopping, so he was able to take the VW. She offered him some food, but he declined and told her that he was going to Ree's for a cookout. She told him to put some gas in the car. He went back upstairs, to his room and got his wallet, he checked and found that he still had twenty one dollars in it. He put the wallet in his back pocket and went back downstairs. He said "good bye" to his folks and went out to the driveway, got into the VW and headed to the gas station and then to Ree's.

The gas cost him five dollars, The tank was almost empty. He pulled up in front of Ree's house. Turned off the car and got out, locked it and started up the front steps, to the front walk. Ree must have heard him pull up. She came around the right side of the house, across the driveway and ran up to him, threw her arms around him and planted a long, wet kiss, with tongue, on his lips. He put his arms around her, while they kissed. When they broke apart, he gasped, "Wow! What a greeting! But what about the neighbors?" he asked. "Don't care!" She said and grabbed him by the arm and led him across the lawn, the driveway and around the side of the house, to the backyard. Her mom was sitting in a lawn chair, her dad was standing over the coals, in the grill,.he was wering a long, white apron, that said, "Master Chef" on it. Ree brought him to her dad, first and introduced him. He said he was pleased to meet him and ended it with "Sir." Her dad said "likewise" and had a big grin on his face. She, then brought him to her mom. She was about to get out of her chair, when he told that she didn't have to do that. He shook her hand and she, quickly, said, "Don't call me maam." He grinned and said, "okay."

A badminton set was 'set up' away from the table and grill. He asked Ree, if she would play. They picked up the rackets and tried to play, Ree was terrible, kept missing the "birdie". Finally her little sister came up to Ree and took the racquet from her and she and he began to play. She was a "formidable opponent." She beat him two out of three games. Every game went right down to wire. He conceded defeat to her. Ree was sitting at the table, nursing a coke, when he came over to her and sat down. Her sister handed him a coke. He thanked her and turned his attention to Ree. She was wearing white, tight, Bermuda shorts and a green polo shirt, that accented her dark auburn hair and red lips. Her sister leaned into him and told him that it was not nice to stare. He looked at her sister, on his left, and told her he couldn't help and that some day boys were going to stare at her soon. "Not too soon" he heard her father, say. Everyone was seated at the long wooden picnic table. Her dad asked him what he was going to study, at Emerson. "Broadcasting" he said, "Broadcast Journalism". "Ah", said her dad, "another Walter Cronkite." Ree leaned in and said, "but much better looking." "Agreed!" her mom said.

The cookout went well. He seemed to score a big hit with Ree's family. He helped clean up, afterwards. Then, Ree's mom asked if she and he would go to Brigham's and get a gallon of Vanilla ice cream. Ree grabbed his hand and pulled him off the bench, at the table. They were, almost, around the side of the house, when her dad yelled, "You forgot the money."

"I got it!" he yelled and they ran. When they got to the VW, he unlocked the car and let her in her side. He went around to his side and got in. He leaned towards the dash, to insert the ignition key, when two hands, grabbed the sides of his head, turned his face towards her and, once again, their lips met in a long, wet passionate kiss. When, at last, their lips separated, she said, "My family loves you!" he gleamed at those words and then thought. "oh no!". Ree asked him what was wrong. He told her that, he heard, when a girl's family liked the guy, his relationship with the girl was "doomed." "Not in this case, baby!" She declared. "I hope not!" He said. "Trust me!" I'm going to love you forever and ever." "Me, too!" he said. He started up the car and drove away from the house, going through the gears. Elvis was on the radio singing "Are You Lonesome Tonight?" "Not me!" She said. "Nor me!" He said. Sandy Nelson was next with "Let There Be Drums". She slid over to him as close as she could. Her left arm, around his shoulders, her right hand resting on his right thigh. As they rode along, she moved her hand, to his zipper and moved it around until she "located" the slight bulge of his penis. She began to stroke it, ever so lightly. Even underneath his briefs and jeans, it began to respond. "Oh! someone likes what I'm doing. Doesn't take much to make it grow, does it!" She exclaimed. "You keep that up and I'm going to pull over and rape you!" He warned. "Can't rape a willing participant." She laughed. "DAMN!" He exclaimed, "you're driving me crazy!" She brought her hand back to his thigh and he looked at her. She was pouting! He never saw the pout before. Then, he realized that she was "putting him on".

He pulled up to the curb at Brigham's. he turned off the cat and they both exited the car. "Damn!" he said." I can't go in there, like this. His erection was so obvious. "Oh my!" She exclaimed. "it does show!" He turned back towards the car and reached into his left rear pocket, took out his wallet and extracted a five dollar bill and gave it to her. She was still chuckling as she went inside the store. He pressed himself against the side of the car, to see if that would help, it didn't. He began to think of 'things" that would help the swelling go down. He thought of Black beauty and the horrendous wreck. That seemed to work. He turned back around and started for the front door of the parlor, when Ree emerged with the ice cream. They got back in the car and Ree took the two remaining one dollar bill and stuck them down inside the top of her bra. He stared at her. "You don't really think they are safe there, do you?" he asked. "I hope not!" she said. Then, "it" started to "grow "again. She laughed all the way back to her house. "How the hell am I supposed to get out of this car and face your family?" he asked. "I'll tell them you can't find the change and are looking for it." She chuckled. He sat in the car and, once again, began to think of the Ford and the wreck. It worked, again, and he got out of the car, vowing to get even with her. He still adored her foolishness. When he arrived in the backyard, her mom asked if he had found the change. He told her "No! but he knew where it was. Ree patted the area just below her neck. Her mom knew exactly where it was and laughed. Her mom asked him if the money was safe there. He felt the rush come to his cheeks, Her sister cried out "He's blushing!" He said "yes" the money was safe there. Her dad said "good." Her mom went into the back door, of the house and asked, "who wants ice cream?" Everyone said they did. Ree went into the house, to help her mom spoon the ice cream into 5 bowls. Her Dad asked him, if he had any plans for the summer, after graduation. He told him that he started his summer job, at the country club, the week after his graduation. Her dad told him that Ree starts her summer job, at about the same time. Just then, Ree called everyone into the kitchen, to get their ice cream. They all took the bowls back outside and sat at the long wooden picnic table and began to eat the ice cream. Ree was sitting next to him and handed him, his "crumpled" bills. "Your change, sir." She said. He thanked her and stuck the bills in his pocket. Ree turned to him and told him that Janet had called, while she was in the kitchen. They were going to get together that evening, to look at prom gowns. She asked him, if he wanted to go to Janet's with her. He declined. He said that he would drive her, there, but looking at dresses was not his thing. She put her left hand under the table and gave his thigh a squeeze. He helped clean up the paper dishes and put the bowls away. Her dad said that the coals were far enough away from the house, to just burn out. He thanked them, for inviting him and said it was a pleasure to, finally meet them.

He and Ree left the backyard and walked hand in hand to the VW. Darkness had settled in. When they got into the car, she told him that he had been a big "hit" with her folks. She said that her sister told her, that if she were a little older, she'd go after him. He laughed. He reached for the dash and inserted the ignition key, started the car and put it in gear and they drove off to Janet's house. He told her that he had hoped for some alone time with her. She said, "I know, baby! Me, too, but I need to look at gowns, I want to look good for you." "oh?" he asked, "Am I your date for your prom?" "You better be!" She said. "Okay" he said, with a smile. They pulled up in front of Janet's house. He left the car running, Roy Orbison was on the radio with "Only The Lonely". They shared a passionate kiss and a tight embrace. When their lips parted, he, again, told her that he loved her. She exclaimed, "Oh baby, I love you so very much". They shared another kiss and then they parted and she got out of the car. She walked up the walk to Janet's front door, turned, waved and blew him a kiss. He blew one back and proceeded to drive away. Lee Dorsey was on the radio, singing "Ya Ya", followed by the Dubs and "Could This Be Magic". As he drove home, he wondered what he was going to do? It had been a real long time, since he was home on a Saturday night. He hoped that there were some good shows on TV. He knew his parents were going to be shocked that he was home.

He drove into the driveway and parked the car, got out and locked it. He went up the back stairs, to the back door. He stopped in the kitchen and grabbed a bottle of coke out of the fridge. He went down the hall and into the den. It was 8:30 PM. His folks were watching "Leave It To Beaver." They couldn't believe he was home. "You and Ree didn't have a fight?" His mom asked. "No!" he said, "She and her girlfriend are, looking at Prom dress magazines. "Oh, good." His mom said. He sat down in one of the easy chairs and finished watching the show. His folks said that he probably wouldn't want to watch the next show, with them. He asked "What is it?" His dad said, "Lawrence Welk!" he told his folks that they were right. He finished his coke and went back into the kitchen and put the empty bottle in it's cardboard package. He, then, went back down the hall and up the stairs, to his room. He turned on Arnie Ginsburg's "Night Train Show and lay down, on his bed. It was "dedication night" on the show. He wasn't really paying attention until he heard his name. "The Platters, "Only You" from Ree, with all her love. He lay back and listened to the words, for the very first time. When the song ended, he wanted to call her, but didn't know Janet's phone number. He listen to Arnie, for the dedication number and once he heard it, he wrote it down and got off the bed and ran down the hall, he dialed the number and got a busy signal. He tried and tried again. Finally, on the sixth try, the phone rang through. A voice that wasn't Arnie's asked who his dedication was for? He said "Ree" The guy said, "wait a minute we don't do that here." He said, no she's a girl!" "okay," the voice said and from? He gave his name and said the song was by Elvis, "Loving You." The voice thanked him and hung up. He waited and waited and then just around 9:15 he heard the dedication. He hoped she heard it too. He heard the phone ring, on the landing, soon after. He raced down the hall and picked up the receiver. "You are so very sweet and I love you so much!" Ree said. "Thank you!" he thanked her, for her dedication and asked if she was still at Janet's. She said "no" that she had left, just after making the dedication. They blew each other a kiss over the phone and said "goodnight" and hung up.

Sunday, he had to go with his folks, after church, to visit his Aunt and Uncle. It was a boring day. He wanted to spend the day with Ree. He arrived, back home, around six that evening and immediately went up the stairs, to the landing phone and called her. "We get our prom tickets on Tuesday, at school" She told him. He told her that he would see if he could get the car, Monday, so he could pick her up, after school, and give her the money for the prom tickets. Before she could say anything, he called down the stairs and asked his mother, if he could have the car Monday. His mom told him to wait, while she checked her grocery list and calendar. Ree told him that she was buying the tickets for her prom. He was her guest and she did not want him to pay. "But" she said, "if he wanted to come over, anyway, she would love to see him." His mom called up, to him, and said that she really needed the car, but that she could pick him, up after school, and drop her off, at home, and then go to Ree's. He was about to tell Ree, what his mom said, "I heard her." Ree said, and asked if he still was able to get out of his last period study?" he said, "of course." He said that would still give him time to pick her up her up, after school. She was excited and asked him when his prom was going to be. He told her that he would find out all the information, on Monday, at school. They ended their conversation with expectations of seeing each other the next afternoon.

His first three classes were cancelled that Monday morning for a senior assembly. He and his fellow classmates filed into the auditorium. They were told of the following events, for the end of their senior year. First, on the agenda was the "senior outing". That was going to be on May 6th. They would be bussed to Ipswich Beach, at 9 AM. They would need to bring a bathing suit, a beach towel, some extra cash and plenty of sun tan oil. They would leave the beach at 1:30 PM and be back at the school, by 3PM, at the latest. He wrote all the information down in his English notebook. Their Prom was set for May 20th at the Totem Pole Ballroom. They should plan on having dinner, somewhere else, before the prom. They said that tickets would go on sale, during homerooms, the rest of the week. Tickets were forty dollars a couple. He wrote it down. Last day of classes would be the 16th of May. Senior "night" would be, in the gym, the night of the 14th. Yearbooks would be passed out, during homeroom on the 16th. Graduation practice would take place on the 8th, 9th, and 10th of June, with Graduation on the 11th of June, outside in the football stadium. Each senior was to get 5 tickets. The last record hop would be that coming Friday, in the gym, at 7PM. They were looking for a D.J. He, immediately, raised his hand and said that he would do it. The class President saw his hand and another student's and said "great!" we'll use you both!". Final exams were scheduled for the 17th.18th. and 19th. Then came the surprising news that anyone who had a "B" or better in a class, did not have to take a final exam, in that class, unless they wanted to. He was excited! That meant he only had to take his math final. He left the auditorium a very happy guy! He couldn't wait to tell Ree the good news.

The rest of the day, "flew by." He told his mom to pick him up in front of building one at 1:30PM. The bell rang at 1:25. He grabbed his books and headed out the door. He saw the VW parked by the curb. He ran to the car. His mom was already, sitting in the passenger seat, he got in, closed the driver's side door and turned on the car and, slowly, went through the gears.

"Well, hello to you, too!" His mom said. "oh, I'm sorry, Hi" he said. He told her about the day and all the activites. She asked him, if he knew what color, Ree's dress was. He said that she hadn't gotten one yet. His mom told him that the color was important for her corsage. He told her that he would try and find out that afternoon.

He dropped his mom off at the house, at 2PM. He had just enough time to get over to Ree's school and pick her up. He drove up, just as the bell rang dismissing classes, for the day. He, again, strained his eyes, scanning the horde of people coming out the big wooden doors. She saw him, first. His eyes picked up her waving hand. She wearing a light green blouse and a black tight skirt. God! He loved the color of her dark auburn hair. She always wore it just long enough to cover her ears and, barely, touch her shoulders. She was, also, sporting bangs, which added to her "cuteness."

He reached over the passenger seat and opened her door, as she hiked up her skirt and slid into the seat. She, again, threw her books into the back seat. "Same place, as last time?" he asked, "uhuh" she said,before she leaned towards him and greeted him with a wet passionate kiss. Some kid parked behind him hit the horn. They parted their lips as he waved to the car behind him and put the VW in gear and drove away from the school. When they, reached the clearing, they found that they weren't the only car, full of couples, there. He found a spot near some bushes and turned off the car and put it in reverse gear. He left the emergency brake,off. She took her small notebook, out of her pocketbook. "We had our last assembly this morning." He looked at her and said, "So did we!" They smiled at each other. "This is so exciting isn't it?" She said. He agreed. She went over her "dates". May 6th was her prom. She said that she and her mom are going shopping for her gown on Wednesday. Her Graduation was on the 4th of June. There were some other activites planned for her class, but she wasn't sure she was going to attend any of them. He asked "why not?" She answered, "Because I can't bring you. Silly!" "oh!" he replied. He, then, told her of his dates. Everything fit into place. She was concerned about her prom. She hoped that he would be back in time. He assured her that he would. She told him that Janet's folks were going to have a "pre-prom party, at Janet's house. That the party would begin around 7 and the prom was supposed to begin at 8. "Plenty of time!" he said. He told her, as soon as she knew the color of her dress, she would have to tell him, so, he would know what color the corsage would be. "You're getting me a corsage?" She asked. "Of course!" he replied. She, also, told him that she would really like it, if his tuxedo had a white coat, with it. "No problem!" he said. Then, she added, that she would really like it, if the tie, cummerbund and suspenders matched her dress. He said "okay" as long as it wasn't pink. "I don't wear pink," She said. They found out that they were going to be getting their yearbooks same day. They made plans to meet that day, to sing each other's yearbook. He told her that he was "co-DJing" the last record hop, at the school, that Friday night. He asked her if she wanted to come to it, with him. They would be able to dance some dances, together. She said that she'd feel "funny" standing or sitting around, while he spun the records. He understood. They made plans for the drive in, that Saturday night, instead. Once they got their dates set up, they put their notebooks away and wrapped themselves up in each other's arms. He was "lost" in her perfume and her lips tasted like cherries. His head was spinning! He took his left arm. From her back and brought it to her right leg, just above her knee. He felt her stocking and was a little disappointed that it wasn't her soft flesh. Her tongue jabbed into his mouth. He moved his hand up farther. He felt the snap of her stocking, to her girdle. She spread her legs apart, just enough for his fingers to move up and under her girdle. She was not wearing panties. His fingers caressed her pubic area. She brought her right hand from his back and to his crotch and zipper. She unzipped it and moved her hand to his briefs and found the opening, felt his hardening flesh. Their lips went "wild"; their tongues "dancing around each other. She slid down farther in her seat, as he slid his middle finger inside her. She began to groan, through their mouths. She began to stroke his hard member. She brought her hand out of his pants and unbuttoned the buttons, on her blouse. With her left hand, she put it on the back of his head and directed his mouth and lips from hers, to the tops of her heaving breasts. Her head was thrown back against the seat as his finger explored her inner depths and his lips kissed her breasts. Her hand, once again, found the opening in his pants and briefs. He pushed himself against her hand, as thrusted her pelvis against his finger. As his middle finger, probed, his other fingers moved against her "outer lips". The poor, little, VW was rocking like the baby's cradle in the "lullabye". A loud siren blasted the stillness of the air, followed by the loudspeaker, telling everyone to clear out and go home!" "Damn cops!" they said, together. They disengaged themselves and he zipped up, as she buttoned up. He put his foot on the brake and the other on the clutch. He turned on the car and slowly backed, then turned around and put the car in the forward gears and drove out of the clearing, with all the other cars.

She asked if he was coming to her graduation on the 4th of June and he said he would, if she would come to his the next Saturday. She cuddled up next to him and said she wouldn't miss it, for the world. He dropped her off at her house with her promising him, to let him know what color her gown was going to be, as soon as she got it. They shared one more "goodbye" kiss, in the car, in front of her house. She got out of the car, got her books from the back seat and closed the door and went up her walk to her front door, and was gone. He put the VW back into first and then sped through the gears. Brook Benton was on the radio, singing, "It's Just A Matter Of Time." He sang along, as he headed home. He was wishing that some day and night, he could wake up, with her again, in the morning. He got home, just in time, for supper. His folks had just turned off the TV, after watching "The Texaco Huntley-Brinkley Report." His folks asked him how things went at school. He got up from the table and went to the chair, in the hall, where he had "dumped" his books. He found his English notebook and brought it back, to the dining room table. He read the list of "events." He couldn't wait to get to the part about grades and exams. His folks were very pleased. He told his mom about Ree getting her prom gown, the next day and that he asked her to tell him the color, so he could get the right color corsage. She was pleased that he remembered things like that. The conversation took a different turn. His parents were deciding what shows, they wanted to watch, that night. His dad wanted to watch "To Tell The Truth" followed by "Pete and Gladys". Then switch over to "Wells Fargo" and then back to "Danny Thomas." His mom said that was okay as long as she could watch "Andy Griffith at 9:30. His dad said, "All right!" He decided to watch TV with them. They looked at him in shock. "Are you sure?" his mom said. "Yeah!" he said, "been awhile. "They finished eating and got up and put their dishes in the dishwasher and left the kitchen for the den. It was 7:30PM. He just settled himself on the couch, when the phone rang. "It's probably for you!" His dad said. He got off the couch and went to the hall phone and picked up the receiver, "Charlie Brown?" The voice said. "Just a minute!" He said, "Dad, it's for you!" His dad came into the hall and took the receiver from him. "Hello?" his dad said. There was a pause. He started back into the hall. His dad slammed the receiver into it's cradle and yelled at him. "Tell your friends, I'm not amused!" he looked at his dad and asked what was it all about. His dad said that some kids called him and then, when he answered, they would play that record of "Charlie Brown" over the phone. He said, "Oh that's the new one by the Coasters." His dad looked at him and said "I don't care who sings it, when someone asks you for my name, just hang up." He said, "okay" with his hand over his mouth, trying to stop laughter from escaping from his lips. His mom was biting her tongue, to keep from laughing.

The phone rang, again, when "Pete and Gladys" came on. He got up, once again, and went to answer it. He picked up the receiver and said, "Hello?" "Hi baby, remember me?" "Of course, "he replied. "I thought you might call tonight." He replied, "Well, I would have, if we hadn't seen each other this afternoon." "I'm just pulling your leg." Ree said. "You can do that as long as you want to." He said. She began to laugh and it took her a minute or so to control herself.

"you got me, with that one" She said. "We are going to look at a light green and white gown, tomorrow afternoon. I'll let you know, if the color changes." "okay" he said. She said, "I really enjoy our times together." He responded," so do I!" Then, he held the phone very close, to his mouth and told her how much he would love to wake up every morning, with her by his side. There was a pause, on her end. Then she whispered, "Me, too." He told her that, at the least, he could hold her in his dreams. She responded by telling him the she dreams of him every night. They wished each other "sweet dreams", and said "good night."

The next day, he got to drive the VW, to school. He gave Joan and Fred a ride, with him. Chuck Berry was on the radio singing about "Johnny Be Good," followed by The Forum and "The River Is Wide." Fred started asking him a lot of questions about him and Ree, so, he turned down the radio. Joan wanted to know all about his new girlfriend. Fred took pride in introducing him and Ree. Joan asked him if he was taking her to his senior prom. He told her that he was. Fred told him that he and June broke up. He asked Fred, "why?" Fred told him that June was becoming to "bossy" and she was talking as if he and her would get married someday. Fred said that he just wasn't ready for that type of commitment. Then, he paused and gave the real reason, he met someone else. Her name was Cathy and she was a lot nicer and better looking than June. Joan told Fred that he went through girls, the way her father goes through new cars. Her father bought a new car every six months, whether he need to or not. He said that he thought his dad was bad. His dad got a new car every two years. Fred just shrugged. Joan asked him, if he was taking Cathy to the senior prom. He said "No!" he couldn't afford it, and she couldn't afford to buy a gown. He felt bad, for Fred. He thought to himself, "I'm going to two proms and two graduations!" He felt so happy and lucky. He could not imagine himself, ever breaking up with Ree. He just loved her too much. He turned the radio back up as they neared the student parking area on Elm road. Elvis was on the radio, singing "Too Much." He smiled, to himself and thought "how ironic!", even though so e of the words, in the song, did not apply to him and Ree.

He parked the car, turned it off, let Joan and Fred out and locked it. He checked his wallet to make sure he had enough money to buy the prom tickets. He was glad that his class dues took care of his yearbook, senior outing, senior supper and the record hop. The only other thing, he had to buy, was the tassle and cape, for his graduation "gown". When he got to home room, someone had drawn, in colored chalk, a rocket ship, with the letters, "Class of 1960" written on it, ready to "blast off."

The bell, signaling the beginning of Home room rang. Their teacher had just took attendance when their "rep" walked in and asked if anyone wanted to buy their prom tickets. He was third in line. He handed the "rep" two twenty dollar bills and signed his name next to his printed name and wrote "guest". He was handed the two prom tickets. He looked at them and then took his wallet back out of his pants and put the tickets in it, and put his wallet back into his left rear pocket. He went back to his seat. He sat and thought how wonderful life was, for him, at that moment. Two proms and two graduations. Two more milestones.

His classes were nothing but reviews of the year's work. He really paid attention, in Math class. That was the only exam, he would have to take. He met Fred and Bert, during lunch. Bert, also, told him that he, too, was not going to the prom. They did say they were doing the other events. They decided to "buddy up" at the outing and 'senior supper". He felt a little disappointed with them, about the prom. He was still going to go, even if it meant that he and Ree would be going alone.

On the way home, he pondered if he should go straight home or surprise Ree, by picking her up, at school. Then, he remembered that she and her mom were going to look at prom dresses. So, he turned up the radio and sang along with Hank Ballard and The Midnighters singing "Finger Popping Time." Once in a while, he would replace "popping" with something else. He arrived home and turned the keys to VW over to his mom and went up to his room, to check on his finances. He looked in his "bank" and was surprised that he had, at least, two hundred dollars left. He hoped that money would last until he started his summer job. He lay down on his bed and thought of Ree and all the things they would do, once school was out. He was glad that Blinstrub's with Johnny Mathis, was at the end of June. He would have several pay checks by then. "Yes," he said, to himself, "life is good!".

It was around five o'clock, when the phone rang. It was Ree. She found her prom dress. She had a color "swatch" that she wanted him to have, so when he got hiss tuxedo, he could get the right color, for his tie, etc. He asked her to wait, for a minute. He called downstairs, to his mom and asked if her could borrow the car, for a while. She said, "okay." He told Ree that he would be over to her house, to pick up the "swatch". She said "good, see you in a bunch, baby". He, then, called the tuxedo rental store. When they answered, he asked their hours. "We're open till 9 PM tonight. Is this about renting a tuxedo for the high school prom?" They asked. He said "yes." They said that normally they close at 6, but because of the prom, they are staying open. He told them that he would be there, within the hour. He got the keys from his mom, went back to his room and picked up some money, for the rental, and went downstairs and out through the kitchen to the VW.

He arrived at Ree's about 6 o'clock. He ran up the walk and rang the bell. She came to the door, dressed in black slacks and a short sleeve polo shirt. He told her that he was going to the "tux" store, then, to rent the tux. She turned and yelled into the house that she and him were going to the rental store, in town. She went back in and got her pocket book and came back, closed the front door, behind her. The two of them, practically, ran, hand in hand, down the walk to the car. They got in. He started the VW and as he went to put it in first gear, she grabbed his head with her hands and brought his lips to hers. It was a long wet, passionate kiss. "I just can't get enough of you!" She said. "Oh Ree!" he said, "if we weren't in such a hurry, I'd head for out parking area." He drove to the center of town. He parked in the municipal parking lot across the street, from the store. They walked across the street, hand in hand, and entered the store. There were four other guys looking at tuxes. Ree took out the 'swatch" and held it in her hand. Finally, after about 15 minutes, a clerk approached them. He told the man that he needed a tuxedo, with a white dinner jacket, shirt, shoes and then, she showed him her "swatch". He showed them where the tuxedos were and took the swatch into the back room. He was gone for about five minutes. Ree was concerned that he wouldn't be able to find a cummerbund, tie, and suspenders to match. The man came back out with a box, in his hand. He showed them the contents. Inside the box were a tie, hankerchief, cummerbund and suspenders that were an exact match of the swatch. Ree was thrilled! He was happy. The man, then proceeded to measure his neck size, waist, inseam and arm length. He wrote down the measurements. He showed him a tuxedo, in his size. He tried on the white coat, it fit. He, then took the pants to a dressing room and tried on the pants, they fit. He came out of the room and handed the pants to the man. He, then, sat down and tried on a pair of satin leather shoes, they fit. The man got out his order pad and wrote everything down, including his name, address and phone number and then wrote "High school prom" on it. "you'll pick the clothes up, when?" he asked. He told the man that it would be best, if he could pick everything up the Thursday before the prom, instead of the prom day. "Are you wearing the tuxedo that Thursday night, as well?" he asked. "No!" he told him, but he was afraid that if he waited to Friday, that he might be too late, for the prom. The man told him, since he was wearing it just for Friday night, that he would only charge him for the one night, provided, he got it back, before noon, the next day. He said that he would. The man wrote on the order slip "Thursday afternoon pickup". The charge for everything was thirty five dollars. He took out his wallet and handed the man two twenty dollar bills. The man left them, to ring up the sale and bring him his change. Ree grabbed his left arm with both of hers. She was so very happy.

They walked out of the store, with the receipt, in his hand. He stopped at the curb and took out his wallet and stuck the receipt and a five dollar bill, in his wallet. He, then, took out his two prom tickets and showed them to her. She looked at them and then gave him a kiss on his right cheek. They crossed the street, hand in hand. When they reached the car, he unlocked her side door and opened it. She gave a quick glance around and seeing no one, embraced him and planted her lips to his. They must have stood their, hugging and kissing each other for a good ten minutes. When, at last they let go of each other, she got in the car and he went around the front and unlocked his door and got in. "I wish we could go somewhere and park, but I've got to get home, baby!" He heaved a heavy sigh and said "I know! Me,too!" They drove back to her house. Johnny and The Hurricanes, were on the radio, playing "Red River Rock".

They sat in the car, in front of her, house and exchanged many, many kisses. Finally, she told him that she had to go in. He told her that he would try and call her later. She opened her door and closed it and walked up her walk. She exaggerated her "swing" and looked over her left shoulder, with a wide grin and blew him a kiss. He waited until she was in her house, before he put the car in gear and drove off, towards home. Lloyd Price was singing "Lawdy Miss Clawdy" on the radio.

He called her, after supper. There wasn't any answer. He went back to his room and tried to study for the math exam, that he would have to take. He couldn't concentrate. He kept checking his watch. It was 8 o'clock, when he, again, called Ree, still no answer. He knew that she and her family must have gone out, for the evening. He was just getting ready for bed, when the phone rang. It was 9:30 PM. His folks weren't happy. "Who the hell calls, after nine, in the evening?" His father yelled. He walked down the hall and picked the phone up on the sixth ring. It was Ree! She just wanted to tell him that she and her folks went out for dinner and had just returned. He told her that he called, at least twice, before he realized that she was out. She called, to tell him and to wish him a "good night." He thanked her and wished her a good night, too. They promised to talk to each other, the next day. He hung up the phone and went back to his room, thankful, that nothing bad had happened.

Wednesday, Thursday, and Friday were uneventful, at school. He picked up his tickets for the "outing" and the 'senior supper/night, in the gym. He and Ree talked a lot about their upcoming plans, for their respective proms. He told her how Fred and Bert weren't going and that Fred and June had split up. She told him that she didn't care, if the others weren't going. That it gave them more time for each other. She, also, wasn't surprised that June and Fred broke up. She mentioned that June had trouble holding on to a guy. June had a reputation, at school. of being too "easy." June's nickname, at school, was "peanut butter" thighs, because they easily spread open. Still, she was grateful that June and Fred had introduced them. He told her, that he would always be thankful for that. He didn't tell Ree, but he was also, thankful, that he felt no "feelings" of jealousy, around her. She, always, made a point of letting other guys know, that he was her man. Something Abby never did. Then, he and Abby were a lot younger.

The Friday night record hop went well. He and the other D.J. worked well together. He would "do" a set and take as break and then the other guy would take a break and he would "work". The dance started at 7:30 and didn't get over till 11:00 PM. He wore his "Spanish madras" sport coat. They played Ray Anthony's "The Bunny Hop". The other D.J. played somebody's "Hokey Pokey". He played The Diamonds, "The Stroll". All the kids joined in that dance, so he had to keep playing it until all the couples had a chance to go the center. The other DJ played Danny and The Juniors, "At The Hop". The last hour, of the dance, they played all slow numbers, such as Johnny and Joe's "Over The Mountain, Across the Sea", The Chimes, "Once

In A While", The Capris, "There's A Moon Out Tonight", and others. They ended the dance, with Earl Grant's "The End." He enjoyed doing the "work", but he missed Ree and wished she had changed her mind and been there.

He called her, around 10 AM, Saturday. They decided to meet at her house around five and go to the drive in. She told him that she wished she had gone with him Friday night. Especially, since he told her that they could have danced a lot of dances together. He told her that he really missed her and couldn't wait to see her and hold her in his arms, again. She felt the same. They chatted for over an hour. He got off the phone and sat down for his "usual" lunch. Afterwards, he went out to the VW and cleaned the interior. After doing that, he drove it to the gas station and filled it up. When he got back home, he walked in the door and his mom told him that Ree had called and wanted him to call her back. He was hoping all was okay and that the date, was still on. He called her back. Her sister answered the phone and when she discovered it was him, said "Hi sexy!" He was not expecting that greeting. Then he heard Ree take the phone from her. "Hey baby!" "Hey!" he said. "My sister thinks you are a dreamboat!" "Oh?" he replied, "and what does her older sister think?" "I know you are!" She said. "Good! "he said. "Cause you are my dreamboat!" She chuckled and then told him she had some news that he might not care for. He braced himself for the cancelled date. She told him that Janet and John wanted to come with them and that John would drive. At first, he wasn't too happy with the news. He really wanted to be alone with her Ree. He agreed, when Ree whispered into the receiver, "we'll have the back seat and they won't bother us, I promise." He would still drive over to her house and they would go in John's car. He felt the excitement grow in his pants, knowing they were going to be together, for the evening. She, then, added to his excitement, when she asked, "Want me to wear something sexy?" He told her that no matter what she wore, it was sexy!" She laughed and told him that he was "cute" and that she adored him. They hung up the phone and he, immediately, went up to his room and looked for something to wear, that she thought was sexy. He remembered she liked guys in jeans and a white shirt.

He arrived at her house, just after 5 Pm. John, Janet and Ree were standing outside the Plymouth. He parked right behind John's Plymouth. They had decided to stop at the new McDonald's on the way. John asked him, if he had eaten, there, yet. He replied that he hadn't. He would have offered his opinion, to go to the car hop, but Ree's lips got in his way. They got into the car and started on their way. Janet turned her head to ask Ree something, but turned her head back to the front. He and Ree were sharing their first passionate kiss, of the evening. They parted their lips, to take a breath. Ree asked him if he liked what she was wearing. She was. She was wearing a white peasant blouse, off the shoulder, showing just a little cleavage and plaid Bermuda shorts that were cut well above her knees. He nodded his approval. She pit her head to his neck and "drank" in his "old Spice". I really like your cologne, she said, but you are no longer at 14 or 15 year old, it's time for you to move up. You have a birthday coming up and I know what to get you." He was about to tell her that all he wanted for his birthday, was her! When Janet turned around and started talking about the upcoming prom. Janet told him that Ree's dress would not fit in the VW. He looked at Ree and she shook her head, no! He told them, that he might be able to get his brother's 1949 Mercury sedan. "That would be much better" said Janet. He and Ree settled back down in the seat. He bought his head to hers and, again, their lips pressed together. The kiss began, sweetly, with lips touching lips and then they began to move their lips over and around each other's lips. Soon, the opened their mouths, just enough, to let their tongues "dance" together. Her arms and hands were around his shoulders and his were on her bare shoulders, slowly moving her small sleeves down her arms. She realized what he was trying to do and wrenched her lips from his. With a heavy breath, she gasped, softly, "not yet, wait till dark, at the show." He nodded "okay" and they went back to embracing and kissing.

They pulled into the McDonald's parking lot. It was full. John drove around and, finally, found a place to park. They excited the car and went inside. The menu consisted of mainy burgers, fries, cold drinks, or frappes. The food was very inexpensive. They ordered cheese burgers, fries and frappes. The girl behind the counter, asked if they wanted onion rings or French fries. Ree stepped forward and told the girl, "French fries, No onions, we're going to the drive in." The girl smiled a knowing smile and said "gotcha!" They got their food and went and sat at a booth. He wasn't too impressed with his two cheeseburgers, but liked the fries. John said that he didn't think the place would "catch on" unless the added more to their menu. Janet said that the low prices made her think where they get their beef. They all agreed it was better than the food at the drive in. Once they finished, they got back in the car and headed for the show. When he and John paid, they found a spot in the back row. He told them that it was only his second time at the drive in, as a passenger. Ree insisted that he tell John and Janet the story of his first time, at the drive in. He could barely finish the story, everyone was laughing so hard. The girls decided that they had to use the restroom. John said, "you know, you never see two guys go to the restroom. How come girls have to go in pairs?" Janet answered, "because, we need to talk and we need to hold each other's hands." The guys laughed, as the two girls got out of the car and headed to the ladies room. John asked him, if he and Ree had been invited to the all night party, after the prom. He said that he hadn't heard about it. John said that he was sure that they had been. The guy, hosting it, has a huge house and is offering breakfast,too. John advised him to bring an extra pair of clothes, so he wouldn't have to spend the entire night and morning, in his tuxedo.

When the girls returned, he asked Ree, about the party, after the prom. She said she hadn't mentioned it, because she wasn't sure he would want to go. He told her, he would go anywhere she wanted to go, again, as long as she doesn't abandon him. John laughed and said, "That girl is not going to let you out of her sight. She might even follow you into the bathroom." They all laughed. Ree snuggled up to him and said that they had been invited and she really wanted to go. He brought her face, up to his and said, 'then we're going." Then. He kissed her, lightly, on her lips.

Dusk hadn't settled in yet, so they talked about the prom and Janet's pre-party. Ree told her that she would come over in the afternoon and help her set it up. Janet asked what he was doing? Ree answered, "he has a senior outing at some beach, that day." Janet told him, "better not come to the prom with a major sunburn." He told her and Ree that he would stay out of the sun, as much as possible.

Darkness set in around them. The newsreel came on the screen. He drew her to him and told her, "I'm not wasting time with the newsreel and cartoon and part of the first movie, this time" Ree chuckled and told him "you better not!" They slid, side by side on to the backseat. She positioned him, with his back towards the front. They began to kiss. Sweetly, at first and then very hot and heavy. She brought her left hand to his crotch and zipper. She pulled the zipper, down, slowly and inserted her hand inside, to his briefs. She found the opening and slipped her fingers inside to his manhood. He let out a gasp as her fingers touched him and his penis began to grow to her touch. "SHHH! Baby!" She whispered and closed her lips on his, again. He brought his right hand to her shoulder and slowly brought the small sleeve, off and down her arm. "Wait a minute!" She whispered and brought her hand out of his pants. She used her elbows to raise herself up slightly off the seat. She leaned against him and reached behind her back and unsnapped her bra strap. He brought his hands to her chest, as she repositioned herself to give him greater access to her breasts. Her hand returned to the place, she had taken it out. He used his hands to move her blouse down off her shoulders and then brought her bra straps off her shoulders and off her breasts. With her free hand, she removed her bra, the rest of the way and he took it from her and placed it on the floor of the car. Her blouse was bunched around her waist. In the dim light he could see that she was very excited. Her nipples were hard as erasers on brand new pencils. He moved his lips and tongue to them, first one breast and then the other. While his mouth paid homage to her left breast, his left hand massaged her right one. She began to softly moan. She increased her caresses on his penis. He repositioned himself, by putting his right leg over her hips and left leg. He brought his right hand from around her waist and put it, between her legs, resting on her inner right thigh. He moved his hand up her thigh to that "special juncture" between her thighs. He massaged her over her shorts. She began to press her pelvis against his hand. He looked up from her heaving breast and saw her head moving from side to side. Her right hand began to "rake "his side and back . . . Breathing heavy, she softly asked him to open the front of his shirt. He withdrew his hand from her breast and moved away just enough to unbutton his shirt. He didn't stop there, he stripped his shirt from his chest, so he laid open his bare chest. He took his mouth, from her breast and nipple and found her lips. She moved, in such a way that their naked chests pressed against each other. His hand continued to massage her pubic region as her hand continued to stroke his naked flesh. He pushed his finger against the 'crevice" between her "lips". He could feel wetness on the cloth of her shorts. She was softly babbling incoherently. He loved the feel of her nakedness against his. He could feel the hardness of her nipples against his. She was writhing "uncontrollably "against him. She brought her hand out from his pants and with both hands, she wrapped her arms and hands around him. He brought his left leg off her hip and leg. She opened her legs and wrapped them around his legs, trapping his hand between them. He was still able to move his finger over her moistness. Her breath was coming in short gasps. She, again, "raked his back with her fingernails. She thrust herself back and forth against his hand and pelvis. She put her head against his right shoulder, nipping his flesh and moaning, at the same time. She gave one strong thrust against him, cried out against him and., then her body released it's tension. She held onto him as she "seemed' to go "limp." She brought her hand back down to his pants and slipped her fingers inside. He knew he would make a "mess" if she continued her strokes. Through a gasping breath, he begged her to ease off. She gave his penis a very tight squeeze. It almost hurt, but it was enough to cause his "hardness" to ebb. She brought her hand back out, as they lay, holding each, very, very tight. He brought his face up to hers. She 'rained" kisses all over his face and neck. Bright lights brought them back from "their own little world. They pulled apart. She brought her blouse back over her breasts, but left her bra, off. He buttoned just the three bottom buttons of his shirt and zipped up his pants. They were both breathing quite heavily. Janet and John raised their heads from the bottom of the front seat. The girls said that they, again, had to use the ladies room. He said that it would be a good idea, if he went to the mens room. John agreed. The girls both said, "wait a minute! You two are going together to the mens room?" They said, "yeah!" The girls began to laugh. "Macho men going to the mens room, together. John realized what they were getting at and said, "okay. This time you got us." They all got out of the car. Ree covered up her chest with the blouse and crossed her arms across her chest. Janet asked if she was all right. She whispered to Janet, "no bra". Janet said, "oh, I'll walk ahead of you and help cover." Ree thanked her as the four of them headed for the rest rooms.

The guys came out of the their restrooms, first and waited, in front of the concession stand for the girls. Janet was walking in front of Ree. When they reached the guys, they parted. John started walking with Janet. He turned and waited for Ree to reach him. The spotlights made her top look almost invisible. He quickly stepped up to her and had her walk just ahead of him. She turned her head back over her right shoulder and asked why he was walking behind her and not beside her. He told her. She gasped! He told her that he was blocking the light. She thanked him. When they reached the car, the two of them climbed into the back seat. She took four sheets of paper towels from her purse, and put them on the "shelf" behind the back seat. He was confused. She put her finger to his lips and said, "trust me!" He nodded "okay". He, then. Realized he was quite thirsty. He asked if anyone else was thirsty. Everyone was. He offered to go get cokes. John said he would accompany him and help him bring them back.

As they walked to the concession stand, John said, "you do realize that Ree is absolutely crazy about you. If you, two survive college, you'll probably get married. She told Janet that was her plan. He beamed, at those words. Then he asked John about him and Janet. John said that they had already talked about it. He told him that he and Janet would probably get engaged next Christmas. He congratulated John. He, silently wished that he and Ree could do the same, but both of them were facing college.

They got back to the car, with the four cokes, just as intermission came to a close. They all sipped their drinks and talked some more about the prom. When they had finished their cokes, they put the bottles on the floor of the car. She lay down on the seat and took off her blouse. He lay down, almost on top of her and put his left hand to her right breast and his right hand to her left breast. She took her hands, unbuttoned his shirt and stripped it off him. She drew him to her and their lips crushed together. There was no sweet kiss, this time, just raw lust! Her fingers continued to rake his back! They broke the kiss and gasped for air. Then, he bought his lips and hands to her breasts. He raised himself off her just enough for her to get at his zipper. This time, she undid his belt, as well. Sliding his pants down to just below his buttocks. She put both her hands around his penis and began to stroke him. He brought his left hand from her right breast and moved it to the area, between her thighs. He stroked and massaged her, as she did the same to him. She increased her strokes, as he placed her '"rock hard" nipple between his lips and gently sucked it. She moaned, loudly and softly asked him to put "it ": between his teeth, but not to bite." He did as ordered. She felt his member grow, dramatically in width. He knew that if she kept it up, that he would create a mess. "Baby, you're going to bring me off!" he whispered. "That's what the paper towels are for, my sweet baby!" She whispered. "You brought me off, now it's my turn."

She rolled him onto his back. He had his back on the seat. She lay on top of him, still stroking him. He reached up and began to massager her hanging breasts, sliding his other hand up and down the sides, over the tops, down to the very bottom where they meet her chest bone, then back up again, teasing her nipples, all the while his other hand was causing her to get very 'wet". She brought her head down and he brought his lips from her nipple, Their tongues thrashed together! He could feel that he was about to "let go". She reached up and came back with the paper towels in her hand. She lifted herself up off him just enough. He gazed at her beautiful breasts and magnificent nipples. She began to "pump" him. "OH MY GOD!" he cried. She stifled his cries with her mouth, once again and covered him with the paper towels as he "soaked' them. She wiped him off and pulled his briefs and pants back up. She didn't zip him up, but instead, kept fondling him. They, once again, lay side by, his right hand slipped between her thighs and went back to caressing her. She put her head against his chest, OH sweet baby!" she cried into his chest. He slipped his hand up under the edge of her shorts, on her leg, up until he felt her panties. She "assisted him in lowering her shorts and panties, to her knees. His finger massaged her "outer lips" and then slipped in between. He explored around inside. She was thrusting herself against his hand. He found the "sensitive spot" and massaged it. She began to thrash and writhe against him. He could barely keep his finger inside her. She bit into his chest as her body gave another big thrust against him and then, once again, went "limp." They lay side by side, fondling each other. Her hand on his member; his hands on her breasts and nipples. They shared sweet, short kisses on each other's lips. They lay liked that through the rest of the show. Brightness showered the lot. They lay on their backs and pulled on their clothes. He reached down to the floor and retrieved her bra. They managed to get themselves dressed. John and Janet, apparently were in the throws of "passion" when the lights came on.

The Proms

"Queen Of The Senior Prom" (Vaughn Monroe)

He and Ree attempted to stifle their laughter as John and Janet struggled to get dressed, as other cars passed them by. While they were getting there last piece of clothing on, he opened his side window and deposited the four coke bottles and paper towels on the ground, beside the car. John, almost, in haste, to leave, forgot to put the speaker, back on the stand. He stopped the car, just in time. By now, he and Ree, were holding each other tight and laughing. Janet realized the humor, in it all, joined in. Pretty soon, the laughter was contagious and caught John. Rosie and The Originals were on the radio, singing," Angel Baby".followed by "Till" by the Angels.

Ree had swung her legs over his and positioned herself on his lap. Her arms encircled his neck and she nestled her cheek against his. He moved his mouth to her ear and whispered, "My heart, mind, soul and body are bursting with so much love for you." She squeezed her arms, tighter and whispered into his ear, "Oh my sweet baby, I love you with my whole heart and being and pray our love will last forever and ever." They continued to hold each very tight, the rest of the way, home.

He did not realize that they would not see each other until the night, of her prom. When he woke up that Sunday morning, he found excited noise, coming from downstairs. He got up out of bed and got into his jeans and a T-shirt. He went right down the hall, down the stairs, and into the living room. "Look who's home!" his mother yelled. Both of his brothers were standing in the middle of the living room, with their "bags". Dave had his suitcase and Phil, in uniform, had his seabag. He realized that Dave was home, from college, for the summer and Phil had been discharged from the Navy. His status, as being the "only child" was over. He shook both their hands and welcomed them home. His dad decided that they should all go "out" for breakfast. They were going to skip church. That would be a "first' for his folks. He was told to go back upstairs and get cleaned up and change clothes and get back downstairs, as soon as he could. He went, as he was told. While going up the stairs, he thought of the bible story of the "Prodigal son."

Later that afternoon, Dave attempted to start the Mercury. It had a dead battery. He came into the house and confronted him. "I thought I could trust you to run my car every other day!" he yelled. His mother came to his defense and told Dave that he had been very busy with school and his new girlfriend. Dave didn't seem to care and ranted about how he was having to buy a new battery. His heart sank. The idea of using the Mercury for the prom, seemed to "die". Dave said that he could never trust him to do anything, again. Phil didn't say anything, in fact, Phil hardly ever said anything. But he must have overheard him telling Ree, on the phone, that he probably couldn't get the Mercury, for the prom. He suggested that maybe the two of them could ride with John and Janet. Ree asked him, how was she supposed to get over to Janet's? He promised her, he would try and come up with a solution. When he hung up the phone, Phil came up to him. Seems Phil had a girlfriend. Someone, he had been seeing and writing to. She lived on the other side of town. Phil told him that he'd let him use the Jeepster, but it needed a lot of work and might not be the safest vehicle to take to the prom. He had an idea and picked up the phone. His girlfriend's name was Nan. He went downstairs, while Phil talked with Nan. Even when he was a little kid, Phil had a way of fixing things. Toys, bikes,model airplanes that had somehow gotten broken. Phil had fixed. He was sitting, in the den, listening, to his records, when Phil walked in. "Nan said you can use her 1951 Chevy coupe. Phil had done it again! He jumped up off the couch and grabbed his hand and shook it. Phil asked him when the prom was and he told him that it was that Friday. He, also, mentioned that he was going to be on a senior outing that day and wouldn't be back, at school until around 1:30PM. Phil said that he would pick him up and bring him home and he could, then, take Nan's car. He. Immediately called Ree and told her the good news. She was so happy. She told him that if he culd come over, she would show him her gratitude. He told her that he wish he could, but that his two brothers had just come home from the service and college. She understood and told him to call, when he could.

Monday, after school, he met Phil's girlfriend, Nan. He thanked her, profusely, for letting him use her car. Her only requirement, was that he return it "unscathed" and full of gas. He promised that he would. Dave was still upset about the Mercury and barely acknowledged his existence. He called Ree. Her sister answered the phone and said that Ree and her mother were at the seamstress's house, working on her prom gown. He asked her to let Ree know that he had called. When he got off the phone, he heard a big truck stop in front of the house. He looked out the living room window and saw Phil talking with the driver. They went to the back of the truck, opened the back doors and began to pull sheets and beams of lumber out of it. He went to the front door, opened it, and went out to see what was going on. He heard his brother Dave, slam the front door, behind him. He went to the truck. Phil asked if he could help unload it. He said sure and began to help. They carried the lumber down the driveway and deposited it inside the garage. It took about a half hour to completely unload the truck. When the truck had departed, he asked Phil what the lumber was for. Phil told him it was for his 18 foot cabin cruiser that he was going to build. He told Phil that he would be glad to help him. Phil thanked him and said that he would probably get started on Tuesday.

He would call Ree every night and see how she was doing. She complained that her dress wasn't exactly the way, she wanted it and that she was going to be with the seamstress every afternoon, till Friday. He told her that he felt bad, for her, having to go through all that trouble. He told her that she would look good and very sexy in a burlap bag. She laughed and told him that might be what she would be wearing, if things didn't go right.

He told her about, helping his brother, build his boat. She thought that was exciting and that she would like to see it. "You will!" he said, "it's going to be able to sleep two people." "Hmmm, she said, "that could be fun!" He told her that he would like to sail away somewhere, just the two of them. She told him that she liked that idea, very much. They wished they could see each other, before the prom, but it didn't look like that was going to happen.

When Thursday afternoon arrived, he asked his mom, if he could use the VW to go and get Ree's corsage and his tuxedo. Dave complained that if he hadn't wrecked his car, he wouldn't have the problems, he was having. He told his brother, that he thought about that every time, he borrowed his mom's car. She gave him the keys. He, first, went to the florist, in town, and told her that he needed a corsage. The woman asked what color was the girl's dress. He told her. She went in the back and ten minutes later came out with a beautiful wrist corsage that looked like it would be perfect. It was a big white flower, surrounded by little light green and yellow flowers. He paid her the ten dollars. She put the corsage in a plastic case and he left the store, beaming. Everything was coming together. He drove to the Tuxedo rental shop. He found a parking spot, right in front. He turned off the car, got out, closed the door and walked into the shop. He handed the clerk his "paid" receipt. The clerk went into the back and came out with the tuxedo, shirt, shoes and box. He opened the box, to check and make sure everything was there. He thanked the man and left the shop. He laid the tuxedo on the back seat of the car and drove home. When he arrived, he put the tux and shirt, and shoes, in his closet and the corsage, in the fridge. He called Ree, after supper, and told her that he had the tux and her corsage, and all he needed, was her. She told him that her dress was "perfect." They were both very excited and couldn't wait to see each other. She asked him to please come over to her house by 5PM. She was so excited to see how he would look in a tuxedo. He knew she was going to be a "vision" in her wait to see each other. She asked him to please come over to her house, by

5PM. Her folks wanted to take pictures. He said he would do his best. She, also, reminded him to bring extra clothes, casual, but no jeans. He said that he said he wanted some "alone time." She said, "absolutely!" They went over a check list for each other, one more time, to be sure they were set for Friday. Everything seemed to hinge on his getting back from his outing on time.

He awoke, early, on Friday. Took care of business, put on a fresh pair of underwear, jeans, socks, polo shirt and his Keds. He found a large bath towel and a pair of "old" bathing trunks. His new ones were at the cottage. He wrapped the trunks in the towel. He went back to the bathroom and looked under the sink and located a bottle of tanning oil. He tightened the cap and unrolled the towel and wrapped the oil in his trunks and then wrapped everything back up in the towel. Phil was up and offered to drive him to the school. He told Phil that he would help him with the boat on Sunday. Phil dropped him off, in front of building three, where there were about twenty yellow school buses. "How many kids are going?" Phil asked. He said that he didn't know, but was told that his senior class was the largest class ever, in the history of the school. Phil said that he would be back between one and one thirty, to pick him up. He thanked Phil and got out of the car. He walked towards the buses and found Fred and Bert. The three of them waited with others for the teachers, to arrive. They only had to wait five minutes. Mr. McDonald, the class advisor began to read the list in alphabetical order. Telling them, that when they heard their name, they were to go to one of the buses and hand the teacher, at the bus door, their ticket and get on board. The whole process took about a half hour. Then, they were on their way. Fred and Bert somehow managed to get on the same bus, as he. A girl, that was in his French class, sat in the aisle seat, next to him. They became good friends, duringschool and even flirted a lot. He leaned forward and looked over the back of his seat and talked with Fred and Bert. Betty was adamant in getting his attention, to talk with her. He sat back and gave in. Betty was kinda cute. She didn't look like the other Jewish girls, he knew. She laughed and said it was because her father was Italian. She had black hair, cut short, about the same length as Ree's. She had a nice sized bust, but not as big as Ree's. She wasn't fat and she wasn't skinny. If someone were to ask, he would say "normal". She liked to talk. He tried to ignore her and every now and then, would actually "tune in" to what she was saying. The ride to Ipswich beach lasted about an hour. When they arrived, they were told they could go anywhere they wanted; lunch would be served at the pavilion. They were to listen for the whistles, that would tell them when lunch was ready and when it was time to leave. He went to the dressing huts and quickly changed into his bathing suit. He kept his sneakers on, but rolled his jeans,shirt,socks and wallet into his towel. He carried the towel in one hand and the suntan oil in the other. He walked over the dunes and searched for Fred and Bert. Once he found them,he spread out his towel, put his clothes in a pile at one end, along with the oil. He took off the Keds and put them with his clothes. He stuck his wallet in the rear pocket of his jeans, out of anyone's sight. He proceeded to rub the oil, on his arms, face, hands and legs and his chest,too. Fred and Bert forgot to bring suntan lotion. They asked to borrow some. "Only if you'll give it all back." He said. They all laughed. When both of them were finished, they handed the bottle back to him. He put it with his clothes. Some guy came running up to them and said the volley ball net was up and they were being challenged by the girls. They got off their towels and went to join the game. Most of the girls were wearing two piece suits. The distraction of their 'bouncing" breasts, caused the guys to lose every game. The girls were getting tired of winning, but the guys wanted to keep on playing, for obvious reasons. The May sun was heating him up. He left the game and ran down to the water. He "tested" the water and found it too be 'cool" but not" ice" cold. He ran back up the sand, found a spot, turned around and ran into the water, until his feet could no longer move and he dove in. When he broke the surface, he began to spit out the salt water from his mouth. He knew, then, why he liked fresh water better. He was about to start swimming, when he saw Fred and Bert racing through the water, at him. Their splashed nearly blinded his eyes with the salt. The three of them swam for a little bit and he realized that he was going to have to put more oil on, after swimming.

The three of them came out of the water, walked to their towels and dried off, in the sun and then put more oil on. It was then that they heard the "lunch" whistle. Lunch consisted of hot dogs, bags of chips and cokes. Several tables had been set up to accommodate everyone. Mr. McDonald warned them, through a bull horn, not to go in the water, right after eating. Fred turned to him and Bert and said, "sounds just like my mother!"

After lunch, they rested on their towels, again, until they heard that another volleyball game was going on. Of course, they got up and joined. Again, the guys were, too distracted, to win. They must have played about six games. He found himself sweltering in the afternoon sun and decided to go back in the water.

He came out of the water and went up to his blanket and this time, he took the towel and dried himself off. He put the blanket back down on the sand and replaced his clothes back on it. He took the oil and began to put it on his arms, face, legs and chest. A female voice, from behind him, said "give me the bottle and I'll rub it on your back. He didn't even turn around to see who it was. He handed the bottle, to whoever it was. She instructed him to lay down on his towel. He felt her "bare" legs straddle his hips. Her hands felt so good as she massaged the oil onto his back. She got off and then he felt her hands slide over the backs of his legs. He was beginning to get excited. He was afraid to roll over and let everyone know about his "condition". "Okay", the girl said, "my turn." She lay down on his towel, next to him. He looked over as she handed the bottle to him. It was Betty. She wore a two piece suit that left very little to his imagination. He couldn't stop staring at her breasts. She smiled and then lay down on her stomach. He poured a little amount of oil on her back and proceeded to massage it on. He worked it on her shoulders and onto her back, pouring small amounts and working it into her skin. "OOOh!" she said, your hands are like velvet on my skin." "That's what my girlfriend says!" He told her. "Lucky girl!" She said. He had just finished the small of her back, right above her suit. "Now my legs" She ordered. He poured more on each leg and worked it in, on her ankles, calves, behind her knees and up to her thighs. She began to softly moan. "Damn!" He thought. "She's getting hot and bothered." When he finished, he capped the bottle and put it by his clothes. Fred and Bert were still playing volleyball. He lay back down, on his stomach. She put her arm across his back and leaned in and gave him a kiss on his cheek. Then, she whispered, in his ear, "why don't we go into the dunes and I'll really thank you!" He couldn't believe what he was hearing! He turned to face her and she moved in and pressed her lips to his and jabbed her tongue against his teeth, until he opened his mouth. She pressed her breasts against his arm. He attempted to free himself from her. As he pulled away, he saw that her nipples were straining against her top. She saw how "excited" he was and reached out and put her hand on him. She traced him over his suit. "Come on, sweetie, I've wanted to fuck you for a long time." He was in shock! That was the first time, he had ever heard a girl use that word. He tried to resist! She was adamant! He fell on his back, trying to escape! She was on him like flies on flypaper! Her lips pressed against his, her body lay on top of his, writhing, thrusting against him. "Hey!" said a man's voice, "Knock it off!" it was Mr. McDonald! She was all over him, with her hands until Mr. McDonald, literally pulled her off him. He looked up at the class advisor and thanked him, profusely and then got up and ran into the water, waist high and hoped no one saw his enraged erection. He turned and saw Mr. McDonald taking Betty, by the arm, somewhere. He relaxed and stood still, in the water. He could feel the sun's reflection heating him up. The cool water settled him down. he was coming out of the water, when he heard the whistle blow, telling them, it was time to leave. He ran up to the towel, dried himself off, grabbed his 'stuff" and was about to leave when Bert and Fred arrived to get their stuff. "Did you hear?" Fred said, "some girl sexually attacked one of the guys and that's why we're leaving early. Bert wondered aloud" hmm wonder who it was?" They both said, "lucky guy! She must have really had the "hots" for him, to do it right here on the beach, in front of everyone." All he said was "yeah!" as they gathered their gear and headed to the changing huts. Once, on the bus, he was glad, Betty was not on it.

Before the bus, they were on, began to move. Mr. McDonald came on the bus and walked up to him. He sat next to him and told him that the girl confessed that it was all her fault. He said, "apparently, she is quite taken with you. We won't mention this to anyone, okay?" He said. Bert and Fred were silent, in the seat, in front of him, but they, obviously overheard everything. Mr. McDonald got out of the seat and looked at Bert and Fred and said, "You guys won't say anything either, will you boys?" "No sir!" They said, in unison. The class advisor got off the bus and told the driver to start it up and get going. Fred and Bert, both put their heads up over the back of their seat and looked at him. "You will tell us all the horny details!". "later!" he promised. He lay his head back against the seat and felt his eyes get sleepy.

"Hey!" We're back!" His eyes flew open, when he heard Bert and Fred. He gathered up his stuff and, finally, got off the bus. He asked Fred, what time it was. Fred told him that it was only 1:15PM. He sighed a sigh of relief. He looked for his brother. He wasn't there, yet. Fred and Bert stood next to him and said "okay, so what happened on the beach?" He told them. They stood there, their eyes, wide open and mouths a gape! He didn't need to add anything. Then, he saw Phil drive up. He said "goodbye' to the guys and ran to his brother's car.

Phil looked at him, as he got in the car, "you got some sun. hope it doesn't hurt." He replied that he was fine and he thanked him, again, for picking him up. Phil turned off his radio. He liked to listen to Country and Western Music. He asked him what had happened to his car. He told him the whole story, as Phil drove. They both said it was a stupid thing for him to do. He wished he still had the car, then, he wouldn't have to keep borrowing his mom's car or Nan's. Phil was a lot more understanding than Dave.

It was just after 2PM, when they arrived at their house. The Chevy was not there! Phil said, "relax, she'll be here at three!" He thanked Phil, again, and went into the house, straight up the stairs, to his room. He stripped off his clothes. He took a fresh pair of briefs out of his dresser, along with fresh black socks. He looked out his door and made sure no one around and ran, naked, down the hall, to the bathroom. He ran the water in the tub and once it was at the right level, turned it off and put the stopper over the drain and climbed in. He soaked in it, until the water turned cold. He got out brushed his teeth, dried himself off. Put the deodorant on under his arms and splashed some "Old Spice" on his cheeks, the sides of his cheeks and even some on his pubic hairs, for "luck". He wrapped a towel around his waist and walked back down to his room. He went to his closet and withdrew the white tuxedo shirt. He took off the plastic and to his "horror" found it had "French cuffs". He, immediately, went down the hall, to the top of the stairs. He hollered to his mom and said the shirt has French cuffs. His mom yelled back, up to him. "Your dad thought it might. Look on the top of your dresser, he left some cuff links for you! Slide the pin part through the holes with the flat part, facing out." You'll be fine!" he sighed a sigh of relief and went back into his room. There, on the top of his dresser were two sets of cufflinks. One set was black and the other, gold. He looked at both and wasn't sure which ones, he liked best. So,he put on the shirt and tried, first one set and then the other. He decided that the black ones would match the black pants. He took the shirt off and laid it on the bed. His Mom yelled back up at him, that if the shirt didn't have buttons, there were "studs" on the dresser, as well. He looked at the shirt and realized he couldn't have buttoned it, if it didn't have buttons. "It's got buttons!" he yelled down to her. "Good!" She yelled back. He put a pair of polished chino slacks and a red and white pinstriped shirt on hangers and laid them on the bed, next to the tux,shirts socks and the box. He looked at his watch 3:10PM. "Nan should be here," he thought. He threw on the jeans, that he wore, for the outing and a fresh T-shirt. He went down stairs and looked out the living room window, no Chevy! He went out the back door, across the driveway, to the garage. Phil was setting up a "steam box". He asked him what it was and how it worked. Phil told him, on Sunday, with his help, they will heat up the steam box and put the beams in it. The steam will wet the wood and make it easy to bend. Phil went back to work and he watched. When he had the box "set up" he looked at his watch. 3:45PM. He wondered out loud, what was keeping Nan? Phil said, to him, I'll go call her." They walked up the driveway, together, just as the Chevy pulled up. He sighed a heavy sigh of relief. "Had to get gas" She said, as she climbed out of the car. "it's and automatic, so it's real easy to drive, except that it doesn't have power steering." He thanked her, as she handed over the keys. "Just remember, return it with a full tank and no scratches." He promised and thank her, again. He looked at his watch and realized he had just enough time to get dressed and get over to Ree's.

He ran into the house, up the stairs and into his room. He got out another fresh pair of briefs and took off the "old" ones and put the others on. He sat on the bed and took off the Keds, which he had thrown on, just to go outside sans socks. He found the, still damp, towel by the foot of the bed, on the floor and "wiped" feet, with it and deposited it back where he found it. He sat on the bed and donned the black socks. Then came the shirt, with the black cuffs. He turned and opened the box and took out the "cheater" bow tie and fastened it around his neck and under the collar of the shirt. He finished buttoning the rest of the buttons. Next came the pants. He put in one leg after another and brought them up to his waist. He buttoned them and zipped up the zipper. He noticed that they had loops for a belt. "better safe than sorry" he said. He took a black belt out of his closet and looped it through and "fastened" it. He went to the box and took out the suspenders. It took him a while to get them right, so there were no twists in them. He finally had them 'right' and snapped each strap to his pants. He, then, brought out the cummerbund and fastened it around his waist. He fastened it, in front, and then moved the snap around to his back. He looked in the mirror and was glad that the belt was hidden. He went back to the box and found the "pocket napkin". The top was real, but the bottom was cardboard. He placed it in the breast pocket of the jacket and it fit in beautifully. He just hoped that Ree would not need to use it. He put on the coat and looked at himself in the mirror. "You handsome devil!" he said. He took the jacket off and put it back on the hanger and placed the plastic wrap over it. He, then, sat down and put on the shiny shoes. After he tied the laces, he went to his bank and took out 45 dollars. He placed it with the other money, in his wallet. He, then put some Brylcreem in his hair and combed it. He combed it four times, before he was satisfied with his looks. He noticed that the day's sun had lightened it. He was almost, a blonde! He picked up the chinos and shirt, along with the white coat. He reached under the plastic and put his wallet in the inside breast pocket. He smoothed the plastic wrap over it and walked down the hall, down the stairs, to the living room. His mom had the camera ready and took his picture, as he walked into the room. Everyone, including his brothers liked the way he looked. He froze, for a moment. He forgot the keys to the Chevy. He put the clothes over the back of a chair and ran up to his room. He put his hand in the jeans, he had worn and fished out the keys. He put them in the front pocket of the pants. He checked his watch. 4:25PM. He went downstairs and picked up the clothes from off the back of the chair and proceeded out of the house. Everyone wished him "good luck" and a good time and "have fun!". He hung the clothes on the back hook, inside the car, near the side window. He was about to get in the car, when he heard his mom yell. He looked back at the house and saw her holding Ree;s corsage. Damn! She came up to him, out of breath and handed it to him. He thanked her so much. He placed it on the seat, next to where he would sit. He got in and put the car in neutral and turned the key and started it up. He put it in "D" and drove off towards Ree's. Perry Como was on the radio, singing "Magic Moments". Followed by Sonny Knight and "Confidential". That was followed by Elvis and "Stuck on You." He prayed that he hadn't forgotten anything else.

He arrived at Ree's two minutes after 5. He turned off the car and put it in "P" for park. He got out. Reached behind the front seat and took the white jacket off it's hanger. He put it on. He reached into the front seat and picked up the corsage, Thanking his mom, silently. He took the keys out of the ignition and put them, in his pocket and closed the door. He walked up the front walk, towards the front door. Her sister came around the side of the house and gave a low wolf whistle. He smiled and she told him that everyone was in the backyard, waiting on him. He followed her around the house and came to a "dead" stop, when his eyes fell on Ree. He almost dropped the corsage! "Beautiful! Gorgeous! Stunning! Lovely!" There were no words to describe her looks. Her hair was perfect, and the dress, the dress, was amazing!" He walked up to her and handed her the corsage. He took it out of the plastic and then placed it on her wrist. Her Mom and Dad, both had their cameras and were snapping pictures, like crazy! Her dad went into the house, but came back out a few minutes later. Her mom was still taking pictures. Her Dad walked up to them and addressed him. "What do you think of my little girl? Beautiful, right? He was tongue-tied. Finally he spoke, to her. "you are a princess! The most beautiful girl in the entire world. I feel so very proud to be your escort tonight!" Her father said, "well put, son! Don't you think that you, two, are too good looking, she is too pretty, to be riding to her prom, in an old Chevrolet?" His heart sank. "You're right, sir, but it was the best I could do." Ree looked at him, sadly. Then her dad handed him the keys to his 1959 Ford Galaxy. "Take my car, you two need to ride in style, tonight." He looked at the keys, in his hand, and then at her dad. He gulped, "Thank you, just doesn't seem to say enough,sir" her dad just said "Have a great time, tonight!" Ree took his arm and looked at hiswatch, "we need to go!" She said, "Thanks Daddy, I love you!" They walked to the back door, of the garage and he opened it for her. They entered the garage and walked to the passenger side of the car, he opened it and held her pocketbook as helped her into the car. He handed her the pocketbook and closed the door, slowly, to make sure her dress wouldn't get caught. He went around to the driver's side and got in. He closed his door and put the key in the ignition; started the car and slowly backed it out of the garage, down the driveway and into the street. He stopped and put it in "D" and they went, on their way, to Janet's. "I'm impressed! My father has never done THAT before! He must really like you!" As he slowly, drove the Galaxy, he noticed the red leather-like interior that went so well with the black exterior. "I'm still in shock!" he said, "I'm sitting next to the most beautiful girl In the world, driving a gorgeous car!" I feel like I've died and gone to heaven!" He pulled up in front of Janet's, behind John's Plymouth. He turned off the car, put it in "P" and got out and went around to her side, opened her door, took her small pocketbook and helped her out of the car. He closed the door. He made sure both doors were locked and then escorted her to Janet's front door. Janet must have seen them pull up. She opened the door and exclaimed how pretty Ree looked and gave a low grrr to him. "If you weren't with her, I'd dump John and go after you." Then she looked at the car. Is that your Dad's car?" She exclaimed. "uh huh" said Ree. "He let you drive it tonight?" She said to him. "He must think the world of you! No one else ever got to go near that car, not even Ree!" She exclaimed. He was feeling so proud! He could not have been happier. They went into the house and he was introduced to everyone. He was starved! He saw the long table with finger sandwiches and pink punch in a large bowl. Janet's mother ushered everyone outside, to take a group picture. There were five couples. Not one girl could even come to close, to Ree. John saddled up to him. After the pictures were taken and wanted to know how he got Ree's dad to let him drive the car. "He just offered it and gave me the keys." He said. They went back inside and were standing around the punch bowl. He ate three small chicken salad finger sandwiches. He poured some punch into the small plastic cup and was about to drink it, when, out of nowhere, Ree's right arm came up and made contact with the cup, sending its' contents up and over the edge, into the air and on to the right pocket of his white tuxedo jacket. He and Ree star4ed in disbelief as the red splotch seemed to grow before their very eyes. Janet's mother saw the "accident" and rushed up to him, "take the coat off, right away, I can fix it!" he did as she said. Now, he was the only guy standing without a tuxedo jacket. Ree was, almost crying, she was so upset. She was afraid that he was going to walk out and never see her again. Janet took her into another room to console her. John said," I hope for everyone's sake, her mom can get that stain out." His "euphoric" state of mind had just "crashed". He wanted to go to Ree, to let her know he would not leave her for something like that. The other couples started to leave the party and head for the prom. John stayed with him and asked if he and Janet could ride with them to the prom. He said, he guessed they could, if in fact, the coat can be cleaned. He poured another cup of punch and stepped away from John and drank it. "HALLELUJAH!!! Janet's mom came back into the room with the white coat. it was spotless! Janet and Ree came back in from the other room. Ree's eyes were a little puffy, but she had applied enough makeup to cover them up. Her mom handed the coat to him and told him it might still be a little damp, but the stain was gone! He was so appreciative! He put on the coat and stepped forward and Janet's mom a kiss on the cheek, as did Ree. "Time to go!" said Janet. John told her that she and he were riding in style that night! Ree grabbed his right arm and squeezed it very tight. The four of them walked to the galaxy and he went and unlocked the doors, for the girls. John helped Janet in and he helped Ree in. Ree looked up at him and whispered "I love you!" he smiled at her and whispered the same thing back to her. He and John went around to their side of the car. He unlocked their doors and they both got in. doors were closed he put the key in the ignition and started the car and put it in "D" and pulled out from behind John's Plymouth and off they went to the prom. The Safaris were on the radio,singing "The Image of A Girl." Fats Domino followed with "Blueberry Hill." He told Ree that he didn't know her dad liked Rock and Roll. She said that he didn't and that he must have changed the station, for them. Before he gave him the keys. He pulled the galaxy up to the side door, of the school, the door, all the kids were going in. he put the car in park. He opened his door and went around and opened Ree's door and then Janet's. Once they were out of the car, he closed the doors and went around and got in his side. John stayed with the girls, while he went and parked the car. He found a spot, away from all the other cars. He put the car in park and turned it off, taking the keys from the ignition, and dropping them in his right pocket of his coat. He sat in the car, for a moment. He was about to embark on yet another milestone, a senior prom, with an amazingly beautiful girl. That and practically being raped by another girl on the beach, earlier, sure made this a day for milestones.

He got out of the car and made sure the doors were locked. He walked back to the where Rees, Janet and John were waiting. As he approached them, he couldn't take his eyes off her. Again, he felt that she was out of his class. With her heels on, she was about an inch taller than him. He didn't care, he was in love. As they walked in the building, the sounds of the Drifters singing "Save The Last Dance For me" echoed down the large hall. They came to a table, where two younger girls were sitting, Ree opened her pocketbook and produced the tickets. The girls had a list and checked off her name and "guest." They went through large doors into what is usually a large gym. Tonight, it looked like a large ballroom. There were tables and chairs all around a large dance floor. A D.J. was atop a large platform that had four very large speakers. He told her that he was impressed. Ree told him not to be, that her class did not have a lot of money and had to make "do." They found a table for four and took their seats. There was a small buffet table set up with a variety of appetizers and bowls of punch, or bottles of cokes. He opted for a bottle of coke, saying that he had his "full" of punch that night. Ree was the only one that didn't find that funny. "I said I was sorry, baby!" She said. He put his arm around her and told her that he was just trying to make her laugh. The Everly Brothers were on the turntable, singing "Dream," He asked her to dance. They got up from the table and moved to the dance floor. They held each other very tight and swayed to the music. He told her that she was THE most beautiful girl at the entire prom. She brought her cheek, from his and pressed her lips to his.

They danced every slow dance and only jitterbugged a couple of times, because of her gown. They stayed for the entire dance. It was well past 11:00 PM, when the king and queen and their courts were announced. After their dances, there was time for two more slow dances. During their last dance, Ree wrapped her arms around his neck and they shared a long, passionate kiss that lasted the entire song.

The four of them met at the table and made plans for the "after prom" party. He would drop Janet and John off at Janet's and then he and Ree would drive to her house. He would park the car in her garage and change into his other clothes, in the garage and meet her and they would go to the party, in the Chevy. They would meet Janet and John, at the party.

He and John went to get the galaxy. They rode together, back to the same door, that he dropped everyone off at. The guys got out of the car and helped the girls back into the car and they drove off into the night. Ree, no longer cared about the condition, of her gown, slid up next to him and put her left arm over his shoulders and her right hand rested on his right thigh. She whispered in his ear, how handsome he looked, in the tuxedo and how she wanted to rip off his clothes, on the dance floor and make "mad passionate love" with him. He told her he wanted to do the same thing with her.

They dropped John and Janet off and headed to Ree's. He drove the car into the garage, turned it off and took the keys out of the ignition and handed them to Ree. They turned and faced each other and wrapped their arms around each other and crushed their lips together. "pent up passion" drove them into a kissing "frenzy". When they separated, to breathe, Ree, breathing heavily, gasped, "not in a car, especially my dad's." He, through, panted breath agreed. He got out of the car, closedhis door and walked around and opened her door. He helped her out. Again, they embraced and lops crushed against lips, tongues lashed with tongues, he pressed her against the Galaxy's right fender. His right leg went between her legs, crushing the her gown. Her arms held him tight around his neck. Once, again, the need to breathe, separated their lips. Ree was the strongest of the two. "We need to change and go to the party." She gathered herself together and gave him a short kiss and went into the house. He closed 'her' door to the car and went to the Chevy. He grabbed his clothes, that were hanging in the car and brought them up to her garage. He took off the jacket and placed it on the hood of the car, took of the tie and put it in one of the coat's pockets, next came the cummerbund. It went into a pocket. He took off the cuff links and placed them on the coat. He took off the shirt, and replaced it with the red and pink striped shirt. He undid the suspenders and took off the belt. He was glad he included the belt, because he would have had a difficult time, keeping the chinos up. He unlaced his shoes and took them off. The floor of the garage was cold to his stocking feet. He took off the pants and hung them on the hanger, his shirt was on, then, put the shirt on the hanger. He put on the chinos, put on the belt and put on the shoes and laced them. He put the cuff links in his pants pocket and put the coat on the hanger that the chinos were on. He took the Chevy's keys out of the left hand pocket of the coat. he did all this in the dark. He hoped he had done everything well and left nothing behind. He took the hangered clothes to the Chevy and put them on the hook, that his other clothes had been on. He turned and started back to see if Ree was ready. He looked up and saw her running towards him. She had on a white shirt, probably one of her dad's and jeans. She still looked gorgeous! She rushed into his arms, pressed him against the driver's side door and crushed her lips to his, with her arms around his neck. He put his arms around her back and the passion of their kiss, grew like gasoline being thrown on an open flame. They went wild in their desire, for each other. Then reason began to take over and they disengaged themselves from each other. They were, both, breathing quite heavily, as he opened her door. She got in and moved over to the be close to him. He went around the front, a little unsteady, on his feet. He opened his door and got in behind the wheel. He wanted, so much, to grab her and throw her down on the seat and rip her clothes off and love her! He put the key, in the ignition and started the car. She laid her back against the back of the seat and let out a large, audible, sigh. "I think there is more than one motor running, right now." She said. He looked at her and they both began to laugh. Their laughter seemed to ease the sexual tension between them.

She gave him directions to the party. When he pulled onto the road, he couldn't believe all the cars that were parked on either side, of the street. He, slowly, cruised along and then he saw John getting out of the Plymouth, and that there was a space, just in front of the car. He pulled in and parked the Chevy. John and Janet waited for them, to get out of the car. He turned off the car and got out, closed his door and walked around the front, to help Ree out. She was already out of the car. He walked up and closed the door and locked it, as Ree walked up to John and Janet. He went back to his side of the car and locked that door and then joined the others. John had hoped that the two of them would stick together, if the girls decided to migle with their friends. Ree put her right arm around his waist and told John that she was not letting go of him. He put his left arm around her waist as they walked up the front walk to the screened in porch. They opened the door and went in. The front door was wide open. The walked into the front room that was "loaded" with kids, drinking, dancing and some making out as they stood. It was a sea of humanity. Ree let go of his waist and pulled him by his hand towards what she assumed was the dining room. Janet and John followed them. When they entered the room, the came upon a very large table, that had many, many, different foods on it. There was Chinese, pizzas, different types of sandwiches, different types of snacks and paper plates and plastic utensils. He was ready to stop and grab something to eat, but Ree pulled him along to what they discovered was a kitchen. On one counter was six different bottle of whiskey, run and vodka. On another counter were four large kegs of beer. Large plastic cups were piled high on yet, another counter. He whispered in Ree's ear, This is what I would, call a party!" She laughed, as he "tapped" a keg and filled up two cups with beer. He made sure that they wouldn't just get a lot of foam. They went back into the dining room and he put six slices of pepperoni pizzas on a large plate. He had both hands full, as he followed Ree, to find a place to sit and consume their food and beer. They waded through more kids, she stopping to say hi and introducing him to "faceless and "nameless' people. She spied a chaise lounge on a side porch, that appeared to be "kidless". They moved to it and sat down, sharing it. Next to it, was another one. John and Janet shared that one. The noise level was not as high, as inside the house. They never got to meet the host/hostess. They ate their food and drank the beer. Through the "din" of the crowd, inside, he heard Elvis, on the hi fi singing "Hound Dog." He surmised it had to be an album, because next came "Loving You", followed by "All Shook Up." When they finished, they left their "trash" in a barrel by the door and went back into the "fray". Again, Ree held his hand and pulled him through the crowd. They came upon a door. She opened the door, that led to a dimly lit room. They entered the room. John and Janet right behind them. When their eyes adjust to the "darkness", they discovered it was a "make out" room. She saw an empty, easy chair and dragged him to it. She turned and pulled his arm around and pushed him into it. His back went up against the back of the chair, causing it to "level out." She put her hands on his legs and pushed them together and then she maneuvered herself on him, straddling his legs and waist. He didn't know if Janet and John had found similar accommodations or not. He really didn't care. Ree leaned in and unbuttoned her shirt and then his shirt. She was breathing very heavy, as she took his hands and placed them on her bra covered breasts. She leaned in closer to his face and he leaned up. Her hands snaked around his neck, as their lips met in unbridled passion. It was as if there had been no respite from their kisses beside the Chevy. When their lips parted, she took her hands from his chest and reached behind her back and undid the clasp on her bra strap. His hands pushed the loosened bra over her breasts. "Oh baby!" she whispered," please put your lips and tongue on them, the way you've done before." Her hands went to the back of his head and guided him to her breasts. When his lips reached their destination, she brought her left hand from the back of his head and moved down to his waist, between them. She raised her pelvis, just enough to give her hand room to find his zipper. She, slowly unzipped him, so as not to "alert" anyone else as to what she was doing. She snaked her hand between the teeth of the opened zipper and found the opening of his briefs. She moved her hands all over his flesh. He began to grow, quickly, in her hand. His lips, on one nipple, began to suck a little harder. He brought his right hand to her right breast and caressed every inch, moving closer to the nipple. His left hand massaged the bottom of her left breast, as his lips and tongue brought it to complete hardness. She moved her upper torso, closer to his chest, giving him more access to her breasts. He brought his mouth of her left nipple and was moving over to her right one, when her right hand came around and brought her hand to his chin and tilted his face up to hers. She stabbed her tongue inside his mouth, her lips crushing his. They were completely lost, in their passion. They were alone in the world. No one else even mattered. The world could have come to a crashing end, wiping out all man and womankind. They didn't care! She would run her hand, all over him, from shaft to head and back again. When she 'felt' him begin to "swell", she would squeeze him. Extremely hard, causing a little bit of pain, but preventing him from making a mess. They lost all meaning of time and space. When they separated their lips, she whispered in his ear, "I want to climax, baby, please make me go off." He brought his left hand from her breast, down past the brim of her jeans. He unbuttoned the buttons on them and found her panties. He slipped his hand, under the cloth and moved it down over her pubic hair, to that wet, warm cleft. She buried her head against his right shoulder, her teeth sank into his flesh. He slipped his middle finger inside her. She began to thrust her pelvis against his hand. He moved his finger slowly, in a circular motion. He found the spot that seemed to be the most sensitive to her. He moved his mouth back to her right breast and put his lips on her "erect" nipple. His mouth, on her breast and nipple and his finger massaging inside her and on her 'spot." She began to writhe against him, thrusting her pelvis back and forth against his hand. It didn't take long. She gave one big push, against him, so hard, that the chaise lounge creaked and groaned and nearly tipped over. He felt "juices" awash his finger and even come out on the rest of his hand. She seemed to collapse against him. She brought her hands up and around his neck. He brought his lips and tongue, from her breast and up from below. They gave each other a tight embrace. She, again, rained short kisses all over his face, muttering how wonderful a lover, he was and how she was never going to let him go. He expressed how much he loved her and would never let her go, either.

Before they knew it, they could smell bacon frying in a skillet. She raised her self up and refastened her bra and buttoned up her shirt and jeans. She, also, buttoned his shirt and zipped him up. They got off the chaise lounge and went to investigate. They couldn't believe, when they left the dim room, that the rest of the house was engulfed in sunlight. They went into the dining room and found big platters of scrambled eggs, bacon, toast and a large coffee urn. The size of the crowd had diminished, greatly. They got their food and coffee and walked out of the dining room and out onto the front porch. John and Janet were already sitting in a couple of deck chairs, eating. They found two empty chairs and sat down. Janet giggled and told Ree, "you really need to control your moans and groans, you two." He felt the warmth creep up his face. Ree just made a face, at Janet. They looked at him and Ree said "Aw Poor baby, you're blushing! You've nothing to be ashamed of, at least my lover makes me moan!" Janet stuck her tongue out at her and then they all laughed. He, thought to himself," wonder how my prom could even compare with this."

Once they had finished their breakfast, their bodies began to tell them, that they needed rest. He told Ree that he really needed to get the Chevy back to his brother's girlfriend. They got up and deposited their "trash" in the trash can, on the porch. They said "Good morning" to John and Janet and went out through the screen door. When they reached the Chevy, Ree was starting to lose it. He opened the door and helped her into the car, and closed it. She moved over towards his side and put her head back against the back of the front seat. He got in and closed his door and put the key in the ignition and started the car. He put it in "D" and made a "u-turn" and headed back down the road, to Ree's house. He glanced over to her. She was asleep. He said "I love you." She mumbled something, inaudible.

He pulled up into her driveway. He turned off the car, put it in park and reached over and stroked her cheek, with his right hand. She began to stir. He said, "Hey! Sleeping beauty! You're home! She began to stir, some more, He shook her shoulder and, once again, urged her to wake up. The third shake, did the trick. "Where are we?" She mumbled. "You're home," he said. "Okay!" She said and opened both eyes. She apologized for falling asleep. He told her not to be silly, that she, obviously, was very tired. He got out of the car and went around to her side and opened the door. She, slowly, saddled over and swung her legs out of the car. He grabbed her arms and pulled her, cautiously, from the car. Once, the cool morning air hit her in the face, she blinked and was fully conscious. They walked into the garage, to the garage door. He took his left arm and hand away from her waist and opened the door, to the kitchen. Her mom was at the kitchen sink. Her mom looked at the both of them and quickly surmised that they had been up all night. Ree turned to him and gave him a kiss on the cheek and said "Goodnight." He chuckled, as she walked past her mom and disappeared into another room. He said "good bye" to her mom. Her mom told him to put the windows down in the car and turn up the radio, so he wouldn't fall asleep, at the wheel. She offered him some coffee, but he declined and assured her, he was fine. He turned and went out the door, to the garage. He went over to the passenger side and closed the door and then went to his side. He got in, closed the door and turned the ignition key and started the car and backed it down the driveway.

He did, as her mom directed, rolled down his window and turned the radio volume up. Elvis was on the radio, singing, "Don't Be Cruel." He sang along.

He parked Nan's car in front of his house. He turned off the motor and put the car in park. He opened the door and got out and closed the door behind him, and locked the car. He went into the house and deposited the keys, to the Chevy on the front hall table. He, slowly, walked up the stairs, down the hall, to his room. Once inside, he closed the door and walked to the bed. He turned and sat down and took off the shoes and lay back down on the bed. He didn't remember his head hitting the pillow.

For some reason, he bolted awake! He suddenly remembered that he had to get the rentals back to the store, before noon. He got off the bed and went to grab the shoes. They were gone! He ran out of the room, in his stocking feet, down the hall, down the stairs, into the kitchen. No one was there! He looked in the living room, empty! He looked in the den, no one! He was beginning to panic. He looked out the window, in the den, to the street, in front of his house, the Chevy was gone! He looked at his watch, 2:35PM! He paced around the house. He just knew that he was going to have to pay for a "lost" tuxedo, shirt, pants, and the rest. He sat at the kitchen table and put his head on the top of it. He heard a noise and looked up. His mom came through the back door and said, "Well, I see you finally came back to the world of the living." He responded by saying, he wished he was dead. His mom asked him if all was all right with him and Ree. He said, "of course, never better, but, I lost the tuxedo, shirt, shoes, pants, and all the rest of the stuff and even his dad's cufflinks." His mom reached into her purse and withdrew the cufflinks. "You mean these?" She asked. He looked up at her with a questionable look. "I realized that, since you were sound asleep, the clothes had to be back before noon. I went to Nan's car and got them out, then to your room and picked up the shoes, rolled you over on to your stomach and fished your wallet out of your pocket and got the receipt and took everything back." He jumped out of the chair and gave his mom a great big hug and a tremendous "Thank you!".

He spent the rest of the day, slipping in and out of sleep, on the couch, in the den, in front of the TV. His mom and brothers kept trying to get him to get up and go to his room and go to sleep. It was after supper, that he, decided to go to bed. But, first he wanted to call Ree. When she came to the phone, she sounded, like she always did, cheerful and happy. As he began to talk, she realized that he was still groggy. He apologized for not being able to see her on a Saturday night. She completely understood and wished he would get some sleep. He told her that he would, but that he wanted to talk to her, first. "Oh my poor baby! Please got to bed and call me tomorrow, okay?" he said "okay." They hung up their phones and he went down the hall and into his room, shed his clothes on to the floor and climbed under the covers. He knew he would have to pleasure himself, in the morning, before he got out of bed or his groin would be in severe pain.

Sunday morning, he awoke very early. He got up and went and closed his bedroom door. He could feel a slow ache begin, in his groin. He found an old towel and got back under the covers of his bed. He put the towel over his "nakedness" and closed his eyes and dreamed of him and Ree. It didn't take long. He got out of bed and deposited the towel in his "dirty clothes" bag, that hung, on the inside of his closet door. The "ache" soon faded away. He got a pair of clean briefs, socks and jeans and went down the hall, into the bathroom. After cleaning himself up, he went back to his room and found a fresh T-shirt. He went downstairs and into the kitchen. He got two pieces of breads and put them into the toaster. He found the peanut butter jar and went to the fridge and got some butter. He went back to the counter, just in time for the "toast' to pop up. He spread the butter on the two pieces and then spread the peanut butter. He put the toast on a small plate that he got from the cabinet. He went to the fridge and got a bottle of milk and went back to the counter. He got a small glass, from the same cabinet as the plate. He poured the milk into the glass and took the bottle back to the fridge. As he put the bottle back on the shelf, in the fridge, he noticed a big bowl of freshly made egg salad. A "trail" appeared right across and deep into the salad. It was, obviously, made by two fingers. "Yup!" he said, "Dave is home." He was about to close the door, when his mom came into the kitchen. She came up next to him and looked inside the fridge. "Oh NO!" She shrieked. "Yep." He said. "That was supposed to be for finger sandwiches, after church, today. He said, "not now." He went back to the counter and picked up his breakfast and went and sat down, at the table. His mom offered to make him some French toast. He declined and said he was happy with what he had. She, then, mentioned his birthday, coming up on Friday and asked him what he wanted. In between bites of hiss toast, he said, "money." She said, "okay." She left the kitchen, to go and get ready for church, as she had done every Sunday morning. He finished his breakfast and sat, at the table, for a minute and pondered about his birthday. Eighteen years old. It meant that he had to get his "draft card," and renew his driver's license. In the eyes of the law, he was no longer a child. He would even have voting rights. Eighteen was quite an age to be. Another milestone.

He spent the rest of the day, helping Phil, build his boat. The work consisted of "bending" a lot of the beams. It didn't look like any boat he had ever seen. Phil explained that the boat was "upside down" that they were looking at the bottom of the hull. He turned his head and then he could envision it.

After supper, he went upstairs to call Ree. "Hey! Sleepy head!" She said, when she picked up the phone. He apologized for not being able to talk with her, Saturday. She apologized for being such a "zombie" when they got to her home, after the prom. They both chuckled and started to talk about his upcoming prom. She was looking at light blue, as the color, for her next dress. "Why don't you wear the one, you wore at yours?" he asked. "NO!" She said. "Why not?" he asked. "You looked incredible in it, very beautiful and very sexy." "Oh you! I can't. You've already seen me in it!" He didn't understand. She attempted to tell him that she wanted him to see her in a completely different dress. "Okay," he said." I guess I understand. She was going with her mom, this week, to look for one. That meant he wouldn't see her. She asked," Am I invited to your birthday party on Friday?" He said "of course" and then told her that it was just going to be his family. His two brothers and their girlfriends, his aunt and uncle and his folks. She sounded excited about meeting his brothers, their girlfriends and his aunt and uncle. She said, she would tell him about the dress color when she picked out a dress. "Please don't feel you have to have a white coat, again. A black tuxedo will be fine. We don't need any accidents with punch. This time." He agreed and told her that he would still wear a tie and cummerbund that matched her dress. He told her that the prom was going to be at the Totem Pole Ballroom and that they don't serve food. So, he told her that he was going to make a reservation at a nice restaurant, for them. He, also, told her that he would try and get the Chevy, again. He didn't think her father would let him drive the Galaxy, out of town. They ended their conversation, hoping to see each other, before Friday.

School was beginning to be such a drag. No one wanted to do anything. English class was a review for the final exam. Joan looked at him and "mimed" the words, "lucky you." He hadn't walked home from school, in a very long time. He didn't want to sit in the last period 'study hall" and he didn't want to hang around and wait for the bus. So, he put his books, in his locker, and set out for "hour" walk home. He would be home just as the other kids were getting on the bus.

He had a lot to think about, as he walked along the sidewalks. He thought about Ree and wondered if the passion that they felt for each other, would subside, or grow into the ultimate conclusion, intercourse! He hoped it would be intercourse. He decided to find a drugstore where he could purchase "protection". He knew that a pregnancy would destroy both their goals of a higher education. He was on the last leg of his trek, when he felt the presence of a car, slowing down. he turned and looked, it was Phil. Phil stopped the Jeepster and told him to get in. he opened the door and got in the seat of the convertible. As Phil drove them home, he said that he had to do something about his collection of rock and roll records. His 45's were getting mixed up with his collection of C&W 45's. he told Phil, he would sort them out and separate his from Phil's.

When he got home, he went into the den and the living room and began to sort out whose records were whose. He separated Phil's from his and put them in two separate racks. He would have liked to have a travel case for his records. He realized he should have told his mother, that he would like to have one. He went to the phone and called the tuxedo rental store. He spoke to the clerk and identified himself. The clerk did not remember him, until he told him that his mom brought his tux back. The clerk said that they already had his measurements and they just need to know what he needed and when. He told him that he wanted a black tux, no white coat, shirt, and shoes. He, also, mentioned a light blue bowtie and cummerbund. The clerk told him that here were many shades of light blue and that he should bring in a swatch, when he can. He said that he would, as soon as he got one. The clerk reserved his tuxedo, for him. He thanked the clerk and said he would be in to pay, that week. His mom called them to supper, early, because she and his dad were going out that night. After supper, he asked his mom, if he could "bum" a couple of cigarettes, because he was "out." She gave him two. The only non-smoker, in the family, was Phil.

He, finally, got to call Ree around 6PM. She had just finished eating and was excited to hear from him. He told her that he reserved the tuxedo, but all he needed was a swatch of color. She told him that she and her mom were going to look at gowns, Tuesday. They told each other how boring school was, for both of them. She was getting ready to take all five of her exams. He was about to tell her that he didn't have to take, but one. He decided against telling her. Then, Ree got serious. "Are you and I moving too fast?" He was blindsided by her question. He paused and tried to find the 'right" answer. He said, "I love you, everything about you. Your hair, your smile, your sense of humor and yes, your figure drives me crazy!" She paused and said, but you didn't answer my question. "Baby, if you want to slow things down, I will.

It'll be difficult, but I'll do whatever you want. I respect you and would do nothing to ruin that respect." This time, she was silent. He, almost, thought the phone connection was lost. Then she said," I don't want to lose you, if we ever should go too far. It scares me! I love you so much!" He said he wished he was with her, so, he could hold her and assure her that his love for her was very strong and nothing that they might do, would change his feelings for her. Again, silence, on the other end. He waited, patiently, for her response. He realized he could hear some sniffling on her end of the line. She said, "I hope your being honest with me. It would kill me, if you weren't." He told her that if she wanted to slow down and take their love relationship slower, He would be glad to oblige, though he really loves to hold her and have her hold him. She said, "me, too." She composed herself and then told him that she had to go and study. She asked him to call her the next night. He promised her, he would.

School was really winding down. His math teacher told him that if he took the final exam, he would pass with a "D". If he managed to get a D plus or C minus, he would give him a c minus for the year. He told his teacher, that he was studying hard and would try his very best. His teacher said, that was all he could hope for. The rest of the classes were review, review, review and review. He went into the gym, for gym class, they were told they didn't have to change into their gym clothes. They were given a softball, bats and gloves and told to go out on the ball field and start a "pick up" game. They were, also, told to bring clean out their lockers and take their gym clothes home or just throw them away. He did not want to put a "dirty" jock strap in with his books, so he just threw everything in the trash.

He continued to meet Fred and Bert for lunch. Bert told him that his mom got rid of the Plymouth and bought a Studebaker "Golden Hawk." He had driven it to school, that day, and offered to drive the two of them home. He told Bert that he couldn't wait to see it. Fred was impressed that Bert's mom would buy such a "sporty" car. Bert said that he had something to do with picking it out.

The rest of the day dragged, as usual. His history teacher had the seniors, rearrange the book closet. His Problems of Democracy teacher spent the period talking about the upcoming senior events and especially the prom. It was a senior class. He liked that teacher. Then, the bell rang, signifying the beginning of the last period. He went to his locker and proceeded to clean it out, of the year's trash that had accumulated. He left his books in it, except his math book, that he brought home. He locked the locker back up and went out of the building. He ran into Mr. Sparks, his speech teacher. Mr. Sparks congratulated him, on being accepted to Emerson College. It was Mr. Sparks's alma mater. He didn't know, until then, that Mr. Sparks gave him a very high recommendation. He thanked him, profusely, and promised him that he wouldn't let Mr. Sparks down. Mr. Sparks asked him to bring his yearbook, by, when he got it and he would sign it. He said he would. He, then, proceeded to walk down Elm Road and looked for the Golden hawk. He didn't have to look very long. It was coming down the road, towards him. He stepped aside as the sleek, low slung car came to a stop. Fred opened the door and he got into the back seat. Bert "peeled out". He thought that Bert must have left at least an inch of burned rubber on the asphalt. Bert asked if everyone really had to go home. They said, "no". So, they headed for the car hop. Fred said that it was still too early for anyone to be there. The car hop didn't have any real "action" until the night. Bert said, "I know. We'll just get some cokes. Maybe we can cruise up there, again, tonight." They said that would be "cool."

When they pulled into the car hop, there were about four cars there. He pulled up to the front row. They had to order their cokes through a speaker, on the pole, beside the car. There were only two car hops working that afternoon. One of the four cars, was a blue 1951 baby blue Ford convertible. There were three girls, sitting in it, sipping on drinks. They kept exchanging glances, with them and smiles. The girls acted like they knew them. They drove the car around and cam up next to the "Hawk". When they parked next to them. He recognized the girl, on the passenger side as a girl in his home room. They began to talk, back and forth between the two cars, about school and how "cool" it was to be seniors. They asked the guys if they were going to any of the events. They said they were going to the senior night/supper. The girls said they were, too. Then the girl, in the back seat suddenly shouted, "Hey you were the D.J. at the last record hop." He rolled down the window, closest to their car and said, "yeah!" She, then, added "you're really cute!" He felt the "flush" came up his face. One of the other girls cried out, "oh look! You made him blush!". Fred and Bert were trying really hard to pick the girls up, but they would have nothing of it. The driver started up the Ford and put it in gear, the girls waved and said 'see you in school" as the driver burned a little rubber pulling out of the parking lot. The car hop girl brought out their cokes. Fred and Bert asked him, when they go to the "supper" to point the girls out to them. He said, "okay." They made plans to come back to the car hop, that very evening.

When he got home, he changed clothes and went down the driveway, to help his brother Phil. He was amazed that Phil had started bending the large sheets of plywood, to be placed on the beams. The hull was really starting to take shape. They worked together, until their Mom called them into supper. They cleaned up and walked into the house and into the living room. He didn't eat a lot. His mom asked him, if he felt all right. He told the family that he was going out that night with Bert and Fred. His dad asked, "On a school night?" He told them, that school was practically over, for the seniors. His brothers said that they remembered how it was just before they graduated.

He took his plate and went into the kitchen and rinsed it off, in the sink and put it in the dishwasher. He went upstairs to the landing and called Ree. She hadn't found the "right" gown yet. She and her mom were going again, the next day, after school. She, then asked to speak

213

with his mom. He said, "What? Why?" She told him that it was none of his "beeswax". He called to his mom, to pick up the phone in the front hallway. He waited a bit and then heard his mom say "hello?" Ree's voice told him to hang up the phone. He did so, reluctantly. After a few minutes, his mom told him to pick up the phone, again. Ree asked him why he was going out that night. He told her that Bert had the new car and that Fred and he were going to the car hop. Ree sounded a little "perturbed." She asked him, "point blank" if he was going there to meet other girls. He told her, emphatically, "NO!" He told her that Bert wanted to be part of the "parade." He could tell that she was suspicious. He, again, told her that she was the only one for him. That he wasn't looking for anyone else. She said, "what if Janet and I decide to go out tonight and go up there.?" He said, "That would be wonderful! I'd love to see you!" She said, "well, maybe we will." Just then, he heard the horn on the car. "They're here!" "Fine! she said, if you rather be with them, than talk with me, go!" He begged her not to be upset; that he would make it up to her. She said, "you better!" Then she giggled and told him to go and have a good time and that she would call Janet and see if they could get to the car hop, too. He said that he hoped so and said, "hope to see you there!" They whispered their love for each other and hung up.

He went out the front door, down the walk, to the "Hawk" and got into the back seat. Jimmy Jones was on the radio, singing "Handy Man", as they drove off to the car hop. He was excited. I had been a long time, since he went "cruising" with the guys. Fats Domino followed Jimmy Jones with "Walking To New Orleans." Fred turned towards him and said that they decided to all go together, to "Senior Night/Supper." He said that he was "in". Bert said, "of course you are, you have to point out those girls, for us." They laughed and joked as Conway Twitty came on the radio with "Lonely Blue Boy." He was followed by Jerry Lee Lewis and "Breathless".

They found a parking spot, the last one, on the front row. "This is a good spot, to see the "parade". Fred said. Bert flashed his headlights, signaling they would wait for service. Neil Sedaka was on the radio with "Calender Girl". Bert told Fred, "I guess we should feel honored that Ree let him come out with us tonight." They laughed as he said, "very funny" sarcastically. The car hop waitress came to the driver's side, of the car, and took their orders. The car, next to them had just pulled out when a customized Mercury pulled in next to them. He and the guys were singing along with Arnie "Woo Woo" Ginsburg and the Adventure car Hop gingle, "Oh Adventure car Hop is the place to go for food that's allways right, toot toot. Out on rout One in Saugus, come dressed just as you are, the food is great and you'll never get out of your car." Bert turned and noticed that the passenger side window, of the Mercury was down and that the driver was trying to get their attention. Bert leaned out of his window. The kid asked him if this was the car hop, where he would say "Woo Woo" to get a 'free' chicken in a basket? He leaned forward, in his seat, to tell them "No!" But Bert beat him to it. "Yes it is. You have to push the red button, on the speaker and yell it, real loud!" He sunk back in his seat. Fred turned his head to his passenger side window. The kid, in the Mercury thanked him. They all heard him yell, real loud, "WOO WOO!" It didn't take the cop, who was sitting in his cruiser, long to walk over to the Mercury and "kick" them out of the lot. The kid leaned over past his date and glared at them. They heard him start the Mercury. He "peeled out" from his parking place and burned rubber in all three gears, right out of the lot. A few seconds later, the police cruiser, with top lights, flashing sped out of the lot, after the Mercury. Bert said, "I think that kid is pissed off." He said, "you think? Hope he doesn't have a bunch of friends and they came back here to "get" us. Fred responded, "Yeah, that's all we'd need."

The waitress skated up to the car and attached the tray to the top of Bert's window and braced it against the driver's side door. Bert passed out the burgers, fries and cokes. The girl waited for the money. He reached forward and gave Bert a ten dollar bill and told the girl it was on him and to keep the change. "Wow!" said Bert, "had we known, we would have ordered the steak sandwiches." Fred leaned forward and asked the girl, if he could change his order to steak. She just laughed and took the tray and gave them a grateful "thank you!" They settled back and began to eat. Joe Jones was on the radio, which was "piped" over the speakers, across the lot, singing "You Talk Too Much." Followed by Billy Bland and "Let The Little Girl Dance."

They were too busy eating and talking, to notice the black Chevy pull into the empty spot next to them. He happened to glance over, at the car, and noticed a cute blonde, sitting next to the passenger window of the Chevy. Her window was down and she was trying to get Bert's attention. He couldn't see anyone else, in the car. He told Bert that the girl, in the car, next to them, was trying to get his attention. Bert took a bite of his burger and looked, at the blonde. He lowered his window and, gulping down the last bite, said "hi." The Blonde leaned back and unbuttoned four buttons on her blouse, then leaned forward, showing expansive cleavage. He thought Bert was going to have a coronary. She said, "I hope you can ditch your friends and come over here. I'm very horny and could use a good looking guy like you, honey!" Fred sprayed his coke all over the inside of the windshield. He nearly choked on his fries. Bert just stared at her with half of his burger, hanging out of his mouth. He turned to Fred, who was trying to wipe up the spilled coke. "Get out!" he screamed, at Fred. "What?" said Fred. Bert screamed louder, "I haven't been laid, since the party! Get out!" He was still sitting in the back seat, in shock. Then they heard laughter come from the Chevy. He looked and recognized Janet, behind the wheel and Ree sitting in the center. All three were laughing hysterically! "Shit!" said Bert. He just realized that he had been "had."

The blonde introduced herself as "Sue." They invited the guys into their car. Sue got out of the Chevy and let Ree get out. She climbed into the back seat of the Chevy and "crooked" her finger, at him, to join her. He got out of the "Hawk" and went to the Chevy and joined her, in the back seat. Sue went to the "Hawk" and changed places with Fred, who went to the front seat of the Chevy and sat in the front passenger seat with Janet. Everyone was laughing and talking, except he and Ree, who were locked in a passionate embrace. Ray Peterson was on the speakers, singing "Corinna Corinna." He and Ree, finally, disengaged themselves and joined in the laughter and talk. They must have "enjoyed" each other's company for well over an hour. They guys finished their food, The girls just ordered cokes and Bert paid for them. Bert told them that he had to be going. He and Ree enjoyed one last passionate kiss and embrace. He got back into the Hawk. He blew her a kiss as, Bert pulled out of the parking space and out of the lot. As they drove down the road, he kept looking for the kid in the Mercury.

On the way home from school, he realized that, in two days, he would be the ripe old age of 18!! He remembered how excited he would get when he a "kid." This was exciting, too, but in a different way. He was on the threshold of "adulthood." In many ways, he was no longer considered a "kid." He felt good about himself. He was "lean", not fat, he was of average height, not short, nor tall, his sandy brown hair was thick, not thin, his skin was "clear" not with acne. He was circumsized. That never really mattered to him, until girls came along, in his life. Those that had touched and seemed him, appeared very happy, that he did not have foreskin, and, most important, of all, girls called him "handsome, cute and good looking. Yes, He felt very good about himself. Bert and Fred dropped him off, at home again. He thanked them and Bert said that he would be driving to school, the next day, as well, if he wanted a ride. He said "sure" and as he exited the car, said that he would see them tomorrow.

He went into the house and up to his room and changed into jeans and a T-shirt and Keds. He went out the back door and down the back stairs, across the driveway and into the garage One side of the hull was completed. He saw that Phil still needed help with "bending" more plywood sheets. Again, they worked up to supper time. As he was washing up for supper, the phone rang. It was Ree. She had the swatch and wanted to know if he could pick her up, from school tomorrow, so they could go to the tuxedo store. He put her on "hold" and asked his mom. She said that was not a problem. He told her that he would see her, in front of the school. She, then told him not to eat any supper, that night, John and Janet wanted to double date to Nantasket Beach. Sort of a pre-birthday date. He said "okay". Then, she said", go eat and I'll see you tomorrow."

At supper, he informed his family, that, he would not be home for supper Thursday night. His mom asked him that he would be home for his birthday supper. He said "of course!" "Don't forget to bring Ree!" He told her that he would certainly remember. The day before his birthday use to be full of anticipation. This birthday was different, from all the others and he was very happy to be sharing this one with the most wonderful girl, in the world. It wasn't about any gifts, it was about sharing his birthday with Ree. He knew hers was on July 22nd. And he prayed that they would still be together, for hers. He went to the phone and called Bert to let him know that he wouldn't have to pick him up, for school. Bert said he was "cool" with it and that he would see him, at lunch.

The early morning sun streaked through the blinds covering his bedroom window, warming up his eyelids and causing them, to open. He, literally, jumped out of bed. He grabbed fresh briefs, socks and chinos and ran down the hall, to the bathroom. He 'freshened up" and went back to his room and picked out a white polo shirt. He took his math book with him, checked his wallet and made sure he enough money to rent the tuxedo. He went downstairs and sat down to eat breakfast. His mom handed him the set of keys, to the VW. "Sure you remember how to drive it?" She asked, "it's been awhile." "That's the kind of car, you never forget how to drive." He said.

Breakfast finished, he went out the back door, to the driveway and unlocked the beetle and got in. He put it in neutral and started it up. He put in the clutch and pushed down and moved the gear shift towards him and to the right. It went into reverse, easily. He backed it up, turned around and headed out of the driveway. He saw Joan, walking to the bus stop, he pulled up next to her and offered to drive her to school. She accepted. He told her that she would have to find another way home, that afternoon. She said that it was okay, because she was going over to her new boyfriend's after school. This one's name was Billy. Patti Page was on the radio, singing "How Much Is That Doggie In The Window?". Joan made a "dislike" face to him. He told her that he hadn't driven the VW for a while and that his mom must have changed the station. He reached over and switch the dial to WMEX. Jim Lowe was singing "The Green Door." Joan asked him, if he was still dating Ree. He replied that he was. "Sounds serious, you've been with her a while." "Yep!" he replied, "since the middle of March." "Sounds like love" sighed Joan. "Uh huh." He said. She asked him, "What happened with us?" He reached and turned down the radio and Lloyd Price, singing "Personality". "Joan, we were a lot younger and I did fall for you, but you told me that you didn't feel the same." "I lied." She said. ":Why?" he asked. "I was scared. As you said, we were barely teenagers." "Well, we both seem to be doing okay." He said. "guess so." She said. He reached and turned up the radio. Frankie Ford was singing "Sea Cruise." Joan reached over and gave him a kiss, on his right cheek and wished him a happy birthday. He thanked her.

He pulled the beetle into a spot near building one. He turned off the car and they both got out.

He locked the VW and they started walking towards the building. They came upon the "Golden Hawk." Fred and Bert were just getting out of it. Fred said, "uh oh, this doesn't look good." "Does Ree know?" He just looked at them and said, sarcastically, "very funny!". Joan gave them both the "finger". The four of them walked along to their homerooms. Joan sighed and said, "you guys are so lucky, your last day is Monday." He looked at her and said, "don't fret, your time is coming. Don't rush it! Lot of mixed emotions about these last days." She looked at him and he actually saw tears beginning. "I'm going to miss the rides, to and from school." She said. She turned to the door that led to her homeroom. She turned and waved and he watched her walk away. Fred looked at him. "You had her living across the street from you and never realized that girl is in love with you." He looked at Fred. "We tried it, a few years ago. We were both kinda young. I got over her." He said. Bert said, "Well, you may have gotten over her, but it's obvious she didn't get over you." Fred looked at him, "What is it about you, that makes girls fall in love with you?" He looked at both of them. "Don't know." He said. Bert said that when he ever finds out, he should bottle it. They all laughed and went into their different homerooms.

Again, the school day dragged on. He was looking forward to next Monday and the last day. When, finally the day was over, he got into the VW and headed to Ree's school. He got there, early and was able to park, by the curb, in front of the front door. He was listening to "Venus" by Frankie Avalon, on the radio, followed by "Honeycomb" by Jimmy Rodgers. Just as Fabian began to sing, "Turn Me Loose", Ree opened the passenger door and slid into the passenger seat. She slid over to him and put her hands on both sides of his head, turned it towards her and planted a wet, passionate kiss, on his lips. He said that he would give her 24hours to stop. She laughed and said, "Just one day?" They laughed, as he pulled away from the curb. They drove to the tuxedo shop and he paid for the rental. Ree showed the clerk the "swatch" and, once again, he returned from the back room, with same color tie and cummerbund. Ree was pleased. The clerk said that he thought the prom was over. They both said that it was his prom that they were going to." Lucky you, two. There aren't too many people that can go to two proms, their senior year." He looked at Ree and said," guess we are unique." She wrapped her arms around his right arm and told the clerk that they were unique.

They left the store and headed for the VW. They got into the car and he asked, "where to?" "where do you think?" She asked. He turned on the car, put it first gear and pulled out onto the street. They headed for "their" spot, by the river. She was wearing a yellow and green sun dress. He was still in his "school" chinos and white polo shirt. He pulled the VW off the road and down the dirt road to the clearing. As soon as he turned off the car and pulled the emergency brake, she was on him like bees on honey. Their lips met, softly and exploring, at first. He wrapped his arms around her. Her arms enveloped him. Their kisses began to be more passionate. She was getting "hotter" and moaned his name over and over, through their kisses. He noticed her hips moving under her dress. He brought his left hand from her back and put it on her right knee. Her tongue stabbed his mouth. Her hands left his back and her right hand went to his crotch. She traced his penis, through the cotton of his chinos, his hand sneaked up, massaging her thigh, on the way, under her dress. Their lips parted, he drew a breath and moved his lips to her neck. Her left hand moved from his back, to the back of his head. He slipped his hand over her damp, cotton covered vagina.He massaged her, while he brought his lips from her neck to her lips She pushed her pelvis against his hand, urging him on. She increased her stroking. They were, both, moaning and groaning, kissing and stroking each other, to a feverous pitch. They were on a path, to ultimate "completion". It was Ree who put the "brakes" on. "Baby!" She gasped, "we got to stop!" he gasped, too and agreed. They pulled apart and shared sweet kisses. They took their hands away and replaced them around each other. He told her that he loved her so very much. She expressed her love for him, as well. He checked his watch and said they had to go, if he was going to get the car, back home. She asked if he could leave the car, at her house. She knew where there was a public phone, in town. He started the car and backed it up, turned it around and drove up the dirt road to the paved road and headed back to town.Her left arm remained around his shoulders and her right hand rested on his right thigh. They pulled up to the public phone booth. Ree gave him a dime and he called home. After talking with his mom, he came back and told her that it was okay. Ree said that they should drive to her house, because John and Janet would be at her house, waiting for them. They got in the VW and headed to Ree's. He felt a little strange, in his school clothes. When they got to Ree's. John and Janet were there. He parked behind John and turned off the car, Ree jumped out and wanted to go in and change clothes. She gave him a short kiss on his lips and then ran up the walk and into her house. John was in jeans and a T-shirt. John asked him, if he felt overdressed for Nantasket beach. He said he did feel uncomfortable, but he could live with it. John laughed. Janet said that he looked very nice. It didn't take Ree long to change. He looked up to see her walking down the walkway towards them. She was wearing a white blouse and plaid Bermuda shorts. She came up to him and "fell" into his arms. They got into John's Plymouth and headed to the park. He had never been to the park, with a girl. It wasn't a a big milestone, but one, to him, anyway.

Ree positioned herself over his lap. She swung her beautiful legs over and wrapped her arms around his neck. He turned to face her and their lips met. The kisses, at first, were short and sweet and then, after the fourth one, got more serious. Their lips parted, just enough, for their tongues to get involved. She began to squirm on his lap. He moved his left hand from her back and brought it around and cupped her right breast, over the cotton fabric of her blouse. "Geez! Can't you two give it a rest, for just a little while?" Janet asked. They separated and Ree said," Sorry, I just can't get enough of this guy. After all it's almost his birthday." Janet said, to John, "I guess we know what he's getting for his birthday." "OH That's nasty!" Ree said as she laughed. He was hoping Janet was right.

John pulled into the parking lot, across from the park. They decided to eat, before they went in. John turned of the ignition, as they got out of the car. They walked into the restaurant and sat at a large booth. Ree sat next to him, on his left and placed her right hand on his upper thigh. He loved the feeling, he got, when she did that. They ordered one large pepperoni pizza and four small bowls of spaghetti, with four cokes. As they waited, for their order, John told him that he was paying. He told John that he didn't have to do that. John said that it was his and Janet's birthday gift. He thanked them both. Ree squeezed his thigh. They talked about the Johnny Mathis show at Blinstrub's. He wondered if he had to rent another tuxedo. They laughed and said that a suit and tie would be sufficient. As they were eating, Ree would, occasionally, move her hand to his crotch and rub him, over the chinos. He leaned over to her and asked her not to do that, because he would never be able to leave the table. She giggled and "patted" him. When they had finished eating, John paid the bill; he left the tip. They proceeded to go across the street, to the park. He and Ree walked with their arms intertwined across each other's lower back. John said that it was too bad that he and Ree didn't like each other. They all laughed.

Once, in the park, they proceeded to the midway, where all the games were. They resisted most of the barkers, until they came upon one game, that included rifles. For fifty cents, they got ten shots with the rifle. The targets were ducks swimming, bears crossing, through trees. Rabbits popping up out of holes. He paid the money and took aim. He hit 9 out of 10 targets. The barker asked what he wanted, for a prize. He asked Ree. She pointed to a pink teddy bear. It wasn't huge, but big enough for her to carry, in the crux of her arm. John was next and he got 10 out of 10! Janet got a larger purple teddy bear. The girls said they had to use the rest room. The guys volunteered to take the teddy bears, back to the car. They met, again, at the entrance.

The girls wanted to go on the rides. So, once again, arm in arm, they walked over to the rides. The first ride was a "joke". They rode on the Merry Go Round, then, they rode in the bumper cars. They left the bumper cars and came upon the "Tunnel of Love". They bought the tickets and proceeded to get into the "boats". Each couple had their own boat. Once inside the tunnel, he and Ree turned to each other like two animals in "heat". Lips explored lips, tongues lashed tongues and hands roamed over bodies. When they emerged from the tunnel, they were both "panting' like two dogs. He and Ree decided to go in the ride again. No sooner did they enter the tunnel, then they were at each other, again. This time, they "generated" more "heat". When they came out of the tunnel, this time, his shirt was out of his pants and her blouse was buttoned wrong. Janet helped Ree out of the boat and told her to rebutton her blouse. He left his shirt hang out over his waist. They, literally, had to drag him, on to the ferris wheel. His stomach began to ache. When they got off the wheel. They, next, went, to the dreaded twirling coffee cups. His stomach was not doing well. As the cups picked up speed, his stomach got worse. He knew what was going to happen. Each time their cup came up next to the operator, he yelled," Stop The Ride!" On the sixth time, the operator heard him and stopped the ride. He leaped out of the cups and ran to the walkway and the rail. Everything, he had eaten, at the restaurant, including the garlic breadsticks, erupted out of his stomach. He heard Ree ask the operator, where he went. The guy told Ree, he was "over the rail." She came up behind him and put her hands on his shoulders. When he was finished, he apologized, profusely, to Ree. She helped down the walkway. He went into the men's room to clean his face. He was thankful that he hadn't hit his clothes or even his shoes. When he emerged from the men's room, Ree asked he was okay. John started singing, "This Time, There'll be No Good Night Kiss" the song by Troy Shondell. Janet told John to "shut up". Ree looked at John and said, "Not true!" She opened her pocket book and brought out two packs of Dentyne gum. She gave him one whole pack. He unwrapped all the small pieces and put them in his mouth and began to chew. She laughed and hugged him and said, "if those don't get rid that taste in your mouth, nothing will!" She told him, that they would test it out, on the way, home.

Janet and John wanted to go on the roller coaster. He looked at Ree and told her to go ahead, that he would opt out. She didn't want to leave him. He told her that it was never his favorite ride, but that she should go. She gave him a kiss on the cheek and went and joined John and Janet. He went over at sat on a bench, nearby, cursing his 'weak' stomach. "You don't care for the roller coaster, either." A voice said. He turned in the direction from which it came. She was a cute brunette with long hair, to her shoulders. Her tight polo shirt, accentuated her large breasts. All the buttons of the shirt were open, revealing nice cleavage. He doubted she could have buttoned the shirt, if she wanted to. The yellow shirt was in sharp contrast to the white short shorts, she wore. Sitting down, she showed a lot of her tanned legs and thighs. He said, "No! Don't care for heights and sure don't want to throw up." He omitted "again." She said, "your girlfriend would rather leave and go without you?" "Guess so." He said. "My boyfriend does the same thing. Most of the time, I sit by myself, while he goes on the 'wild" rides." He said that it sounded kind of selfish on his part, and that, to leave a pretty girl like her alone, was kind of stupid. She replied that, if she were my girlfriend, she sure wouldn't such a good looking guy alone, either. He was afraid where this conversation was headed. He took out am L&M. he offered her one. She took it. He bent his way to light her cigarette. She took a deep drag and let out the smoke, just enough, and inhaled it back up her nose. He recognized that as a "French inhale." She was coming on to him. He was flattered and was about to move closer to her, on the bench, when an angry voice interrupted them. "What the hell are you doing? You got to flirt with every guy, when I leave you alone?" Obviously, it was her boyfriend. The guy grabbed her by the hand and pulled her away. He watched them walk away and couldn't help notice how her hips seem to sway, one at a time. He sighed and took a deep drag on his L&M. "You must be feeling better!" Ree said, as they walked up to him. He was glad that the other girl's boyfriend came up to her, first. Ree took the cigarette from him and put it to her own lips. She told him that she missed him. They decided to go and get an ice cream cone. He spit out the gum and said that a vanilla cone would probably be just what he needed. She put her arms around his neck and they shared a short intimate kiss. She brought her lips from his and said, to the others, "the gum worked, of course the cigarette didn't hurt either. He got up off the bench and the four of them went off to get their cones.

Even though, darkness had replaced the light, the bright spotlights made the park seem like daytime. They sat at a benchs that surrounded a table and ate their ice cream cones. John, Janet and Ree ate chocolate. He ate vanilla. They asked him how he felt. He said he felt fine. That it was the motion of the cups that caused his stomach, to regurgitate. Ree leaned forward and pressed her lips to his for a wet, passionate kiss. When they parted. She said," I like vanilla, too." He said, "your chocolate was good, too." John asked if there were any more rides to do, or games, to play." They said no and so, they decided to head on out. Janet whispered to Ree, if he would be okay to go parking. Ree turned to him and asked if he wanted to go parking. "Is the Pope a catholic?" They laughed and headed for the car. He and Ree, once again, walked with their arms around each other's backs. As they neared the car, he saw the brunette, with her boyfriend, walking towards them. As they passed, the brunette winked at him and said "hi." Ree stopped "dead" in her tracks. She swung him around to face her. There was 'fire' in her eyes! "Who the hell is that?" She demanded. He told her, just a girl, who sat on the bench, next to him, while her boyfriend was on the roller coaster, like she was. She looked at him and asked, "really?" he said "really!" She grabbed hold of him and told him and John and Janet, "That's that, next time we come here. He's not to get out of our sight." He felt like a little kid whose "mommy" was scolding him. He told her so. She said that it wasn't meant to sound that way, but she didn't want to lose him. He told her, again, that wasn't going to happen. She stepped up to him and put her hands on both sides of his head and kissed him full on the lips. When they parted, this time, she said "let's go. I'm going to show you what you would miss, if you ever decide to leave me."

They got into the car and drove out of the parking lot. Buddy Knox was on the radio, singing "Party Doll". Followed by Sonny James and "Young Love". Phil Phillips followed him with "Sea Of Love." They all sang along. Ree was hugging and kissing him, all the way, down the road. Once again, her long legs were on his waist as she sat, on his lap. He massaged her legs and thighs, as they savored each other's lips.

They found an abandoned cul de sac, near Janet's street. John pulled in, turned the car around and had it face out towards the end of the street. He turned off the headlights and turned off the car, just as the Fleetwoods sang "Come Softly To Me." Ree repositioned herself on him. By swing her right leg over and straddling him. She unbuttoned her blouse and loosened her bra. He stripped off his white polo shirt. She crushed her lips to his, as she pulled open her blouse and moved her nakedness to his. Their kisses grew hotter and hotter. His hands cupped her breasts and fingers teased her nipples. Her right hand was between their writhing bodies as she unzipped his pants and pushed her hand inside, parting the cotton briefs and slowly stroking him. Once again, they were in their own little world, locked in passion and unadultered lust! The Plymouth's springs and shocks were being tested, once again.

After about an hour, John mentioned that they should leave. He said the cops would be coming by soon. He and Ree untangled their arms and legs. She moved off him and "fixed "her bra and buttoned her shirt. He put his shirt back on. In a "raspy" voice, he said, to Ree. "I thought you wanted to slow things down a little." She looked, at him, the lust still lingering, in her eyes. "I can't help myself, you drive me crazy!" He told her, he felt the same. That, he never felt that way about anyone, the way he loves her. They wrapped their arms around each other and rode home, without another word.

John and Janet dropped them off at Ree's and wished him a very happy birthday. He thanked them and said that they need to plan the Blinstrub's night. They agreed and then, John drove

235. off. He walked Ree, to her front door. They shared a long, lingering, embrace and kiss. When, at last, they parted, he told her that he would be over, to get her around five, the next day. Dinner, at his house, would be at 6. She, again, she couldn't wait to meet his brothers and the rest of his family. They shared another lingering "good night" kiss. She turned and went into her house and closed the front door, behind her. He walked down the walkway, to the VW. He unlocked it and got in, closed the door and turned it on. The four Lads were on the radio singing "Standing On The Corner." He checked the station, to be sure it was on WMEX. It was. The next singer, on the station was Guy Mitchell and "Heartaches By The Number." He was ready to turn the channel, when he heard Arnie "Woo Woo" Ginsburgh say, after "Heartaches" that it was time to get back to Rock and Roll. Jody Reynolds sang "Endless Sleep." That was followed by Wanda Jackson and "Let's Have A Party." He headed home and wondered what kind of birthday he was going to have.

As he pulled into the driveway. The Tune Weavers were on the radio singing "Happy, Happy Birthday, Baby." He wondered if Ree had called in the request. He listened to the words and realized it was sung, by a girl, who was apart from her boyfriend and that he was with someone else. He parked the VW and turned it off, got out and locked it and went in the back door, of the house. He had a difficult time, getting to sleep. So, he got out of bed and went to the closet and found his "towel" and masturbated. He thought that would help, but the "guilt" of throwing up, on his date with Ree, haunted him. Even though, he apologized and she accepted it. He was still bothered by it. He didn't want her to think he was a "weakling." It took a long time for him to finally "drift off."

Friday, the 13th was a cool, cloudy, gray day. He slept past his usual "wake up" time. When he did, finally "come to", it was too late, to go to school. he scrambled out of bed, threw on a pair of jeans and no shirt and in bare feet, went out of his room and down the hall, downstairs, to the kitchen. "Good morning Birthday Boy!" His mom said. "I'm late!" he mumbled. "Not to worry!" his mom said. "I called the school and told them that you weren't feeling good and were staying home, today." He gave her an incredulous look. "Wow! Thanks! "he said. He sat down and ate his breakfast. After which, his mom asked him to, at least, go upstairs and put on a shirt. He went back upstairs, after breakfast, and got cleaned up. He emptied his clothes hamper and along with "his' towel, brought them down into the basement and put them in the "Bendix." He added a cup of soap powder and closed the door and turned it on. Even at 18, he liked to look in the window and watch the water fill up the washer. He went back upstairs, to his room and put on a T-shirt and white socks and his Keds. Once dressed and cleaned up, he went outside, to the garage. Phil was not there. He went back in the house. His mom said that his Dad and Phil went into the city. Phil was applying to a technical school. it was a college for students with technical abilities, rather than "liberal arts" studies. He was kind of "lost." His girlfriend was in school, his "buddies" were in school, even his neighbor, across the street, was in school. He thought about going for a drive, but, by the time, he decided to do that, it was too late. His mom was already, driving out of the driveway, in the VW. He really began to miss his "Black Beauty." He went back up to his room and went through his top drawer, of his dresser. Even though that drawer held his underwear and socks, it also had a box of photographs. Pictures of when he was a kid, a cub scout, a boy scout, other birthday pictures, a picture of Abby and then, he found it. A picture of him, standing next to the Ford. He remembered Joan had taken it one Saturday morning. He went over to his bed and sat down and stared, at the picture. A flood of memories came back. He reached over and took his wallet off the night stand and opened it up and slid the picture in one of the compartments. He knew that someday, he was going to have to tell Ree all about "Black Beauty."

It was his birthday. But, he knew that his brother Dave would do "something" to try and "upstage" his day. Last year, it was Dave's acceptance to college. The year, before that, he called, in the middle of his party, to tell everyone about an award, he got. He was still in the Army, then. Abby had thought it strange, that his brother had waited, until that very day, to call and tell his folks. But, it didn't really bother him, that much, then, because he had turned 16! This year, he wondered what he would do. It happened around noon. Dave drove into the yard in a sparking, baby green 1954 Ford convertible! He had traded in the '49 Mercury for the convertible. It was a real nice car! He had the top down, even though, the weather looked like it could rain, at any minute. He wished it would rain. Sure enough, when his mom came home, she couldn't believe her eyes! Not too soon after, his dad and Phil came home. Everyone "gushed" over Dave's "New" car. He took his mom and dad for a drive. Phil stayed behind with him. They walked down the driveway, to the garage. Phil looked at him and wished him a happy birthday and added "Well, he's done it again. He just can't stand to be out of the "limelight." But tonight is your night, no matter what!" He thanked Phil and started to help him with the boat. When Dave pulled the ford back into the driveway, his mom got out and in her hand was a large bag of burgers and fries. "Lunch!" She cried. He and Phil put down "their" tools and went into the house and washed up. They all sat at the kitchen table, as his mom "divvied" up the food. His dad had gone to the fridge and came back with four cokes. His mom always drank tea with her lunch. Dave made a big 'deal" about him missing school, that day. Said it wasn't right and that he shouldn't be allowed to go to the "senior thing" Saturday night. Phil told him to "shut up", that it was no business of Dave's. The rest of the lunch was consumed in silence. As they finished eating, his wish was granted. They all heard the torrents of water pouring from the sky. "OMIGOD!" shouted Dave, "My new car!" Dave jumped up from the kitchen table and ran for the back door, urging his brothers to help him. He and Phil sat still and finished eating their fries. His mom looked, at them and asked if they were going to help him put the top up. Phil said, "all he has to do, is put the key in the ignition, start the car up and pull on the button, on the dashboard. The top will come up automatically. Then, he just snaps the lever, in place. It's very easy and we would just be in the way."

Through the "teeming" water, they could hear Dave's cries for help. They got up and went to the back window and watched as Dave tried to pry the top out of the back of the car, with his hands. Phil started to laugh and said "he can't be that stupid!" He started to laugh, as well. Their mom pleaded with them to help him. Finally, Phil put on a raincoat and went out the back door. When he got to the "soaked "Ford. He could see Phil ask Dave, for the keys. Dave, still struggling to pry the top up, tossed Phil the keys. Phil got in the car and put the key, in the ignition and started the car. He, then, pulled on the button. The top raised up out of the back, nearly taking Dave with it. The top came up, over the car and Phil snapped it in place on the top of the windshield. Dave ran over to the driver's side door, as Phil exited the car and gave him back his keys. Then a miracle happened! The sun broke through the clouds! He, his mom, and Dad began to laugh! The look on Dave's face was "priceless." Dave got into the car and unsnapped the top from the top of the windshield and pulled the button. The top, slowly, retracted into the back of the car. The damage had been done! The interior was completely soaked, as was Dave and Phil. When Phil came back into the house, to change, he said that it was worth, getting soaked. They all laughed, again. Dave spent the rest of the early afternoon, running a towel over the inside of his car. He told Phil, his mom and dad, that watching Dave try to pry the top up, with his bare hands was a wonderful birthday present!

He checked his watch, it was 4PM. He went upstairs and changed into a fresh pair of jeans and a blue buttoned down collar shirt. He combed his hair, brushed his teeth, dabbed on some Old Spice and headed out of his room. Down the hall. Down the stairs, and out the back door, to the VW. He got to Ree's house, at just after 5. She must have been standing just behind the door. When he knocked, the door opened and there she was! She had on a light green blouse and dark slacks. The blouse made her auburn hair, really shine. She was holding two cards and two small gift wrapped boxes. He took the boxes, from her, and offered his arm. She closed the door, behind her and they "strutted" to the VW. Once in the car, he put the cards and boxes, in the back seat and drew her to his arms. They embraced and shared a sweet kiss, full of love!

Oh, how he wanted to just sit in the car, hold and kiss her! But, they knew that his family was waiting for them. He turned on the "bug" and put it in gear and headed out towards his house. The Ponytails were on the radio with "Born Too Late." Sam Cooke followed with "Cupid." Ree had her left arm around his shoulders and her right hand on his right thigh. Just as they neared his town, she slid her hand over to his crotch. "OH! I love to feel it grow, under my touch!" She said. He begged her to move her hand back to his thigh, or he would not be able to get out of the car. The Platters were on the radio, singing, "I'm Sorry," as he pulled up to the front of the house. Ree looked at him and said, "looks like it hasn't gone down too much." He groaned. They sat in the car, while he tried to think of things, other than making love with Ree. He "conjured" up the vision, of wrecking Black Beauty. It worked before and was working then. "Yup!" She said. "Whatever you're thinking of, is working."

He turned off the car and they both got out. She was, again, carrying two cards and two gifts. His mom opened the front door and greeted them. She was "genuinely" happy to see Ree, as was his dad. Dave and his girlfriend, Trudy, along with Phil and Nan introduced themselves as he introduced Ree. His dad ushered everyone into the dining room. His dad sat at one end of the table, his mom at the other end. He and Ree sat beside each other and Dave and Trudy, sat beside each other on the other side. Phil and Nan sat across from each other. Ree started the conversation by stating what a powerful range of showers they had, that went through, earlier that day. She had no idea, what she started. His mom and dad began to snicker, followed by Phil and Nan and Trudy. He was having trouble containing his laughter. Dave was not amused. Ree looked around the table and asked what was so funny about a soaking rain. That caused everyone to burst out laughing. When he was able, he explained to Ree, why everyone was laughing so hard. "Really?" She asked Dave, "you really didn't know that the car had an automatic top?" She joined in on the laughter. She said that her dad had a convertible, like that, years ago and that was the main selling point, the automatic top. His family, except, Dave were laughing almost hysterically. When the laughter, finally, subsided, the continued to eat the roast beef dinner. Ree was the first to compliment his mom, on the meal. She offered to help 'clean off" the table. All the ladies took the dishes and followed his mom, into the kitchen. His dad looked at him and said, "I said it before and I'll say it again, I wish you two had met, after college. That girl is definetly a "keeper." He told his dad and brothers he was going to do his best, not to lose her. When they returned to the dining room, the girls were carrying small plates and forks, behind his mom, who was carrying a birthday cake, gloriously in flame!

Nineteen candles afire! They all sang happy birthday, to him. His mom told him to make a wish. He did and blew out all the candles! Ree asked him what he wished for. He told her that his wish came true, the night they met. Then, it was her turn to blush! He cut up the cake and made sure everyone got a piece and those that wanted ice cream, got that, too. Then, his mom brought up the presents from underneath her chair.

From his brother, Dave, a carton of L&M's, from his brother, Phil, a carry case for his 45 pm records. He thanked Phil and Dave and told Phil that, now their records wouldn't get mixed up, together. From his dad, a card. With a hundred dollar bill in it. He did not show the money, but kept it in the card, and from his mom, another card with a hundred dollar bill, in it. Ree had seen the money. But didn't say anything. Ree handed him, the card, with the smallest box. He opened it and found, a silver plated I.D. bracelet, with his name engraved on it. He attempted to put it on his left wrist. As he fumbled with the clasp, he saw the engraving, on the underside, "Love, Ree." He, finally, got it on his wrist. He looked at her. She could see the "love" in his eyes. He whispered, "Thank you." His mom said, A gift like that and all she gets is a "thank you." He leaned over to her and pressed his lips to hers. A short kiss. His mom said, "that's better!" He read the card, that accompanied it, out loud, "To an amazing, brilliant guy! Who is only as amazing and brilliant as the girl, he is with . . . Happy Birthday, Love, Ree." They all laughed. He looked at the other box and card. She whispered, "later." Everyone had "seconds" on the cake and ice cream and, again, the ladies "cleared "the table.

It was close to 8PM. Ree told them that she had to be getting home. She had been a big hit with his family, especially, Nan, Trudy, and his mom. They said goodnight and walked out the front door, to the VW. He opened the door, for her and she got in. He walked around the front of the car and got in the driver's side. "I really wish you didn't have to go home, so soon!" He said. "I don't!" She said, "I lied, I just want to be alone with you." He told her that would be the best birthday present of all. They headed for the Duck Feeding Area, a popular place for "parkers". The Countrymen were on the radio, with "I. Know Where I'm Going." Followed by Jerry Keller and "Here Comes Summer."

He pulled the VW into a pace overlooking the river. Darkness had just set in. He turned off the headlights and was about to turn of the motor, Ree said, "Wait a minute! Have you ever heard the end of this song?" he replied that he had. They listened to Eddie Cochran, anyway, sing "Just Sitting In The Balcony." When the song ended with the popping sound of a kiss, echoing out. She handed him another birthday card. It was from her parents. The note, inside, said, "To a very special boy, who has brought such happiness to our daughter, Happy birthday, Love, "and it was signed by her folks. He felt a lump, in his throat. Inside the card was twenty five dollars. He told her that she needed to thank her folks, for him and that the card, alone, was enough. She told him that her parents couldn't help it, they liked him. She, leaned down and opened her pocketbook and took out, yet, another card. This was a "serious" card from her. He opened it up and his eyes, filled up, as he read, "I am so glad to be with you, on your birthday, and I pray, that I will be with you on many, many, many more. My heart is so full of love, for you! I wouldn't want to go on living without you!!! All My LOVE!!!! Ree. He dropped the card, in his lap and reached for her. Their embrace and kisses were full of pure love, for each other. He told her that the day, he met her, was the happiest day of his life, and every day, he thanks God, for her. She brought up her hands to his chest and held him off, while she gave him the second gift. He opened it up and saw it was a bottle of "Stetson" Cologne. She told hin that while she "liked" Old Spice" she really loved the smell of "Stetson." He opened the bottle and put a little on his cheeks, behind his ears and on both sides of his neck. He closed up the bottle and made sure the cap was tight; put it back in the box. She nestled her face to his neck and emitted a loud "hmmmm, oh yeah, baby, oh God,yes . . . no more Old Spice!" Their kisses started off sweet and short and then, like any other time, their passion started to "rise". Once, when they separated their lips, to take a breath and hug each other, tightly, she noticed bright lights across the river. She asked him what they were. "That's where we are going a week from tonight, to my prom, the Totem Pole Ballroom. She seemed impressed. "What kind of food do they serve?" She asked. "They don't!" he said, "I made reservations at "The Meadows." She pulled away and looked at him. "The Meadows?" She said. "Wow! That's quite ritzy and expensive!" He reached out to her, "nothing is too good for the lady I'm in love with!" They cuddled against each other. "I hope you like you like the bracelet and the cologne." "Oh baby! I love them. If the cologne does something for you, then I'll wear it, whenever we are together and the bracelet, I'll keep forever!" She smiled and they embraced and began to press their lips together, in another sweet kiss. The rich food appeared to "tire" them both out. As much as they wanted to kiss, stroke and 'steam up" the windows, they just didn't have the "energy". So, they embraced, a lot, and watched the lights, from across the river, sparkle like little diamonds on the water. "Amazing" he thought, "when they are too exhausted to "drive each other crazy, with passion", no cops show up".

He knew that it was getting late and in the dim light, her eyes were losing their battle with consciousness. She put her head on his shoulder and her arms around his neck. He started up the car and turned on the headlights. He backed up the car and turned it around and headed out of the area, as Domenico Modugno sang, "Nel Blu Di Pinto Di Blu" on the radio. he tried to sing along, but the Italian lyrics "threw' him. He heard Ree mumble that she loved his singing. They got to her house, a little after 11PM. He woke her up and, again, helped her out of the car.

She, again, apologized for being so tired. He told her that she didn't have to apologize. They walked to the front door. She turned to face him and their arms entwined around each other. She wished him a happy birthday and the shared their last kiss of the night.

She told him to behave himself at his senior night, the next night. He promised her that he would. He asked, if maybe they could have lunch, tomorrow. She told him that she was going to be at the seamstress's most of the day and that she, Sue, and Janet had planned to go to the movies. At the local theatre, not the drive in, to see "A Summer Place." She told him that movie was more of a "girl's show. So, they would, both, be busy Saturday night.

During the day, Saturday, he helped Phil with the boat. The hull was nearly completed. They would be bringing it out of the garage, soon, much to his dad's delight. He couldn't wait to put his car back in the garage, again. Bert called him, during their "lunch break" to tell him that they would pick him up around 6:30 that evening. Before, going back out to the garage, he went up to his room and picked out a pair of tan polished chino pants, a blue pinstriped shirt, black socks and black loafers. He thought about wearing his white bucs, both thought they would stand out too much. He wanted to look "cool." Ree had been after him to get his hair cut in an "Ivy League" look. He thought that he would go to the barber shop and do that.

He and Phil worked until about two o'clock that afternoon. Phil and Nan were going to the beach. So, he went in the house and got cleaned up, took two bucks, out of his bank and walked downtown, to the barber shop. The shop had quite a few ahead of him, so he sat down and looked at several of the "Hot Rod" magzines. Then, he heard Vic say, "okay, Barnaby, you're up!" He smiled and got up and went and sat in the chair. Vic had been cutting his hair, ever since he was in junior high school. It was Vic who gave him his "Flattop", and Vic, who practically shave it all off, so he could go back to his regular "look." "What are we doing this time, Barnaby?" he said. He told Vic that his girlfriend wanted him to have an "Ivy league "look. Vic laughed and said, "I've been cutting hair a long time and I'll tell you, from first time, a little boy comes, it's mom who tell me how to cut his hair. Then, when the same kid meets a girl, it's her who designates what kind of haircut, he gets. We have to please our women, don't we Barnaby." He replied, "guess so!" As Vic cut his hair, he told him about Robert Morse and the TV shows, he was doing and the movies, he was in. Vic showed him a picture, in the newspaper, of Vic cutting Robert's hair, backstage at a show, a few weeks back. He told Vic, if he made it big, he would continue to have him cut his hair, too.

When Vic was done, he looked in the mirror. The "Elvis" look was gone. Instead, the" George Hamilton" look was there. The same style as George had in the movie, "Where The Boys Are."

He like it. He gave Vic his two dollars and Vic thanked him for the tip. He left the shop and walked home. He couldn't wait to see Ree's reaction to his new "look."

When he walked in the door, of his house, he met his mom, coming out of the kitchen. She stopped "dead" in her tracks. "I like it!" She said. "Please keep this style, don't go back the "old' one. He looked, in the hall mirror, and decided that he liked it, too. He went up to the landing phone and called Ree. Her mom and answered that they had just returned from the seamstress. He thanked her for his birthday card and gift. Ree came on the line. "Hi baby! This is a surprise!" He told her, he just wanted to say "hi" before he went out. He wished she was going with him, and she said "I know. Me, too. But, you have fun, just don't pick up any girls." He vowed that he wouldn't. he told her to enjoy the movie.

Bert and Fred were right on time. He heard Bert's horn, outside his house, right at 6:30PM. He said goodnight to his family and went out of the house, down the walk and got into the "hawk". As he settled into the back seat. Fred turned around and handed him a "birthday gift." He told Fred that he didn't expect anything from the two of them, because his party was a "family affair." They knew, but Bert and Fred felt that they had to get him something. Something he wouldn't need right away, at least that night, but later on, maybe. He opened the box and inside were 10 condoms, each one wrapped individually. He began to laugh, so did the guys. "You guys are something else." He said. "I can't carry these in my pocket, into the gym!" Fred said. "just leave them in the car." Duane Eddy was on the radio, playing "Rebel Rouser" as Bert hit the gas and they headed for the school.

Bert parked the car, in the faculty parking lot, next to the gym. Fred wondered if he shouldn't have parked somewhere else. Bert replied, "What are they going to do? Suspend Me?" They laughed, got out of the car. Bert turned off the motor, lights and got out and locked it. They started for the gym. As they got closer, they could hear the music, "Great Balls of Fire" by Jerry Lee Lewis. As they entered the gym, The Crests were on the turntable singing "Sixteen Candles." He had just started walking towards the bleachers, with Fred and Bert, when his left arm was grabbed and he was pulled back. "Come on! Let's dance!" he turned and saw who had his arm, it was Betty. She was in a very tight sweater and tight skirt. She pulled him onto the gym floor and spun him to her and wrapped her arms around him, tightly and laid her head against his chest. He could hardly move and so they swayed to the music. When they song ended, Johnny Preston was next with "Cradle of Love". He pulled her arms away from him and practically ran to the bleachers. Fred and Bert were already "chompin down" on three slices of pizza. He asked where they got it and they pointed. He went over to the large table, got his slices and a coke. He joined the other two, on the bleaches. "So?" asked Fred, "seen the girls from the car hop yet?" "nope!" he replied. Bert asked him why he wasn't with them, to get the pizzas? He said one word "Betty." They both said, "oh." Thurston Harris was singing "Little Bitty Pretty One." On the turntable. The three of them, finished their food and drinks and began to walk around the gym. There was a "makeshift" midway, with all kinds of games and chances to win "worthless junk" as Bert called it. Fred kept looking around, for the girls.

They found a table with a popcorn machine and each took a bag of popcorn and another coke. "Hey guys!" Fred turned around. It was three girls, from the car hop. "How come you aren't dancing?" One of the girls asked. Bert was just about to tell them that he didn't dance, when "The Stroll" by the Diamonds was on the turntable. The girls too each one of them by the hand and led them to the floor. The D.J. was smart. He played it over and over, until everyone had gone down the middle. He must have "hurt" Betty's feelings, because he didn't see her for the rest of the night. All of them continued to dance to Ferlin Husky's "Gone." Afterwards, they got more cokes, with the girls and went back and sat on the bleachers. The girls wanted to leave the gym and go into the city, to a "Beatnik coffee house". Bert and Fred weren't keen on the idea and he certainly didn't want to go. The girls bid their goodbyes and left. It was already 9:30PM and they were 'bored". They decided to leave and go watch the "hot Rod Parade" at the car hop.

When they arrived at the car hop, the found a spot, in the front row. They ordered three frappes and waited for the "show." The girl brought their order and Bert asked her where the hot rods were. As she collected their money and her tip, she said they were there earlier and left. Bert was really angry. He told the guys that the whole night was a "bust." Fred agreed. He told them that he'd had better nights, too. They decided to call it a night and go home.

When they dropped him off at his house, he thanked them and went inside, with his "birthday presents". He went right to his room and put the box, in the drawer of his night stand. He made sure to hide them under his "Car and Driver Magazines". He went into the bathroom and got ready for bed. As he got back into his bed, he wondered if he was ever going to actually use them.

The next morning, his mom went around the house, waking everyone up. It was Sunday and she wanted her whole family, in church, with her. He could hear Phil and Dave grumble over his own grumbling. He had to wait to use the bathroom. Something, he wasn't use to. Once they were all cleaned up and dressed, his mom made breakfast. After which. They all got into their dad's Mercury and headed to church. His Mom sang, in the church choir. She beamed, as she looked out and saw them, in the pew.

After church, they went out for lunch. His mom kept exclaiming how happy she was, that her whole family was in church and that it wasn't even Christmas or Easter! They got home, shortly after 2:30, in the afternoon. His dad exclaimed that he was glad that they, all, didn't go to church that often, because, he couldn't afford to take everyone to eat, afterwards. He went up to his room and changed into jeans, a t-shirt and sneakers. Before, he went out, to help Phil, with the boat, he decided to call Ree. She must have been sitting next to the phone. She picked it up on the first ring. There was the sound of anxiety, in her voice. She asked if everything was "okay" with the two of them. He replied "of course." She asked him about the previous night and he told her how boring it was and that he had come home early. He asked her about the movie. She said that it was good, but she would have enjoyed it more, if he had been with her. He told her the same thing about the senior supper/night. She mentioned that the new Hitchcock film, "Psycho" was playing at the theatre, next Saturday night. He said that if they weren't too tired, from the prom, that they should go. The sound of happiness returned to her voice. She confided, in him, that when she hadn't heard from him, till the afternoon, that maybe he met someone else. He reassured her that no one would ever take her place. She said the same thing, about him. He told her that tomorrow, Monday, was his last day of school and that he was getting his yearbook. He was going to take the car. She told him that she, too, was getting her yearbook. They made plans to meet, after school, and sign each other's yearbooks.

For the first time, in his years of public school, he went to school, wearing jeans and a dress shirt. His mom thought they might send him home, early, to change. He reminded her that it was the last day, of school. His final math exam would be on the Wednesday, the 17th. After breakfast, he went out and got into the VW and headed out to school. He parked in his usual place and as he sat in the car, he listened to The Drifters, on the radio, "There Goes My baby." Followed by Paul Anka and "Diana", that was followed by Frankie Avalon and "Dee Dee Dinah." He turned off the car, as Frankie Lyman and the Teenagers began to sing "Why Do Fools Fall In Love." He was one of the first to enter his home room, for the last time. His home room teacher came in and put her briefcase on her desk and looked at him, "May I help you?" She asked. He looked at her and then she recognized him. "Wow! I didn't know it was you! I like the new haircut, but I never thought I'd see you in blue jeans." He laughed and told her since it was his last day, that he would put them on. She replied, "Why not?"

After the morning announcements, which included a good bye to the class of 1960, Two class reps came into the homeroom and passed out the yearbooks. They were told, when the bell rang, ending home room, they were to report to the gym. He heard Jay, the guy sitting behind him, that they were not attending classes. Jay heard that they were going to a "yearbook signing party." He opened his book and turned to the "senior" section and looked at his picture. He didn't like it and he knew he was going to have to explain his "suppressed desires." The bell rang and the whole room got up out of their seats, as they normally did, all year. Except this time, the excitement permeated the class. They made their way out of the building, for the last time, and walked across Elm Rd, to Building three and the gym. As they made their way into the gym, they were each handed a pen. Chairs were set up for them as well as the bleachers, from Saturday night. He went looking for a place to sit. He saw Fred and Bert sitting on one of the bleachers, each signing the other's book. He went over and joined them. The three of them exchanged books and began to write. He decided to write his name on the inside cover, so he would know and others would know whose book, they were signing.

As soon as they were finished, others had joined them and soon books were exchanged and stillness enveloped the gym, as people were busy writing. One book, he got, was Betty's. He wrote, that if he wasn't "attached" he would have loved to spend some time with her. He passed that book, along, after writing in it. He did write, under his name, that the inside cover was "reserved." He had no idea, where his book was, as he looked at each book's owner and mostly wrote, "all the best," and signed his name. A lot of the people, he didn't know, after all there 1260 kids in his class. He looked up, from writing, and noticed all the senior class teachers had arrived, in the gym, and were 'caught up" signing student's books. He hoped that Mr. Sparks would sign his, along with his English and "Problems of Democracy" teacher; his homeroom teacher.

The senior class president got up in front of a microphone, that was set up by the doors, to the gym. The room got silent, as he spoke and reminded everyone, about finals, the prom and most important, graduation rehearsals. When he finished, he was surrounded by girls wanting him to sign their yearbooks. He noticed that some folks were walking around with cokes, in their hands. He got off the bleachers and went to find where the cokes were. As he picked up a cup, he was handed a book, to sign, by someone, he had no idea, who it was. He wrote "All the best" and signed his name. Those people he had classes with, got more than "all the best." If one was a pretty girl, he wrote something about how he wished they had gotten to know each other better. If it was a guy, he would write something about the fun they had, in class.

Time seemed to "fly." At one point, the class treasurer went to the microphone and announced that pizzas were on their way. The most important news, was that as soon as people were done, they could go home. Classes were suspended for the rest of the day. That news generated a loud "whoop" from the kids. He was walking back, towards the bleachers with another coke, in hand, when he was handed yet another book. He opened it up, to look and see whose book it was and it was his! He put the pen back in his pocket and tucked the yearbook, under his right arm and made his way through the horde, to the bleachers. He sat down to read, what people had written. Mr. Sparks wrote "congratulations on going to Emerson and hoped to see him on the stage or TV or on radio, in four years." His English teacher wrote how she enjoyed having him in class and was waiting with baited breath to see him on stage. His "Problems" teacher called him "an excellent actor and student." His homeroom teacher said that she would miss him. Then, he turned to the "seniors section". He was absolutely amazed at how many girls really liked him. One real good looking one called him "sexy and a swinging actor". A lot of the guys, he knew, said how they were going to miss him. Bert said that they would always be friends, but he had to dump the 'Ivy League haircut." He, also, said how he hoped that he a good time at the "all night party", but that he really didn't. Fred said how he'll miss the fun together and that maybe next time, he'll buy some condoms. He laughed at those words and knew he couldn't let his folks or Ree read that comment. Another comment, that no one else would read, came from Betty. She wrote her phone number, under her picture, and told him to call her, that she was waiting with her legs open, for him. He turned that page, very quickly and began to look at others. There were a lot of "best of luck" on his book, as well. Almost every page had a comment from at least three or four people. He was "dumbfounded!" Bert looked over, at him, and said" I never knew you were that popular!" he replied that he didn't either.

The pizzas arrived and the three of them headed over to the tables. They each got the allotted "two slices" and a coke and went back to sit down. for the first time, he was able to 'really" see the members of his class. He knew that day, was the last real social event, for all of them. Sure, they would be the prom, but not everyone would attend. Graduation was an "individual" event to be shared with family. He felt a, lump in his throat as he saw others come to the same realization, that he had. Girls started sobbing and hugging each other. Guys shook hands and some had tears welling up. Another chapter, in their lives, was coming to a close. This was a major milestone, in his life.

It was around 1PM, when he left the gym. Fred and Bert also left. He told them he had to drive to Ree's school, but first, he had to go to the post office and register for the draft. Fred and Bert, both said, "There is no draft!" he reminded them, at the age of 18, he had to, at least, sign up and get a 'draft card." They said that they did not know that. The three of them walked to the "hawk" and the "bug" and drove to the post office, to register.

Once inside, they went to the appropriate window and were handed forms. They sat on a bench and filled out the forms. They went back to the window. The man, behind the counter took each form, looked at it and then handed each one of them, their very own draft card. It was a permanent card and could only be surrendered if one, they were drafted, or two, they enlisted, in one of the services. He looked at the card and, for the first time, in his life, felt that he was no longer a kid.

He stepped outside and lit up an L&M. "Guys!" he said, "We are no longer considered "boys" in the eyes of our government. We are men!" Bert said, "yeah, well, this is one man, that needs to get home and study for his English exam, tomorrow." Fred said "me, too." They parted their ways. He got into the VW and headed for Ree's school. Gene Vincent was on the radio, with "Be Bop A Lula." He sang along. Mickey and Sylvia followed with "Love Is Strange." When he pulled up in front of Ree's school, Jerry Butler was singing, "He Will Break Your Heart." She was standing on the steps, waiting for him, with her yearbook, being signed by some other guy. She waved to him. He waved back, at her. Bonnie Lou was on the radio singing, "Daddy-O". The guy handed her book back to her and she came down the steps, towards him. He leaned over the passenger seat and opened the door. She jumped in. She put her yearbook on the floor, next to his and they embraced each other, as if they hadn't seen or heard from each other, for months. He didn't want to stop! She gasped, from their kisses, "Let's go to our 'spot." Quickly."

He put the car in gear and pulled away from the curb. The Billy Williams Quartet was on the radio, singing "A Crazy Little Palace (That's My home)." He kept his eyes out for cops, as he sped to that clearing by the river. Ree had on a blue dress shirt and gray Bermuda shorts. Her shirt was not tucked in. her arm was around his shoulders, her right hand on his thigh and her lips were against the side of his neck and on his cheek. He, desperately, wanted to slam on the brakes and take her in his arms. She had to know the effect she was having on him. She moved her hand from his thigh and unbuttoned the three top buttons, on his shirt, and stuck her hand inside and began rubbing his chest, slowly. He mumbled that he would like to do the same, with her. She gave him a big grin and took her hand away and unbuttoned her the same buttons on her shirt. "Damn, babe!" he said. He stole a glance, from the road, to her chest. "keep your eyes on the road, baby, we'll be there, in a minute." He, reluctantly, turn his attention, back to the road. He turned off the main road and drove down the dirt road, and parked by the river. Russ Hamilton was on the radio, singing, "Rainbow." Ree reached down on the side of her seat and moved the lever, so the back of the seat, moved down, almost level with the floor, of the car. She looked up at him and said, "well? Are you going to just look at me or are you going to kiss me?" He put the car in reverse gear and turned off the engine. He leaned over, across the brake and gear shift, towards her. She put her right hand behind his head and pulled him to her lips. Her left hand went back inside his shirt. He stuck his left hand inside her shirt. Their hungry lips caressed each other's and her tongue thrust inside his mouth. Her breasts heaved under his touch. When they broke apart from the kiss, he moved his lips to the base of her neck and then

248. MILESTONES lower, to the tops of her heaving breasts. Both of her hands were on the back of his head, "guiding" him. His left hand had moved from the inside of her shirt, to her leg and thigh. She spread her legs apart, inviting his hand to move higher. She moved one of her hands from the back of his head, to his belt. He felt her unfasten it and unbutton the top button, of his jeans, She slipped her hand down inside his jeans, under his briefs and softy "grasped the shaft of his manhood. He was rubbing and caressing her, between her thighs. "Oh My sweet baby!" She moaned. "You make me so wet and hot!" He responded by saying how "hard" she made him. He brought his lips from her chest and up to hers. They 'crushed' their lips together, tongues swirling in each other's mouths. Even, in the warmth of the sun on that day in May, the windows, of the car, began to cloud up. Then they heard the car, slowly, come down the dirt road. "Damn cops!" he said, as their lips parted. They, both, buttoned up their shirts and he buttoned his pants. Ree reached down and brought her seat to the upright position. She reached down and, quickly, brought up the yearbooks. They were still breathing heavy, when the cop made him roll down his window. The cop saw the yearbooks and sighed "okay. You have 30 minutes to continue looking at them and then I'll be back." He thanked the officer. They watched the cop leave. She opened his book and he gave her the pen from his pocket. She saw the "reserved" sign on the inside cover. "Who is this reserved for?" She

asked. "You!" he replied. She reached over and gave him a kiss. She began to write. She handed him, her book. He noticed that her inside page was without any writing. She told him that she did the same, reserved it for him. When she was done writing, she handed him the pen. He began to write., "My sweet darling Ree. The happiest day of my life was when I met you. You have taken over my heart, my mind, and my soul. I have never, ever loved anyone as I love you! I pray that we will always be as close as we are now! You are the keeper of my love and no matter wha,t I will always love you!!" Then he signed it, with just his first name. When he had finished, he noticed that she was "thumbing" through his book. She giggled when she saw what Bert had written. "Poor Bert". She said. He tried to give her back her book in exchange for his. He saw the look on her face when she, obviously, read what Betty had written. She closed the book and held it against her chest and stared out the windshield. He knew he was in trouble. She began by saying, "We have never lied to each other, so please don't start now. Talk to me about this "Betty." He told her everything. He gave Ree the pen and asked her to cross out not only the phone number, but everything else she wrote. He explained that she meant absolutely nothing to him and would never mean anything to him. That Ree was the only girl, in the world,for him. If they happened to break up, he still wouldn't want anything to do with her. He begged her to please believe him. She turned from the windshield and looked him in his eyes. Hers had filled up with tears. He stuck out his arms, to her. She didn't move. She took the pen and crossed out, not only Betty's words and number, but her picture, as well. He pleaded with her, not to take Betty seriously, she was just a big pest, to him. She gave him back his book and took hers. They both opened the books up and read what they, each, had written to each other. She wrote, "My darling, my sweetheart, my love, my world! I have loved every minute we have been together, the drive ins, the parties, the proms, I am so very much in love with you and pray. every night that we will always be together!!!!! I will never, ever, let you go!!! I hope, and pray, with all my heart, that we will be together until the day, we die!!!! All My Love, Ree."

They looked at each other, both had tears in their eyes. They put the books down and reached for each other. Their embrace and kisses were full of love, for each other. It seemed as if they would never let go of each other. Then, they heard the cops returning. They pulled apart and he started up the car, backed it up and shifted into first gear and drove up the road, right past the cops. He was shifting into third gear, when he reached the pavement. Ree turned her head and looked out the rear window, she was sure the cops would come after them. But they were alone, on the road. Reg Owens was on the radio playing "Manhatten Spiritual." They headed for Ree's house. Ree moved closer to him and put her head on his right shoulder and her left hand on his thigh. They talked about the upcoming prom. They would not be able to see each other until that Friday. She had exams all week. They decided to go to the beach Friday morning; spend the day, together and then get ready for the prom.

He pulled up, in front of her house. He turned off the motor. They shared one last kiss and then he got out and walked around and opened her door. She got out and they walked up her walk, hand in hand and with her yearbook. They shared another short kiss and she was gone inside the house. He walked back to the VW, got in and started it up and headed home. Paul Evans was on the radio singing "Happy Go Lucky Me." He sang along. Next was Bill Black's Combo and "White Silver Sands." He hoped that he had assured Ree that she had nothing to worry about, where his love, for her, was concerned. He couldn't wait to get home and go to his room and look through his yearbook.

His mom was in the kitchen, when he walked into the house. She wanted to know how his last day, in the public school system, went. He told her that it went good and that he got his yearbook. She asked if he was going to be home, for supper. He told her that he was. He left the kitchen and went up to his room. He turned on the ceiling light and lay down on his bed and opened his yearbook. He read and reread what Ree had written. His heart was beating fast, knowing that he was truly loved! He, then, read what his teachers had written. After that, he went to the senior's section. He was surprised how many of his classmates knew him! He got through the senior section and started to look at all the pictures. He was in a lot! The Senior Play, D.J.ing, various events around school. even the freshman hockey team, he was on. He got to the various club and organization pictures. His eyes nearly bugged out of his head.He saw a picture of the cheerleaders and in the middle, on the floor, with legs spread apart in a split was Betty. She drawn a "penis" between her legs and an arrow pointing to her "crotch" with his name on it. Again, she had written her phone number. He was so very happy that Ree had not seen that! She probably would have broken up with him, on the spot! He hoped that he would never get near Betty again. He flipped back through the senior section and began to read all "his" messages. Seemed everyone 'just knew" he was going to be a famous actor. He got off his bed and took the yearbook and put it in the bottom drawer of his nightstand. He went to his desk and sat in the chair and opened his math book; turned on the radio. Brian Hyland was singing the song about the "Itsy Bitsy Teenie Weenie Yellow Polka Dot Bikini." He sang along and wondered if Ree would wear a bikini. That song was followed by Jean Knight and "Mr. Big Stuff." He turned off the radio and really began to study. He figured that if he studied a little bit each day, he's be ready for Wednesday's exam.

He and Ree spoke every night that week. He told her that he would pick up his tuxedo on Thursday afternoon. She said that she was getting her prom gown on Thursday. He made plans to pick her up on Friday morning around 9:30AM and they would drive to the beach in Ipswich. She said that she would pack a "picnic" lunch for them. He was getting excited about their beach date. He said he would bring a blanket and towels. Ree asked if the beach had any large dunes. He told her that it did. She hinted that maybe they could get "lost" in the dunes. He told her that he liked the sound of that and he hoped they would.

Tuesday, he helped Phil, with the boat. When they paused, for lunch, he got in the VW and drove to the florist. The same clerk waited on him. He told her the color of Ree's dress. She said that she would take care of it and he told her that he would pick it up Thursday afternoon. She said that it would be ready. When he got home, he called restaurant and made the reservation for 6:30PM. The Maitre 'D asked him. If it was for the high school prom. He replied that it was. The man said they were preparing a "special menu" for the prom "goers." He told the man that he really didn't need a special menu and then he "name dropped" the owner's name and that he was a friend of the family. The man asked his name and he gave it. The man put him on hold, for a few minutes. The next voice he heard was that of the owner. He recognized his name. "You're a friend of my daughter's." the owner said. He replied "yes." He told him that they would reserve a special table near the entertainment, for him and his date. He thanked the owner, profusely. Everything was in place, for the prom. He was ready to go back out, to help Phil, once again. The phone rang. It was Ree. "I am so sorry!" She said. "I forgot to tell you how much I like your new haircut! I really didn't expect you to get it cut. Baby! You were good looking before, but now!! Wow!!!" He could feel the redness creep into his cheeks. He thanked her and informed her that everything was all set for dinner and the prom. They ended the conversation by exclaiming how they miss each other and can't wait for Friday. They hung and he went back out to the garage, to finish helping his brother. He asked him, if Nan would let him borrow her car, again, on Friday, for his prom. He said that he didn't see a problem, but would check anyway.

They took a break, for supper. Afterwards, Phil called Nan and told him that he could borrow her car, again, she needed to know what time to have the car at their house. He told Phil to tell her, at least 5PM. Phil relayed the message and told him she said okay. Now, he had to wait for Phil to get off the phone, so he could call Ree and let her know that he had the Chevy for Friday. Phil, finally, got off the phone. He called Ree. She was in the middle of studying and he kept the call short and told her that he had the Chevy for Friday. Ree said that her dad was going to let him drive the Galaxy, again. He couldn't believe it, but said he'd be there in the Chevy, anyway. They wished each other "good luck" on their respective exams and hung up.

He went down the hall, to his room, to study. Again, he sat at his desk and opened the math book. He turned on the radio to Arnie" WooWoo" Ginsburg's "Night Train Show". Dorothy Collins was singing "My Boy Flattop." That was followed by Neil Sedaka and "Stairway to Heaven." He finally turned off the radio, after Donnie Brooks sang "Mission Bell." He read the math book and did the work on his "work sheet." It was after 11:00 PM, when he finally put the book and worksheet away.

He woke up at 6AM, that Wednesday. His exam began at 9:00. He got up and got cleaned up and went downstairs for breakfast. He wore a purple polo shirt and tan chino pants. He decided to wear his new "white" bucs. His mom let him drive the VW to school, because he would be home before noon. After breakfast, he got in the VW, started it up and headed out of the driveway and down the road to school. His math book was on the passenger seat. The book cover was off of it and the book was ready to be turned in. Skip and Flip were on the radio singing "Cherry Pie." They were followed by Harold Dorman and "Mountain of Love." Carl Dobkins Jr was next with "My Heart Is An Open Book." Then came a bunch of commercials, so he turned off the radio. He had trouble finding a parking spot. Seemed a lot of people had exams that morning. He, finally, found one, at the end of the road. He turned off the car and got out, locked it and headed for building two, to take his one and only exam.

It took him the entire two hours, as he struggled through the exam. When, at last, he passed it in, he felt that he had at passed the test. At least it was over and so was school. Now, all he had to do was concentrate on his and Ree's beach "party" and his prom. As he walked to the VW, he ran into Bert and Fred. They suggested he follow them to Ho-Jo's for lunch. He thought, why not? He unlocked the VW, got in, and rolled back the sunroof, turned on the motor and put "her' in gear and headed out to the main road. Elvis was on the radio, singing, "Stuck On You". He pulled into the parking lot, of the restaurant, next to the "hawk". The guys were already in a booth, when he entered the place. "How was the math exam?" Fred asked. "I aced it! "he replied. "Yeah, right!" said Bert. They laughed. The waitress came over to their booth and took their orders. Fred asked him, "Don't you ever get tired of burgers and fries?" "Nope!" he answered. Bert made the comment, "Bet when he and Ree go to the fancy restaurant on Friday, that he'll order burgers and fries." "No guys, then I'll order something else." Fred mused, "sure you will". Again, laughter. He, again, shared the wish that he hoped the guys were going to the prom, too. His wish fell on deaf ears. Someone had put some nickels in the jukebox. First, was Steve Lawrence with "Foot Steps." Then, Charlie Rich sang "Lonely Weekends." Next came, Larry Hall and "Sandy." When their orders arrived, Little Willie John was singing "Sleep." The song ended as they consumed their food.

They paid their bills and exited the restaurant. They stood, between both bars, and talked for quite a while. It was, as if, they sensed that, perhaps, this might be the last time the three of them would be together, for a long time. They did a lot of reminiscing. He was the one that said he had to leave. He had to get home and help his brother, with the boat, but, most important, he wanted to call Ree. They, even, shook hands, as they parted. Something they had never done, before. He unlocked the "bug", got in, rolled back the sunroof, and backed out, swung the car around and headed out of the lot. Bobby Rydell was on the radio, singing, "Wild One."

Just as he pulled onto his street, the sun disappeared behind very dark clouds. He slowed down and pulled the sunroof shut and turned the latch, locking it securely. He just ruined into the driveway, when they "heavens" opened up. The rain poured down in "sheets." He was glad that he was not on the road, as it was nearly impossible to see, even with the wipers going full speed. He parked the VW. Turned off the motor and counted to three and jumped out. He locked it, quickly, but not quick enough, buy the time, he got to the back door, he was completely soaked! He knew that there wouldn't be any work on the boat, while the storm raged on! He took off his shoes and socks and walked barefoot through the kitchen, down the hall and up the stairs, down the hall, and into his room. He took off his wet clothes and put them over a chair, in his room. He put on a pairv of fresh briefs and jeans and walked down the hall, to the bathroom. He took off the briefs and jeans and grabbed a bath towel and dried himself off. He put on the, slightly damp briefs and jeans and walked back to his room. He put on a fresh shirt and socks and walked out of his room, down the hall, down the stairs, to the living room. Everyone else was in the den, watching TV. He took some 45's out of his new case and placed them on the large spindle and turned on the record player. He, usually, played it loud, when no one was home, but kept the volume low, this time. The first record was Frankie Avalon and "Why." He cupped his right hand, like holding a microphone, looked at his reflection in the mirror, and sang along. The next record was Fats Domino and "My Girl Josephine." The third record to drop down on the turntable, was Johnny Burnette and "Dreamin'". The record had just ended when, his brother opened the living room door. "Hey, Elvis!" he said, "Ree's on the phone." He walked over to the hi fi and turned it off and went out of the living room, up the stairs, to the landing phone. He called down and yelled, "I've got it!" He didn't say a word, until he heard the downstairs phone "click" telling him that they were alone on the phone. "Hi baby!" he said. "Hi yourself." She replied. They talked about exams and that she was picking up her prom dress, Thursday. He told her that he was picking up the tuxedo and her corsage. "Another corsage?" She asked. "You really don't have to." "You will not be the only girl at my prom, without one" he said. They, then made plans for Friday and the beach. He said that he would pick her up around 9:30 AM, so they could spend most of the day, together and still get back, in plenty of time, for dinner and the prom. She said, "are you going to tell me what time you are going to be here, on Friday, again?" They laughed and he said, 'guess not." They were both so very happy to be out of school and looking forward to their graduations and then the summer, together.

Thursday morning was spent helping Phil with the boat. The hull was finished. Phil had constructed a raft like structure with wheels from old lawn mowers, he had found, in a junkyard. He put a rope to a metal hook, he, also found in a junkyard and attached the end of the rope around the back bumper of his car. The other end was attached to the "raft". Between the two of them, they "hoisted" the front end of the hull, onto the front of the raft. They proceeded, each one on either side of the hull, to put the rest of the hull on the raft. Once, the entire hull was on the raft, Phil, slowly, pulled it out of the garage and onto the driveway. They moved it across the driveway to an area, next to the back porch. Then, they, slowly pulled the raft out from under the hull. Once that was done, they turned the hill over. For the first time, the boat sat on the keel. It looked like a boat. Phil got the garden hose and put the nozzle "end" in the boat and went to the spigot and turned on the water. He asked Phil why he was filling up the hull, with water. Phil told him that the water would "seal" the beams and make the boat "sea-worthy". It would take a while to fill up the hull, he said. So, he went inside the house, into the kitchen and ate his lunch. Afterwards, he went out to the driveway and got into the VW, turned it on and headed out to pick up his tuxedo and Ree' corsage. Lloyd Price was on the radio, singing "Lady Luck." He was followed by Connie Stevens, singing "Sixteen Reasons." Duane Eddy followed with "Because They're Young."

He pulled the VW to the curb, in front of the tuxedo rental store, turned off the motor, gout out of the car, locked it and went inside. The clerk, once again, handed him the tuxedo and a small box. He opened the box and saw that the tie, cummerbund, suspenders, and "false" hankerchief matched her dress. He paid the man the 45 dollars and with everything in hand, left the store. He unlocked the VW and carefully hung the tuxedo on the hook, over the backseat. He placed the box, on the backseat. He got in the car and turned it on and headed off to the florist shop. Steve Lawrence was on the radio, singing about "Blue Eyes." He was followed by Ron Holden singing, "Love You So." Next came Brenda Lee with "That's All You Gotta Do." Elvis followed her with "A Fool Such As I."

He pulled into a parking spot right in front of the florist shop. He, again, turned off the VW, got out and locked it and went inside the shop. He brought the small box, from the tuxedo shop, with him. The woman came up behind the counter and he told her his name and that he was there to pick up a corsage. She went into the rear of the store and came out with a corsage, in a plastic case. He opened the small box and took out the tie. They looked at the color of the tie and then the corsage. He was pleased. She said that the two white flowers, accompanied by the small light blue flowers would be perfect with her dress. He paid her the ten dollars and took the corsage and small box out of the store and unlocked the VW and placed both items on the backseat. He got back in the VW, turned on the engine and backed out of his spot and headed home with his "treasures". Wilbert Harrison was on the radio singing about "Kansas City." He was followed by Dodie Stevens and "Pink Shoe laces." Jerry Wallace was next, singing about "Primrose Lane."

He pulled u [in front of his house, turned off the VW and with both hands and arms full, went up the walk and attempted to open the front door. He, finally, rang the front door bell, with his right elbow. The door opened and Dave stood there and looked at him and said "We don't want any!" Dave shut the door in his face. He, again, put his right elbow against the door bell and this, time Phil opened the door and let him in. He went right upstairs, to his room, and hung up the tuxedo, in his closet. He put the dress shirt and box on top of his dresser and the shoes, in front of the dresser, on the floor. He went back downstairs and put the corsage, on the top shelf, of the fridge. He closed the door and went back to his room. He opened up his "piggy bank" and found that he had one hundred and fifty dollars, in it. He would take that money, for the prom. He looked in his wallet and realized he still had forty dollars in it. He was use that for the beach. He went and lay down on his back, on the bed. He was one very happy young man. He, realized that he had another milestone to his credit, helping to build a cabin cruiser. He had never done that before, either.

He heard the telephone ring, and hid mom answered it. She called out his name. He got up and walked down the hall, hoping it was Ree. He picked up the phone. It was someone, he'd only known for a short time. Someone, he had met, at the barber shop, while waiting to get his "joe college" haircut. His name was Donny. He remembered the guy as a real "greaseball". He liked to use Brylcreem, but he thought that Donny must use axle grease on his hair. Donny asked him, if he was interested in racing boats. Seems he had just moved into their house and in the garage was an 8 foot hydroplane. His dad told him to get rid of it. He was about to ask Donny, how he got his phone number, when Donny said that his friend Fred had told him. Now, he wondered how this guy knew Fred. He said that he and Fred took the same math exam, yesterday, and afterward, Donny asked him, if he knew anyone that might be interested in buying a racing boat. Now that he knew the connection, he said that he would like to look at it. Donny told him where he lived. It was a short walk, just on the other side of the town square. He got off the phone and went downstairs and out the front door, shutting it behind him.

When he got to Donny's, they walked up the gravel driveway to the old wooded garage. Donny walked over to an old Army tarp and pulled it off, revealing a faded red, racing hydroplane. It was just a hull, with one small seat. He fell in love with it and asked Donny how much he wanted for it. Donny said "ten bucks cash and it's yours." He thought, for a minute and wondered how he was going to get the boat out of Donny's garage and over to his house. "How soon does it have to be out of here?" he asked Donny. He'd like it out of here by, at the latest, next Monday." He reached into his wallet and extracted ten dollars. "Great!" said Donny.

He walked home and went to talk with his brother, Phil. He knocked on Phil's bedroom door and when he had heard "enter", he walked in. He told Phil what he had done and wanted to know, if he could help him get the boat, over to the house. "Where are you going to put it?" Phil asked. He said "under the back porch, by the wood pile, for now." Phil said, "let me make some phone calls. How soon does it have to be out of the kid's garage?" "By Monday." He said. Phil said that they could probably get it out of the garage and over to their house on Sunday afternoon. He and Phil walked down the hall, to the landing phone. He paced up and down the hall, while Phil made some calls. He, finally, heard Phil say "great!" He turned and looked at him and told him that his chuck had a station wagon and would be over Sunday afternoon, to help them with the boat. He thanked Phil and went down the stairs and back over to Donny's and told him that they would be over Sunday afternoon, to get the boat. Donny thanked him and said that he would let his father know. He hoped that he would have better luck, racing a boat than racing a car.

When he called Ree, he wasn't sure that he would tell her about the boat. He figured that she would find out, sooner or later. He told her that everything was set for Friday. She giggled as she asked him, "What time are you picking me up?" He, almost, said it, and then checked himself and said "very funny." She laughed and told him how cute he was. They were both excited about tomorrow. They both hoped and prayed that the weather would be good. They wished each other a good night's sleep and, always, ended their phone conversations with "I love you!"

He woke up around 7:30, Friday morning. The morning sun, streaking through the blinds over the windows, in his bedroom, caught him right in the eyes. "yes!" he said, to himself. He got up and went down to the bathroom, in his pajamas. He got cleaned up and went back into his room and put on a fresh pair of briefs, jeans and a fresh T-shirt, socks and his Keds. He left his room, went down the hall, down the stairs and into the kitchen. He told his mom, about the day's plans and she okayed the use of the car, as long as he would have it back by two o'clock that afternoon. He said he would. He went back upstairs, to his room, combed his hair and grabbed his bathing suit and beach towel. On the way out, he stopped by his mom's closet and picked out a large 'beach blanket." He headed out the door, to the VW. He unlocked it, got in and started it up and headed out of the driveway. Edd Byrnes and Connie Stevens were on the radio, singing "Kookie Kookie Lend Me Your Comb." Followed by David Seville and the Chipmu nks with "The Chipmunk Song." After that came Jackie Wilson and "Night."

He rolled back the sun roof on the VW and opened his window. The May sun beated down on his head; the wind blowing through his hair. Dion and the Belmonts were singing, on the radio. ":Where or When". They were followed by Connie Francis and "Vacation". He sang along with Connie.

When he arrived at Ree's house, Anita Bryant was on the radio, singing "Paper Roses." He turned off the car and got out and ran up her walk to the front door. Her sister came to the door and opened it and came out and said, "ok! I'm ready, let's go!" he stopped dead in his tracks. He was still staring through the open door, when Ree came out. She yelled at her sister to get back in the house. She turned, and pouted at them and went back in. Ree grabbed him by the left arm and they walked down the walk to the car. She put her things and the small picnic basket in the back seat next to his towel and blanket. They got in the car and headed for Ipswich beach. She snuggled up next to him, as he headed for the highway. Her left hand caressed his right thigh. Connie Francis was back on the radio singing, "Mama". She was followed by The Champs and "Tequila," They came to a stop sign, before heading on to the main road. He turned to her and she brought her lips to his. They shared a nice, sweet, kiss and then he got onto the road. Little Richard was on the radio, singing "Baby face." He sang along and glanced at her, so she would know he was singing to her.

They pulled into the parking lot. He turned off the car, rolled the sunroof shut and rolled up his window. They gathered their "things" and got out of the car. He locked it up and they walked up the wooden steps and walkway, to the beach. The first place they went to was the bath houses. She went into the ladies, he into the men's. They met outside, in their bathing suits, and walked down the beach. They walked past a bunch of people, already lying on the beach, obviously covered in sun tan oil. They looked around and headed for the dunes. They came over a large dune and found a valley, with a small clearing that was just right for their blanket. The valley had large dunes all around it. It was like Switzerland, surrounded by the Alps. They were alone. He spread the blanket out on the sand. He put his clothes and towel, at the foot of the blanket, with hers. She put the picnic basket at the head of the blanket. She wore a dark green two piece suit, that not only accentuated her figure, but her beautiful dark auburn hair, as well. They sat down on the blanket. She handed him the bottle of suntan oil and asked him to put it on her. She turned her back to him. He opened the bottle and squirted some on his hands and began to massage the oil on her shoulders, working his way down her back around her sides. She repositioned herself and lay face down on the blanket. He continued to pour some on his hands and massage it into her skin, on her back, then the backs of her legs. Once the backs were done, he moved to the outside of her legs, then along the insides. Slowly working his hands up her past her knees, to her thighs. She squirmed a little, but didn't stop him. He massaged the oil deeply into the insides of her thighs, to the edge of her bathing suit. She moaned, softly and her legs trembled, a little. He brought his hands up one side of her torso and down and then up the other side and down. Right up to the cups of her top. She rolled over onto her back. She smiled through her dark red lips. He began at the base of her neck and poured a little oil onto his hands and massaged it into the tops of her breasts, which began to heave, at his touch. Her breath was coming in short gasps. He moved his hands back to the front of her shoulders. She started to 'pout". So he returned to her breasts. He, lightly, brought his hands over her bathing suit, bra and started to massage the flesh at the bottom edge of the cups. He moved his hands slowly over her stomach, lightly massaging in the oil. He moved down to the edge of her bottom suit. He poured some more oil onto his hands and started to massage the tops of her thighs. Every now and then, he move his hands to the insides of her thighs. He moved his hands, slowly down her legs, over her knees and to her ankles and feet. He could hear her panting. She opened her eyes and told him that he had the best pair of hands, in the world. She, also, told him that girls don't do each other's backs as well as he does. He could tell that he made her "hot and bothered." She said, huskily,

"Now it's my turn." He lay on his stomach as she began to massage his legs, with the oil. She, quickly, did the back of his legs and his back, near his shoulders. Then, she proceeded down his back, massaging slowly, around to his rib cages and back to his back, moving to the edge of his suit. His hips began to slowly girate into the blanket, as she massaged his inner thighs and the the edge of his suit. She, huskily, told him to turn over. She began at the base of his neck and went to his shoulders, then to his arms and hands. He grunted that he forgot to do her arms and hands. "I'll do them later, "she gasped. She moved to his chest and nipples and moved down, down, to the edge of his suit. Her hand brushed his manhood as she massaged the front of his legs and then came back to his inner thighs. She brushed his manhood, with her hand, once again. She whispered, "someone likes my touch. I seem to make it grow, don't I?" His eyes were closed; his mouth open. She placed the bottle of oil next to him, on the blanket and put some on her own arms and hands. He was still stretched out on the blanket, on his back. She moved on top of him, bringing her lips to his. Her right hand tossled his hair, on his head. Her left hand sneaked under his bathing suit and began to softly touch him, rubbing and stroking. Her tongue stabbed into his mouth. He brought his hands around to her back. She placed her legs on either side of his waist and brought herself up. His hands came around from her back. She grabbed his wrists and brought his hands to her bra. She undid the snap on the back and let her bra fall off, revealing, to him, her magnificent, beautiful breasts. She lowered herself to him, as he brought his lips and tongue to her breasts. He kissed every inch of her firm breasts and then settled on her 'hardened" nipples. He ran his lips around each one and then softly sucked on one and then the other. She pressed her chest against his mouth, moaning how much she liked what he did to her breasts and nipples. Her left hand had brought his manhood to a large hardened stage, as well. They both knew that if they didn't stop, they would probably get arrested. She panting heavily, rolled off him and reached over and retrieved her bra. He was having difficulty breathing, as well. They knew they had to "cool off". They got up off the blanket and he grabbed their towels and strategically placed them over his waist as they headed for the cool waters of the North Atlantic ocean. When they got to the water's edge, he dropped the towels on the sand and raced into the water, up to his waist. Ree stood at the water's edge and laughed at him. He looked at her and pointed at her chest. She looked down and noticed that her nipples were standing at attention and straining at the cloth of her bra. She cried "oops!" and joined him. Quickly, in the water. While the cool water "calmed "him down, it did nothing but increase her "excitement". She moved farther into the water, to where she was covered from the neck down. He was giggling at her. He moved over to her and they stood there and stole a sweet, loving kiss.

When they decided that they had been in the water, long enough, they emerged onto the sand. Ree, immediately, bent over and picked up her beach towel and wrapped it around herself from neck to thighs. He toweled himself off and wrapped his towel around his waist. They walked hand in hand back to their blanket. Ree opened the basket and they ate their sandwiches and drank their cokes. Once they finished eating, he leaned over to his clothes and took out his watch. It was 12:45PM. The sun dried the salt water off them. He could feel the noon day sun begin to heat up his flesh. She felt it too. They applied more suntan oil on each other. This time, they did it, quickly. Ree said that they had the whole summer to enjoy the dunes and that she really needed to go home and get ready for his prom. They picked up their stuff and headed out of the dunes. They walked to the bath houses and went their separate ways. He stepped into the fresh water shower, before going inside and changing. He heard the fresh water shower running, on the females side and guessed that Ree did the same thing. He toweled off and changed quickly into his clothes. He only had to wait a few minutes, before Ree joined him. They walked across the parking lot, which had filled up. He unlocked the VW. They put their stuff, again, on the back seat and got in. They reached for each other and shared a long, sweet. Kiss. When they separated, she cuddled up next to him and put her left hand on his thigh, as he started the car and they headed out of the parking lot. Don Robertson was on the radio with "The Happy Whistler." Followed by The Monotones with "The Book Of Love." The Royal Teens followed them with "Short Shorts." They sang along. He asked her, when the song ended, why she never wore short shorts. She said that first, her dad wouldn't let her and two, she didn't think she had the legs for them. He assured her that she definetly had the legs for them. She squeezed his thigh and reached up and gave him a kiss, on his right cheek. "I so do love you!" She said. He told her that he loved her, too. They were on the main road, heading to her house. Kay Starr came on the radio with "The Rock And Roll Waltz."

They pulled up, in front of her house. He turned off the motor. They got our of the car. She grabbed her things and they walked up the walk. He opened the front door, for her. She leaned over her right shoulder and they shared a short, sweet kiss." See you later." They said.

He ran down her walk, to the VW. He got in and turned the motor on, put it in gear and headed home. Paul Evans was on the radio, singing "Seven Little Girls Sittin In The Back Seat." He sang along. Sanford Clark followed with "The Fool." He was followed by Don Rondo and "White Silver Sands." He sang along with that one, too. Going down the highway, he sang along with The Kalin Twins and "When."

It was 2:45PM, when he drove into the driveway. He had to be back at Ree's at 5, for pictures and then, to the restaurant by 6PM. He wanted to get there early, in case there was a problem with the reservation. He went into the house, with his bathing suit and towel, under his arm. He gave his mom the keys to the VW and went upstairs to get ready.

He went into his room and stripped off his clothes and wrapped the beach towel around him and went into the bathroom. He ran the tub, with lukewarm water and slid in. He soaked until the water began to cool, then he soaped himself up and slid under the surface and rinsed. He pulled the plug and got out of the tub; dried himself off and went back to his room. It was 3:30PM. He went to the closet and took out his tuxedo and shoes. He took the shirt off the top of the dresser and took it out of the plastic wrap. He laid it out on the bed and realized, once again, it had French cuffs. He threw on a pair of jeans and went downstairs. His mom had taken her car and gone shopping. He went into his mom and dad's bedroom, to his dad's dresser. On top was a black box that held his dad's "jewelry." He opened the box and found the pair of black onyx cuff links. He picked them out of the box, closed the lid and went back upstairs to his room. He laid everything out on his bed. His watch read 3:45PM. He decided to get ready. He took his time. He stripped off the jeans and put on a fresh pair of briefs. Next, he put on the fresh pair of black socks. He took the shirt off the bed and put it on. He took the tie out of the box and put it on. Then, he put the cuff links on. He put on the pants, zipped them up and grabbed his black belt, from the closet, and put it on. Then, he had to take off the pants and attach the suspenders. He attached the back snaps and got back into the pants and fastened the belt. Next came, the contortionist, to bring the front straps over his shoulders and attached the front snaps. He, then, got the cummerbund and put it on. He sat on the bed and put on his shoes. He got off the bed. Went to his "old" jeans and took the wallet out of his left back pocket. He went to the "piggy bank" and withdrew 150 dollars. He put the money in his wallet and put the wallet inside the inside left pocket of the coat. He went back to the dresser and got his wristwatch and put it on. Then he put "her" I.D. bracelet on his left wrist. He went to the closet and took an empty hanger and put the coat on it. He heard Phil holler to him that Nan was there, with the Chevy. He splashed some Stetson cologne on and combed his hair. He used just a little dab of Brylcreem. He went down the hall and into the bathroom, to relieve himself.

When finished, he went back into his bedroom and checked himself out in the mirror. He picked up the coat and went down the hall, down the stairs, and to the kitchen, opened the fridge door and took out the corsage. Nan came into the kitchen and gave him her car keys. "Same rules as last time." She said. "right!" he said. He bade goodnight to all and went out the front door and hung up the coat on the back hook, by the backseat. He put the corsage, next to him, on the seat and started up the Chevy and headed to Ree's. His watch read 4:15PM. Eddie Fisher was on the radio singing "Cindy Oh Cindy." He reached over to the radio and turnedthe dial to WMEX. The Chordettes were singing "Lollipop." Followed by the Crescendos and "Oh Julie." Patience and Prudence came after them with "Tonight you Belong To Me."

He pulled up in front of Ree's house. Turned off the Chevy and got out. He unhooked his jacket and put it on. He reached into the front seat and picked up her corsage. He started up the walk, to the front door. Her sister must have seen him coming. She opened the door and signaled him to go around back, of the house. Once again, her beauty "blew him away!". Her dark auburn hair contrasted well with the strapless gown that adorned her beautiful body. He was mesmerized! He went up and handed her the corsage. She gave him a peck on his cheek. Her folks snapped a lot of pictures and, once again, her father handed him the keys to the Galaxy. They stayed, in the backyard, for quite a while. Janet had come over and, also, took pictures. She commented on what a perfect couple they made.

They left Ree's at approximately 5:35PM. He was very cautious driving her dad's car. She sat as close to him as she possibly could, without wrinkling her dress. She reached over to the radio and turned it on and switched the dial to WMEX. Jay P. Morgan was on the radio, singing "That's All I want From you." Ree sang along and pointed at him. The Ventures followed with "Guitar Boogie Shuffle." Guy Mitchell was next with "Singing The Blues."

They pulled up to the front door of the restaurant. Valets came over and opened both doors. The valet, next to him, gave him a ticket, and he went around the car and gave her his arm. They entered the restaurant and walked up to the maitr'd. He gave the man his name. it was 6:05PM. He told the man, they were early. The man looked down at the reservation list and said "no problem." The Maitre'D took two large brown menus, with tassles hanging off each one and directed them to a table just to the right of the stage. He pulled Ree's chair out and seated her and then him. He wished them and enjoyable evening. Ree took his hand and leaned over the table, giving him a wonderful view of her cleavage. She wanted to know, who he knew, to get such a great table. He leaned towards her and said, "the owner." She gave him a strange look and sat back, as the waiter brought them crystal stemmed glasses of water. The waiter took their orders. He ordered a medium steak, mashed potatoes and peas. She asked him. If she could order the two lobster tails. He told her "of course." She gave him a sweet smile and did so. He looked around the restaurant and noticed other kids from his school were there, too. They were looking at him and Ree. He, finally, gave a little wave and they waved back. He told Ree that he bet the others were wondering how they got such a great table. She giggled and said, "we won't tell them." Their orders arrived, quickly. The waiter said that instead of cokes, he brought ginger ales, in champagne glasses. They both thanked him, and ":clinked" their glasses together, like they were drinking champagne. He knew the others were watching them, with envy. They both finished their meals around 6:55PM. The waiters came over and quickly removed their empty dishes. The lights dimmed and a spotlight appeared on the stage, a microphone was put on the stage. A tall, distinguished, man with graying temples and wearing a tuxedo, stepped into the spotlight. It was the owner. In his deep rich Baratone voice, he said ":Good Evening, and welcome. Tonight we have some young folks dining with us, before going to their senior prom. This first song is dedicated to them." The seven piece orchestra, behind him began to play. Then the owner sang his latest hit record, "Queen Of The Senior Prom." As he sang, he motioned with his hand, for the spotlight to follow him, he took the microphone off the stand. He came over to their table and stuck out his right hand and took Ree's hand and bid her to stand up. She did and he, slowly turned her around, while singing. He paused for a moment and said, to the crowd, "isn't she just the loveliest lady in the hall." Ree blushed, as the audience applauded, he began to sing again. He let go of her hand and she sat back down. The owner looked at him and he "mouthed the words" Thank you. The owner made a slight bow and went back to the stage. The audience loudly applauded, when he had finished. The band struck up the notes for the next song and the owner sang, "There I Said It Again." He sang two more songs, after that and then his "set" was over. He looked at his watch and it read 7:15PM. He asked the waiter, for the bill. The waiter handed it to him and waited. He looked at the bill. He was expecting it to be around 45 dollars. He noticed the twenty dollar "owner's discount." At the bottom, of the bill. He, still, took out 45 dollars and gave it to the waiter. The waiter tried to give back twenty. He told the waiter," no!" The waiter bowed and thanked him. They left the table and went out to the front to wait for the galaxy. While they were waiting, another couple came out. It was Billy, a "super" jock, at the school. He was with Janice, who was the head cheerleader. Two people who were definetly out of his class. They came over and, though, Janice didn't know him, he was amazed that Billy did. Billy began lauding him on his acting talents and how he admired a guy who could get up on stage, in front of a large audience and do what he does, and do it well. He thanked Billy and introduced Janice. He told Billy that what he does, in front of large crowds, is something he couldn't do. Seemed, to him, like a mutual admiration society. Bill, then asked, if they could join them, at the Totem Pole. The "booths sat six, but they did not want to sit with a bunch of jocks and cheerleaders. Billy said that all they would do was talk about sports, all night long. He said that if the four of them shared a booth, then the others would leave them alone. Ree shook her head "yes" and he said "okay." The valet brought the Galaxy to them and opened both doors. Ree got in and he close her door and came around to him. He tipped the valet ten dollars. The valet thanked him and closed the door. They drove away and headed for the prom. Billy Williams was on the Radio, singing "I'm Gonna Sit Right Down And Write Myself A Letter." He was followed by the Bonnie Sisters and "Cry Baby." Then came the Paris Sisters and "I Love How You Love me." When Tommy Sands cam on with "Teenage Crush." He sang along. Ree looked at him and said, "you sound just like him."

They pulled the Galaxy into the parking lot, across the street from the park. Link Wray was playing "Rumble" on the radio. He turned off the motor; and opened the door and got out of the car. He went around to Ree's side and opened her door and helped her out. He closed the door and locked the car. A police officer had been hired to protect the crosswalk. When they got across the street, he heard a whistle. They turned around and saw Billy and Janice heading towards them. They waited. The four of them walked up the long walk, through the park, to the front door of the Totem Pole Ballroom. Once inside the door, he handed the tickets to a teacher, who was behind the card table. She checked off his name and "guest." She, then, handed the tickets back to them. Ree asked if she could have them. He said, "okay." She opened her small purse and put them inside. The four of them walked down the middle aisle until they came to an empty "booth." The booth had a wrap around couch of crushed velvet. The sides and back were over six feet in height and had a small coffee like table in front, for refreshments. The girls sat down, first, then the guys. They left enough space between the two couples, but the girls would slide closer together, in case some other couple tried to sit down. Ree was "beaming." She put her hand on his right thigh and squeezed it. They looked down onto the dance floor. It was empty. The music hadn't started yet. It was just about 8 o'clock when the curtains on the back of the stage, parted and the fifteen piece orchestra began to play. The leader was Bob Batchelder! He gasped and told Ree that that the leader was his seventh grade music teacher. She said that she wasn't surprised, seeing as he knew the owner of the "Meadows" Too. Billy and Janice laughed. Billy said, "So, that's why you two got the "special treatment." He nodded his head and told him that the owners' daughter and he had dated at dancing school and that they were still the best of friends.

The orchestra began to play Glenn Miller's "Moonlight Serenade". Ree looked at him and the two of them got up and went down to the dance floor. They held each other very tight and swayed to the music. He whispered in her ear, that she was the most beautiful girl in the place. She gave him an 'extra' squeeze. They danced all the slow dances up till 9PM. At 9 o'clock, the king and queen and their 'court" were presented on stage. Pictures were taken and Ree asked when the vote was taken. He said they voted at the "senior supper." When the stage was "cleared", The orchestra leader introduced the Four Lads. The "Lads" started off singing "Standing On The Corner", along with the litany of their other hits. Their set lasted about 45 minutes. The orchestra took a "break". During the break, Shelby, one of the most popular girls, in school, went from booth to booth, handing out invitations to her 'after prom' party, along with directions, to her house. He and Ree were cuddling in their booth, when they were handed the invitation. He asked Ree, if she wanted to go; she said "yes." They danced a couple of "slow" jitterbugs" and all the slow ballads.

The orchestra played "Walking My baby back Home" as the last song of the prom. They tightly swayed to the music. When the song ended, they shared a long, passionate kiss, on the dance floor. They said "Good night" to Billy and Janice and left the ball room. They walked hand in hand back to the Galaxy. He unlocked the car and opened the door and let her in. He went around the front and unlocked his door. She had moved all the way over to his side. He squeezed into the car. She turned to him and wrapped her arms around his neck and they shared another long, wet, passionate kiss. He really wanted to go parking, but had promised they would go to the party. She leg of him and he started the car. The Four Preps were on the radio, singing "More Money For You And Me." They laughed, as they listened to the song. He put the car in drive and they headed out of the lot, towards Shelby's house. Charley Gracie was next, on the radio, with "Butterfly" he was followed by Gale Storm and "Dark Moon."

By the time they got to Shelby's, there was not much room to park. So, he parked down the road. When they got in the house. They were people everywhere. They were hungry. So they found the large dining room and the immense table, with all kinds of "snacks", on it. On the sidebar, was beer, whisky, wine and vodka bottles. They both took a glass of red wine and began to walk around. He tried to introduce her to people, but found he really didn't know anyone. Ree wanted to know how many were in his class. He told her over 1200! She said that was why his year book was so thick. He nodded "yes". They didn't stay long, at the party. It was one o'clock when they walked back to the Galaxy. He unlocked the car and helped her back into her side. He went around the front and unlocked his side and slid in. "Now What?" She asked. "What time do you have to home?" he asked. "Oh, probably in about an hour." She said. "Good!" he said. He put the car in drive and headed to the duck feeding area, by the river.

He found a spot that looked out on the river. The lights from the ballroom, still reflected across the water. They fell into each other's arms. When their lips parted, he reached to turn off the car and put it in park. He told her it was a good thing he left his foot on the brake. He turned off the car and Eddie Hodges singing, "I'm Gonna Knock On Your Door." She told him that they couldn't get too involved because she gown was quite stiff and she was wearing a girdle. He sighed, but your lips are still dark red and inviting. She pulled him to her and they continued to make out for about an hour. He could tell she was starting to get tired. He wanted to know if she still wanted to go to the movies that night. She became alert and said "yes." They decided to head for her home. He, finally, released her and reached out and started the Galaxy. Lonnie Donegan was on the radio, singing "Does Your Chewing Gum Lose It's Flavor." They sang along as they drove home.

He pulled the car into her garage, turned the car off and put it in park. He got out and came around to her side and helped her out. He went back and locked the car. They went to the door, that led her into the house, from the garage. They shared a "good night" kiss and she went into the house. He walked through the garage and down the driveway, to the Chevy. He got into the car. He turned on the dome light and checked his wallet. 45 for the waiter, ten for the valet left him with 95 dollars. He was happy. He turned off the dome light and started the Chevy. The radio had nothing but 'static". He surmised that the station was off the air. He drove home.

When he arrived at his house, he parked the Chevy, in the driveway. He went in the front door and put the keys on the hall table and went upstairs to go to bed. It didn't take long for him to fall asleep. The tuxedo, this time, didn't have to be back until five PM.

He woke up around 9:30AM. His mom had already come into his room and picked up the his prom clothes off the floor. He got out of bed and slipped on a pair of jeans and a polo shirt and socks and went down the hall, to the bathroom. He brushed his teeth and then headed downstairs, to have some breakfast. He told his mom that he would take the clothes back, that they didn't have to be back until at least five o'clock. She told him, not to worry that she was going out to do some shopping. He asked if he could have the car that night. He and Ree were going to the movies, to see the new Alfred Hitchcock film, "Psycho." She said he could use the car, but she couldn't understand why he would want to see THAT movie. He just shrugged and said that Ree really wanted to see it. His mom reminded him that he really didn't do well with scary movies. She brought up the time that they went to see the film, "Them." He told her "I know, I know." She said he couldn't sleep for a week. He thought he kept hearing "Giant Ants."

She asked him, if he was going to come with everyone, the next weekend, to "open" up the cottage. It was Memorial Day weekend. She, also, mentioned that Phil and Nan, Dave and Trudy were going and that he could invite Ree. He said that he would ask. She mentioned that there wasn't enough room, for everyone to sleep over and that the guys could draw straws to see who gets to stay over. Again, he told her that he would ask Ree.

Phil came into the kitchen and said he needed help with the boat. He had just finished his breakfast. He said that he had to go upstairs and put on some shoes and that he would be right back, to help. When he got outside, Phil had rigged up some sort of pump, with the garden hose, to "suck" the water out of the hull. They worked on it for most of the day, with the only break for lunch. He called Ree, during the lunch break to find out which show they were going to see. She said 7:30. He said "Okay," he would be by to pick her up around 6:30. That would give them plenty of time. He, asked her about the following weekend. She sounded intrigued. He said that it might be for just the day. She said that she would ask her folks and let him know when he picked her up. He ate his soup and English muffins and went back out to help Phil get the rest of the water out of the hull.

They quit working at five. He went into the house and up to his room. He grabbed fresh black chino pants, a light red pin striped shirt, white socks and his "dirty' bucs, along with fresh underwear. He went down the hall and into the bathroom. He took a quick bath and dried himself off and got dressed. He threw hie T-shirt and jeans in the hamper, along with the briefs and socks. He went back to his room and combed his hair, splashed a little Stetson on and put 75 dollars back in his piggy bank. He went down the hall, down the stairs and into the kitchen. His was cooking beans and hot dogs, for their usual Saturday night supper. He sat down, at the kitchen table and had one hotdog and no beans. His mom tried to talk him into the beans, and he told her that she should know what her beans do to him. The others laughed. Phil said that would ruin a romantic evening. They laughed, again. She made him eat, at least, another hot dog.

It was just after 6PM, when he left the house and headed over to Ree's. He, quickly, went through the gears as he travelled down the road. Neil Sedaka was on the radio, singing "Little Devil". He was followed by Don Gibson and "Sea Of The Heartbreak." When he pulled on to her street, The Fleetwoods were singing "Tragedy." He pulled up in front of her house. He turned off the car and got out. He walked up their walkway, to the front door. An aroma of barbeque sauce wafted through the air and caught his attention. He walked off the walkway and around the house. Ree and her family were having a cookout. Her dad was standing over the grill and said, "just in time." Ree told her dad that they had to go if they were going to get good seats for the movie. He thanked her dad, for the loan of the car. Her dad gave a wave of his hand, as if to say, it's okay. He told her folks that he had already had something to eat. Ree grabbed one of her dad's "famous' cheeseburgers and they started to leave. Her mom asked him, if he was sure that Ree was invited to their cottage, next weekend. "Absolutely!" he said. "Okay!" She said. Ree had a big grin on her pretty face, as they walked around the side of the house, to the VW. She was wearing a green V neck sweater and white Bermuda shorts. Every time he saw her, he fell more in love with her and still felt that he was out of her class.

They got in the VW and he turned it on and started down the road, to the theater. Freddy "Boom Boom" Cannon was on the radio with "Tallahassee Lassie". She cuddled right up next to him, as he drove. Her left arm across his shoulders, her right hand on his thigh. She asked him, if they weren't spending too much time together, that maybe he was getting a little tired of her. He pulled the car over to the curb, put the car in neutral and pulled up the brake. "I wish we could spend every minute of every day together, morning, noon, and night. I love you!" She looked into his eyes and smiled, "I love you, too." Then he asked her, that maybe she was getting tired of him. "Never!" She said, adamantly. He said, as he put the car back into gear and released the emergency brake, "I'm glad that's settled." Annette came on the radio with "Tall Paul". He mentioned that he used to watch her on the Mickey Mouse Club Show. Ree giggled and said, "that' because she was the only girl with a chest." He told her that she was right. They pulled into the small mall parking lot and parked the car. He turned off the motor. They checked their watches and noticed that they had about fifteen minutes before the show started. They got out and he locked the car. They walked, quickly, through the parking lot to the theatre, hand in hand. They got up to the ticket window and he paid. The girl behind the booth, said that the show was just about to start. They knew that meant a newsreel and coming attractions. They went in and stopped at the consession stand and got their popcorn and cokes and went into the theatre. The lights were still on. Ree handed him, her popcorn and coke, as she opened her pocketbook and took out her glasses. She motioned that they would have to sit, at least in the fourth row. He saw two seats; one was an aisle seat. She took the seat farther in and he sat in the aisle seat. He handed her, her popcorn and coke, just as the newsreel started.

Psycho

(Sad Movies Always Make Me Cry . . . Sue Thompson)

He had not one iota, what the movie was about. During the newsreel, he and Ree shared sweet, short kisses, in between hand fulls of popcorn and sips of cokes. The coming attractions did not interest them, because, with the exception of that night, most of the movies they went to see, were at the drive in. They didn't really watch them, either. He groaned and looked at her when, they realized, the main feature, was in black and white. He sat up and took notice, when Janet Leigh was in a bra and skirt. Ree put her left hand on his thigh and squeezed. She leaned over and whispered in his ear, "You like this, don't you!" With his eyes transfixed on the screen, he nodded "yes."

He did remember that Hitchcock, always, appeared, somewhere, in his films. They both scanned the scenes, hoping to see him. Then, with Janet Leigh, in her car, stopped at the crosswalk, he thought he saw Hitchcock. Ree said "No, I don't think so!" The movie, was kind of boring, to him. He couldn't believe that a major star, like Janet Leigh, would be on the wrong side, of the law. He and Ree, cuddled closer and held hands, even when, "she" stopped at the motel. The creepy house, on the top of the hill and the music hinted, to him, that something "bad" was about to happen.

He was doing "fine", even a bit excited with Janet Leigh, in the shower. Then, he couldn't believe his eyes! A major star was being stabbed to death! Ree buried her head against his shoulder. He had a hand full of popcorn, that never made it to his mouth! The only "light" part of the show, was when Anthony Perkins began to wrap "her" body. Someone in the audience, yelled out "What's he going to do? Stuff her?" That evoked laughter throughout the theatre. He was still in shock, as the movie progressed. The next scene that grabbed hold of him and scared the crap out of him, was when the detective went into the house and up the stairs.

Again, Ree buried her head into his chest. His eyes bugged out, his mouth dropped, along with the bag of popcorn. It wasn't enough that the detective fell down the stairs, but that the woman came right after him and continued to stab him.

He looked at Ree and asked, "Why did you want to see this movie?" She did not answer him. Her popcorn and coke had disappeared, as well. He was fidgeting around, in his seat. Ree composed herself and giggled at his discomfort. Then, came the scene with Vera Miles going up the long walkway, to that old house, on the hill. The music started and he knew that old lady was going to come back and stab someone else. He told Ree, he couldn't sit in that seat and PSYCHO watch anymore. He begged her to get out of their seats and watch the rest of the movie, from the back. Ree wouldn't move. She told him that he could go, if he wanted to. He did! He walked up the aisle and turned and stood in the small foyer, of the theatre and watched. Vera Miles went down the stairs and into the basement of the house. He just knew that if Janet Leigh could be killed, so could Vera Miles.

When she turned the old woman around, in the rocker and the old woman was a skeleton! he almost peed his pants, and then, came the killer, out of the back of the room, at Vera Miles. The entire audience screamed along with him! He, finally, composed himself, and went back to his seat, beside Ree. It was the scene, in the police station, when they had captured Norman Bates. Ree was not happy with him. He sat beside her, in silence.

The movie over, they walked up the aisle to the front of the theatre. Once outside, he said, "I think we just saw a movie about real people. The scary part of it, is that there are people like that, out there." Ree said, "I think we just saw the beginning of a whole new type of horror show." He agreed. All the way to the car, Ree made soft "clucking" sounds, like a chicken. He did not think she was very funny. "Aw, poor baby!" She said, "I'll protect you." That began to anger him. He always, thought of himself as a protector. She must have realized that her sarcasm was getting to him. She stopped. They got back in the VW. He remarked that the stairs that the detective was killed on, were like the stairs, in his house. Ree did say that she would probably take baths, from then on, rather than a shower. He said that his folks were thinking of installing a shower in the bathroom, on his floor. He would tell them to forget that idea. Ree asked him, if he was too scared, to go parking. He said "very funny" sarcastically. He started the car and they headed out to the duck feeding area. She cuddled up to him and apologized for suggesting the movie. He did tell her, that he would protect her from anything, even a killer like Norman Bates, if he had to. She kissed his cheek and put her arms around his neck and her right hand, on his thigh.

He told her that he would probably never, again, go to an Alfred Hitchcock movie. Ree just laughed. As they drove along, he turned on the radio. the Rockateens were on, playing "Woo

255

Hoo." followed by Lolita and "Sailor." The Crests followed with "And The Angels Listened In." Even with the music, and Ree cuddling him, the scenes of that movie, stuck with him. He just knew that he would not sleep well, that night.

When he got home, and the VW was safely locked up for the night. He went into the house, through the kitchen, down the hall, to the foot of the staircase. He stood, there, looking at it. The image of that knife wielding woman running at the guy, with the knife, in her hand, haunted him. He breathed a heavy sigh and took off, he ran up the stairs, taking two at time, to beat whatever it was, that was going to come at him. Everyone else, in the house, was asleep. He made it to the top of the stairs and ran down the hall, to his room and shut the door. Once, in his room, he realized how stupid he was acting. But, he decided, to go right to bed and skip brushing his teeth until morning. As he lay in bed, he thought that he and Ree had seen a movie, that was going to change horror movies, forever. Another milestone. This one in the film industry.

He woke up around 9:30 AM. Once again, the sun slipped between the slats of the blinds on his window. The taste, in his mouth, reminded him that he failed to brush his teeth, when he came home the night before. That, coupled with the fact, that he did not sleep well. He got out of bed and threw on a pair of jeans and went down the hall, to the bathroom. Refreshed, he went down the hall, back to his room and put on a T-shirt and white socks. He went downstairs and into the kitchen. His mom was all dressed and leaving for church. He popped two pieces of bread in the toaster. Got some butter and milk, out of the fridge and went back to the shelf that bore the toaster. He brought the jar of peanut butter from the cabinet, just as the toast popped up. He got a glass out of another cabinet and filled it with milk. He took the toast out of the toaster and spread the butter and peanut butter on it. He put the milk and rest of the butter back in the fridge. He went back, got his glass of milk and toast and sat down, to eat.

Phil was next, to enter the kitchen. He did the same thing only without the peanut butter. "Today's the day! We get your boat." Phil said. He had, almost forgotten, "Wow! You're right!" he said. "Chuck will be here around 1 this afternoon. That okay with you?" Phil asked. "Fine!" he said. He finished eating his breakfast and put his small dish and glass in the dishwasher. He went back upstairs, to his bedroom and put on his Keds. He went back downstairs and out through the kitchen, through the back door and down the stairs, that led under the back porch. He went under the porch and cleared a spot for the boat. He found two wooden "horses" and put them approximately six feet apart, length wise. He was getting excited. He hadn't been this excited, since he bought Black Beauty. He felt that he had more experience with boats, than with cars and that racing the boat, would be a lot easier.

Phil came down the stairs and asked him, if he would give him some more help with his boat. He said "sure." They trimmed the edges of the hull, to make it easier to attach the deck beams. The hull was dry and Phil, hoped that it was well sealed. They had to set up the apparatus that they used to bend the beams. When it was ready, they hooked it up and waited for the steam to heat up. The deck beams would not have to be as curved as the ones for the hull. They were still working on the boat, when his mom and dad returned from church. As his folks walked up the stairs, to the back door, his mom said, "you might want to have something to snack on, for lunch. Sunday dinner won't be until around six this evening. They both said "okay" and went back to work.

They were placing one of the deck beams across the hull, when a blue and white Chevy beach wagon drove down the driveway. Phil screwed the beam into place as he and Chuck watched. When Phil finished, he introduced he and Chuck. Phil said, "let's go get the boat." They got into SEA CRUISE . . . Frankie Ford) the wagon and headed back out of the driveway, over to Donny's. When they pulled into Donny's driveway, he told them the boat was in the old garage. Chuck decided to pull out of the driveway and back the wagon up to the garage. While he did that, Fe went to the back door and rang the bell. Donny came to the door and saw who it was, came out. They walked to the garage, together and opened the large wooden door. Donny, Chuck, he and Phil walked to the tarp covered boat. Donny pulled the tarp off it. Chuck walked back to the wagon and opened the tailgate. He came back into the garage. With two guys, on each side, they lifted the hydroplane off two wooden horses and "walked" it out of the garage and slid it into the back of the wagon. He shook Donny's hand and Chuck, he and Phil got back in the wagon and, slowly, drove the boat to his house. Chuck could not close the tailgate, because the transom stuck out just enough to prevent it from being done. Chuck and Phil were amazed at how light the boat was. The only real heavy part was the transom. Phil mentioned that he might want to put "something" in the bow, to give it a little weight.

When they arrived back in his driveway, Chuck backed the wagon up, as far as he could, to the back of the house, without hitting the cabin cruiser. They got out of the wagon and, once again lifted the boat out and carried in under the porch up to the two wooden horses. Once they placed it on the horses, he thanked Chuck and Phil, for the help. He went into the basement and found an old blanket and brought it outside and shook all the dust and cobwebs off it and placed it over the hydroplane. He knew he had a lot of work to do in the boat, before "she" would ever see water. "She" was his and he had dreams of racing her on Lake Winnipesaukee.

He and Phil worked on the cabin cruiser, till around 4 PM. They were both tired. He helped Phil cover the boat and then, they went into the house. He went to the first floor bathroom and washed up. He, then, went upstairs, to the second floor landing telephone. He hadn't any problem going up the stairs, this time. One, It was daytime and two, he wasn't alone, in the house.

He dialed Ree's number and it rang four times, before Ree picked it up. "Hello?" She asked. "Hi!" he said. "Hi yourself" she said. "Did you sleep okay?" She asked. "yes!" he said, but going up the stairs last night was a little tricky." "Oh poor baby!" She said. They began to talk about the upcoming week. She started her summer job on Monday and would be going to her school, for senior events and graduation practices. His heart sank, "I thought you said you weren't going to do any of the events!" he said. She told him that She and Janet were going to go to them, together. "So! I guess we won't be seeing each other, this week." He said. He could hear the disappointment in her voice. "I get an hour off for lunch, every day. Can we meet, then?" She asked. "Yeah, guess, we can. An hour is better than nothing." Happiness returned to her voice. She gave him directions to her workplace. He knew, exactly where it was. It was just down the road from their "parking" place. She suggested that he stop and pick up their lunch and then they can go to their "parking place" and eat. He began to get excited. "And?" he asked. She giggled a little. "All depends on how much food you bring. I don't wear a girdle with my "work 'clothes. He thanked her, for that information. He heard her mom, in the background announce "dinner." He told her that he loved her and hung up, with her saying she loved him, too, and that they would see each other tomorrow. He figured two burgers and they would share the fries, with two cokes. That would give them time to "love" each other.

He woke up early, that Monday morning. Gobbled down his breakfast and headed to the basement. He found four large pieces of sandpaper, two very rough and two "fine". He went out the basement door and over to the boat. He took off the blanket and laid it on the cement floor. He began to sandpaper the deck, with the rough paper. He wanted to smooth out the rough edges and remove as much of the old paint, as he could. It took most of the morning and both sheets of rough paper, but the top and sides, of the hull, were done. He used the "fine" sandpaper to smooth it out even more. He checked his watch, it read 11:15 AM. He put down the paper and went up the stairs to the back door and through the kitchen, up the other stairs to the landing and down the hall, to his room. He grabbed a fresh pair of jeans, briefs, socks, and polo shirt and headed to the bathroom. He, quickly, cleaned him self up, changed clothes and headed to the stairs. He, practically, ran to the VW. Once in, he rolled down the windows, and rolled back the sunroof. He combed his hair, in the rearview mirror. He reached into the glove box and took out the Stetson cologne, splashed some on and with is I.D. bracelet on, he headed to McDonald's and then to Ree's work. The Fireflies were on the radio with "You Were Mine." They were followed by Clarence "Frogman" Henry and "But I do."

It was 11:45AM, when he walked out of McDonald's with their lunch. He had just enough time to get to Ree's work. He got into the VW and put the food on the floor, in front of the passenger seat. He "fired" up the car and headed to meet her. Preston Epps was on the radio with "Bongo Rock." He pulled up in front of her office building with minutes to spare. At 12:10, she came out the door. She was wearing a sun dress that skirted out from her hips, as she walked towards him. "God!" He said, to himself, "She is so damn beautiful!" he reached over the passenger seat and opened the door. He grabbed the food and drinks off the floor, as she got into the seat. The hem of her dress hiked up, well over her knees. She did not attempt to cover her legs. He handed her the food and drinks and she put them back down in front of her.

She reached over and grabbed him by his ears and drew him to her. They shared a wet, tongue lashed, passionate kiss. As their lips parted, he put the car in gear and headed for their "spot." The String A longs were on the radio, playing "Wheels." Followed by Gene McDaniels and "A Hundred Pounds Of Clay." He kept glancing at her, as he drove. He was "mesmerized" by her incredible good looks. Her hand on his thigh and her arm around his shoulders. He was in heaven!

They pulled off the main road, down the dirt road to the clearing. She reached down and moved the back of her seat, down. he turned off the car, put the gear in reverse and left the emergency brake "off." He leaned over towards her. His right arm snaked around her shoulders and his right hand nestled on her right shoulder. His left hand found its way to her left leg, just above her knee. Their lips came together, sweetly, at first, then their passion began to take over their senses. Their lips parted just enough for their tongues to "play". Her left hand found its way to his zipper and unzipped it. Her hand slipped in between the metal "gears" of the opened fly. His right hand moved down and under the thin fabric of her dress. To the firm flesh of her breast. His left hand moved up and under the rest of her dress. He slowly caressed her inner thigh, as moved to the 'center" of her being. Her lips crushed his, her tongue lashed his. Her right hand came around joined her left hand. Her left hand was inside his briefs and pants and was stroking his manhood. Her right hand, outside his pants, squeezing what her left hand missed. Their hips girated against each other's hands and fingers. He moved his hand up and found the rim of her panties. He slipped in under the rim, and around her outer lips and then, slowly inserted it inside her. Her right hand left his pants and grabbed his wrist, bringing it towards her, causing his finger to probe deeper. Their lips moved over each other; their tongues swirling faster against each other's. his right hand moved under the edge of her bra and found her nipple and rolled it between his thumb and forefinger. He could feel it harden at his touch. They were "lost" in pure, unadultered lust! His probing finger sought out and found that special area, inside her. He began to caress it. Her legs spread farther apart. Their lips pulled apart, and they were breathing heavy and gasping. He caught his air, first and began to kiss her neck. She was moaning. "Oh God! Oh Baby! Oh Baby!!!" He felt juices swamp his probing finger. She tightly squeezed his throbbing member. She brought her hand from his pants and with her other hand, still squeezing his wrist, brought his hand and finger out of her. They wrapped their arms tightly around each other, in a huge hug. Her lips were next to his cheek and he could hear her. In a heavy breath and husky voice, she said, "You do things to me that I've never experienced before." He told her that she did the same to him. They pressed their lips together in another wet, passionate kiss. As they parted their lips, she asked him what time, it was getting to be. They had been making out, for about 35 minutes. She pouted and said, "Guess we'd better eat our lunches and get me back, to work. He sighed and said that she was right. She adjusted her dress and reached down and picked up her burger. He started the car and backed it up, turned it around and headed up the dirt road. She told him to turn and look at her, as she fed him a piece of burger. They shared some fries. Roy Hamilton was on the radio singing "You Can Have her." Followed by Thomas Wayne and "Tragedy."

He pulled up in front of the front door, of her building. She adjusted her seat and leaned to him and, once again, they shared a wet and passionate kiss. She said that she would call him, when her graduation practice was over. She opened her door, swung her lakes out and with her coke, in her hand, walked up the walk to the front door. At the door, she turned and waved and blew him a kiss and entered the building.

That was the way, the whole week went, right up to the weekend. During the morning and afternoons, he would work on the hydroplane. He had gone to the marine store and bought a half gallon of dark red paint, and brushes. The top, of the hull was finished, before Friday. She had to work, that Friday. He spoke to her, Friday night and said that he would pick her up around 8 Saturday morning.

He got up, before the sun rose, that Saturday morning. His brothers were already on their way, in the cars, to get their girlfriends. His mom and dad were loading up the Mercury with all the things, they needed, to get the cottage ready, for the summer. He got cleaned up and grabbed an extra pair of briefs and socks, jeans and a T-shirt. He went out the back door, to the VW. He got in and started it up. His folks had just left the driveway, in the Mercury. He headed up the driveway and onto the main street, towards Ree's house. The Four Preps were on the radio singing "Big Man." Followed by Bobby Rydell with "Kissin Time. "It was 7:30AM. The sun was just rising above the horizon. He brought the sun visor down just enough, to keep the morning sun from blinding his eyes.

It was just 8 o'clock, when he pulled up in front of Ree's house. She must have been looking for him, through the window of her living room. She came out of the front door. She wore blue Bermuda shorts and a white polo shirt. The shirt was just a little tight and really accentuated her breasts. In her hand was a small case. He reached across the seat and opened her door, as she jumped in beside him. Her dark auburn hair and red lips, with her tanned legs, face and arms, made his temperature rise. They shared a "good morning kiss." He told her, again, that he could not believe that she cared for him, that she was really out of his class. She laughed and said that she felt the same thing about him. He asked her what was in the small case. She said, "my bathing suit and makeup." He told her that he had seen her without makeup and felt that she really didn't need it. She leaned over and gave him a kiss on his right cheek, as he put the car through 'her gears'. As they headed North, Fats Domino was on the radio with "Margie." He was followed by the Kingston Trio and "The MTA Song." They sang along. The four Preps were next with "26 Miles." Ree told him that she hadn't had any breakfast and he told her that he hadn't either. They decided to stop and eat at Ho-Jo's on the way.

The pulled into the restaurant parking lot and he turned off the motor and put the emergency brake on; put the car in reverse. They got out of the car and walked hand in hand across the parking lot, to the front door, of the restaurant. As they entered, he saw his brothers and their girlfriends at a booth. There was room, for two more. They walked over and joined them. They had just gotten there, as well. Dave made a comment that Trudy had not been ready. The waitress came over and took their orders and left. Dave asked him, how the hydroplane was coming. Ree looked at him and asked him what a hydroplane was. "A racing boat." He told her. "I just bought it." "Is it dangerous?" asked Ree. Before he could answer, Dave piped up with, "hopefully not as dangerous as the Ford was." He sank into the seat. He looked at Phil, for help, but Phil was not listening. Ree demanded to know what Dave was talking about. He reached for his wallet and took it out of his pants and opened it up. He took out the picture of him and Black Beauty and showed it to her. She looked at it very carefully and asked him if that was his car and if it was, what happened to it. He proceeded to tell the entire story. She wouldn't look at him. He took the picture back and put it back into his wallet. She took her hands and put them on either side, of his head and turned him, to look at her. She leaned in close. He thought they were going to kiss. She wanted to examine his nose. It was then, that she saw the scars. She released his head. The waitress brought their orders and they ate, in silence. He had a difficult time, controlling his anger, at his brother, Dave.

They finished eating. The girls went to the girls room; the guys to the men's room. Once, in the men's room, he, angrily, thanked Dave, for ruining his day, with Ree. Dave thought that he had told her. Phil chimed in, "obviously not." They left the bathrooms and walked to the cars. Ree took his hand as they walked to the car. They got in and he turned on the motor. Sammy Turner was on the radio with "Lavender Blue." Ree reached over, to the dash, and turned off the radio. She had tears, in her eyes. "You could have been killed. Why did you try it?" She asked. All he could say was "stupidity." Ree, then, told him that she thought the racing boat was another stupid idea. He told her that he would be careful and for her not to worry, because it didn't even have a motor. He did not mention that he was starting to look for one. She seemed to compose herself and slid closer, to him. She wrapped her arms around his right arm, after he went through all the gears, to the last one. In his mind, he would have loved to have stuffed a hot potato in Dave's mouth. The last thing, he wanted, was for Ree, to worry about him. He reached over to the dash and turned the radio, back on. Marty Robbins was singing about a "White Sport Coat And A Pink Carnation." Ree looked up at him and said "I'll bet his coat didn't get pink punch spilled on it." They both laughed. Clyde McPhatter came on next with "A Lover's Question." He was followed by the Platters and "Smoke Gets In Your Eyes." Ray Peterson was next with "Tell Laura I Love Her." Ree, quickly, reached out and turned the radio off. "I hate that song, especially, now!" She said. Then asked, if he didn't mind if she closed her eyes and took a little nap. He told her, to go right ahead and that he would wake her up. When they got to the cottage.

He waited until she was asleep, before he turned the radio back on. He kept the volume very, low. Bobby Darin was singing "Beyond The Sea." He, softly, sang along. He looked down, occasionally, at Ree and told her how very much in love with her, he was. The Kingston Trio came on the radio, with "Scotch And Soda." He noticed that a lot of folk songs were making it onto the top music charts.

As he came down the dirt road, he noticed that someone else was a few minutes ahead. Their dust from the dirt road was just settling, as he drove through. Pat Boone was on the radio, singing, "April Love." Ree began to stir from her "slumber." As she awoke, she took out an L&M and lit from the cigarette lighter, on the dash. She handed it to him and then took another and lit that one, for herself. He told her that they were almost to the cottage. He turned into the dirt driveway. Ree asked him where the rest of the road went to. He told her that it was a "dead end." She looked at him and noted that it was a swamp on both sides, with high, very high bushes. He told her that part of the road was invisible from the cottage. She said, "looks like a great "parking "spot. He agreed.

He pulled the VW up next to Dave's Ford. Dave and Trudy had just gotten out and were walking towards the porch. He told Ree that it was dave that kicked up the dust on the road. That he and Trudy must have stopped downtown. He turned off the car and got out, he went around the front of the car and opened the door for Ree. She grabbed her small bag. He closed the door and they walked hand in hand to the small porch. He advised her to step tall, to avoid all the roots. She stopped and took a deep breath, expanding her chest. His eyes focused on her chest. She exhaled and said that she loved the smell of pine trees. He told her that he did, too. They entered the cottage. His mom stood in the center of the living room and directed Ree to put her small bag in the front bedroom. Then, she said all the "girls" would congregate in the kitchen. She told he and Dave that they were needed to put in the dock. He went into the bedroom as Ree came out. He changed into his bathing suit. He came out and walked through the kitchen, to the side porch and out to the unassembled dock. The girls gave a "wolf whistle" as he walked through. They did the same thing for Dave. Phil and his dad were already starting to put the framework in place, for the first piece. The metal posts were already in the water, resting on their large bases. The bases had holes in them, for the posts, to go in. The posts were then secured by "pins" that went through holes, in the bases and posts.

It was Dave and his turn, to take the next frame and attached it to the first one. It was easy, because it attached to the end of the first one with large bolts and nuts. Next, they had to bring the "dock" part, "the deck" over and slide it into place on the frame. They tried to slide it along the top of the other. It didn't work. It was obvious, someone had to be in the front and pull it along. He knew the water was going to be cold. The ice had only been "out" of the lake, a few weeks. He did a "tightrope" scene, walking, gingerly, along the narrow edge of the frame. At the same time, he slowly pulled the deck, as Dave pushed. It was, almost, perfectly lined up with the frame and was ready to be dropped in, when Dave gave it a huge push. The weight of the deck and the momentum, sent him off the frame and into the frigid water. The deck popped in perfectly, into the frame. Standing in waist high cold water, he had to hold the front up, while his Dad passed him the bases for the other posts. He had to duck down under the water and place the bases on the sandy bottom. Phil threw him a scuba mask. He put it on and stuck his head under the water. A post was handed to him. He positioned the post through the hole, in the frame and placed it in the hole on the base and slipped a pin through it. He had to search for the pin. Dave had thrown it to him and, of course, it missed and sank to the bottom. He did the same, with the other post and base. He was sure that he was as blue as the suit he wore. The next deck piece was slid along the one that was just placed together. Dave was in the position, that he had, when he met "Davy Jones's locker." He watched as Phil, did what Dave had done to him. Dave's entrance into the water was a lot more "theatrical". Instead of just going into the water, on his back, as he had done. Dave's arms and legs were flailing for something to hang onto, to prevent him from getting wet. There was nothing available. Now, he and Dave were both standing in waist high, cold water and they put the last frame together and the deck. His dad came out walking, on the dock, with his American flag, to put in the last post. That was his signal that he was in the cottage, if anyone wanted to visit, from the water. He stepped to the post, to stick the flag in, when the dock, under his feet listed to a steep angle, sending his dad, flag and all, into the water. When he broke the surface, his face was red, not from the sun, or the coldness of the water, but leveled at Dave. "You didn't secure the post, did you!" he shouted. Dave was too busy laughing, to pay much attention, to his dad. Phil. Finally, waded into the water and secured the ladder, so dad and he could get out of the water. Dave dove down, with the scuba mask and secured the last post. He climbed out, with the flag and put the pole into the hole in the last post. He, finally got out of the water and ran onto the porch, to get a towel and dry off. From the porch, he heard the hysterical laughter, coming from the kitchen. Apparently the girls had been watching them. Ree came out onto the porch and helped dry him off. His mom came onto the porch and asked that the water be hooked up, so they could wash the dishes. Phil, had already, thrown the switch for the electricity. His dad and Phil ran the water pipes from under the cottage to the lake. They connected them together and Phil waded out into the water, with the last pipe. The last pipe was resting in the crotch of two, two by fours, nailed into an "X". it was put on the bottom of the lake, about twenty feet from the shoreline. His dad ran the other end into the pump house. He plugged in the pump and threw the switch. He heard his mom yell "Yay! We have water!".

While the ladies were washing the "winter" off the dishes. He and his dad took the grill off the porch and set it up in the barbeque pit, among the rocks. He, loaded the briquettes and his dad squirted the lighter fluid on them. Dave came up, behind them and threw a lighted match onto the coals. A large "WHOOMP" happened as the coals caught fire. His dad glared at Dave, with singed eyebrows and hair. Dave turned and, quickly, left the area. When the girls realized that no one was injured, they began to laugh, hysterically, again. Ree ran to the bathroom.

Now, it was time to put the 16 foot rowboat, in the water. The four men picked it up, two on each side and carried it onto the dock. They turned it over and slid it into the water. He tied to the bow, to the cleat, on the dock and Phil tied the stern rope, to the other cleat, near the stern. Dave came out of the porch, with two oars and the oar locks. He put the oar, locks in the holes on each side of the middle seat and placed the oars along the insides of the boat. Dave wanted to take Trudy out in the boat. He went and got the gas tank, out of the storage shed. Dave followed with the outboard motor. He watched Dave maneuver the outboard to the transom of the boat. He prayed that a giant wave, from a passing boat, would knock him over the transom, like it did him. It didn't happen. The motor was securely fastened to the transom. Dad yelled to the girls that the coals were ready. Ree brought out the burgers, cheese, and rolls. She was still giggling. They all sat, on the porch and ate the burgers, some with cheese; ate from two large bags of chips. His mom had stopped in town and picked up two six packs of cokes.

The sun was really beating down, on the dock. Dave and Trudy had gone out, in the boat. Ree had gone into the bathroom and changed into her bathing suit. His mom and Nan had done the same thing. They all basked in the sunlight, in their respective deck chairs. His dad was pleased that the cottage had gotten opened so well. He started to apply suntan lotion to Ree's back and shoulders. He leaned and whispered in her ear, "wish I could put all over you." She grinned as he handed the bottle to her. She applied it to his back and whispered, in his ear, "me. too." After they applied the oil, they lay back in the lounges and closed their eyes and soaked in the rays of the sun.

After a while, his mom asked if anyone was going to stay the weekend, with them. Phil said "no, because he wanted to go home and do some more work on the cabin cruiser. He said "no." because he was slated to start his summer job, at the country club, the next day. They knew that Dave couldn't stay, because he was going to be going back to college and take some summer courses, plus work at a, local restaurant. "Guess it's just me and Dad." His mom said. Ree looked at him and said, "you didn't tell me, you were starting your job, so soon." He told her that he thought he did, and was sorry. He did tell her that he had her graduation off. She smiled.

The clock, on the kitchen wall, rang five o'clock. He told Ree that they should start to head back. His dad told him to leave the deck chairs and lounges. He went into the bathroom, to change. Ree was in the front bedroom. Phil and Nan had just returned from a walk and decided to leave as well. While they were changing, Dave and Trudy came back, in the boat. He and Ree emerged from their changing rooms. They went out onto the dock and joined the others and said their goodbyes. His mom, told him, that any time, he and Ree wanted to spend the weekend, with them, they were welcome to come. She thanked them and then they walked around the porch, around the cottage, to the parking area. They got into the VW. She put her small bag, in the back seat and cuddled up next to him. He backed the car down the dirt driveway and turned into the dead end part of the road. "Back up a, little bit more." Ree said. He backed up to the end. He put the car in neutral. He turned to face her. She wrapped her arms around his neck and planted a long, wet, passionate kiss, on his lips, he responded. She was, obviously, "hot" for him. He went to put his arms around her; she took his hands and placed them on her shirt covered breasts. She took one of her hands from around his neck and began to rub his penis through his jeans. When she tore her lips from his, she said, "Oh baby, I want you so much!" She had never said that, before. They heard Phil's car start up. He said, 'we'd better go!" He took his hands, reluctantly, from her chest and put the car in gear. They spewed dirt and stones, as he drove past the driveway and headed up the road. He told her that his body aches for her. She told him the same thing.

Young Love . . . (Tab Hunter/Sonny James)

He began his summer job, that Sunday, working 7 to 3. He would work those hours until Wednesday. He had Wednesday off. Ree worked her job from 9 to 5 Monday through Friday. They would get together on the nights that he worked 7 to 3, and meet for lunch on the days he worked 3 to 11. He did have the night, of her graduation off. He spent the day, that Saturday, with her family. Her graduation took place, that Saturday evening, June 4th. Her dad had a "lunch" cookout. John and Janet were there, as well as Ree's family. He gave her a silver charm bracelet with one charm on it. It was a heart, with her name, on the front, and "with all my Love" and his name, on the back. She was thrilled and put it on, right away. She, then, grabbed his left arm and raised it, with her left arm and showed her bracelet, next to his I.D. bracelet. They spent the afternoon, playing badminton in the backyard. Her dad asked him about the hydroplane. Ree dropped her racket and walked back to the picnic table. Her dad apologized and they both knew it was not a subject to discuss around Ree. John was interested and so, the three of them, left the backyard and walked around the front. He described the boat, to them. Ten feet in length. Bright red, with the number "7" painted on the deck, in bold black paint. He was looking for a 17HP outboard motor, preferably, a Mercury. He was going into the city, to a large marine store, to pick up his steering wheel. He told them that it had to be a "special "steering wheel, with the spindle in front of the dash. He, also, was picking up the throttle lever. It had to have a "kill" switch on it. Her dad asked him to be please be careful. "My daughter, obviously, cares very deeply for you and would be devastated if anything happened to you." He told her dad that he, too, cared very deeply for her and that he would be careful. John asked him, when he planned to race it. He said that he had registered for a race in Alton Bay, NH, in August. They finished talking and went back to the backyard. Ree was sitting at the table with Janet and her mother. Her mother asked if the "boys" were through with their 'secret' talk. They said that they were. The graduation was set for seven PM. Ree had to leave by five thirty to get ready. He and John had brought sport coats and ties, and chinos, to change into. Janet had to leave, early, as well, as she and Ree were graduating together. Ree's mom, said that when the time was ready. He could change in the first floor bathroom. He thanked her. John and Janet would go to her house, to get ready.

Ree left, with her mom, to the school. He went into the house and changed his clothes. He put the jeans and polo shirt in the back seat, of the VW. At 6:30, he, her dad, her sister, her mom piled into the Galaxy and headed for the school. It was a hot and muggy evening, that 4th day of June. The graduation was held outside, in the football stadium. Everyone was glad, when all the speeches were over and done with. They waited with deep anticipation, for Ree's name to be called and to see her cross the stage. Janet last name began with "M", so she went across before Ree. Ree's last name began with "W", so it was a while. After it was all over, pictures were taken. He took one with her and her family. Her mother took one with him and Ree. They all went back to Ree's house for cake and ice cream. They "longed" to leave the party and have time, for themselves, but it was not, to be. They did leave her house, to go to a bunch of "open houses". It was a whirlwind night. She 'dragged him from one party to the next. He was introduced to people, he would never meet or see again. John and Janet were with them. John felt the same. He and John were lucky to grab a beer and a sandwich, before they had to go to, yet, another party. The night ended just after midnight. He was tired. They shared a goodnight kiss at her front door, and he headed home, for a good night's rest.

They did not get to spend a lot of time together, the following week. His work and graduation rehearsals took up a lot of his time. They did get to talk on the phone. When, at last, Saturday, June 11th arrived. He went over to Ree's in the early afternoon and picked her up. He was, once again, mesmerized, by her beauty. They drove back to his house. They turned the radio, off and talked. They told each other, how lonely they had been. Their jobs were interfering with their "love lives." They laughed about that. Ree made the cliché about absence making the heart grow fonder. He said that they needed to make plans, so to spend more time together. June was, almost, impossible, to be alone. Her birthday was coming up and then Blinstrub's with Johnny Mathis. He asked her about the 4th of July weekend. She had to work the Friday before, but not Saturday, Sunday, or Monday. He told her that he was supposed to work, but he would tell them, that he had to go to NH, with his folks. He would tell his folks that he had to work. His brother and Nan were going to the Cape. His brother, Dave was in Maine. He would be in the house, alone. Ree smiled and told him that he would not be alone.

His graduation was, also, held outside, in the football stadium. Another very hot and humid evening. His was "soaked" with sweat inside the cap and gown. They were so happy when the speeches were done. Then, they learned, because of the size of their class, they would not cross the stage, individually. They would be dismissed and would go to the card table, set up in the infield, that had their last name. He would go to the table that had "A to B". They were dismissed and pandemonium broke out, They all ran to the tables. The lines were very long.

He, finally, got his diploma. He left the crowd and went to find Ree and his folks. They were waiting by his dad's Mercury. They would take pictures, at home. He and Ree, got into the VW and followed the Mercury, home. He took his tassel and hung it off the rearview mirror. She took her "white" tassel and hung it next to his black one. He turned on the radio and The Four Lads were singing "Moments To Remember." It was dedicated to his class, that had just graduated. Then came Perry Como singing "Magic Moments." Ree said that every moment with them was "magic". He agreed. They arrived, at his house and assembled in the living room, for pictures. Then, they enjoyed ice cream and cake. He drove her home, by way of the duck feeding area. The Platters were on the radio, singing "Smoke Gets In Your Eyes." They couldn't stay long, "parking" because he was working, the next day, from 7 to 3. They did manage to get in some passionate kisses and heavy "petting." They began to talk about her birthday and Blinstrub's.

His folks had, each, given him one hundred dollars, for graduation. Ree had given him a new Speidel, expandable, watch band. It was silver with a gold band in the middle. He couldn't wait to get it pit on and get rid of the old "imitation leather" band. Ree kept pestering him about what he was going to get her, for her birthday. He asked her what she really wanted. "You, with nothing on, but your watch and my I.D. bracelet." She said. He told her that she could have that anytime. They laughed. He really liked to make her laugh.

The next eleven days, in June, seemed to drag along. Her birthday fell on a week day. He wasn't sure he could get the day off. Then, she told him that her folks wanted to celebrate her birthday on the Sunday, before that Wednesday. He checked his work schedule and found that he had that Sunday, off. She told him that her dad was going to cook outside, so he could come in jeans and a polo shirt.

It was a sunny, warm afternoon. John and Janet were there, too. Ree showed him the new clothes, that her folks had gotten her. New sun dresses, Bermuda shorts, and her own set of car keys, to her mom's car. She whispered to him, "My mom, also, got me some real sexy underwear." He told her that he liked that. She laughed. He, then, gave her his gifts. She immediately opened them. He gave her four more silver charms, for her bracelet and a small bottle of Chanel number 5. She gave him a hug and told him she would thank him, later. John and Janet gave her a gift certificate to Lord & Taylor. She was very happy. He heard Janet ask her how it felt to be "legal." Ree laughed and said her favorite saying, "that's nasty!" The four of them sat down and talked about the upcoming date for Blinstrub's. He would drive over to Ree's and meet the others there. They would ride in John's car. If they wanted to eat, they had to be there, by 6:30PM, at the latest. Guys would wear suit and tie; the girls would wear "dinner" dresses. He called her, from work, on her birthday. He had mailed her a birthday card, that expressed his immense love for her. She had just finished reading it, when he called.

Again, they weren't able to spend a lot of time, together. The 25th of June approached, rapidly.

He got his suit, back from the cleaners, on the 24th. He worked all the previous week and was so glad to have that Saturday off and not have to go to work, until 3 that Sunday afternoon. He was excited about going to an actual night club and seeing Johnny Mathis. Saturday morning, he and Phil drove into the city and he purchased the steering wheel and lines and shifter, for the hydroplane. When he got home, it was around noon. He went to his room and checked his wallet and piggy bank. He withdrew a hundred dollars and put it in his wallet. He ate his usual lunch and when done, called Ree. She was so excited. She, too, told him that this was her first time in a night club and seeing a "celebrity." He spent the afternoon, getting ready. He took a long bath, brushed his teeth, again, combed his hair, which needed to be cut, again. He spent a lot of time applying black shoe polish, to his loafers and polishing them. He laid the suit and a white dress shirt out on his bed. He had on fresh briefs and fresh black socks. He looked at his watch with the new watchband. He put on his I.D. bracelet. His watch said 2:35PM. He had at least two hours, before he had to get dressed. He, quickly, put on his jeans and a polo shirt. He went to his bank and found two one dollar bills and two quarters. He ran out of the room and down the hall, down the stairs and out the front door. He ran and walked fast to the square, to the barber shop. He went in and found that he would be next. He said, to himself, that he planned that right. Vic ushered him into the chair. "I was just about to call it a day, Barnaby." He said. He told Vic that he needed the same haircut, he got the last time. Vic was amazing. He remembered the haircut and began to cut it. "You must be dating the same girl." Vic said. He laughed and replied "yup." Vic said that he didn't know this girl, but he admired her taste in haircuts. He also told him that if he ever met a girl that wanted him to have another flattop. That he would have to have some other barber, do it. He laughed and told Vic that his flattop days were over. The haircut cost a dollar and twenty five cents. He gave Vic the whole two dollars and fifty cents. Vic said that he was glad that he waited, before closing up the shop. He thanked Vic and left the shop. He ran and walked quickly back home. It was 3:40PM. Time to rinse the small hairs, from the haircut, off the back of his neck and get dressed. He left the house with time, to spare. He got into the VW and decided that he better put some gas in it. Frank Sinatra was on the radio, singing "All The Way." Buddy Holly followed with "Rave On." Every time he heard Buddy Holly, his mind went back to the awful February day. The Coasters followed Buddy with "Little Egypt."

He stopped at the gas station and filled up the "bug," His watch read 4:42PM, when he pulled out of the gas station. Larry Williams was on the radio, singing about "Short Fat Fanny." He was followed by Laverne Baker and "Jim Dandy." It was ten after five, when he pulled up in front of Ree's house. He turned off the beetle and opened the door and got out. He checked his tie and suit in his reflection of the driver's side window. He turned and walked up the walk to Ree's front door. He rang the bell. Again, Ree's little sister opened the door. "Holy cow!" She said. "Ree, Jim Dandy's here!" He heard Ree walking toward them. "Who?" She asked. She was wearing a tight gray skirt with a blue blouse, that, again, accentuated her breasts. Her lush red lips were "asking" for his to kiss them. "I like your haircut!" She said. She handed him their tickets; he put them in his left breast pocket of his suit coat. He transferred his wallet from his rear left pants pocket to the same pocket of the coat. He heard John's car pull up. They walked hand in hand down the walk towards the Plymouth. He stopped at the VW and locked it. They got into the back seat and headed for Blinstrub's. Sam Cooke was on the radio, singing "Wonderful World." Followed by Johnny Mathis and "Wonderful. Wonderful." Janet said that she hoped he would sing "The Twelfth of Never." tonight. John said that he would probably sing all his hits. Ree and he were snuggled very close to each other. He told her that he loved the fact that she was wearing the Chanel. She nuzzled his neck and said that his Stetson was driving her wild. They looked into each other's eyes and shared a short light kiss. Then Janet had to bring up "Psycho." She wanted to know if they had seen it, yet. She and John saw it the other night. Ree started laughing. Janet said that she didn't think the movie was funny at all. Ree told them how he had to get out of his seat and watch it from the foyer. They all snickered. John said that the part that bothered him was that there were people like that, in the world. He agreed. They kidded him about not being able to stay, in his seat.

They pulled up to the front door of Blinstrub's. The valet wanted to take the car and park it. John said "no!" that he would park it himself. He, Ree, and Janet stood in front of the door and waited for John to park the car. It was 6:15PM. By the time, they were seated, at a stage side table. A waiter came over and took their orders, quickly. He ordered a medium cooked rib eye steak. The others ordered steak, too. Their food arrived in about twenty minutes. A photographer came up to the them and asked if they wanted their picture taken. He said "yes." She took four of them, of all of them huddled together. She took two of them and two of John and Janet. The pictures cost 35 dollars. He picked up the cost of the pictures. He looked at his steak and cut it and took about two bites, when the lights dimmed and a huge spotlight lit up the back of the stage and a big stair case. The announcer's loud voice rang out. "And now, Boston's own Johnny Mathis!" Everyone stood up and applauded and Johnny appeared in the spotlight and descended the stairs, singing "Wild Is The Wind." He went to eat another piece of steak and found the plates were gone! He was not happy. He was hungry!

The show lasted about an hour and a half. Johnny never took a break. When the show was over. He looked down at the table and saw a bill for him and Ree for twenty five dollars.

The photographer returned to them and handed them their pictures. They got up to leave. He mentioned to Ree, as they were leaving that he was still hungry. Ree said that she was, too. When they got back to the car, John and Janet were, also, hungry. John said that there must be a "clause" in the entertainer's contract that no food be allowed to be served or eaten during a performance. John said they could go to the Adventure car hop in Saugus. It was closest. They all agreed. It was 9:30PM.

They pulled into the car hop and John ordered the chicken in a basket. He said the magic words, "Woo, Woo, Ginsburgh" and received the second chicken in a basket, free. He and Ree shared one and John and Janet shared the other. When, they were finished, they paid the bill and gave the tray, back to the roller skating waitress. They saw that it was ten PM. They decided to go and "park" for awhile. Ree moved closer to him and hiked her skirt up above her knees. She, also, unbuttoned four of the buttons, on her blouse. He took off his suit coat and tie and unbuttoned the buttons, on his shirt. They looked at each other and crushed their lips together. Their arms encircled each other. When they parted lips. She lowered her head and began to kiss his naked chest. He moved his left hand up and under her skirt. As he moved his hand up along her inner thigh, he found the spot where the stocking stopped and naked flesh greeted his hand. He moved it further and found, instead of panties, a hard, elastic garment. She raised her head from his chest and brought her lips back to his. "What are you wearing?" he asked. "Sorry Lover, it's my girdle." He groaned. She pressed her lips to his and they grinded their lips together. When their lips parted, a second time. She pushed his head and lips to her breasts.

They never noticed that John had parked the car. Their hands and lips roamed all over their bodies. She had his zipper down and her hand inside his pants. She loved to feel the hardness of his penis. He had pushed her bra cups up and over her breasts and was kissing every inch of them, finally to her nipples. Which he took between his lips and lightly lashed the tip with his tongue. They were lost in their passion and couldn't care less what time, it was getting to be. John broke them up with saying that they had to get home. He was serving, in church, the next morning. They pulled apart and readjusted their clothing. They cuddled, tightly, together, on the trip to her house. The night had been another milestone, for him.

John pulled up in front of Ree's. Janet told her that she would call her tomorrow. He and Ree said good night and then he walked her to her front door. They embraced in one more passionate kiss. He told her that he would call her, before he went to work. She told him, again, how very much in love with him, she was. He told her the same thing. They wished that they could see more of each other, but their summer jobs kept them apart more than together.

The next weekend was the fourth of July weekend. He didn't realize that the fourth was on a Tuesday. He was going to have four days off, in a row. Ree had the same days off. His folks were going to be at the cottage, for the whole four days, as well. Phil would be away all that week. Dave was in Maine, for the summer. He began to get excited. He and Ree talked about the weekend. They could go to the beach, or just hang out with friends. The important thing was that they were going to be together. They both had to work that Friday. She would be off at 5PM. He had to work the 3 to 11 shift. They made plans to get together, that Saturday. She said that they would think of something to do, maybe the beach.

He called her that Friday, during his dinner break. They decided to go to the beach, at Walden Pond. He told her that he couldn't wait to see her. She said the same. After his dinner break, at work and the phone call, to Ree, was over, he was bored. There were no parties, at the club, nothing. It was quiet. He was more of a night watchman. He sat out on the patio, overlooking the dark expanse of the golf course. He checked the pool, to see, if any kidswere trying to sneak in. Nothing was happening. He sat in one of the deck chairs and lit up one of his last L&M's of the night. At ten o'clock, he heard the switchboard operator answer a call. She was about to "lock" it down, for the night. She called him, to the switchboard. "The boss just called and said that you can call it a night, since nothing is going on." He thanked her and went to the closet by the front door stairs and took off his black tie and white jacket. He closed the door and headed out the front door, to the VW. He unlocked the car and got in and turned it on and drove home. Jimmy Dean was the last song, of the night, on the radio, "Dear Ivan." Static filled the airwaves, after the National Anthem. He turned off the radio. His excitement began to mount as he thought of four straight days with Ree.

He pulled into the driveway and realized that the VW was going to be the only car there. His folks had already left for the cottage and so had Phil and Nan. He got out of the car, closed and locked it up and went into the dark and empty house. Thoughts of "Psycho" came back on him. He decided to sleep in his folks bedroom that night, rather than go upstairs. He would not tell anyone that he did that. Sleep did not come easy to him, that night. The excitement of being with Ree, coupled with the noises an empty house makes, made for an uneasy rest.

He woke up to the sound of the phone ringing. He got out of bed and ambled to the phone. "Hello?" he asked. It was Ree. "Hey sleepy head! Remember me? It's beach time. When are you coming over here?" he asked her what time it was. "10: 00!" She said. "Let me get cleaned up and I'll be right over. He hung up the phone and went back into his parent's bedroom and made their bed, as best he could. He went upstairs and took off his briefs and drew a bath. He went back downstairs and retrieved his 'work "clothes. He went back upstairs, naked, and checked on the bath, and then went to his room. He threw his work clothes on the floor and grabbed a fresh pair of jeans, a polo shirt, fresh briefs, white socks, his keds and went back to the bath room. He turned off the water, in the tub, checked the temperature and climbed in. He, quickly, washed and rinsed himself. He climbed out of the tub, grabbed a bath towel and dried himself. He splashed on some Stetson, applied deodorant, pulled on the polo shirt and combed his hair. He put on the briefs and socks and jeans and then his white bucs. He pulled the plug on the bath tub and went down the stairs, down the hall, through the kitchen and out the back door, down the stairs, pass the cabin cruiser and to the VW. He unlocked it and got in. He looked at his watch and it read 10:30 AM. He started up the VW and backed up, turned it around and headed out of the driveway, to Ree's. Elvis was on the radio with "Good Rockin tonight."

He arrived at Ree's at eleven o'clock. He turned off the car and got out and walked up the walk to her front door. She must have been waiting for him. She opened the door and closed it behind her. She had on dark blue Bermuda shorts and a white pleasant blouse. She carried her small bag, in her right hand, as she took his right hand with her left hand. They walked to the VW. He opened her door and watched as she slid her dark tanned legs onto the passenger seat. He walked around to his side and got in. he turned on the car. They leaned towards each other and shared their first, wet, passionate kiss, of the day. Little Willie John was on the radio, singing, "Talk To Me." They pulled away from the curb. Ree mentioned that she was hungry and did not want to eat the "beach" food. He, too, was hungry, as he hadn't eaten yet. They headed for Ho-Jo's. he still had about 40 dollars left, in his wallet. Her hand squeezed his right thigh, as he drove.

He pulled into the parking lot and turned off the car. They got out and walked hand in hand, into the restaurant. They both decided on lobster rolls and fries, with chocolate shakes. He couldn't take his eyes off her. Her blouse was pulled way up and showed absolutely no cleavage at all. He sighed and thought, to himself, what a shame it was to cover up those beautiful breasts.

They finished eating; he paid the tab and left a good tip and they walked back to the car. It was just after twelve noon, when they were headed for Concord and Walden Pond. It took about a half hour, to get there. The parking lot was practically full. He turned off the car as They exited the car. He locked it and they headed for the beach. It was mobbed! They stood there, holding hands and realized that any thought of being alone, was stupid. Then, it hit him! He left his bathing suit, at home. Ree suggested that they go to his house, get the bathing suit and head up to Ipswich. He agreed. Ipswich had large sand dunes, that they could, once again, be alone. They walked back to the car. He unlocked it and they got in. he started up the car. Ree cuddled up next to him and, once again, her hand rested on his right thigh. Billy Vaughn was on the radio, playing "A Swinging Safari." Debby Reynolds followed with "Tammy". Brooke Benton and Dinah Washington were next with "You Got What It Takes." They sang along and pointed to each other. She sang Dinah's part and he sang Brooke's part.

They arrived at his house around 1:35PM. He pulled the VW down into the driveway. He turned it off and they got out. Ree said that she wanted to see the racing boat. He led her under the back porch, to the boat. He took off the blanket and she gasped. "It's so small!" he told

273

her it was ten feet long. She looked in and asked how he could sit down in such a small space. He told her that he would be kneeling and that he was looking for a pad to place on the seat, to cushion his knees. She did say she liked the color. She expressed hope that he would not be able to find an outboard, for it. He looked at his watch and said that they better get upstairs, and get his suit, if they wanted to get to Ipswich, before that beach fills up. He covered the boat back up and they held hands, as they went up the stairs. They walked through the kitchen. She told him that she had to use the bathroom. He led her up the stairs, to the upstairs bathroom. She went in and closed the door. He went down the hall, to his room and grabbed his bathing suit and towel. He started to walk out of his room. Ree was standing at the entrance to his room. The peasant blouse was pulled down her arms, revealing her milky white breasts. That was the first thing he noticed. The second was that she had taken off her shorts and was standing in a pair of sexy, whispy, see through panties. He gasped! She walked towards him. He dropped his bathing suit and towel, on the floor. He reached for her. She came, willingly, into his arms. Their lips crushed against each other. Their arms encircled each other. They swayed against each other. He doesn't know how they managed to get over to the edge of his bed. They fell onto the bed, their arms and legs intertwined. Their searching lips parted as their tongues swirled against each other. "Oh baby!" she moaned, between their lips. His left arm came from around her back to her the supple soft flesh of her inner thighs. She wrenched her lips from his, panting heavily, her breasts heaving against her bra and blouse. They both sat up. He peeled off his polo shirt. She stripped off her blouse and bra. She used both hands to undo his belt and button, of his jeans; she unzipped them and with both hands slid them off his hips. He fell onto his back as she stripped him of his jeans. Once again, their lips pressed together, tongues lashing in each other's mouths, legs and arms intertwined. His member became enraged. His moved her onto her back and put his left hand on her thighs, his right hand on her left breast, massaging it, whil he tore his mouth, from hers and put it on her right breast. His lips encircled every inch, followed by his tongue. He reached her nipple and put it in between his lips, his tongue slowly and gently lashing it. He felt it harden under his touch. His other hand and fingers found the way to that nipple. Gently squeezing it between thumb and forefinger. His left hand snaked under her panties and massaged her "outer lips" and slowly worked it's way inside. She was very wet! He massaged her in a circular motion. He found her sensitive area. Her legs began to thrash, her arms around his back, rubbing it, stroking it. Her fingernails raked his shoulder blades. He glanced up from her breast, her eyes were closed, her tongue hanging out the corner of her mouth. Soft moans and groans escaped her mouth, along with hissing sounds from between her teeth. He took his hand from her breast, and with his mouth still kissing and teasing her inflamed nipple, with both hands, he grabbed the edges of her panties and rolled them down her legs, to her feet and off. He brought his mouth and lips and tongue to her knees and began to slowly work up. His hands went to her both breasts and continued to softly massage and "tease" her rock hard nipples. "OMIGOD!!! She cried. "Oh baby, Kiss me down there!! PLEASE!!!" he moved his mouth, lips and tongue up. With his tongue, he licked her outer lips, in a circular motion. He would stop and tease the little nub with the tip of his tongue. Her pelvis began to push up to meet his lips and tongue. Then, he plunged his tongue, inside, as far as it would go, lapping and licking. Her hands were in his hair, clenching and pulling on it. Her hips were bucking against his mouth like a wild bronc! His tongue was getting washed in her juices! He continued to kiss her. She was screaming, "oh God! Oh God!". Then, she asked if he had anything. He knew what she meant. He replaced his tongue and lips with his right hand fingers inside her. Her reached across her beautiful heaving body and opened his night stand drawer. He fished around and brought out the pack of three condoms. She reached over and ripped open the pack. Then, with both hands, she pulled his briefs off. She put both hands on his member and took the condom and slid it all the way down his shaft. When it was securely on, she began to rub and stroke him. She was completely out of control! "Oh God, baby, I want you inside me!" She spread her legs as he moved between them. He moved up to her and she guided him "home". She gave out a low moan and wrapped her calves around his. She moved her legs up over his thighs. They lay motionless. She groaned how good he felt inside her. Then, nature took over. He began to slowly thrust in and draw himself almost, completely out and then back in as far as he could go. His hands had moved to her breasts. He lowered his mouth to hers. His lips parted and he stuck his tongue, into her open mouth. She began to suck on it, as if it were a popsickle. She began to meet his thrusts with her own. Their tempo increased, dramatically. Their two bodies locked in paradise! He could feel his penis swell. She felt it too. "Don't hold back, baby! Let it happen!" They were out of control! He felt the climax, start to build. He brought his left hand from her breast and put it between them. He placed a finger on her little nub., and began to rub it. She went Wild! Bucking and thrashing! He didn't know what he was touching, only that she really enjoyed it. Her bucking and thrashing made him "start". He told her that he was going to explode! She grabbed his hips, with both hands and they bucked together. She cried out and her body thrust up against him and collapsed! He gave a mighty thrust and he too, reached his climax! They lay, together, for a few minutes and then she asked him to grab hold of the condom, at it's base, so it wouldn't fall off when he pulled out. He did as she asked and pulled out and got off of her. He held onto it and rolled over her and got off the bed. He went to the bathroom and flushed it down the toilet. He took a wash cloth and dampened it and 'washed his member. He wiped it and, quickly, went back to her. She was still lying on the bed, with her legs apart. She slid over and let him lay beside her on her right side. He lay on his left side and slowly stroked her belly, legs, arms, and around her breasts. Her breathing sounded like it was returning to normal. She let out a large sigh. He moved his lips to hers and they shared a "lover's kiss."

They continued to lie side by side, naked, on the bed. She brought her right hand to his penis and slowly massaged the shaft. He continued to gently run his fingers over body. They shared more short kisses. Her hand began to rub his "head" and all around his shaft. He brought his hand, to her breasts and, again, began to "tease" her nipples. After a few minutes of "petting" he was beginning to "respond" to her. She felt it, too. She told him to lie on his back. He did as she said. She increased her slow strokes on him. She brought her mouth to his and, this time, their kiss lasted longer and passion began to 'take over." She rained kisses on his face, neck, shoulders, and chest. All the while, her hand was bringing him to hardness. She leaned across him and reached her hand into the drawer and took out another condom. While she was leaning over him, opening up the packet, he brought his hands to her hanging breasts and, slowly rubbed his hands all over them. She began to moan, softly and leaned further down, giving his lips and tongue access to them. He felt the blood return to his member. Her hand was working "magic" on him. She raised herself up onto her knees and brought her left leg over him and straddled him. Once again, she 'guided "him to her and slowly lowered herself onto him, impaling herself on him. She leaned back down, so he could continue to pay "homage" to her hanging breasts. Slowly, she began to raise and lower herself, on him. He felt his "strength" grow, with each slow thrust. She increased the tempo of her thrusts, actually "pumping him". She leaned back away from his mouth and threw her head back. He reached up with both hands and filled them with her breasts. He began to lift his pelvis off the bed and match her thrusts. Once again, his bed springs cried out in agony. He brought his left hand off her right breast and slid it between them. He moved it from her pubic hair to the little nub. He began to caress it between his fingers. She let out a loud moan and increased the tempo, even more. He never felt her put the new condom on, but knew it was there. She rode him, like he was a bucking horse. It didn't take long for his fingers to work their own magic. She cried out, once again," OH MY GOD!!!! He felt her juices flow around the condom. She continued to "pump" him. It took a little more time for him to reach a climax. She collapsed on top of him, when he finally exploded. She lay on top of him for a few minutes. Their bodies were bathed in perspiration. She rolled off of him, breathing heavy. They didn't speak right away. He really liked having her on top and controlling their love making. After a few minutes, she rolled off and he, again, got off the bed and went to the bathroom and disposed of the condom. Again, he "cleaned" himself. He was just about to return to his room, when she came into the bathroom. She held another condom, in her hand. It was still in the wrapper. She went to the tub and ran the water. "hope you don't like it too hot." She said, in a husky voice. "Nope!" he said. She leaned over and put the stopper over the drain. He told her that he didn't think he'd be ready. For a while. She told him that they would soak in the tub and if he should begin to arise to the situation, they would be prepared. The water reached a level just over half full. He climbed in first. She followed and put her legs on each side of him, with her feet near his head. She grabbed the soap and begin to wash his chest, then his legs and finally, his penis. She washed it very slowly. He took the soap and did the same, with her breasts and nipples and her legs. Especially her inner thighs. When he, slowly, washed her vagina, she began to squirm. "Oh baby! You make me crazy!" Please don't stop!" he said that he would continue until she told him to stop. She laid her head back against the tub and closed her eyes.He put the face cloth aside and put his right hand on her, slipping his finger inside. His left hand reached out to her soap covered breasts. She began to mover her hips against his probing finger. She reached under the water and found his hardening penis. "Oh baby! I'm getting hot!" She moaned. She slid down the tub, closer to him and continued to bring life to his member. She began to rub the head against her. He removed his finger. She reached over the side of the tub and picked up the condom and tore off the wrapper. With both hands, under the water, she rolled it down his now "hard" member. His hands were on her breasts, slowly massaging and softly kneading her nipples. She moved closer and guided him inside her. They both maneuvered each other into a sitting position. Their eyes locked on to each other. They leaned forward and their lips met. They began to move against each other. They moved closer and wrapped their arms around each other. Her hands on his back and his on hers. Their hips took on a mind of their own. Water started sloshing all around them and out of the tub onto the tile floor. They didn't care. Their passion took over! She wrenched her lips from his and threw her head back, "Oh my sweet baby!" She cried. They unwrapped their arms, from each other and grabbed the sides of the bathtub. They were like two pistons slapping against each other. At one point, he became "disengaged" from her. She pulled herself out of the tub and lay on her back, on the cold tile. He jumped out of the tub, holding the condom to his penis as she spread her legs to accommodate him. He slid between them and up to her. Again, she "guided" him inside. They took up where they had stopped. This time, he was the piston! Her eyes closed, her head turning from side to side, loud moans escaping from her lips. It didn't take, long, for his passion to rise to it's inevitable heights. He gave one more huge thrust and cried out and buried his head against her neck. She wrapped her arms around him and rained kisses against his cheek. He, slowly got off her and turned to the toilet and flushed away the condom. He returned to Ree. Her legs were still spread. He lowered his mouth to her and began to kiss her outer lips. She grabbed tuffs of hair on the top of his head. She began to cry out, "Oh, Oh, Oh, don't stop!" He moved his tongue inside, again, as far as it would go and then brought it up to her "nub". He replaced his tongue, with his forefinger of his right hand and moved it around inside, in a circular motion, till he found her sensitive spot. His tongue lashed the top of her nub, while his lips encased it. She began to thrust against him! Gurgling sounds escaped from her mouth, as he continued. He discovered that he enjoyed kissing her "down there." From what he could tell, she "liked" it, too. All, at once, she screamed out his name followed with" OMIGOD!". Then, he felt "juices" against his chin. Her body went limp. He lifted his head and crawled up, next to her, on the tie floor, which had lost it's coldness.

They got up, off the floor and toweled each other dry. He, then, took two bath towels and mopped up the 'standing" water around the tub. He placed the two soaked towels in the tub. They walked, hand in hand, back to his bedroom. She had picked up the wrapper and, when they got back in his room, they found the other wrappers and put them back in the drawer, from which they came. They sat on the edge of the bed and shared short "love" kisses. They decided that they were both quite hungry. He told her that he felt "drained". She laughed and told him that he should. She, too, felt weak. Then, she got a silly idea. She suggested that they get dressed, but without any underwear. He looked at her and laughed. So, she put on her Bermuda shorts sans panties and her blouse sans bra. He, carefully, slipped his jeans on without putting on his briefs. He was amazed at the feeling. He looked at her. She, obviously, was equally 'excited". Her nipples strained against the blouse. They smiled and giggled like two little kids and decided to go to the car hop and get some food.

They walked out of his house, to the VW. He looked at his watch. It read ten minutes, after five PM. They had been "making love" for over three hours. "No wonder, we are hungry!" Ree said. She brushed her hair, as he started up the car. Every time she moved, a little, he noticed her breasts jiggled under her blouse. He tried not to glance, at her. Once, she decided that her hair was "in place" she cuddled up next to him. Her hand, again, on his thigh. Connie Francis was on the radio, singing "Together". He asked her if he satisfied her, as a lover. She straightened up and looked at him. "Are you serious? Baby, you are fantastic!!! What about me?" She asked. He looked at her and told her that she, too, was a fantastic lover! She laid her head on his shoulder and said, "I guess we are compatible, when it comes to sex." He replied, "uh huh, we sure are." She gave his thigh a tight squeeze.

They pulled into the third row, at the car hop. He rolled down the window and touched the speaker button. Ree moved her hand to his zipper and unzipped his jeans and slipped her hand inside. A voice asked "order, please?" he began to speak, just as she squeezed his member. His voice went three octaves higher. Ree began to laugh. He was surprised that the voice heard his order of two cheeseburger baskets and two cokes. The voice said "thank you." He looked at Ree. She had a big grin, on her face. She brought his hand, from the steering wheel and slipped it under her shorts. She began to squirm as he found the wet crevice and slipped his finger inside. They continued to "play" with each other, until they saw the waitress skating to them, with their order. They withdrew their hands, as she skated up to the car. He rolled the window down halfway, so she could place the tray on it and against the side of the car. He paid her and gave her a generous tip. She told him to flash his lights, when they were ready to leave. As she skated away, they both said, what if we just flashed some flesh. They laughed, as he handed a basket, to her. They ate, in silence, as the Lettermen sang, on the radio, "The Way You look Tonight."

They finished their food. He flashed the headlights. His zipper was still undone. Her hand returned to his penis. "Wouldn't she be surprised, if I brought it out into the "open" when she comes back." Ree said. He responded that he would probably get arrested for indecent exposure. Ree said that there was nothing indecent about his penis. She said." I love your penis." He replied that he loved everything about her. They shared a kiss, as the waitress came and retrieved the tray. Her hand was still inside his pants, when the waitress got the tray. He put the car in gear and drove out of the lot and headed back to his house. The Everly Brothers were on the radio, singing, "Walk Right Back." He asked Ree what was she going to tell her folks, about being gone all day. She told him that she would tell them that they drove to his folks cottage, for the day. "Okay." He said. He took his right hand from the steering wheel and put in under the top of her shorts. She slid down, a little, to give him access. Her hand was stroking his penis. It was getting excited. She told him that she "feels so naughty" without underwear on. He told her that he did, too. They both said that the feel of their clothes against their skin was getting them "hot". She lowered her peasant blouse down over her breasts, to just above her nipples. She was squirming, in her seat, as if she had ants in her pants. His finger was caressing her "nub". Her fingers were caressing his "head". He was having extreme difficulty concentrating on driving.

He pulled into the driveway, at a "pretty good clip." He almost hit the cabin cruiser, as he brought the car to a stop. They both exited the car and, quickly, closed the doors and ran up the back steps, to the back door. He threw the door open! He closed it behind them as they ran through the house and up the stairs, to his room. She was ahead of him. As he came through the doorway, she turned and grabbed him by the shoulders and drew his lips, to hers in a frenzy! Lips, tongues moved at a fast tempo. Her hands moved to his jeans and stripped them off him. He put his hands on her shorts and did the same. He took off his shirt as she took off her blouse. They came together, arms around each other. Their naked bodies pressed tightly against each other. They, literally, fell onto the bed. He released his left hand and opened the drawer and brought up, yet another condom. They were writhing against each other. There would be no 'slow foreplay". She spread her legs, begging him to 'get inside me." He ripped open the package and took the condom and rolled it over his "rock hard" penis. He slid in between her legs. She grabbed him and 'put" him inside her. His mouth was "fastened "to her left breast. His right hand on her right one. Their mouths were 'fused" together. They thrust against each other and rolled around on the bed. He would be on top, thrusting into her and she, would be on top, "pumping" him. Their passion was uncontrollable! She was on her back, as his thrusts got stronger and faster. They knew he couldn't last much longer. He let out a loud "Shit!" as he filled the condom. She wasn't finished. Her thrusting pelvis told him that he needed to take care of her. He slid out of her, holding the base of the condom. He brought his mouth down to her and put his tongue, where his penis had been. She grabbed both his ears and arched her back as he probed and licked her. His tongue found the nub and his lips enveloped it. She was thrashing her legs around him. Her thighs closed in on his head. She gave a loud cry, "OOOH!!" her thighs were like a vise on his head. Even, tasting her "juices" he kept on. She cried out again as more juices covered his chin. Then, her whole body went limp. They lay beside each other for what seemed like hours. He finally got up and went to the bathroom and disposed of the condom. He, also, urinated like he hadn't in a month. He cleaned himself up and went back to her. She jumped off the bed and went down the hall, to the bathroom. When she came back. She said that she was a little "sore down there." He said, "baby we made love four times, today." She said, "no wonder I'm sore." He looked at his watch, on the nightstand. It read 7:30PM. She pouted and said that she should go home, so her parents wouldn't worry. They, reluctantly, got dressed. They said that today was only Saturday. They still had three more days. She asked him how many condoms he had left. He told her that they started out with twelve. So, there were, at least eight left. She smiled and said "good,". He told her that he thought she was "insatiable". She laughed and told him that he more than satisfied her and that he was the "sex maniac". They both laughed, as they got dressed. They left the room and walked out, through the house, to the VW.

They cuddled, together, as he drove her home. The Safaris were on the radio, singing, "The Image Of A Girl." She whispered, in his ear, that she hoped she wouldn't be sore, tomorrow. He said that he would not want to hurt her and that if she was, they could wait a while. She raised her head and planted a 'sweet' kiss on his cheek.

He pulled up in front of her house. He turned off the car. They shared another deep, wet, passionate kiss. When their lips parted, she reached into the back seat and got her small bag and got out of the car. He reached over and closed her door. He got out, closed his door and met her in front of the car. They walked hand in hand, up her walk to her front door. They shared another deep, wet, passionate kiss. When they parted their lips, he said he could kiss her all the time, for the rest of his life. She said the same. She told him that she would be going to church, with her family, in the morning. She asked him to call after noon. He said that he would. She turned and went into her house. He walked back down the walk and opened the door, to the VW, started it up and drove home. He couldn't believe the Saturday, he just had. He was, no longer, a virgin! Just thinking about her and the sex, they enjoyed, got him excited. The fact, that they may be doing it all over again, for the next three days, really got him "going." Talk about some milestones!

They, ended up, using all the condoms, over the next two days, at his house and in his room. They just couldn't get enough of each other! They spent Tuesday, washing his bedspread and sheets and bath towels. He threw all the used condom wrappers in the bottom of the trash barrel, under the back porch. They cuddled and kissed, while everything was washing and drying. At one point, she wished that he had one more condom. He did, too. He promised her that he would replenish his "supply."

The rest of the summer was spent working, parties, drive ins, parking. The rest of that July went fast. August came, quickly, as well. They both had the last two weeks of August, off. They planned to make the most of it. His parents invited them to spend a few days, at their cottage. He made sure he had some condoms, for their "vacation". Their love and passion, for each other, kept growing. He could not imagine himself, ever being without her.

When he wasn't working or with Ree, he was working on the hydroplane. Everything, for the boat, was ready. Everything, but a motor. He looked in the papers, nothing. He searched in boating magazines, nothing. He remembered hearing someone say, that the obvious can, usually, be found right under one's nose. He happened to run into two of his "old" club mates from the "Alladin" days. They told him that one of the guys, from the club, had an old Mercury outboard. They gave him Jackie's phone number. He called Jackie, one afternoon, after he and Ree's "lunch." Jackie couldn't believe that he was calling about the outboard motor. He was just thinking of selling it. He described it as an "old" seventeen horsepower motor, with a quick silver lower unit. He told Jackie, that was exactly the motor, he was looking for. Jackie told him, that since it was him, he could have it for 40 dollars. "Sold!" he said. He got into the VW and went right over to Jackie's. They went into the garage and looked under an old tarp. The motor was in good shape. He gave the cash, to Jackie, and told him that he would be over, the next morning, to pick it up. He knew it wouldn't fit in the VW. He went outside to where Phil was working on the cabin cruiser. He wondered if the trunk, in his Jeepster, was big enough to put the outboard in. Phil said that it probably was. They made plans to go to Jackie's the next morning and pick up the motor. He went upstairs and got ready for work.

He was a happy eighteen year old, at work. His co-workers had never seen him so happy. He felt life was fantastic! He and Ree were very happy and, still, very much in love. They would go to parties, either his friends or hers. They would sneak away and "make love" in the back seat of the VW. On his days "off" when he didn't have to be to work until 3 the following afternoon, they would go to the drive in. He was amazed that the VW's shock absorbers and springs weren't damaged. Their "lunches" were nothing more than passionate make out times, accompanied by a couple of sandwiches, from McDonald's. The boat was coming along, better than expected.

He and Phil picked up the motor and took it to the local marine shop. They guys took the motor, out of Phil's trunk and attached it to a large barrel, filled with water, They attached a gas line to it and 'primed" it. They attempted to start it. It refused to 'turn over." One of the mechanics took off the cover and replaced the spark plug. He, pulled the starter cable, again. The motor sputtered and died. He pulled the cord, again and gave it some gas. The motor came "alive" and sounded good. The mechanic kept giving it some gas and then let off. The guy told him that it probably needed a "tune up." He would have to leave it, there, for a couple of days. They said "okay" and got back in the Jeepster and headed home. Phil, then, informed him, that he and Nan were going to get married; that they were turning in the Jeepster and her Chevy for a Nash Rambler station wagon. He was in shock! He wished them both well and asked when they were planning on getting married. "Next year!" he said. Phil told him that he ought to talk with his mom about getting a trailer hitch for the VW and a trailer for the hydroplane. He approached him mom with the idea. She didn't mind, as long as he was willing to pay for them. He went to work, again, a very happy guy.

The next morning, he went to the garage, where his dad had all his car 'work" done. He talked with the owner. He told him that he could put the hitch on the VW with no problem. He, even, told him where to go to find a small boat trailer. His next day off, was in two days. He went to the trailer place and purchased a small boat trailer for one hundred dollars. The guy that he bought it from, said they would bring it to the garage, where the hitch was going to be put on. He arranged for all to be done, on his day off.

Ree was a little upset that they weren't going to be able to see each other that day. She told him that she really didn't care for that "damn" boat. Ree said that, if she could get her mom's car, would he want to spend the day, with her. He answered, "of course." She told him that she would let him know. That would be a "first". Ree driving them. He was just getting ready for work, when she called back," where should I pick you up? He told her the name of the garage and that he would be there at 8AM, to drop off the VW. She told him that she would be there at 8:15 and that he should have a bathing suit, towel and blanket with him. She would bring the sun tan lotion and food. She was, obviously, planning a day, at the beach.

He dropped off the VW, at the garage. The owner took his keys and showed him the trailer, that he bought. He said that he could pick up the car and the trailer, the next morning. The hitch was fifteen dollars and the labor another 45 dollars. He told the owner, "no problem, I'll have the cash for you tomorrow morning. He grabbed his "gear" out of the car and went outside to wait for Ree. She drove up and honked the horn. She was driving a 1956 Ford fairlane sedan. He did not remember seeing that car, at her house. "You're just not very observant." Ree said. He opened the door and jumped in beside her. They drove away from the garage. The car had an automatic transmission. She motioned for him to sit next to her. He did and she put her right hand on his left thigh. The Maguire Sisters were on the radio, singing "Just For Old Times Sake." Followed by Jerry Butler and "He Will Break Your Heart." Dee Clark followed him with "Just Keep It Up." He sat next to her with his left arm around her shoulders. He asked where they were headed. She said she heard of a pond, with a little beach, where they could go. "Janet said it is practically abandoned. No one goes there, except her and John." "Sounds interesting." He said. They stayed on the main road, for about 45 minutes and then she turned right, down a dirt road. They drove up to an old wooden gate that was across the road. He got out and moved the gate. She drove through and stopped. He closed the gate and got back into the car. They drove a little further and came upon an old gravel covered parking lot. It wasn't very big. She parked the car and turned it off. They got out, with their beach stuff and walked to a very small beach. They laid out the blanket and put their things on it. They looked around and realized that they were very much alone. Ree asked if he had ever been "skinny dipping". He said "no!" She said, "me either." They looked at each other and stripped off their clothes and hand in hand ran into the cool water. He was glad that it had a sandy bottom. They stood in the water, waist high. He looked at her nipples. The cold water made them stand at "attention." Their eyes locked together and they waded towards each other. They crushed their lips together and wrapped their arms around each other, tightly. He doesn't remember, if she lost her balance, or he did. They fell, together, into the water. When they surfaced, they moved closer to the beach. She lay, on her back, at the water's edge. He ran to his jeans and reached in his pocket and produced two condoms. He went back to her. They looked like the couple from the movie "From here To Eternity. Laying at the water's edge, making extremely passionate love to each other. He had learned to let her "finish" first and then him. They, next "made love" on the blanket. After which, they cooled off with another skinny dip. They ate the sandwiches, she had made and drank the cokes, she had brought. The sun began to fade behind some dark clouds, which cooled the air. They decided to put their clothes back on and finish eating. They had just finished, when they heard someone walking on the gravel parking lot. They looked up and saw an old man in coverall approached them. He asked what they were doing? He responded that they were just having a picnic. The old man said "okay, but please stay out of the water". He had, recently, filled it with "baby" bass and was trying to keep people away, until the following year. He told them, that the pond was used by Boy Scouts, in the Spring. It was a "fishing hole." Not a swimming hole." They said that they were just finishing eating and would be on their way. He thanked them and turned and walked away. They both fell onto their backs, laughing. Ree wondered if the old man had seen them skinny dipping and making love. He told her that if he had, he probably would have had a heart attack! They began to laugh hysterically. Just then, a bolt of lightning flashed across the pond and seconds later, a loud crash of thunder! They picked up their things and ran to the car. They just got into the car, when heavy sheets of rain pounded the ground and the car. Ree looked at him. Lust had returned to her eyes. She asked if he had any more condoms. He reached into his right front pocket and found one. She, immediately, stripped off her shorts and panties. He stripped off his briefs and jeans. They kept their tops on, in case the old man came back. He pulled her away from the steering wheel and onto the seat. She lay on her back and spread her legs. He, first, put his lips and tongue to her. She moaned, "Oh God, I love having your lips and tongue do that to me!" She began to thrash about on the seat. He could tell, she was about to experience a climax. When she arched her back and screamed!, he took his mouth away and slipped the condom on and slid in between her legs. "Oh, baby! You feel so good!" She cried. It was a 'good" fifteen minutes before he reached his climax. He sat up and took the condom off. He rolled the window down, as the rain came in, and threw the condom out the window. They sat up and hugged each other. She held his head, in her hands and "rained" kisses all over his face, even his chin, that still had 'traces" of her on it. They put their clothes back on and, once again, she got behind the steering wheel and turned the car around. She drove to the gate. He was about to get out of the car and open the gate, when he saw the old man, standing in the pouring rain. He opened the gate and let them drive through.

He waved to them as passed through. They looked at each other and wondered if he saw them, making love, in the car. They laughed and said, "so What!" They would never see him, again. Jimmy Jones was on the radio, singing, "Good timin". They sang along. She drove him home. The rain had subsided enough that it was not difficult to drive in. She asked what shift, he was working the next day. He said 3 to 11. But, he was picking up the car and trailer that morning. He would still meet her for "lunch." She said "good!" They shared a sweet kiss of pure love and then he got out, with his 'gear" and went into the house.

He got up early and ate his breakfast. Phil drove him to the garage. He walked into the dark expanse of the large garage. There were cars of all shapes, sizes and years, on lifts, hoods up and rear ends jacked up. He didn't see the VW. The owner approached him and they went into the office. The owner handed him the bill and he took out his wallet and paid him, in cash. The owner told him that a mechanic was bringing the car around and that it would face the road, so all he had to do was drive it home. The lights were hooked up, but he would have to register it. The owner gave him the proper paper work, to get it registered. He thanked the man and put the paper work in his pocket and walked out to the front. The VW had just pulled up. He thanked the mechanic and got in and began to drive off, onto the street. He was very careful, driving home. He remembered to make large turns and to leave enough space between him and the car ahead of him, to stop. When he got to the driveway, he made a large turn, so as not to take the small wooden fence with him, as he pulled down into the driveway. He hadn't noticed, but Phil was right behind, all the way, home. He stopped the VW, at the end of the driveway and turned it off and got out. He went to the back of the car and unhitched the small trailer. It was not heavy, at all. He moved it over, past the cabin cruiser and parked it on the lawn. He found a large block of wood and put it under the 'tow" of the trailer. Phil helped him "carry" the boat out from under the back porch. Because it was just the two of them. They made several stops, before, finally, getting it to the trailer. They 'tilted" the trailer' front end up, letting the back get near the ground. They slid the boat up onto the trailer. The only lifting they had to do, was in the middle, so the fin, on the bottom of the boat would "clear" the back beam of the trailer. Once on, he put the straps, he had bought, over the hull, the bow and the stern and secured them to the holes, in the frame of the trailer. Now, all he had to do was pick up the outboard. That would not be ready, to be picked up for another couple of days.

He called Ree, from work, during his dinner break. He told her that his folks had invited tem to the cottage for the third week in August. She put him on "hold" while she checked with her parents. She came back to the phone and made sure it was the third week and not the fourth. "Nope, the third." She said that she would love to spend a week with him. "The only thing is that I would have to be home on Saturday of the fourth week. We're going to our cottage in Maine." "Oh." He said, his voice showing disappointment that they were going to be apart that following week. He told her that he was scheduled to race the boat, the last Saturday in August.

She told him that she wouldn't want to watch the race. She'd be too afraid that something bad would happen to him. He told her that he understood her concerns and he repeated, to her, once again, that he grew up around boats and he'll be very careful. She still didn't want to be there, for the race. He told her that he would be miserable, being away from her, for a whole week. She felt the same and wished he could go to Maine, with her, instead of the damn race. They agreed that at least they would be spending an entire week together, in New Hampshire.

He picked her up, early, that third Saturday. He had one small bag, in the front of the VW, under the hood. She had two large bags and one small bag. Those were put on the back seat. She was not happy that he was towing the hydroplane, behind them. She, also, noticed the outboard motor attached to the transom. The boat and motor were secure and hidden under a tarp. When she got into the car, they shared a "good morning" kiss. Brenda Lee was on the radio, with "I'm Sorry." She cuddled up next to him and put her hand on his thigh. The Lettermen came on the radio, next and sang, "When I Fall In Love." When the song ended, Ree reached forward and turned the radio off. That meant she wanted to talk. She was so happy that her summer job was over. He said that he was, too. He was really looking forward to being with her, for the week. She squeezed his thigh. She made him promise her that he would not use or test out the hydroplane while she was there. He promised. She wanted him to tell her all about his "growing up in the summer" at the lake. He told her about Winter Harbor and Danny and Danny's family and about the beach and the cookouts and, oh yeah, the 'troubles" that he and Danny had gotten into. He, then, asked her to tell him about her summers in Maine.

The only thing, they both left out, were "old" boyfriends and girlfriends. She did tell him, that he was the very first boy, she ever had sex with. He told her, that she was his "first", too. She gave him a very "skeptical" look. She asked him how did he, then, know how to make her climax. He told her that his brother had a bunch of "dirty" books. In his closet and he use to go in there and look at the pictures and read them. She gave him a kiss on his cheek and told him, that she was glad, he had read them. He told her that he was glad, too. He, also, asked her that if he ever failed to "please' her, to let him know. She told him not to worry, that she would. But that he really didn't need to worry about that. She, then, asked him, if she was a good lover? "Are you serious?" he asked. "yes!" She said. He told her that she was a fantastic lover and that she never had to worry about not pleasing him. He did want to know, how she knew, to tell him to hold onto the condom. She said that Janet told her, that if they ever had sex, to make sure you hold onto the condom, when you pull out. She said that Janet mentioned that a girlfriend of hers, had the condom still inside her, when her boyfriend pulled out and they had to pull it out, but that some of the guy's sperm came out and the girl got pregnant. He told her that he would always be sure that didn't happen to them. She asked him, why he never asked her to "blow him". He almost went off the road. He told her that it would be her decision, not his. She said that, she thought it was "nasty" and not something she would ever want to do. He told her that it was okay with him. She looked at him and asked, "really? I've been told that most guys really want the girl to" do it" to him. He told her that he would never "pressure" her to do anything that she didn't want to. She asked him, "What if, on our first date, I said NO and slapped your face." He told her that he didn't know how to respond to that question. "I guess we just would have sat and watched the movies." "really? You wouldn't have forced yourself on me?" "No!" he said. She giggled and told him that she thought he was going to rape her, that night. He glanced at her and told her that he would never have done that. She, giggled, again and said "I might have raped you, if you hadn't made the first move." He told her about Fred's rules. She giggled and said that she and June thought up the rules. He glanced at her, again, and told her, how those 'rules' had tortured him. "Oh Poor baby!" She said and gave him another kiss on his cheek. They changed the subject and started to talk about how excited they both were about starting college in a few weeks.

They pulled into the dirt driveway, just around 11:45 AM. It had taken longer, because of the trailer. He had been very careful, not to speed and "lose" it. They pulled up next to his dad's Mercury. She got out of the car, quickly, and said that she had to use bathroom. He said "okay." He watched her practically run up to the small porch and open the screen door. He heard his folks say "hi" and she said "hi" as she ran to the bathroom. He carried her bags, from the car and into the back bedroom. He went back out to the VW and brought in his own bag. His mom told him to put it in the back bedroom, as well, but he would have to get what he needed, at night, before Ree got ready for bed. He put his bag, on the floor of the closet. He went back out to the VW and unhitched the trailer. It was a lot heavier, with the boat and motor on it. He managed to move it just enough, so he could move the VW in and out of the driveway. He went back into the cottage. His dad was sitting, in his favorite chair by the huge fireplace. He looked around and wondered where Ree and his mother, were. Then, he heard their voices, in the kitchen. They were, obviously, making sandwiches for lunch. They all ate their lunches on the porch, looking out on the lake. He and Ree took turns, changing into their bathing suits. His folks and Ree were already on the dock, when he joined them. He brought out two chaise lounges and offered one to Ree. She applied sun tan oil to his back and he to hers. They spent the afternoon, on the dock, talking with his folks and taking in the sun. When they got too hot, she would step down the ladder and dip into the cool water, just enough so her hair didn't get wet. He dove off the end of the dock and swam, a little bit. She was wearing a one piece, white suit, that made him cross his legs, more that once. She was so pretty and so very sexy. The afternoon began to fade into sunset. His folks told them, that they were all invited over to Winter Harbor, for a cookout. Ree asked him to change, first, because she would take longer. He told her that she didn't have to wear anything fancy, it was just Danny and his family. He was going to wear jeans and a T-shirt and sneakers. His mom suggested that he and Ree follow them over, in the VW, in case he and Ree decided that they might want to leave early. When Ree was ready, they went out to the VW and backed out of the driveway and onto the dirt road. His folks were right behind them, in the Mercury. They followed them to Winter Harbor.

He, carefully, followed his folks, down the dirt road to the clearing and the beach and cottage. He parked behind the Mercury. He turned off the car and pulled up the emergency brake, as they exited the car. They followed his folks, to the beach. He and his dad took four "beach chairs" out of the trunk of the Mercury. When they got, to the beach, he introduced Ree to everyone. He thought Danny's eyes were going to drop out their sockets. He was about to sit down, next to Ree, when Danny's mom handed them two paper bags of corn. She told him and Danny to go to the porch, of the cottage and shuck the corn, like they have done for so many years. Danny brought the blue porcelain pot; he carried the bags. They sat on the steps, of the cottage and began their "task." Danny looked at him, "Your girlfriend is gorgeous! What a beauty! That hair, those lips, and that body! Wow! Those tits are amazing! and her legs and ass! Where did you find her?" he glared at Danny. "You are talking about my girlfriend! I would appreciate it, if you stop at "gorgeous." Danny looked at him and said he couldn't understand how such a good looking girl, like Ree would want anything to do with him. His voice showed a hint of anger. "Well, she does!" he declared. They went back to shucking the corn.

Once they were done, he carried the pot full of corn ears down to the beach and placed it on the table. He turned around, to sit next to Ree and saw had taken his seat. He glared at Danny, but Danny was too busy looking at Ree and trying to talk to her. He could tell that she was "uneasy". Danny's mother noticed it, too. She told Danny to get up and go throw the bags of "shuckins" in the trash. Danny. Reluctantly, got up and went back to the cottage. He sat down, in his seat. Ree breathed a sigh of relief. When Danny got back, he went and sat at the picnic table. He got back up and come over to Ree and asked her if she would like a bottle of coke. They both said that they would. Danny went to the ice chest and took out two bottles and brought them back. He handed one to Ree and drank out of the other one. He asked Danny what happened to his coke? Danny told him, to get his own. Ree tried to stop him from getting back up. He no sooner, was off the chair, going to the cooler, when Danny sat down, again, in his chair. Danny's mother was watching "this" and, again, told Danny that he was sitting in his chair, the one he brought from his cottage. Danny, reluctantly, arose from the chair and returned to the table.

He whispered to Ree, that he had never seen Danny act like this. Like s bee, hovering around the prettiest rose, trying to get at it's nectar. Ree told him not to leave his chair, for anything. Just then, Danny's dad announced that the burgers and "dogs" were ready and for those that wanted cheese on their burgers and their buns toasted, to bring them up. Danny jumped off the bench and came over to Ree and asked her what she would like to eat. He couldn't believe what he saw and heard. Ree, sweetly asked him for a cheeseburger, chips and another coke. Danny bowed to her and went to get her food. He looked at her and whispered in her ear, "What are you doing? Why are you flirting with him?" There was the hint of the old jealousy and anger coming back. The same feelings that destroyed his relationship with Abby. Ree leaned in and told him, that she was just fooling around, that Danny didn't have a prayer and could never hold a candle to him. They grinned at each other. He got up to get his food and when he returned, Danny was, once again, in his seat. He leaned over and whispered "something" in Ree's ear. She put her food on her lap and with her left hand, slapped him on the cheek. Everyone heard it! Danny, immediately, got up and walked away from the beach. He, with his food, sat down. Ree picked up her food and began to eat it. They ate, in silence. When they were done, Danny's dad began to stoke the fire. The little kids got their flashlights. Ree apologized to everyone and said that, along with the trip and all the sun, she really didn't feel well. Danny's mom came over to her and apologized for Danny's actions and hoped that she come back, with him, during her stay. He was "dying" to know what Danny had said to her. He picked up their chairs and walked to the cars. He deposited the chairs, in his dad's car. They walked to the VW and got in. He started it up, turned it around and headed up the dirt road. When they were out of sight, of the beach, Ree told him to stop the car. He put it in neutral and set the emergency brake. "Come here" She said. He leaned towards her. She wrapped her arms around his neck and brought his lips to hers. It was another wet, passionate kiss. After a minute or so, she released him. She asked him not to bring her over to the beach, again. He agreed and told her that he had never seen Danny act that way. Ree told him that Danny wanted her to "ditch" him and go up to one of the fields with him. He was furious! She reached, for him, and again, pressed her lips to his. When they part their lips, he threw the car into its forward gears and spewing rocks and dirt, headed up the road and onto the main road, towards his cottage.

"God, I want to be alone with you!" She said, her hand on his thigh, her other hand, running through the thick hair on the back of his head. "I'll think of something," he promised. They pulled into the driveway and parked next to the hydroplane. He turned off the car. She was already out of the car and walking quickly, to the front door. He closed the doors and took off after her. She had run through the living room, past the kitchen and onto the porch. She was lying on her back, on one of the lounges with the thick cushion. He was right behind her. Night had replaced the dim light of dusk. He could just make her out on the chair. He settled in beside her. They wrapped their arms around each other, their legs intertwined with his right leg between her legs. Her lips pressed, tightly against his. When their lips separated, she moaned, "I want you so bad!" he told her that his body was aching for her. It was then that they heard the Mercury come down the driveway. They got up off the couch and went out through the screen door, of the porch, onto the dock. They stood on the edge of the dock, holding hands and looking at the stars, in the August sky. The sensed the porch light come on and heard his mom say that they were home. They turned and walked up the dock and onto the porch and into the kitchen. His mom shook her head and told them how Danny's parents were so apologetic for Danny's actions. She said that it was over. He, suddenly, said that they wanted to go to Bailey's for a chocolate frappe. His mom said that they had ice cream. They told her that they both wanted to go get a frappe and that they would be back, probably in an hour or so. She told them that she and his dad would probably be in bed, reading. They said 'goodnight" and went out the door. His mom turned on the porch light, as they walked to the car. She told him that she wasn't really in the mood, for a frappe. He told her that he wasn't either. He toldher to get in the car. They got in and he started the car. He turned on the headlights and backed the VW down the driveway and onto the dead end part of the dirt road. He put the car in forward and headed up the road, past the driveway. He got up, beyond the next cottage and stopped. He turned off the headlights, turned the car around and put it in neutral and coasted back down the road, past the driveway, all the way to where the dirt road ended. He stopped the car, put it in forward gear and set the emergency brake. Ree had a big smile on her face and told him that she was "tired" of messing with the gear shift and brake. They both got out and climbed into the back seat. She asked him, if he thought to bring anything. He brought his wallet out of his pants and produced two, individually wrapped condoms. She said no more.

He slipped out of his sneakers as she took off hers. She grabbed his T-shirt, with both hands and brought it over his head and up and over his arms. He did the same with her polo shirt and unsnapped her bra. She leaned over and unbuckled his belt and unbutton his jeans and slid everything down his legs and feet. She arched her back and lifted her hips off the seat, so he could slip her shorts and panties off. Their eyes fastened on each other. They came together, in a lustful frenzy. He managed to move the front seats, as far forward, as they would go, giving them more room. They stretch out on the seat, facing each other, arms and legs tangled together. Their lips were open, just enough, for their tongues to intertwine. Her eyes were lust filled, her breathing heavy. She pushed his face, from hers and guided him to her breasts and nipples. He loved kissing her breasts and lightly 'teasing "her nipples, while his lips sucked on them. Her hand was between them, stroking his blood engorged penis. One of his hands found its way to her vagina. He massaged the "outer" lips and, slowly slid his finer inside her. He couldn't get over the fact that she was already "wet." His hands went to her breasts as she pushed his lips down between her thighs. She was thrashing her legs and moaning how could he felt. His tongue found the "nub". He brought his right hand from her 'rock hard" nipple of her left breast and put two fingers inside her. He was ready to move between her thighs. She grabbed his shoulder with her two hands and brought him onto her. She maneuvered herself onto her back, on the seat. He moved on top. She took her hand from his shoulder tore opened the condom; slipped it down his shaft and 'guided" him "home." He could never get used to the feeling he had, inside her. Her hands went to his buttocks, urging him "in". He nestled his lips against her neck. She turned her head, to him and their lips crushed together, in a 'frenzy". He lifted himself, off her and put his hands on the seat, on either side of her and began to thrust, with his pelvis. She soon, matched his thrusts with her own. They were, again, two "souls" locked in paradise. It didn't take him long, this time, to "finish." He knew she wanted more. He kept on with his movements, until he just wasn't "hard" enough. He grabbed the base of the condom and pulled out. He raised himself off her and reached over and lowered the window, just enough, to dispose of the condom. She was still thrusting her pelvis off the seat. He returned to her and began kissing his way, up her legs, to her inner thighs and, finally, to her vagina. He put his tongue inside her and then moved it to her "nub". His fingers took over where his tongue had been. Her legs held his head in a 'vise-like' grip. Her hands grabbing the hair on his head. Her head thrown back against the inside of the car, her eyes closed, her mouth open. His hand returned to her breasts. Her hands covered his, holding them to her. "weird" sounds emanated from her lips. He felt her body stiffen. Her back arched, to the inside of the car. Then, just as before, her body shuddered and she gave out a loud "OH MY SWEET BABY!!" He took out his finger and released her breasts, from his hand and slid up next to her. They wrapped their arms around each other. They were still "lost" in ecstacy. They cuddled for the longest time, till the cool of the night became the cold of the night. They did not want to let go of each other. He felt "wetness" on his cheek. He looked over at her. "Are you crying?" he asked. She told him that she was so afraid that she might "lose" him. He told her that he really wouldn't want to go on living, if she left him. They held each other, even tighter. The August temperature forced them to get dressed and seek shelter in the warmth of the cottage.

He started up the car and turned on the headlights and drove it into the driveway and parked it next to the hydroplane. They embraced, again. He turned off the headlights and the car and they made their way, to the porch and into the cottage. Once inside, he reached behind the door and turned off the porch light and closed and locked the door. They were very quiet. He looked for a light, under the door, of his parent's bedroom. It was dark. His folks were asleep. He checked his watch. 10:30PM. They had been "parking" for over an hour. Ree went in to use the bathroom, while he went into her room and get his bag. She came out, with a puzzled look on her face. He whispered, to her, "What's wrong?" She whispered back that she had "blood" on her panties. She was bleeding. Not a lot, but enough to concern her. He asked if her 'period" was starting early. She said that it shouldn't be. He went into the bathroom and opened the door that his mom kept the towels in. he reached up and found a box of tampons. It, also, had pads, in it. He knew Ree was scared. He handed the box, to her. She took what she usually used and gave him a hug. He told her, that if it got any worse, they would go to the hospital. She really didn't want to do that. He understood and told her that he would do whatever it took, to keep her healthy. They went into the living room. His mother had already prepared his "bed" for him. They couch rolled out and the back made it into a small bed. They embraced again and he kissed her cheek and then their lips met. Their last kiss, of the night, was a sweet, loving kiss. She said she wished they could go to bed together. She wanted, so much, to wake up in his arms. He told her that he would love that. She turned and went into her room and closed the door. He went into the bathroom and washed himself, brushed his teeth, and changed into his pajama bottoms. He turned off the light and walked, softly, to the living room and got into his "bed." He did not sleep well. His concerns for Ree made him toss and turn, most of the night.

The smell of bacon, frying in a skillet filled his nostrils and told his brain, it was time to open his eyes. He opened one and waited for it to get used to the reflection of the sun, on the water. When he opened the other one, they focused on a beautiful face, close to his. Ree gave him a 'good morning" kiss. She was smiling. His voice had not fully engaged his vocal chords yet and a "scratchy" good morning was followed by "Are you okay?" She replied that she was and leaned her mouth, to his ear and said, "It is my period. It is early. I guess our love making messed up my schedule." He heaved a big sigh of relief. She stood up and said in a loud voice. "Come on get up lazy head!" He grinned and checked, under the blanket, to make sure the pajama bottoms were still on. He threw back the covers and jumped out of bed and ran for the bathroom. Ree went and joined his folks at the breakfast nook. He snuck back into the living room and grabbed his bag and went into Ree's room and got dressed.

His folks were still talking about Danny's strange behavior, that last night. She hoped that Danny would not come by, while she was there. His dad told her that Danny and his dad were working all week, "haying." He said that he and Danny were going to have a serious "talk" next week. He told them that in all the years, they've been friends, last night was the first time, he actually thought about "slugging' him. Ree convinced him,to let it go. They finished eating and both had coffee and took their coffee, out onto the dock. They sat, alone, on the edge of the dock, their feet dangling in the water. He told her, he was so glad that she was "okay." She laid her head on his shoulder and said, sadly, guess we won't need that other condom, for a while. He put his free hand around her and told her that it was okay. That just being together was the main thing. She had tears, in her eyes and told him that she was so very happy and so very much in love with him. Again, he expressed his love for her and told her that she was the best thing that ever happened to him. They sat on the end of the dock and drank their coffee, in silence.

They were startled by the his mother's voice. They were going into town, to do some shopping and did they want to come along. Ree put her hand on his shoulder and pushed herself up to a standing position. He got up next to her. She said, to him," might as well. Another chance to be alone and we can't do anything about it." He heaved a heavy sigh and said, back to his mom, "okay." Ree went into the bathroom, to freshen up. He went into her room and put on socks and his pair of "dirty' bucs, that he had brought. He looked in the mirror and combed his hair.

When he came out of the bedroom, they walked out of the cottage, holding hands. They stood by the Mercury and waited for his folks. She looked at him and wondered, if he still wanted to be with her, even though, they were not able to make love for, a few nights. He took her by her shoulders and looked her straight in her beautiful eyes and told her that he was in love with her and as long as they are together and that she still loves him, then that was all that mattered to him. He pulled her to him and held her in his arms. She said that never, in her life, had she ever felt this loved! His folks were walking towards them, His father, jokingly, said, "all right you, two break it up!" They laughed and got into the back seat, of the car. His mom asked him to change places with her. He said "okay" and, reluctantly, got out of the car and joined his dad, on the front seat. His father told him not to change the radio station. He shrugged and turned and looked at Ree. She had that "poor baby!" look on her face. Once everyone was in the car, his dad backed it out, of the driveway and turned and headed up the road, to town. Perry Como was on the radio singing, "Don't Let The Stars Get In Your Eyes." He was followed by the Maguire Sisters and "Something's Gotta Give." They were followed by Nat King Cole and "Unforgettable." He mentioned that he liked Dinah Washington's version better. His dad looked at him and said "who?"

The ride to town was uneventful. At least his dad did not light up one of his cigars, while they rode. He pulled into a parking space by Dockside. He said, that they all should meet there around 11:30 so they could go somewhere for lunch. He and Ree got out of the car and began to walk up to main street and all the shops. It felt so good to be holding hands with her. The first place, she had to go to was the pharmacy. She wanted her own "things" for her period. They walked into the store and she left him to go to "her" section. He was looking at the various types of sunglasses. She came up to him, with her small paper bag. He showed her a pair of sunglasses with "silver lenses" on the outside. He put them on. She told him only "perverts" wore them, so they could look at girls, without anyone seeing his eyes. He put them back on the rack. She grabbed him by his left hand and they walked out of the shop. They were walking along the sidewalk, looking in the shops windows, when they heard a loud whistle. He said, "it's the Mount!" Ree said "the what?" "The Mount Washington!" he said. "Since when does a mountain have a loud whistle!" Ree said. "It's a cruise ship!" he replied. He led her back down towards Dockside. People were walking past them, with cameras and small tote bags. He pointed to the large ship steaming through the water, making "her" turn to come into the dock. Ree was impressed! He knew that he could never get her to go out with him, in the rowboat, but maybe the "Mount."

They stood back a ways and watched the ship slow down and "saddle up" to the dock. Lines were thrown to an elderly man, wearing a "captain's hat". He caught the lines and wrapped them around large globe like structures on the dock. Bigger lines were thrown and tied around large cleats on the dock. He explained to Ree, that the lines, in back, were stern lines and the ones, in front, were bow lines. She was "genuinely" interested in the ship. She asked him, as they watched people walk across the gangplank, into the ship, if, maybe they could go on it. He took her, by her hand, and went into the Dockside restaurant. He took out his wallet and purchased two tickets for the next day's cruise. Ree squeezed his arm. She was excited!

They went back outside and watched the day's passengers get on board. Then, the crew on the ship brought the gangplank onto the ship. The old man went to unhook the lines. He told Ree to hold her ears. The ship blew the loud whistle, as the lines were thrown and the crew pulled them on board the vessel. They watched the ship start her engines. The water behind "her" began to froth wildly as she backed up and pulled away from the dock. Once clear, the ship made a turn and the water, behind her, turned white with turbulence. She headed out of the harbor, bound for Alton Bay. Ree said, "tomorrow, we'll be on it." Then she got a, little sullen. "How many girls have you taken on that trip." She asked. "one," he said," only she took me." "Oh?" asked Ree. He looked at her and smiled, "my mom. I was 7 seven years old." "Oh!" said Ree. They turned away from the dock and walked up the side road, across main street and into the "paper" store. Ree wanted some souveniers, to take home for her sister and her folks. They walked into the store. He showed her where the souveneirs were and he went and looked at some more sunglasses. She came back to him and said that they probably should have sunglasses for the boat trip. He picked out a dark pair and looked into the little the mirror, on the stand. Ree leaned in and whispered that he looked real sexy in the glasses. That was all he had to hear. He took them off and held them. She tried on several pairs and finally settled on a dark pair. He told her that she the glasses really added to her, sexually. She smiled and he took both pairs up to the counter. He gave them to the old man, behind the counter and paid him. They turned and put their glasses on and walked out of the store. He told Ree that the old man behind the counter, was there, when he was a kid and that he was an old man, then, too. She laughed and took hold of his hand, as they crossed the street and headed for the car. He said it was a good thing, they bought the glasses, because his I.D. bracelet and her charm bracelet caught the noon day sun, just right and were "blinding" him.

They were walking down the side road, to the town docks and the Mercury. He noticed his dad was "pacing" around the car and his mom was standing by the passenger door. She turned and saw them, "Here they are!" She said, to his dad. They got to the car, it was the first time that Ree noticed that his dad was not a patient man. They got into the car. This time, his mom got into the front seat. He and Ree settled in the back. They left a small space between them, in respect for his parents. His dad turned and leaned over the back and said to Ree, "I understand you like lobster. Bailey's has a great, large, lobster roll." They all agreed to go to Bailey's for lunch.

When he pulled into the parking lot. Ree liked that the building looked like an old "Maine" restaurant. His mom said, as they exited the car, "you didn't notice it last night?" Ree was quick, "It was kinda dark and hard to tell." He squeezed her hand. They went in the entrance and were escorted to a booth. The entire interior of the restaurant was pine paneled. The waitress came over and took their orders of the large lobster rolls. She bought their drinks, two teas and two cokes. His dad asked Ree, if she were enjoying herself, so far. Ree was sitting beside him, in the booth, facing his parents. Her hand, under the table, reached out and gave his thigh a squeeze as she said, "very much!" She, then, told them how she was looking forward to the boat trip, tomorrow. His mom looked at him. "what boat trip?" he said that they were going to go on the "mount" tomorrow. His mom put down her glass of tea and said, to him, "the last time, you went with me, you were bored, silly." He said, "mom, I was seven years old." She replied, "Oh, that's right." She looked at Ree and told her that the trip was an all day thing. That they wouldn't be back until well after 4PM. Ree, again, squeezed his thigh and said she was still looking forward to it. Their orders arrived and they ate in silence. His dad picked up the "tab". He left the 'tip". When they got back into the car, his mom told them that she had to go to Market Basket and pick up some "perishables."

His dad pulled the Mercury into the Market Basket parking lot. His mom asked his dad to come into the store, with her. His dad gave a big sigh and said "ok". They could tell that he really didn't like food shopping with her. When they got out of the car and walked into the store, he and Ree moved closer to each other. Ree said that she was very sorry that her period came early. He told her that it really didn't bother him; that she was all right, was more important, to him. She put her arms around his neck and their lips met, for the first time, that day. As their lips parted, she looked him straight in his eyes and told him, "I can still take care of you." He smiled.

His mom and dad came out of the store carrying two large paper bags of groceries. He jumped out of the car and went to the trunk and helped them load the groceries into the trunk. His mom said that they needed to get right back to the cottage, before the heat got to the groceries. They got back in the car and headed home. They planned to spend the rest of the day, on the dock and in the water. Ree had a 'pouted' look, on her face and told him that it was best that she stay out of the water. He told her that he would help "cool" her off. Andy Williams was on his dad's car radio, with "Happy Heart." As they drove through town, they slowed down to see what movie was playing in the theatre, that week. It was "A Summer Place". Ree said that she would love to see the movie, again, this time, with him. He said okay and they would plan to go. Ree leaned and whispered, in his ear, "Thursday night." He gave her a "quizzical "look. She said that Thursday would be "good" for her. It took him a few minutes to understand that her period should have run it's course, by Thursday. He smiled and squeezed her thigh.

They spent the rest of the day, on the dock and he, in the water. When he noticed Ree, the first time, feeling uncomfortable with the heat, he got off his chair and went into the boat and retrieved the "bailing" can. He filled it with water and had her lie on her stomach. He tilted the can just enough for a little of the water to pour out on her back. At first, her back tightened up and her shoulders "reared" back, from the cold. She started to get used to it, as he poured more all over her back. She laid her head on her arms, as he continued to pour, until the can was empty. He could tell that it cooled her off. He put the can down beside his chair and sat back down. He told her to let him know, when she needed "cooling down" again.

He felt the mixture of sun and water start to make him sleepy. He lay on his back and "soaked" up the sun. He came "awake" as the first torrent of cold water splashed against his chest and face. His eyes opened to a smiling Ree. She still held the can, in her hand. "Hey, sleepy head, get up! It's around 5PM and your dad is grilling chicken, on the grill." He got off the lounge and shook the cobwebs out of his head. He grabbed her by the hand and pretended that he was going to throw her off the dock. She was laughing and pulling her hand from his at the same time. He stopped, but pulled her close to him. He told her," you may not want to eat my dad's chicken. He doesn't think it's cooked, unless there is an inch of charcoal on it." Ree looked, at him, "What do you do?" he told her that he usually takes his knife and scrapes the "black" off. She laughed and thanked him for the advice.

His mom came out on the dock, with a pot of "unshucked" corn and asked them, if they would "shuck" it. They sat down, as he showed her how to do it. He told her that he was a "champion shucker" from way back. Ree thanked him for his correct pronunciation. They enjoyed a good laugh, as his mother came back out with an empty paper bag, to put the "shuckings" in. he told her to make sure and take off as much of the "silk" as she could. When they had finished, he looked at her corn and then at his and bowed his head, to her and said that she had done a better job than the champ.

He got up off the chair and carried the pot of corn into the cottage and the kitchen. Ree had already changed out of her suit into shorts and a top. He walked out of the kitchen and through the living room, to the bedroom and got his bag. He took it into the bathroom and changed into jeans and a T-shirt. He did not put on briefs. He liked the feel of the denim against him. Ree had put the bag of "shuckings" in the trash barrel by the porch.

He came out of the bathroom, with his bag and put it by the couch, in the living room. The same couch that would turn into his bed. He walked into the kitchen and then went out to the dock and picked up the "outdoor chairs and lounge chairs" and put them on the porch. Ree came out of the kitchen and sat down beside him. She leaned over and whispered in his ear. "You aren't wearing any underwear, are you?" He looked at her, in shock! "How can you tell?" He asked her. "Baby, I know you! I hope your folks don't know." He assured her that they would be oblivious.

His dad yelled that the chicken was "done" and that he needed a large platter to put "it" on. He got up and went into the kitchen. "I heard him!" His mother said. She gave him the empty platter and he went through the porch and out to the "pit" and his dad placed the "blackened" chicken on the platter. He walked up to the screen door, of the porch, and asked Ree to open it for him. He, then, carried the platter into the kitchen. Ree was right behind him, looking at the "black" chicken. His mom told her to do just what he told her to do. His mom turned to him and said, just loud enough, that Ree heard her, "Dear, please go back into the bathroom and put some underwear on." She said it, as if she had to say it a lot. Ree laughed, as he, blushing, tur ned around and went to his bag an took out a pair of briefs and went into the bathroom. "Men!" his mom said, "sometimes, they are like little boys!" he heard Ree laugh, as he closed the bathroom door.

They ate the dinner, on the porch. Ree enjoyed watching the boats pass by, in the channel. His dad told them. That every Sunday evening, all the boats pass their way, getting ready to go home, for the week. Their channel was called "The Barber Pole". He didn't know why and no one had ever been able to tell him how it was so named. It was the main thorough fare between the "broads" and Melvin Village. Ree looked at him and said, "the broads?" His dad said. "Broadest part of the lake You'll be on them tomorrow."

After dinner, he and Ree put the dishes in the dishwasher. His mom cleared off the table, in the kitchen, dinette area and brought out the scrabble game. His dad was already, in his chair, by the fireplace, doing his crossword puzzle. So, it was his mom, his girlfriend, and he. He could not get over his choice of the 'worst' tiles. So, he could only "play" off the others. He was not a happy "camper". When the final score was tallied. His mom had beat Ree by only three points. Ree demanded a recount, she still was three points "shy". He had lost by at least seventy points to Ree. He demanded a recount. They both laughed at him.

Darkness had settled over the water and the woods. His mom gave out a big "yawn" and told his dad that it was time to go to bed. He and Ree put away the game. His parents "bade' them good night. He and Ree got up from the table and went out to the porch. They closed the thick glass door behind them. They both got onto the thick cushioned chaise lounge and facing each other, cuddled and kissed. Ree, again, apologized for having her period. He, again, was glad that that "it" was the reason for her bleeding. She made him reposition himself, so that his back was against the cushion. She lay on his right side, her right leg over his legs. She moved closer, so her chest was close to his lips. Her hand was on his zipper. He raised her shirt up to her neck and reached behind and unclasped her bra. he pushed her bra up to her shirt which was bunched up around the base of her neck. "Be gentle baby, they are kind of sore." He promised that he would. She unzipped him and put her hand inside and parted the opening in his briefs and brought his manhood to face the cool air. Her lips pressed to his. His hands, gently, cupped her breasts. Their 'sweet' kiss began to intensify their passion. She wrenched her lips from his and, panting, asked him if he had 'something". He arched his pelvis, just enough to get his wallet, out of his pants pocket. He put his finger in to the wallet and brought out another condom. He whispered, "Bu,t your period." She said, "oh sweet baby, I said I will take car e of you." He tore open the package and brought out the condom. His hands returned to her breasts as their lips pressed together, again. Her hands stroked and caressed "him" to a "hard" state. She slipped the condom over 'it' and slid it all the way down his shaft. With her left arm repositioned around his neck, she began to, slowly, stroke his manhood. He took his left hand from her breast and raised his head, just enough to put his lips on it. He ran his tongue, gently around the nipple. His other hand still cupping the other breast. She wrenched her lips from his, "Oh sweet baby! God, I love your mouth on me!" She increased the tempo of her strokes on him. He knew it wouldn't take long. He brought his mouth from her breast and looked up at her, she looked down at him and crushed her lips, to him and her tongue stabbed into his mouth. His hips began to push up to her hand. He groaned that he was going to 'burst" She began to "pump" with her hand. He broke free of her lips and cried, "Oh shit!" He exploded into the receptacle at the tip of the condom. She leaned down and placed her cheek against his. "You okay? Baby." He gasped "oh yeah." "good", she, huskily said. She took her leg off his and gave him so room, to get up off the couch. He got off the couch, holding the condom, to him and went to the screen door and stepped out to the barrel. He lifted the lid and deposited the condom into it. He made sure that the bag of the night's dinner, covered it. He zipped up and went back to the couch. He lay down beside her and told her that she was an amazing lover.

She lowered her lips towards his and told him that she will always take care of her man. He told her that he owed her one. She grinned and said "okay". They continued to make out. She had put her bra back on and pulled down her shirt, while he was at the trash can. She was lying on top of him, their hips grinding against each other, their passion increasing, once again, when they heard the crash of the trash barrel! They, practically, fell off the couch. They jumped up and he put on the porch light. A large raccoon had knocked over the trash barrel. He yelled at it and it scurried away. He went out and righted the barrel and made sure everything was back in the barrel, especially, the condom. He put the long metal piece of pipe through the handle of the lid and across the barrel. They decided to go to bed. It was 11:00PM.

They both woke up around 9:15AM. He stayed under the covers, of the 'bed' in the living room until she had come out of the bathroom and gone back to "her' room. He jumped out of the bed and ran to the bathroom, with his bag. He took care of "business" and went back into the living room, in fresh briefs and socks. Again, he waited till Ree was dressed. She came out of the room, dressed in Navy blue Bermuda Shorts and a light blue polo shirt. She looked fantastic! He told her that she better stick with him, so the deck hands and other guys will know that she is with him. She promised she would. He, then, went into the bedroom and changed into light tan polished chinos, a light purple polo shirt. He "splashed' on some Stetson, put on his I.D. bracelet and checked his wallet. He had just over thirty dollars in it. He combed his hair and went out of the bedroom and joined everyone in the breakfast "nook". It was just after 10 o'clock. They had to be at the dock, by 11:15. They ate their breakfast and deposited their dirty dishes in the dishwasher. He went to the table beside the couch, which he took the sheets off, folded them and the blanket and put the couch back together, and picked up his new sunglasses. Ree went back into the bedroom and came out with her sunglasses and a small pocketbook. They were ready. His dad said they looked like a couple of "tourists". Ree was wearing her charm bracelet and her watch. His folks were going to drive them. His mom didn't want the VW sitting downtown, all day. As they walked to the car, he caught a sniff of her chanel #5. He told her she smelled wonderful. She leaned near him and said, "you do too, baby".

His dad pulled the Mercury into a parking space on Main street. It was 11:10 AM. They said goodbye and his folks said that they would be back around 4PM to pick them up. They got out of the car and hand in hand, made their way down the side road to the dock, along with a bunch of other passengers, to be. He checked his wallet and made sure that he had their tickets. They got to the dock, just as the "Mount" blew her whistle and made her turn and slowed towards the dock. Ree squeezed his hand so tight that his knuckles turned "white". They watched the lines thrown from the vessel, to the old man and he slipped the stern line over the cleat. The old man then went towards the bow and waited for the bow line to be tossed. He caught it as it hit the dock and he put that over the other large cleat. They heard the squeaking sound as the steel vessel rubbed against the large wooden posts, of the dock. They saw the deck hands come up to the side and open a small, half sized door. The boys, then, slid the gangplank out and onto the dock. The old man grabbed a rope and pulled it further onto the dock. The boys secured their end to the ship. He and Ree composed of approximately forty people who were lining up to board her. They heard the words, "all ashore!" he was amazed at the number of people who got off, to spend the day in Wolfeboro. When the gangplank was empty, they heard, "all aboard!" It was an "orderly boarding. He held Ree's hand very tightly as they traversed the wooden gangplank. They were told to step down, from the gangplank onto the steel deck. Once on the ship, they moved with the others towards the stern. Once they crowd 'thinned out", Ree wanted to go "topside" to wave "goodbye" to the people on the dock. They made their way up the 'stairs' and got to the top, just as the loud whistle 'fractured" the quiet sunny morning. They got to the rail and looked out at the people, on the dock. Ree spied his folks and hit his arm. They waved and his folks waved back. He thought, to himself, she must feel like they are going on an ocean cruise across the Atlantic ocean. He smiled. He was glad that she was enjoying herself.

They felt the ship "shudder" as her props churned the water, behind them and then stopped. Only to shudder again as the cruise ship turned towards the outer harbor and began to move forward. They went to the stern and watched as the people on the dock grew smaller and smaller. She was "acting" like a little child. She wanted to go to the bow and see where they were heading. They worked their way forward and found a 'spot' on the bow, as an elderly couple gave up their spot at the railing. They stood there, for the longest time. Ree was amazed at the size of the lake. She was glad the water was calm. Her left arm encircled his waist. He put his right arm around hers. She laid her head against his shoulder. As, they left the harbor, a voice told them that they were heading to Alton bay. The island they were passing, on the port side was called little Barn Door. Ree pointed to it and said, "there it is!" He took her by the hand and told her to come to the other side, so she could see how big the lake really was. When they got to the 'starboard' rail, her eyes grew big." Wow! It's huge!"

They had a twenty minute "stay" in Alton bay. They could leave the ship or stay on board. He had to go to the pursers office and turn in their tickets. Ree mentioned that she was getting hungry. They decided to stay on board and go down to the main deck, where they could get lunch. They passed by the purser's office and turned in their tickets and went into a small restaurant type set up. Their were booths set up along each side, so folks can sit, eat, and look out at the lake and its', many islands. She went and sat at a booth and told him that she wanted a ham and cheese sandwich, fries and a coke. He came back a few minutes, later, with their lunch. As they began to eat, music filled the "room." The Four Freshmen sang "Graduation Day". Followed by Brenda lee and "I Want To Be Wanted." She was followed by Ray Anthony and "The Bunny Hop". A bunch of "teeny boppers", all girls, got up and danced the 'bunny hop around the small dance floor.

The rest of the trip was fun, for him as well as Ree. They had an hour stopover at the "Weirs" and went ashore and played games in the arcade. They watched kids 'dive" for quarters, next to the ship, while it was stopped in Centre Harbor. On the long trip back to Wolfeboro. They were in the area with the dance floor and the jukebox. They danced and swayed to Lenny Welch, "Since I fell For You", and Earl Grant's "The End," Johnny Mathis "It's Not For Me To Say." They went to the side of the ship and he pointed out Winter Harbor, just as the "voice" pointed it out. They, quickly walked to the other side and saw the other side of "Rattlesnake Island." They spent the last "leg" of the trip cuddling against a rail, taking in the sun and the wind. Ree was against the rail, he stood behind her, his arms around her with his hands clasped against her waist. Her head leaned back against his cheek. He heard an elderly couple remark how wonderful it was to see young people, obviously, very much, in love.

They stayed at the rail, as long as they could. Even as the ship steamed back into Wolfeboro harbor. They left the rail when the heard the "voice" cry out "All ashore, that's going ashore." They, reluctantly, gathered her small bag and made their way down the stairs, to the side where the gangplank was. Once the gangplank was across the dock, they joined the others, who had boarded with them, that morning, and stepped across and onto the dock. They walked hand in hand to the parking lot. He saw his mom wave at them. He waved back. They got to the Mercury and got in. They sat close together, in the back seat. His mom asked them, "Well, how was it?" he answered, "a lot different and a lot better than the last time." Ree just muttered "wonderful." His mom turned back towards the front and told his dad that maybe they should go, again, sometime. His mom said that they had planned to have spaghetti and meatballs for dinner. They just said "ok". His mom seemed to sense that something "magical" happened between them, on the boat. They rode back to the cottage, in silence.

After dinner, the two of them sat on the couch. His mom was engrossed in the book, she was reading. His dad was concentrating on his crossword puzzle. They got off the couch and went through the cottage, past the kitchen, out the door, onto the porch and out the screen door and down onto the dock. He grabbed a chaise lounge chair, on the way. Once, on the dock, he set up the chair and the two of them, snuggled into it, both on their backs, arms and legs intertwined, facial cheeks together, staring up into the August sky. Every now and then, they would catch sight of a shooting star, stream across the night sky. They didn't say a word. He was so very "love sick" and somehow felt she was, too.

When the events, of the day, started to close in on them, they decided to call it a day. They got off the chair and turned and looked at the cottage. It was dark. His folks had gone to bed. He folded up the chair and they walked hand in hand back into the cottage. He left the chair on the porch. His "bed" was already made and his bag was sitting on the floor, beside it. He had turned on the floor lamp, by the picture window. That was how he knew that everything had been done. Ree let go of his hand and went into her room. He went into the bathroom and changed and brushed his teeth. He left the bathroom light on, as he exited. He went and turned on the table lamp by his bed and then went and turned off the floor lamp. He waited for Ree to finish in the bathroom. She came out and went into the bedroom. He turned off the lamp by his bed. The cottage was dark, except for the small lamp in the bedroom. Then, she turned off the lamp. He was just about to close his eyes, when he felt her presence. She leaned over and pressed her lips to his. They held the kiss for quite a while. When she stood back up, she thanked him for a wonderful day and night. He thanked her, for loving him. Another short kiss and she went to her room.

The next few days were uneventful. They spent a lot of time, on the dock, soaking up the sun's rays and just relaxing. They went to the local bowling alley, to Center Harbor, to the country store. His folks took them to Meredith and Hart's Turkey farm, for dinner. Thursday, while, soaking up some more sun, Ree leaned over and whispered that her period was over. They were both very happy. She go off the chaise lounge and went towards the ladder. He got off his lounge, quickly, and grabbed her around her waist and pulled her with him to the end of the dock. "I 've wanted to do this all week!" he said. Both of them went off the end of the dock, with Ree screaming "MY HAIR!". They hit the water together! When they both surfaced, Ree grabbed his head and pushed him back under. He came up spewing lake water out of his mouth and nose. He was greeted with her splashing him, in the face. He thought she was angry,till he saw her 'toothy' grin. He was no match for her, in the water. He kept surfacing, after her "dunks" and then would get splashed, in the face. He, finally, cried "uncle!" His parents were laughing, at them. They moved closer to the end of the dock, out of his parent's view. Her beautiful, dark, auburn hair, plastered to her scalp and the sides of her face. She looked so beautiful, to him, and he told her so. They wrapped their arms around each other's necks and shared a wet, passionate kiss. It was short, so as not to arouse suspicion, from his folks. She said softly, "tonight, you are mine, all mine!" She let go of him and swam to the ladder and got out of the water. He had an "enraged" erection and opted to stay in the water, a little bit longer. She shook her head, to get rid of the excess water and then wrapped a towel around her head. He looked up from the edge of the dock and said "Ah mighty sahib!" She looked at him and grinned. His mom got off her chaise lounge and took Ree, by the hand and told her that she had one of those new hair drying machines. As they walked off the dock, Ree turned her head over her right shoulder and stuck her tongue out at him. His dad had put down his paper and witnessed it and began to laugh, as did he. He swam around a little bit to "quiet down" his manhood. They had ham and cheese sandwiches for lunch. His dad said that he was going to grill up some small steaks, for supper. He asked him, when he stopped swimming, what time they were going to the movies. He said they would take in the early show and then go to Baileys for ice cream, afterwards. The early show started at 7PM. His dad decided to start the grill around 4:30,so, they would have plenty of time to eat and get to the show. He swam over to the ladder and climbed out onto the dock. He glanced down, at himself, and saw he was back to "normal". He heard his dad say, "That's quite a girl you have son, quite a girl." He grinned and said, "I know." He sat down on a chair and took a towel and dried himself off.

His dad knew how to cook steak. Everyones's was cooked just the way they "ordered' it. They were finished eating and cleaning up around 5:45PM. Ree went into the bedroom, first, to get ready. It took her fifteen minutes. When she emerged from the bathroom, she looked fantastic! She wear a yellow blouse and white Bermuda shorts. Her deep tan and auburn hair, plus dark red lips, reminded him of Debra Paget, the movie star, who had used to have a serious 'crush" on. It took him ten minutes to get ready. His hair had been "bleached" by the sun, into a blondish brown. His skin was, also, deeply tanned. Her wore light blue polished chinos and a white polo shirt, with his white, now scuffed, white bucs. They checked their watches and said good bye to his folks and headed out the door. She put her nose to his cheek and "drank" in his aroma of Stetson. When they got into the car, he leaned over to kiss her and drink in her chanel. They headed to the movie, knowing they would have a difficult time concentrating on the show.

They had to sit in the floor section of the "old church" building, turned "town hall building, turned theatre. The balcony had been closed for some time. They held hands throughout the show. The actors, Troy Donahue and Sandra Dee, did not Impress him. The actress that portrayed Sandra's mother did a "decent" job of thanking him, that he did not have a mother like her. Ree said the same thing. The "story" itself was intriguing to him. He began to wonder, if Ree might find someone else, while away the next week, in Maine.

After the show, they got in the car. He asked her if she wanted to go to Baileys. She reached over and put her hand on "him" and pressed her lips to his. Their lips caressed each other's. Their tongues pried open each other's teeth and swirled together. When they pulled apart, he said, "to hell with Baileys." She laughed. He spared "no horses" in heading back to the cottage and their "spot" beyond the driveway.

As they got closer, on the dirt road, to the cottage, he "killed the headlights" and turned into the driveway of the cottage two "doors" down. he backed out onto the dirt road and with only the brake lights to "guide" him, coasted down the road, past the driveway, to the dead end. He put the car in forward gear and pulled up the emergency brake. They opened the doors and got out of the car and climbed back in to the back seat. He reached down for the levers on the side of the front seats and raised them, one at a time and pushed the front seats forward. She had, already taken off her top and bra. He stretched out against the back of the seat and stripped off his clothes, except his socks. She did the same. They turned to each other. She stretched out next to him as he put his left leg over her left leg and between her left and her right. His left hand went to her right breast. Her left hand went to his penis. Their lips met for their second wet, passionate, tongue lashing, kiss. God! He loved the feel of her nakedness against him. Their kiss 'broke" for air, She gasped, "please kiss me, again, down there." He brought his leg off of hers. She positioned herself against the side of the car and opened her legs, to him. He moved up towards her and brought his lips, to her. He began to kiss and suck on her "nub" and with his tongue, licked her all over, slowly pull and tugging on her lips, with his teeth, then gently kissing her thighs. He brought his lips back to "her' and stuck his tongue inside her As deep as he could go. He added two fingers, where his tongue had been. His tongue returned to her "nub' his fingers began to move in and out at a steady pace; matching his tongue. She was moaning and groaning, husky voice begging him not to stop. He could sense that she was going to climax, he flicked his tongue faster across and up and down on her "nub" her legs shook and stranger sounds emerged from her mouth. Her hands were holding his ears and squeezing them tight. He felt her 'wetness' against his fingers, lips, and tongue. Her body went "limp". She brought his head up to hers and asked if he brought "one" with him. She let go of him as he reached over to the crumpled clothes on the floor and took his wallet out of his pants. He extracted 'one' out of the wallet. She pushed him onto his back and grabbed the condom out his hand and ripped open the package and took out the condom. She reached over and slipped it down over his "head" and down his shaft, to the base of his penis. She began to stroke him, as their lips crushed together. She had him sit up, but in a, sloping position, so she could straddle him. She put her hand on him and then lowered herself down onto him, impaling herself on him. She leaned close to give his hands access to her, slightly hanging, breasts, he cupped each one with a hand. She leaned in further, so their lips could meet. She was in complete control! She began to "pump" him, very slowly, at first. As they, both, ran out of air, their lips broke free, she gasped, 'work your magic on my nipples". He lowered his lip and tongue to them. He surrounded one with his lips and gently sucked on it, while his tongue gently lashed it. When it responded to an "eraser" hardness, he moved his lips and tongue, to the other one. She increased the tempo of her thrusting! He couldn't just lie still, so he began to match her thrusts. His hands left her breasts and went to her hips. One hand on each one, moving with her thrusts. His mouth going from one breast to the next. Her arms encircled his neck. Their passion increased into pure lust! Animal sounds emanated from her mouth. Their bodies began to sweat. The windows of the car were so fogged up, that no one walking by could see them. But the sounds from within and the rocking of the little car, would certainly leave no doubt, as to what was taking place inside.

He moved his right hand, from her left hip and brought it between their "wet" bodies, to her pubic area and her "nub" he caressed it with his finger tip of his forefinger. That caused her to thrust and thrash against him. He knew he was going over the edge, very soon. She was like a wild animal! He could barely keep his mouth on her breasts. Then, he felt it! The feeling that he was going to explode! He took his mouth from her left breast and gasped that he was going to climax! "Oh my sweet, sweet, baby, don't hold back! I love to feel you swell, just before you go off!" That did it! His thrusts got stronger and then he practically lifted them off the seat, as he filled the condom! He continued to massage her "nub." Then, after a few seconds, her body stiffened and she cried out "OH GOD!" She gave one big thrust down onto him. Their arms went around each other, as they collapsed onto the seat. He let go of her and reached forward and lowered the passenger window, just enough to take off the condom and toss it out the window. He rolled the window back up and leaned back to her. They wrapped themselves in each other's arm and lay still, except for Ree. She was showering his forehead and cheeks with tiny kisses.

He had no idea how long they lay, clinging to each other. She began to beg him to go to Maine, with her. He said that he would think about it. He lied. He really wanted to race the boat, that labor Day Weekend, in Alton Bay. He was torn, because he didn't want to be without her. This time, away, would be the longest they had ever been apart.

They began to feel the cold of the August night on their skin. They got dressed and got out of the car and into the front seats. He started the car, turned on the headlights and drove down the driveway. Again, the cottage was dark. They parked the car, turned off the car and headlights and got out. They walked down the path to the porch. They went inside. Ree went to the bathroom, while he turned off the porch light and turned on the lamp by his "bed." Ree came out of the bathroom and went into "her" room. He grabbed his bag and went into the bathroom. He came out, in his pajama bottoms and climbed under the covers. He heard her bedroom door open. She came back into the room and turned off the lamp, by his bed. She squatted down by him. He reached out to her and their lips met for a "good night" kiss. Afterwards, she rose up and said that she would call her dad, in the morning, and make sure it would be all right for him, to come with them, to Maine.

He opened his eyes, in the morning light, to the sound of "sniffling." He opened his left eye and saw Ree, already dressed, sitting in one of the wicker chairs. He found his voice and asked her what was wrong. She told him that she called her dad and asked about him coming to Maine, with them. "Apparently, there isn't enough room. My little sister invited two of her friends." This was a "first" for him. He had never really seen her that sad and angry, at the same time. Inside, he was happy, that he was going to be able to race, but, also, disappointed that they would not be together, for a week. She got up and went to her room, to pack. He got out of his 'bed.' He grabbed his bag and went into the bathroom. When he came out, he was in jeans and a T-shirt. She had already had her breakfast. He asked her what time they had to leave. She said, "about fifteen minutes from now." He went into the kitchen and had some bacon and toast. He washed it down with a small glass of orange juice. His mom asked him to pick up the mail, when he came back up. He said that he would. His mom and dad went over to Ree and each hugged her and said they enjoyed her company and that she was welcome back, any time. She smiled and thanked them. He picked up her bags and they walked out of the cottage, to the VW. He told Ree how sorry he was. He told her that he had never been to Maine. They got to the car and he opened her door and put her bags in the back seat. She got into the front seat and he looked at her. "Hey! Would you like to drive?" he asked. She said that maybe a, little later. He got into the car and turned it on, closed his door. He reached out to her and held her face between his hands and told her that she was the most beautiful girl, in the world, and he loved her very much. She grabbed him and hugged him, tightly, expressing her "undying" love for him. They released each other and he put the car, through her gears, as they headed to her house.

When they crossed into Massachusetts, he pulled into a "rest stop." Ree decided that she wanted to drive the VW. He said "okay" and put the car in neutral. They got out and traded places. They stayed in the parking area, as she "learned" the different gears. He was surprised that she handled the clutch so well. She told him that she learned to drive in her uncle's car. When she felt comfortable, enough, he told her, "let's go!" He was glad to see her smiling, again. Bobby Darin was singing "Splish Splash'" on the radio, as he turned it on. Gogi Grant followed with the "Wayward Wind." They sang along.

She pulled up in front of her house and 'stalled" the car. They both laughed. He got out and reached into the back seats and grabbed her bags. She was out of the car and had closed the door. They walked up the walk, to her front door. Her mom must have seen them pull up. She took the bags, from him, and went inside. She asked Ree, which bag had the laundry, that had to be done. Ree told her.She turned to him and with tears in her eyes, said how much she was going to miss him, the next week. She could tell that his eyes weren't doing well, either. They thought about writing, but by the time, the letters arrived, they would be back together. She said she would write anyway and maybe, he could to. "That way, we'll both know how miserable we were." He said "okay." Just then her dad asked her, from the garage, to go to her room and get whatever she wants, so he can load it in the car. He waved at him and thanked him for letting Ree stay with him, the last week. He waved back and said they had a good time. She held his wrists, with her hands and told him that she had to go. They shared a sweet, loving, good bye kiss. She turned and went into the house. He turned and walked, slowly back to the VW. The keys were still in the ignition. He got in and closed the door and turned on the car and drove away towards his house. He had trouble focusing on the road. He felt his heart had been torn out of his chest. His lips were quivering. He was glad that she wasn't seeing him like that.

It was still the middle of the day, when he arrived home. He picked up the mail, by the front door, under the mail slot, in the foyer. He looked around the house. He went to the kitchen and looked for something to make a sandwich with. Nothing! It appeared that Phil and Nan had eaten all the sandwich stuff. He walked around the house. He checked his wristwatch and saw that it was just before noon. His eyes began to fill up, again. He was lonely and he was really missing Ree. He went up to his room and opened his "piggy bank". He had about fifty dollars left in it. He checked his wallet and found another twenty five dollars. He was good for sometime. Especially since he hadn't anyone to spend the money on. He really began to feel sorry for himself. His heart was breaking. He went to the phone, to call her and see if they might still be home. He called and the phone rang and rang. He hung it up. It was, then, that he decided to head back up North.

He drove without the radio on. He didn't want to listen to songs about broken hearts and loneliness. He rolled down the windows and rolled the sunroof back. He began to think about the upcoming boat race. As soon as he got to the cottage, he would put the boat, in the water. He knew it had to be "tested" before he took it to Alton Bay. He, also, wanted to have that talk with Danny. He could not understand what "that" was all about. It just wasn't like him.

It was around three PM, when he drove into the driveway. He parked, by the boat. He rolled up the windows and the sunroof, turned off the car and got out and walked around the side of the house, by the screened in porch and out to the dock. The water was very rough! White caps topped the hugs waves, that came crashing onto the dock. There would be no test that day. He brought the mail into the cottage and handed it to his mom. She and his dad sat down and began going "through" it. His dad handed him a letter, from Emerson College. He opened it and found a list of "events" for incoming freshmen. Assemblies, mixers, luncheons and dinners. All would begin, the Thursday, after labor Day. He pocketed the letter and went to his room. He lay down and put his head on the pillow. His eyes filled, again. Ree's Chanel #5 was on the pillow, quite strong. He rolled over and found a note on the night table. "I sprinkled my perfume on your pillow, so you would not forget me and dream of me, while we are apart. All my love, Ree." He buried his face in the pillow. His eyes soaking it.

He awoke to his mom calling him. They were going out to eat and did he want to come with them? He answered that he would. He got off the bed and went into the bathroom, to freshen up. He was asked to put on some nice clothes as they were going to the country club, to eat. He went back into the bedroom and got out a dress shirt and clean chinos. He combed his hair and looked into his bag. He brought out the Stetson cologne and put it on the dresser. He wouldn't need to put it on that week. He fingered the I.D. bracelet and left it on his wrist, thinking that a "part" of her was with him. God! He felt miserable! He knew, when he got back from eating, he was going to write his first letter, to her.

During the night, he heard the rain. When he woke up, it was still raining. There would be no test of the hydroplane. Since it was raining, Danny wouldn't be out in the fields. He got dressed, ate some breakfast and drove the VW over to Danny's. He drove into Danny's yard and parked by the barn. He turned off the car and got out and walked up on the porch and knocked on the door. Danny opened the door and jumped back. "you gonna hit me?" Danny asked. "No! he said, "but I should!" Danny told him that he had every right to be mad, at him. He, profusely, apologized over and over. He kept saying he didn't know what came over him. He accepted Danny's apology. They had been friends, since early childhood.

Danny's dad came into the kitchen and greeted him. He was glad that the two of them were friends, again. Danny had chores to do, in the barn. So, he and Danny went out through the rain and into the barn. They were a good team, but, because it was raining, they took their time with the work. When they had finished, they decided to go into town and do some bowling. He needed to do something, he was so "heartsick". Danny didn't talk about Ree, at all.

They bowled three strings and then he drove Danny home. He talked about the hydroplane and the upcoming race. Danny wished he could go with him, but had work to do. He dropped Danny off and drove home. He still didn't turn on the radio. He drove into the driveway and parked the car. He went into the house. His mom said that she was making egg salad, for sandwiches. He told her that, at least, this time, he could have a couple, without seeing Dave's trademark "two finger trail" in the egg salad. He walked into the bedroom and opened up the top drawer of the dresser. He was going to put his briefs and socks, from his bag, into the top drawer. His eyes nearly "popped" out of his head. There, in the top drawer, were a pair of Ree's panties and her high school picture on them. He looked at her picture and turned it over. "I love you now and will always love you, no matter what! Love, Ree". He took the panties and put them in his bag, God forbid, if his mom should find them. He took the picture and put it on the table, by his bed. He would give her, his picture, when she got back. He sat on the bed and wrote his second letter, to her. In the letter, he thanked her for the picture and the "souvenier." He could "hear" her laugh.

He had lunch and afterwards, in the rain, went out on the dock and attempted to fish. He had to do something to pass the time. All he caught were sunfish. His dad came out and told him that he had to go to work, Monday morning. He and his mom would be at the cottage, alone, for the rest of the week. He understood what his dad was saying, even though, he didn't come right out and say, "Take care of your mom." They, also, made plans to go fishing, esrly in the morning, after his swim.

The rains didn't stop until Tuesday. Even though, the sun was out and drying "things" out, the wind picked up and the white capped waves crashed over the end of the dock. Another day without the "test." He had to move the rowboat over to the small beach area by the "pit", to keep it from being rocked against the dock. He sat on the dock, near the back, away from the waves. He wrote another letter to Ree, in the wind. His mom did everything she could, with board games and going into town, shopping, to help him, in his misery. Finally, she left him alone, knowing that, by the following week, all would be back to normal.

Wednesday afternoon, the winds began to "die" down. He hooked the trailer, up to the VW and drove it over the boat ramp at the cottage, next door. He "eased" the trailer into the water. The trailer was, almost, submerged. He turned off the car, set the emergency brake and put the vehicle in first gear. He got out of the car and unstrapped the boat. It floated above the trailer. He shoved it off the trailer, so the fin, on the bottom, would be free of the trailer. He had a small rope attached to the bow. With the rope, he 'towed' the boat away from the trailer and brought it to the beach and secured the rope to a small tree beside the beach. He got back in the car. He started it and released the emergency brake. He brought the car and trailer out of the water and drove it back to his cottage. He walked back to the next door neighbor's and went to the beach and ramp. He untied the boat, from the tree and walked into the water, pulling the small craft, behind him. When the water became too deep, to walk, with rope in hand, he swam towards his dock. He swam past the dock to the mooring. He tied the bow rope, to the mooring. He swam back to the dock and climbed up the ladder. Once on the dock, he went to the screened in porch and got his life jacket and put it on. He reached down and took his helmet off the floor, and put it on. He went back to the dock and climbed into the rowboat, which was tied to the dock. He untied it and rowed it to the mooring. With the bow rope from the rowboat, he climbed into the 'cockpit' of the hydroplane. He tied the bow rope, of the rowboat, to the mooring and released the bow rope, of the hydroplane. The row boat was considerable longer that the hydroplane and it's stern was practically rubbing the end of the dock. The water was smooth as glass, perfect for a "test run".

He reached over and pushed the hydroplane away from the rowboat and reached under the deck and grabbed hold of the gas line and brought it past him and turned and attached it to the gas "receptacles" on the motor. He grabbed the "prime" bubble and began to "prime' the line, sending gas from the ta nk to the motor. When the bubble was 'hard", he reached behind him and found the starter chord. He put the throttle in neutral gear and pulled the rope. The motor responded. It had to be the "sweetest' sound he had heard all week. He pushed the throttle into forward gear and gave the motor some gas. The boat began to move forward away from the row boat and the dock. He positioned himself, on his knees, hands on the steering wheel as he turned the small boat towards the channel. His mom was on the dock, watching, as he gave more gas. The bow raised up as the boat "plowed" through the calm water. He shoved the throttle all the way forward. The boat picked up speed, but still the bow was high. He could barely see over it. He leaned his body forward, his waist against the steering wheel. The bow started to come 'down." he settled back in the seat, as the boat picked up more speed. Finally, the bow was level with the water surface. She was skimming across the water, at full speed. He felt exhilarated! He headed for the area, between Cow island and the little Squirrel island. The "test" so far was a resounding success! He couldn't wait to race her. He slowed just a little as he made the left hand turn and headed back towards the cottage. He pushed the throttle to full speed, again. He was roaring towards the cottage, he slowed it back just a little as he made the pass, in front of the cottage. His mom waved, to him. He "flew" past the row of small cottages, surrounding the small lagoon, just beyond the swamp.he went to the wide area, that lead to nineteen mile bay. He slowed again for a turn back towards the cottage. The boat and motor were "performing" perfectly! He made a "pass" in the channel and slowed to take the turn back in to the cottage. He gave it the "gas" and sped in towards the cottage. He would make the "pass" and take one more turn in the lagoon and slow it down and return to the mooring. He, again, roared past the cottage and started the turn, he left it at full speed. "She' was not making the turn! He pulled on the wheel, turning it as far to the left as it would go! The motor was turned, but the boat began to skip, sideways, across the water! Suddenly, the right side caught an air "pocket and rose up! He and the boat were going over! He reached for the "kill" switch, but it was too late! He was in the water, with the boat on top of him. He heard the motor "screaming" as the rear of the boat was sinking beneath the surface! He pushed himself out of the cockpit and "sprang' to the surface. He was surrounded by men, who had jumped into the water to "save" him. He kept trying to dive down and save the motor, but the life jacket kept springing him back up to the surface. Two of the men pulled him to their beach as two others pulled the "lifeless" motor and boat. Once on the beach, he thanked them. They thanked him for the "after dinner entertainment". Apparently, all the folks in the small cottages had been watching his "test". He got up and walked over to the boat, with the "stricken" Mercury. When she sank, with the motor running, the exhaust got blocked with mud and debris on the bottom. He knew that the inside of the motor was a "mess". He took off his helmet and life vest and put them in the boat. He looked over at the cottage and began to laugh. His mom had gotten into the rowboat and was trying to row to him. The bow rope was still attached to the mooring and she was rowing around in circles! This "milestone" was his first and only operation of a racing hydroplane!

He walked to the road, in bare feet. It wasn't bad, walking on grass. He came to the fence that blocked the road. He went around it and made sure he walked on the "grassy" middle, instread of the dirt and gravel, on the sides. He looked down, as he walked, not wanting t osrtep on anything that might have crawled out of the swamp. As he walked a, little further, he saw the "discarded" condoms. He, immediately, thought of Ree and how and what she was doing? Then, he wondered how he was going to tell her about the "failed' test. Somehow, he knew she would be happy that he wasn't going to race the boat. He got to the driveway and walked around the house, past the screened in porch, to the dock. His mom was still sitting in the rowboat. He lay, on his stomach, on the dock, and reached for the stern of the rowboat. His left hand reached out and caught hold of the back of the Johnson outboard and pulled the boat to him. The boat was close enough to the dock, for him to get up and jump into the boat. His mom looked like she had been through "hell." She looked, at him, and asked if he was all right. He said that he was and that he was sorry, for what he put her through. He "walked" past her to the bow and reached down and untied the bow rope, from the mooring. He took an oar and paddled the rowboat closer to the dock. Once at the dock, he held the boat, so his mom could get out. She turned and look at him and said, "I must have looked pretty silly, trying to get over to you." He lied and told her "no". As she walked up the dock, towards the screened in porch, he pushed the boat away from the dock. He hooked up the gas to the outboard and "primed' the gas. Again, he was glad that the water was like glass. He put the oars along inside the boat, under the seats. He pulled the starter cord and the "dependable." Outboard started on the first pull. He headed over to the lagoon and the beach. He "beached" the rowboat and got out of it. He went to the hydroplane and took off the Mercury outboard and "hefted" it over to the rowboat. He laid it on the bottom, inside, between the seats. He untied the bow rope, from the rowboat and tied it to the back handle on the stern of the rowboat. He took the other end of the rope and tied it to the bow of the hydroplane. When he pushed the hydroplane, off the beach and into the water, he noticed that the mark of the fin, was not in the sand. He knew that somewhere out in that water, on the bottom, lay the fin; that caused him to flip over.

Once the hydroplane was floating, on its own, he pushed the rowboat off the beach and out to deeper water. He climbed in over the side and went to start the Johnson. Again, first pull, he slowly, turned the rowboat and began pulling the hydroplane, home. He was unaware of the girl and others, watching him, in beach chairs. It wasn't until he made the turn, that he noticed her. She gave him a "little" wave and he gave her a "little "wave" back.

He pulled the hydroplane to the mooring. He put the Johnson in neutral and began to "coast" over the mooring. As the mooring "bobbled by" he grabbed the bow rope, from the stern handle, of the rowboat and grabbed the mooring, with his other hand. He braced his feet, against the stern, to prevent him, from once again, being catapulted into the water. He tied the bow rope, to the mooring and let it go. The hydroplane, was fastened by the rope to the mooring. He sat down and put the Johnson in forward gear and went to the dock.

Once he had tied the rowboat to the dock, he "hefted" the Mercury outboard, out of the rowboat and laid it on the dock. He got out of the rowboat and went to the Mercury. He took off the cover and "surveyed" the damage. It was a mess! Mud and dirt "caked" throughout the insides. He heaved a heavy sigh and put the cover back on. He "carried" the motor off the dock and laid it beside the screened in porch. He would have to wait until his dad came back up, for the weekend. He was hoping he would have good news for him, when they went on their "postponed" fishing trip.

The winds returned on Thursday and continued well into Friday, afternoon. He spent most of the time, watching the hydroplane try to sever the rope from its mooring. The rest of the time, he wrote letters to Ree. Thursday night, he and his mom went to the movies, to see "Butterfield 8" with Elizabeth Taylor and Lawrence Harvey. After the show, his mom confessed that the movie was more for "adults". He said he enjoyed some parts of it. They went for ice cream at Baileys and home. He wrote another "lengthy' letter to Ree.

His dad showed up, at the cottage, around 2PM on Friday. After his dad had settled in, they loaded the Mercury into the trunk of his car and took it to the marina. The man who "owned" the marina, was a relative of Danny's. he looked at the motor and told him that it could be fixed, but would take weeks and cost a lot of money. He decided to "scrap" it. Jack, the owner, said that he would by the motor, for parts. He looked at the "quick silver, lower unit" and told him that it was in pretty good shape. He would give him two hundred dollars for the motor and the lower unit. He told Jack, "sold!" Jack went into his office and came back out with two, one hundred dollar bills. When he opened his wallet, to put the money in, he pulled out the bill of sale, from his "former Alladins member". Jack had one of his workers take the motor into the building. They went in and transferred ownership of the outboard, to Jack. When he and his dad got back into his dad's car, his dad asked him, if he made a good or bad deal, on the motor. He said, "a good deal." His dad said, "good!"

The Labor Day Weekend went by, too slow, for him. He did manage to meet the girl, from the beach chair. She was very pretty, with a "cute" figure. Then, he found out she was only thirteen years old! She had given him her address and he did put it in his wallet. When he found out her age, he forgot the "paper" was in his wallet. Before he realized it, Monday had arrived and Ree would be on her way home, from Maine. He found an "old" empty envelope box and put his letters in it. He wondered how many letters, she would have for him.

He packed up the "bug" with his clothes and toiletries and decided to leave the cottage that Monday afternoon. His folks tried dissuade him, saying the traffic was going to be very heavy. He did not care. He wanted to be home, when Ree called. He and his dad put the "motorless" hydroplane back onto the trailer. He hooked up the "safety chain", the lights and hitched it to the VW. He strapped it to the trailer. He had no idea what he was going to do with the boat. He thought he would "handle" that situation, next summer. His mom packed him a couple of egg salad sandwiches, some chips and a couple of bottles of coke, for the trip. They both asked him to drive carefully.

He "hit" the road around 1:45PM. He stopped at Danny's and said "good bye" and told him that he would see him on Columbus Day, when they came to close the cottage, for the winter. Traffic wasn't too bad, going through town and down to the Alton bay circle. He didn't experience any "heavy" traffic, until he hit the main highway. He did a lot of praying, that no one would rear-end him and destroy the boat.

The ride home, took about three and a half hours. Normally, it would take two. He did stop at a rest stop and eat his "dinner". He, only, drank one of the cokes. He turned on the radio and heard Bobby Darin sing "Mack The Knife." Dion followed him with "The Wanderer". Ray Charles was next with "What'd I Say?" parts one and two. After the commercials, came Elvis and "Are You Lonesome Tonight?" He felt his eyes fill up and turned off the radio.

He pulled into the driveway and drove down behind the house. He pulled onto the grass and immediately noticed that the cabin cruiser was gone! He "unhitched "the trailer and taking the front of it, wheeled it very close to the back of the house. He went and got the old blanket and covered the boat and trailer. He, then, unpacked the VW and took his bags up to his room. He left the box of letters in the back of the car. He sorted out the clothes that needed to be washed and took them down to the basement and put them in in the Bendix, with some soap. He ran the washer and went back upstairs. He hoped that Ree would get home, in time, for them to see each other. The next day, he would be at college, registering for his classes. He went back to his room and looked in the drawer, by the nightstand. He searched the drawer and found one "unused" condom. He took it out and put it in his wallet. He went back down into the basement, just as the washer was in the "spin" cycle. He waited for it to stop. When it did, he took out the clothes and put them in the dryer. He went back upstairs. He tried to watch TV. The Jerry Lewis Telethon was on. He watched it for a while and then checked his watch. It read 6:30PM. He wondered if he should call her. He went to the phone and dialed her number. No answer. He went back to the TV. He couldn't concentrate on anything. He went into the kitchen and found some bread and peanut butter, chips and cokes. He made two sandwiches, for dinner. He went back to the TV and ate and watched. His eyes began to get heavy around 7:30PM.

He awoke at the sound of the telephone. He stumbled off the couch and got to the phone, on the ninth ring. He grabbed the receiver. "hello!" It was Ree! He was so happy to hear from her! She was talking so fast, asking so many questions. He looked at his watch. It read 9:10PM. Too late to get together. They had so much to say, to each other! They both had to register for classes, the next day. He asked her if she wrote any letters to him, "Every day!" She said. "Me,too!" he replied. He asked, if they could get together the next evening and talk, over eating their dinner together, somewhere. She said, "Call me, first, around 4PM and we'll plan our evening." He said "okay!" he told her how miserable he was, without her. She said the same thing. They ended the call, by telling each other how much they loved each other and couldn't wait to see each other, again.

He went and turned off the TV and went upstairs, to bed. His dreams were of Ree, of holding her and kissing her and making "love" to her. He drifted off and never heard his brother, Phil come into the house. He would drive to the "T" station and ride the train into the city and begin his first day as a college freshman. Another "milestone."

Registration was a "unique" experience, for him. He arrived at the college at 9AM and wasn't through until after 10:45. Afterwards, he went to the bookstore and bought the books, he needed and a decal strip with the name of the college, on it. He, then, went to the "coffee shop" and ate his usual cheeseburgers, fries, and coke. He met three people, who like him had just "survived" the registration ritual. The boy' name was Rick, and the two girls were Rachel and Justine. With a "full' stomach, he said it was "nice' meeting them and left the coffee shop and headed for the "T" station, for the long ride home.

He called Ree around 3:30PM. She had just returned from her first day at school, as well. They made plans for him to pick her up at 5 and they would go to the "new" Mexican restaurant, in town. She asked him to bring his letters and she would bring hers. They couldn't wait to see each other. He didn't change out of his "school clothes". He did "splash" on some Stetson cologne and combed his hair and sprayed his underarms with deodorant. To do that, he had to unbutton three top buttons of his shirt. He was 'ready" to meet the" love", of his life.

He was just about to leave, when his folks showed up, from the cottage. He told them, of his plans. His mom said "good" because they had stopped for something to eat, on the way home. He told them that the cabin cruiser wasn't there. His dad said that Phil had bought a trailer and had taken it to get an outboard motor "fitted" to it. He was relieved! It was just after 4:30, when he got into the VW and headed over to Ree's.

He pulled up in front of her house. He turned off the car and got out and was halfway up the walk, when he looked up and saw her coming towards him. She had on a white blouse and tight gray skirt. She a big grin on her face, her auburn hair flowing in the wind, that she created, as she walked. She rushed into his arms. They hugged for quite a while. She kept telling him how much she missed him and being in his arms. They, finally, disengaged themselves and walked to the car. He opened her door and then ran around to his side and got in. Again, they leaned to each other and shared a long, wet, passionate kiss. Once their lips separated, he started the car and drove them to the Mexican restaurant.

He parked the car in the small parking lot aside the restaurant and they got out and went in. they were seated at a small candle lit table, off to the side, away from the main dining area. They sat and stared into each other's eyes and held hands. When the waitress came to their table, they gave her their orders and proceeded to hand each other, their letters. His heart was "bursting" with love for her, as he read. She would read one and put it down, her eyes filled with tears. She told him how much she loved him and then would open another. It was like that until she got to Wednesday night's letter. Her smile turned into a frown. She put the letter down and asked if he had been injured when the boat flipped. He told her "no!" She, then, asked, "Are you still going to keep the boat? And what about the motor?" he told her to read Thursday and Friday night's letters. She did and when, she was done, she was happy that he no longer had the motor. He finished her letters. They, again, held hands across the small table and stared into each other's eyes. When, at last, their orders arrived, the waitress had to ask them to let go of their hands, so she could place their plates down.

They talked about their first day of college. They were both excited to be college freshmen. She was excited that their schools were only five blocks away from each other. She took her small college decal out of her parking lot and wanted him to put it above his, on the back window, of the VW. He said that he didn't want people to think he attended a girl's college. She laughed!

She had a way of getting "her" way with him. When they left the restaurant, he took her "decal" and placed in the passenger side, of the rear window, just above his college "decal".

They headed for their spot, by the river. The sun was setting down over the water. They did not notice that. They were too busy, wrapped up in each other's arms and legs. Her right hand was inside his pants; his right hand was between her thighs. Their lips were "fused' together. They managed to bring each other to a climatic finish, without actual intercourse. He was glad that he had used the condom. The mess in his pants were have been quite obvious. Ree asked that they make a "pact" never to be separated again, for any length of time. He agreed. Even though the time was nearing 9PM, they did not want the night to end. They drove to the car hop for a couple of frappes. Again, the waitress, there, had to interrupt their kissing, to give them their frappes. They knew that they would have to wait to the weekend, to see each other, again. He had a full schedule of meetings and mixers, before his classes "officially" began the next week. Her classes would begin in two days. They parted on her front steps and planned to get together, on the weekend.

He enjoyed the first week college. His class were treated like "kings and Queens." They were taken on tours of the campus, to cookouts, afternoon parties, and dances. By the end of the week, he began to notice that he was feeling "tired" a lot. He and Ree, during one of their eve ning phone conversations, planned on going to the drive in. They had to go on Saturday, because he had a "fiesta" at the college, to attend.

He slept in, late, that Saturday morning. When he got up, around noon, he still felt a little tired. Even though, he had plenty of sleep, he still felt "tired". He spent the afternoon, cleaning the car and getting ready for his and Ree's first real "date" since being together, again. He was to pick her up at 6PM. He arrived, at her house, at ten minutes after 6. They got into the VW, embraced and kissed each other "hello". They drove to the drive in as Ricky nelson was on the radio with "Believe What You Say." They sang along and looked at each other.

Ree was wearing her pleasant blouse and blue Bermuda shorts. He was in a light blue dress shirt and jeans. He parked the VW, well in the rear, in the last row. Once the speaker was in place, they got out of the car and went hand in hand, to the concession stand. She went to the ladies room, he got the popcorn and cokes. He had gone to the drugstore, in the next town, that afternoon. The store that Fred went to get condoms. He bought a package of three. He waited for Ree in front of the stand. She came out and met him. She had moved the 'sleeves' of the blouse down over her shoulders, to just above her elbows, revealing a "nice" amount of cleavage. They got into the back seat of the VW and put their food, behind them, in the small storage space behind the back seat. He reached forward and using the lever, pushed the driver's seat. Forward, as far as it would go. He did the same thing with the passenger seat. He sat back and looked at her. She had lowered the sleeves of her blouse, even more. He leaned to his right, to place his lips upon hers. She reached out, with her hands and arms and brought his head, lips and tongue to her exposed chest. He began to kiss and lick every inch of heaving breasts. She arched her back, pushing her breasts against his lips and tongue. She let go of his head and reached behind her back and unclasped her bra and took it off. He brought is lips and tongue back to now heaving breasts. He circled his lips and tongue over inch, the tops, the sides, underneath and, finally, coming to the nipples. He placed his lips around one, gently sucking, with his tongue, softly lashing the top. He loved to feel the "harden" under his tongue and lips. His right hand would massage her right breast, while his mouth was on her left. His mouth and then his left hand would switch to the other. While his left hand was on her left breast, his right hand was between her thighs, also, softly massaging and squeezing. She pushed her pelvis against his hand. Her hands in his hair, moans escaping from her lips. She began to slide down in the seat, with him next to her. She brought his head up from her breasts and her "rock hard" nipples. Their lips crushed together. Both of his hands were massaging her inner thighs and up to her shorts covered vagina. He unbuttoned her shorts. She raised her hips, as he brought the shorts and panties own to her knees and then her ankles. "Oh baby, take them off!" he obeyed. "Please kiss me, there!" She begged. He moved his lips and tongue up the insides of her legs, to her thighs and beyond. He placed his lips around her 'nub' and did the same thing with his tongue that he had done with each of her nipples. Her legs were trembling and thrashing. He brought two of his fingers up and moved them inside her as his mouth continued its "moves" on her clitoris. Her hands were 'wringing" his hair, on the top of his head. She let out a loud "OMIGOD!" and her body went "limp". She "flooded" his fingers. She gasped, huskily, "Inside me, I want you inside me!" he rolled away from her and stripped off his pants and briefs. He took one of the condoms out of his wallet and ripped open the package and rolled over his "steel" penis. He looked at her. Her blouse, bunched around her waist. Her beautiful white breasts and 'swollen" nipples glistening in the dim light. He looked at her tanned legs, with the white place where her bathing suit must have been. "God! Ree, you are so very, very, beautiful!" She looked at him through lust filled eyes, "Come to me, baby, Please!" he slid between her legs, as she took her hands from his head and guided him inside her. Anyone around that VW had to know what was going on. They established a rhythm that tested the shocks of that little car. She was stretched out on the seat, horizontally, with him on top. They could not be seen through the windows. The fogged up windows, also, blocked most of the light from the screen. They began very slow, savoring the feeling of each other.

Their lips, once again fused, their tongues swirling, his hands on her breasts, her hands "raking" his back. Their hips in unison. Their bodies became as one body. Nothing else, in the world, mattered to them, especially, in the movie lot. They were the only ones in the world! Their eyes closed, their breath ragged and "large". They parted their lips, only to get enough air, to continue breathing. The "friction" started to get to him. He picked up the pace of his thrusts. She seemed to feel 'it' too. She began to match his tempo. She wretched her lips from his, her arms around his neck, her lips against his cheek, "Oh my sweet. sweet, baby! Don't hold back! Oh God I Love You So Much!" he grunted, "Me, too! I want to love you, forever!!!" He took his right hand from her breast and brought it between them, to her clitoris and rubbed it with the top of his finger. She went wild! thrusting harder and harder. He could sense she was nearing 'completion." He increased his tempo. He, too, was getting close. Then it happened! It was almost at the same time. She went first and he came, seconds, after. They held on to each other very tightly and lay as one. Lights began to filter into the car, through the fogged up windows. "Intermission" he whispered. They pulled apart, he holding onto the base of the condom, he slipped it off. He reached over the back of the seat and found a paper napkin and took off the condom and with the napkin, wiped himself off. He placed the condom inside the napkin and put both on the food tray. She found her shorts and panties and put them back on and adjusted her blouse and bra. He pulled his briefs and pants back on. Once they had settled back, he reached behind the back of the seat and brought their popcorns and cokes over to them. He left the napkin, where it was. They shared one coke and left the other.

After they had some nourishment, they both had to use the facilities. He put the rest of the popcorn back behind the seat. They had both finished their cokes, so he took the empty cups and put the napkin inside one and they exited the car and headed for the rest rooms. He deposited the cups, wrapper and napkin in the large trash can, on the way.

Again, he waited for Ree, in front of the concession stand. After a while, he went to the ladies room and saw Ree, in line, outside the door. She was fifth in line, just to get into the ladies room. He told her he was going to get a pizza and meet her by the concession stand. The line, at the concession stand, was long, too, but it moved quickly. He got the pizza and went to stand in front, when Ree was coming to him. "Remind me, next time, to go before intermission." She said. He looked at her and grinned. "We were hardly in a position, at the time, to go." She shoved his arm, "you're naughty!" She said. They laughed, as they walked back to the car. The second show was about to start. Something about a creature from the sea. It was in black and white. They finished their food and he put the empty box, in the back, with the popcorn. They shared the other coke. They were still in the back seat. They began to kiss and hug, again.

It didn't take long, for their passions to take over, again. This time, Ree slipped out of her shorts and panties and he slipped out of his briefs and pants. He remained sitting up, in the seat, as Ree straddled him and took another condom and rolled it over 'him". She raised herself up and then lowered herself down, guiding him, with her right hand and slowly impaling herself on him. Once, again, their lips pressed against each other. His hands on her breasts, under her blouse. He was amazed how quickly her nipples responded to his touch. She set the pace. She started very slowly, eleciting groans from his lips, between kisses. She held his head between her hands. She was in complete control! She would speed up and then slow down, then speed up (her thrusts) and then slow, again. She moaned that she wish they could away, somewhere, just the two of them and make love all weekend! He groaned "that would be heaven!" Sometimes, she would stop moving and make sure he stayed hard, by reaching between them and stroking the shaft that wasn't in her. She, also, made sure the condom was still on. They made love through most of the second movie. He knew she was ready to "end" things, when she brought his hand from under her shirt and placed it between them and 'on' her. She, then began to squirm and thrash and increase her tempo, knowing it would bring them to their crescendo. This time he finished first, with her seconds after. She got off and he removed the condom and placed it in the remaining empty coke cup. He reached over and put his hand on her and, slowly, inserted two fingers inside her and his thumb on her clitoris. Her eyes opened wide as he massaged and rubbed. She reached out and grabbed his head and pushed down to where his hand was. He replaced his thumb with his lips and tongue, but kept his fingers 'busy." Her hands stayed on the top of his head. He felt her beginning to respond. Her legs thrashed and trembled as he "lashed" her clit. She cried out, again and again as he felt her body tense up and then release. She tried to bring him "pleasure" with her hands, but something was wrong. He just couldn't get another erection. They didn't want to waste a condom. She was going to place it on him, when he got "hard" again. It didn't happen. She became concerned. She was always able to get him "going". He felt a kind of exhaustion creep over his body. He had not experienced that before. She continued to hold him, hoping he would respond. He said that he still enjoyed her touch and he couldn't understand why "it" wasn't responding to her touch. She let go and decided to get dressed. He put on his briefs and pants. She told him to stay unzipped. Once she was dressed, she put her hand, back on him. They kissed and hugged throughout the rest of the movie. Her hand still on him, massaging and stroking.

It would be another week, before they would get together, again. In the interim, after a couple of days. He masturbated and was able to maintain an erection. But, soon afterward, he would fall asleep, totally exhausted! He found, during classes, he would, almost fall asleep.

At times, during the afternoon, after classes, before dinner, his mom would find him, on the couch, sound asleep. One night, during dinner, he, almost passed out. When he didn't call Ree, she called and his mother told her that he was asleep. Ree said "At 7PM?" That's when his mom told Ree that she was making an appointment with their doctor. Ree asked his mom, to please let her know. He stayed home from classes and went to the doctor. His mom drove. He was too 'tired" to drive. The doctor ran all kinds of tests and then took some blood. They went home. His mom was visibly shaken. The doctor had mentioned the word 'leukemia".

When they returned home, he told his mom, he was "too tired" to eat. He did not hear what the doctor had told his mom. He went into the living room and laid down on the couch. He heard his mom and dad talking. He did not hear the words, just the tone of their voices. Their voices were very somber. He was half asleep, when he heard the phone rang. His mom answered it and was talking to someone about "their knowing more, when the blood tests come back. It should be in a few days." He drifted off to sleep.

He stayed home from college. He missed talking with Ree. His mood began to change. He became more irritable and seemed to get a "don't care attitude" about his family. He knew he still loved Ree, but wasn't sure he "liked" her. He knew that something was drastically wrong with him. He just didn't know what. He lost his appetite for food. When he did eat, the food tasted 'bland", almost like cardboard. His folks were really worried and were talking about "specialists".

Friday morning, the doctor called and told his mom that she needed to bring him into the office, right away. As they drove, he noticed his mom trying to stop tears from flowing down her cheeks. When they arrived, at the doctor's office, they were 'whisked' right in. he sat near the doctor. The doctor began to ask him a series of questions. The doctor wanted to know if his gums were bleeding and if they hurt. He answered "yes." He asked him, if he had been keeping late hours and not getting enough rest. He said 'yes, up till this past week." The doctor looked at his mom and uttered the word "mononucleosis". His mother asked if it was a form of leukemia. The doctor said 'No". he said that it is called the "kissing disease." The doctor told them, that he was to have complete bed rest and no social activities, at all. Most of all, dating. He looked at the doctor and said, "no dating?" The doctor asked him. "What's her name?" He said, "Ree." They doctor looked at his mother with a quizzical look. His mother chimed in "She's a "she" and that's her nickname. The doctor said, "oh, and replied especially her. You don't want to give this disease to her, do you?" "No" he replied. They asked how long he would have to go without seeing her. The doctor said at least a month. He was heartbroken! The doctor told his mom, to get iron pills and then made out a prescription. They left the office. His mom was happy that it wasn't cancer. He was "sullen". How would he tell Ree, that they couldn't see each other for a month! He was sure that she would "dump" him for someone else, who was a lot healthier. The ride home was not a happy one. His mom stopped by the drugstore, on the way home, and picked up a large bottle of iron pills and dropped off his prescription.

When they arrived home, His mom got a glass of water and made him take an iron pill. She went to the phone and began to make calls, to his dad and brothers. He would have to wait until after dinner, to call Ree. He kept going over, in his mind, how he break the news to her. He was becoming quite depressed, though he wasn't aware of it. He, just knew, that he wasn't happy.

He still didn't have much of an appetite. When every had finished eating, he checked his watch and went to the phone. He called Ree and gave her the bad news. "What?" she cried. "What are you saying? Are we breaking up?" He tried to tell her "no". She really thought that he was using his 'illness' to break up with her. He, in desperation, called his mom to the phone and asked her to tell Ree, what the doctor had told them. His mom had quite a conversation, with Ree. When she was done, she handed the phone back to him. "Oh baby! I'm so sorry! I just don't want to lose you! Please do what the doctor says and get well real quick! I love you! At least we can still talk on the phone." She said. "Of course!" was his reply. There were tears in her voice. She told him to tell her as soon as he knew that he was no longer contagious. He told her that he would. His eyes began to fill up as he told her how much he loved her. He hung up the phone and went upstairs to lie down. This illness was a milestone that he would want to forget.

His mom notified the college and they went along with him restarting, the next semester. He spent most of the days and night, resting or sleeping. He did get quite upset one day, when he looked at his "stool" before flushing the toilet and saw that it was "BLACK"! His scream could be heard throughout the house. His mom reassured him, it was caused by the iron pills. Of course, he did not mention 'this' to Ree.

For three weeks, he recuperated, by listening to his records, but he didn't sing along, like he used to. He watched TV, but he wasn't really interested. Even Annette, on the Mickey Mouse Club, didn't interest him. He tried looking at his brother's "girlie" magazines and didn't get a rise. About the only thing, he liked, was talking to Ree. When she started to relate all the things going on in her life, he soon lost interest.

The first week of October, he went to see the doctor. He was told that he was no longer contagious! That meant that he could have visitors, but still no dating. He asked, specifically, about Ree. She could visit, him, at his house. No going out! This was the first exciting news, he had! He couldn't wait to get home and tell Ree.

His appetite was, slowly, coming back. His weight was on the "upside". His body was still "tired." He was told he cut back on the iron pills. He called Ree, after dinner. When he told her, he wasn't contagious anymore, she got excited and wanted to know, when she could come and see him. He told her "anytime." She asked if she could come by that night. He said, "sure! I can't wait to see you." She told him that she loved him and that she would be over soon. He hung up the phone and went upstairs, to his room. He changed out of his jeans, put on fresh briefs, rolled some fresh deodorant under his arms, combed his hair, splashed on some Stetson and put on socks and shoes. He went downstairs and told everyone that Ree was coming by, to visit. They told him to take it easy and they would leave them alone, in the den.

It was after 8PM. He was beginning to think she wasn't coming, after all. He told his folks they could come into the den and watch TV. He was thinking of going to bed. He was at the foot of the stairs, when the doorbell rang. He turned around and opened the door. It was Ree! She was not alone! She had her friend, Sue, with her. She gave him a "small" hug, but no kiss. He ushered them into the living room and closed the door, behind them. She and Sue sat on the couch. He sat in an easy chair. They made "small talk" about how good he looked and how things were going at school. Sue got off the couch and went over to the hi fi and started to "go through" his albums. She found the Johnny Mathis album and put it on the turntable and turned on the record player. Ree got off the couch and held out her hands. He got off the chair and went to her. They wrapped their arms around each other and began to, slowly, sway to "Chances Are." It felt so good to hold her, in his arms. They rested their cheeks against each other. He felt bad for Sue. She just sat there, on the couch, and watched. Halfway through the song, Ree brought her hand from his back and placed it between them, and unzipped his fly. She slipped her hand inside, through the opening, to his flesh. He couldn't believe it! He was responding to her "touch." She brought her face to his and said, with a grin, "someone is glad to see me." He heard Sue laugh. He told her that was the first time, in a month, that he felt some "hardness." She held him tight and told him that he needed to get better, fast. They were "slated" for a date, in two weeks, with John and Janet, to go on a hayride. He told her he would do his best, to be one hundred per cent. She whispered in his ear, "I want my man, back. My lover, my best friend back!" he replied, "Me, too." She leaned her face in toward his and their lips met, for the first time, in a month. The kiss was a loving, sweet kiss, void of any passion.

It lasted through two of the songs, on the album. They were both breathing heavy, when they pulled apart. Sue told Ree that they had to leave. Ree took her hand out of his pants and she zipped him up. He was so thankful that they had come over. Ree whispered, "I'll never stop loving you." He told her "me,too." He ushered them to the front door. His folks came out of the den and said hello and that they were glad that she had stopped over. She introduced them to Sue and they said goodbye and that she would be back, in a couple of days.

He told his mom about the "hayride date" coming up. She told him, only if the doctor says "okay." Every time Ree stopped by, for a visit, he grew stronger. Everything was returning to "normal". A week before the "hayride" date, the doctor gave him the "okay". He was ecstatic! He couldn't wait to call Ree and give her the good news! She was so happy! He still was unable to drive. Ree told him that John would drive, on the date. Finally! He had something to look forward to. Ree told him that they would take "things" slow. She did not want him to have a relapse. He did not want one, either.

Finally, the night of the hayride came. He took a long hot bath. He put on a pair of fresh briefs, a pair of fresh jeans and a dress shirt with a crewneck sweater. He wore white socks and his dirty bucs. He combed his hair and splashed on some Stetson. He hadn't been out of the house, in over a month! He couldn't wait! He had a tuna fish sandwich, to "hold' him over, until they would get something to eat, later. He found a "straw" cowboy hat, in his closet. He thought it would be appropriate for the hayride. He was ready. He couldn't wait to hold and kiss Ree, again.

They were picking him up around 4PM. It was 3:45 and already, the sun was setting. He, actually, felt excited. He did not have any condoms, but he felt that it would be too soon, anyway. He checked his hair, one more time, before putting on the hat. He had just adjusted the hat to a 'rakish" look, when he heard a horn blow, in front of the house. He said good night to his folks and opened the front door and went out, closing the door, behind him. Ree was already halfway up the walk. The cool, October night air, slapped him, in the face. He stopped, for a second, to adjust to the night. Ree came up and took his arm, in hers. She gave him a kiss on the cheek. Then she said, "You've got to get rid of the hat!" he laughed and asked herm if it wasn't appropriate for a hayride. She said, "you look ridiculous!" He took it off, as they got into the back seat of john's car. Both John and Janet were very glad to see him. They hoped he was feeling much better. He said that he was. Ree cuddled up next to him and wrapped her arms around his waist and kissed his cheek. He turned to her and their lips meet in a sweet, kiss.

They kept hugging and kissing, all the way to the farm. A lot of Janet and Ree's classmates were on the hayride, as well. It was like a "mini" reunion. There were approximately ten couples. The wagon was "loaded" with hay and was being pulled by two large horses. John parked the car in a "makeshift" parking lot. They got out of the car and went and joined the others. He paid the 'farmer" the ten dollars for him and Ree. Once they were all set, the farmer told them to get up in the hay and they would be "off". Ree was, also, wearing jeans and a white blouse under a dark crewneck sweater. He got up onto the back of the hay wagon and found a spot for them. He grabbed Ree's hand and pulled her to him. She landed on top of him, laughing. She said "kind sir, please! The ride hasn't even started yet!" Everyone laughed! John and Janet were sitting beside them. Ree moved beside him and they wrapped their arms around each other's waist. Some guy brought a guitar and they all started singing "old" songs, like "Harvest Moon" and "Heart Of My Heart." The horse drawn wagon moved along very slowly. It didn't take long, for guy with the guitar, to realize that the singing had stopped. He and Ree's lips were fused together. All the couples were "involved" with each other. It had been so very long, since he and Ree had been together. They kissed and hugged each other, for the whole ride, which lasted for well over an hour.

As the ride came to a close, Ree whispered in his ear, "now we'll go parking and make up for lost time." He was feeling kind of weak. He wanted to go to parking, but just wasn't feeling up to it. He didn't want to hurt her feelings or turn her away from him. He didn't know how to tell her that he just wanted to go home and go to bed. When they were walking, arm in arm back to the car, she sensed something was not right. She asked him if he was feeling okay. He told her that he wasn't. That he was feeling weak. He could see the look of disappointment on her face. She really wanted to get "passionate" with him, once again. He just wasn't ready.

When they got into the car, he asked John, to please take him home. He could tell that John and Janet were not happy with him. Ree asked that maybe some food might help him. He didn't think so. They drove him home. He could feel Ree's tears on his cheek. He tried to console her, by saying that it might take another week and he would be ready to "really" love her, physically. They shared an embrace and a long, sweet kiss, in front of his house. Then, he got out. He thanked them and walked up the walk, to the door. He turned around to blow her a kiss, but they had already left. He cursed the "damn mono" and went inside the house.

He tried to call Ree, several evenings, but she was always studying. His depression worsened. He was bored, just sitting around the house. Finally, he was able to talk with Ree. He told her that he was feeling better, physically. She sounded happy. She asked if he was up for a visit. He said that he was. They made plans for her to come over, to his house, the next evening.

His folks went up to the camp, to close it for the winter. Phil and Nan went there, too. Ree was going to be coming over, alone, around 6PM. At 5 o'clock, he bathed, put on fresh clothes, combed his hair, which hadn't seen a barber, for a while, and splashed on some Stetson. He was excited! He checked his wallet and nightstand table and was able to "come up" with one more condom. He hoped he would be up to pleasing her.

Ree arrived at 6:10PM. He was standing by the door, when she rang the bell. He opened it and took hold of her arms and brought her to him. They embraced! His lips found hers and they shared a long, sweet kiss that turned into a wet, passionate kiss. When they separated, she said, "oh baby! I've missed you so very much!" They closed the front door, behind them. She surmised that he was the only one home. She gave him a "special look" and he took her hand and they went quickly, up the stairs, to his bedroom. They fell onto his bed. Arms, legs, hands were everywhere! Clothes just disappeared off the bodies. They were like two animals in "heat". He didn't take his time, but practically dove between her thighs. His hands on her breasts as his lips and tongue paid "homage" to her vagina. She was 'writhing" out of control! She was gasping! He reached over to the nightstand and grabbed the unwrapped condom and rolled it down his penis. She reached down and stroked him. He felt 'it' harden. She kept on stroking. He raised his head and brought his lips and tongue to her nipples. Once they harden, he brought his lips to hers. She maneuvered him between her and guided him inside her. That old bed 'creaked' like it had never done,before.! He brought his hand down between them and found her clit. He massaged it with his forefinger. She began to cry out, "Oh my sweet, sweet, baby! I love you so much!" the weeks of abstinence proved to be too much. They both reached "nirvana" at almost the same time. He rolled off her and grabbed the base of the condom. He got off the bed and went to the bathroom, to dispose of the condom. While he was in the bathroom, he heard voices downstairs. It was Phil and Nan! He raced back to the bedroom! Ree had heard them too and was busy getting dressed. He, quickly, threw his clothes on. Ree went down the hall and into the bathroom. He went downstairs. Phil and Nan were in the living room. He walked in and said "hi". Phil wanted to know who's car was parked in front of the house. He told them it was Ree's and she was in the upstairs bathroom. Nan gave him a "funny" look and asked where he had been? He said he was in the downstairs bathroom. Ree came downstairs and into the living room and said "hi". After some "light' conversation, Ree asked him, if he was up to go to the car hop, for a frappe. He said "yes!" They said good bye and walked out the front door, to the car and got in. They both broke out in laughter! Ree said that she believed that his brother and Nan came to the house, for the same reason, she had.

As they drove to the car hop, The Fleetwoods were on the radio with "Mr. Blue". Followed by Laverne Baker and "Shake A Hand." Jackie Wilson was next with "Higher and Higher." They pulled into the last row and ordered two chocolate frappes. Ree turned off the radio and they began to cuddle. He liked the "reversal" with her driving and he sitting next to her. They talked about Halloween. They both were staying in and handing out candy. She asked him, if he were going out, what would he dress up as. He said, "either a soldier or cowboy." He asker her. She said, "well, if we were going to be together, maybe a hooker or French maid." He told her, that if she were to do that, she might never get home until the next morning. Again, she used her favorite term, "you're naughty!" Their frappes arrived. He paid the waitress and gave her a generous tip. They drank their frappes. When they were finished, she unzipped his fly and put her hand inside his briefs. He began to get hard. She grinned, at him, and said she was so happy that he was back to "normal." He reached over and put his hand on her "crotch" and began to rub her through the material of her pants. "Oh baby! I am so glad you are well!" They crushed their lips together! "Hey! Get a room!" He brought his lips from hers and turned in the direction, of the voice. It was Bert and Fred, in the hawk, parked next to them. "Screw you!" he yelled back. Everyone laughed. Ree started the car. There wasn't any tray on the side, as all they had, were frappes. He waved, at the guys, as they pulled out of the parking spot and headed out of the lot.

When they got to his house, they stayed in the car and made out. He wanted her to go in the house, with him, but he was "out' of condoms. She said that it was "okay". She had to get home. They shared one long, wet, "tongue lashing, kiss, and then, he got out of the car and went into the house. As she drove away, he felt the "depression" come back. This time, it didn't go away. He fell deeper and deeper. His mom called the doctor and was told to bring him back into the office.

The doctor gave him a prescription for the depression and told him that depression went along with "mono". He spent the next week, resting, except for a walk to the barbershop. Vic was amazed at how long his hair had grown. He told Vic that he had been sick. It took Vic a while to get his hair, back to the "Ivy League" look. When Vic was done. He paid him and gave him another two dollars. Vic said that he didn't have to, but he insisted and Vic thanked him and told him not to wait so long, next time. He said he wouldn't, as he left the shop.

The Sunday, afternoon, before Halloween, was not a good day, for him and Ree. They were riding around with John and Janet. They parked at a little park, in the next town. John and Janet stayed in the car. He and Ree went for a walk. They walked along a stone path, that had a sto wall alongside it. They sat on the wall, with their arms around each other's waist. He was looking down at the path and not at Ree. She sensed something was wrong. She asked, again, if he was all right. He got off the wall and faced her with his hands on her thighs, just above her knees. He was glad that she was wearing jeans and not shorts. The cool, brisk Autumn day was not good for shorts. He looked at her, his eyes began to fill up. Her body tensed. "I don't know if it's the "mono" or what, but I don't feel "love" for you, anymore. Her eyes got big, her lower lip quivered, "What?" She paused, to take in what he had just said. The tears started flowing down her cheeks. "Please! Please! Don't tell me this! Please, baby, Please! I love you so much! Please don't break up with me!" the tears flowed down his cheeks, too. "I don't want to break up! But the feelings I had, just aren't there right now!" She slid off the wall and they embraced very tightly, tears flowing! She begged him to not break up! He asked her, how could she want to stay with a guy, who is not sure if he loves her or not? She said that she had enough love, in her heart, for the two of them! She told him, that, she would do anything he wanted her to do, if he would stay with her. "Just tell me that you love me, even if you really don't! Just please don't split us up!" She begged. He was astounded! He had never, ever, met anyone like her. They continued to hold on to each other. He told her that he would not break up with her, if she really wanted them to stay, together. She nodded her head, "yes." He told her that he hoped the "love" would return and soon. They walked back to the car, hand in hand, her head on his shoulder. Their tears dried, they got back into the back seat. Janet was telling John, that hers and Ree's friend, Sue had a boyfriend who had trouble with "control". Seemed every time they were going to have sex, she would strip, first and he would ejaculate, just looking at her. They felt bad for Sue, but had to laugh at the "situation". Ree said that he wouldn't need a condom, because he would never get that close to her! John said, "yeah, talk about birth control!" They all laughed, again. Ree said "That certainly isn't a problem for us!" He agreed. John said the same thing. They laughed, again. Larry Williams was on the radio, singing about "Short Fat Fannie." He was followed by Dinah Washington and Brooke Benton and "You've got What It Takes." They sang along, looking at each other. It was, as if, their conversation never took place. He, still, enjoyed her company; knew he still had "feelings" for her. Just wasn't sure it was "love." They continued their phone conversations. They decided not to 'talk' on Halloween, with all the kids coming to their front doors. They would make plans, after Halloween.

Halloween, 1960

"Monster Mash" by Bobby "Boris" Pickett

Night came early, that Halloween. By 6Pm, kids were already knocking on doors. Sounds of "Trick or treat" echoed up and down the street. His folks were wondering, if he was going out. He told them that He and Ree decided to stay in and "hand' out candy. His mom always had a big bowl of some kind of wrapped candy bars. He would swipe one or two, when neither of them were watching. Around 6:45PM, the phone rang. It was Bert. He and Fred were going out riding around and wondered if he wanted to join them. He wasn't too sure that he should, but his folks heard his part of the conversation and told him that he should. It would be good for him, to get out of the house. So, he said "okay." Bert said that they would be by, to pick him up around 7:30. He went up to his room and put on a crewneck sweater over his pink striped shirt. He, also, put on his 'engineer boots", which he hadn't worn, in quite a while. He rubbed some deodorant, under his arms, by pulling his shirt out of the waist, of his jeans and sticking his hand up under his shirt. He, then, tucked his shirt, back inside his pants and combed his hair. He splashed on some Stetson, just in case. He went to his "bank" and withdrew twenty dollars.

He had just come downstairs, by the front door, when he heard the "Hawk's" horn. He told his folks that he wouldn't be late. He opened the door and was confronted by six little munchkins dressed in an array of costumes. He yelled to his mom that there were 'trick or treaters" at the door. He walked down the walk, as he heard his mom greet the kids. He got into the hawk. Fred let him sit up front, because he had been sick. They were going "cruising". Bert said that neighbor's sister was hanging around with three friends and they were looking for someone, with a car, to 'cruise" with. Bert said that they were supposed to be near the lake.

They cruised the neighborhoods around the lake and were about to give up, when Fred saw four girls walking along the sidewalk of a side street. Bert turned down the road and came up on them. The neighbor's sister was called Andrea. He pulled up to the girls, rolled down the window and yelled out her name. One of the girls, turned around and, staying her ground, asked "who wants to know?" Bert said who he was. The girls went up to the driver's side window and were talking with Bert. Fred had moved over to the driver's side and was, also, talking with them. He was leaning against the inside of the passenger side door, his back was against the inside of the door. He was looking at the girls, trying to ascertain if any were good looking. Apparently, the girls wanted to get in the car and ride around with the guys. Unbeknownst to him, one of the girls came around to his side of the car and "yanked" open his door. Before he realized it, he was falling, in what appeared to be "slow motion" out of the car and onto his back. His backside making contact with asphalt. He looked up at the night sky. A face appeared and blocked his "view". He was looking at the cutest girl, he had ever seen. Her long brown hair cascaded down around her head. "Hi! I'm Karen!" She said. "Hi" Karen." He replied and introduced himself. She helped him off the road. She, then climbed into the back seat of the car. Andrea was sitting in the front seat, between him and Bert. She had "flaming" red hair, that was cut short. In the back were the three other girls and Fred. Bert put the car in drive and proceeded to drive down the road. The girls were all talking and laughing. On the radio was Paul Evans and the song "Seven Little Girls Sitting In The Back Seat". Andrea reached to the radio and turned it up. The girls began singing along. He, for the first time in his life, envied Fred. The one named Karen was sitting on Fred's lap.

The girls all said, after the song, that they were hungry and thirsty. Bert said, "Let's go to the car hop!" They all said "Yes!". Bert reached over and turned down the radio, because the girls were making too much noise. He could barely hear himself think. The girls were very excited! Bert pulled into the car hop and found a place. Three of the girls had to get out of the car and use the restroom. In the light, he was able to clearly see the one called Karen. She had a chest that made Ree look "flat," She, also, had one blue eye and one brown eye. He had never seen a girl like her before. He decided that he wanted to know more about her and, maybe, go out on a date, with her. Andrea told him to forget her. That she was already dating someone. He said to Andrea, "if they ever break up, let her know, I'm interested." Andrea told him "okay."

The rest of the night, though he couldn't keep his eyes off her, was pure bedlam! The girls "performed" three "Chinese fire drills". He had never heard of them, before. It was close to 10:30, when the girls decided that they had to go home. That was, when, he found out that they were all sophomores in high school. At first, it bothered him, that Karen was three years younger than him, but after a while, he didn't care. He was having fun. He hadn't had this much fun on Halloween, for many years. Being surrounded by four beautiful young girls was just what the "doctor" ordered, well, not his doctor, but it sure lifted his "spirits". He was hoping that he would see Karen, again. Bert began to drive the girls home. After they dropped everyone off, Bert drove him home. It was on the drive, that Bert told him that he quit the job at the plastics factory and was thinking of joining the "service". Bert asked him, if he would go with him, into the city, for moral support. He said that he would. Fred asked him why he would be "interested" in a fifteen year old girl, when he had a "woman" like Ree? He told Fred that he had "lost" his feelings for Ree. He still cared, deeply, for her, but he wasn't sure, if it was locve or not. Fred said that he was a fool and that he should stay with Ree. He said that they were still 'going out".

John Zacherly was on the radio with "Dinner With Drac". Bert said that he would call him, when he decided what day, to go in town. He said "okay." He got out of the car, in front of his house and thanked them for the ride. He walked up the walk to the front door and went inside.

The next morning, over breakfast, his mom told him that Ree and a friend, someone named "Sue" had dropped by last night. They were dressed as "prostitutes" and were hoping to find him home. They wanted him to go out riding around with them. He stared at his eggs and wondered just what kind of a night he might have had. Riding around with two beautiful girls dressed as "hookers". He could just imagine the cleavage. He felt "excitement grow between his legs. He wished, now, he had stayed home. Last night's decision was one that he would 'regret" for the rest of his life.

He would never have another "Halloween" like the one in 1960.

"Blue, Navy, Blue" (Diane Renay)

He called Ree ,that night, and apologized for not being home. She told him that he missed out on what could have been a fun time! She told him that she would be busy with school, for the next few nights, but that maybe Saturday night, they could go out. He told her that he was given the "green light" to get behind the wheel of the car, again. She was real happy to hear that. He would call her Friday night and discuss what they would do on Saturday. She said that she didn't care, as long as they were together.

Just as he hung up the phone, Bert called and asked him, if they could go into the city, on Friday. He said that he could. Bert said that he would by around 9 in the morning. He wondered if he could leave the car in his yard and they could walk to the train station, from his house. He said that he could and that he would see him Friday. God! He was tired of sitting around the house and doing nothing. There was nothing, for him, to watch on TV. Three channels, to choose from and nothing , for him, to watch. Even the radio was playing the same songs over and over.

That night, around 7, Bert called again and asked him what he was doing. "Nothing! Absolutely, nothing!" he said. Bert said that he would come by and they could go to the car hop. He said, "great!". He went up to his room and put on a shirt and sweater. He didn't change his jeans. It didn't take long, for Bert to get to his house. Apparently, they both were "bored out of their skins." They rode to the car hop and talked about Friday. Bert wasn't sure what "branch" he wanted to join. He knew that he did not want to be a Marine. "Those are the guys that get killed." He said. So, it was between the Army, Coast Guard, Air Force, or the Navy. He was glad that the recruiting offices were close to each other.

They pulled into the car hop and found a spot in the front row. They were just in time for the "hot rod parade." But their attention was focused on the car ,next to them. In the car were two sailors, in uniform. There were girls, in the car, with them, and hanging around the outside of the car. He and Bert looked at each other. Bert wondered if it was the uniform or the fact that the guys were Navy. He rolled down the window and asked one of the girls what was so special about the guys, in the car. She replied that she loved a man in uniform, especially, a sailor! He and Bert looked at each other. He would definetly look into joining the Navy! They ate their burgers and fries and drank their cokes. They kept looking at the sailors, getting all the attention, from the girls.

On the drive home, Bert said that he would still look at the other branches, but that the Navy sure had the "edge." He had to admit that the idea, of joining the Navy, intrigued him , also. He started thinking more and more, about it. He saw Phil, one day, and asked him about the Navy. Phil told him to stay away, from joining any service! He remembered when Dave got drafted and Phil, to avoid the draft, went and enlisted, in the Navy. Dave kept chiding him that he had only two years, to serve and Phil had four. Dave wasn't around, to ask about the Army. His dad had been in the Coast Guard reserve, but he was noncommittal about it. So, it would be his own decision. Did he hang around the house until February. When he could back to college or join the Navy and go back to college, when his hitch was over, like Phil? He thought long and hard about it.

Friday morning came and Bert arrived, right on time. He had on a pair of tan chinos a dress shirt, his keds and a jacket. He put ten dollars, in his wallet and off they went to the train station. Bert just stared at him, when he told him that he was thinking of joining up ,as well. Bert said, "Really? Have you talked it over with anyone? What about Ree? What if Karen were available?" A lot of questions, but he said that he really thought about it.

They got off the train and started walking. Their first stop was the Army. The recruiter asked them to take a test. They passed! He then asked them what area they were interested in Infantry, Tanks, communication? They weren't sure. The recruiter told them that they would probably be put into the infantry. They thanked him and walked out. The next stop would be the Coast Guard. That recruiter told them that there was a 'real" need for forest rangers. He remembered a school mate of theirs, he met at a football game. Who was s forest ranger. The guy hated it! He looked at Bert and they thanked the recruiter and left. Next stop was the Navy. The recruiter, also, had them take a test. Bert was best a being a mechanical engineer. He tested at communications/intelligence. They were intrigued! The recruiter had them weighed and checked their height. They passed that ,too. The next thing ,to do, was sign up. He asked how soon would they have to report. The recruiter told them, that they would be required to have a physical exam, on Tuesday. He told the recruiter that he had just gotten over a "bout" with mononucleosis. The recruiter told him to get a letter, from his doctor, saying he was okay. Bert astounded him, by saying he might have something on his "record." The recruiter told him to visit the local police station and make sure he was "cleared." They signed up!

When he got home, that night, over dinner, he told his folks and Phil what he had done. His mom burst into tears. His dad shook his hand and made him promise that he would go back to college afterwards. Phil just shook his head and told him that he would be sorry. After dinner, he went to call Ree. She was so happy to hear from him, until he told her. She was so upset, she hung up, on him. She called him, right back and screamed, into the phone, "What about us? What about college? Why did you do this?" He began to feel real bad about his decision. Ree, finally calmed down, but he could hear the sadness in her voice. He told her that the recruiter told them, that if all went well, with the physical, he wouldn't leave until the end of January. She said that with his "mono" they probably wouldn't take him. He said that he had to get a note from his doctor. He asked Ree, if she still wanted to get together, the next night. She said, "of course."

He picked her up around 7:30PM. They were going to get something to eat and then go to the drive in's last movie, before closing for the winter. Ree had her hand on his thigh and her arm around his shoulders. She couldn't stop sniffling. He felt real bad, but he knew he couldn't sit around the house, doing nothing, anymore. They barely ate their burgers and fries. He drove to the drive inn and parked in the last row. He told her that he didn't have any condoms. She said that it was okay, that she was having her period, anyway. They wrapped their arms around each other and passion overtook them. She had her hand on his flesh, he had his lips and tongue on her breasts and nipples. Then, she did something, he never expected. She pushed his pants down around his knees and lowered her head to "him." She kissed his shaft, the head and began nibbling on the sides of his shaft. She stroked and sucked on him. He was in heaven! But he really wanted to be inside her! She raised her head and they crushed their lips together, her hand pumping him. He began to groan and pushed his hips against her hand. She had a napkin in her other hand. He moved his hands to her breasts, as she continued her hands on him. He knew he was going to blast off! He groaned and yelled "OH GOD!" She put the napkin over him as he let loose! Her attitude ,then changed. She grinned, at him, and said that the souveniers she left on him, would be interesting to the doctors, at his physical. She pushed him away and said she wasn't feeling well and if he would take her home. He wanted more, from her, but said that he understood. They left the theater and drove home, in silence. When they arrived at her front door, she leaned over and they shared one last ,wet,passionate kiss! When they parted, she began to cry and told him that she still loved him and would miss him, so very much! She ,then, opened the door and jumped out and ran up her walk, before he could react! He reached over and closed the door, he looked up the walk; she was gone! Somehow, he knew that he would never see Ree, again.

Monday, he went to the doctor and got a note, saying he was in "good health". No sign of the mono. Then. Bert picked him up and they went to the local police station. Bert had gotten into trouble a few years back, nothing real serious, but it was on his record. The sergeant, at the desk, looked it up and told him that the charge had been expunged from his record and he was "clean". The sergeant asked him for his name. He said that he was just there ,for moral support. The sergeant "ran" his name anyway and found nothing. They left the station and Bert said that Fred wanted to get together, afterwards, and go eat at Ho-Jo's. They got in the car and headed to pick up Fred. It was just after 11:30AM, when the three of them sat down. to eat. Fred looked at him and asked, "You still interested in taking out Karen?" He thought for a minute and said, "sure, why not? Fred said that she had just broken up with her boyfriend and was really interested in going out with him. Fred asked him about Ree. He told Fred that he still had strong feelings for Ree, but that she, apparently, is not happy with him. Fred said that he got a call from Ree and that she still cared very deeply for him and would hope that he would write her, while in the Navy. He thanked Fred, for that information. Fred told him that if he were serious about taking Karen out, a group of them were going bowling and Karen would really like it, if he came along. Bert was invited, too. He said "okay, set it up." Fred said, "Meet us at the bowling alleys on route 9 around 7PM, on Friday. If all goes well, you can take her home. "swell." He said. Fred , then laughed, and said "no", we'll pick you up around 7, at your house. He asked Fred, if there were any "rules" this time. Fred starting laughing and told Bert what he had done to him, with his first date with Ree. He did say, "remember, Karen is only fifteen, with the body of a twenty year old, but still only 15." He said that he would keep that in mind.

Tuesday morning, around 8 AM, the recruiter arrived, at his house. Bert was in the car, waiting. The recruiter sat down and had a talk with him and his mom. Then, they left the house and he and Bert were taken to the Federal Building in Boston, for their physcials.

Everything was going well, with his physical, until he filled out the form. Where it asked for diseases, he wrote 'mononucleosis". He attached the doctor's note. When he passed back the form, there was a "flurry" of activity between several doctors. One doctor even asked him how long ago he had the disease. When he told them, things seemed to settle down. They were told to strip down to their 'skivvies" (underwear). He was given a piece of paper, with his name and social security number on it. There were a number of "things" on the form with a space for the doctor's comments. The first thing that was to be inspected were "feet." He had flat feet and his uncle told him that he wouldn't get accepted with flat feet. So, for weeks, he rolled his ankles on milk bottles, under his "arches" to build them up. When they inspected his feet, he raised up his arches and the doctor said "Hammer toes." He smiled. The only reason his toes turned in, was he was raising his arches. They checked his heart, his lungs, his eyes, his ears, and his teeth. Then, a doctor told them. It was time to check for a hernia and any polyps. They were standing in a line, side by side. The doctor told them to drop their "skivvies". He looked up at the ceiling, as the doctor came to him. "Oh, what have we here? I sure hope a female gave you those little "love bites"! The doctor said. He felt his whole body turn red as the doctor inspected Ree's "handiwork." For the rest of the physical he was referred to as "Romeo".

Every time., Bert saw him, he began to laugh. He had hoped Ree's "souvenirs" would have disappeared. The physicals took all day. They were given a "break" for lunch. A lot of the guys failed the physical, but he and Bert, apparently, passed with flying colors. Half of him wanted to fail, while the other half was glad that he passed. He and Bert were driven to their homes. The recruiter told them that they would be "shipping out" for basic training, under the "buddy system." They would need to get their affairs in order for the January 20th.

After dinner that night, he informed his folks that all went well, with the physical. He called Ree. She was very inquisitive about how his day went. He told her that he passed, even with the "mono" thing and .yes, even with her "marks". She began to laugh, when he told her, how his nickname for the day was "Romeo". She began to cry and told him that she really missed him and would write to him, if he wanted her to. He, too, felt tears on his cheeks, when he told her he would send her , his address, when he got it. He didn't tell her that he wasn't leaving until the 20th of January. He wanted to see how 'things' went with Karen. He did tell Ree, that he still cared "deeply" for her. Neither of them spoke about "waiting for him." As they finished their conversation, he heard her say "I love you!" before hanging up the phone.

Friday night arrived. He had on a plain white dress shirt, jeans and his boots. Bert, Fred, Andrea and Judy picked him up at his house. He was nervous! Fred told him to just relax and to be himself and if she likes him, she likes him, if not, well there was always Ree. He didn't like the way Fred said that. He still felt that Ree was way out of his class. That, there was nothing "second class" about her. Dion was on the radio, singing "Runaround Sue". Followed by Elvis and "Frankfurt Special" from the film, "G.I .Blues". He sang along with Elvis. The girls liked his voice and one even said that he missed his "calling." He just smiled, his nervousness showing through.

Bert pulled up in front of Karen's house. He was going to honk the horn, he told Bert that he would get out of the car and go get her. He was halfway up her walk, when her front door opened and she came "bounding out". As she ran past her, she grabbed his hand and pulled him to the car. She was ,again, wearing a large sweater and a flowing,pleated, plaid skirt. Her long black hair, flowing behind her , as they ran, to the car.

She let go of his hand and jumped into the back seat. He looked to get into the front seat, with Bert and Andrea, but Andrea shook her head, "no." He was perplexed. The only way he was going to sit in the Hawk, was if he sat on the seat and Karen sat on his lap. She maneuvered her body, so he could do just that. She said, "It's okay, I don't bite." Fred and Bert laughed , hysterically! He just knew that Bert told Fred about the physical. The girls had no idea why the two guys were laughing so hard. He just lowered his head into her side, as she sat herself onto his lap. Jerry Lee Lewis was on the radio with "Breathless." Karen was not a small girl. She was not fat, by any means, but was large boned. She took his arms and put them around her waist, which was small. It was apparent, to all, in the car, whose date she was. Every time she turned her head, to talk with someone, he would get a mouthful of her hair. He wished her hair wasn't so long. But he enjoyed holding her on his lap.

Usually, when he bowled, he took it very seriously, but that night, it was different. Karen's "outgoing" personality was contagious. He was having fun! When she wasn't bowling, she was sitting beside him and when he was bowling, she kept his score and gave him encouragement. When he got his "first strike", She jumped out of the seat and came up to him and gave him a hug! It was as if they had been dating for quite a while. He felt very comfortable with her. Everyone bowled three strings. He had bowled a lot better, before, but didn't really care. When she got a "mark" he would reciprocate and give her a hug.

When they were done, he paid for their bowling and shoe rentals. They ,all, decided to go to Ho-Jo's for something to eat. They 'piled" into the Hawk. She took up her place , on his lap. As Bert was driving to the restaurant, Karen leaned back and whispered in his ear, "I think I like you!" he replied, " I like you, too." When they got to the restaurant, they got out of the car and laughed and joked all the way into the restaurant. They were shown to a booth. She made sure that he sat beside her. It was "tight" quarters, in the booth. Their legs and thighs touched. She didn't seem to mind and he really didn't mind. He did notice that he missed the hand on his thigh. She was so exuberant! He couldn't take his eyes off her. She was really cute! Having large breasts didn't deter his "interest" in her, either.

On the ride home, she ,again, whispered , in his ear. "I had a great time! I hope you did, too! Will you call me? I hope you want to see me again?" He responded, "me, too and yes and yes." She gave him a hug. She lived closest to the restaurant, so Bert dropped her off, first. He walked her up the walkway, to her porch and front door. She gave him a piece of paper, with her number on it. They said 'good night" and she went inside. He was halfway down the walk, when he heard footsteps running towards him, he turned and she "flew" into his arms and pressed her lips to his! The embraced and the kiss, a sweet kiss, lasted a few seconds. She pulled away and without a word, ran back up the walk, leaving him, standing on the walk, "astounded!" Again, she was gone, inside the house. He walked ,slowly, back to the car. As he got in, everyone told him that she had said that she really, really, liked him! He was still tasting her lipstick, and replied that he liked her ,too. The guys dropped the other girls off and seeing that it was only 10:30PM, decided to go a coffee shop and have a cup of coffee. He was perplexed! Here, he was going into the Navy, after the holidays, and now, he hoped, he had two girls to write to. Bert asked him , if he was changing his mind, about enlisting. He said that, if he was, it was a little too late, since they had already signed up. He wondered if Karen knew that he was going into the Navy, soon. Fred said, "she knows!"

He called, the next day, Saturday, around noon. When she came, to the phone, he told her who he was. She laughed and said she 'knew". He was already to ask her out, to go to a movie, that night. She blurted out that a girlfriend, of hers, was having a party and would he want to go with her. He said "sure, I like parties." She said, "good!" he asked her what time he should come by and pick her up. She told him, "around 7." He said "okay, see you, then." They hung up. He heaved a "heavy sigh". He suspected that Karen was ,probably, still a virgin, though he wondered, with a body, like hers, how she managed to keep guys off of her. He decided to take it nice and slow, with her.

He picked her up at 7:05PM.He turned off the VW and got out and walked up the walk, to the large "farmers porch" to the big oaken front door. He rang the bell. A huge man, unshaven, with dark, unruly hair, opened the door and in a rough voice, said "Yeah?" Behind the large man, he heard Karen's voice. "Don't scare him away, daddy!" The man's demeaner changed. His frown turned into a large toothy grin and ushered him into the house. He introduced himself to her father. They were standing in the large foyer, when Karen appeared. She was wearing a black V-neck sweater over a light blue shirt and jeans. He just knew that her father was looking at him, looking at her chest. He raised his eyes, quickly to her cute face. She smiled and invited him into her living room. There, he met her mom and older sister, Pat. They were very nice. She told her family that he was leaving ,for the Navy, in three months. Pat said, "our brother, Daniel, is in the Army, in Kentucky." He asked if Daniel got home very often." Her mother, said ,"not as much as we would like him to." Karen looked at her watch and said that they had to be going. He said "good night" and that he was pleased to have met them. They walked out to the foyer and out the front door, closing it behind them. She took his hand, as they walked to the car. "Oh, I love your car! What's it going to be, when it grows up?" He stopped "dead" in his tracks. She laughed and pulled him along. "I'm only kidding!" He smiled and opened her door and she got in. "Thank you, sir!" She said. "Sir?" he asked, "Sir? I'm not that much older than you." She laughed again. He was going to have to get used to her style of humor. He got into the car, started it, put it into forward gear and off they went, to the party. She "directed" him. She didn't live that far away.

Her friend, Pam, lived in an upstairs apartment, in an old Victorian apartment building. Her parents were out for the evening. He parked the car in the parking lot and turned it off. He helped her out of her side, of the car and locked it. They had to take an elevator to the eighth floor. They got out of the elevator and walked down the hall. They stopped at a door and Karen knocked. A "demure" girl with short black hair, opened the door. Karen introduced him to Pam. Pam ushered them inside and introduced him around to everyone. He believed that he was the "oldest" one there. Pam introduced him to her boyfriend, Steve. He found out that Steve was a freshman in college. He was glad that there was , at least, someone else there, his age.

He and Karen danced to all the slow dances. Then, Pam brought out a broomstick and Chubby Checker was on the turntable with "The Limbo Rock." He and Steve held the broomstick while everyone else, including Karen "danced" the limbo. Karen hit the floor, on the third try under the stick. Pam, who was the thinnest person there, went on to win. He couldn't believe it, but he was ,actually, developing "feelings" for Karen. He knew that she "liked" him, but, he doubted that ,after just two times, together, she felt anything "deeper."

The party over, he drove her home. He pulled up, in front of her house. He turned off the car and opened the door and went around and opened her door. He walked her up the walk, to her front door. They stood, on the porch, for a while, talking "small" talk and then she moved in closer. He took her, in his arms, and their lips met. Another 'sweet" kiss. This kiss lasted a little longer, than the first one. Their lips parted, and she moved right back in pressing his lips with a little more urgency. Their "sweet" kisses began to add "some" passion to them. No tongues, but lips exploring lips. After their 'fourth" kiss, she was having difficulty catching her breath. Finally she gasped, "You sure know how to kiss!" He panted, "you, too." One more, long, sweet kiss and they said their "good nights". She asked him, to call her Sunday night. He said that he would.

He drove home, that night, his mind in a state of confusion. He now realized that he had feelings for both Karen and Ree. Was it possible to "love" two girls, at the same time. Which one did he have 'stronger" feelings for? He wasn't sure. He did think that it was a good time , to go away, for a while.

Thanksgiving arrived and Karen was going to be away, visiting relatives in Wisconsin. Ree invited him to her "old" high school football game. He was happy to see her and she was real happy to see him. She thought that he had already left for the Navy. He said that there was a delay. But, that he could go at any time. She held his hand, during the entire game. When it was over, she had to go home for her dinner. While he was driving her home, her hand was on his thigh. He told her that he missed that. She said "what?' he said, "your hand on my thigh."

"Oh!" She said, "I've missed you!" She looked at her watch and asked him , if he wanted to go to their "old" spot, by the river. He nodded "yes." She said ,"it being Thanksgiving, there won't be any cops bothering us." He wondered how she knew that. He didn't ask.

No sooner had he parked the car and turned it off, then she ,practically, jumped on him! Her arms went around his neck, her lips crushing his! It was like he was being attacked by animal lust! He responded to her. She grabbed his hands and put them under sweater and her shirt, upon her breasts, her tongue was "stabbing" his. Her eyes closed. Suddenly, she pulled away and began to cry, "I want you to love me, Please love me! I am miserable without you!" he had never, ever, been in this situation, before. He wanted to love her, he really did! She grabbed him, again, and held him tight. "Please write to me, I promise that I'll write to you." He said that he would. She opened the front of her pants and slipped them down to her thighs and brought his left hand to her. She opened his fly and stuck her hand inside his pants and brought "him" out of them. She was leaning against the back of the front seat, he was practically on top of her, his fingers inside her, while his thumb rolled her clit around, gently. She was stroking his manhood. Their lips were "fused" in passion. She cried out "Oh God I love you so Much!" he felt her juices flow against his fingers, as they rubbed her magic "spot". She increased her strokes on him and it wasn't long until he told her that he was going to make a mess. She stuck his penis back inside his pants, as he exploded! She held him, tightly, and told him to remember this time, while he is in the Navy. He could only nod "yes". She pulled her pants back up as he zipped up his fly. He was going to ride home, in dampness.

They arrived back, at her house. There were a bunch of cars in front. She said "relatives." She reached for him and gave him a wet, passionate kiss, followed by a sweet, loving kiss. With tears swelling up, in her eyes, she said, "good bye." The huge lump in his throat prevented him from saying anything. She got out of the car and walked up the walk, not looking back at him.

He drove home, from her house, a miserable soul. His father's words, in his mind. "If only you two could have met a little later in life." Elvis was on the radio with "Are You Lonesome Tonight?" He replied to the song, "yes, I am and I've probably just said good bye to the "love" of my life. I might just have made the biggest mistake, ever." He turned off the radio and headed home, wondering how he was going to get by everyone and get upstairs to change, not just his underwear, but his pants, as well.

He did manage to "slip" by his Aunt and Uncle, his brothers, and his folks. He snuck upstairs and quickly changed his underwear and pants. He went back downstairs and joined everyone, in the dining room. This was going to be his last Thanksgiving, at home, for a very long time. The conversation around the table was about the Navy. He had to answer all the questions. When do you leave? January 20th. How long is the enlistment? 4 years. Where will you be stationed? Don't know. Will you be enlisted or an officer? Enlisted. His brother Phil kept shaking his head and saying "you'll be sorry." Dave and his dad agreed that it would be good for him, to go in and get it over with. His mom was having a difficult time dealing with it. It was his aunt that asked what Ree's reaction was? "Not very happy, not happy at all!" he said.

After dinner, the men sat around and watched football. The women, his mom and his aunt, were in the kitchen, cleaning up. As usual, he ate too much turkey and 'stuff" and ended up going to bed, early. It had been quite a day. First, with Ree and then, the family. He was "saddled" with mixed emotions. He was excited about the possibility of a "new" relationship with Karen, yet, at the same time, mourning the possible loss of Ree .Even though they did not "officially" break up, he felt a real sense of loss. He had a difficult time, falling asleep.

He woke up that Friday morning, to his mom ,yelling, that he had a phone call. He ambled to the phone. He knew it wasn't Karen, she was still in Wisconsin. He didn't think it would be Ree. He picked up the phone. The voice , on the other end, was inquiring about the hydroplane. He saw the "ad" in the local newspaper. He had, totally, forgotten that he placed the ad. The guy wanted to come by and look at it. He said, "okay." He gave the guy directions to his house and hung up the phone and went back into his room. He put on a pair of briefs, jeans and a flannel shirt. He never wore an undershirt. He saw a Kirk Douglas movie, where Kirk didn't wear an undershirt and he thought it was "cool". So he decided not to wear one under a shirt. He put on his engineer boots and went downstairs for breakfast. He had just finished eating, when the doorbell rang. He opened the door and met a guy, in his 30's and a 13 year old son. They came to look at the boat. He went out the front door and walked them around the side of the house, down to the backyard and the blanket hiding the boat and trailer. He pulled off the blanket and the boy's eyes lit up, just as his had , when he first saw it. They asked about the motor and he told them it had been sold. He , also, told them that the boat needed a "fin" on the bottom, but that was all it needed. The father asked if the boat and trailer were a "package" deal?

He said, "yes." The dad, then asked him, why he was selling it? He told them that he just enlisted in the Navy and would not be using it, anymore. The father stepped aside and spoke with his son. After a minute, or so, he turned back, to him and offered him $ 350.00 right there, on the spot. He said "sold!" He went into the basement and came out with a screwdriver and took off the license plate, from the trailer. The father went up the driveway and came back down, in his car. He turned it around and backed up to the trailer. Meanwhile, he had gone into the house and up to his room and got the papers, to the boat and trailer. When he came back down, the father gave him the cash. He signed the registration forms and bill of sale, that he had, when he bought it. They shook hands and he watched the boat and trailer, leave the yard. So much had taken place, in his life, in such a short matter of time. He ,again, had money, in his bank, but no longer owned a boat. He noticed a "change" in the wind. It began to blow in from the North. That meant winter weather was headed his way.

Bert called him that afternoon and wanted to know what he was doing? He said, "nothing." Bert told him that he was 'bored", too. He said , that if he got Fred, maybe the three of them could go and do some bowling. That sounded good, to him. Bert said that he would call back. Fifteen minutes passed by, and then, the phone rang. Bert was excited! He said that Fred had broken down and ,finally, bought himself a car. He asked Bert, "what kind?" "A 1956 Ford Fairlane, four door sedan." Bert said, " he's on his way over to pick me up and then we'll be over to get you!" He was excited, as well. They both thought that Fred would never get a car!

When Fred pulled up, in front his house, he was outside, waiting, on the sidewalk. He couldn't believe his eyes. Fred's car was black, with white doors. It was a "used police car!" "Are you serious?" he asked Fred. "Think of all the fun, we can have!" Fred said. He did say that he had to have it repainted within thirty days. Fred told him that it had a 1956 Thunderbird engine and didn't burn a drop oil. The interior was interesting. He could see where the bars had been, separating the front and back seats. "Get in!" Said Fred. He got in the front seat, next to Bert, as Fred, "peeled out". Fred said that he had to stop and get some gas. He pulled into the "Jenny" station and when the attendant came out , he asked him to fill it up and check the oil. The attendant gave him a "funny" look. "Must think I'm a cop." Said, Fred.

The attendant raised the hood and checked the oil. He brought the dipstick around to show Fred that there wasn't any oil in it. Fred had him add two quarts of 10W-30. He paid for the gas and oil and started up the car. A large "plume" of light blue smoke poured out of the exhaust pipe. He and Bert tried to stifle their laughter. Finally, the "air" cleared. Bert said "looks like you need a ring job. He concurred. Fred was not happy.

Bert called him around 9:30 Saturday morning. Fred wanted to have a party, at his house. His folks were going to be away for the night. Bert said that one of the guys, he used to work with, had a way of getting alcohol. Bert wanted to know, if he wanted to come, to the party, and if so, what did he want to drink? He thought about it and whispered into the phone, "Seagram's Seven." Bert said "okay." He told him that Fred and he would pick him up around 7. They were going to meet the guy, with the "booze", in front of the catholic church. He said "fine" and hung up the phone. He went back to his room and threw on some underwear and jeans and a sweatshirt. He went downstairs and had some breakfast. He was feeling lonely and wished Karen would get back in town, soon. He ,even, wondered, if he should call Ree. He knew, if he did, that she might want to go out, that night. He felt so bad, about her; he wished he hadn't fallen "out of love" with her. He promised that he would write her and that was a promise, that he would keep.

The rest of the day, he watched some football, with his dad and brothers. Around 4 PM, he got a phone call. He went to the phone and hesitated to speak, into the receiver. What if it was Ree? What would he say? He took a deep sigh and said, "Hello?" "Hi", it was Karen. She told him that she just got home, from Wisconsin and she got his number from Bert. He was excited to hear from her. She told him that she really missed him and couldn't wait to see him. She, then, told him that she was really tired, from the trip, but could they get together and spend Sunday afternoon, together? He told her that he really missed her, too and would love to spend Sunday afternoon with her. She asked him to come by her house around 1:00PM. He said that he would be there. She hung up the phone by saying "I'll see you in my dreams." He was happy! He didn't know what they would do on Sunday, but it didn't matter, as long as they were together.

Seven o'clock, on the nose. He heard a strange horn, outside, in front of the house. He looked out and saw a black and white "used" police car. Something told him that it wasn't going to be a good night. He bade good bye to his family and went out the door and got into Fred's car. He tried to say that it might have been a better idea, to use Bert's car. Fred said "no, I want to drive." It was dark, as they drove to the catholic church. As they approached the front of the church, they spotted a car parked under a street light. Fred pulled up behind it and "flashed" his headlights at the rear of the car. Just like the cops do, when they want you to pull over. Fred couldn't believe his eyes! Bert screamed "NO!" His mouth dropped open in shock! They guys, in the other car, "peeled out" in front of them and 'raced' away. Fred said 'they won't outrun my motor!' He "gunned" it and took off after them. Then, to their complete horror, they saw bottles and beer cans get tossed out the windows of the car they were chasing. All three of them were hollering out their windows, "STOP! NO! IT'S US!!!!" Fred began honking the horn of the Ford. More and more bottles went out the windows, meeting their "fate" against the asphalt. Beer cans exploded upon impact. Finally, when all the "booze" had been cleared out of the car, did it pull over. Fred pulled up behind them, put the car in park and all three jumped out and ran to the car. The guys inside were shaking like "toothpicks in a gale". Fred was ready to tear the door off the car. Bert was screaming, at them. He sat on the curb and shook his head. He knew that the "used' cop car was not a good idea. They "rounded up" the beer cans that had landed on grass, by the side of the road and "salvaged" what they could. The whisky and vodka bottles were 'victims' of the chase. Then came the discussion of who should pay. That ,almost, became a fight. He ,finally, stepped in and handed the guy, behind the wheel, a twenty dollar bill and that calmed things down. he was unable to go and buy more "booze" It wasn't much of a party. Guys sitting around and drinking ginger ale, Pepsie, Cokes, and about seven undamaged beers. They played cards and he won back his twenty dollars. Bert turned to Fred and told him, "two things, One, get the damn car painted! And two, get a ring job!"

Fred and Bert dropped him off, at his house, around 11:30PM. He had told them, that he and Karen were getting together, Sunday afternoon. He had no idea, what to do? Bert suggested they could all get together, at the bowling alley. He said that sounded like a good idea.

He slept in until ten o' clock., the next morning. He went into the bathroom and got cleaned up, went back to his room and put on fresh briefs, jeans, socks, boots and a dress shirt. He hadn't had a hair cut in a while and knew Vic was not going to be too happy with him. He figured he get one, next week , when Karen was back in school. He combed his hair and splashed on some Stetson. He wondered if Karen liked Stetson. If not, he still had some Old Spice. He went downstairs and had some eggs and toast, juice and milk. He was feeling a lot better! His mom and Dad came home , from church, around 11:30AM. He told them, that he would not be home for Sunday dinner. He knew, that if he were seeing Ree, that day, he would be enjoying the "flesh" of a woman. With Karen, he would have to be satisfied with tender kisses. Maybe a passionate one, every now and then. He kept , agonizing, over the choice, that he made.

At 12:30, he got into VW and headed to Karen's house. He had just pulled up and was about to turn off the car and go up the walk to her front door, when she came "bounding" down the walk. Her hair was a lot shorter, just over her ears, she wore a heavy, bulky sweater that did little to conceal her ample breasts. Her jeans came down to just under her knees. He got out of the car, to go to her side, to open the door, when she "flew" into his arms and wrapped her arms around his neck and "planted" a long sensuous kiss, on his lips. When she pulled away, breathing, very hard, she huskily, said "Hi!" He gasped "Hi" back. They got into the car and turned it back on and they pulled away from her house. "Andrea called and said the gang wants to meet at the bowling alley." "I know." he said. "Is that okay with you?" he asked. "I was hoping we could have some time alone." She said. "We can do that, too." He said. And asked what time she had to be back home. She said, "It's a school night, so I need to be in by nine." He said that would give them plenty of time to be alone. She smiled. She moved a little closer to him. He missed the arm around his shoulders and the hand on his thigh.

Conway Twitty was on the radio singing, "It's Only Make Believe". He was followed by Neil Sedaka and "Calender Girl." Elvis followed him with "Stuck On You." He pulled into the parking lot of the bowling alley. He saw Fred's car. Karen laughed, when he told her that it was Fred's car. They went inside, to the booth and he paid for their shoes. They went over to the lanes and joined the others. He asked Bert, why he didn't drive and Bert told him that the "Lone Ranger" wanted to see how many cars would pull over and let him pass, thinking he was a cop. Apparently, Bert told Andrea about the previous night's misadventures. Andrea told Judy and Karen. He was halfway in his forward stride, when he had to pull up, from the hysterical laughter behind him. Karen got up out of her seat and came up behind him and put her arms around his waist and told him that she would make him feel better. She, also, said that he would never get in trouble, if she were with him. He felt "stirrings" below his belt. He stepped back and started his "stride" again and bowled a good ball, right down the middle of the alley and left a "spare leave". Which he quickly picked up. When he sat back down, Karen leaned up against him and said ,"see. I'm good for you!"

He told her that she did not act like a high school girl, at all. She told him that she was, actually, 18 and years old. That, she had been held back, a few times, in elementary school. "oh." he said, "that explains it!" She asked, with a twinkle, in her eye, "Am I too told for you?" he laughed and said, "not at all!" "Good!" She said.

He spent a lot of time with Bert, since they were, both, unemployed. Karen was in school, during the day, and was not allowed out on school nights. They did spend a lot of time on the phone. Christmas was coming up fast, for him. He and Bert went shopping. While Bert was getting something, for his mom, he bought Karen a silver and gold bracelet (not real, but pretty) and a silver plated cross, on a small chain. Bert got his mom some perfume. He bought his mom, a full set of hankerchiefs with her initial on them. They both got their dads a box of cigars. Phil and Dave would be away, for the holidays. His mom said she would take care of them, for him.

Christmas Eve, Fred, Bert, Andrea, Judy, Karen, Patty, Steve, and he went Christmas caroling, with her church. Afterwards, they ended up at Karen's for cocoa. He gave Karen her gifts. She loved them! With tears in her eyes, she handed him his gift, a small bag, for his toiletries. They shared a sweet, tender kiss. They didn't see each other Christmas Day, but did, for the next week. She was on Christmas vacation. The weather had been so cold, well below freezing over the nights, that the lake she lived by had frozen over. They spent a lot of time ice skating, going to lunch, going out to eat, at night and then going parking. Their kisses became more intense with each night. She told him that she wanted him to be her "first" but not in the back seat of a car. He understood and wished his parents would go away, for the weekend. It didn't happen.

New Years Eve,1960/1961. His folks were going to be in New Hampshire and be staying overnight. The house was his! He told Bert and Fred. Bert would get the 'booze" for them. Everyone else would BYOB. Karen's brother was home from the Army with his girlfriend. Karen got a hold of Andrea, Judy, Patty and they would get dates. He figured there would be 12 people. He and Karen spent, one day, buying food, for snacks. They, also, bought ginger ale, Coke, Pepsi and Seven Up. They figured two six packs of each. They spent the rest of the day, cleaning the den and the living room and making sure the furniture was set up right for a party. He set up the records, by the Hi Fi, with a pen, he marked his records with his initials. He drove Karen home, after some kissing, on the couch. She would be coming with her brother and his girlfriend, which she really didn't care for. Seems the girl liked to show off her body, a little too much. They told their friends to dress very casual. This was to be his first "home" New Years Eve party. Everyone was supposed to arrive between 7 and 8PM. At 5, he went up to his room and picked out a pair of jeans, a dress shirt, fresh briefs, socks and his black loafers. He went into the bathroom and bathed. He looked at himself in the mirror and wished he had time to get a haircut. He 'splashed' on the rest of the Old Spice, rolled on the deodorant and went back to his room to get dressed.

Once dressed, he combed his hair and went downstairs. He put out the "treats" and dimmed the lights in the den. He made sure the downstairs bathroom was clean and with plenty of hand towels. He went into the living room and "loaded' the spindle on the hi fi. He was ready.

Bert and Andrea arrived at 6:15PM. Bert had two bags of "booze." One bag had a bottle of whiskey, rum, vodka and Sloe Gin. The other bag held two six packs of beer. He placed the beer, in the fridge and the bottles on the shelf, in the kitchen, next to the bottles of Coke, Pepsi, Seven Up and ginger ale. Fred was bringing the ice. Bert was in a pair of chinos and a dress shirt. Andrea, with her bright red hair, had on a white blouse and a dark green skirt. The blouse accentuated her "medium sized" breasts, while the skirt hugged her hips, "just right." He asked her if she thought she could do the limbo, in that skirt. "Well, if I have to, I'll just hike it up, so I can." They laughed. Fred showed up at 6;40, with ice chests, two of them, Bert went out to the car and helped bring in one of them. They put as much ice, as they could, in the freezer. The rest, in the chests, they put on the back porch. Fred was with Kathy, a demure girl, with slightly larger than medium sized breasts and small hips, in a black dress that ended at her knees. The top was a V-neck, showing a little cleavage.

Karen, her brother Denny, and his girlfriend arrived around 7. Karen was wearing a light blue blouse, with the top two buttons unbuttoned, showing a "hint" of cleavage and accentuating her ample bust. She wore black slacks. Denny was in a dress shirt an jeans. His girlfriend, Sharon, was a tight, very low cut and short leopard skinned dress. Her large breasts appeared to be trying to escape her bra and dress. Karen was not happy! Deny and Sharon went into the kitchen and put their beer and drinks away. Karen pulled him into the den. "Do you see her?" She demanded. "She wouldn't change! I offered her some of my clothes, but she refused!" he took her in his arms and tried to calm her down. He told her how "Dynamite" she looked. That seemed to help. He told her that he would do his best, not to look at Sharon. "Good Luck to that!" said Karen.

By 7:30, all had arrived. The music was just loud enough, in the living room, for people to talk and others to dance. The party was in full swing. He went into the den and turned off the lights and turned on the TV. He found the station that would be broadcasting from Times Square in

New York City. He left the TV on, with the volume low. Karen was acting like perfect hostess. She made sure that the treats plates didn't get empty. He made sure that there were plenty of glasses and he would refill the freezer, with ice, from the chests on the porch. He was standing next to the hi fi, picking out the next set of records, when he felt a hand grasp the right cheek of his rear end. Thinking it might be Karen, he joked that he would give her 24 hours to stop. He turned around, as her hand 'grazed" his crotch. It was Sharon! She leaned into his ear and propositioned him. He, quickly, looked around to see if Denny were looking. He tried to be polite and joked with her. She was serious! He thanked her and quickly walked away. If he had not been with Karen, he might have taken her up on it. God knew he wanted sex!

The night was going well, except that Patty came up to him and asked him to taste his seven and seven. He did, it was straight ginger ale! She sighed and said that explained Steve's actions. Steve was not a "drinker". Somehow, the glasses got switched and Steve got his drink, probably when he went to "refurbish" the ice. Steve was dancing, by himself, and making strange noises, that almost resembled singing. He went to Steve and took his glass and gave him the ginger ale. It took a while, but Steve, finally, settled down and became his "old "self, again. Patty thanked him with a kiss on his cheek. Karen saw the kiss and came up to him and wrapped her arms around his right arm. She wanted to know about the kiss. He told her. She said that she was going to get a pen and write on his forehead, "I belong to Karen!" he laughed and took her in his arms and they danced to the Platters "Only You."

At 11:35PM, everyone gathered in the den, to watch the new year come in, at Times Square. Guy Lombardo and The Royal Canadians were playing "Sweet Coquette". The only light, in the den, was from the black and white TV. Karen was sitting, on his lap, her arms around his neck, her lips nuzzling his cheek. Over the sound of the TV, he thought he heard something else. He asked Karen to get off his lap, for a minute. He got up out of the chair and went into the small hallway, where the downstairs bathroom, was. He heard the sounds, coming from the downstairs bedroom. He opened the door and saw Sharon, completely nude, bouncing up and down on Denny. His hands on her breasts, both grunting and groaning, on his parent's bed. They turned their heads, in his direction and invited him, to join them. Again, if it had been, for the fact, that Karen was in the Den, he might have. He closed the door, as "anger" began to surge throughout his body. He went back to the den. He wanted to tell Karen, but thought better of it.

The countdown started, everyone, in the den, counted down with the TV. When the clock struck twelve, everyone jumped up and began kissing everyone "happy New Year! Everyone, except Denny and Sharon. One of the guys went over to the TV and turned it off, sending the den into complete darkness, except for the light from the front hallway. Then, in the still of the moment, came the lustfull cries of fulfillment from the downstairs bedroom. Karen stormed out of the den. He followed her. She was livid! The others filed out and went back into the kitchen and the living room. Soon after, Denny and Sharon came out and into the living room. Karen walked up to them and told them, to leave the party! Denny had the nerve to ask "why?" Karen told them, in a loud voice, for everyone to hear, that the two of them were "pigs" and that they violated the trust of him and her. Denny and Sharon gave her the "finger' and left. He said that she would have to come home, with them. She said "no!" that she would get a ride home, from someone else. They left. Karen apologized to everyone, for her brother and his girlfriend. The others said that it wasn't her fault and voiced their support, of her. She thanked them. Someone turned up the volume, on the hi fi and the party "carried on."

Most of the people were gone by 1:30AM. He and Karen had "retired" to the couch, in the dark den. They were alone. They started out sitting, side by side, on the couch. As their kissing intensified in passion, they slid down and ended up lying side by side, on the couch. His right leg, between hers, moving so slowly, rubbing her crotch. She was responding by "grinding" her pelvis against his leg. They didn't care if there was anyone else, at the party. She told him how much she was falling in love with him and that she wished she could spend the night, in his arms. He told her that he wished she could too. Then, his heart guided his words and he told her that he was falling in love with her, too. Their lips crushed together, their bodies thrashing against each other. "Oh God, I want you!" She said, in his ear. "me, too!" he said. They heard voices, in the hall. They pulled apart and sat up. They got up off the couch and went into the hall. Bert, Andrea, Fred and Judy were the only ones left. They said "goodnight." He looked at his watch and saw that it was after 2AM. Karen said that she, too, had to leave. He would clean up the house, before his folks got home.

It was three AM, before his head hit the pillow. He wondered what he might be doing, next New Year's Eve. He would get about six hours sleep, before he had to get up and clean up the mess. He knew he had to take the cover, sheets and pillow cases off his parents bed and throw them in the washer and dryer.

He awoke at nine AM and began the arduous task of cleaning the house. Fred came by, at noon, and picked up the ice chests and the empty bottles and cans, along with those that weren't so empty. He thanked Fred, for the help. He fell asleep, on the couch, in the den.

His folks came home around 6PM. They were amazed that the house looked so good. They asked, if he had a party. He lied and said that he went out to a party. They were pleased. He asked them, if they had a good time and they said that they did. 1961 was going to be an interesting year, for him. In nineteen days, he would be on his way to basic training in Illinois. This was going to be a major milestone, in his life.

The days passed, quickly. He would pick Karen, up from school, in the afternoons. They would try and find a place, to be alone, at least for a little while. They would "make out" and, then, she would cry, a lot. She really did not want him to leave. He told her, that if he knew, before he signed up, he never would have signed up. "Can't you tell them that you changed your mind?" She asked. He said that he wished it was that easy, but that he couldn't. Every day, it was the same, "making out' and the questions. Once, after parking, they went to the local ho-jo's and got something to eat. She excused herself and went to the ladies room. When they finished eating, he took her home. She couldn't go out, at night, on school nights. So, he would spend time with Bert and Fred. They would go bowling and then to the car hop. They were coming up on the last Saturday night, before they would be leaving. He asked them what they had planned for the last Saturday night. Fred told them that they better be going to Karen's house, that night. They weren't supposed to know, but Karen planned a "surprise going away" party, for them. He thought she took a long time, in the ladies room, at ho-jo's.

Karen asked him to come and pick her up, around 7:30PM, that Saturday night. He got to her house around 7:35PM. He knocked on the door and heard "come in." he opened the door, walked in and closed the door, behind him. He walked into the living room and Patty, Steve, Andrea, Judy, Fred and Bert all yelled "Surprise!" he was "overwhelmed". He thanked them all and he and Bert received "toiletries' as gifts. Karen's brother gave him a table top PlayBoy calendar. He said he would look at it later. Everyone laughed. Then, he wasn't sure he was going to do it, but, he thought, all she could do is say "no!". he asked Fred to put the Monarch's record of "Pretty Little Girl" on the turntable. When the song got near the part, he wanted, he took Karen's hand and took off his high school ring and sang along to "Let's go Steady." Her eyes got big and tears filled the bottoms. She shook her head "yes!". He gave her his ring. They embraced, to everyone's applause. Karen ran out of the room and came back in two to three minutes, with the ring on a chain, next to the cross, he had given her. He told her that it wasn't exactly fair to her, to ask her to go steady, since she was going to be around a lot of guys and he wasn't going to be around any girls. She said that she didn't care. She would be 'his girl" for as long as he wanted her to be. When the party ended, and the others had left, they were alone, in the dimmed living room. They started out with tender, loving kisses. Those kisses grew into passionate, tongue lashing kisses. She held him tight and didn't want to let him go. He felt the same. After about an hour and a half, they finally, reluctantly, parted. She hugged him, tightly, again and one last kiss, ran out of the room, in tears. He got up and walked to the front door, opened it and turned around and with tears, in his voice, hollered, "I love you!" He walked out the door and gently closed it behind him. The walk to the car, had to be the loneliness walk, ever. He meant the three words, he left her with. He hoped that she heard them. He was about to get into the car, when he heard a scraping sound, he turned around and looked at the house. From the second floor window, he saw her and heard her yell "I love you, too!". Then, she was gone. He drove home, with tears in his eyes.

His mom cooked him a very special dinner. Roast beef with mashed potatoes, corn and peas mixed, chocolate milk and apple pie with vanilla ice cream, for dessert. His folks asked him to write them, as soon as he got his address. He said that he would. He had no idea, what lay in store for him and Bert. He tried to think of it as a new adventure. But somehow, he had misgivings about it. Bert called him and wanted to go to the car hop, one last time. He said "okay". Bert picked him up around 8PM and they started out. He made Bert pull over to the side of the road. Bert was, obviously, drunk. Bert let him drive. He asked him where he had gotten the booze. Bert said, "from your party." He said, "but Fred took all that stuff home." "Yeah" said Bert, "and gave some to me." They pulled into the car hop. He found a spot, on the front row. He parked the car, by the speaker and went out to use the restroom. As he walked through the restaurant, he heard a voice come over the speaker, "Just one GD hamburger and fries!" it was Bert! He quickly, used the rest room and headed back to the car. Two cops were standing by the car, talking with Bert. They were getting ready to arrest him. He tried to explain to the cops, that they were both "shipping out" with the Navy, in the morning. The cops said that as long as he was driving, and not Bert, they would let them go. They got their burgers and fries and cokes and sat, quietly, in the car. After the car hop, he drove them to a coffee shop. After getting Bert to have three or four cups, he drove them to his house and then, told Bert to drive straight home. He said that he would.

9:00 AM. The recruiter arrived at his house. He was wearing tan chinos, a white dress shirt, dirty bucs, and his winter jacket. In his hand, was his small bag, that Karen had given him for Christmas, inside, were the toiletries that he had gotten at his "going away" party. He kissed his mom good bye and followed the recruiter out the door. His mom stood in the doorway and watched him get into the car, with Bert. They were on their way. He soon learned that the Navy's slogan was "hurry up and wait."

They arrived at the recruiting station and were ushered into a large room, with many seats. All the seats were filled with guys. One group was pretty well "banged up". They were from Nashua, NH and must have been in one hell of a fight! Others were from all over the Northeast. They were handed more paperwork, to fill out. One had the name of their local newspaper. He and Bert filled it out. Then, they were called, one by one to another room. There were lights and a background of a Naval destroyer. He was told, to take off his shirt. When he did, they noticed that he wasn't wearing an undershirt. The recruiter was not happy. He went to find an undershirt, for him to wear. He came back with one and told him to put it on. He, reluctantly, put it on. It was too big, as was the jumper and the white hat. They made him stand in front of the drop. That had the destroyer, on it. His picture was taken, for the local newspaper. Once, that was over, he took off the hat, jumper and undershirt and handed them back to the recruiter. Bert was next. Everything went better with Bert. He was wearing an undershirt. After the pictures were taken, they went back into the large room, and sat back down. They must have sat, there, for about 45 minutes, until all the pictures were taken. The photographer said that he would have "touch up" the pictures of the guys from NH. Everyone laughed about that. As they sat around talking, two flags were brought into the room. A U.S. flag and a Navy flag. A small podium was also brought in. They were told to stand up. A naval officer, with scrambled eggs on the visor, of his hat, stepped into the room. He stepped to the podium and told them to raise their right hands. They were sworn into the United States Navy. The officer left and they were told to sit down. They waited for another hour, for something else to occur. He looked at his watch. He couldn't get over how slow the morning was going! They were told the "smoking lamp was 'lit'" Ash trays that were made from old bomb casings were brought in. Finally, the recruiter came in and ordered them to stand up and file single file out of the room, through the front room and out of the building, into a navy gray bus. They filled up the bus. He thought that this was it. They would, finally, be going to the airport, to fly to Illinois. Wrong! They were bussed downtown to a local restaurant, for lunch. He was glad he brought plenty of money. He didn't need it. Lunch was on the U.S. Navy. They could eat whatever they wanted, as long as they ate everything on their tray. It was buffet style. He ate a "hearty" lunch, because he wasn't sure when he would eat, again. Lunch last for over an hour, though many had finished eating within thirty minutes. They were, then, ordered out of the restaurant and back on the bus and taken back to the recruiting office. Back in the large room, they were told, once again, that the smoking lamp was "lit". After another hour, they were handed large manila envelopes. Inside the envelopes, were each one's individual orders. His name was written in black ink, on the cover. After getting their orders, they waited, in the large room, for another hour. He was running out of L&M's. he never smoked so many cigarettes, in his life. He asked the recruiter, if he could find a machine and get some more. "You can do that at the airport!" The recruiter said. "So much for Mr. "nice guy" he thought. He looked out through the door, past the front room, to the outside. Darkness had replaced the daylight. They had been waiting around all day. He glanced at his watch. It read 6:30PM. Right about now, he should be on the phone with Karen. He heaved a heavy sigh and was about to light another L&M, when they ordered to gather their coats and especially their orders and file single file, once again, out to the bus. He though they were being transported back to the restaurant, for dinner. Wrong! This time they were, actually, going to the airport. It was not a long ride, at all. They were "unloaded" at the airport and "ushered" into a lounge, where they were given sandwiches and chips and cokes. He found a cigarette machine and fed it a quarter and got another pack of L&M's. he got back a nickel, in change. He felt the machine robbed him. Then he saw, that at the airport, cigarettes were twenty cents a pack! A lot of the guys ate their sandwiches, quickly, thinking that they would be getting on the plane, real soon. Wrong! He took his time. Somehow, he knew that the waiting was hardly over. He saw a public phone and thought about calling Karen. He wasn't the only one thinking of calling home. As got off the chair, the line was already thirty guys deep. He sat back down.

He decided to take a nap. He thought he had hardly closed his eyes, when they were ordered to report to the "gate" to begin boarding the plane. Through sleepy eyes, he looked at his watch, 9PM! Once on the plane, a Navy charter, they were told to try and get some "shut eye." They had a three to four hour flight to Illinois. They all heaved a mutual sigh and got comfortable, in their seats. Bert was sitting next to him, by the window. This was another "first" for him. His first commercial airplane ride. Another milestone. As they left the ground, he gripped the arms of his chair. He did not like heights! Bert laughed just laughed! As the plane gained altitude, it suddenly banked hard to the left. He thought, for sure, that they were going straight down into the ground or the harbor. He closed his eyes, tightly! Bert shoved him on the shoulder and made him look out the little window. Below were the lights of the city. He thought he was going to pass out! When the plane, finally, "righted itself" he closed his eyes and tried to sleep. He thought that if he was asleep and the plane crashed, he would never know what hit him! After awhile, he got accustomed to the flight. A stewardess came by and offered them some liquid refreshment. They were only allowed to drink "soft' drinks. He asked her" what time were they going to land in Illinois?" She said "oh around 1AM! He and Bert looked at each other. He told Bert that he was beginning to regret, going into the city, with him, that day, to sign up.

They arrived in Chicago a little after 1:15AM. They were herded into another bus and endured a cold, long ride to the Naval base. The bus stopped and deposited them in front of a large building. They were told to get off the bus and get inside. Inside the large wooden building were metal racks of bunk beds. They were told to pick out a "rack" and put the mattress cover on the small mattress. Get out of their clothes, get in the rack and pull the blanket over them. He looked at his watch, just before the lights were turned off. It was 2:30AM!

Sleep came, quickly, but so did the "wake up" time. He thought he was having a nightmare! A God awful sound echoed into his ear drums and caused them to vibrate "uncontrollably". He did not want to open his eyes. The sound wouldn't stop and the darkness was "shattered "by extreme brightness! He was compelled to open at least one eye. He wished he hadn't! He focused his one opened eye on his watch, 4:30AM! 4:30!! The horrible 'racket' continued, followed by the "bellowing" of a loud male voice! He heard the others, getting up and decided that he better join them. He had never, ever, been told that he had to "function" on just two hours sleep! "GET UP AND GET IN THE HEAD, LADIES, SHIT, SHOWER AND SHAVE AND GET DRESSED AND GET OUTSIDE FOR MUSTER!!!!" His eyes, finally, focused on the short, burley, sailor, with the "loud" voice. The "racket" was produced by running an empty coke bottle around the insides of an empty, metal, trash can! He climbed down from his "rack" and nearly collided with Bert, who was trying to locate his glasses. He asked Bert, "what's a "head?" Bert had no idea. "For you ladies, who don't know that the "head" is the bathroom, you'll never call it a bathroom, again! Now get in there!" He looked at Bert and said "the bathroom." Bert, finding his glasses, said "yeah, bathroom, now called the "head". He grabbed his small bag and followed the others into the head. He had never seen anything like it before. 20 stalls, side by side, no doors. 20 urinals, side by side. 20 sinks side by side, with one huge mirror, the length of the wall. Bare, naked, light bulbs hung from the ceiling, produced a glare that caused his retinas to 'blink". He went to a urinal and took care of "business." He, then went to the sink and brushed his teeth. He was about to comb his hair. Bert asked why he was going to do that. There weren't any girls around and nobody, here, cared what he looked like. He agreed and put everything back in his bag and left the "head" and went back to his "rack" and got dressed. It was still quite dark, when he joined the others, outside, in the cold, Illinois, January morning.

They stood outside, for what seemed, at least an hour, waiting for everyone to finish getting dressed. The short, burly, sailor, with the big voice, stood in front of them, with a clipboard. "Okay!" He said, "Who forgot to bring out the envelope, with his orders in it?" He and a few others, went back into the building and retrieved the large manila folder. Before, he went back out, he opened the small bag and took out the small PlayBoy calendar and began to "x" out the days. "four years of "this"? he thought, as he walked back out, to the front of building. He stood next to Bert and glared at him. When they were all assembled, the "sailor" called out their names. He told them to answer either, "here" or "Yo". He thought he would be an individualist and he answered "present." The sailor repeated his name, three times, he kept answering "present". The sailor, walked up to him and glared up into his face. "here or yo." He began to reconsider his answer, "yo!" he said. The sailor turned and read the rest of the names. He, then, told them to get in line by twos. He marched them away, from the lights of the barracks and into the darkness.

They marched for "blocks" past many old wooden "barracks" where other 'poor souls" were being 'roused' out of a short sleep. The smell of food wafted into his nostrils. They came upon a lighted building that was serving breakfast. They marched inside and stood in line, waiting to eat. The Burley sailor told them where to sit, once they got their food tray.

After breakfast, which consisted of scrambled eggs, toast, bacon, and juice or milk, they were, again marched out, this time, the darkness was replaced with a cold gray, cloudy morning. They marched to another large wooden building. They marched in and were told to sit in the chairs, that were connected to a wooden desk. The burley sailor instructed them to remain silent and do as they were told. Two more sailors came into the building and stood at the front. Behind them was a blackboard. They were pleasant. They welcomed them to the United States Navy. One of the sailors, passed out two sheets of paper and a pencil, to each of them. The "pleasant" sailor wrote, in chalk, on the blackboard, their "new address." They were told to copy it down, on the paper. The sailor waited, while they didst so. Next, he called out their name, one by one and gave each of them a number and told them to write that down, as well, and to memorize it, as that was to be their service number and was as important, if not more, than their social security numbers. When his name was called, he wrote down 903 63 04.

After that was done, they were told that they would be taken to the PX and would be given stationary and their first task was to sit down and write letters home, to their parents, girlfriends, mistresses, wives, anyone, that they wanted to received letters, from and, mostly to let them, at home, know they arrived, safely. He was glad he brought some money. When they got to the PX, he broke from others and bought a box of stationary, stamps and a pack of L&Ms. The burley sailor stepped up in front of him. "You don't listen very well, do you sailor? The Navy gives you your first set of stationary and stamps. You will pay for everything afterwards!" "Oh." he said. He, quickly, left the building and stood, outside, with the others. They were marched back to the "classroom," and spent the next hour, or so, writing letters "home". He wrote to his parents, Karen and Ree. He gave them, his address and told them that the first day of basic, was the "pits." He told Karen how much he loved her and missed her already and hoped the next 9 weeks would pass, quickly, for both of them. He told Ree, that he missed her and still cared a lot for her and hoped that she would write back. The burley sailor came up to his desk and told him, he was not there, to write a book, just give them the "info" he was told to give. He took out the addresses from his wallet and addressed each of the envelopes and put his return address on the top left hand corner, of the envelopes and then put stamps, on them. The burley sailor shook his head and walked away. He yelled to the guys, "The Navy pays for the postage for your first letter!" he looked down at the stamps and sighed. One of the other sailors came by and picked up the letters. They were, then, given a smoke break, outside the building. Bert told him, that he had better start paying attention or it could get a lot worse, for him. He agreed and mentioned that he wouldn't be there, if he had not listened to him, in the first place.

The first week, they stayed, in their civilian clothes. They were in a different barracks and were allowed to smoke, in the head. Their hair grew long and wild. Their clothes began to take on a whole new personality. No matter how many times they showered; changed underwear, they were still in the same clothes. The only saving grace, was smoking in the head. It helped to alleviate the "stink' of the clothes.

Things changed, the second week. They were marched to the barbershop. Where about five passes, of electric clippers eliminated the use of combs and hair brushes. They were, then, marched to another building where they picked up their uniforms. He was given a box. He could either send his civilian clothes home or have them burned. He thought about having them burned, but decided to send them home. He boxed them up and addressed the label. He stepped into Navy boxers, now called "skivvies". He got dressed into a fresh pair of Navy fatigues, wool socks, big black boots, black watch cap and a heavy fatigue jacket. The rest of the uniforms and "things' were packed into a large khaki green bag, called a "sea bag." Once, completely 'outfitted" they were marched to a new barracks and were told to pick out a rack and locker and "stow" their "gear". They, also, were shown how to make up their rack. It had to be so smooth and tight, that they could bounce a quarter off of it. Once they were "squared away." They were marched back to the classroom, where they would meet their new "Company Commander."

He thought his "new" commander would be a "reasonable" man and listen to his "civilian mentality". Wrong! He and the Navy clashed on many subjects and found him shoveling snow off the "gridiron" and drill fields, many a night. He didn't mind the physical training and all the classroom classes, but the mental harassment, got to be a bit much! He was happiest. When the company commander wasn't around, especially on weekends. The last confrontation with commander was over the length of "clothes ties." The Navy says a quarter of an inch above the line, but he thought the clothes would stay on the line better, if the length was a whole inch above the line, Wrong! The basic Navy vocabulary wasn't a problem, well, most of it. The bells "threw" him and he wanted to know why someone just didn't come on a loudspeaker and give the "time." This "reasoning" made him two hours late for their first "Cinderella Liberty."

His liberty was in Chicago, on State Street. They had burgers and fries, and a chocolate milk shake. People in Illinois were unfamiliar with Frappes. They, Bert and two others, took in a burlesque show and a got to meet some "interesting girls." Unfortunately, something that had been 'added" to their meals, during basic, rendered them "useless' with women. Still, they had an interesting time in Chicago.

The next morning was kind of an "enlightenment" for some of the guys. Those that found something, other than soft drinks, to drink, also found "things" from one of the tattoo parlors. As they looked, in the mirror, in the head, to shave, etc. they found big red hearts, black panthers and all kinds of interesting pictures on their arms and chests. He was glad that he had not had anything to drink and that he did not have any tattoos.

After the evening meal, they were given time to go the PX and buy toiletries and stationary. There was a "bank" of public phones. Each man was given two minutes to talk. He wrote his folks that he would be calling home on a certain evening. He could not "pinpoint" the time, but said it would be around 7PM, his time. He made sure he was at the PX by 6:00PM, that night. By 7PM, he was next in line. He got on the phone and called "collect". That was the only way they could make calls. His mom answered and he answered all her questions, truthfully, except the one about a tattoo. She told him not to get one! He responded, "Sorry, you're too late. I've got a big red heart, on my chest that says "mom." She hung up the phone. He called back and when his dad answered, his dad yelled "get rid of it!" he told his dad that he was kidding. He didn't have a tattoo and would prove it when he got home. His dad said, "good" and he heard him tell his mom that he really didn't have a tattoo. He said that he would call again in a few days. His time up, he hung up the phone and waited for Bert. They walked back to the barracks, together.

He had learned a valuable lesson, from his short liberty. Obey the Navy's rules and regulations and don't use any "civilian logic" ever again. The rest of basic training went very well, for him.

He received two letters from Ree. She told him that school was going well. She did say that she missed being with him and hoped that he would call her, when he got home. He wrote back and told her that he would only be home for two weeks, but that he would definetly call her. He, also, received many, many, letters, from Karen. He would get, at least, one a day. They were sprinkled with perfume and had "SWAK" written across the back seal of the envelopes. She really missed him. She, also, wrote about school. She couldn't wait until he was home, again and be held in his arms. He wrote her, every night. He told her how much he loved her and missed her too, very much! He got a letter, from his mother, telling him that he had a new sister in law! He, immediately, thought of Phil and Nan, but was told that it was Dave and a girl named Ellie! He was in shock! So many changes in his life.

Basic training came to an end. Graduation took place, in the morning. After the noon chow, they sat around in a circle with their company commander. He held more manila envelopes, in his hands. He read off their names and told each one of them, where their next "duty station" was going to be. He prayed it would be close to Boston. It wasn't. he was headed for communication/intelligence schools in Bainbridge Maryland and then, to Quantico, Virginia. Bert was going to electrician school in South Carolina. The company commander wished them well and then told them to pack their "gear" and "fall" outside the barracks, to be loaded onto buses and taken to O'Hare Airport, outside Chicago. The bus was filled to capacity. Everyone was excited! His two week leave wouldn't begin, until he arrived back in Boston. As the bus headed for the airport, he couldn't resist it. Bert cautioned him not to do it; he wouldn't be responsible for his well—being. He stood up and yelled, at the top of his lungs, "ATTENTION ON DECK!" Everyone jumped to their feet. It took a few seconds for them to realize that they were on a bus and there weren't any officers on board. He ducked down as white hats came "flying" in his direction. The bus was filled with roars of laughter.

While they were waiting, at the airport, to board their flight home, he noticed two Air force guys walking towards them. They were carrying their uniforms in dry cleaner bags! He stopped them and asked if they just got out of basic training? They had, and all their clothes were washed by professionals and uniforms were dry cleaned! He turned to Bert. Two blocks! Two more blocks! If we had just walked two more blocks, we would not have had to "hand wash" anything! Two blocks! Bert stepped back, expecting him to swing. He apologized and agreed that they sure would have had "dishpan hands" from hand washing everything from socks to skivvies and T-shirts and white hats! Bert managed to keep his distance from him. He was not happy and kept mumbling, "two more blocks." Even as they boarded the plane, he was heard to say "two more blocks!" One thing he had to do in basic training, that he never had to do before was shave! He tried to tell them, that he didn't have any little hairs growing out of his face. They didn't care. He tried shaving without putting a blade in the razor, but they soon caught on. So, he began shaving, with the rest. It became a morning "ritual".

It was seated on the plane, that he realized they were really going home. It had been a long nine weeks, for him. He had lost so much weight, that he had to have a safety pin, clasped behind his waist, on his dress blues, to keep his "thirteen button" pants up. He was hoping that Karen would be at the airport, when he arrived. He knew his folks would be there. He hoped that they would recognize him. He tried to catch some sleep, on the plane, but was too excited about seeing Karen. He asked the stewardess, what time they would be landing, in Boston? She said around 8:30PM. He still wasn't too thrilled with flying. Bert had the window seat.

He kept his white hat on, the whole trip. They had stopped shaving his head a week and a half before graduation, but to him, he still looked "bald". He was afraid Karen would not like his absence of hair. He remembered Vic told him that hair grew faster, at night, while asleep. He thought that if he could get some sleep, maybe his hair would grow back, by the time the plane landed. He tried, real hard, to get some sleep.

His eyes were just starting to get "heavy" when he heard the pilot announce that they would be landing in two minutes. He opened his eyes and looked at his watch. It read 8:20PM! Bert was able to sleep. He nudged Bert's arm and woke him up. "We're landing!" He said. Bert looked at him and asked why he kept his hat on, the whole trip? He said that he didn't want anyone to see his "bald" head. Bert just laughed. Bert said that they would probably be separated, when they landed, so he would call him, in a few days. He said. "okay."

The landing was a little rough, but he didn't care! He was home, if only for two weeks. He adjusted his hat and waited for the plane to come to a complete stop. When it did, all the other sailors got up and got their Peacoats and "ditty' bags out of the overhead compartment. His bag was packed at the top of his seabag. All he had to get was his coat. He got up and put it on and sat and waited, for everyone to deplane. Then, it was his and Bert's turn. They walked down the aisle, to the front and went out the door and down the stairs to the ground and walked to the building. Once through the door, he looked for Karen and his folks. He saw her, in the crowd. She waved her right hand, furiously, at him. He walked as fast as could, towards her. She broke from the crowd and rushed into his arms. They hugged and kissed and hugged and kissed at least four times. She, then grabbed his arm and they walked to greet his parents. He forgot all about Bert. He hugged his mom and shook his dad's hand. His dad was not into hugging another male. Karen was attached to his right arm as they walked to the baggage claim. His mom noticed, right away, how slim he was. Karen grabbed his hat, off his head and put it on her head. She noticed his short hair and ran her right hand through it and laughed and told him that he looked like a little boy in a sailor suit. He wasn't sure how to take that. He did say, "yeah, right!" They waited for almost a half hour, for the bags to come out and on the turnstyle. There were a lot of seabags. He checked all the ones, that came by, until he recognized his. He had a difficult time reaching for it, because Karen was so "attached" to his arm. His dad grabbed it and carried it out of the terminal, to the car. He and Karen occupied the back seat of the Mercury, as they drove home. He asked her how she managed to get to his house. She told him that she walked. He couldn't believe that she walk that far. His mom wanted to know if he wanted to stop and get something to eat. He said that he was okay, but if they wanted to, they could. They asked Karen, if she were hungry. She said "no!, thanks." So, they drove home. It was almost ten o'clock, when they arrived home. They went into the house. He put his seabag at the foot of the stairs and they all went into the living room. They had so many questions. His mom asked him again about the tattoo. He assured everyone, that he hadn't got one. He did tell them about all the guys that did. Some, being so drunk, they didn't remember it, until the next morning, when they went to shave and saw 'it" on their arms. After about 20 minutes. Karen said that she had to get home. That it was a school night, for her. He realized that it was Thursday night. He checked his manila folder, before they got up to take her home. He realized that his two week leave didn't actually start until the following Monday. He had an extra three days! He and Karen liked that! His mom gave him the keys to the VW and they went out the back door, to the car. She gave him back his white hat. He wished that they could have some 'alone time" before he drove her home. She told him that she could always say that his plane was late. He started the car and put "her" through her "gears" and headed for the DFA (duck feeding area) by the river.

He pulled into the parking area, by the river. He turned the car off and put it in reverse gear. She pulled the lever on the side of her seat and moved it back as far as it would go. He leaned over to her, as her arms went around his neck. She drew him in. Their lips met in a long tender kiss. Her perfume swirled around his nose. His lips explored hers and hers explored his. It didn't take long for their "passion" to ignite. They held each other tightly. Her lips parted, enough for his tongue to enter her mouth. She swirled her tongue around his. His parted lips allowed hers to enter his mouth. He moved his hands from her waist, up the sides of her rib cage, to the sides of her breasts. She had unbuttoned her winter coat, as he drove. At a red light, he had shed his peacoat. She moaned as his hands caressed the sides. Her lips and tongue went wild! She began to thrust her pelvis against his. When they parted their lips, for a breath, she moaned, huskily, "I've dreamt about this night, for nine weeks." He mumbled that he was so miserable without her. She moved her hand, down between his thirteen buttons, to the spot between his legs. He was kissing the side of her neck, his hands drifted over her breasts, over her sweater. She asked, why he wasn't excited by her touch? He told her that they put something in his food, to stop any "excitement." She groaned, "I hope it wears off soon." "So do I!" He said. Their lips crushed together as they continued their "petting." She moved her hands from his crotch, to the back of his bell bottom trousers. She felt the safety pin and moved her hands past it inside his pants, rubbing his flesh. he brought his lips from hers and moved them over her sweater covered breasts. She arched her back and pushed against his lips. He groaned through his lips about how much he wanted her. She moaned that she wanted him, too. They kissed, petted and hugged each other, for well over an hour.

They both knew that she had to go home. They left the DFA at around 11:20 and headed to her house. He dropped her off at 11:45. She asked him to pick her up, after school. he said that he would. They shared another deep, tender kiss, on her porch, in front of her front door. He drove home, a very happy sailor. He pulled into his driveway and parked the VW and turned it off, locked it and went up the backstairs to the back door. He took off his uniform and hung it in his closet. He went to get into bed and noticed that his seabag was on the floor at the foot of his bed. It felt so good to get back into a "real" bed. He hadn't any trouble falling asleep.

He, still, woke up at 5AM. It was still dark. He started to get out of bed, when he realized that he was really home. He lay back down, on his back, and just relaxed. Soon, he was back asleep. He slept, again, till 8:45AM. He got out of bed and made his bed. He went to his seabag and opened it up and took out his "ditty" bag and went to the bathroom. When he returned to his room, he, for the first time, in nine weeks, put on "civilian" briefs, jeans and a T-shirt. He went downstairs and sat down, to eat breakfast. His mom sat across from him. Again, she expressed concern about his "weight." He told her that he felt fine. She asked him to raise his T-shirt. She wanted to make sure that he didn't have a tattoo. He raised his shirt, with a grin. She sighed a big sigh of relief. He asked if he could borrow her car, in the afternoon, to pick up Karen. She said "okay." He spent the rest of the time, looking over his civilian clothes. He found a new dress shirt, socks and chinos. He went back downstairs and asked his mom about the new clothes. She told him, that, when she opened the box, he had sent home, the "stench" had been too much, for her to stand, so she threw them out, except for the shoes. He went back upstairs and put on the new clothes, to go and pick up Karen. He looked in the mirror. For a guy, who took care of his "hair", to comb it and comb it, just right, he was very discouraged! To him, he looked bald! He looked in his closet and found a baseball hat and put it on. It looked kind of funny, to him, but was better than not having any hair. He drove to Karen's school and parked in front in the circle. As he waited for her, a couple of parents walked up to his window and wanted him to move, so they could park. He told them he was not a 'student." They didn't seem to care. He did not move the car. When Karen came out, he reached over and opened the door, for her. She reached over to him and their lips met for a long, tender and sweet kiss. Then he put the car in gear and they drove out of the circle. Del Shannon was on the radio, with "Runaway." She was hungry, so they went to Ho-Jo's. The waitress took their orders of burgers and fries and frappes. She said that she had to call her folks and tell them, where she was. She was on the phone, for a long time. He was afraid her food was going to get cold. She came back, just as he was about to ask the waitress to take hers back and warm it up. She pushed her plate next to him, in the booth and slid in next to him. She sat so close, their hips and legs touched. She was so happy, that he was home! He was so happy, to be home, with her.

Back in the car, they hugged and kissed some more. Afterwards, she asked him to come by her house around 7PM. They were planning on going bowling and then parking. He drove her home. The Tokens were on the radio with "The Lion Sleeps Tonight." Followed by Gary U.S. Bonds and "Quarter To Three." He pulled up to the front of her house. They shared another tender kiss and he turned off the car, got out and went to her door and opened it and helped her out, with her books. He closed the door and walked her up the walk to her door. Another kiss and a promise that he would see her in a while. He drove home. Ricky Nelson was on the radio with "Travellin' Man." He was followed by Brenda Lee and "I Want To Be Wanted."

He pulled up, in front of his house, turned off the car and went inside the house, to the kitchen. His mom had made roast beef, with peas and mashed potatoes, for dinner. She was determined to put some "meat" on his bones. At dinner, he answered more questions about boot camp. He answered them, by saying, boot camp sucked! He was glad that it was behind him. He asked about Dave. Dave and his bride were living in Virginia and he was a sales rep for Breck Shampoo. They were, also, expecting a baby. That was all the information, they could give him. After dinner, he went to his room and "freshened "up. That meant he rubbed more deodorant under his arms and put on more cologne. He tried to do something with his hair, it just wasn't growing in fast enough to suit him. He checked his watch. It read 6:15PM. He thanked his mom, for the diner and said he'd be late. He went out the front door and got into the VW. Started it up and pulled away from the curb and headed to Karen's. Troy Shondell was on the radio with "This Time." Followed by Pat Boone and "Moody River."

He pulled up in front of Karen's house at exactly 7PM. He turned off the VW and got and closed the door, after him and walked up the walk to her porch and front door. He knocked on the door and heard her call out "come in." He opened the door and walked into the foyer. She opened the door and yelled "surprise!" All the gang that was at his and Bert's going away party, were there, even Bert. He was surprised! It was great to see everyone. It was a great party! As he and Karen danced to Elvis's "Surrender." He told her, he really wanted the two of them to be alone. "Tomorrow, honey. We'll have the whole day and most of the night, just the two of us." She promised. He held her tight and told her how happy, he was, that they were together. The party lasted well past 11 o'clock. After everyone else had left, he held her in his arms and told her how much he loved her. She held him tight and kissed him and said she was the happiest girl, in the world! One last kiss and he went out the door, with the expectation that he would pick her up around 10:30AM for their picnic at Walden Pond. He drove home, a very happy sailor. The Marcels were on the radio, with "Blue Moon."

He woke up at 9:00 that Saturday morning. He was amazed that he slept so late. He went to take a bath and saw that while he was away, his folks had a shower installed. He showered, shaved, brushed his teeth and tried to brush his hair. He went back to the bed room and put on fresh pair of "Navy" boxers, white socks, a "fresh" long sleeve shirt and jeans. He went downstairs and grabbed a couple of pieces of toast, and a small cup of coffee. His mother was in shock! "Since when did you start drinking coffee." He joked, "about two minutes ago." He went to the hall closet, by the downstairs bathroom and grabbed a blanket. They would pick up food and drinks on the way. He walked out the back door and got into the VW and started it up and drove out of the driveway, to Karen's house. Lawrence Welk's orchestra was on the radio with "Calcutta", followed by Bobby Lewis and "Twistin And Turnin." He got to Karen's house around 10:15AM. He was wearing his engineer boots and a Boston Red Sox ball cap. When he got to her front door, she opened it, before he could knock or ring the bell. She came out and handed him a large wicker basket. It was a little heavy. He put his right arm, through the wooden handle and she took his left arm. They walked down the walk, to the car. He put the basket in the back seat, with the blanket, as she got into the passenger side of the car. Bert Kampfert was on the radio with "Wonderland By Night." Followed by Sue Thompson and "Norman." She was followed by Kathy Linden and "Billy." As they drove to Walden Pond, on the gray, cool, April morning, he asked her what was in the basket. She said her mom fried two pieces of chicken and put in some chips and cokes and cookies. He asked if they should stop and get anything else. Karen snuggled up close to him and asked, "why? We may not even get to eat any food." He felt an "actual" stirring, below his belt.

They arrived at the parking lot, for Walden Pond, around 11:30AM. They got out of the car and took out the basket and blanket. He locked the car and they started to walk in. They were met by a park ranger. She wanted to make sure that they weren't going to start any campfires. They said "no". As they walked away from her. Karen whispered in his ear, "maybe our body heat will cause a fire." He looked at her and grinned. This was the kind of day, he dreamed about, for nine weeks. They walked a good deal into the woods, away from any sign of other people. They found a clearing, on a small ridge, that, if they looked hard enough, they could see the pond. The clearing was well off the "beaten path" and was hidden by a lot of "stately" pines. He spread out the blanket and she put the basket at what was the "head" of the blanket. They lay down, face to face, side by side. He stared into her one blue eye and one brown eye and her luscious red lips. She was wearing a dark blue sweater and jeans. He moved to put his lips on hers. She moved onto her back. He moved on top. His right leg between hers, his hands on the side of her head. Her arms went around his back, as she drew his lips to hers. Their first, few, kisses were sweet and tender. It didn't take long for passion and lust to grow, inside of both of them. The intensity of their kisses increased as their bodies rubbed against bodies. He brought his hands to her sides and began to move up to the sides of her sweater covered breasts. Her tongue stabbed his mouth. When they ran out of breath, they hugged each other, extra, tight. He put his lips to her cheek and then her earlobe and down along her neck. She began to moan and groan. She brought her hands to his head and 'guided" his mouth to her sweater covered breasts. He moved over them, very slowly, trying not to get the fabric in his teeth and mouth. Her hands went around his buttocks and pressed into his jean covered flesh. The sounds of the woods meant nothing to them. They were "lost" in their own little world. She pulled his shirt from his jeans and ran her hands up underneath his shirt. His lips went "crazy" on hers. The next time they "broke' for air, she slid out from under him and took off her sweater and left just her white buttoned shirt on. She "untucked" it from her jeans. She, then, rolled over on top of him, and pressed her lips to his. Her hands were back under his shirt, rubbing his rib cage and moving to his stomach and chest. He followed suit. He ran his hands up under her shirt and rubbed the naked flesh, of her back. He massaged her lower back, moving up to and over her bra strap to her shoulders and back down. She whispered, to him, as her lips moved to his, "unclasp the strap." He never was very good at doing that, but he managed to undo first one and then the others. His hands moved from her back to the sides of her breasts. Her lips "mashed' against his, moans escaping from her mouth. Her flesh was so smooth and pliable. She brought her hands from his chest to his sides and then to each side of him, on the blanket. She brought herself off him just enough for his hands to move to the front of her breasts. Her pelvis was still pressing against his. Her head thrown back, looking skyward, as he massaged her breasts with his hands, all around, top, bottom, sides and, finally to her nipples, which were hard like stones. She ground her pelvis against his, moaning. He wanted to rip off her shirt and place his lips and tongue to her marvelous orbs, but something halted their attention. They both stopped and listened. They heard voices of kids, coming near them. She rolled off him and they, quickly, adjusted their clothing and sat up and took the chips and cokes out of the basket. Just in time, for two boys dressed in cub scout uniforms happened upon "their" clearing. The boys stopped dead in their tracks! They were only there, for a minute and, then, turned and were gone. It was enough to spoil the "moment." They realized that they had to use the restrooms. They packed the basket and the rolled up the blanket. Shirts buttoned and tucked back in, they made their way along the ridge and down towards the beach, where the restrooms were. She took the basket and he took the blanket. They met, once again, outside the building. He realized that it would be getting dark, soon. They decided to go and get something to eat and then, finish their "picnic" at the drive in. He took the basket and they walked hand in hand to the parking lot. He happened to glance in the basket and noticed her bra was in it. He turned and looked at her and smiled and then glanced at her chest and saw her breasts heave and sway, under her shirt, as they walked. He knew that, if anyone, looked at his crotch, they would see the outline of an inflamed male member. When they got to the car, he unlocked it, opened the driver's door and put the basket and blanket back on the floor, of the back seat. She had already got into the passenger's side. He got in, behind the wheel and noticed that she had unbuttoned the top three buttons of her shirt. He turned his attention to her face and eyes. She moved towards him. There was "lust" in her eyes. She wrapped her arms around his neck and their lips met in a 'frenzied" kiss. She broke their kiss and told him to get to the drive in, that they could get a pizza or something there. He started the car, backed it out of the lot, quickly, and slammed the car into the forward gears and headed for the drive in, as the light of the day, turn to the dark of the night.

He pulled up to the gate, just as the newsreel started. They found a spot in the back, near the concession stand. They decided to get a pizza and popcorn. They still had their cokes, in the picnic basket. He turned off the car and put it in first gear. He told her that he would be back as soon as possible. Since the show had just started, there wasn't much of a line. He got the pizza and popcorn and headed back to the car. He got to the passenger side and noticed she wasn't in the passenger seat. She was in the back seat. He opened the door and passed the pizza and popcorn to her. He, then, climbed into the backseat, next to her. He leaned forward and closed the door. He, also, pushed the levers on the front seats and moved them forward, as far as they could go. They cuddled together, as they ate the pizzas and drank their cokes. When they had finished, he put the "trash" behind them in the small storage space, where the basket and blanket were. He hadn't turned completely around, when she was "on" him. She was on fire! Lips crushing his, her hands under his shirt, rubbing his chest. Her legs straddling his waist. Her pelvis pressing down upon him. He ran his hands up under her shirt, along the flesh of her back, around to her sides and, coming to 'rest' on her breasts. Caressing every inch, from the sides, to the tops, the bottoms and, finally, to her nipples. She brought her hands from his chest and tore open the buttons on her shirt. She put her hands on the top of his head and 'guided" his lips to the flesh of her breasts. With his hands, he brushed aside her shirt and began to kiss her breasts, where his hands had started. "Oh my darling!" She moaned, as his lips and tongue found, first one nipple, and then the other. He took "it" between his lips, the tip of his tongue, gently lashing "it" over the top and around the sides. While his mouth, lips, and tongue, paid "homage' to one, his right hand was on the other. His left hand sneaked down, moving up her leg. She was uncontrollable! He had never experienced such passion with her. She had to feel his "excitement" between them. His member was straining against the confines of his underwear and jeans. He raised his head from her breast to reach her lips. Her head was thrown back, her eyes closed, her breath ragged, moans escaped from her lips along with "Oh honey, please don't stop!" he returned to her other breast, switching hands. He brought his hand, that was on her leg, to her inner thigh, and massaged her thigh over her jeans covered leg. She was rubbing back and forth against him, with her pelvis. She was "crazy" with desire! He knew he could rip her clothes off and make passionate love to her! Something held him back.

Then, as quickly as she had started, she began to slow down and stop. "Whew!" She said. He removed his hands and mouth from her breasts. She slid off him and they both sat and "caught" their breaths. She brought her shirt together over her breasts, but did not button up. "Is there any coke left?" She asked. He reached over the back of the seat and brought both bottles to them. She drank what was left from both bottles. "You are a wonderful lover!" She exclaimed. He reciprocated," you are too!" "Really?" she asked. "uh huh" he said. Just then they were "bathed" in light. Intermission! They had been making out through the entire first show. She cuddled next to him and asked "Can we do it again?" he answered, "of course." "better go and get some more cokes." She said. "Okay.' He replied. He got out of the car, buttoning his shirt, and headed to the concession stand. He knew there would be a long line, but it would give them both enough time, to catch their breaths.

He returned to the car with two large cokes. She reached out and opened the door, for him. He handed one of the cokes, to her, as he got into the car. She held his coke, as he reached over the front seat and closed the door. Her shirt front was wide open, revealing her wonderful cleavage and most of her magnificent breasts. He thought, to himself, what a lucky guy he was. They rested, ate some popcorn and sipped their cokes. They exchanged sweet kisses, as they ate and rested.

When the lights went out, they put away their cokes and popcorn and took up where they left off. They began, sitting next to each other and slid down into the seat. She parted her legs just enough to give his hand access to her thighs and beyond. Her hand was between his thighs, too. One of his hands, on a breast, his mouth and lips, and tongue, on the other, and his other hand massaging her vagina, over her jeans. One of her hands was on the back of his head, the other, massaging his member, over his jeans. They did that, until they could, barely, take it anymore and she maneuvered to allow him on top of her. Their passion lasted through the entire second show. As the credits rolled, she reached into the basket and retrieved her bra and put it on. He buttoned his shirt, as she buttoned hers. When they finished, they embraced and shared a sweet, tender kiss. As they got out of the back seat, he took the trash and dumped it in a barrel near the car. She had pushed her seat back into the position, so she could sit, comfortably on the way home. He opened the driver's door and repositioned his seat. He got in, started the car and returned the speaker, to its stand, closed the window and put the car in gear, and headed home. Sheb Wooley was on the radio the "Purple People Eater." He was followed by Chubby Checker and "The Twist." He was followed by Ernie K. Dow and "Mother In Law". He was glad that she must have achieved "satisfaction", but he was a "hurtin puppy." He knew that he would have to take matters into his own hand, when he got home. Still, it had been the best

Saturday, for him, in a long time. Karen put her arm around his shoulders and her head against his right shoulder and told him that this had been a wonderful Saturday. She wished they could spend every day like today.

He pulled up, in front of her house. They shared a good night kiss, in the car, and then he walked her to her front door. She told him that the "gang" was going to Nantasket, tomorrow. He said he would pick her up, after church. He promised his mom, he would go to church, in uniform. They shared another good night kiss and then she went inside. He drove home, listening to Chubby Checker and "Pony time" on the radio. Dion followed with "the Wanderer."

It didn't take him long, once he climbed into the bed, to reach sexual "satisfaction." Just remembering Karen's breasts and her passion, was enough. Sleep came easy, afterwards. He dreamt of the day, when he wouldn't need to "do things' himself. With Ree, he didn't need to.

He woke up to his mom's calling him, from downstairs. He got out of bed. Went into the bathroom and shaved and showered, and did the "other S." he went back to his room and put on a "fresh undershirt and shorts". H put on his uniform and grabbed a clean white hat. He went downstairs and had some toast and juice. He then went out and got into the Mercury and rode with his parents, to church. He was surprised to see Bert, there, too, with his folks. They surmised that their moms must have been talking. They hung around the 'coffee hour" afterwards and said their "hellos" and answered a lot of questions. They both had other places to be that afternoon, so, they told their folks they had to go home. He told Bert that he would see him later as he and his folks walked to the Mercury and headed home.

Once home, he changed out of his uniform, into a pair of chinos and a long sleeved polo shirt and his white bucs. He called Karen and told her that he was on his way. He arrived back at her house around 12:30PM. He stopped the car, in front of her house and got out and went up the walk, to her front door. Her mother answered his "ring." She reminded him that it was a school night and that Karen had to be home, by six. He assured her that she would, maybe earlier. Karen came up to him and took his arm. She was wearing a light blue short sleeve shirt and black Bermuda shorts. They walked, happily, to the car. They were going to meet the others around 1:30PM, at the main gate. They got into the car and he started it up. He told her that he had to get gas. She asked him to stop at a gas station that gave "S&H" green stamps. He did. They got to the main gate at 1: 32PM. Bert and the Fred and the girls were already there. He was still wearing his baseball cap. He looked at Bert and noticed his hair was growing back, at a good clip, better that his. They paid their admission and went in. The first ride Karen wanted to go on was "The Tunnel Of Love." They went on it three times. Each time, he had to wipe her lipstick from his face. They did not get as passionate as they had the night, before. The only ride he would not go on was the "cups." That was the ride that caused him to lose the contents of his stomach, the last time. He did manage to win her a large teddy bear. She was thrilled! They managed to do, almost everything the park had to offer. They left the park around 4:45PM. Karen was "beat." They said "good bye to the "gang" and headed back home, to Karen's. She fell asleep, with her head against his right shoulder, as he drove. She looked so sweet, next to him. He felt his heart swell with feelings for her. He woke her up as they pulled up in front of her house. He told her that he would pick her up, after school, Monday. They went up her walk and shared a sweet kiss, before she opened the door and was gone. He drove home, listening to "Running Scared' by Roy Orbison.

Once home, he realized that he, too, was tired. It had been quite a weekend. For some reason, as he sat, on his bed, he remembered the "passion" on that bed, with Ree. He decided that he better call her. He promised that he would, when he got home from basic training. He got off the bed and walked down the hall to the landing and the phone. He paused and tried hard to remember her phone number. He picked up the phone book and found her number and dialed. Her father answered on the third ring. When he asked for Ree, her father said "hello, Admiral, how are you??" he said "fine sir, and you?" "just fine" her father answered and then had him hold on. She came to the phone and "excitedly" said "Hi baby!" He said "hi". She asked when he got home and he lied and told her "last night." She told him that she would love to see him, but she was studying and could they meet for coffee or something, the next night. He said "sure" that he would love to see her, too. They made plans to get together around 6 Monday night. She asked him to wear his uniform. She wanted to see how he looked, in it. He said that he would. He planned up wearing it, anyway, so he wouldn't be mistaken for a student, in front of the school.

It was a tiring day, for him. Actually, an exhausting weekend. He got off the phone with Ree and decided to go to bed, early. He went down the hall, to his room. He checked his uniform, to make sure it was still clean enough, to wear. He turned on his radio, to hear The Flamingos and "I Only Have Eyes For You." He didn't mind the lyrics as much, but the "she bops she bops" between the lyrics drove him crazy.

He turned off the radio and lay back down on his bed. His mind ran "wild" with thoughts of Karen and Ree. He couldn't understand why he and Ree kept connecting. They, only corresponded twice, while he was in basic. Now, she wanted to see him. He had to admit, that he wanted to see her, as well. He could not figure out why. Other couples drifted apart and stayed apart. He had trouble, trying to do that with Ree. He wanted to move on and be with Karen, but something still cared, very deeply, for Ree. He got off the bed and got a pen and a piece of paper. He put both girl's names at the top and under each one, wrote "pros and cons." For Karen, under pros, he wrote, "cute, sweet, sexy, funny, made him feel good about himself; was deeply in love with him." For cons, he wrote, "still in high school, a little immature, virgin, may not be faithful to him." For Ree, the pros were, "very beautiful, very sexy, great sense of humor, seems to still love him, made him feel good, very passionate, first lover, same age and very mature, lot in common." The cons were, sometimes likes to be in control, has a temper, could be argumentative." He fell asleep on the top of the covers, with the sheet of paper, on his chest. He woke up around 2AM and got undressed and climbed back under the covers. It took him a long time to finally, fall asleep.

He woke up around 10:00 AM. His mind kept playing with the fact that he and Ree, just couldn't seem to close their relationship. Maybe, when they got together, that night, they would be able to. His relationship with Ree was far more serious than with Karen. But, then again, he and Karen, were still, in the "early" stages of their relationship. He remembered, one time, after he and Ree had made love, that she approached him and told him that her period was "late." He didn't even pause and told her that if she was pregnant, they would get married and, somehow, get through it all. That was how he much he loved her. He asked himself, if he and Karen have sex, and she gets pregnant, would he want to marry her. He found himself, having doubts about her and him. With Ree, there wasn't even the hint of not marrying her, but with Karen. He kept wondering why?

He, finally, crawled out of bed, slipped on an undershirt and jeans and went downstairs, to the kitchen. He made himself some toast and had a glass of milk. His mom was out. Probably shopping. He would run his dilemma past her. She was, always, able to help him, in the past. He knew that she liked Ree, very much and never said anything about Karen. He wondered why that was. He had just finished his "breakfast" when he heard the VW pull into the driveway and stop. He went upstairs and put on his sneakers and went back downstairs and out the back door, to help unload the groceries. When all the food was put away, he sat down at the kitchen table with his mom and told her about his problem. His mom was very "forthright". She told him how much she really liked Ree. She said her only concern with Karen was her "immaturity." He thanked her and went back upstairs to "spit shine" his Navy shoes. He had two pairs of dress shoes. One pair was for inspections, only. They were encased in plastic and beautifully shined. The other pair, the ones he wore, regularly, were the ones that he would shine. Once they were "done", he got a fresh pair of boxers, T-shirt, socks and took them, with him to the bathroom. He showered and shaved, put on fresh deodorant, Stetson cologne and attempted to "comb" his hair. It was growing back, just not fast enough, to suit him. He put on his uniform and white hat and went back down stairs. His mom asked why he put his uniform back on and he told her, so parents wouldn't think he was a student, picking up Karen. He went out the back door and down the stairs, out to the driveway and got into the VW. He headed for Karen's school. The Shirelles were on the radio with "Will you Still Love me, tomorrow?" Followed by Dwayne Eddy and "Rebel Rouser."

He pulled into the circle, in front of Karen's school and parked the VW. In the rearview mirror he saw three of them, get out of the cars and approach the car. As they got up to his side, he put on his white hat. He rolled down his window. The three "ladies" stopped walking and stared at him. Before they could speak, he told them that he only had two weeks leave and then he would be gone and they could have their spaces back. All three apologized and thanked him for his service and went back to their vehicles. He was never bothered again.

When Karen came out the front door of the school and got into the car, she was surprised that he was in uniform. He told her why. She laughed, as they headed out to Ho-Jo's. Jan and Dean were on the radio singing about "Dead Man's Curve." Followed by Jody Powers and "Midnight Mary." He turned down the radio, as she talked about her day, at school. She mentioned that they were invited to party on Saturday night. He said "okay." She wondered if he should wear his uniform, to the party. He said that he really didn't want to, but would, if she wanted him to. She said that she would think about it and let him know.

He pulled into the parking lot, behind the restaurant. They shared an embrace and lots of short, sweet, tender, kisses. They, finally, exited the car and went into the restaurant. He was hungry, but decided to eat 'light." He ordered a hot dog and fries and a coke. She ordered a frappe. She turned her attention, from her day at school, to him. "Have you thought, at all, about becoming an officer?" She asked. "police officer?" he asked. "No, silly, and officer in the Navy?" She said. "not really." He replied. "Officers make more money that enlisted guys." She stated. "Yeah," he said, "but the tour of duty lasts a lot longer. About six years, instead of just four." She asked him to look into it, at his next duty station. He said "okay". He couldn't eat all the French fries, so she ate half. As she was eating, she mentioned that next year was her last year, in high school. he almost choked on a fry. "What? But aren't you a Sophomore?" he asked. "No." She said. "Whatever gave you that idea?" He said "Fred." "Well!" She said, "Fred is wrong!" "Great!" he thought, to himself, more misinformation from the great Fred! Now, he began to understand where her line of questioning, was coming from. She told him that he was not really that much older than her. He began to wonder if she was hinting at marriage, by asking him to check into OCS? He began to get an "edgy" feeling. He was going back to college, after the Navy and marriage would not be an option, at this time. She was still talking, but his thoughts and concerns blocked her voice from his ears. She stopped talking and looked, at him. "Are you hearing anything I've been saying?" "I'm sorry." He said, "I was lost in thought about what you said about becoming an officer." "Oh!" She said. "Good!" Then, she told him that he wouldn't be able to meet her after school, the next day. Her mom was picking her up, to go shopping for some new clothes. She said, "Will you call me, tomorrow night, around 7?" he said "of course." They held hands across the table and continued their conversation. It was 4:45PM when they left the restaurant. He was in a bind, he had to meet Ree in about an hour. He drove Karen home, her head resting on his shoulder. Her perfume "wafted" around them.

He pulled up in front of her house and they shared three more sweet kisses. They got out of the car and walked hand in hand up the walk, to her door. They kissed, again, a longer one this time. He handed her books, to her and she gave him a kiss on the check and went inside. He walked very quickly back to the car, jumped in, started it up and headed home. It was after 5PM! He was glad that there weren't any cops around as he sped home. He got home, in record time. He had to get the scent of Karen's perfume, off his jumper. He sprayed some water on it, mixed with a little vinegar. His mom's idea. He went up to his room and found the bottle of Stetson and "splashed" it on his cheeks and his jumper. He went downstairs and his mom said that it was a little strong. He said 'good!". He looked at his watch, 5:25PM! He went out of the house and got into the car and headed for Ree's. Dion was on the radio with "Runaround Sue." He stopped, along the way, at an auto parts store and asked the clerk, for the strongest air freshener, he had. The got an "air wick", in the shape of a Pine tree, and hung it from the rear view mirror. He got to Ree's at 5:36PM.

He pulled up in front of her house. It felt very "strange" to him, to be 'there' again. He turned off the car and got out and put his white hat on and closed the door and walked up the walk to her front door. He rang the bell. Her little sister opened the door and looked at him, "Wow!" She said, "look at you!" Then he heard her mom's voice, "well don't let him stand there, bring him in!" She stepped aside as he entered the foyer. He had never been inside the Ree's house before. He was "ushered" into the living room. He took off his white hat and stood on the "shag" carpet. The living room was large with a good sized fireplace. There was a small couch, on each side, with a coffee table in front of each. Two large easy chairs, were on each side of a couch, facing in. her mom was sitting in one of the chairs. Her dad just got out of the other and came up to him and shook his hand. "Good to see you, again!" he said "You, too, sir." He stepped forward and her mom got up and came up to him and gave him a small hug, "hello." Her little sister exclaimed, "What happened to all your hair?" he knew he was blushing. "They cut it off, but it's slowly growing back." Her dad said, "yeah I remember that. Mine took abolut eight weeks, before I could start combing it again." "8 weeks!" he thought, "I hope not." They told him to sit down and tell them what it was like to be home. He was in the middle of telling them, how much he hated basic training, when he heard footsteps and a voice say "Hi sailor!" He stood up and turned to her. God, she was just as beautiful as ever!" her dark auburn hair was just over her small ears. Her lips were a bright red. She wore a dark blue jersey that really accentuated her breasts and gray Bermuda shorts. She came up to him and said that he looked really nice in uniform. He told her, that she was just as beautiful as ever! She look at her watch and said that they should be going. He said goodnight to them and they walked to the front door. He put on his white hat, she grabbed his hand, as they walked to the car. "God! I'm so glad to see you!" She said. "Me, too!" he said. He walked her to the passenger side and opened the door. She thanked him as she got into the car. He walked around to his side and opened the door and got in. He took off the hat. She said she liked his short hair. He looked at her, "you've got to be kidding!" He said. "No, I really like it, makes you look younger. Boy! Do we really need that air freshener?" She asked. "My mom left something in the car and I guess it went bad." He said. She said "oh." He started up the car and pulled away from the curb. Floyd Cramer was on the radio. playing "Last Date." He turned the radio off and they talked as he drove. She moved over next to him and put her arm around his shoulders and her hand on his right thigh. He smiled. She said that she hadn't been seeing anyone, since he left. That she was really busy with school. She ran her fingers over his short hair, on the back of his head. "I still love you, very much!" She said. He looked at her, for an instant and turned his eyes back to the road. "Do you think you could ever get your love back, for me?" She asked. Tears began to form at the bottom of his eyes. He said, "I want to love you, I really do!" He stopped at a red light. She turned his head to her and pressed her lips to his in a sweet kiss. He loved the taste of her lips on his. The light changed and he turned his head to the road. "Where are we going?" he asked. "Oh, right! "She said. The Italian place, downtown. "Okay!" he said. He pulled into the small parking lot next to the restaurant. He turned off the car and leaned over to pull up the emergency brake. Ree wrapped her arms around his neck and drew him to her lips, again. This kiss had some "passion" to it. He put his arms around her,too. Their kiss lasted a few minutes. They parted for a breath and he pulled up the brake. They got out and he locked the car. They walked hand in hand to the entrance and went inside.

In his mind, was total confusion. Could he, possibly, be in love with two girls, at the same time? They were shown to a small private table, with a tall lighted candle in the middle. He moved the candle, so he could look at her. She noticed how thin he had gotten. He told her that, he ate well, but all the physical "stuff' took the pounds off. She laughed and said that maybe she should join the Navy. He laughed and told her that she looked great and did not need to lose anything. She smiled and reached across the table and took his hands, with hers. They both ordered lasagna. He asked her why she had only written him two letters? Her answer was that she was very busy with school and her studies. He told her that he understood. He asked her if she would want his new address, at his new duty station? She said "of course." He told her that he was going to communications/intelligence school. The first one, in Maryland and the second one in Virginia. She asked if he was going to be able to get home, at all. He said that he hoped so. Their meals came and they made more "small talk" as they ate. They finished their meals with a cup of coffee and a cigarette. When they were done, they got up and walked outside, hand in hand. It was just beginning to get dark. She laid her head against his shoulder, as they walked. They got to the car and he, again, opened her door. She got in and moved over close to his seat. He got in and she thanked him, for dinner, with another long, lingering, passionate kiss. He felt a "stirring" and knew that if they went "parking", they would probably make love. When they parted their lips, she said, "I don't have to be home, for a while." "Good!" he said and asked "what about the drive in?" She said, "the movie has probably, already started." And added, "But who cares? "he started the car and headed for the drive in.

The got to the gate, just as the movies began. He paid the guy, at the gate, and drove to the very back row. He pulled up to the speaker stand. Ree leaned toward him and said, "we won't need the speaker." She got out her side and climbed into the back seat. He got out of his side and joined her. She reached forward for the lever on the passenger seat and pushed it and moved the passenger seat as forward as it would go. He did the same with the driver's seat. He turned to her. She had already taken her jersey off. He took of his tie and then the jumper, followed by the undershirt. He lay his clothes behind the backseat. They looked at each other and their eyes locked. They came together. Her arms encircled his waist as did his, to her waist. Their lips "fused' together, tongues searching tongues. His hands moved up to her back and her bra strap. He hadn't any trouble undoing it. Their naked chests rubbed together. He felt her nipples harden against him. She brought her hands from his waist to his pants. She swore as she undid his thirteen buttons. He lifted his hips, as she pulled his pants and shorts down over his knees. She unzipped her shorts and brought her shorts and panties down over her sneakers. They, completely naked, lunged at each other. Months of longing, overtook any reasoning. She pushed him down on the seat, her lips exploring his chest. He filled his hands with her hanging breasts. Her hand was stroking his, already stiff, member. "God! I hope you have something!" She said, huskily. He could barely talk, but managed to tell her, in his wallet. She let go of his member and searched for his wallet. She found it and searched through it and found two condoms. She tore open the package and brought her hand back to where it was. This time she rolled the condom over it, all the way down. her hand remained there, as her lips moved to his. She climbed on top of him and slowly sank down on him, impaling herself, on him. Her head came away from his, as her head tilted back. "Oh baby, it's been so long, so damn long, too long!" he put his hands on her breasts and massaged them. She leaned in, to give his lips and tongue access to her nipples. One hand massaged one breast and nipple, while his lips and tongue sucked and lashed the other. She began to thrust against him. Rising up and slamming down. She ran her hands through his 'fuzzy' hair, moaning and groaning as she "rode" him. He knew he wouldn't last too long. He brought his right hand down and put it between them and searched for her "nub". Once he found it, he began to massage it, as best he could. Her reactions told him that she would climax soon. He hoped she would 'go" first. He tried to control himself, but it was no use. She went wild on him! He exploded first and then, soon after, she screamed her climax and collapsed on top of him. He held the base of the condom to him. Eventually, she rolled off him. He straightened himself up, enough, to take off the condom. He leaned forward and rolled down the driver's window and threw the condom out, to the ground. There were no other cars around them. He rolled the window back up and sat back against the seat. They held each other tight and began to kiss each other. They began to slide off the seat.

He got off the seat and helped her lie down on the seat. He, then began to stroke her legs from her ankles, to her calves, up to her knees and up to her inner thighs. His lips followed his hands and fingers. He moved up to her wonderful "juncture". His hands moved back up to her breasts, as his tongue caressed her outer lips and slipped inside her. Her eyes were closed, her mouth open just a little. Moans of pleasure, escaped her mouth. Her hips began to gyrate. He brought the tip of his tongue up to her clitoris and gently lashed the end. "Oh my sweet baby" she moaned. His mouth and right hand, traded places. He slipped two fingers inside her as his lips and tongue gently "teased' and sucked on a nipple. He drew back and fumbled for the other condom. He found it and tore open the package. She drew herself up onto the seat. They began kissing each other, furiously! She took the condom from him and rolled it over his penis. She stroked him to "newness". Again, she mounted him and they, once again, repeated their "love making". This time, he made sure that she would "finish" first.

Once they were "done", he, again, disposed of the condom. He told her that he didn't have any more. She cuddled him real tight and said that she was "fine." He leaned down brought his rumpled bell bottoms and shorts back up to his waist, and buttoned them. She put on her panties and shorts and then her bra and jersey. He put on his dog tags, undershirt and jumper and tie. Once, they were both dressed. They hugged and kissed each other. Somehow they both knew that it would be a long time, before they would get together, again. She held him very tight, not wanting to let him go. He felt her tears and knew that his would be 'flowing" as well. He found himself saying, "I love you." She buried her face against his jumper. "If only, I could, really, believe you!" she cried. "I love you so very much!" They hugged and kissed, even as they lights came on for intermission. She looked at her watch and drying her eyes, said, 'we should go." They got out of the car and pushed their respective levers back. Got into the car. They kissed and hugged some more, right through the intermission. As the next movie started, he started the VW and they began to leave the "theater". She had both her arms around his neck, as they drove home. He left the radio turned off.

They pulled in front of her house. It was 10:15PM. She took out her "make up kit" from her purse and reapplied her mascara and lipstick. She asked him, if he could tell, if she had been crying. He turned on this dome light and looked at her and said "no." She asked him to call her, during the week and to please send her, his new address. He promised to do both. She said that he didn't have to walk her up the walk. He did anyway. They held each other tight, at the door. One last kiss and she went in. He walked back down the walk, to the car, and again, wondered if he was making the biggest mistake, of his life. He got in the car and started it and turned up the radio, Billy "Crash" Craddock was singing "One Last Kiss". He sang along, thinking that it was an appropriate song. After the song ended, he turned off the radio and drove home, in silence. One of the things that Ree hoped that he would do was go back to college, after his "hitch" was up. He asked her, if she would "wait' for him. She had asked him, not to ask her that. Four years was a long way off. She was realistic, when she said, "no one knows what is going to happen a few months, from now, let alone, years." He had to agree.

Karen, on the other hand, was "hinting" about the possibility of marriage. He kind of wished, Ree, was the one hinting about marriage.

He heaved a "heavy hearted" sigh and turned the radio back on. The Drifters were singing "Save The Last Dance For Me." They were followed by The Shirelles, "Will You Still Love Me Tomorrow." They were followed by The Regents and "Barbara Ann." As the song ended, he drove into his driveway and parked the VW for the night. At least, tonight, he didn't feel the "need" to pleasure himself. He went into the house, through the back door and up the stairs, to his room and took off the uniform. He made a "mental" note, to take it to the dry cleaners, tomorrow. He wouldn't be wearing it, again, until he had to leave.

He climbed into the bed and had a horrible time, trying to go to sleep. He tried to understand why Ree and he had made love, so quickly, after all the time, that passed between them. He wondered if he and Karen would ever make love. She sure was a passionate girl, but wasn't sure if she wanted to lose her virginity, just yet. But, she did want to lose it, to him. After what seemed like hours, he finally drifted off.

He woke up just a little after ten, the next morning. He didn't get up right away. It dawned on him, that he must be putting on some weight. The safety pin, holding up his bell bottoms had been off the pants, for since Sunday. He got up and went to the closet and looked at the back of the pants and noticed some "new" stitching. He threw on a pair of jeans and a shirt, sans shoes and socks and went downstairs. He sat down at the kitchen table. She was making scrambled eggs. He asked her about his Navy pants. She said that one morning, while he slept in, she came and got the pants and 'took them in'. he just smiled and thanked her. She handed him some scrambled eggs, toast and bacon and juice. She asked him what plans, he had for the day. He told her 'none". She said that Phil had told her that he needed to go to the Department of Motor Vehicles and get his driver's license stamped. He asked why? She said that they do that for the military, so they don't have to worry about getting it renewed, while in the service. He decided to call Bert and the two of them would go and do that. When he finished his breakfast, he went to the front hall phone and called Bert. Bert knew nothing about it. Apparently, all they had to do was show their military I.D. cards and get their licenses stamped. Bert had just finished eating and said that he would come by and pick him up.

They spent most of the rest of the morning, waiting to see someone, that could stamp the back of their drivers licenses. Seems everyone had picked the same day and time to go to the DMV. Finally, their numbers were called and they went to two separate people. He showed the woman, his military I.D. and she reached into her drawer and took his driver's license and turned it over and stamped it. He read the stamp and it "said" no expiration date until 6 months after discharge from the armed services," he asked her how much he owed her.

"nothing." It's a service we give to all servicemen and women." He thanked her and left the office. He met Bert, in the waiting room. They decided to go to the car hop, for lunch. Bert told him, that the woman, he saw, said if they had shown up in uniform, they would not have had to wait. He said that he didn't know that. Then, he remembered that he had to take his to the dry cleaners. On the way, to the car hop, Wayne Cochran was on the radio with "One Last Kiss." They both said how much they hated the "death" songs. Bert said the one he hated the most was "Tell Laura I love her." He agreed. Brenda Lee came on after the "death" song, with "Break It To Me Gently." Johnny Preston followed her with "Running Bear". Bert pulled the Golden Hawk into the lot, of the car hop. There weren't many cars, there. He pulled up to the front row. A roller skating waitress came up to the car and took their orders. Bert was going to South Carolina, for school. his school would last approximately 5 weeks. Bert asked him how he got into communications/intelligence. He said that he didn't know. They both took the same test, in basic. He told Bert that he hated him, because his hair was growing out faster than his. Bert just laughed. The waitress brought out their orders, took her money and skated away. She did not leave the tray, because they said that they didn't need it. As they ate, they both came to the realization that this would probably be the last time, they would see each other for awhile. They would write their parents and make sure each got the other's address, at the their schools. Bert asked him if he had been in contact with Ree. He told him that they went out to eat. He didn't tell him about the drive in. Bert asked if he still had feelings for Ree. He said that he did, but didn't think they would be together, because of her school and other things. She was a busy girl. Bert asked abpout Karen. He told him that Karen and he were going "strong", but he had a feeling she was leaning towards marriage and he just wasn't ready. "Marriage?" Bert said, almost choking on his burger. "you've got to be kidding?" Bert said. "Nope." He replied, "she wants me to apply for OCS, because officers make more money that enlisted." Bert asked him if he was going to apply. He said that he wasn't. Four years was going to be long enough, for him. Bert agreed. They finished their lunch and deposited the trash in the barrel as they drove out of the lot. When Bert dropped him off, at home, they shook hands and wished each other well and vowed to keep in touch.

He walked in the door and went upstairs and got his uniform and was going to take it to the dry cleaners, in town. He heard his mom, on the phone. He came downstairs and found that she was upset. He asked her what was wrong. She said his brother, Dave, had called and said that his wife was having a difficult pregnancy. That she might have to go to Virginia, to help. She knew his dad would not be happy about that. Then, she told him that his brother Phil and Nan were planning on getting married the end of May. She wanted to know if he could get away and be an usher. He said that he didn't know, but would let her know. He told her that he hoped all went well with the Dave and he wished he could help. She said that she would be okay. He left the house and got into the VW and drove to the dry cleaners. He could have the uniform back in three days. He took the slip and drove back home. Doris Day was on the radio with "Everybody Loves A Lover." She was followed by Kay Starr and "Rock And Roll Waltz." Who was followed by Theresa Brewer and "Old Fashioned Girl." He, then, realized that his mom had switched the dial, on the radio. he didn't bother to change it, even with Frank Sinatra singing "Love And Marriage." He parked the car, in front of the house and went inside.

He spent the rest of the afternoon, going through his seabag. He counted five pairs of black socks, five pairs of boxers, four white hats, his dress shoes, wrapped in plastic, for inspections, the other pair of black shoes, two "undress' blue uniforms and two white bellbottoms, two white jumpers and two white short sleeve shirts. he, also, had a black hat, with U.S.Navy on the front. He was told that he could not wear that hat, anymore. Of course, her asked "why not?" and was told "Regulations." He also found a blue baseball cap, a blue work jacket, four blue chambray shirts and four dungaree bellbottoms, a pair of boots, that needed to be shined, and the wool "watch cap" that he wore, during basic. He repacked all the clothes back into the seabag. He, then, sat on the bed and read his orders, from the manila envelope.

His time of departure was drawing near. He had one weekend left. He knew that he would not be seeing Ree, before he left. He hoped Karen would not mention OCS anymore. He would call Karen, after dinner and plan on picking her up, after school, for the rest of the week. He remembered the party, they were going to, on Friday. He would not wear his uniform. Their last "night" together would be Saturday night. He had to leave the following Saturday afternoon. The Navy provided him with a plane ticket to Baltimore, Maryland.

The rest of his two week "leave" went well. His mom did not have to go to Virginia, yet. He and Karen spent a lot of time, making out., especially, at her friend's party. They went to the drive in, that last Saturday night and they, again, failed to see any of the movies. They came very. Very, close to having sexual intercourse, but once again, Karen put on the "brakes." She promised that she would be ready "soon." The last Friday night, together, they went out to eat and then went parking. They spent most of the night, cuddling, kissing and embracing. Her tears flowed like a "waterfall." She was afraid that he would find someone else. He said that if she found someone else, to please not send him a "dear John" letter. He wouldn't be able to stand losing her. They made the "deal" and sealed it with a long, sweet, tender, lover's kiss. She would not go with him and his parents, to the airport. She did not want him to see her crying. He understood. They said their "goodbyes" on her front porch. He did tell her that Maryland was not that far away and that he would come back, as often as he could. She liked that.

He and his folks sat in the restaurant, at the airport. It felt good to be in his "clean" dress blue uniform. He was too nervous to eat anything, so he just sipped on a large coke. His dad looked around the restaurant and said that he hoped the guy, sitting at the corner table, wasn't going on his flight. He glanced over and recognized Jimmy Hoffa, from the news. He said, he hoped he wasn't either. Then, he heard a voice call his flight. He got up and, with his seabag, said goodbye to his folks and headed to the check in counter. He checked his seabag in and gave them his ticket and boarding pass and went through the gate. The plane was scheduled to arrive in Baltimore, at 8:00PM. This was his third time on a plane. He decided to try and sleep, the entire flight.

He did manage to get some sleep. He woke up, when the captain's voice said that they would be landing in Baltimore. After the plane landed, he went to baggage claim and picked up his seabag and walked out into the night air. He found a cab and asked the driver, how far Bainbridge was. The cabbie said that he would take him to the main gate for fifteen dollars. He didn't know any better, so he said "okay." The cabbie took his seabag and put it in the trunk and told him that he could ride up front with him, if he wanted to. He said "okay" and got into the cab. He did not realize how far Bainbridge was from Baltimore. He knew that he would never take a cab ride again, from that city. He arrived at the main gate, gave the cabbie his money and took his seabag out of the trunk of the cab and walked up to the gate. He handed the sailor, on guard duty, his orders. The sailor directed him to a building, a short distance away. He checked in at the desk. The sailor, on duty, had him sign in and then got another sailor to drive him to the barracks. When he got to the barracks, he handed another sailor, his orders and was directed to a "rack" and a locker. It was late. He was tired. He "stowed" his bag and uniform in the locker. He took the padlock off his seabag and put it on the locker. IN his "skivvies" he crawled up onto the top bunk and pulled the blanket over him.

He woke up, Sunday morning, to a lot of noise, around him. Rays of sunlight streaked in through the many windows, on the east side. He climbed down out of his "rack' and went to the, locker and put on the "slippers" his mom had given him. He got his "ditty" bag out of the seabag and went to find the head." He followed some other guys, who looked like they were going to the head. He found an empty sink and proceeded to shave and brush his teeth. He noticed the shower stalls did not have doors, or a shower curtain. That would take some getting used. Just like it did in high school, when everyone showered in the same large room. The toilets did not have doors, either. So much for privacy, he thought. When he came out of the head, he noticed that the others were in their" fatigues". He went ot "his" locker and unpacked his seabag and took out a pair of dungaree bell bottoms and a blue chambray shirt. Once dressed, he walked around the barracks, to familiarize himself with the place. He felt the pangs of hunger start to rumble in his stomach. He asked one guy, when "chow" was being served. The guy told him that the mess hall was closed on Sundays, but the "geedunk" was open. He would have to put on his undress blues, to go there. He went back to his locker and, once again, changed clothes. Once in his other uniform, he asked where the 'geedunk' was? The guy gave him the directions and he headed out of the barracks and up the road.

The "geedunk" was the Navy's name for a coffee shop. He found it and walked inside. There was a large counter and tables and chairs and a dance floor and a jukebox. The Marcels were on the jukebox with "Blue Moon." He walked up to the counter and sat down on a stool and looked at the menu. He ordered his "usual", two cheeseburgers, fries and a large coke. As his order was placed, in front of him of him, he was joined by two other guys. One on his left, the other on his right. They introduced themselves. They, too, had just arrived and were fresh out of boot camp, like him. One was named Stenberger. He was from Michigan. The other was James, from Ohio. After a short conversation, they discovered they were going to be in the same communications class. They took their "meals" and went and sat at a table. Stenberger had driven his 1958 Buick convertible from Michigan, to the base. He had to park it at the base parking lot near the main gate. The Jarmels were on the jukebox, with "A Little Bit of Soap." The three of them seem to "hit it off" right from the start. They would begin their first day of classes, that Monday. They would, also, get their addresses. He did not feel "like a fish out of water." They decided to go to the "rec" building and shoot some pool. One main "rule" they told him, was smoking was only allowed, inside and not outside. He put out the L&M, in the ashtray, as they left the "geedunk."

Communications school was a lot different than basic training. Even though, he had to march to classes and from classes to lunch, back to classes, and back to the barracks, after classes. He was "free" in the evenings, to do, as he pleased, as long as it was on base. During the week, he studied with Stenberger and James. Friday nights, after classes, they went to the E.M. club. Even though, he had plenty of money, there wasn't much to do around the base. Perryville was a "one horse" town. Havre Da Grace was another small town that hadn't grown in over one hundred years. It couldn't, because it had a river on one side of the main road and a large hills, on the other side of the road. Sometimes, he would go into Baltimore, or to Lancaster, Pennsylvania. Once, he and Stenberger rode to Washington D.C. Stenberger parked the car in a parking lot and they, both in uniform, walked along the streets. They had just turned a corner, when they met a couple of "girls". The "ladies" were very friendly and hooked their arms around his and Stenbergers. The four of them went for a drink in the "Rocket Room". They were seated at a booth. He 'sensed" something was not right, but he couldn't figure it out. His "girl" kept putting her arm around his shoulders and squeezing his thigh, the way Ree used to. Stenberger was really getting it "on" with his date. They wrapped their arms around each other and he watched as they 'frenched". Stenberger, then took his arm from the girl's waist and slipped it under the table. He had just raised his mug of beer, when Stenberger brought his hand from under the table and reared back and slugged his 'date' right in the mouth! Stenberger reached across the table, grabbed his arm and yanked him out of the booth, dragged him across the floor and out of the bar. Out on the sidewalk, Stenberger began spitting and spitting! He, finally, asked him, why he hit that girl?" GIRL?" Stenberger yelled," GIRL? They were MEN!" the two of them walked quickly to the parking lot and got into the Buick and headed back to Bainbridge. Stenberger made him take an oath, that he would not breathe a word of what happened, to anyone! He promised.

He received "love letters" from Karen every day. Even though, he gave Ree, his address, he never heard from her. He, soon, realized that "mail call" was THE most important time of the day, in the life of a serviceman. One day, he received four letters from Karen and one letter, from Andrea, Bert's friend. Andrea told him, that Karen was "fooling around" on him. He stared at the letter, in shock! That night, he went to the rec hall and called Karen. She was crying, as he asked her why? She said the guy meant nothing, that she was very lonely and would he please come home to her. She said that all she did was kiss the guy, on a dare, from Andrea and that nothing else happened. He wanted to believe her. He felt the tears build up in his eyes. He told her that he would be home, the next time he had liberty. He would call her and tell her when that would be. She kept telling him that she loved him and only him! He went back to the barracks and sat at the long wooden table in the center of the room. He went to his locker and took out the small Playboy calendar. He looked at the weekends. Memorial Day weekend was coming up. He went to talk with his class leader. Jackson was in charge of liberty cards. He asked Jackson when his next weekend, liberty would be. Jackson said, "matter of fact" everyone was getting a four day liberty that weekend. Four days! He was excited and went back to the calendar. He couldn't believe it! That was the coming weekend! Jackson had said that cards would be given out Thursday night, after chow. He told Stenberger he was going home. Stenberger told him, that, he realized they only had a 500 mile limit. He went to the map, on the wall, by Jackson's office. If he went home, he would be well beyond the 500 mile limit. He whispered to Stenberger that he didn't care. He went out of the barracks and back to the rec hall. He called Karen, again. He told her that he was coming home, that coming weekend! That he would, probably, be late Friday night. She said that she didn't care how late he was going to be! She, also, said that it being Memorial Day weekend, her family was going to be away for the whole weekend. He told her that his folks go up to the cottage, to open it up, that weekend, so they, too, would be away. She started crying and told him that she loved him so very much and was so sorry and that she would show him, how much she loved him. Then she said something that he didn't understand. She said "I'm ready for you, and only you!" They hung up, saying how much they couldn't wait to be in each other's arms again. He called his folks and told them that he was coming home that weekend. His mom said that she would leave the keys under the flower pot, by the back door. She asked if he was going to drive up to the lake. He said he wished he could, but that he was well over the limit, just going home. She understood. After the calls, he went into the pool section, lit up an L&M and joined Stenberger and James at a pool table.

The three of them left the recreation hall and went back to the barracks to go over the day's classes. He had a difficult time, concentrating. His mind kept picturing Karen making out with another guy. The picture tore at his soul. He began to wish that he and Ree, had stayed together. He felt that she would not have done it. Yet, Karen did not send him a "Dear John" letter. He was hurt and confused. He couldn't wait to get back home and see her face. He fell asleep, that night, staring at her picture. She looked so innocent and loving, sitting in front of the fireplace, in her living room, wearing a sweater and pleated skirt, with his ring, on the end of chain, around her neck. Her words of "undying love" written at the bottom of the picture.

He tried to "lose" himself in the next day's classes. It was difficult, but it kept his mind on the tasks, at hand. Thursday night, after chow, he got his liberty card. Stenberger said that he would drive him to the bus depot in Perryville. Stenberger whispered to him, that, he too, was going home. "To Michigan?" he asked. Stenberger said "why not?" He had not seen his girlfriend, for a long time, either. "besides, if I don't get any speeding tickets and obey myself, I'll be all right." He agreed and wished he had his own car.

Thursday morning, at reveille, they were told that, the day was uniform changing day. No more dress blues. Summer uniforms were the order of the day. He went to his locker and was happy that he had the foresight to get his dry cleaned. The pants and jumper was so "loaded' with starch, he had to slide his hand down inside the pants to open the legs. He had to slide his hands inside the jumper and the sleeves, to open them, as well. Once done, he hung the uniform on a hanger. He "dug" his black belt out of his seabag and took the brass buckle out of his "ditty" bag. It needed to be polished. He looked around the barracks. Most of the guys were "spit shining' their black dress shoes. His were still encased in the plastic. He asked Stenberger why everyone was working so hard on their shoes. Stenberger told him that they were having an inspection, that afternoon, after the noon mess. If he did not pass inspection, he would not have liberty. He asked Stenberger, if he had any brass polish. Stenberger gave him a small can. Stenberger asked if he could borrow his shoe polish. They made the exchange and he went and began polishing his buckle. He opened the plastic, after he had polished the buckle. He looked at his "inspection shoes." He looked close and could still see his "detailed" reflection, in the toes and backs. The pants would cover the tops and sides.

They marched from the barracks to the mess hall. He wore another white uniform and his regular shoes. Stenberger looked at him, over the table and told him that he would never pass inspection, in that uniform. He agreed and said that his inspection uniform was hanging in his locker. After lunch, they marched back to the barracks and were told to meet on the drill field, for inspection. He, quickly, changed into his "inspection uniform" and he and Stenberger went out of the barracks to the drill field. They joined the rest of the class and Jackson had them line up in two rows, facing West. They stood an arms length apart, at ease. He was in the second row and was still able to see the gray car with the Admiral flags, drive up. They were going to be inspected by a full Admiral! Jackson stood in front of the class and as the Admiral approached, yelled "Attention on Deck!" They all went from "at ease" to full attention. As the Admiral and his aide walked along, in front of the first line. He watched, in horror, as the sailor, in front of him. Lifted his right leg and buffed his right shoe against his white bell bottoms. He put that leg back down and did the same thing with his left leg. The Admiral must have seen him. He walked up to the "hapless" sailor and asked him what uniform he was wearing. He heard the sailor say "Oh shit!" "Yes indeed!" said the Admiral, as he looked behind the sailor, at the black smudges on the bottom of his whites. The Admiral asked the sailor, if he had another pair of whites, in his locker, that he could wear, for the weekend. The sailor said, "Yes sir!" The Admiral said "good. Put them on, before you leave the base tomorrow." The sailor, showed a sign of huge relief and told the Admiral he would and thanked him. He began to sweat, as the Admiral came up and along the line, he was in. The Admiral stopped in front of Stenberger and asked where he was from. Stenberger told him. The Admiral said that it was too bad Michigan was so far away. The Admiral came to him and looked at him, for the longest time. He thought his liberty was doomed. He stepped back and turned and looked at the sailor, in front of him. He turned back to him and asked him if he saw the sailor, in front, buff his shoes? He said in a weak voice, that he had. The Admiral asked him what went through his mind, when he saw the sailor do it. He said that he wished he could have stepped out of line and stopped him. The Admiral said "good." He went down the line, looking at the rest of the class, the n he and his aide walked back towards the car. He stopped and wished them all a good and safe liberty. He, then, surprised them saying. That classes would resume at 0800 Wednesday morning. He gulped and thought, "wow! Just got another whole day!" The Admiral left and Jackson dismissed them and said, "liberty will commence at 0700 tomorrow. All of them let out a large "whoop!" Stenberger came up to him and said, "Did you hear that, we got another whole day off!"

When he woke up and went to the head, he had to wait for a "free" sink. Afterwards, he had to wait for a "free" stall. Finally, all three 'S's were taken care of. He went back to his locker and pit on all "fresh clothes, except his shoes. His inspection shoes went back into the plastic wrapping, and into this locker. He looked in his wallet and counted his money. He had more than enough for the trip North. His hair was long enough, to comb, now, that made him happy. Stenberger was just about ready. He didn't have to wait too long, for him. When Stenberger was ready, he checked around his rack and his locker and made sure everything was put away. He and Stenberger walked out of the barracks and headed for the main gate, parking lot. It was 8:30AM, by the time they got to the Buick. They got in and drove to the gate. They showed the guard their liberty cards and I.D. cards and drove on out. He was in the Perryville bus station in ten minutes. He bought a bus ticket, for Port Authority, New York City. He was a little disappointed that the next bus wouldn't be there until 9:45AM.

Since he and Stenberger hadn't had chow, he sat at the counter, in the station, and ordered breakfast. When he had finished, he spent the rest of the time, reading magazines. As he finished, the last magazine, he opened his "ditty" bag and reached for his pack of L&M's. he found two packs of condoms! Each one had three in it. There was a note from Stenberger, "Happy Memorial Day". He laughed, as he thought, to himself, "if he was heading home to Ree, he would probably use all of them, but not with Karen. He took two packs pout and put them in his wallet. He, then, took out the pack of L&M's and put them in his breast pocket, of his jumper. He just lit up one, when the guy, behind the counter, announced the arrival of his bus. He closed up the "ditty" bag and got up out of his seat and headed outside, to the bus. He handed the driver, his ticket. The driver stamped it and he got on board and found a window seat. There weren't a lot of people on the bus. He liked that. After about five minutes, the driver got on and closed the door and started the bus. He was headed home! He figured that they would get to New York City around one, in the afternoon, Wrong! The bus was going into Baltimore, first. Then, would go on to New York. He was not too happy. He would have to find a way to call Karen and let her know that he would be a little bit later than he thought.

The traffic, getting into Baltimore was very heavy. It was stop and go, for quite a while. They, finally got to the bus station. But, the bus wasn't leaving, again, for twenty minutes. He got off the bus and ran to a public phone and, though he knew Karen would be at school, he would leave a message with her mom, or whoever else might be "home". He heard the phone ring and then Karen answered! He told her, he was on his way, but it would probably be more like 9 o'clock before he would be there. He, then, asked why she was home? She took a "sick day", to get ready for him. He told her, that the Admiral had given him an 'extra" day off. That he didn't have to be back until Wednesday morning. Karen was thrilled to hear that. He told her that he loved her and would see her that night. She told him that she would pray that the bus would "fly" him to her. They hung up and he went back and got on the bus.

He got back into his seat, just as more passengers boarded. He hoped that no one would sit next to him. An old man took the seat, next to him. He wore a "funny looking" wide brim, black hat. He had long "stringy "hair where his sideburns should have been. As the bus backed up and headed for New York City, the old man took out a large bag of peanuts and began cracking shells and eating the peanuts, inside. He stretched his head above the back of the seat, to see if they were any vacant seats he could switch to. There weren't any, the bus was filled to capacity. He heaved a huge sigh and pulled his white hat down over his eyes and tried to get some sleep. It wasn't easy, with the old man cracking the peanut shells.

Traffic was even heavier, getting into New York City. The bus, finally, pulled into Port Authority at 4:35PM. The driver said that "all passengers going further, to Boston, would have to go to gate 12." He heaved another huge sigh and got off the bus. He hoped that the old man was not going to Boston. He hurried to gate 12 and saw that there was a long line, waiting to board the bus. He got in line behind a young girl, who looked like she was going home, from college, for the weekend. The dark windows, to his right, acted like a mirror. He checked himself out, to make sure he didn't look too "disheveled". A soldier was behind him and behind them was an Air Force guy. While he was looking, his eyes caught hold of "them". An MP, SP and an AP, walking towards them. They were all military police! His heart sank deep into his chest. He felt nausea overcome him. If they wanted to see his liberty card, he would be arrested and sent back to Bainbridge. He would not be with Karen, for the weekend! He stared into the dark glass. The cops went to the Air force guy and he heard them ask for his papers. His knees went weak! He couldn't believe he got this far, only to be turned around, at the last minute. Just then, the driver called "all aboard for Boston". The line moved quickly. He practically pushed the girl, in front of him. He got to the driver and got his ticket stamped and, practically, jumped onto the bus and found the first empty seat and plopped himself down. He was "bathed' in sweat! He looked out the window, of the bus, into the terminal, and saw the cops escorting the Air force guy away. He breathed a huge sigh of relief! The soldier, who had been standing behind him, sat down in the seat, next to him and asked if he was all right? He said, "yeah." The soldier said that he noticed when the cops came, he turned as white as his uniform. He explained that he was only well over the 500 mile limit, on his liberty card. The soldier whistled and told him that he was lucky. He agreed. The bus backed up and then headed out of Port Authority, bound for Boston. With any luck, he thought, he would be home by at least 10PM.

The last "leg' of the trip was far more pleasant than the first one. Both he and the soldier "napped". He woke up, when he felt the bus stop. He looked out the window and saw that they had stopped by a Ho-Jo's. The driver told them that they had a twenty minute "rest stop" before heading into Boston. He got off the bus and lit up an L&M. he asked the driver what time they might get into Boston. The driver told him that he couldn't take the Mass Pike all the way in because of construction, that he would have to go onto Route 128, to Route 9, to get into Boston. He asked the driver, that when he got to Newton, on Route 9, if he could stop and let him off, as he lived in Newton. The driver asked him, if he had any luggage under the bus. He told him that he didn't. The driver told him, to let him know ahead of time, and he would let him off. He thanked the driver and went and got a "cold' sandwich and a coke. He was reaslly getting excited! He looked at his watch and realized that he should be in Karen's arms, by 10 PM.

He was too excited, to sleep! His eyes were "peeled" on the road, through the bus's windshield. Once they were on route 9, he looked for "Echo bridge". He saw it coming up and he got up out of his seat and went to the driver and told him to please let him off, right after the bridge. The driver did so. He thanked the driver and got off the bus. The bus pulled away and he began to walk along Chestnut street to his home. He hadn't walked very far, when he noticed a black Ford pull up alongside him. He kept on walking, not wanting to look at the car. Then the driver of the car, honked his horn. He stopped and went to the car and looked in the window, it was Fred! He opened the door and jumped into the passenger seat. They shook hands and asked each other what they were doing out this hour of the night? Fred was heading home a date. He told him that he was home, for the weekend. Fred dropped him off at his house. Fred wanted to double date, sometime over the weekend. He wanted to be alone with Karen, so he lied, and told Fred that they were going to the cottage. Before, he got out of the car, he gave Fred his address.

Once, he was home, he ran down the driveway, to the back porch, up the stairs, and got the keys out of the flower pot. He opened the back door, went into the kitchen and to the phone, in the hall. He called Karen. A sleepy voice answered the phone, "Where are you?" She asked. "home! I'm on my way!" he said. "Don't change! Just get over here!" She demanded, "and park in the driveway, behind the house." "okay!" he said, "on my way!" He picked up his "ditty "bag and went out the back door, locking it behind him. He went down the stairs, to the driveway and unlocked the VW and got in and started it up and headed for Karen's.

As he approached her house, he turned off the headlights and the motor, and 'coasted "onto the driveway. He stopped just before the garage doors. He got out of the car, locked it, and with "ditty' bag, in hand. He walked to the back door. It was locked. He looked in the door window. The house was dark. He wondered if she had gone back to sleep. He walked around the farmer's porch, to the front door. He looked in the living room window and noticed a small light. He went to the front door and knocked. He heard her voice say "get in here!" he opened the door. The front hall was dark, except for the light, emanating from the living room. He stepped into the living room and stopped, dropping his "ditty" bag on the floor. He couldn't believe his eyes! She was standing in the center, of the room, wearing a sheer, see—through "teddy". She had placed a blanket on the living room floor. The light, from the table lamp, in the corner, of the room, shown through her 'garment" as if she was naked! The light outlined her ample breasts, showing the dark tip. His eyes followed down and saw that the light illuminated that dark patch between her legs. He gasped! and went to her. She moved towards him. He was quicker. Their arms embraced each other. Their lips met in a soft, sensual kiss. He could feel every inch of her beautiful body against him. Lips explored lips, as their passion increased. His hands roamed over her back, down to her buttocks, tops of her legs, her thighs, then up her sides, to the sides of her breasts. Her hands rubbed his back. Their lips parted, but neither said a word. He stepped back and removed his tie, jumper, and undershirt. He stepped to her, again. She moaned as they embraced, again. His lips went to her neck. She rubbed her hands through his "grown back" hair. His lips left her neck and trailed down to her shoulders and then to the tops of her breasts. She brought her hands down to his belt buckle and undid it. He stepped back, once again and stepped out of his bell bottoms. He, sat down, on the blanket and took off his shoes and socks. She was all over his back, as he took them off. She was on her knees, behind him, her arms around him, her hands on his chest, rubbing him. She pressed her breasts to his naked back. All he had on were his boxers. He turned around and they fell to the blanket, face to face, arms around each other, lips on lips. He gently, lay her on her back. His right hand went to her legs, just above her knees and began to massage first one and then the other. She parted her legs, as his hand moved up. His left hand and arm cradled her the back of her neck. They began to kiss harder and longer! Tongues swirled against each other, lips 'fused' together. She wasn't wearing any underwear, under the teddy. His hand moved farther up and began to lightly stroke her pubic hairs. She moaned through their kisses. His fingers caressed her outer lips and then, gently probed her "entrance". Her hands left his back and guided his head to her heaving breasts. He kissed each one over the thin fabric of the teddy. She began to squirm and move her hips against his probing finger. Her hands left his head and moved down his back to his buttocks. She moved her hands under the fabric and squeezed and massaged his cheeks. She was dampening his probing finger. Her moans grew louder and louder! She brought her hands out from his 'rear' to the waistband of his shorts and started to push the shorts off him. She sat up just enough for his left hand to help her remove her teddy. He, then, lay on his back and removed the last of his clothing. She went wild as his finger returned to its "treasure". His lips and left hand to her breasts. She moaned, "I'm ready to be yours!" he removed his finger, from her, and with his hand, "fished "around, for his wallet and once he found it, extracted one of the condoms from it. With both hands, he tore open the package and rolled the condom all the way down his shaft. With the condom, "safely attached", he went back to his "foreplay." Her beautiful body "shined" in the dim light. She parted her legs, even more. Her hands went to his manhood. She stroked it. He crushed his lips to hers, their tongues swirling against each other. His hands massaging her "taught" nipples. He moved to her. She guided him in, slowly. He felt her hands let go of him as he started to enter. He knew it was her first time and he didn't want to hurt her. He moved, slowly, as he continued his entrance. He was in a good way, when he felt her "hymen". She began to moan louder. He asked if she was okay. Her lips "tightlipped", she nodded "yes." He began to move against her. He looked into her eyes. He could tell she was in pain. He stopped and "rested". He asked if she was still in pain? She murmured "no". he began to push again. She cried out! He stopped. There were tears in her eyes, but she urged him on. He gave another gentle push. She screamed and clamped her teeth against his shoulder, giving him extreme pain, as well. He pushed again and felt her teeth dig in even more! One more push and he no longer felt resistance! Her hymen had been "breached". He stopped pushing and waited for her 'pain" to subside. After what seemed like an eternity, she released her teeth from his right shoulder and began to kiss it, "better". He began to slowly thrust forward and back. At first, she just lay beneath him, like a "limp rag". Soon, his thrusts began to awaken 'something' in her and she began to math his thrusts. "Oh My God!" She screamed! He stopped and asked if he was still hurting her? She yelled "NO!, don't stop!" His hands returned to her breasts and nipples. He brought his lips to hers as they found a rhythm!

Their tempo increased! She was thrusting harder and harder, against him. They were locked together in paradise! He brought one of his hands, down between them and managed to find her clitoris. He began to massage it! She went absolutely wild! "Oh God, Oh God!" She yelled "Oh Honey!" She gave one final push against him, bringing her hips off the blanket covered floor. Her whole body went limp, underneath him. He began to increase his thrusts against her. It didn't take long for him to "finish." They lay together, him still on top, for a few minutes. She finally released her 'hold" on him and he rolled off her. He made sure that the condom was still on him. In a weak voice, she asked him, "why did we wait so long?" He asked her, if she were all right and, if her "first time' was okay? "Okay? Okay?" Honey, it was wonderful! Very painful, at first, but once the pain was gone, it was fantastic! He smiled. She asked him, if she was a good lover? He told her she was a wonderful lover! She leaned over and their lips met in a soft, sensual manner. When she lay, back down. He told her that he had to use the bathroom. She told him where it was. She asked him to bring her a towel. He disposed of the condom and brought her a towel. She asked him not to look at her, as she placed the towel, between her legs. She got up and went to the bathroom. She was in there a while. She came out and told him that she had bled some, but not as much as she expected to. She said her girlfriends told her that she would bleed like the first day of her period. They both decided that every girl is different. They cuddled together. She had found a damp spot on the blanket and put another towel over it. They lay in each other's arms and, almost fell asleep. She reached over and began to caress his manhood. "Can we do it again?" She asked. He told her that if she kept touching him, like she was doing, it wouldn't take long. "good," She said. "I like to touch you" she said. "I enjoy touching you, too." He said. He couldn't believe that "they" had made love. It was completely unsuspected. He told her what a wonderful surprise, it was. Her touch was beginning to 'work". He leaned on his left side and ran his right hand up her left leg, beyond her knew and upward. She opened her legs to give him access. He leaned his lips to hers. The kiss started off, as a soft, sensual kiss and grew into pure passion! She maneuvered her back against his chest. He brought his lips to her back. His left hand snaked around her side and cupped her left breast. "I love your hands on me and in me." She said, huskily. Her hand increased its strokes on him. His finger slipped back inside and explored in a circular motion. She repositioned herself, so his lips and tongue could work "their magic" on one breast, while his other hand massaged the other one and his finger could continue its exploration. She was reacting to him and her legs began to tremble. He brought his finger out, just enough, to join his thumb at her clitoris. She really began to moan and groan! His hips began to react to her manipulations. He brought his hand away and searched around them, for the other condom. It took a little while, but he found it. She released him and asked him, if she could put it on. He groaned "yes." She, slowly, rolled it down, stroking as she did it. He fell on his back. She turned and climbed on top of him, lowering herself onto him, impaling herself. She leaned in on him, giving his lips, tongue and hands access to her hanging, heaving, breasts. She began to "ride "him, as if he were a bucking bronco, in a rodeo! They rolled around on the blanket, sharing different positions. Her on top, then, him and then, back to her. All the time, he managed to stay inside. Again, when he was on top, he brought his hand, between them and found her clitoris and massaged her to another "finish." When he knew she was "done", he began to thrust harder and faster than before. Grunts, groans, moans, and some other sounds, he was unfamiliar, with escaped her mouth. They were as one, as he, finally came to a conclusion.

They lay close to each other, after he rolled off her. Her eyes were closed, her breathing, a little ragged, a big smile on her face. They had no idea what time it was; they didn't really care. He, finally, told her, that he had to dispose of the condom. He got up and went to the bathroom. She chose to stay on the blanket. He cleaned himself, with tissue paper, in the bathroom. He did, finally, check his watch. It read 1:45AM! He went back into the living room and lay down beside her. They wrapped their arms around each other. His face against hers, their bodies tightly entwined. They napped for a while. When they awoke, the dawn of a new day made its way through the living room windows and 'splashed" across the floor on their naked bodies. She, slowly, opened her eyes and looked at him and kissed his eyes open. "You better get dressed and move the car around to the front of the house. Drive it around the block and park it." He understood. She didn't want the neighbors to know that he had been there all night. He got up and put his uniform, back on and walked out the back. He got into the car and rolled it down her driveway, into the street. He started it up and drove it around the block and parked in front. She had taken the time, to throw on a pair of Bermuda shorts and a jersey. She came out the front door and ran down the walk and got into the car. She had his "ditty" bag in her hand. As she got in the car, she threw it onto the back seat. She leaned into him and wrapped her arms around his neck and gave him a "good morning" kiss. Afterwards she said, "I'm hungry, can we get something to eat?" he said, "of course!" They decided to drive back to his house, so, he could change clothes and 'freshen up." She wanted to "freshen up" too. She had put her toothbrush and other things in his "ditty' bag. She, also, noticed that he had four more condoms. She asked him, if he knew they were going to make love? He said that he had no idea. That a friend, of his, in the barracks, gave them to him, as a present. She told him to be sure and thank him, when he got back.

He pulled into the driveway, of his house, and down behind the back of the house. They got out of the car. He carried his "ditty" bag, in one hand and held her with the other. They went up the back stairs and into the house. Karen said she really would like to shower. He said that he could use one, too. Their eyes locked! He took her by the hand and they ascended the stairs, to the upstairs bathroom. He showed her how to start the shower. He went to his bedroom and took off his whites and hung the jumper and bell bottoms in his closet. He walked back to the bathroom, with only his "skivvies' on. She had already "shed' her clothes and was in the shower. "Save some water, for me!" He said. She opened the shower curtain and said "you better join me!" he was out of his shorts, in a New York minute! He took the soap and began to apply it to her. He started with her back, then her lower back, to her buttocks and her thighs, down her legs and back up. Water cascaded over them! She turned around and he applied the soap to her face, neck, down to her shoulders, then her breasts, spending considerable time, on each one and each nipple, then to her stomach and down to her pubic region, which until the weekend, had really been "off limits." He spent considerable time "there" as well. Then down her thighs, and legs. He even soaped her feet. He came up and handed her the soap. Her eyes were half closed, her nostrils 'flared"; her breath, ragged! In a, lusty, voice, she said, "my turn." She did exactly as he had done. First his back, all the way down to his feet and back up. He turned around and she started on his face, to his neck, chest, stomach, pubic area and she spent a lot of time, on his penis, creating another 'erection". She left his penis and soaped his thighs, then legs, ankles and feet and came back up to his penis. "I think it wants to have some fun!' She said, huskily. They rinsed themselves off and stepped out of the shower. He leaned in and turned off the water. He got a large bath towel and began to dry her off. He followed the same "procedure" as the "soaping." He could see that she was getting more and more excited! Then she dried him off, the same way. She picked up her clothes and he picked up the "ditty" bag. They walked, quickly, to his bedroom. He took the last condom of the first three pack and put it on the night stand, as Karen lay on her back, on the bed. He stood, by the bed, and looked at her. Even with her damp hair, she was absolutely gorgeous! He told her so. She opened her arms to her and they made love for the third time. Each time, she got wilder and wilder! He disposed of the condom, in the toilet. They brushed their teeth together over the bathroom sink and, then got dressed, to go and get something to eat. Another milestone had been reached. Taking a shower with a girl and, actually knowing, that he was her "first" real lover. The best part of this milestone, was that he appeared to do it "right". That he listened to her and did his best to keep her pain, at a minimum.

They drove to Ho-Jo's, for breakfast. Neil Sedaka was on the radio with "Hey Little Devil." He was followed by Bobby Vee and "Devil or Angel." He was followed by The Marvellettes and "Please Mr. Postman". He pulled into the parking lot. He turned off the cat, they got out, and he locked the car. They walked hand in hand, into the restaurant. They both ordered large breakfasts. They held hands over the table, waiting for their orders. Karen got a "pensive" look, on her face. He asked her if she was all right. She asked him, "Now, that we've taken our, love to the ultimate step, are you still in love with me? "He looked into her eyes and held her hands very tight and told her, "Now, more than ever!" She smiled. "I love you, with my whole heart and now, with my whole body!" She said. "Me,too!" he said, "we are one and I pray that we will be "one" forever!" She grasped his hands and said, "Me, too." Their orders arrived and they ate, in silence.

Breakfast over, they drove back to his house. They sat on the couch, in the den, and started to watch TV. They cuddled real close and put their arms around each other. Karen asked him where his little bag was. "Upstairs." He said. "Maybe you should go and get it, just in case."

He looked at her and she grinned at him. He jumped off the couch and went upstairs, to his room and retrieved the bag. When he came back, downstairs, to the den. She was lying on her back on the couch. Her legs were open just enough. The top of her shorts were undone and her bra was lying on the seat of one of the easy chairs. She gave him a very seductive look! She raised her jersey and revealed the bottom of her breasts. She kept raising her jersey, slowly. He, quickly, stripped off his shirt and jeans and joined her on the couch. They made love, for the fourth time. She was out of control with her passion. They ended up on the floor, rolling around, legs, arms, entwined and lips, feverishly locked! He, barely, found a "break" to put the condom on.

When they had both "finished", they lay on the carpeted floor, of the den, completely exhausted! He rolled onto his side, away from her and took off the condom and put it on the small towel, he had brought with him, when he went and got the bag. He rolled back towards her. They lay, side by side, her hand resting on his manhood; his hand cupping one of her breasts. He was beginning to think he 'created" a sex maniac, a sexual "monster". He asked himself, if she would be able to control her urges for sex, while he was away? He wanted to ask her, but was afraid of the answer. She gave him the answer, without him having to ask her. "How many of those "things' have you left?" She asked. "Two," he replied. "can you buy some more?" She asked. He said, "think so." "Good!" she said, "If we make love, up to Monday night, I should be 'good" until you come home, again." He looked at her and said, "I don't want to even imagine you with someone else!" She said, "Don't worry, honey, I don't think there will ever, ever be anyone who could hold a candle to you, when it comes to making love." He smiled and prayed, to himself, that he hoped she was right. As they lay, there, on the carpet, her fingers began to have an effect on him. "Hmmm, looks like "someone" wants to have a party." She said. He groaned, "you're impossible." She giggled, "No, I just love you so very much. If I wear you out, then you won't go looking for another girl, while you're away. I want you to remember this weekend, until you come home again. I want you to come home, often." He told her that he would try and get home, as much as he could. He asked her if she would consider, letting him kiss her "all over"? She replied, "you mean?" "uh huh" he replied. "Why would you want to kiss me there?" he said, "I think you would really enjoy it." She said, matter of factly, "I don't think so!" he said "okay." She, then, asked "would you want me to kiss you there, too?" He replied, "only, if you would want to.' She said that she would have to think about it. He said "okay."

It didn't take long for her, to get 'him" ready, once again. They made love, once again. He wondered if they set some kind of record, five times, in less than twenty four hours. He just knew that he had nothing "left". They realized that it must be time for lunch, because stomachs were growling. They got up off the floor. She "freshened "up first and then he went into the downstairs bathroom and did the same. They got dressed and went out to the VW and got in. He started it up and they pulled away from the curb. They decided on Chinese food, for lunch. She knew of a restaurant in Newtonville. They headed for it.Fats Domino was on the radio with, "Blueberry Hill." Followed by The Temptations and "Barbara". He would later find out, from a D.J. that they were a white groups from Long Island and not confused with the Temptations of the 70's. They were followed by Joe Jones and "You Talk Too Much."

He pulled the VW into a small parking lot in front of the restaurant. He turned off the car and they got out. He locked the car and they went in. They were shown to a corner booth. They both ordered tea and they got a large "Poo Poo platter", which they shared. She apologized about only getting him a card, for his birthday. He told her that he didn't expect anything, but wanted to get her more than just a card, too. He told her about the cake, his mom had sent him. When he opened it, all that was left was a "pink blob" with what looked like candles around it. He had to call her and ask her what it was supposed to be. He couldn't stop laughing when she told him. He was glad the money ($50.00) made it through. Karen thought that was really funny! He had an idea. When they finished eating, he was going to get her, her birthday gift. One, that he wanted to get her, for a long time. She asked," what was it?" He said "never mind, you'll have to wait a while." She gave him her "pretty little pout". It used to make him give in to her, but not this time. She told him, that she wanted to get him a gift, too. They decided to drive out to "Shoppers World."

They left the restaurant, full of food, and headed out to the mall. She kept trying to guess her gift. He wouldn't budge! She even tried "twenty questions." That didn't work, either. He, turned it around and asked her what his gift was. She refused to tell him, too. When they got to the mall, the parking lot was "loaded" he drove around and around. He was making his second "pass" when Karen saw a car's break lights come on. He stopped the VW! Sure enough, a car was backing out of a space. He waited and when the car drove away, he pulled in. They did not have very far to walk. He told her that whenever he had to go somewhere, like a mall, he was going to bring her with him. She said "You better!" he turned off the car, they got out, he locked the car and they met in front of the car and walked to the mall entrance, hand in hand. God! It felt so good to him, to be in love and to be loved!

They walked into the mall and looked at the many shops. He, finally, found the one he wanted. A jewelry store! She gave him a "funny" look. He thought that she might think he was buying her an engagement ring! They walked up to a counter and began looking into the cases. A man came up, to them, behind the counter and asked if he could help them. He asked him about "Clatter Rings". Karen stared at him! "I've always wanted one! I love Clatter Rings! The man brought out a tray and showed it to them. He told her to pick out the one she liked the best. She saw one that she, absolutely adored! The man picked it out of the tray and showed it to her. It was solid silver! He asked the man to "size" her finger. He did so. The man, then said, that today was their "lucky day". Everything in the store was 25% off! When

Karen heard the price, she tried to tell him, that it was too expensive! Both she and the clerk were surprised, when he withdrew the money, from his wallet. The man put his hand up and stopped him and said that he would go and see if they had one, in her size, in stock. Karen asked him, "where did you get the money?" He told her that they only thing he spent his 'service pay" on was cigarettes and toiletries. She grabbed his arm and squeezed it! The clerk came back with a small velvet box. He opened it and showed them the ring. He asked her, if she wanted to have it gift wrapped? She said "no, I'll wear it." She took the ring and put it on the third finger of her left hand. There were tears in her eyes, as he handed the clerk the cash. He left to get him a receipt. She looked at him and told him that she couldn't possibly match his gift. He told her that he didn't expect her to. He whispered in her ear, "You gave your complete self, to me. That in itself was the best gift of all." They left the store. She couldn't stop looking at the ring. She loved the way the lighting made it 'sparkle". They were walking by a perfume shop, when she grabbed his arm and made him stop. They turned and went inside. She went up the aisle that had men's cologne. She found the bottle of English Leather. He liked the wooden top on it. They went to the counter, with it. She, also, got a discount. She paid the clerk and handed him the bag with his cologne. The girl, behind the counter asked him, if he ever used it before. He said "no". She had a small spray bottle and told him to hold out his hand. She sprayed a little, on the back of his hand. He brought his hand, to his nose. "Wow! That's nice!" Karen was pleased. They went out of the store. He said that they needed to make one more stop, before they went back to either her house or his. "Yours!" She said. They walked out of the mall and to the car. Once inside the car, she drew his lips to hers and they kissed for a while. He noticed, when the drew apart, that there was a car, waiting for their 'spot'. As he backed out and drove out of mall parking lot, she kept holding her ring, up to the sun light and turning it on her finger. She said "I still can't believe that you bought this for me!" He answered, "Honey, you deserved it!" I wanted to get you one last Christmas. She was still wearing the cross and his high school ring. A "nagging" thought came to him. He wondered if she was wearing his ring and the cross, when she kissed that other guy. He shook his head, to get rid of that thought. She was with him and said she really loved him and would be true to him, forever!

They drove to the town, that had the drugstore, where Fred bought his condoms. He parked the car, in front of the store and said that it would be best, if she waited in the car. She said "okay" with a smirk on her face. She knew what he was going to buy. He was only gone a few minutes and came back out with a small paper bag, in his hand. He got back in the car and put the bag, on the floor, at her feet. She leaned down, to look inside the bag, as he backed the car out of the parking space and headed home. "Do these things come in different sizes?" She asked. He said he didn't know, but he supposed so. She asked him what size he got? He told her extra large! They both laughed. She said" that's better than petite!" They laughed again. He said that he hoped that his size was good for her. She said that he was "perfect." He smiled and turned up the radio. Jimmy Bowen was on the radio with "Party Girl", followed by Elvis and "Don't". He was followed by Link Ray and "Rumble." Link was followed by David Rose and his orchestra with "The Stripper." Karen said that maybe she would do a strip tease for him. He told her that he would really like that. She said that he would have to do "one" for her. He laughed and said that wouldn't be much of a "tease". He said, "you girls have a lot more to work with, to get a guy "worked up." She agreed.

It was just after 4PM, when they arrived back, at his house. He parked the car, back down behind the back of the house and they went in the back door. Karen had to use the rest room. He went into the den and put the contents of the white paper bag, in his "ditty" bag. He heard the phone ring. He went to the phone, in the front hall and picked it up. It was his mom! She said that she had been trying to reach him, all afternoon. He said that he was at Karen's. She told him that she and his dad really missed him! But, she knew what he meant about not going any further, than he had to. She, also, told him that Phil and Nan were there and that there probably wasn't any place for him to sleep, anyway. Then it hit him! "Weren't they supposed to be married this weekend?" "They couldn't get the church, because of the holiday." She said. "It's been moved to the third weekend in June. I hope you can get it off." He told her that he would try. His mom told him that his brother Dave would be driving in from Virginia and would pick him up at the main gate, that Friday. He told her that he would put in for it, when he got back. She said 'good". She, then, asked, "Why are you home, now?" he told her that he came back to change, that he and Karen were going to the movies. "Okay, well, I'll let you go. Call us, if you need anything, we love you, bye." "love you, too, bye". Karen was standing next to him, when he hung up the phone. "I was really tempted to start stripping, while you were on the phone." She said. "Oh yeah!" he said, "My mom would have loved that!" They laughed and hugged! She said, that while he was on the phone, she checked the fridge and found plenty of food and soft drinks. He told her that there were bags of chips in one of the cabinets, too. She said that she could make them some sandwiches, or burgers, or hot dogs, for supper. He said that he did not expect her to do anything like that, while he was home. She said that she would like to do that, for her man. He liked the sound of that "her man."

He told her that he was thinking of ordering a pizza. She gave him that "pout" again and he caved in! "Okay! You want to rustle us up some grub, then, fine!" "Okay, cowboy!" She said. "But first, I want some sugar!" She took him, by his hand, into the den. She picked up his "ditty" bag and they went up the stairs to his bedroom. "Surely", he thought, "six times, must be some sort of record! Talk about another milestone!"

They finally came out of his bedroom about 7:30PM. He was really dragging! He went into the bathroom and disposed of another condom. Their love making was really growing in intensity! He hoped that they would just crash and sleep, that night. When he came out of the bathroom, she was already in the kitchen, making their supper. She was boiling hot dogs and had out the hot dog rolls and chips and cokes. As they ate, she said that she really should go home, in case her folks called, to check up on her. He said that he understood. She wished they could sleep together. He said, "me, too." Then it "hit" her! Her folks would never call her, after nine PM! If he took her home, after they ate, she could clean up her house and then would call him, after nine and he could come over and pick her up and they could spend the night, together! He told her that there was a little "larceny" in her. "Don't you want to spend the night, together? "She asked. "More than ever!" he replied. "Good!" She said.

They finished eating and he drove her home. She gave him a soft tender kiss, at her front door and told him, again, she would call, as soon as she hung up from them. He told her he would be waiting, buy the phone. He drove home, a happy, but "drained" sailor. He couldn't believe the weekend, he was having. Never, in his wildest dreams, did he imagine that she would be so sexual! She couldn't get enough of him! And vice versa! Elvis was on the radio with "Surrender." He sang along and then turned the radio off.

When he got home, he set about "straightening" up the house. He made sure all the condom "wrappers" were buried deep into the trash barrels, out by the back door. He threw any and all towels that may have been "used' into the washing machine, in the basement. He couldn't believe that he might be sleeping with Karen. He hadn't slept with anyone, since Ree. Once, he was satisfied that the house looked good. He went into the basement and put the towels in the dryer and started it. He, then, went back upstairs, to the kitchen and found the opened bag of chips; grabbed a coke, out of the fridge and went into the den and turned on the TV. He caught the tail end of "Bonanza" and was hallway through "The Tall Man" when Karen called. She had just got off the phone with her folks. They were planning on being home, sometime, on Monday. That meant that they had all day Sunday and Sunday night. She told him to "come and get me." He hung up the phone and turned off the TV. He went into the basement and took the towels out of the dryer and brought them to the upstairs bathroom. He went downstairs and out the front door, to where the parked the VW. He got in, turned it on and headed to Karen's.

She was standing on her porch, by the front door, when he pulled up in front. He didn't even have time to turn off the motor and get out of the car. She ran down the walk, with a small overnight bag, in her hand. When she got to the car, she opened the door, jumped in and tossed her bag, into the back seat. She wrapped her arms around his neck and gave him a big kiss. When she withdrew, he put the car, through her forward gears, and headed back to his house. When he shifted into the last forward gear, she took his right hand and put it between her legs. She sat close enough, to him, to put her left hand, between his legs. "So much for a good night's, sleep." He thought. Tommy Roe was on the radio with "Sheila." Followed by Neil Sedaka and "Calender Girl".

Once again, he pulled the "bug" down the driveway and parked behind the house. He turned off the car, got out and reached into the back seat and got her bag. They both ran up the back stairs and into the kitchen, through the front hall and up the stairs, to his bedroom. He dropped her bag on the floor. She was ahead of him. She turned around and faced him. They walked towards each other. They embraced and shared a long sensuous kiss! Their hands caressed each other's backs as their kisses grew in intensity. They unbuttoned each other's shirts as they continued to kiss. Shirts off, he unfastened her bra. She moved her hands up to her shoulders and 'shrugged' the straps off. The cups fell to the floor. He filled his hands with her breasts. They moved slowly to his bed. When the backs of her knees reached the edge of the bed. She reached down and unbuckled his pants, unzipped his pants and 'tore open" the top button. With both hands, she stripped his pants and shorts, from him. He did the same with her Bermuda shorts and panties. Once naked, they, slowly, fell onto the bed, still kissing.

When their lips parted, he lowered his lips and tongue to her breasts. Her hands seeked out and found his manhood. She must have seen the wrapped condom on the bed stand. Before he knew it, she had unwrapped it and rolled it all the way down his member. He began to lower his head downward, but her hands stopped him and guided him back to her breasts. He did bring his hand and fingers to her pubic region and continued to move inside and "probe". It didn't take her long to get wet. She rolled him over onto his back and crawled on top and guided him "home." They made love, again, for the seventh time. This time, after he disposed of the condom, they fell asleep, like two naked 'spoons." Somewhere in the night, one of them, pulled the bedspread over them. His arms were around her and his hands cupped her breasts.

He woke up, to her stroking him, softly and slowly. He was on his back. Her head was very close to his "head". She seemed to be examining him. He moved his hand underneath her and found her vagina and with his right hand, massaged and probed her very "being". She turned and face him and leaned in towards him and pressed her lips to him. It didn't take her long to get him "aroused." When their lips parted, he gasped, "ditty' bag. She showed him her left hand. In it was an unwrapped condom. The bedspread had been removed from on top of them. She was breathing heavy. He wondered how long she had been awake and "ministering" to him. She, again, rolled the condom over and down "him". She, once again, climbed on top of him and straddled his waist, lowering herself down on top of him. She leaned forward and gave his hands, lips and tongue access to her hanging breasts. As she moved, he wondered just how much more, he could take? Would she, always, be like this? She was like a child, discovering a brand new 'toy" and wouldn't leave "it" alone. Once again, he brought his fingers to her clitoris and massage her to "completion." He raised his hips and began his thrusts. It didn't take him long. She rolled off him and he got up and went and disposed of the condom. He went back and lay down next to her. They wrapped their arms around each other and cuddled. She murmured that she would never let him go, that she loved him, so very, very, much! He told her that she was his world! His everything! That, he, too, would never ever leave her! They lay cuddled tightly against each other for quite a while. They both whispered, together, that hunger was taking over their bodies. They got off the bed and got dressed. She admitted that she felt "soreness" between her legs. He said that he, too, felt some discomfort. They admitted that they better give each other some "rest." They went into the bathroom and brushed their teeth together. She kicked him out of the bathroom, so she could 'use' it. He went downstairs and used the one, by his folk's bedroom. They met at the foot of the stairs and decided to go and get some breakfast.

They drove, again, to Ho-Jo's. She laid her head against his shoulder, as he drove them to the restaurant. He pulled into the parking lot and they got out of the car. He locked it and they walked, to the front entrance, with an arm around each other's waist. Being a Sunday, the place was packed with people! They waited, for a short time, and then were shown to a booth. They sat side by side. They were looking at a menu, when he heard a voice. He looked up and it was Fred! He was with Kathy! They sat down opposite him and Karen. Fred assumed that he and Karen had just got back from New Hampshire. He lied and said "yeah, we wanted to beat tomorrow's traffic." He told them, that he had to leave Monday afternoon. Fred and Kathy decided to join them, for breakfast. Fred had just started a new job as manager of a new motel. Kathy still worked at a bank. Karen said that she was ending her junior year, in high school. Fred asked them, what they were doing for the rest of the day? He didn't think Karen would appreciate it, if he told them, that they were waiting for the 'soreness" to go away, so they could make love, one more time. So, he said that they were thinking of going to the beach, but thought better of it, because the beach would be crowded. Fred said that he could arrange for the four of them to relax by the motel pool, for the afternoon. Karen looked at him; he looked at her. They said "great!" He said that they would have to meet Fred and Kathy, there. He left his good bathing suit, at the cottage. Karen said she wanted to go home, first. Fred and Kathy said that would be good, so they could go and get their suits. They made plans to pick up their, suits, as they ate and would meet at the motel, in an hour. They paid for their breakfasts and went out to the parking lot.

Once in the car, Karen said that she really didn't care for each of them, but the pool sounded nice. He said that he didn't know Kathy, that well, but that he agreed, as much as he wanted to spend the rest of the day, alone with her, perhaps they could have fun and cool off, at the same time. She leaned in and pressed her lips to his cheek and said "I don't want to cool off. I want to get hot, very hot with you!" That caused a 'stirring' where he really didn't need a 'stirring' at that time. He told her that, just looking at her, in a bathing suit, would probably make him stay in the cool water, of a pool, just so no one would know what he was thinking of. Karen laughed and asked him, if it would help, if she were in the water, with him. He said "No! that would probably make it worse." She laughed.

They drove to her house; she got out of the car, ran up the walk and in the front door. She was back inside of three minutes. They drove to his house. Fred said they could change in the motel's rest rooms. He left her, in the car, and ran up the back stairs and up to his room and got his suit. He was back in two minutes. They drove to the motel. Fred showed them where the restrooms were and they went in and changed. When she came out and joined him, at the pool, he jumped in the cold water! She was absolutely beautiful! She wore a white one piece suit that did little to the imagination. It accentuated her breasts and legs and buttocks, as if she had nothing on! She was the center of attention, of every guy, young and old, at the pool! She "knew' the effect, he had on him, when she saw he leap into the water. She found an empty chaise lounge and lay down on it. He, quickly, got out of the water and lay down on the chaise lounge, next to her! There was very little space between each lounge. They leaned in and their lips met in a long, soft sensuous kiss. Afterwards, they leaned back on the lounges and 'soaked" up the sun's rays. Fred and Kathy joined them. Fred pulled up a lounge, next to him and Kathy was next to Fred. Kathy wasn't any "slouch" in a bathing suit, either. She wore a green two piece that left very little to the imagination. Fred leaned over to him and said, "How's it feel to be the envy of every man and teenage boy at the pool?" He said, "We should be angry, but I'm not, are you?" Fred said "nope!" He leaned back to Karen and asked her how it felt to have guys mentally undress her? She said "the only one that I care about is you!" She, then, said, "and what about you? A lot of women and girl's eyes are on you, as well." He said, "they are?" "honey, your flat stomach and rippling muscles, with your light brown wavy hair are driving them mad!" "You're kidding?" he asked. "Nope!" She said. They both smiled and laid back against the back of the chaise lounges. He asked her, if her suit were to get wet, would it reveal too much? She said, "we'll never know. I'm not going to get it wet." He replied, "good." Kathy and Fred got off their lounges and went into the water. Fred tried to coax them in, but they declined. They both closed their eyes and took well deserved naps.

It was around three o'clock, in the afternoon. They both opened their eyes and notice that the pool area was practically empty. Fred and Kathy were seated at the bar, at the far end of the pool area. He looked around and noticed that there weren't any guys at the pool. They decided to go in the water and cool off. They went down the steps, at the shallow end and waded into the deeper part. They immersed themselves into the cool, clear, blue water. They swam around a little and she asked him to 'duck" down and let her know, if the suit was "revealing." He went under the surface and opened his eyes. The suit was clinging to every part of her, but did not "reveal" her nipples nor her pubic area. He came back up and reported. She asked him to get out of the pool, before her and bring her a towel, when she climbed up the ladder. He swam away and climbed out. He went to the chaise and got her beach towel and brought it to her. She swam over to the ladder and climbed out. He, immediately, wrapped the towel around her. They went back to the chaise and lay down, she kept the towel around her.

Fred and Kathy came over to them and wanted to know if they wanted to go and get something to eat. It was well past lunch time. They said "sure." He got off his chaise, first and then helped her off her lounge chair. They went back to the restrooms and changed back into street clothes. They met Fred and Kathy in the lounge and as they sipped on cokes, decided where to go to eat. Fred knew of a great 'steak house' down the road. He said the food was great and inexpensive. They finished their cokes and headed out. Fred thought they would go in one car, but he told Fred they would follow him, because Karen's folks would be worried, if they stayed out longer. Fred and Kathy agreed. They got into the VW and proceeded to follow Fred. Chubby Checker was on the radio with "The Twist." Followed by Buddy Holly and "Maybe Baby" he was followed by the Everly Brothers and "I Wonder If I Care As Much." They were followed by The Marvellettes and "Please Mister Postman."

They pulled into the parking lot of the steak house and walked hand in hand to front entrance. They were escorted to a corner table. A waitress came up to them and they gave her their orders. Fred and Kathy asked him all kinds of questions about the Navy. Kathy asked Karen, what she had planned to do, after high school? Karen said that she would find a job and work for a couple of years and then, hopefully, get married and settle down. He swallowed his coke very fast! His eyes began to water! This was the first time that the word "marriage" had entered into their conversation. She gave him a "hurt" expression. He said that when he got out of the service, he would go back to college and that it might be tough, for the two of them, but that they would make it work. Fred looked at him and said, "Then, it's official, you two are going to tie the knot? They both nodded "yes." He said that he and Kathy were talking about it, too. Kathy said, in jest, "We could have a double wedding!" Karen looked at him and he said "maybe." Their orders arrived and he and Karen ate "theirs" as if they hadn't eaten in months. "You two must be real hungry!" Kathy said. They made "small talk" as they ate.

Once finished, he asked for the check. Fred and Kathy were still eating. He looked at his watch. He thanked Fred for letting them use the pool and said that they really had to be leaving. Fred asked him to call him, before he went back. He said that he would and they left. They practically ran to the VW and got in and left the parking lot, in a hurry. They headed back to his house. Elvis was on the radio with "Stuck On You." He sang along and looked at her, from time to time, to let her know that he was 'stuck' on her.

As they drove, she took his right hand and put it between her thighs. She put her hand between his and traced "him" with her fingers, as he massaged her. She asked him, if he was still sore. He said that it didn't feel as if it were. She opened her legs and unzipped her "fly" and he gently slid his fingers over her pubic hair and inside her. He asked if she was still sore. "No!" She moaned. "Oh honey, you are making me very warm, very, very, warm." She groaned. "Oh God!"

He grunted! He stepped on the gas and hoped that there weren't any cops between where they were and his house. Their hands were still "busy" as he drove down the driveway, to the back of the house. They jumped out of the car, as he turned it off, slammed both doors, and ran up the back stairs, through the kitchen, up the stairs, down the hall, to his room. Clothes were "flying off them, as they ran. They only slowed down to take off shorts, pants and underwear, and shoes. They both landed on the bed, in his room, with only their socks on.

Hands, arms, legs, lips, tongues were all over each other. They were on fire! He only stopped, to get a condom and unwrap it and slip it on. She stroked him, slowly as he "slowly probed" her. His other hand and his mouth, lips and tongue "made love" to her breasts. They both sensed that this was the last time, this weekend, that they would be able to "make love". They took their time and savored each other. She still was not ready for "oral." He didn't really care! They were "lost" in each other's arms. No one else existed in their world!

It was well after 8PM, when they, totally exhausted, got dressed and left his house. He would have to open his windows, when he got back, from taking her home. The "scent" of "sex" permeated his room. He would check the den, too. Now, they were really sore! They walked "gingerly" down the stairs, out through his kitchen and out the back door. They slowly, got into the VW and he drove her home. As they pulled up to the front of her house. Troy Shondell was on the radio with "This Time". They got out of the car. He carried her towel, bathing suit and small overnight bag with them, as they made their way up the walk to her door. He told her that his brother was getting married the end of June and that he would be back. She was, of course, invited to the wedding. She said, "That's only four weeks! I should be over my "soreness" by then!" "God, honey, I hope so!" They laughed. She hoped that they could still see each other Monday, even though their families would be home. He would call her. They shared a long, wet, passionate kiss, 'good night." They both said that they would miss holding each other through the night. He handed her, her things. She turned and unlocked the door and went inside. He turned and walked down the walk, to the VW. He got in and started it up and made a "mental note" to get gas, on the way, home.

He was exhausted! But, he managed to go through the house and make sure that all was the way he found it, before he and Karen were there. When he felt, all was okay, he went upstairs and crawled into bed. Her "scent" was all over the bed. He "felt" as if she was still with him. He would have to wash the bed sheets and bedspread in the morning. He left the windows "open" in the bathrooms and the den and his bedroom. He hoped that the scent of "sex" would dissipate before his folks got home.

He woke up 'early" the next morning and, again, went through the house. The "scent" was gone from the upstairs bathroom. He went back to his room and 'stripped" his bed and carried sheet, pillow cases and the bedspread down to the basement and put them in the washer. He put in the soap and started the washer. He went back upstairs, to the first bathroom and closed the window. The den still had an "odor". He found a bottle of "Air Wick" and put it in the den, with the wick up, as far as it would go. He went upstairs and found a bottle in the upstairs bathroom and put it in his room, with the wick up as far as it would go. He, then, went back to his bedroom and put on an old pair of jeans and a T-shirt, socks and sneakers and went down to the kitchen and was ready to make himself some breakfast. It was ten after eight. His folks wouldn't be home until after noon. He went to the phone and called Karen. A "sleepy" voice answered the phone. "How about breakfast?" he asked. "What?" She asked, "You want me to come over there and make you breakfast?" "No!" he laughed, "How about I pick you up and we go and get some breakfast?" She was awake and said, "give me about twenty minutes, honey!" he said "okay". They hung up. He went to the basement and put the wet things in the dryer and turned it on. He went back upstairs, to the den. The "scent' had dissipated. He closed the Air Wick bottle and put it back in the bathroom cabinet. He went back upstairs, to his bedroom and took a 'deep" breath. There was still a "hint" of sexual activity, in the room. He left the bottle open and the windows, too. He went into the bathroom and 'freshened up". He, then, went downstairs and out the back door and got into the VW and drove over to pick up Karen.

When he pulled up in front of her house, she walked, very slowly, to the car. He could tell she was still sore. He felt bad for her. "Aren't you sore?" She asked. "A little bit." He replied. They shared a short, sweet, good morning kiss. As he drove to the restaurant, she said "You are a sex maniac!" he laughed and told her, all she had to do was say "no." She laughed and said "Now, you tell me!" She laid her head against his shoulder, as he drove.

They each had another large breakfast. Afterwards, they settled back, in their seats, and sipped their coffees and enjoyed an L&M. She looked at him, as she exhaled, and told him that she hoped the next four weeks would "fly by." "of course, if I'm still sore, it won't matter much.

She said. He told her that he was sorry, for her 'soreness". She said that it was okay and that it reminded her of the wonderful weekend, they had.

He dropped her off at her house and walked her up to the front door. They shared another deep, sweet "lover's kiss." She still had to "clean up "the house, before her family got home. He said that he did, too. They kissed and embraced each other and she turned and went into the house. He walked back to the VW and got in and drove home. Bobby Vee was on the radio, singing, "Take Good Care Of My Baby."

When he got home, he took the sheets, pillowcase and bedspread out of the dryer and went back to his room. He took another deep breath. The only "scent" was the air wick. He made the bed and capped the air wick and put it back in the bathroom cabinet. He made another "check" of the house. Everything checked out! He sat down on the back porch and lit up another L&M and closed his eyes and thought about his "fantastic" girlfriend and the "great" weekend, they had together. A weekend, that was not anticipated. It all started with her and that see through teddy. She had planned it all. He was glad that he was able to make her first time as less painful as possible. Just as he put out the cigarette, he heard the Mercury pull down into the driveway. He got up and went down the stairs, to greet his folks. Phil and Nan pulled into next to the Mercury. He got to greet, them, too.

He helped them with their bags. His mom said that they could make their own sandwiches, for lunch. She asked him what he had eaten. He told her that he had some sandwiches and hot dogs and chips, that he and Fred had been together, most of the time and had eaten "out". They were sitting on the back porch, talking, when Nan gestured to him, to comer into the living room. She was holding a lipstick, in her hand. She told him that it wasn't hers and that she noticed it under the bathtub. "You might want to give this to Karen, before you have to go back." She said, with a smile. He, sheepishly, took it and said "thanks." She said that she wouldn't say anything, that it was their "secret." Again, he thanked her. When he called her that night, after 6, he told her that Nan had found her lipstick, in the downstairs bathroom. "Oh honey, I am so sorry. I've been looking all over for it!" He said, he could bring it over, if she really needed it. She didn't think that would be a good idea. She asked him to hold onto it and bring it with him, when he returned, in four weeks. He said that he would. She said that the only one, she would wear lipstick for, was him, anyway. They said good night and good bye over the phone.

He, again, woke up early, that Tuesday morning. His mom had been in his closet and told him that she was washing his uniform and would iron it. He asked if she washed his white hat, as well. She said, "of course." He checked his "ditty' bag and made sure the remaining condoms were well hidden, in the bottom of the bag. His bottle of English leather was in an upright position, so none would spill. He went to the bathroom and put his toothbrush, toothpaste, deodorant and shaving gear along with his Brylcreem and comb and brushes, back into the bag. He kept out the shoe polish and began to spit shine his shoes.

He and his uniform were ready. He had a couple of peanut butter sandwiches and some chips and a coke, for lunch. After which, he went to his room, and got dressed back into his uniform. His mom and Phil drove him to the bus depot, in Newton. He was taking the two o' clock bus, back. He told his mom that he would put in for early liberty, that Friday, in June, so Dave could pick him up and they could get back, for the rehearsal and rehearsal dinner. "Don't forget to invite Karen and give her enough time, if she wants to buy a dress. He promised!

He boarded the bus and took a window seat, after he showed the driver, his ticket. He went to wave good bye, from the window, but the VW had already left the parking lot. He settled back and closed his eyes and took a nap. It would be a five hour ride to Port Authority in New York City. He smiled, as his thoughts drifted back to the past weekend. It felt so good, to be loved and to be "in love."

He saw Jackson, the next morning, at muster and told him the 'circumstances" for an early liberty in June. Jackson made him a "deal." They needed another "hand" on the waxing and buffing crew, in the school buildings. If he joined the crew, he could have 'early liberty" every weekend. He jumped on! Jackson thanked him and he started that night, after the evening mess. They had two floors and every classroom floor, to do, every night. They would get through around 8:30PM and still have time to study. Stenberger joined the crew, too.

He called home the next Saturday and told his mother, that it was all set for the wedding! She was happy. He, then, called Karen and told her, too. She, too, was happy and said that she was feeling much better. He was very happy about that,too. She told him that she found just the dress, for the wedding. He told her that if she needed any help, with the money, for it, to let him know and he would "wire "it to her. Again, they expressed their love for each other. He hung up and walked back to the barracks, to write his "daily" love letter, to her.

He and Stenberger had become good friends. Seems Stenberger had gotten engaged over the Memorial Day Liberty. He congratulated him and wished them well. Stenberger asked him if he found his "presents" that he had left for him, in his 'ditty" bag. He replied that he had and had to purchase more. They, both laughed and thanked the Navy for the extended liberty!

The next four weeks consisted of intense studying. He and Stenberger studied hard and passed all the tests. They were told that they would be going into "intelligence training, the end of July, if they continued to work as hard as they were. He had to take the June 23rd test on Thursday, the 22nd. Because he had the early liberty on the 23rd. he wouldn't know the results, of the test, until the following Monday.

He got up, at the sound of reveille, that Friday. He ran to head and completed the three "S's" and got back to his locker and dressed into dress whites. He packed his "ditty" bag and remembered Karen's lipstick and, of course, the condoms, along with his 'toiletries.' He got to the Main gate, with liberty card, in hand, at exactly 7:30AM. He had missed "morning chow". His brother was not there. He started to pace around. Finally, at 7:45AM, Dave showed up in a gray, 1961 Chevrolet Stationwagon. He jumped in, said "hi" and they took off down the road, and headed North. Dave had, always been so cool, so calm, so "collected". Now, he was practically shaking, he was so nervous and worried about his wife and the upcoming birth of his first child. He had never seen his brother, like this! It worried him! Dave said that he needed to stop and get gas. He began looking for the cheapest gas. Dave asked him, if he had any money. He said that he did. Dave said "good! You can help with the gas and take care of your own food!" He replied, "okay!" They stopped for gas and something to eat, just before entering the New Jersey Turnpike. They wouldn't stop, again, until Connecticut. Dave was making him nervous, as well. All he did was talk about how his wife's pregnancy wasn't going well. He felt for him, and thought that if it were him, he would feel the same way.

It was 3:45PM, when they stopped and gassed up and had a sandwich and something, to drink. They had to be at the church, for rehearsal, by 6PM. He told Dave, they had plenty of time to spare. Dave didn't care. He stayed five to ten miles over the speed limit. He thought that they were sure to get "pulled over". They didn't! They arrived at the house at 5:15PM. There was 'bedlam" in the house! He was beginning to become a "nervous wreck" just being around everyone. He went to the phone and called Karen. She wanted to know what to wear to the church and the rehearsal dinner. He put her on "hold" and went and asked his mom. She said any dress would do. He came back and told her. She said that she could be ready in ten minutes. He told her that he had her lipstick and was on his way, to get her. He got the keys to the VW and told his mom, that he and Karen would meet them at the church. She said "okay." When he pulled up in front of her house, she was walking towards him on the walk. She didn't look like she was feeling "sore" anymore. He jumped out and opened the door, for her and she got into the passenger's side. He walked around the front of the car and got in. They shared a long, sweet kiss and embrace! He handed her, the lipstick. She turned the rearview mirror, to her and applied her lipstick. She turned the mirror, back to him and he readjusted it. He looked at his watch, they had about ten minutes to get to the church. He got there, with time to spare. He parked the car, in the church parking lot and they got out. Karen asked him, if she looked all right and he told her she was absolutely beautiful, in her flowery sundress. He couldn't wait until they could be alone. They walked hand in hand into the church. Everyone was there, but Nan and her parents! His mother was pacing around with Dave! He thought to himself, "what a pair!" he and Karen sat in a pew, in the back of the church and held hands. Finally, the bride and her folks arrived at 6:10PM. They lined up for the rehearsal. All he had to do was ask people, friend of the bride or groom. It was, also, his "job" to usher his mom and dad, and Karen.

He would not be able to sit with her. He had to stand with the other ushers and bridesmaids. There wasn't a bridesmaid that could hold a candle to Karen. He told her that. He was, also, instructed to watch the back of the best man's feet, when they would walk down the aisle. This was to be another major milestone, in his life. He had never been a part of a wedding, before.

The rehearsal didn't take long. It was over by 6:30PM. His dad said they had to hurry to the Pillar House, for the rehearsal dinner. The reservation for a private room, was for 7 PM. He and Karen got back into the VW and, again, embraced and shared a deeper, more sensual kiss than the one before. The rehearsal dinner was quite extravagant! His dad had gone all out! Before the food arrived, his dad stood up and made a champagne toast, to the bride and groom. Everyone sipped the champagne, except his brother Dave. He gulped it down, like water! He and Karen decided that they didn't really care for the taste of champagne. The dinner was nice, with lots of jokes and laughter. He looked at his watch, it read 8:30PM. He asked Karen if she was done eating. She laughed and said "no, I might want to eat my cigarette!" Oh" he said and then noticed she put it out. He announced that he was tired and that he was taking Karen home. His mom said, "Don't be too late, you have to get your tuxedo in the morning. "He replied that he knew. They said good night and that they would see everyone the next day. They walked out of the restaurant and headed to the VW. Karen said that they could have stayed and sampled more champagne. He stopped and looked at her. "Are you serious? Do you really want to go back in?" She said, of course not!" She dragged him by the arm across the parking lot, to the VW. The sun was just settling, in the West, when they arrived at the DFA.

He parked the car and looked around. There weren't too many cars there, yet. They got out of the car and climbed into the backseat, after he had set the emergency brake and put the car in reverse gear. She lifted her hips and said "wait a minute." She rolled a large garment down her legs; her stockings came with it. "My girdle" she said. He told her that the guy who invented girdles should be shot! She agreed! Even though, he left his "ditty" bag, at home, he still managed to put "one" in his wallet. They embraced and began with sweet, loving kisses. The sweetness soon gave way to "raw" passion. She leaned forward, so he could unzip her dress. The dress had cups built into it. He had never seen that before. She wasn't wearing a bra. He brought his lips and tongue to her breasts. She had both her hands at his pants buckle and zipper. He brought one his hands down and placed it between her thighs. She, with him raising his hips, brought his pants and boxers down below his knees. It didn't take her long, with her hands, to make him "strong." So, too, his lips and tongue brought her nipples to attention and wetness between her thighs. She moaned and moaned how she missed him and wanted him. She put her right leg over him and 'straddled" him and guided him "home.", after he had placed the condom, from his wallet, on him. His hands on her breasts, mouth and lips caressing her nipples, she began her thrusts. He was glad the cops didn't arrive and 'interrupt them". He brought his left hand from one of her breasts and placed it on her "nub" and began to massage it. She went absolutely Wild!!! Moaning and groaning and thrusting! It didn't take too long for her to finish first, followed by him. They hugged and kissed and kissed and hugged. She finally got off him, so he could roll the passenger side window down and dispose of the condom. Once that was accomplished, they went back to kissing and hugging. He couldn't keep his hands off her breasts. She didn't mind at all! She said she loved "feel' of his penis, even when not at full strength. They happened to notice a car cruising around the DFA. It was a cop. She held up the front of her dress, as he zipped it up. He zipped up and buckled his pants. She reached down and struggled to get her girdle up. She did it, just as the flash light beam tried to penetrate the fogged up window. He climbed over the seat and got into the driver's seat and rolled down the window. The cop looked to be around Phil's age. He asked him for his driver's license and registration. He reached over to the glove compartment and brought it out and handed both to him. "Where are you stationed, sailor?" he asked. "Bainbridge," he replied. "kind of over the limit aren't you?" the cop asked. "I have special permission. I'm ushering at my brother's wedding tomorrow." The cop shined the light at Karen, "and the young lady?" he asked. Karen was smoking an L&M. "Bridesmaid" he answered. The cop shined light in his face and asked "Phil's wedding?" He gulped and said "yes!" The cop said, "I'll see you there. Your brother and I are old friends. I would suggest you take the young lady home and get some rest. You have a big day tomorrow." He said that he would and thanked the cop. The cop gave him back his "papers and Karen got out of the car and into the front seat. He started the car and they drove out of the area. Karen laughed and he said "What's so funny?" She said that if the cop had come up to the car a few minutes earlier, he might have had some "evidence" on the toe of his shoes. They both laughed very hard, as he drove her home.

He and Dave got up early and went to the tuxedo place and got their suits. It took over an hour to get fitted and get the right shoe size. Dave was still very nervous, like a cat with a long tail in a room full of rocking chairs. They, finally had their clothes in hand and drove home. He wanted to call Karen, right away and tell her what time he would pick her up, but Dave monopolized the phone, talking with his wife. After a half hour on the phone, he said she was doing all right. He, finally, got to the phone and called Karen. She said that she was trying to call him, but the line was busy. He told her why. She understood. He told her that the wedding was at 6PM and that he had to be there at 5:15PM. He said that he would pick her up at 5. She said that she would be ready. She whispered, "I won't wear the girdle. My dress is just above my ankles, so I don't need stockings, okay?" He told her that was fantastic and that he would see her at 5.

The wedding went off without a hitch and was very well attended. The little church was filled. There was a small reception, in a hall, on the other side of the church. He and Karen stayed around while pictures were taken. He was glad that she was included in the family photos. A guy about Phil's age was talking with him and Nan and gestured in the direction of he and Karen. Then, he came over to them. He recognized the cop! The cop made no mention of the previous night. Phil and Nan came up to them, too. Phil introduced the cop as "Barry", his best friend in high school. Barry told Phil that they had met earlier. Phil and Nan left them to mix with others. Barry said that the best time to be at the DFA is between 8 and 10PM. After that, he said the cops patrol the area. They do that to prevent any rapes or abuse. He thanked Barry. It was around 8:30, when the newlyweds ran from the church to get to their car. Everyone chased them. Everyone, but he and Karen. They got in the VW and headed for the DFA.

They made love, twice that night and were on their way home at 10PM. She asked him when he would be home again. He told her the 30th of June, for the July 4th weekend. She looked at him. "Two weeks!" That's two weeks from now! She said. "uh huh." He said. He, then asked her if she would like to spend the weekend with him at the cottage? She said "sure". She also said that her folks were going to be away Friday and Saturday of that weekend. She told him that she didn't care what time he arrived, Friday, she and her "teddy" would be waiting.

They hugged and kissed each other good night on her front porch, by her front door. She asked him to call her, when he got up. He said he would. Little did they know that Dave would get him up at 5AM and they would be on the road, South, by 5:45AM! He was not happy! There was no way to tell her why he didn't call! Dave was a real basket case! Dave wanted to leave, right after the wedding reception, but couldn't find him. He was glad that he and Karen got away! His heart was aching! He really wanted to spend some more time with her.

Dave dropped him off, in front of the main gate and drove away, as fast as he came. He looked at his watch, 2:20PM. He wasn't due back until Monday morning. He walked onto the base, with "ditty" bag, in hand. He went right to the rec hall and to the bank of public phones. He called Karen. She answered on the second ring! "Where are you? She asked. "Maryland" He said, "My damn brother woke me up at 5 and we got on the road at quarter to six! I am so sorry! I, so, wanted to spend some of today, with you." "Me. Too!" She said. "But, honey, you'll be back this coming weekend!" he said, "you're right!" he began to feel better. They talked for a while and then she said that she started her summer job on Monday, but that she was getting Saturday, Sunday, Monday and Tuesday off, the next week. He told her that he might be pretty late on Friday. She said that she didn't care! They hung up.

He started to leave the rec hall, when he saw Stenberger at one of the pool tables. He was alone. He challenged Stenberger to a game. They played three, and then, decided to go to the geedunk for a couple of burgers. Norma Jean was on the jukebox with "Let's Go All The Way." The Chiffons followed her with "One Fine Day." Skeeter Davis was next with "The End Of

The World." Sue Thompson followed Skeeter, with "Sad Movies." They ate their food and decided to go back to the barracks and study.

He was glad that he had saved almost all of his Navy pay. Travel, was getting expensive. He was, almost, glad that he wouldn't be doing much, for the next months. He wished that Karen could find a way, to come to him. The Fourth of July weekend started out, much like Memorial Day. He arrived at her house, after ten PM, that Friday night. He had to walk from spot where the bus dropped him off, to his house. He went up the back stairs and got the keys and went into the house and packed a small bag of civilian clothes, for the cottage. He ran down the stairs, to the back door, out the back door, locked it and ran down the back stairs to the VW. He got in, started it and headed for Karen's. Ray Charles was on the radio with "Hit The Road, Jack".

He pulled up in front of Karen's, stopped the car, turned it off, and got out and ran up her walk. He knew her parents weren't home. He rang the bell, twice; no response. He looked through the small window, of the front door and saw her descending the stairs. She was wearing that see-through teddy! He could "make out" every detail of her magnificent body! She opened the door and pulled him inside and closed the door, behind them. She wrapped her arms around him and "greeted" him with a long, passionate, sexual kiss! Then, she took him by his hand and pulled him up the stairs, to her room. They made love as if they hadn't seen each other for months! He was glad that he had thought to put a condom, in his wallet. When they both had "finished," he went to the bathroom and flushed down the condom. She got dressed.

She had packed her "overnight" bag, earlier. He told her that as much as he really, really liked her "sexy" white bathing suit. It would be best, if she packed a more 'conservative' suit. She knew his mother would not like the white one, so, she packed one that was very conservative. Once, they were both dressed. They went down the stairs, to the front door, opened it and went out to the front porch. She locked the door, behind them and with her bag, in his hand, walked to the VW.

They made love every night, they were at the cottage. Only once, did they, actually use "his' bed. That was Saturday afternoon, when his folks left to go visit friends. The rest of the time, they made love in the backseat of the VW. In the same location, that he and Ree were parked in. He was not happy, that he had to get back to the base, by Wednesday morning, the 5th of July. He had to travel on the 4th. Karen wanted to know, when he would be able to get home, again. He told her that he wasn't sure, he would try as soon as he could. They spent a good deal of Monday night, in each other's arms.

He and Stenberger, graduated from Communications school, the third Friday, in July. They got no time off between duty stations. They had to be in Virginia, the following Monday, to start "intelligence" training. He called Karen, when he arrived at the new base and told her his "new' address. He, also, called his folks and told them. From that night on, he was only allowed to write to Karen and his folks. He could not discuss his training with them at all. He wrote the bad news, to Karen, that he would not be home again until his training was over. That would be a week, before Christmas. The good news was that he would be home for a whole three weeks! Her letters showed her disappointment, but she said that she waited for nine weeks before, she could do it, again.

The training was quite intense, both physically and mentally. Out of a class of 25, only 15 graduated. He was very proud to be a member of an "elite" team. That Friday, before Christmas, after graduation, he got his orders. He was to report to the Brooklyn Navy Yard on Friday, January 6th at 4PM. From there, he would be taken to McGuire AFB and flown by Military Air transport Service to Prestwick AFB in Scotland and then flown to Belfast Northern Ireland, where he would board a train to Londonderry, Northern Ireland. He asked his commanding officer, who handed out the orders, "We have a base there?" The captain told him "Yes, a small communications base. It is the sole link between Europe and Washington D.C." He was having mixed emotions! How was he going to tell Karen! Yet, he was going to have an opportunity to see Europe!

"Travelling Man" by Rick Nelson

This time, he flew home and was greeted at the airport, by his folks and Karen. It was an early Friday evening. He and Karen spent some time with his folks. He had stowed his seabag, in his room. By nine o'clock, he and Karen were getting "antsy". He said it was time, to drive her home. They left his house and drove right to the DFA. She had stripped of her slacks and sweater and crawled over into the back seat, before he even brought the car to stop. He turned off the motor and slammed the gear into reverse and, in record time, had his thirteen buttons unbuttoned and bell bottoms off. He climbed over the back seat, quickly. He had taken a condom out of his wallet, as he stripped off his pants. There was very little "foreplay". They went at each other like two rabbits, in the throes of heat!

When they each had "finished" they reached over the seat and brought their clothes back and got dressed. They climbed back over the seat and, then, cuddled and kissed "hello." They hugged and kissed, until the cops arrived and then he drove her home. The "only proof", that they were there, was the "used" condom, lying on the asphalt. Percy Sledge was on the radio with "When A Man Loves A Woman." They kissed good night, at her front door. She was off, from school, the entire week. They would go Christmas shopping together and go to parties, together, and spend Christmas Eve, together. They exchanged their gifts on Christmas Eve. She gave him a 8 by 12 picture of herself, in a silver frame. On the bottom were her words of "love forever" Karen. He gave her a silver bracelet. She absolutely loved it!

The New Years Party was spent at the home, of one of her girlfriends. The friend's parents were away. They spent the night together, in a guest bedroom. They were both quite "sore" in the morning. Little did he know, that would be the last holidays, they would spend together. He drove home, alone. For him to drive Karen home, would have been a "dead giveaway" to her parents that they had spent the night together.

She was in school, the following week. They did not get to see each other until the Thursday night, before he was to leave. The spent the time from 6 to 9PM, in the backseat of the VW. She did a, lot of crying, about not being together for the next eighteen months. They held each very tight, not wanting to let go. When the time came, at her front door, the last embrace lasted a very long time. When, at last, they parted, she went into her house, in tears and he walked back to the VW, in tears.

He arrived at the Brooklyn Navy Yard at 4PM. He checked in at the main gate and was shown to his "new" barracks. He found an empty locker and stowed his gear, in it.

He was told to get a good night's sleep. He would be going to New Jersey, right after morning chow. He went to the head and ran into Stenberger. After they cleaned up, they decided, since it was only five o'clock, they would find the rec hall and play some pool. They both felt miserable about leaving their loved ones behind. They both played the 'worst" game of pool, they had ever played. He realized that he just couldn't concentrate. They went back to the barracks. He went into the head and brushed his teeth. He sat down on his rack and wrote a letter to Karen.

The next morning, after chow, they were herded onto a bus and driven to the Air Force Base in New Jersey. Again, they learned the meaning of the words, "hurry up and wait." He spent a lot of money, on the phone, with Karen. They both prayed that the next 18 months would pass quickly. It was seven o'clock that night, they finally boarded the MATS flight. His father had given him a new 35mm camera, to take pictures of "leaving" the country and arriving in Europe. Unfortunately, it was quite dark, when he took off.

The first stop was in Iceland, for refueling. The pilot told, the fifteen of them, to get off the plane and "run like hell" to the first quanset hut, they see. The temperature was 45 degrees below zero! Once refueled, they took off for Prestwick AFB in Scotland. The "old Prop" plane took over 15 hours to go across the Atlantic. They landed in Prestwick, the next day. They were told that they had a 12 hour "lay over", before heading to Belfast, Northern Ireland. Stenberger talked him into going into Edinburgh, to see the sights. He brought his new camera, with him. He took a lot of pictures. When he had to use a public restroom, he found that the toilet paper was a lot like sandpaper. He was glad that he was in dress blues. He wouldn't want any blood stains showing through his "bottom." He just couldn't get "use" to cars driving on the left side of the road. Riding In the passenger side of a cab, was quite an experience!

They got back to the base and boarded the plane for the last "plane ride" of his journey. It was late afternoon when they landed in Belfast. They were "ushered" to the train depot and had to wait for a half hour, to take the train to Londonderry. The train conductor was very nice, to them and help stow their seabags in an empty compartment. He and Stenberger and two others sat in one compartment. He wished it was "daytime" so he could take some more pictures. They were resting and talking when one of them noticed that they were the "center of attention". Several girls were in the aisle, looking through the window, at them. Stenberger got up and opened the door. Three of the girls came into the compartment and sat down. It was tight sitting, but they seemed to enjoy it! He made the mistake of asking what school they went to. They laughed and said they were "working' girls. Stenberger thought they were prostitutes!

When he asked one, "how much?" he, immediately, got his face slapped and the girls got up and left the compartment. They said that they would have to learn the differences in language!

They arrived at the Londonderry station around 9PM, by his watch. He forgot to set it to Irish time. He looked around at the row of houses and their chimneys with the thick black, smoke pouring out. It reminded him of the old black and white English movies. They were, again, ushered to a van that had U. S. Navy emblazoned on the side. It seemed, to him. That every place, every new station, he, always, seemed to arrive, at night. The van drove right through the main gate and around a building and stopped in front of a new, large, modern building. They got their "gear" out of the back of the van and went through the large glass doors. They were greeted by a large, burly built First Class Boatswain's Mate. They, each, handed him their orders. He assigned them, each to a compartment. His was just down the hall, on the first floor. He stepped in and was shown to an empty bunk. No rack, an actual bed! The locker was taller than him. He could actually hang clothes in it! He had to be quiet, as his three other bunk mates were sleeping. He, quickly undressed and, in his skivvies, went down the hall to the head and prepared himself, for bed. As he, finally, climbed in, under the covers, he noticed his throat was a little painful.

When he awoke, the next morning, he had a "full blown" sore throat! The "boats" as he wanted to be called, got him up and took him to a quanset hut that had "sickbay" over the door. The Corpsman looked at his throat and gave him some antibiotics and told him to go eat breakfast and then get back into bed, until he felt better. He had to wear undress blues, to meals and then went right back to bed. He was sick, for the first three days. While, in bed, he got to write letters home, giving everyone his new address. He, also, wrote many "love" letters to Karen.

On the fourth day, he was "directed" to a building and given his assignment. His first watch was the "midwatch." It began at 11PM and ran until 7AM! He spent the "watch" receiving and transmitting teletype messages from all over Europe and 'routing' them to Washington D.C.

The time on watch, went quickly. He found, that, when he got off watch and ate breakfast, in the mess hall, he went to sleep, very fast and would sleep till two, sometimes 3PM.

While stationed in Northern Ireland, he bought his first motorcycle, an AJS 500 twin. He had it insured with Lloyd's of London. It took three minor accidents to get him off 'two wheels" forever. All three involved women! The first one took place, with a girl riding on the back, who leaned in the wrong direction, causing him to go off the road, no injuries. The second, he was riding behind his "bunk mates" when a young lady came out of a store with her blouse wide open, exposing her breasts. He ran into the back of his "buddy's "bike. He hadn't noticed that his buddy had stopped. He rode his bike, for the longest time, without a front fender. That made riding, in a rain shower, very interesting! The third occurred when he and another buddy met two beautiful twin colleens in town one day. They said that their parents were going to be away, the next Saturday night and they lived out in the country and would like some company. He and Jeff were supposed to ride by the house and honk their horns, turn around and ride back up, park the bikes and go on in the house. All went, according to plan, until the girls, hearing the horns, came running out of the house in nothing, but bras and panties! He drove the bike, past the house and off the road! He bent the frame of the bike and bruised his lower back. Needless to say, there wasn't any party! He stopped riding after that.

A major milestone occurred, for him, when he sat on the "circuit" that 7th day of July 1962 and listened and communicated with the U.S.S. Skate and U.S.S. Sea Dragon, two nuclear submarines, as they rendezvoused under the North Pole. He was surrounded by many officers and men as they listened to the two subs greet each other. It was an historical moment, not only for him, but for the Navy.

His second major milestone was not a "happy" one. It was April 10th 1963. He sat on the circuit and listened to the U.S.S. Skylark, a sub rescue vessel communicate with a new nuclear submarine, called the U.S.S. Thresher. The sub was running a 'test". He was proud to be on the circuit. He would respond with "RAR" when the Skylark would "tell" him about "her" contacts with the sub. He knew he had a couple of friends, from communications school, on the sub. It was sometime around 5PM, "their time", when the half hour report did not come through. He sent a message, asking why the Skylark had not heard from the sub. There was no response. 5:30PM, again no message from the surface vessel. One of the communications officers looked at his log and demanded to know why there wasn't anything written, after 5. He said "Sir, I messaged the Skylark, as you can see by the log, but there hasn't been any response from the Thresher!" The officer took off the headset from him and told him to get out of the chair. That he had, obviously, been "asleep". He denied it! The officer, also, tried to contact the Skylark. At 6:30PM, the Skylark reported that they had lost contact with the Thresher. That they had not from her, since they received a "garbled message". The officer took off the headsets and handed them back to him, with an apology. He asked him to continue to "monitor" the circuit. Silence filled the room. The officer asked everyone to bow their heads and say a prayer for the crew of the U.S.S. Thresher. Tears filled his eyes as his mind pictured the two "mates" he knew, in school.

He did get "emergency leave" just before Christmas of 1962. His mom had suffered a "heart attack". By the time, he got home, she was out of the hospital and doing okay. She told him that if she did what the doctor told her to, she would live another twenty years. He told her to "do whatever the "doc" says." She said that she would.

It was during that short "leave", that he and Fred went into Boston, while Karen was in school. She was a senior. The two of them, Fred and he, decided to buy engagement rings. Fred came out of the city, with his ring, for Kathy. His ring had to be 'sized.' He had the receipt in his pocket. They took the girls bowling that night. It was his turn to bowl. Fred took Kathy outside of the building. He knew that he was going to propose to her. He bowled his first three balls and didn't do well. Before he bowled the nest three, he emptied his pockets of loose change, car keys and wallet. He did not realize the receipt was sticking out of his wallet. Karen was keeping score. His arm was back and coming forward, when he heard her scream! He turned around as she rushed into his arms. He dropped the ball on the alley. He knew that she had seen the receipt. With her arms wrapped around his neck, he asked her. She screamed, so the whole crowd could hear her, YES!!!! Kathy and Fred came back into the building. Kathy had been crying. She was wearing her ring. Both girls hugged and congratulated each other. Fred came up to him and asked, "what happened? I thought you were going to wait until you two were alone!" he said that she saw the ring receipt, in his wallet. The girls even talked about the possibility of a double wedding. Fred and Kathy were going to get married that next summer, while he was still in Ireland. Karen didn't care, she was so very happy!

He went back to Ireland a happy man! His mom was all right. His girlfriend, now fiancée was still in love with him and could not wait to be his wife and bear his children. He had only nine months left in Ireland. They could do "that" easy. He wasn't counting on depression to 'hit' him. The "Thresher" disaster didn't help; may have been the 'cause".

She had written him a letter, in April, telling him that she had been invited to her senior prom. He wrote back that engaged women don't go out dancing with another guy. His "mates" reminded him what he did on his senior prom. He remembered the wonderful sex that he and Ree had enjoyed. She wrote back, that she would not do anything to jeopardize their relationship; that he should be able to trust her. The problem was trust. He trusted her and then, received THAT letter from Andrea, telling him about her "trysts" with another guy. The letters got worse. He was afraid of losing her! It, seemed, to him, no matter what he said, she would be mad enough, to "dump' him. It wasn't too long, after that, the duration of her letters, to him, grew longer and longer. He would spend a lot of time, at the EM club. One night, in an angry, drunk, state, he wrote her a letter, saying that if she really wanted to go to the prom, to go ahead, but take off the ring! That was the last of the correspondence between them. His depression and drinking got worse. His work was not impacted, but, out of work, he tried to be the "life' of the party. His "buddies" kept fixing him up with "willing" colleens. Most of them were looking for a "ticket" to the states. He made up his mind that he would not bring home an "Irish" wife.

His "tour" in Ireland ended the second week of July, 1963. His "buddies" gave him a 'rousing" going away party. It was so good, that he missed the train to Belfast, the next morning and had to "hitch" a ride with a farmer, in a small pickup truck, who was on his way to Belfast, to sell some sheep. His leave did not start until he arrived "stateside".

Once, in Belfast, he hailed a cab, to the airport. This time, he flew by commercial airline back to Prestwick AFB, in Scotland. When he arrived at the demarcation point, he was told that there wouldn't be any planes leaving for a couple of days. He was directed to a barracks and he, once again, stowed his gear. He met up with two "airmen" at the "em" club. Being a Petty Officer, he was told that he should be at the "noncom" club. He didn't really care, which club, he drank at. The three of them "striked" up a friendship. They changed into their civvies and went into town. There, they met up with three "willing" Scottish girls. He did not return to the base, for four days. He was in "limbo". He was not under orders to any place nor anyone.

When he, finally, reported back, to the base. The sergeant was "livid! Where you been? The Red Cross has been screaming at me! Your folks are worried sick! You were supposed to be out of here, three days ago! You sit right down on that bench! "The sergeant directed an airman to go to his barracks and pick up his gear and get back. He processed him right away and within two hours, he was back on a MATS flight, headed back to New Jersey!

The plane, home, was not a "prop" job, but a jet! It only took 5 hours. When he arrived at McGuire AFB, the outside temperature was 93 degrees! He was I "wool" dress blues. He hadn't worn whites for over 18 months! He got off the plane and headed to a rest room and changed into dress whites. Then, he caught a bus to Port Authority, New York City. From there, he bought a ticket to Boston. Again, he was able to talk the driver, into letting him off in Newton. It felt good, to be walking along Chestnut street, in his home town, again.

His mom came out the front door and hugged him, as he walked up the front walk. She asked where his bag was? He told her that the driver said that he could pick it up in Boston, later that day, in fact, his dad could get it, on the way home. She wanted to know what happened? That he wasn't home days ago? He told her that he couldn't get a plane and so he visited the countryside and took lots of pictures, that he would have to get developed. It was July 20ᵗʰ 1963. The first day of his 30 day leave. He went up to his room and, quickly, changed out of his uniform and into his "old" civilian clothes. He relaxed on the back porch with an L&M and a glass of iced tea, with his mom. He asked her about her 'health" and she told him that she was doing everything the doctor told her to do. He was glad, to hear that. The conversation soon got around to Karen. He told her what happened. His mom said that she was sorry, but that Karen was probably too young to get engaged.

His dad got home around 5PM, with his seabag. He had to produce identification, to prove that he was, who he said he was. They laughed and enjoyed a nice dinner out on the screened in back porch. After dinner, he went into the hall and called Fred. Fred was real happy to hear from him. He was living in an apartment, in Brighton and gave him the directions. He asked his mom, for the keys to the VW and drove over to Fred's. They popped open a couple of beers and Fred filled him on the many changes that had taken place, since he left. For one, thing Folk music had just about replaced rock and Roll. Clothing styles had really changed! Fred looked at him and asked if he had any money. "Some." He said. He didn't want anyone to know, that despite his drinking and carousing, he had managed to "stow" away over a thousand dollars. Fred told him that the next morning, they were going clothes shopping, for him. He laughed and finished his beer. Fred asked him, "when was the last time, you heard from Karen?" "April." He replied. Fred said "that would be about right. She came to Kathy, crying her eyes out." He began to feel real bad. "I guess I really 'blew" it with her. Wonder if I'll ever see her, again or for that matter, if she'll ever want to see me, again." Fred asked him," would you want to get back with her?" he answered, "doubt that she would want to, after the way I treated her." Fred said "who knows? Stranger things have happened." They shook hands, again, and made plans the next morning, to go and buy him some "up to date" clothes.

He picked Fred up around ten, the next morning. Fred no longer had the Ford. They went a store called "Mal's". When they walked into the store, a clerk approached them. "Can I help you?" the man said. Fred responded, "He needs everything, the "works"! The clerk must have thought his "ship" came in. The guy probably cursed the fact that he had to work on a Saturday, until that moment. He bought shirts, pants, shoes, even two pair of Bermuda shorts. He tried to tell Fred that he didn't like shorts and never wore them! Fred said "you can't go to a hootnanny and not be in shorts and sandals, it just isn't done!" "A what?" he asked. "A hootnanny said Fred." It's a folk music concert. There's one this afternoon at Normbega Park. He dropped over five hundred dollars at Mal's. He never saw such a happy clerk, as when he rang up the total sale, and he handed the guy, cash!

They went back to Fred's apartment. He went into Fred's bathroom and changed into the white polo shirt and blue Bermuda shorts, and brown sandals. He told Fred that he felt "naked". The rest of his "new" clothes were still in the back of the VW. As they were sitting on his porch, overlooking the street, Kathy showed up. She was glad to see him and greeted him with a hug. She grabbed a beer and joined them on the porch. She told him that he looked good, in shorts. He just grunted. Fred said, "he feels naked in them." She asked how long he was home for? He told her August 20th. She said "good". They finished their beers and headed to the hootnanny.

All through the concert, his eyes scanned the large crowd, hoping that "she" might be there. It was well after 6PM, when the concert ended. He asked Fred what was next in store? Fred said that they should drop Kathy back to the apartment. She did not like stock car races. He said, "the stocks? I can't go to the stocks, dressed like this!" "Relax," said Fred, "You won't know anyone there, besides, we don't have time to eat and change." He, reluctantly, agreed. The three of them went to the "old hang out", the car hop. After they ate their food, he drove back to the apartment. He and Fred headed to the stock car races. He never realized it, but, whenever he was home, he always parked the VW, in front of his house. He never realized that he was the only that did it. His mom always parked it in the driveway. The only time, he parked it in the driveway, was at night. He never thought that it might be a "signal" that he was home.

It was during the fourth race, it was Fred's turn to buy the beer. He was sitting, by himself, when he noticed Carolyn, Karen's friend. She was the one, whose house, the last New Year's Eve party was at. Carolyn was waving, frantically, at him. He waved back and she ascended the wooden benches and sat down next to him and gave him a "welcome home" hug. She asked him how long was he going to be home. "just a month" he said. "Then, where to?" She asked. "An aircraft carrier, out of Norfolk Virginia." He said. "Well, that's not very far away. Guess we'll see a lot of you, from time to time,." She said. "depends", he said, "not sure I'll want to be home, that much." Carolyn said that it was good seeing him and for him to take care. "You, too." He said. He was just beginning to wonder what was taking Fred so long with the beers. He looked and saw Fred walking back. He was talking with someone, but he couldn't see who, because of a tall guy, in front of them. He lit up an L&M. he, nearly, burned his fingers, when he saw who Fred was with, Karen!

She bounded up the wooden planks and gave him a big hug! He responded. She sat down between him and Fred. She was wearing jeans and a sweatshirt. Her hair was cropped real short. She looked wonderful to him! His heart was rejuvenated at the sight of her. She seemed happy to see him. "I knew you were home. When Carolyn reported that the VW was parked in front of the house. Oh my God! You are wearing shorts!" He felt the redness form in his cheeks. She, then, got a little serious and asked if they could get together and talk. She said that she really missed him! He said that, maybe, they could get together tomorrow night, get something to eat and talk. She said, pick me up at 6PM. Then she leaned in and kissed him on the lips and jumped down the wooden planks and waved up at him and left. He looked at Fred. Fred, then, told him that her brother was in the next race and she was part of his "pit crew". Fred made it sound as if he had just run into her. Somehow, he thought it was a set up. One, that he wasn't unhappy with.

It was exactly 6PM, when he pulled the VW, up in front of her house. He turned it off, set the emergency brake and got out. As he got out of the car, he noticed an old "beat up" Plymouth sedan, slowly "cruise' by. He walked up her walkway, stepped onto the front porch and knocked on the door. She opened the door. She was in a white jersey and black Bermuda shorts. He was in one of his new shirts and pants. She gave him her "pout" and said. "Oh, I was hoping you would wear your new shorts. He just smiled. She let him and they went into the kitchen. Her folks were there and welcomed, warmly, welcomed him back. It felt "strange" to him, being in that house, again. Almost, like he really shouldn't be there.

They said "good night" to her folks and went through the hall and out the front door. He noticed that old Plymouth go by, again. He asked her if she knew the guy driving the car. She, emphatically, said "no." They got into the VW and headed out. She said that it felt good to be sitting in the VW again, next to him. He said that it felt good to have her next to him, too. He turned on the radio and heard Trini Lopez sing "If I Had A Hammer." She said that she liked Peter, Paul & Mary's version better. He said that he didn't know who they were. He told her that Bobby Vinton's big hit, overseas, was "Roses Are Red." They continued to make small talk, as he drove to the Italian restaurant, that he and Ree used to go to. Maybe, he was hoping to run into her, too. He pulled into the parking lot next to the restaurant. They got out of the car and went inside. They were seated across from each other, at a small candle lit table. She put both hands on the table, stretched out, towards him. He knew she wanted to hold hands. He kept his to himself. He could see she was feeling some pain. She asked him, "what went wrong? You should know that I did not go to my prom, after all." His mood softened. He told her that he had no right to interfere with her school life. She told him that she was being foolish and that he had every right to tell her not to go. She told him that she was so hurt, so distraught, she felt like killing herself. He brought his hands up and reached out and took hers. He told her that he was so drunk and so angry in the last letter. He, also, told her that he never stopped loving her. That he saw her face in every girl, he looked at. Tears filled her eyes. She told him that she felt so alone, so hurt, that she "gave" herself to a guy on the cape, last May. His head went down to the top of the table. She continued, "I didn't like it. It wasn't you! He didn't care about me, not the way, you did." His heart was breaking all over, again. With tear filled eyes, he looked at her." I still love you and will, until the day I die, no matter what!" he wanted to reach across the table and hold her face in his hands and kiss her.

The waitress came, to take their order. She saw the expression on their faces and said that she would come back later. They both stopped her and ordered spaghetti and meatballs. The waitress left. She asked him to please, please, forgive her and give her another chance. He told her that it was all his fault and that he should ask her for forgiveness. She said, with a smile, "I forgive you, if you'll forgive me?" he said he would. When, their food and cokes arrived. They ate it, fast.

They left the restaurant and went to the VW. He unlocked it and they got in." Can we take up where we left off, last year? "she asked. "Guess so." He said. She moved over to him and put her arms around his neck. Their lips met, for the first time, since before Christmas. There wasn't any passion, just a sweet, loving kiss. She asked if they could go to the DFA? He put the car in forward and shifted through the gears.

He pulled into the DFA and found a spot by the back. It was just turning dark. Thoughts of her, in the arms of some other guy, haunted him. They embraced and hugged and kissed for a very long time. He was not ready to make love to her, not yet. He sensed that she wanted to. But, seemed to obey his wishes. It was a sweet, loving, homecoming. She had to be at work, at the luncheonette, in Newtonville. She asked if he would pick her up, after work. He said that he would be glad to.

Fred worked at the reservation desk, at a motel, just down the road from his apartment. He worked from 7AM to noon, Monday through Friday. Karen got off work at 2PM. Their schedules worked well for him. He would sleep "in" until nine or ten, get up, freshen up and meet the day. He would visit with Fred and then go and pick up Karen. No one worked on the weekends. Kathy, even worked close to Fred's place. When he picked Fred up, that Monday, Fred had all kinds of questions. "How did the date go with Karen?" he told him that it went well, that he had to pick her up, after work, that afternoon. Fred said that the four of them should get together. He said that he would ask her, when he picked her up.

It was one o' clock, when he decided to go to the luncheonette. He hadn't had lunch and Fred had laundry to do. He pulled into the parking lot, next to the luncheonette and noticed the same old beat up Plymouth sedan, in the lot. He turned off the car, as Peter, Paul & Mary were singing about "Puff, The Magic Dragon" on the radio. he got out of the VW and locked it and went into the restaurant. He thought he recognized the guy, who passed by him, as he entered. He turned to say something, but the guy was already out the door. Karen had a surprised look, on her face, when she saw him. She looked at her watch and gestured that she wasn't off work, yet. He went up to the counter and sat down on a stool. She came to the counter in her waitress uniform and told him that he was early. He said that he knew, but thought he'd have a sandwich, while he waited, for her. He didn't mention the guy, who drove the Plymouth. He noticed, she was wearing his engagement ring. He smiled at her.

The "timing" was good. He finished the sandwich, as she finished her shift. They walked out of the restaurant together. She reached for his hand and held it, as they walked to the car. He unlocked it and they got in. he turned the car and backed it out of the lot. The Kingston Trio was singing about "Tom Dooley" on the radio. They were followed by some guy named Alan Sherman who "sang" a funny song called "Hello Mudda, Hello Fadda." He listened and couldn't stop laughing at the "lyrics." Karen asked him if he ever heard the song, before. He said, "No, I haven't. It's really funny." He asked her, if she wanted to go with him to Fred's apartment. She said, "sure."

Fred put on some of the old 45's, on his stereo record player. It had two separate speakers, each one, strategically placed in a corner, to give the ultimate sound. He felt like a "fish out of water." So much had changed in the few months, he was away. He and Karen sat on the couch, next to him. She sat so close, she was practically on top of him. As they listened to the records, they reminisced about the "old days". Fred kept checking his watch. Finally, he said that he had to go and get his laundry out of the dryer and fold the clothes. He would be back, in a while. He told them to make themselves comfortable. As soon as he was out the door, Karen threw her leg over his waist and straddled him. They began to make out. She was like a "bitch" in heat. He couldn't help, but respond. She unbuttoned his shirt and her blouse and took his hands and put them on her breasts. Her hands roamed all over his, semi hairy chest. Their lips roamed over each other's lips. His head was spinning! He wanted to throw her off him and onto the floor and rip her clothes off and make passionate love to her, but he knew Fred wouldn't be gone that long! It was a "noise" on the front door, of the apartment, that separated them. She, immediately buttoned up. He was buttoning his shirt, as Fred, with a large white laundry bag, over his shoulder, came through the door. He got up and took the bag, from Fred's shoulder. Fred told him to just throw the bag on his bed. Fred went into the kitchen and came back with three Budweisers. Fred handed one to Karen, and one to him. He was surprised that Karen took the bottle and, actually, drank from it. They went out to the "porch" and sat in the "lawn chairs" and watched the traffic on the street, below, and talked "small talk." They were still there, when Kathy arrived. She saw that they were having a beer and asked where hers was? Fred got up and got her one. They were all sitting on the chairs, talking. It didn't take long for the questions about the Navy, surfaced. He answered as best as he could. He did tell them, that there was a "war" going on in Southeast Asia and that the U.S. might become more involved. Karen looked at him and hoped that he wouldn't have to go. Kathy butted in and said, that she was getting hungry and they should think about doing something for supper. Fred suggested that the "girls" cook something up. Kathy said "Fine with me, but there's nothing here to cook." He said that he would pay for the food. They finished their beers and got up and went out of the apartment. They got into the VW and headed to the A&P Supermarket, that was just down the road. He told Fred that he found the perfect apartment. It was close to everything.

At the market, he was pushing the carriage. Fred insisted on picking out the meat. They were at the meat counter. Fred was "inspecting" all the different cuts of steaks. He, finally, decided on a large rib eye. Karen, without forethought, said "okay, you've got your meat, now beat it!" The four of them looked at each other and broke out in fits of laughter. He went right to the floor. The only thing holding him up were his hands on the handle of the cart. Fred was leaning against the meat counter, tears flowing down his cheeks. Kathy and Karen were holding onto each other, laughing so hard, they were shaking! When, at last, the laughter subsided, the guys beat a hasty retreat, but not before he gave Karen the cash of three twenty dollar bills and a ten dollar bill. Her eyes bugged out, at the money. He looked at her and said, "well, I do expect some change back." They laughed and Karen winked at him and said "maybe".

Back at the apartment, he and Fred were sitting out on the porch, while the girls cooked dinner. Karen had grown tired of wearing her "uniform". Kathy gave her some clothes to wear. Kathy was smaller than Karen and the clothes were a little tight on her. In fact, she couldn't button all the buttons on the blouse. Which made it difficult, for him, to not look at her cleavage. Kathy noticed that Fred had difficulty as well. She became quite agitated with him and proceeded to unbutton her own shirt. She showed more cleavage than Karen. Fred's attention turned back to Kathy.

The dinner went very well. The guys lifted their glasses of beer and toasted the chefs! As they sat around the table, Kathy said, "okay, guys, we cooked, you get to clean up." He and Fred groaned and got out of their chairs and "cleaned off the small dining room table." They took the dirty dishes to the kitchen and put them in the sink. They flipped a coin and he got to wash, while Fred dried. It made sense, because Fred knew where everything "went." When all was done, they joined the girls back on the porch. The sun was setting and street lights began to glow.

As darkness set in, he didn't notice that Fred and Kathy had left them alone, on the porch. The evening breeze set a slight chill on them and they got up and went inside. The only light, in the apartment, came from the kitchen. He and Karen sat on the couch. He thanked her for a wonderful meal. She said that Kathy had cooked the meat, she cooked the vegetables and "made" the mashed potatoes. She, again, told him, that she was very happy that he was home and that they were, once again, together. They couldn't help but hear the unmistakable sounds of "love making" emanate from the bedroom. They wrapped their arms around each other and slid down on the seats of the couch. Their "making out" was "hot" and "heavy", but still they did not make love. He did not have any condoms and he was not ready to 'father' a child.

The first two and a half weeks of his leave went very well. He, Karen and Fred and Kathy spent a lot of time, together. He and Fred rented Boston Whalers on the lake, and the girls joined them for a day of boating and swimming. He purchased four tickets, to see Peter, Paul & Mary, "live in concert", at the Hampton Beach Casino. It was during his third week, that things began to go "wrong." He found out that the guy who was in the old Plymouth was the same guy, he had purchased the hydroplane from. Karen had asked that they double date with Donny, and his girlfriend. He really didn't care for Donny. There was something about him. First of all, he was a real "grease ball." He looked like he used axle grease on his hair. He didn't seem to care about using "foul language" around people. There was something else. He just couldn't put his finger on it, but something sent shivers up the back of his neck.

They ended up spending a lot more time with Donny and his girlfriend. He wanted to see Fred and Kathy. He was more comfortable with them. But, Karen decided that she and Kathy didn't get along. Then came the weekend, before, he was to leave, for his next "duty station". They had been at the lake and were driving back, alone. They were singing "their" song, "Side By Side." Her hand was between his thighs and his "free" hand was between hers. They were making each other very "hot." His parents would not be home, until the Friday, before he was to leave. By the time, he pulled into the driveway and parked behind the house, he was "rigid" and she was very "damp." It was getting dark. He parked the car and they both got out and practically ran up the backstairs. He, quickly, unlocked the back door and as they ran through the house, clothes began to "fall' off them. By the time they got to his bedroom, they were both naked, as the day they were born. They fell onto his bed, arms and legs entwined, lips passionately "engaged." Then, when they released their lips, for air, she put her hands on the top of his head and pushed him down. He kissed her breasts and nipples, as he had done, in the past. Her breathing became more ragged. Then, she pushed his head down, farther. He couldn't believe that he was finally going to give her kisses, where he had wanted to, for a very long time. He trailed his lips and tongue over her stomach, down to her pubic area. He, purposely, went to her inner thighs, kissing and gently licking them. Then, he moved up and with his tongue, licked her outer lips. He stuck his tongue inside her and moved it around. Then, he slowly withdrew it and pushed it back in. he brought his right hand down and inserted two fingers, as his tongue and lips caressed and gently sucked on her clitoris. Her legs trembled and her hips kept thrusting against his probing tongue and then his fingers. He tasted her 'juices" at least three different times. His left hand was alternating between her breasts and nipples, while he probed and sucked. He was "lost" in her paradise. When he had "given" her the fourth orgasm, he brought his head up and looked at her. Her hands were white knuckled against the headboard, eyes were closed, nostrils flared, mouth opened and he tongue sticking out at the corner of her mouth. He moved up next to her. His left hand, still caressing her left breast and extremely hard nipple. She spoke in a very raspy, husky, voice. "I shouldn't have waited so long! Now, it's my turn!" She pushed him onto his back and lowered her mouth to him. The feeling was incredible! She was "making love "to 'it." With her lips and tongue and her mouth, she did "things" to him, that had never been done before. He was afraid that he was going to mess up her face. He tried to warn her, that he was about to explode! He was all the way, in her mouth when he erupted! She didn't flinch, but seemed to swallow every drop. When he was finished, she "cleaned" him with her lips and tongue. Her hand went to him and began to "lightly" stroke him. While she was making love to "him", he was able to caress her the outside of her breast. They lay beside each other, breathing quite heavy! Her ministrations to his manhood were having a good effect on him. His strength was rapidly returning. He brought his right hand down and inserted two fingers inside her and probed until he found her "sensitive" area. After a few minutes, they were both "ready," She moaned, "I want you inside me." He didn't care that he was without protection. She didn't care, either. He slipped in. It felt so good to be inside her, flesh against flesh. he couldn't wait and began his thrusts. Then, from out of nowhere, she yelled, "I want your baby! Make us a baby! Give me your baby!"

It was as if someone had poured ice cold water down his back! "He" shrank and slipped out of her. There was nothing! Her eyes flew open! "What's wrong? Why did you stop?" She brought her hand to him and desperately tried to 'revive" him. It was over. He rolled off her and lay on his back. The silence, in the room was "deadly." The room temperature, suddenly dipped to "freezing." She got off the bed, without saying a word and left the room. He got up and followed her. She was stopping and putting her clothing back on. When he saw what she was doing, he did the same. Once dressed, they silently walked out of the house and got into the VW. He drove her home, in silence.

When he pulled up to the front of her house, He stopped the car. She, quickly, opened her door, got out and closed it and ran up her front walk, got to her front door and opened it and disappeared!

Once again, he drove home from her house, with tears filling up his eyes and flowing down his cheeks. The next day, he drove over to her work. She wasn't there. She had called in "sick". He drove over to her house. He knew her parents were away. As he drove down the side street, to her house, he saw the Plymouth in her driveway. He pulled over to the side of the street. He turned the car off and got out. He walked across the front lawn of her house and up the front steps to the porch. For some reason, he went to the living room window. He shielded his eyes and looked in. They were on the living room floor! She was on top of Donny, His hands on her naked breasts, as she bounced up and down on top of him! They were both as naked as he and she had been, their first time, on that floor! He staggered back! His mouth wide open, his eyes wide open! He couldn't breathe! His back hit the porch railing, preventing him from falling off the porch and into the bushes! He ran off the porch, across the lawn and got back into the car. He was devastated! He was in shock! His hands trembled on the steering wheel! He was racked in pain! His heart was shattered like a fragile piece of glass! Tears flowed! He couldn't drive! He sat, there, for the longest time. Then, out of the corner of his eye, he saw them walking to the Plymouth. She saw him and stopped. She started to run over to him. Donny stayed behind. Anger took over from grief! He turned the car on and sped away from her, before she could reach the car.

He spent the last few days, with Fred and Kathy. They, too, were in shock! They did their best to console him. He knew the best thing for him, was to get on that bus and head to the next duty station. They were planning their wedding, which was coming in September. He told them that he would try and get back, for it. Kathy assured him that Karen would not be invited.

His folks came home, a few days, early, from the cottage. They, also, were in shock. His mom and dad, talked and his dad, on the Thursday, before he was to leave, took him to a friend's Lincoln Mercury dealership. His dad's friend walked him out to the used car lot and showed him a 1961 Ford Galaxy Convertible. It was dark blue, with duel exhausts, fender skirts and a dark red leather interior. He took it for a "test" drive. Not only did it ride, smooth, but the "twin pipes" sounded loud and rich! When, he brought it back to the lot. He went inside and they 'crunched' some numbers. They payments would be "easy" for him. He paid the man four hundred and fifty dollars 'down". While in the office, dad called his other friend, and got the insurance. The friend at the dealership, told him, he would have the plates and inspection done and he could pick the car up on Friday. That meant he would be able to drive, to his new duty station. Best of all, he would have a couple of days to drive around town, in it. The car took his mind of Karen, for a while. He thought, "too bad, she'll never ride in it!"

He picked up the car, Friday afternoon. He drove it home, to show his mom. She was excited for him and though, she didn't say it, she glad to see him smiling, again. He called Fred and told him that he was taking he and Kathy out to eat. Fred sensed something and told him to pick them up around 4PM. He pulled up. In front, of the apartment and honked the horn. The top was down. he looked up and saw them sitting on the front porch. He honked the horn, again. This time, Fred looked down and yelled, "Is that yours?" he yelled back, "Yeah, come on, let's go!" Kathy and Fred came running out of the apartment building. Kathy opened the door and jumped in beside him. Fred got in and closed the door. "Sure beats the VW" said Fred. "Sure does." He laughed. He pulled away, from the curb. Harold Dorman was on the radio with "Mountain Of Love." Followed by Bobby Darin and "Multiplication". As they cruised around. Fred said that they should go by Karen's and just maybe she would be outside and see what she could have been riding in. Kathy looked at him and said "sweet revenge."

He thought "what the hell". As he turned the corner and proceeded to go by the front of her house, he saw "them" walking to the old Plymouth. He slowed down, waved, and hit the gas! The twin pipes "roared" as he rounded the corner. Fred said "slow down. Let them "catch up". He stopped at the stop sign, at the top of her street. He saw the Plymouth came up behind him. Fred turned and waved, as he hit the gas and peeled out, sending dirt and sand against the grill of the Plymouth. Fred said that he could swear that Karen was yelling at the guy driving the Plymouth. It did help his heart, for a little bit. He said to himself, that dumping him, for the 'grease ball" Donny would be the biggest mistake of her life.

It was a beautiful, August day, with, seabag in the trunk and a suitcase full of civilian clothes, he set out for Norfolk, Virginia. His next and, hopefully, final tour of duty was the U.S.S. Randolph, an aircraft carrier. It was, also, to be the first duty, on a ship. With his 'triptik" from AAA, he was well, on his way. This would, also, be the first time, that he actually arrived, in the daylight. With the top down, the wind in his hair, he was feeling good, except he still had some "pain" left over from Karen. He couldn't get over the fact that she dumped him for Donny. He wondered if not having a condom, that night, was really the reason she dumped him, or just an excuse. He tried to put it out of his mind. He turned up the radio and listened to Bobby Darin, sing "Beyond The Sea."

He arrived at the ferry, that would take him across the waters, to Norfolk and the base, at 7PM. He realized that he might just not make it to the main gate, before the sun went down. He pulled the car onto the ferry and parked it. He raised the top and latched it to the top of the windshield. He turned off the car and locked it. He went up the stairs, to the lounge and had some supper. After which, he stepped out onto the open deck and lit up an L&M. When he finally arrived at the main gate, he pulled the car over beside the building. With his insurance papers, registration, driver's license and orders, he went inside the building. He filled out a form, for the car and received a 'sticker" for the top center of the inside of the windshield. He was told that his ship was at sea and wouldn't be back for a couple of weeks. He was directed to a barracks. He parked and locked the Ford behind the building. He opened the trunk and took out his seabag and went inside. He was directed to a top empty rack. He, also, had a locker, just big enough for his seabag. The "receiving station" was his "home" until the ship came back.

Being a Petty Officer, he was assigned to Shore Patrol duties at the base "EM" club. He wasn't allowed to leave the best for five days. It was August 27th. He was given a 72 hour liberty. If he and Karen had still been together, he would have tried to get home. Instead, he and three other guys, he met in the receiving station, decided to drive to Washington D.C., to see the sights. He hadn't been there, since communications school. They drove off the base, in their dress whites and headed for "D.C."

It was August 28th 1963. The traffic going in to "D.C." was horrendous! They, finally, found a parking lot that was just about to close, from being "full." He paid the attendant and parked the car and locked it. They began to walk towards the area, where the Lincoln Memorial was. One of the guys, Wilson, was from Alabama. He was really nervous. They were very conspicuous. Four white guys, in white uniforms, in the midst of a sea of black people! They were a minority!

He kept asking the others, "What the hell is going on?" One of them said that it looked like a huge "sit in", except everyone was not only sitting, but standing around. The closer they got to the Lincoln Memorial, the thicker the crowd of blacks. They surmised that it was some very, very, big demonstration! They heard several voices over speakers, that seemed to be set up everywhere! They got to a point, where they couldn't go any further. A lot of people were saying "Amen" to one particular speaker. He turned to an old black man and asked him, "Who's the speaker?" The old man looked at him. Like, he was from outer space. "Son", he said, "That's the Reverend Dr. Martin Luther King speaking." "Oh" he said, "I've been overseas." "uh huh" the old man said. They began to walk away from the monument as the speaker kept repeating himself, over the speakers, about "having a dream." They finally got away from the area and found their way to the street where most of the bars, were. He heaved a heavy sigh and turned to the others. "Guess they are all closed for the demonstration." They made their way back to the car and got in and drove off the lot. Driving out of D.C. was a lot easier than driving in. What took 4 and a half hours to drive to and find a place to park, now only took about 3 and half hours to get back to the base. It had been quite a day! He would, later learn, that he had heard Dr. King's most famous speech, and he had been there! Another milestone!

Once he boarded the Randolph, he was put in ICU (incoming unit). He stayed there for a few days. He hadn't any duty. He had a difficult time adjusting to his new surroundings. His top bunk was just below a steel eyelet. The eyelet was used to hang his bunk up against the bulkhead, during the day. That eyelet became a source of extreme pain, every morning, when reveille "blasted" over the speaker on the bulkhead, by his head. He would wear his hat down over his forehead to conceal the large red imprint of the eyelet.

One day, he wondered if, by chance, he would have some mail. Though, he didn't know how anyone would have his address. Every morning, while the "sweepers manned their brooms", he would explore the ship. He found where the communications shack was. On this particular day, he snuck into the shack and looked around and found a small stack of letters on top of a file cabinet. He reached for the letters. A hand with an arm full of "hash" marks grabbed his hand! "Been wondering who these letters were for? Where have you been sailor?" it was the Chief Petty officer in charge. "ICU, Chief." He said. "All this time? You get down there and grab your gear and get your ass back up here fast, mister!" The chief demanded. The chief held onto his mail, until he got back to the "com shack".

When he got back, he realized that it wasn't his fault. Someone in ICU screwed up and didn't tell anyone that he was on board. The Lt. Commander, in charge, assigned him to the "back room". That room was "manned" by only those sailors, like him, that had the highest security clearance, the Navy gave. He bunked with the others, of the same clearance. The room was very small and contained a lot of 'sensitive" material. On his first shift, he was introduced to Ensign Barnes. The ensign gave him a short introduction to the various "things" in the room and, then, handed him a 45 automatic pistol, with a belt and a holster. He was told that he would wear the weapon, the whole time, he was in the room. The room had a small door and no windows! The weapon had one "round" of ammunition, in it. He told the ensign, that one round wouldn't stop a bunch of the enemy, coming through the door. The ensign informed him that the "round" wasn't for "them" but for him. That was not what he wanted to hear.

When he got off his "first watch", he went to his 'berth' area and emptied his seabag into his large locker. He "made" his bunk and took off his shoes and lay in the bunk and read the batch of letters. The address only said his name and rate and the name of his ship, and Norfolk VA. He was amazed that the letters got to him. Most of the letters were from his Mom, two from Fred, three from Karen and two from Carolyn, Karen's friend. He read the ones from his mom, first. Dave's wife was still having health problems after his nephew's birth. She spent a couple of days, there, helping out. Fred's letters included the wedding announcement, for September. He read Carolyn's letter. She "disowned" Karen, as a friend, after what she had done to him. The rest of the letter said how much she liked and admired him. She, also, couldn't believe how Karen had "bragged" about his "expertise" in the bedroom. Carolyn mentioned that she was going to school, in Virginia and that she would love to see him. She included her address. The second letter read much like the first, except that she, frequently, spent time in D.C. and how it would be great, if they could spend some time there, together. He put her letters, aside, with Fred's wedding invitation. He heaved a heavy sigh and began to open Karen's letters. The first one was full of apologies, for what she had done. She begged his forgiveness. She still had his rings and would give them back, if he wanted them. The second letter was just "small talk" and hoped they could, at least, be friends. The third letter had stronger language, in it. Apparently, Donny felt "threatened" by Karen's continued feelings towards him. He spread lies about him. He told Karen that he had "fathered" two kids in Ireland! Karen called him all kinds of names and would never write to him, again. He shook his head and ripped up her letters. He kept Fred's, his mom's, and Carolyn's.

Life aboard the Randolph was not "dull". It took him awhile to learn to step over the bottom part of the doors. He had many scars from his knees to his ankles. The work was easy. Only because, he had been well trained, in school. He got along with his shipmates. August turned into September and he was at sea, heading to Bermuda, when Fred and Kathy got married.

He sent them some money and a letter expressing his regret that he couldn't be there. He did carry on correspondence with Carolyn. He seemed to be at sea, every time she wanted to get together.

It was in October, that he noticed "things" were heating up in Viet Nam. Ensign Barnes was concerned that the "crew" might get transferred to a carrier, over there. He didn't pay him much mind. It was the last week in October, that Carolyn sent him a letter, asking if they could get together in November, before she went home for Thanksgiving. He wrote back and said that he would check his calendar and let her know. It turned out that the ship would be "home" in Norfolk the weekend of the 23rd. She wrote back and said how excited she was that they would finally see each other and explore the "sights" of D.C.

The ship got back to Norfolk on the 21st. "She" was anchored in the "stream", because there was any pier space. That meant that he would go ashore by liberty boat. That Friday morning, he was seated at the table, spit shining his shoes. A seaman apprentice knocked on the door to his compartment and asked for him. The seaman handed him a telegram. "So Sorry can't make weekend, explanation in letter, Carolyn." He put down the shoes he was polishing. He wasn't happy. He, actually, was looking forward to seeing her and maybe, just maybe having some sex. He had purchased a box of 12 Trojans. He heaved a heavy sigh and thought, well, he would still leave the ship and drive to Dave's in Richmond, Virginia.

He was halfway down the ladder, to the liberty boat, when the call came out throughout the ship. That all liberty was cancelled. That the Commander in Chief had been shot! They turned around and went back into the ship. He ran down hallways and up ladders to the com shack! Someone had a small black and white TV. They watched the news unfold from Dallas. Walter Cronkite was at the news desk. No one made a sound, everyone listened to the news. He was saying "silent prayers". Then they watched as Walter Cronkite took off his glasses and announced the news that President John F. Kennedy was dead! He had not cried since he was "dumped" by Karen. He found a chair and sat down. The chief led the communications crew in a prayer. Someone said that the Vice President needed our support, now. He thought how ironic it was, that he was going to D.C. and that she cancelled. He never heard from Carolyn, again.

After a few hours, when authorities arrested Lee Harvey Oswald, they must have felt that it was "safe" to grant liberty. He got off the ship and, slowly, walked to the Ford. A front page of a newspaper lay on the ground, of the parking lot. A small breeze from the water, picked it up, and turned it over. The headline read, "Kennedy Assassinated." Then, the paper blew away.

He spent the weekend. At Dave's. Most of it watching the news, unfold. Like, so many others, across the nation, he was in shock and dismayed over everything. He kept thinking, to himself,. "what's next?" In his mind, he knew that Viet Nam would "explode" into a major war and involve many, many, soldiers and sailors. The assassination was a major milestone.

The rest of the year, went by, without incidents, or major events, in his life. Thanksgiving came and went, as did another holiday season, away from home. It was awesome to walk along the piers, during the holidays and see the ships adorned with Christmas lights. Memories of Christmases, long ago, came back, into his mind, as a child. Christmas was a major holiday, in his home, a happy time, with family and friends. He did send out cards, to a lot of folks, including Fred and Kathy, even Karen and Ree. The only ones he heard back from were Fred and Kathy. He even, sent one to Bert's family. His mom sent one, to him, with Bert's address. He and Bert began to correspond.

1964 was his last full year, in the Navy. It started out, uneventful, for him. He and the ensign were becoming more concerned with the "happenings" in Southeast Asia. Most Americans had no idea, what was taking place, in that "corner' of the world. Top Secret communications were "buzzing" about Viet Nam. Soldiers were called "consultants and advisors" and were being killed. They were not allowed to get involved in any "fire" or "aggressive "behavior. If "fired upon" they were to seek shelter and report the coordinates of the "enemy fire." A message went out to all Naval personnel asking for volunteers, to go to Viet Nam. He actually gave it some thought. Unfortunately, it was decided for him and Ensign Barnes. They were involuntarily transferred to the U.S.S. Ranger, in the Gulf of Tonkin, Viet Nam. They were flown to California, then to Hawaii and on to Japan. From the Naval base in Japan, they were flown by helicopter, to the carrier. He and the ensign made it known that they were not happy with their transfer, even if only temporary.

The next milestone, in his life was not a "good one." He was off duty and playing poker with three other "mates" in a room, near one of the elevators on the starboard side. Gerry, a sailor, from Texas, had just got his hand, he looked at it and began to shake. He threw the cards on the table. They all stared at them. Aces and eights, the dead man's hand. It was the hand that Wild Bill Hitchcock had, when he was shot in the back and killed. He got up away from the table and that side of the room and was on the other side of the room, when it happened. A huge, deafening, "blast!" Fire and thick, black smoke, immediately filled the small room. The explosion knocked him to the deck. Facing the bulkhead. His ears were ringing and felt blocked. His eyes and mouth were burning from the acrid smoke. He could not see anything, through the thick, black, smoke. He turned to face the table and the others. He could not see them and he could not open his mouth, with the dense smoke. He crawled on the deck, towards where he knew the door, was supposed to be. He found that the door had been blown open. The door, from what he could tell, was a twisted piece of hot steel! He crawled through the door and into the hallway. Somehow, he knew what direction to crawl to. As the smoke lessened in density, he stood up! He still could not see very well. He used his hands along the bulkhead and, slowly, walked, until he found a ladder. He went up the ladder, to the next deck, down a passageway to another ladder. He finally, made his way to the hanger bay. He knew he had to get to the com shack. The General quarters claxon was 'going off'' throughout the ship. He made it to the com shack and stepped inside. Everyone stared at him. The chief grabbed the phone and screamed into it, for a corpsman! The others laid him down on a blanket that someone had brought. He tried to tell them, that he was okay, but his throat hurt too much. The chief asked him if he was hurt. He shook his head, "no!" Somebody stuck a small mirror in his face. Staring back at him, was a "black" man without any eye brows! His "work shirt had massive tears along the back and back of the sleeves. Somebody said that his shirt probably saved him from being burned. A corpsman arrived and checked him out. The corpsman poured some cold water, slowly down his throat. His voice came back, slowly. The corpsman wiped his face, hands and arms with a cool, damp rag. They said that it was a miracle that he wasn't burned. The "black" was from the smoke! He was helped up, from the deck and placed in a chair. When he could, he asked where the others were? The chief took a roll call and the three, that were with him, were unaccounted for. He lowered his head and muttered "dead man's hand." It took a couple of days for his hearing to completely return to normal. By then, he knew the awful truth. An enemy shell, supposedly from a "gunboat" had hit the ship, as an elevator was bringing a plane, a tractor and two other men down from the flight deck, to the hanger bay. The elevator and the equipment along with the two men, kept right on going, into the sea. There was a large hole, in the bulkhead of the room, where he had been playing cards. Being on the other side of the room, saved his life. The others were not as fortunate. They were never found.

Physically, he was fine. Mentally, he was not. He could not understand why he had been spared! Why was it necessary for him to get up from the table and go and pour another cup of coffee? The ship's chaplain tried to explain, several times. He just couldn't understand. After, a week, from the "hit." He was found to be able to go back to work. Someone found "replacements" for him and the ensign and they were being sent back to the Randolph. They were under strict orders not to say anything about being on the Ranger. It never showed up in their service jackets. For all intensive purposes, they were never on the Ranger! He finished out his tour of duty, on the Randolph. He was promoted to Radioman second class. He guessed it was the Navy's way of saying "sorry." Even though, he passed the test, for it. He was able to go home for the last Christmas, in the Navy. He got the Ford out of "storage" and drove home. He was back on board the ship for New years Eve, but knew it was his last holiday away, from home.

January 5th 1965, he packed his seabag, for the last time. With his orders, releasing him to the U.S. Navy Reserve, he walked off the ship. He couldn't believe that it was over. This time, he was going home and would never have to put on a naval uniform, again.

He had made the trip, home, twice before. Once, to New Hampshire, to see his lifelong friend, Danny, who had been injured in an accident, with a hay baler. The machine had rolled over him and broke his back, but he was going to be all right. He visited Danny, in the hospital and told him it was one "hell of a way" to stay out of the service. It was, then, that the two of them had a "bond" that nothing, not even time could break.

The second time, was for Christmas, 1964. He left most of his civilian clothes, at home, knowing that he would be home, soon, for good. Now, that time, had arrived. He got to the Ford and unlocked the trunk and stowed his seabag in it. He got into the car and was pleased that it started up, oj such a cold January morning. With his orders, beside him, on the front seat, he drove to the main gate and passed through, for the last time. He drove into Norfolk. He stopped at a place called the big "O". it was a bar, but upstairs, above the bar, were lockers, where sailors could change into their civilian clothes and go out on the town. He went to his locker and took out the last set of civvies. He changed and rolled his uniform into two large rolls, one for his jumoer and the other for his bell bottoms. He put the rolls into a large white laundry bag, along with his tie and white hat. He kept his Navy socks and shoes on. He threw the laundry bag over his right shoulder and went the stairs to the bar and handed in his key. The guy behind the bar, took out a ledger and checked his name. He was all "paid up." He thanked the man and walked out to the Ford. He, again, opened the trunk and threw the laundry bag in it. He kept the peacoat on, even though it had his stripes on the left sleeve. He unlocked the Ford and got in and started it up and headed out of Norfolk, for the ride home.

It would only take him 10 hours. The ferry had been replaced by a new "Bay Bridge/tunnel system that took two hours off his travel time. When he got on the highway, he relaxed, lit up an L&M, turned on the radio and sang along with Ray Charles and "Hit The Road, Jack". Ray was followed by Gale Garnett and "We'll Sing In The Sunshine." He sang along with her, too.

She was followed by Manfred Mann and "Do Wah Ditty Ditty" It was a good day, as he sang along with them. Even though he wasn't crazy about the Beatles or the Animals, he still sang along with "Please, Please Me" and "House Of The Rising Sun."

He stopped, only for gas and lunch, as he made the trip, northward. He was thankful that it was a sunny day, though cold. Tears of happiness filled his eyes, when he entered the Massachusetts

Turnpike. He was headed for a new chapter, in his life. He would be sitting in a college classroom in a few weeks. Emerson had welcomed him back, after a four year absence. He would probably be one of the "oldest" freshmen they had, in a long time. He was glad that he had a few weeks to readjust to civilian life. He wondered what it would be like to be home, but without female companionship. That would probably be the toughest adjustment of all.

His folks had moved to a new town. He had been there, only once. That was last Christmas. He pulled into the driveway and parked next to his mom's new VW. He turned off the car and got out. He unlocked the trunk and grabbed his seabag and laundry bag and walked through the garage to the back door. He put down the seabag and opened the door and picked up the bag and went inside. His mom was at the stove, fixing supper. "Just in time." She said and hugged him. He went past the dining room and down the hall and into his "new" room. His old bed was there and his bureau. He deposited the bags on the bed and took off the peacoat and walked back down the hall and into the living room. He shook hands with his dad and sat down. A hockey game was on TV.

After dinner, he went to the hall phone and called Fred. They were the proud new parents of a baby boy! He made plans to go and visit with them, in their new home, in Newton, the next day. He spent that day, relaxing with them. They did a lot of reminiscing. The talk, eventually, got around to Karen. Kathy had heard that she had gotten married to some piano teacher or something. He took them, with little Fred, out to lunch. Fred asked if he ever got his rings back, from her. He told them that she sent them to him. He told Fred that the diamond got him a "whopping" twenty five dollars. She had scratched the hell out of it. Fred wasn't surprised. He didn't see a lot of them, after that day. His dad gave him the 48, 100 dollar bonds, that he had sent to them, every month, during his service. He took them downtown to the local bank. He sat down with a manager, who informed him that he had over four thousand dollars, in bonds. But, some had not matured at all, while some had only a few years to go. He did not want to cash them in, but wanted to know what to do with them. The manager got him a safe deposit box, to put them in, where they would be safe. He thanked the man and turned to leave. As he was walking to the door, a woman passed by him. He stopped and thought he knew her.

She, too, stopped and turned around. It was Ree's mother. They were both surprised to see each other. She asked how he was? He told her that he just finished his "hitch" in the Navy and was going back to college. He asked how she was and she said that she was fine. He asked how Ree was? He hoped that she was still single and that the two of them might get together. He did not relay that thought to her mom. His heart fell, when he was told that Ree was fine. She had been married for a little over a year and was expecting her first child. Though his heart was heavy, he told her to tell Ree, that he was happy for her and wished her well. Her mom that said, "you know, my husband and I were hoping that you two would get married. We really liked you!

She married a nice guy, kinda nerdy, but a nice guy. Ree was and I suspect, still is quite fond of you." That statement cut him deep. They wished each well and said good bye. He went out to the Ford and got in, started it up and drove home.

While he was home, he had to renew his driver's license, his registration, and get the car inspected. He was told at the inspection station, that he needed to have seatbelts installed. It was a new regulation. The station said that they could do it, a hundred and twenty five dollars. He was pondering it, when the owner of the station drove in. He heard him mention his last name as he gave the manager, his information, for the work. The owner asked him if he was related to his dad? He said "yes." The owner shook his hand and told him that his dad was working to get his son into Brown University. He asked the manager what the work order was for? He told him, "seatbelts." The owner said "write it up for 75 dollars." He thanked the man, profusely and would bring the car in, the next day. He had nothing to do, so he would wait for the car. The manager said that it would take a couple of hours. He said that was okay, he would walk around and get acquainted with the town.

The car done, he went home and prepared for his next milestone, College. He had to prepare himself, mentally. He was going to major in broadcast journalism. He wanted to get through college as fast as he could, so that he could begin his career as a broadcast newsman. The next few weeks went by very fast and February arrived, quickly. Before he realized it, he was in Boston and registering for his classes. Getting ready for the next major milestone, in his life.

College days

(In Crowd . . . . Dobie Gray)

Registration was a culture shock! He was dressed in a blue blazer, white shirt, tie and tan slacks. He was, constantly, identified as a professor. Even the registrar thought he was a teacher. When he told her, that he was a member of the second semester freshmen class. She told him that it was nice to see someone dress up, again. He handed her his G.I. Bill papers. He looked around and couldn't believe his eyes! Girls were either dressed in the shortest skirts, he had ever seen (miniskirts) or in dungaree bell bottoms! The strangest thing was that they paid top dollar for the bell bottoms. His were free! Well, almost, they did cost him years of his life and almost his life.

After he registered his major classes, he needed some minor ones. He saw two lines, that were 95% female! He went and stood in both the lines, one after the other and registered for education classes. He realized that he signed up for six, three credit courses. He knew it was a lot, but he was in a hurry, to get through college.

After registration, he went to the book store and purchased his books. He was lucky to have some cash left in his wallet. He went to the car and took a small suitcase and his seabag, full of civilian clothes and Navy work jacket and dungarees, and went into the dorm, across the street, from where he parked. His room overlooked the street. He could see the car and that made him feel good. He unloaded his clothes into a closet and bureau. He put his toiletries in the top drawer, put hibooks on the bed. He changed out of the "registration" clothes and into a pair of dungarees (bell bottoms) and his work jacket. He went to look, for the coffee shop.

After many different directions, he, finally, found it. He made his way through the tables, some empty, some not, to the counter. The short order cook was a brawny guy in an apron that should have been condemned by the board of health, months ago. Even the paper hat had grease stains! The guy wiped his hands on a towel, that was as dirty as his apron and T-shirt. The man had half a cigar hanging out of the corner of his mouth. He, also, looked like he hadn't shaved for days. It wasn't a beard, it was just stubble. He wasn't sure he wanted any food, from this guy, but he was hungry! "Yaah?" the guy asked. He ordered two cheeseburgers, a side of fries and a large coke. The man turned around and threw two thick raw slabs of meat on the grill along with two pieces of cheese, on a plate next to the grill. "cokes are in the machine" he growled. He went and took out a bottle of coke and returned to the counter. He sat down. As the burgers turned a dark brown, he threw the cheese on them, and toasted the bread.

The "cook" turned around and put the cheeseburgers on a paper plate and put it in front of him. He then went to a bin and scooped out a bunch of fries and put them in a paper cup and brought them to him. For the first time, the cook actually looked at him. "You Navy?" he asked. "yeah!" he replied, "just got out," The cook wiped his burly right hand on the aforementioned apron and stuck it out, to him. Inside he cringed as he shook it. "I'm Frank. The meal's on the house, this time. Next time, you pay." He thanked him and Frank then said "we Navy guys stick together." Frank told him that he was the cook on a Destroyer, in the South Pacific, during Korea. Frank leaned forward and the distinct odor of his body wafted over his food. He, quickly, moved his plate to his right side. Frank said, softly," if you was in Nam, don't tell anyone. These punk kids will be all over you! These sniffling brats don't know nothing about war! Theys all stinking pinko doves!" he leaned back, almost off the stool! Frank, again, said, "We Navy guys stick together!" Frank had to go down the counter to wait on a couple of girls. He, quickly, grabbed his food and moved to an empty table. He was sitting, there, eating, when three young girls sat down across from him. They were so busy talking about what a pain registration was and they paid him no attention. He finished his meal. He had to admit that Frank cooked a "mean" burger! He sat back, in his seat, and took out an L&M and lit it. He drew the smoke deep into his lungs and let out a long exhale. A cigarette always tasted best, after a good meal. The three girls had stopped talking and looked at him. They each asked him for a cigarette. He gave one to each of them. He passed his zippo to them. The conversation was very friendly, until he told them that he had just got out of the Navy. They glared at him, picked up their books and left the table. He looked at the counter. Frank was leaning over it. "Told them you were Navy, didn't ya?" he sighed and got up from the table and went back to the dorm.

He thought dorm life would be somewhat like life in the barracks. It wasn't. he was the only person over 21 and all the others wanted him to buy them booze. The other thing, about dorm, life, was he was not allowed to have female companionship in his room. After two months, he was ready to move out, to either a room, in a boarding house, or his own apartment. Rooms were hard to come by and apartments weren't cheap.

One evening, over dinner, in the college dining room, he discussed his dilemma with a guy, the had met a few days earlier. Chet, was, also, in the dorm. Chet felt the same, as him. While they were discussing their "problem", they were joined by two other friends, Robbie and Rick. It seemed that all four of them had the same feelings. They wanted to get out of the dorm.

It was the beginning of March, Chet and he had double dated to see the new James Bond film. He was with a short, plump girl who seemed scared to death of him. Chet was with Rachel, a slim, athletic type girl with a nice figure. It was after the show, as they all walked back towards the dorms, that he mentioned the cottage on the lake. He decided that he was going to go there, the weekend after the next one. Chet and Rachel said that they wished they could go. Rachel loved the mountains and the outdoors! He said, "why not!" Rachel said that she would ask around and see if she could get another girl to come with them. Chet felt that he had a "sure thing" with Rachel.

Rachel tried hard to find someone, for Chet! No one was interested! So, when the weekend approached, he was surprised to find that Rachel, still wanted to go. It wasn't until they were at the cottage and she tried to get the fire going, that he found out that Rachel wanted to be with him and not Chet. He took the poker and matches from her and said that he would take over. She looked at him and said "I hope so!" Chet was "hurt" when he found out that he really didn't have a "sure thing." Each of them spent the night, huddled around the fire, in the fire place in their own sleeping bags. It was in the middle of the night, that he felt the zipper of his bag unzip. He was half awake and hoped the body that joined him in his bag, was Rachel and not Chet. It was Rachel. He turned to her and she put her arms around his neck and their lips met. When their lips separated, she said, "I don't want to be a one night stand." He said he didn't like one night stands. They kissed several times and then fell asleep in each other's arms.

The next morning, the three of them drove back, in the Ford, to school. Chet was sleeping in the back seat. Rachel was sitting right next to him. They sang along to Jewel Atkins "Birds and Bees." And The Rolling Stones song, "I Can't Get No Satisfaction." Afterwards, Rachel began expressing the wish that he had his own apartment. He told her that he was looking into it.

He was sitting in the coffee shop, drinking coffee and smoking an L&M, while studying. Chet, Robbie and Rick sat down at the table. They were excited! They found an apartment. It was at the base of Beacon Hill, It was spacious, had four bedrooms, a breakfast nook, kitchen, large living room, one bathroom and was only 240 dollars a month. It was furnished and the cost of heat and electricity was included! He quickly divided four into 240. He said "that's sixty dollars a month, for each of us. "Right! "They said. "I can swing it, but can you guys?" he asked. They had already talked to their parents and their parents would co-sign for them. He wanted to go and look at it. They grabbed him out of his seat and he left a buck on the table, as they left the shop. They would have to sign a 12 month lease. The realtor office on the first floor handled the rent. They would pay him, the first of each month. He was reluctant to sign. He asked the realtor, what would happen if two or more of them dropped out of the lease. "You would be responsible for the whole 240 dollars." The realtor assured them, that if, for some reason, they should opt out of the lease, they only had to come to him and he would find subletters. The realtor said that he does it all the time. The others pushed him to sign. He did! The apartment would be empty the middle of May. They could move in then. The rent would not start until the first of June.

He and Rick drove to his house, in Needham, one evening, to get some of his things. Things, that he would want in the apartment. They loaded up his trunk and on the way back to Boston, they decided to stop at ho-Jo's for dinner. He parked the car, next to a light green VW beetle. He turned off the Ford and the two of them got out of the car. He locked the car and they went inside. He turned to his left and started walking to a booth. The first one he saw, was Janet. He looked at who she was with, it was Ree! He was in shock! He managed to say "hi". They were shock, but pleased to see him. Ree had a baby with her. She moved the baby seat, closer to the wall and invited he and Rick, to join them. They hadn't ordered yet. He sat beside Ree and Rick sat beside Janet. A waitress came and took their orders. Ree guessed that he still ate cheeseburgers. He smiled and said that some things never change. She ordered a lobster roll. They did a lot of catching up. Inside, his heart was aching. She looked fabulous! He told her that he wished he knew her secret, for looking so good. Janet caught on something, between them and tried to prevent it from going any further. Ree couldn't take her eyes off him and he couldn't take his eyes off her. He learned the baby's name was Doug. He learned that she had been married since 1963. She said that he would like her husband. That her husband was a lot like him. Inside, he hated the man and envied him. He told Ree that her husband was a very, very, lucky man. She wanted to know how he was doing? When did he get out? What was he doing now? He told her everything except what he wasn't suppose to tell anyone. They all finished eating. Ree and Janet had to leave. He and Rick walked with them out to Ree's car. It was the Beetle he parked beside. She said that it was because of him, that she knew how to drive the car. She put the baby into the backseat and strapped him in. She turned around and said that it was great seeing him again. He wished her all the happiness, that she deserved. He watched her get in, start the car, close the door. Janet got in the other side and they drove away. When he and Rick got into the Ford, Rick asked him who were those beautiful women. He told him. Rick looked at him and said "I think you made a big mistake, not staying with her." He replied, "I do to, too."

School was going well. He studied hard and even though he carried six courses, he managed to keep his grades at C+ and above. March quickly ended and April went by fast, as well. Rachel was getting impatient with him. She wanted a "sex life" with him. It seems that every time they would get to the point, where intercourse was inevitable, they would be interrupted!

One evening, they were shooting pool, on the third floor, of the student union. He had a very easy shot lined up. The shot that would beat her. She was wearing a low cut blouse. She stood by the corner hole, the hole that he was aiming his shot at. She had unbuttoned the buttons on her blouse. She was not wearing a bra. Her breasts hung out over the hole. He looked at her breasts as he attempted to make the shot. He "scratched" horribly! He threw the cue on the table and came around the side. She was walking towards him, her blouse wide open. As they embraced, one of his teachers came through the door, with two potential students, on tour. He held Rachel tight against his chest, so no one could see her chest. She giggled as the teacher and the "guests" left the room. She told him that she was having a hard time, waiting for the apartment. He said that he was too.

In fact, all four of them were getting "antsy". They couldn't wait to get into their new "digs". They had parties all lined up for the first three weekends. Chet was dating Ingrid, a statuesque blond. Rick was dating Rhonda, a hippie guitar player, with long brown hair, all the way down her back to her lower back. Robbie had "designs" on Michelle, a short black haired girl from Mississippi. They just knew that college life was going to get a lot better, once they were out of the dorm and into their own place. He, especially, was excited, because he was going to be the "caretaker" of the place, while the others were away, for the summer. The large apartment was in effect, going to be his! He would be alone in it!

Saturday, May 22nd was moving day! He made several trips with the Ford, between the dorm and Charles Street. Chet had a sports car and had gone home, to get it, over the Spring break. He helped move stuff as well. The girlfriends were already in the apartment. They helped clean it and helped with the small things. Small things like wall pictures and paintings, lamps and a small stereo. It took all morning. The girls stayed in the apartment, while the guys jumped into the Ford and drove to the Stop&Shop supermarket to buy and stock up on food and cleaning supplies.

The rear end of the Ford was quite low to the ground, as they drove "home". The girls came down to the street and everyone "pitched in" and unloaded the Ford. He went around the block, several times until he found a parking space. Rick wanted to know why he didn't park across the street. There were plenty of parking spaces. He showed Rick that it was a "taxi stand." He showed him the phone attached to the brick siding of the building. The cabs would pull up, during the weekdays and when the phone rang, a driver would get out of his cab, walk up to the building and pick up the phone and then go and get his "fare".

By four PM, they were in! By six PM, the beer was cold, the wine chilled; the party on!

The Apartment

(Theme from The Apartment . . . Ferrante & Teicher)

He was glad that the apartment just below them was vacant. Their party went on well past midnight. It was about two thirty AM, when the last "guests" left. He and Rachel had snuck into his bed around 12:30 and made up for "lost time." They were under the covers and totally exhausted, when he heard Chet and Ingrid come into the room. The noises caused by Chet and Ingrid, ignited their passion, again. No one seemed to notice or even care that both couples were having sex, in the same room. He and Rachel couldn't get enough of each other! She told him that she had never had a boyfriend tend to her needs over his, before. He doesn't remember when he and Rachel, finally fell asleep.

The next morning, Sunday, everyone slept in till around ten AM. He got out of bed, after slipping on his briefs, under the covers. He bent down beside the bed and carefully picked up two "used' condoms, off the floor. Rachel was still asleep. He looked over at Chet and Ingrid. They, too were asleep, in each other's arms. He crept out of the bedroom, into the living room and into the back bedroom. Rick and Rhonda were asleep, in each other's arms, as well. Robbie and Michelle were asleep, too. He crept into the bathroom and flushed the condoms down the toilet. He was walking back through the kitchen, when he heard the buzzer. Someone, at the street level wanted to come up to the apartment. The noise woke everyone up. No one was dressed! The girls were walking around in bras and panties and the guys, like him, were in undershorts, and briefs.

There was a knock on the door. He opened it and stood face to face with two Nuns! They were just about to speak to him, when Rachel and Ingrid walked up behind him, in their bras and panties. He didn't get a chance to say anything, either. The Nuns quickly turned around and went back down the stairs. He closed the door as everyone burst into laughter! Chet said that he felt bad, for them. He asked him, "why?" he said, "because I'm Catholic!" Then, even he joined in the laughter. Chet said "They probably think we are too deep in sin and can't be helped." All the rest, with his exception, were Jewish! He was the only Protestant. That was the first and last time, religion was talked about, in the apartment.

Rick, being the "cook" in the group began to crack eggs and put bread in the toaster. He offered to make the coffee. The only ones that got dressed were Robbie and Michelle. The rest of them spent most of the day, lounging around the apartment. Every once in a while, Chet and Ingrid would slip back into the bedroom. When they emerged, he and Rachel would go back in.

Rachel had a way of sitting on his bed, on the back of her legs, her underwear off, covered only by one of his T-shirts. The bottom hiked up to her thighs, her shoulder and one breast exposed, with the sexiest look on her face. That drove him absolutely wild!

Weekends in the apartment, were just like the first one, right up to finals. Then everyone spent the time, studying. There was still a lot of sex, but most of the time was in the books. There was one big party, when finals were over. Rachel was leaving, to go home. She told him about a party in New York City on the fourth of July. She would write him about the time and the place. They would have their own room. He was interested and said he would check the mail and for her to include a phone number. She said that she would. Rick was the first of the "four" guys, to leave. Rick walked out with his suitcase and told him that he would send the rent money every month, to the realtor. He wished Rick a good summer. Rick said, as he left, that Rhonda was still asleep in his bed. Robbie left with Michelle and told him that his rent checks would, also be sent to the realtor. All that was left, by 11AM, were Chet and Ingrid. He grabbed a beer from the fridge and a chair and sat in the front window and "people watched". He lit up an L&M and watched the people scurrying around in the street, below. Chet and Ingrid had retreated to the couch and were making plans, to meet over the summer. Rhonda appeared from the bedroom, wearing a little teddy and nothing underneath. Her long, dirty blonde hair cascading down her back to her buttocks. She walked up to him and took the L&M from his mouth; put it in hers and took a long drag. She stuck it back in his mouth and took the can of Miller Light, from him and took a sip. All this without saying a word! She, then took the cigarette from his lips and crushed it out in the ash tray, next to him. She put the beer can on the floor and took his hand and pulled him from the chair. "I'm horny!" was all she said, as she pulled him along, across the living room and into his and Chet's bedroom.

She was wild! She liked everything! Especially oral! He learned some new positions from her. They spent over an hour in the room. He used up three more condoms. She left him, lying on his back, on the bed and left the room. He was still lying there, when she dressed and with her guitar slung over her shoulder, left the apartment. He crawled off the bed and put on a pair of cutoff jeans and practically staggered out into the living room. Chet and Ingrid, had obviously, just finished having sex on the couch. He went back to the chair and sat down, drank the rest of the, now warm, beer and lit up another L&M.

"How can you do it? How can you spend the night, with a girl, who is obviously crazy about you and then not a few hours later, have sex with another girl?" Ingrid was furious with him! He turned around and told her that he had just been through" hell" the last few months of the Navy! He had come close to being killed. He made a vow, that he was going to live life to the fullest. As if every day was going to be his last. If a young, beautiful girl wanted to have sex with him, he would not refuse her! Ingrid tried to understand.

Chet and Ingrid left the apartment, together. Chet wished him a good summer and to take care of the apartment. He said that he would. He would even clean it up, for them. They said their good byes and then he was alone. He went back to the window and watched as Chet and Ingrid drove off in Chet's sports car. He went into the bedroom and, again, picked up the "evidence" of his and Rhonda's "escapades."

When he came out of the bathroom, he went back into the bedroom and made his bed. He was glad that the others made their beds, before they left. He went into the kitchen and cleaned up the dirty dishes and pots and pans and put everything away. He threw on a pair of jeans and a T-shirt, sneakers sans socks, found his keys with the apartment key and with his wallet, in his back pocket, went down the stairs and onto the street. He walked along until he found a pizza shop. He went inside and ordered a small cheese and pepperoni pizza. He paid for the pizza and walked back to the apartment. Once back in, he sat at the window, with his pizza, a Miller Lite and said to himself" Life is good; he only hoped that the summer would be as good as the way it was starting out. He would start his summer job, Monday.

He arrived at the garage at 8AM. He parked the Ford alongside the building and went into the office. Seven of the "roughest" looking men were sitting around on small chairs, facing a large desk. He had to stand and lean against a wall. No one said a word, to him. At five minutes after eight, a small, stocky, bald headed man walked into the office and sat down behind the desk. He looked at him and asked if he was the "summer" kid. He said "yes." Though, he hardly thought of himself as a kid. When he glanced around the room, he guessed that he was the youngest one there. The boss's name was Daley. He was introduced to all the others. He was assigned to ride with a guy they called "Dago." The man was not happy. He told the boss that he enjoyed being alone. The man told him to "come on". He followed the "Dago" outside and climbed up into the cab of a large dump truck. Their job was to go to the high school and find some empty classrooms and take apart old desks and throw them into the dump part of the truck. Summer school was in session, so they had to be careful and pick the right rooms.

They did that for the whole week. He remembered picking up Ree, at that very school and attending her senior prom, there. He couldn't get over that, five years had passed since that time. Dago asked if he was married. He said "no." he did tell Dago that he had just gotten out of the Navy. Dago's attitude, towards him, softened. So did the attitudes of the others, when they found out that he was a veteran, like them. After that Monday, he was told to just go and park his car, in the high school parking lot and meet Dago and the others, there. Friday morning, the boss came into one of the rooms they were in. he had just finished dismantling an old desk, when the boss handed him his first paycheck. Daly, then told them, that the work, for the week, ended at noon. He went to the boss and said that he was expecting a full check, for the week. That he really needed a full pay check. Daley took him aside, away from the others and told him, that because of his friendship with a member of the school board, he would receive a full check. He told him, for his own good, to keep his mouth shut. He did as he was told.

Thursday, he went to his folks house, for lunch. His mom wanted to know, if he was going to spend the weekend, with them, at the cottage. He hadn't thought about it, but after thinking about it, said "sure!" He told her that he would be off work that Friday, at noon. She said, for him to drive up, right from work. He went home that night and packed some clothes into a small bag.

Summer school was over. They had to dismantle all the old desks and out them in the dump truck. Now that school was over, they were allowed to open the windows and throw the parts out the windows, into the truck. He said that he always wanted to tear apart a school desk and throw it out a window. Dago and the others laughed and said, "us to."

They left the building, at noon. Dago drove the truck back to the garage. He got into the Ford. His bag of clothes, were in the trunk. The June, noonday, sun shone down. He unlatched the top and pushed the button that lowered the top. He stopped at the gas station, where he got the seat belts and "fueled up." With a full tank of gas and the oil checked, he headed North. He had no idea, what kind of a weekend, he was going to have.

He didn't even stop, for lunch. He arrived at the cottage, around two thirty. He took his bag, and entered the cottage and went into the his room, at the cottage. His mom was in the kitchen; his dad was at the grill, cooking some hot dogs. He changed into his bathing suit and walked out onto the end of the dock and dove into, the crystal clear, blue water. The cool water felt so soothing on his skin. He floated on his back, did the back stroke and turned over and swam back towards the dock. Dripping wet, he climbed up the ladder and sank his wet body into a chaise lounge chair. In no time, the hot sun dried his unruly hair and body. For the first time, in a long time, he didn't care what his hair looked like. In fact, he didn't have a care, in the world. It had been a very long time, since he had felt that good, about himself. He was ready to take a nap, when his dad yelled that the hot dogs and rolls were "ready."

He got off the chair and went to the porch and got himself two hotdogs, a bunch of chips and a coke. He told his mom, that he dreamed of being there, in the summer, many times. She asked him, if he had made sure that everything was off and locked up in the apartment. He told her it was "secure." He went back out to the dock and sat back in the chair and proceeded to eat his lunch. When done, he got off the chair and went into the kitchen and got rid of his "trash" in the kitchen trash barrel. He went back out and onto the dock, to his chair and laid back down and closed his eyes. He felt like he was on paradise!

He never heard the speedboat pull up to the dock. He did hear a man's voice say, "guess we're working him too hard." He opened his left eye and put his hand over it, to shield the sun. It was the gas station owner, who had helped him get the job. He used both eyes to look at the blonde girl sitting next to him, in the boat. His dad was holding the bow rope. The girl stood up and he got off the chair and stood up. They were introduced. The girl's name was Constance. She said "Hi and it's Connie." He said "hi" and told her his name. Next to her was a short, stocky brunette, in a one piece bathing suit. She was Jessie. His attention went back to the slim, well toned, long haired blonde in the light blue bikini. She had the type of body that bikinis were meant for. Her breasts were large, but not too large. Her body was also well tanned. There wasn't an ounce of fat on her! Her long legs and flat stomach, added to his excitement. That excitement faded fast, when her dad said that she was there, at their place, with her husband and Jessie, the stocky brunette. He heaved a heavy sigh and thought to himself, 'too bad, she's married." He thanked her dad, for getting him the job. He said nothing about the full week's pay. As they talked, Jessie had a great sense of humor. She made everyone laugh!

As they were about to leave, Connie asked him, if he wanted to come over to their place that night? He tried not to sound too eager and said "sure, what time?" They said around 7PM. He said "okay!" They pushed the boat away, from the dock. He looked at Connie, through the windshield. She ran her tongue across her white teeth and lips and waved to him. He gave a short wave back. He sat back down on the chaise. He wished his hair had been combed!

His mom said, after they left, "better do something about tonight's dinner, early, so he can get over to their place." His dad said that he thought they would go out to eat. His mom told his dad that, in that case, they should leave around five, so they could get back, in time. He told them, that he probably didn't have to be there right at 7. He closed his eyes and tried to imagine what a night, it could be. If only the blonde wasn't married. Jessie wasn't too bad looking, a little on the "earthy" side. She was funny, though.

They went to the Wolfeboro Inn, to eat. Instead of his usual cheeseburgers, he had a lobster dinner. For the first time, in his life, he had a before dinner drink, with his folks. His dad liked manhattans, his mom had gin and he had a rum and coke. He was glad that he had packed some "nice" clothes. He had on a light blue dress shirt and tan slacks with black loafers. He decided that when he got back to the cottage, he would not change his clothes. He knew that he was going to be 'paired" with Jessie. He didn't care. It wasn't as if they were going to make out or anything. They would probably just sit around and talk.

He and his parents got back to the cottage around 6:40PM. He wondered, to his folks, if he should bring something, with him, to their cottage. His mom had an unopened bottle of wine, in the cabinet. He would bring that. His dad told him to tell them, that they might want to chill it in ice before opening it. He said he would mention it.

His mom wanted him to wear a jacket. She said the night gets cool. He said that his long sleeved shirt was good enough. He went into the bathroom and combed his hair and splashed some English leather on. He checked himself, out in the mirror and decided he looked "okay." He came out of the bathroom and went into the kitchen and picked up the bottle of wine and walked through the living room. His mom was reading a book, his dad was listening to the Red Sox, on the radio and doing a crossword puzzle. He said that he probably would be back in a couple of hours. His mom, without looking up, from her book, told him to have fun and that they would leave the porch light on. His dad told him to take the flashlight off the hutch. He did, as he headed out the door.

He walked out the driveway, turned to his left and walked to the end of the road. He went around the fence. Past the small cottages and onto the driveway, behind a large cottage. The cottage had a large farmers porch. He walked around to the front, that faced the lake. As he approached the front, they were all sitting in chairs, on the porch. He walked up the steps. He said hello to Mr. Gorman and introduced himself to Mrs. Gorman. He handed the bottle of wine, to her and said that it should be chilled. He said 'hi" to Jessie. Connie was not on the porch. He was invited to have a seat. Mr. Gorman explained to the others, that he had just got out of the Navy and was back in college. As Mr. Gorman was talking, yelling was heard from within the house. Mr. Gorman winced and said that things were not good with Connie and her husband, Joe. Mrs. Gorman said the 'boy" was a drunk! The yelling went on for a while, and then subsided. Connie soon appeared at the screen door. She looked out at them, straightened her long blonde hair and opened the door. When she stepped onto the porch, she took his breath away! She was in a white shirt, with the two top buttons unbuttoned. The shirt was tucked into a pair of white short shorts. Her dark tan was in sharp contrast with her clothes.

Jessie was in a dark blue sweatshirt and black Bermuda shorts. He surmised that they were two totally different women. He got out of his seat and said "hi." She had obviously been crying. Her folks were concerned and asked if she was all right. She said "Herb is stinking drunk, again!" She looked at him and Jessie and asked if they could go for a walk. He said "sure, why not!" The three of them stepped off the porch and walked around the side of the house, to the back driveway. They began to walk up the road, away from the house. Connie did most of the talking. She had been married for three years and said that Herb had been constantly drunk for most of those years. She said that had she known he was a drunk, she never would have married him. He learned that Connie was three years older than him. Jessie was a year younger than him. He didn't say anything, just listened. Connie soon apologized for doing all the talking. Jessie soon began to 'crack" a few jokes and pretty soon all three of them were laughing. When they got back to the cottage, they went out and sat on the dock, to watch the sunset.

They stayed on the dock, well past the sunset. Their chairs were close together. Every now and then one of them would see a "shooting star." It was quite peaceful, on the dock. He was sitting between Jessie and Connie. Connie made the remark that he was like a thorn between two roses. They laughed. Connie asked him if he liked to dance. He said that he loved to dance. She asked "jitterbug?" he said "yup!" Jessie mocked him "yup!" Connie said that three of them should go out the next night, downtown to the "Pirates Den." She explained that it was an inn that was on the water. It had three floating docks. One dock was a bandstand, with a "Live" band and the other docks were put together for a dance floor. He said, "Let's do it!" Jessie did not know how to Jitterbug, but said that she would dance the "slow" dances with him. They made plans to go, the next night. It was getting late and Connie said that Herb should be "passed out." They said "good night' and parted.

The girls picked him up around 7:30PM. Connie drove them in her white 1962 Ford Galaxie, hardtop sedan. She parked in front of the inn. They walked down a driveway, to the back of the inn. He brought a bottle of Seagram's. Connie was concerned that he might end up like her husband. He promised her that he was more of a dancer, than a drinker.

They found an empty table. The band was just getting set up. A waitress brought them three bottles of Seven Up and three glasses. He poured more Seven up into the glasses, than the whiskey. He and Connie danced every jitterbug. She was a natural! They were a perfect match! Everyone stopped dancing and watched them. They knew and danced all the moves, smoothly and to the music. They got more applause than the band. He danced the waltzes with Jessie. They barely touched the "booze." They were having too much fun!

Jessie was dressed in a pair of slacks and a sweater. Connie was in a pleated dress that flared out like a poodle skirt. The top was cut just low enough to share a little cleavage. Towards the end of the evening, Jessie made him dance a couple of slow dances with Connie. When he did, she held him so tight, he thought his back and ribs might crack! He danced almost every dance! When they, finally, called it a night. He was exhausted! He left the whisky bottle on the table. It was full! Jessie said that he and Connie danced as if they had been dancing together, all their lives. He had never had a dancing partner, like her.

On the way back to the cottages, Connie asked if he was living at home. He told her that he had an apartment in Boston, at the base of Beacon Hill, on Charles Street. In the dim light, he saw her smile. They made a "pact" that when the two of them were at the lake, on a weekend, they would get together and go dancing at the Pirates Den. Jessie commented, "only if you bring me with you!" They agreed.

When they dropped him off at his cottage, Jessie gave him, her phone number. They did date for a week or so. Then something 'strange" happened. Jessie began to act rather strange. She was a "Brenda Starr" fan. "Brenda Starr" was a comic strip character. The boyfriend, in the strip, was a "mystery man." He wore a patch over one eye. Jessie wanted him to wear a patch over one eye. He said that he wouldn't. Jessie was not happy.

One weekend, Connie's car wouldn't start. He drove them home. The three of them were in the front seat, of his car. A "passed out drunk" was lying in the backseat. He drove Jessie home, first. Then, he drove Connie and Herb home. Herb woke up, enough, to go into the house. Connie stayed behind and was talking with him, in her driveway. She noticed that things had "cooled off" between him and Jessie. He told her why. She was not surprised. Connie wanted to know if he and Jessie had made love. He told her, "No!" They had shared a couple of kisses. Connie then asked, if maybe his kissing wasn't up to par. He replied that he didn't know. "let's see." Said Connie. She moved up to him and pushed him against the side of the house. Their lips met in a sensual, long, wet kiss. She stepped back. "Wow! Nothing wrong with your kisses! You are a great kisser! I want some more!" She stepped in, again. This time was more intense and more passionate than the first! When, at last, she stepped away. She looked him in the eye and said, "to hell with Jessie! I want you!" He stammered "what about Herb?" She answered that Herb hadn't 'touched" her in months! That she wanted a "real" man and that she found him! She told him that she would be moving back in with her parents by the middle of the week. He never saw Jessie again!

(You Were On My Mind . . .
The Wee Five)

I t started off innocently enough. She would find out where he was working, in town, and drive up to the site, in her white Ford, and have two bags of sandwiches and cokes, with her. He would get in the car and they would drive to a park, or some remote place, and have lunch, together. After lunch, they would share a couple of kisses. Then, she would drive him back to the work site.

After she moved out on her husband and started divorce proceedings, their meetings took on a more serious note. It was a weekend in NH. They had "double dated" with her brother and his girlfriend, at the Pirates Den. She drove, that night. She drove her brother and his girlfriend home, first. Then, she told them that she was going to drive him home. She didn't want him walking to his cottage, without a flashlight. She turned the car around and sped out down the road. She was really speeding! They got to his dirt road and turned into the mile and a half dirt road to his cottage. Halfway in, she found an overgrown road, that didn't go very far. She backed the car into it, far enough, so anyone coming down the road would not see them. She turned off the car and the headlights and pushed the front seat, as far back as it would go. She turned to him. "I hope you are as good as your kisses!" They embraced in a kissing frenzy! How their clothes came off as fast as they did, he didn't know, or cared. The first time, there wasn't any foreplay! Her back was on the seat, her legs splayed apart, him between them. Her arms around his back, her nails "raking" his back! She could not have children, so there wasn't any need for a condom. It felt so wonderful for him to be inside her, without a condom! Their passion was unstoppable! She matched him thrust for thrust! She was grunting and screaming like a wild animal! The first time, he finished first and she didn't finished at all. They lay together, with him on top, for a long time. In the moonlight, he could just see her beautiful body. He got off her and they sat up, in the seat. He lit two

442

L&Ms and handed one to her. She put her hand on him and began to slowly stroke him back to life. He crushed out his cigarette and moved his lips and tongue over to her breasts. His left arm around her neck, his right hand between her thighs. She leaned forward and put out her cigarette, then threw he head back against the back of the seat. "Oh My God! You feel so good on my breasts and nipples and your fingers!" he wanted to make sure that she finished, the second time, they made love. He was getting stronger, from her ministrations. She was getting quite damp. Then, he found her "nub" with his the tip of one of his fingers. Her hips began to thrust against his fingers. In one quick move, she was on him, straddling him and putting him inside her. He moved his fingers to her clitoris. His mouth, lips and tongue and his "free" hand were caressing her breasts ad nipples. She grabbed his head with her hands and brought their lips together. Her mouth opened and her tongue stabbed through his slightly opened lips. Her scream almost shattered his ear drums as he felt her finish, the first time. He kept caressing her clitoris, as she thrust up and down on him, covering his face with kisses and fusing her lips to his. She kept right on thrusting and thrusting. Finally, he could not take it anymore and exploded inside her, again. His fingers didn't stop, nor her thrusting, even though he was finished. He had never experienced such passion, such animal lust! She,again, finished! After a few minutes, as he, "limped" out of her, she climbed off him. They didn't say a word, as they dressed. Once their clothes were back on, he, again, lit two cigarettes and handed one to her. She laid her head on his shoulder. She broke the silence. "I wish I met you, before Herb. Now, that I found you. You are not getting away!" He asked her how long it had been, for her? She said, "seven months!" Then she said," I can't believe that you are single, or, at least have a girlfriend! Sweet one, you do now!" She turned on the car and the heater, as the cool New Hampshire night air, filtered into the car. When the radio came on, The Wee Five were singing "You Were On My Mind." "That's our song," she said, as she turned on the headlights and drove him to the cottage. She parked in his driveway and ended the night with a long sensual, wet, tongue lashing kiss. "Good night, sugar, I hope I didn't wear you out!" he got out of the car and looked back in and said to her, "not a chance!" She laughed, as he closed the car door. She was down the driveway and gone, by the time he let himself into the cottage.

It didn't take her long to find her way to the apartment. One night, after work, he had just arrived at the apartment and was in the shower, cleaning off the day's work. He was "toweling off" when the buzzer sounded. He wrapped the towel around him and went to the intercom, by the door. He was surprised to hear her voice! He buzzed her up. He forgot that he was still in just a towel. He opened the door. She looked at him, ran her tongue around her teeth and lips and stepped out of the hall, into the apartment, turned and closed the door and stripped him of the towel. She, not knowing, which bedroom was his, literally pushed him into the nearest one. It just happened to be his. She pushed him onto the bed and quickly "tore" off her clothes and jumped on him. It was nine o'clock, when they emerged from the bedroom.

She was hungry. He went to the phone and ordered a pizza. They were still in their underwear, when the pizza arrived. She went to the kitchen, while he answered the door and paid for the pizza. They sat at the small kitchenette and devoured many slices!

For the rest of the summer, they danced, went sightseeing around New Hampshire, sailed her sailboat, which always ended up at some uninhabited beach. Most of all, they had sex! A lot of sex! It was quite another milestone! First of all, a divorcee, second, an older woman, third, unable to have children, meant no condoms, to buy. Quite a milestone.

She would show up at the apartment, for only one reason and that reason ended up in his bed, or the couch and once, on the living room floor! It was a summer like no other. Even his summer with Ree didn't compare, except that Connie was not into "oral". She was a very sexual lady! They spent the Labor Day weekend together. He knew, with the fall, his roommates would return.

Even though college wouldn't begin until the middle of September, one by one, Chet, Rick, and Robbie came back to the apartment. He was thankful that Connie did not show up, the night the four guys got together. They sat around the kitchenette table and swapped "summer stories". It was Robbie that asked how the "sex" party in New York City went with Rachel. He explained that it didn't. He did not have a key to their mailbox. He couldn't get one, until after the July weekend. He wrote Rachel and explained what had happened, but never got a response. He found out, later, that Rachel was not coming back to college, until the second semester. Chet and Ingrid had broken up as had the others and their girlfriends. They asked him about his summer. He told them. They decided to throw a 'welcome back" party.

He was at the mailbox, when he noticed three very good looking girls coming up the steps to the building, they were carrying boxes. He opened the door and let them in. The first one to enter, was a short brunette with a petite body, but well rounded. Her name was Gina. The others, a redhead with a real nice figure, was Theresa and the third, was a small blond with an ample chest, named Jackie. He helped them move their boxes and lamps and things into the apartment, below his. They thanked him and were glad to meet their neighbor. As they were talking, the other three returned with groceries and booze for the party. Introductions were made and he found out the girls were nurses. They guys invited them to their party. They said that they would think about it.

He called Connie and told her that his roommates had returned. She was not happy, but said that she hoped they could have some "alone time". He invited her to the party. She said that she would come and wear her sexiest little black dress. He got excited just imagining her in it.

The party was a huge success! A lot of people showed up! Even the nurses from the apartment below theirs. Connie looked gorgeous in her little black dress. It was very short and showed just enough cleavage to "peak' the imagination. Sometime during the night, the two of them snuck into the bedroom. She locked the door. Her little black dress brought out the "animal" in him! When they finally emerged from the room, Chet stormed past them! He didn't put too much into Chet's attitude. Rick got together with Susan, a sophomore. He had been trying to date her, for a long time. Susan and Connie hit it off, right away. Rick and Susan had "disappeared" into his bedroom, about the same time, that he and Connie did. Robbie wasn't too happy, either. The four of them, double dated a couple of times.

September moved quickly into October. The nurses, downstairs, became "fixtures" in the apartment, though, much to Chet's chagrin, nothing romantic developed. His studies were going well. He and Connie spent many weekends in New Hampshire, at their respective cottages. They spent even more time, in the back seat of either her car or his. Even though, his folks had "closed" the cottage, for the winter, it was still warm enough, during the day, to spend some time there.

It was Columbus Day weekend. The four of them, he and Connie, Rick and Susan, after spending the night, in the apartment, decided to spend the day at the cottage, in New Hampshire. They left, in his car, with the top down, at 7AM. Chet and Robbie were not happy about sleeping on the couches, in the living room. The four of them stopped along the way and had breakfast and then arrived at the cottage. It did not take but a few minutes, for each pair to adjourn to a bedroom and spend the rest of the daylight hours, in bed. On the way, back they stopped for dinner. He dropped Connie off, at her folk's house and proceeded back into Boston with Rick and Susan. He parked in front of the apartment building. Rick walked Susan back to the girl's dorm. When he got inside the apartment, he was 'hit" with the news that Chet was going to "move out" and find his own apartment. Chet had talked with another guy, from school, who was willing to move in. Robbie was more forgiving. Robbie said that if it was him with a girl, in his bed, and she wanted privacy, then he would expect Rick to oblige. When Rick returned, he said "of course." Chet didn't care and was quite "adamant" about leaving.

Connie continued to 'visit" him, at the apartment. The "new" guy was from the Cape and was not at the apartment, on weekends, when Connie stayed over. After Connie would leave, Gina, one of the nurses, from the apartment below, would "tease" him, about Connie's "visit. She would say things like "sure you can walk? You must be exhausted!, or You're going to wear that penis out!" He tried not to blush, but took her comments in stride. Then, came Halloween.

He was not expecting Connie to visit him. Rick and Susan had gone to a party. Robbie was doing some work at the college library, for a paper. He was loafing around the apartment, in a pair of cutoff jeans. The new guy, Jim, was home, on the Cape. He was lying on the couch, a beer in one hand and an L&M, in the other. There was a knock, on the door. For some reason, he left the door unlocked, so Robbie could get in. Robbie, sometimes, left his key on his bureau. He yelled, "come on in, it's unlocked. He heard the high heels "clack" across the floor. He looked up and saw Gina! She stood in front of him, her legs, slightly apart, wearing a black mini skirt, that really showed off her legs! She, also, was wearing a blonde wig! He couldn't believe his eyes! She was acting a little "tipsy". She came closer and said "trick or treat". Before he could answer, she threw herself on top of him and covered his lips with hers. She was all over him! Her hands roamed over his naked chest and legs and brushed the crotch of his shorts! Her lips moved all over his lips as her tongue stabbed between his teeth and into his mouth. She grabbed his hands and brought them to her breasts. Instinct took over, followed by weakness of the flesh. he never heard the buzzer. How she got buzzed into the building, he never knew. He and Gina were on the couch, she was on top of him, desperately trying to get him "inside" her. Connie's scream reverberated off the ceiling, floor and walls of the room! Gina jumped up and off him, and ran out of the apartment. The fight that ensued was horrific! After what seemed like an eternity, Connie stopped yelling and informed him that she was going to go back to the drunk! She told him that there wasn't any future with him! He wasn't ready for marriage! He didn't help matters, by telling her, that she was right! He wasn't ready for marriage! Connie stormed back out of the apartment, tears flowing. He, then, realized that Connie had fallen in love with him. He felt bad for her. Karen had turned his heart into "stone". He doubted that he would ever really find "love" again.

He and Gina "dated" over the holidays. He realized that she, too, wanted marriage. He avoided sexual relations with her, because, he felt that she would take 'sex" as the path to matrimony. He, still, was not ready for that kind of commitment. He and Robbie lost Jim as a roommate. Jim dropped out of school. Rick flunked out and went home, to join the Air Force. That left Him and Robbie, holding the bag, as far as rent went. Jim and Rick were "nice" enough to pay their share of the rent, through February. He and Robbie went to the realtor and explained their situation. The realtor said that with only three months left on the lease. He would let them out of the lease, if he could get it rented, again, beginning the first of March. They thanked him and realized they had a month's "reprieve". It was during the month of February, that he was looking for a new place to live, that Robbie showed up at the apartment with Rachel! She was far more forgiving of him, than the letter she had sent him, when he missed the party in New York City. She, obviously, wanted to get back together. She made it quite clear, when she joined him on the couch and began to kiss him and rub the crotch of his pants. Robbie left the apartment and he and Rachel, ended up in his bed, again.

The 'end" of his apartment life was, quickly, coming to an end. He was sitting in the college coffee shop lamenting his situation to a guy, he had only known for a little while, Tim. Tim said that he might have a solution to his situation. Tim mentioned that he lived in a boarding house, on the top of Beacon Hill. Time would introduce him to Maggie, the manager, and see if there was a vacancy and maybe he could have the empty room. They finished their coffee and he paid for Tim's as well as his own. They left the shop and made the long trek up the hill to the boarding house. They met with Maggie. Maggie told him that the rent was 14 dollars a week and no loud noises after 11:00PM. Maggie was a striking redhead, about the same age as he and Tim. He had learned that he and Tim were both Navy veterans. He gave Maggie the first week's rent and she handed him a front door key. She showed him the room. It was very small, but furnished with a bed and desk. Much, like the dorm room. It did have a closet.

He went back to the apartment and told Robbie that he found a place to live. Robbie said that he was moving back into the dorm. He loaded his stuff into the trunk of the Ford. He wished Robbie well. He and Rachel rode up the hill to the boarding house, on Joy Street. They unloaded the Ford and moved his "stuff" into the small room. He went back out to the Ford and moved it to a parking space. When he returned to the room, Rachel was sitting on the bed, her legs tucked underneath, wearing one of his T-shirts, and nothing else. They didn't leave the room for, at least three hours! She was insatiable! She only left his arms, when she realized that she would miss "curfew." He drove her back to her dorm and returned to the top of the hill and searched for another parking place. Forty five minutes, later, he was back in the room.

The next day was a Sunday. He had everything 'stowed" away and decided to play some music, on the small stereo that Robbie had given him. He placed the two separate speakers in the open, screened windows, one on each side of his desk. Ferlin Husky's Greatest hits was the album, he chose. For some reason, he was unable to hear the music. He kept turning up the volume, but the music didn't get any louder. Finally, he turned the volume all the way up and, still, though he could hear it. The music was "muffled". He was trying to figure out what was wrong, when there was a loud knock on his door. He opened it and it was Maggie, the manager. She walked into the room and went to the stereo and turned it off. "You haven't been here a week and already, the neighbors across the courtyard are complaining that your music is too loud, especially for a Sunday morning!" He was confused, until she went to the windows and turned each of the speakers, around and faced them into the room. Ferlin Husky had been serenading the neighbors and not him. He apologized for his stupidity. Maggie accepted his 'stupidity" and reminded him about the pot luck lunch/dinner, every Sunday, in Nancy's room. He, immediately, left the room and went to Tim's on the third floor. Tim was a devout Catholic and was just leaving for church. He asked Tim about the "dinner" thing. Tim told him, to bring chips, and a dip, or make a salad. He opted for the chips and a dip.

Tim said everyone gathered in Nancy's room around one thirty. He had plenty of time, to get the chips and dip, at the corner grocery store. He went back to his room, and "marveled" at good luck, at running into Tim and getting his new "digs." He made his bed and picked out a nice shirt and jeans. He got dressed and went to "explore" the "hill", as everyone called it. He found a coffee shop a few blocks away and went in and sat at the counter and had breakfast. On his way back to the room, he stopped at the corner grocery store and purchased the chips and dip and a few other snacks, for him. He did not have the means to cook anything, in his room, so snacks it would have to be. He was looking forward to meeting the others.

He picked up the two bags of chips and two different dips and headed down to the second floor. The door, to Nancy's room was open. He soon learned that if your door was open, people could just walk in. If the door was closed, one must knock and wait to be invited in. Tim was there and introduce him to everyone. Nancy was his age, with strawberry blonde hair and a nice figure. She was from England and worked for the director of the local hospital. George, was a student at one of the local universities and worked in the ER of the local hospital. His girlfriend, Madge worked as a receptionist for a lawyer. There was an elderly gentleman that everyone, simply, called 'Mr. R". he was a retired chemical engineer. Most of those assembled, were his own age or close to it. Nancy had a very large room, with a kitchenette, much like Tim's. Maggie mentioned that he had serenaded the neighbors. Everyone laughed! Then Nancy asked him and Tim to relate some of their funniest stories, while in the Navy. He told them the story of the "milk".

Their ship was moored in New York Harbor. They had been at sea for about two months. He explained that after two weeks, at sea, fresh food was just about gone. They ate powdered eggs and powdered milk. Coffee was about the only fresh beverage. He was in charge of the communications shack. It was during a midwatch (11PM to 7AM). Everyone was complaining about the coffee. One of the seaman apprentices, his messenger, stated that a friend in the mess deck, told him that they had just received some fresh milk, from shore. Everyone stared at the kid. They messenger said that he could probably get some. They all said, "well that are you standing around for? Get going!" The messenger took the other messenger with him. The two of them returned about twenty minutes later, with a large plastic sack, filled with fresh milk! They had been given the inside container, of one the big metal containers. They had no idea how many gallons it held. The night crew drank fresh milk all night long. At around four AM, they realized they had not made the slightest "dent" in the contents of the sack. Everyone had pretty much had their "fill" of the milk. He ordered the two messengers to take the sack back to the mess deck and thank his friends. The messenger said the mess deck would not take it back. He ordered the two messengers to get rid of the milk. If the morning watch came on and found the milk, they would all be in a mess of trouble! The two took the sack and left the "shack".

The messengers and the milk were gone for about an hour. He was beginning to get concerned that they may have been caught with the milk. The two, finally, burst through the door, of the 'shack" and told him, if anyone calls, he knows nothing about any milk. He looked at them and asked them what they had done? They told him that they couldn't get rid of the milk and so they went up to the flight deck and with each one holding an end of the sack, they heaved it off the ship. They watched as the sack made its way to the sea, when to their dismay, a gust of wind sent the sack, back towards the ship and right onto the quarter deck! They saw it explode on the deck, sending its contents everywhere!

It was just as they finished talking, that the Officer of The Day called. It was his job to answer the phone. "Milk sir? Did you say milk? No sir I don't know anything about any milk. We drink coffee, here, sir. Yes sir. Understood, sir!" he hung up the phone. He looked at the two "idiots" and said the OOD is going to investigate the milk. He, also, told them that OOD knows he'll never find out where it came from. The thought was it might have come from a plane or another passing ship. They were off the hook.

When he finished the story, everyone was laughing quite hard. Nancy said that she could just image that officer looking though his binoculars and watching the milk coming at him. That evoked more laughter. He, also, told them about the time, the Randolph was visiting Quebec, Canada. They were all on the flight deck, in their dress whites, as the ship approached the city pier. They saw all the dignitaries standing on the pier. There was even a large marching band assembled, to welcome them. They couldn't believe their eyes as the ship sailed past the pier and ran aground, some seventy yards away from the pier. Again more laughter. He was accepted into the group. Tim said that he didn't have any funny stories. He did not tell them about "life" on the Ranger.

The dinner was wonderful. They all chipped in five dollars and gave the money, to Nancy, to pay for the chicken, she had bought and fried. He watched Tim and realized that Tim had a "thing" for Nancy. Though, he believed, that Nancy had no idea, that Tim did.

He only resided in the small room, for about three weeks. Tim told him, as they walked down the hill to school, that the room next to him, the same size as his and Nancy's was going to be available in about a week. It was seventeen dollars a week. He would put his "dibs" in on it, to Maggie.

The Ford was starting to give him a lot of trouble. He was told that it would cost over a thousand dollars to fix it. He decided to look for another car. He had, always, wanted a sports car. He started to look around. He found a dealer that dealt only in sports cars, in Wellesley. He drove out to the dealer, the next Saturday. The dealer looked at the Ford and said that they could make a good deal. The dealer like that he had "babied" the Ford. He showed him MG's,

Sunbeam's and a couple of Triumphs. He didn't see anything that he really liked. Then the dealer remembered a TR3 that had just come in the day before. It hadn't been "prepped" yet, but they went to take a look at it. It was white, with a red leather interior. The top was white canvas as were the side windows. The side panels and top had to be taken off and on, by hand. They snapped into place. He loved it! The dealer said they would take his car and five hundred dollars. He made the deal! Monday's classes didn't start till 1PM. He drove the Ford out to the bank, in the town, where his folks lived. He withdrew eight hundred dollars from his bonds and cashed them in. He drove to the dealership. Papers were signed. He would come back, tomorrow, with the Ford and they would transfer the plates.

Tuesday's classes were over just before noon. He was having lunch, with Tim, in the coffee shop. Tim asked if he could go with him, to pick up the car. He said "sure". His dad had talked with the insurance agent and everything was set for the transfer. He and Tim rode to the dealership with the top down. Inside of an hour, they were riding back to Boston, his 1961 Triumph TR3! He left the car, at his folks, during the week. He had the car, in Boston, on the weekends.

Maggie gave him the good news, that the room next to Tim's was his. He moved his stuff into it, in record time. Rachel never saw that room. She had, again, flunked out, halfway through the semester. His new room had a large couch that turned into his bed, two easy chairs and a large kitchenette, like Nancy's. Two large windows looked out, onto the street and at the restaurant, across the street. He had the car, of his dreams, a room, that he absolutely, loved! They only thing missing was female companionship. Even with the Sunday dinners, and the constant visitors, through his open door, he was lonely!

He and Tim spent a lot of time, riding around in the Triumph. They went to the Cape, to New Hampshire and out to the countryside near, where his folks lived. They had become good friends. The door between their rooms was always open. The shared a lot of the same broadcasting courses and would study together. The third floor, that they inhabited, had just their room, a bathroom and a small room next to his. There was a door that opened between his room and the small one. Four the next three months, the small room had been vacant. Maggie said that she, probably, would never rent it.

His birthday arrived on Friday the thirteenth. He thought no one knew about it.

He forgot that Maggie had the information on the rental agreement. Still, the day came and went, without fanfare. Then, came the Sunday dinner. It turned into a "surprise" party. He received many "small' gifts, like cologne, pens, for studying, a polo shirt from George, Madge and Tim. Five dollars from Mr. R. he thanked them, profusely, and blew out the candles on the chocolate cake. While he was reading the card, Nancy sat down next to him and told him not to leave, until after the others. She had a "special" gift for him.

It was well, after five PM. The dinner dishes were cleaned and put away. Nancy was sitting on the couch. He had just put his gifts in a small paper bag. Nancy got up and closed her door. She took his hand and brought him to the couch. They were sitting side by side, when she whispered "Happy birthday" and put her arms around him and pressed her lips, to his. He was pleasantly surprised. She pushed him down onto the couch and kept on kissing him. He began to respond. They "made out" for over an hour. She didn't want him to leave, but he had an exam the next morning, that he and Tim had to study for.

They, quickly, became a "couple". Unfortunately, for Tim, Nancy became his riding partner, in the Triumph. She had a wonderful sense of humor. He enjoyed being with her. She accompanied him when he went and helped his folks open the cottage, for the summer. His folks liked her, too. Their "love making" got more intense, with each day. He would no sooner, enter her room, than he had to close the door, because their clothes would disappear! He had "performance" issues with her. Every time, they would try to make love, "it" refused to rise to the occasion. It became very frustrating for the two of them. As much as they enjoyed their foreplay, he was unable to follow through. Their frustration, led to arguments and distrust. She accused him of unfaithfulness. No matter how he denied it. She didn't believe him!

Their "brief" romance ended, after four weeks. He avoided the Sunday dinners. Tim seemed happy that things had cooled off with him and Nancy. School ended for the summer. He went to work for a moving company, outside of Boston. He would come back to the boarding house and take a quick shower and prepare to go out for dinner. On one particular evening, after a difficult day, at work, he wrapped a towel around him and walked out of his room and down the small hall, to the bathroom. There was a telephone in the hall, between his and Tim's room. Tim wasn't home! He just stepped out of the shower and was toweling off, when he heard Maggie's voice, on the first floor, yelling up that there was a call, for Tim. He went to the phone and picked up the receiver. It was Tim's mom! He had spoken to her, many times. While talking with her, he had trouble keeping his towel on! Thinking that he and Tim were the only residents on the third floor, he finally, lost the fight with the towel and let it drop. He did not notice the pair of eyes, staring at him, through the partially opened door, of the small room. He heard a "gasp!" and turned and saw the eyes! He bent down and grabbed the towel and attempted to cover himself. He told Tim's mom that something just came up and he had to go! He hung up the phone and ran into his room. He checked the door between his room and the small one and made sure it was bolted on his side.

That night, he and Tim were awakened by strange noises and crashing sounds coming from the small room! The noises were followed by large screams that echoed throughout the building. Someone, finally, called the police! The cops came and began to knock on the door, of the small room. Maggie and the cops tried to calm down the person within the room. He and Tim had gotten dressed and were in the hall. It seemed that Maggie had rented the room and failed to notify he and Tim! It was rented to someone named "Betsy"! The cops were finally able to get Betsy to open the door. She looked like a wild animal! Her hair looked like she had stuck her finger in an electric light socket! Her bedclothes were hardly on her. She was grunting like an animal! The cops wrapped her in a blanket and assisted her down the stairs and out of the building.

The next day, Maggie informed them that she tried to tell them that they had a new tenant, but that neither of them were home. He said, "a note stuck to the door, would have worked!" Maggie, then explained that the girl had just been released from an institution. She was treated for "nymphomania." He felt sick! Maggie said that something must have triggered a relapse! He made a mistake about telling Tim. In a few days, it was all over the building, that he had been the cause of Betsy's relapse. The guys thought it was hysterical. The girls giggled, but felt bad for Betsy. It was the last time, he went to and from the bathroom, with just a towel on.

Lorraine

(Going To The Chapel . . . The Dixiecups)

He developed a routine. He would get home from work. Take a long warm shower. Put on his cutoff jeans and a T-shirt, pop open a Miller Lite, light up an L&M, put the Beach boys on the stereo, open his door, and sing along with the album.

He did this, even after some woman, failed to stop at the stop sign, he was at and smashed the entire rear end of the Triumph up to the back of his seat. The cops said he was lucky that the gas tank didn't explode. It took many weeks, for the Triumph to be returned to its original state. His ragged top and side curtains were in the trunk and he got a brand new black top and side curtains, out of the deal. It was while the car was in the body shop, and he was driving his mom's VW, that he met Lorraine.

A typical evening, after work. He was standing by his door, a beer in one hand, a cigarette in the other. He heard the footsteps running up the stairs, toward the floor above him. He looked out in the direction of the sound and saw the most beautiful, tanned, well-proportioned legs, he had ever seen! He had never considered himself to be a "leg" man, but those legs were absolutely gorgeous! He stood by his door and waited for the owner of the legs to come back down the stairs. It was two beers later and another Beach Boys album, before his eyes were, once again, rewarded! This time he got to see where the legs ended! In a pair of blue denim, extremely short shorts! He never saw the rest of her or her face. He went back into his room and through the open door, to Tim's room. He told Tim that there were new tenants in the building. Tim said he knew. One, a dark redhead was from Nebraska and the other one a dark black haired girl, from somewhere down South. The Southerner was living in George's old first floor apartment with a blonde. The redhead had moved into the room, above theirs.

Apparently, he said that the two, the one from Nebraska and the one from the South were friends. He wondered how old they were. Tim said that he didn't know.

He attended one of the Sunday dinners, but the new tenants did not. He left early, before he and Nancy began to argue, again. His evenings consisted of watching that girl, with the fantastic legs run up and down the stairs. He made up his mind that he was going to meet her. He didn't know how or where, but he was going to.

He got home from work around 5:30 that Friday, July the first. He checked his mail, at the front table and saw an announcement on the hall bulletin board. There was to be a "roof" party that evening at 7PM. Snacks would be provided, but BYOB. He rushed up the stairs and opened hi room. Tim was home and was cooking some hotdogs on his burner. Tim asked him, if he could cook some as well, for the party. He said that he would. He looked in his small fridge and saw that he had three cans of Miller Lite left. He put a pot of water on the burner and got six hot dogs from Tim and put them in the pot. He grabbed a towel, some soap and his pair of cutoffs and headed for the shower. He, quickly, got out of the shower, toweled off and put on the cutoffs and ran back into his room. He asked Tim, if he thought the new tenants were going to be there. Tim said that they were the ones that set it up! He was glad that he was, finally, going to meet them!

The roof looked like an Hawaiian luau! Tiki lights illuminations out lined the area. He had to walk through the fourth floor room, to climb out onto the roof. A record player was set up at a window, with soft music whispering across the gravel. Tables were set up with the snacks. The hot dogs were in a bowl next to a plate of rolls alongside the "fixins." It was a cool July night! The girls wore slacks. He still didn't know the owner of the fabulous legs. The one from Nebraska, Brenda, had the dark red hair. Lorraine had the dark black hair and a real cute face. She, almost, reminded him of Ree. The short haired blonde, who shared the first floor room with Lorraine was Debby. She apparently had a boyfriend, on the South Shore of Boston. George and Madge were there, also. The only ones missing were Mr. R and Nancy! He was, first, attracted to the redhead, until he learned that she was engaged to be married, later on that summer, in Nebraska. But there was something about Lorraine, that intrigued him.

They all spent the fourth of July, on the esplanade, listening to the Boston Pops, directed by Arthur Fiedler. They had a great time with some wine and snacks, on a blanket. He got to know more about the new tenants and they learned more about him and Tim. There were many more parties. Some, in their first floor room. Then, one night, while sitting and listening to the Doors, Lorraine asked if she could come up to his room and listen to his collection of Elvis albums. He said, "sure." They left the party and went up the stairs. He recognized the footsteps. She was the one with the gorgeous legs. He noticed that she was short, compact with an athletic figure. She was well rounded in all the right places and very firm in all the other places. They sat beside each other, on his couch and began to listen to the records. She made the first move and leaned in and pressed her lips to his. They never really listened to the rest of the records. They spent much of the time just kissing and hugging. He began to feel 'things' he hadn't felt in a very long time, not since Karen. They began to go "out" together. He had to drive his mom's VW, for a while and then one day, he arrived at the building, in the Triumph, completely restored! They went for a ride. His "after work" routine was disrupted by the short Southern girl.

It was a Saturday night. He asked her out for dinner. She was wearing a light colored sun dress. He had on a short sleeved button down dress shirt and pair of tan chinos. They went across the street to the restaurant. They sat out on the patio and had Italian food. He found out she was from Louisiana. He had never met anyone from Louisiana, before. They had a nice dinner and afterwards, they sat back and he lit up two L&Ms. He handed one to her. It was a starlit July evening. Not too cool with just the slightest breeze.

They walked back across the street to the boarding house. She suggested they go to his room, because her roommate was home. They walked, slowly, up the stairs. They entered his room. He closed the door, to the hall and for the first time, he locked it. He went to the door, between his and Tim's room and did the same. His heart was pounding! He sat down beside her on the couch. Their arms wrapped around each other as their lips met. They ended up lying on the couch. Her sun dress was hiked up well over her knees. While their lips were locked, he couldn't resist. He had to put his hands on those beautiful legs and thighs! Her response was immediate! She opened her legs, inviting his hands to travel further. It had been so long since he had any feeling for someone else! His hands caressed her dampness. He brought his fingers to the top of her panties and began to, slowly, slide them down her legs. Afterwards, he stripped off his pants and briefs. Their fused together, he slipped between her thighs as if they had made love many times before. He knew it wasn't just sex, they were having. They were making love, like he never made love before, in his entire life!

They spent the night, together. Somehow, the couch became the bed. Their clothes had completely disappeared! They were wrapped in each other's arms. He had pulled out, in time. It felt so natural, to be in each other's arms. They became a "couple". They did everything, together. He felt so comfortable with her. They could discuss anything. They drove to his folks cottage for a weekend, in August. His folks went crazy over her. His father was very impressed her. His dad told him, when she was in the kitchen, helping his mom, that for a young girl, she was very mature. That Saturday afternoon, they went to the beach, to see Danny. He hadn't seen Danny, since he drove well over the limit, of another liberty, to visit Danny, in the hospital. Danny had an accident with a hay baler, that ended up breaking his back.

While at the beach, Danny introduced them to his fiancé, Sally. Danny was getting married in September! He congratulated both of them. Sally was a knockout! He pulled Danny aside and asked him where had met such a beautiful girl. Danny thanked him and asked the same about Lorraine! Before he knew it, he and Lorraine were not only invited to the wedding, but Lorraine was invited to the bachelorette party and he was invited to the bachelor party! The parties were going to be on the same night, in August. With both of them invited, he really felt like they were a 'couple."

It was a whirlwind romance! He discovered that they both shared the same strong sex drive! But they were very careful. Still, it was a miracle that she did not get pregnant! He would sneak into her bed, every morning, after her roommate left, for work. Afternoons found them in his bed, after their work. Of course, evenings, were spent in his room, too.

They were back in New Hampshire, in August, for the parties. He, finally, realized that he was feeling a kind of "love" for Lorraine. He really felt that they were, indeed, meant to be together. The wedding was very nice. Keith was there with his "new" bride, Sarah. When he got back to the cottage, Keith and Sarah showed up with Keith's parents. He couldn't get over how 'taken" everyone was with Lorraine. Keith and Sarah were planning a New Year's Eve party. They told him that he could not come, unless he brought Lorraine.

The "bombshell" came at the end of September. Lorraine informed him that she was going home! He was confused! His first thought was, "here we go again. I meet a girl that I love with being with, not only as a wonderful lover, but as a friend, as well and she's going to leave!" They had never really said that they "loved" each other. He knew that if he didn't say something soon, she would, too, be gone. He would miss her greetings, on the sidewalk, after doing one of his college broadcasts. She would walk down the hill, to meet him walking up the hill, and race into his arms. She would, actually leap into his arms, and wrapped her "white booted" legs around his waist. He would miss her smile, her laughter, yes, even her tears.

He knew that they had to talk. He told her that he would drive her home. She told him that she couldn't expect him to. She was still adamant that she would be going, before the first snow storm. They still made love like she was leaving him, the next day. He tried and tried to talk her out of it. They spent Christmas together. They exchanged matching sets of winter clothes. Christmas Eve, saw the biggest snowstorm, of the year. They drove to his folks. He was "white knuckle "driving, while she exclaimed how beautiful the snow was. She was still in Boston, with him. They drove out to Keith and Sarah's for New Year's. It was during that time, that Sarah sat down with Lorraine and planned a wedding! Lorraine, at one point, looked at him and asked him, if he loved her. Without hesitation, he answered that he did. It was, then, that he knew that he really did love her! She and Sarah talked wedding plans, the rest of the day.

It was on the way home, in his mom's VW, (his car was in the shop) that he said, "seems like you two have our wedding all planned." "Not really. "She said. He pulled the VW over to the breakdown lane and took her hands in his and asked her to marry him. He was ready and he did not want to lose her. She said "yes" and they embraced and kissed. She laid her head on his shoulder as he drove them home, to his parent's house. This was a major milestone!

His family was thrilled! First thing his mom asked Lorraine, if she could help her plan the wedding. Lorraine said that she would love to have his mom's help. His mom told her that she always wanted a daughter, so she could help plan a wedding! Everyone in the boarding house was happy for them. He realized that he didn't have much to say or do. The wedding was planned for the 10th of June. Another major milestone!

They began to attend an Episcopal Church, in Boston. After a month or two, they approached the ministers. One of the Priests sat down with them and took down the information. He took hers, first. He wrote down the address and the phone number and a lot of "her" information. Then, he started with his information. The Priest put down his pen, after getting "his" address and phone number. The Priest looked at them and asked "how soon does this wedding have to be?" He explained that it was a boarding house. The Priest sighed some relief, and was even happier, when he found out the wedding was set for June.

They were so very happy! He never felt so loved! Not even with Ree and Karen! Lorraine couldn't believe how everything was coming together. His mom found a wedding dress, for her. She picked out her bridesmaids. His brother, Phil, was his best man. Dave was an usher, as well as Keith and Danny. Tim volunteered to tape record the ceremony. Her Mom and her two "baby" sisters attended the wedding. George gave her away, for her dad, who was unable to attend.

The wedding went off without any problems! They honeymooned at his folk's cottage. Needless to say, with both of them having a strong sex drive, they were late for every dinner.

They moved out of the boarding house and into a small apartment in Cambridge. It was a predominately black neighborhood. They felt fine with it and got along very well with their neighbors, until the night, Dr. Martin Luther King was shot and killed. His folks were very worried for their safety, though they weren't. But they "caved' to the pressure from his folks and spent a few nights at their house. King's assassination was another major event, in his life, followed by Robert Kennedy's assassination.

They moved from Cambridge, to Worcester, to be near Keith and Sarah and they were living in the top floor of a huge house. They had been living there, when Lorraine told him that they were going to be a family! Again his folks were thrilled! Their daughter was born on August 5th. The same year that man walked on the moon and that Kennedy's chances as President were "quashed' on Martha's Vineyard. He was not allowed in the delivery room, but was able to see his daughter, shortly after her birth. Besides, his wedding, she was the biggest miracle and milestone! He was a senior in college, when she was born. He earned his degree in Jan. 1969.

The family, of three, move to Louisiana in early December of 1969. He began his broadcasting career at a small, daytime radio station, in Sulphur. They stayed there for two years and then at Lorraine's insistence, they moved back to the Northeast. He got a newswriting job at one of the local TV stations. He worked there for one day! Then AFTRA went out on a nationwide strike! He heard that a radio station on the South Shore was hiring. He went to see the manager and was hired, immediately! He worked there, for a few weeks and then was transferred to their sister station, on the North shore! He hosted a big band Jazz show from 4 to 10PM. Another milestone for him!

Then, in February of 1974, his son was born. This was a huge miracle and milestone. This time, he got to stay in the delivery room and stand at Lorraine's head and watch the birth of their son. His son was, practically, born "on the air." Now, they were a family of four!

They lived in a small brick home in the inner city. A far cry from the large homes he had lived in, as a child. Money was very "tight". He decided to ask around about any part-time jobs. There weren't any! He met a man, at their church, who was high up in the hierarchy of the local public schools. The man asked him to bring him a copy of his college transcripts.

Upon reading his transcripts, the man hired him, full time, as a Special Ed" teacher. The extra income was just what they needed! Soon, it was apparent that his family life was in jeopardy! He worked holidays and weekends and was hardly ever home. He had to make a drastic decision! One of the jobs would have to go! He decided to leave the radio station.

The station manager was upset! He had the most popular nighttime program, they had ever had! He offered him a part-time position. He asked him to start his program at 7PM and go to 10PM, no weekends and a raise in his salary! He talked it over with Lorraine. She got off work at 5PM, they would have, at least an hour with the kids, together and weekends. She told him to take it. He went to school, with the kids and came home with them. It worked out. Perfectly!

He took time off, one morning, to go to his son's class. It was show and tell. A lot of the kids dads were there, talking about their different jobs. When it was his turn, his son was asked what kind of work, did his dad, do? He answered that his dad doesn't work, he's on the radio!

Even with the evening work and the weekends off, the jobs started to get to him. In order to get interviews with celebrities, he would have to wait until their "set' was over. Sometimes, it would be one or two o'clock in the morning, before he got home. He decided to give up the radio, all together. At first, the kids were disappointed, but they enjoyed having him around, in the evenings, especially, holidays! He wasn't completely out of radio and would "fill" in from time to time.

There was the night, when the station was having a "live" broadcast for some charity. All he had to do was "man" the "board." His fellow announcer, Chip happened by, to do some production work. Chip asked him, if he would help him. He said "sure". They were going through a sound effects library and found the sound of a "dying" chicken. They played it over and over. They put it aside, thinking they could use it for something. A few minutes later, they found the sound of a very large gun, firing! He and Chip looked at each other and knew what they must do!

The morning man began his show at 5AM with the sound of a rooster crowing! He went out of the production room and got the "cassette" out of the "rack" that held all the commercials and PSAs and sound effects. It took most of the evening to put the tape together. They recorded it on the morning man's cassette. By mistake, they put it back in his rack. They went home, after the broadcast and, literally, forgot what they had done.

The next morning, at 5AM, the stations listeners heard the rooster crow and then, BLAM!!! The roar of a mighty shotgun! What followed was classic! The long, drawn out sound of someone choking the life, out of the rooster. The dying sounds last a good three minutes, with the last "aaaarrrrghhhh" and then, silence!

They both received calls from the station, that the owner wanted to see them, both, in his office at 10AM sharp! He got someone to 'cover" for him, at school.

When they both arrived in the parking lot, at the station, they looked at each other and realized that they put the wrong cassette in the morning man's rack. They walked in the front door of the station. The secretaries were trying very hard to stifle their giggles. The sales staff was in the sales office, holding their sides. They were ushered into the office, and told to sit down. The owner was very angry! He told them that they had "ruined" a wonderful announcer, with a great reputation! The poor man had to be carried out of the station on a stretcher! It was a wonder that he didn't suffer a heart attack! They both knew that they would never work for that station again! The owner gave them paper and pencil and demanded they write a sincere letter of apology, to the man. The owner left the office and the building. They began to write the letter, when the manager burst into laughter! They weren't fired? The manager told them what had happened. The morning man opened his microphone and was about to wish everyone a good morning, when the rooster was shot in the middle of the crowing and the long drawn out death rail, did the morning man in. He was in a state of shock! He couldn't utter a sound! He just sat there, in his chair, with his mouth wide open and his eyes bulging out of his head! EMTS were called and carried him out of the station on a stretcher to the local hospital. He would be okay! He was just "shell shocked!"

The manager, then, told them, that they received many, many, phone calls! People laughing, others saying it was about time that rooster "'croaked". Not one call was sad to hear it "go!"

There was one other time, he came close to never working in radio, again. It was Saint Patrick's Day. They were doing a "live" broadcast. He had to work the broadcast and then return to the station to do the rest of his shift. Someone had slipped him a couple of rum and cokes. When he got to the station, the news director had put together his newscast. He went into the studio and saw that the "Red tide Organism" had struck the shoreline, north of Boston. The news director had circled the word "organism" in red. It was a minute to go, before the newscast. He looked up through the window. Everyone, from sales people, to engineers, even the secretaries were crowded into the control room. He hit the intercom and told them he was a professional and would not mess it up and that they should all go back to work! No one moved!

The red light came on and he introduced himself with the latest news. He got through the entire cast without a single problem, or so he thought. He looked up at the clock, to give the time and his eyes caught the sight, in the control room. The engineer's feet were straight up in the air, the secretaries were holding each other, their mascara running down their faces. Sales people were doubled over with laughter. The news director had tears of laughter streaming down his cheeks. That was when he realized that he had informed the entire listening area, that the "Red Tide Orgasm had struck the North shore of Boston." Every now and then when he was asked to fill in, a listener would call in and tell him how much they enjoyed the death of the rooster. Some would even call in and ask if he had seen the red tide orgasm. He left behind quite a legacy!

He spent 12 years in Special Education. Then, one day, he was called to the high school, after school. The Superintendent, the Principal, and several school board members asked him, if he would be interested in teaching broadcasting at the high school level, especially TV production. They had seen his transcripts and noted that he could be certified, easily. They would get him started with some equipment. He would have to decide what textbook, he wanted. He accepted!

He started off, in the school auditorium, with minimal equipment. Soon, with the help of grants, he was able to get more equipment. He found an easy textbook. He founded a TV club. They would videotape all the sports events and other events, at the school. He was in his element. It wasn't long, before there were TV sets in every classroom and his "kids" were broadcasting "live" every morning, throughout the school. When the school was being renovated, he was asked to design a "state of the art" studio. He obtained news and sports desks, from his friends in the industry. The kids loved it! They would broadcast two local news stories, two sports stories, with clips, the morning announcements, the menu of the day and the weather, complete with a "blue" screen. Of course there were some "glitches" like the time a young lady announced that the meal of the day was "breast on a bulkie roll". Then,there was the time that a young lady was applying her lipstick and did not see the floor manager signaling her. She looked up at the monitor and realized she was on the air and said "SHIT!" He remembers when, for some unknown reason a bra strap would mysteriously "appear' from under a blouse and a hand would come across the shirt and try to put it back where it was supposed to be. All while the young lady kept right on delivering the news, as if nothing was amiss! Good memories! Great milestones!

2003

Sifting through the box, he found the I.D. bracelet, that Ree had given him, for his 18th birthday. He found her senior picture, with words of "undying' love, written on the back. He searched deeper into the box and extracted the black, metal, miniature VW beetle that Karen had given him. He found her picture, sitting in front of the fireplace, in her home, wearing his high school ring around her neck, words of love written on the bottom. There were senior pictures of all his students, from the past. The box was filled with a lot of personal items and a lot of wonderful memories. He couldn't understand why he brought them to school and put them in his desk. Maybe he didn't want to have to explain them to Lorraine, or he wanted "alone" time with them.

He continued to look through the contents, of the box. There were pictures of the kids. His son in his Spiderman pajamas. He remembered that he had just convinced his son that Spiderman was a fictional character, when they went to the mall and found "Spiderman" signing autographs! He had a tough time, convincing his son of anything, after that. There was the picture of his daughter, the first time, she wore pigtails! She was now a married lady, with her own children. He had pictures of them, too.

There were copies of all the senior "video" yearbooks that he and Tony had produced. It was quite a box! He found a picture of his first dog, a Beagle named "Mike." There were several pictures of Lorraine, from when they were first married, to the present, holding their grand daughter, by his son. In the bottom, of the box, was another box. Inside that box, were reel to reel tapes of the various people, he had interviewed and met, during his years, as a broadcaster. Politicians, such has Amb. Henry Cabot Lodge, Massachusett's Senators Leverett Saltonstall and Edward Kennedy; jazz musicians, Jerry Fuller (Dukes of Dixieland), Benny Goodman, Teddy Wilson, Bobby Hackett, Earl "Fatha" Hynes, Count Basie, Anita O'Day, Roy Elderidge. Country music stars such as, Jean Shepard, Buddy Allen, Tommy Cash, Skeeter Davis, Bobby Bare, George Hamilton IVth. Musicians from the 50's such as Fats Domino, Jerry Lee Lewis, Conway Twitty. His one regret was not meeting Duke Ellington.

He found the tape of 911! He remembered, he was teaching the class about how TV impacted the everyday lives of Americans. He turned on the TV, in the classroom, to find something that would illustrate his point. The channel was on CNN. The first tower was on fire. Then, they all watched in horror as the second plane hit the second tower! He didn't realize that he had a tape, in the VCR and was recording! When he realized what was happening, he ran into the control room and threw the switch that turned on all the TV's in the school! They continued to watch, as first, one tower came crashing down and then later, as the second one crashed to the ground. The bells, signaling the end and beginning of classes were silent. No one moved. All eyes were on the TVs!

It was shortly after, when the bells started, again, and classes moved from one room to another. His cell phone rang. It was Lorraine, telling him that their son was in the area, of the twin towers. They did not hear from him, until after 8 that night. He was in a hospital. He was all right, physically, but, mentally, he was a mess! He had been there, when bodies were falling around him. That was a milestone, he would like to forget! But, probably never would!

He picked up the box and his newspaper. He put the paper in the box. He went to the door and stopped. He put the box on the top of the desk, nearest the door. He went back and took one last walk through the studio, control room, production room and store room. He made sure that he had everything, he wanted. He went to the door of the studio and reached up and took down the plaque that one of his classes, had given him. It read "This studio is dedicated to (his name). for his strong work ethics, the admiration of all those around him, that he was more than a teacher, but a father figure, friend, mentor and role model. Next to the fine words, is a picture taken some years ago. He stood in the doorway and read and reread the words. A lump appeared in his throat. He decided to take the plaque home. The next teacher may not appreciate seeing his picture and reading the words. He went back to the classroom and the box and put the plaque, on top. He felt humbled by the words on the plaque.

He continued to walk through the studio and the rooms. He knew it was time, to leave, but he took his time. He remembered how he started, with practically nothing and now, he was leaving behind a state of the art TV studio! Something he had envisioned from day one!

He turned off the lights in the studio, then the control room, then the production room and the store room. He went back to the classroom and stood by the door and with one last look at what he had accomplished, over the years, he turned off the classroom lights and opened the door, to the hall. He picked up the box of memories and went out into the hall. He put the box down and closed the door and took his keys and locked it, for the very last time.

He hooked the keys to his belt and bent down and picked up the box and proceeded down the hall, to the rear door. He got to the door, when Tony appeared. "Where the hell do you think you're going?" he asked. "Just going to put the box in my truck." He said. "I'll come with you."

Tony said. They went out the door and to the red Ram pickup. He unlocked the passenger door. Tony opened it and he put the box on the seat. He closed the door and locked the truck. "Come on, you've got business in the office!" said Tony.

They walked back into the building, down the halls and into the office. There an awful lot of people milling about. The Superintendent of schools was there, along with two principals, two school board members, teachers from his days in SPED and members of the "present" faculty. Several of his "former" students along with present students. He was very surprised! They were standing around a large cake with his name on it and the words, "Good luck and Good health". They asked him for a speech and all he could say, was "Thanks for coming and thanks for caring." The Superintendent remembered when they taught together, ay one of the middle schools. The principals remembered how he "begged" them for, money, to purchase equipment. It was his friend, Tony who told them all that, he, not Tony, was instrumental in getting his courses noticed and accepted by a local technical school. That his "history" course offered 3 college credits to any incoming freshman, from his course. Tony, also, reminded them, that he was the one that put their high school on national TV.

After all the applause and hand shaking, he was presented with a yearbook, signed by everyone, in the office. The English teacher that taught down the hall, said she would miss the sound of his cowboy boots in the hall, every morning. His good friend, now a principal of the other high school, said that the school system was losing one hell of a good teacher. Everyone thanked him and soon there was just Tony and him. They walked out of the office, he with his many gifts and Tony with two large pieces of cake. One of his 'former" students asked him, at his age, besides retirement, what was there left to look forward to, in his life. He stopped and looked at the young man. He paused before answering him. "Tommy, I really don't know. There have been many, many milestones, in my life. I certainly hope that there are many more to come. Life is a journey and just because I'm not working anymore, I'm sure the good Lord will find something for me to do. I do know this. I'm looking forward to some time off and then we'll see what is coming around the corner, before that one last, big milestone."

Tony said, "well put!" The two of them walked back down the halls, to the back door and out through the back door, to the truck. Once again, he unlocked it and they put the gifts next to the box, on the front seat. He closed the passenger side door. He turned around and thanked Tony with a hug. They had been friends for a very long time. They both said, at the same time, "see you at the races!" Then he climbed into the truck, closed the door and started it up. He took one last look at the building, before he put the truck in drive and headed out of the parking lot. He, already, had plans for tomorrow. He was going to the lake, get into his boat and go fishing!

Epilogue

A few years have passed, since that day. A lot has transpired. He, now has five healthy grand children. He has "dabbled in real estate, been a flower delivery man, greeted folks at a "super store"; been a substitute teacher. He and Lorraine have been together for over forty years. She is still his confidante, lover, best friend, and companion. Though they lead totally different lives, they still manage to find "time" to enjoy each other's company.

The "highlights" have been travelling together, seeing their grand children, and remaining somewhat healthy. What "ailments" he has, are under control. Type 2 Diabetes, high blood pressure, enlarged prostrate and acid reflux disease. Even though, he takes a lot of pills, he feels good and is still very active with various volunteer work. He even finds time to chase a little white ball around.

The "lowlights" are those he's lost. People, who were a major influence, in his life. His mom, dad, and two brothers. His folks lived well, into their 80's. His brothers didn't reach 60. He lost Ree, Keith and Sarah, to alcoholism, Karen to COPD, Tim to a massive heart attack; George to, he doesn't know! He's been told that as he grows older, he'll continue to lose people and friends. He doesn't like those milestones.

Bert is doing well, retired, married and living in the Southwest. The last time, he saw Fred, was at a NASCAR event. He looked good with a full, though gray, beard. His wife Kathy was a shock, to behold! She was crippled with arthritis and in a wheel chair. Tony is retired. He has lost contact with him, but keeps in touch, with Tony's family on the wonderful technological advance called the "internet." Danny is battling cancer and appears to be holding his own. He talks with him on the phone and corresponds via email. Danny's wife is doing well. Danny lost his folks, soon after he did. They still carry on the tradition of the cookouts, with the family, on the beach, in Winter Harbor.

It's been quite a journey! Lots and lots of milestones. Most have been good and some have not. He sighs a lot and sometimes wishes he could return to the past. When he looks in the mirror, he realizes that the "senior citizen" was once a very good looking kid and young man. He only weighs fifteen pounds more that he did, in high school. But, the nose and ears have grown and what used to be a full head of thick, light brown hair, is now a little thinner. He has "picked up" new friends along the way without forgetting the "old." He is in the Autumn of his life. He hopes that there will be many, many more good milestones, to come, before the greatest milestone of all.

مبـادئ

محاسبـة التكـاليف

تأليف

الدكتور " محمد تيسير " عبد الحكيم الرجبي

أستاذ مشارك – قسم المحاسبة

جامعة الكويت

(الجامعة الأردنية سابقاً)

دار وائل للنشر

الطبعة الخامسة

٢٠١٠

رقم الايداع لدى دائرة المكتبة الوطنية : (2003/9/2079)

الرجبي ، "محمد تيسير" عبد الحكيم

مبادئ محاسبة التكاليف / "محمد تيسير" عبد الحكيم الرجبي .

- عمان: دار وائل ، 2004.

(490) ص

ر.إ. : (2003/9/2079)

الواصفات: محاسبة التكاليف / البيانات المالية / الإدارة المالية / المحاسبة

* تم إعداد بيانات الفهرسة والتصنيف الأولية من قبل دائرة المكتبة الوطنية

****

رقم التصنيف العشري / ديوي : 657.42

ISBN 9957-11-461-1 (ردمك)

* مبادئ محاسبة التكاليف
* الدكتور "محمد تيسير" عبد الحكيم الرجبي
* الطبعة الخامسة 2010
* حقوق الطبع والنشر والتوزيع محفوظة للناشر

دار وائـل للنشر والتوزيع

* الأردن – عمان – شارع الجمعية العلمية الملكية – مبنى الجامعة الاردنية الاستثماري رقم (2) الطابق الثاني
هـاتف : 5338410-6-00962 : فاكس : 5331661-6-00962 : ص. ب (1615 – الجبيهة)
* الأردن – عمان – وسط البلد – مجمع الفحيص التجاري- هـاتف: 4627627-6-00962
www.darwael.com
E-Mail: Wael@Darwael.Com

الإهـــداء

إلى روح والدي ووالدتي

إلى

زوجتي وأولادي

مقدمـــة

لقد قمت بكتابة هذا الكتاب لتغطية متطلبات مساق مادة محاسبة التكاليف التي يتم تدريسها في أقسام المحاسبة بالجامعات الأردنية، ولقد راعيت في إعداده الاتجاهات الحديثة في مجال محاسبة التكاليف حتى يفيد الطلبة والعاملين في مجالات المحاسبة المختلفة.

وتهدف محاسبة التكاليف إلى تقديم معلومات لمساعدة الإدارة في اتخاذ القرارات الاقتصادية الرشيدة ومنها تحديد تكاليف الإنتاج اللازمة لأغراض إعداد القوائم المالية وهذه تهدف إلى خدمة أغراض قرارات عدة جهات مهتمة بشؤون المنشأة ولتحقيق أهداف محاسبة التكاليف يلزمنا تناول العديد من الموضوعات وهذه يصعب وضعها في مؤلف واحد من حجم هذا الكتاب، لذلك اقتصر هذا الكتاب على دراسة المبادئ والإجراءات المحاسبية اللازمة لتحديد تكلفة الإنتاج والرقابة عليها، وقد تم الاهتمام بهذا الهدف لأنه نقطة البداية في خدمة الأغراض الإدارية الأخرى.

ويمكن تقسيم هذا الكتاب إلى أربعة أجزاء، الأول ويحتوي على الفصلين ١-٢ وهذه تهدف إلى التعريف بأهمية محاسبة التكاليف وتطورها وعلاقتها بفروع المحاسبة الأخرى، وكذلك التعريف بالمصطلحات المختلفة اللازمة لأغراض محاسبة التكاليف. والجزء الثاني ويضم الفصول ٣-٥ وهذه تهدف إلى تناول المبادئ الأساسية لأنظمة محاسبة التكاليف الفعلية في المنشآت التي يختلف إنتاجها حسب طلبات التشغيل المقدمة من الإدارة والعملاء وفي المنشآت التي لا يختلف إنتاجها من كمية إلى أخرى. ومعالجة مشكلة الإنتاج غير الجيد، أما الجزء الثالث ويضم الفصول من ٦-٩ وهذه تهدف إلى دراسة مشكلة توزيع التكاليف وإعداد قوائم التكاليف المختلفة، إذ تم تناول المشكلات المحاسبية الخاصة بعناصر التكاليف الصناعية غير المباشرة لذلك تم معالجة طرق تحميلها على المنتجات المستفيدة، وعرض مشكلات توزيعها عندما يتم إنتاج عدة منتجات معاً من استخدام مادة أو عدة مواد خام، وغطى الفصل الأخير محاسبة تكاليف الأنشطة

وهذا يعتبر من احدث التطورات للمحاسبة على الأعباء الإضافية. وفي الجزء الأخير ويتضمن الفصول من ١٠-١٣ وهذه تهدف إلى تناول الموضوعات المختلفة الخاصة بالتكاليف المعيارية والتي تشمل مواضيع أعداد معايير التكلفة وتحليل انحرافات عناصر التكاليف والإيرادات والطرق المحاسبية اللازمة لتشغيل أنظمة التكاليف المعيارية.

ولقد احتوى كل فصل من فصول هذا الكتاب على مجموعة من الأسئلة والتمارين التي تناولت الجوانب النظرية والعملية المختلفة التي وردت فيه، وضمت هذه الأسئلة مجموعة من الأسئلة التي وردت في امتحانات المجمع الأمريكي للمحاسبين القانونيين وامتحانات جمعية المحاسبين الإداريين وامتحانات مجلس مهنة تدقيق الحسابات الأردني وامتحانات المجمع العربي للمحاسبين القانونيين، كما هي منشورة في كتيبات وأسئلة امتحانات هذه الهيئات العلمية.

وفي الطبعتين الثانية والثالثة حاولت بقدر الامكان مسايرة التطورات التي ظهرت في هذا الحقل من المعرفة ومعالجة بعض القصور الذي وجدته. وفي هذه الطبعة قمت بمراجعة كل فصول الكتاب وعملت على تحسين عرض المادة وغيرت الكثير من الأمثلة التي استخدمت في شرح الفصول حتى تزيد من إيضاح المادة. كما قمت بإضافة فصل جديد هو محاسبة تكاليف الأنشطة لمراعاة التطورات العلمية في هذا المجال. كما وجدت انه من الضروري أن يتم كتابة الفواصل الخاصة بالآلاف لتسهيل عملية فهم القارئ.

ولتحسين مستوى الاستفادة من الكتاب قمت بحل التمارين وطباعتها ولذا يمكن للأستاذ الذي يخصص هذا الكتاب على طلبته أن يتصل بالناشر لتزويده بالحلول مع الرجاء بان لا ينشر هذه الحلول الى طلبته. وكان لطلابي في الجامعات الأردنية وجامعة الكويت الفضل في إعادة صياغة الكثير من الأفكار حتى تصبح في متناول أيدي القارئ.

وما كنت لأنجز هذا المؤلف بصورته النهائية دون تعاون الزملاء في أقسام المحاسبة، ومن السيد محمود عبد الرحيم الرجبي ومحمد سلامة اللذين ساهما بالتدقيق اللغوي، فلهم مني جميعاً كل الشكر والتقدير.

المؤلف

المحتويات

الصفحة	الموضوع
١٣	**الفصل الأول: التعريف بمحاسبة التكاليف وأهميتها** ....
١٥	- مقدمة ....
١٧	- التعريف بمحاسبة التكاليف ....
١٨	- المقارنة بين المحاسبة المالية ومحاسبة التكاليف ....
٢٢	- التنظيم الإداري وأثره على محاسبة التكاليف ....
٢٦	- وظائف الإدارة ودور محاسبة التكاليف ....
٢٨	- المدير المالي ....
٢٩	- زمالة جمعية المحاسبين الإداريين ....
٣١	- أسئلة وتمارين ....
٣٣	**الفصل الثاني: طبيعة وتصنيفات التكاليف** ....
٣٥	- مقدمة ....
٣٧	- تبويب عناصر تكاليف الإنتاج ....
٤٤	- تدفق التكاليف في المنشآت الصناعية ....
٥١	- تبويب التكاليف حسب سلوكها ....
٥٥	- تبويب التكاليف من وجهة نظر الرقابة ....
٥٦	- تبويب التكاليف لأغراض اتخاذ القرارات الإدارية ....
٥٩	- أسئلة وتمارين ....
٦٧	**الفصل الثالث: محاسبة تكاليف الأوامر الإنتاجية** ....
٦٩	- مقدمة ....
٧٠	- محاسبة الأوامر الإنتاجية ....
٧١	- الإجراءات المستخدمة في محاسبة التكاليف المباشرة ....
٧٧	- التكاليف الصناعية غير المباشرة ....

الموضوع	الصفحة
- تحميل التكاليف الصناعية غير المباشرة على الأوامر	٧٧
- أوامر الإنتاج المنتهية	٨١
- معالجة التكاليف الصناعية غير المباشرة المحملة بالزيادة أو	٨٣
بالنقص	
- مثال محلول	٨٦
- أسئلة وتمارين	٩٤
الفصل الرابع: محاسبة المراحل الإنتاجية	١٠٧
- مقدمة	١٠٩
- تدفق الإنتاج	١٠٩
- حسابات التكاليف في صناعة المراحل	١١٠
- تقرير تكاليف المرحلة	١١٢
- طريقة المتوسط المرجح	١١٣
- طريقة الأول في الأول	١١٩
- حالة تعدد المواد	١٢٤
- التحويل بين المراحل	١٢٦
- مثال محلول	١٣١
- أسئلة وتمارين	١٣٧
الفصل الخامس: التالف والفاقد والوحدات المعيبة والخردة ..	١٥١
- مقدمة	١٥٣
- الوحدات غير الجيدة	١٥٣
- التالف العادي وغير العادي	١٥٤
- الإنتاج الجيد	١٥٥
- معالجة التالف في صناعة المراحل	١٥٨
- معالجة التالف في صناعة الأوامر الإنتاجية	١٦٩
- المعالجة المحاسبية للانتاج المعيب	١٧٢

الصفحة	الموضوع
١٧٣	- المعالجة المحاسبية للخردة ....
١٧٦	- أسئلة وتمارين ....
١٨٩	**الفصل السادس: التكاليف الصناعية غير المباشرة** ....
١٩١	- مقدمة ....
١٩٢	- مراكز الإنتاج ومراكز الخدمات ....
١٩٥	- تبويب عناصر التكاليف غير المباشرة ....
١٩٩	- توزيع تكاليف مراكز الخدمات ....
٢٠٢	- طريقة التوزيع المباشر ....
٢٠٤	- طريقة التوزيع التنازلي ....
٢٠٧	- طريقة التوزيع التبادلي ....
٢١٠	- تحميل تكاليف مراكز الإنتاج على المنتجات ....
٢١٤	- أسئلة وتمارين ....
٢٢٣	**الفصل السابع: تكاليف المنتجات الرئيسية والمنتجات الفرعية** ...
٢٢٥	- مقدمة ....
٢٢٥	- تعريف المنتجات الرئيسية والفرعية ....
٢٢٦	- التكاليف المشتركة والتكاليف الخاصة ....
٢٢٧	- المحاسبة على المنتجات الفرعية ....
٢٣١	- توزيع التكاليف المشتركة ....
٢٤١	- التكاليف المشتركة واتخاذ القرارات ....
٢٤٤	- أسئلة وتمارين ....
٢٥٥	**الفصل الثامن : نظام تكاليف الأنشطة** ....
٢٥٧	- مقدمة ....
٢٥٩	- نظام التكاليف التقليدي ....
٢٦١	- معدل تحميل الاعباء الاضافية ....

الموضوع	الصفحة
- نظام تكاليف الانشطة	٢٦٢
- تحديد الاعباء المحملة على الانتاج	٢٦٦
- مقارنة تكلفة الوحدة في الانظمة البديلة	٢٦٨
- الخاتمة	٢٧٢
- أسئلة وتمارين	٢٧٣
الفصل التاسع : طرق تحميل التكاليف الكلية والمتغيرة	٢٨٣
- طريقة التكلفة الكلية	٢٨٥
- طريقة التكلفة المتغيرة	٢٨٦
- سلوك التكاليف	٢٨٧
- قائمة الدخل حسب طريقتي التكلفة الكلية والمتغيرة	٢٨٧
- دورة حسابات طريقة التكلفة المتغيرة	٢٩١
- قائمة الدخل حسب طريقة التكلفة الكلية	٢٩٥
- قوائم الدخل حسب التكاليف المعيارية	٢٩٧
- تقييم طرق التكاليف الكلية والمتغيرة	٢٩٩
- أسئلة وتمارين	٣٠٣
الفصل العاشر: التكاليف المعيارية للمواد والأجور والأعباء الإضافية.	٣١١
- مقدمة	٣١٣
- أنواع المعايير	٣١٧
- معايير المواد المباشرة وتحليل انحرافاتها	٣١٨
- معايير الأجور المباشرة وتحليل انحرافاتها	٣٢٢
- معايير عناصر التكاليف غير المباشرة وتحليل انحرافاتها	٣٢٧
- طريقة الاربعة انحرافات	٣٣٠
- طريقة الثلاثة انحرافات	٣٣٥
- طريقة الانحرافين	٣٣٦

الصفحة	الموضوع
٣٣٨	- مثال محلول ....
٣٤٣	- أسئلة وتمارين ....
٣٥٥	**الفصل الحادي عشر: التكاليف المعيارية: الدورة المحاسبية ...**
٣٥٧	- مقدمة ....
٣٥٨	- طريقة التكاليف المعيارية الجزئية ....
٣٦٢	- تعديل طريقة التكاليف الجزئية ....
٣٦٣	- طريقة التكاليف المعيارية الكاملة ....
٣٦٧	- المعالجة المحاسبية للانحرافات ....
٣٧٣	- قائمة تكلفة البضاعة المباعة المعيارية ....
٣٧٥	- تطبيق التكاليف المعيارية في صناعة المراحل ....
٣٨٠	- أسئلة وتمارين ....
٣٨٩	**الفصل الثاني عشر: مواضع خاصة في تحليل انحرافات التكاليف....**
٣٩١	- مقدمة ....
٣٩٣	- انحرافات مزيج المواد المباشرة ....
٣٩٨	- انحرافات عائد المواد ....
٤٠٣	- انحرافات الأجور المباشرة ....
٤٠٤	- انحراف العائد الكلي ....
٤٠٧	- انحراف التالف ....
٤١٣	- أسئلة وتمارين ....
٤١٥	**الفصل الثالث عشر: تحليل انحرافات الإيرادات ....**
٤١٥	- مقدمة ....
٤٢٠	- تحليل انحرافات منتج واحد ....
٤٢٠	- تحليل انحرافات المبيعات في حالة تعدد المنتجات ....
٤٢٧	- مثال محلول على تحليل الانحرافات ....

الموضوع	الصفحة
- أسئلة وتمارين	٤٣٢
المراجع العربية	٤٣٥
المراجع الأجنبية	٤٣٦

الفصل الأول
التعريف بمحاسبة التكاليف وأهميتها

يهدف هذا الفصل إلى تحقيق الآتي:

١. إعطاء لمحة تاريخية عن تطور محاسبة التكاليف.

٢. مقارنة محاسبة التكاليف مع المحاسبة المالية.

٣. تعريف بعض مصطلحات محاسبة التكاليف.

٤. تحديد الوضع التنظيمي لمحاسبة التكاليف.

٥. بيان دور محاسبة التكاليف في خدمة الوظائف الإدارية.

٦. بيان وظائف المراقب المالي وأمين الخزينة في المنشآت الكبيرة.

٧. عرض الملامح الرئيسة لزمالة المحاسبين الإداريين الأمريكيين.

المقدمــة:

تحتاج المنشآت على اختلاف أنواعها إلى توفير المعلومات التي يطلبها المهتمون في شؤونها، لتساعدهم في اتخاذ القرارات الاقتصادية الرشيدة، وتضم هذه الجهات الإدارة، والمستثمرين الحاليين والمتوقعين، والدائنين، والوكالات والهيئات الحكومية، واتحادات العمال. إذ بدون توفير المعلومات المناسبة لهذه الجهات تزداد نسبة قراراتهم الخاطئة. لذلك تقوم كل منشاة بوضع الأنظمة المحاسبية والمالية لتوفير المعلومات اللازمة لإخلاء مسؤولية الادارة تجاه الأطراف الأخرى ومساعدتها في القيام بعملها على أحسن صورة، ومن هذه الأنظمة نظام محاسبة التكاليف ونظام المحاسبة المالية.

يقوم نظام المحاسبة المالية على تشغيل المعلومات المالية التي يتم التعبير عنها بوحدات نقدية مثل: تكلفة الأجور، وتكلفة المواد الخام، وقيمة المصروفات الصناعية، والتسويقية والإدارية، والإيرادات، وبهذا تبقى المعلومات غير المالية خارج نطاق السجلات المحاسبية. ويعرف نظام المحاسبة المالية على أنه نظام يعمل على تجميع وتشغيل الأحداث والعمليات المالية، وتقديم التقارير التي تساعد الإدارة والأطراف الاخرى على اتخاذ القرارات الاقتصادية الرشيدة. وتضم تقارير المحاسبة المالية الميزانية وقائمة الدخل وقائمة التدفق النقدي. ويتم توزيع هذه التقارير على الأطراف الخارجية.

في البداية كانت المحاسبة تهتم بعملية تقديم تقارير مالية سنوية لإخلاء مسؤولية الإدارة ، والعمل على تزويد الأطراف المهتمة بالمعلومات التي تساعدها في اتخاذ القرارات الاستثمارية. مع مرور الزمن ، وتطور الأنشطة الاقتصادية ، وكبر حجم المشروعات، وتنوع الإنتاج، واشتداد حدة المنافسة في الأسواق [1] أصبح من الضروري تطوير الأسس والأساليب المحاسبية لزيادة دقة التقارير المالية وتقديم المعلومات اللازمة للقرارات الإدارية المختلفة. وهذا أدي الى ظهور محاسبة التكاليف لتهتم بتحديد تكلفة وحدات الإنتاج لرفع دقة التقارير المالية عن طريق زيادة دقة أرقام تكلفة البضاعة المباعة وتكلفة بضاعة آخر المدة . وفي نهاية القرن التاسع عشر ظهرت عدة طرق لزيادة

---

[1] Sidney Davidson, and Roman L. Weil, <u>Handbook of Cost Accounting</u>, (McGraw - Hill, Inc., ١٩٧٨), P. ١ - ١٠.

دقة أرقام تكاليف الإنتاج، فتم استخدام طرقاً لتوزيع التكاليف الصناعية غير المباشرة ومعالجة تكاليف الطاقة العاطلة، وهنا ذكر ألكزندر هاميلتون شيرش عام ١٩٠٠، بأن معظم الشركات الصناعية‌حينها كان لديها طرقاً لتحديد تكاليف المواد والأجور التي تصرف على أوامر الإنتاج. وشهد النصف الأول من القرن العشرين عدة محاولات لتطوير أنظمة التكاليف، منها استخدام أنظمة التكاليف المعيارية‌والموازنات التخطيطية وهذه الأنظمة‌عملت توسيع نطاق اهتمام محاسبة‌التكاليف من موضوع تحديد‌تكلفة‌الإنتاج إلى موضوع الرقابة‌على التكاليف.

وفي الفترة من ١٩٥٠ - ١٩٦٠ اكتشف المحاسبون بأن بيانات التكاليف التي يعدونها لأغراض تحديد تكلفة الإنتاج يتم استخدامها من قبل المديرين في اتخاذ قرارات إدارية مثل: التسعير، وتحديد خطة الإنتاج، واستغلال المصادر النادرة. وعندها قام المحاسبون بدراسة بعض القرارات الإدارية فتم إنشاء عدة نماذج محاسبية للعديد من هذه القرارات لتحديد التكاليف والإيرادات المناسبة التي يتوقع حدوثها عند اتخاذ تلك القرارات أو يتم تجنب حدوثها عند عدم اتخاذ تلك القرارات. وهذا أدى إلى توسيع نطاق اهتمام محاسبة التكاليف من تحديد تكلفة الإنتاج إلى خدمة القرارات الإدارية، مما دفع البعض الى أن يطلق على محاسبة التكاليف اسم "المحاسبة الإدارية". [١]

وفي سنة ١٩٧٠ تم تكوين مجلس معايير محاسبة التكاليف في الولايات المتحدة، بهدف تحقيق التوحيد والتطبيق المنظم لمبادئ محاسبة التكاليف من قبل مقاولي صناعة الأسلحة. وتم حل هذا المجلس سنة ١٩٨٠ بعد أن أنجز أهدافه. وخلال فترة وجوده أصدر عدة معايير تحكم تحديد وتوزيع التكاليف على المنتجات وأوامر الإنتاج[٢]. وهذا أثرى محاسبة التكاليف لأنه قدم حلولا للمشكلات الصعبة التي كانت تواجهها عملية تحديد تكلفة الإنتاج، وخصوصاً توزيع التكاليف الصناعية غير المباشرة. ومن التطورات الحديثة استخدام نظام تكاليف الأنشطة بهدف زيادة دقة توزيع التكاليف الصناعية غير المباشرة واستخدام نظام المخزون عند الحاجة Just –in Time .

---

[١] Kaplan S. R., Advanced Management Accounting, Prentice - Hall, Englewood cliffs, NJ, ١٩٨٢ m pp ١-١٠.

[٢] Matz Usery, cost Accounting Planning and Control, south - Western Publishing Co -, Cincinnali, Ohio, ١٩٨٤, pp, ١١-١٤.

التعريف بمحاسبة التكاليف:

تعرف التكلفة على أنها قيمة الموارد التي يتم التضحية بها للحصول على سلعه أو تقديم خدمة. ويتم قياس التضحية بالمبالغ التي يتم دفعها أو يتم التعهد بدفعها مستقبلاً عند المبادلة، وهذه تعرف بالنفقات. وتعرف النفقة على أنها التضحيات النقدية أو العينية التي وقعت فعلاً أو تلك التي يتم التعهد بوقوعها مستقبلاً من أجل الحصول على سلعة أو خدمة. [1] لذا تكون تكلفة الأصل عبارة عن مجموع النفقات التي تتحملها المنشأة في سبيل الحصول على الأصل، فإذا كان الأصل مثلاً عبارة عن سيارة فإن تكلفتها تتكون من: ثمن شرائها زائد قيمة الرسوم الجمركية وتكاليف تسجيلها في دائرة السير(المرور). وبالمثل فإن تكلفة الإنتاج تتمثل في تكلفة المواد الخام، وأجور العمال، والمصروفات اللازمة لإنتاج المنتج.

ويمكن تعريف محاسبة التكاليف على أنها مجموعة من الأسس والإجراءات المنظمة بطريقة معينة للقيام بتجميع وتخصيص وتوزيع التكاليف على أهداف التكلفة [2]. وكما يمكن تعريفها على أنها نظام محاسبي يعمل على تجميع المعلومات، وتصنيفها، وتلخيصها، وتحليلها، والتقرير عنها إلى الإدارة لمساعدتها في أنشطة التخطيط والرقابة واتخاذ القرارات [3] . لقد أعطى هذا التعريف أهمية خاصة لدور محاسبة التكاليف في خدمة الأغراض الإدارية بالمقارنة مع هدف تحديد تكلفة الإنتاج الذي ركز عليه التعريف الاول. وعليه نستطيع القول أن نظام التكاليف يحتوي على مجموعة من المبادئ والإجراءات الرسمية اللازمة لتحقيق أهداف النظام، وأنه يعمل على تجميع وتخصيص وتحليل تكاليف الإنتاج أو النشاط، لتحديد تكلفة وحدات الإنتاج، وتحديد التكاليف التي تحدث في الوحدات الإدارية المختلفة، وتقديم معلومات مفيدة للأغراض الإدارية، بما فيها رقابة وتخطيط تكاليف الإنتاج [4].

---

[1] محمد عادل إلهامي، محاسبة التكاليف الفعلية: الأسس العلمية والعملية، مكتبة عين شمس، القاهرة، ١٩٨٧، ص ٣٦.

[2] تشارلز، ت، هورنجرن، محاسبة التكاليف مدخل إداري، ترجمة أحمد حامد حاج(دار المريخ ١٩٨٧)، ص٢٣-٢٥.

[3] Robert S. Kaplan, Op. Cit, PP ١ -١٠.

[4] مجدي عمارة ،آخرون، دراسات منهجية معاصرة في محاسبة التكاليف الفعلية، ص ٤٥-٥٠.

تقوم المحاسبة المالية بإعداد تقارير مالية تحتوي على الميزانية، وقائمة الدخل، وقائمة التدفق النقدي، وتوزيع هذه التقارير على الأطراف المهتمة خارج المنشأة، أما محاسبة التكاليف (الإدارية) فتقوم بإعداد التقارير الخاصة بتحديد تكاليف الإنتاج أو الخدمات وتقديم المعلومات التي تطلبها الإدارة لاتخاذ القرارات الإدارية اللازمة لتسيير أعمال المنشأة.

المقارنة بين المحاسبة المالية ومحاسبة التكاليف:

للتعمق في فهم طبيعة محاسبة التكاليف من المفيد مقارنتها مع المحاسبة المالية وهنا نجد بينهما بعض الاختلافات أهمها الآتي: [1]

(أ) الالتزام بالمعايير المحاسبية:

يلتزم المحاسب المالي بتطبيق المعايير المحاسبية المقبولة قبولاً عاماً عند إعداد التقارير المالية، فهذه المعايير تهدف إلى توحيد المعالجات المحاسبية في النواحي التي تغطيها، وهذا يؤدي إلى الحد من مرونة المحاسب المالي في اختيار الطرق المحاسبية وزيادة إمكانية مقارنة التقارير المالية المنشورة ومن ثم زيادة فائدتها. وعلى الجانب الآخر، فان هذه المعايير غير موجودة (نوعاً ما) في محاسبة التكاليف (المحاسبة الإدارية)، ولذا تستطيع كل منشأة أن تحدد محتويات، وشكل تقاريرها بما يتلاءم وطبيعة نشاطها واحتياجات قراراتها الإدارية.

(ب) الإلزامية:

تتطلب قوانين أغلب بلدان العالم أن تمسك منشآت الأعمال حسابات مالية منتظمة وخاصة الشركات المساهمة العامة. وعلى الجانب الآخر، لا تعتبر محاسبة التكاليف إجبارية على هذه المنشآت، وبالتالي فإن استخدام محاسبة التكاليف يتوقف على شعور الإدارة بأهمية المعلومات التي تقدمها محاسبة التكاليف، وعلى كفاءتها في توفير المعلومات اللازمة، وعلى قدرة المحاسب على إقناع الإدارة بضرورتها.

---

[1] Titard, P, L., Managerial Accounting, (The Dryden Press, ١٩٨٧), Pp. ٥-٧.

(د) نوع المعلومات:

تقـوم المحاسبة الماليـة بتشـغيل البيانـات التاريخيـة. وعـلى الـرغم مـن الانتقادات الموجهة إلى هـذه الأرقام مـن مـؤدي الطرق المحاسبية الاخرى مثل طريقة التكاليف الجارية، أو طريقة التكاليف التاريخية المعدلة بالأرقام القياسية ، فإنه لم يتم استبدالها بطرق قياس أخرى

أما محاسبة التكاليف، فلا تقتصر على استخدام أرقام التكاليف التاريخية، إذ يمكنها تقديم تقارير تعتمد على التنبؤات، كـما هـو الحـال عنـد إعـداد الموازنـات التخطيطية، وإعداد بيانات لاتخاذ قرارات إدارية مثل: قـرار الاستمرار في تشغيل أحد أقسام المنشأة أو إيقافه، وقرارات الإنفـاق الرأسـمالي. فـاهم صـفات البيانـات اللازمة لهذه القرارات أنها مستقبلية ومن ثم فهي غير مسجلة في الدفاتر، وبالتـالي فهي أقل موضوعية من بيانات التكلفة التاريخية. وكذلك تعتبر محاسبة التكاليف تكلفة الفرص المضاعة من ضمن التكاليف المناسبة للقرارات الإداريـة عـلى الـرغم من عدم تسجيلها في الدفاتر المحاسبية.

(هـ) موضوع التقرير:

تغطي تقاريـر المحاسبـة الماليـة المنشـأة كوحـدة واحـدة ولذلـك لا يمكـن استخدامها في تقييم أداء الأقسام المختلفة التي تتكون منها المنشأة، وعـلى الجانـب الآخر تقـوم محاسبة التكاليف بإعـداد تقاريـر بعضـها يتعلـق بوحـدات الإدارة التشغيلية، وبعضها يتعلق بوحدات الإدارة الوسطى، وبعضها يتعلق بالإدارة العليا، وبعض هذه التقارير يحتوي على بيانـات تاريخيـة، وبعضـها يحتـوي عـلى بيانـات تقديرية. إضافة إلى ذلك، تكون تقارير محاسبة التكاليف أكـثر دوريـة مـن تقاريـر المحاسبة الماليـة التي تكون في الغالب سنوية أو فصلية[1]. ويمكن تلخيص الفرق بين المحاسبة المالية ومحاسبة التكاليف كما في الجدول[2] رقم (١-١).

---

[1] مجدي عماره، دراسات منهجية معاصره في محاسبة التكـاليف الفعليـة، (كليـة المحاسـبة، غربان، ليبيا، ١٩٩٢)، ٤٩ - ٦٩.

[2] Wilson R., Chua, W. ff., "Managerial Accounting", (VNR, ١٩٨٨, P,١٢).

جدول (١-١)
المقارنة بين المحاسبة المالية ومحاسبة التكاليف

محاسبة التكاليف	المحاسبة المالية	وجه الاختلاف
غير موجودة	موجودة وملزمة	المعايير
غير إلزامية	إلزامية	الإلزامية
- بيانات مالية وكمية تفصيلية تحليلية	- بيانات مالية وإجمالية عامه	صفات المعلومات
- بيانات عن تكاليف الماضي الحاضر والمستقبل	- بيانات إجمالية عن النفقات والإيرادات التي حدثت	الإطار الزمني للبيانات
- تتسم بالمرونة والسرعة	- موضوعية وقابلة للتحقق	طبيعة البيانات
- تحديد تكلفة الوحدات المنتجة وتكلفة إنتاج تحت التشغيل والرقابة على التكاليف وخدمة القرارات الإدارية	- تحديد نتائج أعمال المنشأة ومركزها المالي وتدفقاتها النقدية	الهدف من تقديم البيانات
إدارة المشروع نفسه	المستثمرون والمقرضون والدائنون وذوي العلاقة من خارج المشروع	المستفيد من البيانات
قصيرة نسبياً ومتكررة	سنة مالية أو فصلية	فترة التقرير

على الرغم من الاختلافات السابقة بين محاسبة التكاليف والمحاسبة المالية، فإنهما يكملان بعضهما البعض حيث أن كل نظام يقدم معلومات للنظام الآخر. ففي مجال الدفاتر، نجد أن بعض الدفاتر والسجلات التي تمسكها المحاسبة المالية تستخدم من قبل محاسبة التكاليف مثل سجلات الأجور، والمواد، والمصروفات فهذه السجلات توفر المدخلات الرئيسة لمحاسبة التكاليف واللازمة لتحديد تكاليف الإنتاج. كما تقدم محاسبة التكاليف معلومات لإعداد القوائم المالية ومنها تكلفة البضاعة المباعة وتكلفة مخزون آخر المدة. نظراً لهذه السمات يمكن دمج هذين النظامين معاً، بدلاً من تصميم كل نظام مستقلاً عن الآخر، فمثلاً ما هي جدوى أن تقوم المحاسبة المالية ومحاسبة التكاليف بتسجيل تكاليف شراء المواد وأجور العمال والمصروفات في مجموعتها الدفترية كل على حده ، أن الجواب - بطبيعة الحال - لا توجد جدوى من وراء ذلك . وقد زاد من قوة هذا الاتجاه

في أيامنا الحالية، وجود آلات التشغيل الإلكترونية (الحاسوب)، إذ تستطيع هـذه الآلات أن تقوم بالتسجيل والترحيل إلى عدة حسابات وعدة سجلات بعملية إدخال واحدة للمعلومات.

التعريف بالمنشأة الصناعية:

تعمـل المنشـأة الصناعيـة عـلى تحويـل المـواد الخـام إلى منتجـات نهائيـة، ولتحقيـق ذلـك تقـوم بشـراء المـواد الخـام وتخضعهـا لعمليـة تصنيـع لتحولهـا إلى منتجات نهائية. بعض المواد الخام تدخل في المكونات المادية للمنتج النهائي فتكون جزءاً منه مثل: حبيبات البلاستيك في صناعة أكياس البلاستيك، والأخشاب في صناعة الأثاث ولكن بعض المواد الاخرى لا تدخل في التركيبة النهائية لوحدات الإنتاج مثل: زيوت تزييت آلات الإنتاج، والوقود البترولي، ومواد الصيانة، والقرطاسية. وتحتاج عملية تحويل المواد إلى استخدام مجهود العمال الذين يعملون بصورة مباشرة أو غير مباشرة على الإنتاج، وبالإضافة إلى ذلك، يحتاج الإنتـاج الى اسـتخدام خدمات الآلات الصناعية والكهرباء، والاستهلاك، والإيجار، والرسوم، والرخص، وتعرف جميع هذه التكاليف باسم التكاليف الصناعية.

ولتحديد تكلفة الوحدة المنتجة يجب حصر ـ عـدد هـذه الوحدات وحصر ـ تكاليف المواد والأجور والمصروفات الصناعية المستخدمة في الإنتاج، ثم بقسمة إجمالي التكاليف الصناعية على عدد هذه الوحدات يتم التوصل إلى متوسط تكلفة الوحدة المنتجة. وتحدد تكلفة الوحدات المباعة بضرب عـدد الوحدات المباعة في تكلفة الوحدة المنتجة. وقد يتم تحديد تكلفة الوحـدات المباعـة بطريقة اخرى وذلك بجمع بضاعة أول المدة وتكلفة البضاعة التامة الصنع خلال الفـترة الجاريـة وطرح تكلفة مخزون آخر المدة من المجموع السابق. وتمثل تكلفة الوحدات التي لم يتم بيعها حتى نهاية الفترة الماليـة مخزون آخر المـدة وهـذا الـرقم يظهـر في الميزانية. وهنا يجب أن نلاحـظ أن التكاليف التـي تحمـل عـلى وحدات الإنتاج تقتصر على التكلفة الصناعية أما المصروفات التسويقية والمصروفات الإدارية فانه لا يجوز تحميلها على الوحدات المنتجة وسيتم دراسة سبب ذلك في الفصل القادم.

التنظيم الإداري وأثره على محاسبة التكاليف:

يتم تغطية موضوع التنظيم الإداري في كتب إدارة الأعمال، ولذلك سيتم التعرض لهذا الموضوع بالقدر الذي يبين دور محاسبة التكاليف في هذه التنظيمات. يمكن تعريف المنظمة على أنها مجموعة من المصادر المادية والبشرية التي تنظم معاً بصورة معينة بهدف تحقيق هدف معين [١]. ومن المنظمات من يهدف الى تحقيق أقصى ربح ممكن وهذه تعرف بمنشآت الأعمال، في حين يسعى بعضها الآخر إلى تحقيق أهداف اجتماعية، أو سياسية أو علمية مثل: الإدارات الحكومية، الجامعات، والمستشفيات الحكومية، وجمعيات الهلال الأحمر والجامعات. وعلى الرغم من أهمية محاسبة التكاليف لكل أنواع الوحدات إلا أن دورها أكثر وضوحاً في منشآت الأعمال، لذلك تركز أغلب الكتب الجامعية في أمثلتها وتطبيقاتها على منشآت الأعمال على أمل أن يتم تعميم ذلك على المنظمات الأخرى.

وكما تختلف منشآت الأعمال عن بعضها البعض من حيث العمل، فقد تقوم منشأة بالأعمال الصناعية، أو الزراعية، أو التجارية، أو الخدمية، ولكنها تشترك معاً في أن هدفها هو تحقيق أقصى ـ أرباح ممكنة لتعظيم ثروة أصحاب المنشأة في الأجل الطويل [٢] لأنه يهمل مصالح الأطراف الأخرى التي تتعامل مع المنشأة ومنها الإدارة، فهل يعقل بأن تقوم الإدارة بتعظيم ثروة أصحاب المنشأة وتنسى نفسها؟!! إن هذا أمراً غير مقبول، لذا تسعى نظرية الوكالة إلى وضع الشروط اللازمة لتعظيم ثروة أصحاب المنشأة والإدارة في آن واحد. يزداد الأمر صعوبة عند اخذ مصالح الأطراف المختلفة الأخرى في الحسبان مثل: العمالة والدولة. وللتغلب على هذه المشكلة اقترح البعض أن هدف منشآت الأعمال هو ترضية مصالح الأطراف المهتمة بالمنشأة [٣].

[١] Ray H. Garrison "Managerial Accounting", 5th. Ed.. (Homewood Illinois, ١٩٨٨), P.٣

[٢] Pappas, J. L., and Brigham, E. F., "Managerial Economics" (The Dryden Press, ١٩٧٩), P.١٧.

[٣] Pappas and Brigham, Op. Cit, PP. ١٧ - ٢٢.

التنظيم الإداري:

يتم التعبير عن التنظيم الإداري باستخدام الخريطة التنظيمية، ويتم إعدادها بتجميع الموارد على أساس وظيفي أو جغرافي، ويكون ترتيبها على شكل هرم، وتقع الإدارة العليا في قمة الهرم التنظيمي، في حين تقع الإدارات التشغيلية في قاعدته، وتعرف كل مجموعة متجانسة بالوحدة الإدارية، وتجمع الوحدات التي تقوم بوظيفة معينة في إدارة معينة مثل: إدارة الإنتاج، وإدارة المبيعات، وإدارة الشؤون المالية. وترتبط هذه الإدارات بالإدارة العليا وترتبط مع الوحدات الإدارية التابعة لها بعلاقة سلطة ومسؤولية، وهذا يعني أن مدير الإدارة له سلطة على الوحدات الإدارية التابعة له فمثلاً إذا رجعنا إلى الشكل (1-1) نجد أن مدير الإنتاج في مصنع الأثاث له سلطة على رؤساء خطوط الإنتاج، والصيانة، وأفران التجفيف، وبالتالي يكون رؤساء هذه الأقسام مسؤولين أمامه، وبالمثل يكون مدير الإنتاج مسؤولاً أمام المدير العام.

يفيد وجود الخريطة التنظيمية المحاسب عند قيامة بتحديد الوحدات الإدارية أو الأقسام أو مراكز التكاليف اللازمة لحصر وقياس التكلفة والرقابة على التكاليف. فالتكاليف التي تحمل على قسم معين يمكن تحميلها على وحدات الإنتاج الذي يمر في ذلك القسم، ومعرفة تكاليف القسم تحدد مسؤولية رئيس ذلك القسم. وهذه الأمور ضرورية لتصميم نظام محاسبة التكاليف. وهنا يجب مراعاة مستوى التفاصيل التي تحتويها التقارير لأن حاجة الوحدات الإدارية إلى البيانات يختلف عن بعضها البعض، فبعضها يحتاج الى بيانات مجمعة بينما يحتاج بعضها الآخر الى بيانات تفصيلية ومتكررة.

الإدارات التنفيذية والإدارات الاستشارية:

يتم تقسيم الوحدات الإدارية التي تتكون منها المنشأة إلى مجموعتين: الأولى وتشمل الإدارات التنفيذية، والثانية وتشمل الإدارات الاستشارية. تقوم الإدارات التنفيذية بالأعمال التي يتطلبها تحقيق الهدف الذي تسعى إليه المنشأة. ففي المنشآت الصناعية يكون الهدف هو إنتاج المنتجات وبيعها، لذا تكون إدارة الإنتاج، وإدارة المبيعات إدارات تنفيذية، أما الإدارات الأخرى مثل إدارة المصادر البشرية، والشؤون القانونية، والإدارة المالية، فهي إدارات استشارية لأنها تقوم بتقديم النصح والمشورة إلى الإدارات التنفيذية

لتمكنها من تحقيق الهدف الرئيسي ـ للمنشأة[1]. وهذا التقسيم يؤدي إلى عدم وجود سلطة للإدارات الاستشارية على الإدارات التنفيذية، وبالتالي لا يجوز لها أن تصدر الأوامر لها.

وللتغلب على هذه المشكلة تم ابتكار ما يسمى بالسلطة الوظيفية[2] والتي بموجبها يسمح لمديري الإدارات الاستشارية بإصدار تعليمات إلى مرؤوسي الإدارات التنفيذية للطلب منهم القيام بعمل يقع في حدود سلطة تلك الإدارة، وهنا ينظر الى الأوامر التي تصدرها الإدارات الاستشارية إلى الإدارات التنفيذية كأنها طلبات قدمت إلى الإدارة العليا وأن الأخيرة قامت بتوجيهها إلى الإدارات التنفيذية. ومن هذا المنطلق، يمكن للمدير المالي أن يطلب من الإدارات التنفيذية القيام ببعض الأعمال التي تتطلبها العمليات المحاسبية مثل: استخدام أذون صرف المواد الخام وتوقيعها قبل إرسالها للصرف من المخازن، وحصر ـ ساعات العمل المباشر وساعات تشغيل الآلات وحصر عدد وحدات الإنتاج وحالتها وعمل الجرد المفاجئ للمخزون وغيرها من المعلومات اللازمة لأغراض التقارير المحاسبية.

---

[1] Koontz and others, "Management", (McGraw - Hill, ١٩٨٠) PP, ٦٠-٦٥.

[2] Ibid, PP. ٦٠ - ٦٥.

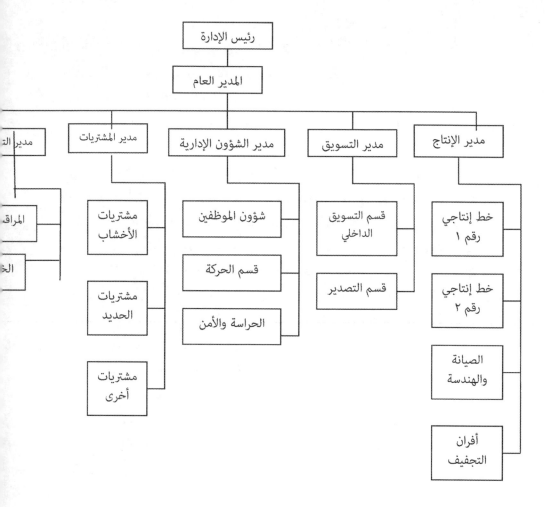

شكل (١-١) الخريطة التنظيمية لشركة الأثاث الأردنية

وظائف الإدارة ودور محاسبة التكاليف:

تقسم الأنشطة التي تقوم بها الإدارة إلى وظائف متعددة منها: التخطيط، والتوجيه، والتنظيم، والرقابة، واتخاذ القرارات [1]. وسيتم شرح مضامين هذه الوظائف لبيان دور محاسبة التكاليف في خدمة الإدارة.

أولاً: التخطيط (Planning):

يهدف التخطيط إلى وضع خطط العمل التي يجب التمسك بها خلال فترة العمل المقبلة، والتي تكون في الغالب سنة مالية، ويتم وضع الخطة بدراسة الظروف المتوقعة خلال فترة العمل المقبلة. وتغطي الخطط تقديرات الإيرادات والمصروفات اللازمة للوصول إلى أهداف المنشأة. ويتم ترجمة هذه الخطط على شكل جداول تعرف باسم الموازنة. تساهم محاسبة التكاليف في توفير الكثير من البيانات اللازمة لإعداد هذه الموازنة، حيث تستطيع توفير بيانات على مستوى الوحدات الإدارية المختلفة وعلى مستوى المنشأة ككل، إضافة إلى ذلك يمكن للمحاسبة المساهمة في تعديل الخطط الموضوعة عن طريق تقديم التقارير الدورية التي تعمل على مقارنة الإنجاز الفعلي مع الخطط، وبهذا يمكن لمحاسبة التكاليف المساعدة في وضع الخطط وتعديلها.

ثانياً: التنظيم والتوجيه (Organizing and Directing):

يهدف التنظيم إلى ترتيب العمال في مجموعات وظيفية هي إدارات الانتاج، والتسويق، والإدارات الاخرى مثل الادارة المالية والإدارة القانونية والمشتريات وإدارة المصادر البشرية. وكل من هذه الإدارات تنظم داخليا بطريقة لتسهيل قيامها بالأهداف المناطة بها واللازمة لتحقيق أهداف المنشأة، ويتم تنظيم هذه المجموعات بطريقة تبين سلطات ألأفراد في المنشأة، يتم التعبير عن التنظيم بصورة رسمية باستخدام الخريطة التنظيمية، وفي هذا المجال، تقوم محاسبة التكاليف بمراعاة التنظيم الإداري الموضوع وتعمل على تجميع وقياس وتخصيص تكاليف تشغيل كل وحدة إدارية، مما يسهل على الإدارة قياس أداء هذه الوحدات الإدارية.[2] إضافة إلى ذلك إذا وجدت المحاسبة أن التنظيم الإداري لتضارب السلطات فإنها تقترح إجراء التعديلات اللازمة على التنظيم الإداري.

---

[1] Ibid, PP. ٧٩-٨٨.

[2] Garrison R. H., op. Cit.

ويهدف التوجيه إلى استغلال المصادر الاقتصادية المتاحة بما فيها مجهود العمال في تحقيق هدف المنشاة، وللنجاح في ذلك يجب أن تحدد واجبات العاملين بصورة واضحة، والعمل على حل مشكلاتهم اليومية، وتوفير الحوافز المناسبة لهم. وعلى الرغم من أن أغلب أنشطة التوجيه تعتمد على الملاحظة الشخصية للمشرفين ورؤسائهم، إلا أن التقارير التي تقدمها المحاسبة الإدارية تـترجم الأداء الفعلي الى أرقام مالية وغير مالية مما يمكن كل مدير من معرفة نجاحه في توجيـه مرؤوسيه بطريقة أكثر موضوعية.

ثالثاً: الرقابة (Controlling):

تتم مزاولة الرقابة عن طريق مقارنة، التكاليف الفعلية للأنشطة بـالخطط الموضوعة لكشف الانحراف بيـنهما ومعرفـة أسباب ذلك والتقريـر عنـه للإدارة، ولذلك تعرف الرقابة على أنها مجموعة من الأنشطة التي تسعى إلى التأكد مـن أن المنشأة تسير في الطريق المرسوم لها، وهذا بدوره يتطلب وجود خطط (موازنة) تحكم مسار عمل المنشأة، لأنه بدون ذلك يصعب الحكم علـى كفاءة الأداء. (١) وقد جرت العادة في حالـة عـدم وجود خطط أن تـتم مقارنـة التكاليف الفعليـة للفترة الجارية مع تكاليف الفترة السابقة لها، وتحديد التغير الـذي طـرأ بينهما، وهذا يساعد الإدارة في معرفة الاتجاهات إلا أن ذلك لا يعتبر مقياساً سـليماً للأداء لأن أرقام التكاليف الفعلية للفترة السابقة تكون قد تأثرت بظروف العمل في الفترة السابقة وهذه قد تختلف عن ظروف العمل في الفترة الجارية، مـما ينعكس سـلباً على قدرة أساس المقارنة (٢) . ولفعالية الرقابة يفضل مقارنة التكلفة الفعليـة مـع التكاليف المخططة الـواردة في الموازنـات التخطيطيـة لان الأرقام الأخيرة تعكس الظروف المتوقعة في الفترة الجارية.

وتوفر محاسبة التكاليف المعلومات على مستوى وحدات الإنتاج والأقسـام والإدارات اللازمـة لإنشـاء الموازنـات ولإعـداد تقاريـر الرقابـة. فعنـد تـوفير هـذه المعلومات عـن الأنشطة والإدارات المختلفة إلى الإدارة العليا يمكن تطبيـق نظام محاسبة المسؤولية والذي يعمل على ربط الأداء بالأشخاص المسؤولين في المنشأة. ومن المعروف فان الرقابة الفعالة هي التي تعمل على ربط الأداء بالأفراد.

---

(١) Ibid, P.٦.

(٢) Wilson and Chua, Managerial Accounting Methods and Meaning١٩٨٨و, P.١٣.

رابعاً: اتخاذ القرارات *Decision Making*:

تهدف عملية اتخاذ القرارات إلى المفاضلة بين البدائل المتاحة واختيار أنسبها. وتقوم الإدارة بالمفاضلة بين البدائل في كل الوظائف الإدارية السابقة فمثلاً في مجال التخطيط تتم المفاضلة بين المنتجات التي ستتعامل معها المنشأة خلال فترة الموازنة، والمفاضلة بين الأسواق التي سوف يتم تغطيتها، وفي مجال الرقابة تتم المفاضلة بين مجالات العمل اللازمة لمعالجة الانحراف، وكذلك يتم المفاضلة بين القرارات المتعلقة بمسائلة الأفراد، وفي كل الحالات السابقة يجب اختيار أحد البدائل الممكنة للقرار. وتقوم الإدارة باتخاذ قرارات روتينية مثل أي المنتجات يجب إنتاجها اليوم، وأي المنتجات يجب إنتاجها غداً، وما هو المكان الذي يعمل فيه العامل س اليوم وغداً. وما هو ظاهر تعتمد الكثير من هذه القرارات على خبرة الإدارة.

وعلى الجانب المقابل تتخذ الإدارة قرارات غير روتينية من وقت لآخر، مثل قرارات الإنفاق الرأسمالي والقرارات الإدارية قصيرة الأجل مثل قرارات الإنتاج الداخلي أو الشراء من مورد، وقرار الاستمرار في تشغيل خط إنتاجي أو إيقافه. هذه القرارات تحتاج إلى معلومات غير متوافرة في السجلات المحاسبية التقليدية، ولتوفيرها تقوم محاسبة التكاليف بتقدير الإيرادات والتكاليف المناسبة أي المرتبطة بهذه القرارات. مما سبق نجد أن محاسبة التكاليف لديها طاقات يمكن تسخيرها لخدمة الوظائف الإدارية المختلفة ولمساعدتها في اتخاذ القرارات الروتينية وغير الروتينية الرشيدة. [1]

المدير المالي *Vice President of Finance*:

يوجد في المنشآت الكبيرة إدارة تعرف بالإدارة المالية، وهذه الإدارة تقسم أنشطتها إلى قسمين هما المحاسبة والتمويل. ويرأس النشاط المحاسبي شخص يسمى بالمراقب المالي ويرأس نشاط التمويل شخص يعرف برئيس الخزينة.

يقوم المراقب المالي (Controller) بإعداد القوائم المالية في نهاية كل فترة مالية وتقديم معلومات تساعد الإدارة في اتخاذ قراراتها الإدارية، وتشمل مسؤوليته: تجميع المعلومات المالية وإعداد التقارير اللازمة لسد احتياجات الأطراف الداخلية والخارجية

---

[1] هورنجرن، ت. تشارلز، مرجع سابق، ص ٣٥.

وتفسيرها، والتعامل مع إدارة الضريبة، وتجهيز التقارير للجهات الحكومية، وحماية الأصول. أما الشخص الآخر الذي يتبع المدير المالي فهو رئيس الخزينة Treasurer ويعمل على بتوفير رأس المال، وإنشاء العلاقات الاستثمارية مع الممولين، وتوفير التمويل قصير الأجل، وتطوير العلاقات مع البنوك وتجميع النقدية، والحصول على الائتمان والتحصيل، وعمل الاستثمارات، وإجراء التأمين على الأصول.

زمالة جمعية المحاسبين الإداريين

نظراً للدور الهام الذي تلعبه المحاسبة الإدارية في القرارات الإدارية فقد ارتأت الجمعية القومية للمحاسبين في أمريكا (National Association of Accountants) في شهر آذار سنة ١٩٧٧، إصدار شهادة زمالة للمحاسب الإداري الذي يجتاز امتحان الزمالة ويغطي الامتحان المواضيع الآتية: [1]

١. الاقتصاد الإداري والتمويل.

٢. الاعتبارات التنظيمية والسلوكية وشرف المهنة.

٣. التقارير العامة الموجة إلى الجمهور.

٤. التقارير الدورية الموجهة إلى الجهات الداخلية وللأغراض الخارجية.

٥. تحليل القرارات بما فيها أنظمة المعلومات.

يعقد امتحان الزمالة في عدة دول منها الأردن، الكويت، السعودية ومصر ــ وللحصول على الزمالة يجب على الشخص إتباع الآتي

١. أن يتقدم لبرنامج المحاسبين الإداريين القانونيين (Certified Management Accountants) وأن يسجل للامتحان.

٢. أن يجتاز أجزاء الامتحان الأربعة خلال فترة ثلاث سنوات.

٣. أن يستوفي شروط الخبرة قبل أو خلال سبع سنوات من اجتياز الامتحان.

٤. أن يلتزم بميثاق شرف مهنة المحاسبين القانونيين.

وحتى يتم الاحتفاظ بالزمالة يجب على حاملها أن يخضع لمتطلبات التعليم المستمر وعلى أساس منتظم.

---

[1] For More Information Write to, Institute of Management Accountant, ٥٧٠, City Center Building Ann Arbor, Mi, ٤٨-١١٠.

الخاتمـــة

تقوم محاسبة التكاليف بجمع وتصنيف وتخصيص التكاليف على المنتجـات والأنشطة، بقصد تقديم المعلومات التـي تستخدم في ترشيد القـرارات وفي إعـداد التقارير المالية السنوية. وتستطيع محاسبة التكاليف تقديم معلومـات تساعد الإدارة في أعمال التخطيط والتنظيم والتوجيه والرقابـة وفي مجـال اتخـاذ القرارات تقدم المعلومات لخدمة أغراض القرارات الروتينية وغير الروتينية.

وكذلك تبين لنا أن محاسبة التكاليف والمحاسبة الإدارية هما أسماء مترادفة في الوقت الحالي، ولكـن هـذا الكتـاب سيقوم باستخدام اللفـظ الأول لأن تركيـزه ينصب على الإجراءات والأسس المستخدمة في تحديد التكلفـة والرقابـة عليهـا، وان للمؤلف كتابا آخر يركز على استخدام البيانـات في القرارات الإداريـة لـذلك اسماه المحاسبة الإدارية.

السؤال الأول: ما هو المقصود بالتكلفة والمصروف والنفقة.

السؤال الثاني: ما هي أوجه الشبه والاختلاف بين المحاسبة المالية ومحاسبة التكاليف؟

السؤال الثالث: تستطيع محاسبة التكاليف تقديم معلومات كثيرة إلى الإدارة، ما هي أهم الوظائف الإدارية التي تخدمها محاسبة التكاليف ؟

السؤال الرابع: عـرف المقصود بالرقابة وكيـف يمكـن لمحاسبة التكاليف خدمـة أغراضها؟

السؤال الخامس: عرف المقصود بالتخطيط، وما هي أهم أنواع الخطط؟

السؤال السادس: تختلف تقارير المحاسبة المالية ومحاسبة التكاليف مـن حيـث الشكل والمضمون. اشرح ذلك.

السؤال السابع: ما هـو الفـرق بين الإدارات التنفيذية والاستشارية ومـاذا يقصـد بالسلطة الوظيفية؟

السؤال الثامن: تصر إدارة إحدى الشركات على أن تتبع وحدة محاسبة التكاليف مدير الإنتاج. هل توافق على هذا الاقتراح ولماذا؟

السؤال التاسع: قارن بين وظائف المراقب المالي ورئيس الخزينة وهل يمكن تحقيق ذلك في الشركات الصغيرة والمتوسطة الحجم؟

السؤال العاشر: ما هي العوامل التي يجب أخـذها في الاعتبار عند تصميم نظـام التكاليف؟

السؤال الحادي عشر: تقوم إحدى الشركات بتجارة السيارات وقد نظمت أعمالهـا في أربع إدارات هي:
١. السيارات الجديدة.
٢. السيارات المستعملة.
٣. الكراج والصيانة.
٤. الإدارة والمحاسبة.

وقد لاحظت الشركة أن مبيعاتها في السنوات الثلاثة الأخيرة قد انخفضت بدرجة كبيرة، ولذلك طلبت منك أن تصمم لها نظام معلومات يساعدها في اتخاذ القرارات الإدارية.

المطلوب: ما هي المعلومات التي يستطيع نظام المحاسبة الإدارية أن يقدمها لهذه الشركة.

السؤال الثاني عشر: يوجد في إحدى الشركات الوحدات الإدارية التالية:

١. المدير العام، ٢. المراقب المالي ٣. إدارة المبيعات ٤. إدارة الإنتاج ٥. منطقة مبيعات أ ٦. منطقة مبيعات ب ٧. قسم إنتاجي أ ٨. قسم الصيانة ٩. قسم الحسابات المالية ١٠. قسم الحسابات الإدارية ١١. قسم تجميع الإنتاج ١٢. قسم مراقبة الجودة ١٣. قسم الرقابة الداخلية.

المطلوب:

تصميم خريطة تنظيمية لهذه الشركة.

الفصل الثاني
طبيعة وتصنيفات التكاليف

يهدف هذا الفصل إلى :

١- التعريف بمفهوم التكلفة والمصروف.

٢- التعريف بتبويب التكاليف حسب وظائف المشروع.

٣- تبويب التكاليف إلى تكاليف منتج وتكاليف فترة.

٤- التعريف بالعناصر المباشرة الصناعية وغير المباشرة.

٥- التعريف بقوائم التكاليف وتكلفة البضاعة المباعة.

٦- التعريف بتبويب التكاليف حسب سلوكها تجاه حجم الإنتاج.

٧- التعريف بالتكاليف الخاصة بمحاسبة المسؤولية.

٨- التعريف بتبويب التكاليف لأغراض اتخاذ القرارات الإدارية.

المقدمة:

تهتم الإدارة في جميع أنواع المشروعات باستغلال الموارد الاقتصادية المتاحة بأفضل صورة ممكنة، وهذا يتحقق بزيادة الإيرادات على التكاليف. لهذا فإن على الإدارة إعطاء أهمية خاصة للتكاليف حتى لا تزيد عن الإيرادات ومن ثم تفشل الإدارة في تحقيق أهدافها. ولقد اهتمت الإدارة في البداية بدقة أرقام تكلفة البضاعة المباعة والمصروفات التشغيلية ولكن هذه الأرقام لا تغطي إلا جانباً من اهتمامات الإدارة في الوقت الحالي، لأنه أصبح عليها الإجابة عن العديد من الأسئلة مثل، ما هي تكلفة وحدة المنتج؟ وما هي التكاليف الملائمة لاتخاذ قرار الإنتاج في مصانع الشركة؟ وما هي التكلفة التي سيتم تحملها عند التوسع في حجم الإنتاج ؟ وما هي التكاليف التي يجب مراقبتها على مستوى إداري معين؟.

وتشير كلمة التكاليف Cost إلى قيمة الموارد ألتي يتم التضحية بها في سبيل الحصول على سلعة أو خدمة معينة. فمثلاً تشمل تكلفة السيارة كل ما تدفعه أو تعد المنشأة بدفعه لامتلاك السيارة، وتسمى هذه المبالغ بالنفقات[1]. على أية حال، يختلف هيكل التكلفة حسب طبيعة أعمال المنشأة، ففي المنشآت الصناعية مثلاً تتكون تكلفة البضاعة التامة الصنع من تكاليف المواد المباشرة وتكاليف الأجور المباشرة والمصروفات الصناعية غير المباشرة. بينما تتكون تكلفة البضاعة في المنشآت التجارية من ثمن شرائها.

التكاليف والمصروفات والخسارة: *Cost، Expense and Loss* :

تقوم المحاسبة بتسجيل التكاليف في الدفاتر على أساس قيمة التضحية الفعلية التي تتحملها المنشاة في سبيل الحصول على السلعة أوالخدمة.ويتم تقسيم التكاليف إلى تكاليف مستنفذةللحصول على إيرادفي الفترةالجاريةوتعرف هذه التكلفة بالمصروفات ومثال ذلك : الإيجار ، والصيانة ،والضرائب والرسوم ،والأجور ، ويتم طرح قيمة هذه

---

[1] مجدي عمارة، مرجع سابق الذكر، ص ص ٤٥- ٦٠.

المصروفـات مـن إيرادات الفـترة الماليـة قبل التوصل إلى رقم صافـي الربح. أمـا المجموعة الأخرى، فهي التكاليف غير المستنفذة عند حدوثها وتشمل التكاليف التي يكون لها منافع مستقبلية. وهذه تعرف بالأصول وتظهر في الميزانية إذا بقيت حتى نهاية السنة المالية، وبهذا فالتكاليف تعتبر أصلاً إذا كان من المتوقع أن تكون لها قيمة في المستقبل، وتعتبر مصروفاً إذا تم استنفاذها في تحقيق الـدخل ولم يعـد لها قيمة بعد نهاية الفترة الجارية. وقد جرت العادة أن يتم رسملة تكاليف المـواد الخام، وتكاليف أجور العمال الذين يعملون في إدارة الإنتاج، والمصروفات الصناعية الأخرى مثل الاستهلاك، والإيجار، ومصروف الكهرباء المرتبطة بالإنتاج. وتتم رسملة هذه التكاليف بتحميلها على وحدات الإنتاج لان لهذه الوحدات قيمـة مستقبلية تتمثل في ثمن بيعها. وإذا تم بيع بعض هذه الوحدات خلال الفترة الجارية يتم تحويل تكلفة الوحدات المباعة الى مصروف يسمى تكلفة البضاعة المباعـة ويتم طرحها من إيرادات الفترة، وإذا لم يتم بيعها حتى نهايـة المـدة فإنهـا تظهـر ضمن الأصول في الميزانية.

أما الخسارة فهـي تكـاليف مستنفذة ولكـن بـدون تحقيـق إيراد بصـورة مباشرة أو غير مباشرة. وفي القيـاس المحاسبي نجـد أن الخسارة تحـدث إذا كان الإيراد أقل من التكاليف، أو عندما تحدث التكاليف، ولا تؤدي إلى تحقيق إيرادات مثل الفاقد الصناعي أو سرقة بعض البضائع من قبل العمال أو الزبائن.

تكلفة البضاعة المباعة:

تحدد تكلفة البضاعة المباعة حسب طبيعة نشاط المنشأة، ففي المنشآت التجارية تتحدد تكلفة البضاعة المباعة بجمع تكلفة بضاعة أول المـدة مـع تكلفة المشتريات وطرح تكلفة بضاعة آخر المدة منهما. وتتحدد تكلفة المخزون آخر المدة بضرب عدد الوحدات بالمخازن في تكلفة الوحدة، وهذه يتم تحديدها في ضوء طريقة تسعير المخزون ونظام الجرد الذي تتبناه المنشأة. وهذه التكاليف تعرف بتكاليف المنتج فهي ترتبط مباشرة بتكلفة البضاعة المشتراة، وتتضمن قيمـة المصروفات التي تتحملها المنشأة حتى تصل البضاعة إلى المخازن. وفي هذه المنشآت يتم قسمة تكاليف المشتريات على عـدد الوحدات المشتراة لتحديـد تكلفة الوحدة الواحدة . وحسب المعايير المحاسبية المقبولة قبولا عاما لا يتم إضافة

المصروفات التسويقية أو الإدارية إلى تكلفة البضاعة المباعة، لأنها تعتبر تكاليف فترة، حيث يتم خصمها من رقم مجمل الربح في قائمة الدخل.

وتتكون تكاليف المنتج في المنشآت الصناعية من تكلفة المواد الخام المستخدمة في الإنتاج، وتكاليف أجور عمال الإنتاج، والمصروفات الصناعية الأخرى مثل: الاستهلاك والوقود، والقوى المحركة، والصيانة والإيجار، ولان هذه التكاليف تحمل على وحدات المنتج أطلق عليها تكلفة منتج Product cost، وهي تناظر تكلفة المشتريات في المنشآت التجارية. وتتكون تكلفة البضاعة المباعة في المنشآت الصناعية من تكلفة الإنتاج التام أول المدة زائد تكاليف الإنتاج التام خلال المدة ناقص تكاليف الإنتاج التام آخر المدة. ومرة أخرى تعتبر مصروفات التسويق والمصروفات الإدارية مصروفات فترة Period cost. ويتم خصمها من رقم مجمل الربح في فترة حدوثها.

ونستنتج مما سبق أنه يتم تبويب التكاليف إلى تكاليف منتج، وتكاليف فترة، وتشمل الأخيرة مصروفات التسويق والمصروفات الإدارية. وتتطلب المعايير المحاسبية المقبولة قبولاً عاماً، عدم تحميل المصروفات التسويقية والإدارية على تكاليف وحدات المخزون.[١]

لا يوجد في شركات الخدمات مثل شركات التأمين والمستشفيات، ومكاتب تدقيق الحسابات والفنادق، تكاليف منتج ذات أهمية لأن هذه المنشآت تحصل على معظم إيراداتها من بيع خدماتها وهذه الخدمات لا يتم تخزينها من فترة لأخرى، لذلك تعتبر كل تكاليفها تكاليف فترة، أي تعتبر مصروفات منذ حدوثها ولذلك يتم طرحها من إيرادات السنة المالية التي تحدث فيها.

تبويب عناصر تكاليف الإنتاج (المنتج)

التبويب هوتجميع منهجي للعناصرالمتشابهة وفقألخصائصهاالمشتركة.[٢]

وتعمل عملية تبويب عناصرالتكاليف على تقسيمها الى مجموعات مختلفة يكون لكل

---

[١]   Heitager, L. E. and Marulich, S.., <u>Managerial Accounting</u>, 2nd . ed (McGraw - Hill, ١٩٨٧), P ٣٦.

[٢] مجدي عمارة، مرجع سابق الذكر، ص٨١.

مجموعة صفات مشتركة ومختلفة عن المجموعات الأخرى. ويوجد في الحياة العملية عدة أسس للتبويب أهمها:

١. التبويب النوعي.

٢. التبويب الوظيفي.

٣. التبويب حسب علاقة العنصر بهدف التكلفة.

٤. التبويب حسب سلوك العنصر تجاه التغيرات في حجم النشاط.

٥. التبويب حسب قابلية العنصر للرقابة.

٦. التبويب حسب القرار الإداري.

يقوم التبويب النوعي للمصروفات بقسمتها إلى ثلاث مجموعات هـي المواد، والأجور، والمصروفات. ويقوم التبويب الوظيفي على قسمة التكاليف حسب الوظائف الرئيسية في المنشأة لذلك نجد أن التكاليف تقسـم إلى ثلاث مجموعـات حسب هذا التبويب هـي: تكـاليف الإنتاج أو التكاليف الصناعية، ومصروفات التسويق والمصروفات الإدارية، وسيتم التعـرف علـى طبيعـة هـذه التكـاليف عند دراسة طرق التبويب الأخرى والتي سيتم دراستها على التوالي.

التبويب حسب علاقة العنصر بهدف التكلفة:

يعرف هدف التكلفة على انه أي شيء يتم قياس تكلفته، وقد يكون وحـدة منتج أو قسم من أقسام المنشأة أو أي نشاط من أنشطتها. وبدراسة علاقة عناصر التكاليف مع هدف التكلفة يمكن تبويبها في ثلاث مجموعات هي:

أ- المواد المباشرة Direct material

ب- الأجور المباشرة Direct Labor

جـ- التكـاليف الصناعية غيـر المباشـرة (الأعبـاء الإضافية) Manufacturing overhead.

ولأن هذا الكتاب يركز على قياس تكلفة وحدات الإنتاج لـذلك سيعطي هذه العلاقة أهمية اكبر من علاقة التكلفة مع الأهداف الاخرى للتكلفة. وفيما يلي شرحاً لطبيعة هذه البنود:

المواد المباشرة:

وتشمل المواد التي يسهل تتبعها وتخصيصها على وحدات المنتجات لأنها من المكونات المادية للوحدات التي يتم إنتاجها ومثالها الأخشاب، والقماش، والأسفنج في صناعة الأثاث، والقطن في صناعة المنسوجات القطنية، والأقمشة في صناعة الملابس، والورق في صناعة الكتب. فهذه المواد يتم تتبعها الى وحدات المنتجات النهائية ويمكن تحديد الكمية التي استخدمتها كل وحدة منها، وبالتالي يسهل تخصيص تكاليفها على وحدات المنتج.

وهناك بعض المواد التي يمكن تتبعها إلى وحدات المنتجات النهائية ولكن تعتبر مواداً غير مباشرة لقلة أهميتها النسبية مثل: الغراء والمسامير في صناعة الأثاث، والخيطان في صناعة الكتب، والنشرات الطبية في صناعة الدواء. إضافة الى ذلك، هناك بعض المواد مثل زيوت التزييت ومواد النظافة والقرطاسية تعتبر مواد غير مباشرة لأنها لا تدخل ضمن التركيب المادي لوحدات الإنتاج

الأجور المباشرة:

هي أجور العمال الذين يعملون بصورة مباشرة على وحدات الإنتاج مثل: أجور العمال الذين يقومون بتشغيل آلات التفصيل، والتغريز، والتشطيب في صناعة الأثاث، وأجور العمال الذين يشرفون على آلات صب البلاستيك. أما أجور العمال الذين لا يعملون بصورة مباشرة على وحدات الإنتاج لأن مجهوداتهم لا تبذل على منتج واحد، بل على عدة منتجات مثل أجور المهندسين والمشرفين فتعتبر أجوراً غير مباشرة، ، وللسبب نفسه، تعتبر أجور عمال الصيانة، والنظافة، والحراسة، وأجور مدير إدارة الإنتاج، أجوراً غير مباشرة، لأنها تفيد أكثر من منتج.

وتقسم أجور العمال الذين يقومون بالإنتاج إلى قسمين: الأول: ويمثل أجرة الوقت الذي يبذل مباشرة في الإنتاج، وتعتبر هذه الأجور أجوراً مباشرة، والثاني: ويمثل أجرة الوقت الذي لايصرف على الإنتاج،وتعتبرهذه الأجورغيرمباشرة.وفي حالة الطلب من العمال العمل خارج ساعات الدوام الرسمية تصرف لهم علاوة تعرف باسم علاوة الوقت الإضافي،وعادة ما تحدد هذه العلاوة بنسبةمؤية من معدل الأجرالعادي، وتعتبر

هذه العلاوة ضمن الأجور غير المباشرة حتى لا يتم التمييز بين تكلفة الوحدات المنتجة خلال الوقت العادي والوقت الإضافي.

التكاليف الصناعية غير المباشرة (الأعباء الصناعية الإضافية):

Manufacturing overhead

تضم هذه المجموعة كل عناصر التكاليف الصناعية فيما عدا المواد المباشرة والأجور المباشرة، وتشتمل على العديد من العناصر التي تختلف في طبيعتها وأهميتها وسلوكها تجاه تغيرات حجم النشاط، ويتم تبويبها حسب طبيعتها في ثلاث مجموعات هي:

أولاً: المواد غير المباشرة:

وتشمل هذه المجموعة المواد التي لا يمكن تتبعها وتخصيصها على وحدات الإنتاج مثل: مواد الصيانة وقطع الغيار، والوقود والقوى المحركة، وكذلك تشمل المواد المباشرة ضئيلة القيمة التي لا تبرر اعتبارها مواداً مباشرة.

ثانياً: الأجور غير المباشرة:

وتشمل هذه المجموعة أجور العمال الذين لا يعملون بصورة مباشرة على الوحدات المنتجة مثل : أجور المشرفين والمهندسين، وأجور عمال المناولة، وأجور عمال الصيانة، والحراسة وأجور الإجازات العادية والمرضية، ومساهمة المنشأة في التأمينات الصحية والاجتماعية للعمال الذين لا تعتبر أجورهم أجورا مباشرة.

ثالثاً: المصروفات الأخرى:

وتشمل المصروفات الصناعية التي تتحملها المنشأة في سبيل القيام بمهمتها الصناعية ولم تدرج ضمن المجموعتين السابقتين. وتشمل على سبيل المثال مصروفات الكهرباء، والهاتف، والضرائب، والرسوم، والإيجارات، والاستهلاك. ويجب أن نلاحظ أن هذه التكاليف تنحصر فقط في التكاليف الخاصة بوظيفة الإنتاج ولا تحتوي على أي من المصروفات التسويقية والإدارية، لذلك يعتبر إيجار مبنى المصنع ضمن التكاليف الصناعية غير المباشرة بينما يعتبر إيجار مبنى الإدارة من ضمن المصروفات الإدارية.

ومن ضمن مصطلحات التكاليف المستخدمة في المنشآت الصناعية التكلفة الأولية Prime cost وتستخدم للتعبير عن مجموع تكلفة المواد الأولية والأجور المباشرة، وكذلك

تكلفة التحويل Conversion cost وتستخدم للتعبير عن مجموع تكلفة الأجور المباشرة، والتكاليف الصناعية غير المباشرة.

تكاليف الإنتاج وتكلفة الوحدة:

يتم تحديد إجمالي التكاليف الصناعية للإنتاج عن طريق استخدام حساب الإنتاج تحت التشغيل، ويسمى مجموع تكاليف المواد المباشرة والأجور المباشرة والتكاليف الصناعية غير المباشرة المحملة على حساب إنتاج تحت التشغيل بالتكاليف الصناعية للفترة الجارية. وتكون صورة حساب الإنتاج تحت التشغيل، وباستخدام بعض الأرقام الافتراضية كالتالي:-

حـ / الإنتاج تحت التشغيل

تكلفة الإنتاج التام	١٠٠,٠٠٠		رصيد أول المدة	١٥,٠٠٠	
رصيد آخر المدة	٥,٠٠٠		مواد مباشرة	٢٠,٠٠٠	
			أجور مباشرة	٣٠,٠٠٠	
			أعباء صناعية	٤٠,٠٠٠	
	١٠٥,٠٠٠			١٠٥,٠٠٠	

من دراسة حـ / الإنتاج تحت التشغيل نجد أن تكلفة البضاعة التامة الصنع تساوي ١٠٠,٠٠٠ د، وإذا تم إنتاج ٢٠,٠٠٠ وحدة خلال المدة فإن تكلفة الوحدة التامة الصنع تساوي:

$$\text{تكلفة الوحدة} = \frac{\text{التكاليف الإنتاج التام}}{\text{عدد وحدات الإنتاج التام}} = \frac{١٠٠,٠٠٠ \text{ دينار}}{٢٠,٠٠٠ \text{ وحدة}}$$

$$= ٥ \text{ دنانير للوحدة.}$$

ويتم إعادة عرض حساب الإنتاج تحت التشغيل على شكل قائمة كما في الشكل (٢-١).

		قائمة تكلفة البضاعة التامة الصنع
	*	مواد خام أول المدة
	*	زائد: مشتريات مواد خام
	*	تكلفة المواد الخام المتاحة للاستخدام
	(*)	ناقص: مواد خام آخر المدة
*	————	مواد مباشرة مستخدمة في الإنتاج
*		الأجور المباشرة
		التكاليف الصناعية غير المباشرة:
*		مواد غير مباشرة
*		أجور غير مباشرة
*		الإيجار
*		الاستهلاك
*		مصروفات نقل ومناوله
*	————	إجمالي التكاليف الصناعية غير المباشرة
**		التكاليف الصناعية للفترة الجارية
*		زائد : رصيد إنتاج تحت التشغيل أول المدة
*		ناقص: رصيد إنتاج تحت التشغيل آخر المدة
*		تكلفة البضاعة التامة الصنع خلال الفترة الجارية

شكل (٢-١) قائمة تكلفة البضاعة التامة الصنع

مكونات المخزون في المنشآت الصناعية:

يختلف المخزون في المنشآت الصناعية عنه في المنشآت التجارية، ففي المنشآت التجارية يتم شراء البضاعة وبيعها على حالتها الراهنة دون إدخال أي تغييرات عليها، لذلك يكون مخزون بضاعة آخر المدة وأولها مـن نفـس نـوع الأصناف البضاعة المشتراة. وعلى الجانب الآخر، تقوم المنشآت الصناعية بشراء المواد الخام بقصد إخضاعها

لعمليات التصنيع، وتحويلها إلى منتجات تامة الصنع. لذلك يتكون المخـزون في الشركات الصناعية من البنود التالية:

١. **مواد خام:** وتمثل المواد الخام التي لم يتم استخدامها في الإنتاج حتى نهاية الفـترة المالية.

٢. **إنتاج تحت التشغيل:** ويمثل تكلفة الوحدات التي بدأ إنتاجها ولكن لم ينته ذلك مع نهاية الفترة المالية.

٣. **إنتاج تام الصنع:** ويمثل تكلفة الوحدات التي تم إنتاجها ولكن لم يتم بيعها حتى نهاية الفترة المالية.

وسيتم في الفصـول التاليـة بيـان الإجراءات والأسـاليب المحاسبية اللازمـة لتحديد وحدات الإنتاج تحت التشغيل ووحدات الإنتـاج التـام الصنع، ولتحديـد تكلفة بضاعة آخـر المـدة فقد يتم استخدام أسـلوب الجـرد المسـتمر أو الجـرد الدوري، ففي حالة الجرد المستمر تسجل عملية استلام وصرف البضاعة في الـدفاتر أولاً بأول لذلك يمكن تحديد تكلفة المخزون من واقع السجلات، أما في حالة الجـرد الدوري فيتم تحديد تكلفة مخزون بضاعة آخر المدة عن طريـق الجـرد الفعلـي في نهاية السنة المالية أو أي جزء منها وتسعير المخزون حسب طريقة تسعير المخزون التي تختارها الإدارة. ولتحديـد تكلفـة البنـود الموجـودة في قائمـة تكلفـة البضاعة التامة الصنع يمكن استخدام معادلات الجرد التالية :

تكلفة المواد المباشرة = مخزون مواد خام أول المدة + مشتريات مواد خام - مخزون مواد خام آخر المدة.

تكلفة الإنتاج التام = تكلفة إنتاج تحت التشغيل أول المدة + التكلفة الصناعية للفترة الجارية - تكلفة إنتاج تحت التشغيل آخر المدة.

تكلفة البضاعة المباعة = إنتاج تام الصنع أول المدة + تكلفـة الإنتـاج التـام الصنع خلال الفترة الجارية - إنتاج تام الصنع آخر المدة.

تدفق التكاليف في المنشآت الصناعية:

يختلف نمط تدفق التكاليف في المنشآت الصناعية عنه في المنشآت التجارية، ففي المنشآت التجارية تحدث التكاليف لشراء البضاعة ليتم بيعها على حالتها دون إدخال أية تعديلات على البضاعة المشتراة، أما تدفق التكاليف في المنشآت الصناعية فيتبع نمط تدفق أعقد، حيث يتم شراء المواد الخام لإخضاعها لعمليات صناعية لتحويلها إلى منتجات نهائية، وتحتاج عملية التحويل الى استخدام الأجور المباشرة والمصروفات الصناعية غير المباشرة (الأعباء الصناعية الإضافية). لمتابعة تدفق تكاليف البضاعة يتم عادة استخدام ثلاثة حسابات مراقبة تخصص لتسجيل تكاليف المواد الخام وتكاليف الإنتاج تحت التشغيل وتكاليف الإنتاج التام، وتكلفة البضاعة المباعة. وبالإضافة إلى ذلك يتم استخدام حسابات لتسجيل وتحليل تكلفة الأجور والمصروفات الصناعية غير المباشرة.

ويمكن وصف دورة تدفق التكلفة في الشركات الصناعية كما في الشكل رقم (٢-٢). من دراسة هذا الشكل نجد أن المواد الخام التي يتم صرفها من المخازن تحمل على حساب الإنتاج تحت التشغيل، ولكن إذا كانت غير مباشرة فإنها تحمل على حساب مراقبة الأعباء الإضافية، والوضع نفسه بالنسبة لمراقبة الأجور، ويتم تجميع المصروفات الصناعية الأخرى في حساب الأعباء الإضافية وبعدها يتم تحميل هذه الأعباء على حساب الإنتاج تحت التشغيل. ويحمل حساب تكلفة البضاعة التامة الصنع بتكلفة الإنتاج التام، وبالتالي يمثل رصيد حساب الإنتاج تحت التشغيل آخر المدة تكلفة البضاعة التي لم ينته إنتاجها حتى نهاية الفترة. وتحول تكلفة البضاعة المباعة من حساب تكلفة الإنتاج التام إلى حساب تكلفة البضاعة المباعة ومن ثم فإن رصيد

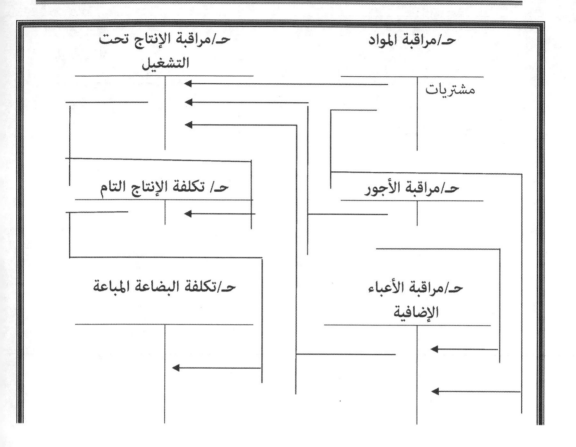

الشكل (٢-٢) دورة تدفق التكاليف في المنشأة الصناعية

الحساب الأول يمثل قيمة البضاعة التي لم يتم بيعها حتى نهاية الفترة. لاحظ في هذا الشكل أن رأس السهم يشير إلى الجانب المدين من قيد اليومية ونقطة نهاية خط السهم تشير إلى الجانب الدائن من قيد اليومية اللازم لإثبات حركة التكلفة.

التكاليف غير الصناعية:

يشير هذا اللفظ الى المصروفات التسويقية والإدارية، وهذه المصروفات تعتبر تكاليف فترة يتم خصمها من الإيرادات قبل التوصل إلى رقم صافي الربح. وتشتمل المصروفات التسويقية على كل المصروفات التي تتحملها إدارة المبيعات لخلق الطلب على المنتجات وبيعها، وتتكون هذه المصروفات من مرتبات موظفي إدارة المبيعات، وعمولات البيع، ومصروفات نقل المبيعات، ومصاريف الانتقال والسفر، والهاتف

والاتصالات، والحملات الإعلانية. أما المصروفات الإدارية فتشمل جميع المصروفات التي تتحملها المنشأة فيما عدا التكاليف الصناعية، والمصروفات التسويقية، وتضم مصروفات الإدارة العليا، وإدارة الشؤون الإدارية، وإدارة التمويل، ويمكن أن يتم تبويب تكاليفها إلى رواتب، وأجور، وإيجار، واستهلاك، واتصالات، وسفر، ومبيت.. الخ. ولتوضيح الدورة المحاسبية سيتم الاعتماد على البيانات الآتية:

مثال (١):-

كانت أرصدة حسابات البضاعة في أول المدة كالتالي:

- المواد الخام ١٥,٠٠٠ دينار وحساب الإنتاج تحت التشغيل ٢٠,٠٠٠ د، وحساب البضاعة التامة الصنع ٢٥,٠٠٠ دينار، وخلال الشهر الجاري تمت العمليات الآتية:

- تم شراء مواد خام بمبلغ ٧٠,٠٠٠ د، على الحساب وصرف منها للإنتاج ٦٥,٠٠٠ د.

- بلغت الأجور المستحقة خلال الشهر ٨٠,٠٠٠ د، منها ٤٥,٠٠٠ د أجوراً مباشرة والباقي يعتبر أجوراً غير مباشرة.

- بلغت التكاليف الصناعية غير المباشرة الأخرى ٥٥,٠٠٠ د، وتتكون من : ١٢,٠٠٠ مواد غير مباشرة اشتريت واستخدمت بدون إدخالها إلى المخازن، ١٧,٠٠٠ إيجار، ٢٠,٠٠٠ د استهلاك، ٦٠٠٠ د مصروفات أخرى. وجميع هذه المصروفات عدا الاستهلاك كانت على الحساب.

- بلغ رصيد حساب الإنتاج تحت التشغيل آخر المدة ١٥,٠٠٠ د، وبلغت تكلفة البضاعة المباعة خلال المدة ٢١٠,٠٠٠ د ، وثمن بيعها ٣٤٠,٥٠٠ دينار.

- بلغت المصروفات التسويقية ٣٥,٠٠٠ د، كما بلغت المصروفات الإدارية ٤٥,٠٠٠ د.

المطلوب:

١. عمل قيود اليومية اللازمة لإثبات العمليات السابقة وتصوير الحسابات اللازمة علماً بأن المصروفات غير المباشرة تحمل على حساب الإنتاج تحت التشغيل على أساس فعلي.

٢. إعداد قائمة تكلفة البضاعة المباعة و إعداد قائمة الدخل.

الحـــل: أولاً: قيود اليومية

٧٠,٠٠٠		حـ/ مراقبة المواد الخام
	٧٠,٠٠٠	حـ/ الموردين (١)
		إثبات شراء المواد الخام على الحساب
٦٥,٠٠٠		حـ/ الإنتاج تحت التشغيل
	٦٥,٠٠٠	حـ/ مراقبة المواد الخام (٢)
		إثبات صرف المواد الخام إلى الإنتاج
٤٥,٠٠٠		حـ/ الإنتاج تحت التشغيل
٣٥,٠٠٠		حـ/ التكاليف الصناعية غير المباشرة (٣)
	٨٠,٠٠٠	حـ/ مراقبة الأجور
		تحليل تكاليف أجور إدارة الإنتاج

٥٥,٠٠٠		حـ/ التكاليف الصناعية غير المباشرة
	٣٥,٠٠٠	حـ/ الموردين (٤)
	٢٠,٠٠٠	حـ/ مخصص الاستهلاك
		تسجيل المصروفات الصناعية غير المباشرة

وخلال الفترة يتم تجميع التكاليف الصناعية غير المباشرة في حساب مراقبـة التكاليف الصناعية غير المباشرة، وهي خطوة وسيطة، وفي نهاية الفترة يتم تحميـل رصيد الحساب على حساب الإنتاج تحت التشغيل. ويتم تحميـل الرصيـد الفعـلي بموجب القيد التالي:

٩٠,٠٠٠		حـ/ إنتاج تحت التشغيل
	٩٠,٠٠٠	حـ/ التكاليف الصناعية غير المباشرة (٥)
		إقفال التكاليف غير المباشرة في حساب الإنتاج تحت التشغيل

وبعد ترحيل قيود اليومية السابقة وترصيد حساب الإنتاج تحت التشغيل تحدد تكلفة الإنتاج التام وتبلغ ٢٠٥,٠٠٠ د وبعدها إثبات تحويل تكلفة الإنتاج التام بقيد اليومية التالي:

٢٠٥,٠٠٠		حـ/ تكلفة بضاعة تامة الصنع	
	٢٠٥,٠٠٠	حـ/ إنتاج تحت التشغيل	(٦)
		تحويل تكلفة الإنتاج التام خلال الفترة الى المخازن	

يتم اثبات تكلفة البضاعة المباعة بموجب القيد التالي:

٢١٠,٠٠٠		حـ/ تكلفة بضاعة المباعة	
	٢١٠,٠٠٠	حـ/ تكلفة البضاعة التامة الصنع	(٧)
		اثبات تكلفة البضاعة المباعة	

ومن واقع هذه القيود وأرصدة حسابات بضاعة أول المدة وآخرها تكون الحسابات اللازمة لإظهار حركة تكلفة البضاعة كالتالي:

حـ/ مراقبة المواد الخام

الرصيد	١٥,٠٠٠	(٢)	٦٥,٠٠٠
(١)	٧٠,٠٠٠	الرصيد	٢٠,٠٠٠
	٨٥,٠٠٠		٨٥,٠٠٠

حـ/ الإنتاج تحت التشغيل

الرصيد	٢٠,٠٠٠	(٦)	٢٠٥,٠٠٠
(٢)	٦٥,٠٠٠	الرصيد	١٥,٠٠٠
(٣)	٤٥,٠٠٠		
(٥)	٩٠,٠٠٠		
	٢٢٠,٠٠٠٠		٢٢٠,٠٠٠

حـ/ مراقبة التكاليف الصناعية غير المباشرة

(٣)	٣٥,٠٠٠	(٥)	٩٠,٠٠٠
(٤)	٥٥,٠٠٠		
	٩٠,٠٠٠		٩٠,٠٠٠

حـ/ تكلفة البضاعة المباعة

(٧)	٢١٠,٠٠٠		

ح/ تكلفة البضاعة   التامة الصنع

(٧)	٢١٠,٠٠٠	رصيد	٢٥,٠٠٠		
الرصيد	٢٠,٠٠٠	(٦)	٢٠٥,٠٠٠		
	٢٣٠,٠٠٠		٢٣٠,٠٠٠		

ثانيا: قائمة تكلفة البضاعة المباعة:

ومن واقع البيانات الظاهرة في الحسابات أعلاه يتم إعداد قائمة تكلفة البضاعة التامة كما في الشكل (٢-٤). نلاحظ من دراسة هذا الجدول بأن الجزء الخاص بالمواد المباشرة قد تم

قائمة تكلفة البضاعة التامة الصنع		
مواد خام أول المدة	١٥,٠٠٠	
يضاف : مشتريات مواد خام	٧٠,٠٠٠	
المواد الخام المتاحة للاستخدام	٨٥,٠٠٠	
يطرح : مواد خام آخر المدة	٣٠,٠٠٠	
المواد المباشرة		٦٥,٠٠٠
الأجور المباشرة		٤٥,٠٠٠
التكاليف الصناعية غير المباشرة:		
أجور غير مباشرة	٣٥,٠٠٠	
مواد غير مباشرة	١٢,٠٠٠	
إيجار	١٧,٠٠٠	
استهلاك	٢٠,٠٠٠	
مصروفات أخرى	٦,٠٠٠	
إجمالي التكاليف الصناعية غير المباشرة		٩٠,٠٠٠
التكلفة الصناعية للفترة الجارية		٢٠٠,٠٠٠
يضاف: رصيد إنتاج تحت التشغيل أول المدة		٢٠,٠٠٠
يطرح : رصيد إنتاج تحت التشغيل آخر المدة		١٥,٠٠٠
التكلفة الصناعية للبضاعة التامة الصنع		٢٠٥,٠٠٠

شكل (٢-٤) قائمة تكلفة البضاعة التامة الصنع

الحصول عليه من حساب مراقبة المواد المباشرة وهو أول رقم في حساب الإنتاج تحت التشغيل، ثم بإضافة الأجور المباشرة والمصروفات الصناعية غير المباشرة نصل إلى التكلفة الصناعية للفترة الجارية ، بعض هذه التكاليف انفق لإتمام وحدات الإنتاج تحت التشغيل أول المدة وبعضها أنفق على وحدات بدأت وتم إنتاجها وبعضها لم ينتهي إنتاجها حتى نهاية الفترة، لذلك تقوم هذه القائمة على إضافة رصيد حساب الإنتاج تحت التشغيل أول المدة الى تكاليف الفترة الجارية ثم تطرح رصيد حساب الإنتاج تحت التشغيل آخر المدة من المجموع السابق ليكون الناتج هو تكلفة الإنتاج التام.

ثالثا قائمة الدخل :

يتم إعداد قائمة الدخل في المنشآت الصناعية كما في الشكل (٢-٥). وهنا نجد أن رقم تكلفة البضاعة التامة الصنع قد حل محل رقم صافي المشتريات في قائمة الدخل الخاصة بالمنشآت التجارية.

قائمة الدخل لمنشأة صناعية		
المبيعات		٣٤٠,٥٠٠
يطرح تكلفة البضاعة المباعة:		
بضاعة تامة الصنع أول المدة	٢٥,٠٠٠	
تكلفة البضاعة التامة الصنع خلال المدة	٢٠٥,٠٠٠	
تكلفة البضاعة المتاحة للبيع	٢٣٠,٠٠٠	
ناقص بضاعة تامة الصنع آخر المدة	٢٠,٠٠٠	
التكلفة الصناعية للبضاعة المباعة		٢١٠,٠٠٠
مجمل الربح		١٣٠,٥٠٠
ناقص: المصروفات التشغيلية:		
مصروفات تسويقية	٣٥,٠٠٠	
مصروفات إدارية	٤٥,٠٠٠	
إجمالي المصروفات التشغيلية		٨٠,٠٠٠
صافي الربح التشغيلي		٥٠,٥٠٠

شكل (٢-٥) قائمة الدخل لمنشأة صناعية

رابعاً: تبويب التكاليف حسب سلوكها:

يقوم هذا التبويب بدراسة استجابة عناصر التكاليف للتغير في حجم النشاط فيتم تبويب التكاليف في ثلاث مجموعات هي: التكاليف المتغيرة Variable Cost، والتكاليف الثابتة Fixed Cost، التكاليف المختلطة Mixed Cost، أو التكلفة شبة الثابتة أو شبه المتغيرة، فقد يكون ضمن تكاليف الإنتاج أو المصروفات التسويقية والإدارية تكاليف متغيرة وتكاليف ثابتة وتكاليف مختلطة، وفيما يلي سيتم دراسة مفاهيم هذه التكاليف.

١. التكاليف المتغيرة: Variable Cost:

تعرف التكاليف المتغيرة بأنها التكاليف التي يتغير مجموعها طردياً مع التغير في حجم النشاط، فإذا زاد حجم النشاط مثلاً بنسبة ١٠٪ يزداد مجموع التكاليف المتغيرة بنسبة ١٠٪ وإذا زاد حجم النشاط بنسبة ٢٥٪، تزداد التكاليف بنسبة ٢٥٪ فعند إنتاج السيارة مثلاً يلزمنا ٥ إطارات، فإذا افترضنا أن سعر الإطار الواحد ٢٠ ديناراً لذا تكون تكلفة الإطارات للسيارة الواحدة ١٠٠ دينار وإذا تم إنتاج ٥ سيارات تكون تكلفة الإطارات ٥٠٠ د ، وهذا بدوره يعني أن التكلفة المتغيرة للوحدة ثابتة، فكل سيارة في مثالنا تحتاج إلى ١٠٠ دينار تكلفة إطارات، وبالتالي فان إجمالي التكلفة المتغيرة عند إنتاج ٢٠٠ سيارة يساوي ٢٠٠ سيارة ×١٠٠د =٢٠,٠٠٠ دينار. ويتم تمثيل دالة التكاليف المتغيرة كما في الشكل (٢-٦). وهنا يقيس المحور الأفقي وحدات النشاط بينما يقيس المحور الرأسي التكاليف.

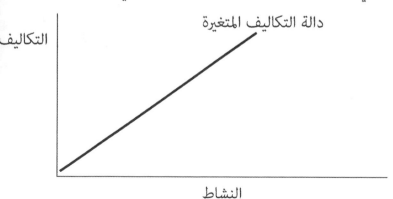

الشكل (٢-٦) دالة التكاليف المتغيرة

٢. التكاليف الثابتة: *Fixed Cost*

تعرف التكاليف الثابتة على أنها التكاليف التي لا يتغير مجموعها مع التغير في حجم النشاط طالما كان التغير ضمن المدى الملائم، وعليه فإذا زاد حجم النشاط أو نقص تبقى هذه التكاليف على حالتها ويتم تمثيل دالة هذه التكاليف بيانياً كما في الشكل (٢-٧).

من الرسم البياني يظهر لنا أن التكاليف الثابتة ستبقى عند مستوى ٥,٠٠٠ ديناراً سواء كان عدد وحدات النشاط ١,٠٠٠ وحدة أو ٤,٠٠٠ وحدة، وهذا يعني أن متوسط تكلفة الوحدة سوف يرتبط عكسياً مع حجم النشاط لأنه عند إنتاج ١٠٠٠ وحدة تكون تكلفة الوحدة ٥د (٥٠٠٠ د ÷ ١٠٠٠ وحده) أما عند إنتاج ٢٠٠٠ وحده تكون تكلفة الوحدة ٢,٥د، هذه التكاليف تشمل الاستهلاك، الإيجار والأجور والرواتب الإدارية، الضرائب والرسوم السنوية.

بدأت هذه الدالة من نقطة الصفر عند عدم وجود إنتاج ثم انحدرت الى أعلى عند زيادة النشاط. وهذا يعني انه كلما زادت وحدات النشاط زادت التكاليف. ويشير ميل دالة التكاليف إلى التكلفة المتغيرة للوحدة. ويحدد إجمالي التكاليف المتغيرة بضرب عدد الوحدات في التكلفة المتغيرة الوحدة. ومن هذه التكاليف المواد المباشرة والأجور المباشرة وبعض المصروفات الصناعية غير المباشرة وبعض المصروفات التسويقية والإدارية.

ويمكن تقسيم التكاليف الثابتة إلى تكاليف ثابتة اختيارية وتكاليف ثابتة الزامية. وتشتمل المجموعة الأولى على البنود التي يمكن للإدارة التأثير في قيمتها في الأجل القصير مثل : بند الرواتب والأجور، وتكاليف الإعلان المتعلق بالتعريف بالمنشأة، وتشمل المجموعة الثانية على البنود التي يصعب على الإدارة التخلص منها في الأجل القصير بدون الأضرار بمصالح المنشأة والتأثير على قدرتها على الاستمرار وهي مثل: الاستهلاك، والإيجار، والرسوم والضرائب السنوية ورواتب الوظائف الإدارية الرئيسية.

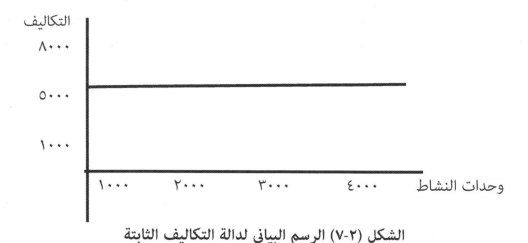

الشكل (٢-٧) الرسم البياني لدالة التكاليف الثابتة

٣- التكاليف شبه الثابتة : *Semi-fixed Cost*

تعرف هذه التكاليف بعدة مسميات منها التكاليف شبه المتغيرة، أو شبه الثابتة، أو المختلطة، وهي التكاليف التي تحمل صفات من التكاليف المتغيرة وصفات من التكاليف الثابتة في آن واحد. فمثلاً نجد أن الكثير من الآلات تحتاج لتسخين لدرجة حرارة مئوية معينة قبل استخدامها في الإنتاج مثل آلات صب أكياس النايلون والأفران، لذلك تكون كمية الوقود اللازمة لذلك تكلفة ثابتة أما كمية الوقود المستخدمة بعد ذلك فإن تكلفتها تكون متغيرة لأنها تعتمد على عدد الوحدات المنتجة، وبنفس المنطق نرى أن تكلفة الكهرباء المستهلكة في تشغيل الآلات فهي تكلفة متغيرة لأنها تعتمد على عدد الوحدات التي يتم إنتاجها.

ويزيد من صعوبة الأمر، أن تصميم الأنظمة المالية يسمح بتخصيص حسابات لتجميع العمليات المالية المتشابهة وليس المتماثلة. [1] وهذا يؤدي إلى اختلاط التكاليف

---

[1] Hirsch, M. L., and Louder Back, J. G., Cost Accounting Accumulation, Analysis, and Use, 2nd, ed., (PWS - Kent Publishing Co-. ١٩٨٦), P. ٩٠.

الثابتة والمتغيرة معاً، فمثلاً بفتح حساب للكهرباء ويجعل مـديناً بقيمـة الكهربـاء المستخدمة في الإنارة والكهرباء المستخدمة في التشغيل.

ويمكن تمثيل دالة التكاليف شبه الثابتة بيانياً بعـدة أشـكال منهـا مـا تـم إبرازها في الشكل (٢-٨). وفي هذا الشكل فإن التكاليف عند نقطة الصفر تساوي (أ) وهذا المبلـغ يسـاوي قيمـة التكاليف الثابتـة ولكـن إذا زاد حجم النشاط إلى مستوى ك تصبح عنده إجمالي التكاليف ص وبالتالي تكون التكـاليف المتغيـرة هـي ص-أ وأن التكاليف الثابتة هي (أ).

ويمكن فصل هـذه التكـاليف إلى شقين هـما التكـاليف المتغيـرة والتكاليف الثابتة، ويتم ذلك باستخدام أحد الطرق التالية:[1]

- طريقة الخبرة الشخصية.
- طريقة التقدير الهندسية.
- النقطة العالية المنخفضة.
- الطرق الإحصائية. عند عدم وجود إنتاج
وسيتم شرح هذه الطرق في الفصل الثالث.

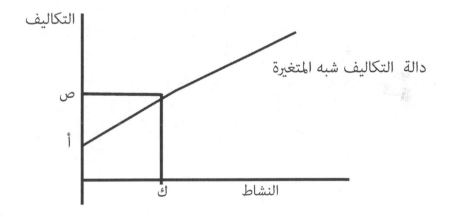

الشكل (٢-٨) الرسم البياني الدالة التكاليف شبه الثابتة

[1] Ibid, PP. ٦٩ - ٧٦.

خامساً: تبويب التكاليف من وجهة نظر الرقابة

تقسم التكاليف من وجهة نظر الأشخاص المسؤولين عن الرقابة إلى مجموعتين هما: التكاليف القابلة للرقابة Controllable Cost والتكاليف غير القابلة للرقابة Uncontrollable Cost فتكون التكاليف قابلة للرقابة من وجهة نظر الشخص المسؤول عنها إذا كان يمكنه التأثير فيها، وحتى يتحقق ذلك ليس من الضروري أن يمتلك الشخص سلطة التخلص من البند كلية بل يشترط لذلك أن تتوفر للشخص إمكانية تخفيض تكلفته، فمثلاً يستطيع مدير مركز إنتاج معين أن يزاول الرقابة على كمية المواد غير المباشرة والأجور غير المباشرة التي يستخدمها مركزه ولكن لا يستطيع أن يزاول الرقابة على أسعار المواد أو رواتب رؤسائه أو حتى رواتب مرؤوسيه. إذن تتوقف القابلية للرقابة على سلطة الشخص وليس على طبيعة البند فبعض البنود غير قابلة للرقابة عند مستوى إداري معين إلا أنها تصبح قابلة للرقابة عند مستوى إداري أعلى، فرئيس قسم إداري معين يعتبر مسؤولاً عن كمية المواد الخام التي يستخدمها في الإنتاج، ورئيس قسم آخر يكون مسؤولاً عن الأسعار، وقد لا يستطيعون الرقابة على تكلفة استهلاك الآلات والمعدات التي يستخدمونها. وبالتالي يكون الشخص مسؤولاً عن البنود التي يتصرف بها والبنود التي يفوض سلطة استخدامها إلى مرؤوسيه. لذلك عند تقديم تقارير الأداء يتم تبويب التكاليف فيها إلى تكاليف قابلة للرقابة وتكاليف غير قابلة للرقابة لكل مستوى إداري في المنشأة وعند كل مستوى إداري يتم جمع التكاليف القابلة للرقابة لمسئول ذلك المستوى والتكاليف القابلة للرقابة للمرؤوسين تحته، فمثلاً بالرغم من أن تكاليف الصيانة الشاملة غير قابلة للرقابة عند مستوى الإشراف الأول إلا أنها قابلة للرقابة على مستوى مدير إدارة الإنتاج لذلك تدرج ضمن تقدير أدائه، وإذا نظرنا إلى التكاليف في المدى البعيد نجد أنها تقع ضمن رقابة إدارة المنشأة ولكن بعد حدوثها وخصوصاً التكاليف الثابتة تصبح غير قابلة للرقابة.

بالنسبة للتكاليف المتغيرة ليس من الضروري أن تكون قابلة للرقابة في مركز مسؤولية واحد لأن هذه التكاليف لها شقين هما السعر والكمية حيث تقع مسؤولية كل منهما ضمن نطاق مسؤولية قسم معين بالمنشأة، وكذلك يزداد نطاق قدرة الشخص على

الرقابة كلما ارتفع مستواه التنظيمي. وللنجاح في مزاولة الرقابة يجب تقسيم المنشأة إلى مراكز مسؤولية وأن تحدد سلطات ومسؤوليات كل قسم بصورة واضحة.

سادساً: التكاليف لأغراض اتخاذ القرارات الإدارية:

يتطلب اتخاذ القرارات الإدارية تحديد التكاليف المرتبطة بهذه القرارات، وهذه التكاليف تعرف باسم التكاليف المناسبة، ويتم تعريفها بأنها التكاليف التي سوف تحدث نتيجة اتخاذ القرار ويتم تجنب حدوثها بعدم اتخاذه. [1] فمثلاً إذا قررت المنشأة زيادة حجم الإنتاج فإن ذلك سوف يؤدي الى زيادة تكلفة المواد المباشرة الأجور المباشرة وبعض - المصروفات الصناعية الأخرى، ولكن ذلك قد لا يؤدي إلى زيادة مصروف الاستهلاك أو الإيجار أو الرسوم والضرائب. لذلك تسمى تكلفة المواد المباشرة والأجور المباشرة والمصروفات الأخرى التي يتوقع حدوثها نتيجة للقرار بالتكاليف المناسبة لأنها سوف تحدث عند اتخاذ القرار الإداري الخاص بزيادة الإنتاج وأنها سوف لا تحدث إذا لم يتم اتخاذ ذلك القرار. ومن صفات هذه التكاليف أنها سوف تحدث في المستقبل. تعتبر التكاليف التاريخية غير مناسبة لأنها تكون نتيجة قرار سابق لذلك يتم وصفها بأن غارقة sunk cost فهي لن تتأثر باتخاذ القرارات التي ستنتج في المستقبل، فمثلاً تعتبر تكاليف البحث والتطوير تكاليف غارقة فيما يتعلق باتخاذ قرار تطبيق نتائج هذه الأبحاث لأنه سواء تم تطبيق النتائج أو لم يتم ذلك تكون المنشأة قد تحملت هذه التكاليف.

التكاليف الفعلية والمعيارية: Actual and Standard Cost:

تعرف التكاليف الفعلية بأنها التكاليف التي حدثت فعلاً في سبيل إنتاج السلع والخدمات التي تقدمها المنشأة وبالتالي فهي تعكس الأداء الفعلي بما يحتويه من كفاءة أو عدم كفاءة. ومن ناحية أخرى تعرف التكاليف المعيارية بأنها تكاليف محددة مقدماً لما يجب أن تكون عليه التكاليف خلال فترة العمل المقبلة. فهي لم تحدث بعد وتعكس التكاليف التي يتوقع حدوثها إذا تم العمل وفق الظروف التي تتوقعها الإدارة ويتم إعداد التكلفة المعيارية للوحدة وعلى مستوى الإنتاج ككل. ويمكن وضع التقديرات الخاصة

---

[1] Garrison, R, H., op. Cit., Pp ٥٨٥-٥٨٦.

بحجم النشاط الذي تتوقعه الإدارة في جدول تعرف باسم الموازنة التخطيطية. على أية حال، لا تعتبر هذه التكاليف متنافسة بحيث إذا تم استخدام التكاليف الفعلية نستغني عن استخدام التكاليف المعيارية وعلى العكس من ذلك نعتبر أن الواحـدة مكملة للأخرى. فالتكاليف المعيارية تستخدم كأسـاس لمقارنـة التكـاليف الفعليـة للحكم على كفاءة الأداء، كما أن لكل نوع من هذه التكاليف استخدامات متعددة. فمثلاً تستخدم التكـاليف الفعليـة في تحديـد تكلفـة مخـزون آخـر المـدة، وتكلفـة البضاعة المباعة، وتستخدم التكاليف المعيارية في اتخاذ القرارات الإداريـة المختلفـة ومنها تقديم المناقصات.

الخاتمـــة

تـم في هـذا الفصـل مناقشـة مصطلحات محاسبة التكاليف التـي سـيتم استخدامها في هـذا الكتـاب، وقد تـم البـدء بالمصطلحات المسـتخدمة في أغـراض تحديـد تكلفـة الإنتـاج، ولهـذا الغـرض تـم تبويـب التكاليـف إلى تكاليف إنتـاج (صناعية) ومصروفات تسويقية ومصروفات إدارية، ووجدنا أن التكاليف الصناعية هي التكاليف الوحيدة التي يتم تحميلهـا عـلى وحـدات الإنتـاج، ولتسـهيل تحديـد تكلفة هذه الوحـدات يتم تبويـب التكاليـف الصناعية إلى مـواد مباشرة وأجـور مباشرة وتكاليف صناعية غير مباشرة وقد تم إعـداد قائمـة تكلفـة البضاعة التامة الصنع وقائمة الدخل الخاصة بالمنشآت الصناعية.

إضافة إلى ذلك، فقد تمـت مناقشـة المفاهيم الأساسية التـي تستخدم في أغـراض الرقابة والتخطيط واتخـاذ القرارات، وتـم التعـرف عـلى طبيعـة التكاليف المتغيرة والتكاليف الثابتة والتكاليف المختلطة، وفي مجـال الرقابـة تـم تقسـيم التكاليف إلى قابلة للرقابة وغير قابلة للرقابة من وجهة نظر المستوى المسؤول عـن رقابة عناصر التكاليف وتبين أنه يجب أن يحمل الشخص بمسؤولية العناصر التـي يمكنه هو أو مرؤوسيه الرقابة عليها، ولأغراض اتخاذ القرارات الإداريـة فإنـه يجب أن يـتم تحديـد التكلفـة المناسبة التي تمثل التكاليف التـي يتوقع حـدوثها في المستقبل وبالتالي تكون التكاليف التاريخية غير مناسبة لاتخاذ القرارات الإدارية إلا بمقدار ما توفره من معلومات تساعد في عملية التنبؤ بالتكاليف المناسبة.

أسئلــة وتماريـــن

السؤال الاول: ما هو الفرق بين تكاليف المنتج وتكاليف الفترة والتصنيفات المناسبة لكل منهما، وبين متى يصبح كل منهما مصروفاً؟

السؤال الثاني: قارن بين الأجور المباشرة وغير المباشرة، والمواد المباشرة والمواد غير المباشرة.

السؤال الثالث: ما هي مكونات تكلفة البضاعة المباعة؟

السؤال الرابع: ما هو المقصود بالتكلفة الأولية وتكلفة التحويل؟

السؤال الخامس: قارن بين التكلفة المتغيرة والتكلفة الثابتة من حيث مجموع التكاليف وتكلفة الوحدة؟

السؤال السادس: أذكر الطرق المختلفة التي يمكن استخدامها في فصل التكاليف المختلطة؟

السؤال السابع: عرف المقصود بالتكاليف المناسبة ومتى تكون كل التكاليف قابلة للرقابة؟

السؤال الثامن: ما هو المقصود بالتكاليف المناسبة ومتى تكون تكلفة الأصول الثابتة مناسبة لاتخاذ القرار؟

السؤال التاسع: التكلفة التاريخية هي تكلفة غارقة ولكن ما هو شرط اعتبارها تكلفة مناسبة؟

السؤال العاشر: هناك تكاليف مختلفة للأهداف المختلفة، ناقش هذه العبارة مع إعطاء الأمثلة على ذلك.

السؤال الحادي عشر: حدثت التكاليف التالية في إحدى الشركات الصناعية خلال السنة المالية ٢٠٠٨

٤٠,٠٠٠ د مواد مباشرة

٥٠,٠٠٠ د أجور مباشرة

٧٥,٠٠٠ د تكاليف صناعية غير مباشرة

المطلوب :

الإجابة على البدائل المستقلة التالية:-

أ- افترض أن مخزون إنتاج تحت التشغيل أول المدة يساوي ٢٥,٠٠٠د وأن مخزون إنتاج تحت التشغيل آخر المدة يساوي ٣٥,٠٠٠ د فما هي تكلفة البضاعة التامة الصنع؟

ب- افترض أن هناك زيادة في تكلفة مخزون الإنتاج تحت التشغيل آخر المدة مقدارها ١٥,٠٠٠ د، ونقصاً في مخزون الإنتاج التام بمبلغ ٢٠,٠٠٠ د. فما هي تكلفة البضاعة المباعة؟

السؤال الثاني عشر: الآتي بعض المعلومات المتوافرة في سجلات إحدى الشركات الصناعية:

مخزون مواد مباشرة أول المدة ٢٠,٠٠٠د، ومشتريات مواد خام ٧٥,٠٠٠د، ومخزون مواد خام آخر المدة ١٥,٠٠٠د، وبلغت الأجور المباشرة ٣٠,٠٠٠د، وإيجار المصنع ٤٠٠٠ د، واستهلاك الآلات ١٢,٠٠٠ د، ومرتبات وأجور إدارة الإنتاج ١٨,٠٠٠د، المدينون ٨٣,٠٠٠د، والدائنون ٧٥,٠٠٠د، المبيعات ٢٠٠,٠٠٠د، والإنتاج تحت التشغيل أول المدة ١٣,٠٠٠د، إنتاج تحت التشغيل آخر المدة ١٨,٠٠٠د، والبضاعة التامة الصنع آخر المدة ١٩,٠٠٠د. ولا يوجد مخزون إنتاج تام أول المدة.

تقوم الشركة بتحميل التكاليف الصناعية غير المباشرة الفعلية على الإنتاج في نهاية كل فترة.

المطلوب:

(١) تحديد تكلفة البضاعة التامة الصنع عن طريق تصوير الحسابات المناسبة.

(٢) حساب قيمة المخزون الذي يظهر في الميزانية.

(٣) حساب التكلفة الأولية وتكلفة التحويل للفترة الجارية.

السؤال الثالث عشر: الآتي معلومات مستخرجه من سجلات إحدى الشركات الصناعية:-

التغير في مخزون المواد الخام بالنقص	٥٠٠٠ د
مشتريات المواد الخام	١٨٠,٠٠٠ د
الأجور المباشرة	٢٢٠,٠٠٠د
التكاليف الصناعية غير المباشرة	١١٠,٠٠٠د
النقص في مخزون الإنتاج تحت التشغيل	٣٠,٠٠٠د

المطلوب:

إعداد قائمة تكلفة البضاعة التامة الصنع.

السؤال الرابع عشر: كانت أرصدة المخزون في شركة بلاستيك الشرق تتكون مـن : ٤٥,٠٠٠ د مواد خام، ٧٧,٠٠٠د إنتاج تحت التشغيل، ٦٤,٠٠٠ د مخزون إنتاج تـام، وخلال شهر آذار تمت العمليات الآتية:-

- تم شراء مواد خام بمبلغ ٢٥٠,٠٠٠ د على الحساب.
- تم صرف مواد خام من المخازن تكلفتها ٢٨٠,٠٠٠ د إلى الإنتاج.
- بلغت الأجور الخاصة بإدارة الإنتاج ١٤٠,٠٠٠ منها ١٠٠,٠٠٠ أجوراً مبـاشرة، والباقي يعتبر أجوراً غير مباشرة، وتم دفع هذه الأجور نقداً.
- تتضمن المصروفات الصناعية غير المباشرة الآتي:

زيوت ووقود	١٩٠٠٠ د
إيجار مبنى المصنع	٨٠٠٠د
استهلاك الآلات	١٤٠٠٠د
تأمين على الآلات والبضائع	٣٠٠٠د

وجميعها دفعت نقداً عدا الاستهلاك

- بلغ المخزون آخر المدة مـن إنتاج تحـت التشغيل ٢٥,٠٠٠ د ومـن البضاعة التامة الصنع ٢٠,٠٠٠ د.

المطلوب:

إجراء قيود اليومية اللازمة لإثبات العمليات السابقة وتصوير الحسابات المناسبة.

السؤال الخامس عشر: الآتي بعض حسابات التكاليف والمطلوب تبويبها إلى تكاليف فترة أو تكلفة منتج وتبويبها حسب سلوكها إلى متغيرة وثابتة.

البند	منتج / فترة	متغيرة / ثابتة
المواد الخام المصروفة للإنتاج		
مرتب مدير الإنتاج		
مرتبات مشرفي الإنتاج		
الأجور المباشرة		
استهلاك الآلات الصناعية		
كهرباء تشغيل الآلات		
استهلاك مبنى الإدارة		
راتب المدير العام		
الضرائب على المصنع		
صيانة الآلات الإدارة		

السؤال السادس عشر: الآتي بيانات مالية مستخرجة مـن دفاتر إحـدى الشركات الصناعية في ٣١/١٢

	٢٠٠٨	٢٠٠٧
مخزون إنتاج تام أول المدة	٤٠,٠٠٠	٣٥,٠٠٠
التكلفة الصناعية للإنتاج التام	١٨٠,٠٠٠	١٤٠,٠٠٠
مخزون الإنتاج التام آخر المدة	٣٥,٠٠٠	٤٠,٠٠٠
المبيعات	٣١٠,٠٠٠	٢١٠,٠٠٠
مصروفات تسويقية وإدارية	١٢٠,٠٠٠	٦٠,٠٠٠

المطلوب:

(١) ما هي التكلفة الصناعية للبضاعة المباعة؟

(٢) إعداد قائمة الدخل لكل سنة من السنوات الظاهرة أعلاه؟

السؤال السابع عشر: الآتي معلومات مستخرجة من دفاتر إحدى الشركات الصناعية:

اسم الحساب	دينار
مواد مباشرة	١٨٠,٠٠٠
مخزون تحت التشغيل آخر المدة	٤٠,٠٠٠
أجور مباشرة	١٤٠,٠٠٠
مواد غير مباشرة	٢٥,٠٠٠
استهلاك مباني المصنع	١٥,٠٠٠
استهلاك آلات المصنع	١٥,٠٠٠
استهلاك مباني ومعدات الإدارة	٥٠٠٠
مخزون إنتاج تام أول المدة	٨٠,٠٠٠
تأمين على البضاعة وآلات المصنع	٥٠٠٠
الإيجار (٧٠٪ المصنع ٣٠٪ الإدارة)	٢٠,٠٠٠
تكاليف صناعية غير مباشرة أخرى	٢٥,٠٠٠
مرتبات إدارية	٢٥,٠٠٠
مرتبات تسويقية	١٥,٠٠٠
عمولة مبيعات	٦٠٠٠
مبيعات	٥٢٥,٠٠٠
مردودات مبيعات	٥,٠٠٠
نقدية	١٥,٠٠٠
دائنون	٨٠,٠٠٠
مخزون تحت التشغيل أول المدة	٤٥,٠٠٠
مخزون إنتاج تام آخر المدة	٩٠,٠٠٠
مخزون مواد خام آخر المدة	٦٠,٠٠٠

والمطلوب: (١) إعداد قائمة تكلفة الإنتاج التام الصنع.

(٢) إعداد قائمة الدخل.

السؤال الثامن عشر: الآتي حالات منفصلة والمطلوب استبدال علامة الاستفهام بالرقم المناسب مع العلم بأن المصروفات الصناعية غير المباشرة تساوي ٧٥٪ من الأجور:

	حالة (٣)	حالة (٢)	حالة (١)
مبيعات	٧٠٠,٠٠٠	٧٠٠,٠٠٠	٥٠٠,٠٠٠
إنتاج تام أول المدة	١٢٠,٠٠٠	١٠٠,٠٠٠	٥٠,٠٠٠
إنتاج تحت التشغيل أول المدة	٥٧,٥٠٠	١٢٠,٠٠٠	٧٥,٠٠٠
مواد مباشرة	٢٢٠,٠٠٠	؟	١٨٠,٠٠٠
أجور مباشرة	١٥٠,٠٠٠	٢٠٠,٠٠٠	؟
تكاليف صناعية أخرى	١١٥,٠٠٠	١٥٠,٠٠٠	؟
إنتاج تحت التشغيل آخر المدة	٦٠,٠٠٠	٧٠,٠٠٠	٤٠,٠٠٠
إنتاج تام آخر المدة	؟	٩٠,٠٠٠	٨٠,٠٠٠
مجمل الربح	٢٠٠,٠٠٠	١٠٠,٠٠٠	٦٥,٠٠٠

السؤال التاسع عشر: الآتي بعض الحسابات غير المكتملة التي رحلت إليها بعض المبالغ وأرقام القيود فقط.

حـ/ مراقبة المواد الخام

رصيد ١٠,٠٠٠		٨٠,٠٠٠	(٢)
(١) ١٠٠,٠٠٠			
الرصيد ٣٠,٠٠٠			

حـ/ مراقبة الأجور

النقدية (٣) ١٠٠,٠٠٠			(٤)
١٠٠,٠٠٠			١٠٠,٠٠٠

حـ/ إنتاج تحت التشغيل

رصيد ١٥,٠٠٠	(٧)
(٢)	
الأجور ٨٠,٠٠٠	
(٤)	
(٦)	

حـ/ التكاليف الصناعية غير المباشرة

(٢) ١٠,٠٠٠		٨٠,٠٠٠	(٦)
(٤)			
أخرى (٥) ٥٠,٠٠٠			

ح/ تكلفة البضاعة المباعة		ح/ بضاعة تامة الصنع	
(٨)	٢٠٠,٠٠٠	رصيد ٢٥,٠٠٠	
(٨)		(٧) ٢٢٠,٠٠٠	

المطلوب: إجراء قيود اليومية وترحيلها بصورة صحيحة، وتحديد أرصد الحسابات السابقة في آخر المدة.

السؤال العشرون: (CMA معدل) يخص الأسئلة الثلاثة التالية:

الآتي معلومات مستخرجة من سجلات إحدى الشركات الصناعية.

المخزون	٤/ ١	٤/٣٠
مواد مباشرة	١٨,٠٠٠د	١٥,٠٠٠د
إنتاج تحت التشغيل	٩,٠٠٠د	٦,٠٠٠د
إنتاج تام	٢٧,٠٠٠د	٣٦,٠٠٠د

والآتي بعض المعلومات الإضافية عن شهر ٤:-

مواد مباشرة مشتراة	٤٢,٠٠٠د
أجور مباشرة	٣٠,٠٠٠د
معدل الأجر المباشر بالساعة	٧,٥د
معدل تحميل الأعباء الإضافية	١٠ د / س ع م

- فإن التكلفة الأولية هي :-

(أ) ٧٥,٠٠٠ د	(ب) ٦٩٠٠٠ د
(جـ) ٤٥,٠٠٠ د	(د) ٣٩,٠٠٠ د

- كانت تكاليف التحويل في شهر ٤ هي:

(ب) ٤٠,٠٠٠د   (أ) ٣٠,٠٠٠ د

(د) ٧٢,٠٠٠ د   (جـ) ٧٠,٠٠٠ د

- تكلفة البضاعة التامة الصنع في شهر ٤ هي:

(ب) ١١٥,٠٠٠ د   (أ) ١١٨,٠٠٠ د

(د) ١٠٩,٠٠٠ د   (جـ) ١١٢٠٠٠ د

- تكلفة البضاعة المباعة في شهر ٤ هي:

(ب) ١١٢,٠٠٠   (أ) ١١٨,٠٠٠

(د) ١٢٧,٠٠٠   (جـ) ١٠٩,٠٠٠

السؤال الحادي والعشرون: المواد المباشر تعتبر:

	تكلفة تحويل	تكلفة صناعية	تكلفة أولية
أ	نعم	نعم	لا
ب	نعم	نعم	نعم
جـ	لا	نعم	نعم
د	لا	لا	لا

الفصل الثالث
محاسبة تكاليف الأوامر الإنتاجية

أهداف الفصل:

بعد دراسة هذا الفصل يتوقع معرفة الآتي:

١- صفات أنظمة المراحل والأوامر الإنتاجية.

٢- الدورة المحاسبية لمحاسبة الأوامر.

٣- قيود اليومية المستخدمة في صناعة الأوامر.

٤- النماذج والحسابات المختلفة في صناعة الأوامر.

٥- طريقة تحميل الأعباء الإضافية على الأوامر.

٦- معالجة تكاليف الأوامر المنتهية.

٧- معالجة تكاليف البضاعة المباعة.

٨- معالجة الأعباء الإضافية المحملة بالزيادة أو النقص

مقدمـة :

يستخدم نظام محاسبة الأوامر الإنتاجية في المنشآت التي تختلف مواصفات الإنتاج أو الخدمات التي تقدمها من طلبية الى أخرى أو أمر تشغيل الى آخر وهذا يؤدي الى تباين إجمالي تكاليف الطلبيات ومن ثم الوحدات المنتجة أو الخدمات المقدمة. تسود هذه الظروف في صناعات مثل صناعة الكتب وصناعة السينما والأثاث وصناعة السفن وتشييد المباني وصناعة الآلات المتخصصة. يتميز إنتاج هذه المنشآت بأنه يتغير من طلبية إلى أخرى، فمثلاً في صناعة الكتب تختلف متطلبات إنتاج كل كتاب عن الآخر حسب حجم الكتاب وطريقة طباعته ولون حبره ورسومه البيانية ونوعية غلافه، ومن ثم يجب اعتبار كل كتاب أمراً إنتاجياً مستقلاً. تعرف الطريقة المحاسبية التي تستخدم في المحاسبة على تكاليف الأوامر باسم محاسبة الأوامر الإنتاجية. ونظراً لاختلاف مواصفات الإنتاج من طلبية إلى أخرى تقوم هذه الطريقة المحاسبية بفتح حساب خاص لكل طلبية عمل لحصر تكاليفها ويعرف هذا الحساب باسم حساب الأمر الإنتاجي. يتم فتحه في دفتر أستاذ مساعد الأوامر الإنتاجية. وتتم مراقبة هذه الحسابات باستخدام حساب إجمالي(حساب مراقبة) يفتح في دفتر الأستاذ العام ويعرف بحساب إنتاج تحت التشغيل Work in Process.

وعلى الجانب الآخر، إذا كانت مواصفات الإنتاج لا تتغير من كمية لأخرى وأن الإنتاج ينساب بصورة مستمرة فإنه لا يوجد ما يبرر فصل تكاليف كل كمية عن الأخرى لأن الوحدة تحتاج إلى استخدام نفس كمية الموارد الاقتصادية التي تحتاجها الوحدة الأخرى. لذلك يلزم للمحاسبة على تكاليف الإنتاج في هذه الحالة حصر التكاليف التي تحدث خلال فترة زمنية معينة وقسمتها على الوحدات التي استفادت من تكاليف الفترة. تعرف هذه الطريقة المحاسبية باسم طريقة محاسبة المراحل الإنتاجية. وتستخدم هذه الطريقة في صناعة البلاستيك، والزجاج، وصناعة الطوب، والبلاط، وصناعة الأغذية المعلبة، وصناعة النسيج، وصناعة إنتاج وتكرير البترول، وصناعة الأسمنت، وصناعة الفوسفات والبوتاس، فجميع هذه الصناعات تنتج وحدات إنتاج متماثلة. وسيتم في هذا الفصل تغطية محاسبة الأوامر الإنتاجية بينما سيتم في الفصلين التاليين دراسة محاسبة المراحل الإنتاجية.

محاسبة الأوامر الإنتاجية:

تقوم محاسبة الأوامر الإنتاجية بصورة رئيسية على تتبع تكاليف كل أمر إنتاجي على حدة، ولتحقيق ذلك يتم فتح حساب مستقل لكل واحد منها في دفتر أستاذ مساعد الأوامر الإنتاجية. ويجعل حسابه مدينا بما يصرف له من مواد مباشرة وأجور مباشرة ومصروفات صناعية غير مباشرة. يصمم حساب الأمر الإنتاجي بعدة طرق منها على سبيل المثال بطاقة الأمر الإنتاجي الواردة في الشكل (٣-١). وتحتوي هذه البطاقة على بيانات منها: رقم الأمر الإنتاجي، وتاريخ بدء العمل عليه، وتاريخ تسليمه المتوقع، وتاريخ تسليمه الفعلي وحقول لحصر عناصر التكاليف المباشرة وغير المباشرة التي يحصل عليها من كل قسم إنتاجي يستفيد من خدماته. وللتبسيط سيتم استخدام حساب حرف T في شرح هذا الفصل. وكذلك أيضا سيتم تطبيق الشرح على منشأة صناعية صغيرة لذلك سيتم استخدام حساب إنتاج تحت التشغيل لحصر تكاليفها الصناعية ولكن عندما يكون في المنشأة عدة أقسام صناعية يتم فتح حساب إنتاج تحت التشغيل لكل واحد منها لحصر تكاليفه وهذا يتطلب أيضاً تقسيم بطاقة الأمر الإنتاجي إلى عدة مناطق ليتم استخدام كل واحدة منها لحصر التكاليف التي يحصل عليها الأمر الإنتاجي من كل قسم يستفيد من خدماته، لذلك قسمت بطاقة الأمر الإنتاجي الوارد في الشكل (٣-١) إلى منطقتين: الأولى، وتخصص لحصر تكاليف قسم التفصيل والثانية وتخصص لحصر تكاليف قسم التشطيب.

بطاقة أمر إنتاجي								

اسم العميل

تاريخ البدء   /   /   رقم الأمر: ....

تاريخ التسليم المتوقع   /   /   تاريخ التسليم الفعلي   /   /

مواصفات الأمر ....

....

قسم التفصيل:

الأعباء الإضافية			الأجور المباشرة			مواد مباشرة		
القيمة	الرقم	التاريخ	القيمة	رقم الصرف	التاريخ	القيمة	رقم الصرف	التاريخ

قسم التشطيب:								
الأعباء الإضافية			الأجور المباشرة			المواد المباشرة		
القيمة	رقم الصرف	التاريخ	القيمة	رقم الصرف	التاريخ	القيمة	رقم الصرف	التاريخ
								الملخص
الإجمالي		قسم ٢			قسم ١			

مواد مباشرة:
أجور مباشرة:
أعباء إضافية:
الإجمالي

شكل (٣-١) بطاقة الأمر الإنتاجي

الإجراءات المستخدمة في محاسبة الأوامر الإنتاجية:

مما سبق يتبين لنا أن كل أمر إنتاجي سيخصص له حساب مستقل في دفتر أستاذ مساعد الأوامر الإنتاجية وتتم مراقبة هذه الحسابات باستخدام حساب الإنتاج تحت التشغيل. ولتوضيح علاقة هذه الحسابات بعناصر التكاليف سيتم دراسة الإجراءات المحاسبية للمواد المباشرة والأجور المباشرة والتكاليف الصناعية غير المباشرة على التوالي:

المواد المباشرة :

تعرف المواد المباشرة على أنها المواد التي يتم صرفها خصيصاً للأمر الإنتاجي. ويتم تحديد تكلفتها من واقع سندات صرف المواد التي تحررها إدارة الإنتاج وتحمل رقم الأمر الإنتاجي. ويحتوي الشكل(٣-٢) على نموذج لسند صرف المواد Material requisition.

سند صرف المواد	
الرقم	
التاريخ...............	القسم
....	المستفيد...............
توقيع المفوض بالصرف	رقم الأمر الإنتاجي...............

يرجى صرف المواد التالية: ....

البيان	التكلفة	سعر	وحدة القياس	الكمية	رقم المادة

توقيع المستلم........................ توقيع أمين المخزن ......

الشكل (٣-٢) طلب صرف مواد من المخازن

ومن دراسة هذا النموذج نرى أنه يحتوي على اسم القسم الذي صرفت له المواد وبالتالي تعتبر هذه المواد مواداً مباشرة على القسم المعني ولذلك تحمل على حساب إنتاج تحت التشغيل الخاص به وكذلك ترحل تكلفتها على الأمر الإنتاجي المستفيد عليه لأنها مواد مباشرة عليه. أما أذونات الصرف التي لا تحتوي على رقم إنتاجي فتعتبر مواداً غير مباشرة وتحمل تكاليفها على حساب مراقبة التكاليف الصناعية غير المباشرة للقسم. يتم تسجيل سندات صرف المواد يومياً أو أسبوعياً أو لأية فترة أخرى تحددها الشركة. ولتسهيل ذلك يتم استخدام كشوفات تحليلية لتلخيص أذون الصرف كما في الشكل (٣-٣).

أعباء إضافية	الأوامر					الإجمالي	رقم الأذن	التاريخ
	٢١٥	٢١٤	٢١٣	٢١٢	٢١١			
			١٤,٠٠٠	١٨,٠٠٠	٢٨,٠٠٠	٦٠,٠٠٠		الإجمالي

شكل (٣-٣) كشف تحليل سندات صرف المواد

فمثلاً إذا تبين أن المواد التي تم صرفها خلال الفترة تخص الأوامر الإنتاجية التالية:

الأمر رقم ٢١١   ٢٨,٠٠٠د

الأمر رقم ٢١٢   ١٨,٠٠٠د

الأمر رقم ٢١٣   ١٤,٠٠٠د

فإنه يتم تسجيلها في دفتر اليومية باستخدام القيد التالي:

	حـ/ إنتاج تحت التشغيل	(١)	٦٠,٠٠٠
	الأمر رقم ٢١١	٢٨,٠٠٠	
	الأمر رقم ٢١٢	١٨,٠٠٠	
	الأمر رقم ٢١٣	١٤,٠٠٠	
	حـ/ مراقبة المواد الخام	٦٠,٠٠٠	

ويرحل المبلغ الإجمالي إلى حساب الإنتاج تحت التشغيل وحساب مراقبة المواد الخام في دفتر الأستاذ العام. كما ترحل المبالغ الخاصة بالأوامر الإنتاجية إلى بطاقاتها. على أية حال، للاختصار سوف نهمل المبالغ التفصيلية الخاصة بالأوامر الإنتاجية في قيود اليومية التالية.

المواد غير المباشرة:

تشمل المواد غير المباشرة المواد التي يتم صرفها الى الأقسام الإنتاجية لخدمة أغراضها العامة وليس لأمر إنتاجي معين، وهي مثل زيوت التزييت ومواد النظافة. تحمل تكلفة المواد غير المباشرة على حساب مراقبة التكاليف الصناعية غير المباشرة (الأعباء الإضافية) للقسم ليتم تحميلها لاحقا على الإنتاج تحت التشغيل. ولنفرض أنه خلال الفترة تم صرف مواد غير مباشرة من المخازن بمبلغ ٢,٧٥٠ د إلى القسم الإنتاجي فإنها تسجل بقيد اليومية التالي:

	حـ/ مراقبة التكاليف الصناعية غير المباشرة	٢,٧٥٠
(٢)	حـ/ مراقبة المواد	٢,٧٥٠

بموجب هذا القيد يتم فتح حساب للتكاليف الصناعية غير المباشرة ويجعل مدينا بمبلغ ٢,٧٥٠د، وهذا الحساب يخصص لكل قسم على حده.

الأجور المباشرة:

الأجور المباشرة هي أجور العمال الذين يعملون مباشرة على الأوامر الإنتاجية مثل أجور العمال الذين تكون مهامهم استخدام الآلات لتنفيذ الأوامر الإنتاجية، وأجور العمال الذين ينقلون الإنتاج من آلة إلى أخرى ضمن الخط الإنتاجي، أما أجور العمال الذين يشرفون على عدة منتجات، وأجور عمال الصيانة، وأجور عمال التنظيف والحراسة فإنها تعتبر أجوراً غير مباشرة لأنها تصرف لمصلحة كل الأوامر.

لتحديد تكلفة الأجور يجب أن يتم تحديد الوقت الذي يقضيه العمال في المنشأة ويتم ذلك بطرق منها: التوقيع على سجل الحضور والانصراف أو استخدام ساعة الوقت أو بطاقات الدوام. وبعد تحديد إجمالي الوقت الذي يقضيه العمال في العمل يتم قسمته الى وقت عادي ووقت إضافي وعلى أساس ذلك تحدد أجور ومرتبات العمال وتدفع لهم ويتم تحميل قيمتها على حساب مراقبة الأجور. وعلى افتراض أن إجمالي الأجور المستحقة للعمال خلال إحدى الفترات هي٣٥,٠٠٠د. فإنه يتم تسجيلها بموجب قيد اليومية التالي:

٣٥,٠٠٠		ح/ مراقبة الأجور الصناعية	
	٣٥,٠٠٠	ح/ الأجور المستحقة أو النقدية	(٢)

بطاقات وقت العمل:

حتى تتم معرفة الأجور المباشرة يجب حصر الوقت الذي يقضيه العمال المباشرون في العمل على الأوامر الإنتاجية المختلفة ويتم ذلك باستخدام بطاقة وقت العمل الواردة في الشكل (٣-٤). تخصص هذه البطاقة لحصر وقت العمل الذي يقضيه العامل على كل أمر إنتاجي يعمل عليه خلال يوم عمله وفي نهاية كل يوم يتم تفريغ هذه البطاقات في كشف العمل اليومي لعمال القسم الوارد في الشكل (٣-٥). يتم حساب معدل أجر الساعة لكل عامل على حدة أو للقسم أو لإدارة الإنتاج ككل. ويؤدي استخدام الأسلوب الأول إلى زيادة دقة المعلومات لأن أجور عمال القسم تختلف من عامل إلى آخر ، ويؤدي استخدام معدل واحد لكل عمال إدارة الإنتاج إلى تبسيط الإجراءات المحاسبية وتقليل تكاليف تشغيل نظام

التكاليف. ويفضل استخدام معدل لكل قسم على حدة. ويحدد معدل أجر الساعة للعامل بقسمة راتبه السنوي

القسم	رقم الأمر	ساعات العمل	وقت الانتهاء	وقت البدء

شركة الخليل الصناعية

التاريخ / /

معدل أجرة ساعة العمل = ٢ د

ملاحظات

اسم العامل : أحمد علي

ساعات العمل العادي.............

ساعات العمل الإضافي.............

إجمالي ساعات العمل.............

توقيع العامل

....

....

توقيع المشرف

....

.....

شكل (٣-٤) بطاقة عمل يومية

على ساعات عمله السنوية وهذه تحدد بضرب عدد أيام العمل الرسمية في السنة في عدد ساعات العمل اليومية. ويفضل المعدل السنوي على المعدل الشهري لأن الأول يتجنب التغير في أيام العمل الشهرية. ويحدد معدل أجر الساعة على مستوى القسم بقسمة إجمالي رواتب الإدارة أو القسم على ساعات عمل العمال في القسم.

الإجمالي	أمر ٢١٦	أمر ٢١٣	أمر ٢١٢	أمر ٢١١	اسم العامل
١٣,٥٥٠		٢,٧٥٠	٤,٨٠٠	٦,٠٠٠	الإجمالي

كشف (٣-٥) كشف العمل اليومي لعمال القسم

فإذا كانت ساعات العمل المباشرة للأوامر الإنتاجية هي كما ظهرت في سطر الإجمالي من الشكل (٣-٥) وأن معدل أجر الساعة في القسم هو ٢ د / س ع م تكون الأجور المباشرة الخاصة بالأوامر (١٣٥٥٠ ساعة × ٢د) = ٢٧,١٠٠ د. وعليـة تكون تكلفة الأجور غير المباشرة للقسم خلال الشهر هي الفرق بـين إجـمالي أجـور القسم والأجور المباشرة وتساوي (٣٥٠٠٠ - ٢٧١٠٠) ٧,٩٠٠ د.

ويتم إثبات توزيع أجور القسم في دفتر اليومية بالقيد التالي:

	ح/ إنتاج تحت التشغيل	٢٧,١٠٠
	ح/ تكاليف صناعية غير مباشرة	٧,٩٠٠
٣٥,٠٠٠	ح/ مراقبة الأجور	

وبعد ذلك يتم ترحيل الأجور المباشرة على بطاقات الأوامر وتحسب كالتالي:

الأمر رقم ٢١١ = ٢ × ٦,٠٠٠ ساعة = ١٢,٠٠٠د

الأمر رقم ٢١٢ = ٢ × ٤,٨٠٠ ساعة = ٩,٦٠٠د

الأمر رقم ٢١٤ = ٢ × ٢,٧٥٠ ساعة = ٥,٥٠٠د

المجموع = ٢٧,١٠٠

التكاليف الصناعية غير المباشرة:

تشمل التكاليف الصناعية غير المباشرة كل التكاليف الصناعية التي لا تعتبر مواداً وأجوراً مباشرة وتتضمن على سبيل المثال لا الحصر، المواد غير المباشرة والأجور غير المباشرة، واستهلاك الآلات ومعدات المصنع، والقوى المحركة والتأمين والرسوم والرخص. تسجل هذه البنود عند حدوثها في الجانب المدين لحساب مراقبة التكاليف الصناعية غير المباشرة. ويتم تحليلها في دفتر أستاذ مساعد أو في كشوف تحليلية لمعرفة قيمة بنودها الفرعية. تسجل بعض هذه البنود عندما ترد فواتيرها من مصادر خارجية مثل الإيجار والمياه والكهرباء والهاتف ويتم تسجيل بعضها الآخر بناء على مستندات داخلية مثل أذون صرف المواد غير المباشرة والأجور غير المباشرة والاستهلاك. وافترض الآن أن تكلفة هذه البنود تساوي ٢٨,٨٥٠ د فإنها تسجل بجعل حساب تكاليف صناعية غير مباشرة مدين وحساب موردين والنقدية ومجمع الاستهلاك دائنا حسب ظروف الحال.

تحميل التكاليف الصناعية غير المباشرة:

لا يتم معرفة هذه التكاليف إلا في نهاية السنة المالية مما يجعل من المحال تحميل هذه التكاليف على الأوامر لحظة الانتهاء من إنتاجها. ويتطلب هذا الأمر تقدير التكاليف المتوقع حدوثها خلال السنة المقبلة وتقدير مستوى النشاط عند مستوى النشاط التقديري لتلك السنة ثم قسمة التكاليف التقديرية على عدد وحدات النشاط التقديرية كما في المعادلة التالية:

$$\text{معدل التحميل الأعباء الإضافية} = \frac{\text{التكاليف التقديرية}}{\text{عدد وحدات النشاط عند الطاقة العادية}}$$

مما سبق نجد أن تحديد معدل التحميل يتطلب تقدير التكاليف الصناعية غير المباشرة التي يتوقع حدوثها مقدما أي قبل بدء السنة المالية، ويتم استخدام فترة السنة للتغلب على مشكلة التغيرات الموسمية التي قد يتعرض لها نشاط المنشأة [١] ويتم قياس وحدات النشاط باستخدام أحد المقاييس الآتية: [٢]

١. ساعات العمل المباشرة.

٢. ساعات دوران الآلات.

٣. تكلفة الأجور المباشرة.

٤. تكلفة المواد المباشرة.

٥. التكلفة الأولية.

تتميز ساعات العمل المباشرة وساعات الدوران بأنها مقاييس مادية لا تتأثر بالتغير في الأسعار ويتم الحصول عليها من بطاقات العمال والآلات على التوالي، أما تكلفة الأجور المباشرة والمواد المباشرة والتكلفة الأولية فهي مقاييس مالية وبالتالي فإنها عرضه لأثر تقلبات الأسعار وهذا قد يؤثر على نصيب الوحدة من التكاليف غير المباشرة لذلك يفضل استخدام ساعات العمل المباشرة إذا كانت المنشأة تعتمد على الأيدي العاملة بصورة رئيسية في عملياتها لأن أغلب التكاليف غير المباشرة ستكون مرتبطة بساعات العمل، أما إذا كانت المنشأة تعتمد على الآلات بصورة رئيسية فإنه يفضل [٣] استخدام ساعات دوران الآلات لأن أغلب عناصر التكاليف الصناعية غير المباشرة تكون مرتبطة بتشغيل الآلات. وعلى أية حال، مع التقدم التكنولوجي الذي تشهده أيامنا الحالية تزايدت أهمية التكاليف غير المباشرة المرتبطة بالتجهيزات الآلية على حساب التكاليف المرتبطة بالأيدي العاملة وهذا يتطلب ازدياد الاهتمام بساعات دوران الآلات. [٤]

---

[١] تشارلز. هورنجرن،مرجع سابق، ص ص ١٥٨-١٧٤.

[٢] Bierman and Dyckman, <u>Managerial Accounting</u>, ٢nd. Ed., (Macmillan Publishing Co - ١٩٧٦), Pp. ٤٨ - ٥١.

[٣] Rayburn, L. G., Principles of cost Accounting. ٤th, ed.

[٤] Horngren and Foster, Cost Accounting: A Managerial Emphasis (Prentice Hall. INC. ١٩٨٢)., Pp. ٤٥٠ - ٤٥٢.

تمتاز الأساليب الثلاثة الأخيرة بسهولتها لتوفرها في دفاتر وسجلات المنشأة وبالتالي لا يؤدي استخدامها إلى حدوث تكاليف تشغيل إضافية لتجميعها كما هو الحال عند استخدام ساعات العمل وساعات الدوران. وعلى الرغم من الانتقادات الموجهة إليها فإنها قد تلائم توزيع تكاليف رواتب وأجور المهندسين وتكاليف إدارة الإنتاج أكثر من غيرها لأن هذه التكاليف غير مرتبطة بعلاقة سببية مع ساعات العمل المباشرة أو مع ساعات دوران الآلات. على أية حال، عند المفاضلة بين هذه الأسس، يمكن للمنشأة اختيار أكثر من أساس حسب مدي ارتباطها بالتكاليف التي سيتم توزيعها وبقدر الإمكان عند المفاضلة بين هذه الأسس يجب مراعاة السبب والنتيجة ومراعاة التكلفة والمنفعة قبل التوصل إلى قرار نهائي.

تحميل التكاليف الصناعية غير المباشرة على الأوامر:

لتوضيح الإجراءات المحاسبية التي يجب استخدامها لتحميل التكاليف الصناعية غير المباشرة على أوامر الإنتاج سوف نفترض أن معدل تحميل التكاليف الصناعية غير المباشرة يبلغ ٣د/س ع م وأن ساعات العمل المباشرة التي حصلت عليها الأوامر (٢١١، ٢١٢، ٢١٣) هي ٦,٠٠٠، ٤,٨٠٠، ٢,٧٥٠ ساعة على التوالي، وهي نفس الساعات التي استخدمت في حساب تكلفة الأجور المباشرة سابقا، وعليه تكون التكاليف غير المباشرة التي يجب تحميلها على الأوامر كالتالي:

المبلغ (بالدينار) =	معدل التحميل	ساعات العمل المباشرة ×	رقم الأمر
١٨,٠٠٠	٣	٦,٠٠٠	٢١١
١٤,٤٠٠	٣	٤,٨٠٠	٢١٢
٨,٢٥٠	٣	٢,٧٥٠	٢١٣
٤٠,٦٥٠		١٣,٥٥٠	الإجمالي

ويتم تسجيل مبلغ التكاليف الصناعية غير المباشرة على الأوامرالإنتاجية باستخدام قيد اليومية التالي:

٤٠,٦٥٠	حـ/ إنتاج تحت التشغيل	
(٥)	حـ/ تكاليف صناعية غير مباشرة محملة	٤٠,٦٥٠

يؤدي ترحيل هذا القيد الى فتح حساب جديد اسمه حساب التكاليف الصناعية غير المباشرة المحملة لحصر ما يتم تحميله من هذه التكاليف على الأوامر الإنتاج المنتهية، وهو حساب مقابل لحساب التكاليف الصناعية غير المباشرة الفعلية، وبالتالي يجب أن يقفلا معاً عند إعداد الحسابات الختامية. وبعد ترحيل قيود اليومية الخاصة بتسجيل التكاليف الصناعية المباشرة وغير المباشرة على حساب إنتاج تحت التشغيل وإلى بطاقات الأوامر تصبح حسابات الأوامر وحساب إنتاج تحت التشغيل كالتالي:

من دراسة الحسابات نلاحظ أن مجموع المواد المباشرة المرحلة على حسابات (بطاقات) الأوامر الإنتاجية تساوي قيمة المواد المحملة على حساب إنتاج تحت التشغيل. وهكذا بالنسبة لتكاليف الأجور المباشرة والتكاليف الصناعية غير المباشرة.

حـ/ الأمر ٢١٢		حـ/ الأمر ٢١١	
١٨,٠٠٠ مواد مباشرة (١)		٢٨,٠٠٠ مواد مباشرة (١)	
٩,٦٠٠ أجور مباشرة (٤)		١٢,٠٠٠ أجور مباشرة (٤)	
١٤,٤٠٠ ت ص غ ش (٥)		١٨,٠٠٠ ت ص غ ش (٥)	
٤٢,٠٠٠		٥٨,٠٠٠	

حـ/ الإنتاج تحت التشغيل		حـ/ الأمر ٢١٣	
٦٠,٠٠٠ مواد مباشرة (١)		١٤,٠٠٠ مواد مباشرة (١)	
٢٧,١٠٠ أجور مباشرة (٤)		٥,٥٠٠ أجور مباشرة (٤)	
٤٠,٦٥٠ ت ص غ ش (٥)		٨,٢٥٠ ت ص غ ش (٥)	
		٢٧,٧٥٠	

حـ/ أعباء صناعية محملة		حـ/ أعباء صناعية فعلية	
٤٠,٦٥٠ (٥)			
		٢,٧٥٠ (٢)	
		٧,٩٠٠ (٤)	
		٢٨,٨٥٠ أعباء فعلية	
		٣٩,٥٠٠ الرصيد	

أوامر الإنتاج المنتهية:

عندما ينتهي تصنيع الأمر الإنتاجي يتم تحويل تكلفته من حساب الإنتاج تحت التشغيل إلى حساب تكلفة البضاعة التامة الصنع وتبقى فيه الى أن يتم التصرف به أما بتسليم البضاعة إلى العملاء أو بتخزينها في مخازن المنشأة لاستخدامها في إنتاج منتجات أخرى أو بيعها في السوق. وقبل أن يتم أقفال بطاقة الأمر الإنتاجي يجب التأكد من تحميله بكل عناصر التكاليف وخصوصاً التكاليف الصناعية غير المباشرة. وللمحاسبة على الأوامر المنتهية، افترض أن الأمر رقم ٢١١ قد انتهى إنتاجه وتم تحويله إلى مخزن

المنتجات التامة الصنع وان رصيد تكلفته كما في دفتر أستاذ مساعد الأوامر تبلغ ٥٨,٠٠٠ د فإنه يتم إثبات تكلفته بقيد اليومية التالي:

(٦)	حـ/ الإنتاج التام بالمخازن	٥٨,٠٠٠
	حـ/ إنتاج تحت التشغيل	٥٨,٠٠٠

وإذا كان هذا الأمر يحتوي على وحدات متجانسة أو وحدات يمكن قياسها بوحدات قياس عامة مثل الكيلو غرام أو الجالون فإنه يتم حساب تكلفة الوحدة منه بقسمة إجمالي تكلفة الأمر على عدد الوحدات التي يتكون منها. فمثلاً إذا كان الأمر الإنتاجي ٢١١ يحتوي على ٥,٠٠٠ وحدة فإن تكلفة الوحدة منها تكون ١١,٦ د

(٥٨,٠٠٠ ÷ ٥,٠٠٠ وحدة).

تكلفة البضاعة المباعة:

تمثل تكلفة البضاعة المباعة تكلفة أوامر الإنتاج التي تم تسليمها إلى العملاء أو تكلفة الوحدات التي تم بيعها في السوق. ويتوقف إثباتها في الدفاتر على طريقة الجرد التي تتبعها المنشأة. فإذا كانت تستخدم طريقة الجرد الدوري فإن تكلفة البضاعة المباعة سوف تحدد في نهاية الفترة بعد الجرد الفعلي للبضاعة التامة الصنع، ويتم تحديد قيمتها بطرح تكلفة الإنتاج التام الصنع آخر المدة من تكلفة الإنتاج التام المتاح للبيع، والرقم الأخير يمثل مجموع تكلفة الإنتاج التام أول المدة زائد تكلفة الإنتاج التام خلال الفترة الجارية.

أما إذا كانت المنشأة تتبع طريقة الجرد المستمر ففي هذه الحالة يخصص حساب لحصر تكلفة البضاعة المباعة، ويتم إثبات عملية البيع باستخدام قيدين أحدهما لإثبات إيرادات المبيعات والآخر لإثبات تكلفة البضاعة المباعة. ولتوضيح ذلك افترض انهَ تم بيع الأمر الإنتاجي ٢١١ والذي تكلفته تساوي ٥٨,٠٠٠ د بمبلغ ٧٥,٠٠٠ د، فإن قيود اليومية اللازمة لإثبات هذه الحقائق هي كالتالي:

أولا: قيد اليومية لإثبات إيرادات المبيعات:

حـ/ العملاء أو النقدية		٧٥,٠٠٠
(٧)	حـ/ المبيعات	٧٥,٠٠٠

ثانيا: قيد اليومية لإثبات تكلفة البضاعة المباعة

حـ/ تكلفة البضاعة المباعة		٥٨,٠٠٠
(٨)	حـ/ الإنتاج التام بالمخازن	٥٨,٠٠٠

معالجة التكاليف الصناعية غير المباشرة المحملة بالزيادة أو النقص:

سبق وأن ذكرنا أن هذه التكاليف تحمل على الأوامر باستخدام معدل تحميل محدد مقدماً وأن التكاليف المحملة تسجل في الجانب الدائن من حساب تكاليف صناعية غير مباشرة محملة، وان التكلفة الفعلية لهذه المصاريف يتم تسجيلها في حساب التكاليف الصناعية غير المباشرة الفعلية. وفي نهاية الفترة تتم مقارنة أرصدة هذه المصروفات وهنا قد نجد أن التكاليف التي تم تحميلها على الأوامر الإنتاجية أكبر من التكاليف الفعلية ويسمى الفرق بالتكاليف المحملة بالزيادة Overapplied Cost أو أن تكون التكاليف المحملة أقل من التكاليف الفعلية ويسمى الفرق بالتكاليف المحملة بالنقص Underapplied Cost. وبالتالي فان ظهور هذه الفروقات بالزيادة أو النقص يشير الى حدوث خطأ في تكاليف البضاعة وهذا يتطلب عمل قيود يومية لتصحيح الخطأ.

المحاسبة على فروقات التحميل:

يمكن إقفال فروقات التحميل بالزيادة أو بالنقص البسيطة في حساب تكلفة البضاعة المباعة على اعتبار أن رصيدها هو أكبر أرصدة البضاعة التي تحتوي على تكاليف صناعية غير مباشرة محملة[1]. ولكن إذا كانت هذه الفروقات جوهرية فانه يجب توزيعها على حسابات البضاعة المختلفة التي تحتوي أرصدتها على أعباء اضافية محملة وهي حساب الإنتاج تحت التشغيل وحساب الإنتاج التام بالمخازن، وحساب تكلفة البضاعة

---

[1] Matz, A., and Usry, M. F., <u>Cost Accounting Planning and Control</u>, ٨[th]. ed., (South - Western Publishing Co., ١٩٨٤). Pp. ١٥٨ - ١٦٠.

المباعة. وفي هذه الحالة قد يتم التوزيع على أساس ألأرصدة النهائية لهذه الحسابات أو على أساس ما تحتويه هذه الحسابات من تكاليف صناعية غير مباشرة. وتعتبر الطريقة الأخيرة أكثر دقة ولكنها تحتاج إلى مجهودات وتكاليف أكبر[1] من طريقة الأرصدة النهائية. ولتوضيح المعالجات المحاسبية الممكنة افترض أن أرصدة التكاليف الصناعية غير المباشرة المحملة والفعلية هي ١٢٩,٠٠٠د، ١٢٤,٠٠٠ على التوالي، كما بلغت أرصدة حسابات تكاليف البضاعة كالتالي:

اسم الحساب	الرصيد بالدينار
إنتاج تحت التشغيل	٢٤,٠٠٠
إنتاج تام بالمخازن	٦٦,٠٠٠
تكلفة البضاعة المباعة	٢١٠,٠٠٠

المطلوب: معالجة الفرق بين الأعباء الإضافية الفعلية والمحملة على افتراض أنها غير مهمة ثم على اعتبار أنها مهمة.

الحل:

عند مقارنة أرصدة الأعباء الإضافية المحملة والأعباء الفعلية نجد أن الأعباء محملة بأكثر من اللازم مما يؤدي الى زيادة أرصدة تكاليف البضاعة بمبلغ ٥٠٠٠د لأن التكلفة المحملة ١٢٩,٠٠٠ د بينما كانت التكاليف الفعلية ١٢٤,٠٠٠ د. وسيتم توزيع المبلغ المحمل بالزيادة كالتالي:

أولا: اعتبار الفرق غير مهم:

عندما يعتبر أن هذا الفرق غير مهم يتم إقفاله في حساب تكلفة البضاعة المباعة لان رصيدها عادة أكبر من أرصدة البضاعة الأخرى. ويتم بالقيد التالي.

ح/ أعباء إضافية محملة			١٢٩,٠٠٠
ح/ تكلفة البضاعة المباعة	٥,٠٠٠		
ح/ أعباء إضافية فعلية	١٢٤,٠٠٠		

---

[1] Calvin Engler, Managerial Accounting, (IRWIN, ١٩٨٧), P. ١٠٠.

يعمل القيد السابق على إقفال حسابات الأعباء الفعلية والمحملة لأنها حسابات اسمية وقد سجل الفرق في الجانب الدائن من تكلفة البضاعة المباعة. فكالعادة يتم إقفال رصيد الحساب الاسمي الدائن بجعله مدينا والعكس صحيح بالنسبة للحساب الدائن.

ثانيا: اعتبار الفرق مهماً

في هذه الحالة يجب توزيع المبلغ المحمل بالزيادة على حسابات البضائع التي تحملت بالأعباء الإضافية ولقد حددت النسبة المؤية في الجدول التالي على أساس قسمة رصيد حساب البضاعة على مجموع ارصده حسابات البضائع، وتم التوصل إلى أن المبلغ يوزع بنسبة ٨%: ٢٢%: ٧٠%. ويتم تحديد حصة كل صنف من البضاعة بضرب المبلغ المحمل بالزيادة في النسبة المؤية كالتالي:

إنتاج تحت التشغيل ٥٠٠٠ × ٨%	=	٤٠٠ د
الإنتاج التام بالمخازن ٥٠٠٠× ٢٢%	=	١,١٠٠
تكلفة البضاعة المباعة ٩٠٠٠ × ٧٠%	=	٣,٥٠٠
إجمالي المبلغ الذي تم توزيعه		٥,٠٠٠

ويتم إثبات المبالغ الموزعة وإقفال حسابات التكاليف غير المباشرة باستخدام قيد اليومية التالي:

ح/ التكاليف الصناعية غير المباشرة المحملة		١٢٩,٠٠٠
ح/ التكاليف الصناعية غير المباشرة الفعلية	١٢٤,٠٠٠	
ح/ إنتاج تحت التشغيل	٤٠٠	
ح/ إنتاج تام بالمخازن	١,١٠٠	
ح/ تكلفة البضاعة المباعة	٣,٥٠٠	

مثال محلول:

يعتمد إنتاج إحدى الشركات على الطلبات التي تستلمها من العملاء وتستخدم طريقة محاسبة الأوامر الإنتاجية وكانت أرصدة حسابات تكلفة البضاعة في أول شهر آذار كالتالي: ٢٥,٨٠٠ د إنتاج تحت التشغيل ويمثل تكلفة الأمر رقم ٢٢١، ٣٥,٤٠٠ د إنتاج تام، ١٨,٦٠٠ د مواد خام. وخلال شهر آذار حدثت العمليات التالية:

١. تم شراء مواد خام بمبلغ ١٢٥,٩٠٠ د على الحساب.

٢. تم صرف مواد خام من المخازن إلى الأوامر الإنتاجية خلال الفترة كالتالي:

أمر ٢٢١	٢٨,٤٠٠د
أمر ٢٢٢	٢٢,٨٠٠د
أمر ٢٢٣	٩,٤٥٠د
أمر ٢٢٤	٢٩,٦٠٠د

٣. بلغت رواتب وأجور موظفي عمال إدارة الإنتاج ٢٤٠,٠٠٠ د وتبين من تحليل بطاقات العمل أن قيمة الأجور المباشرة التي تخص الأوامر السابقة هي كالتالي:

أمر ٢٢١	١٣٠,٠٠٠د
أمر ٢٢٢	٦٠,٠٠٠د
أمر ٢٢٣	٣٠,٠٠٠د
أمر ٢٢٤	١٥,٠٠٠ د

٤. تتكون التكاليف الصناعية غير المباشرة (الأعباء الصناعية الإضافية) من ٨٠,٠٠٠ د قيمة فواتير متنوعة تم قيدها على الحساب كما بلغ الاستهلاك عن الفترة ٣٦,٠٠٠د.

٥. معدل تحميل التكاليف الصناعية غير المباشرة نصف دينار لكل دينار من الأجور المباشرة.

٦. انتهت الأوامر ٢٢١,٢٢٢ ، ٢٢٤ ، وسلمت إلى العملاء كما بلغ ثمن بيع هذه الأوامر ٥١٧,١٤٨د.

٧ تقوم الشركة بإقفال التكاليف المحملة بالزيادة أو بالنقص في حساب تكلفة البضاعة المباعة.

المطلوب:

١ عمل قيود اليومية اللازمة لإثبات الحقائق السابقة وتصوير حسابات الأوامر المختلفة.

٢ إعداد قائمة تكلفة البضاعة المباعة وإقفال الأعباء الإضافية المحملة بالزيادة أو النقص في حساب تكلفة البضاعة المباعة.

الحل:

أولا: قيود اليومية:

١- اثبات شراء المواد الخام

ح/ مواد خام بالمخازن		١٢٥,٩٠٠
(١) ح/ الموردين	١٢٥,٩٠٠	

٢- إثبات صرف المواد الخام لأوامر الإنتاج

ح/ إنتاج تحت التشغيل		٩٠,٢٥٠
٢٨,٤٠٠ أمر ٢٢١		
٢٢,٨٠٠ أمر ٢٢٢		
٩,٤٥٠ أمر ٢٢٣		
٢٩,٦٠٠ أمر ٢٢٤		
(٢) ح/ مواد خام بالمخازن	٩٠,٢٥٠	

٣- إثبات تكلفة الأجور

ح/ مراقبة الأجور		٢٤٠,٠٠٠
(٣) ح/ الأجور المستحقة	٢٤٠,٠٠٠	

٤- تحميل الأوامر بالأجور المباشرة

وهنا يتم تحميل الأجور المباشرة التي بذلت على الأوامر على حساب الإنتاج تحت التشغيل ويحمل الباقي على حساب الأعباء الإضافية.

	حـ/ إنتاج تحت التشغيل		٢٣٥,٠٠٠
	١٣٠,٠٠٠ أمر ٢٢١		
	٦٠,٠٠٠ أمر ٢٢٢		
	٣٠,٠٠٠ أمر ٢٢٣		
	١٥,٠٠٠ أمر ٢٢٤		
(٤)	حـ/ مراقبة الأجور	٢٣٥,٠٠٠	

٥- إثبات الأجور غير المباشرة

	حـ/ أعباء إضافية فعلية		٥,٠٠٠
(٥)	حـ/ مراقبة الأجور	٥,٠٠٠	

٦- تسجيل قيمة المصروفات الصناعية غير المباشرة

	حـ/ أعباء إضافية فعلية		١١٦,٠٠٠
	حـ/ الموردين	٨٠,٠٠٠	
(٦)	ح/ مخصص استهلاك	٣٦,٠٠٠	

٧- تحميل الأعباء الإضافية على أوامر الإنتاج

	حـ/ إنتاج تحت التشغيل		١١٧,٥٠٠
	٦٥,٠٠٠ أمر ٢٢١		
	٣٠,٠٠٠ أمر ٢٢٢		
	١٥,٠٠٠ أمر ٢٢٣		
	٧,٥٠٠ أمر ٢٢٤		
(٧)	حـ/ أعباء إضافية محملة	١١٧,٥٠٠	

٨- تسجيل تكاليف الأوامر المنتهية

			٤١٤,١٠٠
	حـ/ مخزون إنتاج تام		٤١٤,١٠٠
	حـ/ إنتاج تحت التشغيل	٤١٤,١٠٠	
	٢٤٩,٢٠٠ أمر ٢٢١		
	١١٢,٨٠٠ أمر ٢٢٢		
(٨)	٥٢,١٠٠ أمر ٢٢٣		

٩- إثبات قيمة المبيعات

			٥١٧,١٤٨
	حـ/ المدينين		٥١٧,١٤٨
(٩)	حـ/ المبيعات	٥١٧,١٤٨	

١٠- إثبات تكلفة البضاعة المباعة

			٤١٤,١٠٠
	حـ/ تكلفة البضاعة المباعة		٤١٤,١٠٠
(١٠)	حـ/ مخزون الإنتاج التام	٤١٤,١٠٠	

١١- إقفال حسابات الأعباء الإضافية وتحميل الفرق على تكلفة البضاعة المباعة

			١١٧,٥٠٠
	حـ/ أعباء إضافية محملة		١١٧,٥٠٠
(١١)	حـ/ تكلفة البضاعة المباعة		٣,٥٠٠
	حـ/ أعباء إضافية فعلية	١٢١,٠٠٠	

حسابات دفتر الأستاذ مساعد الأوامر الإنتاجية:

حـ/ أمر ٢٢٢		حـ/ أمر ٢٢١	
(٢) ٢٢,٨٠٠	(٨) ١١٢٨٠٠	رصيد ٢٥,٨٠٠	(٨) ٢٤٩,٢٠٠
(٤) ٦٠,٠٠٠		(٢) ٢٨,٤٠٠	
(٦) ٣٠,٠٠٠		(٤) ١٣٠,٠٠٠	
		(٦) ٦٥,٠٠٠	

حـ/ أمر ٢٢٤		حـ/ أمر ٢٢٣	
(٢) ٢٩,٦٠٠	(٨) ٥٢,١٠٠	(٢) ٩,٤٥٠	٥٤,٤٥٠
(٤) ١٥,٠٠٠		(٤) ٣٠,٠٠٠	
(٧) ٧,٥٠٠		(٧) ١٥,٠٠٠	

حسابات دفتر الأستاذ العام

حـ/ إنتاج تحت التشغيل		حـ/ مواد خام بالمخازن	
رصيد ٢٥,٨٠٠	(٨) ٤١٤,١٠٠	رصيد ١٨,٦٠٠	(٢) ٩٠,٢٥٠
(٢) ٩٠,٢٥٠		(١) ١٢٥,٩٠٠	
(٤) ٢٣٥,٠٠٠			
(٧) ١١٧,٥٠٠			
٥٤,٤٥٠		٥٤,٢٥٠	

ح/ مراقبة الأجور				ح/ إنتاج تام بالمخازن			
(٧)	٢٤٠,٠٠٠	(٤)	٢٣٥,٠٠٠	(١٠)	٤١٤,١٠٠	رصيد	٣٥٤٠٠
		(٥)	٥٠٠٠			(٨)	٤١٤,١٠٠
							٣٥٤٠٠

ح/ أعباء صناعية فعلية				ح/ تكلفة البضاعة المباعة			
أجور (٥)	٥٠٠٠	(١١)	١٢١٠٠٠			رصيد	٤١٤,١٠٠
(٦)	١١٦,٠٠٠					(١١)	٣٥٠٠
							٤١٧,٦٠٠

ملاحظات على الحل:

١. ورد في قيود المواد المباشرة والأجور المباشرة والأعباء المحملة نصيب كل أمر في الخانة الجزئية من قيد اليومية لتذكرك بان هذه المبالغ يجب ترحيلها إلى بطاقات الأوامر.

٢. تشير الأرقام التي بين الأقواس في الحسابات إلى رقم قيد اليومية.

ثانيا: قائمة تكلفة البضاعة المباعة

باستخدام البيانات الظاهرة في الحسابات السابقة يتم إعدادها كالتالي:

قائمة تكلفة البضاعة المباعة

مواد خام أول المدة	١٨,٦٠٠	
يضاف: مشتريات مواد خام	١٢٥,٩٠٠	
المواد الخام المتاحة للاستخدام	١٤٤,٥٠٠	
يطرح : مواد خام آخر المدة	٥٤,٢٥٠	
المواد المباشرة		٩٠,٢٥٠
الأجور المباشرة		٢٣٥,٠٠٠
أعباء صناعية محملة		١١٧,٥٠٠
التكلفة الصناعية للفترة الجارية		٤٤٢,٧٥٠
يضاف : إنتاج تحت التشغيل أول المدة		٢٥٨٠٠
يطرح : إنتاج تحت التشغيل آخر المدة		٥٤,٤٥٠
تكلفة البضاعة التامة الصنع خلال المدة		٤١٤,١٠٠
يضاف: مخزون إنتاج تام أول المدة		٣٥٤٠٠
يطرح: مخزون إنتاج تام آخر المدة		٣٥٤٠٠
تكلفة البضاعة المباعة قبل التعديل		٤١٤,١٠٠
يضاف: التكاليف المحملة بالنقص		٣,٥٠٠
تكلفة البضاعة المباعة		٤١٧,٦٠٠

الخاتمــة

في هذا الفصل تم عرض طريقة محاسبة الأوامر الإنتاجية وتبين أنه يجب إتباعها عندما تختلف مواصفات الإنتاج من طلبية تشغيل الى أخرى. ووجد أن طريقة محاسبة الأوامر الإنتاجية تخصص حساب مستقل في دفتر أستاذ مساعد الأوامر لكل طلبية تشغيل ليتم تحميله بكل ما يستخدمه الأمر من مواد مباشرة وأجور مباشرة وتكاليف صناعية غير مباشرة (أعباء إضافية) ويتم ربط حسابات الأوامر بحساب إجمالي في دفتر الأستاذ العام يعرف بحساب الإنتاج تحت التشغيل ليسجل فيه مجموع المبلغ الذي سجل في حسابات الأوامر بصورة تفصيلية.

يتم تحميل الأعباء الصناعية الإضافية على أوامر التشغيل باستخدام معدل تحميل محدد مقدماً، حيث يتم تحديد هذا المعدل، بقسمة التكاليف التقديرية لفترة العمل المقبلة على عدد وحدات النشاط المتوقعة لتلك الفترة. ويتم قياس وحدات النشاط بعدة مقاييس. على أية حال يجب أن يرتبط المقياس الذي يتم اختياره بعلاقة سببية مع التكاليف غير المباشرة وأن يراعى التكلفة والمنفعة من استخدامه.

أسئـلة وتمـارين

السؤال الأول: ميز بين طريقة محاسبة الأوامر الإنتاجية وطريقة محاسبة المراحل الإنتاجية من حيث طبيعة الإنتاج وطريقة حساب تكلفة الوحدة المنتجة.

السؤال الثاني: بين كيف يتم حصر وتحميل تكلفة المواد المباشرة على أوامر الإنتاج.

السؤال الثالث: أذكر مزايا وعيوب استخدام معدل الأجر على مستوى القسم بالمقارنة مع المعدل المحسوب على مستوى المصنع وعلى مستوى كل عامل.

السؤال الرابع: لماذا يتم تحميل أوامر الإنتاج بالتكاليف الصناعية غير المباشرة باستخدام معدل التحميل؟

السؤال الخامس: هل تفضل تقدير معدل التحميل على أساس شهري أو على أساس سنوي ولماذا؟

السؤال السادس: ما هو المقصود بالتكاليف غير المباشرة المحملة بالزيادة؟

السؤال السابع: ما هو أثر نظام الجرد الذي تتبعه المنشأة على طريقة حساب تكلفة البضاعة المباعة؟

السؤال الثامن: أعط أمثلة على الصناعات التي يمكن أن تستخدم طريقة محاسبة الأوامر الإنتاجية.

السؤال التاسع: ناقش مدى مسايرة معالجة التكاليف المحملة بالزيادة أو النقص التي وردت في هذا الفصل مع المبادئ المحاسبية المتعارف عليها.

السؤال العاشر: استخدمت شركة الصناعات الأردنية التكاليف التالية خلال إحدى فترات التكاليف:

مواد مباشرة	٢٢٨,٠٠٠ د
أجور مباشرة	٢٤٠,٠٠٠ د وتمثل تكلفة ١٢٠,٠٠٠ ساعة
تكاليف صناعية غير مباشرة فعلية	٣٦٥,٠٠٠ د

وتقوم الشركة بتحميل التكاليف الصناعية غير المباشرة على الإنتاج بواقع ٣ د لكل ساعة عمل مباشرة.

المطلوب:

١. تصوير حساب الإنتاج تحت التشغيل.

٢. تحديد التكاليف الصناعية غير المباشرة المحملة بالزيادة أو النقص.

٣. عمل قيد اليومية اللازمة لإقفال حسابات التكاليف الصناعية غير المباشرة ومعالجة الفرق في حساب تكلفة البضاعة المباعة.

السؤال الحادي عشر: تم الحصول على المعلومات الآتية من سجلات إحدى الشركات الصناعية:

حسابات البضاعة	مواد	أجور	تكاليف غير مباشرة محملة	إجمالي
إنتاج تحت التشغيل	٥٠,٠٠٠	٥٩,٧٥٠	٤٤,٢٥٠	١٥٤,٠٠٠
إنتاج تام الصنع	١١٠,٠٠٠	١٦٨,٠٠٠	١١٨,٠٠٠	٣٩٦,٠٠٠
بضاعة مباعة	٥٤٠,٠٠٠	٦٨٢,٢٥٠	٤٢٧,٧٥٠	١٦٥٠,٠٠٠
الإجمالي	٧٠٠,٠٠٠	٩١٠,٠٠٠	٥٩٠,٠٠٠	٢,٢٠٠,٠٠٠

وكانت التكاليف الصناعية غير المباشرة محملة بالزيادة بمبلغ ٣٣,٠٠٠ دينار.

المطلوب:

١. تحديد قيمة الأعباء الإضافية الفعلية وعمل قيد اليومية اللازم لإقفال الحسابات إذا اعتبر أن الفرق السابق غير جوهري.

٢. توزيع الفرق السابق على جميع حسابات البضاعة باستخدام الرصيد النهائي.

٣. توزيع الفرق السابق على جميع حسابات البضاعة باستخدام التكاليف غير المباشرة المحملة.

السؤال الثاني عشر: تقوم إحدى الشركات الصناعية باستخدام نظام الأوامر الإنتاجية وتعمل على تحميل الأوامر الإنتاجية بالأعباء الإضافية باستخدام معدل تحميل يستند على ساعات العمل المباشرة وخلال عام ٢٠٠٧ كان معدل التحميل يساوي ٤د/س ع م (١٢٠,٠٠٠ دينار على ٣٠,٠٠٠ ساعة عمل مباشرة). وخلال العام عملت الشركة على الأمر الإنتاجي رقم ١٠٨ وحصل هذا الأمر على ٢٠٠٠ د مواد مباشرة، ١٥٠ ساعة عمل مباشر بمعدل ٣ د للساعة. ويحتوي الأمر على ٦١٠ وحدات.

المطلوب:

١. عمل قيود اليومية اللازمة لتحديد تكلفة الأمر وتحويله إلى المخازن.

٢. تحديد تكلفة وحدة المنتج.

السؤال الثالث عشر: الآتي بعض العمليات التي جرت خلال شهر آذار في إحدى الشركات الصناعية:

- تم شراء مواد خام مباشرة بمبلغ ١٧٠,٠٠٠ د نقداً.

- تم صرف ١٤٥,٠٠٠ د مواد مباشرة إلى أوامر الإنتاج.

- بلغت الأجور الفعلية خلال الشهر ٨٤,٠٠٠ د منها ٧٠,٠٠٠ د أجوراً مباشرة والباقي أجوراً غير مباشرة. وتم دفع هذه الأجور نقداً في نهاية الشهر.

- بلغت المصروفات الصناعية غير المباشرة الأخرى خلال الشهر ١٠٤,١٨٠د. بما فيها الاستهلاك وقدره ٢٠,٠٠٠ د وجميع المصروفات الأخرى سجلت على الحساب.

- تقوم الشركة بتحميل المصروفات الصناعية غير المباشرة على أساس الأجور المباشرة وبمعدل مقداره ١,٨ ديناراً لكل دينار من الأجور مباشرة.

- كانت أرصدة أول المدة تتكون من: ٣٠,٠٠٠ د مواد خام مباشرة، ٤٠,٠٠٠ د إنتاج تحت التشغيل و ١٠,٠٠٠ د بضاعة تامة الصنع وأن رصيد حساب إنتاج تحت التشغيل آخر المدة ٥٠,٠٠٠ د.

- وكانت تكلفة البضاعة المباعة ٣٢٠,٠٠٠ د وتحقق الشركة نسبة مجمل ربح على مبيعاتها مقدارها ٢٥%.

المطلوب:

١. عمل قيود اليومية اللازمة لإثبات العمليات السابقة.

٢. تصوير حسابات الأستاذ العام.

٣. تحديد قيمة المخزون التي يجب أن تظهر في الميزانية إذا اعتبر فرق التحميل جوهرياً وأنه يوزع على أساس الأرصدة النهائية لحسابات البضاعة.

السؤال الرابع عشر: تتكون إحدى الشركات من قسمين وتستخدم نظام محاسبة الأوامر الإنتاجية وتقوم بتحميل الأوامر بنصيبها في الأعباء الإضافية باستخدام معدل تحميل محدد مقدماً حيث تستخدم ساعات العمل المباشر في المركز أ وساعات دوران الآلات في مركز ب لحساب معدلات التحميل، وفي بداية العام تم إعداد التقديرات الآتية لمراكز الإنتاج:

	مركز ب	مركز أ
الأجور المباشرة	١٨٠,٠٠٠	١٥٠,٠٠٠
المواد المباشرة	٢٠٠,٠٠٠	٢٥٠,٠٠٠
الأعباء الإضافية	٢٠٠,٠٠٠	١٦٥,٠٠٠
ساعات دوران الآلات	٢٥,٠٠٠	٢٦٣,٠٠٠
ساعات العمل المباشر	١٢,٠٠٠	٦٠,٠٠٠

وخلال السنة تم العمل على الأمر الإنتاجي رقم ١٧٢ وتم الحصول على المعلومات الآتية من بطاقة هذا الأمر.

	مركز ب	مركز أ
ساعات دوران الآلات	٣٠٠	١٠٠٠
ساعات العمل المباشر	٢٥٠	٢٢٨
المواد المباشرة	٢٨٧٥	٣٥١٢
الأجور المباشرة	٤٥٨٠	٢٥٦٠

المطلوب :

١. تحديد معدل التحميل لكل قسم من الأقسام.

٢. تحديد الأعباء المحملة على الأمر من القسمين.

٣. تحديد التكلفة الكلية لهذا الأمر الإنتاجي.

السؤال الخامس عشر: يتم تنظيم العمل في الشركة المتحدة للأثاث باستخدام طريقة الأوامر الإنتاجية وكان لديها في أول المدة الأوامر ٢٢١، ٣٢١ وتكاليفهما ٢١,٠٠٠ د ٢٣,٠٠٠ د على التوالي، وخلال فترة التكاليف الجارية تم العمل على الأمر رقم ٤٢١، وبلغت التكاليف التي تم تحميلها على الأوامر الإنتاجية خلال الفترة الجارية كالتالي:

	الأمر ٢٢١	الأمر ٣٢١	الأمر ٤٢١
مواد مباشرة	٩,٠٠٠	١٠,٠٠٠	٨,٠٠٠
أجور مباشرة (بواقع ٢ د ساعة)	٢,٨٠٠	٦,٣٠٠	٤,٢٠٠

- وكانت الشركة تقوم بتحميل التكاليف الصناعية غير المباشرة على أساس ٣د/س ع م وبلغت التكاليف غير المباشرة الفعلية للفترة الجارية ٢٠,٠٠٠ دينار.
- وفي نهاية المدة بقي الأمر ٤٢١ تحت التشغيل وانتهى إنتاج الأوامر الأخرى.

المطلوب:

١. تحديد رصيد حساب الإنتاج تحت التشغيل آخر المدة.

٢. تحديد التكاليف غير المباشرة المحملة بالزيادة أو النقص.

٣. تحديد تكلفة كل أمر من الأوامر على حدة.

السؤال السادس عشر: تتبع إحدى الشركات طريقة محاسبة الأوامر الإنتاجية وتوفرت في سجلاتها البيانات التالية:

- يتم تحميل التكاليف الصناعية غير المباشرة باستخدام ساعات دوران الآلات، وبلغت الموازنة التقديرية لهذه التكاليف ٧٥,٠٠٠ د. كما بلغت ساعات دوران الآلات التقديرية لمستوى الطاقة العادية ٢٥,٠٠٠ ساعة.

- بلغ رصيد حساب الإنتاج تحت التشغيل أول المدة ٩,٣٥٠ د. وتمثل ٤,٥٠٠د تكلفة الأمر ٢١١، ٤,٨٥٠د تكلفة الأمر ٢١٢ وخلال الفترة الجارية جرت العمليات التالية:

- تم بدء العمل على الأمر رقم ٢١٣.

- تم شراء مواد مباشرة بمبلغ ٢٥,٠٠٠ د على الحساب وصرف منها المبالغ التالية للأوامر الإنتاجية:

د٤٠٠٠	أمر٢١١
د٣٥٠٠	أمر٢١٢
د٤٨٠٠	أمر٢١٣

- بلغت الأجور المباشرة للأوامر ٢١١، ٢١٢، ٢١٣ خلال الفترة ٣,٠٠٠د، ٤,٠٠٠د، ٥,٠٠٠د على التوالي.

وبلغت ساعات دوران الآلات التي استفادت منها الأوامر ٢١١، ٢١٢، ٢١٣ ٢٠٠٠ ساعة، ٣٠٠٠ ساعة، ٥٠٠٠ ساعة على التوالي.

- تم بيع الأمر ٢١١ إلى العميل بمبلغ ٢٢,٥٠٠ د نقداً.

- تم تحويل الأمر ٢١٢ إلى المخازن وهو يتكون من ١٠٠٠ وحدة وقد تم بيع ٦٠٠ وحدة منها بسعر ٢٦ د للواحدة.

المطلوب:

١. عمل قيود اليومية اللازمة لإثبات الحقائق السابقة.

٢. تصوير حسابات الأوامر وحساب الإنتاج تحت التشغيل.

٣. إعداد قائمة تكلفة البضاعة المباعة.

٤. تحديد رقم مجمل الربح.

السؤال السابع عشر: تقوم إحدى الشركات بتحديد تكاليف وحدة المنتج بقسمة إجمالي تكاليف الإنتاج على عدد الوحدات المنتجة والتي يتم تحديدها كل ثلاثة أشهر وأستغرب مدير الشركة من ذبذبة تكلفة الوحدة والتي تم حسابها كما يلي (البيانات بالألف).

	الربع الأول	الربع الثاني	الربع الثالث	الربع الرابع	الإجمالي
مواد مباشرة	١,٨٠٠	١,٢٠٠	١,٥٠٠	٢,١٠٠	٦,٦٠٠
أجور مباشرة	١,٢٠٠	٨٠٠	١,٠٠٠	١,٤٠٠	٤,٤٠٠
أعباء صناعية متغيرة	٩٠٠	٦٠٠	٧٥٠	١,٠٥٠	٣,٣٠٠
أعباء صناعية ثابتة	٢,٠٠٠	٢,٠٠٠	٢,٠٠٠	٢,٠٠٠	٨,٠٠٠
إجمالي التكاليف	٥,٩٠٠	٤,٦٠٠	٥,٢٥٠	٦,٥٥٠	٢٢,٣٠٠
÷ عدد الوحدات	٦٠٠	٤٠٠	٥٠٠	٧٠٠	٢,٢٠٠
= تكلفة الوحدة	٩,٨٣	١١,٥	١٠,٥	٩,٣٤	١٠,١٤

المطلوب:

ما هي اقتراحاتك بخصوص هذه الشركة وما هي تكلفة وحدة الإنتاج حسب الطريقة التي تقترحها.

السؤال الثامن عشر: تستخدم إحدى الشركات طريقة الأوامر الإنتاجية وخلال عام ٢٠٠٨ كانت سجلاتها تحتوي على الأرقام التالية:

	الأوامر المنتهية	الأوامر تحت التشغيل آخر المدة	البضاعة المباعة
المواد	٢٠٠,٠٠٠	١٠٠,٠٠	٢٠٠,٠٠٠
الأجور المباشرة	٦٠٠,٠٠٠	٢٥٠,٠٠٠	٣٠٠,٠٠٠

وكانت الشركة تستخدم قيمة الأجور المباشرة كأساس لتحميل الأعباء الإضافية، وإن معدل التحميل يبلغ ٨٠٪ من قيمة الأجور المباشرة. وقد بلغت الأعباء الإضافية الفعلية خلال العام ٩٥٠,٠٠٠ دينار.

المطلوب:

١. تحميل حسابات البضاعة بنصيبها من الأعباء الإضافية ثم تحديد أرصدة هذه الحسابات.

٢. توزيع الأعباء الإضافية المحملة بالزيادة أو النقص على أساس الأرصدة النهائية لحسابات البضاعة.

السؤال التاسع عشر: ترغب شركة في إعداد معدل تحميل مستقل لكل مركز من مراكزها، لذلك أعدت التقديرات التالية لمستوى الطاقة العادية للمراكز.

المنشأة	مركز ب	مركز أ	
٣١,٠٠٠	٥,٠٠٠	٢٦,٠٠٠	مواد غير مباشرة
١٩,٠٠٠	١,٠٠٠	١٨,٠٠٠	أجور غير مباشرة
٧,٠٠٠	٣,٠٠٠	٤,٠٠٠	إيجار
٢,٥٠٠	١,٠٠٠	١,٥٠٠	تأمين
١٤,٥٠٠	١٢,٠٠٠	٢,٥٠٠	وقود وقوى محركة
٣٤,٠٠٠	٢٦,٠٠٠	٨,٠٠٠	إستهلاكات
١٠٨,٠٠٠	٤٨,٠٠٠	٦٠,٠٠٠	الإجمالي
	٢٥,٠٠٠	٣٠,٠٠٠	ساعات العمل المباشرة
	١٢,٠٠٠	١٠,٠٠٠	ساعات دوران الآلات

المطلوب:

١- حساب معدل تحميل مستقل لكل مركز وللمنشأة باستخدام:
(أ) ساعات العمل المباشرة.
(ب) ساعات دوران الآلات.

٢- أي من هذه الأسس أفضل لتحميل الأعباء الإضافية؟

السؤال العشرون: افترض أن المنشأة في السؤال السابق قررت تحميل تكاليف المركز أ باستخدام ساعات العمل المباشرة وتحميل تكاليف المركز ب باستخدام ساعات دوران الآلات وأن أحد الأوامر الإنتاج استخدم ٥٠٠ ساعة عمل مباشرة من مركز أ، ١,٢٥٠ ساعة دوران آلة من مركز ب.

المطلوب: تحديد قيمة الأعباء الإضافية التي سيتم تحميلها على الأمر الإنتاجي من المركزين المذكورين.

السؤال الحادي والعشرون: تتبع شركة طريقة محاسبة الأوامر الإنتاجية وتقوم الشركة بإقفال الأعباء الإضافية المحملة بالزيادة أو النقص في حساب تكلفة البضاعة المباعة. وتقوم بتحميل الأعباء الإضافية بمعدل ٣ د لكل ساعة عمل مباشرة وأجرة ساعة العمل المباشر ٤د. والآتي معلومات من دفاتر هذه الشركة.

الأعباء الإضافية الفعلية	؟
الأعباء الإضافية المحملة	؟
أرصدة بضاعة (مخزون) أول المدة:	
إنتاج تحت التشغيل	١٠٠,٠٠٠
بضاعة تامة الصنع	١٠٠,٠٠٠
أرصدة بضاعة آخر المدة:	
إنتاج تحت التشغيل	٣٠٠,٠٠٠
بضاعة تامة الصنع	١٥٠,٠٠٠
تكلفة بضاعة مباعة بعد طرح ١٠,٠٠٠ د أعباء إضافية محملة بالزيادة	٦٤٠,٠٠٠
مواد مباشرة	٣٠٠,٠٠٠
تكلفة بضاعة تامة الصنع خلال الفترة الجارية	؟

المطلوب: تحديد قيمة الأرقام المجهولة في القائمة السابقة.

السؤال الثاني والعشرون: تقوم شركة الهندسة المعمارية بتصميم المباني والإشراف عليها أثناء البناء وتخصص حساب مقاولة (أمر إنتاجي) لكل مبنى تقوم بالإشراف عليه يعرف باسم صاحب المقاولة. يتم تحميل الأوامر بنصيبها من الأجور باستخدام كشف العمل الأسبوعي الذي يعده المهندس يثبت فيه ساعات العمل التي قضاها على كل مشروع، يقوم بالإشراف عليه ويتم تسعير ساعات عمل الإشراف بقسمة الراتب السنوي لمهندس الإشراف على ساعات عمله الرسمية ومقدارها ٢٤٠٠ ساعة (٣٠٠ يوم عمل بواقع ٨ ساعات يومياً)، وفي نهاية كل أسبوع يقوم المحاسب بتحديد ساعات الإشراف للمهندسين على المشروعات وتحميلها عليهم أما المهندسون الذين يشرفون بصورة دائمة على مشروع معين فتحمل رواتبهم على تلك المشاريع (الأوامر) مباشرة.

أما الأعباء الإضافية فيتم تحميلها على مشروعات الإشراف وعلى التصميم حسب قيمة الأجور المباشرة وهي أجور المشرفين والمقيمين في المواقع وفي إحدى السنوات قدرت المصروفات غير المباشرة للمكتب بمبلغ ٦٠,٠٠٠ دينار كما قدرت الأجور المباشرة بمبلغ ٤٠,٠٠٠ د وبلغ معدل أجر الساعة للمهندسين ٥ دنانير. وخلال الفترة حصلت الشركة على ثلاثة مشروعات وتم تجميع المعلومات التالية عنها:

المشروع	١	٢	٣
مواد مباشرة	١٠٠	٢٥٠	٤٠٠
أجور مشرفين ومقيمين	٢,٠٠٠د	٣,٠٠٠د	٤,٠٠٠د
ساعات المهندسين	١٥٠	٢٠٠	٣٠٠

وقد تم الانتهاء من العمل على المشروعين ١، ٢ وبقي المشروع ٣ تحت التشغيل.

المطلوب:

١. إعداد قيود اليومية اللازمة لإثبات الحقائق السابقة وتصوير الحسابات المناسبة.

٢. تحديد تكلفة المشاريع التامة.

السؤال الثالث والعشرون: تستخدم إحدى الشركات معدل تحميل للأعباء الإضافية وتقوم بتوزيع الأعباء الإضافية المحملة بالزيادة على حسابات البضاعة حسب أرصدتها النهائية.

والآتي بعض الأرصدة المتعلقة بالبضاعة والأعباء المحملة وذلك قبل توزيع الفرق بين الأعباء الفعلية والمحملة.

تكلفة البضاعة المباعة   ٨٠٠,٠٠٠د

المخزون في آخر المدة:

مواد مباشرة   ١٠٠,٠٠٠د

إنتاج تام   ١٥٠,٠٠٠د

إنتاج تحت التشغيل   ٥٠,٠٠٠د

أعباء فعلية   ٦١٠,٠٠٠د

أعباء محملة   ٦٥٥,٠٠٠د

فإن تكلفة البضاعة المباعة التي سوف تظهر في قائمة الدخل هي:

أ- ٨٣٦,٠٠٠ د   ب- ٧٦٤,٠٠٠ د

جـ- ٨٤٥,٠٠٠ د   د- ٧٥٥,٠٠٠ د

السؤال الرابع والعشرون: تستخدم شركة النيل معدل تحميل للأعباء الإضافية باستخدام ساعات العمل المباشر. وفي نهاية السنة كانت الأعباء المخططة ٥٠٠,٠٠٠ د وحجم الإنتاج المخطط يساوي ٥٠,٠٠٠ ساعة عمل مباشر وأن أجرة ساعة العمل المباشر ٥ دنانير. وقد بلغت الأعباء الفعلية ٤٨٠,٠٠٠ دينار والأجور الفعلية ٢٤٥,٠٠٠ دينار ولم يتغير معدل الأجور عن المعدل المخطط، **فإن الأعباء الفعلية كانت خلال العام كالتالي:**

أ- محملة بالنقص بمبلغ ١٠,٠٠٠ د   ب- محملة بالنقص ٥٠٠٠ د

جـ- محملة بالزيادة بمبلغ ٥٠٠٠ د   د- محملة بالزيادة بمبلغ ١٠,٠٠٠د

السؤال الخامس العشرون: . تستخدم شركة نظام محاسبة الأوامر الإنتاجية وأظهر حساب الإنتاج تحت التشغيل المعلومات الآتية:

رصيد أول المدة	١٤,٠٠٠د	
مواد مباشرة	٦٠,٠٠٠د	
أعباء صناعية وأجور	١٥٢,٠٠٠د	
بضاعة تامة ومحولة	٢٢٠,٠٠٠د	

ويتم تحميل الأعباء الإضافية بنسبة ٩٠٪ من تكلفة الأجور المباشرة. وقد بقي في آخر المدة أوامر تم تحميلها بمبلغ ١,٨٠٠ دينار أعباء إضافية لذلك **فإن تكلفة المواد المباشرة المحملة على هذه الأوامر هي:**

أ- ٢٨٥٠   ب- ٢٥٨٠

جـ- ٢٢٠٠   د- ٢٥٠٠

الفصل الرابع
محاسبة المراحل الإنتاجية

اهداف الفصل:

بعد دراسة هذا الفصل يجب أن تكون قادرا على:

١- معرفة السمات الرئيسة لصناعة المراحل الإنتاجية.

٢- حساب الوحدات المكافئة.

٣- استخدام طريقة المتوسط المرجح وطريقة الوارد أولاً صادر أولاً عند حساب تكاليف وحدات الإنتاج في صناعة المراحل.

٤- إعداد تقارير تكاليف المراحل الإنتاجية حسب طريقة المتوسط المرجح وطريقة الوارد أولاً صادر أولاً.

٥- معرفة الدورة المحاسبية لمحاسبة تكاليف المراحل.

٦- أثر استخدام عدة مواد على محاسبة المراحل.

٧- اثر تحويل الوحدات بين المراحل على محاسبة المراحل.

مقدمـــة :

يتم استخدام طريقة محاسبة المراحل الإنتاجية Process costing عندما يكون الإنتاج مستمراً وتكون الوحدات المنتجة متماثلة، وهذه الصفات تجعل كل وحدة تحتاج إلى نفس ما تحتاجه الوحدة الأخرى من التكاليف. ولذلك تقوم هذه الطريقة بحصر التكاليف التي تحدث خلال فترة زمنية معينة في قسم إنتاجي وقسمتها على عدد الوحدات التي تستفيد من تكاليف هذه الفترة للتوصل إلى تكلفة الوحدة، يتم عادة تقسيم المصنع إلى مناطق عمل متخصصة تعرف كل واحدة منها باسم المرحلة، بحيث يكون لكل مرحلة هدف معين، ففي صناعة الأسمنت مثلاً هناك مرحلة للطحن ومرحلة للتحميص ومرحلة للتعبئة، وفي صناعة تكرير البترول هناك مرحلة لتقطير البترول الخام ومراحل أخرى لتحسين البنزين، وإنتاج الزيوت المعدنية.

تدفق الإنتاج

يقصد بالتدفق الحركة فقد يتحرك الإنتاج في صناعة المراحل بين عدة أقسام إنتاجية متتالية فيبدأ في المرحلة الأولى، وبعدها يحول إلى المرحلة الثانية ثم إلى المرحلة التي بعدها وهكذا حتى يصل الإنتاج إلى مخازن المنتجات التامة الصنع. وفي حالات أخرى يمر الإنتاج في مراحل متوازية أو عشوائية وفي النهاية يتم تجميعه في مرحلة التجميع النهائي ليحول إلى مخازن المنتجات التامة الصنع. على أية حال، لا تؤثر طريقة حركة أو تدفق وحدات الإنتاج على إجراءات المحاسبة على تكاليف المنتجات بصورة جوهرية، لأن كل مرحلة تعتبر وحدة محاسبية مستقلة. ففي كل مرحلة يتم حصر الوحدات التي عملت عليها المرحلة وحصر تكاليف تشغيل المرحلة خلال الفترة. وإذا تم تحويل الوحدات التامة الصنع إلى مرحلة أخرى يتم تحويل تكلفتها معها إلى تلك المرحلة، تعرف التكاليف الوحدات التي تحول الى مرحلة تالية باسم التكاليف المستلمة أو التكاليف المحولة.

سمات نظام تكاليف المراحل:

تتميز طريقة محاسبة المراحل عن طريقة محاسبة الأوامر بما يلي:

(١) تستخدم طريقة المراحل الإنتاجية في حالة تجانس الوحدات المنتجة، بينما تستخدم طريقة الأوامر الإنتاجية في حالة تنوع المنتجات واختلاف مواصفاتها من أمر إنتاجي إلى آخر.

(٢) تركز محاسبة المراحل على تكاليف المرحلة الإنتاجية خلال فترة التكاليف بينما تركز محاسبة الأوامر الإنتاجية على التكاليف التي تخص الأمر الإنتاجي.

(٣) تحدد تكلفة الوحدة في صناعة المراحل بقسمة تكاليف المرحلة خلال فترة معينة على عدد الوحدات الانتاج المكافئ التي تستفيد من تكاليف تلك الفترة، بينما يتم تحديد تكلفة الوحدة في طريقة الأوامر بقسمة تكلفة الأمر الإنتاجي على عدد الوحدات وهذه الوحدات تختلف من أمر الى آخر .

(٤) تستخدم طريقة المراحل تقرير التكاليف لتلخيص تكاليف المرحلة ، بينما تستخدم طريقة محاسبة الأوامر بطاقة تكلفة الأمر لتلخيص التكاليف المحملة على كل امر.

(٥) لاستخدام الاجور المباشرة والأعباء الصناعية بصورة منتظمة في الانتاج يتم دمجهما في مجموعة واحدة تعرف بتكاليف التحويل.

حسابات التكاليف في صناعة المراحل:

ولتوضيح الإجراءات المحاسبية سيتم عرض قيود اليومية التي يتم استخدامها لتسجيل تكاليف هذه المراحل من مواد مباشرة وأجور ومصروفات غير مباشرة.

المواد المباشرة:

يتم صرف المواد المباشرة من المخازن بموجب إذن صرف مواد، ويحتوي هذا الإذن على حقول تبين الكمية التي يتم صرفها والجهة أو المرحلة المستفيدة، وبعد صرف المواد يتم إرسال نسخة من إذن الصرف إلى محاسب التكاليف ليقوم بتسعير المواد المصروفة وتحميل تكلفتها على المرحلة المستفيدة بموجب قيد اليومية التالي:

حـ/ الإنتاج تحت التشغيل مرحلة أ		×
حـ/ الإنتاج تحت التشغيل مرحلة ب		×
حـ/ مراقبة المواد	×	

قد يتم عمل هذا القيد من واقع اذونات الصرف مباشرة أو بعد تلخيصها في كشف تفريغ أذونات صرف المواد المباشرة الذي يصمم لهذا الغرض.

الأجور المباشرة:

يتم تحميل المرحلة بتكاليف أجور العاملين فيها سواء كانوا يعملون على الإنتاج بصورة مباشرة أو بصورة غير مباشرة، وهذا يجعل أنه ليس من الضروري مسك بطاقات وقت العمل لتتبع الأعمال التي يقوم بها العمال خلال اوقات العمل كما هو الحال في صناعة الأوامر الإنتاجية، وهنا يتم حصر دوام العمال عن طريق التوقيع على سجلات الحضور والانصراف أو بطاقات الدوام، ولتسهيل تحميل الأجور على المراحل يتم إعداد أجور كل مرحلة على حدة، وبعد إعدادها يتم تسجيل هذه الأجور بقيد اليومية التالي:

حـ/ الإنتاج تحت التشغيل مرحلة أ		×
حـ/ الإنتاج تحت التشغيل مرحلة ب		×
حـ/ مراقبة الأجور	×	

التكاليف الصناعية غير المباشرة:

يتم تقسيم التكاليف الصناعية غير المباشرة (الاعباء الاضافية) في محاسبة المراحل إلى مجموعتين: الأولى وتشمل العناصر التي تعتبر مباشرة على المرحلة مثل: استهلاك آلاتها ومعداتها، والمواد والمهمات المصروفة خصيصاً لها، أما المجموعة الثانية فإنها تضم عناصر التكاليف التي تصرف لخدمة أكثر من مرحلة إنتاجية مثل: إيجار المباني

التي تقع فيها المراحل، ونصيبها من تكاليف اقسام الخدمات مثل قسم الصيانة، والهندسة والنظافة وإدارة الإنتاج. ولحساب تكلفة الانتاج يجب توزيع مجموعة التكاليف الأخيرة على المراحل المختلفة المستفيدة ويتم تحميل هذه التكاليف على المراحل المستفيدة بقيد اليومية التالي:

حـ/ الإنتاج تحت التشغيل مرحلة أ		×
حـ/ الإنتاج تحت التشغيل مرحلة ب		×
حـ/ مراقبة التكاليف الصناعية غير المباشرة	×	

تقرير تكاليف المرحلة:

يستخدم تقرير تكاليف المرحلة لتلخيص تكاليف المرحلة وحصر الوحدات التي استفادت من نشاط المرحلة خلال فترة التكاليف وتحديد تكاليف الإنتاج التام وتكاليف الإنتاج تحت التشغيل، ويمكن تقسيمه إلى خمس خطوات كالتالي: [١]

(١) التدفق المادي.

(٢) الإنتاج المكافئ.

(٣) تكاليف المرحلة.

(٤) تكلفة الوحدة المكافئة.

(٥) تكلفة الإنتاج التام والإنتاج تحت التشغيل آخر المدة

يتم إعداد تقرير تكاليف المرحلة بطريقتين هما طريقة المتوسط المرجح وطريقة الأول في الأول. تقوم طريقة المتوسط المرجح بإضافة رصيد حساب الإنتاج تحت التشغيل أول المدة الى تكاليف الفترة الجارية وإضافة الوحدات تحت التشغيل اول المدة الى الوحدات التي يتم إضافتها ويبدأ تشغيلها خلال الفترة الجارية. أما في طريقة الأول في الأول فلا يتم عمل ذلك حيث تتم المحاسبة على الوحدات تحت التشغيل أول المدة بصورة مستقلة عن الوحدات الأخرى التي اضيفت الى المرحلة خلال الفترة الجارية . ولتوضيح كيفية

─────────
[١] هورنجرن، تشارلز، ص ص. ٦٤١-٦٥٠.

إعداد تقرير تكاليف المرحلة حسب طريقتي المتوسط المرجح وطريقة الأول في الأول سيتم الاعتماد على البيانات التالية:

مثال (١):

كانت حركة الوحدات المادية والتكاليف خلال إحدى فترات التكاليف كالتالي:

وحدات تحت التشغيل أول المدة	٥,٠٠٠ (٦٠٪)
وحدات بدأت الإنتاج خلال الفترة	١٥,٠٠٠
وحدات تامة محولة	١٦,٠٠٠
وحدات تحت التشغيل آخر المدة	٤,٠٠٠ (٧٥٪)

يتكون رصيد حساب الإنتاج تحت التشغيل أول المدة من ٢٢,٥٠٠ د مواد مباشرة ٤٢,٤٠٠د تكاليف تحويل (أجور مباشرة زائد تكاليف صناعية غير مباشرة). وبلغت تكاليف الفترة الجارية كالتالي:

مواد مباشرة	٦٠,٠٠٠د
تكاليف تحويل	١٨٥,٦٠٠ د

وتضاف المواد الخام في بداية المرحلة وتضاف تكاليف التحويل بانتظام.

المطلوب: إعداد تقرير تكاليف المرحلة أ حسب طريقة المتوسط المرجح ثم باستخدام طريقة الأول في الأول.

أولاً: طريقة المتوسط المرجح

الحل: سيتم عرض خطوات إعداد تقرير تكاليف المرحلة حسب الخطوات السابقة على التوالي.

الخطوة الأولى: حصر الوحدات المادية:

يمكن بيان حركة التدفق المادي باستخدام شكل حرف Z الكبيرة.

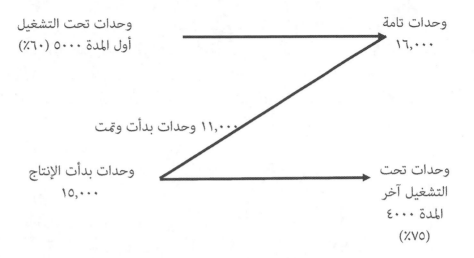

وحدات تامة
١٦,٠٠٠

وحدات تحت التشغيل أول المدة ٥٠٠٠ (٦٠٪)

١١,٠٠٠ وحدات بدأت وتمت

وحدات بدأت الإنتاج
١٥,٠٠٠

وحدات تحت التشغيل آخر المدة ٤٠٠٠ (٧٥٪)

الشكل (٤-١) تدفق وحدات الإنتاج

نرى من الشكل (٤-١) أن مجموع وحدات الإنتاج تحت التشغيل أول المدة والوحدات التي بدأت الانتاج خلال المدة يساوي عدد تحت التشغيل آخر المدة والوحدات التامة الصنع. وان الوحدات التامة الصنع تتكون من وحدات، تحت التشغيل اول المدة زائد وحدات بدات وتمت (٥٠٠٠= اول المدة + ١١,٠٠٠ بدات وتمت). وان الوحدات التي بدات الانتاج تحولت الى مجموعتين الاولى وهي وحدات بقيت تحت التشغيل آخر المدة وعددها ٤,٠٠٠ وحدة، والمجموعة الثانية وهي الوحدات التي بدات وتمت وتساوي ١١,٠٠٠ (١٥,٠٠٠= – ٤,٠٠٠) وحدة. مما سبق نجد أن الوحدات المادية التي تستفيد من تكاليف تشغيل المرحلة تقع في مجموعتين هما: الوحدات تحت التشغيل أول المدة، والوحدات الجديدة التي يبدأ إنتاجها خلال الفترة الجارية، ويعرف مجموع هذه الوحدات باسم الوحدات التي سيتم المحاسبة عليها. يطلق على مجموع الوحدات التامة الصنع ووحدات تحت التشغيل آخر المدة، اسم الوحدات التي تم المحاسبة عليها. ولذلك يجب أن يتساوى مجموع الوحدات التي سيتم المحاسبة عليها مع مجموع الوحدات التي تم المحاسبة عليها. وقد ظهرت هذه الارقام على يسار ويمين الشكل ٤-١على التوالي. وتظهر حركة الوحدات في تقرير تكاليف المرحلة كالتالي:

وحدات تحت التشغيل أول المدة	5,000 (60%)
وحدات بدأت الإنتاج خلال المدة	15,000
وحدات سيتم المحاسبة عليها	20,000
وحدات تامة محولة	16,000
وحدات تحت التشغيل آخر المدة	4,000 (75%)
وحدات تم المحاسبة عليها	20,000

تشير النسبة المئوية المرتبطة بوحدات الإنتاج تحت التشغيل أول المدة أو آخر المدة إلى مستوى إتمامها الذي وصلته في نهاية الفترة السابقة والجارية على التوالي. وعليه فإن الوحدات تحت التشغيل آخر المدة حصلت على 75% مما تحتاجه الوحدة التامة من عناصر تكاليف التحويل (أجور مباشرة وأعباء إضافية). وحصلت على 100% من المواد المباشرة، لأن المواد المباشرة تضاف في بداية عملية التشغيل. ففي صناعة الأقمشة مثلاً يتم إضافة الخيوط في بداية عملية الإنتاج، اذن هنا تضاف المواد في بداية عملية التشغيل.

ثانياً: الوحدات المكافئة:

لتحديد متوسط تكلفة الوحدة، يجب تحديد عدد الوحدات التي سيتم قسمة التكاليف عليها، والمشكلة التي تواجهنا هي أن استفادة الوحدات من تكاليف التشغيل خلال الفترة الجارية تختلف عن بعضها، حيث نجد أن الوحدات التي بدأت وتمت تحصل على كل ما تحتاجه من مواد وتكاليف أخرى خلال الفترة الجارية، أما وحدات تحت التشغيل آخر المدة فإنها تحصل على نسبة أقل من ذلك. ولذلك لا نستطيع القسمة على مجموع هذه الوحدات بدون عمل الاجراءات اللازمة. وللتغلب على هذه المشكلة يتم تحويل هذه الوحدات الى ما يسمى بالوحدات المكافئة وذلك بضرب كل نوع من هذه الوحدات في نسبة إتمامه ، وباستخدام بيانات المثال رقم (1) يتم حساب الوحدات المكافئة كالتالي:
الوحدات المكافئة = وحدات الإنتاج التام× 100% + وحدات تحت التشغيل آخر المدة × نسبة إتمامها.

المواد   =   ١٦,٠٠٠× ١٠٠٪ + ٤٠٠٠ × ١٠٠٪ = ٢٠,٠٠٠ وحدة

تكاليف تحويل= ١٦,٠٠٠ × ١٠٠٪ + ٤٠٠٠ × ٧٥٪   = ١٩,٠٠٠ وحدة

ولان الضرب في ١٠٠٪ لا يؤثر على الرقم لذلك سيتم إغفاله. وتظهر هذه العمليات الحسابية في تقرير تكاليف المرحلة كالتالي:

	إجمالي	مواد	تكاليف تحويل
وحدات تامة الصنع(× ١٠٠٪)	١٦,٠٠٠	١٦,٠٠٠	١٦,٠٠٠
وحدات تحت التشغيل آخر المدة (٧٥٪)	٤,٠٠٠	٤,٠٠٠	٣,٠٠٠
الوحدات المكافئة	٢٠,٠٠٠	٢٠,٠٠٠	١٩,٠٠٠

ثالثا تكاليف المرحلة:

لاحظ أنه قد تم إضافة وحدات تحت التشغيل أول المدة إلى الوحدات التي بدأت وتمت وكأنها بدأت العمل خلال الفترة الجارية. ولذلك تتكون تكاليف المرحلة عند إتباع طريقة المتوسط من مجموع رصيد حساب إنتاج تحت التشغيل أول المدة وتكاليف الفترة الجارية، ويظهر هذا الجزء في تقرير تكاليف المرحلة كالتالي:

	الإجمالي	المواد	تكاليف التحويل
رصيد إنتاج تحت التشغيل أول المدة	٦٤,٩٠٠	٢٢,٥٠٠	٤٢,٤٠٠
تكاليف الفترة الجارية	٢٤٥,٦٠٠	٦٠,٠٠٠	١٨٥,٦٠٠
إجمالي التكاليف	٣١٠,٥٠٠	٨٢,٥٠٠	٢٢٨,٠٠٠

رابعاً: تكلفة الوحدة:

يتم تحديد تكلفة الوحدة في الخطوة الرابعة في تقرير تكاليف المرحلة بقسمة تكاليف المواد وتكاليف التحويل على عدد وحدات الانتاج المكافئة، وتكون تكلفة الوحدة المكافئة الوحدة كالتالي:

المواد المباشرة = ٨٢,٥٠٠ ÷ ٢٠,٠٠٠ = ٤,١٢٥ د للوحدة

تكاليف التحويل= ٢٢٨,٠٠٠ ÷١٩,٠٠٠ = ١٢د للوحدة

تكلفة الوحدة التامة الصنع = ٤,١٢٥ د + ١٢ د = ١٦,١٢٥ دينار

خامساً: ملخص التكاليف:

بعد تحديد تكلفة الوحدة المكافئة يتم تلخيص تكاليف المرحلة في قسمين: الأول: ويمثل تكاليف الإنتاج التام الصنع، ويساوي عدد الوحدات التامة الصنع ضرب تكلفة الوحدة المكافئة التامة الصنع ويساوي (١٦,٠٠٠ × ١٦,١٢٥ =) ٢٥٨,٠٠٠ دينار. وفي القسم الثاني تم تحديد رصيد حساب الإنتاج تحت التشغيل آخر المدة وذلك بضرب الوحدات المكافئة الخاصة بالإنتاج تحت التشغيل آخر المدة في تكلفة الوحدة المكافئة. وفي ضوء البيانات السابقة تحدد تكلفته كالتالي:

المواد المباشرة = ٤,١٢٥ د × ٤,٠٠٠ د = ١٦,٥٠٠ د

تكاليف تحويل = ١٢ د × ٣,٠٠٠ د = ٣٦,٠٠٠ د

الإجمالي = ٥٢,٥٠٠د

بعد إنجاز الخطوات الخمس السابقة سيكون تقرير تكاليف المرحلة حسب طريقة المتوسط المرجح كما في الجدول (٤-١). ومن دراسة هذه الجدول نجد أنه قد تم دمج خطوة التدفق المادي مع خطوة تحديد الإنتاج المكافئ لأنهما ظهرا في تقرير تكاليف المرحلة في منطقة واحدة، وتم إضافة رصيد حساب الإنتاج تحت التشغيل أول المدة على تكاليف الفترة الجارية، وتم تحديد تكلفة الإنتاج التام بضرب عدد الوحدات التامة الصنع في تكلفة الوحدة التامة الصنع، وكذلك تم تحديد تكلفة الإنتاج تحت التشغيل آخر المدة كما في المثال السابق. وبعد تجهيز تقرير تكاليف المرحلة علي النحو السابق، يتم عمل قيد يومية لجعل حساب إنتاج تحت التشغيل للمرحلة أ دائناً بتكلفة الإنتاج التام، وإذا تم تحويل هذا الإنتاج إلى مرحلة ب يكون قيد اليومية كالتالي:

٢٥٨,٠٠٠	ح/ الإنتاج تحت التشغيل مرحلة ب	
	ح/ الإنتاج تحت التشغيل مرحلة أ	٢٥٨,٠٠٠

وبعد أن يتم ترحيل هذا القيد إلى حساب إنتاج تحت التشغيل مرحلة أ، يجب أن يتطابق رصيد هذا الحساب مع تكلفة الإنتاج تحت التشغيل الظاهرة في تقرير تكاليف المرحلة، ويتم ترحيل تكلفة الإنتاج التام إلى حساب إنتاج تحت التشغيل

جدول (٤-١)
تقرير تكاليف المرحلة حسب طريقة المتوسط المرجح

تكاليف تحويل	مواد مباشرة	الإجمالي	بيان
		٥,٠٠٠ (٦٠)	وحدات تحت التشغيل أول المدة
		١٥,٠٠٠	وحدات مضافة خلال الفترة الجارية
		٢٠,٠٠٠	وحدات سيتم المحاسبة عليها
١٦,٠٠٠	١٦,٠٠٠	١٦,٠٠٠	وحدات تامة محولة
٣,٠٠٠	٤,٠٠٠	٤,٠٠٠ (٧٥%)	وحدات تحت التشغيل آخر المدة
١٩,٠٠٠	٢٠,٠٠٠	٢٠,٠٠٠	وحدات تم المحاسبة عليها
			التكاليف:
٤٢,٤٠٠	٢٢,٥٠٠	٦٤,٩٠٠	رصيد إنتاج تحت التشغيل أول المدة
١٨٥,٦٠٠	٦٠,٠٠٠	٢٤٥,٦٠٠	تكاليف الفترة الجارية
٢٢٨,٠٠٠	٨٢,٥٠٠	٣١٠,٥٠٠	إجمالي تكاليف المرحلة
١٩,٠٠٠	٢٠,٠٠٠		تقسيم: عدد الوحدات المكافئة
١٢	٤,١٢٥	١٦,١٢٥	متوسط تكلفة الوحدة المكافئة
			ملخص التكاليف:
		٢٥٨,٠٠٠	تكلفة الإنتاج التام (١٦,١٢٥× ١٦,٠٠٠)
			تكلفة الإنتاج تحت التشغيل آخر المدة:
		١٦,٥٠٠	مواد مباشرة (٤,١٢٥ × ٤,٠٠٠)
		٣٦,٠٠٠	تكاليف تحويل (١٢ ×٣,٠٠٠)
		٥٢,٥٠٠	
		٣١٠,٥٠٠	تكلفة المرحلة

للمرحلة ب وأن هذه التكاليف تسمى بالتكاليف المستلمة أو المحولة في المرحلة ب. وبهذا يكون حساب الإنتاج تحت التشغيل للمرحلة أ كالتالي:

حـ / الإنتاج تحت التشغيل للمرحلة أ			
٢٥٨,٠٠٠	إنتاج تحت التشغيل مرحلة ب	٦٤,٩٠٠	رصيد أول المدة
٥٢,٥٠٠	رصيد آخر المدة	٦٠,٠٠٠	المواد المباشرة
		١٨٥,٠٠٠	تكاليف التحويل
٣١٠,٥٠٠		٣١٠,٥٠٠	

ثانيا طريقة الوارد أولاً صادر أولاً:

تقوم هذه الطريقة على التمييز بين أنشطة الفترة السابقة وأنشطة الفترة الجارية، لذلك تعالج وحدات تحت التشغيل أول المدة بصورة مستقلة عن الوحدات الجديدة عند حساب الوحدات المكافئة للفترة الجارية، وبالتالي لا يضاف رصيد حساب إنتاج تحت التشغيل أول المدة إلى تكاليف الفترة الجارية عند تحديد تكاليف المرحلة.

الإنتاج المكافئ :

لحساب وحدات الإنتاج المكافئ نجد ان الحركة المادية للوحدات كما في شكل رقم٤-١ تتكون من وحدات تحت التشغيل أول المدة وعددها ٥,٠٠٠ وحدة ومستوى إتمامها ٦٠٪. ووحدات بدأت الإنتاج وتمت وعددها ١١,٠٠٠ وحدة، ووحدات اخر المدة وعددها ٤,٠٠٠ وحدة. فبالنسبة لوحدات تحت التشغيل أول المدة تكون قد حصلت على ١٠٠٪ من المواد المباشرة وعلى ٦٠٪ من تكاليف التحويل أيضا خلال الفترة السابقة، لذلك سوف لا تحتاج إلى مواد مباشرة خلال الفترة الجارية، ولكن سوف تحتاج إلى ٤٠٪ من تكاليف التحويل حتى تصبح وحدات تامة الصنع. أما الوحدات الجديدة التي بدأت وعددها ١٥,٠٠٠ وحدة فقد بقي منها ٤,٠٠٠ وحدة تحت التشغيل آخر المدة لذاك تم منها ١١,٠٠٠ وحدة. فالوحدات التي بدأت الإنتاج وتمت فتكون قد حصلت على ١٠٠٪ من المواد، وعلى ١٠٠٪ أيضا من تكاليف التحويل خلال الفترة الجارية. أما وحدات تحت

التشغيل آخر المدة وعددها ٤,٠٠٠ وحدة فتكون قد بدأت الإنتاج خلال الفترة الجارية وبالتالي حصلت على ١٠٠٪ من المواد المباشرة وحصلت على ٧٥٪ من تكاليف التحويل لأنها وصلت إلى مستوى إتمام ٧٥٪ خلال الفترة الجارية. وفي ضوء التحليل السابق يمكن استخدام المعادلة التالية لحساب إجمالي الوحدات المكافئة من كل عنصر من عناصر التكاليف:

الوحدات المكافئة = وحدات تحت التشغيل أول المدة × النسبة المؤية اللازمة لإتمامها + وحدات بدأت وتمت + وحدات تحت التشغيل آخر المدة × نسبة إتمامها. وبالتعويض في هذه المعادلة باستخدام بيانات المثال ١ يكون الناتج كالتالي:

وحدات مكافئة مواد مباشرة = ٥٠٠٠ × صفر + ١١,٠٠٠ × ١٠٠٪ + ٤,٠٠٠ × ١٠٠٪ = ١٥,٠٠٠ وحدة

وحدات مكافئة تكاليف تحويل= ٥,٠٠٠ × ٤٠٪ + ١١,٠٠٠ × ١٠٠٪ + ٤٠٠٠ × ٧٥٪ = ١٦,٠٠٠ وحدة

ويظهر عدد الوحدات المكافئة في تقرير تكاليف المرحلة كالتالي:

	عدد الوحدات	مواد مباشرة	تكاليف تحويل
وحدات تحت التشغيل أول المدة	٥,٠٠٠ (٦٠٪)	--	٢,٠٠٠
وحدات بدأت وتمت	١١,٠٠٠	١١,٠٠٠	١١,٠٠٠
وحدات تحت التشغيل آخر المدة	٤,٠٠٠ (٧٥٪)	٤,٠٠٠	٣,٠٠٠
الوحدات المكافئة	٢٠,٠٠٠	١٥,٠٠٠	١٦,٠٠٠

عند مقارنة الوحدات المكافئة لطريقة الأول في الأول نجدها أقل من الوحدات في طريقة المتوسط والسبب هو معالجة وحدات تحت التشغيل أول المدة، فهذه الوحدات حصلت على المواد كاملة في الفترة السابقة، وكما حصلت على ٣,٠٠٠ وحدة (٥,٠٠٠ × ٦٠٪ مستوى إتمام) من تكاليف التحويل خلال الفترة السابقة ، لذلك لو أضفنا الى مجموع الانتاج المكافئ في طريقة الاول في الاول ٥,٠٠٠ وحدة على الوحدات المكافئة للمواد و ٣,٠٠٠ وحدة مكافئة على مجموع الوحدات المكافئة لتكاليف التحويل لوصلنا إلى مجموع الوحدات المكافئة حسب طريقة المتوسط، وكما أنه إذا طرحت هذه الوحدات من الوحدات

المكافئة في طريقة المتوسط لوصلنا إلى عدد الوحدات المكافئة في طريقة الأول في الأول.

تكاليف المرحلة:

تتكون تكاليف المرحلة من كل ما يصرف الى المرحلة خلال الفترة الجارية فقط، ولا يضاف رصيد أول المدة الى هذه التكاليف. ولذلك تشتمل تكاليف المرحلة على ٦٠,٠٠٠ د تكلفة المواد المباشرة و ١٨٥,٦٠٠ د تكاليف التحويل.

تكلفة الوحدة المكافئة:

تحدد تكلفة الوحدة المكافئة بقسمة تكاليف الفترة الجارية على عدد الوحدات المكافئة للفترة الجارية، وتكون كالتالي:

تكلفة الوحدة المكافئة من المواد المباشرة = ٦٠,٠٠٠ ÷ ١٥,٠٠٠ = ٤ د

تكلفة الوحدة المكافئة من تكاليف التحويل= ١٨٥,٦٠٠ ÷ ١٦,٠٠٠ =١١,٦ د

أذن تكلفة الوحدة التامة الصنع = ٤ د +١١,٦ د = ١٥,٦ دينار.

ملخص التكاليف:

يهدف هذا القسم إلى تحديد تكلفة الإنتاج التام وتكاليف الإنتاج تحت التشغيل. ونحن نعلم أن الإنتاج التام يتكون من شقين هما: وحدات تحت التشغيل أول المدة، ووحدات بدأت وتمت، لذلك فإن تكلفة الإنتاج التام تتكون من تكلفة هذين الجزيئين، وتتكون تكلفة الإنتاج تحت التشغيل أول المدة من رصيد أول المدة زائد التكاليف التي تم الحصول عليها من تكاليف الفترة الجارية لإتمام هذه الوحدات وهي في مثالنا الحالي عبارة عن ٢٠٠٠ وحدة مكافئة من تكاليف التحويل، وبهذا تحسب تكلفة الإنتاج التام كالتالي:

رصيد حساب الإنتاج تحت التشغيل أول المدة =٦٤,٩٠٠ د

تكاليف تحويل لإتمام وحدات أول المدة (٢,٠٠٠ × ١١,٦) = ٢٣,٢٠٠ د

وحدات بدأت وتمت ١١,٠٠٠ × (٤ + ١١,٦) =١٧١,٦٠٠د

اجمالي تكلفة الانتاج التام = ٢٥٩,٧٠٠ د

رصيد الإنتاج تحت التشغيل آخر المدة:

مواد مباشرة   ٤,٠٠٠ × ٤د   = ١٦,٠٠٠د

تكاليف تحويل ٣,٠٠٠ × ١١,٦ = ٣٤,٨٠٠د

الإجمالي   =٥٠,٨٠٠د

يمكن حساب إنتاج تحت التشغيل آخر المدة بطريقة أخرى كالتالي:

٤٠٠٠ (٤ × ١٠٠% + ١١,٦ × ٧٥%) = ٥٠,٨٠٠

في داخل القوس تم ضرب تكلفة الوحدة المكافئة للمواد المباشرة بنسبة ١٠٠% لان المواد تضاف في بداية المرحلة وتم ضرب تكلفة الوحدة المكافئة لتكاليف التحويل في نسبة إتمام هذه الوحدات ثم تم ضرب الناتج في وحدات تحت التشغيل آخر المدة.

تقرير تكاليف المرحلة حسب طريقة الأول في الأول:

جدول ٤-٢

مرحلة أ : تقرير تكاليف المرحلة بأتباع طريق الأول في الأول

تكاليف تحويل	مواد مباشرة	الإجمالي	بيان
			التدفق المادي والإنتاج المكافئ:
		٥,٠٠٠	وحدات تحت التشغيل أول المدة(٦٠)
		١٥,٠٠٠	وحدات مضافة خلال الفترة
		٢٠,٠٠٠	الوحدات التي سيتم المحاسبة عليها
٢,٠٠٠	-	٥,٠٠٠	وحدات تامة من وحدات أول المدة
١١,٠٠٠	١١,٠٠٠	١١,٠٠٠	وحدات بدأت وتمت
٣,٠٠٠	٤٠٠٠	٤,٠٠٠	وحدات تحت التشغيل آخر المدة (٧٥%)
١٦,٠٠٠	١٥,٠٠٠	٢٠,٠٠٠	وحدات تمت المحاسبة عليها والمكافئة
			التكاليف:
-٠-	-٠-	٦٤,٩٠٠	رصيد أول المدة
١٨٥,٦٠٠	٦٠,٠٠٠	٢٤٥,٦٠٠	تكاليف الفترة الجارية

إجمالي التكاليف	٣١٠,٥٠٠	٦٠,٠٠٠	١٨٥,٦٠٠
تقسيم : عدد الوحدات المكافئة		١٥,٠٠٠	١٦,٠٠٠
تكلفة الوحدة المكافئة	١٥,٦	٤	١١,٦
ملخص التكاليف:			
١. وحدات تامة محولة:			
أ- وحدات أول المدة:			
رصيد تحت التشغيل أول المدة	٦٤,٩٠٠		
تكاليف تحويل (٢,٠٠٠ × ١١,٦)	٢٣,٢٠٠		
إجمالي تكلفة وحدات تحت التشغيل أول المدة	٨٨,١٠٠		
ب- وحدات بدأت وتمت (١١,٠٠٠ × ١٥,٦)	١٧١,٦٠٠		
تكلفة الإنتاج التام المحول	٢٥٩,٧٠٠		
٢. وحدات تحت التشغيل آخر المدة:			
مواد (٤,٠٠٠ وحدة × ٤د)	١٦,٠٠٠		
تكاليف تحويل (٣,٠٠٠ وحدة ×١١,٦د)	٣٤,٨٠٠		
تكلفة الإنتاج تحت التشغيل آخر المدة	٥٠,٨٠٠		
إجمالي تكاليف المرحلة	٣١٠,٥٠٠		

بدراسة الجدول ٤-٢ الخاص بطريقة الاول في الاول يمكن ملاحظة الأمور التالية:

١- لقد تم تقسيم الإنتاج التام إلى مجموعتين: الأولى وتمثل الإنتاج التام الذي بدأ الإنتاج خلال الفترة السابقة والثانية وتمثل الوحدات التي بدأت وتمت خلال الفترة الجارية.

٢- لم يتم تحميل الإنتاج تحت التشغيل أول المدة بتكاليف مواد مباشرة خلال الفترة الجارية لأن المواد تضاف في بداية الإنتاج، وبالتالي تكون هذه الوحدات قد حصلت على احتياجاتها من المواد المباشرة خلال الفترة السابقة.

٣- عند تحديد تكلفة الوحدة المكافئة تم تقسيم تكاليف الفترة الجارية على عدد الوحدات المكافئة للفترة الجارية فقط.

٤ - تتكون تكلفة الانتاج التام من رصيد حساب إنتاج تحت التشغيل أول المدة، زائد تكاليف التحويل اللازمة لإتمام هذه الوحدات في الفترة الجارية. اضافة الى تكلفة الانتاج الذي بدأ وتم. وبقسمة مجموع هذين البندين على عدد الوحدات التامة والمحولة، نتوصل إلى متوسط تكلفة الوحدة التامة، وهذا الرقم قد يختلف عن تكلفة الوحدة التامة المكافئة خلال الفترة الجارية إذا كانت تكاليف الفترة السابقة مختلفة عن تكاليف الفترة الجارية.

وبعد الانتهاء من إعداد تقرير تكاليف المرحلة وتحويل إنتاجها إلى المرحلة ب يتم إثبات تكلفة الإنتاج التام المحول بالقيد التالي:

ح/ الإنتاج تحت التشغيل مرحلة ب		٢٥٩,٧٠٠
	ح/ الإنتاج تحت التشغيل مرحلة أ	٢٥٩,٧٠٠

حالة تعدد المواد المباشرة

قد يتم في استخدام عدة مواد في الانتاج ويتم اضافة هذه المواد عند مستويات اتمام مختلفة. فقد يتم إضافة المواد المباشرة في بداية العملية الإنتاجية كما في حالة الكثير من الصناعات الكيماوية، أو قد يتم إضافتها بعد ذلك المستوى، ولكن يتم إضافة عناصر تكاليف التحويل بانتظام.

عند إضافة المواد في بداية المرحلة يكون مستوى إتمام الوحدات الجديدة ١٠٠٪ لأن هذه الوحدات سوف تحصل على المواد سواء تمت أو بقيت تحت التشغيل آخر المدة. ولكن عند استخدام عدة مواد فانه يجب معرفة متى وكيف يتم إضافة هذه المواد، وهل أن الوحدات تحت التشغيل أول المدة وآخر المدة قد وصلت إلى مستوى إضافة هذه المواد أم لا. فالوحدات التامة تكون قد حصلت على ١٠٠٪ من كل المواد، أما الوحدات تحت التشغيل آخر المدة أو أولها فيتوقف ذلك على مستوى إتمامها وعلى مستوى إضافة كل مادة من المواد الخام، فإذا تجاوز مستوى إتمامها مستوى إضافة مادة معينة يكون مستوى إتمامها من تلك المادة ١٠٠٪، ولكن إذا لم تتجاوزه يكون مستوى إتمامها منها صفراً، وإذا كانت المواد تضاف بانتظام فتعامل معاملة تكاليف التحويل.

مثال (٢):

ولتوضيح حساب الوحدات المكافئة افترض أنه لا يوجد إنتاج تحت التشغيل أول المدة، وأنه تم بدء العمل على ٣,٠٠٠ وحدة خلال الفترة، وانتهى إنتاج ٢,٥٠٠ وحدة وبقي ٥٠٠ وحدة تحت التشغيل آخر المدة ومستوى إتمامها ٦٠٪. ويستخدم في الإنتاج المواد أ، ب، جـ والتي تضاف كل منها الى الإنتاج دفعة واحدة عند مستوى إتمام صفر، ٤٠٪، ٧٠٪ على التوالي، أما تكاليف التحويل فتضاف بانتظام.

المطلوب: حساب عدد الوحدات المكافئة لعناصر التكاليف

الحل:

نعلم ان الوحدات التامة الصنع قد حصلت على ١٠٠٪ من كل عناصر التكاليف ولكن يختلف الأمر بالنسبة لوحدات تحت التشغيل آخر المدة فهذه قد وصلت إلى مستوى إتمام ٦٠٪ مما يعني إنها تجاوزت مستوى إضافة المادتين أ و ب لذلك يتم ضرب هذه الوحدات بنسبة ١٠٠٪، أما بالنسبة للمادة ج والتي تضاف عند مستوى ٧٠٪ لذلك فإنها لم تضاف الى وحدات تحت التشغيل آخر المدة.

وعليه يتم حساب الوحدات المكافئة كالتالي:

المادة أ = ٢,٥٠٠ × ١٠٠٪ + ٥٠٠ × ١٠٠٪   = ٣,٠٠٠ وحدة

المادة ب = ٢,٥٠٠ × ١٠٠٪ + ٥٠٠ × ١٠٠٪   =٣,٠٠٠ وحدة

المادة جـ = ٢,٥٠٠ × ١٠٠٪ + ٥٠٠ × صفر   =٢,٥٠٠

تكاليف التحويل = ٢,٥٠٠ × ١٠٠٪ + ٥٠٠ × ٦٠٪   = ٢,٨٠٠ وحدة

وتظهر هذه الأرقام في تقرير تكاليف المرحلة كالتالي:

تكاليف تحويل	مادة جـ	مادة ب	مادة أ	
٢,٥٠٠	٢,٥٠٠	٢,٥٠٠	٢,٥٠٠	وحدات تامة الصنع × ١٠٠٪
				وحدات تحت التشغيل آخر المدة:
			٥٠٠	مادة أ ٥٠٠ × ١٠٠٪
		٥٠٠		مادة ب ٥٠٠ × ١٠٠٪
	--			مادة جـ ٥٠٠ × صفر٪
٣٠٠	==	==	==	تكاليف التحويل ٥٠٠ ×٦٠٪
٢,٨٠٠	٢,٥٠٠	٣,٠٠٠	٣,٠٠٠	الوحدات المكافئة

لاحظ أن الوحدات التامة الصنع قد أدرجت بالكامل، لأنها استفادت بنسبة ١٠٠٪ من كل عناصر التكاليف، أما وحدات تحت التشغيل آخر المدة، فقد تم ضربها بالنسبة للمواد أ، ب، في ١٠٠٪، لأن هذه المواد تضاف قبل مستوى إتمام ٦٠٪، أما المادة جـ فتم ضربها بصفر لأنها تضاف إلى الإنتاج عند مستوى ٧٠٪ وأن وحدات تحت التشغيل آخر المدة وصلت إلى مستوى إتمام ٦٠٪ فقط.

التحويل بين المراحل :

فيما سبق تم التركيز على طرق تقرير تكاليف المرحلة الأولى من مراحل الإنتاج، وسنقوم الآن بعرض طريقة المحاسبة على تكاليف مرحلة تالية للمرحلة أ وهي المرحلة ب. فهنا سوف يظهر عنصر تكاليف جديد هو التكاليف المحولة (المستلمة)، وبطبيعة الحال فان هذه التكاليف تضاف في المرحلة الجديدة في بداية عملية التشغيل ولذلك نحتاج الى تخصيص عمود جديد في تقرير تكاليف المرحلة للمحاسبة على هذه التكاليف. ولتوضيح عملية إعداد التقرير سيتم الاعتماد على بيانات المثال التالي:

مثال (٣):

افترض أن إنتاج المرحلة أ - التي سبق دراستها - يتم تحويله إلى المرحلة ب، وأن البيانات الخاصة بهذه المرحلة هي كالتالي:

وحدات تحت التشغيل أول المدة ٦,٠٠٠ وحدة ومستوى إتمامها ٤٠٪ وتكلفتها ١١٨,٠٩٨ وتتكون من: ١١١,٧٩٨ د تكلفة محولة، ٦,٣٠٠ د تكاليف تحويل. وحدات تحت التشغيل آخر المدة = ٢,٠٠٠ وحدة ومستوى إتمامها ٥٠٪ وبلغت تكاليف المرحلة للفترة الجارية كالتالي:

- مواد مباشرة ٢٥,٠٠٠ د وتضاف عند مستوى إتمام ٧٥٪

- تكاليف تحويل ٦٥,١٠٠ د وتضاف بانتظام

والمطلوب :

(١) إعداد تقرير تكاليف المرحلة حسب طريقة المتوسط المرجح.

(٢) إعداد تقرير تكاليف المرحلة حسب طريقة الأول في الأول.

أولاً: تقرير تكاليف المرحلة حسب طريقة المتوسط المرجح:

في هذه الحالة يستمر وضع وحدات تحت التشغيل أول المدة وآخرها في جدول التدفق المادي كما تم ذكره بالنسبة للمرحلة الأولى والاختلاف الوحيد هو أن الإنتاج الذي يبدأ العمل عليه في هذه المرحلة ليس جديداً لأنه يتم استلامه من المرحلة أ ويطلق عليه اسم وحدات مستلمة.

عند حساب الوحدات المكافئة لعنصر التكاليف المحولة (المستلمة) يجب مراعاة أن هذه التكاليف قد حدثت في المرحلة أ لذلك يمكن النظر إليها وكأنها مواد مباشرة يتم إضافتها الى الإنتاج في بداية المرحلة ب. وهذا يعني أن وحدات تحت التشغيل آخر المدة تستفيد منها بنسبة ١٠٠٪ خلال الفترة الجارية، أما وحدات تحت التشغيل أول المدة فإنها استفادت منها بنسبة ١٠٠٪ خلال الفترة السابقة ولا تستفيد منها بشيء خلال الفترة الجارية، أما بالنسبة لعناصر التكاليف الأخرى فتبقى معالجتها حسب ما تم ذكره في حالة المرحلة الأولى.

بالنسبة للمواد في هذه المرحلة نجد أن وحدات تحت التشغيل أول المدة كانت في أول المدة عن مستوى إتمام ٤٠٪ مما يعني أنها لم تحصل على هذه المواد خلال الفترة السابقة لأن المواد تضاف عند مستوى ٧٥٪ وكذلك نجد أن وحدات تحت التشغيل آخر المدة وهي عند مستوى إتمام ٥٠٪ لم تصل هي الأخرى إلى مستوى إضافة المواد المباشرة وبالتالي تكون استفادتها من المواد المباشرة خلال الفترة الجارية لا شيء. وفي ضوء هذه المعلومات يظهر تقرير تكاليف المرحلة ب عند إتباع طريقة المتوسط المرجح في الجدول (٤-٣). ويكون قيد تسجيل الإنتاج التام الذي يتم تحويله إلى المخازن كالتالي:

	حـ/ مخازن الإنتاج التام	٤٢٩,١٨٠
٤٢٩,١٨٠	حـ/ إنتاج تحت التشغيل مرحلة ب	

وبترحيل هذا القيد إلى حساب الإنتاج تحت التشغيل يصبح رصيده في آخر المدة ٣٧,٠١٨د.

		حـ/ إنتاج تحت التشغيل مرحلة ب	
إنتاج تام	٤٢٩,١٨٠	الرصيد	١١٨,٠٩٨
		مواد مباشرة	٢٥,٠٠٠
		تكاليف تحويل	٦٥,١٠٠
		تكلفة مستلمة	٢٥٨,٠٠٠
		الرصيد	٣٧,٠١٨

جدول (٤-٣)
تقرير تكاليف المرحل ب حسب طريقة المتوسط المرجح

تكاليف تحويل	مواد مباشرة	تكلفة مستلمة	الإجمالي	بيـان
				التدفق المادي والوحدات المكافئة:
			٦,٠٠٠(٤٠%)	وحدات تحت التشغيل أول المدة
			١٦,٠٠٠	وحدات تم استلامها من المرحلة أ
			٢٢,٠٠٠	وحدات سيتم المحاسبة عليها
٢٠,٠٠٠	٢٠,٠٠٠	٢٠,٠٠٠	٢٠,٠٠٠	وحدات تامة محولة
١,٠٠٠	--	٢٠٠٠	٢,٠٠٠(٥٠%)	وحدات تحت التشغيل آخر المدة
٢١,٠٠٠	٢٠,٠٠٠	٢٢,٠٠٠	٢٢,٠٠٠	وحدات تم المحاسبة عليها ومكافئة
				التكاليف:
٦,٣٠٠	---	١١١,٧٩٨	١١٨,٠٩٨	رصيد إنتاج تحت التشغيل أول المدة
٦٥,١٠٠	٢٥,٠٠٠	٢٥٨,٠٠٠	٣٤٨,١٠٠	تكاليف الفترة الجارية
٧١,٤٠٠	٢٥,٠٠٠	٣٦٩,٧٩٨	٤٦٦,١٩٨	إجمالي تكاليف الفترة
٢١,٠٠٠	٢٠,٠٠٠	٢٢,٠٠٠		تقسيم : عدد الوحدات المكافئة
٣,٤	١,٢٥	١٦,٨٠٩	٢١,٤٥٩	تكلفة الوحدة المكافئة
				ملخص التكاليف:
				تكاليف الإنتاج التام
			٤٢٩,١٨٠	٢٠,٠٠ وحدة ×٢١,٤٥٩
				الإنتاج تحت التشغيل آخر المدة:

				بيان
			٣٣,٦١٨	تكلفة محولة (٢,٠٠٠ × ١٦,٨٠٩)
			صفر	مواد مباشرة (صفر × ١,٢٥)
			٣,٤٠٠	تكاليف تحويل (١,٠٠٠ × ٣,٤د)
			٣٧,٠١٨	الإجمالي
			٤٦٦,١٩٨	إجمالي تكاليف المرحلة

تقرير تكاليف المرحلة بطريقة الأول في الأول:

بنفس المنطق - الذي تم ذكره تحت طريقة المتوسط تبقى كل الأمور المتعلقة بإعداد تقرير تكاليف المرحلة الأولى على حالها عند إعداد تقرير تكاليف المرحلة الثانية لذلك عند معالجة الوحدات تحت التشغيل أول المدة يجب اعتبار أنها قد حصلت على التكلفة المحولة خلال الفترة السابقة، وبالتالي لا تتحمل بشيء منها خلال الفترة الجارية. ولأنه لم يصل مستوى إتمام هذه الوحدات الى مستوى إضافة المواد خلال الفترة السابقة فإنها لم تحصل على شيء من المواد المباشرة لذلك حصلت على ١٠٠٪ من المواد المباشرة خلال الفترة الجارية.

جدول (٤-٤)
تقرير تكاليف المرحلة ب باستخدام طريقة الأول في الأول

تكاليف تحويل	مواد مباشرة	تكلفة مستلمة	الإجمالي	بيان
				التدفق المادي والوحدات المكافئة:
			٦,٠٠٠ (٤٠٪)	وحدات تحت التشغيل أول المدة
			١٦,٠٠٠	وحدات تم استلامها من المرحلة أ
			٢٢,٠٠٠	وحدات سيتم المحاسبة عليها
٣,٦٠٠	٦,٠٠٠	-٠-	٦,٠٠٠	وحدات تامة من إنتاج أول المدة
١٤,٠٠٠	١٤,٠٠٠	١٤,٠٠٠	١٤,٠٠٠	وحدات بدأت وتمت
١,٠٠٠	---	٢,٠٠٠	٢,٠٠٠	وحدات تحت التشغيل آخر المدة
١٨,٦٠٠	٢٠,٠٠٠	١٦,٠٠٠	٢٢,٠٠٠	وحدات مادية والوحدات المكافئة

				التكاليف:
---	---	---	١١٨,٠٩٨	إنتاج تحت التشغيل أول المدة
٦٥,١٠٠	٢٥,٠٠٠	٢٥٩,٧٠٠	٣٤٩,٨٠٠	تكاليف الفترة الجارية
٦٥,١٠٠	٢٥,٠٠٠	٢٥٩,٧٠٠	٤٦٧,٨٩٨	إجمالي التكاليف
				تكلفة الوحدة المكافئة :
١٨,٦٠٠	٢٠,٠٠٠	١٦,٠٠٠		تقسيم: عدد الوحدات المكافئة
٣,٥	١,٢٥	١٦,٢٣١	٢٠,٩٨١	تكلفة الوحدة المكافئة

ملخص التكاليف:

(أ) تكاليف إنتاج تام:

- إنتاج تحت التشغيل أول المدة

١١٨,٠٩٨	- رصيد أول المدة
٧,٥٠٠	- مواد (٦,٠٠٠ × ١,٢٥)
١٢,٦٠٠	- تكلفة تحويل (٣٦٠٠ × ٣,٥)
١٣٨,١٩٨	تكلفة وحدات أول المدة
٢٩٣,٧٣٨*	- وحدات بدأت تمت ١٤,٠٠٠ × ٢٠,٩٨١
٤٣١,٩٣٦	تكلفة الإنتاج التام المحول

(ب) تحت التشغيل آخر المدة:

٣٢,٤٦٢	تكلفة محولة ٢,٠٠٠ × ١٦,٢٣١
صفر	مواد (صفر وحدة × ١,٢٥د)
٣,٥٠٠	تكاليف تحويل (١,٠٠٠ × ٣,٥د)
٣٥,٩٦٢	الإجمالي
٤٦٧,٨٩٨	إجمالي تكاليف المرحلة

* هناك فرق في التقريب

مثال محلول:

تقوم شركة صناعية بإنتاج إحدى منتجاتها في مرحلة تشغيل واحدة تسمى بمرحلة الخراطة تضاف المواد الخام في بداية عملية التشغيل في المرحلة الأولى، أما تكاليف التحويل فتضاف بانتظام. وكانت رصيد حساب إنتاج تحت التشغيل أول المدة ١٧,٥٠٠د ويتكون من ١٢,٢٥٠ د تكاليف مواد مباشرة و ٥,٢٥٠ د تكاليف تحويل، وعدد الوحدات تحت التشغيل أول المدة ٥,٠٠٠ وحدة ومستوى إتمامها ٥٠٪.

وخلال الفترة الجارية تم إضافة ١٦,٠٠٠ وحدة إلى مرحلة الخراطة وبقي منها تحت التشغيل آخر المدة ٣,٠٠٠ وحدة ومستوى إتمامها ٦٠٪ وكانت تكاليف الفترة الجارية للمرحلة كالتالي:

	مرحلة الخراطة
مواد مباشرة	٤٠,٠٠٠
تكاليف تحويل	٣٤,٦٠٠

المطلوب:

(١) إعداد تقارير تكاليف للمرحلة باستخدام طريقة الأول في الأول.

(٢) إعداد تقارير تكاليف للمرحلة باستخدام طريقة المتوسط المرجح

(٣) تصوير حسابات الإنتاج تحت التشغيل للطريقتين السابقتين.

(٤) عمل قيود اليومية اللازمة لإثبات تحويل تكاليف الإنتاج التام للمراحل السابقة.

الحل:

طريقة الأول في الأول

بدراسة الشكل التالي نجد أن وحدات تحت التشغيل أول المدة هي عند مستوى إتمام ٥٠٪ لذلك سوف لا تحتاج الى مواد مباشرة خلال الفترة الجارية وحتى تكتمل تحتاج الى ٥٠٪ تكاليف تحويل. وبالنسبة للوحدات المضافة الى المرحلة وعددها ١٦,٠٠٠ وحدة فقد انتهى إنتاج ١٣,٠٠٠ وحدة منها وبالتالي حصلت هذه الوحدات على ١٠٠٪ من كل عناصر التكاليف، إضافة الى ذلك بقي من الوحدات المضافة تحت التشغيل آخر المدة

٣,٠٠٠ وحدة وهذه حصلت على ١٠٠٪ من المواد المباشرة وعلى ٦٠٪ من تكاليف تحويل. وعليه يكون تقرير تكاليف المرحلة كما في الجدول رقم (٤-٥).

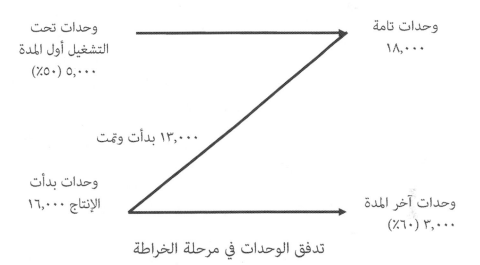

تدفق الوحدات في مرحلة الخراطة

جدول (٤-٥) تقرير تكاليف مرحلة الخراطة

تكاليف تحويل	مواد	إجمالي	
			التدفق المادي والوحدات المكافئة
		٥,٠٠٠	وحدات تحت التشغيل أول المدة
		١٦,٠٠٠	وحدات مضافة خلال الفترة الجارية
		٢١,٠٠٠	الوحدات التي سيتم المحاسبة عليها
٢,٥٠٠	---	٥,٠٠٠	وحدات أول المدة
١٣,٠٠٠	١٣,٠٠٠	١٣,٠٠٠	وحدات بدأت وتمت
١,٨٠٠	٣,٠٠٠	٣,٠٠٠ (٦٠٪)	وحدات تحت التشغيل آخر المدة
١٧,٣٠٠	١٦,٠٠٠	٢١,٠٠٠	وحدات تم المحاسبة عليها ومكافأة

			التكاليف:
----	----	١٧,٥٠٠	رصيد أول المدة
٣٤,٦٠٠	٤٠,٠٠٠	٧٤,٦٠٠	تكاليف الفترة الجارية
٣٤,٦٠٠	٤٠,٠٠٠	٩٢,١٠٠	إجمالي التكاليف
١٧,٣٠٠	١٦,٠٠٠		عدد الوحدات المتجانسة
٢	٢,٥	٤,٥	تكلفة الوحدة المتجانسة
			ملخص التكاليف: وحدات تامة:
		١٧,٥٠٠	رصيد أول المدة
		٥,٠٠٠	تكاليف تحويل ٢٥٠٠ × ٢
		٥٨,٥٠٠	وحدات بدأت وتمت ١٣٠٠٠ ×٤,٥
		٨١,٠٠٠	تكلفة الإنتاج التام المحول
			إنتاج تحت التشغيل آخر المدة:
		٧,٥٠٠	مواد مباشرة ٣,٠٠٠ × ٢,٥
		٣,٦٠٠	تكاليف تحويل ١,٨٠٠ × ٢
		١١,١٠٠	حساب إنتاج تحت التشغيل
		٩١,٢٠٠	إجمالي التكاليف

ويكون حساب الإنتاج تحت التشغيل لمرحلة الخراطة بعد إعداد تقرير التكاليف كالتالي:

حـ/ إنتاج تحت التشغيل مرحلة الخراطة

مرحلة التشطيب	٨١,٠٠٠	رصيد	١٧,٥٠٠
		مواد مباشرة	٤٠,٠٠٠
		تكاليف تحويل	٣٤,٦٠٠
		الرصيد	١١,١٠٠

ويتم إثبات تحويل الإنتاج من مرحلة الخراطة الى مخازن المنتجات التامة الصنع بموجب قيد اليومية التالي.

	حـ/ مراقبة إنتاج تام الصنع		٨١,٠٠٠
	حـ/ إنتاج تحت التشغيل مرحلة الخراطة	٨١,٠٠٠	

طريقة المتوسط المرجح

بموجب هذه الطريقة ستضاف وحدات تحت التشغيل اول المدة الى الوحدات الجديدة كما يضاف رصيد حساب الانتاج تحت التشغيل اول المدة على تكاليف الفترة الجارية. وسوف تكون الوحدات المكافئة كالتالي:

وحدات مكافئة مواد = وحدات تامة الصنع + وحدات تحت التشغيل اخر المدة ضرب مستوى اتمامها

= ١٨,٠٠٠ وحدة + ٣,٠٠٠ × ١٠٠% =٢١,٠٠٠ وحدة

وحدات مكافئة تكاليف تحويل = ١٨,٠٠٠ وحدة + ٣,٠٠٠ × ٦٠% = ١٩,٨٠٠

تكاليف المرحلة= رصيد اول المدة + تكاليف الفترة الجارية

المواد المباشرة = ١٢,٢٥٠ + ٤٠,٠٠٠   = ٥٥٢,٢٥٠

تكاليف التحويل= ٥,٢٥٠ + ٥٣,٦٠٠   =٤٨,٨٥٠

تكلفة الوحدة = تكاليف المرحلة على عدد الوحات المكافئة

من المواد المباشرة + ٥٢,٢٥٠ ÷ ٢١,٠٠٠ = ٢,٤٨٨

من تكاليف التحويل = ٤٨,٨٥٠ ÷ ١٩,٨٠٠ = ٢,٤٦٧

تقرير تكاليف المرحل ب حسب طريقة المتوسط المرجح

تكاليف تحويل	مواد مباشرة	الإجمالي	بيـان
			التدفق المادي والوحدات المكافئة:
		٥,٠٠٠(٥٠%)	وحدات تحت التشغيل أول المدة
		<u>١٦,٠٠٠</u>	وحدات تم استلامها من المرحلة أ
		٢١,٠٠٠	وحدات سيتم المحاسبة عليها
١٨,٠٠٠	١٨,٠٠٠	١٨,٠٠٠	وحدات تامة محولة
<u>١,٨٠٠</u>	<u>٣,٠٠٠</u>	<u>٣,٠٠٠</u>(٦٠%)	وحدات تحت التشغيل آخر المدة

١٩,٨٠٠	٢١,٠٠٠	٢١,٠٠٠	وحدات تم المحاسبة عليها ومكافئة التكاليف:
٥,٢٥٠	١٢,٢٥٠	١٧,٥٠٠	رصيد تحت التشغيل أول المدة
٤٣,٦٠٠	٤٠,٠٠٠	٨٣,٦٠٠	تكاليف الفترة الجارية
٤٨,٨٥٠	٥٢,٢٥٠	١٠١,١٠٠	إجمالي تكاليف الفترة
١٩,٨٠٠	٢١,٠٠٠		تقسيم : عدد الوحدات المكافئة
٢,٤٦٧	٢,٤٨٨	٤,٩٥٥	تكلفة الوحدة المكافئة
			ملخص التكاليف:
			تكاليف الإنتاج التام
		٨٩,١٩٠	١٨,٠٠٠ وحدة ×٤,٩٥٥
×١,٨٠٠	×٣,٠٠٠	١١,٩١٠	الإنتاج تحت التشغيل آخر المدة:
٢,٤٦٧	٢,٤٨٨		
		١٠١,١٠٠	إجمالي تكاليف المرحلة:

الخاتــمــة

يتم استخدام طريقة محاسبة المراحل عندما ينساب الإنتاج بصورة مستمرة ويحدث ذلك عندما تكون وحدات الإنتاج متجانسة، لذلك يتم حصر تكاليف مرحلة الإنتاج خلال فترة معينة وقسمتها على عدد الوحدات المكافئة للإنتاج للوصول إلى متوسط تكلفة الوحدة المكافئة.

يتم تحديد الإنتاج المكافئ لوحدات الإنتاج تحت التشغيل آخر المدة بضرب عدد وحداته في مستوى إتمامها بالنسبة للمواد ولتكاليف التحويل وهذه تضاف إلى عدد الوحدات المكافئة للإنتاج الذي بدأ وتم خلال الفترة. أما بالنسبة لوحدات تحت التشغيل أول المدة فتتوقف طريقة معالجتها على طريقة المحاسبة المتبعة، فعند إتباع طريقة المتوسط المرجح، تعامل هذه الوحدات نفس معاملة الوحدات التي بدأت وتمت وتكلفتها والمتمثلة في رصيد حساب الإنتاج تحت التشغيل أول المدة إلى تكاليف الفترة الجارية قبل التوصل إلى تكلفة الوحدة المكافئة، أما عند إتباع طريقة الأول في الأول فلا تضاف الوحدات المكافئة الموجودة في إنتاج تحت التشغيل أول المدة إلى الوحدات المكافئة للفترة الجارية، وكذلك لا تضاف تكلفتها إلى تكاليف الفترة الجارية، تتحمل هذه الوحدات من تكاليف الفترة الجارية على أساس الوحدات اللازمة لإتمام صناعتها.

في حالة تحويل إنتاج إحدى المراحل إلى مرحلة أخرى فإنه يجب تحويل تكلفة ذلك الإنتاج إلى المرحلة التي تم التحويل إليها، وتسمى هذه التكاليف بالتكاليف المحولة أو المستلمة، وفي حالة المرحلة التي تستلم إنتاجها من مراحل أخرى يجب حساب الوحدات المكافئة لعنصر التكلفة المحولة بالإضافة إلى الوحدات المكافئة لعناصر التكاليف الأخرى التي يتم استخدامها في المرحلة.

أسئلة وتمارين

السؤال الأول: ما هي الظروف الفنية التي تتطلب استخدام طريقة محاسبة المراحل؟

السؤال الثاني: لماذا تعتبر الإجراءات المحاسبية في طريقة محاسبة المراحل الإنتاجية أسهل من الإجراءات المحاسبية في طريقة محاسبة الأوامر الإنتاجية؟

السؤال الثالث: قارن بين محاسبة المراحل الإنتاجية ومحاسبة الأوامر الإنتاجية.

السؤال الرابع: عدد الخطوات الرئيسية لإعداد تقرير تكاليف المرحلة.

السؤال الخامس: ما هو المقصود بالوحدة المكافئة وكيف يتم حسابها بالنسبة لوحدات تحت التشغيل آخر المدة؟

السؤال السادس: ما هي الظروف التي تسمح بإهمال وحدات تحت التشغيل أول المدة عند إعداد تقرير تكاليف المرحلة؟

السؤال السابع: قارن بين أثر وجود وحدات تحت التشغيل آخر المدة في طريقة الأول في الأول وطريقة المتوسط المرجح.

السؤال الثامن: قارن بين أثر وجود وحدات تحت التشغيل أول المدة في طريقة الأول في الأول وطريقة المتوسط المرجح.

السؤال التاسع: أشرح كيف يتم تحديد تكلفة الإنتاج التام في طريقة الأول في الأول وما هي مكوناته.

السؤال العاشر: الآتي بيانات خاصة بتشغيل المرحلة الإنتاجي أ في إحدى الشركات الصناعية عن شهر آذار .:

إنتاج تحت التشغيل أول المدة	صفر
وحدات تامة محولة	١٨,٠٠٠
وحدات تحت التشغيل آخر المدة	٢,٠٠٠

يستخدم في إنتاج هذه الوحدة مادتين هما س، ص حيث تضاف المادة س في بداية عملية التشغيل وتضاف المادة ص عند مستوى ٧٠٪ بينما تضاف تكاليف التحويل بانتظام وأن وحدات تحت التشغيل آخر المدة وصلت إلى مستوى إتمام ٥٠٪.

المطلوب : تحديد عدد الوحدات المكافئة للمرحلة أ بإتباع:

أ- طريقة المتوسط المرجح.

ب- طريقة الأول في الأول.

السؤال الحادي عشر: بالرجوع إلى بيانات السؤال السابق ولكن بافتراض أن وحدات تحت التشغيل أول المدة بلغت ٥،٠٠٠ وحدة عند مستوى إتمام ٦٠٪. وان وحدات تحت التشغيل آخر المدة ٤٠٠٠ وحدة ومستوي إتمامها ٤٠٪

المطلوب:

(١) حساب الوحدات المكافئة حسب طريقة الأول في الأول.

(٢) حساب عدد الوحدات المكافئة حسب طريقة ألمتوسط المرجح.

(٣) تحديد عدد الوحدات المكافئة الموجودة في وحدات تحت التشغيل أول المدة.

السؤال الثاني عشر: تتبع شركة طريقة المتوسط المرجح في المحاسبة عن تكاليف مراحل الإنتاج والمعلومات التالية مستخرجة من سجلاتها عن فترة المنتهية في ٣١/٣.

تكاليف تحويل	مواد مباشرة	
٨٢٥٠د	٩،٦٠٠ د	رصيدحساب الإنتاج تحت التشغيل
٣٠،٠٠٠د	٢٠،٤٠٠د	تكاليف الفترة الجارية
	٧٠،٠٠٠	الوحدات التامة المحولة للمخازن
	٢٠،٠٠٠	وحدات تحت التشغيل آخر المدة

تضاف المواد في بداية المرحلة أما تكاليف التحويل فتضاف بانتظام وأن وحدات تحت التشغيل آخر المدة عند مستوى إتمام ٧٥٪.

المطلوب:

١. تحديد تكلفة الإنتاج تحت التشغيل آخر المدة.

٢. تحديد تكلفة الإنتاج التام الذي حول إلى مخازن الإنتاج التام.

السؤال الثالث عشر: يتم الإنتاج في إحدى الشركات بإضافة المادة أ في بداية عملية التشغيل وإضافة المادة ب عند مستوى إتمام ٧٥٪ والآتي بعض المعلومات المتعلقة بإنتاج إحدى فترات التكاليف.

- كان عدد الوحدات تحت التشغيل أول المدة ٥,٠٠٠ وحدة ومستوى إتمامها ٣٠٪ وتكاليفها تتكون من ٩,٥٠٠ د مواد و ٤,٨٠٠ د تكاليف تحويل.

وخلال شهر آذار تم إضافة ١٩,٠٠٠ وحدة إلى الإنتاج، وانتهى إنتاج ١٧,٥٠٠ وحدة وبلغ مستوى إتمام وحدات تحت التشغيل آخر المدة ٦٠٪ وبلغت تكاليف شهر آذار كالتالي:

٣٨,٠٠٠ د تكاليف المادة أ، ٤٣,٧٥٠ د تكاليف المادة ب، ٥٩,٧٠٠ د تكاليف تحويل.

المطلوب: إعداد تقرير تكاليف المرحلة باستخدام طريقة الأول في الأول وإعداد قيد تحويل الإنتاج التام إلى المخازن.

السؤال الرابع عشر: المعلومات الآتية تخص الأسئلة الأربعة التالية:

تقوم شركة صناعية بإنتاج التلفاز وتستخدم في المحاسبة طريقة محاسبة المراحل الإنتاجية، تقوم بإضافة الأجزاء المختلفة في بداية المرحلة وتكاليف التحويل بانتظام، وخلال إحدى الفترات توفرت لديك المعلومات الآتية:

- وحدات تحت التشغيل أول المدة ٣,٥٠٠ وحدة ومستوى إتمامها ٨٠٪.
- وحدات مضافة خلال الفترة الجارية ١٢,٠٠٠ وحدة.
- وحدات تحت التشغيل آخر المدة ٤,٠٠٠ وحدة ومستوى إتمامها ٦٠٪.

(١) عند إتباع طريقة الأول في الأول في المحاسبة على الوحدات تحت التشغيل أول المدة فإن **الوحدات المكافئة بالنسبة لعنصري المواد وتكاليف التحويل للفترة هي:**

	تكاليف تحويل	مواد مباشرة
أ	١٣,٢٠٠	١٢,٠٠٠
ب	١٣,٨٠٠	١٣,٩٠٠
جـ	١١,١٠٠	١٢,٠٠٠
د	١٣,٢٠٠	١٥,٥٠٠

(٢) عند إتباع طريقة المتوسط المرجح في محاسبة المراحل فإن **الوحدات المكافئة بالنسبة لتكاليف التحويل هي:**

أ- ١١,١٠٠ وحدة   ب- ١٣,٩٠٠ وحدة

جـ- ١٢,٠٠٠ وحدة   د- ١٣,٨٠٠ وحدة

(٣) إذا كانت تكلفة الوحدة المكافئة من المواد المباشرة هي ١ دينار خلال الفترة الجارية والفترة السابقة وكانت تكلفة التحويل خلال الفترة الجارية ٠,٧ د ولكن هذه التكلفة كانت خلال الفترة السابقة ٠,٨٥ د وبغض النظر عن إجابة الأسئلة السابقة وكانت الوحدات التامة ١٠,٠٠٠ وحدة منها ٢٠٠٠ وحدة كانت تحت التشغيل عند مستوى إتمام ٥٠% وعليه فعند إتباع **طريقة التوسط المرجح فإن تكلفة الإنتاج التام تبلغ:**

أ- ١٨,٥٠٠ د   ب- ١٧,٦٠٠ د

جـ- ١٦,٧٥٠د   د- ١٧,٥٠٠ د

(٤) بالرجوع إلى البيانات الأصلية، فإذا عملت أن تكلفة الوحدة المكافئة من المواد للفترة الجارية هي ديناران فإن **تكلفة المواد التي يتضمنها حساب إنتاج تحت التشغيل آخر المدة هي:**

أ- ٣,٢٠٠ د   ب- ٤,٨٠٠د

جـ- ٨,٠٠٠ د   د- ٤,٢٨٠ د

(جمعية المحاسبين الإداريين - معدل)

السؤال الخامس عشر: فيما يلي بيانات عن إحدى مراحل الإنتاج في شركة البلاستيك عن شهر كانون ثاني: وحدات تحت التشغيل أول المدة ٢,٠٠٠ وحدة وتكلفتها تتكون من ٤,٨٠٠ د مواد مباشرة و ٢,٧٠٠ د تكاليف تحويل وكانت عند مستوى إتمام ٥٠% والوحدات المضافة إلى المرحلة ٨,٠٠٠ وحدة، والوحدات تحت التشغيل آخر المدة ٣,٠٠٠ وحدة عند مستوى إتمام ٦٠% وبلغت تكلفة الوحدة المتجانسة من المواد ٣,٥ ومن الأجور ٢,٢٥ د من الأعباء الإضافية ١,٧٥ د وتتبع طريقة المتوسط والمرجح.

المطلوب:

(١) حساب عدد الوحدات المكافئة.

(٢) تصوير حساب الإنتاج تحت التشغيل.

السؤال السادس عشر: تتبع شركة طريقة المراحل وتستخدم طريقة الأول في الأول عند تحديد تكلفة الوحدة. ويحتاج إحد منتجاتها إلى مادتين هما أ و ب حيث تضاف المادة أ في بداية عملية التشغيل وتضاف المادة ب عندما تصل الوحدة إلى مستوى إتمام ٦٠٪ وقد توفرت المعلومات الآتية عن فترة التكاليف المنتهية في ٦/٣٠.

أن الوحدات تحت التشغيل أول المدة عددها ٦,٠٠٠ وحدة ومستوى إتمامها ٣٠٪ وقد تم إضافة ٢٤,٠٠٠ وحدة خلال الفترة الجارية إلى التشغيل بقي منها تحت التشغيل في ٦/٣٠ ٤,٠٠٠ وحدة متوسط مستوى إتمامها ٧٠٪ وكانت التكاليف المحملة على حساب الإنتاج تحت التشغيل كالآتي:

تكاليف تحويل	مادة ب	مادة أ	
٣٩٦٠	---	٩,٠٠٠	رصيد أول المدة
٥٤,٠٠٠	٤٥,٠٠٠٠	٣٨,٤٠٠	تكاليف الفترة الجارية

المطلوب:

(١) إعداد تقرير المرحلة حسب طريقة الأول في الأول.

(٢) تصوير حساب الإنتاج تحت التشغيل لهذه المرحلة.

السؤال السابع عشر: يمثل حساب إنتاج تحت التشغيل في أول شهر نيسان ٢٠٠٨، ١٧٠٠ وحدة نسبة إتمامها ١٠٠٪ بالنسبة للمواد، ٦٠٪ بالنسبة لتكاليف التحويل. ويتكون رصيده من ٧,٥٠٠ د موادًا مباشرة، و ٧,٢٩٠ د تكاليف تحويل، تستخدم المنشأة طريقة المتوسط المرجح، وخلال شهر نيسان جرت العمليات الآتية:

- تم شراء مواد خام تكلفتها ٧٥,٠٠٠ د، وصرف منها إلى الإنتاج ٦٦,٠٠٠ د فأدت إلى إضافة ١٣,٠٠٠ وحدة جديدة إلى المرحلة.

- بلغت الأجور المباشرة ٥٤,١٢٠ د والتكاليف الصناعية غير المباشرة ٣٣,٣٠٠ د وتتألف هذه التكاليف من :

استهلاك	١٥,٠٠٠د
وقود وقوى محركة دفعت نقداً	١٢,٠٠٠د
مواد غير مباشرة صرفت من المخازن	٢,٣٠٠د
إيجار	٤٠٠٠ د

- يتم تحميل التكاليف الصناعية غير المباشرة على أساس ٦٠٪ من الأجور المباشرة، وتقفل أية فروقات تحميل في تكلفة البضاعة المباعة.

- تم إنتاج ١٤,٠٠٠ وحدة وبقي ٧٠٠ وحدة تحت التشغيل آخر المدة عند مستوى إتمام ٥٠٪.

المطلوب:

(١) إعداد تقرير المرحلة.

(٢) إثبات قيود اليومية اللازمة لإثبات الحقائق السابقة.

(٣) تصوير حساب إنتاج تحت التشغيل للمرحلة.

السؤال الثامن عشر:. تم تجميع المعلومات الآتية بخصوص إحدى المراحل:

- وحدات تحت التشغيل أول المدة   ١٠,٠٠٠ وحدة (٤٠٪)
- وحدات تامة   ٥٠,٠٠٠
- وحدات تحت التشغيل آخر المدة   ١٠,٠٠٠ (٦٠٪)

وقد كانت تكلفة الوحدة المكافئة كالتالي:

	تكاليف تحويل	مواد
الفترة الجارية	٣د	٢د
الفترة السابقة	٢,٨د	٢,٢د

وتستخدم الشركة طريقة الأول في الأول

المطلوب:

١. تحديد الوحدات التي بدىء الإنتاج عليها خلال الفترة الجارية.

٢. تصوير حساب الإنتاج تحت التشغيل حسب الأصول.

٣. إذا قامت الشركة بالتحول من طريقة الأول في الأول إلى طريقة المتوسط فما هو قيد التعديل اللازم لتصحيح تكلفة المخزون التام.

السؤال التاسع عشر: (تخص الأسئلة ١،٢) الآتي معلومات عن المرحلة ب في إحدى الشركات الصناعية: **أولا : حركة الوحدات المادية**

	وحدات
إنتاج تحت التشغيل أول المدة	٥,٠٠٠
وحدات مضافة خلال الفترة	٣٥,٠٠٠
وحدات سيتم المحاسبة عليها	٤٠,٠٠٠
وحدات تامة محولة	٣٧,٠٠٠
وحدات آخر المدة	٣,٠٠٠
وحدات تم المحاسبة عليها	٤٠,٠٠٠

ثانيا : التكاليف

	تكلفة محولة	مواد	تكاليف تحويل	الإجمالي
رصيد أول المدة	٢,٩٠٠	---	٣,٤٠٠	٦,٣٠٠
تكلفة الفترة الجارية	١٧,٥٠٠	٢٥,٥٠٠	١٥,٠٠٠	٥٨,٠٠٠
الاجمالي	٢٠,٤٠٠	٢٥٥٠٠	١٨,٤٠٠	٦٤,٣٠٠

وكان نسبة إتمام وحدات تحت التشغيل أول المدة ٢٠٪ ونسبة إتمام وحدات تحت التشغيل آخر المدة ٤٠٪ وتضاف المواد في نهاية المرحلة وتستخدم الشركة طريقة المتوسط المرجح.

(أ) تبلغ تكلفة الوحدة من تكاليف التحويل مقربة لأقرب خانتين عشريتين الآتي:

أ- ٠,٤٤ د   ب- ٠,٤٦

جـ- ٠,٤٨ د   د- ٠,٥٠ د

(ب) المبلغ المحمل على إنتاج تحت التشغيل آخر المدة من التكاليف المستلمة هو:

أ- صفر   ب- ١,٥٠٠

جـ- ١٥٣٠   د- ١,٦٥٠

(المعهد الأمريكي للمحاسبين القانونيين أيار ١٩٧٨)

السؤال العشرون: كان لدى إحدى الشركات الصناعية ٨,٠٠٠ وحدة تحت التشغيل في ٢٠٠٣/١٠/١ وكان نسبة إتمام هذه الوحدات ٦٠٪ بالنسبة لتكاليف التحويل، وتضاف المواد في بداية المرحلة وخلال شهر تشرين أول (١٠) تم إضافة ٤٣,٠٠٠ وحدة وتم الانتهاء من إنتاج ٣٦,٠٠٠ وحدة، وكان مستوى إتمام وحدات تحت التشغيل آخر المدة ٨٠٪ بالنسبة لتكاليف التحويل. وعليه فان مقدار زيادة الوحدات المكافئة عند استخدام طريقة المتوسط المرجح بالمقارنة مع طريقة الأول في الأول بالنسبة للمواد وتكاليف التحويل.

	تكاليف تحويل	مواد
أ	٣,٢٠٠	٠
ب	٤,٨٠٠	٠
جـ	٣,٢٠٠	٨,٠٠٠
د	٤,٨٠٠	٨,٠٠٠

(المعهد الأمريكي للمحاسبين القانونيين/ تشرين ثاني ١٩٧٨)

السؤال الحادي العشرون: الآتي معلومات مستخرجة من سجلات التكاليف في إحدى الشركات التي تقوم باستخدام طريقة محاسبة المراحل الإنتاجية:

	إنتاج تحت التشغيل	الفترة الجارية
مواد مباشرة	٦,٥٠٠د	٢٣,٦٠٠د
تكاليف تحويل	١,٨٠٠د	٣٩,٠٠٠د

وخلال الفترة انتهى إنتاج ٢,٥٠٠ وحدة وحولت جميعها إلى المرحلة التالية وبقي ٣٠٠ وحدة تحت التشغيل آخر المدة عند مستوى إتمام ٣/١.

فإنه عند استخدام طريقة المتوسط المرجح تكون تكلفة الوحدة المكافئة من تكاليف التحويل هي:

أ- ١٦,٢٨ د   ب- ١١,٩٠

جـ- ١٥,٠٠د   د- ١٥,٦٩ د

ب- بالاعتماد على بيانات السؤال السابق إذا كانت تتبع المنشأة طريقة الأول في الأول وكان من ضمن الوحدات التامة ٥٠٠ وحدة تحت التشغيل أول المدة وعند مستوى إتمام ٦٠%. فإن نصيب الوحدة المكافئة من تكلفة المواد في الفترة الجارية مقربه لأقرب خانتين عشريتين هي:

أ- ١٣,١٤ د   ب- ١٤,٨٣د

جـ- ١٢,٠٠ د   د- لا شيء مما ذكر

السؤال الثاني العشرون: تقوم شركة بإنتاج إحدى المنتجات باستخدام الصودا الكاوية والسيلفونيك أسيد حيث يضاف السيلفونيك أسيد في بداية المرحلة وتضاف الصودا الكاوية عند مستوى إتمام ٥٠% وقد توفرت البيانات التالية عن هذه المرحلة الإنتاجية عن فترتين متتاليتين.

	الفترة الثانية	الفترة الأولى
وحدات تحت التشغيل أول المدة	؟	٥٠٠٠ (٤٠%)
وحدات بدأت الإنتاج	٢٥,٠٠٠	٢٥,٠٠٠
وحدات تحت التشغيل آخر المدة	٤٠٠٠ (٤٠%)	٦٠٠٠ (٦٠%)

وكانت التكاليف كالتالي:

رصيد أول المدة يتكون من مواد سلفونيك	؟	٧٥٠٠د
تكاليف تحويل	؟	٢٢٠٠د
تكاليف الفترة الجارية:		

د٣٦,٢٥٠	د٣٥,٠٠٠	سلفونيك أسيد
د٣٥,٧٠٠	د٥١,٠٠٠	صودا
د٣٢,٥٠٠	د٣٠,٧٢٠	تكاليف تحويل

وتستخدم الشركة طريقة الأول في الأول في المحاسبة على تكاليف المرحلة.

المطلوب:

إعداد تقرير تكاليف المرحلة في الفترة الأولى والفترة الثانية.

السؤال الثالث العشرون: تتبع إحدى الشركات طريقة محاسبة المراحل الإنتاجية وتستخدم طريقة المتوسط المرجح وقد حصلت منها على المعلومات الآتية عن الفترة المنتهية في ٢٠٠٨/٣/٣١.

- وحدات تحت التشغيل أول المدة ٨,٠٠٠ وحدة ومستوى إتمامها ٧٥٪ ووحدات تحت التشغيل آخر المدة ٦,٠٠٠ وحدة ومستوى إتمامها ٦٠٪.
- ثم بدأ العمل على ٣٤,٠٠٠ وحدة خلال الفترة.
- بلغ رصيد أول المدة من المواد ٣٣,٦٠٠ د ومن تكاليف التحويل ٢٢,٢٠٠ د.
- بلغت تكلفة الفترة الجارية: مواد ١٤٢,٨٠٠ د تكاليف تحويل ١٢٨,٢٨٠ د **فإن عدد الوحدات المكافئة للفترة الجارية هي:**

	تكاليف تحويل	مواد	
أ	٣٩٦٠٠	٣٦,٠٠٠	
ب	٤٠,٠٠٠	٤٢,٠٠٠	
ج	٣٩٦٠٠	٤٢,٠٠٠	
د	٢٨,٠٠٠	٤٠,٠٠٠	

تكلفة الإنتاج التام للفترة الجارية هي:

أ- ٢٨٠,٨٠٠   ب- ٢٥٩,٢٠٠

جـ- ٢٨٨,٠٠٠   د- ٢٧٨,٠٠٠

تكلفة الإنتاج تحت التشغيل آخر المدة:

أ- ٣٨,٨٨٠   ب- ٣٨,٦٨٢

جـ- ٣٩,٧٧٢   د- لا شيء مما ذكر

عدد الوحدات المكافئة في وحدات تحت التشغيل أول المدة

	ت	مواد
		تحويل
أ-	٢٠٠٠	٨٠٠٠
ب-	٥٦٠٠	٨٠٠٠
جـ-	٦٠٠٠	٨٠٠٠
د-	إجابة أخرى أذكرها	

عند إتباع طريقة المتوسط المرجح فإن عدد الوحدات المكافئة هو:
أ- وحدات مكافئة أول المدة زائد وحدات مكافئة للفترة الجارية.
ب- وحدات مكافئة تامة الصنع زائد وحدات تحت التشغيل آخر المدة.
جـ- وحدات مكافئة للفترة الجارية زائد وحدات مكافئة في وحدات تحت التشغيل آخر المدة.
د- وحدات أول المدة زائد وحدات بدأت وتمت ناقص وحدات مكافئة أول المدة.

السؤال الرابع العشرون: تستخدم إحدى الشركات طريقة محاسبة المراحل الإنتاجية ووفرت إليك المعلومات الآتية:
وحدات تحت التشغيل أول المدة ١٠,٠٠٠ وحدة ومستوى إتمامها ٥٠٪ ووحدات بدأت ٢٥,٠٠٠ وحدة ووحدات تحت التشغيل آخر المدة ١٠,٠٠٠ ومستوى إتمامها ٥٠٪ وتقوم الشركة باستخدام مادتين هما أ ، ب ، ويتم إضافة المادة أ عند بداية المرحلة أما المادة ب فتتم إضافتها عند مستوى إتمام ٦٠٪ وبلغ متوسط تكلفة الوحدة المكافئة كالتالي:

مادة أ	= ١,٦ د
مادة ب	= ١,٤
تكاليف تحويل	= ٣
تكلفة الوحدة التامة	٦

وتستخدم الشركة طريقة المتوسط المرجح في حساب تكلفة الوحدة وأن متوسط تكلفة الوحدة لم يختلف في هذه الفترة عن الفترة السابقة وعليه فإن:

١- **التكلفة الخاصة بالمرحلة والتي حملت على حساب الإنتاج تحت التشغيل خلال الفترة الجارية فقط هي:**

أ- ١٨١,٠٠٠ د   ب- ١٥٨,٠٠٠

جـ- ١٤٢,٠٠٠   د- ١٥٠,٠٠٠د

٢- **عدد الوحدات المكافئة في المادة ص هي:**

أ- ٣٠,٠٠٠   ب- ٢٥,٠٠٠

جـ- ٣٥,٠٠٠   د- ٤٠,٠٠٠

٣- **فإن تكلفة الإنتاج تحت التشغيل آخر المدة هي:**

أ- ٣١,٠٠٠د   ب- ٤٥,٠٠٠د

جـ- ٢٩,٠٠٠د   د- لا شيء مما ذكر

٤- **تكلفة الإنتاج التام للفترة الجارية هي:**

أ- ١٢٥,٠٠٠ د   ب- ١٥٠,٠٠٠ د

جـ- ١٤٠,٠٠٠   د- لاشيء مما سبق.

السؤال الخامس العشرون: يتم الإنتاج في مرحلتين هما أ، ب فبعد أن يتم الإنتاج في مرحلة أ يحول إلى مرحلة ب ويتم المحاسبة على تكاليف الإنتاج باستخدام طريقة الأول في الأول. والآتي المعلومات المستخرجة من الدفاتر عن شهر نيسان.

	المرحلة ب	المرحلة أ	
وحدات تحت التشغيل أول المدة	٥٠٠٠(٢٠%)	٦٠٠٠(٦٠%)	
وحدات بدأت الإنتاج	؟	٢٠,٠٠٠	
وحدات تحت التشغيل آخر المدة	٣٠٠٠ (٤٠%)	٤٠٠٠ (٣٠%)	
رصيد إنتاج تحت التشغيل أول المدة			
تكلفة مستلمة	١٢٧٥٠	-٠-	
مواد		٥١٠٠	
تكاليف تحويل	٤٥٠٠	٦١٢٠	
تكاليف الفترة الجارية			
تكلفة مستلمة	؟	-٠-	
مواد	٥٠,٤٠٠	١٦,٠٠٠	
تكاليف تحويل	٧٢,٦٠٠	٣٦,٠٠٠	

تضاف المواد في المرحلة أ في بداية المرحلة أما في المرحلة ب فتضاف المواد عند مستوى إتمام ٥٠%.

المطلوب:

إعداد تقارير تكاليف المراحل أ، ب.

الفصل الخامس
التالف والفاقد والوحدات المعيبة والخردة

أهداف الفصل

بعد دراسة هذا الفصل يجب أن تكون قادرا على:

١- المحاسبة على الإنتاج الجيد والإنتاج غير الجيد.

٢- تحديد تكاليف التالف الطبيعي وغير الطبيعي.

٣- بيان أثر وجود التالف في محاسبة المراحل.

٤- معالجة تكاليف التالف في صناعة الأوامر الإنتاجية.

٥- معالجة تكاليف إصلاح الإنتاج المعيب.

٦- بيان طرق معالجة تكاليف الخردة والفاقد.

مقدمــــة :

ينتج عن العمليات الصناعية وحدات غير مطابقة للمواصفات الفنية الموضوعة، فمثلاً في صناعة الزجاج يتم إنتاج ألواح من الزجاج بها فقاعات هوائية مما يجعلها غير مطابقة للمواصفات، وفي صناعة البلاط الصيني قد تنكسر بعد البلاطات. وهذا يؤدي إلى تقليل عدد وحدات الإنتاج الجيدة المطابقة للمواصفات وهذا يؤدي الى زيادة متوسط تكلفة الوحدة الجيدة.

الوحدات غير الجيدة:

يتم تقسيم الوحدات غير الجيدة إلى أربع مجموعات هي: [١]

١. الوحدات التالفة Spoiled Units

وهي وحدات لا تساير معايير الجودة الموضوعة وليس من الممكن إصلاحها كي تصبح وحدات جيدة ويمكن بيعها بسعر منخفض نسبياً بالمقارنة مع سعر بيع الوحدات الجيدة، ويترتب على حدوثها خسارة تتمثل في الفرق بين تكلفة إنتاجها وثمن بيعها إذا كان أقل من تكلفتها.

٢. الوحدات المعيبة Defective Units:

وهي وحدات لا تساير معايير الجودة الموضوعة ولكن يمكن إصلاحها وبعد ذلك تصبح وحدات جيدة يتم بيعها مع المنتجات الأخرى، فمثلاً قد تصطدم بعض السيارات الجديدة في مصانع السيارات مما يتطلب إصلاح تلك السيارات، ويحدث الشيء نفسه في صناعة الثلاجات والتلفاز، والأدوات الكهربائية الأخرى وبعد اكتشاف ذلك يتم إصلاح هذه الوحدات وبيعها مع الوحدات الجيدة الأخرى. وتتمثل الخسارة في التكاليف التي تتحملها المنشأة لإصلاح عيب هذه الوحدات. [١]

---

[١] تشارلز ت. هورنجرن، مرجع سابق الذكر، جـ٢، ص ٤٢٧ - ٤٢٨.

[٢] Kilough, L. N., and Leininger, W. E., Cost Accounting Concepts and Techniques for Management, (West - Publishing Co., ١٩٨٤), Pp. ١١٦-١١٧.

٣. الخردة Scrap:

وهي مخلفات الإنتاج وتكون على شكل مواد خام مثل قصاصات القماش في صناعة الملابس ونشارة الخشب في صناعة الأثاث، والبرادة في صناعة المعادن. في بعض الحالات يتم بيع الخردة بقيمة منخفضة بالمقارنة مع ثمن شراء المواد الخام وفي حالات أخرى لا يمكن بيعها، وقد تتحمل المنشأة بعض المصارف لإزالتها.

٤. الفاقد Waste:

ويمثل المواد الخام التي يتم فقدها أثناء العملية الإنتاجية مثل الغازات التي يتم حرقها في صناعة البترول، والمواد المتبخرة في الصناعات الكيماوية وصناعات المواد الغذائية. وبطبيعة الحال، لا توجد قيمة للفاقد، وقد تتحمل المنشأة بعض التكاليف لتخفيضه للحفاظ على البيئة.

مما سبق يتبين لنا أنه يتم التمييز بين الوحدات غير الجيدة والوحدات الجيدة على أساس قيمتها البيعية ويتم اكتشاف الوحدات غير الجيدة بفحص الإنتاج وهذا قد يتم مرة واحدة في نهاية العملية الإنتاجية، أو يتم بصورة متكررة، ولاختيار الطريقة الأفضل منهما يجب الموازنة بين تكلفة ومنفعة الفحص.[٢]
ولدراسة المعالجة المحاسبية للوحدات غير الجيدة سيتم دراستها على التوالي:

التالف العادي وغير العادي Normal and Abnormal Spoilage:

يتم تصنيف الوحدات التالفة إلى مجموعتين هي وحدات التالف العادية ووحدات التالف غير العادية. وتشمل وحدات التالف غير العادية الوحدات التي تلفت نتيجة عدم كفاءة التشغيل وكان يمكن تجنب حدوثها إذا ما بذلت العناية الضرورية أثناء عملية التشغيل، لذلك تعتبر غير ضرورية للحصول على الإنتاج، ومن ثم تعتبر خسارة، أما وحدات التالف العادي فتعتبر من ضروريات العملية الصناعية لأنه لا يمكن تجنب حدوثها في ظل كفاءة التشغيل الحالية التي تعيشها المنشأة. لذلك تحمل تكاليفها على تكاليف الإنتاج الجيد ويتم التعبير عن الوحدات التالفة العادية على شكل نسبة مئوية من وحدات

(1) Fischer, P. M., and Frank, W. G., Cost Accounting. Theory and Application, (South - Western Publishing Co - ١٩٨٥), Pp. ٣٣٦ - ٣٣٨.

الإنتاج الجيد أو وحدات المدخلات. وإذا زاد عدد وحدات التالف الفعلي عن وحدات التالف العادي فإن هذه الزيادة تعتبر وحدات إنتاج تالف غير عادي.

الإنتاج الجيد:

يعرف الإنتاج الجيد على أنه الإنتاج الذي يتم فحصه خلال الفترة الجارية ويكون مطابقاً للمواصفات الفنية الموضوعة، فإذا كانت المنشأة تقوم بالفحص عند نهاية العملية الإنتاجية عندها يتساوى الإنتاج الجيد مع الإنتاج التام أما إذا كانت المنشأة تقوم بفحص إنتاجها قبل وصوله إلى نهاية المرحلة فقد يختلف إجمالي الإنتاج الجيد عن إجمالي الإنتاج التام، ولتحديد الإنتاج الجيد في صناعة المراحل فإنه يجب أن يقسم الإنتاج إلى أربعة مجموعات هي:

١. وحدات تحت التشغيل أول المدة.

٢. وحدات بدأت الإنتاج وتمت.

٣. وحدات تحت التشغيل آخر المدة.

٤. وحدات تالفة.

تكون الوحدات الجيدة هي مجموع الوحدات التي تم فحصها خلال الفترة الجارية، ولتوضيح ذلك سيتم الاعتماد على الأمثلة التالية:

مثال (١):

تقوم إحدى المنشآت بفحص إنتاجها عند مستوى إتمام ٦٠٪ وتتوقع أن تبلغ نسبة التالف العادي ٥٪ من الإنتاج الجيد. وقد توفرت البيانات التالية عن إحدى مراحل الإنتاج:

- وحدات تحت التشغيل أول المدة ٥,٠٠٠ وحدة ومستوى إتمامها ٧٠٪

- وحدات بدىء بإنتاجها خلال الفترة ١٥,٠٠٠ وحدة.

- وحدات تحت التشغيل آخر المدة ٣,٠٠٠ وحدة ومستوى إتمامها ٤٠٪

- وحدات تالفة فعلية ٨٠٠ وحدة.

المطلوب: تحديد وحدات التالف العادي.

من دراسة هذه البيانات نجد أن مستوى إتمام وحدات تحت التشغيل أول المدة قد بلغ ٧٠٪، ولأن الفحص يتم عند مستوى ٦٠٪ إذن يكون قد تم فحص هذه الوحدات خلال الفترة السابقة وأدرجت ضمن الوحدات الجيدة لتلك الفترة، وبالتالي لا تعتبر ضمن الوحدات الجيدة للفترة الجارية. أما بالنسبة لوحدات تحت التشغيل آخر المدة فلم يتم فحصها هي الأخرى خلال الفترة الجارية لأنها لم تصل الى مستوى الفحص، لذلك لا تعتبر ضمن الوحدات الجيدة. وبناء على ذلك تكون الوحدات الجيدة هي الوحدات التي بدأت وتمت فقط. ويمكن أن تحسب كالتالي:-

وحدات سيتم المحاسبة عليها (١٥,٠٠٠ + ٥٠٠٠)	= ٢٠,٠٠٠
ناقص: وحدات تحت التشغيل آخر المدة	(٣,٠٠٠)
ناقص: وحدات تحت التشغيل أول المدة	(٥,٠٠٠)
وحدات تم فحصها	(١٢,٠٠٠)
ناقص: وحدات تالفة	(٨٠٠)
وحدات الإنتاج الجيدة	١١,٢٠٠

لقد تم طرح وحدات تحت التشغيل أول المدة وآخر المدة لأنهما لم تفحصا خلال الفترة الجارية، وبعد ذلك تم طرح وحدات التالف الفعلي لتحديد وحدات الإنتاج الجيد. وبعد إنجاز ذلك يتم حساب وحدات التالف كالتالي:

وحدات التالف العادي = ١١,٢٠٠× ٥٪ = ٥٦٠ وحدة
وحدات التالف غير العادي = ٨٠٠ - ٥٦٠ = ٢٤٠ وحدة،

مثال (٢):

افترض أن بيانات المثال (١) بقيت على ما هي عليه فيما عدا أن مستوى إتمام وحدات تحت التشغيل آخر المدة كان عند مستوى ٧٥٪

في هذه الحالة يكون عدد الوحدات التي تم فحصها خلال المدة هو ١٥,٠٠٠ وحدة، لأنه تم فحص الوحدات التي بدأت وتمت والوحدات تحت التشغيل آخر المدة. ثم بطرح وحدات التالف من الرصيد تحدد الوحدات الجيدة، ويحدد التالف العادي بضرب وحدات الإنتاج الجيد في نسبة التالف العادي ويتم حسابه كالتالي:

الإنتاج الجيد = (١٥,٠٠٠ - ٨٠٠)   =   ١٤,٢٠٠ وحدة

التالف العادي = ١٤,٢٠٠ × ٥%   =   ٧١٠ وحدة

وحدات التالف غير العادي = ٨٠٠ - ٧١٠   =   ٩٠ وحدة

توزيع تكاليف التالف العادي:

يتم توزيع تكاليف التالف العادي بين الإنتاج التام والإنتاج تحت التشغيل آخر المدة إذا تم فحصه وبنسبة عدد وحدات كل منهما. فالوحدات الجيدة في المثال السابق كانت ١٤,٢٠٠ وحدة وتتكون من ٣,٠٠٠ وحدة تحت التشغيل آخر المدة و١١,٢٠٠ وحدة بدأت وتمت خلال الفترة الجارية، لذلك توزع تكاليف التالف العادي على هذه المجموعات بنسبة عدد الوحدات أي بنسبة (٣: ١١,٢)، ويتم استخدام عدد الوحدات لأنه عند نقطة الفحص كانت كل الوحدات بنفس الحالة وأن التغير الذي حدث بعد نقطة الفحص لم يؤثر على كمية التالف.

مثال (٣):

افترض أن بيانات المثال (٢) بقيت على حالها فيما عدا أن وحدات تحت التشغيل أول المدة كانت عند مستوى إتمام ٤٠% وكانت وحدات تحت التشغيل آخر المدة عند مستوى إتمام ٧٠%

في هذه الحالة سوف تخضع كل الوحدات التي سيتم المحاسبة عليها لعملية الفحص لأن وحدات تحت التشغيل أول المدة وآخر المدة يتم فحصها خلال الفترة الجارية، ولذلك يتكون الإنتاج الجيد من ٥,٠٠٠ وحدة تحت التشغيل أول المدة، ١١,٢٠٠ وحدة بدأت وتمت و ٣,٠٠٠ وحدة تحت التشغيل آخر المدة لاحظ أن بهذا يكون التالف الفعلي قد تم طرحه من الإنتاج الذي بدأ خلال الفترة. مما سبق نجد أن:

الإنتاج الجيد = ٥٠٠٠ + ١١,٢٠٠ + ٣,٠٠٠   =   ١٩,٢٠٠ وحدة

التالف العادي = ١٩,٢٠٠ × ٥%   =   ٩٦٠

ونظراً لأن هذا العدد أكبر من التالف الفعلي والذي يساوي ٨٠٠ وحدة لذا يكون التالف العادي هو التالف الفعلي وتوزع تكاليفه على الإنتاج التام والإنتاج تحت التشغيل بنسبة ١٦,٢٠٠: ٣,٠٠٠ على التوالي.

مما سبق نتوصل إلى أن الإنتاج الجيد هو عبارة عن الوحدات التي سيتم المحاسبة عليها ناقص وحدات تحت التشغيل أو المدة ناقص وحدات تحت التشغيل آخر المدة إذا لم يتم فحصهما وناقص وحدات التالف العادي.

معالجة التالف في محاسبة المراحل:

ركزت الأمثلة السابقة على كيفية حساب عدد وحدات التالف العادي وما هي مجموعة الوحدات الجيدة التي يجب أن تتحمل بتكاليف التالف العادي ورأينا أن ذلك يتوقف على مستوى إجراء الفحص ومستوى إتمام وحدات تحت التشغيل أول المدة وآخرها. ولزيادة الإيضاح سنقوم ببيان أثر التالف الفعلي على تقرير تكاليف المرحلة باستخدام البيانات التالية.

مثال (٤):

يتم الإنتاج في إحدى الشركات الصناعية باستخدام المواد س، ص حيث يتم إضافتهما في بداية عملية الإنتاج، ويتم فحص الإنتاج في نهاية العملية الإنتاجية وتقدر نسبة التالف العادي بـ ٢٪ من الإنتاج الجيد والآتي البيانات الخاصة بإحدى مراحل الإنتاج:

-وحدات تحت التشغيل أول المدة	١٠,٠٠٠ وحدة (٦٠٪)
- وحدات مضافة خلال الفترة الجارية	٤٠,٠٠٠ وحدة
- وحدات تامة	٣٦,٠٠٠ وحدة
- وحدات تحت التشغيل آخر المدة	١٢,٠٠٠ وحدة (٧٠٪)
- وحدات تالفة فعلية	٢,٠٠٠ وحدة

ويتكون رصيد إنتاج تحت التشغيل أول المدة من: ١٠,٠٠٠ د مواد مباشرة و ٦,٥٠٠ د تكاليف تحويل.

وتم تحميل هذا الحساب خلال الفترة الجارية بالمبالغ التالية:
٥٠,٠٠٠ د تكاليف مواد مباشرة س و ص، ٥١,٥٠٠ د تكاليف تحويل.

المطلوب:

إعداد تقرير تكاليف المرحلة حسب طريقة المتوسط المرجح.

الحل:

الوحدات التي ستتم المحاسبة عليها تساوي ١٠,٠٠٠ + ١٠,٠٠٠ = ٤٠,٠٠٠ = ٥٠,٠٠٠ وحدة، وهذه تساوي مجموع الوحدات التامة والوحدات تحت التشغيل آخر المدة والوحدات التالفة، ويمكن عرض هذا التدفق المادي باستخدام حرف Z الكبيرة مع تعديلها وهي كما في الشكل (٥-١).

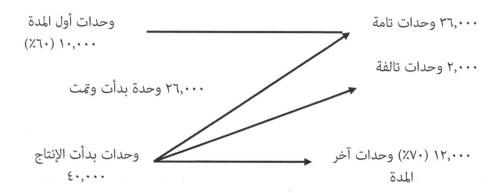

شكل (٥-١) تدفق وحدات الإنتاج

بدراسة الشكل (٥-١) نرى أن وحدات تحت التشغيل آخر المدة لم يتم فحصها لأنها لم تصل الى مستوى ١٠٠٪ خلال الفترة الجارية إذن لا تدخل ضمن وحدات الإنتاج الجيد أما وحدات تحت التشغيل أول المدة فقد تم فحصها خلال الفترة الجارية حيث كان مستوى إتمامها ٦٠٪ في بداية الفترة وأن الفحص يتم عند مستوى ١٠٠٪ إذن تعتبر ضمن الوحدات الجيدة، وهذا يعني أن الوحدات التامة تعتبر هي الوحدات الجيدة وأن الإنتاج الجيد يساوي ٣٦,٠٠٠ وحدة.

إذن التالف العادي = ٣٦,٠٠٠ × ٢٪ = ٧٢٠ وحدة
التالف غير العادي = ٢٠٠٠ – ٧٢٠ = ١٢٨٠ وحدة

تقرير تكاليف المرحلة حسب طريقة المتوسط المرجح:

لقد تم إعداد تقرير تكاليف المرحلة حسب طريقة المتوسط المرجح كما في الجدول (5-1) وفي هذا التقرير قمنا بإدراج وحدات التالف بعد تقسيمها إلى تالف عادي وتالف غير عادي، وتم معاملتها لأغراض حساب الإنتاج المكافئ نفس معاملة الوحدات التامة لأن فحص الإنتاج يتم في نهاية المرحلة، وهذا يعني أن هذه الوحدات قد حصلت على 100% من المواد المباشرة اللازمة للوحدة الجيدة، و 100% من تكاليف التحويل اللازمة للوحدة الجيدة، ويتحمل الإنتاج التام بخسائر التالف العادي ولا يتحمل الإنتاج تحت التشغيل آخر المدة بشيء منها لأنه لم يتم فحصه.

جدول (5-1)
تقرير تكاليف المرحلة حسب طريقة المتوسط المرجح

تكاليف تحويل	مواد	الإجمالي	
			التدفق المادي:
		10,000(75%)	وحدات تحت التشغيل أول المدة
		40,000	وحدات مضافة إلى المرحلة
		50,000	وحدات سيتم المحاسبة عليها
36,000	36,000	36,000	وحدات تامة
720	720	720	وحدات تالف عادي
1280	1280	1280	وحدات تالف غير عادي
8,400	12,000	12,000(70%)	وحدات تحت التشغيل آخر المدة
46,400	50,000	50,000	وحدات تم المحاسبة عليها
			والمكافئة:
			التكاليف:
6,500	10,000	16,500	رصيد أول المدة
51,500	40,000	91,500	تكاليف الفترة الجارية
58,000	50,000	108,000	إجمالي التكاليف
46,400	50,000		÷ عدد الوحدات المكافئة
1,25	1	2,25	تكلفة الوحدة المكافئة
			ملخص التكاليف:

		٨١,٠٠٠	وحدات تامة ٣٦,٠٠٠ × ٢,٢٥
		١,٦٢٠	وحدات تالفة عادية ٧٢٠ ×٢,٢٥
		٨٢,٦٢٠	
		٢,٨٨٠	وحدات تالفة غيرعادي١١٢٨ ×٢,٢٥
١,٢٥× ٨,٤٠٠	١×١٢,٠٠٠	٢٢,٥٠٠	إنتاج تحت التشغيل آخر المدة
		١٠٨,٠٠٠	الإجمالي

مثال (٥):

افترض أن المعلومات الواردة في المثال رقم (٤) بقيت على ما هي عليه فيما عدا أن الفحص يجري عند مستوى إتمام ٥٠٪ يتم تمثيل حركة التدفق المادي للوحدات كما في الشكل رقم (٢-٥) التالي:

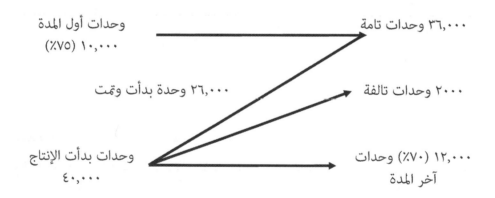

شكل (٢-٥) تدفق وحدات الإنتاج

من دراسة الشكل (٢-٥) نجد أن وحدات بدأت وتمت تبلغ ٢٦,٠٠٠ وحدة وهذه تم فحصها خلال الفترة الجارية وكذلك بالنسبة لوحدات تحت التشغيل آخر المدة فقد تم فحصها هي الأخرى خلال الفترة ألجارية لأنها وصلت الى مستوى إتمام ٧٠٪ وهذا يزيدعن مستوى الفحص والذي يتم عندمستوى ٥٠٪، أماوحدات تحت التشغيل أول المدة

يكون قد تم فحصها خلال الفترة السابقة لأنها كانت عند مستوى ٧٥٪ في أول المدة. لذلك فإن عدد الوحدات الجيدة يتكون من:

٢٦,٠٠٠ وحدة بدأت وتمت + ١٢,٠٠٠ وحدة تحت التشغيل آخر المدة
= ٣٨,٠٠٠ وحدة

الوحدات التالفة العادية = ٣٨,٠٠٠ × ٢٪ = ٧٦٠ وحدة.

الوحدات التالفة غير العادية = ٢,٠٠٠ - ٧٦٠ = ١,٢٤٠ وحدة.

جدول (٥-٢)

جدول الإنتاج المكافئ حسب طريقة المتوسط المرجح

	تكاليف تحويل	مواد
وحدات تامة خلال الفترة الجارية	٣٦,٠٠٠	٣٦,٠٠٠
وحدات تالفة عادية	٣٨٠	٧٦٠
وحدات تالفة غير عادية	٦٢٠	١٢٤٠
وحدات تحت التشغيل آخر المدة	٨٤٠٠	١٢,٠٠٠
الوحدات المكافئة	٤٥٤٠٠	٥٠,٠٠٠

لاحظ أنه عند حساب الوحدات المكافئة للوحدات التالفة قد تم ضربها بنسبة ١٠٠٪ في حالة المواد المباشرة وبنسبة ٥٠٪ بالنسبة لتكاليف التحويل لان فحص الإنتاج يتم عند مستوي ٥٠٪، وان المواد المباشرة تضاف في بداية المرحلة، وعليه يتم تحديد تكلفة الوحدة المكافئة لهذه المرحلة كالتالي:

تكلفة الوحدة من المواد = ٥٠,٠٠٠ ÷ د ٥٠,٠٠٠ = د١

تكاليف التحويل = ٥٨,٠٠٠ ÷ ٤٥,٤٠٠ = د ١,٢٧٨

توزيع خسائر التالف:

تكلفة التالف العادي تساوي:

المواد المباشرة: ٧٦٠ × ١ = ٧٦٠

تكاليف تحويل: ٧٦٠ × ٥٠٪ × ١,٢٧٨ = <u>٤٨٥,٦</u>

الإجمالي ١٢٤٥,٦

وإذا لم تكن للتالف قيمة بيعيه فإن كل تكلفته تعتبر خسارة تحمل على الإنتاج الجيد ولان الإنتاج الجيد في هذا المثال يتكون من الإنتاج التام والإنتاج تحت التشغيل آخر المدة، لذلك توزع بنسبة ٢٦,٠٠٠: ١٢,٠٠٠ على الإنتاج التام والإنتاج تحت التشغيل على التوالي. وبهذا يكون نصيب كل مجموعة من خسائر التالف كالتالي:

$$\frac{١٢٤٥,٦ \times ٢٦,٠٠٠}{٣٨,٠٠٠} = ٨٥٨,٤ \text{ دينار}$$

$$\frac{١٢٤٥,٦ \times ١٢,٠٠٠}{٣٨,٠٠٠} = ٣٩٦,٢ \text{ دينار}$$

معالجة التالف في الدفاتر:

يمكن معالجة التالف في الدفاتر بأحد طريقتين: الأولى وتعمل على إثبات التالف بصافي قيمته البيعية عند إنتاجه وتسمى هذه الطريقة بطريقة الإنتاج. والطريقة الثانية ولا تقوم بإثباته في الدفاتر إلا عند بيعه لذلك يتم كتابة مذكرة به وتعرف هذه الطريقة بطريقة البيع.

طريقة الإنتاج:

فإذا أثبت التالف العادي عند الإنتاج تحمل صافي خسارته بفتح حساب للتالف يجعل مدينا بالقيمة البيعية لوحدات التالف وهي الفرق بين تكلفته وصافي قيمته البيعية فتحمل على حساب الإنتاج الجيد. ولتوضيح ذلك سوف نعتمد على البيانات الواردة في الجدول (١ - ٥) ومنها نجد أن تكاليف التالف العادي ١٦٢٠ د. والآن افترض أن صافي القيمة البيعية للوحدة هي ١,٥ د. إذن سيتم حساب خسائر التالف كالتالي:

القيمة البيعية لوحدات التالف العادي = ٧٢٠ × ١,٥ = ١٠٨٠ دينار
خسائر التالف العادي   = ١٦٢٠ - ١٠٨٠ = ٥٤٠ دينار.

وفي هذه الحالة تحمل الخسارة على حساب الإنتاج التام لأن وحدات تحت التشغيل آخر المدة لم يتم فحصها فتصبح تكلفته ٨١,٥٤٠ د (= ٨١,٠٠٠ د + ٥٤٠د). ويتم تسجيلها في الدفاتر باستخدام قيد اليومية التالي:

٨١,٥٤٠		حـ/ مخزون الإنتاج التام
١,٠٨٠		حـ/ مخزون الإنتاج التالف
	٨٢,٦٢٠	حـ/ إنتاج تحت التشغيل

بموجب هذا القيد تم تحميل حساب مخزون الإنتاج بخسائر التالف العادي ومقدارها ٥٤٠ د وتم تحميل حساب مخزون الإنتاج التالف بصافي القيمة البيعية للوحدات التالفة الصناعية غير المباشرة. وفي الوقت نفسه يجب إثبات تكاليف التالف غير العادي باستخدام قيد اليومية التالي:

١٩٢٠		حـ/ مخزون الإنتاج التالف (١٢٨٠×١,٥ د)
٩٢٠		حـ/ خسائر الإنتاج التالف
	٢٨٨٠	حـ/ إنتاج تحت التشغيل (١٢٨٠ ×٢,٥ د)

٢- طريقة البيع:

إذا قررت المنشأة إتباع طريقة البيع عندها يتم إثبات قيمة التالف العادي عند البيع وتعتبر تكاليفه خسارة عند الإنتاج وتحمل على تكلفة الإنتاج الجيد فتصبح تكلفته ٨٢٦٢٠ د (٨١,٠٠٠ + ١٦٢٠). وعند بيع وحدات الإنتاج التالف تعتبر صافي قيمة البيعية إيرادات متنوعة أو قد يتم توزيعها على حسابات البضاعة.

ب- تقرير تكاليف المرحلة حسب طريقة (الأول في الأول):

للتبسيط عند إعداد تقرير تكاليف المرحلة في هذه الطريقة سوف نفترض أن وحدات التالف تعزى إلى الوحدات التي بدىء بإنتاجها خلال الفترة الجارية وهذا يعني أن وحدات تحت التشغيل أول المدة لم تؤدي الى حدوث وحدات تالفة. وعلى الرغم من أن هذا الافتراض يؤدي إلى تبسيط إجراءات إعداد تقرير التكاليف لكنه لا يتمشى مع الواقع العملي. (١)

مثال ٦:

افترض أن وحدات تحت التشغيل أول المدة ١٠,٠٠٠ وحدة (٦٠٪)، - وحدات مضافة خلال الفترة الجارية ٤٠,٠٠٠ وحدة بقي منها وحدات تحت التشغيل آخر المدة ١٢٠٠٠ وحدة (٧٠٪) ، ويتم الفحص عند مستوى إتمام ٥٠٪ واكتشف عند الفحص وجود وحدات تالفة فعلية ٢٠٠٠ وحدة. وأن رصيد إنتاج تحت التشغيل أول المدة يتكون من: ١٠,٠٠٠ د مواد مباشرة و٦,٥٠٠ د تكاليف تحويل. وخلال الفترة تم تحميل هذا الحساب بمبلغ ٤٠,٠٠٠ د تكاليف مواد مباشرة ومبلغ ٥١,٢٢٠ د تكاليف تحويل.

المطلوب: إعداد تقرير تكاليف المرحلة حسب طريقة الأول في الأول

الحل:

في ضوء البيانات المعطاة تم إعداد تقرير تكاليف المرحلة في الجدول (٥-٢) وفيما يلي الملاحظات الخاصة بتقرير تكاليف المرحلة.

١. حددت وحدات التالف العادي بنسبة ٢٪ من الإنتاج الجيد الذي هو عبارة عن:

وحدات سيتم المحاسبة عليها	٥٠,٠٠٠
(ناقص) وحدات تحت التشغيل أول المدة	١٠,٠٠٠
وحدات تم فحصها	٤٠,٠٠٠
(ناقص) وحدات تالفة	٢,٠٠٠
وحدات الإنتاج الجيد	٣٨,٠٠٠

---

(1) Fischer and Frank. Op. Cit, Op. ٣٧٠-٣٧١.

لقد تم طرح وحدات تحت التشغيل أول المدة من رقم وحدات سيتم المحاسبة عليها خلال الفترة الجارية لأنه تم فحصها خلال الفترة السابقة أما وحدات تحت التشغيل آخر المدة فقد تم فحصها خلال الفترة الجارية.

وحدات التالف العادي تساوي (٣٨,٠٠٠ × ٢) = ٧٦٠ وحدة

وحدات التالف غير العادي =(٢٠٠٠ -٧٦٠) =١٢٤٠ وحدة.

جدول (٥- ٢)
تقرير تكاليف المرحلة حسب طريقة الأول في الأول

تكاليف تحويل	مواد	الإجمالي	
			التدفق المادي:
		١٠,٠٠٠(٦٠%)	وحدات تحت التشغيل أول المدة
		٤٠,٠٠٠	وحدات مضافة إلى المرحلة
		٥٠,٠٠٠	وحدات سيتم المحاسبة عليها
٤٠٠٠	---	١٠,٠٠٠	وحدات أول المدة (٦٠%)
٢٦,٠٠٠	٢٦,٠٠٠	٢٦,٠٠٠	وحدات بدأت وتمت
٣٨٠	٧٦٠	٧٦٠	وحدات تالف عادي (٣٨,٠٠٠×٢%)
٦٢٠	١٢٤٠	١٢٤٠	وحدات تالف غير عادي
٨٤٠٠	١٢,٠٠٠	١٢,٠٠٠(٧٠%)	وحدات تحت التشغيل آخر المدة(٧٠%)
٣٩٤٠٠	٤٠,٠٠٠	٥٠,٠٠٠	وحدات تم المحاسبة عليها ومكافئة التكاليف:
		١٦,٥٠٠	رصيد أول المدة
٥١,٢٢٠	٤٠,٠٠٠	٩١,٢٢٠	تكاليف الفترة الجارية
٥١,٥٠٠	٤٠,٠٠٠	١٠٧,٧٢٠	إجمالي التكاليف
٣٩,٤٠٠	٤٠,٠٠٠		÷ عدد الوحدات المتجانسة
١,٣	١	٢,٣	تكلفة الوحدة المتجانسة
			ملخص التكاليف:

			إنتاج تام:
		١٦,٥٠٠	رصيد أول المدة
١,٣×٤٠٠٠		٥,٢٠٠	تكاليف تحويل
٢,٣×٢٦,٠٠٠		<u>٥٩,٨٠٠</u>	وحدات بدأت وتمت
		٨١,٥٠٠	تكلفة الإنتاج التام
١,٣×٣٨٠	١×٧٦٠	١٢٥٤	تكلفة التالف العادي
١,٣×٦٢٠	١×١,٢٤٠	٢,٠٤٦	تكلفة التالف غير العادي
١,٣×٨,٤٠٠	١×١٢,٠٠٠	٢٢,٩٢٠	إنتاج تحت التشغيل آخر المدة
		١٠٧,٧٢٠	

٢. عند حساب الوحدات المكافئة لوحدات التالف العادي ووحدات التالف غير العادي تم ضربها بنسبة ١٠٠٪ بالنسبة للمواد وضربها بنسبة ٥٠٪ بالنسبة لتكاليف التحويل لأن المواد تضاف في بداية المرحلة بينما تضاف تكاليف التحويل بانتظام وأن الفحص يتم عند مستوى ٥٠٪ .

٣. تم تحديد تكاليف التالف العادي على أساس تكاليف الفترة الجارية لأنه افترضنا أن الوحدات التالفة هي من ضمن الوحدات التي بدىء بإنتاجها خلال الفترة الجارية لذلك اعتبرت وحداته المكافئة ضمن الوحدات المكافئة للفترة الجارية. ويتم توزيع تكاليف هذا التالف على الإنتاج تحت التشغيل آخر المدة، والإنتاج التام بنسبة ٢٦:١٢ على التوالي ويكون نصيب كل منهما كالتالي:

الإنتاج التام ١,٢٥٤ × (٢٦ ÷ ٣٨)   = ٨٥٨ دينار

الإنتاج تحت التشغيل آخر المدة ١,٢٥٤ × (١٢ ÷ ٣٨) = <u>٣٩٦</u> دينار.

الإجمالي   = ١,٢٥٤ دينار

وبعد إعداد تقرير تكاليف المرحلة وتوزيع تكاليف التالف العادي يتم تحديد تكاليف الإنتاج التام وتكاليف التالف باستخدام الطرق التالية:

طريقة الإنتاج:

حسب هذه الطريقة يتم فتح حساب للإنتاج التالف ويحمل بصافي القيمة البيعية لوحدات الإنتاج التالف. فمثلا إذا كان صافي القيمة البيعية لوحدة التالف هي ١,٥ دينار وأن سياسة المنشأة تتطلب إثبات خسائر التالف عند الإنتاج فإن علينا تحديد الآتي:

القيمة البيعية للتالف العادي = سعر بيع الوحدة × عدد الوحدات

$$= ١,٥ × ٧٦٠ = ١,١٤٠$$

خسائر التالف العادي = تكاليف التالف – القيمة البيعية للتالف

$$= ١,٢٥٤ – ١,١٤٠ = ١١٤د.$$

ويوزع هذا المبلغ بنسب التوزيع السابقة نفسها كالتالي:

$$الإنتاج التام: ١١٤ × \frac{٢٦}{٣٨} = ٧٨د$$

$$لإنتاج تحت التشغيل آخر المدة: ١١٤ × \frac{١٢}{٣٨} = ٣٦د$$

تكلفة الإنتاج التام = تكلفة الإنتاج التام قبل التالف + حصته في تكاليف التالف

تكلفة الإنتاج التام: ٨١,٥٠٠ + ٧٨ = ٨١,٥٧٨ د

ويكون قيد اليومية اللازم لإثبات تحويل تكلفة الإنتاج من حساب المرحلة كالتالي:

٨١,٥٧٨		حـ/ مخزون الإنتاج التام
١,١٤٠		حـ/ مخزون الإنتاج التالف (٧٦٠ × ١,٥)
	٨٢,٧١٨	حـ/ إنتاج تحت التشغيل

ويسجل التالف غير العادي بقيد اليومية التالي:

١,٨٦٠		حـ/ مخزون الإنتاج التالف (١٢٤٠ ×١,٥)
١٨٦		حـ/ خسائر الإنتاج التالف (متمم حسابي)
	٢,٠٤٦	حـ/ إنتاج تحت التشغيل

وعليه يكون حساب إنتاج تحت التشغيل كالآتي:

حـ/ الإنتاج تحت التشغيل

مذكورين	٨١,٥٧٨		الرصيد	١٦,٥٠٠
مذكورين	٢,٠٤٦		مواد مباشرة	٤٠,٠٠٠
الرصيد	٢٢,٩٥٦		تكاليف تحويل	٥١,٢٢٠
(٢٢,٩٢٠ +٣٦)				
	١٠٨,٠٠٠			١٠٧,٧٢٠

طريقة البيع:

إذا كانت سياسة الإدارة إثبات التالف العادي عند البيع عندها لا يتم فتح حساب للتالف وتعتبر تكلفة التالف العادي خسارة تحمل على الإنتاج الجيد. ومن واقع تقرير تكاليف المرحلة نجد أن تكاليف التالف العادي هي ١٢٥٤د ويتم توزيعها بنسبة ٢٦: ١٢ بين الإنتاج التام والإنتاج تحت التشغيل آخر المدة ويكون نصيب كل منهما ٨٥٨ د و ٣٩٦د على التوالي. ويسجل الإنتاج التام باستخدام قيد اليومية التالي:

	حـ/ الإنتاج التام (٨١,٥٠٠ + ٨٥٨)		٨٢,٣٥٨
	حـ/ إنتاج تحت التشغيل	٨٢,٣٥٨	

وتعتبر تكاليف التالف غير العادي خسارة وتسجل بقيد اليومية التالي:

	حـ/ خسائر التالف غير العادي)		٢,٠٤٦
	حـ/ إنتاج تحت التشغيل	٢,٠٤٦	

معالجة التالف في صناعة الأوامر الإنتاجية:

كما قد يحدث التالف في صناعات المراحل يحدث أيضاً في صناعة الأوامر الإنتاجية، وتتأثر معالجة هذا التالف بالطريقة المحاسبية التي يتم اختيارها وفي هذا

الخصوص قد يتم استخدام إحدى طريقتين الأولى وتعرف بالطريقة المباشرة. [1] وتقوم بتحميل تكاليف وحدات التالف العادي على الأوامر التي أدت إلى حدوثها. والثانية وتعرف بالطريقة غير المباشرة وتعالج تكاليف التالف العادي كأحد بنود التكاليف الصناعية غير المباشرة وبالتالي يتم تحميل تكاليف وحدات التالف العادي على كل الأوامر الإنتاجية بواسطة معدل تحميل التكاليف الصناعية غير المباشرة. [2] . ولتوضيح المعالجة المحاسبية لهذه الطرق سنقوم بافتراض المعلومات الآتية:

مثال (٥):

تحمل أحد أوامر الإنتاج بمبلغ ٨,٠٠٠ ديناراً مواد مباشرة، ٦,٠٠٠ دينار أجور مباشرة وكان معدل تحميل التكاليف الصناعية غير المباشرة هو ١,٥ ديناراً لكل دينار أجوراً مباشرة. ويتكون الأمر من ١٠٠٠ وحدة تلف منها ٥٠ وحدة واعتبرت ضمن حدود التالف المسموح به وتم اكتشاف ذلك عند انتهاء العمل على الأمر الإنتاجي، والمطلوب معالجة التالف العادي حسب الطريقة المباشرة والطريقة غير المباشرة علماً بأن سعر بيع وحدة التالف هو ١٠ دنانير.

أولاً: الطريقة المباشرة:

بموجب هذه الطريقة يتحمل الأمر الإنتاجي بخسائر الوحدات التالفة العادية ويتم تحديد هذه الخسائر كالتالي:

تكلفة الوحدة = (٨,٠٠٠ مواد + ٦,٠٠٠ أجور + ٦,٠٠٠ × ١,٥ تكاليف غير مباشرة) ÷ ١,٠٠٠ وحدة = ٢٣ ديناراً.

خسائر التالف = ٥٠ وحدة × (٢٣ د التكلفة - ١٠ د سعر البيع)

= ٦٥٠ د

تكلفة الإنتاج الجيد = تكلفة الأمر الإنتاجي- القيمة البيعية للتالف

[1] أحمد الخطيب، التكاليف في المجال التطبيقي، ١٩٨٨، ص ٢٣٧.
[2] Horngren and Foster, Op. Cit, Pp. ٥٥٤ - ٥٥٥.

هنا يتم تحميل تكاليف التالف العادية على حساب الأمر ضمنيا عند تحميله بالتكاليف الصناعية لذلك لا نحتاج إلى عمل قيود جديدة لها وكل ما نعمله هو أن نقسم تكاليف الأمر على عدد الوحدات الجيدة فيه بعد طرح صافي القيمة البيعية لوحدات التالف العادية من التكاليف الإجمالية للأمر الإنتاجي، ويكون قيد إقفال هذا الأمر الإنتاجي كالتالي:

حـ/ مخزون الإنتاج التام		٢٢,٥٠٠
حـ/ مخزون الإنتاج التالف		٥٠٠
حـ/ إنتاج تحت التشغيل - أمر رقم	٢٣,٠٠٠	

تؤدي هذه المعالجة المحاسبية إلى معرفة التكاليف التي تحملتها المنشأة في سبيل إنتاج الأمر محل الاعتبار وهذا يخدم أغراض الرقابة والتخطيط.

ثانياً: الطريقة غير المباشرة:

حسب هذه الطريقة تحمل خسارة الوحدات التالفة العادية على حساب مراقبة التكاليف الصناعية غير المباشرة الفعلية. وبهذا يتم تحميل كل الأوامر بنصيبها من تكاليف التالف العادي عند تحميله المصروفات الصناعية غير المباشرة لان تكلفة التالف العادي تدخل ضمن مكونات معدل التحميل، لذلك فإن خسائر التالف المتوقعة تستقر في الجانب الدائن في حساب الأعباء الإضافية المحملة. وبالتالي لا يجوز تحميل تكاليف التالف الفعلي على حساب الإنتاج تحت التشغيل لأن ذلك سوف يؤدي إلى تكرار تحميل الإنتاج بتكاليف التالف بل يجب تسجيلها في حساب مراقبة التكاليف الصناعية غير المباشرة الفعلية. ويكون قيد إقفال حساب الأمر الإنتاجي في المثال السابق كالتالي:

حـ/ مخزون الإنتاج التام		٢١,٨٥٠
حـ/ مخزون الإنتاج التالف		٥٠٠
حـ/ التكاليف الصناعية غير المباشرة - فعلية		٦٥٠
حـ/ إنتاج تحت التشغيل	٢٣,٠٠٠	

لاحظ أنه بموجب هذا القيد سجلت التكلفة الفعلية لخسائر التالف في حساب مراقبة التكاليف الفعلية.

المعالجة المحاسبية للإنتاج المعيب:

ذكرنا أن الإنتاج المعيب يمثل الوحدات التي لا تساير المواصفات الفنية الموضوعة للإنتاج ولكن يمكن إصلاحها فتصبح وحدات جيدة. يتم تصنيف الوحدات المعيبة إلى وحدات عادية ووحدات غير عادية وتعتبر الأخيرة خسارة وبالتالي لا يجوز تحميل تكلفة إصلاحها على وحدات الإنتاج الجيد أما الوحدات المعيبة العادية فتحمل خسارة إصلاحها على وحدات الإنتاج الجيد سواء بطريقة مباشرة أو بطريقة غير مباشرة، وتقوم الطريقة المباشرة بتحميل تكاليف إصلاح الإنتاج المعيب على الوحدات، التي اكتشف الإنتاج المعيب ضمنها أثناء الفحص وتقوم الطريقة غير المباشرة، بتحميل خسائر التالف التقديرية على الإنتاج ولذلك تسجل تكاليف الإصلاح الفعلي على حساب مراقبة التكاليف الصناعية غير المباشرة. ولتوضيح هاتين الطريقتين افترض أن المنشأة قد تحملت ٣٠٠ د مواد مباشرة، ٤٠٠ د أجوراً مباشرة و ٣٠٠ د تكاليف صناعية غير مباشرة لإصلاح وحدات الإنتاج المعيب العادي التي تم اكتشافها خلال الفترة.

والمطلوب:

معالجة هذه التكاليف حسب الطريقة المباشرة والطريقة غير المباشرة.

أولاً الطريقة المباشرة:

تقوم هذه الطريقة بتحميل تكاليف الإصلاح على حساب الإنتاج تحت التشغيل بموجب قيد اليومية التالي:

١,٠٠٠		حـ/ إنتاج تحت التشغيل
	٣٠٠	حـ/ مراقبة المواد
	٤٠٠	حـ/ مراقبة الأجور
	٣٠٠	حـ/ تكاليف صناعية غير مباشرة محملة

ثانياً: الطريقة غير المباشرة: تقوم هذه الطريقة بتحميل تكاليف الإصلاح على حساب التكاليف الصناعية غير المباشرة باستخدام قيد اليومية التالي:

١٠٠٠		حـ/ تكاليف صناعية غير مباشرة (فعلية)
	٣٠٠	حـ/ مراقبة المواد
	٤٠٠	حـ/ مراقبة الأجور
	٣٠٠	حـ تكاليف صناعية غير مباشرة محملة

لاحظ أننا لم نذكر أن المعالجة السابقة تخص المراحل الإنتاجية أو الأوامر الإنتاجية لأن ذلك لا يؤدي إلى تغيير في شكل قيد اليومية السابق.

المعالجة المحاسبية للخردة:

الخردة هي مادة خام تم استخدامها ولكنها لم تدخل في التكوين المادي للسلع المنتجة مثل النشارة في صناعة الأثاث، وبرادة المعادن في الصناعات المعدنية، والزجاج المكسور في صناعة الزجاج. وقد يتم بيع الخردة بقيمة بيعيه منخفضة بالمقارنة مع سعر شراء المواد الخام.

تتوقف المعالجة المحاسبية على أهميتها ونظرة الإدارة إليها، فإذا كانت مهمة وترغب الإدارة في مزاولة رقابة عليها، يتم إثباتها في السجلات المحاسبية عند إنتاجها وتسجل على أساس صافي قيمتها البيعية، وهنا إذا كانت صافي القيمة البيعية للخردة تساوي ١٠٠ دينار مثلا يتم تسجيلها بموجب قيد اليومية التالي:

١٠٠	حـ/مخزون الخردة
	حـ/ الإنتاج تحت التشغيل ١٠٠

وإما إذا اتبعت الطريقة غير المباشرة فيكون الجانب الدائن من قيد اليومية هو حساب مراقبة التكاليف الصناعية غير المباشرة، وهنا يجب أخذ قيمة الخردة في الحسبان عند القيام بإعداد معدل تحميل التكاليف الصناعية غير المباشرة، ويتم إثباتها في الدفاتر بالقيد التالي:

	حـ/مخزون الخردة		١٠٠
١٠٠	حـ/ تكاليف صناعية غير مباشرة فعلية		

وإذا رأت الإدارة أن قيمتها البيعية منخفضة نوعاً ما، وترغب في مراقبتها عن طريق تتبع كمياتها فقط، ففي هذه الحالة يتم كتابة مذكرة عن كمياتها التي يتم توريدها إلى المخازن، ويعتبر ثمنها عند بيعها إيرادات عرضية.

بيع الخردة:

عند بيع الخردة بمبلغ ١٠٠ دينار واستخدام أي من القيدين السابقين تسجل قيمة المبيعات باستخدام قيد اليومية التالي:

	حـ/ النقدية أو المدينين		١٠٠
١٠٠	حـ/ مخزون الخردة		

وإذا حدث فرق بين ثمن بيع الخردة وصافي قيمتها البيعية المقدرة يحمل الفرق على حساب إيرادات أو خسائر أخرى. أما في حالة كتابة مذكرة عند إنتاجها فإنه يتم إثبات البيع باستخدام أحد القيود التالية:

	حـ/ النقدية		١٠٠
١٠٠	حـ/ إنتاج تحت التشغيل		

أو

	حـ/ النقدية		١٠٠
١٠٠	حـ/ تكاليف صناعية غير مباشرة فعلية		

يستخدم القيد الأول في حالة الطريقة المباشرة ويستخدم القيد الثاني في حالة الطريقة غير المباشرة.

وبدراسة الطرق السابقة نجد أن إثبات القيمة البيعية للخردة عند الإنتاج يساعد في حمايتها من التلاعب ولكن للأسف تعتبر طريقة عدم إثباتها عند الإنتاج هي أكثر استخداماً. (١)

(١) Horngren and Foster, Op. Cit., P. ٥٥٦.

الخاتمـــــــة

في هذا الفصل تمت دراسة المعالجة المحاسبية للوحدات غير الجيدة، وقسمت إلى أربع مجموعات هي: وحدات التالف والوحدات المعيبة والخردة والفاقد. وعند التعرض للتالف وجدنا أنه من الضروري أن يتم إدراجه في جدول الإنتاج المكافئ وأن يعتبر مستوى إتمامه بالنسبة لتكاليف التحويل وأما المواد فيجب أن تعالج حسب المستوى الذي تضاف عنده وما إذا استفادت الوحدات التالفة منها أم لا. و يجب أن تقسم الوحدات غير الجيدة إلى وحدات عادية ووحدات غير عادية واعتبار تكاليف الوحدات العادية، ضمن عناصر تكاليف الإنتاج واعتبار الأخيرة خسارة، وقد تم التعرض لمعالجة التالف محاسبياً عند الإنتاج أو عند البيع.

يتم تحميل الإنتاج الجيد بتكاليف إصلاح الوحدات المعيبة العادية وذلك بجعل حساب إنتاج تحت التشغيل مديناً عند إتباع الطريقة المباشرة أو بتحميل هذه التكاليف على حساب التكاليف الصناعية غير المباشرة عند إتباع الطريقة غير المباشرة، أما بالنسبة للخردة والفاقد فيجب عدم تحميلها بأية تكاليف ويمكن إثبات الخردة عند الإنتاج أو عند البيع. ومن ناحية الرقابة يفضل إثباتها محاسبياً عند الإنتاج وللتسهيل يمكن الاكتفاء بمذكرة عنها وإثباتها محاسبياً عند البيع فقط.

أسئلة وتمارين

السؤال الأول: ميز بين الوحدات التالفة والوحدات المعيبة.

السؤال الثاني: ما الفرق بين التالف الطبيعي والتالف غير الطبيعي وما أثر ذلك على تكاليف الوحدات الجيدة؟

السؤال الثالث: تعتمد تكلفة التالف العادي على مستوى الفحص علل ذلك؟

السؤال الرابع: ما هي عيوب الطريقة المباشرة المستخدمة في معالجة التالف في صناعة الأوامر الإنتاجية؟

السؤال الخامس: إذا تم إهمال وحدات التالف العادي عند حساب الوحدات المكافئة، هل نصل إلى تكلفة صحيحة للوحدات المنتجة؟

السؤال السادس: هل تفضل إثبات صافي القيمة البيعية للخردة عند الإنتاج أو عند البيع ولماذا؟

السؤال السابع: إذا طلب إليك معالجة تكاليف إصلاح التالف في مصنع لصناعة الثلاجات وتقديم تقرير عن ذلك، فما هي الأمور التي يجب أخذها في الحسبان؟

السؤال الثامن: إذا لم توافق على افتراض أن الوحدات التالفة تعود إلى الوحدات المضافة خلال الفترة في طريقة الأول في الأول ما هو اقتراحك للتغلب على هذا العيب؟

السؤال التاسع: تضاف المواد في بداية المرحلة وتضاف تكاليف التحويل بانتظام، ويتم فحص التالف عند مستوى إتمام ٥٠٪ وفيما يلي بالتدفق المادي.

	تكاليف تحويل	مواد	وحدات	
وحدات تحت التشغيل أول المدة	٤٠٪	١٠٠٪	٧,٠٠٠	
وحدات مضافة خلال المدة			٣٠,٠٠٠	
وحدات تامة محولة			٣٠,٠٠٠	
وحدات تحت التشغيل آخر المدة	٦٥٪	١٠٠٪	٦,٠٠٠	

وأن نسبة التالف العادي هي ٢٪ من الوحدات الجيدة.

المطلوب:

(١) إعداد جدول الوحدات المكافئة بطريقة الأول في الأول مع التمييز بين وحدات التالف العادي ووحدات التالف غير العادي.

(٢) تحديد نسبة توزيع التالف العادي بين حسابات البضاعة.

السؤال العاشر: بالرجوع إلى بيانات السؤال السابق افترض أن الشركة تستخدم طريقة المتوسط المرجح وتقوم بفحص الإنتاج في نهاية المرحلة.

المطلوب:

١- إعداد جدول الوحدات المكافئة مع التمييز بين وحدات التالف العادي ووحدات التالف غير العادي.

٢- بيان نسب توزيع التالف بين الإنتاج التام والإنتاج تحت التشغيل آخر المدة.

السؤال الحادي عشر: إذا كانت تكلفة الوحدة التالفة ٣ دنانير وتتكون من دينارين مواداً والباقي تكاليف تحويل ويتم الفحص عند مستوى ٥٠٪ وبلغت وحدات التالف العادي ١,٥٠٠ وحدة، ووحدات الإنتاج التام ٣٠,٠٠٠ وحدة ووحدات الإنتاج تحت التشغيل آخر المدة ٥,٠٠٠ وحدة ومستوى إتمامها ٧٠٪، ولا يوجد إنتاج تحت التشغيل أول المدة، وتبلغ القيمة البيعية للوحدة التالفة ٢,٥ د، تضاف المواد في بداية المرحلة وتضاف تكاليف التحويل بانتظام.

المطلوب:

١. تحديد عدد وحدات التالف العادي.

٢. تحديد تكلفة الإنتاج التام عند إثبات التالف بطريقة الإنتاج؟

٣. تحديد تكلفة الإنتاج تحت التشغيل إذا كانت الشركة تتبع طريقة البيع؟

السؤال الثاني عشر: تستخدم إحدى الشركات طريقة محاسبة المراحل الإنتاجية وتتبع طريقة الأول في الأول، وتستخدم مادتين في الإنتاج هما س، ص حيث تضاف المادة س في بداية العملية الإنتاجية وتضاف المادة ص بعد الفحص مباشرة وتقوم بفحص إنتاجها

عند مستوى إتمام ٧٠٪ وتتوقع أن تبلغ نسبة التالف العادي ٢.٥٪ من الإنتاج الجيد. والآتي معلومات مستخرجة من سجلات وتقارير الشركة.

- وحدات تحت التشغيل أول المدة ١٣,٠٠٠ وحدة وكان تفاصيل إتمامها كالتالي:

٢,٠٠٠ وحدة عند مستوى ٤٠٪

٤,٠٠٠ وحدة عند مستوى ٧٥٪

٧,٠٠٠ وحدة عند مستوى ٨٠٪

- وحدات بدأت الإنتاج ٣٣,٠٠٠ وقد تم منها ١٩,٠٠٠ وحدة والباقي يعتبر تحت التشغيل آخر المدة أو وحدات تالف.

- وحدات تحت التشغيل آخر المدة ١٢,٠٠٠ وحدة منها ٧,٠٠٠ وحدة عند مستوى إتمام ٦٠٪ و ٥,٠٠٠ وحدة عند مستوى إتمام ٨٠٪

وقد اعتبر باقي الوحدات تالفاً، وتفترض الشركة بأن الوحدات التالفة من الوحدات التي أضيفت للمرحلة.

المطلوب:

١. حساب عدد الوحدات الجيدة وتحديد عدد وحدات التالف العادي.

٢. إعداد جدول الوحدات المكافئة بإتباع طريقة الأول في الأول.

٣. إذا كانت تكلفة الوحدة التالفة مؤلفة من ٣ دينار وأنه يمكن بيع الوحدة بمبلغ ١.٥ دينار وتقوم المنشأة بإثبات التالف حسب طريقة الإنتاج. عمل القيود الضرورية في هذه الحالة.

السؤال الثالث عشر: الآتي معلومات مستخرجة من دفاتر إحدى الشركات الصناعية خلال شهر نيسان:

	وحدات	مواد	تكاليف تحويل
إنتاج تحت التشغيل أول المدة	٥,٠٠٠	١٠٠٪	٧٥٪
وحدات مضافة إلى المرحلة	١٤,٠٠٠		
وحدات تامة محولة	١٤,٠٠٠		
وحدات تحت التشغيل آخر المدة	٤,٠٠٠	١٠٠٪	٤٠٪

| %٥٠ | %١٠٠ | ١,٠٠٠ | وحدات تالفة |

التكاليف:

| ١١,٠٠٠ | ١٥,٠٠٠ | رصيد أول المدة |
| ٣٧,٣٠٠ | ٦٠,٥٠٠ | تكاليف الفترة الجارية |

وتتبع الشركة طريقة المتوسط المرجح ويقدر التالف العادي بنسبة ٤% من الإنتاج الجيد.

المطلوب:

١. إعداد تقرير تكاليف المرحلة.

٢. عمل قيود اليومية اللازمة إذا كان سعر بيع وحدة التالف هو ٣ دنانير في حالات:

أ- إثبات التالف حسب طريقة الإنتاج.

ب- إثبات التالف حسب طريقة البيع.

السؤال الرابع عشر: المطلوب حل السؤال السابق باستخدام طريقة الأول في الأول.

السؤال الخامس عشر: تستخدم شركة طريقة المتوسط المرجح وتقوم بفحص الإنتاج عند مستوى ٥٠% ويقدر التالف العادي بنسبة ٥% من الإنتاج الجيد. وكانت التدفقات المادية للوحدات كالتالي:

وحدات تحت التشغيل أول المدة	١,٠٠٠ (٤٠%)
وحدات مضافة خلال الفترة الجارية	١٢,٠٠٠
وحدات تامة محول	١٠,٠٠٠
وحدات تحت التشغيل آخر المدة	٢,٠٠٠ (٦٠%)
وحدات تالفة	١,٠٠٠

تضاف المواد في بداية عملية الإنتاج أما تكاليف التحويل فتضاف بانتظام وبلغت تكلفة الوحدة المكافئة خلال الفترة ٥ دنانير منها ٣ دينار مواد ٢ دينار تكاليف تحويل، ويتوقع أن تباع وحدة التالف بمبلغ ٢ دينار.

المطلوب:

توزيع تكاليف التالف العادي على الوحدات الجيدة في حالة:

أ- إثبات التالف عن الإنتاج.

ب- إثبات التالف عن البيع.

السؤال السادس عشر: تتبع إحدى الشركات نظام محاسبة الأوامر الإنتاجية وتأخذ التالف العادي في الحسبان عند إعداد معدل تحميل التكاليف الصناعية غير المباشرة. وخلال الفترة عملت الشركة على عدة أوامر إنتاجية وبلغت تكلفة الوحدات التالفة العادية ٦٠٠ دينار وتفاصيلها ٣٠٠ مواد مباشرة، ٢٠٠ أجور مباشرة ١٠٠ تكاليف صناعية غير مباشرة، وتبلغ صافي القيمة البيعية لهذه الوحدات ٤٠٠ دينار. علماً بأن تكلفة الإنتاج التام قبل توزيع التالف تبلغ ٥٨,٠٠٠ دينار.

المطلوب:

١. إثبات قيمة التالف في الدفاتر إذا كانت الشركة تقوم بإثبات قيمة التالف عند الإنتاج.

٢. إثبات قيمة التالف في الدفاتر إذا كانت الشركة تتبع الطريقة المباشرة وترغب في إثبات التالف عن الإنتاج.

السؤال السابع عشر: تتبع شركة طريقة محاسبة المراحل وخلال الفترة التكاليف المنتهية في ١٢/٣١ توفرت في سجلاتها البيانات التالية:

	وحدة
وحدات تحت التشغيل أول المدة	٢,٠٠٠ (٦٠%)
وحدات تامة محولة	١٨,٠٠٠
وحدات تحت التشغيل آخر المدة	٤,٠٠٠ (٨٠%)
وحدات تالفة	٢,٠٠٠

وتبلغ نسبة التالف ٥% ويتم الفحص عند مستوى ٧٠%

وكانت التكاليف كالتالي:

	ت تحويل	مواد
رصيد حساب إنتاج تحت التشغيل أول المدة	٥,٣٨٨	٥,١٠٠
تكاليف الفترة الجارية	٩٦,٣٠٠	٥٥,٠٠٠

واكتشفت الشركة وجود ٢٠٠ وحدة معيبة في نهاية عملية التشغيل تم اعتبارها وحدات معيبة عادية ولزم لإصلاحها ٢٢٠ مواد مباشرة ١,٠٥٠ تكاليف تحويل، ولم تحمل هذه التكاليف على حساب الإنتاج تحت التشغيل وتتبع المنشأة الطريقة المباشرة عند المحاسبة على تكاليف الإصلاح.

المطلوب:

(١) إعداد تقرير تكاليف المرحلة حسب طريقة الأول في الأول.

(٢) عمل قيود اليومية لإثبات تكاليف الإصلاح حسب الطريقة المباشرة.

(٣) عمل قيود اليومية اللازمة في حالة استخدام الطريقة غير المباشرة في معالجة تكاليف الإنتاج المعيب.

(٤) عمل قيد اليومية عند إثبات التالف عند البيع.

السؤال الثامن عشر: (CMA معدل):

يمر الإنتاج في إحدى الشركات الصناعية بثلاث مراحل هي الصب والتجميع والتشطيب وبعدها يحول الإنتاج إلى مخازن المنتجات التامة والمعلومات التالية تخص إدارة التشطيب عن شهر أيار:

	الوحدات
مخزون تحت التشغيل أول المدة	١,٤٠٠
وحدات محولة من مرحلة التجميع	١٤,٠٠٠
وحدات تالفة	٧٠٠
وحدات تامة محولة إلى المخازن	١١,٢٠٠

تضاف المواد الخام في بداية المرحلة بدون أن تؤدي إلى تغير في عدد الوحدات وتضاف تكاليف التحويل بانتظام وكان مخزون إنتاج تحت التشغيل أول المدة عند مستوى إتمام ٧٠٪ أما مخزون تحت التشغيل آخر المدة فقد كان عند مستوى إتمام ٤٠٪ ويتم اكتشاف التالف في نهاية المرحلة وقبل تحويل الإنتاج إلى المخازن، ٥٦٠ وحدة من التالف كانت عادية والباقي غير العادية. تستخدم المنشأة المتوسط المرجح. وكانت الوحدات المكافئة وتكلفة الوحدة المكافئة لكل عناصر التكاليف كالتالي:

تكاليف الوحدة المكافئة	وحدات مكافئة	
٥د	١٥,٤٠٠	تكاليف محولة
١د	١٥,٤٠٠	مواد مباشرة
٣د	١٣,٣٠٠	تكاليف تحويل
٩د		المجموع

المطلوب: الإجابة على أسئلة التالية:

١. تكلفة الإنتاج التام بعد المحاسبة على التالف والمحول إلى المخازن هي:

أ- ١٠٠,٨٠٠ د   ب- ١٠٥,٨٤٠د

جـ- ١٠٧,١٠٠ د   د- ١٠٢,٠٦٠ د

هـ- لا شيء مما ذكر

٢. تكلفة الإنتاج تحت التشغيل آخر المدة هي:

أ- ٢٨,٠٠٠ د   ب- ٣١,٠٠٠ د

جـ- ٢٥,٢٠٠ د   د- ٣٠,٢٤٠ د

هـ- لاشي مما ذكر

٣. إذا كانت التكلفة المستلمة التي يحتويها رصيد حساب إنتاج تحت التشغيل أول المدة في هذه الإدارة هو ٦,٢٠٠ دينار، فإن التكلفة المستلمة من إدارة التجميع خلال الشهر هي:

أ- ٧٠,٠٠٠ د   ب- ٦٢,٣٠٠ د

جـ- ٧٠,٧٠٠ د   د- ٦٣,٧٠٠ د

هـ- لاشي مما ذكر

٤. تكلفة التالف غير العادي هي:

أ- ٦,٣٠٠ د   ب- ١,٢٦٠ د

جـ- ٥٦٠ د   د- ٨٤٠ د

هـ- لاشيء مما ذكر

السؤال التاسع عشر: تستخدم إحدى الشركات نظام تكلفة الأوامر وتعتبر تكلفة العمل المعيب عند إعداد معدل تحميل التكاليف الصناعية غير المباشرة المحددة مقدماً. وخلال شهر آذار انتهى الأمر رقم ٢٠١ المتعلق بإنتاج ٢,٠٠٠ وحدة من المنتج أ وبلغت تكلفة الوحدة كالتالي:

٥ دنانير مواد مباشرة

٤ دنانير أجور مباشر

٦ دينار تكاليف صناعية غير مباشرة محملة بنسبة ١٥٠٪ من الأجور.

وتبين من فحص هذا الأمر عند الانتهاء من إنتاجه أن هناك ١٠٠ وحدة معيبة تم إعادة تشغيلها وبلغ متوسط تكلفة تصليح الوحدة ٢ دينار أجور مباشرة بالإضافة إلى حصتها من الأعباء الإضافية ولم يحتاج إصلاحها إلى أية مواد. وتقع الوحدات المعيبة المكتشفة ضمن المجال العادي، فما هو إجمالي تكلفة التصليح وما هو الحساب الذي تحمل عليه:

تكاليف الإصلاح	الحساب المدين
أ- ٢٠٠	إنتاج تحت التشغيل
ب- ٢٠٠	مراقبة التكاليف الصناعية غير المباشرة
جـ- ٥٠٠	إنتاج تحت التشغيل
د- ٥٠٠	مراقبة التكاليف الصناعية غير المباشرة

(مجمع المحاسبين القانونيين سنة ١٩٨٢)

السؤال العشرون: تقوم شركة صناعية بإضافة المواد المباشرة في بداية عملية التشغيل والآتي معلومات تتعلق بالمواد المستخدمة في الإنتاج خلال شهر نيسان.

	وحدات
وحدات تحت التشغيل في ¼	١٠,٠٠٠
وحدات مضافة خلال شهر نيسان	٥٠,٠٠٠
وحدات تامة محولة إلى الإدارة التالية	٣٦,٠٠٠
وحدات تالف عادي	٣٠٠٠
وحدات تالف غير عادي	٥٠٠٠
وحدات تحت التشغيل في ٤/٣٠	١٦٠٠٠

وتعتبر الشركة أن تكاليف التالف العادي هي جزء من تكاليف الوحدات الجيدة التي يتم إنتاجها، أما تكاليف التالف غير العادي فتعتبر ضمن التكاليف غير المباشرة. وباستخدام طريقة المتوسط المرجح ما هو عدد الوحدات المكافئة لعنصر المواد المستخدمة في حساب تكلفة الوحدة خلال شهر نيسان؟

أ- ٤٧,٠٠٠   ب- ٥٢,٠٠٠

جـ- ٦٠,٠٠٠   د- ٥٧,٠٠٠

(مجمع المحاسبين القانونيين الأمريكي معدل)

السؤال الحادي والعشرون: المعلومات التالية تخص الأسئلة (أسئلة امتحانات سابقة) التالية:

يتم فحص الإنتاج عند مستوى إتمام ٧٥٪ وكانت وحدات تحت التشغيل أول المدة عند مستوى إتمام ٨٠٪ وعددها ٣,٠٠٠ وحدة، والوحدات التي بدأت وعددها ١٥,٠٠٠ قد بقي منها ٢,٠٠٠ وحدة تحت التشغيل آخر المدة عند مستوى إتمام ٧٠٪ وعدد الوحدات التالفة التي اكتشفت نتيجة الفحص هي ٢,٠٠٠ وحدة. وأن نسبة التالف العادي ٥٪ وتكلفة الوحدة التالفة هي ٢د. وتتبع الشركة طريقة الأول في الأول في المحاسبة على تكاليف المراحل. وتضاف كل التكاليف بانتظام.

أ- فإن عدد وحدات التالف العادي هي:

أ- ٨٥٠ وحدة   ب- ٦٥٠ وحدة

جـ- ٥٧٥ وحدة   د- ٧٥٠ وحدة

هـ- لا شيء مما ذكر

ب- نصيب الإنتاج التام من تكاليف التالف العادي هي:

أ- ١,٧٠٠ د   ب- ١,٣٠٠ د

جـ- ١,١٥٠ د   د- ١٥,٠٠٠ د

هـ- لاشيء

جـ- إذا كان الفحص يتم في نهاية المرحلة مع بقاء المعلومات المعطاة في السؤال على ما هي عليه فإن نصيب وحدات تحت التشغيل آخر المدة من تكاليف التالف العادي هي:

أ- ١٠٠ د   ب- ٧٠٠ د

جـ- ٨٠ د   د- صفر

هـ- لا شيء مما ذكر

السؤال الثاني والعشرون: لقد تم تجميع المعلومات الآتية في سجلات إحدى الشركات الصناعية عن السنة المنتهية في ١٢/٣١. يوجد في الشركة مرحلتين إنتاجيتين هما التصنيع والتشطيب وإدارة للخدمات، وفي مرحلة التصنيع يتم إنتاج المنتج أ من خلط مادتين هما س، ص. أما في مرحلة التشطيب فإن كل وحدة من ا يتم تقسيمها إلى ٦ وحدات من المنتج عن ٣ وحدات من المنتج ط. وتقوم إدارة الخدمات بتقديم خدمات لقسمي الإنتاج تضاف المواد في بداية عملية التصنيع.

- تستخدم الشركة محاسبة التكاليف الفعلية في تحميل الأعباء الإضافية ويتم تقسيم تكاليف قسم الخدمات على أساس فعلي وأن التالف العادي يقدر بنسبة ٢٪ ويتم الفحص بانتظام. يتم توزيع تكاليف قسم الخدمة كالتالي:

المصروف	أساس التوزيع
صيانة واستهلاك المباني	المساحة المربعة
الموظفون والأعمال الكتابية	عدد الموظفين
أخرى	بالتساوي

يتم تسعير المواد الخام والإنتاج باستخدام طريقة الأول في الأول وتم الحصول على المعلومات الآتية من إدارة التصنيع عن شهر ١٢.

الكميات (وحدات المنتج أ)	العدد
تحت التشغيل في ١٢/١	٣,٠٠٠ (١٠٠%، ٤٠%)
مضافة إلى التشغيل خلال شهر ١٢	٢٥,٠٠٠
محولة إلى إدارة التشطيب	١٩,٠٠٠
تحت التشغيل آخر المدة	٦,٠٠٠ (١٠٠%، ٧٥%)
تالفة	٣,٠٠٠

وكانت التكاليف كالتالي:

	الإجمالي	مواد	أجور	تكاليف تحويل
الرصيد في ١/١	٥٢,٠٠٠	١٣,٠٠٠	١٧,٥٠٠	٢١,٥٠٠
أجور شهر ١٢			١٥٤,٠٠٠	١٣٢,٠٠٠

وقد تم الحصول على المعلومات التالية من سجلات المخازن

	المادة س		المادة ص	
	الكمية	القيمة	الكمية	القيمة
الرصيد في ١/١	٦٢,٠٠٠	٦٢,٠٠٠د	٢٦٥,٠٠٠	١٨٥,٠٠٠
المشتريات:				
١٢/١٠	٣٩,٥٠٠	٤٩,٣٧٥د		
١٢/٢٥	٢٨,٥٠٠	٣٤,٢٠٠د		
المصروف للإنتاج	٨٣,٢٠٠		٥٠,٠٠٠	

وكانت تكاليف قسم الخدمات كالتالي:

صيانة المبنى واستهلاكه	٤٥,٠٠٠د
الموظفين	٢٧,٥٠٠
أخرى	٣٩,٠٠٠
الإجمالي	١١١,٥٠٠

والمعلومات الأخرى:

	المساحة المربعة	عدد الموظفين
التصنيع	٧٥,٠٠٠	١٨٠
التجميع	٣٧,٥٠٠	١٢٠

المطلوب:

(١) حساب عدد الوحدات المكافئة من المنتج أ.

(٢) إعداد تقرير تكاليف المرحلة لقسم التصنيع.

(٣) إثبات التالف عند الإنتاج إذا كانت القيمة البيعية لوحدة التالف ٣ دنانير.

الفصل السادس
توزيع تكاليف مراكز الخدمات الصناعية

بعد دراسة هذا الفصل يتوقع معرفة الآتي:

١. طبيعة ومفهوم التكاليف الصناعية غير المباشرة.

٢. مشاكل تصنيف التكاليف الصناعية غير المباشرة.

٣- طرق تحميل التكاليف الصناعية غير المباشرة على وحدات الإنتاج.

٤. مراكز التكاليف وأهميتها في المحاسبة على التكاليف الصناعية غير المباشرة وتحميلها على وحدات الإنتاج.

٥. معايير وأسس توزيع التكاليف الصناعية غير المباشرة على المراكز المختلفة.

٦. طرق توزيع تكاليف مراكز الخدمات على مراكز الإنتاج.

٧. مفهوم مستوى الطاقة اللازم لتوزيع التكاليف الصناعية غير المباشرة.

مقدمـــة:

تشمل التكاليف الصناعية غير المباشرة (الأعباء الصناعية الإضافية) Manufacturing Overhead على كل عناصر التكاليف التي يصعب تتبعها وتخصيصها على الهدف النهائي للتكلفة، والذي قد يكون وحدات الإنتاج أو مراكز التكاليف أو المسؤولية. فإذا كان الهدف النهائي للتكلفة هو تحديد تكلفة وحدة الإنتاج، فإن التكاليف الصناعية غير المباشرة هي التكاليف الصناعية التي يصعب ربطها وتخصيصها على وحدة الإنتاج النهائية. وإذا كان الهدف النهائي للتكلفة هو تحديد تكلفة تشغيل قسم أو مركز معين، فإن التكلفة غير المباشرة للقسم تشتمل على تكاليف الخدمات التي تقدمها له المراكز الأخرى، أو عناصر التكاليف التي يشترك فيها مع مراكز أخرى مثل: تكلفة الإيجار، والضرائب والرسوم، ومصروفات نقل العاملين. لذلك تواجه المحاسب عند التعامل مع هذه المجموعة عدة مشكلات تعود للأسباب الآتية:

١- إن هذه المجموعة تضم العديد من العناصر التي تختلف عن بعضها من حيث الطبيعة والسلوك، فهي تشتمل على سبيل المثال، على المواد غير المباشرة، والأجور غير المباشرة، والخدمات الصناعية الأخرى. وكل بند منها يتميز عن غيره من حيث الاستجابة للتغير في حجم النشاط، فبعضها لا يتغير عند تغير حجم النشاط إذا كان التغير ضمن مدى معين، وبعضها الآخر يتغير طردياً مع التغير في حجم النشاط مثل الكهرباء المستخدمة في تشغيل الآلات. وبعض العناصر الأخرى يجمع بين الصفتين السابقتين.

٢- لا توجد هناك علاقة واضحة بين هذه العناصر ووحدات الإنتاج، وهذا يؤدي الى صعوبة في تحديد قيمة الكمية التي تخص كل وحدة من هذه العناصر ويزيد من تعقيد هذه المشكلة أن بعض البنود تحدث في مراكز غير إنتاجية لا تعمل بصورة مباشرة على وحدات المنتج النهائي.

٣- تحدث في كل إرجاء المنشأة وهذا يؤدي إلى تعقيد تخطيطها، ومزاولة الرقابة الفعالة على حدوثها.

تبويب عناصر التكاليف الصناعية غير المباشرة:

حتى تتم المحاسبة على عناصر التكاليف الصناعية غير المباشرة يجب البدء في تحديد حساباتها لتستخدم في تسجيلها بالدفاتر، وهنا جرت العادة على تبويب هذه العناصر في ثلاث مجموعات فرعية هي:-

أولاً: المواد غير المباشرة،

ثانياً: الأجور غير المباشرة،

ثالثاً: المصروفات الصناعية الأخرى،

ولقد تم شرح طبيعة هذه البنود في الفصل الثاني من هذا الكتاب.

مراكز الإنتاج ومراكز الخدمات:

ولزيادة دقة تحميل التكاليف غير المباشرة على وحدات الإنتاج، ولتحقيق أغراض الرقابة، يتم تقسيم المنشأة إلى أقسام تعرف بمراكز التكاليف، وهذه يتم تعريفها على أنها وحدات إدارية أو فنية تقوم باستخدام عناصر تكاليف معينة لتحقيق هدف أو أهداف معينة، وتهدف جميع هذه الوحدات إلى تحقيق الهدف النهائي للمنشأة الذي هو تعظيم ثروتها في الأجل الطويل. بعض هذه الوحدات الإدارية أو الفنية يسند إليه هدف إنتاج منتج معين أو منتجات معينة، وبعضها الآخر يسند إليه تقديم خدمة للوحدات الأخرى مثل: الصيانة، والخدمات الهندسية، وتوليد البخار، وبعضها يسند إليه القيام بأعمال التسويق وهكذا. وحتى ينجح النظام المحاسبي في تحقيق أهدافه يجب أن يراعي طبيعة أعمال المنشأة وحجمها، ونوع إداراتها وتنوع المنتجات التي تقدمها.

وفي إطار وظيفة الإنتاج يمكن التمييز بين نوعين من المراكز هما: مراكز الإنتاج، ومراكز الخدمات الإنتاجية، وتقوم مراكز الإنتاج بالعمل على إنتاج المنتجات النهائية للمنشأة، وقد تقوم بعملها بصورة مستمرة، كما هو الحال في صناعات المراحل، أو تقوم بعملها على منتجات ذات مواصفات خاصة، كما هو الحال في صناعات الأوامر الإنتاجية. ولأن المنتجات تستفيد من خدماتها مباشرة نجد علاقة واضحة نوعا ما بين تكاليفها ووحدات الإنتاج التي تستفيد من أنشطة التشغيل التي تقوم فيها هذه الأقسام [1].

---

[1] Hirsch and Louder, Back, Op. Cit, Pp. ٤٨٥-٤٨٨.

وعلى الجانب الآخر تقوم مراكز الخدمات الإنتاجية بتقديم العون والمساعدة إلى أقسام الإنتاج ولذلك لا تمر المنتجات من خلالها. وبالتالي يجب توزيع تكاليفها على أقسام الإنتاج حتى تضاف الى التكاليف غير المباشرة الخاصة بمراكز الإنتاج وبعدها توزع على وحدات المنتجات. ويمكن توضيح هذه العلاقة كما في الشكل رقم (٦-١).

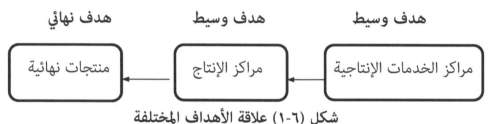

شكل (٦-١) علاقة الأهداف المختلفة

دورة توزيع تكاليف مراكز الخدمات الإنتاجية على المنتجات النهائية.

أهمية مراكز التكاليف :

يؤدي تقسيم المنشأة إلى مراكز تكاليف إلى زيادة الأعباء المحاسبية لأن كل قسم تتم معاملته كوحدة محاسبية مستقلة له علاقات مع مراكز تكاليف أخرى. ويمكن النظر إلى القسم على أنه منشأة تتعامل مع البيئة الخارجية التي تحتوي على العديد من المنشآت الأخرى التي من ضمنها مراكز التكاليف الأخرى في المنشأة، ويتم تبرير تحمل تكاليف تشغيل هذا النظام، لأنه يؤدي إلى زيادة دقة تكلفة الوحدات، وزيادة فعالية أنظمة الرقابة والتخطيط [١]. فعدم تقسيم المنشأة إلى مراكز تكاليف يتم اعتبارها مركز تكلفة واحد، وهذا يؤدي الى تحميل عناصر التكاليف الصناعية غير المباشرة بصورة إجمالية على المنتجات، ولكن إذا تم تقسيم المنشأة إلى عدة مراكز تكاليف، فيتم توزيع هذه التكاليف على مراكز التكلفة أولاً وبعد ذلك يتم تحميلها على الإنتاج حسب العلاقة بين التكاليف وطبيعة نشاط المركز وهذا يؤدي إلى زيادة دقة توزيع التكلفة.

ولتوضيح ذلك افترض أن إحدى المنشآت تتكون من مركزين هما: مركز أ، ومركز ب، وكانت بياناتهما كالتالي:

---

[1] Ibid., P. ٤٨٩.

مثال (١):

المنشأة	مركز ب	مركز أ	
٤٥,٠٠٠	٢٥,٠٠٠	٢٠,٠٠٠	التكاليف الصناعية غير المباشرة
١٥,٠٠٠	٥,٠٠٠	١٠,٠٠٠	ساعات العمل المباشرة
٣د	٥د	٢د	معدل التحميل لساعة العمل المباشر

افترض بأن المنشأة تقوم بإنتاج منتجين هما: س، ص، يحتاج المنتج س إلى ٢٠ س ع م منها ٥ ساعات في المركز أ و ١٥ ساعة في المركز ب، وان المنتج ص فيحتاج إلى ٢٠ س ع م منها ١٥ ساعة في المركز أ و ٥ ساعات في المركز ب.

المطلوب: تحديد الأعباء المحملة على المنتج س، والمنتج ص.

أولاً: تحميل الأعباء عند عدم تقسيم المنشأة إلى مراكز تكاليف

هنا إذا اختارت المنشأة تحميل الأعباء الإضافية على المنتجات باستخدام ساعات العمل المباشر، فيكون المعدل حينئذن ٣ د لساعة العمل المباشرة وتكون الأعباء المحملة على المنتجين كالتالي:

المنتج س = ٢٠ × ٣ = ٦٠ د

المنتج ص = ٢٠ × ٣ = ٦٠ د

وبهذا تتحمل وحدة المنتج س ووحدة المنتج ص بمبلغ ٦٠ د على الرغم من اختلاف درجة استفادتهما من التسهيلات الفنية والإنتاجية التي توفرها مراكز التكاليف أ، ب. ويطلق على معدل التحميل المستخدم في هذه الحالة اسم معدل التحميل الإجمالي.

ثانياً: تحميل الأعباء عند تقسيم المنشأة إلى مركز تكلفة:

عند تقسيم المنشأة إلى عدة مراكز تكلفة، فإن الأمر يتطلب أن تحدد المنشأة أساساً لتوزيع تكاليف كل مركز من هذه المراكز، ولنفرض أن المنشأة تستخدم ساعات العمل المباشرة لتحميل تكاليف هذه المركز على وحدات المنتجات وبالتالي يكون نصيب س، ص من هذه التكاليف كالتالي:

المنتج س:

مركز أ = 5 ساعات × 2د = 10د

مركز ب = 15 ساعة × 5 د = 75د

الإجمالي = 85د

المنتج ص:

مركز أ = 15 ساعة × 2د = 30 د

مركز ب = 5 ساعات × 5 د = 25د

الإجمالي = 55 د

وهذا يشير إلى أنه عند استخدام المعدل التحميل الإجمالي تحملت المنتجات س ص بنفس المبلغ، ولكن عندما تم استخدام معدلات مستقلة للأقسام اختلفت هذه المبالغ. وهنا نجد أن المعدل الإجمالي قد لا يراعي طبيعة عناصر التكاليف لأنه يفترض أن أساس التوزيع له نفس قوة العلاقة مع كل بنود الأعباء الإضافية. فقد تكون ساعات العمل المباشر مناسبة لتوزيع تكاليف المركز أ ولكنها قد لا تكون مناسبة لتوزيع تكاليف المركز ب، إذن يفضل أن يعامل كل مركز على حده.

تبويب عناصر التكاليف غير المباشرة:

ويمكن تبويب عناصر التكاليف الصناعية غير المباشرة - عند النظر إليها من ناحية مراكز التكاليف في مجموعتين هما:

أ- التكاليف الخاصة:

وتشمل التكاليف التي يمكن ربطها وتخصيصها على مركز معين دون غيره، وتشمل المواد واللوازم التي تصرف خصيصاً له، وأجرة مشرفي العمال، واستهلاك الآلات والمعدات الموجودة بالمركز، والتأمين على الأصول والبضاعة.

ب- التكاليف العامة أو المشتركة:

وتشمل التكاليف التي تخص أكثر من مركز، ومثال ذلك، الإيجار، وتكاليف الكهرباء والمياه، والهاتف، الرسوم، والرخص، ومرتب مدير المصنع والفنيين الذين يقدمون خدماتهم لعدة مراكز، وكذلك استهلاك الآلات والمعدات التي تفيد أكثر من مركز.

وعليه يجب توزيع هذه التكاليف على المراكز المستفيدة. وهنا يجب مراعاة طبيعة النفقة، مدى استفادة الأقسام منها. وفي الحياة العملية يتم استخدام عدة أسس لتوزيع عناصر التكاليف المشتركة بين الأقسام المستفيدة، ومثالها كما في الجدول رقم (٦-١).

جدول (٦-١)
أسس توزيع التكاليف العامة

أساس التوزيع	عنصر التكلفة
المساحة الأقسام بالمتر أو القدم المربعين	الإيجار
ساعة التشغيل مرجحة بالحصان	القوى المحركة
قيمة مواد الصيانة على أساس فعلي أما البنود الاخرى فتوزع على أساس ساعات التشغيل	الصيانة
عدد العمال المرضى أو عدد العاملين	النفقات الطبية
قيمة الأجور أو عدد العمال	التأمين الاجتماعي والصحي
قيمة الأصول الرأسمالية	الاستهلاك
المساحة أو عدد العمال	الرسوم والرخص
كمية الانتاج او ساعات الفحص	مركز رقابة الجودة
عدد العمال	مركز الاتصالات
المساحة	التدفئة والإنارة
عدد العمال	السفر والانتقال

ولتوضيح كيفية توزيع هذه التكاليف على مراكز التكلفة سيتم الاعتماد على البيانات التالية:

مثال (٢):

الآتي عناصر التكاليف غير المباشرة من سجلات إحدى الشركات الصناعية.

أولاً: التكاليف الخاصة:

	مراكز الإنتاج		مراكز الخدمات		إجمالي
	أ	ب	ج	د	
مواد غير مباشرة	١٥,٠٠٠	٩,٠٠٠	٤,٠٠٠	٨,٠٠٠	٣٦,٠٠٠
أجور غير مباشرة	١٢,٠٠٠	٦,٥٠٠	٤,٠٠٠	٧,٠٠٠	٢٩,٥٠٠
استهلاك الآلات	٢,٥٠٠	١,٨٠٠	٤٠٠	٦٥٠	٥,٣٥٠

ثانياً: وكانت التكاليف غير المباشرة المشتركة كالتالي:

١. مصروفات الكهرباء والمياه ١,٠٥٠ د.

٢. مرتبات مهندسي الإنتاج ١٢,٠٠٠ د.

٣. إيجار المبنى وصيانته ٤,٠٠٠ د.

٤. تكاليف الصيانة والتدفئة والتبريد ٣,٠٠٠ د.

٥. تبلغ مساحة المراكز السابقة بالمتر المربع: ٤٠٠، ٤٠٠، ١٠٠، ١٠٠ على التوالي.

٦. يبلغ عدد العمال في المراكز السابقة: ٤٠، ٣٠، ٢٠، ١٠ على التوالي.

٧. تقوم المنشأة بتوزيع إيجار المبنى وصيانته على أساس المساحة، وتوزيع مرتبات مهندسي الإنتاج على أساس عدد العمال الذين يعملون في مراكز التكاليف، وتوزع الكهرباء والمياه على أساس المساحة، ويستخدم الأساس نفسه في توزيع تكاليف الصيانة، والتدفئة، والتبريد، وإيجار المبنى.

وفي ضوء المعلومات السابقة توزع تكاليف المراكز كالتالي:

ملاحظات على الحل:

تم توزيع مرتبات مهندسي الإنتاج على أساس عدد العمال، وكانت نسب العمال في هذه المراكز هي: ٤٠٪، ٣٠٪، ٢٠٪، ١٠٪، وحسبت نسبة العمال في المركز بقسمة عدد العمال في المركز على إجمالي عدد العمال في المنشأة. وعليه تم حساب نصيب كل مركز من بند مرتبات مهندسي الإنتاج بضرب هذه المرتبات في نسبة عدد العمال في القسم وأصبحت التكاليف الموزعة كالتالي:

$$مركز أ = ١٢,٠٠٠ × ٠,٤٠ = ٤,٨٠٠$$

$$مركز ب = ١٢,٠٠٠ × ٠,٣٠ = ٣,٦٠٠$$

جدول (٦-٢)
توزيع التكاليف العامة والخاصة

بيان	أساس التوزيع	مراكز الإنتاج		مراكز الخدمات		الإجمالي
		أ	ب	جـ	د	
تكاليف خاصة:						
مواد غير مباشرة		١٥,٠٠٠	٩,٠٠٠	٤,٠٠٠	٨,٠٠٠	٣٦,٠٠٠
أجور غير مباشرة		١٢,٠٠٠	٦,٥٠٠	٤,٠٠٠	٧,٠٠٠	٢٩,٥٠٠
استهلاك الآلات		٢,٥٠٠	١,٨٠٠	٤٠٠	٦٥٠	٥,٣٥٠
تكاليف عامة:						
مرتبات المهندسون	عدد العمال	٤,٨٠٠	٣,٦٠٠	٢,٤٠٠	١,٢٠٠	١٢,٠٠٠
الإيجار	المساحة	١,٦٠٠	١,٦٠٠	٤٠٠	٤٠٠	٤,٠٠٠
الكهرباء والمياه	المساحة	٤٢٠	٤٢٠	١٠٥	١٠٥	١,٠٥٠
صيانة وتدفئة	المساحة	١,٢٠٠	١,٢٠٠	٣٠٠	٣٠٠	٣,٠٠٠
التكاليف		٣٧,٥٢٠	٢٤,٠١٥	١١٧١٠	١٧,٦٥٠	٩٠,٩٠٠

$$مركز جـ = ١٢,٠٠٠ × ٠,٢٠ = ٢٤٠٠$$

$$مركز د = ١٢,٠٠ × ٠,١٠ = ١٢٠٠$$

أما البنود الأخرى فقد تم توزيعها على أساس مساحة كل مركز وأن نسبة مساحة المراكز من أ وحتى د هي ٤٠٪ : ٤٠٪ : ١٠٪ : ١٠٪ على التوالي. لذلك حسب نصيب المراكز من تكاليف بند الإيجار كالتالي:

$$مركز أ = ٤,٠٠٠ × ٤٠٪ = ١,٦٠٠ د$$

$$مركز ب = ٤,٠٠٠ × ٤٠٪ = ١,٦٠٠ د$$

مركز جـ = ٤,٠٠٠ × ١٠% = ٤٠٠ د

مركز د = ٤,٠٠٠ × ١٠% = ٤٠٠ د

وبالطريقة نفسها تم توزيع بقية بنود التكاليف المشتركة عن طريق تحديد النسب المئوية الخاصة بالقسم وضربها بتكلفة البند.

توزيع تكاليف مراكز الخدمات:

تعرف هذه المراكز على أنها المراكز أو الأقسام أو الوحدات الإدارية التي لا تعمل بصورة مباشرة على المنتجات الخاصة بالمنشاة وتقدم خدماتها لمساعدة مراكز الإنتاج. وعلية لا توحد علاقة مباشرة بين وحدات الإنتاج وتكاليف هذه المراكز، وحتى يتم تحميل تكاليفها على المنتجات النهائية يجب توزيعها أولاً على مراكز الإنتاج، وبعد ذلك تضاف الى التكاليف غير المباشرة لمراكز الإنتاج ومنها توزع على وحدات المنتجات. ولتوزيع تكاليف مراكز الخدمات يجب الاتفاق على الأمور الآتية:

أ- قياس نشاط مراكز الخدمات.

ب- إختيار طريقة توزيع التكاليف.

وسيتم مناقشة هذه الأمور على التوالي:

أولاً: قياس نشاط مراكز الخدمات:

يتم قياس وحدات نشاط مراكز الخدمة حسب نوع النشاط الذي يقدمه المركز. وفي الحياة العملية هناك سهولة في قياس نشاط بعض مراكز الخدمات كما في حالة مركزي البخار والكهرباء في مصافي تكرير البترول حيث يقاس إنتاجهما بالطن المتري من البخار والكيلووات ساعة على التوالي. وعلى الجانب الآخر، هناك صعوبة في قياس نشاط مراكز أخرى لتنوع نشاطها لذلك يتم استخدام مقاييس تقريبية لقياس نشاطها، فمثلاً يقاس نشاط مركز العيادة الصحية باستخدام عدد المرضى مع انهم يختلفون من حالة إلى أخرى. على أية حال، لقد نمت في الحياة العملية عدة أسس لقياس أنشطة مراكز التكاليف وهي كما في الجدول رقم (٦-١) الذي تم عرضه سابقاً.

وبعد تحديد طريقة قياس نشاط مركز الخدمة يجب تحديد كمية استفادة المراكز الاخرى من خدمات هذا المركز. فمثلا إذا تم استخدام ساعات دوران الآلات لقياس نشاط مركز القوى المحركة يجب تحديد ساعات الدوران التي استفادت منها المراكز الاخرى الموجودة في الشركة وبجمعها نحدد نشاط مركز القوى المحركة. وبقسمة نشاط كل مركز على مجموع نشاط كل المراكز تحدد نسبة استفادة كل مركز من نشاط مركز الخدمة.

ثانيا : طرق توزيع تكاليف مراكز الخدمات:

يمكن توزيع تكاليف مراكز الخدمات على مراكز الإنتاج باستخدام إحدى الطرق التالية:

أ- طريقة التوزيع المباشرة   Direct Method

ب- طريقة التوزيع التنازلي   Step-down Method

جـ- طريقة التوزيع التبادلي   Mutual Method

ولتوضيح هذه الطرق يتم الاعتماد على البيانات التالية:

مثال (٣):

تتكون شركة الصناعات المعدنية من قسمين للإنتاج هما: قسم التصنيع وقسم التشطيب ومن قسمين للخدمات هما: القوى المحركة، والصيانة، ويتم قياس نشاط مراكز الخدمات باستخدام الكيلوات ساعة، وساعات الصيانة على التوالي، وكانت أرصدة تكاليف هذه الأقسام: ٧٠,٠٠٠ د، ٩٠,٠٠٠ د، ٣٠,٠٠٠ د، ٤٥,٠٠٠ د على التوالي. وان أقسام الخدمات قدمت الخدمات التالية: قام قسم القوى المحركة بتوليد ٢٤٠,٠٠٠ كيلو وات استهلك منها ٤٠,٠٠٠ كيلووات في أغراضه الخاصة، وقدم: ٨٠,٠٠٠ كيلووات الى قسم التصنيع، ٧٠,٠٠٠ كيلووات الى قسم التجميع، والباقي وقدرة ٥٠,٠٠٠ كيلووات قدمه الى قسم الصيانة.

بلغت ساعات عمل مركز الصيانة ١٠,٠٠٠ ساعة، حصل منها قسم التصنيع على ٤,٠٠٠ ساعة، وقسم التجميع على ٥,٠٠٠ ساعة، وقسم القوى المحركة على ١,٠٠٠ ساعة.

والمطلوب: توزيع تكاليف مراكز الخدمات على مراكز الإنتاج باستخدام:

أ- طريقة التوزيع المباشرة

ب- طريقة التوزيع التنازلي

جـ- طريقة التوزيع التبادلي

الحل:

عند توزيع تكاليف مراكز الخدمات لا يجوز تحميل مركز الخدمة بتكلفة الخدمات التي يستهلكها من إنتاجه، لذلك لا يتحمل مركز القوى المحركة بتكلفة الكهرباء التي استهلكها في أغراضه الخاصة لذلك تطرح هذه الكمية من إجمالي الكمية التي أنتجها، وتستخدم الكمية الباقية كأساس لتوزع تكلفة هذا المركز علي المراكز الأخرى. وكذلك هو الحال بالنسبة لمركز الصيانة. ولتسهيل عملية التوزيع يتم حساب النسبة المئوية للخدمات المقدمة للأقسام الأخرى كما في الجدول رقم (٤-٦). يتم حساب النسب المؤية بقسمة الكمية التي استهلكها مركز التكاليف الى إجمالي كمية نشاط المركز. فمركز الكهرباء أنتج ٢٤٠,٠٠٠ كيلووات استهلك منها ٤٠,٠٠٠ كيلووات إذن فان نشاطه المستخدم كأساس للتوزيع هو ٢٠٠,٠٠٠ كيلووات. حصل قسم التصنيع منها على ٨٠,٠٠٠ كيلووات وهذه تمثل نسبة ٤٠% (= ٨٠,٠٠٠ ÷ ٢٠٠,٠٠٠) من نشاطه. وهكذا يتم حساب بقية النسب الظاهرة في الجدول.

جدول (٤-٦)
النسب المئوية للخدمات المقدمة من مراكز الخدمات الإنتاجية

الإجمالي	مراكز الإنتاج		مراكز الخدمات		
	التجميع	التصنيع	الصيانة	القوى المحركة	الخدمات مقدمة من:
١٠٠%	٣٥%	٤٠%	٢٥%	---	قسم القوى المحركة
١٠٠%	٥٠%	٤٠%	--	١٠%	قسم الصيانة

من دراسة الجدول (٤-٦) نرى أن قسم الصيانة قد حصل على ٢٥٪ من خدمات قسم القوى المحركة، كما حصل قسم التجميع على ٣٥٪ من خدمات هذا المركز أيضاً.

١- طريقة التوزيع المباشر:

بموجب هذه الطريقة يتم توزيع تكاليف مركز الخدمة على مراكز الإنتاج فقط، وبالتالي لا يتم تحميل مراكز الخدمات بأية تكاليف عن الخدمات التي تحصل عليها من مراكز الخدمات الأخرى، وهذا يتطلب شطب الكمية التي تحصل عليها مراكز الخدمات من إنتاج مراكز الخدمات الاخرى قبل البدء في عملية التوزيع. وعليه لا يتم تحميل قسم الصيانة بتكاليف الكهرباء التي يحصل عليها من قسم القوى المحركة، ولا يتم تحميل قسم القوى المحركة بتكاليف الصيانة التي يحصل عليها من قسم الصيانة، وهذا يتطلب حساب نسب مؤية لتوزيع تكاليف مراكز الخدمات غير تلك الظاهرة في الجدول ٦-٤ ومع ذلك فانه يمكن حسابها منها. ويمكن تمثيل عملية التوزيع كما في الشكل التالي:-

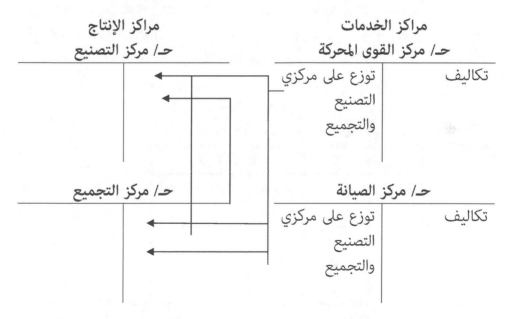

شكل (٦-٢) توزيع تكاليف أقسام الخدمات - طريقة التوزيع المباشر

بدراسة جدول (٤-٦) نجد أن مركز التصنيع حصل على ٤٠٪ من خدمات مركز القوى المحركة وأن التجميع حصل منها على ٣٥٪ أيضاً، لذلك توزع تكاليف مركز القوى المحركة على مركزي التصنيع والتجميع بنسبة ٤٠: ٣٥ على التوالي، والنتيجة نفسها يتم الوصول اليها حيث يظهر في بيانات التمرين ان قسم التصنيع قد حصل على ٨٠,٠٠٠ كيلووات وحصل قسم التجميع على ٧٠,٠٠٠ كيلووات من انتاج قسم القوى المحركة وعلية توزع تكاليف هذا القسم بنسبة ٨:٧ بين قسمى التصنيع والتجميع على التوالي. ويحسب نصيب كل مركزمن التكاليف كالتالي:

التكاليف = نسبة الاستفادة × المبلغ الموزع

$$\text{قسم التصنيع} = \frac{٤٠}{٤٠+٣٥} \times ٣٠,٠٠٠ = ١٦,٠٠٠ \text{ دينار}$$

$$\text{قسم التجميع} = \frac{٣٥}{٤٠ + ٣٥} \times ٣٠,٠٠٠ = ١٤,٠٠٠ \text{ دينار}$$

ويتم توزيع تكاليف مركز الصيانة هو الآخر على مركزي التصنيع والتجميع بنسبة ٤٠ : ٥٠ ويكون نصيب كل مركز منها كالتالي:

$$\text{قسم التصنيع} = \frac{٤٠}{٤٠+٥٠} \times ٤٥٠٠٠ = ٢٠,٠٠٠ \text{ دينار}$$

$$\text{قسم التجميع} = \frac{٥٠}{٤٠ + ٥٠} \times ٤٥٠٠٠ = ٢٥,٠٠٠ \text{ دينار}$$

ويأخذ كشف توزيع التكاليف الشكل الوارد في الجدول رقم (٥-٦)

جدول (٦-٥)
توزيع تكاليف مراكز الخدمات باستخدام طريقة التوزيع المباشر

	القوى المحركة	الصيانة	التصنيع	التجميع	الإجمالي
تكاليف مباشرة	٣٠,٠٠٠	٤٥,٠٠٠	٧٠,٠٠٠	٩٠,٠٠٠	٢٣٥,٠٠٠
القوى المحركة(٣٥:٤٠)	(٣٠,٠٠٠)	--	١٦,٠٠٠د	١٤,٠٠٠	صفر
الصيانة(٤٠:٥٠)	---	(٤٥,٠٠٠)	٢٠,٠٠٠د	٢٥,٠٠٠	صفر
إجمالي	صفر	صفر	١٠٦,٠٠٠	١٢٩,٠٠٠	٢٣٥,٠٠٠

وبدراسة الجدول (٦-٥) نجد أن مركزي التصنيع والتجميع قد تحملا بمبلغ ٣٦,٠٠٠ د ٣٩,٠٠٠ من تكاليف مراكز الخدمات على التوالي. ويتم إثبات توزيع تكاليف مراكز الخدمات على مراكز الإنتاج باستخدام قيد اليومية التالي:

٣٦,٠٠٠		حـ/مركز التصنيع	
٣٩,٠٠٠		حـ/ مركز التجميع	
	٣٠,٠٠٠	حـ/ مركز القوى المحركة	
	٤٥,٠٠٠	حـ/ مركز الصيانة	

يمكن انتقاد هذه الطريقة لأنها تهمل الخدمات التي يقدمها مركز الخدمة إلى مراكز الخدمات الأخرى، وهذا يؤثر على التكاليف التي تحمل على مراكز الإنتاج ومن ثم تكلفة وحدات الإنتاج. كما انها لا تستطيع توزيع تكاليف مركز الخدمة اذا كان لا يقدم خدمات لمراكز الخدمات الاخرى.

طريقة التوزيع التنازلي: Step-down Method

تعمل طريقة التوزيع التنازلي على معالجة الانتقاد الموجهة للطريقة السابقة جزئياً حيث تبدأ بتوزيع تكلفة مركز الخدمة الذي يقدم أكبر نسبة من نشاطه إلى مراكز الخدمات الأخرى، ففي مثالنا السابق نجدأن مركزالقوى المحركةيقدم ٢٥% من خدماته إلى

مركز الصيانة، بينما نجد أن مركز الصيانة يقدم ١٠٪ فقط من خدماته إلى مركز القوى المحركة، لذلك يتم البدء بتوزيع تكاليف مركز القوى المحركة. وبعد ذلك يتم توزيع تكاليف مركز الصيانة.

وفي حالة وجود أكثر من مركز للخدمة يتم جمع نسب الخدمة التي يقدمها كل مركز خدمة إلى جميع مراكز الخدمات الأخرى، والبدء بتوزيع تكاليف المركز الذي يقدم الكبر نسبة من خدماته الى مراكز الخدمات الاخرى. وعندما تتساوى نسب الخدمة التي يقدمها مركزان أو أكثر الى مراكز الخدمات الاخرى يتم البدء بتوزيع تكاليف المركز الذي تكون تكلفته أعلى.

وحسب هذه الطريقة بعد أن يتم توزيع تكلفة مركز معين على المراكز الأخرى لا يتم فتحه ثانية لتحميله بتكاليف من مراكز الخدمة التي توزع بعدة، لذلك نجد أنه في مثالنا السابق بعد أن تم توزيع تكلفة القوى المحركة لأنه لم يتم إعادة فتح حسابه ثانية لتحميله بتكاليف من قسم الصيانة. ويتم التوزيع بموجب هذه الطريقة كما في الشكل (٦-٣).

بالاعتماد على البيانات الواردة في جدول (٦-٤) نجد أن مراكز التصنيع والتجميع والصيانة قد استفادت من خدمات مركز القوى المحركة بنسب ٤٠٪ : ٣٥٪ : ٢٥٪ على التوالي. ولذلك يتم توزيع تكاليف هذا المركز كالتالي:

نصيب القسم المستفيد= نسبة استفادته من الخدمة × تكاليف المركز

قسم الصيانة = ٢٥٪ × ٣٠,٠٠٠ = ٧,٥٠٠د

قسم التصنيع = ٤٠٪ × ٣٠,٠٠٠ = ١٢,٠٠٠د

قسم التجميع = ٣٥٪ × ٣٠,٠٠٠ = ١٠,٥٠٠د

وبعد توزيع تكاليف مركز القوى المحركة تصبح تكلفة مركز الصيانة ٥٢,٥٠٠ دينار = (٤٥,٠٠٠ د + ٧,٥٠٠د)، وهذه يتم توزيعها على مركزي التصنيع والتجميع بنسبة ٤٠٪ : ٥٠٪ أو بنسبة ٤:٥ ولا يتم تحميل مركز القوى المحركة بأية تكاليف منها، لأنه سبق توزيع تكاليفه. ويتم توزيع تكاليف هذا المركز حسب نسب الخدمات كالتالي:

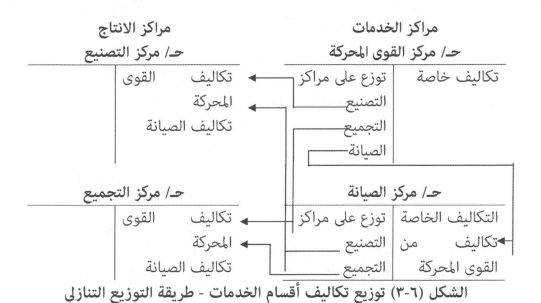

الشكل (٦-٣) توزيع تكاليف أقسام الخدمات - طريقة التوزيع التنازلي

نصيب القسم المستفيد= نسبة استفادته من الخدمة × تكاليف المركز

قسم التصنيع = (٤ ÷ ٩) × ٥٢,٥٠٠ = ٢٣,٣٣٣د

قسم التجميع = (٥ ÷ ٩) × ٥٢,٥٠٠= ٢٩,١٦٧د

وبالتالي يكون جدول توزيع التكاليف بطريقة التوزيع التنازلي كالتالي:

جدول (٦-٦)

توزيع تكاليف مراكز الخدمات باستخدام طريقة التوزيع التنازلي

الإجمالي	مراكز الإنتاج		مراكز الخدمات		
	التجميع	التصنيع	الصيانة	القوى المحركة	
٢٣٥,٠٠٠	٩٠,٠٠٠	٧٠,٠٠٠	٤٥,٠٠٠	٣٠,٠٠٠	تكاليف مباشرة
صفر	١٠,٥٠٠	١٢,٠٠٠	٧,٥٠٠	(٣٠,٠٠٠)	القوى المحركة بنسبة (٢٥:٤٠:٣٥)
صفر	٢٩,١٦٧	٢٣,٣٣٣	(٥٢,٥٠٠)	---	الصيانة بنسب (٤:٥)
٢٣٥,٠٠٠	١٢٩,٦٦٧	١٠٥,٣٣٣	صفر	صفر	الإجمالي

بمقارنة جدول (٦-٦) مع جدول (٦-٥) نجد أن تكاليف المحملة على مركز التجميع قد ازدادت والتكاليف المحملة على مركز التصنيع قد انخفضت في طريقة التوزيع التنازلي مقارنة مع طريقة التوزيع المباشر، والسبب أن قسم الصيانة قد تحمل بتكلفة الخدمات التي حصل عليها من قسم القوى المحركة. تعطي هذه الطريقة نتائج أفضل من طريقة التوزيع المباشر، ولكن يعاب عليها أنها لا تحمل بعض مراكز الخدمة تكاليف الخدمات التي تحصل عليها من مراكز الخدمات الأخرى عندما يتم توزيع تكاليفها قبل غيرها. ويتم إثبات التوزيع في الدفاتر بقيد اليومية الاتي:

حـ/مركز التصنيع		٣٥,٣٣٣
حـ/ مركز التجميع		٣٩,٦٦٧
حـ/ مركز القوى المحركة	٣٠,٠٠٠	
حـ/ مركز الصيانة	٤٥,٠٠٠	

طريقة التوزيع التبادلي Simultaneous Solution Method:

تعترف هذه الطريقة بتكلفة الخدمات التي يحصل عليها مركز الخدمة من مراكز الخدمات الأخرى. وبالتالي تتكون تكلفة مركز الخدمة من جزئين التكلفة المباشرة لمركز الخدمة زائد نصيبه من تكاليف مراكز الخدمات الاخرى. ويحدد نصيب مركز الخدمة من تكاليف المراكز الاخرى بضرب نسبة استفادته من خدمات المراكز الأخرى في تكاليف تلك المراكز. ولان تكاليف مركز الخدمات غير معروفة لحتى الآن فانه يفترض أن مجموعها هي ألفاظ جبرية وتحدد تكاليفها في المعادلات الاتية:

ق = ٣٠,٠٠٠ + ٠,١٠ ص .... (١)

حيث أن ق = هي تكلفة مركز القوى المحركة

ص: تكلفة مركز الصيانة، و١٠٪ : نسبة الخدمات التي قدمها مركز الصيانة لمركز القوى المحركة.

وتكون تكاليف مركز الصيانة كالتالي:

ص = ٤٥,٠٠٠ د + ٠,٢٥ ق .... (٢)

وبهذا تحول الوضع إلى معادلتين من الدرجة الأولى بمجهولين الأول وهو ق ويمثل إجمالي تكلفة مركز القوى المحركة، والثاني هو ص ويمثل إجمالي تكلفة مركز الصيانة، وبحل المعادلتين يتم تحديد قيمة كل من س، ص. وفي حالة زيادة عدد المراكز عن ثلاثة يمكن اللجوء لحل تلك المعادلات إلى الحاسوب. والآن بالتعويض في المعادلة ١ بقيمة ص من المعادلة ٢ تصبح المعادلة ١ كالتالي:

$$ق = ٣٠,٠٠٠ + ٠,١٠ (٤٥,٠٠٠ + ٠,٢٥ ق)$$

$$ق = ٣٠,٠٠٠ + ٤٥٠٠ + ٠,٠٢٥٠ ق$$

$$٠,٩٧٥ ق = ٣٤٥٠٠$$

$$ق = ٣٥٣٨٥ د$$

وبتعويض قيمة ق في المعادلة رقم ٢ نصل إلى أن:

$$ص = ٤٥,٠٠٠ + ٠,٢٥ × ٣٥,٣٨٥$$

$$ص = ٥٣,٨٤٦ د$$

وباستخدام النسب الواردة في جدول (٤-٦) يتم توزيع تكاليف مركز القوى المحركة كالتالي:

المراكز المستفيدة	نسبة الخدمة	التكاليف الموزعة
الصيانة	٢٥%	٣٥,٣٨٥ × ٢٥% = ٨,٨٤٦ د
التصنيع	٤٠%	٣٥,٣٨٥ × ٤٠% = ١٤,١٥٤ د
التجميع	٣٥%	٣٥,٣٨٥ × ٣٥% = ١٢,٣٨٥
الإجمالي		٣٥,٣٨٥ د

كما يتم توزيع تكاليف مركز الصيانة كالتالي:

المراكز المستفيدة	نسبة الخدمة	التكاليف الموزعة
القوى المحركة	١٠%	٥٣,٨٤٦ × ١٠% = ٥,٣٨٥ د
التصنيع	٤٠%	٥٣,٨٤٦ × ٤٠% = ٢١,٥٣٨د
التجميع	٥٠%	٥٣,٨٤٦ × ٥٠% = ٢٦,٩٢٣
الإجمالي		٥٣,٨٤٦ د

لاحظ أن أقسام الإنتاج قد تم تحميلها بنسبة الخدمات نفسها التي حصلت عليها من مراكز الخدمات، ولأنه تم تعديل تكاليف المراكز الأخيرة اختلفت التكاليف التي حملت على هذه المراكز، وظهرت نتيجة التوزيع في الجدول (٦-٧).

الجدول (٦-٧)

توزيع تكاليف مراكز الخدمات على مراكز الإنتاج بطريقة التوزيع التبادلي

إجمالي	مراكز انتاج		مراكز خدمات		
	تجميع	تصنيع	صيانة	قوى محركة	
٢٣٥٠٠٠	٩٠٠٠٠	٧٠٠٠٠	٤٥٠٠٠	٣٠,٠٠٠	تكاليف مباشرة
صفر	١٢,٣٨٥	١٤,١٥٤	٨٨٤٦	٣٥,٣٨٥-	قوى محركة بنسبة ٢٥:٤٠: ٣٥
صفر	٢٦٩٢٣	٢١٥٣٨	٥٣٨٤٦-	٥٣٨٥	الصيانة وبنسبة ١٠: ٤٠ :٥٠
٢٣٥٠٠٠	١٢٩٣٠٨	١٠٥٦٩٢	صفر	صفر	الإجمالي

لقد كان إجمالي تكاليف مركز القوى المحركة ٣٥,٣٨٥د، وتكاليف مركز الصيانة ٥٣,٨٤٦ د وهذه المبالغ أكبر من التكاليف المباشرة لهذين المركزين، وهي نتيجة تحميل هذه المراكز بتكاليف الخدمات التي حصلت عليها من مراكز الخدمات الأخرى. لاحظ أن هذه الطريقة أدت إلى تحميل مراكز الإنتاج بتكلفة تساوي إجمالي تكلفة مراكز الخدمات ومقدارها ٧٥,٠٠٠د، وهذا يساوي مجموع تكلفة مراكز الخدمات قبل تحميلهما بتكاليفهما من مراكز الخدمات الأخرى، ويتم إثبات توزيع هذه التكاليف باستخدام قيد اليومية التالي:

٣٥,٦٩٢		حـ/ قسم التصنيع (١٤١٥٤ + ٢١,٥٣٨)	
٣٩,٣٠٨		حـ/ قسم التجميع (١٢٣٨٥ + ٢٦٩٢٣)	
٥,٣٨٥		حـ/ قسم القوى المحركة	
٨,٨٤٦		حـ/ قسم الصيانة	
	٣٥,٣٨٥	حـ/ قسم القوى المحركة	
	٥٣,٨٤٦	حـ/ قسم الصيانة	

لاحظ أننا جعلنا أقسام الخدمات دائنة بتكلفتها المباشرة وغير المباشرة أي بالتكلفة التي تم توزيعها على المراكز الأخرى، وفي الوقت نفسه تم جعلها مدينة بتكاليف الخدمات التي حصلت عليها من مراكز الخدمات الأخرى.

مقارنة طرق توزيع تكاليف مراكز الخدمات:

يتبين لنا من دراسة الطرق السابقة أن طريقة التوزيع المباشر هي أسهلها، ولكنها تغفل تكلفة الخدمات التي حصلت عليها مراكز الخدمات من بعضها البعض، وهذا بدوره يؤدي إلى أن تكون تكلفة مراكز الإنتاج غير معبرة عن التكلفة الواقعية لمراكز الخدمات. وأدى هذا العيب إلى ظهور طريقة التوزيع التنازلي وطريقة التوزيع التبادلي. وتعالج طريقة التوزيع التنازلي بعضاً من عيوب طريقة التوزيع المباشر، إلا أنها تهمل أيضاً جزءاً من تكاليف مراكز الخدمة، لأن القسم الذي توزع تكاليفه أولاً لا يتم تحميله بالتكاليف التي يحصل عليها من مراكز الخدمات الأخرى، لذلك تؤدي طريقة التوزيع التبادلي إلى نتائج أفضل، وعيبها الوحيد هو تعقيدها خصوصاً إذا كان في المنشأة عدداً كبيراً من مراكز الخدمة. على أية حال، لا يعتبر هذا الأمر عقبة أمام استخدامها في الوقت الحالي بعد أن أصبح الحاسوب متوافراً ويمكنه حل المصفوفات الكبيرة الحجم.

تحميل تكاليف مراكز الإنتاج على المنتجات:

بعد أن يتم توزيع تكاليف مراكز الخدمات على مراكز الإنتاج نصل إلى المرحلة الأخيرة، وهي تحميل هذه المراكز على المنتجات التي استفادت من خدماتها، ويتم - بطبيعة الحال - حصر التكاليف غير المباشرة لمركز التكاليف باستخدام حساب مراقبة التكاليف الصناعية غير المباشرة، ويجعل هذا الحساب مديناً بالمصروفات الخاصة بالمركز، وبنصيبه من التكاليف الموزعة عليه من تكاليف مراكز الخدمات.

وإذا تم توزيع التكاليف غير المباشرة الفعلية على الإنتاج يحول رصيد هذا الحساب إلى حساب الإنتاج تحت التشغيل الذي يمثل تكاليف إنتاج المنتجات التي قام بتصنيعها خلال الفترة. ويعاب على هذه الطريقة أنها تؤدي الى تأخير تحديد تكلفة الوحدات المنتجة إلى نهاية فترة التكاليف، وهذا الأمر غير مقبول خصوصاً في حالة صناعة الأوامر

الإنتاجية، إضافة إلى ذلك فإن تكلفة الوحدات المنتجة قد ترتفع أو تنخفض بناءً على عدد الوحدات المنتجة، نظراً لسلوك التكاليف الصناعية غير المباشرة الثابتة.

وللتغلب على هذه المشكلات يفضل محاسبو التكاليف تحميل التكاليف الصناعية غير المباشرة باستخدام معدلات تحميل محددة مقدماً أي باستخدام طريقة التكاليف العادية. تحتاج هذه الطريقة الى تقدير قيمة التكاليف الصناعية غير المباشرة المتوقعة خلال فترة العمل المقبلة ونسبة هذه التكاليف إلى حجم النشاط المخطط عند مستوى الطاقة العادية. يتم قياس الطاقة بعدة مقاييس منها ساعات العمل المباشرة، وساعات دوران الآلات، وقيمة الأجور المباشرة، والتكلفة الأولية وهناك عدة مستويات للطاقة تختلف عن بعضها من حيث المسموحات الخاصة بالعطلات، ومدى الفترة الزمنية التي تشملها، وسيتم مناقشة المستويات المعروفة في الحياة العملية على التوالي: [1]

أولاً: مستوى الطاقة النظرية أو القصوى:

يمثل هذا المستوى أقصى قدر لمجهودات الآلات والعمال، وبالتالي لا يقوم بالسماح بأية عطلات لا تقتضيها الطبيعة الفنية للعناصر المادية أو التعاقدية للعناصر البشرية، لذلك فهو صعب التحقيق إلا في حالات نادرة، وعند استخدامه لأغراض الرقابة لا بد من عمل موازنة للانحرافات التي تنتج حتماً من جراء استخدامه. [2]

الطاقة العملية:

وتمثل الطاقة النظرية ناقص المسموحات العادية التي لا يمكن تجنب حدوثها في ظل ظروف التشغيل السائدة في المنشأة، فمثلاً يأخذ هذا المفهوم للطاقة الوقت اللازم لإصلاح الآلات وصيانتها، وأثر عدم مطابقة مواصفات المواد والتأخير في تسليمها، والوقت الذي يقضيه العمال في العبادة وغياباتهم المتوقعة. وهذا يعني أن مستوى الطاقة يحدد بناءً على ظروف العمل داخل المنشأة، ولكنه يهمل الظروف الخارجية مثل: توافر الطلب على المنتجات، وقد يتساوى هذا المستوى مع مستوى الطاقة العادية إلا أن الأخير غالباً ما يكون أقل منه، لأنه يأخذ طلبات العملاء في الحسبان.

---

[1] Rayburn, Op, Cit., Pp. ٢٢٠ - ٢٢٣.

[2] Fischer and Frank, Op. Cit., P. ٣٠٢.

الطاقة الفعلية المتوقعة:

تمثل الطاقة الفعلية المتوقعة حجم الإنتاج الضروري لمواجهة الطلب على المبيعات خلال فترة العمل المقبلة. ويركز هذا المفهوم للطاقة على الأجل القصير، ولا يحاول أخذ المتغيرات الموسمية طويلة الأجل في الحسبان، ويرفض مؤيدو هذا المستوى فكرة الطاقة العادية، لأنهم يرون بأنه يجب معاملة كل سنة مالية بصورة مستقلة عن غيرها، وتحميل تكاليفها على الوحدات التي يتوقع أن يتم إنتاجها فيها.

من دراسة هذه المستويات نجد أن مستوى الطاقة النظرية لا يحتوي على مسموحات بقدر كاف، وبالتالي فهو غير واقعي، وعلى الجانب الآخر يحتوي مستوى الطاقة الفعلية المتوقعة على قدر وافر من المسموحات، مما يجعله هو الآخر غير عادل، وبين هذين الطرفين تقع مستويات الطاقة العملية والطاقة العادية. ويفضل استخدام الطاقة العادية، لأنها تراعي طاقات العمل وظروف الطلب على المنتجات. فالمنشأة لن تقوم بالإنتاج طالما أنه لا يوجد لديها طلب على منتجاتها، على أية حال، يجب مراعاة المسموحات الحتمية في كل الأحوال قبل اختيار اساس التوزيع.

الخاتـمـة

في هذا الفصل تمت مناقشة التكاليف الصناعية غير المباشرة، والتعرض لمفهومها، وكيفية تبويبها، وقد تم التعرض إلى طرق توزيع تكاليف مراكز الخدمات الإنتاجية على مراكز الإنتاج، ووجدنا أبسط الطرق هي الطريقة المباشرة، لأنها توزع تكاليف مراكز الخدمات على مراكز الإنتاج فقط، وهذا اعتبر انتقاداً لها لأن مراكز الخدمات لا تتحمل بتكاليف الخدمات التي تحصل عليها من مراكز الخدمات الأخرى، فقامت طريقة التوزيع التنازلي بمعالجة هذا الموضوع جزئياً عن طريق ترتيب مراكز الخدمات تنازلياً على أساس نسبة الخدمات التي يقدمها كل مركز خدمة إلى مراكز الخدمات الأخرى، وتوزيع تكاليف المركز الذي يقدم خدمات أكثر من غيره أولاً. أما طريقة التوزيع التبادلي فتقوم بتحميل مراكز الخدمات بتكلفة الخدمات التي تحصل عليها من مراكز الخدمات الأخرى قبل توزيع تكاليفها، وهذا يجعل تكاليف مراكز الخدمات أكثر دقة من المراكز السابقة.

السؤال الأول: ما هو المقصود بالتكاليف الصناعية غير المباشرة.

السؤال الثاني: أذكر أهم أنواع عناصر التكاليف الصناعية غير المباشرة.

السؤال الثالث: ما هو الفرق بين مراكز تكاليف الإنتاج ومراكز تكاليف الخدمات الإنتاجية.

السؤال الرابع: أشرح أهمية استخدام مراكز التكاليف ودورها في تحديد تكلفة المنتجات.

السؤال الخامس: أيهما أفضل استخدام معدل واحد لتحميل التكاليف الصناعية غير المباشرة على مستوى المنشأة، أو استخدام معدل مستقل لكل مركز على حدة؟ مع تبرير ذلك بإعطاء أمثلة رقمية.

السؤال السادس: أذكر المعايير التي يمكن الاستناد عليها عند توزيع عناصر التكاليف غير المباشرة.

السؤال السابع: ما هو المقصود بالقدرة على تحمل التكاليف، وكيف يمكن قياس هذه القدرة.

السؤال الثامن: أذكر أهم صفات طريقة التوزيع التبادلي وطريقة التوزيع التنازلي.

السؤال التاسع: أذكر ثلاث طرق لتحميل التكاليف الصناعية غير المباشرة على وحدات الإنتاج.

السؤال العاشر: تحتوي إحدى الشركات الصناعية على ثلاثة أقسام إنتاجية، وتقوم بتحميل الأعباء الإضافية على أوامر التشغيل باستخدام معدل تحميل محدد مقدماً، والآتي البيانات التقديرية التي أعدتها الشركة في بداية السنة المالية.

الأقسام	الإجمالي	أ	ب	جـ
الأعباء الإضافية (بالإلف)	١,٣٠٠	١٧٠	٩٢٠	٢١٠
ساعات العمل المباشرة (بالإلف)	١٣٢	٣٢	٣٠	٧٠

وخلال الفترة تم العمل على الإنتاج، وحصلت على معلومات عن أربعة من هذه الأوامر حيث حصلت على ساعات العمل المباشر التالية:

ساعات العمل في	أمر ١٠١	أمر ١٠٢	أمر ١٠٣	أمر ١٠٤
مركز أ	١٥٠	١٦٠	١١٨	١١٥
مركز ب	٢٠٠	١٧٠	٨٢	١٣٥
مركز جـ	٢١٠	٩٥	١٢٠	٦٥

المطلوب:

(١) حساب معدل التحميل الإجمالي للأعباء الإضافية وتحديد المبالغ المحملة على كل أمر إنتاجي.

(٢) حساب معدل تحميل مستقل لكل قسم من الأقسام ثم حدد المبالغ المحملة على كل أمر إنتاجي.

السؤال الحادي عشر: يوجد في إحدى الشركات أربعة أقسام هي: قسم التفصيل، وقسم الخياطة، وهذه تعتبر أقساماً إنتاجية، وقسم الصيانة، وقسم الحركة، وهذه تعتبر أقسام خدمات. وبدراسة أنشطة أقسام الخدمات تبين أنها تقوم بتقديم خدماتها على النحو التالي:

قسم الصيانة   ٤٠٪ إلى قسم التفصيل

     ٥٠٪ إلى قسم الخياطة

     ١٠٪ إلى قسم الحركة

قسم الحركة   ٢٥٪ إلى قسم التفصيل

     ٦٠٪ إلى قسم الخياطة

     ١٥٪ إلى قسم الصيانة

وخلال الفترة كانت التكاليف المحملة على أقسام الشركة الأربعة كالتالي:

الحركة	الصيانة	الخياطة	التفصيل	
٦٤٥	١,٠٠٠	٣,٠٠٠	٦,٠٠٠	مواد مباشرة
١,٤٠٠	٨٠٠	٨,٠٠٠	٢,٠٠٠	أجور مباشرة
٢٥٠	٧٢٠	١,٥٠٠	١,٢٠٠	تكاليف غير مباشرة
٢,٢٩٥	٢,٥٢٠	١٢,٥٠٠	٩,٢٠٠	

المطلوب:

توزيع تكاليف مراكز الخدمات على مراكز الإنتاج باستخدام:

١. طريقة التوزيع المباشر مع بيان جدول التوزيع.

٢. طريقة التوزيع التنازلي مع بيان جدول التوزيع.

٣. طريقة التوزيع التبادلي مع بيان جدول التوزيع.

٤. عمل قيد اليومية اللازمة لإثبات التكلفة الموزعة في الحالات السابقة.

السؤال الثاني عشر: قامت إحدى الشركات بتحليل أنشطة أقسامها الإنتاجية والخدمية وتوصلت إلى تكوين المصفوفة التالية:

خدمات٣	خدمات ٢	خدمات ١	إنتاج٢	إنتاج ١	من / إلى
--	--	--	--	١٠٠%	إنتاج ١
--	--	--	١٠٠%	--	إنتاج ٢
١٠%	٢٠%	--	٤٠%	٣٠%	خدمات ١
١٠%	--	١٠%	٤٥%	٣٥%	خدمات ٢
--	١٠%	٢٥%	٤٠%	٢٥%	خدمات ٣
٨,٠٠٠	٧,٠٠٠	٥,٠٠٠	٥٨,٠٠٠	٦,٠٠٠د	إجمالي التكاليف

المطلوب: توزيع تكاليف مراكز خدمات ١ وخدمات ٢، وخدمات ٣ باستخدام:

أ- طريقة التوزيع المباشر.

ب- طريقة التوزيع التنازلي.

السؤال الثالث عشر: تتكون إحدى الشركات الصناعية من ثلاثة أقسام إنتاجية وأربعة أقسام للخدمات، وكانت البيانات الخاصة بهذه الأقسام (الساعات بالألف) كالتالي:

إجمالي	أقسام خدمات				أقسام انتاج			
	ز	و	هـ	د	جـ	ب	أ	
٥,٠٠٠	٥٠٠	٥٠٠	٧٥٠	٧٥٠	٥٠٠	١,٠٠٠	١,٠٠٠	المساحة بالمتر
١٤٥	٥	١٠	١٥	١٥	٢٠	٤٠	٤٠	عدد العمال
٣٠	٢	٣	٢	٣	٥	٨	٧	ساعات العمل المباشر
٤٠	٢	٣	٧	٤	٨	٦	١٠	ساعات دوران الآلات

وخلال الفترة كانت التكاليف غير المباشرة الخاصة، والتكاليف العامة وأسس توزيعها كالتالي:

أساس التوزيع على المراكز	المبلغ	
الأجور المباشرة	٣٤,٤٥٠	الأجور غير المباشرة
المتر المربع	١٥,٠٠٠	الإيجار
ساعات العمل المباشر	٣,٠٠٠	التأمين
ساعات الدوران	٢٠,٠٠٠	الاستهلاك
عدد العمال	٢٩,٠٠٠	الكهرباء والهاتف والنقل

وكانت التكاليف الخاصة بالمراكز كالتالي (المبلغ بالألف)

إجمالي	ز	و	هـ	د	جـ	ب	أ	
١١,٥	٥،	١	٢	١	١	٢	٤	مواد غير مباشرة
٥٣	٣	٧	٦	٤	٨	١٢	١٣	أجور مباشرة
١٩	١	٣	٢	٣	٣	٣	٤	استهلاك
٣٠	٢	٦	٤	٥	٣	٤	٦	مصروفات أخرى
١١٣,٥	٦,٥	١٧	١٤	١٣	١٥	٢١	٢٧	الإجمالي

وكانت مصفوفة النسبة المئوية للخدمات التي تقدمها مراكز الخدمة كالتالي:

	أ	ب	جـ	د	هـ	و	ز
قسم د	١٥	٢٥	١٥	--	٢٠	١٠	١٥
قسم هـ	٣٠	١٠	٢٥	١٠	--	١٥	١٠
قسم و	٢٠	٣٠	١٥	١٥	١٥	--	٥
قسم ز	٢٠	٢٠	١٠	١٥	١٥	٢٠	--

المطلوب:

(١) توزيع التكاليف العامة على المراكز المستفيدة.

(٢) توزيع تكاليف مراكز الخدمات باستخدام طريقة التوزيع التنازلي.

(٣) حساب معدل تحميل الأعباء الإضافية لمراكز الإنتاج باستخدام ساعات العمل المباشر ثم باستخدام ساعات الدوران.

السؤال الرابع عشر: يوجد في إحدى كليات الجامعة أربعة أقسام علمية وقسمان للخدمات هما، عمادة الكلية، وقسم التزويد، وتوافرت لديك المعلومات الآتية عن هذه الأقسام عن السنة المنتهية في ٢٠٠٨/١٢/٣١.

	الأجور المباشرة	عدد العاملين	المساحة بالمتر	عدد طلبة التخصص
مكتب العميد	٢٥	١٥	٤٠٠	
تزويد ومكتبة	١٠	٥	٤٠٠	
قسم ١	٢٠	٤	١٢٠٠	٨٩٠
قسم ٢	١٨	٦	٨٠٠	٨١٠
قسم ٣	٢٢	٧	١٢٠٠	٨٥٠
قسم ٤	٣٠	٨	١٠٠٠	٧٥٠

وقامت الإدارة المالية في الجامعة بتحديد البنود التالية لنفقات الكلية:

البند	المبلغ	أساس التوزيع
- قرطاسيه ومطبوعات	٥٤,٠٠٠ د	عدد العاملين
- تدفئة وكهرباء	١٢٦,٠٠٠	المساحة
- استهلاك أثاث ومباني	١١٠,٠٠٠	المساحة
- صيانة	٢٣,٩٢٥	عدد الطلبة
- أعباء عمومية وإدارية	٦٠,٠٠٠	عدد العاملين
الإجمالي	٣٧٣,٩٢٥	

المطلوب:

١. توزيع التكاليف العامة على المراكز المختلفة.

٢. توزيع التكاليف العامة على مراكز الإنتاج علماً بأن ٥% من نشاط مكتب العميد وان تكاليف هذه الاقسام توزع على الاقسام الأخرى حسب عدد العمال، هو لخدمة قسم التزويد، وأن ١٠% من نشاط قسم التزويد لخدمة مكتب العميد، وأن الجامعة تستخدم طريقة التوزيع التنازلي.

٣. تحديد تكلفة الطالب في كل قسم من أقسام الكلية.

السؤال الخامس عشر: يتكون أحد مصانع الأثاث من ثلاثة مراكز للإنتاج هي أ، ب، جـ ومركزين للخدمات هي د، هـ ويتم الإنتاج في هذا المصنع حسب طلبات العملاء. والآتي بيانات الإنتاج والتكاليف التي حملت على الأوامر والمراكز خلال إحدى فترات التكاليف.

المركز	أمر ١٠١	أمر ١٠٢	أمر ١٠٣	أمر ١٠٤	أعباء إضافية
أ	١٥,٠٠٠	١,٠٠٠د	٧٥٠د	٨٠٠د	٣٥٠د
ب	٢,٥٠٠	٢,٠٠٠	١,٧٥٠	١,٢٠٠	٤٠٠
جـ	١,٨٠٠	١,٧٠٠	٣,٢٠٠	٨٠٠	٥٠٠
د	--	--	--	--	٦٠٠
هـ	--	--	--	--	٥٠٠
					٢,٣٥٠

ثانياً: الأجور:

أ	٨٠٠د	٧٠٠د	٦٠٠د	٨٠٠	٤٥٠
ب	١٢٠٠	١٠٠٠	٩٠٠	١٠٠٠	٨٠٠
جـ	١٣٠٠	٨٥٠	٨٠٠	٩٠٠	٧٠٠
د	--	--	--	--	١٠٠٠
هـ	--	--	--	--	٨٠٠
					٣٧٥٠

ثالثاً: المصروفات الأخرى:

قسم أ- ٨٠٠ ، قسم ب- ٦٠٠، قسم جـ- ٧٠٠ ، قسم د-٢٠٠٠، قسم هـ- ١٢٠٠

- يتم تحميل التكاليف غير المباشرة للمركز أ باستخدام ساعات الدوران، وللمركز ب باستخدام ساعات العمل المباشر، والمركز جـ باستخدام الأجور المباشرة، وتبلغ أجرة ساعة العمل المباشر في أقسام الإنتاج ٢ دينار.

- يتم توزيع تكاليف مراكز الخدمات على مراكز الإنتاج باستخدام طريقة التوزيع التبادلي، وكانت مصفوفة الخدمات التي تقدمها أقسام الخدمات كالتالي:

الأقسام المقدمة للخدمة	الأقسام المستفيدة				
	أ	ب	جـ	د	هـ
د	٢٥%	٣٠%	٥٥%	--	٣٠%
هـ	٣٠%	١٥%	٢٠%	٣٥%	--

- كان معدل تحميل الأعباء الإضافية في مركز أ هو ٣,٧ د/ ساعة دوران، وفي مركز ب هو ١,٩ د/ س ع م، وفي مركز جـ هو ٠,٩٠ د/١ دينار أجور مباشرة، وقد حصلت الأوامر الإنتاجية على الساعات التالية في مركزي أ، ب على التوالي:

	ساعة دوران	ساعة عمل مباشرة
أمر ١٠١	٣٦٠	٦١٠
أمر ١٠٢	٢٤٠	٥٢٠
أمر ١٠٣	٢٥٠	٤٥٠
أمر ١٠٤	٢٥٠	٥١٠
الإجمالي	١١٠٠	٢٠٩٠

- انتهى إنتاج الأوامر ١٠١، ١٠٢، ١٠٣، وحولت إلى المخازن، أما الأمر ١٠٤ فقد بقي تحت التشغيل. ولم يكن هناك أية أوامر تحت التشغيل في أول المدة.

المطلوب:

(١) عمل قيود اليومية اللازمة لتسجيل التكاليف خلال الفترة.

(٢) توزيع تكاليف مراكز الخدمات على مراكز الإنتاج بطريقة التوزيع التنازلي.

(٣) تصوير حسابات الإنتاج تحت التشغيل وحسابات الأوامر الإنتاجية.

(٤) أعتبر أن التكاليف الصناعية غير المباشرة المحملة بالزيادة أو النقص غير مهمة، وأنها تقفل في تكاليف البضاعة المباعة، وأن الأوامر جميعها قد تم تسليمها إلى العملاء، والمطلوب: تحديد تكلفة البضاعة المباعة.

السؤال السادس عشر: (أسئلة امتحانات سابقة).

تستخدم إحدى الشركات محاسبة التكاليف في تحديد تكاليف إنتاجها، وتقوم بتحميل الإنتاج بالأعباء الإضافية باستخدام معدل تحميل مقداره ١٢٠٪ من قيمة الأجور المباشرة، وتقفل الأعباء الإضافية المحملة بالزيادة أو النقص في تكلفة البضاعة المباعة. وقد بلغت الأعباء المحملة بالزيادة عن الفترة المنتهية في ٢٠٠٧/٦/٣٠ مبلغ ١٠,٠٠٠ دينار، وتم فعلاً أقفالها في حساب تكلفة البضاعة المباعة وتوافرت لديك المعلومات الأخرى التالية:

المخزون في	٢٠٠٧/١/١	٢٠٠٧/٦/٣٠
مواد خام	٢٠,٠٠٠	٤٠,٠٠٠
إنتاج تحت التشغيل	٢٦,٠٠٠	؟
إنتاج تام	؟	٥٠,٠٠٠

وبلغت مبيعات الشركة خلال الفترة المذكورة ٧٥٠,٠٠٠ دينار، وحققت نسبة مجمل أرباح مقدارها ٤٠٪ وخلال الفترة تم شراء مواد خام بمبلغ ٢١٠,٠٠٠ دينار، وتم دفع ١٢٠,٠٠٠ د أجور مباشرة. وكذلك حدث نقص في مخزون إنتاج تحت التشغيل آخر المدة بمبلغ ١٦,٠٠٠ د، ولكن زاد مخزون الإنتاج التام بمبلغ ١٠,٠٠٠ دينار.

المطلوب: الإجابة عن الأسئلة من ١-٤.

١. المواد المباشرة هي:

أ- ١٨٠,٠٠٠   ب- ١٩٠,٠٠٠

جـ- ٢٢٠,٠٠٠   د- ٢١٠,٠٠٠

٢. تكلفة البضاعة المباعة بعد التعديل بالزيادة في الأعباء الإضافية:

أ- ٤٦٠,٠٠٠   ب- ٤٥٠,٠٠٠

جـ- ٤٨٠,٠٠٠   د- ٤٥٤,٠٠٠

٣. تكاليف الفترة الجارية هي:

أ- ٤٤٤,٠٠٠   ب- ٤٦٠,٠٠٠

جـ- ٤٥٠,٠٠٠   د- ٤٥٤,٠٠٠

٤. الأعباء الإضافية المحملة على إنتاج الفترة الجارية:

أ- ١٠٠,٠٠٠ د   ب- ١٤٤,٠٠٠ د

جـ- ١٤٨,٠٠٠   د- ١٥٤,٠٠٠ د

الفصل السابع
تكاليف المنتجات الرئيسية والمنتجات الفرعية

اهداف الفصل

بعد دراسة هذا الفصل يجب ان تكون قادرا على معرفة:

01. طبيعة المنتجات المشتركة والفرعية.

02. اهداف توزيع التكاليف المشتركة.

3. طرق توزيع التكاليف المشتركة على المنتجات الرئيسية.

04. معالجة التكاليف الخاصة بأحد المنتجات.

5. معالجة تكاليف المنتجات الفرعية.

06. معرفة أهمية توزيع التكاليف المشتركة في القرارات الادارية.

المقدمـة:

في بعض الصناعات يتم استخدام مادة خام او عدة مواد خام معا وينتج عن ذلك أكثر من منتج كما هو الحال في صناعة تكرير البترول وصناعة تعليب اللحوم والكثير من الصناعات الكيماوية، فهنا لا يمكن التحكم في انواع المنتجات النهائية على الرغم من امكانية التأثير كمية بعض المنتجات، وهـذا يعني أنـه إذا رغبت منشأة في انتاج منتج معين فإنها سوف تنتج حتما جميع المنتجات الأخرى، فمثلا، في صناعة تكرير البترول إذا رغبت الإدارة في إنتاج البنـزين، فإنهـا سـوف تحصـل حتما على المنتجـات البتروليـة الأخرى، كالكيروسين والسـولار والإسفلت، وتعرف المنتجات التي يتم انتاجها مـن عمليـة صناعيـة واحدة باسم المنتجات المشتركة Joint Products. وتعرف التكاليف التي تحدث حتى تتميز المنتجات عـن بعضها باسم التكاليف المشتركة Joint cost.

تعريف المنتجات الرئيسية والمنتجات الفرعية:

يـتم تصنيف المنتجـات المشـتركة في مجموعتين: الأولى وتشـمل مجموعـة المنتجـات الرئيسية: Main or Joint Products وهـي المنتجات التي تهدف المنشأة الى إنتاجها. والثانيـة مجموعـة المنتجات الفرعيـة By-Product وهـي المنتجات التي يتم انتاجها بصورة عرضية أثنـاء عمليـة الإنتاج. وفي العـادة تكون كميات المنتجات الرئيسية اكبر من كميات المنتجات الفرعيـة، وقد يتغير تصنيف المنتجات المشتركة مع مرور الزمن، فبعد أن تكون بعض المنتجات منتجات فرعية تصبح منتجات رئيسية، فمثلا بعد ان كان الكـاز (الكيروسين) المنتج الرئيسيـ في بداية عهد صناعة البترول والمنتجـات البتروليـة الأخرى منتجـات فرعيـة اصبحت المنتجات الاخرى بعد اختراع السيارات والطائرات والآليـات التي تعمـل بالوقود البترولي منتجات رئيسية. لذلك على الادارة ان تراجـع منتجاتها المشـتركة كلما اقتضت الظروف ذلك.

المنتجات الفرعية والخردة By Product and the Scrap:

تشترك الخردة والمنتجات الفرعية بانخفاض قيمها البيعية النسبية بالمقارنة مع قيمة المنتجات الرئيسية مع أنهما ينتجان من نفس المادة الخام ومن عملية انتاجية واحدة، وتختلف الخردة عن المنتجات الفرعية في ان الخردة تمثل مخلفات مواد خام مثل قصاصات القماش في صناعة الملبوسات، فالقصاصات هي منتج مشترك مع الملابس ولكن لا تحتوي على عنصري الاجور والمصروفات الصناعية غير المباشرة، ويكون لها قيمة بيعية اقل من أسعار الملابس، أما المنتجات الفرعية فإنها تحتوي على مواد خام ولكنها خضعت الى عمليات التشغيل، وبالتالي فهي تختلف عن المواد الخام لأنها حصلت على عنصري الأجور والمصروفات الصناعية غير المباشرة، ومع ذلك تكون قيمتها البيعية منخفضة نسبيا بالمقارنة مع أسعار بيع المنتجات الرئيسية. ونظرا لانخفاض القيمة البيعية للخردة والمنتجات الفرعية فانه يمكن المحاسبة عليهما باستخدام نفس الاجراءات المحاسبية التي تم عرضها في الفصل الخامس من هذا الكتاب وهذه الاجراءات تختلف عن تلك المطبقة على المنتجات الرئيسية.

التكاليف المشتركة والخاصة: Joint and Separable Costs

التكاليف المشتركة هي التي تتحملها المنشأة في سبيل انتاج المنتجات المشتركة، وتحدث قبل انفصال هذه المنتجات عن بعضها، ويسمى المستوى الإنتاجي الذي تتميز عنده المنتجات عن بعضها بنقطة الانفصال Split- off point . وتشمل التكاليف المشتركة على تكاليف المواد المباشرة والأجور المباشرة والأعباء الإضافية اللازمة لإنتاج المنتجات المشتركة، وعلى الجانب الآخر قد تضطر المنشأة الى الاستمرار في عملية تصنيع احد المنتجات المشتركة بعد نقطة الانفصال ومن اجل ذلك تحدث التكاليف الخاصة Separable cost. ولأن هذه التكاليف تحدث في سبيل استكمال إنتاج منتج معين لذلك تخصص هذه التكاليف عليه مباشرة إذا أمكن ذلك.

أهداف توزيع التكاليف المشتركة:

هناك إجماع بين المحاسبين على ان كل طرق توزيع التكاليف المشتركة هي طرق شخصية، ومع ذلك يقومون بتوزيعها على المنتجات لتحقيق اهداف عدة من أهمها:[1]

1- المساعدة في تقييم المخزون لأغراض التقارير المالية الخارجية فهذه التقارير تتطلب ان يتم تقييم المخزون بالتكلفة او السوق ايهما اقل، وهذا يعني انه يسمح فقط باستخدام اسعار السوق، والتي تعبر عن التكلفة الاستبدالية، إذا كانت هذه القيمة اقل من التكلفة التاريخية، وبالتالي يجب تحديد تكلفة المنتجات لمقارنتها مع سعر السوق، وقد يتم انتقاد التكلفة الموزعة لعدم موضوعيتها إلا أن هذا الانتقاد مألوف في المحاسبة لأنه يتم انتقاد الارقام التقديرية الأخرى مثل رقم الاستهلاك ورقم مخصص الديون المشكوك في تحصيلها.

2- خدمة أغراض التأمين، حتى يمكن تقدير قيمة الأضرار التي تلحق بالمؤمن تقوم شركة التامين بالاتفاق مع المؤمن على الطريقة التي سيتم استخدامها لتوزيع التكاليف المشتركة.

3- المساعدة في تحديد أسعار التحويل الداخلية من قسم إلى آخر وخصوصا عندما يتم تقييم أداء الأقسام على أساس رقم صافي الربح.

4- المساعدة في تحديد الأسعار إذا كانت الاتفاقيات تربط الأسعار وأرقام التكلفة.

المحاسبة على المنتجات الفرعية:

تتوقف المعالجة المحاسبية على المنتجات الفرعية على السياسة التي تتبعها المنشأة عند تحديد تكلفة المخزون. وفي هذا المجال، قد تقوم المنشأة بإثبات صافي القيمة البيعية للمنتجات الفرعية عند الإنتاج أو تأجل ذلك حتى يتم بيع هذه المنتجات، تعرف الطريقة الأولى بطريقة الإنتاج، وتعرف الطريقة الثانية بطريقة البيع، وسيتم مناقشة هذه الطرق على التوالي:

---

[1] Deakin and Maher, " Cost Accounting , (IRWIN, ٢ nd ,.ed), pp.٣٠٥-٣٠٦.

أولا: طريقة الإنتاج

بموجب هذه الطريقة يتم تحميل حساب مخزون المنتج الفرعي بمبلغ يساوي صافي قيمته البيعية وهي عبارة عن ثمن بيع المنتج الفرعي ناقص التكاليف الصناعية والتسويقية والإدارية اللازمة لبيعه، لتوضيح ذلك سيتم الاعتماد على البيانات التالية:

مثال (١):

بلغت كمية المنتج الفرعي التي تم إنتاجها خلال الفترة ١,٠٠٠ كغم ويقدر سعر بيع الكيلو غرام منه بمبلغ ١ دينار، وتقدر المصروفات البيعية والإدارية اللازمة لبيع الوحدة ٥٪ من قيمة المبيعات، وتم خلال الفترة تم بيع ٦٠٠ كغم من هذا المنتج حسب الأسعار والمصروفات المقدرة.

المطلوب:

عمل قيود اليومية المتعلقة بإثبات المنتج الفرعي في الدفاتر استخدام: طريقة الإنتاج، ثم طريقة المبيعات.

الحل:

صافي القيمة البيعية للمنتج = ١,٠٠٠ × (١-٠,٠٥) = (٠,٠٥-١) = ٩٥٠د.

ويتم إثبات هذه القيمة بقيد اليومية التالي:

حـ/مخزون الإنتاج الفرعي		٩٥٠
حـ/إنتاج تحت التشغيل	٩٥٠	

بترحيل هذا القيد الى الجانب الدائن من حساب إنتاج تحت التشغيل يتم تخفيض قيمة التكاليف المشتركة بمبلغ ٩٥٠د وفتح حساب مخزون المنتجات الفرعية يجعل مدينا بنفس المبلغ. ولإثبات عملية البيع تحدد قيمة مبيعات المنتج وقيمة المصروفات البيعية والإدارية المرتبطة بعملية البيع. فعند إتباع نظام الجرد المستمر وبيع وحدة المنتج بسعر ١دينار، تكون قيود اليومية اللازمة لإثبات هذه الحقائق كالتالي:

حـ/النقدية		٦٠٠
حـ/مبيعات المنتج الفرعي	٦٠٠	

حـ/مصروفات تسويقية وإدارية/ منتج الفرعي		٣٠
حـ/النقدية	٣٠	

حـ/تكلفة مبيعات المنتج الفرعي		٥٧٠
حـ/مخزون المنتج الفرعي	٥٧٠	

قائمة الدخل الخاصة بالمنتج الفرعي

المبيعات (٦٠٠× د١)		٦٠٠
تكلفة الإنتاج	٩٥٠	
ناقص: مخزون آخر المدة (٤٠٠كغم × ٠,٩٥ د)	٣٨٠	
تكلفة البضاعة المباعة (٦٠٠ كغم × ٠,٩٥ د)	-------	٥٧٠
مجمل الربح		٣٠
ناقص: مصروفات تسويقية وإدارية		٣٠
صافي الربح		صفر

مما سبق يتبين لنا أن المنتج الفرعي لم يحقق أية أرباح، لأن التكاليف المشتركة التي تم تحميلها عليه كانت تساوي قيمته البيعية المتوقعة. ولكن إذا تم بيع المنتجات الفرعية بأسعار مختلفة عن الأسعار المستخدمة في تحديد تكلفتها يظهر رقما للربح أو للخسارة في قائمة دخل المنتجات الفرعية ، ويحول هـذا الـرقم الى قائمة الدخل الرئيسية تحت عنوان حساب إيرادات (خسائر) أخرى.

ثانيا: طريقة المبيعات:

حسب هذه الطريقة لا يتم تحميل المنتج الفرعي بأية تكلفة عند إنتاجه، ويتم تأجيل معالجته المحاسبية إلى أن يتم بيعه. ولمتابعة الكميات المنتجة منه، يتم كتابة مذكرة تبين الكمية التي تم إنتاجها منه. وعند بيع المنتج الفرعي يتم إثبات قيمة مبيعاته بقيود اليومية التالية:

حـ/النقدية		٦٠٠
حـ/مبيعات المنتج الفرعي	٦٠٠	
حـ/ مصروفات تسويقية وإدارية/ منتج الفرعي		٣٠
حـ/النقدية	٣٠	

من واقع هذه القيود تكون صافي إيرادات المنتجات الفرعية ٥٧٠ د . ويتم اعتبار مبيعات المنتج الفرعي ضمن الإيرادات الأخرى إذا كان مبلغها غير مهم (أو غير جوهري) ولكن إذا كان مبلغها جوهريا فانه يفضل توزيعه على حسابات تكلفة البضاعة المباعة ومخزون الإنتاج التام الصنع والإنتاج تحت التشغيل بنفس طريقة توزيع التكاليف غير المباشرة المحملة بالزيادة أو النقص التي تمت دراستها في الفصل الثالث. والأمر الذي يجب ملاحظته أن قيمة التكاليف المشتركة لم تتغير في طريقة المبيعات كما حدث في طريقة الإنتاج.

اختيار الطريقة المناسبة:

للمفاضلة بين طريقتي الإنتاج والبيع للمحاسبة على المنتجات الفرعية يجب الأخذ في الحسبان أهمية القيمة البيعية للمنتجات الفرعية وموضوع الرقابة الداخلية على الأصول. فإذا كانت قيمة المنتج أو المنتجات الفرعية مهمة نسبيا يجب أن تثبت تكاليفها في الدفاتر لأنه بدون ذلك لا تظهر بعض أصول المنشأة من سجلاتها المحاسبية، وتكون المقابلة بين الايرادات والمصروفات غير سليمة ولذلك في هذه الحالة يفضل استخدام طريقة الإنتاج.

وعلى الجانب الآخر، على أية حال، يمكن انتقاد طريقة الإنتاج لأنها تدعي بان المنتجات الفرعية لا تحقق أية أرباح لأنه يتم تحميلها بتكلفة تساوي صافي قيمتها البيعية، مما يجعل المنتجات الرئيسية تحقق الأرباح. فإذا تم تحميل هذه المنتجات بتكاليف اقل من صافي قيمتها البيعية كما في حالة المنتجات الرئيسية لأظهرت نتائج أعمالها اربحا هي الأخرى[1]. أما إذا كانت قيمة المنتجات الفرعية ضئيلة ولا تبرر تكاليف القيام بالمحاسبة عليها عند الإنتاج فإنه يمكن استخدام طريقة المبيعات.

توزيع التكاليف المشتركة:

سبق وأن ذكرنا أن التكاليف المشتركة تخص إنتاج المنتجات المشتركة وبالتالي يجب توزيعها على هذه المنتجات. وتعرف التكاليف المشتركة على أنها كل التكاليف التي يتم تحملها عند إنتاج المنتجات المشتركة حتى نقطة الانفصال مخصوما منها التكلفة المشتركة المحملة على المنتجات الفرعية. ويمكن أن يتم توزيع هذه التكاليف على المنتجات الرئيسية (المشتركة) باستخدام أحدى الطرق التالية:

١-   طرق كمية المنتجات.

٢-   طرق القيمة البيعية للمنتجات.

وفيما يلي شرحا لهذه الطرق:

أولا: طرق كمية المنتجات:

تعمل هذه الطرق على توزيع التكاليف المشتركة على المنتجات الرئيسية المشتركة على اساس كمية هذه المنتجات. ولوجود انتقادات على هذه الطريقة هناك اقتراح بتوزيع التكاليف المشتركة على اساس كمية المنتجات بعد ترجيحها بعوامل تعكس أهميتها النسبية. ولإيضاح هذه الطرق سيتم استخدام البيانات التالية:

---

[1] محمد تيسير الرجبي، التكاليف المعيارية كأداة للرقابة على تكاليف تكرير البترول، رسالة ماجستير غير منشورة، جامعة القاهرة، ١٩٧٢، ص ص ٣٧-٥٢.

مثال (٢):

تنتج إحدى الشركات ثلاثة منتجات هي أ، ب، ج، وتوفرت عنها البيانات التالية:

القيمة البيعية بالدينار	السعر	الكمية بالكيلوغرام	اسم المنتج
٦٠,٠٠٠	٣	٢٠,٠٠٠	أ
٣٠,٠٠٠	٢	١٥,٠٠٠	ب
٧,٥٠٠	٠,٧٥	١٠,٠٠٠	ج
٩٧,٥٠٠		٤٥,٠٠٠	الإجمالي

وبلغت التكاليف المشتركة بعد خصم القيمة البيعية للمنتجات الفرعية ٥٨,٥٠٠ دينار.

والمطلوب: توزيع التكاليف المشتركة على أساس كمية المنتجات.

الحل:

١- طريقة الكميات:

يتحدد نصيب كل منتج من التكاليف المشتركة على اساس نسبة كمية المنتج الى إجمالي كمية المنتجات والتي تساوي ٤٥,٠٠٠ كغم. فبعد أن يتم تقسيم التكاليف المشتركة على إجمالي كمية المنتجات تتحدد تكلفة الوحدة، وبهذا تكون تكلفة الوحدة (٥٨,٥٠٠ د ÷ ٤٥,٠٠٠كغم = ١,٣د/كغم). ولتحديد تكلفة المنتج يتم ضرب تكلفة الوحدة في عدد وحدات المنتج، وقد ظهرت نتائج هذه العمليات الحسابية في جدول (٧-١).

جدول رقم (٧-١)

توزيع التكاليف المشتركة على أساس كمية المنتجات

نسبة مجمل الربح	سعر الوحدة	تكلفة المنتج	التكاليف	كمية المنتج	المنتج
٥٦,٧%	٣	٢٦,٠٠٠	١,٣	٢٠,٠٠٠	أ
٣٥%	٢	١٩,٥٠٠	١,٣	١٥,٠٠٠	ب
(٧٣,٣%)	٠,٧٥	١٣,٠٠٠	١,٣	١٠,٠٠٠	ج
		٥٨,٥٠٠		٤٥,٠٠٠	الإجمالي

تم تحديد تكاليف المنتج بضرب كميته في تكلفة الوحدة. وتم حساب نسبة مجمل الربح لكل منتج باستخدام المعادلة التالية:

$$\text{مجمل الربح} = \frac{\text{سعر بيع الوحدة} - \text{تكلفة الوحدة}}{\text{سعر بيع الوحدة}}$$

$$\text{مجمل الربح (أ)} = \frac{٣ - ١,٣}{٣} = ٥٦\%$$

ونفس الطريقة تستخدم لحساب مجمل ربح المنتجين ب ، ج.

تؤدي هذه الطريقة إلى تحميل كل كيلو غرام بمبلغ ١,٣د، بغض النظر عن نوعه أو سعره، مما أدى إلى وجود اختلاف في نسبة مجمل ربح المنتجات حيث كانت بعضها موجبة وبعضها سالبة، وهذا يعني أن هذه الطريقة لا تراعي قدرة المنتجات على تحمل التكاليف، وتعطي الانطباع أن المنتج ج غير جدير بالإنتاج.

٢- طريقة الكميات المرجحة:

ولمعالجة بعض عيوب الطريقة السابقة يتم ترجيح الكميات باستخدام أوزان لتعكس الأهمية النسبية للمنتجات، وعند استخدام هذه الأوزان يتم حساب كمية المنتج المرجحة بضرب كميته في وزنه النسبي. فمثلا إذا قررت الإدارة أن الأهمية النسبية للمنتجات أ، ب، جـ هي ٥، ٤، ٣,٥ على التوالي فإنه يتم حساب الكميات المرجحة للمنتجات كالتالي:

كمية المنتجات المرجحة = ٢٠,٠٠٠ × ٥ + ١٥,٠٠٠ ×٤ + ١٠,٠٠٠ × ٣,٥

= ١٩٥,٠٠٠

تكلفة الوحدة المرجحة = التكاليف المشتركة ÷ كمية المنتجات المرجحة

=٥٨,٥٠٠د. ÷ ١٩٥,٠٠٠ = ٣٠,٣د. للوحدة المرجحة.

وتتحدد تكلفة المنتج بضرب كميته في تكلفة الوحدة المرجحة وتم ذلك كما في الجدول رقم (٧-٢). وبدراسة هذا الجدول نجد أن تكلفة الوحدة تم الحصول عليها

بقسمة تكلفة المنتج على عدد الوحدات المنتجة منه، و تم حساب نسبة مجمل الربح حسب المعادلة المذكورة أعلاه.

توزيع التكلفة المشتركة باستخدام الأوزان النسبية للمنتجات

نسبة	سعر البيع	تكلفة الوحدة	تكلفة المنتج	الكمية المرجحة	الوزن النسبي	الكمية	المنتج
٥٠%	٣	١,٥	٣٠,٠٠٠	١٠٠,٠٠٠	٥	٢٠,٠٠٠	أ
٤٠%	٢	١,٢	١٨,٠٠٠	٦٠,٠٠٠	٤	١٥,٠٠٠	ب
(٤٠%)	٠,٧٥	١,٠٥	١٠,٥٠٠	٣٥,٠٠٠	٣,٥	١٠,٠٠٠	ج
			٥٨,٥٠٠	١٩٥,٠٠٠		٤٥,٠٠٠	الإجمالي

على الرغم من أن هذه الطريقة حاولت التغلب على مشاكل الطريقة السابقة إلا أنها لم تراعي قدرة المنتجات على التحمل، لأن بعضها أظهر أرباحا وبعضها الآخر أظهر خسائر، إضافة إلى ذلك، تتوقف الأوزان على وجهة نظر الإدارة مما يجعلها غير موضوعية.

ثانيا: طرق القيمة البيعية للمنتجات:

تعمل هذه الطرق على تحميل المنتجات بتكاليف مشتركة على أساس قدرتها على التحمل والتي يتم قياسها باستخدام رقم صافي قيمتها البيعية، وهذه تتكون من ايرادات بيع المنتجات ناقص التكاليف الصناعية والتسويقية والإدارية اللازمة حتى تكون المنتجات قابلة للبيع. وتحدد القيمة البيعية لكمية الإنتاج وليس للكمية المباعة. ومن الأمور التي يجب أخذها في الحسبان أنه إذا توافرت أسعار بيع للمنتجات المشتركة عند نقطة الانفصال عندها يجب استخدام هذه الأسعار في توزيع التكاليف المشتركة أما إذا لم تتوفر أسعار بيع لبعض المنتجات أو كلها، وان المنشأة تضطر الى تشغيلها (لإكمال عملية تصنيعها) بعد نقطة الانفصال حتى يمكن بيعها عندها لا بد من اعتبار التكاليف الخاصة عند القيام بالتوزيع . فالتكاليف الخاصة تعمل على زيادة منفعة المنتجات التي خضعت

لعملية التشغيل الإضافي وتؤدي إلى زيادة قيمها البيعية. ولذلك سيتم التعرض لموضوع توزيع التكاليف حسب الحالات السابقة على التوالي:

١ - القيمة البيعية عند نقطة الانفصال:

إذا توفرت قيمة بيعية للمنتجات المشتركة عند نقطة الانفصال يجب استخدامها في توزيع التكاليف المشتركة على المنتجات الرئيسية وإهمال التكاليف الخاصة لأنها لم تساهم في إنتاج المنتجات المشتركة. وتتحدد حصة كل منتج من التكاليف المشتركة حسب نسبة صافي قيمته البيعية إلى صافي القيمة البيعية لكل المنتجات. وتتحدد صافي القيمة البيعية بضرب عدد الوحدات التي تم إنتاجها من كل منتج في سعر بيعة وطرح المصروفات التسويقية والإدارية اللازمة لبيعه. وبالرجوع إلى البيانات الموجودة في جدول (٧-١) يتم ضرب كمية كل منتج في سعر بيعه ثم تحدد نسبة صافي القيمة البيعية للمنتج إلى صافي القيمة البيعية لكل المنتجات وبعد ذلك يتم ضرب النسبة المحسوبة في التكاليف المشتركة. ولتحديد تكلفة الحدة المنتجة يتم قسمة حصة المنتج من التكاليف المشتركة على عدد الوحدات التي تم إنتاجها منه. وفي الجدول (٧-٣) بلغت القيمة البيعية للمنتجات ٩٧,٥٠٠ د وان القيمة البيعية للمنتج أ ٦٠,٠٠٠د فإن نسبة استفادة المنتج أ من التكاليف المشتركة هي ٦٠/٩٧,٥. وبعد تحديد نسبة استفادة المنتجات الأخرى يتم توزيع التكاليف المشتركة كالتالي:

$$\text{منتج أ :} \quad \frac{60}{97,5} \times 58,500 \quad = 36,000\text{د}$$

$$\text{منتج ب:} \quad \frac{30}{97,5} \times 58,500 \quad = 18,000\text{د}$$

$$\text{منتج ج:} \quad \frac{7,5}{97,5} \times 58,500 \quad = 4500\text{د}$$

وقد ظهـرت نتيجـة التوزيـع في الجـدول (٧-٣). ويمكـن اسـتخدام طريقـة أخـرى للتوزيع تقوم على حساب نسبة التكاليف إلى إجمالي الإيرادات وهي تساوي:

$$\text{نسبة التكاليف الى الإيرادات} = \frac{\text{التكاليف المشتركة}}{\text{إجمالي الإيرادات}} = \frac{٥٨,٥٠٠}{٩٧,٥٠٠} = ٠,٦ \text{ د}$$

تشير هذه النسبة إلى أن كل دينار من الإيرادات يجب أن يـتم تحميلـه بمبلـغ ٠,٦ دينار من التكاليف المشتركة. لذلك فإن المنتج أ يجب تحميله بمبلغ ٣٦,٠٠٠ دينار (= ٦٠,٠٠٠ × ٠,٦) من التكاليف المشتركة. وهو نفس المبلـغ الـذي تحمـل بـة في الطريقة السابقة.

جدول رقم (٧-٣)
توزيع التكاليف المشتركة باستخدام صافي القيمة البيعية للمنتجات المشتركة الرئيسية

مجمل الربح	تكلفة الوحدة	التكاليف	نسبة التوزيع	القيمة البيعية	السعر	الكمية	المنتج
٤٠%	١,٨	٣٦,٠٠٠	٩٧,٥/٦٠	٦٠,٠٠٠	٣	٢٠,٠٠٠	أ
٤٠%	١,٢	١٨,٠٠٠	٩٧,٥/٣٠	٣٠,٠٠٠	٢	١٥,٠٠٠	ب
٤٠%	٠,٤٥	٤,٥٠٠	٩٧,٥/٧,٥	٧,٥٠٠	٠,٧٥	١٠,٠٠٠	جـ
		٥٨٥٠٠		٩٧,٥٠٠			الإجمالي

تعطي هذه الطريقة نفس نسبة مجمل الربح للمنتجـات الثلاثـة، وهـذا أمـر منطقي، فطالما أنه من الصعب تحديد حصة كل منتج من التكاليـف المشتركة فعلى الأقل يجب أن نفترض بأن التكاليف تحقق نفس نسبة مجمل الـربح بغـض النظـر عن المنتج الذي تحملها، وهذا يتمشى مع الافتراض الذي يدعى بأن التكاليـف هـي أساس تحديد الأسعار.

٢ - عدم توفر أسعار بيعية عند نقطة الانفصال (التكاليف الخاصة):

في حالة عدم توفر أسعار بيع لبعض أو لكل المنتجات عند نقطة الانفصال او عدم إمكانية تقدير هذه القيمة، عندها يجب استخدام أسعار البيع بعد نقطة الانفصال لتوزيع التكاليف، والتي تعرف بالأسعار النهائية. والمشكلة هنا هي كيفية معالجة التكاليف الخاصة. وهنا قد نفترض بأن الأرباح تتحقق من التكاليف المشتركة فقط أو تتحقق من كل التكاليف. ففي الحالة الأولى نفترض بان التكاليف الخاصة لا تحقق أية أرباح ولذلك يتم طرحها من القيمة البيعية النهائية للمنتجات للتوصل إلى صافي القيمة البيعية للمنتجات المشتركة عند نقطة الانفصال، أما في الحالة الثانية فيتم جمع التكاليف المشتركة والتكاليف الخاصة معا وتوزيع إجمالي التكاليف على المنتجات المشتركة على أساس قيمتها البيعية النهائية. ولتوضيح هذه الطرق سنقوم باستخدام المعلومات التالية:

مثال (٣):

يتم الإنتاج في إحدى الشركات الصناعية في ثلاثة أقسام، يقوم القسم الأول بتشغيل المواد الخام ويفصلها إلى ثلاثة منتجات هي أ، ب، ج، وخلال شهر آذار استطاع هذا القسم إنتاج الكميات الآتية: ٢٠,٠٠٠ كغم من المنتج أ، ١٥,٠٠٠ كغم من المنتج ب، ١٠,٠٠٠ كغم من المنتج ج. ولعدم إمكانية بيع المنتجات أ، ب، مباشرة عند نقطة الانفصال يتم تشغيل المنتج أ في القسم الثاني وبعدها يباع بسعر ٤,٧٥ د/كغم، ويتم تشغيل المنتج ب في القسم الثالث، وبعدها يباع بسعر ٣,٥ د/كغم، أما المنتج ج فيتم بيعه مباشرة عند نقطة الانفصال بسعر ٠,٧٥د/كغم.

وبلغت تكاليف تشغيل هذه الأقسام خلال هذه الفترة كالتالي:

القسم الأول	٥٨,٥٠٠د
القسم الثاني	٢٠,٠٠٠د
القسم الثالث	٣٠,٠٠٠د

والمطلوب:

توزيع التكاليف على المنتجات الثلاث:

أ – طريقة صافي القيمة البيعية:

في هذه الطريقة تكون تكاليف تشغيل القسم الأول هي التكاليف المشتركة ومن ثم هي التكاليف يتم توزيعها على المنتجات المشتركة لأن هذه الطريقة تفترض بأن التكاليف المشتركة هي التي يمكنها تحقيق الأرباح أما التكاليف الخاصة فلا تستطيع ذلك وبالتالي يتم خصمها من القيمة البيعية للمنتجات أ،ب، قبل التوصل إلى صافي قيمتها البيعية. وبعد تحديد صافي القيمة البيعية للمنتجات يتم توزيع التكاليف المشتركة للقسم الأول كما في الجدول رقم (٤-٧).

جدول رقم (٤-٧)

طريقة توزيع التكاليف باستخدام طريقة صافي القيمة البيعية

نسبة التوزيع	صافي القيمة	التكاليف الخاصة	القيمة البيعية	السعر	الكمية	المنتج
١٠٥/٧٥	٧٥,٠٠٠	٢٠,٠٠٠	٩٥,٠٠٠	٤,٧٥	٢٠,٠٠٠	أ
١٠٥/٢٢,٥	٢٢,٥٠٠	٣٠,٠٠٠	٥٢,٥٠٠	٣,٥	١٥,٠٠٠	ب
١٠٥/٧,٥	٧,٥٠٠		٧,٥٠٠	٠,٧٥	١٠,٠٠٠	ج
	١٠٥,٠٠٠					الإجمالي

تابع جدول (٤-٧)

نسبة مجمل الربح	تكلفة الوحدة	إجمالي التكاليف	التكاليف الموزعة	المنتج
٪٣٤,٩٧	٣,٠٨٩	٦١٧٨٦	٤١,٧٨٦	أ
٪١٨,٩٧	٢,٨٣٦	٤٢٥٣٦	١٢,٥٣٦	ب
٪٤٤,٢٧	٠,٤١٨	٤١٧٨	٤,١٧٨	ج

في الجدول (٤-٧) تم ضرب كمية المنتجات بأسعارها لتحديد إجمالي القيمة البيعية لها،وبعدذلك تم خصم التكاليف الخاصةمنها للتوصل إلى صافي القيمةالبيعية للمنتجات

ومقدارها ١٠٥,٠٠٠ د، وبعدها تم حساب نسبة التوزيع بقسمة صافي القيمة البيعية للمنتج على إجمالي القيمة البيعية لكل المنتجات. ولتحديد نصيب المنتج من التكاليف المشتركة تم ضرب نسبة المنتج في التكلفة المشتركة وبعد تحديد نصيب المنتج من التكلفة المشتركة تم إضافة التكلفة الخاصة للمنتج للتوصل إلى إجمالي تكاليف المنتج.

تؤدي هذه الطريقة إلى اختلاف نسبة مجمل ربح المنتجات، وأن السبب في ذلك يعود إلى أن التكاليف الخاصة لا تحقق اية أرباح وهذا افتراض بطبيعة الحال غير منطقي، لأن التكاليف الخاصة يجب أن تكون مبررة اقتصاديا وبالتالي يجب أن تحقق تقريبا نفس الأرباح التي تحققها التكاليف الأخرى، وبالإضافة إلى ذلك، فإن هذه الطريقة ستكون غير مقبولة من قبل مدير القسم (٢) ومدير القسم (٣) عند استخدام رقم صافي الربح كأساس في تقييم الأداء، لأن تكاليف أقسامهم لا تحقق أية أرباح، أما رئيس القسم ١ فسيكون سعيدا لأن الأرباح سوف تتجمع في قسمه لأن تكاليفه اعتبرت تكاليف مشتركة.

ب – طريقة القيمة البيعية المعدلة:

نظرا للانتقادات الموجهة إلى الطريقة السابقة فإن هذه الطريقة تفترض أن التكاليف الخاصة والمشتركة تحقق نفس نسبة مجمل الربح، لذلك تقوم بجمع هذه التكاليف معا وتوزيعها على المنتجات المشتركة على اساس قيمتها البيعية النهائية، وتظهر نتائج التوزيع حسب هذه الطريقة كما في الجدول رقم (٥-٧).

جدول رقم (٥-٧)
توزيع إجمالي التكاليف حسب طريقة القيمة البيعية المعدلة

التكاليف المشتركة	التكاليف الخاصة	التكاليف الموزعة	نسبة التوزيع	القيمة البيعية	المنتج
٤٦,٥٠٠	٢٠,٠٠٠	٦٦,٥٠٠	٩٥/١٠٠	٩٥,٠٠٠	أ
٦,٧٥٠	٣٠,٠٠٠	٣٦,٧٥٠	٥٢,٥/١٠٠	٥٢,٥٠٠	ب
٥,٢٥٠		٥,٢٥٠	٧,٥/١٠٠	٧,٥٠٠	ج
٥٧٥٠٠	٥٠,٠٠٠	١٩٨٥٠٠		١٠٠,٠٠٠	
		نسبة مجمل	تكلفة الوحدة	المنتج

		%٣٠	٣,٣٢٥	أ
		%٣٠	٢,٤٥	ب
		%٣٠	٠,٥٢٥	ج

للتوصل إلى توزيع التكاليف تم حساب الأمور الآتية:

$$\text{أولا: نسب التوزيع} = \frac{\text{إجمالي القيمة البيعية للمنتج}}{\text{إجمالي القيمة البيعية لكل المنتجات}}$$

ثانيا: إجمالي التكاليف = التكاليف المشتركة + التكاليف الخاصة

ثالثا: نصيب المنتج = إجمالي التكاليف × نسبة التوزيع

ويمكن اتباع أسلوب آخر للتوزيع يقوم على تحديد نسبة مجمل الربح ثم تحديد مجمل الربح لكل منتج وطرح ذلك من مبيعات كل منتج لتحديد تكلفته، وبطرح التكاليف الخاصة للمنتج من تكاليفه المحددة بالخطوة السابقة يتحدد نصيبه من التكاليف المشتركة. وبتطبيق ذلك على المنتج (أ) تكون خطوات تحديد تكلفته كالتالي: [1]

$$\text{نسبة مجمل الربح} = \frac{١٠٨,٥٠٠ - ١٠٠,٠٠٠}{١٠٠,٠٠٠} = ٣٠\%$$

إذن نسبة تكلفة البضاعة إلى المبيعات = ١-٣٠% = ٧٠%

تكلفة المنتج أ = ٩٥,٠٠٠ × ٧٠% = ٦٦,٥٠٠

التكاليف المشتركة للمنتج أ = ٦٦,٥٠٠ – ٢٠,٠٠٠ = ٤٦,٥٠٠ دينار.

ومن مزايا هذه الطريقة أنها تجاوزت الانتقاد الموجه إلى الطريقة السابقة لأنها عاملت التكاليف المشتركة والخاصة نفس المعاملة، وعلى الجانب الآخر، يمكن انتقادها

---

[1] هورنجرين ت. تشارلز، مرجع سابق الذكر، ص ص ٦٠٦-٦٠٧.

على اساس أن التكاليف قد لا تحقق نفس نسبة مجمل الربح، وهذا الانتقاد يذكرنا بأن كل طرق توزيع التكاليف المشتركة هي طرق تحكمية.[٢]

التكاليف المشتركة واتخاذ القرارات:

لقد تم التعرض لأهداف توزيع التكاليف المشتركة في مقدمة هذا الفصل، وهنا سوف نهتم بموضوع اتخاذ القرارات المتعلقة بتشغيل المنتجات المشتركة، فمثلا قد يقدم اقتراح يتعلق بإمكانية تشغيل أحد المنتجات المشتركة في مرحلة تشغيل إضافية أو حتى هل يجب أن يتم القيام بالصناعة في المقام الأول، لاتخاذ هذا النوع من القرارات الإدارية لا نحتاج إلى توزيع التكاليف المشتركة، لأنه بدلا من ذلك تتم نحتاجه الإيرادات المضافة والتكاليف المضافة المرتبطين بقرار التشغيل المقترح، فالإيرادات المضافة هي الزيادة في الإيرادات الناتجة عن قرار التشغيل الإضافي، وكذلك فإن التكاليف المضافة هي الزيادة في التكاليف التي تتحملها المنشاة نتيجة لقرار التشغيل المقترح.

فمثلا إذا أردنا اتخاذ قرار يتعلق بإنتاج المنتجات المشتركة في القسم الإنتاجي الأول الوارد في المثال رقم (٢) من هذا الفصل نجد أن الإيرادات المضافة هي مجموع القيمة البيعية للمنتجات الثلاثة وقدرها ٩٧,٥٠٠ دينار وهذه الإيرادات تعتبر جميعها مضافة لأن الإيرادات كانت قبل بدء التشغيل تساوي صفراً، وأن التكاليف المضافة ٥٨,٥٠٠د للسبب نفسه وبالتالي يكون قرار البدء في التشغيل مبرراً من ناحية اقتصادية لأن الإيرادات المضافة أكبر من التكاليف المضافة. لاحظ أنه لاتخاذ هذا القرار لم يتم توزيع التكاليف المشتركة وعلى العكس تم جمع القيمة البيعية للمنتجات الثلاثة ومقارنتها مع التكاليف المشتركة.

إذا تم تطبيق التحليل السابق على حالة أقسام التشغيل الأخرى الواردة في المثال رقم (٣) فإنه يجب التركيز على الإيرادات والتكاليف التي تعزى إلى قرار استمرار التشغيل بعد نقطة الانفصال في الأقسام ٣,٢ والتي تعرف بالإيرادات المضافة (التفاضلية) والتكاليف المضافة(التفاضلية)وإذا تبين لنا أن الإيرادات المضاف قدزادت عن التكاليف المضافةسيكون القراري صالح الاستمراربالتشغيل،أما إذا كانت التكاليف المضافة

---

[٢] Thomas L. Arthur, O.P. cit., pp٦-١٥.

أكبر من الإيرادات المضافة فيجب بيع المنتج عند نقطة الانفصال، ومرة أخرى، فإننا لا نحتاج إلى توزيع التكاليف المشتركة لاتخاذ هذا القرار الإداري.

ولتوضيح ذلك افترض أن اسعار بيع المنتجات أ، ب عند نقطة الانفصال هي ٣د، ٢د، على التوالي مع بقاء البيانات الأخرى الواردة في المثال (٣) على ما هي عليه، فإن الإيرادات المضافة تقيس التغير في الإيرادات المترتبة على القرار المقترح والتكاليف المضافة تقيس أيضا التغير في التكاليف المترتبة على القرار المقترح وهي تعرف بالتكاليف الخاصة وسيتم حسابهما كما في جدول رقم (٦-٧).

جدول رقم (٦-٧)
الإيرادات المضافة والتكاليف المضافة للمنتجات أ،ب

التكاليف الخاصة	الإيرادات المضافة	الكمية المنتجة	فرق السعر	سعر البيع النهائي	سعر البيع عند الانفصال	المنتج
٢٠،٠٠٠	٣٥،٠٠٠	٢٠،٠٠٠	١،٧٥	٤،٧٥	٣	أ
٣٠،٠٠٠	٢٢،٥٠٠	١٥،٠٠٠	١،٥	٣،٥٠	٢	ب

لقد تم تحديد الإيرادات المضافة بضرب فرق السعر بكمية المنتجات. وبالتركيز على المنتج أ نجد أن إيراداته المضافة تساوي ٣٥،٠٠٠د وهذا المبلغ أكبر من تكاليفه الخاصة وبالتالي فان قرار تشغيل المنتج أ في مرحلة تشغيل إضافية يؤدي إلى زيادة أرباح المنشأة بمبلغ ١٥،٠٠٠د. أما المنتج ب فإن تشغيله في القسم الإنتاجي ٣ يؤدي إلى تحمل خسارة مقدارها ٧،٥٠٠ دينار لأن إيراداته المضافة تساوي ٢٢،٥٠٠د وتكاليفه المضافة تساوي ٣٠،٠٠٠د. ومرة أخرى لم نحتاج إلى توزيع التكاليف المشتركة لأنها غير موجودة في هذه الحالة. ولذلك يجب عدم الاستمرار في تشغيل المنتج ب بعد نقطة الانفصال إذا كان يمكن بيعه بسعر ٢ دينار للوحدة لان ذلك يؤدي الى تحميل المنشأة لخسارة مقدارها ٧،٥٠٠ د.

الخاتمـــة

لقد قمنـا في هـذا الفصـل بمناقشـة مشاكـل توزيـع التكاليـف المشتركة على المنتجات المشتركة، وتبين لنا أن المنتجات المشتركة الرئيسية هي التي تهدف المنشأة إلى إنتاجها، أما المنتجـات المشتركة الفرعية فهي التي يتم إنتاجها عرضـا، ولا تهدف المنشأة إلى إنتاجها في المقام الأول، لذلك لا تظهر ايـة ارباح منهـا، وتتم معالجتها محاسبيا بإحـدى طريقتين همـا طريقـة الإنتاج وطريقـة المبيعـات، ففي حالة استخدام طريقة الإنتاج يتم تحميل المنتجات الفرعية بتكلفة مشتركة تساوي صافي قيمتها البيعية، أما في حالة استخدام طريقـة المبيعـات فلا يتم تحميل المنتجـات الفرعية بأية تكلفة مشتركة وتعتبر قيمتها البيعية إيرادات عرضية، أو يتم توزيعهـا على حسابات تكاليف البضاعة.

وعلى الجانب الآخر يتم توزيع التكاليف المشتركة على المنتجات الرئيسية باستخدام طريقة الكميات أو باستخدام صافي القيمـة البيعيـة، وتفضل الطريقـة الثانية على الأولى لمراعاتها قدرة المنتجـات على تحمل التكاليف، ولـذلك تعطي المنتجات عند استخدام طريقـة صافي القيمـة البيعيـة نفس نسبة مجمل الـربح، ومعالجة التكاليف الخاصة قد يتم طرحها من القيمـة البيعيـة للمنتج المستفيد وتوزع بعد ذلك التكاليف المشتركة بنسبة صافي القيمـة البيعيـة للمنتج إلى صافي القيمـة البيعية للمنتجات أو أن تضاف التكاليف الخاصة إلى التكاليف المشتركة، ويتم توزيعهما معا على المنتجات على اساس مقـدرتهما على الـدفع والتي تقـاس بنسبة إجمالي القيمـة البيعية للمنتج إلى إجمالي القيمـة البيعيـة لكل المنتجات، يفضل استخدام الطريقة الثانية على الطريقة الأولى لأنها تسمح للتكاليف المشتركة والخاصة بتحقيق نفس نسبة مجمل الربح.

أسئلة وتمــارين

السؤال الأول: ميز بين المنتجات الرئيسية والمنتجات الفرعية.

السؤال الثاني: ميز بين التكاليف المشتركة والتكاليف الخاصة.

السؤال الثالث: لا تسمح التكاليف المشتركة للمنتجات الفرعية بتحقيـق الأربـاح، ناقش ذلك.

السؤال الرابع: قـارن بيـن طريقـة الكميـات وطريقـة القيمـة البيعيـة المعدلة المستخدمتان في توزيع التكاليف المشتركة.

السؤال الخامس: أذكر أوجه الاختلاف الرئيسية بيـن طريقـة صافي القيمـة البيعيـة وطريقة القيمة البيعية المعدلة وأي الطرق تنصح باستخدامها؟

السؤال السادس: إذا كانت قيمة المنتج الفرعي مرتفعة نسبيا فهل تفضل استخدام طريقة الإنتاج أو طريقة المبيعات ولماذا ؟

السؤال السابع: ما هي أوجه الاختلاف بين الخردة والمنتجات الفرعية.

السؤال الثامن: تقـوم إحدى الشركات الصناعية بإنتاج الرصاص والزنك مـن أحـد مناجمها ويتم إنتاج هذه المنتجات بنسبة ٢٠٪، ٣٠٪ على التوالي مـن المواد الخـام المستخرجة من المنجم والباقي ونسبته ٥٠٪ لا يتم الاستفادة منه، وتكلفة استخراج طن المواد الخام هي ٦٥ دينار وسعر بيع طن الرصاص ٢٠٠ دينار وسعر بيع طن الزنك ١٥٠ دينار. وخلال السنة تم استخراج ١٠,٠٠٠ طن مـن المناجم وتحققت نفس نسب المنتجات والتكاليف، وبقي مـن هـذه المنتجات في المخازن في آخر السنة ٢٠٪ من كمية الإنتاج ولم يكن هناك أي مخزون في بداية السنة.

المطلوب:

١- تحديد تكلفة الزنك والرصاص باستخدام طريقة الكميات الماديـة مـع تحديد نسبة مجمل ربح كل منتج منها.

٢- إعداد قائمة الدخل للشركة.

السؤال التاسع: تنتج إحدى الشركات ثلاثة منتجات من عملية صناعة واحدة وكان بيان الوحدات المنتجة والمباعة وأسعار بيعها خلال المدة كالتالي:

سعر البيع	الكمية المباعة	الكمية المنتجة	المنتج
١٠	١٢٠	٢٠٠	أ
٨	١٦٠	٣٠٠	ب
٥	٨٠	١٠٠	ج
	٣٦٠	٦٠٠	الإجمالي

وكانت التكاليف المشتركة للشركة ٣٦٧٢ دينـار، يتم بيع المنتجات السـابقة بعـد نقطة الانفصال مباشرة.

المطلوب:

١- توزيع التكاليف المشتركة باستخدام طريقة الوحدات الكمية.

٢- توزيع التكاليف المشتركة على أساس الكميات المرجحـة بالأهميـة النسبية إذا كانت الأهمية النسبية للمنتجات أ، ب، ج هي ٥، ٤، ٣، على التوالي.

٣- توزيع التكاليف المشتركة باستخدام طريقة صافي القيمة البيعية.

السؤال العاشر: تنتج إحدى الشركات الصناعية ثلاثة منتجات هي أ، ب،ج، ويعتبر المنتج ج منتجا فرعيا أما المنتجات أ،ب فهي منتجات رئيسية والآتي البيانات الخاصة بهذه المنتجات.

– بلغت الكمية المنتجة من أ = ٣٠,٠٠٠كغم، ومـن ب= ٤٠,٠٠٠ كغـم. ومـن ج ٥٠٠ كغم، وسعر بيع هذه المنتجات هي ٥د، ٤د، ١د على التوالي.

– تقدر المصروفات التسويقية والإداريـة اللازمـة لبيـع المنتـج الفرعـي ٥% مـن مبيعاته.

– بلغت التكاليف المشتركة ١٩٢,٦٧٥ دينارا.

وتتبع الشركة طريقة الإنتاج في المحاسبة على المنتجات الفرعية.

المطلوب:

١- عمل قيود اليومية اللازمة لإثبات الحركة التي طرأت على حساب مخزون المنتجات الفرعية، مع العلم بأنه قد تم بيع ٨٠٪ من كمية المنتج ج بأسعاره وتكاليفه المخططة حسب طريقة الإنتاج.

٢- توزيع التكاليف المشتركة باستخدام طريقة القيمة البيعية.

٣- افترض أنه حتى يتم بيع المنتج الفرعي يجب تصنيعه في مرحلة تشغيل إضافية ومتوسط تكلفة التشغيل فيها ٣د/كغم وبعدها يتم بيعه بسعر ٤,٥ دينار /كغم. ما هو نصيب المنتج ج من التكاليف المشتركة إذا كانت المنشأة تتبع طريقة الإنتاج في المحاسبة على المنتج الفرعي.

السؤال الحادي عشر: تنتج إحدى الشركات ثلاثة منتجات مشتركة وتقوم بتوزيع التكاليف المشتركة باستخدام طريقة القيمة البيعية عند نقطة الانفصال. والآتي معلومات عن عملياتها خلال شهر آذار.

ج	ب	أ	الإجمالي	البيــــان
؟	٨٠٠	؟	٣,٠٠٠	القيمة البيعية عند نقطة الانفصال
٣٠٠	؟	؟	١,٨٠٠	التكاليف المشتركة الموزعة
؟	١,٣٠٠	٢,١٠٠	٤,١٥٠	القيمة البيعية بعد التشغيل الإضافي
١٠٠	٤٠٠	٥٠٠	١,٠٠٠	التكلفة الخاصة

المطلوب:

١- تحديد قيمة الأرقام المجهولة.

٢- تحديد قيمة مجمل الربح الذي حققته الشركة.

السؤال الثاني عشر: تحتوي إحدى المنشآت على ثلاثة أقسام إنتاجية حيث يبدأ الإنتاج في القسم الأول ويترتب عليه ظهور ثلاثة منتجات هي س، ص، ع، يتم بيع المنتج س بعد ذلك مباشرة أما المنتج ص فيتم تحويله إلى القسم الإنتاجي الثاني ويتم تحويل المنتج ع إلى القسم الإنتاجي الثالث ويقدر التالف العادي في الأقسام الثلاثة بنسبة ٥٪ من المواد

وتكون نسبة الناتج من المنتجات س، ص، ع في نهاية التشغيل في القسم الأول هي ٣٠٪، ٤٠٪، ٣٠٪ على التوالي.

وخلال فترة التكاليف تم تشغيل ٣٠٠,٠٠٠ كغم من المواد الخام وتحقق منها نفس نسب المنتجات المتوقعة وتقدر أسعار بيع المنتجات كالتالي:

س = ٣د/كغم، ص =٥د/كغم، ع=٦د/كغم، وكانت تكاليف الأقسام الإنتاجية الثلاث كالتالي:

القسم الأول ٤٣٤,٥٦٨د.

القسم الثاني ١٨٠,٠٠٠د.

القسم الثالث ٢٠٠,٠٠٠د.

المطلوب:

١- توزيع التكاليف باستخدام طريقة صافي القيمة البيعية.

٢- توزيع التكاليف حسب طريقة القيمة البيعية المعدلة.

السؤال الثالث عشر: تقوم شركة الأردن بإنتاج المنتجات س، ص، ع، ي من عملية إنتاج مشتركة والآتي معلومات إضافية أخرى.

القيمة البيعية النهائية	التكلفة الخاصة	القيمة البيعية عند الانفصال	الوحدات المنتجة بالكيلو غرام	المنتج
٩٠,٠٠٠	٧,٥٠٠	٨٠,٠٠٠	٦,٠٠٠	س
٧٠,٠٠٠	٦,٠٠٠	٦٠,٠٠٠	٥,٠٠٠	ص
٥٠,٠٠٠	٤,٠٠٠	٤٠,٠٠٠	٤,٠٠٠	ع
٣٠,٠٠٠	٢,٥٠٠	٢٠,٠٠٠	٣,٠٠٠	ي
٢٤٠,٠٠٠	٢٠,٠٠٠	٢٠٠,٠٠٠	١٨,٠٠٠	

افترض أن إجمالي التكاليف المشتركة ١٦٠،٠٠٠ دينار ويتم توزيعها باستخدام طريقة صافي القيمة البيعية عند نقطة الانفصال، فإن التكاليف المخصصة على المنتجات الأربعة هي:

	ي	ع	ص	س
أ	٤٠،٠٠٠	٤٠،٠٠٠	٤٠،٠٠٠	٤٠،٠٠٠
ب	٢٦،٦٦٧	٣٥،٥٥٦	٤٤،٤٤٤	٥٣،٣٣٣
ج	١٦،٠٠٠	٣٢،٠٠٠	٤٨،٠٠٠	٦٤،٠٠٠
د	٢٠،٠٠٠	٣٣،٣٣٣	٤٦،٦٦٧	٦٠،٠٠٠

(المجمع الأمريكي للمحاسبين القانونيين سنة ١٩٧٨)

السؤال الرابع عشر: تقوم شركة بإنتاج المنتجات س، ت من عملية إنتاج مشترك وكانت القيمة البيعية عند نقطة الانفصال لهما ٥٠،٠٠٠ دينار من ٦،٠٠٠ وحدة من المنتج س، ٢٥،٠٠٠ دينار من ٢،٠٠٠ وحدة من المنتج ت، افترض أن التكاليف المحملة على المنتج س باستخدام القيمة البيعية هي ٣٠،٠٠٠ دينار. ما هو إجمالي التكاليف المشتركة.

أ. ٤٠،٠٠٠   ب. ٤٢،٥٠٠د.
ج. ٤٥،٠٠٠   د. ٦٠،٠٠٠د.

(المجمع الأمريكي للمحاسبين القانونيين سنة ١٩٧٨)

السؤال الخامس عشر: تقوم إحدى الشركات الصناعية بإنتاج المركبات الكيماوية التي تدخل في صناعة الأسمدة ويستخدم أحد خطوط الإنتاج كلوريد الصوديوم وحامض الكبريتيك بنسبة ٩٨ :١١٦ وينتج عن ذلك كبريتات الصوديوم وحامض الكلوريك وبنسبة ١٤٢:٧٢ ونتيجة العملية الصناعية يتم فقد ١٠٪ من كمية المدخلات وهذه النسبة تعتبر طبيعية في هذه الصناعة.
وخلال إحدى الفترات قد حصلت على المعلومات التالية:

- تم استخدام ٦٩٦ طن من كلوريد الصوديوم و ٥٨٥ طن من حامض الكبريتيك وكان سعر الطن من هذه المواد ٢٥د، ٧٠د على التوالي، وتم الحصول على المخرجات بنفس النسب المحددة. بلغت تكاليف تشغيل هذا الخط الإنتاجي خلال الفترة كالتالي:

استهلاك آلات الخط الإنتاجي	٢٥,٠٠٠د
أجور العمل	٤٥,٠٠٠
صيانة ووقود وقوى محركة	١٢,٠٠٠
إيجار وهاتف وكهرباء	٨,٠٠٠
مصروفات أخرى موزعة	٥٨,٠٠٠
الإجمالي	١٤٨,٠٠

- يبلغ سعر بيع الطن من كبريتات الصوديوم ٢٢٠د، ومن حامض الكوريك ٢٥٠د، وتقوم الشركة بتوزيع التكاليف المشتركة باستخدام طريقة صافي القيمة البيعية.

- لم يكن هناك مخزون أول المدة من المنتجات النهائية ولكن بقي ٢٥طن من كبريتات الصوديوم و ٣٠طن من حامض الكلوريك في المخازن آخر المدة.

المطلوب:

١- توزيع التكاليف المشتركة على المنتجات المشتركة باستخدام طريقة صافي القيمة البيعية.

٢- إعداد قائمة الدخل للخط الإنتاجي.

السؤال السادس عشر: تقوم إحدى الشركات الصناعية بتحليل المواد الكيماوية ويترتب على ذلك إنتاج منتجين هما: أ، ب. ويعتبر المنتج أ منتجا رئيسيا لأنه يدخل في صناعة عدة منتجات أخرى أما المنتج ب فيعتبر منتجا فرعيا وقبل أن يتم بيعه يتم إخضاعه لعملية صناعية لتحويله إلى مادة قابلة للبيع، وخلال إحدى الفترات بلغت الكمية المنتجة من أ ٢٥,٠٠٠كغم ومن المنتج ب ٥٠٠٠ كغم وتحملت الشركة مبلغ ٤,٠٠٠ دينار في سبيل تشغيل المنتج ب وبعدها يتم بيع الوحدة منه بسعر ١,٢ دينار. أما تكاليف المرحلة التشغيل الأولى فقد بلغت ٥٢,٠٠٠ دينار وأن القيمة البيعية للمنتج أ هي ٣د/كغم. وقد تم بيع المنتج بنفس السعر التقديري له.

المطلوب:

1- عمل قيود اليومية اللازمة لإثبات حركة المنتج الفرعي عند إتباع طريقة الإنتاج وما هي تكلفة المنتج أ.

2- عمل قيود اليومية اللازمة لإثبات حركة المنتج الفرعي ب عند إتباع طريقة البيع وما هي تكلفة المنتج ب.

السؤال السابع عشر: تقوم شركة صناعية بإنتاج ثلاثة منتجات هي س، ص، ع، في القسم أ ويتم بيع المنتج ص مباشرة ويحول المنتج س إلى قسم ب ويحول المنتج ع الى قسم ج، وكانت تكاليف هذه الأقسام كالتالي:

قسم ج	قسم ب	قسم أ	
١,٠٠٠	٣٠,٠٠٠	١٢٠,٠٠٠	مواد مباشرة
١,٠٠٠	٦٠,٠٠٠	٨٠,٠٠٠	أجور مباشرة
٢٠٠	٦٠,٠٠٠	٨٠,٠٠٠	غير مباشرة
٢,٢٠٠	١٥٠,٠٠٠	٢٨٠,٠٠٠	الإجمالي

والآتي بيانات المبيعات والمخزون

المنتج ع	المنتج ص	المنتج س	
٢,٠٠٠	٤٠,٠٠٠	٦٠,٠٠٠	الوحدات المباعة بالكيلو غرام
-	١٠,٠٠٠	١٠,٠٠٠	وحدات بالمخازن آخر المدة
٤	٧	٦	سعر بيع الوحدة

لم يكن هناك لدى الشركة مخزون أول المدة. وتعتبر الشركة المنتج ع منتجا فرعيا وتقوم بإثباته في الدفاتر عند إنتاجه وتحدد تكاليفه على أساس قيمته البيعية ناقص ١٠٪ مقابل المصروفات التسويقية والإدارية أما المنتجات س، ص، فهي منتجات رئيسية.

المطلوب:

1- توزيع التكاليف المشتركة باستخدام طريقة الكميات المادية.

2- توزيع التكاليف المشتركة باستخدام طريقة القيمة البيعية المعدلة.

3- إذا اعتبرت صافي القيمة البيعية للمنتج ع إيرادات عرضية المطلوب توزيع التكاليف المشتركة باستخدام طريقة صافي القيمة البيعية.

4- إذا أمكن تشغيل المنتج ص في القسم د وكانت تكلفة هذا القسم ٧٥,٠٠٠د وخلال الإنتاج يتم فقد ٥% من كمية المنتج ص التي يستلمها وبعد انتهاء التشغيل يباع المنتج بسعر ٨,٥ دينار /كغم والمطلوب هل تنصح بتشغيل القسم د أم لا مع إظهار العمليات الحسابية التي اعتمدت عليها على افتراض أن كمية المنتج ص هي ٥٠,٠٠٠ كغم.

السؤال الثامن عشر: تنتج إحدى الشركات ثلاث منتجات من تشغيل إحدى المواد الخام في إحدى أقسامها الإنتاجية س، ص، ع، ويتم تشغيل المنتج ع في مرحلة تشغيل إضافية أما المنتجات س، ص، فيتم بيعها عند نقطة الانفصال. وبلغت التكلفة المشتركة خلال إحدى فترات التكاليف ٤٠٠,٠٠٠ دينار ويمكن للشركة بيع كل منتجاتها في السوق المحلية حسب البيانات المعطاة. وتقوم الشركة في الوقت الحالي بشراء إحدى المنتجات من السوق بسعر ٧ دنانير للوحدة، ويرى مدير الإنتاج أنه يمكن تطوير المنتج ع واستخدامه في الإنتاج بدلا من هذا المنتج وتحتاج علمية تطوير المنتج ع إلى تشغيله في مرحلة التشغيل إضافية تكلفة الوحدة فيها ١,٥ دينار وتعيين موظفين رواتبهم الشهرية ٢٠,٠٠٠ دينار وأن الشركة تحتاج إلى ٢٥,٠٠٠ وحدة شهريا من هذا المنتج. والآتي معلومات عن المنتجات س، ص، ع.

ع	ص	س	الإجمالي	
٣٥,٠٠٠	٣٠,٠٠٠	٣٥,٠٠٠	١٠٠,٠٠٠	عدد الوحدات
١٧٥,٠٠٠	٣٦٠,٠٠٠	٣١٠,٠٠٠	٨٤٥,٠٠٠	الإيرادات
١٤٠,٠٠٠	٢٠٠,٠٠٠	٢٠٠,٠٠٠	٥٤٠,٠٠٠	تكلفة البضاعة المباعة

ويرى مدير الإنتاج أن تكلفة وحدة المنتج الجديد الذي سيتم تقديمه كالتالي:

تكلفة مشتركة موزعة	٤
تكلفة إنتاج خاصة	١,٥
تكلفة ثابتة مضافة	٠,٨٠
الإجمالي	٦,٣٠

ولأن الشركة تحتاج إلى ٢٥,٠٠٠ وحدة من المنتج ع المعدل. لـذلك يعتقـد مـدير الإنتاج بأن الشركة سوف توفر في حالة الإنتاج الداخلي بدلا من الشراء مـن المـورد دينار عن كل وحدة وتتضمن التكاليف المشتركة عـلى ١٠٠,٠٠٠د تكاليف ثابتة لا يمكن التخلص منها.

المطلوب:

هل توافق على الإنتاج الداخلي ولماذا ؟

السؤال التاسع عشر: يمر إنتاج إحدى الشركات في ثلاثة مراحل هـي مرحلة الفـرز ومرحلة التحليل ثم مرحلة التصنيع حيث يبدأ الإنتاج في المرحلة الأولى وتهدف إلى تخليص المواد الخام من الشوائب ويتم تجميع هذه الشوائب وبيعها بسعر ٧دينار /كغم ثم تنقل المواد بعد ذلك إلى مرحلة التحليل حيث يتم فصلها إلى منتجين هما أ، ب وعندها يمكن بيع المنتج أ بسعر ١,٥ دينار للوحدة وبيع المنتج ب بسعر ٦ د للوحدة. وبدلا من بيع المنتج أ عند نقطة الانفصال يتم تحويله إلى مرحلة التصنيع حيث يتم إضافة بعض المواد الكيماوية عليه وخلطه وبعدها يتم بيع الوحدة منـه بسعر ٩,٥ دينار، وخلال إحدى فترات التكاليف تـم تجميع البيانات التالية عـن هذه المراحل:

	التصنيع	التحليل	الفرز
وحدات أول المدة	--	--	٣٠٠٠ (٤٠%)
وحدات مضافة	١٤,٥٠٠ وحدة	٨,٩٠٠طن	١٠,٠٠٠
وحدات تحت التشغيل آخر المدة	--	--	٤,٠٠٠ (٨٠%)
وحدات تامة			٩,٠٠٠ طن

ومن ضمن الوحدات التامة في مرحلة الفرز ١٠٠ طن شوائب صافي قيمتها البيعية ٧٠٠ دينار والباقي وقدره ٨,٩٠٠ طن تـم تحويلها إلى مرحلـة التحليل ونتج عـن هذه الكمية ١٤,٥٠٠وحدة من المنتج أ تم تحويلها إلى مرحلـة التصنيع ونتج عـن هذه الكمية ٤٢,٠٠٠وحدة من المنتج المعروف باسم ب وحولت إلى المخازن وتم فقد ٣٥٠ كغم من هذه الوحدات اعتبرت فاقد عادي، وفي مرحلة التصنيع تم إنتاج كل الكمية التي تم استلامها من المنتج أ.

وكانت التكاليف المحملة على حساب الإنتاج تحت التشغيل لهذه المراحل كالتالي:

	التصنيع	التحليل	الفرز	
	--	--	٩,٦٠٠	رصيد اول المدة
	٢٠,٠٠٠	٤٠,٠٠٠	٢٢,٠٠٠	مواد مباشرة
	٢٣,٥٠٠	٣٢,٥٠٠	٢٧,٥٠٠	تكاليف تحويل
	؟	؟	--	تكلفة مستلمة

ومن سياسة الشركة إثبات قيمـة الشوائب عنـد الإنتـاج وتخفيض تكلفتها مـن التكاليف المشتركة وأن الفاقـد في المرحلة الثانية يعتبر فاقدا عاديا وهو نتيجـة التبخر الناتج عن التفاعلات الكيماوية وأن الشركة تطبق طريقة الأول في المحاسبة على تكاليف المراحل.

المطلوب:

إعداد تقارير المراحل الثلاثة وتحديد تكلفة الإنتاج تحت التشغيل آخـر المـدة إن وجد لهذه المراحل. وعمل قيود اليومية اللازمة لإثبات تحويل تكاليف الإنتـاج في مرحلة أخرى.

السؤال العشرون: تنتج إحدى الشركات الكيماوية ثلاثة منتجات من استخدام مادة خام واحدة وهي أ، ب، ج. وتعتبر الشركة المنتج ج منتجا فرعيا وتقوم بخصـم صافي قيمتـه البيعية القابلة للتحقق من التكاليف المشتركة قبل توزيعها على المنتجات الرئيسية أ، ب. وخلال إحدى الفترات تم إنتاج ٤٠,٠٠٠ كغم مـن المنتج أ و ٥٠,٠٠٠كغم مـن المنتج ب. ويتم تشغيل هذه المنتجات في مراحل تشغيل إضافية حيث بلغت التكلفةالخاصة للمنتج أ

خلال الفترة ٢٠،٠٠٠ دينار والتكلفة الخاصة للمنتج (ب) خلال الفترة ٣٠،٠٠٠ دينار. وبعد توزيع التكاليف المشتركة على أساس صافي القيمة عند نقطة الانفصال وبلغت نسبة مجمل الربح ٢٥٪، ٣٠٪ النسبة للمنتجات أ، ب، على التوالي.

وبالنسبة للمنتج ج فقد تم إنتاج ٥٠٠٠ وحدة منه خلال الفترة وتقدر صافي القيمة البيعية للوحدة ١,٥ دينار، وقد بلغت التكلفة المشتركة ٨٧،٥٠٠ دينار وكان نصيب المنتج أ منها ٣٤،٠٠٠ دينار.

المطلوب:

١- تحديد صافي القيمة البيعية للمنتجات أ، ب.

٢- تحديد إجمالي تكاليف المنتج ب.

الفصل الثامن
نظام تكاليف الانشطة

Activity-Based Costing

الأهداف التعليمية للفصل:

بعد دراسة الفصل يتوقع معرفة الامور الاتية:

١- الملامح الرئيسية لأنظمة محاسبة التكاليف التقليدية

٢- الاهداف الرئيسية لنظام تكاليف الانشطة

٣- ضرورة تقسيم المصروفات غير المباشرة الى اقسام كل منها يتبع نشاط معين

٤- مقارنة معالجة التكاليف المباشرة في كل من نظام التكاليف التقليدي ونظام تكاليف الانشطة

٥- معرفة أسباب الفرق بين تكلفة الوحدة عند استخدام نظام التكاليف التقليدي ونظام تكاليف الانشطة

مقدمــة :

يعتبر نظام تكاليف الأنشطة تطورا جديدا في مجال محاسبة التكاليف وبدأ الاهتمام به في العقدين الأخيرين مـن القرن المـاضي. ويهـدف الى توزيـع تكاليف المصادر الاقتصادية للمنظمة على أنشطتها ومنها على المنتجات أو الخدمات التي تقدمها. ويعتبر النظام اداة لقياس الاداء وتحديد وتوصيف وتوزيع التكاليف على الانشطة ووحدات الانتاج والخدمات. يفيد استخدام نظام التكاليف بالتركيز على الانشطة اللازمة لتحقيق هـدف التكاليف وهـذا يـؤدي الى تحسـين دقـة حسـاب تكلفة الوحدات المنتجة. ويعرف النشاط على انه حدث، عمل، وحدة عمل بهدف محـدد[1] ، ومثـال ذلك تصميم المنتج وإعـداد الالات للإنتاج، وتشغيل الآلات، المنتجات. ويعطي هذا النظام أرقاما أكثر دقة من نظام التكاليف التقليدي لأنه يقوم بربط التكلفة مع مسبب حدوثها، ويعمل على تحديـد مناطق العمل التي يمكن فيها ادخال التحسينات على اداء المنشاة واستبعاد الانشطة التي لا تـؤدي الى خلق قيمة إضافية للمنشأة. على أية حال، يتفق نظام تكاليف الأنشطة مع النظام التقليدي في المحاسبة عـلى عنصري المـواد المباشرة والأجـور المباشرة حيث يتم تتبعهما على وحدات الانتاج ولكن يختلف عنه في الامور الاتية:

أولا: استهلاك المصادر مقابل استهلاك الانشطة

ويعمل نظام تكاليف الانشطة على استخدام مقاييس الأنشطة ومـن ثـم يربط التكاليف بالأنشطة وهذا يؤدي الى تحسين الانتاجية. فعن طريق فحص مـا يحدث في أنشطة المنشاة بطريقة منتظمة يمكن تحديد الطاقة الفائضة وخطأ تقديرات التكاليف وتوزيع التكاليف، وهـذا يسـاعد في اعـادة توزيـع الطاقـة الى الأنشطة التي تحتاج الى ذلك. بينما نجد ان نظام التكاليف التقليـدي يـري ان اهداف التكلفة هي التي تستهلك المصادر الاقتصادية.

Horgren et. Al., ٢٠٠٣

ثانيا: استخدام عوامل مرتبطة بالحجم والأنشطة

يستخدم نظام التكاليف التقليدي ساعات العمل المباشر او ساعات دوران الالات كأساس لتوزيع التكاليف غير المباشرة، ولكن مع تنوع المصروفات غير المباشرة اصبحت العناصر المرتبطة بهذه الاسس محدودة، وبالتالي فان استخدامها يؤدي الى ارتفاع نسبة اخطاء توزيع التكاليف. ولكن عند استخدام نظام تكاليف الانشطة فانه يتم التركيز على علاقة السبب والنتيجة عند اختيار مسببات التكلفة Cost drivers التي هي أساس توزيع التكاليف. لذلك يمكن القول بان مسببات التكلفة Cost drivers ترتبط بصورة أقوى مع عناصر التكاليف غير المباشرة مقارنة مع أسس توزيع التكاليف المستخدمة في النظام التقليدي. وبدراسة علاقة مسببات التكلفة Cost drivers بالعمليات الفعلية يتم تصنيف التكاليف الى المجموعات الاتية:

١- مستوى الوحدة Unit Level وهنا تبدأ مسببات التكلفة Cost drivers مع اي وحدة يتم انتاجها. فمثلا عند إنتاج الوحدة يتم استخدام الآلات وهذا يؤدي الى استهلاك الوقود لتشغيل الآلات وصيانتها وأجور العمال الذين يقومون بتشغيل هذه الآلات . وبالتالي يؤثر عدد الوحدات على هذه التكاليف لذلك يمكن استخدام عدد الوحدات أو ساعات دوران الآلات في توزيع هذه التكاليف.

٢- مستوى الكمية Batch Level وتبدأ مسببات التكلفة Cost drivers في الحدوث عند كل كمية يتم انتاجها ومثال ذلك اعداد جداول الإنتاج أو تجهيز الآلات لإنتاج المنتجات أو شراء المواد. ففي حالة البدء بالإنتاج بغض النظر عن حجم الكمية المنتجة سوف تحدت في كل مرة يتم إعداد جداول الإنتاج وإعداد الآلات للإنتاج.

٣- مستوى المنتج Product level وهنا يبدأ مسبب التكلفة مع حدوث المنتج بغض النظر عن عدد الوحدات او الكميات التي يتم انتاجها منه. ومثال ذلك ساعات العمل اللازمة لتطوير المنتج. وبالتالي عند زيادة عدد المنتجات يزداد عدد ساعات التطوير وكلما كانت عملية الانتاج معقدة كلما ازدادت ساعات العمل اللازمة للتطوير.

٤- مستوى المصنع او التسهيلات الصناعية Facility level وهذه المسببات التكاليفية لا ترتبط بحجم الانتاج أو بعدد الوحدات أو الكميات المنتجة وإنما ترتبط بوجود الشركة ككل، ومثالها تكاليف إدارة الإنتاج ويمكن توزيعها باستخدام ساعات العمل المباشر.

ثالثا : الارتباط بالهيكل التنظيمي مقابل الارتباط بالعملية

يعطي نظام التكاليف التقليدي أهمية كبيرة للخريطة التنظيمية مقارنة مع العمليات التشغيلية لذلك فان الشخص في هذه الحالة لا يستطيع ان يتساءل عما يمكن عمله لان العملية غير معروفة. وعلى الجانب الآخر، فإن نظام تكاليف الانشطة ينطلق من العملية ويعمل على تجميع البيانات عن العمليات لذلك يمكن استخدامه في تحديد ما الذي يجب ان يعمل، وكيف يمكن توزيع المصادر بطريقة اكثر كفاءة. وهذا يساعد الادارة على مقابلة المصادر المطلوبة مع المصادر المتاحة مما يحسن مستوى الإنتاجية في الشركة. ولذلك نرى أن نظام التكاليف التقليدي لا يعطي دعما للقرارات الادارية المتعلقة بتوزيع المصادر بين الأنشطة المحتاجة لها، إضافة الى ذالك، فان الدراسة اللازمة لتطبيق نظام تكاليف الانشطة توجه الانظار الى سبب حدوث التكلفة

نظام التكاليف التقليدي :

لتوضيح طريقة عمل هذا النظام سوف نفترض وجود شركة صناعية تقوم بإنتاج ثلاثة منتجات هي أ، ب، جـ ويتم الإنتاج باستخدام طريقة الكميات Batch method حيث يتم تجهيز الآلات لإنتاج كمية من احد هذه المنتجات وبعد الانتهاء من ذلك يتم تنظيف الآلات والمعدات وإعدادها لإنتاج كمية من منتج آخر وتعرف هذه بعملية إعداد الآلات Setup، ويقوم موظف أو أكثر بالتعامل مع الآلة أثناء عملية الإنتاج، وتقوم الشركة بشحن المنتجات إلى العملاء بصناديق تختلف في حجمها حسب نوع المنتج، وأخيرا يقوم مندوبي الشركة بترتيب المنتجات وعرضها في محلات الشركات التي اشترت المنتجات. وفي النظام التقليدي يتم تحميل المصروفات الصناعية غير المباشرة على أساس ساعات العمل المباشرة وهذه تم حسابها كما في الجدول رقم (٨-١)

جدول رقم (٨-١) ساعات العمل المباشر

المنتج	عدد الوحدات	زمن إنتاج الوحدة	إجمالي الساعات
أ	٤٠,٠٠٠	١,٥ ساعة	٦٠,٠٠٠
ب	٢٠,٠٠٠	١,٢٥ ساعة	٢٥,٠٠٠
جـ	١٥,٠٠٠	١ ساعة	١٥,٠٠٠
الإجمالي			١٠٠,٠٠٠

من دراسة الجدول رقم (٨-١) نجد أن حجم الإنتاج من المنتج (أ) هو الأكبر مقارنة بالمنتجات الأخرى، كذلك فان ساعات العمل المباشر اللازمة لإنتاجه هي الأكبر لذلك من المنطقي أن يتحمل من المصروفات الصناعية غير المباشرة أكثر من المنتجين (ب، جـ) معا، وهذا بدوره سوف يرفع من متوسط تكلفة الوحدة. ولتوضيح هذه الفكرة افترض أن المواد المباشرة والأجور المباشرة اللازمة للإنتاج هي كما في الجدول رقم (٨-٢). بدراسة هذا الجدول نجد أنه قد تم حساب نصيب وحدة المنتج من الأجور المباشرة بضرب معدل اجر الساعة في ساعات العمل المباشر اللازمة لإنتاج الوحدة، فلما كان المنتج (أ) يحتاج إلى ١,٥ ساعة وان معدل اجر الساعة هو ٧ د لذلك تم تحميل هذه الوحدة بمبلغ ١٠,٥ د. وبالمثل تم حساب نصيب الوحدة من الأعباء الإضافية بضرب معدل تحميل الأعباء الإضافية ومقداره ٨د لساعة العمل المباشر في ساعات العمل المباشر للوحدة، فتم حساب الأعباء المحملة على وحدة المنتج (ب) بضرب ساعات العمل المباشرة اللازمة لإنتاجها وقدرها ١,٢٥ ساعة في معدل الأعباء الإضافية وقدره ٨ دنانير.

جدول (٨-٢) تكاليف وحدة المنتج

المنتجات	أ	ب	جـ
مواد مباشرة	٦	٥	٨
أجور مباشرة (٧د للساعة)	١٠,٥	٨,٧٥	٧
مصروفات أعباء إضافية	١٢	١٠	٨
تكلفة وحدة المنتج	٢٨,٥	٢٣,٧٥	٢٣

معدل تحميل الأعباء الإضافية:

حتى يتم تحميل الأعباء على وحدات المنتجات يتطلب الأمر تحديد هـل يتم تحميلها على أساس فعلي أو على أساس تقديري، ففـي حالـة الإنتاج المستمر يمكن تحميلها على أساس فعلي لان وحدات الإنتاج متجانسة أمـا في حالة الإنتاج غير المستمر فانه يفضل تحميلها على وحدات الإنتاج علـى أسـاس تقديري. وبعد ذلك يلزم اختيار أساس لتوزيع هذه التكاليف والذي قد يتم التعبير عنه باستخدام ساعات العمل المباشر أو ساعات دوران الآلات أو التكلفة الأولية. وقررت الشركة استخدام ساعات المباشر وعددها ١٠٠,٠٠٠ ساعة وهي كما ظهرت في جـدول رقم (٨-١)، وإذا تم تقدير الأعبـاء الإضافية للفترة بمبلـغ ٨٠٠,٠٠٠ د. يكون معدل تحميل الأعباء الإضافية لساعة العمل المباشر كالتالي:

$$\text{معدل تحميل الاعباء} = \frac{\text{الأعباء الاضافية}}{\text{ساعات العمل المباشر}} = \frac{٨٠٠,٠٠٠}{١٠٠,٠٠٠}$$

= ٨ د / ساعة عمل مباشر (س.ع.م).

وعند حساب نصيب الوحدة من هـذه الأعبـاء يتـم ضرب معـدل تحميل الأعباء الإضافية في عدد ساعات العمل المباشر اللازمة لإنتاجها. ويحتوي الجـدول (٨-٢) على ساعات العمل المباشر وإذا لم تتوفر يتم تحديدها بقسمة أجور العمـل المباشر على معدل اجر الساعة.

تكلفة الإنتاج وتكلفة الوحدة:

بعد أن تم تحديد تكلفة الوحدة في الجدول (٨-٢) فانـه يتـم تحويلها إلى إجمالي التكاليف بضرب تكلفة الوحدة في عدد وحدات الإنتاج وتظهـر النتيجـة في الجدول رقم (٨-٣) لذلك أضيف إلى هذا الجدول مقارنة مـع جـدول (٨-٢) عمـود جديد لخانة الإجمالي.

جدول رقم (٨-٣)

تكلفة الوحدة وتكاليف الإنتاج

	منتج (جـ)		منتج (ب)		منتج (أ)	
	الإجمالي	الوحدة	الإجمالي	الوحدة	الإجمالي	الوحدة
مواد مباشرة	١٢٠,٠٠٠	٨	١٠٠,٠٠٠	٥	٢٤٠,٠٠٠	٦
أجور مباشرة	١٠٥,٠٠٠	٧	١٧٥,٠٠٠	٨,٧٥	٤٢٠,٠٠٠	١٠,٥
أعباء إضافية	١٢٠,٠٠	٨	٢٠٠,٠٠٠	١٠	٤٨٠,٠٠٠	١٢
الإجمالي	٣٤٥,٠٠٠	٢٣	٤٧٥,٠٠٠	٢٣,٧٥	١,١٤٠,٠٠٠	٢٨,٥

نظام تكاليف الأنشطة :

يتم البدء بتطبيق نظام تكاليف الأنشطة باختيار فريق للقيام بدراسة الأنشطة المختلفة الموجودة في المنشأة، وهذا الفريق يحتوي على أعضاء من جهات العمل المختلفة وتكون مهمته الرئيسية حصر الأنشطة المختلفة في المنشأة. ولنجاح هذا الفريق يجب أن يحظى بدعم الإدارة العليا. ولتحديد الأنشطة يقوم هذا الفريق بمقابلة الأشخاص الذي يعملون في إدارات المصروفات غير المباشرة للحصول على ملخص للأعمال التي يقومون بها، وعادة تكون هذه الملخصات مطولة وعلى الفريق أن يختصرها حتى يصل إلى أنشطة ذات دلالة عملية، فمثلا في مجال تصميم المنتجات يتم عمل الخرائط وإنشاء النماذج وتجربة عملها والحصول على المواد وتدريب العمال على تنفيذ نماذج المنتجات إذا لزم الأمر، فهذه التفاصيل يمكن اختصارها بنشاط واحد هو تصميم المنتج، ويمكن رؤية الأنشطة التالية في المنشأة الصناعية [٢].

١) تصميم المنتجات.

٢) إعداد الآلات.

٣) تشغيل الآلات.

٤) توزيع المنتجات.

٥) إدارة العمليات.

---

٢   Horngren, et. Al., ٢٠٠٣

وهنا يجب مراعاة تجانس الأنشطة بقدر الإمكان، وبعد ذلك يتم إنشاء حساب خاص لكل نشاط يعرف باسم وعاء التكاليف Cost Pool ليجعل مدينا بتكلفة القيام بالنشاط، فمثلا تجمع تكاليف الصيانة في مجمع تكاليف واحد لأنها ترتبط مسبب تكلفة Cost driver هو ساعات دوران الآلات، ويتم تجميع تكلفة اللف والحزم والتغليف ومناولة المبيعات في وعاء واحد واعتبار أن مسبب التكلفة هو عدد الطلبيات أو كميتها المستلمة من العملاء. وعندما يمكن تتبع بعض المصروفات غير المباشرة إلى أهداف التكلفة مثل تنظيف الآلات ونماذج الإنتاج قبل بدء العمل الإنتاجي فان تكلفة ذلك تحمل مباشرة على المنتجات المستفيدة وهنا قد نجد أن بعض التكاليف قد يتم تخصيصها مباشرة على أنشطة معينة بينما يحتاج بعضها إلى تخصيصها على أكثر من منتج ومن المشاكل في هذا المجال أن نظام المحاسبة يعمل على دمج أكثر من نوع من المصروفات في حساب واحد وهذا يؤدي إلى عدم دقة تحميل هذه المصروفات.

مما سبق تكون الخطوة الأولى في تطبيق نظام تكاليف الأنشطة هي تحديد الأنشطة التي يتكون منها عمل المنشأة وبعد ذلك يخصص حساب لكل نشاط يطلق علية اسم وعاء تكلفة لتجميع تكلفة النشاط ، وبعد ذلك يجب تحديد مسبب التكلفة Cost driver وهنا يجب مراعاة السبب والنتيجة عند الاختيار، وهنا قد نجد علاقة قوية بين عدد مرات إعداد الآلات للإنتاج وتكاليف إعداد الآلات للإنتاج، كما نجد علاقة قوية بين ساعات دوران الآلات وتكاليف صيانة الآلات ووقودها. وبعد اختيار مسببات التكلفة وتحديد التكلفة الخاصة بكل نشاط يتم حساب معدل تحميل تكاليف النشاط وذلك بقسمة تكاليف النشاط الواردة في وعاء التكاليف على عدد وحدات مسبب النشاط. ولتوضيح هذه إجراءات تطبيق النظام سيتم الاعتماد على بيانات المثال التالي.

مثال: تطبيق نظام تكاليف الأنشطة:

أظهرت دراسة نظام الشركة الصناعية والتي استخدمت في دراسة نظام التكاليف التقليدي بأنها تنتج ثلاثة منتجات هي (أ، ب، جـ)، ويحتاج تصميم هذه المنتجات إلى ١٢٠ ساعة، ٢٠٠ ساعة، ٢٨٠ ساعة تصميم في السنة على التوالي، وأن الشركة تنتج هذه

المنتجات بكميات Batches حيث يتم إنتاج ٤,٠٠٠ وحدة من المنتج (أ) في كل مرة ومن ثم يحتاج الأمر إلى ١٠ مرات إنتاج سنويا، ويتم إنتاج ٢,٥٠٠ وحدة من المنتج (ب) في كل مرة ومن ثم يحتاج الأمر إلى ٨ مرات إنتاج سنويا، كما يتم إنتاج ١,٥٠٠ وحدة من المنتج في كل مرة ومن ثم يحتاج الأمر إلى ١٠ مرات إنتاج سنويا، ويستغرق إنتاج وحدات المنتجات أ، ب، جـ ٣٠ دقيقة، ٤٥ دقيقة، ٥٠ دقيقة للوحدة على التوالي من عمل الآلات، لذلك فان ساعات عمل الآلات اللازمة لإنتاج هذه المنتجات يحدد كما يلي:

الزمن/ساعة	وحدات الإنتاج	الزمن / دقيقة	المنتج
٢٠,٠٠٠	٤٠,٠٠٠	٣٠ دقيقة	أ
١٥,٠٠٠	٢٠,٠٠٠	٤٥ دقيقة	ب
١٢,٥٠٠	١٥,٠٠٠	٥٠ دقيقة	جـ

ولتجهيز الطلبيات فان الطلب على المنتج (أ) يكون بمكرر ٢٠٠ وحدة وأن المنتج (ب) فيتم طلبه بمعدل ٥٠ وحدة في كل مرة وان المنتج (ج) فيتم طلبه بمعدل ٥٠وحدة. ولأن طبيعة المنتجات وحجمها وحساسيتها للنقل فان تغليف هذه الكميات له نفس التكلفة وعليه فان عدد الطلبيات التي سيتم تغليفها خلال الفترة هي ٢٠٠ مرة للمنتج (أ = ٤٠,٠٠٠ وحدة ÷ ٢٠٠)، وأن عدد الطلبيات من منتج (ب) هي ٤٠٠ (= ٢٠,٠٠٠ وحدة ÷ ٥٠)، وأن عدد الطلبيات من المنتج (ج) هي ٣٠٠ (= ١٥,٠٠٠ وحدة ÷ ٥٠)، ومن ثم يكون مجموع الطلبيات خلال السنة ٩٠٠ طلبيه (٢٠٠ + ٤٠٠ + ٣٠٠).

وتوزع تكاليف الإدارة باستخدام ساعات العمل المباشر وكما ورد سابقا فان وحدة المنتج (أ) تحتاج إلى ١,٥ ساعة عمل مباشر، وان وحدة المنتج (ب) تحتاج إلى ١,٢٥ ساعة، وأن وحدة المنتج (ج) تحتاج إلى ١ ساعة، وقد تم حساب عدد ساعات العمل المباشر في الجدول (٨-١) وسيتم إعادتها هنا وهي كالتالي:

منتج (أ)   =   ١,٥ × ٤٠,٠٠٠ وحدة   =   ٦٠,٠٠٠ ساعة

منتج (ب)   =   ١,٢٥ × ٢٠,٠٠٠   =   ٢٥,٠٠٠ ساعة

منتج (ج)   =   ١ ×١٥,٠٠٠ وحدة   =   <u>١٥,٠٠٠</u>

الإجمالي   =   ١٠٠,٠٠٠ ساعة.

وللتسهيل سيتم تلخص الأنشطة من حيث مسبباتها ومدي استفادة المنتجات من الأنشطة في الجدول رقم (٨-٤).

جدول رقم (٨-٤)
ملخص لأنشطة الشركة

عدد الوحدات	منتج ج	منتج ب	منتج أ	مسبب التكلفة	النشاط
٦٠٠	٢٨٠	٢٠٠	١٢٠	ساعة التصميم	التصميم
٢٨	١٠	٨	١٠	مرة إعداد	إعداد الآلات للإنتاج
٤٧,٥٠٠	١٢٥٠٠	١٥,٠٠٠	٢٠,٠٠٠	ساعة عمل آلة	إنتاج المنتجات
٩٠٠	٣٠٠	٤٠٠	٢٠٠	عدد الطلبيات	تجهيز طلبات العملاء
١٠٠,٠٠٠	١٥٠٠٠	٢٥٠٠٠	٦٠٠٠٠	ساعة عمل مباشر	الإدارة

من دراسة جدول (٨-٤) يظهر لنا أن الشركة قد قسمت إلى خمسة أنشطة وان لكل نشاط منها مسبب تكلفة، وفي الأعمدة ٣، ٤، ٥ من الجدول ظهرت وحدات كل مسبب التي حصلت عليها المنتجات وفي العمود الأخير ظهر إجمالي وحدات مسبب التكلفة كل نشاط. وفي الجدول (٨-٥) ظهرت تكاليف كل نشاط وان مجموعها يساوي مبلغ الأعباء الإضافية الذي قام نظام التكلفة التقليدي بتوزيعه على المنتجات. وحدد معدل تحميل النشاط بقسمة التكاليف الظاهرة في العمود ٢ على عدد الوحدات الظاهرة في العمود ٣. ويظهر معدل تحميل الأنشطة كما في العمود ٤.

جدول رقم (٨-٥)
حساب معدلات تحميل الأنشطة

معدل التحميل للأنشطة	عدد الوحدات النشاط	التكلفة	النشاط
١٥٠ د للساعة	٦٠٠	٩٠,٠٠٠	التصميم
٦٢٥ د للمرة	٢٨	١٧,٥٠٠	إعداد الآلات للإنتاج
٨,٦ د للساعة	٤٧,٥٠٠	٤٠٨,٥٠٠	إنتاج المنتجات
٨٠ د للطلبية	٩٠٠	٧٢,٠٠٠	تجهيز طلبات العملاء
١٢و٢ د للساعة	١٠٠,٠٠٠	٢١٢,٠٠٠	الإدارة
		٨٠٠,٠٠٠	الإجمالي

تحديد الأعباء الإضافية المحملة على الإنتاج:

في هذه الخطوة يتم ضرب مقدار مسبب التكلفة الذي استهلكه كل منتج، كما ظهر في جدول (٨-٤)، في معدل تحميل التكلفة لهذا المسبب والذي تم حسابه في جدول (٨-٥) وتظهر النتيجة كما في **جدول (٨-٦)**

جدول (٨-٦)
توزيع الأعباء الإضافية على المنتجات

الإجمالي	منتج (ج)	منتج (ب)	منتج (أ)	
				١- نشاط التصميم
١٨,٠٠٠			١٨,٠٠٠	منتج أ = ١٥٠ د × ١٢٠
٣٠,٠٠٠		٣٠,٠٠٠		منتج ب = ١٥٠ × ٢٠٠
٤٢,٠٠٠	٤٢,٠٠٠			منتج ج = ١٥٠ × ٢٨٠
				٢- إعداد وتجهيز الآلات
٦,٢٥٠			٦,٢٥٠	منتج أ = ٦٢٥ × ١٠
٥,٠٠٠		٥,٠٠٠		منتج ب = ٦٢٥ × ٨

٢٦٦

٦٬٢٥٠	٦٬٢٥٠		منتج ج = ٦٢٥ × ١٠

٣- العمل الصناعي

١٧٢٬٠٠٠			١٧٢٬٠٠٠	منتج أ = ٨٬٦ × ٢٠٬٠٠٠
١٢٩٬٠٠٠		١٢٩٬٠٠٠		منتج ب = ٨٬٦ × ١٥٬٠٠٠
١٠٧٬٥٠٠	١٠٧٬٥٠٠			منتج ج = ٨٬٦ × ١٢٬٥٠٠

٤- تجهيز وشحن الطلبات

١٦٬٠٠٠			١٦٬٠٠٠	منتج أ = ٨٠ × ٢٠٠
٣٢٬٠٠٠		٣٢٬٠٠٠		منتج ب = ٨٠ × ٤٠٠
٢٤٬٠٠٠	٢٤٬٠٠٠			منتج ج = ٨٠ × ٣٠٠

٥- الإدارة والإشراف

١٢٧٬٢٠٠			١٢٧٬٢٠٠	منتج أ = ٢٬١٢ × ٦٠٬٠٠٠
٥٣٬٠٠٠		٥٣٬٠٠٠		منتج ب = ٢٬١٢ × ٢٥٬٠٠٠
٣١٬٨٠٠	٣١٬٨٠٠			منتج ج = ٢٬١٢ × ١٥٠٠٠
٨٠٠٬٠٠٠	٢١١٬٥٥٠	٢٤٩٬٠٠٠	٣٣٩٬٤٥٠	**الإجمالي الأعباء الموزعة**
	١٥٬٠٠٠	٢٠٬٠٠٠	٤٠٬٠٠٠	÷ عدد وحدات الإنتاج
	١٤٬١٠٣	١٢٬٤٥٠	٨٬٤٨٦	تكلفة الأعباء الإضافية للوحدة

يضاف التكلفة المباشرة :

	٨	٥	٦	مواد مباشرة للوحدة
	٧	٨٬٧٥	١٠٬٥	الأجور المباشرة للوحدة
	٢٩٬١٠٣	٢٦٬٢٠	٢٤٬٩٨٦	**التكلفة الكلية للوحدة**

لقد تم تحديد نصيب كل منتج من تكاليف كل نشاط بضرب معدل تحميل أعباء النشاط في كمية النشاط الذي استهلكها المنتج، ففي تكاليف التصميم وجدنا أن المنتجات أ، ب، ج قد استهلكت ١٢٠، ٢٠٠، ٢٨٠ ساعة تصميم على التوالي وبضرب هذه الساعات في معدل التحميل ومقداره ١٥٠ د نتوصل إلى نصيب كل منتج منها.

مقارنة تكلفة الوحدة في الأنظمة البديلة

لقد تم حساب تكلفة وحدة المنتج في النظام التقليدي في الجدول (٨-٢) كما تم تحديد تكلفة الوحدة في تكاليف أساس النشاط في الجدول (٨-٧) وأن ملخص هذه النتائج تظهر في الجدول (٨-٧).

جدول (٨-٧)
تكلفة الوحدة في النظامين التقليدي وأساس النشاط

	منتج (ج)	منتج (ب)	منتج (أ)
تكاليف أساس النشاط	٢٩,١٠٣	٢٦,٢٠	٢٤,٩٨٦
التكاليف التقليدي	٢٣	٢٣,٧٥	٢٨,٥٠

من دراسة هذا الجدول يظهر لنا بأن تكلفة المنتج (أ) في النظام التقليدي كانت أعلى من نظام أساس النشاط والعكس صحيحا بالنسبة للمنتجين ب، ج حيث كانت أعلى في أساس النشاط عنها في النظام التقليدي. ولأننا نعرف بأن نظام تكاليف أساس النشاط يستخدم مسببات تكلفة ترتبط بعلاقة سبب ونتيجة مع عناصر التكاليف الموجودة في مجمعات التكلفة تكون تكلفة الوحدة أكثر دقة من النظام التقليدي، لذلك فان النظام التقليدي يعمل على زيادة تكاليف المنتجات ذات الحجم الكبير، وهذا قد يؤثر على أسعارها وعلى الموقف التنافسي- للشركة، فمثلا إذا افترضنا أن الشركة قد سعرت المنتج ج على أساس إعطاء ربح مقداره ٢٠% أي بسعر مقداره ٢٧,٦ وتحقيقها لهذا السعر يجعلها راضية عن هذا المنتج ولكن في واقع الحال فانه عند هذا السعر فانه لا تسترد الشركة تكاليف إنتاج هذا المنتج وذلك حسب نتائج نظام تكاليف أساس النشاط.

مثال محلول :

يتكون نشاط إحدى الشركات من التصميم، والهندسة، والإنتاج وتقوم بإنتاج ثلاثة منتجات هي أ١، أ، أ، وتستخدم الشركة في تحميل الأعباء الإضافية حاليا ساعات دوران الآلات وان هذه المنتجات تحتاج إلى ساعات الدوران كالتالي:

المنتج أ₁	١,٤٠٠ ساعة
المنتج أ₂	١,٨٠٠ ساعة
المنتج أ₃	٨٠٠ ساعة
الإجمالي	٤,٠٠٠ ساعة

وقررت الشركة تقسيم العمل فيها إلى أنشطة التصميم، والهندسة والإنتاج وكانت مجمعات التكلفة ومسببات التكاليف كالتالي:

النشاط	الأعباء الإضافية	مسبب التكاليف
التصميم	٩,٠٠٠	ساعة التصميم
الهندسة	٦٣,٠٠٠	ساعة الهندسة
الإنتاج	١٦٨,٠٠٠	ساعة الآلة
الإجمالي	٢٤٠,٠٠٠	

وخلال الفترة تم تحديد استخدام المنتجات الثلاثة مـن أنشطة الشركة كالتالي:

النشاط	مسبب التكلفة	منتج (أ₁)	منتج (أ₂)	منتج (أ₃)	الإجمالي
التصميم	ساعة تصميم	١٠٠	١٢٠	٨٠	٣٠٠
الهندسة	ساعة الهندسة	٤٠٠	٦٠٠	٨٠٠	١٨٠٠
الإنتاج	ساعة الآلة	١٤٠٠	١٨٠٠	٨٠٠	٤٠٠٠

المطلوب :

١) تحديد معدل تحميل الأعباء الإضافية لكل نشاط.

٢) ما هي تكلفة كل منتج من المنتجات في حالات:

أ- استخدام النظام التقليدي.

ب- استخدام نظام تكاليف النشاط

الحل : أولا: نظام التكاليف التقليدي

الأعباء الإضافية   ٢٤٠,٠٠٠

$$\text{معدل تحميل الأعباء الإضافية} = \frac{\text{الأعباء الإضافية}}{\text{ساعات العمل المباشر}} = \frac{٢٤٠,٠٠٠}{٤,٠٠٠}$$

$$= ٦٠ \text{ د /س}$$

الأعباء المحملة على المنتجات في حالة النظام التقليدي

أ₁ = ٦٠ د × ١٤٠٠ = ٨٤٠٠٠ د.

أ₂ = ٦٠ د × ١٨٠٠ = ١٠٨٠٠٠ د.

أ₃ = ٦٠ د × ٨٠٠ = ٤٨٠٠٠ د.

تطبيق نظام تكاليف الأنشطة

معدلات التحميل لأعباء الأنشطة :

$$\text{التصميم} = \frac{٩٠٠٠}{٣٠٠} = ٣٠ \text{ د/س}$$

$$\text{الهندسة} = \frac{٦٣,٠٠٠}{١,٨٠٠} = ٣٥ \text{ د/س}$$

$$\text{الإنتاج} = \frac{١٦٨,٠٠٠}{٤,٠٠٠} = ٤٢ \text{ د/س}$$

وبعد تحديد معدلات تحميل تكاليف الأنشطة يتم تحديد المبالغ التي يتم تحميلها على كل منتج كما في الجدول التالي.

المنتج	أ₁	أ₂	أ₃	
التصميم ٣٠ × ١٠٠	٣,٠٠٠			٣,٠٠٠
٣٠ × ١٢٠		٣,٦٠٠		٣,٦٠٠
٣٠ × ٨٠			٢,٤٠٠	٢,٤٠٠
الهندسة ٣٥ × ٤٠٠	١٤,٠٠٠			١٤,٠٠٠
٣٥ × ٦٠٠		٢١,٠٠٠		٢١,٠٠٠
٣٥ × ٨٠٠			٢٨,٠٠٠	٢٨,٠٠٠
الإنتاج ٤٢ × ١٤٠٠	٥٨,٨٠٠			٥٨,٨٠٠
٤٢ × ١٨٠٠		٧٥,٦٠٠		٧٥,٦٠٠
٤٢ × ٨٠٠			٣٣,٦٠٠	٣٣,٦٠٠
إجمالي الأعباء	٧٥,٨٠٠	١٠٠,٢٠٠	٦٤,٠٠٠	٢٤٠,٠٠٠

الخاتمــــة

في هذا الفصل تم تغطية نظام تكاليف الأنشطة وهـذا النظام يعتبر أحـد التطورات الهامة في محاسبة التكاليف، وقد تم في البداية عرض أهم أسس تصـميم النظام وبيان أنه يعتمد على تحديد الأنشطة وحساب معدل تحميل للمصروفات غير المباشرة لكل نشاط على حـده. وكل نشاط اعتبر كوحدة محاسبية مسـتقلة حيث خصص له مجمع تكلفـة Cost driver وتم تحميل كل منتج أو هـدف تكلفة على أساس مقدار ما استنفذه من وحدات مسبب التكلفة وقد تمت مقارنـة النتائج النهائية لهذا النظام مع النتائج التي يتوصل إليها نظام التكاليف التقليدي وتبين أن النظام الأخير يتحيـز ضد المنتجات ذات الحجـم الكبير حيـث يحملها بتكاليف أعلى من المنتجات ذات الحجم الأقل لأن مقياس الحجم الذي يتبناه عادة لا يتأثر بما تستنفذه المنتجات قليلة الحجم، كما تبين أن أرقام التكاليف المستخرجة باستخدام تكاليف الأنشطة قد تغير من مدى ربحية المنتجات التي تظهر في نظام التكاليف التقليدي.

أسئلة وتمارين

السؤال الأول: أي من عناصر التكاليف التي يتم معالجتها بنفس الطريقة في نظامي تكاليف الأنشطة والتكاليف التقليدي.

السؤال الثاني: أذكر أهم الاعتبارات التي يستخدمها نظام التكاليف التقليدي عند توزيع الأعباء الإضافية.

السؤال الثالث: عرف المقصود بالأنشطة وما هي أهم الاعتبارات في تحديدها.

السؤال الرابع: هل تختلف وظيفة الحساب عن مجمع التكلفة

السؤال الخامس: اذكر بعض الأنشطة التي يمكن أن تراها في شركة صناعية.

السؤال السادس: اذكر أهم أنواع التكلفة في نظام تكاليف الأنشطة.

السؤال السابع: ما هو الاختلاف الرئيسي بين التكلفة على مستوى الوحدة والتكلفة على مستوى المصنع.

السؤال الثامن: هل يتم توزيع التكلفة على مستوى المنظمة عند استخدام نظام تكاليف الأنشطة.

السؤال التاسع: قارن بين التكلفة على مستوى الوحدة والتكلفة على مستوى الكمية.

السؤال العاشر: هل هناك ضرورة للتفرقة بين التكاليف المتغيرة والتكاليف الثابتة عند استخدام تكاليف مستوى النشاط.

السؤال الحادي عشر: تم تجميع المعلومات الاتية عن نشاط احد فروع البنك العربي:

النشاط	التكاليف
استقبال العملاء	١٨٠,٠٠٠
الإشراف الإداري	٦٠,٠٠٠د
الإدارة العليا للفرع	٨٥,٠٠٠

وكانت أنشطة هذه الفئات خلال إحدى الفترات كالتالي:

النشاط	فتح الحسابات	عمليات مصرفية	عمليات أخرى	أنشطة أخرى
استقبال العملاء	٥%	٦٠%	٢٥%	١٠%
الإشراف الإداري	١٥%	٤٠%	٣٥%	١٠%
الإدارة العليا للفرع	٥%	٣٠%	٤٠%	٢٥%

المطلوب: توزيع تكاليف الأنشطة على العمليات المصرفية.

السؤال الثاني عشر: بالإضافة إلى بيانات السؤال السابق تم توفير المعلومات الاتية عن أنشطة الفرع:

النشاط	مسببات التكاليف
فتح الحسابات	٤٠٠ حساب جديد
عمليات مصرفية	٥٠,٠٠٠ عملية
عمليات أخرى	٨٠٠ عمليات اعتمادات وقروض

المطلوب: حساب معدل تحميل الأعباء الاضافية لأنشطة الفرع.

السؤال الثالث عشر: تقوم إحدى الشركات بإنتاج منتجين يعرف احدهما بالمنتج الممتاز ويعرف الثاني بالمنتج العادي. وتتزايد مبيعات المنتج الممتاز باطراد، وتقوم الشركة بتوزيع الأعباء الإضافية على المنتجات على أساس ساعات العمل المباشر، وقدرت الأعباء الإضافية بمبلغ ٣ مليون دينار، كما تتوقع الشركة أن تنتج ١٥,٠٠٠ وحدة من المنتج الممتاز، مع ١٢٠,٠٠٠ وحدة من المنتج العادي. يلزم لإنتاج الوحدة من الممتاز ٢ ساعة عمل مباشر كما يلزم لإنتاج وحدة المنتج العادي إلى ١ ساعة عمل مباشر. وكانت تكاليف الوحدة من المواد المباشرة والأجور المباشرة كالتالي:

	منتج ممتاز	منتج عادي
مواد مباشرة للوحدة	١٦٠ د	١١٥ د
أجور مباشرة للوحدة	٢٠د	١٠د

وقررت الشركة البدء في استخدام نظام تكاليف الأنشطة لتوزيع الأعباء الإضافية ووفرت المعلومات الاتية:

النشاط	مسببات التكلفة	الأعباء الإضافية التقديرية
الشراء	عدد أوامر الشراء	١٠٠,٠٠٠
نشاط التشغيل	عدد أوامر التشغيل	٣٠٠,٠٠٠
فحص جودة الإنتاج	عدد الفحوصات	١,٠٥٠,٠٠٠
تشغيل الآلات	ساعات دوران الآلات	١,٥٥٠,٠٠٠

وكانت مسببات التكلفة المستخدمة كالتالي:

	مسببات التكلفة المتوقعة		
	الممتاز	العادي	الإجمالي
عدد أوامر الشراء	٨٠٠	١,٦٠٠	٢٤٠٠
عدد أوامر التشغيل	٦٠٠	٤٠٠	١,٠٠٠
عدد الفحوصات	٩,٠٠٠	١٢,٠٠٠	٢١,٠٠٠
ساعات دوران الآلات	١٠,٠٠٠	٢١,٠٠٠	٣١,٠٠٠

المطلوب:

١- حساب معدلات تحميل الأعباء الإضافية للأنشطة المختلفة عند استخدام نظام التكاليف التقليدي ونظام تكاليف الأنشطة.

٢- حساب تكاليف الوحدة عند استخدام نظام تكاليف الأنشطة ونظام التكاليف التقليدي.

السؤال الرابع عشر: وفرت إحدى الشركات التي تستخدم تكاليف الأنشطة البيانات التالية:

الأنشطة	معدل تحميل تكاليف الأنشطة
عدد الوحدات	٢٥ د لساعة العمل المباشر
تشغيل الأوامر	١٨٠د للأمر
تصميم الإنتاج	١٥٠د لكل تصميم يقدمه العميل
خدمة العملاء	٢٥٠د لكل عميل منتج

وترغب الإدارة في تقييم تعاملها مع عميل من عملائها والذي يشتري المنتج العادي والمنتج المعدل. والآتي بيانات عن عمليات هذا العميل عن السنة المالية المنتهية في ١٢|٣١

	المنتج العادي	المنتج المعدل
عـــدد الوحــدات المباعــة للعميل	٢٠٠	٥٠
عدد أوامر الشراء	٥	٢
عدد تصاميم الإنتاج	٠	٢
ساعات العمل المباشر للوحدة	١٦	١٨
سعر بيع الوحدة	١,٥٠٠د	٢,٣٠٠د
تكلفة المواد المباشرة للوحدة	٥٦٠د	٢,٠٢٠

المطلوب: تحديد الربح الناتج عن التعامل مع هذا العميل.

السؤال الخامس عشر: تستخدم شركة نظام تكاليف الأنشطة وان أعبائها الإضافية تحتوي على ٣٠٠,٠٠٠ د أجور غير مباشرة و ٢٠٠,٠٠٠ د مصروفات أخرى. وانه تم تحديد الأنشطة ومعدلات تحميلها لإحدى الفترات كالتالي:

النشاط	وحدة قياس النشاط	عدد وحدات النشاط
مصروفات مرتبطة بالوحدة	ساعات العمل المباشر	٢٠,٠٠٠ س ع م
مصروف مرتبطة بالمبيعات	عدد أوامر المبيعات	٤٠,٠٠٠ طلبية
مصروفات دعم العملاء	عدد العملاء	٥٠٠
أخرى	لا توزع لأنها غير مرتبطة بالمنتجات أو العملاء	لا تنطبق

وان الشركة وزعت تكاليف الأعباء الإضافية خلال الفترة كالتالي:

	مصروفات مرتبطة بالوحدة	مصروف بالمبيعات	مصروفات دعم العملاء	أخرى	الإجمالي
أجور غير مباشرة	٣٠٪	٤٠٪	٢٠٪	١٠٪	١٠٠٪
مصروفات أخرى	٤٠٪	٢٠٪	٢٠٪	٢٠٪	١٠٠٪

وكانت المعلومات الخاصة بأحد العملاء الذي طلب الشراء مرة واحدة كالتالي:

عدد الوحدات المشتراة	١٥ وحدة
ساعات العمل المباشر	٢ ساعة للوحدة
سعر البيع	٢٥٠د للوحدة
المواد المباشرة	١٥٠د للوحدة
الأجور المباشرة	٤٠د للوحدة

المطلوب:

١- حساب معدلات تحميل أعباء الأنشطة

٢- حساب ربح الأمر

السؤال السادس عشر: تنتج إحدى الشركات نوعية من التلفزيونات هما نوفا وبلازما. يحتاج المنتج الأخير إلى ٢ ساعة عمل مباشر لإنتاج الوحدة والى فحص لأكثر من مرة

أثناء العملية الإنتاجية، أما إنتاج نوفا فإنه ابسط من المنتج السابق حيث يحتاج إنتاج الوحدة إلى ساعة عمل مباشرة وفحص لمرة واحدة. توزع التكاليف في نظام التكاليف التقليدي باستخدام ساعات العمل المباشرة، وان التكاليف المباشرة للوحدة كالتالي:

	نوفا	بلازما
المواد المباشرة	٨٠	١٢٠
الأجور المباشرة بواقع ٤ د للساعة	٤٠	٨٠

تتوقع الشركة ان تنتج ٩٠,٠٠٠ نوفا و ١٥,٠٠٠ بلازما خلال السنة القادمة وان تبلغ الأعباء الإضافية ١,٨٠٠,٠٠٠ د خلال السنة القادمة. ورغبت الادارة في تطبيق نظام تكاليف الأنشطة ووفرت لك البيانات الاتية:

	الأعباء الإضافية	إجمالي مسبب التكلفة	نوفا	بلازما
الاحتفاظ بالمخزون(عدد القطع)	٢٠٠,٠٠٠د	٢٥,٠٠٠	١٠,٠٠٠	١٥,٠٠٠
مصروفات الشراء(عدد الأوامر)	٣٦٠,٠٠٠	٤,٥٠٠	٣,٠٠٠	١,٥٠٠
جودة الإنتاج (عدد الفحوصات)	٤٢٠,٠٠٠	١٢,٠٠٠	٣,٠٠٠	٩,٠٠٠
تشغيل الآلات (ساعة آلة)	٨٢٠,٠٠٠	٨٢,٠٠٠	٣٥,٠٠٠	٤٧,٠٠٠
إجمالي الأعباء الإضافية	١,٨٠٠,٠٠٠			

المطلوب:

١- ما هي تكلفة وحدة المنتج عند استخدام نظام التكاليف التقليدي.

٢- ما هو معدل تحميل الأعباء الإضافية للأنشطة المختلفة.

٣- ما هي تكلفة الوحدة عند استخدام نظام تكاليف أساس الأنشطة.

٤- برر أسباب الاختلاف في تكلفة الوحدة عند استخدام نظام التكاليف التقليدي عند استخدام تكاليف أساس الأنشطة.

السؤال السابع عشر: تستخدم شركة نظام التكاليف التقليدي وتستخدم ساعات الدوران في توزيع الأعباء الإضافية، وتنتج الشركة ثلاث منتجات هي أ، ب، ج واستخدمت ١,٦٠٠ ساعة ، ١,٠٠٠ ساعة، ١,٤٠٠ ساعة دوران آلة على التوالي . وبلغت الأعباء الإضافية

خلال السنة ٢٦١,٦٠٠ د. وقررت الشركة استخدام نظام تكاليف الأنشطة ووفرت إليك البيانات الآتية:

مسبب التكلفة	التكلفة	النشاط
ساعة تصميم	١٦,١٥٠د	التصميم
ساعة الهندسة	٢١,٤٥٠د	الهندسة والإشراف
ساعة دوران الآلات	٢٢٤,٠٠٠ د	عمل الآلات
	٢٦١,٦٠٠د	الاجمالي

وكان استخدام المنتجات للأنشطة كالتالي:

الإجمالي	منتج ج	منتج ب	منتج أ	
٩٥٠	١٥٠	٤٥٠	٣٥٠	التصميم
١٤٣٠	٤٤٠	٦٢٠	٣٧٠	الهندسة والإشراف
٤,٠٠٠	١,٤٠٠	١,٠٠٠	١,٦٠٠	عمل الآلات

المطلوب:

١- تحديد قيمة الأعباء الإضافية المحملة على كل منتج عند استخدام النظام التقليدي.

٢- تحديد قيمة الأعباء الإضافية المحملة على كل منتج عند استخدام نظام تكاليف الأنشطة.

السؤال الثامن عشر: أسئلة اختيارات متعددة من ١,-٤

١- أي من الامور التالية اكثر دقة لقياس نشاط إدارة المشتريات:

١- ساعات العمل المباشرة

٢- ساعات دوران الآلات

٣- أوامر الشراء

٤- تكلفة المواد المشتراة

٢- تشغيل أوامر الإنتاج هو مثال على:

1- التكاليف على مستوى الوحدة
2- التكاليف على مستوى المنشأة
3- التكاليف على مستوى المنتج
4- التكاليف على مستوى الكمية

تستخدم شركة نظام تكاليف الانشطة وحصلت منها على البيانات الاتية:

النشاط	مجموع وحدات النشاط
التصنيع	٤٠,٠٠٠ وحدة
تشغيل أوامر العملاء	١٣,٠٠٠ أمر
أخرى	غير مستخدمة

وتستخدم الأنشطة الاخرى لتجميع تكاليف الطاقة العطلة والتكاليف التي على مستوى الشركة وكانت التكاليف غير المباشرة واستخداماتها في الشركة كالتالي:

	التكاليف	التصنيع	تشغيل أوامر العملاء	أخرى	الاجمالي
الأجور والمرتبات	٤٨٠,٠٠٠د	٤٠%	٥٠%	١٠%	١٠٠%
الاستهلاك	٢٨٠,٠٠٠	٢٥%	٤٠%	٣٥%	١٠٠%
التشغيل	٣٢٠,٠٠٠	٣٥%	٤٠%	٢٥%	١٠٠%

٣- فان معدل تحميل الوحدة من نشاط التصنيع هو:

1- ٧,٢٥ د   2- ٧,٦٠د

3- ١٠,٤٠د   4- ٩,٣٥د

٤- فإن تكلفة الأمر الواحد خلال الفترة هي:

1- ٣٦,٩٢د   2- ٢٨,٣١د

3- ١٢٢,٦٧د   4- ٣٣,٢٣د

السؤال التاسع عشر: CMA معدل:

تستخدم شركة نظام التكاليف التقليدي وتقوم بتوزيع تكاليف رقابة الجودة بنسبة ١٥٪ من تكلفة الأجور المباشرة ، وان تكلفة الأجور المباشرة لمنتج رئيسيـ خلال الشهر هي ٣٠,٠٠٠ د . وقررت الشركة التحول لتطبيق نظام تكاليف الأنشطة وحددت ثلاثة أنشطة هي (١) فحص المواد الخام، (٢) فحص الإنتاج تحت التشغيل، (٣) وإصدار شهادات جودة المنتجات. وتم توفير البيانات التالية عن نظام تكاليف الأنشطة:

كمية المنتج الرئيسي	معدل التكلفة	مسبب التكلفة	النشاط
٢٠ نوع	١٤د لكل نوع	عدد أنواع المواد الخام	١
١٧,٠٠٠ وحدة	٠,١٤د للوحدة	عدد الوحدات	٢
٣٠ أمر	٧٥ د/أمر	عدد الأوامر	٣

فان التكاليف التي تحمل على المنتج الرئيسي باستخدام تكاليف الأنشطة هي:

- ١٥٠ د لكل أمر.

- ٤٠٤د لكل من استخدام نظام تكاليف الأنشطة والنظام التقليدي.

- ٤٥٠٠ د.

- ٤١٠ د أعلى من تكاليف النظام التقليدي.

الفصل التاسع
طرق التكاليف الكلية والمتغيرة

أهداف الفصل:

بعد دراسة هذا الفصل يجب أن تكون قادرا على:

١. تعريف التكلفة الكلية والتكلفة المتغيرة للوحدة.

٢. إعداد قائمة الدخل حسب طريقة التكلفة الكلية الفعلية والمعيارية.

٣. إعداد قائمة الدخل حسب طريقة التكلفة المتغيرة الفعلية والمعيارية.

٤. معرفة دور طريقة التكاليف المتغيرة في القرارات الإدارية.

٥. معرفة أهم الانتقادات الموجهة إلى طريقة التكاليف المتغيرة.

٦. معرفة دور طريقة التكلفة الكلية.

المقدمـة :

توجد في الحياة العملية طريقتان تستخدمان في تحديد تكاليف الانتاج وإعداد قائمة الدخل هما: طريقة التكاليف الكلية، وطريقة التكاليف المتغيرة. ولقد شاع استخدام لفظ نظريات التكاليف بدلا من لفظ طرق التكاليف في المؤلفات العربية، كما أطلق على هاتين الطريقتين تسميات [1] أخرى حيث أطلق البعض على طريقة التكلفة الكلية اسم طريقة التكلفة المستغلة أو المستوعبة، وكما أطلق البعض أيضا على طريقة التكلفة المتغيرة اسم طريقة التكلفة المباشرة، وطريقة هامش المساهمة، وطريقة التكلفة الحدية. على أية حال، فان هذه الأسماء من وجهة نظرنا مترادفة، وحتى لا يعيقنا اختلاف الأسماء عن جوهر الموضوع سوف نركز على سمات هاتين الطريقتين، ولذلك سوف يتم شرح طريقة التكاليف الكلية، وطريقة التكاليف المتغيرة ومقارنتهما معا من حيث أثرهما على تكلفة وحدات الإنتاج وتكلفة اجمالي الانتاج.

طريقة التكلفة الكلية   Full Absorption Costing

تقوم هذه الطريقة على تصنيف عناصر التكاليف إلى ثلاث مجموعات هي: التكاليف الصناعية (الإنتاجية)، والمصروفات التسويقية، والمصروفات الإدارية. تعتبر التكاليف الصناعية التكاليف الوحيدة التي يتم تحميلها على الوحدات المنتجة ولذلك تسمى تكاليف قابلة للتخزين أو تكاليف منتج. وتتكون هذه التكاليف من التكاليف الصناعية المتغيرة والتكاليف الصناعية الثابتة. وتتألف التكاليف الصناعية المتغيرة من تكاليف المواد المباشرة، وتكاليف الأجور المباشرة، والتكاليف الصناعية غير المباشرة المتغيرة.

أما المصروفات التسويقية والإدارية فتعتبر تكاليف فترة، وبالتالي لا يتم تحميلها على وحدات الانتاج ، ويتم طرحهما من رقم مجمل الربح قبل تحديد رقم صافي الربح . ويتم إعداد قائمة الدخل حسب هذه طريقة على مرحلتين، الأولى وبها يتم طرح وتكلفة البضاعة المباعة من الإيرادات ويعرف الفرق باسم مجمل الربح ، ويتم في المرحلة الثانية طرح المصروفات التسويقية والإدارية من رقم مجمل الربح للتوصل الى رقم صافي

---

[1]Hirsh and Louderback, op.cit., P.٤٨.

الربح، وبهذا فإن إعداد قائمة الدخل لا تحتاج الى التميز بين المصروفات الصناعية غير المباشرة المتغيرة والثابتة. ويطلق على قائمة الدخل حسب هذه الطريقة اسم قائمة الدخل الوظيفية أو التقليدية، لأنه يتم إعدادها حسب الوظائف الرئيسية في المنشأة، وهي وظيفة الإنتاج ووظيفة البيع، ووظيفة الإدارة.

تعتبر قائمة دخل الطريقة الكلية مقبولة لأغراض التقارير المالية المنشورة لأن المعايير المحاسبية المقبولة قبولا عاما تتطلب تقييم مخزون آخر المدة على أساس إجمالي التكاليف الصناعية. ولكن ينتقد مؤيدو طريقة التكلفة المتغيرة هذه الطريقة لأن قائمة الدخل التي تعدها طريقة التكلفة الكلية لا تساعد الأطراف المستفيدة في التنبؤ، فمثلا إذا توقعنا زيادة المبيعات بنسبة ١٠٪ فإن هذه القائمة لا تمكننا من معرفة أثر هذه الزيادة على الارباح لعدم قيامها بفصل التكاليف المتغيرة عن التكاليف الثابتة. فالتكاليف المتغيرة تتغير بنفس نسبة الزيادة في المبيعات أما التكاليف الثابتة فتبقى على ما هي عليه بدون تغيير إذا كانت زيادة المبيعات ضمن مدى معقول.

طريقة التكاليف المتغيرة   Variable Costing

تقوم هذه الطريقة بتحميل الوحدات المنتجة بتكاليف المواد المباشرة والأجور المباشرة والمصروفات الصناعية غير المباشرة المتغيرة فقط، أما التكاليف الصناعية غير المباشرة الثابتة فتعتبرها تكلفة فترة، ولذلك فان هذه الطريقة لا تعتبر تكاليف استهلاك الآلات الصناعية، وإيجار المصنع، ومرتبات وأجور المشرفين ضمن تكاليف الإنتاج، لأنها تكاليف ثابتة، وتبرر هذه المعالجة على اساس ان هذه المصروفات تحدث نتيجة لمرور الزمن ولإعداد الطاقة للإنتاج وليس بسبب حدوث النشاط، وهذا لا يجعل وحدات الإنتاج مسؤولة عنها. ولذلك تتكون تكلفة الإنتاج التام ومخزون إنتاج تحت التشغيل من التكلفة الصناعية المتغيرة فقط.

وعند إعداد قائمة الدخل حسب هذه الطريقة يتم إضافة المصروفات التسويقية والإدارية المتغيرة إلى التكلفة الصناعية المتغيرة للبضاعة المباعة. ويعرف الرقم الناتج باسم التكلفة المتغيرة للبضاعة المباعة، ويطرح هذا الرقم من الإيرادات للتوصل الى رقم

هامش المساهمة Contribution Margin. ثم يطرح من هذا الرقم المصروفات الصناعية والتسويقية والإدارية الثابتة للتوصل إلى رقم صافي الربح.

سلوك التكاليف Cost Behavior

حتى يمكن إعداد قوائم التكاليف المتغيرة، يجب تبويب التكاليف إلى متغيرة وثابتة، حيث إن التكاليف المتغيرة هي التكاليف التي يتغير مجموعها طرديا مع التغير في حجم النشاط، وأن نصيب الوحدة منها ثابت، أما التكاليف الثابتة فهي التكاليف التي يبقى مجموعها ثابتا، إذا كان التغير في حجم النشاط، ضمن المدى الملائم. ومن الناحية العملية نجد أن هناك مجموعة أخرى من عناصر التكاليف تحمل صفات التكاليف الثابتة والمتغيرة معا، حيث لا تتغير مع التغير في حجم النشاط إذا كان ذلك التغير يقع ضمن مجال معين وبعد ذلك يزداد مبلغها إذا تخطى حجم الإنتاج ذلك المستوى وبعدها تثبت ثم تعود إلى التغير مثل أجور عمال الصيانة، ومصروف الكهرباء، وأجور المشرفين وتعرف هذه المجموعة من التكاليف بعدة مسميات منها التكلفة شبه المتغيرة، أو شبه الثابتة أو المختلطة. وهذه التكاليف يجب فصلها الى تكاليف متغيرة وتكاليف ثابتة. واهم الطرق المستخدمة في هذا المجال هي:

١. الطريقة الشخصية.

٢. طريقة النقطة العالية والمنخفضة.

٣. طريقة الرسم البياني.

٤. طريقة التحليل الإحصائي.

ولدراسة هذه الطرق يمكن الرجوع الى كتاب المحاسبة الادارية للمؤلف.

قائمة الدخل حسب طريقتي التكلفة الكلية والمتغيرة:

ولتوضيح هذه الطرق سيتم الاعتماد على البيانات التالية:

مثال (١) الآتي بيانات مستخرجة من سجلات إحدى الشركات الصناعية

فبراير	يناير	الوحدات
٣٠٠٠	صفر	مخزون إنتاج تام أول المدة
١٥,٠٠٠	١٥,٠٠٠	وحدات الإنتاج التام خلال الشهر
١٨,٠٠٠	١٢,٠٠٠	الوحدات المباعة خلال الشهر
صفر	٣٠٠٠	وحدات مخزون إنتاج تام آخر الشهر
صفر	صفر	إنتاج تحت التشغيل أول وآخر الشهر

وكان متوسط تكلفة الوحدة خلال شهري الدراسة كالتالي:

مواد مباشرة ٦ دنانير

أجور مباشرة ٤ دنانير

تكاليف صناعية غير مباشرة متغيرة ٥ دنانير

تكاليف صناعية غير مباشرة ثابتة ٤ دنانير(٦٠,٠٠٠ ÷ ١٥,٠٠٠ وحدة)

مصروفات تسويقية متغيرة ٢ دينار

وبلغت التكاليف الصناعية غير المباشرة الثابتة الفعلية ٦٠,٠٠٠د لكل شهر ويتم تحميلها على الإنتاج بمعدل تحميل مقداره ٤د للوحدة. وكما بلغت المصروفات التسويقية والإدارية الثابتة لكل شهر ٤٠,٠٠٠د.

وتقدر طاقة الإنتاج الشهرية للشركة بإنتاج ١٥,٠٠٠ وحدة، وأن سعر بيع الوحدة ٣٠د.

والمطلوب: حساب تكلفة الوحدة وإجمالي تكاليف الانتاج وإعداد قائمة الدخل حسب طريقة التكلفة الكلية وطريقة التكلفة المتغيرة.

الحـل:

يتم تحديد تكلفة الوحدة وتكلفة حسب طريقتي التكاليف المتغيرة والكلية كالتالي:

الكلية	المتغيرة	طريقة التكلفة
		تكلفة الوحدة:
٦د	٦د	مواد مباشرة
٤	٤	أجور مباشرة
٥	٥	أعباء إضافية متغيرة
٤	صفر	أعباء إضافية ثابتة
١٩د	١٥ د	إجمالي التكلفة الصناعية للوحدة
١٥,٠٠٠	١٥,٠٠٠	ضرب عدد وحدات الانتاج
٢٨٥,٠٠٠	٢٢٥,٠٠٠	اجمالي التكاليف الصناعية للإنتاج

١- تدفق تكاليف الإنتاج حسب طريقة التكلفة الكلية :

يمكن أن يتم التعبير عن الحسابات التي تبين تكاليف الإنتاج لشهر يناير (شهر كانون ثاني) كما في الشكل (٩-١) التالي:

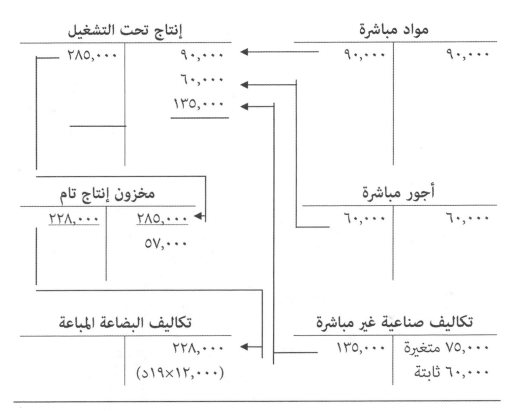

إنتاج تحت التشغيل		مواد مباشرة	
٢٨٥,٠٠٠	٩٠,٠٠٠	٩٠,٠٠٠	٩٠,٠٠٠
	٦٠,٠٠٠		
	١٣٥,٠٠٠		

مخزون إنتاج تام		أجور مباشرة	
٢٢٨,٠٠٠	٢٨٥,٠٠٠	٦٠,٠٠٠	٦٠,٠٠٠
	٥٧,٠٠٠		

تكاليف البضاعة المباعة		تكاليف صناعية غير مباشرة	
	٢٢٨,٠٠٠	١٣٥,٠٠٠	٧٥,٠٠٠ متغيرة
	(١٢,٠٠٠×١٩د)		٦٠,٠٠٠ ثابتة

٢- تكاليف فترة

مصروفات تسويقية وإدارية	
	٤٠,٠٠٠ ثابتة
	٢٤,٠٠٠ متغيرة

شكل (٩-١) دورة حسابات التكاليف حسب طريقة التكلفة الكلية لشهر يناير

من البيانات السابقة وجدنا ان تكلفة وحدة الانتاج حسب طريقة التكلفة الكلية تساوي ١٩ د، وعلية فانه يتم حساب تكلفة الانتاج التام وتكلفة البضاعة المباعة وبضاعة آخر المدة كالتالي:

تكلفة الانتاج التام = عدد وحدات الإنتاج التام X تكلفة الوحدة

= ١٥,٠٠٠ X١٩د = ٢٨٥,٠٠٠د

تكلفة البضاعة المباعة = ١٢,٠٠٠ X١٩د = ٢٢٨,٠٠٠د

تكلفة مخزون الإنتاج التام آخر شهر يناير= ٣,٠٠٠ X ١٩د = ٥٧,٠٠٠د

وحسب هذه الطريقة تكون تكاليف الفترة عبارة عن المصروفات التسويقية والإدارية الثابتة ومقدارهما ٤٠,٠٠٠د زائد المصروفات التسويقية والإدارية المتغيرة ومقدارها ٢٤,٠٠٠ (١٢,٠٠٠ وحدة × ٢دينار) على التوالي.

دورة حسابات التكاليف المتغيرة:

مما سبق نجد ان التكلفة الصناعية المتغيرة للوحدة تساوي ١٥ دينار وعلية فانه يتم حساب تكلفة الانتاج التام وتكلفة البضاعة المباعة وبضاعة آخر المدة كالتالي:

تكلفة الإنتاج التام = عدد وحدات الإنتاج التام X تكلفة الوحدة

= ١٥,٠٠٠ X١٥د = ٢٢٥,٠٠٠د

تكلفة البضاعة المباعة = ١٢,٠٠٠ X١٥د = ١٨٠,٠٠٠د

تكلفة مخزون الإنتاج التام آخر يناير= ٣,٠٠٠ X ١٥د = ٤٥,٠٠٠د

وأن أعباء الفترة تساوي مجموع التكاليف الصناعية الثابتة وقدرها ٦٠,٠٠٠د والمصروفات التسويقية والإدارية الثابتة وقدرها ٤٠,٠٠٠د.

من دراسة الاشكال (٩-١) و (٩-٢) نجد ان الحسابات مربوطة معا في خطوط وتبدأ من عند رأس السهم وذلك الحساب يكون هو الحساب المدين في قيد اليومية وينتهي في حساب آخر هو الحساب الدائن. ففي الشكل (٩-١) تم تحميل حساب الانتاج تحت التشغيل بالمواد المباشرة والأجور المباشرة والأعباء الاضافية المتغيرة والثابتة. ولكن في الشكل (٩-٢) لم تحمل الاعباء الصناعية الثابتة على حساب الانتاج تحت التشغيل بل اعتبرت تكاليف فترة.

قائمة الدخل حسب طريقة التكلفة الكلية:

لقد تم إعداد قائمة الدخل حسب طريقة التكلفة الكلية في الجدول (٩-١) وهي تشبه القائمة التي تعودنا على إعدادها لأغراض التقارير المالية المنشورة، وتم إعداد قائمة الدخل حسب طريقة التكلفة المتغيرة في الجدول (٩-٢) ومن مقارنة هذين الجدولين يتضح لنا الآتي:

١- التكاليف الصناعية المتغيرة:

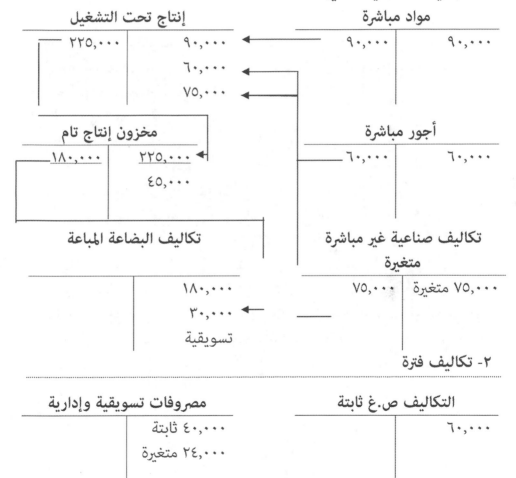

شكل (٩-٢) دورة حسابات التكاليف حسب طريقة التكلفة المتغيرة لشهر يناير

1- لم تميز قائمة الدخل المعدة على أساس التكلفة الكلية بين التكاليف الصناعية المتغيرة والثابتة وبلغت التكلفة الصناعية للبضاعة المباعة خلال شهر يناير ٢٢٨,٠٠٠ (=١٢,٠٠٠ ×١٩د) دينار، أما عند استخدام طريقة التكلفة المتغيرة لنفس الشهر فقد بلغت التكلفة الصناعية للبضاعة المباعة ١٨٠,٠٠٠ (=١٢,٠٠٠ ×١٥د) دينار ويرجع السبب في انخفاض تكلفة البضاعة المباعة في طريقة التكلفة المتغيرة بالمقارنة مع التكلفة الكلية إلى أن طريقة التكلفة المتغيرة لا تعتبر التكاليف الصناعية الثابتة ضمن تكاليف الانتاج.

2- تكلفة بضاعة آخر المدة في طريقة التكاليف الكلية أعلى من طريقة التكاليف المتغيرة لأنها تحتوي على نصيب وحدات آخر المدة من التكاليف الصناعية الثابتة، وهذا المبلغ يساوي عدد وحدات آخر المدة ضرب نصيب الوحدة من التكاليف الثابتة. ويساوي: ٣,٠٠٠وحدة × ٤ دنانير = ١٢,٠٠٠ دينار.

الجدول (٩-١)

قائمة الدخل حسب طريقة التكلفة الكلية للفترات المنتهية في نهاية شهر

الإجمالي	فبراير	يناير	
٩٠٠,٠٠٠	٥٤٠,٠٠٠	٣٦٠,٠٠٠	المبيعات
			تكلفة المبيعات:
٥٧,٠٠٠	٥٧,٠٠٠	صفر	بضاعة أول المدة
٥٧٠,٠٠٠	٢٨٥,٠٠٠	٢٨٥,٠٠٠	التكلفة الصناعية للفترة الجارية
٦٢٧,٠٠٠	٣٤٢,٠٠٠	٢٨٥,٠٠٠	تكلفة البضاعة المتاحة للبيع
٥٧,٠٠٠	صفر	(٥٧,٠٠٠)	ناقص: بضاعة آخر المدة
٥٧٠,٠٠٠	٣٤٢,٠٠٠	٢٢٨,٠٠٠	تكلفة البضاعة المباعة
٣٣٠,٠٠٠	١٩٨,٠٠٠	١٣٢,٠٠٠	مجمل الربح
٦٠,٠٠٠	٣٦,٠٠٠	٢٤,٠٠٠	مصروفات تسويقية متغيرة
٨٠,٠٠٠	٤٠,٠٠٠	٤٠,٠٠٠	مصروفات إدارية وتسويقية ثابتة
١٩٠,٠٠٠	١٢٢,٠٠٠	٦٨,٠٠٠	صافي الربح

٣- لقد تم طرح المصروفات التسويقية المتغيرة من الإيرادات في طريقة التكلفة المتغيرة قبل تحديد رقم هامش المساهمة. وبالتالي يعرف هامش مساهمة الوحدة على أنه الفرق بين سعر البيع ناقص التكلفة المتغيرة الصناعية زائد المصروفات التسويقية والإدارية المتغيرة.

لقد كان صافي الربح في طريقة التكلفة الكلية أعلى من صافي الربح في طريقة التكلفة المتغيرة لشهر يناير والعكس صحيحا بالنسبة لشهر فبراير، والسبب في ذلك أن طريقة التكلفة المتغيرة قامت في كل شهر بتحميل كل التكاليف الصناعية الثابتة ومقدارها ٦٠٬٠٠٠ دينار على إيرادات الشهر نفسه بغض النظر عن عدد الوحدات المنتجة بينما قامت طريقة التكلفة الكلية بتحميل جزء من هذه التكاليف على بضاعة آخر المدة مبلغه ١٢٬٠٠٠ د في شهر يناير وباقي التكاليف الصناعية الثابتة ومقداره ٤٨٬٠٠٠ دينار وتم تحميله على البضاعة المباعة وهذا المبلغ ظهر في قائمة الدخل، وحسب كالتالي (١٢٬٠٠٠وحدة مباعة × ٤ دنانير للوحدة). وتغيرت الصورة في شهر فبراير فقد تم إنتاج ١٥٬٠٠٠ وحدة وتم بيع ١٨٬٠٠٠ وحدة وبالتالي أصبحت وحدات آخر المدة أقل من وحدات أول المدة، مما جعل التكاليف الثابتة التي تمت معالجتها في قائمة الدخل في طريقة التكلفة الكلية تساوي ٧٢٬٠٠٠د. (= ١٢٬٠٠٠د تكاليف ثابتة في بضاعة أول المده زائد ٦٠٬٠٠٠ د تكاليف ثابتة للفترة الجارية - صفر تكاليف ثابتة محملة على بضاعة آخر المدة). وبكلمات أخرى يمكن تفسير هذا الوضع بأن الشركة قد باعت كل إنتاج شهر فبراير في الشهر نفسه وهذا تحمل بالتكاليف الثابتة لشهر فبراير ومقدارها٦٠٬٠٠٠د. وبالإضافة الى ذلك تم بيع ٣٠٠٠ وحدة من المخزون أول المدة وهذه تحمل جزءا من التكاليف الثابتة لشهر يناير ومقدارها ١٢٬٠٠٠د (٣٬٠٠٠ ×٤د). إذن تصبح التكاليف الثابتة التي تخصم من إيرادات شهر فبراير ٧٢٬٠٠٠د (=٦٠٬٠٠٠ + ١٢٬٠٠٠د).

قائمة الدخل حسب طريقة التكاليف المتغيرة للفترات المنتهية في نهاية شهر

الإجمالي	شباط	يناير	
٩٠٠,٠٠٠	٥٤٠,٠٠٠	٣٦٠,٠٠٠	المبيعات
			تكلفة المبيعات:
٤٥,٠٠٠	٤٥,٠٠٠	صفر	مخزون أول المدة
٤٥٠,٠٠٠	٢٢٥٠٠٠	٢٢٥,٠٠٠	التكلفة الصناعية للفترة الجارية
٤٩٥,٠٠٠	٢٧٠,٠٠٠	٢٢٥,٠٠٠	تكلفة البضاعة المتاحة للبيع
(٤٥,٠٠٠)	صفر	(٤٥,٠٠٠)	ناقص: بضاعة آخر المدة
٤٥٠,٠٠٠	٢٧٠,٠٠٠	١٨٠,٠٠٠	التكلفة الصناعية للبضاعة المباعة
٦٠,٠٠٠	٣٦,٠٠٠	٢٤,٠٠٠	زائد: مصروفات تسويقية متغيرة
٥١٠,٠٠٠	٣٠٦,٠٠٠	٢٠٤,٠٠٠	التكلفة المتغيرة للمبيعات
٣٩٠,٠٠٠	٢٣٤,٠٠٠	١٥٦,٠٠٠	هامش المساهمة
			ناقص: المصروفات الثابتة:
١٢٠,٠٠٠	٦٠,٠٠٠	٦٠,٠٠٠	تكلفة صناعية ثابتة
٨٠,٠٠٠	٤٠,٠٠٠	٤٠,٠٠٠	مصروفات تسويقية وإدارية ثابتة
١٩٠,٠٠٠	١٣٤,٠٠٠	٥٦,٠٠٠	صافي الربح

أما في طريقة التكلفة المتغيرة يتم تحميل إيرادات شهر فبراير بالمصروفات الصناعية غير مباشرة الثابتة لشهر فبراير بدون زيادة أو نقص ومقدارها ٦٠,٠٠٠ دينار. لذلك تكون التكاليف الصناعية في هذه الطريقة اقل من طريقة التكاليف الكلية وبالتالي سوف تكون أرباح هذه الطريقة أعلى من أرباح طريقة التكلفة الكلية بمبلغ ١٢,٠٠٠ دينار.

٥- وفي ضوء ما سبق، نستطيع تحديد أرباح أية طريقة إذا عرفنا أرباح الطريقة الأخرى والتغير في التكاليف الثابتة المحملة على المخزون، فمثلا إذا تم إعداد قائمة الدخل حسب طريقة التكلفة الكلية لشهر يناير ولم نرغب في اعداد قائمة الدخل حسب طريقة التكلفة المتغيرة، ورغبنا في تحديد أرباح هذا الشهر باستخدام طريقة التكلفة المتغيرة فإنه يمكن استخدام المعادلة التالية:

أرباح التكلفة المتغيرة = أرباح التكلفة الكلية + التكاليف الثابتة في بضاعة أول المدة – التكاليف الثابتة في بضاعة آخر المدة.

ارباح التكلفة المتغيرة لشهر يناير = ٦٨,٠٠٠ + صفر – ١٢,٠٠٠ = ٥٦,٠٠٠ د

أرباح التكلفة المتغيرة لشهر شباط = ١٢٢,٠٠٠+ ١٢,٠٠٠ -صفر =١٣٤,٠٠٠د

افترضت المعادلة السابقة أن التكاليف الثابتة المحملة على وحدة المنتج لم تتغير من شهر إلى آخر، وإذا كان هذا الافتراض لا يمثل الواقع فإنه يجب الرجوع إلى السجلات المحاسبية، لتحديد قيمة التكاليف الصناعية الثابتة المحملة على مخزون الإنتاج التام أول المدة وآخرها.

يمكن القول أنه إذا زاد حجم الإنتاج عن حجم المبيعات فإن ارباح طريقة التكلفة الكلية تكون أعلى من طريقة التكلفة المتغيرة لأن جزءا من التكاليف الثابتة في الطريقة الكلية تحميله على وحدات مخزون آخر المدة ومن ثم يتم تأجيل الاعتراف به كمصروف إلى الفترة المقبلة ، والعكس صحيح بالنسبة لزيادة المبيعات عن حجم الإنتاج. وبالرجوع الى البيانات السابقة نجد ان ارباح طريقة التكلفة الكلية في الجدول (٩-١) تساوي ٦٨,٠٠٠ د بينما ان ارباح التكلفة المتغيرة من جدول (٩-٢) تساوي ٥٦,٠٠٠ لان الانتاج في هذا الشهر اعلى من المبيعات. وعلى الرغم من اختلاف الأرباح الشهرية حسب طريقة التكلفة المتبعة، فان مجموع أرباح الشهرين متساوي، لأن بضاعة أول المدة تساوي بضاعة آخر المدة وهما يساويان صفرا.

٧ - تتوقف قيمة الأرباح في طريقة التكلفة الكلية على الإنتاج والمبيعات معا وهذا يعني أنه بإمكان المنشأة زيادة أرباحها بزيادة مبيعاتها أو بزيادة الإنتاج وهذا يؤدي إلى نقص تكلفة الوحدة المنتجة والمباعة أو بزيادتهما معا، أما عند إتباع طريقة التكلفة المتغيرة فإن الأرباح تتوقف على حجم المبيعات فقط.

قوائم الدخل حسب التكلفة المعيارية:

يمكن إعداد قوائم الدخل حسب طرق تحميل التكاليف الكلية والمتغيرة باستخدام التكاليف الفعلية أو المعيارية ولتوضيح ذلك سوف يتم الاعتماد على البيانات التالية:

مثال (٢):

حجم الإنتاج	٢٠,٠٠٠ وحدة
حجم المبيعات	١٥,٠٠٠ وحدة
بضاعة آخر المدة	٥,٠٠٠ وحدة
التكلفة الصناعية المتغيرة المعيارية للوحدة	١٥ دينار
التكلفة الصناعية الثابتة المعيارية للوحدة	٥ دنانير
المصروفات التسويقية والإدارية الثابتة المخططة	٥٠,٠٠٠ دينار
سعر بيع الوحدة	٣٠ دينار

ولقد تم حساب نصيب الوحدة من التكاليف الثابتة على أساس أن الطاقة الإنتاجية تساوي انتاج ٢٥,٠٠٠ وحدة. وخلال الفترة لم يحدث أي اختلاف بين التكاليف الفعلية والمعيارية.

المطلوب:

إعداد قائمة الدخل حسب طريقة التكلفة الكلية وطريقة التكلفة المتغيرة

قائمة الدخل حسب طريقة التكلفة الكلية:

سيتم إعداد هذه القائمة في الجدول (٩-٣).

جدول رقم (٩-٣)
قائمة الدخل باستخدام طريقة التكاليف الكلية

المبيعات		٤٥٠,٠٠٠
يطرح: تكلفة البضاعة المباعة:		
تكلفة الإنتاج التام (١٥+٥) × ٢٠,٠٠٠	٤٠٠,٠٠٠	
- تكلفة بضاعة آخر المدة (٥,٠٠٠×٢٠)	(١٠٠,٠٠٠)	
التكلفة المعيارية للبضاعة المباعة	٣٠٠,٠٠٠	

	٢٥,٠٠٠	زائد: انحراف الحجم
٣٢٥,٠٠٠	————	تكلفة البضاعة المباعة
١٢٥,٠٠٠		مجمل الربح
٥٠,٠٠٠		ناقص: مصروفات إدارية وتسويقية
٧٥,٠٠٠		صافي الربح

تم حساب انحراف الحجم كالتالي:

انحراف الحجم = (مستوى الطاقة العادية – حجم الإنتاج الفعلي) × معدل تحميل الأعباء الإضافية الثابتة.

انحراف الحجم = (٢٥,٠٠٠ – ٢٠,٠٠٠) ×٥ = ٢٥,٠٠٠ د (غير مفضل)

لقد تم إضافة انحراف الحجم إلى تكلفة البضاعة المباعة لأنه غير مفضل وتم اعتباره غير جوهري، وإذا تم اعتبار أن قيمة هذا الانحراف مهمة يمكن استخدام نفس الاجراءات المستخدمة في توزيع الاعباء الاضافية المحملة بالزيادة او النقص التي تم تغطيتها في الفصل الثالث.

قائمة الدخل حسب طريقة التكلفة المتغيرة:

سيتم إعداد قائمة الدخل حسب طريقة التكلفة المتغيرة كما في الجدول (٩-٤).

جدول رقم (٩-٤)
قائمة الدخل حسب طريقة التكلفة المتغيرة المعيارية

٤٥٠,٠٠٠	المبيعات
٢٢٥,٠٠٠	يطرح التكلفة الصناعية المتغيرة للمبيعات
٢٢٥,٠٠٠	هامش المساهمة
(١٢٥,٠٠٠)	يطرح: التكاليف الصناعية الثابتة
(٥٠,٠٠٠)	يطرح: التكاليف التسويقية والإدارية
٥٠,٠٠٠	صافي الربح

لم ينتج انحراف الحجم في طريقة التكلفة المتغيرة لأن التكاليف الثابتة تعتبر تكاليف فترة ولا تحمل على الإنتاج.

تقييم طريقتي التكاليف الكلية والمتغيرة:

لقد دار نقاش حاد في الأدبيات المحاسبية حول طرق تحميل التكاليف الكلية والمتغيرة واستقر الوضع على أنه لكل طريقة منهما مزايا وعيوبا واستخدامات معينة [1]. ولتوضيح ذلك سيتم مناقشة مزايا وعيوب طريقة التكلفة المتغيرة والانتقادات التي يوجهها لها مؤيدوا طريقة التكلفة الكلية.

مزايا طريقة التكلفة المتغيرة:

أولا: سهولة فهم التكاليف المتغيرة لأن تكلفة الوحدات المنتجة تقتصر على التكاليف الصناعية المتغيرة. وهذه تسهل فهم تكلفة البضاعة المباعة وتكلفة المخزون وتزيد من فعالية الرقابة على عناصر التكاليف الثابتة، حيث أن التكاليف الأخيرة يتم رقابتها على أساس قيمتها الإجمالية وليس على أساس نصيب الوحدة المنتجة.

ثانيا: عدم التلاعب في الأرباح لأن الإرباح تتوقف على عدد الوحدات المباعة. أما في طريقة التكاليف الكلية فتعتمد الأرباح على عدد الوحدات المباعة وعدد الوحدات المنتجة. ففي طريقة التكلفة الكلية تحمل التكاليف الثابتة على وحدات الإنتاج وهذا قد يؤدي الى التلاعب في رقم الربح. فمن المعروف أنه إذا زادت وحدات آخر المدة عن أول المدة يتم تحويل جزء من التكاليف الثابتة إلى الفترة القادمة وبالتالي تزداد أرباح طريقة التكاليف الكلية عن أرباح طريقة التكاليف المتغيرة فمثلا، إذا تم الاتفاق مع مدير على أن يحصل على نسبة مئوية من الأرباح فإن هذا المدير يستطيع زيادة مكافأته عند إتباع طريقة التكاليف الكلية بزيادة المبيعات أو بزيادة الإنتاج أو بكليهما. [1]

---

[1] Gayle Rayburn, Op., cit., Pp.٧٢٦-٧٣٠.

[1] Hirsch and Louderback., Op. Cit., P.٤٦٠.

ثالثا: تحليل علاقة التكلفة والحجم والأرباح:

يعتبر تحليل علاقات هذه العوامل من الأمور الهامة في تخطيط الربحية، وللقيام بذلك لا بد من فصل التكاليف إلى متغيرة وثابتة وتحديد هامش مساهمة الوحدة أو نسبة هامش المساهمة، لذلك فإن أعداد قائمة الدخل حسب طريقة التكلفة المتغيرة يعتبر نقطة البداية في إجراء هذا التحليل.

رابعا: اتخاذ القرارات الإدارية قصيرة الأجل:

تشمل هذه المجوعة من القرارات على العديد من القرارات مثل قرار الاستمرار في إنتاج منتج أو إيقافه، الإنتاج الداخلي أو الشراء من مورد، قبول طلبات الشراء بأسعار خاصة. هذه القرارات تحتاج إلى تحديد ما يسمى بالتكاليف المناسبة، وهي التكاليف التي ترتبط بالقرار محل الاعتبار، أو هي التكاليف التي يمكن تجنبها عند عدم اتخاذ القرار، وتشتمل هذه التكاليف على التكاليف المتغيرة وتكاليف الفرص البديلة والتكاليف الثابتة المضافة، وفي كثير من الأحوال تقتصر التكاليف المناسبة على التكاليف المتغيرة لأنه لا توجد تكلفة فرص بديلة لاستخدام كثير من الأصول التي يتم استخدامها لأغراض تنفيذ القرارات المذكورة سابقاً، وكذلك لا تؤدي القرارات الجديدة في أغلب الأحيان إلى إضافة تكلفة ثابتة جديدة. لذا يمكن القول بان التكاليف المتغيرة هي اساس اتخاذ القرارات الادارية قصيرة الاجل.

ينتقد مؤيدوا طريقة التكلفة الكلية هذا الأسلوب، ويرون أن الاعتماد على التكاليف المتغيرة في التسعير يؤدي في كثير من الأحيان إلى تحديد أسعار غير عادلة ومنهم من يعتقد بأن استخدام طريقة التكلفة المتغيرة في القرارات العادية والمتكررة يؤدي إلى عواقب سيئة [1]. لذلك يرون بأن طريقة التكلفة المتغيرة تصلح لمجموعة من القرارات الإدارية فقط وليس لكل القرارات الإدارية.

---

[1] Belkaoui, A., Op. Cit., ٣٨١-٣٨٧.

التقارير الخارجية:

تتطلب المعايير المحاسبية المقبولة قبولا عاما أن تم إعداد التقارير المالية الخارجية بالاعتماد على طريقة التكلفة الكلية، فمبدأ مقابلة الإيرادات والمصروفات ومبدأ الاستحقاق. يشترط لإجراء المقابلة أن يكون قد تم استنفاذ الخدمات المتوقعة في إنتاج الإيرادات، وفي حالة عدم توفر هذا الشرط يتم تأجيل الاعتراف بالمصروف إلى المستقبل. فالآلات مثلا تعتبر ضمن الأصول لأنه يتوقع أن يكون لها خدمات أو منافع مستقبلية، وتتناقص هذه الخدمات سنة بعد أخرى لذلك يتم استهلاكها. وهنا نجد أن للاستهلاك فوائد متوقعة لأنه يؤدي إلى زيادة قيمة الوحدات المنتجة، لذلك يجب عدم اعتباره مصروفا إلا عندما يتم بيع الوحدات التي أدى إلى إنتاجها، وبالمثل يمكن تبرير معالجة بقية المصروفات الثابتة.

ومن ناحية أخرى، يرى مؤيدوا التكلفة المتغيرة أنه طالما أن التكاليف المتغيرة مفيدة لأغراض التقارير الداخلية فلماذا لا يتم السماح باستخدامها في التقارير المالية المنشورة.

الخاتمــة

في هذا الفصل تمت دراسة طريقة التكلفة الكلية وطريقة التكلفة المتغيرة، وهاتان الطريقتان تختلفان عن بعضهما بصورة أساسية في معاملة التكاليف الصناعية غير المباشرة الثابتة، فتقوم طريقة التكلفة الكلية على اعتبارها ضمن التكلفة الصناعية للوحدة المنتجة، أما طريقة التكلفة المتغيرة فتعتبر هذه التكاليف ضمن الأعباء الدورية للفترة وبالتالي لا تحملها على الوحدات المنتجة، وتبرر ذلك أن حدوث هذه التكاليف خلال الفترة الجارية لا يؤدي إلى تجنب حدوثها خلال الفترة المقبلة، وهذا يعني أنه لا يوجد لهذه التكاليف خدمات مستقبلية متوقعة وبالتالي لا يجوز رسملتها على شكل تكلفة مخزون آخر المدة.

تستطيع طريقة التكاليف المتغيرة تقديم معلومات مناسبة لخدمة أغراض إدارية كثيرة منها: الإنتاج الداخلي أو الشراء من الورد، الاستمرار في تشغيل بعض المنتجات أو إيقافها وتحليل التعادل وخدمة أغراض تخطيط الإنتاج والرقابة على التكاليف، ولكن يسمح باستخدامها في أغراض التقارير المالية الخارجية.

أسئلة وتمارين

السؤال الأول: ما هي عناصر التكاليف الصناعية التي تتكون منها تكلفة الوحدة عند إتباع طريقة التكلفة المتغيرة وطريقة التكلفة الكلية؟

السؤال الثاني: ما هو هامش المساهمة وكيف يتم تحديده ؟

السؤال الثالث: إذا كان حجم الإنتاج أكبر من حجم المبيعات فهل تعطي طريقة التكلفة المتغيرة أرباحا أعلى من طريقة التكلفة الكلية.

السؤال الرابع: بين أثر تحميل التكاليف الصناعية غير المباشرة الثابتة على الإنتاج وعلى صافي الربح.

السؤال الخامس: ما هو انحراف الحجم وكيف يتم حسابه؟

السؤال السادس: قارن بين مساهمة كل من طريقة التكلفة الكلية والتكلفة المتغيرة في اتخاذ القرارات الإدارية قصيرة الأجل ؟

السؤال السابع: هل تفضل استخدام طريقة التكلفة الكلية أو طريقة التكلفة المتغيرة لأغراض التسعير العادي ولماذا ؟

السؤال الثامن: ما هي المبررات التي تؤدي إلى استخدام طريقة التكلفة الكلية في التقارير الخارجية؟

السؤال التاسع: في المدى الطويل ما هي الطريقة التي تؤدي إلى تقرير أرباح أعلى هل هي طريقة التكلفة الكلية أم طريقة التكلفة المتغيرة (مع ذكر شروط تحقيق ذلك) ؟

السؤال العاشر: الآتي بيانات مستخرجة من دفاتر إحدى الشركات الصناعية وتتعلق بالمنتجات (أ)، (ب):

المنتج ب	المنتج أ	الوحدات
١٩,٥٠٠ وحدة	١٨,٥٠٠ وحدة	الإنتاج
٢٠,٠٠٠ وحدة	١٧,٥٠٠ وحدة	المبيعات
٥,٠٠٠ وحدة	٤,٥٠٠ وحدة	مخزون أول المدة
٤,٥٠٠ وحدة	٥,٥٠٠ وحدة	مخزون آخر المدة
		وكانت البيانات المالية للوحدة كالتالي:
١٤ دينار	١٦ دينار	سعر بيع الوحدة
٤ دينار	٥ دينار	تكلفة أولية
١ دينار	٣ دينار	تكاليف صناعية غير مباشرة متغيرة
١,٢	١,٨	التكاليف الصناعية الثابتة (على أساس إنتاج ٢٠,٠٠٠ وحدة من كل من أ، ب)

وتدفع المنشأة عمولة مبيعات مقدارها ٢٪ من قيمة المبيعات، وبلغت المصروفات التسويقية والإدارية الثابتة للشركة ٧٠,٠٠٠ دينار، وهذا المبلغ يتم توزيعه على المنتجين بنسبة قيمة المبيعات.

المطلوب:

إعداد قائمة الدخل للمنتجين وللمنشأة حسب:

١. طريقة التكلفة المتغيرة.

٢. طريقة التكلفة الكلية.

السؤال الحادي عشر: بدأت إحدى الشركات أعمالها الإنتاجيه في ٢٠٠٤/١/١ وحتى نهاية السنة أتمت الشركة إنتاج ٩٨,٠٠٠ وحدة وباعت منها ٩٠,٠٠٠ وحدة بسعر ٢٠د للوحدة، وبقي في حساب إنتاج تحت التشغيل ١٠,٠٠٠ وحدة وقد حصلت هذه الوحدات على ١٠٠٪ من المواد وحصلت على ٥٠٪ من تكاليف التحويل وبلغت التكاليف المحملة على حساب إنتاج تحت التشغيل خلال السنة الآتي:

مواد مباشرة   ٥٤٠,٠٠٠د

أجور مباشرة   ٣٦٠,٥٠٠د

تكاليف صناعية أخرى متغيرة   ٢٥٧,٥٠٠

تكاليف صناعية ثابتة   ٥١٥,٠٠٠د

وبلغت المصروفات التسويقية المتغيرة ١د للوحدة وبلغت المصروفات التسويقية الثابتة ٨٥,٠٠٠ دينار وبلغت المصروفات الإدارية الثابتة ٧٥,٠٠٠ دينار وتستخدم الشركة طريقة التكاليف المتغيرة.

المطلوب:

١. إعداد قائمة الدخل للشركة.

٢. بيان أثر ذلك على الميزانية العمومية.

السؤال الثاني عشر: المطلوب استخدام طريقة التكلفة المتغيره وإعداد

١. قائمة الدخل للشركة.

٢. بيان أثر ذلك على الميزانية العمومية.

السؤال الثالث عشر: بدأت إحدى الشركات الصناعية أعمالها ١/١ وتقوم بإنتاج منتج واحد وتبيعه بسعر ٧ دنانير للوحدة. وتبلغ طاقتها المعيارية ١٠٠,٠٠٠ وحدة في السنة ونجحت في إنتاج ١٠٠,٠٠٠ وحدة خلال السنة ولكن قامت ببيع ٨٠,٠٠٠ وحدة منها خلال السنة الأولى من حياتها.

وكانت التكاليف الصناعية والمصروفات التسويقية والإدارية كالتالي:

	الثابتة	المتغيرة
مواد خام	-	١,٥ للوحدة المنتجة
أجور مباشرة	-	١د للوحدة المنتجة
أعباء صناعية	١٥٠,٠٠٠	٠,٥ للوحدة المنتجة
مصروفات تسويقية وإدارية	٨٠,٠٠٠	٠,٥ للوحدة المباعة

ولا توجد أية انحرافات عن التكلفة المتغيرة. وأن أية تكاليف محملة بالزيادة أو بالنقص يتم إقفالها في حساب تكلفة البضاعة المباعة.

أ. عند عرض البضاعة في الميزانية في نهاية السنة المالية فإن تكلفة الوحدة باستخدام طريقة التكلفة الكلية هي:

أ – ٢,٥د   ب – ٣د

ج – ٣,٥ د   د – ٤,٥د

ب – ما هو صافي الربح خلال سنة ٢٠٠٧ باستخدام طريقة التكلفة المتغيرة

أ – ٥٠,٠٠٠د   ب – ٨٠,٠٠٠د

ج – ٩٠,٠٠٠د   د – ١٢٠,٠٠٠د

(المجمع الأمريكي للمحاسبين القانونيين)

السؤال الرابع عشر: الآتي معلومات عن التكاليف والإنتاج الفعلي لشركة الشرق الصناعية عن الربع الأول لسنة ٢٠٠٨:

- المواد المباشرة الفعلية	٦٠٠,٠٠٠ دينار
- الأجور المباشرة الفعلية	٥٢٥,٠٠٠ دينار
- الأعباء الصناعية المتغيرة	٣٠٠,٠٠٠ دينار
- الأعباء الصناعية الثابتة	٤٥٠,٠٠٠ دينار
- المصروفات التسويقية والإدارية:	
متغيرة	١٢٥,٠٠٠ دينار
ثابتة	٣٧٥,٠٠٠ دينار

وخلال هذا الربع تم إنتاج ١٥٠,٠٠٠ وحدة بيع منها ١٢٥,٠٠٠ وحدة ومتوسط سعر بيع الوحدة ١٨ دينار ولا يوجد مخزون في أول المدة ولكن هناك ٢٥,٠٠٠ وحدة في اخرها.

المطلوب:

١. تحديد تكلفة الوحدة المنتجة باستخدام:

أ. طريقة التكلفة المتغيرة   ب. طريقة التكلفة الكلية

٢. إعداد قائمة الدخل باستخدام طريقة التكاليف الكلية.

٣. عمل تسوية لتحديد ارباح طريقة التكلفة المتغيرة

السؤال الخامس عشر: الآتي معلومات مستخرجة من دفاتر إحدى الشركات عن الأشهر: ٤، ٥، ٦ والمتعلقة بإنتاج أحد المنتجات. وتستخدم الشركة نظام محاسبة التكاليف الفعلية.

	٦	٥	٤
الإنتاج بالوحدة	٤٠,٠٠٠	٦٠,٠٠٠	٥٠,٠٠٠
المبيعات بالوحدة	٦٠,٠٠٠	٥٠,٠٠٠	٤٠,٠٠٠
مخزون وحدات آخر المدة	٨,٠٠٠	٢٨,٠٠٠	١٨,٠٠٠
مخزون وحدات أول المدة	٢٨,٠٠٠	١٨,٠٠٠	٨,٠٠٠
سعر بيع الوحدة	٢٢	٢٤	٢٥
التكاليف الصناعية المتغيرة للوحدة	١٣	١٢	١٢
التكاليف الصناعية الثابتة للفترة	٤٠٠,٠٠٠	٤٠٠,٠٠٠	٤٠٠,٠٠٠
المصروفات التسويقية المتغيرة للوحدة	٠,٥٠	٠,٥٠	٠,٥٠
المصروفات التسويقية والإدارية الثابتة	٨٠,٠٠٠	٨٠,٠٠٠	٨٠,٠٠٠

وتستخدم الشركة طريقة الأول في الأول في المحاسبة على المخزون. وكان مخزون الإنتاج التام أول المدة ١٦٨,٠٠٠ دينار منها ٧٢,٠٠٠ دينار أعباء ثابتة، ولا يوجد إنتاج تحت التشغيل أول المدة أو آخر المدة خلال الفترات الثلاث ويتم تحميل التكاليف الثابتة على أساس فعلي في طريقة التكلفة الكلية.

المطلوب: إعداد قائمة الدخل للفترات الثلاث باستخدام:

أ – طريقة التكلفة المتغيرة.

ب – طريقة التكلفة الكلية.

وعمل تسوية لأرباح الطرق السابقة لشهر٥.

السؤال السادس عشر: تقوم إحدى الشركات بإنتاج الورق الصحي وتبلغ طاقتها الإنتاجية ١٥٠,٠٠٠ طن في السنة ولكن خلال السنة المالية الماضية قامت بإنتاج وبيع ٧٥,٠٠٠طن ورق صحي فقط ونظرا لعدم استغلال الطاقة الإنتاجية للشركة تم انتخاب مجلس إدارة جديد وفي نهاية السنة الجارية وتم تجهيز التقرير المالي التالي للشركة:

قائمة الدخل عن السنة المنتهية في ١٢/٣١

	٤	٣
المبيعات (٢٠ دينار للطن)	١٨٠٠,٠٠٠	١٥٠٠,٠٠٠
يطرح: التكلفة الصناعية للبضاعة المباعة	١١٤٠,٠٠٠	١١٥٠,٠٠٠
مجمل الربح	٦٦٠,٠٠٠	٣٥٠,٠٠٠
ناقص: المصروفات التسويقية والإدارية	٢٠٠,٠٠٠	٢٠٠,٠٠٠
صافي الربح	٤٦٠,٠٠٠	١٥٠,٠٠٠

وقد بلغت التكلفة الصناعية الثابتة في كل من سنة ٣، ٤، مبلغ ٤٠٠,٠٠٠ دينار وأن متوسط التكلفة المتغيرة للوحدة في كل من السنتين المذكورتين أعلاه هو ١٠ دنانير وقد استطاعت إدارة الشركة مضاعفة حجم الإنتاج حتى وصل إنتاجها إلى ١٥٠,٠٠٠ طن عام ٤ وقد باعت من هذه الكمية ٩٠,٠٠٠ طن وفي رسالة مجلس الإدارة ركزت الإدارة على أنها حققت نموا في الأرباح مقداره ٢٠٥%.

المطلوب:

مناقشة أداء الإدارة الجديدة، وهل توافقها على خطتها التي استخدمتها في توليد الأرباح وما سبب هذه الزيادة الكبيرة في الأرباح.

السؤال السابع عشر: الآتي معلومات من إحدى الشركات الصناعية:

تكلفة أولية	٦٠٠,٠٠٠د
أعباء صناعية متغيرة	٨٠,٠٠٠د

استهلاك بطريقة القسط الثابت:

للآلات الصناعية	٧٠,٠٠٠
لمبنى المصنع	٥٠,٠٠٠

وتتبع طريقة التكلفة الكلية فإن التكلفة القابلة للتخزين هي:

أ. ٦٨٠,٠٠٠ دينار   ب. ٧٣٠,٠٠٠ دينار

ج. ٧٥٠,٠٠٠ دينار   د. ٨٠,٠٠٠ دينار

(المجمع الأمريكي للمحاسبين القانونيين)

الفصل العاشر
التكاليف المعيارية للمواد والأجور والأعباء الإضافية

أهداف الفصل

بعد دراسة هذا الفصل يجب أن تعرف الآتي:

١- أهمية التكاليف المعيارية للمنشآت الصناعية.

٢- فوائد التكاليف المعيارية.

٣- وصف طرق معايرة عناصر التكاليف.

٤- أنواع المعايير.

٥- حساب التكلفة المعيارية للإنتاج.

٦- تحليل انحرافات المواد المباشرة.

٧- تحليل انحرافات الأجور المباشرة.

٨- تحليل انحرافات الأعباء الإضافية حسب طرق التحليل المختلفة.

٩- تحديد الجهة المسؤولة عن الانحرافات المختلفة.

مقدمــــة :

التكاليف المعيارية هي مقياس لما يجب أن تكون عليه تكلفة وحدة المنتج. لذلك ينظر إليها على أنها مقياس، أو نمط، أو أداة لمقارنة التكاليف الفعلية لمعرفة مدى كفاءة وفعالية الأداء الفعلي، ولا تعتبر هذه التكاليف بديلا عن التكاليف الفعلية، لأنها تستخدم لمقارنة التكلفة الفعلية لتحديد الفرق (الانحراف) بينهما، ومعرفة أسبابه وتقديمه للإدارة، لتستخدم نتيجة هذا التحليل في الحكم على كفاءة وفعالية الأداء. ويقصد بالفعالية تحقيق الأهداف المحددة. ويقصد بالكفاءة العلاقة بين المدخلات والمخرجات، وتعتبر تقارير الانحرافات الوسيلة التي تستخدم لتوصيل المعلومات عن كفاءة وفعالية الأداء.

وبهذا المفهوم تعتبر التكاليف المعيارية أداة لتوصيل الأهداف إلى رؤساء الوحدات الإدارية ومرؤوسيها، وبالتالي يصبح هؤلاء في موضع يعرفون به توقعات الإدارة منهم، ويحاولون قدر استطاعتهم تحقيق هذه التوقعات.

ويعتبر استخدام التكاليف المعيارية للحكم على أرقام تكاليف الفترة الجارية أفضل من استخدام التكلفة الفعلية للفترة السابقة للحكم على أرقام التكلفة الفعلية للفترة الجارية، لأن التكلفة المعيارية تعكس توقعات الإدارة حول كفاءة وفعالية أداء الفترة الجارية، أما عند استخدام التكلفة الفعلية للفترة السابقة فإن ذلك يؤدي إلى استخدام أهداف إدارية قديمة، لأن التكلفة الفعلية للفترة السابقة تعكس الأداء الذي حدث في الفترة السابقة وبالتالي قد تحتوي التكلفة الفعلية لتلك السنة على إسراف فعلي، مما يجعل هذه الأرقام غير قادرة للتعبير عن الأداء المرغوب فيه للفترة الجارية، ولذلك فإن مقارنة التكلفة الفعلية للفترة الجارية مع التكلفة الفعلية للفترة السابقة لا يقدم معلومات مفيدة عن أداء الفترة الجارية وكل ما يقدمه هو معرفة اتجاه أو التغير الذي لحق بتكاليف الفترة الجارية بالمقارنة مع تكاليف الفترة السابقة. وكذلك تفشل مقارنة التكاليف الفعلية مع بعضها في إعطاء معلومات مفيدة خصوصا إذا تغيرت أنشطة المنشأة من فترة لأخرى.

عند استخدام أنظمة التكاليف المعيارية نقوم بتحديد تكلفة المواد المباشرة، والأجور المباشرة، والمصروفات الصناعية غير المباشرة مقدما، أي قبل بدء فترة التكاليف، ولهذا يمكن تعريف التكاليف المعيارية على أنها تكاليف محددة مقدما لما يجب أن تكون عليه

تكلفة وحدة المنتج خلال فترة العمل المقبلة، ويتم تحديدها باستخدام بعض الأساليب العلمية والعملية وتهدف إلى مساعدة الإدارة في أغراض التخطيط، والرقابة، واتخاذ القرارات. وحتى تستطيع التكاليف المعيارية خدمة أغراضها لا بد أن تكون المعايير مسايرة لظروف العمل في المنشأة في الحاضر والمستقبل ودون ذلك تكون هذه المعايير غير مناسبة وكأنها معايير منشأة أخرى [1].

ويتم تحديد معايير لكل عناصر التكاليف المستخدمة في إنتاج وحدة المنتج وتتكون التكلفة المعيارية لكل عنصر من شقين: الأول: ويبين الكمية اللازمة من العنصر لإنتاج وحدة المنتج، وتسمى بالكمية المعيارية Standard Quantity، ويتم التعبير عنها باستخدام وحدة قياس كمية العنصر مثل: الكيلو غرام من المواد الخام، والمتر المكعب من الخشب، وساعة العمل المباشر، أما الشق الثاني فهو معيار السعر Standard Price وهذا يمثل سعر وحدة قياس الكمية مثل ثمن الكيلو غرام من المواد، ومعدل أجر ساعة العمل المباشر، وتتحدد التكلفة المعيارية Standard Cost لعنصر التكلفة بضرب الكمية المعيارية في معيار السعر. فمثلا، إذا كانت الكمية المعيارية للمواد الخام اللازمة لإنتاج وحدة المنتج هي ٣ كغم والسعر المعياري للكيلو غرام هو ٢ دينار فتكون التكلفة المعيارية للمادة اللازمة لإنتاج وحدة المنتج هي ٦ دنانير (٣ كغم × ٢ دينار).

وتتحدد التكلفة المعيارية لحجم الإنتاج بضرب عدد وحدات الإنتاج الفعلي في التكلفة المعيارية للوحدة. فمثلا إذا بلغ حجم الإنتاج الفعلي ٢٠،٠٠٠ وحدة، وكانت التكلفة المعيارية للمواد المباشرة للوحدة ٦ دنانير تكون التكلفة المعيارية للمواد المباشرة (٢٠،٠٠٠×٦=) ١٢٠،٠٠٠د. مما سبق نلاحظ أن التكلفة المعيارية للمواد المباشرة للوحدة هي ٦د، ولحجم الإنتاج الفعلي هي ١٢٠،٠٠٠د. وأن الرقم الأخير هو ناتج ضرب التكلفة المعيارية للوحدة في عدد وحدات الإنتاج الفعلي.

---

[1] محمد توفيق بلبع، التكاليف المعيارية لأغراض قياس وضبط التكاليف الفعلية، دار الشباب، القاهرة، ١٩٧٢، ص ٤٣-٤٤.

فوائد استخدام التكاليف المعيارية:

يساعد استخدام التكاليف المعيارية الإدارة في الحكم على كفاءة وفعالية الأداء الفعلي للمنشأة، ويتحقق ذلك عن طريق مقارنة التكاليف الفعلية مع التكاليف المعيارية وتحديد الانحراف بينهما، ويمكن أن يؤدي استخدام التكاليف المعيارية إلى تحقيق الفوائد التالية [1]:

١- المساعدة في التخطيط، ويتم ذلك عن طريق تقديم البيانات اللازمة لإعداد جداول الموازنة التخطيطية، فالموازنة هي تعبير كمي عن الأهداف التي تسعى الإدارة إلى تحقيقها، وتحتوي على تقدير للإيرادات والمصروفات والمركز المالي والنقدي وقائمة الدخل للمنشأة خلال فترة الموازنة، وهذه التقديرات يمكن تقديمها من قبل التكاليف المعيارية على مستوى وحدة المنتج وكمية الإنتاج وذلك لإعداد الموازنة.

٢- المساعدة في الرقابة ويتم ذلك عن طريق تقديم الأساس اللازم لمقارنة التكلفة الفعلية وكشف ما بينهما من انحراف ودراسة أسباب حدوث الانحرافات وتسليط الضوء على الانحرافات الهامة، وبهذا تسهل التكاليف المعيارية تطبيق مبدأ الإدارة بالاستثناء. فتقارير الانحرافات تعتبر تغذية عكسية ضرورية للإدارة للتأكد من أن أنشطة المنشأة تسير حسب الخطط المرسومة.

٣- المساعدة في اكتشاف مناطق عدم الكفاية في استخدام التكاليف ومعالجة أسباب وجودها، وبالتالي تحقق التكاليف المعيارية أهداف برامج خفض التكاليف.

٤- المساعدة في تحقيق وفر في الأعمال الكتابية، فعند إمساك بطاقات مخزون المواد الخام مثلا بالتكلفة المعيارية يتم مسك هذه البطاقات بالكمية فقط بدلا من الكميات والقيم كما في حالة التكلفة الفعلية.

٥- المساعدة في تسهيل عمليات تسعير المنتجات والخدمات لأن تكاليف هذه المنتجات قد حددت مقدما عند إعداد التكاليف المعيارية وعلى أسس علمية، وبالتالي يمكن استخدامها في تسعير أوامر الشراء الخاصة التي تقدم إلى المنشأة

---

[1] J. Batty. <u>Standard Costing</u>, (Macdonald and Evans Ltd,١٩٦٨), Pp.١٠-١١.

وتحديد الأسعار العادية في حالات الاحتكار مثل تسعير قطع غيار السيارات في وكالات تجارة السيارات.

التكاليف المعيارية والموازنات:

تشترك التكاليف المعيارية والموازنات التخطيطية في انهما يعدان مقدما لغرض مقارنة التكلفة الفعلية وأنهما عبارة عن تقديرات لما يجب أن تكون عليه التكاليف، إلا أنهما يختلفان عن بعضهما في أن التكاليف المعيارية تركز على وحدة المنتج أما الموازنة فتركز على حجم النشاط. وقد تحتوي الموازنة على بيانات تقديرية تعد بالاعتماد على الخبرة وتحليل البيانات التاريخية مما يجعلها أقل دقة من التكاليف المعيارية التي تعتمد على تحليل المدخلات والمخرجات بأساليب علمية[1]. على أية حال، كما سنرى فيما بعد، فإن معايرة الكثير من عناصر التكاليف وخصوصا غير المباشرة منها لا تقبل عملية تحليل المدخلات والمخرجات، وبالتالي تتم معايرتها بالاستناد إلى الخبرة وتحليل البيانات التاريخية مما يجعل التكاليف المعيارية والموازنات تحتوي على بيانات تقديرية، وهنا يجب الانتباه إلى أن وصف البيانات بالتقديرية لا يقلل من قيمتها [2] فهي جزء من التكاليف المعيارية، وتستخدم لأغراض مقارنة التكاليف الفعلية، ولكن لزيادة فاعلية البيانات التقديرية في التخطيط والرقابة يجب بذل العناية اللازمة في إعدادها وإلا من الأفضل عدم القيام بذلك.

تعد الموازنة إما لمواجهة حجم النشاط واحد في هذه الحالة تسمى بالموازنة الساكنة Static Budget أو تعد لعدة مستويات نشاط وفي هذه الحالة تعرف بالموازنة المرنة – Flexible Budget ولإعداد هذا النوع من الموازنات لا بد من فصل التكاليف إلى متغيرة وثابتة، فالتكاليف الثابتة هي التي يبقى مجموعها على ما هو عليه بغض النظر عن التغير في حجم النشاط طالما بقي النشاط ضمن المدى المناسب. أما التكاليف المتغيرة فهي

---

[1] عبد الحي مرعي، محاسبة التكاليف لأغراض التخطيط والرقابة، مؤسسة شباب الجامعة ١٩٨٥، ص٤٥٠.

[2] محمد توفيق بليغ، مرجع سابق الذكر، ص ٤٥-٤٧.

التكاليف التي يتغير مجموعها طرديا مع التغير في حجم النشاط ويكون نصيب الوحدة منها ثابتا ويتحدد مبلغها بضرب عدد وحدات النشاط في التكلفة المعيارية لوحدة النشاط [3].

أنواع المعايير:

يوجد في الحياة العملية عدة أنواع من المعايير تختلف عن بعضها من حيث درجة المسموحات الخاصة بالتلف العادي للإنتاج وتعطل الآلات والاعتراف بالعوامل الإنسانية وأهم هذه المعايير هي:

أولا: المعايير النظرية Ideal Standard:

وتعد هذه المعايير في ضوء أقصى درجة كفاءة يمكن تحقيقها ومن ثم تكون المسموحات السابقة عند حدها الأدنى، وهذا يعني بأن هذه المعايير لا تسمح بأي توقف للآلات نتيجة العطل إلا تلك التي تسمح بها المواصفات الفنية للآلات، ولكن لا تسمح بتعطل الآلات المترتبة على عدم توفر الطلب على الإنتاج وتهمل المتطلبات الإنسانية للعمال، مثل السماح لهم بمزاولة العبادة أثناء الدوام الرسمي، وإذا تم اعتبار هذه العوامل تحدد عند مستواها الأدنى. وعندما تستخدم المنشأة هذه المعايير يعلم العمال أنها وضعت لخلق روح التحدي عندهم ويعلمون بأن الإدارة لا تتوقع منهم تحقيقها ومن ثم قد يؤدي استخدام هذا النوع من المعايير إلى خلق حوافز سلبية لدى العمال. مما سبق نرى أن هذا النوع من المعايير غير واقعي وعند استخدامه يجب أن تحتوي الموازنات والمعايير على مخصصات للانحرافات التي ستظهر أثناء التشغيل [1].

ثانيا: المعايير العادية Normal Standards:

هي معايير تستند على مفهوم الطاقة في الأجل الطويل بهدف التغلب على آثار الذبذبات الموسمية في الإنتاج أو التسويق، وهي قابلة للتحقيق إذا تم القيام بالعمل وفقا للظروف المتوافرة في المنشأة وهي تحتوي على قدر واقعي من المسموحات العادية التي لا يمكن تجنب حدوثها في ظل التشغيل وكفاءة العمال المتوقعة.

---

[3] Matz and Usry, op. Cit, p470.

[1] Fishcher and Frank, cost Accounting, Theory and Applications, (south – western Publishing Co.1985), p302.

ثالثا: المعايير المتوقعة Expected Standards:

وهي معايير تعد على أساس ما يتوقع تحقيقه في المستقبل وغالبا ما تعد باستخدام نتائج العمل الفعلية، وبالتالي تحتوي على عوامل عدم الكفاءة والإسراف التي كانت سائدة في الماضي وكان بالإمكان تجنب حدوث بعضها.

من دراسة أنواع المعايير السابقة نرى أن المعايير النظرية والمتوقعة تشكلان طرفي النقيض فالمعايير المثالية لا تعتبر المسموحات الحتمية، أما المعايير المتوقعة فتحتوي على المسموحات بنوعيها المسموح به وغير المسموح به وبين هذين الطرفين تقع المعايير العادية. فالمعيار يعد بناء على ظروف العمل في المنشأة ويحتوي على المسموحات الحتمية التي لا يمكن تجنب حدوثها في ظل ظروف العمل السائدة في المنشأة، وفي هذا المجال يجب أن لا ننساق وراق التسميات العديدة التي وردت في المؤلفات العلمية، بل علينا التركيز على المسموحات التي تجعل المعيار واقعيا.[١]

معايير المواد المباشرة وتحليل انحرافاتها:

تتألف التكلفة المعيارية للمواد المباشرة من معيار كمية ومعيار سعر، لإعداد معيار الكمية تتم دراسة المواصفات الفنية لوحدة المنتج لتحديد احتياجاتها من المواد الخام، وقد يتم ذلك بإجراء القياسات الفنية والهندسية وتدعيم ذلك بإجراء عمليات التشغيل الاختباري لأخذ الظروف العملية السائدة في الحسبان، وفي بعض الحالات قد يتم الاعتماد على الأسلوب الأخير لصعوبة تقدير الكمية بالطرق الهندسية، وهنا يجب أخذ عادم المواد والتالف في الحسبان، فمثلا في صناعة الأثاث، فإنه على الرغم من إمكانية قياس كمية الخشب المستخدمة في صناعة أية قطعة أثاث بدقة إلا أنه يصاحب عملية الإنتاج فقد كمية من الأخشاب أثناء عملية التفصيل، فمثل هذه الكمية المفقودة يجب أن تعتبر ضمن الكمية المعيارية للمواد المباشرة.

في صناعة الشبس مثلا، يتم فقد كمية من البطاطا من جراء عملية التقشير والقلي، لذلك يجب اعتبار هذه الكمية ضمن الكمية المعيارية،ففي هذه الصناعةقد نحتاج عند

---

[١] محمد توفيق بلبع، مرجع سابق الذكر، ص ٥٠.

إنتاج ٥ كغم من الشبس إلى ٧ كغم من البطاطا وهذا يعني بأن الكمية المعيارية تبلغ ١،٤ كغم بطاطا لكل ١ كغم من الشبس وهذا يعني أن فرق وزن المواد وقدره ٠،٤ كغم قد تم اعتباره ضمن الكمية المعيارية لأنه لا يمكن تجنب حدوثه إذا أردنا إنتاج هذا المنتج.

يتم تحديد معيار السعر لوحدة المواد الخام بدراسة أسعار أحدث الكميات المشتراة وتعديل ذلك إذا لزم الأمر لمسايرة الظروف الاقتصادية المتوقعة خلال فترة سريان المعيار فهنا يجب مراعاة التغير في الأسعار الخاصة بالمواد الخام والتغير في القوة الشرائية للعملة.

بعد تحديد معيار الكمية ومعيار السعر تحدد التكلفة المعيارية للمواد المباشرة للوحدة وهي حاصل ضربهما معا. ويتم تحديد التكلفة الفعلية للإنتاج كما سبق ذكره في الفصول السابقة، وفي نهاية كل فترة تتم مقارنة التكلفة الفعلية للإنتاج مع تكلفته المعيارية لكشف الانحراف بينهما. وهنا قد نجد أن سبب حدوث الانحراف يعود إلى أن الكمية الفعلية للمواد مختلفة عن الكمية المعيارية وهذا الانحراف يعرف بانحراف الكمية أو إنحراف الاستخدام Quantity or Usage Variance. وقد يعود الانحراف إلى اختلاف السعر الفعلي عن السعر المعياري وهذا الانحراف يعرف بانحراف السعر Price Variance [1] بطبيعة الحال، إذا كانت الكمية الفعلية أكبر من الكمية المعيارية أو كان السعر الفعلي أكبر من السعر المعياري، تكون الأمور قد سارت في غير صالح المنشأة، لذلك توصف الانحرافات في هذه الحالات بأنها غير محببة، والعكس إذا كانت الكميات والأسعار الفعلية أقل من المعيارية [1] ولتوضيح تحليل انحرافات عنصر المواد المباشرة سيتم الاعتماد على البيانات التالية:

مثال (١):

تبلغ الكمية المعيارية للمواد المباشرة اللازمة لإنتاج الطاولة ٢ مترا مربعا من الخشب ويبلغ السعر المعياري للمتر منه ١،٢٥د. خلال الفترة تم إنتاج ٢،٠٠٠ طاولة واستخدم في سبيل ذلك ٤،١٠٠ متر مربع من الخشب تكلفتها الفعلية ٤،٩٢٠د.

---

[1] Stanely B. Henrici, standard costs Manufacturing, (McGraw-Hill Book Co., ١٩٦٦) Pp.٩٩-١٠٥.

[1] Fisher and Frank, Op. Cit, P. ٣٠٣.

المطلوب: تحليل انحرافات المواد المباشرة.

الحل:

انحراف السعر أو الإنفاق:

يتطلب حساب انحراف سعر المواد المباشرة تحديد النقطة الزمنية التي يتم عندها حساب هذا الانحراف، وجرت العادة أن يتم حسابه عند شراء المواد أو عند استخدام هذه المواد.

يعتبر الأسلوب الأول أكثر فعالية في خدمة غرض الرقابة لأنه يؤدي إلى معرفة الانحراف عند حدوثه بدلا من تأجيل ذلك إلى أن يتم استخدام تلك المواد، إضافة إلى ذلك، يؤدي استخدام الأسلوب الأول إلى وفر في الأعمال الكتابية للمحاسبة على مخزون المواد الخام لأن ذلك يساعد على مسك بطاقات المواد بالكميات فقط بدلا من الكميات والأسعار والقيم، وفي هذه الحالة يتم تعريف انحراف السعر على أنه الفرق بين السعر الفعلي والسعر المعياري ضرب الكمية المشتراة ويحدد باستخدام المعادلة التالية:

انحراف السعر = (السعر الفعلي – السعر المعياري) × الكمية المشتراة

= (س ف – س م) × ك ف

حيث أن:

س ف = السعر الفعلي

ك ف = الكمية الفعلية

س م = السعر المعياري

وبفك القوس تصبح المعادلة السابقة كالتالي:

= س ف × ك ف – س م × ك ف

س ف × ك ف وتساوي التكلفة الفعلية، س م × ك ف وتساوي كمية فعلية مضروبة في السعر المعياري. وبالتعويض نصل الى:

$4,920 - (1,25 \times 4100)$

= 205د (مفضل)

يحدد السعر الفعلي بقسمة التكلفة الفعلية على السعر الفعلي. ووصف انحراف السعر بأنه مفضل لأن سعر الشراء الفعلي كان أقل من سعر الشراء المعياري حيث بلغ السعر الفعلي (٤١٠٠/٤,٩٢٠) ١,٢٠ دينار. وأن السعر المعياري ١,٢٥ دينار. تقع مسؤولية انحراف السعر على عاتق إدارة المشتريات لأنها المسؤولة عن شراء المواد بأقل الأسعار الممكنة مع المحافظة على جودة المواد المشتراة. وفي حالات معينة عندما تضطر هذه الإدارة إلى الشراء المفاجئ نتيجة لضغط إدارة أخرى عندها تتحمل الأخيرة مسؤولية انحراف السعر.

وعند حساب الانحراف عند استخدام المواد يتم استبدال الكمية المستخدمة بدلا من الكمية المشتراة في المعادلة السابقة.

انحراف كمية (استخدام) المواد Quantity Variance:

يقوم هذا الانحراف بقياس الفرق بين كمية المواد الفعلية المستخدمة في الإنتاج وكمية المواد المعيارية اللازمة للإنتاج الفعلي وتسعير الفرق بالسعر المعياري للمواد. ويتم حسابه بموجب المعادلة التالية:

انحراف كمية المواد = (الكمية الفعلية – الكمية المعيارية) × السعر المعياري

$$= (ك ف - ك م) × س م$$

$$= (٤,١٠٠-٢,٠٠٠×٢) ×١,٢٥$$

$$= ١٠٠×١,٢٥ =١٢٥ (غير مفضل)$$

حددت الكمية المعيارية للمواد بضرب عدد وحدات الإنتاج الفعلي في الكمية المعيارية لوحدة المنتج.

وصف الانحراف بأنه غير مفضل لأن الكمية الفعلية المستخدمة في الإنتاج كانت أكبر من الكمية المعيارية اللازمة للإنتاج، وعادة تقع مسؤولية هذا الانحراف على عاتق إدارة الإنتاج لأنها المسؤولة عن كفاءة استخدام المواد المباشرة عندما يتم توفيرها حسب الجودة المحددة، أما إذا كانت جودة المواد الخام غير مطابقة للمواصفات فإن المسؤول عن شراء هذا المواد هو الذي يتحمل مسؤولية هذا الانحراف.

الانحراف الكلي:

ويمثل هذا الانحراف الفرق بين التكلفة الفعلية للمواد المباشرة المشتراة والتكلفة المعيارية للمواد المباشرة المستخدمة في الإنتاج. تحدد التكلفة المعيارية للمواد بضرب الكمية المعيارية لوحدة الإنتاج في عدد الوحدات المنتجة في السعر المعياري لوحدة قياس الكمية.

وهذه تساوي (٢ متر × ٢,٠٠٠ وحدة × ١,٢٥)   = ٥,٠٠٠ دينار.

الانحراف الكلي للمواد = ٢ × ٢,٠٠٠× ١,٢٥- ٤,١٠٠×١,٢=٨٠د (مفضل).

ويتم تعريف الانحراف الكلي على أنه مجموع انحراف السعر وانحراف الكمية.

٢٠٥= د (مفضل) +١٢٥د (غير مفضل) = ٨٠ د (مفضل)

ويمكن إيضاح تحليل انحرافات المواد المباشرة كما في الشكل (١٠-١)

ك م × س م	ك ف × س م	ك ف × س ف
١,٢٥×٤,٠٠٠	٤,١٠٠	١,٢٠×٤,١٠٠
= ٥,٠٠٠	١,٢٥×	٤,٩٢٠=
انحراف الكمية = -٥,١٥٢	٥,١٢٥ = ٤,٩٢٠- = انحراف السعر	٥,١٢٥
٥,٠٠٠		
(م غ) د ١٢٥=		(م) د ٢٠٥=
انحراف كلي = ٤,٩٢٠ – ٥,٠٠٠ = ٨٠ د (م)	

شكل (١٠-١) تحليل انحرافات المواد المباشرة

من دراسة البيانات السابقة نجد أن كمية المواد الخام المشتراة تساوي الكمية الفعلية المستخدمة في الإنتاج لذلك قمنا بحساب الانحراف الكلي.

معايير الأجور المباشرة وتحليل انحرافاتها:

تتكون التكلفة المعيارية للأجور المباشرة من معيار الكمية الذي يعكس ساعات العمل المباشرة اللازمة لإنتاج وحدة المنتج، ومعيار معدل الأجر الذي يمثل معدل أجرة ساعة

العمل المباشرة. يتم تحديد ساعات العمل المباشرة بالوقوف على قدرة التجهيزات الآلية المستخدمة وخبرة وكفاءة العمال. ويقدر الوقت اللازم إما بدراسة الحركة والزمن أو بالتشغيل الاختباري. وعند استخدام هذه الأساليب يجب الاعتماد على عمال من ذوي خبرة تزيد عن المستوى المتوسط حتى يحتاج تحقيق المعيار إلى جهد وكفاءة أعلى من المستوى السائد حاليا [1]. وكذلك يجب الأخذ في الحسبان الوقت الضائع نتيجة للحاجات الشخصية وتوقف الإنتاج، فمثلا عند تقدير الزمن المعياري اللازم لإنتاج الطاولة يجب أن يتم تقدير الزمن اللازم لتنفيذ كل عملية لازمة لإنتاجها، وذلك بقياس الزمن الذي يستغرقه العمال في تنفيذها، وبتكرار العملية يمكن اعتبار متوسط الزمن معيار الزمن اللازم لإنجاز تلك العملية وبجمع ما تستغرقه كل العمليات يتم التوصل إلى الوقت المعياري اللازم لإنتاج الطاولة وهذا الوقت يمثل معيار الكمية.

ويتحدد معدل أجر ساعة العمل المباشرة بقسمة إجمالي الأجر المباشر على عدد ساعات العمل المعيارية خلال العام، ويشتمل الأجر المباشر على إجمالي الأجر بالإضافة إلى مساهمة المنشأة في التأمينات الاجتماعية والصحية. ويمكن أن يتم حساب معدل لكل عامل على حدة أو لكل فئة مهارة على حدة أو لكل قسم، وغالبا ما يفضل استخدام الأسلوب الثاني أو الأخير لتوفير الأعمال الكتابية، وعند استخدام عدة فئات من العمال يتم اعتبار المتوسط المرجح لأجورهم كمعيار لمعدل أجر ساعة العمل المباشرة، ولحساب المتوسط المرجح يتم ضرب عدد ساعات عمل كل فئة في معدل أجرها وقسمة المبلغ الناتج على عدد ساعات العمل لكل الفئات. ولتوضيح ذلك افترض توفر البيانات التالية:

تكلفة الأجور	معدل أجر الساعة	ساعات العمل	الفئة
٧د	١,٧٥د	٤	أ
٦د	٣د	٢	ب
٧د	٣,٥د	٢	ج
٢٠د		٨	المجموع

[1] Fisher and Frank, op. cit, Pp.٣٠٥-٣٠٧.

المتوسط المرجح لمعدل أجر الساعة = ٢٠د ÷ ٨ = ٢,٥ د لكل ساعة عمل مباشرة (س ع م). ويتحدد معدل أجر الساعة لعمال مركز التكاليف كما في الجدول (١٠-١). لقد تم استخدام ساعات العمل المباشرة السنوية والأجور المباشرة السنوية لتجنب الذبذبات الشهرية في ساعات العمل، وخصم من ساعات العمل أيام الجمع، والعطلات الرسمية، وتخفيض ساعات العمل في شهر رمضان الكريم، بالإضافة إلى اعتبار أوقات تعطل العمل.

جدول (١٠-١)
تقدير معدل أجرة الساعة المباشرة كمركز إنتاج (أ)

فئة (ج)	فئة (ب)	فئة (أ)	
٩	٧	٨	١- عدد العمال
١,٩٩٠	١,٩٩٠	١,٩٩٠	٢- عدد ساعات العمل السنوية للعامل
١٧,٩١٠	١٣,٩٣٠	١٥,٩٢٠	٣- عدد ساعات العمل المباشرة السنوية
٥٣,٧٣٠	٣٥,٥٢٢	٢٢,٢٨٨د	٤- الأجور التقديرية السنوية
٣د	٢,٥٥د	١,٤٠د	٥- أجرة الساعة
٠,٥٠د	٠,٤٥د	٠,٣٥د	٦- المزايا النقدية والعينية
٣,٥د	٣د	١,٧٥د	٧- معدل أجر الساعة

ولبيان طريقة حساب انحرافات الأجور المباشرة يتم الاعتماد على البيانات التالية:

مثال (٢):

بالإضافة إلى المعلومات الواردة في المثال (١) افترض أن ساعات العمل المعيارية لإنتاج الوحدة هي ٨ س ع م. وأن معدل أجر الساعة المعياري هو ٢,٥د/س ع م. وخلال فترة التكاليف تم استخدام ١٥,٥٠٠ س ع م وبلغت تكلفتها الفعلية ٤٠,٣٠٠د أي أن معدل أجر الساعة الفعلي هو ٢,٦د/س ع م.
المطلوب: تحليل انحرافات الأجور المباشرة.

الحل:

يتم تحليل انحرافات الأجور المباشرة بنفس طريقة تحليل انحرافات المواد المباشرة ولكن بعد استبدال كلمة المواد بساعات العمل المباشرة وأسعار المواد المباشرة بمعدلات الأجور المباشرة. ويحدد الانحراف الكلي بمقارنة الأجور الفعلية مع الأجور المعيارية اللازمة لكمية الإنتاج الفعلي. وقد يعزى وجوده إلى وجود فرق بين معدل الأجر الفعلي ومعدل الأجر المعياري وبين ساعات العمل الفعلية وساعات العمل المعيارية وتحسب هذه الانحرافات كالتالي:

الانحراف الكلي للأجور المباشرة:

يمثل هذا الانحراف الفرق بين التكلفة الفعلية والتكلفة المعيارية للأجور المباشرة ويساوي:

٤٠,٣٠٠ – (٢,٠٠٠ وحدة × ٨ ساعات × ٢,٥ د)

= ٤٠,٣٠٠ – ٤٠,٠٠٠   =٣٠٠د (غير مفضل)

ولأن التكلفة الفعلية أكبر من التكلفة المعيارية لذلك يكون الانحراف في غير صالح المنشأة.

انحراف معدل (إنفاق) الأجور المباشرة:

ويمثل هذا الانحراف الفرق بين معدل الأجور الفعلية ومعدل الأجور المعيارية مضروبا في عدد ساعات العمل الفعلية، وإذا كان المعدل الفعلي أقل من المعدل المعياري سيكون الانحراف مفضلا، والعكس صحيح إذا كان المعدل الفعلي أعلى من المعدل المعياري ويحسب هذا الانحراف كالتالي:

انحراف معدل الأجر = (معدل الأجر الفعلي – معدل الأجر المعياري) × ساعات العمل الفعلية

= (م ف – م م) س ع ف

وبفتح القوسين نجد أن: م ف × س ع ف – م م × س ع ف

= ٤٠,٣٠٠ – (٢,٥×١٥٥٠٠)

= ١,٥٥٠د. (غير مفضل)

انحراف كمية (كفاءة) الأجور المباشرة:

يقيس هذا الانحراف أثر اختلاف ساعات العمل المباشرة الفعلية عن ساعات العمل المعيارية للإنتاج الفعلي ويتم حسابه بموجب المعادلة كالتالي:

انحراف كمية الأجور = (ساعات العمل الفعلية – ساعات العمل المعيارية) × معدل الأجر المعياري

= (س ع ف – س ع م) م م

= (١٥,٥٠٠) – ((٨×٢,٠٠٠)) ×٢,٥ = ١٢٥٠ (مفضل).

لقد تم تحديد ساعات العمل المعيارية بضرب عدد وحدات الإنتاج الفعلي في ساعات العمل المعيارية للوحدة. وان ساعات العمل الفعلية قد وردت في السؤال. هذا الانحراف مفضل لأن ساعات العمل الفعلية كانت أقل من ساعات العمل المعيارية. تقع مسؤولية هذا الانحراف على عاتق إدارة الإنتاج لأنها المسؤولة عن توجيه العمال أمام مسؤولية انحراف معدل الأجور فتقع على عاتق الجهة التي تقوم بتعيين العمال.

الانحراف الكلي = انحراف معدل الأجور + إنحرا ف كمية الأجور

= ١,٠٥٠د (غ م) + ١,٢٥٠د (م) = ٣٠٠= د (غ م)

ويمكن توضيح انحرافات الأجور المباشرة كما في الشكل (١٠-٢):

س ع ف × م ف	س ع ف × م م	س ع م × م م
١٥,٥٠٠ ×٢,٦	٢,٥× ١٥,٥٠٠	٢,٥×٨×٢,٠٠٠
=٤٠,٣٠٠	= ٣٨,٧٥٠	= ٤٠,٠٠٠
انحراف الإنفاق =		انحرا ف الكفاءة =
٤٠,٣٠٠ –٣٨,٧٥٠		٤٠,٠٠٠-٣٨,٧٥٠
١,٠٥٠د(غ م) =		=١,٢٥٠ د (م)
الانحراف الكلي = ٤٠,٣٠٠ – ٤٠,٠٠٠ =٣٠٠د(غ م)		

الشكل (١٠-٢) تحليل انحرافات الأجور المباشرة

معايير عناصر التكاليف غير المباشرة وتحليل انحرافاتها:

لقد تمت التعرف على طبيعة هذه العناصر في الفصول من هذا الكتاب، ورأينا أنها تضم العديد من العناصر التي يختلف سلوكها تجاه تغيرات حجم الإنتاج، ومنها من لا يتغير مع تغير حجم الإنتاج ومنها من يتغير طرديا مع التغير في حجم الإنتاج، ومنها من يجمع بين الصفتين السابقتين، لذلك يلزم لتقدير قيمتها الاعتماد على الخبرة الشخصية والأساليب الإحصائية ومراعاة ظروف العمل خلال فترة سريان المعايير. وهنا يجب التمييز بين التكاليف الصناعية غير المباشرة (الأعباء الإضافية) المتغيرة والثابتة، لأن ذلك يساعد في إعداد الموازنة المرنة، تعد الموازنة المرنة لأي حجم نشاط بضرب وحدات النشاط التي تمثله في معدل تحميل الأعباء الإضافية المتغيرة ثم إضافة إجمالي قيمة الأعباء الإضافية الثابتة. وتأخذ الموازنة المرنة شكل المعادلة التالية:

إجمالي التكاليف غير المباشرة = الأعباء الإضافية الثابتة +معدل تحميل الأعباء الإضافية المتغيرة × وحدات النشاط

وهذه المعادلة تعني أن الأعباء الإضافية الثابتة في أي موازنة لاي مستوى نشاط لا تتغير طالما أن هذه المستويات تقع ضمن المدى الملائم.

ولتوضيح ذلك افترض أن التكلفة المتغيرة لوحدة المنتج هي ٥ دنانير وأن التكاليف الثابتة لمستوى الطاقة العادية هي ٥٠,٠٠٠ دينار وأن المدى الملائم لحجم الطاقة يتراوح بين ٢٠,٠٠٠ ساعة إلى ٣٠,٠٠٠ ساعة وأردنا أن نعد موازنة لهذين المستويين ومستوى ٢٥,٠٠٠ ساعة فإن الموازنة المرنة ستكون كما في الجدول (١٠-٢). لاحظ أن الأعباء الإضافية الثابتة بلغت ٥٠,٠٠٠د عند كل مستوى من المستويات الثلاثة. وتم تحديد التكاليف المتغيرة تحت كل مستوى بضرب عدد الوحدات في ٥ دنانير. والآن أفترض أن مستوى الطاقة (حجم المقام) هو ٢٥,٠٠٠ وحدة فإن معدل تحميل الأعباء الإضافية سيكون كالتالي:

الموازنة المرنة للسنة التقديرية المنتهية في ١٩٩٠/١٢/٣١

بيان	الوحدة	٢٠,٠٠٠	٢٥,٠٠٠	٣٠,٠٠٠
تكاليف متغيرة	٥	١٠٠,٠٠٠	١٢٥,٠٠٠	١٥٠,٠٠٠
تكاليف ثابتة		٥٠,٠٠٠	٥٠,٠٠٠	٥٠,٠٠٠
إجمالي التكاليف		١٥٠,٠٠٠	١٧٥,٠٠٠	٢٠٠,٠٠٠

$$\text{معدل تحميل الأعباء الإضافية المتغيرة} = \frac{١٢٥,٠٠٠}{٢٥,٠٠٠} = ٥\text{د وحدة}$$

$$\text{معدل تحميل الأعباء الإضافية الثابتة} = \frac{٥٠,٠٠٠}{٢٥,٠٠٠} = ٢\text{ وحدة}$$

معدل تحميل الأعباء الإضافية الكلي = ٥ + ٢ = ٧د للوحدة

لقد تم فصل المعدل الكلي إلى معدل للأعباء المتغيرة وآخر للأعباء الثابتة لتسهيل تحليل الانحرافات.

تحليل انحرافات الأعباء الإضافية:

يتم تحليل انحرافات الأعباء الإضافية بعدة طرق تأخذ أسمائها من عدد الانحرافات التي يتم حسابها، لذلك نجد طريقة الأربعة انحرافات وطريقة الثلاثة انحرافات وطريقة الانحرافين، ولتوضيح هذه الطرق سيتم الاعتماد على البيانات التالية:

مثال (٣):

الآتي بيانات تخص إحدى المنتجات الصناعية.

أولا: البيانات المعيارية:

ساعات العمل المباشرة	= ٨ ساعات / وحدة
معدل تحمل الأعباء المتغيرة	٥د/س ع م
معدل تحميل الأعباء الثابتة	٢د/ س ع م

وكانت الأعباء الثابتة التقديرية ٥٠,٠٠٠ دينار والطاقة العادية للشركة ٢٥,٠٠٠ ساعة عمل مباشرة. ومعادلة الموازنة المرنة هي:

إجمالي التكاليف = ٥٠,٠٠٠ د + ٥ د /س ع م

ثانيا: البيانات الفعلية:

حجم الإنتاج الفعلي	٢,٠٠٠ وحدة
ساعات العمل المباشرة	١٥,٥٠٠ ساعة
الأعباء الإضافية المتغيرة	٨٠,٦٠٠ د
الأعباء الإضافية الثابتة	٥٤,٠٠٠ د

المطلوب:

تحليل الانحرافات الخاصة بالأعباء الإضافية.

الانحراف الكلي:

يعمل هذا الانحراف على بيان الفرق بين الأعباء الإضافية الفعلية والأعباء الإضافية المعيارية المحملة على الإنتاج الفعلي. ونحدد الأعباء الإضافية الفعلية بجمع الأعباء الإضافية المتغيرة الفعلية والأعباء الإضافية الثابتة الفعلية وهي في هذا المثال تساوي ١٣٤,٦٠٠ د (٨٠,٦٠٠ + ٥٤,٠٠٠ د) وتحدد الأعباء الإضافية المعيارية المحملة على الإنتاج حسب المعادلة الآتية:

الأعباء المعيارية المحملة = عدد وحدات الإنتاج الفعلي × ساعات العمل المباشرة المعيارية للوحدة × معدل التحميل الكلي للأعباء الإضافية

= ٢،٠٠٠ وحدة × ٨ ساعات × (د٥ + د٢) = ١١٢،٠٠٠ دينار

لاحظ أن هذا المبلغ يتكون من ٨٠،٠٠٠د أعباء متغيرة معيارية (= ٢،٠٠٠× ٨ × ٥ د). والباقي وقدره ٣٢،٠٠٠ د تكاليف ثابتة معيارية (٢٠٠٠ وحدة ×٨ × د٢)

وعليه فإن الانحراف الكلي للأعباء الإضافية يساوي:

= الأعباء الفعلية – التكاليف المعيارية للأعباء الإضافية

= ١٣٤،٦٠٠ – ١١٢،٠٠٠

= د٢٢،٦٠٠ (غ م)

وكان الانحراف غير محبب لأن الأعباء الفعلية أكبر من الأعباء المعيارية. ويمكن تحليل هذا الانحراف الى أربعة انحرافات كالتالي:

أولا: طريقة الأربعة انحرافات:

بموجب هذه الطريقة يخصص انحرافان للأعباء المتغيرة وانحرافان للأعباء الثابتة، وسيتم حسابها على التوالي:

١ – انحرافات الأعباء المتغيرة:

يتم تحميل الأعباء المتغيرة على الإنتاج الفعلي باستخدام معدل تحميل الأعباء المتغيرة وعليه تكون الأعباء المحملة على الإنتاج الفعلي كالتالي:

٢،٠٠٠ وحدة × ٨ ساعات × د٥ = ٨٠،٠٠٠ دينار

وعليه يكون الفرق بين الأعباء الإضافية المتغيرة الفعلية والأعباء الإضافية المتغيرة المعيارية المحملة على الإنتاج ٦٠٠ دينار (= ٨٠،٦٠٠ - ٨٠،٠٠٠). ويعرف باسم انحراف الموازنة أو الانحراف الكلي. ويتم تحليل الانحراف الكلي للمصروفات المتغيرة إلى انحرافين هما انحراف الإنفاق وانحراف الكفاءة. ولأن هذه الانحرافات تتعلق بالمصروفات المتغيرة لذلك فإن طريقة حساب هذه الانحرافات تشبه تماما طريقة حساب انحرافات المواد المباشرة والأجور المباشرة.

انحراف السعر أو الإنفاق:

يشير السعر هنا إلى معدل تحميل الأعباء الإضافية، وبالرجوع إلى انحرافات المواد المباشرة والأجور المباشرة فإنه يمكن تعريف هذا الانحراف على أنه الفرق بين معدل التحميل الفعلي ومعدل التحميل المعياري ضرب ساعات العمل الفعلية. ويحدد معدل التحميل الفعلي للأعباء بقسمة الأعباء الإضافية الفعلية على ساعات العمل الفعلية ويساوي (٨٠,٦٠٠ د ÷ ١٥,٥٠٠ ساعة = ٥,٢ د/س ع م. ويحدد الانحراف بموجب المعادلة التالية:

انحراف الإنفاق = (معدل التحميل المعياري – معدل التحميل الفعلي) × ساعات العمل الفعلية

= (م ت م – م ت ف) م ع ف

= (٥ - ٥,٢) × ١٥,٥٠٠ = ٣,١٠٠ د(غير مفضل)

يعرف ناتج ضرب معدل التحميل المعياري بساعات العمل الفعلية بمبلغ الموازنة للأعباء المتغيرة لساعات العمل الفعلية، لذلك يمكن تعريف انحراف الإنفاق على أنه الفرق بين التكلفة الفعلية ومبلغ الموازنة المرنة لساعات العمل الفعلية فالموازنة المرنة تساوي (١٥,٥٠٠ ساعة × ٥د = ٧٧,٥٠٠ د) وأن الأعباء الفعلية تساوي ٨٠,٦٠٠ د لذلك فإن انحراف السعر يساوي (٨٠,٦٠٠ – ٧٧,٥٠٠=٣,١٠٠د (غير محبب). هذه المعادلة أسهل من السابقة لأنها لا تتطلب حساب معدل التحميل الفعلي للأعباء الإضافية.

يحدث انحراف الإنفاق نتيجة اختلاف أسعار البنود غير المباشرة المتغيرة عما هو مخطط لها. نتيجة لاختلاف معدلات الأجور، أو اختلاف أسعار المرافق والخدمات، أو اختلاف تكاليف قطع الغيار..الخ.

انحراف الكفاءة:

يقوم هذا الانحراف بتقييم أثر اختلاف ساعات العمل الفعلية المستخدمة كأساس لقياس النشاط عن ساعات العمل المعيارية المطلوبة للإنتاج الفعلي وتسعير هذا الفرق

بمعدل التحميل المعياري للأعباء الإضافية المتغيرة، لاحظ أن هذا الانحراف يستخدم ساعات العمل التي استخدمت في حساب انحراف كمية الأجور المباشرة لأن الأعباء الإضافية المتغيرة يتم تحميلها باستخدام ساعات العمل المباشرة. ويتم حساب هذا الانحراف بموجب المعادلة التالية:

انحراف الكفاءة = (ساعات العمل الفعلية – ساعات العمل المعيارية) × معدل تحميل الأعباء الإضافية المتغيرة

= (س ع ف – س ع م) م م ت م

= (١٥,٥٠٠ - ٢,٠٠٠ ×٨) ×٥ = ٢,٥٠٠ د (مفضل)

وحددت ساعات العمل المعيارية بضرب عدد وحدات الإنتاج في ساعات العمل اللازمة للوحدة. وبجمع انحراف الإنفاق وانحراف الكفاءة نتوصل إلى الانحراف الكلي أو انحراف الموازنة. [١] ويمكن إيضاح تحليل انحرافات الأعباء الإضافية المتغيرة كما هو وارد في الشكل (١٠-٣). لاحظ أن العمود الأيمن ضرب الكمية الفعلية في السعر الفعلي وان العمود الأوسط ضرب الكمية الفعلية في السعر المعياري وان العمود الأخير ضرب الكمية المعيارية في السعر المعياري.

الموازنة المرنة لساعات العمل المعيارية	الموازنة المرنة لساعات العمل الفعلية	التكلفة الفعلية
= س ع م × م م	= س ع ف × م م	= س ع ف × م ف
= ١٦,٠٠٠ × ٥	= ١٥,٠٠٠ ×٥	= ١٥,٥٠٠ × ٥,٢
= ٨٠,٠٠٠	= ٧٧٥٠٠	= ٨٠,٦٠٠
انحراف كفاءة = = ٨٠,٠٠٠- ٧٧,٥٠٠ =٢٥٠٠د(م)		انحراف الإنفاق =٨٠,٦٠٠-٧٧,٥٠٠ ٣,١٠٠د(غ م)
انحراف كلي (موازنة) = ٨٠,٦٠٠ -٨٠,٠٠٠ = ٦٠٠ د(غ)		

شكل (١٠-٣) تحليل انحرافات الأعباء الإضافية المتغيرة

---

[١] Morsse and Rath, Cost Accounting, (Addison-Wesley Publishing Co, ١٩٨٦),Pp. ٤٦٤-٤٦٦.

٢ - تحليل انحرافات الأعباء الثابتة:

يتم تحميل الأعباء الثابتة على وحدات الإنتاج باستخدام معدل التحميل المعياري وخلال الفترة تم تحميل الإنتاج الفعلي بالتكاليف المعيارية التالية:

٢,٠٠٠ وحدة × ٨ ساعات × ٢ د = ٣٢,٠٠٠ دينار

ويعرف الانحراف الكلي للأعباء الثابتة على أنه الفرق بين التكلفة الفعلية الثابتة والتكاليف الثابتة المعيارية التي تم تحميلها على الإنتاج ويساوي:

٥٤,٠٠٠ - ٣٢,٠٠٠ = ٢٢,٠٠٠ د (غير مفضل)

وعند تحليل هذا الانحراف يصعب تطبيق النموذج السابق المستخدم في تحليل انحرافات الأعباء المتغيرة لأن التكاليف الثابتة عند مستوى ساعات العمل المعيارية وساعات العمل الفعلية متساوية، ومن ثم يكون انحراف كفاءة الأعباء الإضافية الثابتة صفرا[1]. ومع ذلك يمكن تقسيم الانحراف الكلي للأعباء الثابتة إلى انحرافين هما انحراف الإنفاق، وانحراف الحجم، وسيتم مناقشة هذه الانحرافات كالتالي:

انحراف الإنفاق:

يشير انحراف الإنفاق إلى اختلاف معدل التحميل الفعلي عن معدل التحميل المعياري لساعات العمل الفعلية لذلك فهو يساوي الفرق بين الأعباء الثابتة الفعلية والأعباء الثابتة المخططة لمستوى ساعات العمل الفعلية ويساوي:

٥٤,٠٠٠ - ٥٠,٠٠٠ = ٤,٠٠٠ د (غير مفضل)

لاحظ أن التكاليف المخططة لمستوى ١٥,٥٠٠ ساعة هي نفسها المخططة لأي مستوى نشاط آخر ضمن المدى الملائم لذلك تشبه طريقة احتساب هذا الانحراف الطريقة التي استخدمت في حساب معدل انحراف إنفاق الأعباء المتغيرة وأن الفارق الوحيد بينهما هو أن المعدل المعياري يحسب بقسمة الأعباء الثابتة المخططة وقدرها ٥٠,٠٠٠ د على عدد ساعات العمل الفعلية وليست المعيارية. وهذا الانحراف قد ينتج عن زيادة معدلات

---

[1] Morese and Rath, <u>Cost Accounting</u>, (ÖÖÖAddison- Wesley Publishing Co, ١٩٨٦), Pp. ٨٥٠-٨٥٤.

الأجور غير المباشرة أو نتيجة التغير في الاستهلاك الناتج عـن شراء آلات جديـدة أو لارتفاع أجرة مبنى المصنع..الخ.

انحراف الحجم:

ويحدد انحراف الحجم لمعرفة الفرق بين التكاليف الثابتة المخططة ومقدارها ٥٠,٠٠٠ د والتكاليف الثابتة التي تم تحميلها على الإنتاج ومقدارها ٣٢,٠٠٠د كما تم حسابها أعلاه وهذا يعني أن انحراف الحجم يسـاوي ١٨,٠٠٠د (غير مفضل)، لقد كان هذا الانحراف غير مفضل لأن الشركة لم تستطع استغلال طاقتها العاديـة وبالتالي كانت التكاليف الثابتة المحملة على الإنتاج أقل مـن التكاليف المخططة عند مستوى الطاقة العادية. وقد يحسب انحراف الحجم باستخدام المعادلة الآتية:

انحراف الحجم = (ساعات العمل للطاقة العادية – ساعات العمل المعيارية للإنتاج) × معدل تحميل الأعباء الإضافية الثابتة

= (٢٥,٠٠٠ – (٢,٠٠٠ ×٨))×٢د = ١٨,٠٠٠د (غير مفضل)

ويتم تحليل انحرافات التكاليف الثابتة كما في الشكل (١٠-٤)

أعباء ثابتة محملة	أعباء ثابتة مخططة	أعباء فعلية
	= ٥٠,٠٠٠	
= س ع م × م ت م		= س ع ف × م ت ف
= ٣٢,٠٠٠		= ٥٤,٠٠٠
انحراف الحجم=٥٠,٠٠٠-٣٢,٠٠٠		انحراف إنفاق = ٥٤,٠٠٠-٥٠,٠٠٠=
= ١٨,٠٠٠د (غ م)		٤,٠٠٠د (غ م)
انحراف كلي = ٥٤,٠٠٠– ٣٢,٠٠٠ = ٢٢,٠٠٠د (غ م)		

شكل (١٠-٤) تحليل انحرافات الأعباء الثابتة

ثانيا: طريقة الثلاثة انحرافات:

تقوم هذه الطريقة بجمع انحراف إنفاق الأعباء المتغيرة وانحراف إنفاق الأعباء الثابتة التي تم حسابهما في طريقة الأربعة انحرافات معا. أما الانحرافات الأخرى وهي انحراف الكفاءة وانحراف الحجم فتبقى على ما كانت عليه تحت طريقة الأربعة انحرافات، وبالاعتماد على بيانات المثال (٣) الواردة أعلاه تكون انحرافات الأعباء الإضافية حسب طريقة الثلاثة انحرافات كالتالي:

١ - انحراف الإنفاق:

يعرف هذا الانحراف على أنه الفرق بين الأعباء الإضافية الفعلية والموازنة المرنة لساعات العمل الفعلية. وباستخدام معادلة الموازنة المرنة تحسب التكاليف غير المباشرة لموازنة ساعات العمل الفعلية كالتالي:

الموازنة المرنة لساعات العمل الفعلية = التكاليف الثابتة + د٥ × ساعات العمل الفعلية

$$= \text{٥٠,٠٠٠} + \text{٥} \times \text{١٥,٥٠٠} = \text{١٢٧,٥٠٠د}$$

أما التكاليف غير المباشرة الفعلية فإنها تتكون من مجموع التكاليف الثابتة الفعلية والمتغيرة الفعلية وتساوي (٨٠,٦٠٠ تكاليف متغيرة + ٥٤,٠٠٠ د تكاليف ثابتة) ١٣٤,٦٠٠ دينار.

انحراف الإنفاق = ١٣٤,٦٠٠ – ١٢٧,٥٠٠ = ٧,١٠٠د (غ م).

وعند مقارنة هذا المبلغ مع انحرافات طريقة الأربعة انحرافات نجد أنه عبارة عن٤,٠٠٠ دينار انحراف إنفاق الأعباء الثابتة و٣,٠٠٠ دينار انحراف إنفاق الأعباء المتغيرة.

٢ - انحراف الكفاءة: وهو كما تم حسابه تحت طريقة الأربعة انحرافات.

٣ - انحراف الحجم: وهو الآخر كما تم حسابه تحت طريقة الأربعة انحرافات ويمكن بيان الانحرافات المستخدمة في طريقة الثلاثة انحرافات كما في الشكل (١٠-٥).

التكاليف المعيارية للإنتاج الفعلي	موازنة مرنة لساعات العمل المعيارية	موازنة مرنة لساعات العمل الفعلية	تكاليف فعلية
٨٠,٠٠٠	٨٠,٠٠٠	٧٧,٥٠٠	متغيرة = ٨٠,٦٠٠
٣٢,٠٠٠	٥٠,٠٠٠	٥٠,٠٠٠	ثابتة = ٥٤,٠٠٠
١١٢,٠٠٠	١٣٠,٠٠٠	١٢٧,٥٠٠	الإجمالي = ١٣٤,٦٠٠
انحراف الحجم =١٣٠,٠٠٠- ١١٢,٠٠٠=١٨,٠٠٠ (غ م)		انحراف الكفاءة =١٢٧,٥٠٠- ١٣٠,٠٠٠ =٢٥٠٠ (م)	انحراف الإنفاق = ١٣٤,٦٠٠- ١٢٧,٥٠٠=٧١٠٠ غ م
الانحراف الكلي = ١٣٤,٦٠٠-١١٢,٠٠٠=٢٢٦٠٠د (غ م)			

شكل (١٠-٥) تحليل انحرافات الأعباء الإضافية حسب طريقة الثلاثة انحرافات

لاحظ أن انحراف الكفاءة والذي هو الفرق بين العمود الثاني والعمود الثالث كان نتيجة الاختلاف الأعباء الإضافية المتغيرة الفعلية والأعباء الإضافية المتغيرة المعيارية لأن الأعباء الإضافية الثابتة قد وردت بنفس الرقم في العمودين لذلك بقي هذا الانحراف على ما كان عليه في طريقة الأربعة انحرافات.

ثالثا: طريقة الانحرافين:

تقوم هذه الطريقة بجمع انحراف الإنفاق وانحراف الكفاءة التي تم حسابها في طريقة الثلاثة انحرافات، وبالنظر إلى الشكل (١٠-٥) نرى أنه عند دمج هذه الانحرافات معا نقارن بين التكلفة الفعلية في العمود الأول مع الموازنة المرنة لساعات العمل المعيارية في العمود الثالث ويسمى هذا الانحراف بانحراف الموازنة أو الانحراف القابل للرقابة، ويعرف على أنه الفرق بين الأعباء الإضافية الفعلية والموازنة المرنة لساعات العمل المعيارية. ويتم حسابه كالتالي:

١٣٤,٦٠٠ – ١٣٠,٠٠٠ = ٤,٦٠٠ د (غير مفضل).

والانحراف الثاني في هذه الطريقة هو انحراف الحجم يتم حسابه كما في الطرق السابقة وهو يساوي ١٨,٠٠٠ د (غير مفضل).

مقارنة طرق تحليل الانحرافات:

لتسهيل مقارنة طرق تحليل انحرافات الأعباء الإضافية تم تلخيص معادلات الانحرافات ومبالغها في الجدول (١٠-٢).

جدول رقم (١٠-٢)
مقارنة طرق تحليل انحرافات الأعباء الإضافية

طريقة الانحرافين	طريقة الثلاثة انحرافات	طريقة الأربعة انحرافات
انحراف الموازنة = الفرق بين مجموع التكاليف الثابتة والمتغيرة الفعلية والموازنة المرنة لساعات العمل المعيارية = ١٣٤,٦٠٠ - ١٣٠,٠٠٠ =٤,٦٠٠د(غ م)	انحراف الإنفاق = الفرق بين مجموع التكاليف الثابتة والمتغيرة الفعلية والموازنة المرنة لساعات العمل الفعلية = ١٣٤,٦٠٠ - ١٢٧,٥٠٠ =٧,١٠٠د(م غ)	١- انحراف إنفاق الأعباء المتغيرة = الفرق بين التكاليف المتغيرة الفعلية والموازنة المرنة لساعات العمل الفعلية ويساوي: ٨٠,٦٠٠ - ٧٧,٥٠٠ = ٣,١٠٠د(غ م)
لا يتم حسابه	لا يتم حسابه	٢- انحراف إنفاق الأعباء الثابتة = الفرق بين التكاليف الثابتة الفعلية والتكاليف الثابتة المخططة = ٥٤,٠٠٠-٥٠,٠٠٠ =٤,٠٠٠د (غ م)
لا يتم حسابه	انحراف الكفاءة = نفس الرقم كما في طريقة الأربعة انحرافات = ٢٥٠٠د (م)	٣- انحراف الكفاءة = الفرق بين الموازنة المرنة لساعات العمل الفعلية والموازنة المرنة لساعات العمل المعيارية للأعباء المتغيرة ويساوي: ٨٠,٠٠٠ - ٧٧,٥٠٠ = ٢,٥٠٠د (م)
انحراف الحجم = نفس الرقم في طريقة الأربعة انحرافات ويساوي ١٨,٠٠٠د (غ م)	انحراف الحجم = نفس الرقم في طريقة الأربعة انحرافات ويساوي ١٨,٠٠٠د (غ م)	٤- انحراف الحجم = الفرق بين التكاليف الثابتة المحملة على الإنتاج والتكاليف الثابتة المخططة= ٣٢,٠٠٠ – ٥٠,٠٠٠ =١٨,٠٠٠ د (غ م)
إجمالي الانحرافات ٢٢,٦٠٠د	إجمالي الانحرافات ٢٢,٦٠٠د	إجمالي الانحراف ٢٢,٦٠٠د

مثال محلول:

كانت بطاقة التكاليف المعيارية لإحدى المنتجات الصناعية تبين الآتي:

مادة مباشرة أ (٢م٠,٦ صاج بسعر ١٠د للمتر المربع)   ٦د =

مادة مباشرة ب (٢م مواسير بسعر ٢,٥ د للمتر)   ٥د =

مادة مباشرة ج (٤ قطع بسعر ١,٢٥د للقطعة)   ٥د=

أجور مباشرة (٦ساعات بمعدل ٢د للساعة)   ١٢د=

أعباء إضافية متغيرة (٦ ساعات بمعدل ٠,٥د للساعة)   ٣د =

أعباء إضافية ثابتة ٦ ساعات بمعدل٥د للساعة   ٣٠د =

(حسب على أساس أن الطاقة العادية ١١,٠٠٠ وحدة)

الإجمالي   ٦١د =

وخلال الفترة تم إنتاج ١٠,٠٠٠ وحدة وكانت بيانات التكاليف الفعلية كالتالي:

تم شراء واستخدام المواد التالية:

٦,٢٥٠ ٢م صاج وتكلفتها   ٥٩,٣٧٥د

١٩,٥٠٠ م مواسير وتكلفتها   ٥٠,٧٠٠د

٤١,٠٠٠ قطعة بسعر ١,٢٧د تكلفتها   ٥٢,٠٧٠د

بلغت ساعات العمل المباشرة ٥٨,٥٠٠ ساعة وتكلفتها ١١٨,٩٠٠د.

وبلغت الأعباء الإضافية الفعلية: ٢٩,٠٠٠د متغيرة، ٣١٥,٠٠٠د ثابتة.

المطلوب:

تحليل انحرافات المواد المباشرة والأجور المباشرة والأعباء الإضافية. وبقدر ما تسمح به البيانات السابقة.

أولا: انحرافات المواد المباشرة:

١- انحراف سعر المواد المباشرة

انحراف السعر = (السعر الفعلي – السعر المعياري) × الكمية المشتراة

الانحراف	الكمية الفعلية	السعر المعياري	السعر الفعلي*	المادة
٣,١٢٥د (م)	٦,٢٥٠	١٠	٩,٥	أ
١,٩٥٠د (غ م)	١٩,٥٠٠	٢,٥	٢,٦	ب
٨٢٠د (غ م)	٤١,٠٠٠	١,٢٥	١,٢٧	ج
٣٥٥د (م)	إجمالي انحراف السعر			

* تم تحديد السعر الفعلي بقسمة تكلفة المادة على الكمية المشتراة والمستخدمة، وتم الحصول على السعر المعياري للمواد من بطاقة التكلفة المعيارية.

٢ – انحراف كمية (كفاءة) المواد المباشرة ويساوي:

(الكمية الفعلية – الكمية المعيارية للإنتاج الفعلي) × السعر المعياري للمواد
ويحسب كالتالي:

الانحراف	السعر المعياري	كمية معيارية (عدد وحدات× كمية معيارية)	كمية فعلية*	المادة
٢,٥٠٠د (غ م)	١٠د	٠,٦×١٠,٠٠٠	٦,٢٥٠	أ
١,٢٥٠د (م)	٢,٥د	٢×١٠,٠٠٠	١٩,٥٠٠	ب
١,٢٥٠د (غ م)	١,٢٥د	٤×١٠,٠٠٠	٤١,٠٠٠	ج
٢,٥٠٠د (غ م)				إجمالي الانحراف

الانحراف الكلي للمواد المباشرة = الفرق بين التكلفة الفعلية للمواد المباشرة والتكلفة المعيارية لهذه المواد.

التكلفة الفعلية = ٥٩,٣٧٥+٥٠,٧٠٠+٥٢,٠٧٠   = ١٦٢,١٤٥ د

التكلفة المعيارية = (كمية معيارية × سعر معياري)

مادة أ = ٦,٠٠٠ × ١٠د =	٦٠,٠٠٠د
مادة ب = ١٠,٠٠٠ × ٢ × ٢,٥ د =	٥٠,٠٠٠د
مادة ج = ١٠,٠٠٠ ×٤ × ١,٢٥د =	٥٠,٠٠٠د

التكلفة المعيارية للمواد المباشرة   ١٦٠,٠٠٠د

الانحراف الكلي   ٢,١٤٥د

ثانيا: انحرافات معدل الأجور = (المعدل الفعلي – المعدل المعياري) × ساعات العمل المباشرة الفعلية

$$= ((\frac{١١٨,٩٠٠}{٥٨,٥٠٠}) - ٢) × ٥٨,٥٠٠$$

$$= ١١٨,٩٠٠ - ٢ × ٥٨,٥٠٠ = ١,٩٠٠ د (غ م)$$

انحراف كمية (كفاءة) الأجور = (ساعات العمل الفعلية – ساعات العمل المعيارية) × معدل الأجر المعياري

$$= (٥٨,٥٠٠ – ١٠,٠٠٠ ×٦) × ٢ = ٣,٠٠٠د (م)$$

٣ – الانحراف الكلي = الأجور الفعلية – الأجور المعيارية للإنتاج الفعلي

$$= ١١٨,٩٠٠ – ١٠,٠٠٠ وحدة × ٦ ساعات × ٢د = ١,١٠٠ د (م)$$

ثالثا: انحرافات الأعباء الإضافية

سيتم تحليل الانحرافات حسب طرق الانحرافات الثلاث المذكورة في الفصل

الأربعة انحرافات	الثلاثة انحرافات	الانحرافين
١- انحراف إنفاق أعباء متغيرة التكلفة الفعلية ناقص الموازنة المرنة لساعات العمل الفعلية = ٢٩,٠٠٠-(٠,٥ × ٥٨,٥٠٠)= ٢٥٠ د م	(١) انحراف الإنفاق هو الفرق بـين الأعباء المتغيـرة والثابتـة والفعلية والموازنة المرنة لساعات العمــل الفعليـة (٢٩,٠٠٠ + ٣٣٠,٠٠٠) – (٣١٥,٠٠٠ -٣٤٤,٠٠٠ = (٠,٥× ٥٨,٥٠٠ (م) ١٥,٢٥٠ = ٣٥٩,٢٥٠	(١) انحراف الموازنة القابل للرقابـة ويساوي الفرق بين الأعباء الإضافية (المتغيرة والثابتة) الفعلية والموازنة المرنة لساعات العمل المعيارية التكاليف الفعلية = ٣٤٤,٠٠٠ الموازنة المرنة=٣٣٠,٠٠٠+٦٠,٠٠٠ ٣٦٠,٠٠٠ = ٠,٥× ١٦,٠٠٠ = د (م)
٢- انحراف إنفاق الأعباء الثابتة = التكلفـة الثابتـة الفعليـة – التكاليف الثابتة المخططة =٣٣٠,٠٠٠ - ٣١٥,٠٠٠ ١٥,٠٠٠د (م)	لا يوجد	لا يوجد
٣- انحراف الكفاءة = الفرق بين ساعات العمل الفعلية وساعات العمل المعيارية × في معدل تحميل الأعباء المتغيرة = = ٠,٥×(٦٠,٠٠٠-٥٨,٥٠٠) ٧٥٠م.		
٤- الانحراف الحجم :الفرق بين الأعباء الثابتة المخططة والأعباء المحملة على الإنتاج =٥×٦ × ١٠,٠٠٠ - ٣٣٠,٠٠٠ ٣٠,٠٠٠د (غ م)	انحراف الحجم ٣٠,٠٠٠ غ م	انحراف الحجم ٣٠,٠٠٠ غ م
الانحراف الكلـي = ٢٥٠(م) + ١٥٠٠٠(م) + ٧٥٠(م) - ٣٠,٠٠٠(غ م) =١٤,٠٠٠	الانحراف الكلـي = ١٥٢٥٠ +٧٥٠(م) - ٣٠,٠٠٠ (م) غ = (م) ١٤,٠٠٠د غ م	الانحراف الكلـي = ١٦٠٠٠ (م) - ٣٠,٠٠٠ (غ م) = ١٤,٠٠٠

الخاتمــة

في هذا الفصـل تمت دراسـة التكـاليف المعياريـة وبينا أنها محـددة مقـدما وتستخدم لأغراض التخطيط والرقابة، وحتى تحقق هذه الأهداف يجب أن تحتوي المعايير على المسموحات الحتمية التي تجعل المعايير قابلـة للتحقيـق خـلال فـترة سريانها.

وتـم التعـرض إلى طـرق معـايرة تكـاليف المـواد المبـاشرة والأجـور المبـاشرة والتكاليف الصناعية غير المباشرة (الأعباء الصناعية الإضافية). وبالنسبة لانحرافات المواد والأجور فقد تم تعريف انحراف السعر على أنه الفرق بين السعر الفعلـي والسعر المعياري مضروبا في كمية المواد المباشرة في حالة المواد ومضروبا في ساعات العمل المباشرة الفعلية في حالة الأجور.

وعرف انحراف الكميـة على أنه الفرق بين الكميـة الفعليـة والكميـة المعياريـة ضرب السعر المعياري بالنسبة للمواد ومعدل الأجر بالنسبة للأجور المباشرة، أمـا بالنسبة للتكاليف الصناعية غير المباشرة فقد تم تحليلها بثلاث طرق هـي طريقـة الأربعة انحرافات وطريقـة الثلاثة انحرافات وطريقـة الانحرافين وفي نهايـة الفصـل تمت مقارنة طرق تحليل انحرافات الأعباء الإضافية في الجـدول (١٠-٢).

أسئلة وتمارين

السؤال الأول: عرف التكاليف المعيارية وما هي فوائد استخدامها؟

السؤال الثاني: ما هي أنواع المعايير ومزايا وعيوب كل منها؟

السؤال الثالث: يعتقد البعض أن الموازنة التقديرية أقل دقـة مـن التكاليف المعيارية، ناقش ذلك.

السؤال الرابع: اشرح كيـف يمكـن وضـع معـايير كميـة المـواد المباشرة والأجور المباشرة

السؤال الخامس: ما هو الفرق بـين طريقـة الأربعـة انحرافـات وطريقـة الثلاثـة انحرافات المستخدمة في تحليل انحرافات التكاليف الصناعية غير المباشرة؟

السؤال السادس: ما هو الفرق بين انحراف الإنفاق في طريقـة الأربعـة انحرافات وانحراف الموازنة في طريقة الانحرافين ؟

السؤال السابع: اشترى مصنع البسكويت الأردني ٥,٠٠٠كغم من الطحين بمبلغ ٩٠٠ دينار وصرفت جميعها للإنتاج وتشير بطاقة التكلفة المعيارية للكرتونه أن معيار الكمية للكرتونة هو ٦ كغم طحين بواقع ٠,١٧٥د /كغم. وخلال الفترة تم إنتاج ٧٥٠ كرتونة بسكويت.

المطلوب:

١ - ما هي الكمية المعيارية للطحين المستخدمة في الإنتاج ؟

٢ - ما هو انحراف السعر ؟

٣ - ما هو انحراف الكمية؟

السؤال الثامن: تسـتخدم إحـدى الشـركات الصـناعية التكـاليف المعياريـة وكانـت البيانات المعيارية المتعلقة بالأجور المباشرة كالتالي:

الوقت المباشر لإنتاج الوحدة يساوي ٣ ساعات، وأن معدل أجر الساعة ٢د، وخلال الفترة تم إنتاج ٢,٠٠٠ وحدة واستخدم في سبيل ذلك ٦,٥٠٠ ساعة عمل مباشرة فعلية وبلغت تكلفتها الفعلية ١١٧,٠٠ دينار.

المطلوب:

تحليل انحرافات الأجور التي يمكنك حسابها من البيانات السابقة.

السؤال التاسع: بالإضافة إلى المعلومات الواردة في السؤال السابق إذا علمت أن الأعباء الإضافية يتم تحميلها على الإنتاج كالتالي:

الأعباء المتغيرة (٣ ساعات بواقع ٣د/س ع م)   = ٩د.

الأعباء الثابتة (٣ ساعات بواقع ٢,٥د/ س ع م)   = ٧,٥د

إجمالي الأعباء الصناعية لوحدة المنتج   = ١٦,٥د

تبلغ الطاقة العادية للشركة ٧,٠٠٠ ساعة عمل مباشرة.

وبلغت الأعباء الصناعية المتغيرة خلال الفترة ١٧,٠٠٠د كما بلغت الأعباء الثابتة ١٦,٨٠٠د.

المطلوب:

١ — تحليل انحرافات الأعباء الإضافية باستخدام طريقة الأربعة انحرافات.

٢ — تحليل انحرافات الأعباء الإضافية باستخدام طريقة الانحرافين.

السؤال العاشر: أعدت إحدى الشركات الصناعية بطاقة التكلفة المعيارية لإحدى منتجاتها وكانت كالتالي:

مواد مباشرة (٥كغم بواقع ٣د/كغم)   = ١٥د

أجور مباشرة (٥ ساعات بواقع ١,٥د/س ع م)   = ٧,٥د

أعباء إضافية متغيرة (٥ ساعات بواقع ٤د)   = ٢٠د

أعباء صناعية ثابتة (٥ ساعات بواقع ٥د)   = ٢٥د

الاجمالي   ٦٧,٥د

وتوفرت لديك المعلومات التالية:

— بلغ عدد الوحدات المنتجة خلال الفترة ٦,٠٠٠ وحدة وأن حجم الطاقة ٧,٠٠٠ وحدة.

- تم شراء ٣٥,٠٠٠ كغم من المواد المباشرة بمبلغ ١٠٠,٠٠٠ دينار واستخدام منها في الإنتاج ٣١,٢٠٠ كغم وتقوم الشركة بتحديد انحراف السعر عند الشراء.

- بلغت الأجور المباشرة ٤٤,١٠٠ دينار وتمثل تكلفة ٣١,٥٠٠ ساعة عمل.

- بلغت الأعباء الصناعية الإضافية الفعلية ٢٦٥,٠٠٠ دينار.

المطلوب:

تحليل الانحرافات بالقدر الذي تسمح به المعلومات المتوفرة.

السؤال الحادي عشر: الآتي معلومات مستخرجة من دفاتر إحدى الشركات خلال شهر آذار:

- معدل أجر معياري   ١,٥د
- معدل الأجر الفعلي للأجور المباشرة   ١,٤د
- ساعات العمل المعيارية   ١,٥٠٠
- انحراف معدل الأجور   ١,٦٠٠د (مفضل)
- انحراف كفاءة الأجور   ١,٥٠٠ (غير مفضل)

المطلوب:

١- تحديد ساعات العمل الفعلية خلال شهر آذار.

٢- تحديد التكلفة المعيارية للأجور.

السؤال الثاني عشر: صنفت شركة عمالها لأغراض إعداد التكاليف المعيارية إلى ثلاث فئات من الكفاءة وكانت بيانات الأجور المعيارية لإنتاج الوحدة كالتالي:

معدل أجر الساعة	ساعات العمل للوحدة	فئة
٢	٥	١
٢,٥	٦	٢
١,٢٥	٤	٣

وخلال الفترة المالية أنتجت الشركة ٩,٠٠٠ وحدة واستخدمت في سبيل ذلك ١٤٠,٠٠٠ ساعة عمل مباشرة تكلفتها ٢٨٥,٠٠٠ دينار. وكان استخدام فئات العمل كما هو مخطط لها.

المطلوب:

١- حساب انحرافات الأجور المباشرة.

السؤال الثالث عشر: تستخدم إحدى الشركات مادتين هما أ، ب في إنتاج إحدى منتجاتها وتم استخدام المواد التالية:

مادة أ (١٠ كغم وسعرها المعياري ٢د/كغم) = ٢٠ د

مادة ب (٦ م والسعر المعياري ٣د/م) = ١٨ د

تكلفة المواد المباشرة للوحدة ٣٨ د

وخلال الفترة تم إنتاج ٥,٠٠٠ وحدة من هذا المنتج وتم استخدام المواد التالية:

المادة (أ) (٥٢,٠٠٠ كغم بسعر ٢,١٠د) =١٠٩,٢٠٠ دينار

مادة (ب) (٢٩,٠٠٠م بسعر ٢,٨٠د) =٨١,٢٠٠ دينار

المطلوب:

حساب انحرافات المواد المباشرة بافتراض أن الكمية المستخدمة من كل مادة لا تؤثر على كمية المادة الأخرى.

السؤال الرابع عشر: تقوم أحد المصانع الصغيرة بإنتاج أقفاص للعصافير وكانت بطاقة التكلفة المعيارية لإنتاج القفص رقم أ٣ كالتالي:

خشب زان (١قدم٢ بسعر ١,٨) ١,٨د

سلك حديد (٢/١ ربطة بسعر ٢,٤٠د للربطة) ١,٢٠د

عمل مباشر (٢ ساعة بمعدل ٢د للساعة) ٤ د

وخلال إحدى الفترات حدث الآتي:

١- تم إنتاج ٥٠٠ قفص من هذا النوع.

٢- تم شراء ١,٠٠٠قدم٢ من الخشب بسعر ١,٨٥٠د.

٣- تم شراء ٢٠٠ ربطة سلك وصرف للإنتاج ٢٤٥ربطة بعضها من مخـزون أول المدة.

٤- بلغت تكلفة الأجور المباشرة ٢,١٨٥د.

وقام محاسب التكاليف بتحديد الانحرافات الآتية:

١. انحرف كفاءة العمل المباشر ٣٠٠د (غ م)

٢. انحراف سعر المواد المباشرة ٣٠د (غ م)

٣. انحراف كمية المواد المباشرة ١٥د (غ م)

المطلوب:

إعادة حساب الانحرافات المختلفة التي قـدمها لـك محاسب التكاليف ومـا هـي كمية الخشب المستخدمة في الإنتاج.

السؤال الخامس عشر: الآتي بطاقة التكلفة المعيارية لإنتاج أحد المنتجات الصناعية مع العلم بأن الشركة تستخدم نظام التكاليف المعيارية وكانـت التكلفـة المعياريـة لوحدة المنتج كالتالي:

المواد المباشرة (٧كغم بسعر ١د/كغم) = ٧د

أجور مباشرة (٢ ساعة بمعدل ١د/ س ع م) = ٤د

أعباء إضافية ٦٠% من الأجور المباشرة = ٢,٤د

وقد تم الحصول على المعلمات التالية من دفاتر الشركة عن شهر كانون ثاني:

كمية الإنتاج ٨,٠٠٠ وحدة

المشتريات ٦٠,٠٠٠ كغم بمبلغ ٦٦,٠٠٠د

انحراف سعر المواد ٦,٠٠٠د (غ م)

انحراف كمية المواد ٢,٠٠٠د (غ م)

انحراف معدل الأجور ١,٥٣٠د (غ م)

انحراف كفاءة الأجور ١,٤٠٠د (م)

الانحراف الكلي للأعباء الإضافية ٣,٥٠٠د (غ م)

المطلوب:

١- تحديد الكمية المعيارية للمواد المباشرة المستخدمة.

٢- تحديد ساعات العمل المباشرة المعيارية.

٣- تحديد ساعات العمل المباشرة الفعلية.

٤- تحديد قيمة الأعباء الإضافية الفعلية.

السؤال السادس عشر: الآتي معلومات مستخرجة من دفاتر إحدى الشركات: كان حجم الطاقة المخطط ٥٠,٠٠٠ وحدة منتج (١٠٠,٠٠٠ ساعة عمل مباشر) وتحتوي بطاقة التكاليف المعيارية للوحدة على المعلومات الآتية:

أعباء إضافية متغيرة	٦د للوحدة
أعباء إضافية ثابتة	٨د للوحدة

والمعلومات التالية تخص شهر آذار:

الإنتاج الفعلي	٣٨,٠٠٠ وحدة
ساعات العمل المباشرة الفعلية	٨٠,٠٠٠ ساعة
الأعباء الإضافية الفعلية:	
متغيرة	٢٥٠,٠٠٠ د
الثابتة	٣٨٤,٠٠٠د

المطلوب: الإجابة على الأسئلة الأربعة التالية:

١- يبلغ انحراف إنفاق الأعباء المتغيرة في شهر آذار الآتي

أ- ٦,٠٠د   ب- ١٢,٠٠٠د

ج – ١٠,٠٠٠د   د- ٢٢,٠٠٠د

٢- يبلغ انحراف حجم الأعباء الإضافية في شهر آذار الآتي:

أ – ٩٦,٠٠٠د (غ م)   ب – ٨٠,٠٠٠د (غ م)

ج – ٩٦,٠٠٠د (م)   د – ٨٠,٠٠٠د (م)

٣ - يبلغ انحراف كفاءة الأعباء الإضافية في شهر آذار الآتي:

أ - ١٢,٠٠٠د (غ م)   ب - ١٨٠٠٠د (غ م)

ج- ١٢,٠٠٠د (م)   د - ١٨٠٠٠د (م)

٤ - يبلغ انحراف الموازنة في شهر آذار الآتي:

أ - ٨,٠٠٠د (غ م)   ب - ٦,٠٠د (غ م)

ج - ٨,٠٠د (م)   د - ٦,٠٠د (م)

السؤال السابع عشر: كانت الموازنة المرنة لإحدى الشركات الصناعية كالتالي:

إجمالي التكاليف = ٩٠,٠٠٠ + ٥ د / س ع م

ومعدل التحميل الكلي للأعباء الإضافية هو ٨ د/ س ع م.

وبلغ حجم الإنتاج الكلي خلال شهر آذار ٢٥,٠٠٠ وحدة وتحتاج كل وحدة إلى ١,١ ساعة عمل مباشرة ولكن تم استخدام ٢٨,٠٠٠ ساعة عمل مباشرة خلال هذا الشهر.

وبلغت الأعباء الإضافية الفعلية ٢٣٥,٠٠٠ دينار.

وتتبع الشركة طريقة الثلاثة انحرافات عند تحليل انحرافات الأعباء الإضافية.

المطلوب: الإجابة على الأسئلة الثلاث التالية:

١ - انحراف إنفاق الأعباء الإضافية

أ - ٥,٠٠٠د(غ م)   ب - ٥,٠٠٠د (م)

ج - ١١,٠٠٠د (غ م)   د - ١١,٠٠٠د (م)

٢ - انحراف كفاءة الأعباء الإضافية يساوي:

أ- ٢,٥٠٠د (غ م)   ب - ٢,٥٠٠د (م)

ج - ٤,٠٠٠د (غ م)   د -٤,٠٠٠د (م)

٣ - انحراف الحجم يساوي:

أ - ٤,٠٠٠د (غ م)   ب - ٤,٠٠٠د(م)

ج - ٢,٠٠٠د (م)   د- غير ذلك

(مجمع المحاسبين القانونيين الأمريكيين)

السؤال الثامن عشر: تقوم إحدى الشركات بتصنيع مكاتب وكانت تكلفة المواد المباشرة المعيارية للمكتب الواحد ٢٧ دينار على أساس استخدام ١٢ قدم مربع من الفورمايكا، وخلال الفترة تم إنتاج ١,٠٠٠ مكتب وتم استخدام ١٢,٦٠٠ قدم مربع من الفورمايكا في إنتاجها وبلغ السعر الفعلي ٢ دينار للقدم المربع أي أن إجمالي تكلفتها ٢٥,٢٠٠ دينار وعليه يكون انحراف كمية المواد المباشرة خلال الفترة:

أ – ١,٢٠٠د (غ م)   ب – ١,٣٥٠د (غ م)

ج – ١,٨٠٠د (م)   د – ٣,١٥٠د (م)

(مجمع المحاسبين القانونيين الأمريكيين)

السؤال التاسع عشر: لقد كانت التكلفة المعيارية لإحدى المنتجات كالآتي:

مواد مباشرة = (٤ لتر بسعر ٢د/لتر)	= ٨د
أجور مباشرة (١ ساعة بمعدل ٣د /س ع م)	=٣د
أعباء إضافية متغيرة (١ ساعة بمعدل ٢د/س ع م)	= ٢د
إجمالي التكلفة المتغيرة المعيارية للوحدة	١٣د

وكانت البيانات الفعلية كالتالي:

عدد الوحدات المنتجة ١٥,٠٠٠ وحدة.

ساعات العمل المباشرة ١٥,٨٥٠ ساعة.

معدل الأجر الفعلي ٣,١٠د/د/س ع م.

المواد المشتراة ٧٠,٠٠٠ لتر بمبلغ ١٣٣,٠٠٠ دينار.

وانحراف كمية المواد ٤,٠٠٠د (غير مفضل).

الأعباء الإضافية الفعلية ٤٠,٠٠٠د.

المطلوب:

تحليل انحرافات التكاليف المتغيرة.

السؤال العشرون: تقوم شركة صناعات علاء الدين وهي إحدى الشركات المساهمة العامة الأردنية بإنتاج المدافئ المعروفة باسم صوبة علاء الدين وتستخدم هذه الشركة التكاليف المعيارية، وكانت البيانات المعيارية اللازمة لإنتاج الصوبة كالآتي:

مواد مباشرة: صاج سمك ٢ملم (٠,٥م٢/بسعر ٣,٥ دينار للمتر)	١,٧٥د
شبك معدني (٠,٤م٢ بسعر ٥ دنانير للمتر المربع)	٢د
قوائم معدنية (١,٥م بسعر ٤ دنانير)	٦د
الأجور المباشرة (٦ ساعات بمعدل ٢د/ س ع م)	١٢د
أعباء صناعية متغيرة (٦ ساعات بمعدل ١,٢٥د/ س ع م)	٧,٥٠د
أعباء صناعية ثابتة (٦ ساعات بمعدل ١د/س ع م)	٦د
إجمالي التكاليف الصناعية المعيارية للوحدة	٣٥,٢٥د

وتقوم الشركة بحساب انحرافات سعر المواد عند الشراء.

والطاقة العادية للشركة ١١٨,٠٠٠ ساعة عمل مباشرة وخلال الفترة قد تم إنتاج ٢٠,٠٠٠ صوبة.

وكذلك توفرت الحقائق الفعلية التالية:

تم شراء ١٢,٠٠٠م٢ صاج سمك ٢ملم وتكلفتها ٤٠,٨٠٠ دينار صرف منها للإنتاج ١٠,٢٠٠م٢.

تـم شراء ١٠,٠٠٠م٢ شبك معدني وتكلفتها ٤٩,٥٠٠ دينار صرف منها للإنتاج ٨,٣٠٠م.

تـم شراء ٢٠,٠٠٠م قوائم معدنية وتكلفتها ٨٤,٠٠٠ دينار صرف منها للإنتاج ٣١,٠٠٠م.

وبلغت ساعات العمل الفعلية ١١٥,٠٠٠ ساعة وتكلفتها ٢٣١,٠٠٠ دينار.

وبلغت الأعباء المتغيرة ١٤٦,٠٠٠ دينار وكما بلغت الأعباء الثابتة١٢٥,٠٠٠د.

المطلوب:

تحليل انحرافات عناصر التكاليف بالقدر الذي تسمح به البيانات المعطاة.

السؤال الواحد والعشرون: تقوم شركة مصانع الأثاث الأردنية باستخدام التكاليف المعيارية وتتخصص بإنتاج غرف السفرة وكانت بطاقة التكلفة المعيارية لإحدى طاولاتها كالتالي:

خشب بلوط (٣٦ قدم٢ بسعر ٠,٤٥د)	١٦,٢د
عمل مباشر (٤ ساعات بمعدل ٥د)	٢٠د
التكلفة الأولية	٣٦,٢د

وخلال شهر آذار تم شراء ٦٠,٠٠٠قدم٢ من خشب البلوط بمبلغ ٢٨,٨٠٠د صرف منها للإنتاج ٥٤,٥٠٠ قدم٢ لإنتاج ١,٥٠٠ طاولة. وقد بلغت ساعات العمل المباشرة المستخدمة في الإنتاج ٦,٣٥٠ ساعة وأن تكلفة أجور العمال خلال الفترة ٣٣,٦٠٠ دينار وأن ٨٠% من هذه الأجور مباشرة والباقي غير مباشرة.

المطلوب:

حساب انحرافات المواد والأجور.

السؤال الثاني والعشرون: كانت بطاقة التكلفة المعيارية لإحدى المنتجات تتكون من الآتي:

معدل أجر ساعة العمل المباشرة	٣,٢د
ساعات العمل المباشرة للوحدة	٣ ساعات
معدل تحميل الأعباء المتغيرة	١,٨٠ لكل س ع م
معدل تحميل الأعباء الثابتة	٥,٥ لكل س ع م
الطاقة العادية	٨,٠٠٠ وحدة

وخلال إحدى الفترات تم إنتاج ٧,٨٠٠ وحدة واستخدمت الشركة ٢٣,٦٥٠ ساعة عمل مباشرة، وأن معدل أجر الساعة قد بلغ ٣,١٥د، وكذلك بلغت الأعباء المتغيرة الفعلية ٣٨,٠٠٠د، وبلغت الأعباء الثابتة ١٤٢,٠٠٠د.

المطلوب:

١- تحليل الانحرافات السابقة باستخدام طريقة الانحرافين.

٢- تحليل الانحرافات السابقة باستخدام طريقة الثلاث انحرافات.

السؤال الثالث والعشرون: أعدت شركة موازنتها المرنة الخاصة بإنتاج إحدى المنتجات:

الطاقة	%٩٠	%٩٥	%١٠٠
عدد الوحدات	٢٢,٥٠٠	٢٣,٧٥٠	٢٥,٠٠٠د
الأعباء المتغيرة	٦٧,٥٠٠د	٧١,٢٥٠د	٧٥,٠٠٠د
الأعباء الثابتة	٩٥,٠٠٠د	٩٥,٠٠٠د	٩٥,٠٠٠د
الإجمالي	١٦٢,٥٠٠د	١٦٦,٢٥٠د	١٧٠,٠٠٠د

وكانت بطاقة التكلفة المعيارية لوحدة المنتج تحتوي على الآتي:

مواد مباشرة (١٥ كغم بسعر ٣د)	= ٤٥د
أجور مباشرة (٤ ساعات بمعدل ٢,٥د)	= ١٠د
أعباء متغيرة (٤ ساعات بمعدل ١,٧٥د)	= ٧د
إجمالي التكلفة الصناعية	٦٢د

تستخدم الشركة الطاقة العادية وقدرها ٢٣,٧٥٠ وحدة لحساب معدل تحميل الأعباء الإضافية، وقد استغلت الشركة نسبة ٩٠% من الطاقة وأنتجت ٢٢,٥٠٠ وحدة وتحملت التكاليف التالية:

المـواد المبـاشرة: اشتـرت الشركـة ٣٤٠,٠٠٠ كغـم وتكلفتهـا ١,٠٤٦,٢٥٠ دينـار واستخدمت جميعها في الإنتاج.

الأجور المباشرة: بلغت ساعات العمل المباشرة ٩١,٠٠٠ ساعة وتكلفتها ٢٤٣,٠٠٠ دينار.

الأعباء المتغيرة: ٧٢,٠٠٠د

الأعباء الثابتة: ١٠٠,٠٠٠د

المطلوب:

١ - حسابات انحرافات الأعباء الإضافية باستخدام.

أ- طريقة الانحرافين.

ب- طريقة الأربعة انحرافات.

الفصل الحادي عشر
التكاليف المعيارية: الدورة المحاسبية

أهداف الفصل:

بعد دراسة هذا الفصل يجب أن تكون قادراً على معرفة:

١- تحديد الانحرافات الخاصة بعناصر التكاليف الصناعية.

٢- الدورة المحاسبية للتكاليف المعيارية.

٣- قيود اليومية المستخدمة في أنظمة التكاليف المعيارية الجزئية والكاملة.

٤- طرق توزيع انحرافات التكاليف على حسابات البضاعة.

٥- طرق إعداد قوائم تكلفة البضاعة بالتكاليف المعيارية.

٦- طريقة تحويل قوائم التكلفة المعيارية إلى قوائم تكلفة فعلية.

٧- تحليل الانحرافات باستخدام الوحدات المكافئة في صناعة المراحل.

مقدمــة :

في الفصل السابق تناولنا طرق إعداد معايير التكلفة وكيفية تحليل انحرافات عناصر التكاليف الصناعية، وفي هـذا الفصـل سـيتم دراسـة الإجـراءات المحاسبية اللازمة للمحاسبة علـى التكلفـة المعياريـة، وكذلك سـيتم دراسـة طرق معالجـة الانحرافات لغرض إعداد الحسابات الختامية وبيان كيفية استخدام نظام التكاليف المعيارية في صناعة المراحل الإنتاجية.

تتوقف القيود المحاسبية علـى الطريقـة التـي تسـتخدمها المنشـأة في تجميـع التكلفة المعيارية، وفي هـذا المجـال، يوجد في الحياة العملية طريقتان هـما [1]: طريقـة التكـاليف المعياريـة الجزئيـة Partial Plan، وطريقـة التكلفـة المعياريـة الكاملة :Standard Cost Single Plan. ويقع الاختلاف بـين هـاتين الطـريقتين في المبالغ التي تسجل حساب الإنتاج تحت التشغيل.

ففي حالـة طريقـة التكـاليف المعياريـة الجزئيـة يجعل هـذا الحسـاب دائنـاً بالتكلفة المعيارية للبضاعة التامة الصنع فقط أما تكاليف المـواد المباشرة والأجـور المباشرة فتحمل على أساس فعلي، وبالتالي يتكون رصيد نهاية المدة لحساب الإنتاج تحت التشغيل من انحرافات عناصر هـذه التكـاليف والتكلفـة المعياريـة للإنتاج تحت التشغيل آخر المدة، أما في الطريقـة الثانيـة فيحمـل حسـاب الإنتاج تحت التشغيل بالتكلفة المعيارية لعنـاصر التكـاليف ويجعل دائنـاً بالتكلفـة المعياريـة للإنتاج التام المحول وبالتالي تحدد الانحرافات وتحمل لحساباتها عند تسجيلها في الدفاتر. ويمكن أن يوجد بين هاتين الطريقتين طرقـاً تقـف في أيـة نقطة بـينهما [2]. وسيتم دراسة هذه الطرق باستخدام بيانات المثال التالي:

(1) Cecil Gillespie " Standard and Direct Costing", (Prentice – hall of India, New Delhi, ١٩٦٥). Pp. ٦-٤٧.

(2) Bhabat osh Banerjee. "Cost Accounting", Vth . ed (world press Calcutta, ١٩٨٦), Pp. ٦٩٨-٧١٠.

مثال (١):

تحتوي بطاقة التكلفة المعيارية لوحدة المنتج (أ) على المعلومات الآتية:

مواد مباشرة (٥ كغم بسعر ٣ د/ كغم)   = ١٥ د

أجور مباشرة(٦ ساعات بمعدل ١,٥ د/ س ع م)   = ٩ د

أعباء متغيرة (٦ ساعات بمعدل ٢ د/ س ع م)   = ١٢ د

أعباء ثابتة (٦ ساعات بمعدل ٣ د/ س ع م ، وتم
حساب المعدل باستخدام الطاقة العادية وقدرها   = ١٨ د
٣٥,٠٠٠ ساعة)

التكلفة الصناعية المعيارية لوحدة المنتج   = ٥٤ د

وخلال الفترة حدثت العمليات التالية:

١- تم إنتاج ٦,٠٠٠ وحدة.

٢- تم شراء ٣٥,٠٠٠ كغم من المواد المباشرة بمبلغ ٩٩,٧٥٠ دينار على الحساب، وصرف منها للإنتاج ٢٩,٠٠٠ كغم.

٣- بلغت الأجور المباشرة ٥٦,٥٧٥ دينار، وتمثل أجرة ٣٦,٥٠٠ ساعة عمل مباشر.

٤- بلغت الأعباء الإضافية المتغيرة ٦٥,٧٠٠ دينار، وكما بلغت الأعباء الإضافية الثابتة ١٠٥,٨٥٠ دينار.

٥- لم يكن هناك أي إنتاج تحت التشغيل أول المدة أو آخرها.

المطلوب:

قيد العمليات السابقة في سجلات التكاليف حسب طريقة التكاليف المعيارية الجزئية ثم قيدها حسب طريقة التكاليف المعيارية الكاملة.

أولاً: طريقة التكاليف المعيارية الجزئية:

حسب هذه الطريقة يجعل حساب الإنتاج تحت التشغيل مديناً بالتكاليف الفعلية للمواد المباشرة الأجور والأعباء الإضافية، وفيما يلي قيود اليومية اللازمة لإثبات العمليات السابقة.

(١) شراء المواد:

ح/مراقبة المواد		٩٩,٧٥٠
ح/ الموردين	٩٩,٧٥٠	
شراء ٣٥,٠٠٠ كغم بسعر ٢,٨٥ د / كغم		

(٢) صرف المواد إلى الإنتاج:

ح/الإنتاج تحت التشغيل		٨٢,٦٥٠
ح/ مراقبة المواد	٨٢,٦٥٠	
شراء ٣٥,٠٠٠ كغم بسعر ٢,٨٥ د / كغم		

(٣) تحميل الأجور المباشرة:

ح/إنتاج تحت التشغيل		٥٦,٥٧٥
ح/ مراقبة الأجور	٥٦,٥٧٥	
أجرة ٣٦,٥٠٠ ساعة بواقع ١,٥٥ د/ س		

(٤) تحميل الأعباء الإضافية:

ح/الإنتاج تحت التشغيل		١٧١,٠٥٠
ح/ مراقبة الأعباء الإضافية	١٧١,٠٥٠	
أعباء متغيرة ٦٥,٧٠٠ زائد أعباء ثابتة ١٠٥,٨٥٠ وتم تحميلها على أساس فعلي		

أعباء إضافية		إنتاج تحت التشغيل	
متغيرة ٦٥,٧٠٠	١٧١,٠٥٠ (٤)	٨٢,٦٥٠ (٢)	٣٢٤,٠٠٠
			(٥)
ثابتة ١٠٥,٨٥٠		٥٦,٥٧٥ (٣)	
		١٧١,٠٥٠ (٤)	
		١٣,٢٢٥ رصيد	

(٥) تسجيل الإنتاج التام:

حـ/مخزون الإنتاج التام		٣٢٤,٠٠٠
حـ/ إنتاج تحت التشغيل	٣٢٤,٠٠٠	
٦٠٠٠ وحدة تامة الصنع بواقع ٥٤ د للوحدة		

من دراسة القيود من ٢-٤ نجد أنها حملت التكاليف الفعلية على حساب الإنتاج تحت التشغيل، ولأن هذا الحساب قد جعل دائناً بالتكلفة المعيارية للبضاعة التامة الصنع ولعدم وجود رصيد في هذا الحساب أول وآخر المدة، لذلك فإن رصيده الدائن والبالغ ١٣,٢٢٥ د يبين رصيد انحرافات عناصر التكاليف الصناعية. ولكن إذا كان هناك وحدات تحت التشغيل آخر المدة فإن رصيد هذا الحساب يمثل التكلفة المعيارية للإنتاج تحت التشغيل آخر المدة بالإضافة إلى انحرافات عناصر التكاليف، والآن سنقوم بحساب الانحرافات الموجودة في هذا الحساب.

أولاً: انحرافات المواد المباشرة:

(أ) انحراف السعر = (السعر الفعلي – السعر المعياري) × الكمية المستخدمة

= (٢,٨٥ – ٣) × ٢٩,٠٠٠   = ٤,٣٥٠ د (م)

(ب) انحراف الكمية = (كمية فعلية – كمية معيارية) × سعر معياري

= (٢٩,٠٠٠ – ٦,٠٠٠ ×٥) × ٣   = ٣,٠٠٠ د (م)

ثانياً: انحرافات الأجور المباشرة

(أ) انحراف معدل الأجور= (معدل أجر فعلي – معدل أجر معياري)× ساعات عمل فعلية

=(١,٥٥ – ١,٥٠) × ٣٦,٥٠٠   = ١,٨٢٥ د (غ م)

(ب) انحراف كمية الأجور = (ساعات فعلية – ساعات معيارية)× معدل أجر معياري

= (٣٦,٥٠٠ – ٣٦,٠٠٠) × ١,٥   = ٧٥٠ د (غ م)

ثالثاً: انحرافات الأعباء الإضافية – طريقة الثلاثة انحرافات

(أ) انحراف الإنفاق = التكاليف الفعلية – الموازنة المرنة لساعات العمل الفعلية

$$= ١٧١,٥٠٠ - [١٠٥,٠٠٠ + ٣٦,٥٠٠ ×٢]$$

$$= ١٧١,٥٠٠ - ١٧٨,٠٠٠ \qquad = ٦,٤٥٠ \text{ د (م)}$$

(ب) انحراف الكفاءة = (ساعات فعلية – ساعات معيارية)× معدل تحميل الأعباء المتغيرة

$$(٣٦,٥٠٠ - ٣٦,٠٠٠)×٢ \qquad = ١,٠٠٠ \text{ د (غ م)}$$

(جـ) انحراف الحجم = (ساعات الطاقة – ساعات معيارية) × معدل تحميل الأعباء الثابتة

$$(٣٥,٠٠٠ - ٣٦,٠٠٠) ×٣$$

$$١٠٠٠ × ٣ \qquad = \underline{٣,٠٠٠} \text{ د (م)}$$

إجمالي الانحرافات (المواد + الأجور – الأعباء)   ١٣,٢٢٥

وبعد تحديد الانحرافات السابقة يتم تحويلها إلى حساب ملخص الانحرافات بجعله مديناً بالانحرافات غير المفضلة ودائناً بالانحرافات المفضلة ويأخذ هذا الحساب الشكل التالي:

إجمالي (ملخص) الانحرافات

انحراف سعر المواد	٤,٣٥٠		انحراف معدل الأجر	١,٨٢٥	
انحراف كمية المواد	٣,٠٠٠		انحراف كمية الأجور	٧٥٠	
انحراف إنفاق الأعباء الإضافية	٦,٤٥٠		انحراف كفاءة الأعباء الإضافية	١,٠٠٠	
انحراف الحجم	٣,٠٠٠				
الرصيد	١٣,٢٢٥				

ويعتبر حساب ملخص الانحرافات من الحسابات الاسمية، وبالتالي يجب أقفاله في نهاية السنة المالية، ويتوقف ذلك على مدى أهمية الانحرافات ووجهة النظر تجاه التكاليف المعيارية، فإذا كانت هذه الانحرافات غير مهمة نسبياً فيتم أقفالها في حساب تكلفة البضاعة المباعة، أما إذا كانت مهمة فيجب توزيعها على حسابات البضاعة بناء على تكلفتها المعيارية [1]، وهذا الموضوع سيتم مناقشته بالتفصيل في نهاية هذا الفصل.

---

(١) J. Batty, Op.cit., Pp. ٣٠٢ – ٣٠٨.

تعديل طريقة التكاليف الجزئية:

يمكن إدخال بعض التعديلات على حركة القيود السابقة، وتشمل هـذه التعديلات مثلاً، إثبات المواد الخام المشتراة بالسعر المعياري وبالتالي يتم تحديـد انحراف سعر المواد عند الشراء بـدلاً مـن الانتظار حتـى تاريخ استخدام المـواد، والتعديل الثاني ويشمل تحميل حساب الإنتاج تحت التشغيل بالأعباء الإضافية باستخدام معدل تحميل على أساس ساعات العمل الفعلية، وبهذا تستقر بعض انحرافات الأعباء الثابتة في حساب مراقبة التكاليف الصناعية غير المباشرة، ويتم إثبات هذه التعديلات بموجب قيود اليومية التالية:

(١) شراء المواد المباشرة:

حـ/ مراقبة المواد		١٠٥,٠٠٠
حـ/ الموردين	٩٩,٧٥٠	
حـ/ انحراف سعر المواد	٥,٢٥٠	
شراء ٣٥,٠٠٠ كغم مواد بسعر ٢,٨٥ د / كغم		

(٢) صرف المواد الخام للإنتاج :

حـ/ إنتاج تحت التشغيل		٨٧,٠٠٠
حـ/ مراقبة المواد	٨٧,٠٠٠	
إثبات صرف ٢٩,٠٠٠ كغم بسعر ٣ د / كغم		

ونتيجة لهذه القيود يوجد في حساب الإنتاج تحت التشغيل انحراف كفاءة المواد فقط. وان رصيد حساب مراقبة المواد يمثل التكاليف المعيارية لمخزون المواد.

(٣) تحميل الأعباء الإضافية على أساس ساعات العمل الفعلية:

في هذه الحالة يتم تحميل حسـاب إنتاج تحت التشـغيل بالأعباء الإضافية باستخدام معدل تحميل محدد مقدماً مقداره ٥ دنانير لكل ساعة عمل مباشرة فعلية. لذلك يتم تحميله بمبلغ ١٨٢,٥٠٠ د (٣٦,٥٠٠ ×٥=) ويسجل هذا المبلغ بموجب قيد اليومية التالي:

	حـ/ الإنتاج تحت التشغيل	١٨٢,٥٠٠	
حـ/ مراقبة الأعباء الإضافية			١٨٢,٥٠٠

وبموجب هـذا القيد تحمـل حسـاب الإنتاج تحت التشغيل بمبلغ يسـمى انحراف التحميل (١) ويعرف على أنه الفرق بين ساعات العمل المعيارية وسـاعات العمل الفعلية في معدل تحميل الأعباء الإضافية الكلي ويساوي:

(٣٦,٥٠٠ ساعة فعلية – ٣٦,٠٠٠ ساعة معيارية) × ٥د = ٢,٥٠٠ دينار.

يتم ترحيل هذا الانحراف إلى حساب مراقبة الأعباء الإضافية ليـدخل ضـمن الانحرافات التي سيتم حسابها بالنسبة للأعباء الإضافية، وبموجب هـذا التعديل يكون حساب مراقبة الأعباء الإضافية كالتالي:

حـ/ مراقبة الأعباء الإضافية

أعباء متغيرة	٦٥,٧٠٠	إنتاج تحت التشغيل	١٨٢,٥٠٠
أعباء ثابتة	١٠٥٨٥٠		
إنتاج تحت التشغيل	٢,٥٠٠		
		الرصيد	٨,٤٥٠

يتكون رصيد حساب الأعباء الإضافية أعلاه من ٦,٤٥٠ د (م) انحراف الإنفاق ناقص ١,٠٠٠ د (غ م) انحراف كفاءة زائد ٣,٠٠٠ د (م) انحراف حجم وهذه الانحرافات بقيت كما تم تحديدها في الحالة السابقة عند تحميل حساب الإنتاج تحت التشغيل بالتكاليف الفعلية، ويتم إقفال حساب الأعباء الإضافية بموجب قيد اليومية التالي:

	حـ/ الأعباء الإضافية		٨,٤٥٠
	حـ/ انحراف الكفاءة		١,٠٠٠
حـ/ انحراف الإنفاق		٦,٤٥٠	
حـ/ انحراف الحجم		٣,٠٠٠	

وتقفل حسابات الانحرافات بطبيعة الحـال في حساب إجمالي (ملخص) الانحرافات ويتم إدخال التعديلات السابقة إلى خطة التكـاليف المعيارية الجزئية لأنها تؤدي إلى :

١- تخفيض تكلفة الأعمال الكتابية، لأنها تسمح بمسك بطاقـات مخزون المـواد بالكميات بدلاً من الكميات والقيم.

٢- زيادة فعالية الرقابة، لأنها تحدد انحراف سعر المواد عند الشراء.

٣- تؤدي إلى تحميل الإنتاج بتكاليفه عند الانتهاء من إنتاجه بدلاً من الانتظار حتى يتم تجميع التكاليف الإضافية الفعلية.

ثانياً: طريقة التكاليف المعيارية الكاملة:

حسب هذه الطريقة يتم إثبات المواد الخام المشتراة بسعرها المعياري، ومـن ثم يتحدد انحراف سعر المواد عند الشراء، وكذلك يتم تحميل حساب الإنتاج تحت التشغيل بالتكلفة المعيارية لعناصر التكاليف، ومـن ثـم تسجيل انحراف الكميـة للمواد والأجور والأعباء لحظة تحميل حساب الإنتاج تحت التشغيل بالتكاليف المعيارية، وبالتالي فإن أي رصيد يظهر في هذا الحسـاب يمثل التكلفة المعيارية للإنتاج تحت التشغيل آخر المدة، وكما كان عليه الحال في طريقة التكاليف الجزئية يتم مسك حساب مخزون الإنتاج التام وتكلفة البضاعة المباعة بالتكاليف المعيارية [١]. ولإبراز قيود اليومية وحسابات البضاعة تحت هذه الطريقة سيتم الاعتماد على بيانات المثال رقم (١).

حـ/ مراقبة المواد (٣٥,٠٠٠ كغم×٣د)		١٠٥,٠٠٠
حـ/ الموردين	٩٩,٧٥٠	
حـ/ انحراف السعر (٣٥,٠٠٠ (٢,٨٥ - ٣))	٥,٢٥٠	

---

(١) Matz and Usry, Op.cit, Pp. ٥٠١-٥١٠.

٢- إثبات صرف المواد إلى الإنتاج :

حـ/ إنتاج تحت التشغيل ٦,٠٠٠×٥×٣		٩٠,٠٠٠
حـ/انحراف كمية (٢٩,٠٠٠-٣٠,٠٠٠)×٣	٣,٠٠٠	
حـ/ مراقبة المواد (٢٩٠٠٠ ×٣)	٨٧,٠٠٠	

٣ - إثبات تحميل الأجور:

حـ/ الإنتاج تحت التشغيل (٦,٠٠٠×١,٥)		٥٤,٠٠٠
حـ/ انحراف معدل الأجور (١,٥٠ – ١,٥٥) × ٣٦,٥٠٠		١,٨٢٥
حـ/ انحراف كفاءة الأجور (٣٦,٥٠٠ – ٣٦,٠٠٠)×١,٥		٧٥٠
حـ/ مراقبة الأجور	٥٦,٥٧٥	

٤- إثبات الأعباء الفعلية:

حـ/ مراقبة الأعباء الإضافية		١٧١,٠٥٠
حـ/ مذكورين	١٧١,٠٥٠	

٥- إثبات تحميل الأعباء المتغيرة:

حـ/ الإنتاج تحت التشغيل (٦,٠٠٠×٦×٢)		٧٢,٠٠٠
حـ/ مراقبة الأعباء الإضافية (٣٦,٠٠٠×٢)	٧٢,٠٠٠	

٦- إثبات تحميل الأعباء الثابتة:

حـ/ الإنتاج تحت التشغيل ٣٦,٠٠٠ ×٣		١٠٨,٠٠٠
حـ/ مراقبة الأعباء الإضافية	١٠٨,٠٠٠	

٧- إثبات تكلفة البضاعة التامة الصنع:

حـ/ مخزون الإنتاج التام (٦,٠٠٠× ٥٤د)		٣٢٤,٠٠٠
حـ/ الإنتاج تحت التشغيل	٣٢٤,٠٠٠	

٨- إثبات انحرافات الأعباء الإضافية – طريقة الأربعة انحرافات:

ويعد حساب انحرافات الأعباء الإضافية كما ورد في الفصل السابق يتم قيدها في الدفاتر كالتالي:

حـ/ مراقبة أعباء إضافية		٨,٤٥٠
حـ/ انحراف كفاءة الأعباء الثابتة		١,٠٠٠
حـ/ انحراف إنفاق الأعباء الثابتة		٨٥٠
حـ/ انحراف إنفاق الأعباء المتغيرة	٧,٣٠٠	
حـ/ انحراف الحجم	٣,٠٠٠	

إقفال حساب الأعباء الإضافية وتحويله إلى حساب إجمالي الانحرافات:

مراقبة المواد الخام		الإنتاج تحت التشغيل	
(١) ١٠٥,٠٠٠	(٢) ٩٠,٠٠٠	(٢) ٩٠,٠٠٠	(٧) ٣٢٤,٠٠٠
		(٣) ٥٤,٠٠٠	
		(٥) ٧٢,٠٠٠	
		(٦) ١٠٨,٠٠٠	

الأعباء الإضافية		البضاعة التامة الصنع	
(٤) ١٧١,٥٥٠	(٥) ٧٢,٠٠٠	(٧) ٣٢٤,٠٠٠	
(٨) ٨,٤٥٠	(٦) ١٠٨,٠٠٠		

إجمالي الانحرافات			
(١)	٥،٢٥٠	(٣)	١،٨٢٥
(٢)	٣،٠٠٠	(٣)	٧٥٠
(٨)	٧،٣٠٠	(٨)	١،٠٠٠
(٨)	٣،٠٠٠	(٨)	٨٥٠
	١٤١٢٥ الرصيد		

لقد قمنا بترحيل الانحرافات إلى حساب إجمالي الانحرافات فهذا الحساب هو حساب مراقبة عامة، وكذلك تم تحميل انحرافات الأعباء الإضافية حسب طريقة الأربعة انحرافات وهذه الانحرافات – كما رأينا – كانت مستقرة في حساب مراقبة الأعباء الإضافية لأن حساب الإنتاج تحت التشغيل يتم تحميله باستخدام معدل التحميل وعلى أساس ساعات العمل المعيارية. وسيتم معالجة هذه الانحرافات لغرض إعداد القوائم المالية فيما بعد.

المعالجة المحاسبية للانحرافات:

تختلف المعالجة المحاسبية للانحرافات حسب وجهات النظر تجاه التكاليف المعيارية، فالبعض يرى أن التكاليف المعيارية هي التكاليف الحقيقة للإنتاج وأن الانحرافات تمثل عدم كفاية وإسراف التي كان يمكن منع حدوثهما لو تم التمسك بالإجراءات التي تم تحديدها عند وضع التكاليف المعيارية، ولذلك يدافعون عن عدم جواز إقفال هذه الانحرافات في حسابات تكلفة البضاعة، وبالتالي فإن الانحرافات من وجهة نظرهم هي تكاليف فترة يجب أن تحمل على قائمة الدخل في فترة حدوثها، أما وجهة النظر الأخرى فترى أن التكاليف الفعلية هي التكاليف الحقيقية، وبالتالي تدافع عن ضرورة توزيع الانحرافات على حسابات تكلفة البضاعة حتى تعكس هذه الحسابات التكلفة الحقيقية لحسابات البضاعة [١].

---

(١) J. Batty, "Standard Costing", ٢nd. Ed., (Macdonald and Evans ١٩٦٦), Pp. ٣٢٧-٣٣٢.

وفي هذا المجال يمكن التمييز بين الانحرافات عن المعايير الممكن تحقيقها والانحرافات الناتجة عن استخدام معايير مثالية، واعتبار الأخيرة ضمن تكاليف الإنتاج لأن المعايير المثالية لا يمكن تحقيقها[1]. أما الانحرافات الأولى فيجب أن تعتبر ضمن تكاليف الفترة، فمثلاً إذا كان المعيار المثالي يسمح باستخدام ٣ ساعات عمل مباشرة في حين أن المعيار الممكن تحقيقه يسمح باستخدام ٣,٥ ساعة عمل مباشر، وأثناء التنفيذ تم استخدام ٥ ساعات عمل، فبموجب هذه المعلومات يكون الانحراف عن المعيار المثالي مقداره ٢ ساعة عمل منها ٠,٥ ساعة تمثل انحراف عن المعيار الممكن تحقيقه وهذه تحمل على الإنتاج، أما الساعة والنصف الأخرى والتي تمثل الفرق بين الوقت الفعلي والمعيار الممكن تحقيقه فتعتبر ضمن تكاليف الفترة، وبين هذين الأسلوبين قد نجد وجهات نظر تتطلب معالجة الانحرافات في ضوء أهميتها النسبية وهنا إذا كانت الانحرافات غير مهمة فلا تحتاج إلى توزيع وعليه يتم تحميلها على قائمة الدخل أو يتم أقفالها في حساب تكلفة البضاعة المباعة، وهذا هو موقف مجلس معايير التكاليف[2]، والذي يرى أن يتم أقفالها في تكلفة البضاعة المباعة إذا لم تكن قيمتها جوهرية بدلاً من تحميلها على قائمة الدخل.

وفي دراسة أجريت على مجموعة من الشركات في الولايات المتحدة الأمريكية تبين أن ٥٣,١% من الشركات تقوم بإقفال الانحرافات في حساب تكلفة البضاعة المباعة، ١٠,٥% تقوم بإقفال الانحرافات في قائمة الدخل، ٣٣,٦% تقوم بإقفال الانحرافات بحسابات تكلفة البضائع، وأن ٢,٨ تتبع معالجات أخرى أو لم تقم برد الاستبانة[3]، من هذه الدراسة نجد أن الأقلية هي التي تقوم باعتبار الانحرافات تكاليف فترة، أما الأغلبية فتعتبرها من ضمن تكلفة البضاعة المباعة أو ضمن تكاليف حسابات البضاعة، وهذا يعني أن الأغلبية تعتبر التكاليف الفعلية هي التكلفة الحقيقية للإنتاج، وبطبيعة الحال يعتبر تحميل الانحرافات على تكلفة البضاعة المباعة أمراً سهلاً ويمكن تبريره على أساس أن هذا

(١) Horngren and Foster, Op.cit., P. ٢١٧.

(٢) Matz and Usry, Op.cit, P. ٥١٤.

(٣) Horngern and Foster, Op.cit., P. ٢٧٥.

الحساب هو أكبر حسابات البضاعة، لـذلك سـيركز بقيـة هـذا القسـم علـى توزيع الانحرافات على حسابات تكلفة البضاعة.

توزيع الانحرافات:

يتم توزيع الانحرافات – كما ذكرنا سابقاً – علـى حسـاب البضاعة التـي يـتم إمساكها بالتكلفة المعيارية، وهي مراقبة المـواد الخـام، وإنتاج تحـت التشغيل، والبضاعة التامة الصنع وتكلفة البضاعة المباعة، ويجـب أن يـتم التوزيع أمـا علـى أساس أرصدتها النهائية، أو على أساس ما يحتويه الحساب من تكاليف معيارية في ذلك العنصر [1]. ولتوضيح إجراءات التوزيع سيتم الاعتماد على البيانات التالية:

مثال (٢):

أدى تحليل أرصدة حسابات البضاعة إلى ظهور البيانات التالية:

أعباء إضافية	أجور مباشرة	مواد مباشرة	الرصيد	اسم الحساب
١,٥١٢	٢,١٦٠	٤,٠٠٠	٧,٦٧٢	إنتاج تحت التشغيل
١,٢٦٠	١,٨٠٠	٣,٠٠٠	٦,٠٦٠	بضاعة تامة
٥,٦٢٨	٨,٠٤٠	١٣,٠٠٠	٢٦,٦٦٨	بضاعة مباعة
٠٠	٠٠٠	١٠,٠٠٠	١٠,٠٠٠	مواد خام
٨,٤٠٠	١٢,٠٠٠	٣٠,٠٠٠	٥٠,٤٠٠	المجموع

وكانت انحرافات التكاليف الصناعية كالتالي:

انحراف سعر المواد	١,٩٥٠ د (غ م)
انحراف كمية المواد	٦٠٠ د (غ م)
انحراف الأجور	١,٥٠٠ د (غ م)
الانحراف الكلي للأعباء الإضافية	٥٠٠ د (غ م)

والمطلوب:

توزيع الانحرافات على حسابات البضاعة بنسبة ما يحتويه كـل منهـا مـن تكاليف معيارية.

---

(١) Fisher and Frank, Op.cit., Pp. ٣٣٩ – ٣٤٤.

الحل:

للبدء في الحل يجب إعداد مصفوفة النسب المئوية للتوزيع، حيث تبين النسبة قيمة البند في حساب البضاعة إلى إجمالي تكلفة البند، فمثلاً تكون نسبة المواد الخام في حساب مخزون البضاعة التامة الصنع ١٠% وهي عبارة عن ((٣,٠٠٠ دينار ÷ ٣٠,٠٠٠) × ١٠٠%) وتكون نسبة المواد في حساب البضاعة المباعة ٤٣,٣% (١٣,٠٠٠= ÷ ٣٠,٠٠٠) وهكذا بالنسبة لبقية البنود الواردة في عمود سعر المواد، وبنفس الطريقة يتم حساب النسب الأخرى وتظهر مصفوفة النسب المئوية كالتالي:

الأعباء الإضافية	الأجور	كمية المواد	سعر المواد	اسم الحساب
١٨%	١٨%	٢٠%	١٣,٣%	إنتاج تحت التشغيل
١٥%	١٥%	١٥%	١٠%	بضاعة تامة الصنع
٦٧%	٦٧%	٦٥%	٤٣,٣%	تكلفة بضاعة مباعة
٠٠	٠٠٠	٠٠٠	٣٣,٣%	مواد خام
١٠٠%	١٠٠%	١٠٠%	١٠٠%	الإجمالي

وفي هذه المصفوفة خصص للنسب المئوية لتوزيع انحراف سعر المواد وعمود آخر لتوزيع انحراف كمية المواد والسبب في ذلك هو أن مخزون مواد الخام لا يساهم في حدوث انحراف كمية المواد، ولكن لهذه المواد تأثير على انحراف سعر المواد، لذلك يجب ألا يتحمل حساب مخزون المواد الخام بأي نصيب من انحراف الكمية، وبالنسبة لأعمدة الأجور المباشرة والأعباء الإضافية فهما يحتويان على نفس النسب المئوية لأن الأعباء الإضافية تحمل على أساس الأجور المباشرة، وبضرب النسب المئوية الظاهرة في مصفوفة الانحرافات في الانحراف المعني نتوصل إلى توزيع تكاليف فمثلاً يتم توزيع انحراف سعر المواد كالتالي:

مواد خام = ١,٩٥٠ × ٣٣,٣%	= ٦٥٠ د
بضاعة مباعة = ١,٩٥٠ × ٤٣,٣%	= ٨٤٥ د
بضاعة تامة الصنع = ١,٩٥٠ × ١٠%	= ١٩٥د
إنتاج تحت التشغيل = ١,٩٥٠ × ١٣,٣%	= ٢٦٠د

وهكذا يتم توزيع باقي الانحرافات.

جدول (١١-١)

توزيع الانحرافات على حسابات تكلفة البضاعة

انحراف	الإجمالي	مواد خام	إنتاج تحت التشغيل	بضاعة تامة	بضاعة مباعة
سعر المواد	١,٩٥٠	٦٥٠	٢٦٠	١٩٥	٨٤٥
استخدام المواد	٦٠٠	...	١٢٠	٩٠	٣٩٠
الأجور	١,٥٠٠	...	٢٧٠	٢٢٥	١,٠٠٥
الأعباء الإضافية	٥٠٠	...	٩٠	٧٥	٢٣٥
المجموع	٤,٥٥٠	٦٥٠	٧٤٠	٥٨٥	٢,٥٧٥

وعليه يمكن إثبات توزيع هذه الانحرافات كالتالي:

ح/ مخزون المواد الخام		٦٥٠
ح/ إنتاج تحت التشغيل		٧٤٠
ح/ بضاعة تامة		٥٨٥
ح/ تكلفة البضاعة المباعة		٢,٠٧٥
ح/ ملخص الانحرافات	٤,٥٥٠	

وبعد عمل هذا القيد يتم ترحيله إلى الحسابات المعنية فيقفل حساب ملخص الانحرافات وتعدل حسابات البضاعة بنصيبها من الأعباء الإضافية، وبالرجوع إلى المثال رقم (٢) وفتح حسابات للبضاعة بأرصدتها المعيارية وترحيل القيد السابق إلى تلك الحسابات تصبح أرصدتها الفعلية كالتالي:

بضاعة تامة الصنع

٦،٠٦٠ رصيد	
٥٨٥ انحراف	
٦،٦٤٥ رصيد	

المواد الخام

٣٠،٠٠٠ رصيد	
١،٩٥٠ انحراف سعر	
٦٠٠ انحراف كمية	
٣٢،٥٥٠ رصيد	

بضاعة مباعة

٢٦،٦٦٧ رصيد	
٢،٥٧٥ انحراف	
٢٩٢٤٢ رصيد	

الإنتاج تحت التشغيل

٧،٦٧٢ رصيد	
٧٤٠ انحراف	
٨،٤١٢ رصيد	

الأعباء الإضافية

٨،٤٠٠ الرصيد	
٥٠٠ انحراف	
٨،٩٠٠ الرصيد الفعلي	

الأجور

	١٢،٠٠٠
	١،٥٠٠
	١٣،٥٠٠

مواد خام آخر المدة

١٠،٠٠٠ رصيد	
٦٥٠ انحراف	
١٠،٦٥٠	

قائمة تكلفة البضاعة المباعة المعيارية:

في ضوء البيانات المعطاة في المثال رقم (٢) تكون قائمة تكلفة البضاعة المباعة بالتكاليف المعيارية كالتالي:

مواد خام متاحة للإنتاج	٣٠,٠٠٠
ناقص: مواد خام آخر المدة	١٠,٠٠٠
تكلفة المواد المباشرة	٢٠,٠٠٠
الأجور المباشرة	١٢,٠٠٠
التكاليف الصناعية غير المباشرة	٨,٤٠٠
التكلفة الصناعية للفترة الجارية	٤٠,٤٠٠
زائد إنتاج تحت التشغيل أول المدة	-.-
ناقص: إنتاج تحت التشغيل آخر المدة	(٧,٦٧٢)
تكلفة البضاعة تامة الصنع خلال الفترة	٣٢,٧٢٨
زائد: تكلفة بضاعة تامة الصنع أول المدة	-.-
ناقص: تكلفة بضاعة تامة الصنع آخر المدة	٦,٠٦٠
التكلفة المعيارية للبضاعة المباعة	٢٦,٦٦٨

قائمة تكلفة البضاعة المباعة الفعلية:

يتم تحويل قائمة البضاعة المباعة بالتكلفة المعيارية إلى قائمة بالتكلفة الفعلية، وذلك بإضافة الانحرافات الخاصة بالمواد المباشرة والأجور المباشرة والأعباء الإضافية للتوصل إلى التكلفة الصناعية الفعلية للفترة الجارية، وكذلك يتم تعديل تكالي ف مخزون الإنتاج تحت التشغيل والبضاعة تامة الصنع بترحيل نصيبها من الانحرافات كما يظهر في جدول تحليل الانحرافات ، فمثلاً بإضافة الانحرافات الخاصة بالمواد تصبح التكلفة الفعلية للمواد المباشرة (٣٠,٠٠٠ د زائد ١,٩٥٠ د انحراف سعر المواد زائد ٦٠٠ انحراف كمية المواد =) ٣٢,٢٥٠ د ثم بطرح التكلفة الفعلية للمواد المباشرة آخر المدة وقدرها ١٠,٦٥٠ د (١٠,٠٠٠ د زائد ٦٥٠ د نصيبها من الانحرافات) ولتسهيل فهم العملية يجب

فتح حسابات التكلفة المعيارية وترحيل الانحرافات الموزعة عليها وبعد ذلك يتم أعداد قائمة تكلفة البضاعة المباعة الفعلية من تلك الحسابات، وفي ضوء ما سبق يمكن إعداد قائمة التكلفة الفعلية للبضاعة المباعة كالتالي:

قائمة تكلفة البضاعة المباعة الفعلية:

مواد خام متاحة للإنتاج	٣٢,٥٥٠	
ناقص: مواد خام آخر المدة	١٠,٦٥٠	
تكلفة المواد المباشرة		٢١,٩٠٠
الأجور المباشرة (١٢٠٠٠ + ١٥٠٠)		١٣,٥٠٠
تكاليف صناعية غير مباشرة فعلية (٨٤٠٠ + ٥٠٠)		٨,٩٠٠
التكلفة الصناعية للفترة الجارية		٤٤,٣٠٠
ناقص: إنتاج تحت التشغيل آخر المدة (٧٦٧٢+٧٤٠)		٨,٤١٢
تكلفة البضاعة تامة الصنع		٣٥,٨٨٨
ناقص: بضاعة تامة الصنع آخر المدة (٦٠٦٠+٥٨٥)		٦,٦٤٥
التكلفة الفعلية للبضاعة المباعة		٢٩,٢٤٣

يمثل رقم تكلفة البضاعة المباعة تكلفتها المعيارية زائد نصيب هـذه البضاعة من الانحرافات وتساوي: ٢٦,٦٦٨ + ٢,٥٧٥ = ٢٩,٢٤٣ د.

توزيع الانحرافات على أساس الأرصدة النهائية:

للتسهيل وتجنب تحليل الحسابات – كما في الطريقـة السابقـة – يمكن استخدام الأرصدة النهائية لحسابات البضاعة كأساس لتوزيع إجمالي الانحرافات، وبالرجوع إلى بيانات المثال رقم ٢ يتم توزيع الانحرافات فيما عدا انحراف سعر المواد بنسبة ٧,٦٧٢: ٦,٠٦٠: ٢٦,٦٦٨ على حسابات إنتاج تحت التشغيل وحساب البضاعة التامة الصنع وحساب تكلفة البضاعة المباعة على التوالي.

تطبيق التكاليف المعيارية في صناعة المراحل:

يمكن استخدام التكاليف المعيارية عند إتباع طريقة محاسبة المراحل وطريقة محاسبة الأوامر الإنتاجية، ويعتبر تطبيقها في صناعة المراحل أسهل بكثير من صناعة الأوامر لأن الإنتاج في المراحل يتدفق بانتظام وتكون الوحدات متماثلة. أما في صناعة الأوامر فتكون وحدات الإنتاج غير متماثلة، مما يتطلب وضع معايير لكل طلبية يتم استلامها وتحليل انحرافاتها، على أية حال، ستبقى إجراءات محاسبة التكاليف الفعلية والمعيارية هي نفسها التي تم شرحها في الفصول السابقة، ولإيضاح إجراءات محاسبة التكاليف المعيارية سوف نقتصرـ تطبيقها على منشأة تعمل في صناعة المراحل.

في محاسبة المراحل تحدد معايير عناصر التكاليف المختلفة اللازمة لإنتاج وحدة المنتج، وفي نهاية كل فترة يتم قياس عدد وحدات الإنتاج المكافئ وضربها بالتكلفة المعيارية لوحدة المنتج لتحديد التكلفة المعيارية لحجم الإنتاج الفعلي، ويتم استخدام التكلفة المعيارية لتحليل الانحرافات بالأسلوب نفسه الذي سبق شرحه في الفصل التاسع ولتوضيح تحليل الانحرافات في صناعة المراحل سيتم الاعتماد على البيانات التالية:

مثال (٣):

تحتوي بطاقة التكلفة المعيارية لوحدة المنتج على الآتي:

مواد مباشرة (٥ كغم بمعدل ٢د / كغم) = ١٠ د

أجور مباشرة (٤ ساعات بمعدل ١,٥ د / س ع م = ٦ د)

أعباء متغيرة (٤ ساعات بمعدل ١ د / س ع م) = ٤د

أعباء ثابتة (٤ ساعات بمعدل ٢ د/ س ع م) = ٨ د

وكانت الطاقة العادية هي ٨٠,٠٠٠ ساعة عمل مباشر. وخلال شهر آذار كانت النتائج الفعلية كالتالي:

وحدات تحت التشغيل أول المدة	٢٠٠٠ عند مستوى إتمامها ٦٠%	
وحدات مضافة خلال الفترة	٢٠,٠٠٠	
وحدات تامة خلال الفترة	١٨,٠٠٠	
وحدات تحت التشغيل آخر المدة	٤,٠٠٠ مستوى إتمام ٤٠%	

وتضاف المواد في بداية عملية التشغيل بينما تضاف تكاليف التحويل بانتظام
وبلغت التكلفة الفعلية لمرحلة الإنتاج كالتالي:

مواد مباشرة (٩٨,٠٠٠ كغم بسعر ٢,٢ د)   =   ٢١٥,٦٠٠ د

الأجور المباشرة (٧٨,٢٠٠ ساعة عمل بمعدل ١,٦٠د)   =   ١٢٥,١٢٠ د

الأعباء المتغيرة (٧٨,٢٠٠ ساعة بمعدل ٠,٩٥)   =   ٧٤,٢٩٠د

الأعباء الثابتة   =   ١٥٨,٧٥٠

المطلوب: تحليل انحرافات تكاليف المرحلة عند استخدام طريقة الأول في الأول في
المحاسبة على تكاليف المرحلة.

الحل:

قبل البدء في التحليل يجب تحديد عدد الوحدات المكافئة وهي كالتالي:

تكاليف تحويل	مواد		
		٢,٠٠٠	وحدات تحت التشغيل أول المدة
		(٦٠%)	
		٢٠,٠٠٠	وحدات مضافة
تكاليف تحويل	مواد	٢٢,٠٠٠	وحدات سيتم المحاسبة عليها
٨٠٠	٠٠٠	٢,٠٠٠	وحدات تحت التشغيل أول المدة
١٦,٠٠٠	١٦,٠٠٠	١٦,٠٠٠	وحدات بدأت وتمت
١,٦٠٠	٤,٠٠٠	٤,٠٠٠	وحدات تحت التشغيل آخر المدة
---	---	٢٢,٠٠٠	وحدات تم المحاسبة عليها
١٨,٤٠٠	٢٠,٠٠٠		وحدات متجانسة (متكافئة)

ويتكون رقم تكاليف التحويل من الأجور المباشرة والأعباء الإضافية. وبالاعتماد
على البيانات المثال ٣ والبيانات الفعلية الواردة في تقرير تكاليف المرحلة يتم
تحليل انحرافات المرحلة كالتالي:

أولاً: انحرافات المواد المباشرة:

إذا تم تحديد انحرافات سعر المواد عند الشراء تكون انحرافات المواد المباشرة
كالتالي:

(أ) انحراف سعر المواد = (سعر المعياري – سعر الفعلي)× كمية فعلية مشتراة

= (٢ - ٢,٢) × ٩٨,٠٠٠ كيلو

= ١٩,٦٠٠ د (غ م)

(ب) انحراف كمية المواد = (كمية فعلية – كمية معيارية) × ٨ د سعر معياري

= (٩٨,٠٠٠ – ٢٠,٠٠٠×٥) ×٢

= ٤,٠٠٠ د (م)

ثانياً: انحرافات الأجور المباشرة:

(أ) انحراف معدل الأجور = (المعدل المعياري – المعدل الفعلي) × ساعات العمل الفعلية

= (١,٥ – ١,٦) × ٧٨,٢٠٠ ساعة

= ٧,٨٢٠ د (غ م)

(ب) انحراف كمية (كفاءة) الأجور = (ساعات العمل المعيارية – ساعات العمل الفعلية) × معدل الأجور المعياري

= (١٨,٤٠٠ × ٤ - ٧٨,٢٠٠)× ١,٥

= ٦,٩٠٠ د (غ م)

ثالثاً: انحرافات الأعباء الإضافية في طريقة الأربعة انحرافات:

أ- انحراف إنفاق الأعباء المتغيرة =الأعباء الفعلية – الموازنة المرنة لساعات العمل الفعلية

= ٧٤,٢٩٠ – ٧٨,٢٠٠ ×١

= ٣,٩١٠ د (غ م)

ب- انحراف إنفاق الأعباء الثابتة = الأعباء الثابتة الفعلية – الأعباء الثابتة المخططة

= ١٥٨,٧٥٠ – ٨٠,٠٠٠ ساعة × ٢

= ١,٢٥٠ د (م)

جـ- انحراف كفاءة الأعباء الإضافية = (ساعات العمل المعيارية – ساعات العمل الفعلية) × معدل تحميل الأعباء المتغيرة

= (١٨,٤٠٠ × ٤ - ٧٨,٢٠٠) ×١

= ٤,٦٠٠ د (غ م)

د- انحراف الحجم = (ساعات العمل المعيارية – ساعات الطاقة العادية)× معدل تحميل الأعباء الثابتة

$= (٧٣,٦٠٠ - ٨٠,٠٠٠)×٢$

$= ١٢,٨٠٠$ د (غ م)

كانت الانحرافات التي تم حسابها في الفصل التاسع ومقدمة هـذا الفصل تفترض – ضمنا – أن لا يوجد وحدات تحت التشغيل آخر المـدة أو أولهـا. وهـذا الافتراض غير عملي. ولكن هذا الجزء فقد افترض وجـود وحدات تحـت التشـغيل آخر المدة وأخذها في الحسبان عند تحليل انحرافات عناصر التكاليف.

الخاتمـة

لقد قمنا في هذا الفصل بدراسة طرق محاسبة التكاليف المعيارية ووجدنا أنه يمكن إتباع طريقتين رئيسيتين هما: طريقـة التكاليف الجزئيـة وطريقـة التكاليف المعيارية الكاملة، ووجدنا أن الاختلاف الرئيسي بينهما يكمن في طبيعة المبالغ التي تحمل على حساب الإنتاج تحت التشغيل، ففي الطريقة الجزئية كان يتم تحميل حساب الإنتاج تحت التشغيل بالتكاليف الفعلية، أمـا عنـد استخدام طريقـة التكاليف المعيارية الكاملة فانه يتم تحميل هذا الحساب بالتكاليف المعيارية لعناصر التكاليف، وفي الطريقة الجزئية وجدنا أن كل الانحرافات توجد في حساب الإنتاج تحـت التشغيل، بينما في الطريقة الكلية تسجل الانحرافات في حساب إجمالي الانحرافات لحظة تحميل حساب الإنتاج تحت التشغيل بالتكاليف المعيارية لعناصر التكاليف، وبين هاتين الطريقتين قد نـرى بعض التعديلات التي تتطلب تسجيل المواد الخام المشتراة بالأسعار المعيارية وتحميل الأعباء الإضافية باستخدام ساعات العمل المعيارية أو باستخدام ساعات العمل الفعلية، مضروبة في معدل التحميل المحدد مقدماً. وقد غطى هـذا الفصل أيضاً طرق معالجة الانحرافات، وتبين أن أغلب الشركات أما أنها تقفل الانحرافات في حساب تكلفة البضاعة المباعة، أو أنها توزعهـا عـلى حسابات تكلفة البضاعة المباعـة، وتكلفـة مخزون الإنتاج التام، وتكلفة الإنتاج تحت التشغيل، وتكلفة مخزون المواد الخام، وفي نهاية الفصل تم عرض أسلوب تحليل الانحرافات في صناعة المراحل، وبينا أنه عند حساب انحرافات التكلفة المعيارية لعناصر التكاليف يجب استخدام عـدد وحدات الإنتاج المكافئ لكل عنصر تكلفة.

أسئلة وتمارين

السؤال الأول: أذكر الملامح الرئيسية لطريقة التكلفة المعيارية الجزئية وطريقة التكلفة المعيارية الكاملة.

السؤال الثاني: عند تحليل الانحرافات حسب طريقة التكلفة المعيارية الجزئية أين ستوجد انحرافات التكاليف؟

السؤال الثالث: من الأفضل طريقة التكلفة المعيارية الجزئية أم طريقة التكلفة الكلية لغرض الرقابة ولماذا؟

السؤال الرابع: تختلف طرق معالجة الانحرافات عن بعضها، اذكر أهم هذه الطرق والأساس النظري الذي تستند عليه كل منها؟

السؤال الخامس: إذا كانت التكاليف المعيارية هي التكاليف الحقيقية بين كيف يتم إقفال حسابات الانحرافات.

السؤال السادس: أذكر مزايا وعيوب توزيع الانحرافات على أساس الأرصدة النهائية لحسابات البضاعة.

السؤال السابع: تستخدم شركة صناعية التكاليف المعيارية وكانت تكلفة وحدة المنتج كالآتي:

مواد مباشرة (٣ كغم بسعر ٢ د/ كغم)	٦د
أجور مباشرة (٢ ساعة بمعدل أجرة ١,٢٥ د / س ع م)	٢,٥ د
أعباء متغيرة (٢ ساعة بمعدل ١,٥ د / س ع م)	٣د
أعباء ثابتة (٢ ساعة بمعدل ٣ د / س ع م ، باستخدام طاقة مقدارها ٢٥,٠٠٠ ساعة)	٦ د
التكلفة المعيارية للوحدة	١٧,٥ د

وخلال الفترة حدثت الوقائع التالية:
- تم إنتاج ١٠,٠٠٠ وحدة وحولت إلى مخازن المنتجات التامة الصنع.
- تم شراء ٤٠,٠٠٠ كغم من المواد المباشرة بمبلغ ٨٢,٠٠٠ دينار على الحساب.
- تم صرف ٣١,٠٠٠ كغم من المواد المباشرة إلى الإنتاج.
- بلغت الأجور المباشرة ٣٠,٠٠٠ د وتمثل تكلفة ٢٣,٠٠٠ ساعة عمل مباشرة.
- بلغت الأعباء المتغيرة ٣٢,٠٠٠ دينار.
- بلغت الأعباء الثابتة بما فيها الأجور غير المباشرة ٧٣,٥٠٠ دينار.

المطلوب:

(١) تحليل عناصر التكاليف بأقصى ما تسمح به البيانات والمعلومات المعطاة أعلاه وتقوم الشركة بإثبات تكلفة المواد المباشرة بموجب الأسعار المعيارية عند الشراء. إثبات قيود اليومية المتعلقة بشراء المواد وصرفها للإنتاج.

السؤال الثامن: بالرجوع إلى البيانات الواردة في السؤال السابع افترض أن الشركة تستخدم طريقة التكاليف المعيارية الجزئية.

المطلوب:

١- عمل قيود اليومية اللازمة لإثبات الوقائع السابقة.
٢- تصوير حسابات البضاعة بطريقة أصولية.
٣- تصوير حساب إجمالي الانحرافات.

السؤال التاسع: بالرجوع إلى البيانات الواردة في السؤال السابع وبافتراض أن الشركة تقوم باستخدام طريقة التكاليف المعيارية الكلية.

المطلوب:

١- عمل قيود اليومية اللازمة لإثبات الوقائع السابقة.
٢- تصوير حسابات البضاعة بطريقة أصولية.

السؤال العاشر: المعلومات الآتية مستخرجة من دفاتر إحدى الشركات الصناعية:

المخزون:

إنتاج تحت التشغيل أول المدة ٢,٠٠٠ وحدة ونسبة إتمامه ٧٠% بالنسبة لتكاليف التحويل و ١٠٠% بالنسبة للمواد المباشرة، وإنتاج تحت التشغيل آخر المدة ٥,٠٠٠ وحدة ونسبة إتمامه ٤٠% بالنسبة لتكاليف التحويل ١٠٠% بالنسبة للمواد وتستخدم الشركة طريقة المتوسط المرجح.

وعدد الوحدات التي بدأت التشغيل خلال المدة ٢٠,٠٠٠ وحدة، ولم يكن هناك أية بضائع تامة الصنع أول المدة وآخرها، والآتي التكلفة المعيارية لوحدة المنتج.

مواد مباشرة (٤ كغم بسعر ١,٥ د)	٦د
أجور مباشرة (٣ ساعات بمعدل ٢د)	٦د
أعباء إضافية (٣ ساعات بمعدل ٣د/س ع م، ٦٠% منها	
أعباء ثابتة خصصت على أساس إنتاج ٢٠,٠٠٠ وحدة)	٩د
التكلفة المعيارية للوحدة	٢١د

وخلال الفترة حدث الآتي:

- صرف للإنتاج ٨٢,٠٠٠ كغم وتكلفتها الفعلية ١٢٠,٠٠٠ وهي كمية المواد المشتراة فعلاً.

- تم استخدام ٥٢,٠٠٠ ساعة عمل مباشرة وبلغت أجورها الفعلية ١٠٢,٥٠٠ دينار.

- بلغت الأعباء الإضافية الفعلية ١٦٤,٦٠٠ دينار.

المطلوب:

١- عمل القيود اليومية بافتراض استخدام طريقة التكاليف المعيارية الكاملة.

٢- تحديد تكلفة البضاعة المباعة بافتراض أن الانحرافات يتم أقفالها في تكلفة البضاعة المباعة.

السؤال الحادي عشر: بالرجوع إلى بيانات التمرين (١٠) وبافتراض أن الشركة تقوم بتوزيع الانحرافات على حسابات البضاعة على أساس ما يحتويه كل حساب من تكلفة معيارية لعناصر التكاليف.

المطلوب:

١- توزيع الانحرافات على حسابات تكلفة البضاعة.

٢- تحديد تكلفة البضاعة المباعة حسب التكلفة الفعلية.

السؤال الثاني عشر: تتبع إحدى الشركات طريقة التكاليف المعيارية الكاملة والآتي بيانات عن البضاعة الموجودة لديها:

تكاليف التحميل	المواد المباشرة	الإجمالي	اسم الحساب
٠٠٠٠	١٠,٠٠٠	١٠,٠٠٠	مواد خام
٨,٠٠٠	١٢,٠٠٠	٢٠,٠٠٠	إنتـــــاج تحـــــت التشغيل
١٨,٠٠٠	١٢,٠٠٠	٣٠,٠٠٠	بضاعة تامة الصنع
١٤٤,٠٠٠	٩٦,٠٠٠	٢٤٠,٠٠٠	بضاعة مباعة
١٧٠,٠٠٠	١٣٠,٠٠٠	٣٠٠,٠٠٠	الإجمالي

وكانت انحرافات عناصر التكاليف الصناعية كالتالي:

١- انحراف سعر المواد المباشرة ٦,٥٠٠ د (مفضل).

٢- انحراف كمية المواد المباشرة ٦,٠٠٠ د (غير مفضل).

٣- انحرافات تكاليف التحويل ١١,٩٠٠ د (غير مفضل).

المطلوب:

١- توزيع الانحرافات على حسابات البضاعة على أساس التكاليف المعيارية لعناصر التكاليف.

٢- إعداد قائمة التكاليف المعيارية للبضاعة المباعة.

٣- إعداد قائمة التكاليف الفعلية للبضاعة على أساس توزيع الانحرافات كما تم التوصل إليه في المطلوب في رقم (١).

السؤال الثالث عشر: بـدأت إحـدى الشركات أعمالها في ١/١/من السـنة الجاريـة وتمسك حساباتها باستخدام الحاسوب وبطريقـة التكـاليف المعياريـة الكاملـة، وفي ٣/٣١ من السنة الجارية وهو تاريخ نهاية فترة التكـاليف الأولى، أصيب الحاسوب بفيروس أدى إلى تلف كافة قيود اليومية التي سبق تسجيلها، وبالاتصال بمصادر التوريد وجرد مستودعات المـواد الخـام، ومتابعة سـندات صرف المـواد وبطاقات العمل الإضافي وبعض الأوراق المتوافرة لدى المحاسب تم تصوير الحسابات التالية (المبالغ بالألف).

حـ/ تكلفة البضاعة المباعة		حـ/ مراقبة المواد		حـ/ الموردين	
٨٠ ٣/٣١	٨٠ ٣/٣١	٢٨ ٣/٣١	٣٨ ٣/٣١	٤٠ ٣/٣١	٣٥ ٣/٣١
حـ/ انحراف كفاءة الأجور		**حـ/ الأجور المستحقة**		**حـ/ الإنتاج تحت التشغيل**	
٣ ٣/٣١		٢٩ ٣/٣١		١٥ آخر المدة	٢٦ مواد
					٣٠ الأجور
					٤٥ أعباء

وكانـت الشركـة تقـوم بتحميـل الأعبـاء الإضـافية بنسـبة ١٥٠% مـن الأجـور المباشرة وحسب معدل تحميل الأعباء الإضافية على أساس ان الأجور المعيارية هي ٣٥ دينار، وأن ٦٠% من هذه الأعباء ثابتة، وقد بلغت الأعباء الفعلية ٤٨ منها ٨ د استهلاك والباقي دفع نقداً.

المطلوب:

١- إعـادة إثبات قيـود اليوميـة اللازمـة لإثبـات إجمالي عمليـات الشركـة عـن الفترة المنتهية في ٣,٣١

٢- تصوير حساب إجمالي الانحرافات.

السؤال الرابع عشر: تستخدم شركة الأردن الصناعية التكاليف المعيارية في المحاسبة على تكاليف إنتاجها من أفران الغاز. وكانت بطاقة التكلفة المعيارية لإنتاج فرن الغاز ماركة رم ٣١٥ كالتالي:

دينار	مواد مباشرة
٦	صاج سمك ١,٥ ملم ٢م١,٥ بسعر ٤ د للمتر المربع
٦	مواسير نحاسية ٤ متر بسعر ١,٥ دينار للمتر
٢	زجاج ٠,٤ متر مربع بسعر ٥ دنانير للمتر
١٠	رؤوس نحاسية عدد ٥ متوسط تكلفة الرأس ٢ دينار
٤٠	أجور مباشرة (١٠ ساعات بمعدل ٤ د للساعة)
٣٥	أعباء صناعية متغيرة (١٠ ساعات بمعدل ٣,٥ د/ س ع م)
<u>٢٠</u>	أعباء صناعية ثابتة (١٠ ساعات بمعدل ٢ د / س ع م)
١١٩	التكلفة الصناعية المعيارية

وتم حساب معدل تحميل الأعباء الصناعية الثابتة على أساس أن الطاقة العادية للشركة هي ٥٠,٠٠٠ ساعة عمل وخلال الفترة تمت العمليات التالية:

- تم إنتاج ٤,٨٠٠ فرن غاز ماركة (أ) ٣١٥.

- تم شراء ٨,٠٠٠ م٢ من الصاج سمك ١,٥ ملم بمبلغ ٣٣,٦٠٠ دينار صرف منها للإنتاج ٧,٥٠٠ م٢.

- وتم شراء ٢٠,٠٠٠ متر مواسير نحاسية بمبلغ ٢٦,٨٨٠ دينار واستخدمت جميعها في الإنتاج.

- صرف ١,٩٥٠ م٢ من الزجاج من المخازن إلى الإنتاج حيث قد تم شراء الزجاج سابقاً بسعر ٥ د للمتر المربع.

- تم شراء ٢٥,٠٠٠ رأس نحاسية بمبلغ ٤٨,٠٠٠ دينار صرف منها للإنتاج ٢٤,٠٠٠ رأس.

- بلغت ساعات العمل المباشرة الفعلية ٥٠,٠٠٠ ساعة وكان معدل الأجور ٣,٧٥ د للساعة.
- بلغت الأعباء الإضافية المتغيرة ١٦٥,٦٠٠ دينار.
- بلغت الأعباء الإضافية الثابتة ٩٦,٠٠٠ دينار.
- كان رصيد حساب الإنتاج تحت التشغيل أول المدة ٣٠,٠٠٠ د كما وبلغ رصيد هذا الحساب في آخر المدة ٣٠,٠٠٠ د.
- كان رصيد حساب البضاعة التامة الصنع أول المدة ٥٠,٠٠٠ د، وأصبح هذا الرصيد في نهاية المدة ٧٦,٠٠٠ د.

تستخدم الشركة طريقة التكاليف المعيارية الكلية.

المطلوب:

(١) إعداد قيود اليومية اللازمة لإثبات العمليات السابقة.

(٢) تصوير حسابات البضاعة.

(٣) إعداد قائمة تكلفة البضاعة التامة الصنع مع تحميل الانحرافات على تكلفة البضاعة المباعة.

السؤال الخامس عشر: يوجـد في شركـة سي. جي. سي الأردنيـة لصناعة الملابس الجاهزة خط إنتاجي يتخصص في صناعة القمصان الرجالي، ونظراً لتخصص العمل في هذا الخط وقيامه بالإنتاج بكميات كبيرة لسد حاجة السوق المحلي والدولي فإنه يتم استخدام طريقة محاسبة المراحل ونظام التكاليف المعيارية الجزئية في إثبات تكاليف الإنتاج وكانت تكلفة القميص المعيارية كالتالي:

مواد مباشرة (١,٢٥ يرد بسعر ٢ د / يرد)	٢,٥٠
أجور مباشرة (١ ساعة بمعدل ١,٥ د / س ع م)	١,٥٠
أعباء إضافية (١ ساعة بمعدل ٢ د / س ع م)	٢,٠
التكلفة المعيارية للقميص الواحد	٦,٠

وقد حسبت الأعباء الإضافية على أساس ٣٠,٠٠٠ ساعة عمل وأن الأعباء الإضافية الثابتة التقديرية عند هذا المستوى تبلغ ٢٧,٠٠٠ دينار، وبالرغم من اختلاف ألوان القمصان فإن التكلفة المعيارية للقميص تبقى واحدة.

وخلال فترة التكاليف المنتهية في ٣/٣١ حدثت الأمور الآتية:

كان رصيد حساب الإنتاج تحت التشغيل في ١/١ يتكون من ١٠,٠٠٠ د مواد مباشرة و ٤٥٠٠ د أجور مباشرة و ٦٠٠٠ د أعباء إضافية، ويمثل تكلفة ٥٠٠٠ قميص عند مستوى إتمام ٦٠%. أما وحدات تحت التشغيل آخر المدة فتتكون من ٤٠٠٠ قميص عند مستوى إتمام ٧٥%.

- تم تفصيل ٢٥,٠٠٠ قميص خلال الفترة واستخدام في ذلك ٣٢,٠٠٠ يرد قماش تكلفتها الفعلية ٦٥,٦٠٠ دينار.

- بلغت ساعات العمل المباشرة الفعلية ٢٧,٠٠٠ ساعة وأجورها المستحقة هي ٣٩,١٥٠ دينار.

- بلغت الأعباء الإضافية ٥٥,٩٠٠ دينار.

المطلوب:

(١) إعداد تقرير تكاليف المرحلة باستخدام بيانات التكاليف المعيارية.

(٢) تحليل انحرافات التكاليف واستخدام طريقة الانحرافين في حالة الأعباء الإضافية.

السؤال السادس عشر: تقوم إحدى الشركات الكيماوية بخلط مادتين من المواد الخام عند إنتاج أحد منتجاتها وبنسبة ٦٠% للمادة (أ) : ٤٠% للمادة (ب)، ويبلغ سعر الكيلو غرام من هذه المواد ٣ دنانير و ٤ دنانير على التوالي وتبلغ نسبة العائد المعياري للإنتاج ٩٥% من كمية المدخلات وخلال إحدى الفترات تمت العمليات الآتية:

- تم إنتاج ١٠,٠٠٠ كغم من المنتج النهائي واستخدم في ذلك ٦٨٠٠ كغم من المادة (أ)، ٤٢٠٠ كغم من المادة (أ).

المطلوب:

١- تحديد انحراف مزيج المواد المباشرة.

٢- تحديد انحراف عائد المواد المباشرة.

٣- تحديد التكلفة المعيارية للمواد المباشرة اللازمة لوحدة المنتج.

الفصل الثاني عشر
مواضيع خاصة في تحليل انحرافات التكاليف

أهداف الفصل :

بعد دراسة هذا الفصل يجب أن تكون قادراً على معرفة:

١- أثر استبدال وإحلال المواد المباشرة محل بعضها.

٢- أثر استبدال فئات العمال وتحويلهم من عمل لآخر.

٣- طريقة حساب انحراف مزيج المواد.

٤- طريقة حساب انحراف مزيج الأجور.

٥- طريقة حساب انحراف العائد الكلي للمواد والأجور والأعباء الإضافية.

٦- طريقة حساب انحراف التالف غير العادي.

مقدمـــة :

في الفصلين السابقين تمت دراسة التكاليف المعيارية وتحليل الانحرافات عند استخدام مادة مباشرة واحدة وفئة مهارة عمل واحدة، وفي هـذا الفصل سـنقوم بدراسة تحليل الانحرافات عند تعدد المواد المباشرة وتعدد فئات العمل، لأن ذلك يؤدي الى ظهور مشاكل جديدة عند تحليل الانحرافات نتيجـة إحلال مـادة خـام محل أخرى وإحلال فئة عمل محل أخرى، وهـذا يـؤدي إلى إضافة عنصرـ جديد للانحرافات التي تم دراستها سابقاً يعرف بـانحراف المـزيج، وهو نتيجـة اختلاف المزج الفعلي عن المزج المعياري للمواد والأجور، ويتم التعبير عـن المـزج بالنسـب المئوية. إضافة إلى ذلك، سوف نتعرض إلى انحراف جديد آخر هـو انحراف العائـد والذي ينتج عن اختلاف كمية المخرجات الفعلية عن كمية المخرجات المعيارية.

انحراف مزيج المواد المباشرة:

يحدث انحراف مزيج المواد عندما يتم إنتاج منتج معين باستخدام عدة مواد يتم مزجها بنسب مئوية مع بعضها، وهنا قد تضطر المنشأة عند التشغيل الفعلي الى إحلال مادة خام محل أخرى للاستفادة مـن فروقـات الأسعار أو التغلب عـلى مشكلة توافر المواد. وهذا يـؤدي إلى حـدوث اختلاف بـين نسـب المـزج المعياريـة ونسب المزج الفعليـة للمـواد المباشـرة[1]، ولتحديـد هـذا الانحراف يجب إتبـاع الخطوات الآتية:

١- تحديد نسبة المزج المعياري للمواد وهي تمثل نسبة وزن كـل مـادة الى إجمالي أوزان المواد

٢- تحديـد إجـمالي كميـة المـدخلات الفعليـة وذلك بجمـع كميـة المـواد الخـام المستخدمة من كل صنف.

٣- تحديد الكمية الفعلية المعدلة وتساوي إجمالي كمية المدخلات الفعلية ضرب نسبة المزج المعيارية لكل مادة.

---

(١) Fischer and Frank, op.cit., Pp. ٣٣١-٣٣٥.

٤- ضرب الفرق بين الكمية الفعلية والكمية الفعلية المعدله في السعر المعياري للمواد الخام.

مثال (١١):

تشير بطاقة التكلفة المعيارية إلى أن إنتاج إحدى المنتجات يحتاج إلى المواد الآتية:

مادة أ	(٦ كغم × ١,٥ د)	= ٩ د
مادة ب	(٣ كغم ×٢، د)	= ٦ د
مادة جـ	(١ كغم × ٣، د)	= ٣ د
الاجمالي		١٨ د

وخلال إحدى الفترات كانت كمية المواد المستخدمة في الإنتاج كالتالي:

مادة أ	=	٥٥,٠٠٠
مادة ب	=	٣٣,٠٠٠
مادة جـ	=	١٢,٠٠٠
إجمالي كمية المواد		١٠٠,٠٠٠ كغم

المطلوب:

تحديد انحراف مزيج المواد.

الحل:

لتحديد قيمة هذا الانحراف يجب إتباع الخطوات الثلاث السابقة:

١- تحديد إجمالي كمية المواد وهو يساوي ١٠٠,٠٠٠ كغم.

٢- الكمية الفعلية المعدلة = إجمالي كمية المواد × نسبة المادة في المزيج المعياري والتي هي نسبة وزن المادة اللازم لإنتاج الوحدة إلى وزن كافة المواد وتكون ٦: ٣: ١ أو بنسبة ٦٠٪ : ٣٠٪: ١٠٪ وعليه تكون كمية المدخلات المعدلة كالتالي:

المادة	الكمية	نسبة المزج	الكمية الفعلية المعدلة
أ	١٠٠,٠٠٠×	٦٠٪	٦٠,٠٠٠

ب	١٠٠,٠٠٠×	٣٠%	٣٠,٠٠٠
جـ	١٠٠,٠٠٠×	١٠%	١٠,٠٠٠

لقد تم تحديد نسبة المزج من بطاقة التكلفة المعيارية، ولتحديد قيمة الانحراف سيتم استخدام المعادلة الآتية:

انحراف المزيج = (الكمية الفعلية المعدلة – الكمية الفعلية) × السعر المعياري للمادة وعليه تكون قيمة هذا الانحراف كالتالي:

أ	(٦٠,٠٠٠ – ٥٥,٠٠٠)	×	١,٥د	= ٧٥٠٠ (م)
ب	(٣٠,٠٠٠ – ٣٣,٠٠٠)	×	٢	= ٦,٠٠٠ (غ م)
جـ	(١٠,٠٠٠ – ١٢,٠٠٠)	×	٣د.	= ٦,٠٠٠ (غ م)

انحراف المزيج = (٤٥٠٠) (غ م)

انحراف عائد المواد المباشرة   Material Yield Variance:

يحدث انحراف العائد عندما يتم فقد جزء من المواد الخام أثناء عملية التشغيل نتيجة لعمليات والانكماش والتفاعلات، وبالتالي تكون الكمية الفعلية للمخرجات أقل من الكمية الفعلية للمدخلات. وفي العادة يتم التعبير عن العائد بقسمة كمية المخرجات المتوقعة على كمية المدخلات المتوقعة، فمثلاً إذا كانت العملية الصناعية تحتاج إلى ١٠٠ كغم من المدخلات لإنتاج ٩٠ كغم من المخرجات، فإن ذلك يعني أنه يتم فقد ١٠ كغم من المدخلات أثناء عملية التشغيل. وأن نسبة العائد تساوي ٩٠%، ولضبط كمية الفاقد تقوم المنشأة بمعايرته وتحديد نسبة الفاقد المسموح بها ومن ثم تحدد نسبة العائد المعيارية.

ولتحديد التكلفة المعيارية لوحدة المنتج النهائي في حالة استخدام عدة مواد خام فإنه يجب تحديد التكلفة المعيارية للمواد المباشرة حسب نسب المزج المعيارية، فمثلاً، إذا كان يلزم لإنتاج وحدة المنتج ٦ كغم من المادة أ، و ٤ كغم من المادة ب وكانت أسعارهما المعيارية هي ٢د، ١,٥ د على التوالي، فإن التكلفة المعيارية لمدخلات الإنتاج حسب نسب المزج المعياري ستكون: (٦ كغم من أ × ٢د + ٤كغم في ب × ١,٥ د =) ١٨ ديناراً. والآن افترض أن نسبة العائد ٩٠% فإن ذلك يعني أن كمية المخرجات المعيارية التي يتم

الحصول عليها من كل ١٠ كغم من المدخلات ستكون: (١٠ كغم × ٠,٩) = ٩ كغم، وبهذا فإن تكلفة الكيلو غرام من المخرجات تساوي (١٨ د ÷ ٩ كغم) ٢ د/ كغم.

ويتم تعريف انحراف العائد على أنه الفرق بين العائد الفعلي والعائد المعياري وضرب التكلفة المعيارية لوحدة العائد الفعلي، ولتوضيح تحليل الانحرافات السابقة سيتم الاعتماد على البيانات التالية:

مثال (١٢-٢)):

يقوم مصنع الأعلاف بتصنيع نوع من العلف الحيواني باستخدام ثلاث مواد والآتي بيانات عن مزجها المعياري وتكلفتها المعيارية:

مادة أ	(٧٠ كغم بسعر ١,٤٥)	= ١٠١,٥ د
مادة ب	(٢٥ كغم بسعر ١,٦٠ د)	= ٤٠د
مادة جـ	(٥ كغم بسعر ٢,١ د)	= ١٠,٥د
التكلفة المعيارية للمواد المباشرة		= ١٥٢د

وتبلغ نسبة العائد المعياري ٩٥%، وخلال شهر آذار تم استخدام المواد التالية:

مادة (أ) : ٩٢,٠٠٠ كغم وتكلفتها ١٣٨,٠٠ د.

مادة (ب) : ٣٠,٢٠٠ كغم وتكلفتها ٥١,٣٤٠د.

مادة (ج) : ٧,٨٠٠ كغم وتكلفتها ١٥,٦٠٠ د.

وتم إنتاج ١٢٥,٠٠٠ كغم من العلف الجاهز.

والمطلوب: تحديد الانحراف الآتية:

١- انحراف السعر.

٢- انحراف المزيج.

٣- انحراف العائد.

الحل:

أولاً: انحراف السعر:

يتم حساب هذا الانحراف بنفس طريقة تحليل انحرافات السعر التي تم عرضها في الفصول السابقة، وهو يساوي الفرق بين السعر الفعلي والسعر المعياري ضرب الكمية

الفعلية. ويحدد السعر الفعلي بقسمة التكلفة الفعلية للمادة على كميتها، ويتم حساب هذا الانحراف كالتالي:

المادة	سعر فعلي	سعر معياري	فرق السعر	الكمية	الانحراف
أ	١,٥	١,٤٥	٠,٠٥	٩٢,٠٠٠	٤,٦٠٠ د (غ م)
ب	١,٧٠	١,٦٠	٠,١٠	٣٠,٢٠٠	٣,٠٢٠ د (غ م)
جـ	٢,٠٠	٢,١	٠,١٠-	٧,٨٠٠	٧٨٠د (م)
انحراف سعر المواد مباشرة					٦,٨٤٠ د (غ م)

ثانياً: انحراف المزيج:

يعرف هذا الانحراف على أنه الفرق بين الكمية الفعلية للمواد الخام وكمية المواد الخام المعدلة حسب نسبة المزيج المعياري مضروباً بالسعر المعياري، بالنسبة لكل مادة، وأن نسبة مزج المواد هي ٧٠٪: ٢٥٪: ٥٪، ولما كان إجمالي المواد المستخدمة في الإنتاج هو ١٣٠,٠٠٠ كغم يتم حساب كمية المواد الفعلية المعدلة كالتالي:

مادة أ   =   ١٣٠,٠٠٠ × ٧٠٪   =   ٩١,٠٠٠ كغم

مادة ب   =   ١٣٠,٠٠٠ × ٢٥٪   =   ٣٢,٥٠٠كغم

مادة جـ   =   ١٣٠,٠٠٠ × ٥٪   =   ٦,٥٠٠ كغم

	كمية فعلية	كمية فعلية معدلة	سعر معياري	انحراف المزيج
أ	٩٢,٠٠٠	٩١,٠٠٠	١,٤٥	١,٤٥٠ د (غ م)
ب	٣٠,٢٠٠	٣٢,٥٠٠	١,٦٠	٣,٦٨٠ د (م)
جـ	٧,٨٠٠	٦,٥٠٠	٢,١	٢,٧٣٠ د (غ م)
الإجمالي	١٣٠,٠٠٠	١٣٠,٠٠٠	انحراف المزيج	٥٠٠ د (غ م)

ومن ثم يحسب انحراف المزيج كالتالي:

وهنا إذا كانت الكمية الفعلية أكبر من الكمية الفعلية المعدلة يكون الانحراف غير محبب وعند حدوث العكس يكون الانحراف محبباً. إذا تم ضرب عامود الكمية الفعلية المعدلة في عمود السعر المعياري، ستكون النتيجة كالتالي:

	كمية فعلية معدلة	× السعر المعياري		
أ	٩١،٠٠٠	١،٤٥	=	١٣١،٩٥٠ دينار
ب	٣٢،٥٠٠	١،٦٠	=	٥٢،٠٠٠ دينار
جـ	٦،٥٠٠	٢،١	=	١٣،٦٥٠ دينار
				١٩٧،٦٠٠

وهذا المبلغ يساوي: إجمالي كمية المدخلات ضرب السعر المعياري لوحدة المزيج

$$= ١٣٠،٠٠٠ × ١،٥٢ = ١٩٧،٦٠٠.$$

ولذلك يمكن تعريف انحراف المزيج على أنه الكمية الفعلية للمدخلات ضرب سعرها المعياري ناقص إجمالي كمية المدخلات ضرب السعر المعياري لوحدة المزيج المعياري، ويتم حساب الانحراف كالتالي[1]:

التكلفة المعيارية للكمية الفعلية = مجـ (الكمية الفعلية للمواد × السعر المعياري)

$$= ٩٢،٠٠٠ × ١،٤٥ + ٣٠،٢٠٠× ١،٦ + ٧،٨٠٠ × ٢،١$$

$$= ١٩٨،١٠٠ ديناراً.$$

التكلفة المعيارية للمزيج المعياري = الكمية الفعلية ضرب سعر الكيلو حسب المزيج المعياري:

$$= ١٣٠،٠٠٠ × ١،٥٢ = ١٩٧،٦٠٠$$

انحراف المزيج = ١٩٧،٦٠٠ – ١٩٨،١٠٠ = ٥٠٠ د (غير مفضل)

ثالثاً: انحراف عائد المواد:

انحراف العائد = (العائد الفعلي – العائد المعياري) السعر المعياري لوحدة العائد

- فالعائد الفعلي هو ١٢٥،٠٠٠ كغم.

(١) Edward B. Deakin and M.W Maher, op.cit., Pp. ٨٤٢ – ٨٤٦.

- والعائد المعياري = كمية المدخلات × نسبة العائد.

= ١٣٠,٠٠٠ × ٩٥% = ١٢٣,٥٠٠

إذن انحراف العائد = (١٢٥,٠٠٠ – ١٢٣,٥٠٠)× ١,٦

= ٢,٤٠٠ دينار مفضل.

ولقد تم تحديد السعر المعياري لوحدة العائد بقسمة التكلفة المعيارية لكمية المدخلات في المزيج المعياري على كمية المزيج المعياري، وهذا يساوي = ١٥٢ دينار ÷ ٩٥ كغم = ١,٦ دينار لكل كغم.

طريقة أخرى:

يمكن حساب انحراف العائد بطريقة أخرى وذلك بحساب كمية المواد الخام اللازمة لتحقيق كمية المخرجات الفعلية، فنحن نعلم أن كل ١٠٠ كغم تؤدي إلى إنتاج ٩٥ كغم من المنتج النهائي، لذلك فإنه يلزم لإنتاج ١٢٥,٠٠٠ كغم منتج نهائي إلى ١٣١,٥٧٩ كغم

$(١٢٥,٠٠٠ × \frac{١٠٠}{٩٥})$.

وبالتالي يكون التوفير الذي حققته المنشأة أثناء عملية التشغيل هو :

ألتوفير = ١٣١,٥٧٩ – ١٣٠,٠٠٠

= ١,٥٧٩ د

وعليه يكون الانحراف العائد = التوفير في كمية المواد × سعر وحدة المدخلات حسب نسبة المزج المعيارية

= ١٥٧٩ كغم × ١,٥٢

= ٢٤٠٠ د مفضل

لقد كان الانحراف مفضلاً لأن الكمية الفعلية أقل من الكمية المعيارية اللازمة للإنتاج.

رابعاً: الانحراف الكلي للمواد:

ويمثل هذا الانحراف مجموع انحراف السعر وانحراف المزيج وانحرافات العائد، لذلك فهو يمثل الفرق بين التكلفة الفعلية للمواد المباشرة والتكلفة المعيارية للإنتاج التام، فالتكاليف الفعلية للمواد المباشرة: [١٣٨,٠٠٠ د المادة (أ) + ٥١,٣٤٠ د المادة (ب) + ١٥,٦٠٠ المادة (ج)] = ٢٠٤,٩٤٠ دينار.

وتحدد التكلفة المعيارية للإنتاج الفعلي بضرب حجم الإنتاج الفعلي في التكلفة المعيارية لوحدة الإنتاج بعد الفاقد ويساوي (١٢٥,٠٠٠ × ١,٦) ٢٠٠,٠٠٠ د ، وعليه يكون الانحراف الكلي كالتالي:

٢٠٤,٩٤٠ – ٢٠٠,٠٠٠

= ٤,٩٤٠ د (غير مفضل)

وبجمع الانحرافات السابقة يكون الانحراف الكلي هو:

انحراف السعر	٦,٨٤٠ د (غ م)
انحراف المزيج	٥٠٠ د (غ م)
انحراف العائد	٢,٤٠٠ د (م)
الانحراف الكلي	٤,٩٤٠ د (غ م)

انحرافات الأجور المباشرة:

عندما يتم استخدام عمال من فئات مهارة مختلفة في الإنتاج، قد تضطر المنشأة إلى إحلال فئة مهارة محل أخرى[1]، ولهذا يظهر انحراف جديد عند تحليل انحرافات الأجور المباشرة هو انحراف مزيج الأجور المباشرة، ولتوضيح طريقة حساب انحرافات الأجور المباشرة، في حالة وجود فئات مهارة مختلفة سيتم الاعتماد على البيانات التالية:

---

(١) Fischer and Frank, op,c.it, Pp. ٣٦ – ٣٣٩.

مثال (١٢-٢)

بالإضافة إلى المعلومات الواردة في المثال (١٢-١) افترض أن تشغيل كـل مائـة كيلو غرام من المواد الخام يؤدي إلى ٩٥ كغم من الإنتاج النهائي يحتاج إلى استخدام ساعات العمل المباشرة التالية:

فئة مهارة أ (٥ ساعات بمعدل ٢د/ س ع م)	١٠د
فئة مهارة ب (١٠ ساعات بمعدل ١,٨٥ د/ س ع م)	١٨,٥د
إجمالي الأجور	٢٨,٥د

التكلفة المعيارية للأجور المباشرة لوحدة الإنتاج = ٢٨,٥ / ٩٥ كغم   = ٠,٣٠ د

وخلال شهر آذار بلغت الأجور المباشرة الفعلية كالتالي:

فئة مهارة أ (٦,٧٥٠ ساعة بواقع ٢,٢ د / س ع م)	١٤,٨٥٠ د
فئة مهارة ب (١٢,٥١٠ ساعة بواقع ١,٧٥ د / س ع م)	٢١,٨٩٢,٥
الأجور المباشرة الفعلية	٣٦,٧٤٢,٥

المطلوب:

تحليل انحرافات الأجور بقدر ما تسمح به المعلومات:

أولاً: الانحراف الكلي = الأجور الفعلية - الأجور المعيارية للإنتاج الفعلي

= الأجور الفعلية - الإنتاج الفعلي × الأجر المعياري لوحدة الإنتاج التام

= (٣٦,٧٤٢,٥ - ١٢٥,٠٠٠× ٠,٣)

= ٧٥٧,٥ د (مفضل)

لاحظ أن الإنتاج التام قد تم ضربه بالتكلفة المعيارية للأجور المباشرة لوحـدة الإنتاج النهائي لأن تكلفة الفاقد العادي تعتبر من تكلفة الإنتاج التام الجيد.

ثانياً: انحراف معدل الأجور:

يتم حساب هذا الانحراف بنفس الطريقة التـي اسـتخدمت في حسـابه عنـد استخدام فئة عمال واحدة ويعرف على أنه الفرق بين معـدل الأجر الفعلي ومعـدل الأجر المعياري لكل فئة عمال على حده ضرب ساعات العمل المباشرة الفعلية لكـل فئة، ويكون كالتالي:

انحراف معدل الأجور	ساعات العمل الفعلية	معدل الأجر المعياري	معدل الأجر الفعلي	فئة مهارة
١,٣٥٠ د (غ م)	٦,٧٥٠	٢	٢,٢	أ
١,٢٥١ د (م)	١٢,٥١٠	١,٨٥	١,٧٥	ب
٩٩ د (غ م)			انحراف معدل الأجور	

لقد تم تحديد معدل الأجر الفعلي بقسمة تكلفة الأجور الفعلية على عـدد ساعات العمل الفعلية.

ثالثاً: انحراف مزيج الأجور:

ويساوي الأجور المباشرة المعيارية في المزيج المعياري ناقص ساعات العمـل المباشرة في المزيج الفعلي مضروبة بالسعر المعياري، ويساوي ساعـات العمـل المباشرة المعيارية بالمزيج المعياري (ساعات العمل الفعلية المعدلة بالمزج المعياري) نـاقص سـاعـات العمـل المبـاشرة الفعليـة في المـزيج الفعلي ضرب معـدل الأجر المعياري[1]، ويتم حسابه كالتالي:

انحراف المزيج	معدل الأجر	فرق	ساعات العمل الفعلية المعدلة بالمزج المعياري	ساعات العمل الفعلية	فئة العمل
٦٦٠ د (غ م)	٢	-٣٣٠	٦,٤٢٠ = ١٥/٥×١٩,٢٦٠	٦,٧٥٠	أ
٦١٠,٥ د (م)	١,٨٥	+٣٣٠	١٢,٨٤٠=١٥/١٠×١٩,٢٦٠	١٢,٥١٠	ب
٤٩,٥ د (غ م)			١٩٢٦٠ =	١٩,٢٦٠	

(١) عبد الحي مرعي، مرجع سابق الذكر، ص ٤٤٨ – ٤٨٩.

لقد تم تحديد ساعات العمل الفعلية المعدلة بالمزج المعياري بضرب إجمالي ساعات العمل المباشرة الفعلية في نسب المزج المعياري لفئات العمل، ويمكن حساب هذا الانحراف أيضاً بطريقة مناظرة لانحراف مزيج المواد المباشرة باعتباره الفرق بين التكلفة المعيارية للمزيج الفعلي وهذه تساوي ساعات العمل الفعلي لكل فئة ضرب معدل الأجر المعياري لها، وتكلفة الأجور المعيارية لساعات العمل الفعلية، وهي تساوي إجمالي عدد ساعات كل فئة عمالة ضرب معدل الأجر المعياري للساعة لهذه الفئة وقسمة الناتج على عدد الساعات، ويتم حساب المتوسط المرجح كالتالي:

$$\text{المتوسط المرجح المعياري} = \frac{(١,٨٥ \times \text{ساعات} ١٠ + ٢ \times \text{ساعات} ٥)}{١٥ \text{ ساعة}} = \frac{٢٨,٥}{١٥}$$

= ١,٩ د / س ع م حسب المزيج المعياري.

وبهذا يكون انحراف مزيج الأجور كالتالي:
التكلفة المعيارية للمزيج الفعلي= ٦,٧٥٠ ×٢ + ١٢,٥١٠ × ١,٨٥=٣٦٦٤٣,٥ د
ناقص :
التكلفة المعيارية لساعات العمل الفعلية = ١٩,٢٦٠ = ٣٦,٥٩٤ د
× ١,٩
_____
انحراف المزيج = ٣٦,٦٤٣,٥ – ٣٦,٥٩٤ =٤٩,٥د (غ م)

رابعاً: انحراف الزمن (أو الكفاءة):
وهو عبارة عن الفرق بين ساعات العمل الفعلية المعدلة بنسب المزج المعياري وساعات العمل المعيارية لتشغيل المدخلات ضرب معدل الأجر المعياري لفئات العمل، ويحسب كالتالي:
١- ساعات العمل الفعلية المعدلة بنسب المزج المعياري تساوي: = إجمالي ساعات العمل المباشر × نسبة المزج المعياري

فئة أ = ١٩,٢٦٠ × $\frac{٥}{١٥}$ = ٦,٤٢٠ ساعة

فئة ب= ١٩,٢٦٠ × ١٠ = ١٢,٨٤٠ ساعة
١٥

٢- ساعات العمل المعيارية لتشغيل المدخلات تساوي كمية المدخلات في عدد الساعات اللازمة لتشغيل وتحسب كالتالي:

فئة أ = ١٣٠,٠٠٠ كغم × ٥ / ١٠٠ = ٦,٥٠٠ ساعة

فئة ب= ١٣٠,٠٠٠ كغم × ١٠ / ١٠٠ = ١٣,٠٠٠ ساعة

لاحظ أنه قمنا بتحديد ساعات العمل المعيارية التي يقتضيها تشغيل كمية المدخلات من المواد الخام، وبالرجوع إلى البيانات نجد أن تشغيل كل ١٠٠ كغم من المدخلات يحتاج إلى ٥ ساعات من الفئة (أ) وإلى ١٠ ساعات من الفئة (ب) وبتطبيق التعريف السابق يكون انحراف الزمن كالتالي:

انحراف الزمن	المعدل المعياري	فرق الزمن	ساعات العمل المعيارية للمدخلات الفعلية	ساعات العمل الفعلية المعدلة بالمزيج المعياري	فئة العمل
١٦٠ د (م)	٢	٨٠	٦,٥٠٠	٦,٤٢٠	أ
٢٩٦د (م)	١,٨٥	١٦٠	١٣,٠٠٠	١٢,٨٤٠	ب
٤٥٦ د (م)					انحراف الزمن

خامساً: انحراف العائد:

ويعكس هذا الانحراف قيمة ألوفر في تكاليف الأجور المباشرة والناتجة عن كفاءة استخدام المواد المباشرة، فأثناء تحليل انحرافات المواد المباشرة وجدنا أنه قد تم توفير ١,٥٧٩ كغم من المواد الخام، وهذا بدوره يؤدي إلى توفير في تكاليف الأجور المباشرة لأنه بدون زيادة كفاءة تشغيل المواد، تحتاج المنشأة إلى ساعات عمل مباشرة لتشغيل ١,٥٧٩ كغم من المواد الخام، ولذلك يتم حساب انحراف العائد كالتالي[١]:

_____

(١) Fischer and Frank, op,c.it, P. ٣٣٤.

(المدخلات الفعلية من المواد – المدخلات اللازمة لإنتاج المخرجات)× معدل الأجر المعياري

$$= (١٣٠,٠٠٠ - ١٢٥,٠٠٠ / ٠,٩٥) \times \frac{٢٨,٥}{١٠٠}$$

$= ٤٥٠$ د (مفضل)

سادساً: الانحراف الكلي:

الانحراف الكلي = انحراف السعر + انحراف المزيج + انحراف الزمن + انحراف العائد

$= ٩٩$ (غ م) + ٤٩,٥ (غ م) + ٤٥٦ (م) + ٤٥٠ (م)= ٧٥٧,٥ د (م)

انحراف العائد الكلي:

تـم حسـاب انحـراف عائـد المـواد المبـاشرة وانحـراف عائـد الأجـور المبـاشرة باستخدام الفرق بين كميـة المدخلات الفعليـة وكميـة المـدخلات اللازمة لتحقيـق حجم الإنتاج الفعـلي، وضرب هذا الفـرق بالسـعر المعيـاري للكيلـو غـرام حسـب المزيج المعياري بالنسبة للمواد المباشرة ومعدل أجر ساعة العمل المعياري حسب المزيج المعياري بالنسبة للمواد المباشرة ومعدل أجر ساعة العمل المعياري حسب المزيج المعياري بالنسبة للمواد المباشرة ومعدل أجر ساعة العمل المعياري حسب المزيج المعياري بالنسبة للأجور المباشرة، وللاختصار في عمليـة تحليـل الانحرافـات يتم حساب الانحراف العائد الكلي للمواد المباشرة والأعباء الإضافية معـاً بـدلاً مـن حساب انحراف العائد لكل عنصر من العناصر السـابقة كـل عـلى حـدة، فمثلاً إذا إفترضنا أن معدل تحميل الأعباء الإضافية كان ١٥٠٪ من الأجور المباشرة وبالاعتماد على البيانات الواردة في المثالين (٢،١) يتم حساب الانحراف الكلي كالتالي[1]:

٢,٤٠٠ د	انحراف عائد المواد ١,٥٧٩ × ١,٥٢
٤٥٠	انحراف عائد الأجور ١,٥٧٩ × ٠,٢٨٥
٦٧٥ د	انحراف عائد الأعباء الإضافية = ١,٥٧٩ × ٠,٢٨٥ × ١٥٠٪
٣,٥٢٥د	الانحراف الكلي

---

(١) Ibid, P.٣٣٥.

ولأن هناك وفراً في كمية المواد الخام الفعلية، لذلك تكون جميع هذه الانحرافات مفضلة ويكون الانحراف الكلي مفضلاً كذلك.

انحراف التالف:

يقوم هذا الانحراف بإبراز أثر زيادة عدد الوحدات التالفة الفعلية عن عدد وحدات التالف المسموح بها، ويعرف هذا الفرق باسم وحدات التالف غير العادي ويتم تقييمه بضرب وحدات التالف غير العادي في تكلفة الوحدة التالفة[1].

تتوقف تكلفة الوحدة التالفة كما تم ذكره في الفصل الخامس على مستوى فحص الإنتاج لأن ذلك يحدد ما هي التكاليف التي يجب أن تحمل على الوحدات التالفة، فإذا كان الفحص يجرى في نهاية العملية الإنتاجية، عندها تستفيد وحدات التالف من كل عناصر التكاليف بنسبة ١٠٠٪، أما إذا كان الفحص يتم عند مستوى إنتاجي معين، فإن تكلفة الوحدة التالفة يجب أن تحدد على أساس عناصر التكاليف التي استخدمت في الإنتاج لغاية مستوى فحصها، فمثلاً إذا كانت المواد تضاف في بداية المرحلة وتضاف عناصر تكاليف التحويل بانتظام ويجري الفحص عند مستوى إتمام ٦٠٪، عندها تتحمل الوحدة التالفة بنسبة ١٠٠٪ من تكاليف المواد المباشرة وبنسبة ٦٠٪ من تكاليف التحويل، ولتوضيح طريقة حساب هذا الانحراف سيتم الاعتماد على البيانات التالية:

مثال (٣):

كانت بطاقة التكلفة المعيارية لأحد المنتجات الصناعية تحتوي على الآتي:

مواد مباشرة (٤ كغم بسعر ٢د / كغم)	٨ د
الأجور المباشرة (٣ ساعات بمعدل ٢د / س ع م)	٦د
الأعباء الإضافية (٣ ساعات بمعدل ٥د/ س ع م)	١٥د
التكلفة المعيارية لوحدة الإنتاج التام	٢٩د

وكانت نسبة التالف المعيارية ٥٪ من الإنتاج الجيد ويتم فحص عند مستوى إتمام ٦٠٪ وتضاف المواد المباشرة في بداية عملية التشغيل، وتضاف تكاليف التحويل بانتظام.

---

(١) تشارلز. ت. هورنجرن، مرجع سابق، جـ٢، ص ٤٤٩ – ٤٥١.

وكانت البيانات الفعلية كالتالي:

- بلغ الإنتاج التام الجيد ٢٠,٠٠٠ وحدة.
- بلغ عدد وحدات التالف الفعلي ١,٥٠٠ وحدة.

المطلوب:

حساب انحراف التالف.

الحل: نسبة التالف العادي ٥% من الإنتاج الجيد، لذلك فإن وحدات التالف العادي
= ٢٠,٠٠٠ × ٥% = ١٠٠٠ وحدة

التالف غير العادي = ١,٥٠٠ – ١,٠٠٠ = ٥٠٠ وحدة

تكلفة الوحدة التالفة:

مواد مباشرة = ٨ د × ١٠٠%	=	٨د
الأجور المباشرة = ٦د×٦٠%	=	٣,٦د
الأعباء الإضافية = ١٥د×٦٠%	=	٩د
التكلفة المعيارية لوحدة التالف	=	٢٠,٦

ولقد تم ضرب تكلفة المواد المباشرة بنسبة ١٠٠% لأن الوحدة التالفة قد حصلت على المواد اللازمة لإنتاجها كاملة وحصلت على ٦٠% بالنسبة للأجور والأعباء الإضافية.

انحراف التالف = عدد وحدات التالف غير العادي × تكلفة الوحدة التالفة
= ٥٠٠× ٢٠,٦ = ١٠,٣٠٠ دينار (غير مفضل)

وعندما يتم الفحص في نهاية المرحلة، عندها تكون تكلفة الوحدة التالفة ٢٩ ديناراً ويكون انحراف التالف كالتالي:

= ٥٠٠ وحدة × ٢٩
= ١٤,٥٠٠ دينار (غير مفضل)

هنا تكون تكلفة الوحدة التالفة غير العادية مساوية لتكلفة الوحدة الجيدة قبل تحميلها بنصيبها من تكاليف التالف العادي.

الخاتمـــة

في هذا الفصل تم دراسة انحرافات عناصر التكـاليف الصـناعية وتـم التركيـز على انحراف العائد والمزيج، وهذه الانحراف يجب حسابها في حالة إمكانية إحلال مادة محل أخرى أو إحلال فئة مهارة عمل محل أخرى، ويحـل انحـراف العائـد والمزيج محل انحراف الكمية في حالة استخدام مادة واحدة، يقوم انحراف العائـد بحساب أثر كفاءة استخدام المدخلات في إنتاج المخرجات ويقوم انحراف المـزيج بحساب أثر اختلاف نسبة المزيج الفعلية عـن نسـبة المـزيج المعياريـة في الكميـة الفعلية للمدخلات، وللتسهيل فقد تم حساب انحراف العائد الكلي وهو عبارة عن مجموع انحراف عائد المواد المباشرة وعائد الأجور المباشرة وعائد الأعباء الإضافية.

وفي نهاية الفصل تم حساب انحراف التالف ليعكس أثر التالف غـير العـادي. وقد يـتم حساب انحرافـات مماثلـة لوحـدات الإنتاج المعيبة والخردة، وهـذه الانحرافات تمثل الفرق بين الكمية الفعلية والكمية المعيارية والمسموح بها مضروباً في تكلفة إصلاح الوحدة المعيبة أو تكلفة الخردة على التوالي.

أسئلة وتمارين

السؤال الأول: ما هو انحراف المزيج وماذا يفيد حسابه وكيف يتم حسابه؟

السؤال الثاني: ما هو انحراف العائد وماذا يفيد حسابه وكيف يتم حسابه؟

السؤال الثالث: كيف يتم حساب السعر المعياري لوحدة المزيج المعياري؟

السؤال الرابع: ما هو المقصود بنسبة المزيج الفعلية وكيف يتم تحديدها من واقع البيانات الفعلية؟

السؤال الخامس: ما هي الانحرافات التي يتم حسابها بالنسبة للأجور المباشرة في حالة مزج فئات العمل ووجود نسبة عائد معين؟

السؤال السادس: ما هو العائد الكلي وبين طريقة حسابه بالنسبة للأجور المباشرة؟

السؤال السابع: عرف انحراف التالف وكيف يمكن أن تتم معالجة تكاليف وحدات التالف العادي؟

السؤال الثامن: تقوم إحدى الشركات بخلط المواد الخام (أ)، (ب)، (ج) بنسبة ٥:٣:٢ عند إنتاج أحد منتجاتها، وتزن وحدة المنتج منه ٣ كغم وكانت الأسعار المعيارية لهذه المواد هي: ١، ١,٥د، ٢د على التوالي ويلزم لإنتاج الوحدة ساعة عمل مباشرة ومعدل الأجر المعياري ٢د. ويلزم الإنتاج الوحدة ساعة عمل واحدة بمعدل أجر مقداره ٢د/ س ع م وأن نسبة عائد المواد ١٠٠%.

وخلال المدة تم إنتاج ١٥,٠٠٠ وحدة والآتي بيانات التكاليف الفعلية:

مادة (أ)	٢٣,٠٠٠ كغم وتكلفتها	٢٢,٠٠٠ د
مادة (ب)	١٤,٠٠٠ كغم وتكلفتها	٢٣,٠٠٠ د
مادة (ج)	٨,٠٠٠ كغم وتكلفتها	١٧,٦٠٠ د
المجموع		٦٢,٦٠٠

المطلوب:

تحليل انحرافات المواد المباشرة والأجور المباشرة.

السؤال التاسع: بالرجوع إلى السؤال السابق وإذا علمت أن المواد المباشرة تضاف كالتالي:

المادة (أ) تضاف في بداية مرحلة التشغيل.

المادة (ب) تضاف عند مستوى إتمام ٦٠٪ وبعد الفحص مباشرة.

المادة (ج) تضاف عند نهاية مرحلة التشغيل.

وإذا كان فحص الإنتاج يتم عند مستوى إتمام ٦٠٪ وقبل إضافة المادة (ب) مباشرة ويتوقع أن تبلغ نسبة التالف العادي ٥٪ من الإنتاج الجيد.

المطلوب:

١- تحديد التكلفة الأولية المعيارية للوحدة التالفة.

٢- تحديد التكلفة الأولية المعيارية لوحدة الإنتاج التام.

السؤال العاشر: يتم إنتاج بعض أنواع الحلويات باستخدام خلطة من المواد كالتالي:

طحين (٨٥ كغم بسعر ٠,٢٣ د للكيلو)	=	١٩,٥٥د
سكر (١٠ كغم بسعر ٠,٤٢ د للكيلو)	=	٤,٢٠ د
زبده (٥ كغم بسعر ٢,٤٠ د للكيلو)	=	١٢,٠٠د
التكلفة المعيارية للمواد المباشرة	=	٣٥,٧٥د

وخلال شهر نيسان تم تشغيل ٢٠٠ خلطة من المواد واستخدم في ذلك المواد المباشرة التالية:

١٧,٥٠٠   كغم طحين تكلفتها الفعلية ٤٢٠٠ د

١,٩٧٥   كغم سكر وتكلفتها ٨٢٩,٥د

٩٥٠   كغم من الزبدة وتكلفتها ٢,٥١٧,٥د

المطلوب:

تحليل انحرافات المواد المباشرة.

السؤال الحادي عشر: إضافة إلى بيانات السؤال السابق إذا كانت كل خلطة مـن المواد تحتاج إلى ساعات العمل المباشرة التالية:

عمال مهره (٤ ساعات بواقع ٣د / س ع م)   ١٢د

عمال غير مهره (٣ ساعات بواقع ١،٧٥د / س ع م)   ٥،٢٥د

وخلال شهر نيسان بلغت ساعات العمل الفعلية ومعدلاتها الفعلية كالتالي:

عمال مهره : ٨٥٠ ساعة بواقع ٣،٢٥ د / س ع م .

عمال غير مهره: ٦٥٠ ساعة بواقع ١،٧٠ د / س ع م .

المطلوب:

١- تحديد انحراف معدل الأجور المباشرة.

٢- تحديد انحراف كمية الأجور المباشرة.

٣- تحديد انحراف مزج الأجور المباشرة.

٤- تحديد الانحراف الكلي للأجور المباشرة.

السؤال الثاني عشر: يحتاج إنتاج أحد المنتجات إلى المادتين (أ)، (ب) اللتين تمزجان معاً بنسبة ٦٠٪، ٤٠٪ وكان سعر الكيلو غرام من المادة (أ) هـو دينار واحـد وكـان سعر الكيلو غرام من المادة (ب) هو نصف دينار وتزن وحدة المنتج النهائي ٤ كغم وخلال المدة تم إنتاج ٥٠،٠٠٠ وحـدة، واسـتخدام في إنتاجهـا ١١٣،٠٠٠ كغم مـن المادة (أ)، ٧٥،٠٠٠ كغم من المادة (ب).

أ- يبلغ انحراف كمية المواد

أ- ٧٠٠٠ د (م)   ب- ٩٥٠٠ د (م)

جـ-٧٢٠٠ د (م)   د- ٩٦٠٠د (م)

ب- انحراف مزيج المواد يساوي:

أ- ١٠٠ د (غ م)   ب- ٢٠٠ د (ع م)

جـ-٩٥٠٠ (م)   د- ٩٦٠٠ د (م)

جـ- انحراف العائد ويساوي:

أ- ٧٢٠٠ د (م)   ب- ٩٥٠٠ د (م)

جـ-٩٦٠ (م)   د- إجابة أخرى

(جمعية المحاسبين الإداريين)

السؤال الثالث عشر: تقوم شركة الدهانات الوطنية بإنتاج العديد من الدهانات أحدها يتطلب عند إنتاج ١٠٠ جلون إلى المواد التالية:

التكلفة المعيارية	السعر المعياري	الكمية	المواد
٣٠	١,٥	٢٠	أ
٤٥	٠,٧٥	٦٠	ب
٤٥	١	٤٥	جـ
١٢٠		١٢٥	الإجمالي

وبالتالي فإن نسبة العائد المعياري تساوي ٨٠٪ ويعبأ الإنتاج في عبوات سعة الواحدة منها ٢ جالون، ويلزم لتشغيل هذه الكمية ٣ ساعات عمل مباشرة بواقع ٣ د في الساعة، وكان معدل تحميل الأعباء الإضافية هو ٥ دنانير لكل ساعة عمل مباشرة تم تقديرها على أساس طاقة تشغيل مقدارها ١,٠٠٠ ساعة عمل وتبلغ نسبة الأعباء الثابتة ٥٠٪ من إجمالي الأعباء وخلال الفترة تم تشغيل ٣٦٠ خلطة واستخدم في ذلك المواد التالية:

التكلفة الفعلية	السعر الفعلي	الكمية	المواد
١٠,٠٨٠ دينار	١,٤٠	٧,٢٠٠	أ
١٧,٦٠٠ دينار	٠,٨٠	٢٢,٠٠٠	ب
١٦,٢٨٠ دينار	١,١٠	١٤,٨٠٠	جـ
٤٣,٩٦٠		٤٤,٠٠٠	

- بلغت ساعات العمل المباشرة الفعلية ١,١٠٠ ساعة بواقع ٣,٢٠ د في الساعة.
- وبلغت الأعباء الإضافية المتغيرة ٣,٠٢٤ وكذلك بلغت الأعباء الثابتة ٢,٧٠٠ د.
- بلغ الإنتاج الفعلي ٧,٠٩٧ علبة من الدهان الجاهز.

المطلوب:

١- تحديد انحراف مزيج المواد المباشرة، وانحراف سعر المواد.

٢- تحديد انحراف معدل وكفاءة الأجور المباشرة.

٣- تحديد انحراف العائد الكلي بالنسبة لعنصري المواد المباشرة والأجور المباشرة.

(مجمع المحاسبين القانونيين الأمريكيين)

السؤال الرابع عشر: تستخدم إحدى الشركات نظام تكاليف المراحل وتقوم بتحليل الانحرافات شهرياً، وكانت تصنف عمالها إلى ثلاث فئات حسب مهارتهم وكانت التكاليف المعيارية للأجور المباشرة اللازمة لإنتاج الوحدة كالتالي:

فئة مهارة (أ):‏ (١ ساعة بمعدل ٤ د / س ع م)‏ = ٤ د

فئة مهارة (١ ساعة بمعدل ٣,٥ د / س ع م = ٣,٥ د

(ب):

فئة مهارة (١ ساعة عمل بمعدل ٣ د / س = <u>٣د</u>

(جـ): ع م)

التكلفة المعيارية للأجور المباشرة ١٠,٥ د

السؤال الخامس عشر: تستخدم إحدى الشركات نظام تكاليف المراحل وتقوم بتحليل الانحرافات شهرياً، وكانت تصنف عمالها إلى ثلاث فئات حسب مهارتهم وكانت التكاليف المعيارية للأجور المباشرة اللازمة لإنتاج الوحدة كالتالي:

فئة مهارة (أ):‏ (١ ساعة بمعدل ٤ د / س ع م)‏ = ٤ د

فئة مهارة (ب):‏ (١ ساعة بمعدل ٣,٥ د / س ع م)‏ = ٣,٥ د

فئة مهارة (جـ):‏ (١ ساعة بمعدل ٣ د / س ع م)‏ = <u>٣د</u>

التكلفة المعيارية للأجور المباشرة ١٠,٥ د

وخلال شهر شباط تم إنتاج ١٠٠ وحدة وكانت تكاليف الأجور الفعلية كالتالي:

فئة مهارة (أ): (١١٥٠ ساعة بواقع ٤,١٠د / س ع م)

فئة مهارة (ب): (١١٠٠ ساعة بواقع ٣,٧٥ د / س ع م)

فئة مهارة (جـ): (٩٠٠ ساعة بواقع ٣,١٠ د / س ع م)

المطلوب:

تحليل انحرافات الأجور المباشرة مع العلم بأنه قد تم إحلال فئات عمل محل أخرى.

السؤال السادس عشر: تقوم إحدى الشركات الكيماوية بخلط مادتين من المواد الخام عند إنتاج أحد منتجاتها وبنسبة ٦٠٪ للمادة (أ) : ٤٠٪ للمادة (ب)، ويبلغ سعر الكيلو غرام من هذه المواد ٣ دنانير و ٤ دنانير على التوالي وتبلغ نسبة العائد المعياري للإنتاج ٩٥٪ من كمية المدخلات وخلال إحدى الفترات تمت العمليات الآتية:

- تم إنتاج ١٠,٠٠٠ كغم من المنتج النهائي واستخدم في ذلك ٦,٨٠٠ كغم من المادة (أ)، ٤,٢٠٠ كغم من المادة (أ).

المطلوب:

١- تحديد انحراف مزيج المواد المباشرة.

٢- تحديد انحراف عائد المواد المباشرة.

٣- تحديد التكلفة المعيارية للمواد المباشرة اللازمة لوحدة المنتج.

الفصل الثالث عشر
تحليل انحرافات الإيرادات

أهداف الفصل:

بعد دراسة هذا الفصل يجب أن تكون قادراً على معرفة

١- تحليل انحرافات إيرادات المبيعات في حالة بيع منتج واحد.

٢- تحليل انحرافات المبيعات في حالة بيع عدة منتجات.

٣- الإطار العام لتحليل انحرافات الإيرادات والتكاليف.

٤- الإطار العام لإعداد الموازنات المرنة للإيرادات.

المقدمــة :

في الفصلين السابقين تمت مناقشة المعايير والانحرافات المتعلقة بالتكاليف الصناعية، وفي هذا الفصل ستتم مناقشة تحليل انحرافات الإيرادات بقصد تقييم أداء إدارة المبيعات، فهي مسؤولية عن بيع المنتجات بالكميات والأسعار المخططة، تظهر انحرافات الإيرادات نتيجة اختلاف عدد الوحدات التي تـم بيعهـا فعـلاً عـن الوحدات المخطط بيعها والمستخدمة كأسـاس لإعـداد بيانـات الموازنـة الشـاملة أو نتيجة لاختلاف أسعار بيع هذه الوحدات.

وعند تحليل انحرافات الإيرادات يجب أن تخصم التكاليف المتغيرة المعيارية للوحدات المباعـة مـن الإيـرادات ليـتم التركيـز عـلى رقم هـامش المسـاهمة، لأن مسؤولية إدارة المبيعات تنحصر ـ في تعظيم سـعر بيـع الوحـدة، ومـن ثـم تعظيم هامش المساهمة، وحتى يتم القيام بهذا التحليل يجب توفر المعلومات عن سـلوك التكاليف لتحديد رقم هامش المساهمة، وإذا لم يتـوفر ذلـك يمكـن اسـتخدام رقم مجمل الربح [1] بدلاً من هامش المساهمة.

وفي بداية هذا الفصل سيتم تحليل انحرافات الإيرادات في حالة إنتاج وبيع منتج واحد، وبعد ذلك سيتم تحليل الانحرافات في حالة تعدد المنتجات المباعة.

أولاً: تحليل انحرافات منتج واحد:

حتى يمكن تحليل الانحرافات في هذه الحالة سوف يتم الاعتماد على البيانات الآتية:

مثال (١): توفرت المعلومات التالية عن مبيعات إحدى الشركات الصناعية.

---

(1)Robert S. Kaplan, Advanced Management Accounting, (Prentice – Hall, INC., ١٩٨٢), ٢٩٥ – ٢٩٧.

موازنة شاملة	فعلية	
١٥د	١٦د	سعر البيع
١٥,٠٠٠ د	١٤,٠٠٠ د	عدد الوحدات المباعة
٦	٧	التكاليف الصناعية المتغيرة للوحدة
١	١,٥	المصروفات التسويقية المتغيرة للوحدة
٣٠,٠٠٠	٣١,٢٠٠	التكاليف الصناعية الثابتة
٤٠,٠٠٠	٤٢,٠٠٠	المصروفات التسويقية والإدارية الثابتة

المطلوب: تحليل انحرافات الإيرادات:

الحل:

يتطلب الحل أن نقارن بين الأداء الفعلي والمخطط للشركة كالتالي:

الانحراف	الموازنة	الفعلي	
١,٠٠٠ (غ م)	٢٢٥,٠٠٠	٢٢٤,٠٠٠	المبيعات (عدد الوحدات× سعر البيع)
١٤,٠٠٠ (غ م)	١٠٥,٠٠٠	١١٩,٠٠٠	تكاليف متغيرة (صناعية وتسويقية)
١٥,٠٠٠ (غ م)	١٢٠,٠٠٠	١٠٥,٠٠٠	هامش المساهمة
١,٢٠٠ (غ م)	٣٠,٠٠٠	٣١,٢٠٠	يطرح: تكاليف صناعية ثابتة
٢,٠٠٠ (غ م)	٤٠,٠٠٠	٤٢,٠٠٠	يطرح: مصروفات تسويقية وإدارية ثابتة
١٨,٢٠٠ (غ م)	٥٠,٠٠٠	٣١,٨٠٠	صافي الربح

من التحليل السابق يتبين أن صافي الربح الفعلي قد انخفض عـن الـربح المخطط بمبلغ ١٨,٢٠٠ د وسبب ذلك عـدة عوامل منهـا مـا يتعلق بالتكاليف الصناعية، ومنها مـا يتعلق بالمصروفات الإدارية، ومنهـا مـا يتعلق بالمصروفات التسويقية، فمثلاً بفحص انحراف رقم هامش المساهمة نجـده يعـود إلى انحراف التكاليف الصناعية المتغيرة وإلى انحراف سعر البيع وعـدد الوحدات المباعة عـن الأسعار والوحدات المخطط بيعها على التوالي.

وبدراسة انحراف التكاليف الصناعية المتغيرة وقدره ١٤,٠٠٠ د نجده يتكون من جزئين: الأول ويعود إلى اختلاف تكلفة الوحدة، فقد كانت التكلفة المتغيرة المخططة ٧ دنانير (٦+١) ولكن التكلفة الفعلية بلغت ٨,٥ د (٧+ ١,٥) وهـذا أدى إلى وجود انحراف في التكاليف المتغيرة ومقداره:

(٧-٨,٥)×(١٤,٠٠٠ وحدة = ٢١,٠٠٠ دينار (غير مفضل)

إضافة إلى ذلك، فقد أدى انخفاض حجم المبيعات الفعلي عـن المخطط إلى عدم بيع ١٠٠٠ وحدة (١٥,٠٠٠=) وحدة مخططة – ١٤,٠٠٠ وحدة فعلية) وهـذا أدى إلى توفير في التكاليف المتغيرة مقداره ٧,٠٠٠ د، وبجمع الانحـرافين السـابقين معاً يكون انحراف التكلفة المتغيرة ١٤,٠٠٠ د (غير مفضل)، على أية حال، لقد تمت دراسة هذه الانحرافات بالتفصيل عند تحليل انحرافات التكاليف الصناعية في الفصول السابقة، لذلك سـنقوم في هـذا الفصـل بتحميل إدارة المبيعـات بالتكلفـة المعيارية للوحدات المباعة لأن إدارة الإنتاج وليس إدارة المبيعات هي المسؤولة عن حدوث انحرافات التكلفة المتغيرة، وبالتـالي سـوف لا نـدرس انحرافـات التكـاليف المتغيرة في هذا الفصل.

ويعرف هامش المساهمة الفعلي عـلى أنه الفـرق بـين سعر البيع الفعلـي والتكاليف المتغيرة المعيارية للوحدة، ويعرف هامش المساهمة المعياري عـلى أنه سعر البيع المخطط ناقص التكاليف المتغيرة المعيارية للوحدة، ومـن ثـم يعرف الانحـراف الكلـي للمبيعـات عـلى أنـه هامـش المساهمة الفعلـي ناقص هامـش المساهمة المخطط للمبيعات الفعلية والمخططة على التوالي ويساوي:

هامش المساهمة الفعلي = ١٤,٠٠٠ (١٦-٧)   = ١٢٦,٠٠٠
ناقص: هامش المساهمة المخطط = ١٥,٠٠٠ (١٥-٧) = ١٢٠,٠٠٠د
الانحراف الكلي   ٦,٠٠٠ د (م)

حيث أن السبعة دنانير تمثل التكلفة المتغيرة المعيارية.

انحراف السعر:

يطلق على هذا الانحراف عـدة مسميات منها : انحـراف الموازنـة المرنـة وانحراف هامش المساهمة، ويعمل على تحديد أثر انحراف هامش المساهمة على الانحراف الكـلي

للمبيعات، ويتم تحديده بضرب الفرق بـين هـامش المساهمة الفعلي والمخطط للوحدة في عدد الوحدات الفعلية المباعة ويحسب كالتالي:

(هامش المساهمة الفعلي – هـامش المساهمة المخطط)× عـدد الوحـدات المباعة

= (٩-٨) × ١٤,٠٠٠ = ١٤,٠٠٠ دينار (مفضل)

وهذا يعني أن ارتفاع الأسعار أدى إلى ارتفاع رقم هـامش المساهمة وهـذه الزيادة نابعة من الظروف السوقية العامـة وليس مـن كفـاءة إدارة المبيعـات لأن التكاليف المتغيرة قد ارتفعت الى١,٥ د للوحـدة، أمـا أسـعار البيـع فقـد ارتفعت بدينار واحد فقط فكان انحراف السعر محبباً إلا أن هذه الظاهرة الاقتصـادية قـد أدت في النهاية إلى الضغط على أرباح المنشأة.

انحراف الحجم:

يعمل هذا الانحراف على قياس أثر تغير عدد الوحدات على هـامش المساهمة الإجمالي، ويعرف بعدة مسميات منها انحراف نشاط المبيعـات أو انحراف كميـة المبيعات، ويتم تحديده بموجب المعادلة التالية [1]:

انحراف حجم المبيعات = (الوحدات الفعلية المباعة – الوحدات المخطط بيعها)× هامش المساهمة المخطط للوحدة

= (١٤,٠٠٠ – ١٥,٠٠٠) ×٨

= ٨,٠٠٠ دينار (غير مفضل)

الانحراف الكلي = انحراف السعر + انحراف الحجم

= ١٤٠٠٠ د (م) + ٨٠٠٠ (غ م)

= ٦٠٠ د (مفضل)

يمكن تمثيل عملية انحرافات المبيعات كما في الشكل (١٣-١)

---

(١) Edward B. Deakin and M.W. Maher, Op.cit, Pp. ٨٣٧.

(موازنة شاملة)	(موازنة مرنة)	(فعلي)
سعر بيع فعلي ناقص تكلفة متغيرة معيارية × عدد الوحدات المخططة	سعر بيع معياري ناقص تكلفة متغيرة معيارية × عدد الوحدات المباعة	سعر بيع فعلي ناقص تكلفة متغيرة معيارية × عدد الوحدات المباعة
١٥,٠٠٠ ×(١٥-٧)	١٤,٠٠٠ ×(١٥-٧)	١٤,٠٠٠ ×(١٦-٧)
= ١٢٠,٠٠٠	= ١١٢,٠٠٠	= ١٢٦,٠٠٠

انحراف الحجم :	انحراف السعر:
١٢٠,٠٠٠ – ١١٢,٠٠٠	١١٢,٠٠٠ – ١٢٦,٠٠٠
= ٨,٠٠٠ د (غ م)	= ١٤,٠٠٠ د (م)

الانحراف الكلي ١٢٦,٠٠٠ – ١٢٠,٠٠٠ = ٦,٠٠٠ د (م)

(شكل ١-١٣) انحرافات مبيعات منتج واحد فقط

لاحظ أن الموازنة المرنة والموازنة الشاملة قد أعدتا باستخدام أسعار البيع المعيارية والتكاليف المتغيرة المعيارية، ولكن الأولى أعدت لمستوى المبيعات الفعلي وقدره ١٤,٠٠٠ وحدة، أما الثانية فقد أعدت لمستوى المبيعات المخطط وقدره ١٥,٠٠٠ وحدة. وفي ضوء المعلومات السابقة يمكن إعداد تقرير انحرافات صافي الربح كما في الجدول (١-١٣).

جدول (١-١٣)
تقرير تحليل انحرافات صافي الربح

موازنة شاملة	انحراف	موازنة مرنة	انحراف	فعلي	بيان
٢٢٥,٠٠٠	١٥,٠٠٠	٢١٠,٠٠٠	١٤,٠٠٠	٢٢٤,٠٠٠	المبيعات
					تكاليف متغيرة:
٩٠,٠٠٠	٦,٠٠٠م	٨٤,٠٠٠	١٤,٠٠٠ غ م	٩٨,٠٠٠	صناعية
١٥,٠٠٠	١٠٠٠م	١٤,٠٠٠	٧,٠٠٠ غ م	٢١,٠٠٠	تسويقية
١٢٠,٠٠٠	٨,٠٠٠ غ م	١١٢,٠٠٠	٧,٠٠٠ غ م	١٠٥,٠٠٠	هامش المساهمة
٣٠,٠٠٠	صفر	٣٠,٠٠٠	١,٢٠٠ غ م	٣١,٢٠٠	يطرح: تكاليف صناعية ثابتة
٤٠,٠٠٠	صفر	٤٠,٠٠٠	٢,٠٠٠ غ م	٤٢,٠٠٠	يطرح: مصروفات تسويقية وإدارية
٥٠,٠٠٠	٨,٠٠٠ غ م	٤٢,٠٠٠	١٠٢٠٠ غ م	٣١٨٠٠	صافي الربح

ملاحظات من الجدول:

١- لقد تم إعداد تقرير الانحرافات لتحديد مصدرها، وليس لتحديد مسؤولية إدارة المبيعات، لأن هذه الإدارة غير مسؤولة عن التكلفة الصناعية المتغيرة المعيارية والفعلية كما ظهر في التقرير أعلاه، ولذلك فإن انحراف السعر يمثل الفرق بين هامش المساهمة الفعلي وهامش المساهمة المخطط، وتم حسابه كالتالي:

((سعر البيع الفعلي- التكاليف المتغيرة الفعلية)- (سعر بيع المخطط – التكلفة المتغيرة المخططة)) × عدد الوحدات المباعة

لاحظ أن هذا الانحراف يخص التكاليف الصناعية والتسويقية المتغيرة.

٢- تم إعداد عامود الموازنة المرنة على اعتبار أن عدد الوحدات المباعة فعلاً هو ١٤,٠٠٠ وحدة واستخدامها في إعدادها الأسعار والتكاليف المخططة وبنفس الأسلوب تم إعداد عمود الموازنة الشاملة، ولكن على أساس أن عدد الوحدات المخطط بيعها هو ١٥,٠٠٠ وحدة، وهذه الموازنة تعرف بالموازنة الساكنة (الشاملة).

٣- يعتبر انحراف الإيراد مفضلاً إذا كانت الإيرادات الفعلية أكبر من إيرادات الموازنة المرنة وكذلك إذا كانت إيرادات هذه الموازنة أكبر من إيرادات الموازنة الشاملة، والعكس صحيح عند انخفاض الإيرادات الفعلية عن الإيرادات المخططة في الموازنة المرنة والموازنة الشاملة، وهذا عكس ما تم استخدامه عند وصف انحرافات التكاليف.

٤- يمثل انحراف دخل التشغيل محصلة تفاعل انحرافات التكاليف الصناعية والتسويقية والإدارية وانحرافات الإيرادات، فمثلاً نجد أن انحراف سعر المبيعات قد بلغ ١٤,٠٠٠ د (م) ولكن انحرافات التكاليف الصناعية والتسويقية والإدارية قد جعلت انحراف صافي الربح (انحراف الموازنة المرنة) غير مفضل بمبلغ ١٠٢,٠٠ د.

ثانياً: تحليل انحرافات المبيعات في حالة تعدد المنتجات:

عندما تتعامل المنشأة مع عدة منتجات، فإنها تقوم بإعداد موازنتها الشاملة على أساس خلط أو مزج هذه المنتجات بنسب مزج معينة، وتؤدي ظروف العمل إلى زيادة نسبة المبيعات منتج أو منتجات معينة على حساب المنتجات الأخرى [1]، ويؤدي تغير

---

(١) تشارلز. ت، هورنجرن، ص ٤٧٣ – ٤٨٠.

نسب مزج المبيعات الفعلية عن المخططة وحدوث انحراف في إيرادات المبيعات. وللوقوف على اثر ذلك يتم حساب انحراف جديد بالمقارنة مع حالة المنتج الواحد يعرف باسم انحراف مزيج المبيعات، ولتوضيح تحليل انحرافات المبيعات في حالة تعدد المنتجات المباعة سيتم الاعتماد على البيانات التالية:

مثال (٢):

تقوم إحدى الشركات ببيع منتجين هما (أ)، (ب)، والآتي البيانات المخططة والفعلية لهما:

أ- البيانات المخططة :

	منتج أ	منتج ب
عدد الوحدات	٥٠٠٠	١٠,٠٠٠
سعر بيع الوحدة	٢٠د	٢٥د
التكلفة المتغيرة للوحدة المباعة	١٣د	١٥د
هامش المساهمة المخطط	٧	١٠
عدد الوحدات المباعة فعلاً	٥,٧٠٠	٨,٥٥٠
سعر البيع الفعلي للوحدة	٢٢د	٢٧د

المطلوب: تحليل انحرافات الإيرادات.

الحل: سنبدأ بتحليل الانحرافات بحساب الانحراف الكلي ثم تقسيم ذلك إلى انحراف السعر وانحراف الحجم.

أولاً: الانحراف الكلي: وهو الفرق بين هامش المساهمة الفعلي وهامش المساهمة المخطط في الموازنة الشاملة ويتم حسابه كالتالي:

١- هامش المساهمة الفعلي = عدد الوحدات المباعة من كل منتج ضرب هامش المساهمة الفعلي لكل منتج.

المنتج (أ) = ٥,٧٠٠ (٢٢- ١٣) = ٥١,٣٠٠ د

المنتج (ب) = ٨,٥٥٠ (٢٧-١٥) = ١٠٢,٦٠٠ د

الاجمالي   ١٥٣,٩٠٠ د

٢- هامش المساهمة المخطط = عدد الوحدات المخطط بيعها من كل منتج ضرب هامش المساهمة المخطط للوحدة.

المنتج (أ) = ٥,٠٠٠ (٢٠-١٣)   = ٣٥,٠٠٠ د

المنتج (ب) = ١٠,٠٠٠ (٢٥-١٥) = ١٠٠,٠٠٠ د

الاجمالي   = ١٣٥,٠٠٠ د

الانحراف الكلي = هامش المساهمة الفعلي – هامش المساهمة المخطط

= ١٥٣,٩٠٠ – ١٣٥,٠٠٠

= ١٨,٩٠٠ د (مفضل)

انحراف السعر:

يتم حساب هذا الانحراف بنفس الطريقة التي تم اتباعها في حالة تحليل انحرافات المنتج الواحد، لذلك يعرف على أنه الفرق بين هامش المساهمة الفعلي وهامش المساهمة المخطط ضرب عدد الوحدات المباعة فعلاً من كل منتج. تذكر بأن هامش المساهمة الفعلي هو عبارة عن سعر البيع الفعلي ناقص التكاليف المتغيرة المعيارية، لذلك يحسب هذا الانحراف كالتالي:

المنتج (أ) = (٢٢-١٣) – (٢٠-١٣)× ٥,٧٠٠ = ١١,٤٠٠ د (مفضل)

المنتج (ب) = (٢٧-١٥) – (٢٥-١٥) × ٨,٥٥٠ = ١٧١,١٠٠ د (مفضل)

انحراف سعر المبيعات :   ٢٨,٥٠٠ د (مفضل)

لقد زادت أسعار بيع كل من المنتج (أ) والمنتج (ب) بدينارين للوحدة لذلك كان الانحراف مفضلاً.

انحراف الحجم:

ويهدف هذا الانحراف إلى بيان أثر تغير وحدات المبيعات الفعلية للمنتجات عن وحدات المبيعات المخططة، ويتم حسابه لكل منتج بضرب هامش المساهمة المخطط

لوحدة المنتج في الفرق بين الوحدات المباعة فعلاً من المنتج والوحدات المخطط بيعها منه ويتم حسابه بالنسبة للمنتجات (أ)، (ب) كالتالي:

المنتج (أ) = ٧ (٥٠٠٠ – ٥٧٠٠) = ٤٩٠٠د (مفضل)

المنتج (ب) = ١٠ (١٠,٠٠٠ – ٨٥٥٠) = ١٤٥٠٠ د (غير مفضل)

انحراف الحجم ٩٦٠٠ د (غير مفضل)

ويمكن تعريف انحراف الحجم أيضاً على أنه الوحدات الفعلية في المزيج الفعلي ضرب هامش المساهمة المعياري للوحدة ناقص الوحدات المخططة في المزيج المعياري ضرب هامش المساهمة المعياري للوحدة ويساوي =

(١٠×١٠,٠٠٠+٧ ×٥٠٠٠) – (١٠×٨٥٥٠+٧ × ٥٧٠٠)

= ١٣٥,٠٠٠ – ١٢٥,٤٠٠   = ٩٦٠٠ د (غير مفضل)

الانحراف الكلي = انحراف السعر + انحراف الحجم

= ٢٨٥٠٠ د (م) + ٩٦٠٠ د (غ م)   = ١٨٩٠٠ د (م)

ويمكن تجزئة انحراف حجم المبيعات إلى عاملين: الأول ويحدد أثر اختلاف كمية المبيعات، والثاني يحدد أثر اختلاف نسبة مزج المبيعات، ويسمى الانحراف الأول باسم انحراف كمية المبيعات، ويسمى الثاني باسم انحراف مزج المبيعات، وسيتم مناقشة هذين الانحرافين على التوالي[1]:

انحراف كمية المبيعات:

يعرف هذا الانحراف – في بعض الأحيان – باسم انحراف الحجم أو انحراف النشاط، ويهدف إلى تحديد أثر اختلاف وحدات المبيعات الفعلية حسب نسبة المزيج المعياري عن وحدات المبيعات المخططة بالموازنة الشاملة[2] وللتسهيل سوف نسمي وحدات المبيعات الفعلية حسب نسبة المزج المعياري باسم الوحدات الفعلية المعدلة، ويتم

---

(١) Horgren and Foster, Op.cit., Pp. ٨٠٢ – ٨٠٥.

(٢) Deakin and Maher, Op.cit, Pp.٨١٤-٨٤٤.

حساب هذه الوحدات بضرب إجمالي عدد الوحدات المباعة فعلاً في نسبة المزج المعيارية للمبيعات، ويكون كالتالي:

أولاً: عدد الوحدات المباعة من المنتج (أ) زائد عدد الوحدات المباعة من المنتج (ب).

$$= ٥,٧٠٠ + ٨,٥٥٠$$

$$= ١٤,٢٥٠ \text{ وحدة}$$

الوحدات الفعلية المعدلة للمنتج (أ) = ١٤,٢٥٠ × ٥/ ١٥

$$= ٤,٧٥٠ \text{ وحدة}$$

الوحدات الفعلية المعدلة للمنتج (ب) = ١٤,٢٥٠ ×١٠/١٥

$$= ٩,٥٠٠ \text{ وحدة}$$

لقد حسبت نسبة المزيج المعياري على أساس عدد الوحدات المباعة من كل منتج إلى إجمالي عدد الوحدات المباعة من كل المنتجات، ويمكن تحديد الانحراف بضرب الفرق بين الوحدات الفعلية المعدلة والوحدات الواردة في الموازنة الشاملة بهامش مساهمة الوحدة المخطط وعليه يكون هذا الانحراف كالتالي:

انحراف كمية المنتج (أ) = (٥٠٠٠ – ٤٧٥٠)× ٧ = ١,٧٥٠ د (غ م)

انحراف كمية المنتج (ب) = (١٠,٠٠ – ٩٥٠٠)× ١٠ = ٥,٠٠٠ د (غ م)

انحراف كمية المبيعات = ٦,٧٥٠ د (غ م)

لاحظ أنه عند حساب هذا الانحراف، تم استخدام هامش المساهمة المخطط للوحدة، أي أن هذا الانحراف لم ينتج عن تغير هامش المساهمة بل عن تغير عدد الوحدات المباعة حسب المزيج المعياري، وبكلمات أخرى، لو فرضنا أن المبيعات الفعلية قد تمت طبقاً لنسب المزج المعيارية للمبيعات فإن هذا الانحراف ينتج عن اختلاف الوحدات المباعة منه عن الوحدات المخطط بيعها.

ويمكن أن يتم حسابه بطريقة أخرى عن طريق مقارنة الوحدات المباعة فعلاً مع الوحدات المخطط بيعها في الموازنة الشاملة وضرب الفرق بينهما في متوسط هامش المساهمة المرجح (١)، ويتم حساب هذا المتوسط كالتالي:

$$\text{متوسط هامش المساهمة المرجح} = \frac{(٥,٠٠٠ \times ٧) + (١٠,٠٠٠ \times ١٠)}{١٥,٠٠٠ \text{ وحدة}} = ٩ \text{ دينار}$$

وعليه يكون انحراف كمية المبيعات كالتالي:

انحراف كمية المنتج (أ) = (٥,٠٠٠ – ٤٧٥٠) × ٩   = ٢٢٥٠ د (غ م)
انحراف كمية المنتج (ب) = (١٠,٠٠٠ – ٩,٥٠٠) × ٩ = ٤,٥٠٠ د (غ م)

انحراف كمية المبيعات =   ٦,٧٥٠ د (غ م)

لقد تم التوصل – باستخدام هذين الأسلوبين – إلى نفس رقم انحـراف كميـة المبيعات، ولكـن كـان هنـاك اختـلاف في انحـراف كميـة كـل منـتج منهما حسـب الطريقة المتبعة.

انحراف مزيج المبيعات:

يؤدي اختلاف المبيعات الفعلية عن المبيعات المخططة لكل منتج إلى اختلاف متوسط هامش مساهمة المـزيج الفعـلي عـن متوسـط هـامش مساهمة المـزيج المعياري (متوسط هامش المساهمة المخطط)، لذلك يحسب هذا الانحراف بضرب الفرق بين الهامشين المذكورين في عدد الوحدات المباعـة فعـلاً، ولقـد تم حسـاب متوسط هامش المساهمة للمـزج المعياري سـابقاً أمـا متوسط هـامش المسـاهمة المرجح للمزيج الفعلي فهو كالتالي:

$$\frac{٨,٥٠٠ \times ١٠ + ٧,٠٠٠ \times ٧}{٨,٥٠٠ + ٧,٠٠٠} = ٨,٨ \text{ دينار للوحدة}$$

انحراف المزيج = (هامش المساهمة المرجح المخطط – هامش المساهمة المرجح الفعلي) × إجمالي عدد الوحدات المباعة [1].
= (٩ – ٨,٨) × ١٤٢٥٠ وحدة
= ٢,٨٥٠ د (غير مفضل)

---

(١) Elipse lliGliceC, Op.cit, Pp.١٤٥- ١٥٢.

ويمكن حساب هذا الانحراف بطريقة بديلة، وذلك بمقارنة الوحدات المباعة فعلاً مع وحدات المبيعات الفعلية المعدلة وضرب الفرق بينهما في هامش مساهمة الوحدة ناقص هامش المساهمة بالمزيج المعياري [1]، وفي ضوء ذلك يتم حساب انحراف المزيج كالتالي:

انحراف مزيج المنتج (أ) = (٤٧٥٠ – ٧,٥٠٠) × ٧-٩ =   ١,٩٠٠ د (غ م)
انحراف مزيج المنتج (ب) = (٩٥٠٠ – ٨,٠٥٠) × (١٠-٩) = ٩٥٠ د (غ م)

انحراف مزيج المبيعات: ٢,٨٥٠ د (غ م)

لقد تم اعتبار انحراف المزيج للمنتج أ غير مفضل لأنه قد تم بيع وحدات منه أكبر من المخطط لها، ولكن هامش مساهمة أقل من المتوسط المرجح، لذلك فإن نتيجة ضرب هذين الجزئين ستكون سالبة، لذلك أدت زيادة مبيعاته إلى تخفيض متوسط هامش المساهمة الفعلي للمبيعات، وهذا في غير صالح المنشأة، وكذلك حدث الشيء نفسه مع المنتج ب. فعلى الرغم من ارتفاع هامش مساهمة الوحدة المخطط له عن المتوسط المرجح لهامش المساهمة، إلا أنه قد تم بيع وحدات منه أقل من نسبته في مزيج المبيعات المعياري وبالتالي ستكون نتيجة ضرب هذين المتغيرين سالبة، وهذا أيضاً في غير صالح المنشأة، مما يعني أنه لو انخفضت مبيعات المنتج أ عن ٤,٧٥٠ وحدة وزادت مبيعات المنتج ب عن ٩,٥٠٠ وحدة لأصبحت الانحرافات محببة.

وللتأكد من تحليل الانحرافات السابقة يتم جمع انحراف الكمية وانحراف المزيج ويجب أن يساوي مجموعها قيمة انحراف الحجم.

= ٦٧٥٠ د (غ م) + ٢٨٥٠ د (غ م) = ٩٦٠٠ د (غ م)
ويمكن تلخيص تحليل الانحرافات السابقة في الشكل (١٣-٢)

(١) تشارلز، ت. هورنجرن، مرجع سابق الذكر، ص ٤٧٨ – ٤٧٩.

موازنة شاملة	انحراف كمية	موازنة مزيج معياري	انحراف مزيج	موازنة مرنة مزيج فعلي	انحراف سعر	الأرقام الفعلية مزيج فعلي	المنتج
٥٠٠٠×٧ = ٣٥٠٠٠		٤٧٥٠×٧ = ٣٣٢٥٠		٥٧٠٠×٧ = ٣٩٩٠٠		٥٧٠٠×٩ = ٥١٣٠٠	أ
	١٧٥٠ غ م		٦٦٥٠		١١٤٠٠		
١٠٠٠٠×١٠ = ١٠٠,٠٠٠		٩٥٠٠×١٠ = ٩٥٠٠٠		٨٥٠٠×١٠ = ٨٥٠٠٠		٨٥٠٠×١٢ = ١٠٢٦٠٠	ب
	٥٠٠٠ غ م		٩٥٠٠غ م		١٧١١٠٠م		
= ١٣٥,٠٠٠		= ١٢٨٢٥٠		= ١٢٥,٤٠٠		=	الاجمالي
	٦٧٥٠ غ م	٢٨٥٠غ م		٢٨٥٠غ	١٥٣,٩٠٠		

الانحراف الكلي = ١٥٣,٩٠٠ – ١٢٥,٠٠٠ = ١٨٩٠٠ مفضل

شكل (١٣-٢) تحليل انحرافات المبيعات في حالة تعدد المنتجات

من دراسة الشكل (١٣-٢) نرى أنه قد تم تعريف انحـراف المـزيج عـلى أنـه الفرق بين الوحدات المباعة فعلاً والوحدات الفعلية المعدلة ضرب هامش مساهمة المنتج، وبطبيعة الحال كان انحراف المنتج أ مفضلاً لأن مبيعاته الفعليـة أكـثر مـن مبيعاته المعدلة، وعلى العكس كان انحراف المنتج ب.

مثال محلول:

كانت الموازنة الشاملة لإحدى الشركات كالتالي :

الإجمالي	منتج ج	منتج ب	منتج أ	
٧,٩٠٠	٢,٥٠٠	١,٨٠٠	٣,٦٠٠	المبيعات
٥,٥٥٠	٢,١٠٠	١,٣٥٠	٢,١٠٠	ناقص: التكاليف المتغيرة
٢,٣٥٠	٤٠٠	٤٥٠	١,٥٠٠	هامش المساهمة
١,١٧٥	٢٨٠	٢٧٠	٦٢٥	تكاليف ثابتة
١,١٧٥	١٢٠	١٨٠	٨٧٥	صافي الربح
	٢٠٠	٣٠٠	٦٠٠	عدد الوحدات
	٢	١,٥	٢,٥	هامش مساهمة الوحدة

وخــلال الفــترة لم تحــدث انحرافــات في التكــاليف المتغـيرة والثابتـة وكانـت المبيعات كالتالي:

هامش المساهمة للوحدة	التكلفة المتغيرة	سعر البيع	عدد الوحدات المباعة	
٣	٣,٥	٦,٥	٧٥٠	أ
١,٧	٤,٥	٦,٢	٢٥٠	ب
١,٥	١٠,٥	١٢	٣٠٠	جـ

المطلوب:

تحليل انحرافات المبيعات باستخدام رقم هامش المساهمة.

الحل:

أولاً: انحراف السعر = (هامش المساهمة الفعلي – هامش المساهمة المخطط) × عدد الوحدات

وهو كالتالي:

انحراف السعر	الوحدات المباعة	هامش المساهمة المخطط	هامش المساهمة الفعلي	المنتج
٣٧٥ (م)	٧٥٠	٢,٥	٣	أ
٥٠ (م)	٢٥٠	١,٥	١,٧	ب
١٥٠ (غ م)	٣٠٠	٢	١,٥	جـ
٢٧٥ (م)			انحراف السعر	

ثانياً: انحراف الكمية:

يتم مزج المنتجات معيارياً بنسبة من الوحدات كما في الموازنة الشاملة والتي تساوي ٦:٣:٢ وأن الوحدات الفعلية المعدلة للمنتجات تساوي:

$$\text{منتج أ} = ١٣٠٠ \times \frac{٦}{١١} = ٧٠٩ \text{ وحدة}$$

$$\text{منتج ب} = ١٣٠٠ \times \frac{٣}{١١} = ٣٥٥ \text{ وحدة}$$

$$\text{منتج جـ} = ١٣٠٠ \times \frac{٢}{١١} = ٢٣٦ \text{ وحدة}$$

$$\text{وحدة فعلية معدلة} = ١٣٠٠$$

انحراف الكمية = وحدات الموازنة الشاملة ناقص الوحدات الفعلية المعدلة للمنتج ضرب هامش المساهمة المخطط لوحدة المنتج ويساوي:

منتج (أ)	= (٦٠٠ – ٧٠٩)× ٢,٥	= ٢٧٢,٥ د (مفضل)
منتج (ب)	= (٣٠٠ – ٣٥٥)× ١,٥	= ٨٢,٥ د (مفضل)
منتج (جـ)	= (٢٠٠ – ٢٣٦) ×٢	= ٧٢ د (مفضل)
		٤٢٧ د (مفضل)

ويمكن حساب هذا الانحراف أيضاً كالتالي:

$$\text{متوسط هامش المساهمة} = \frac{٦٠٠ \times ٢٫٥ + ١٫٥ \times ٣٠٠ + ٢٠٠}{١٣٠٠} = ٢٫١٣٦٤$$

انحراف الكمية = (إجمالي الوحدات المخطط بيعها – الوحدات المباعة فعلاً) متوسط هامش المساهمة

= (١١٠٠ – ١٣٠٠) × ٢٫١٣٦٤ =

= ٤٢٧ دينار (مفضل)

ثالثاً: انحراف المزيج:

انحراف المزيج = (الوحدات المباعة – الوحدات الفعلية المعدلة) هامش مساهمة وحدة المنتج

ويتم حسابه كالتالي:

المنتج (أ)	= (٧٥٠ – ٧٠٩) ٢٫٥	= ١٠٢٫٥ د (م)
المنتج (ب)	= (٢٥٠ – ٣٥٥) ١٫٥	= ١٠٧٫٥ د (غ م)
المنتج (جـ)	= (٣٠٠ – ٢٣٦) ٢	= ١٢٨ (م)
انحراف المزيج		= ٧٣ د (م)

الخاتمــة

في هذا الفصل قمنا بدراسة تحليل انحرافات الإيرادات وتم التعرض لحالتي المنتج الواحد والمنتجات المتعددة، وفي حالة المنتج الواحد تم حساب انحراف السعر لقياس أثر تغير أسعار المبيعات وحساب انحراف الحجم لبيان أثر انحراف الكمية الفعلية المباعة عن الكمية المخطط بيعها كما في الموازنة، وفي حالة تعدد المنتجات تم حساب انحراف السعر وكان هذا الانحراف يشبه حالة المنتج الواحد في حين تغير انحراف الحجم بتقسيمه إلى انحرافين هما انحراف مزج المبيعات وانحراف كمية المبيعات، ويقيس انحراف مزج المبيعات أثر اختلاف مزج الوحدات المباعة عن الوحدات المخطط بيعها ويقيس الانحراف الثاني أثر اختلاف كمية المبيعات في كل منتج عن مبيعاته الفعلية حسب نسبة المزج المعيارية وقد تم في نهاية الفصل عرض مثال شامل لتحليل الانحرافات.

أسئلة وتمارين

السؤال الأول: عرف المقصود بانحراف حجم المبيعات وبين كيف يتم حسابه.

السؤال الثاني: بين كيف يتم حساب الانحراف الكلي للمبيعات في حالة تعدد المنتجات.

السؤال الثالث: ما هو المقصود بانحراف مزيج المبيعات واشرح طريقتين يمكن استخدامهما في حسابه.

السؤال الرابع: عند تقييم أداء إدارة المبيعات يفضل استخدام التكاليف المتغيرة المعيارية بدلاً من التكاليف المتغيرة الفعلية علل ذلك.

السؤال الخامس: قامت إحدى الشركات بإعداد موازنتها التخطيطية على أساس إنتاج وبيع ٢٥,٠٠٠ وحدة ولكن خلال السنة المالية تم إنتاج ٣٠,٠٠٠ وحدة وتم بيع ٢٠,٠٠٠ وحدة فقط، وبلغ سعر بيع الوحدة ٨ دنانير وبلغت نسبة هامش المساهمة ٤٠% وبلغت التكاليف الثابتة الفعلية ٣٤,٠٠٠.

المطلوب: تحديد المبلغ الذي يستخدم في قياس كفاءة الإدارة.

السؤال السادس: الآتي معلومات تخص أحد المنتجات.

سعر البيع	١٥ د للوحدة
التكاليف الصناعية المتغيرة المخططة	٥ دنانير للوحدة
التكاليف التسويقية المتغيرة المخططة	١ دينار للوحدة

وتخطط الشركة بيع ٣٠,٠٠٠ وحدة خلال فترة الموازنة ولكنها باعت ٢٥,٠٠٠ وحدة فقط بسعر ١٤ دينار للوحدة، وكانت التكاليف المتغيرة الفعلية الآتي:

التكاليف المتغيرة الصناعية	٤,٨ د للوحدة
التكاليف التسويقية المتغيرة	١,٠٥ د للوحدة

المطلوب: ١- تحليل الانحرافات الخاصة بالمبيعات والتكاليف.

٢- إعداد تقرير انحرافات التكاليف الذي يوضح تفاصيل انحراف الربح الفعلي عن المخطط.

السؤال السابع: الآتي قوائم الدخل التقدير والفعلية لإحدى الشركات:

	الفعلي			الموازنة		
الإجمالي	منتج ب	منتج أ	إجمالي	منتج ب	منتج أ	
٧٥٠	٣٠٠	٤٥٠	٧٥٠	٣٥٠	٤٠٠	عدد الوحدات المباعة
١٢٣٠٠	٣٧٥٠	٨٥٥٠	١٢٢٠٠	٤٢٠٠	٨٠٠٠	قيمة المبيعات
٧٠٠٨	٢٢٢٠	٤٧٨٨	٦٥٢٠	٢٥٢٠	٤٠٠٠	يطــرح التكـــاليـف المتغيرة
٥٢٩٢	١٥٣٠	٣٧٦٢	٥٦٨٠	١٦٨٠	٤٠٠٠	هامش المساهمة
١٧٨٠			١٦٨٠			يطرح التكاليف الثابتة
٣٥١٢			٤٠٠٠			صافي الربح

المطلوب: ١- تحديد انحراف مزيج المبيعات.

٢- تحديد انحراف كمية المبيعات.

السؤال الثامن: تقوم إحدى المنشآت بإنتاج المنتج أو الآتي تقريـر الأداء عـن شـهر تشرين ثاني .

	الفعلي	الموازنة
الوحدات المباعة	٥,٠٠٠	٦,٠٠٠
المبيعات (بالدينار)	٢٣٥,٠٠٠	٣٠٠,٠٠٠
التكلفة المتغيرة (بالدينار)	١٤٥,٠٠٠	١٨٠,٠٠٠
هامش المساهمة	٩٠,٠٠٠	١٢٠,٠٠٠
تكاليف ثابتة	٨٤,٠٠٠	٨٠,٠٠٠
صافي الربح	٦,٠٠٠	٤٠,٠٠٠

وتستخدم الشركة الموازنة المرنة في تحليل أدائها ولقياس أثر مختلف العوامل التي تؤثر على الفرق بين الربح المخطط والفعلي والمطلوب الإجابة على الأسئلة الآتية :

١- فإن أثر حجم المبيعات على هامش المساهمة خلال شهر تشرين ثاني هو :

أ- ٣٠,٠٠٠ د (غ م)   ب- ١٨,٠٠٠ د (غ م)

جـ- ٢٠,٠٠٠ د (غ م)   د- ١٥,٠٠٠ د (غ م)

هـ- ٦٥,٠٠٠ د (غ م)

٢- انحراف السعر خلال شهر تشرين ثاني هو :

أ- ٣٠,٠٠٠ د (غ م)   ب- ١٨,٠٠٠ د (غ م)

جـ- ٢٠,٠٠٠ د (غ م)   د- ١٥,٠٠٠ د (غ م)

هـ- ٦٥,٠٠٠ د (غ م)

٣- انحراف الموازنة للتكاليف المتغيرة خلال شهر تشرين ثاني هو:

أ- ٥٠٠٠ د (غ م)   ب- ٥٠٠٠ د (غ م)

جـ- ٤٠٠٠ د (م)   د- ٤٠٠٠ د (غ م)

هـ- ٦٠٠٠ د (م)

٤- انحراف التكاليف الثابتة خلال شهر تشرين ثاني هو :

أ- ٥٠٠٠ د (م)   ب- ٥٠٠٠ د (غ م)

جـ- ٤٠٠٠ د (م)   د- ٤٠٠٠ (غ م)

هـ- ١٠٠٠ د (م)

(جمعية المحاسبين الإداريين CMA)

المراجــــع

المراجع العربية:

- أحمد الخطيب، التكاليف في المجال التطبيقي، القاهرة ١٩٨٧.

- أحمد نور وعبد المقصود دبيان، محاسبة التكاليف الصناعية، مؤسسة شباب الجامعة، الإسكندرية، ١٩٨٩.

- عبد الحي مرعي، في محاسبة التكاليف المبادئ والإجراءات والرقابة، مؤسسة شباب الجامعة، الإسكندرية، ١٩٨٥.

- مجدي عمارة، ميلود خليفة، الهادي المحسيري، دراسات منهجية معاصرة في محاسبة التكاليف الفعلية، جامعة الجبل الغربية، بدون تاريخ.

- محمد توفيق بلبع، التكاليف المعيارية لأغراض قياس وضبط التكاليف الفعلية، دار الشباب، القاهرة، ١٩٧٢.

- محمد تيسير الرجبي، التكاليف المعيارية كأداة للرقابة على تكاليف تكرير البترول، رسالة ماجستير غير منشورة، جامعة القاهرة، ١٩٧٢.

- هورنجرن، ت، تشارلز، محاسبة التكاليف مدخل إداري، ترجمة أحمد حامد حجاج، الجزء الأول والجزء الثاني، دار المريخ، الرياض، ١٩٨٧.

المراجع الأجنبية:

- Anderson Henry R, and B,E. Needles, Jr and J.C Cadwell, Managerial Accounting, Houghton Mifflin Co. ١٩٨٣.

- Anthoy, Robert N. and Welsch, Gelnn, N. Fundamentals of Management Accounting, ٣rd . ed. IRWIN, ١٩٨١.

- Batty, J., Standard Costing, MacDonalds and Evans Ltd., ١٩٦٨.

- Belkaoui, Ahmed, Cost Accounting: A Multidimensional Emphasis, The Dryden Press, ١٩٨٣.

- Bhabatosh Banerhee, Cost Accounting, V th . ed, Calcutta, The World Press Ltd, ١٩٨٦.

- Bierman Harold, Jr and Thomas R. Dykman, Managerial Cost Accounting, ٢nd, ed, MaCmillan Publishing Co. INC., ١٩٧٦.

- Bisk Matham M., CPA Comprehensive Exam Review, Bisk publisher, ٢٠٠٠.

- Bodnar, George H., and W. S. Jopwood, Accounting Information System ٣rd, ed, Allyn and Bacon, Inc, ١٩٨٧.

- Brown, Lweis, J. and Leslie R. Howard, Principles and Practice of Management Accounting, MacDonald and Evans, Ltd., ١٩٦٩.

- Davison S. and R. L Weil, Handbook of Cost Accounting, McGraw – Hill Inc, ١٩٧٨.

- Deakin Edward B, and Michael W. Maher, Cost Accounting, ٢nd, ed. IRWIN, ١٩٨٧.

- Delaney Patric, CPA Examination Review, John Wiley and Sons, ٢٠٠١.

- Engler, Calvin, Managerial Accounting, IRWIN, ١٩٨٧.

- Fisher, Paul M. and Frank, Werner G., Cost Accounting Theory and Applications, South – Western Publishing Co., ١٩٨٥.

- Heitger, Lestary E., and Matulich, Serge, Managerial Accounting, ٢nd, ed McGraw – Hill Book Co, ١٩٨٧.

- Henrici, Stanely B., <u>Standard Costs for Manufacturing</u>, ٣rd, ed., McGraw – Hill Book, Co ١٩٦٠.

- Hilton. R. W., <u>Managerial Accounting Creating Value in a Dynamic Business Environment</u>, McGraw – Hill international Edition, ٥th ed., ٢٠٠٨.

- Hirsch, Maurice, Jr and J. G Louderback, <u>Cost Accounting: Accumulation, Analysis and Use</u>, ٢nd, ed kent Publishing Co, ١٩٨٦.

- Horngren, C. T, S. M. Datar, G. Foster, <u>Cost Accounting: A Managerial Emphasis,</u> Prentice – Hall, Pearson Education International, ١١ ed., ٢٠٠٣.

- Horngren, C. T. and G. L. Sundem, <u>Introduction to Management Accounting</u>, ٥th, ed, Prentice – Hall, INC, ١٩٨٧.

- Horngren, C. T, and G.Foster, <u>Cost Accounting: A Managerial Emphasis,</u> Prentice – Hall, INC., Englewood Cliffs, ١٩٨٧.

- Howe, A, and Squith W., <u>Cost Accounting, International</u> Textbook Co., ١٩٦٩.

- Ijiri Yuji, <u>Historical Cost Accounting and its Rationality, Research Monograph Number</u> ١. The Canadian Certified General Accounting Research Foundation, ١٩٨١.

- Ijiri, Yuji, A Defense for Historical Cost Accounting, Accounting Review, (Oct. ١٩٨٦).

- Garrison, Ray, H., Managerial Accounting: Concepts for Planning, Control Decision Making, ٥th, ed., Homewood, Illinois, ١٩٨٨.

- Garrison, Ray, H., E. W. Noreen., and PC. Brewer <u>Managerial Accounting</u>, ١٢ ed., McGraw-Hill, ٢٠٠٨.

- Gillespie, C., Standard and Direct Costing, Prentice – Hall of India, New Delhi, ١٩٦٥.

- Kaplan, Robert S., <u>Advanced Management Accounting</u>, Prentice – Hall, INC, ١٩٨٢.

- Killough, L. N, and wayne, Leininger, <u>Cost Accounting Concepts and Techniques for Management</u>, West Publishing Co, ١٩٨٤.

- Koontz, Harold, and C. O'donnel and H, Weihrich, <u>Management</u>, McGraw – Hill Book Co, ١٩٨٠.

- Lucey, T., Costing, ٣rd, ed <u>English Language Book</u> Society D P Publication, ١٩٨٩.

- Lucey, T., <u>Management Accounting Planning and Control</u>, ٨th, ed South Western Publishing Co, ١٩٨١.

- Morse, Wayne, J, Naf Harold p. Roth, <u>Cost Accounting: Processing, Evaluating, and Using Cost Data</u>, ٣ th. Ed., Addison – Wesley Publishing Co, ١٩٨٦.

- Rayburn, Gayle L. <u>Principles of Cost Accounting</u>, ٤th, ed, IRWIN, ١٩٨٩.

- Ricketts D., Jack Gary, <u>Managerial Accounting</u>, ٢nd, ed., Houghton Mifflin, Co, ١٩٩١.

- Ryan Bob and J, Hosben, <u>Management Accounting</u>, Pitman, ١٩٨٥.

- Smith, Jack L., and R. M. Keith W.L. Stephens, <u>Accounting Principles</u>, ٢nd, ed., McGraw – Hill Book Co, ١٩٨٧.

- Swaminthan L., <u>Lectures on Costing</u>, S, Chanda and C, ١٩٦٨.

- Thomas, Arthur, L. <u>The Allocation Problem in Accounting, Studies in Accounting Research #٣</u>, AAA, ١٩٦٩.

- Titard, Pierrel L., **Managerial Accounting,** ٢nd, ed. The Dryden Press, ١٩٩٠.

- Wilson, Richard M.S. and Wal Fong Chua, <u>Managerial Accounting Method and Meaning</u>, VNR, ١٩٨٨.

- Wayne, J, Morse, Janes R.R., and All Hartgraves, <u>Management Accounting</u>, ٢nd, ed, Addison, Wesley, ١٩٨٨.